Fodor's

ESSENTIAL
EUROPE

1st Edition

Where to Stay and Eat
for All Budgets

Must-See Sights
and Local Secrets

Ratings You Can Trust

Fodor's Travel Publications · New York, Toronto, London, Sydney, Auckland
www.fodors.com

FODOR'S ESSENTIAL EUROPE

Editors: Matthew Lombardi, lead editor; Linda Cabasin, Robert I. C. Fisher, Maria Hart, Salwa Jabado, Kelly Kealy, Laura Kidder, Rachel Klein, Caroline Trefler

Production Editor: Astrid deRidder

Maps & Illustrations: David Lindroth, Mark Stroud, *cartographers*; Bob Blake, Rebecca Baer, *map editors;* William Wu, *information graphics*

Design: Fabrizio La Rocca, *creative director*; Guido Caroti, Siobhan O'Hare, *art directors*; Tina Malaney, Chie Ushio, Ann McBride, Jessica Walsh, *designers*; Melanie Marin, *senior picture editor;* Moon Sun Kim, *cover designer*

Cover Photo: (Old astronomical clock in the center square of Prague): Fribus Ekaterina/Shutterstock. (Santorini): Apollofoto/Shutterstock. (Guggenheim, Bilbao): Jarno Gonzalez Zarraonandia/Shutterstock. (Guard, Buckingham Palace, London): Bryan Busovicki/Shutterstock. (Acoustic guitar): Luis Pedrosa/iStockphoto. (Ceramic tile): Clara Natoli/Shutterstock. (Sign, Germany): iStockphoto.

Production Manager: Amanda Bullock

COPYRIGHT

1st Edition

ISBN 978-1-4000-0894-0

ISSN 1943-006X

SPECIAL SALES

This book is available at special discounts for bulk purchases for sales promotions or premiums. Special editions, including personalized covers, excerpts of existing books, and corporate imprints, can be created in large quantities for special needs. For more information, write to Special Markets/Premium Sales, 1745 Broadway, MD 6-2, New York, New York 10019, or e-mail specialmarkets@randomhouse.com.

AN IMPORTANT TIP & AN INVITATION

Although all prices, opening times, and other details in this book are based on information supplied to us at press time, changes occur all the time in the travel world, and Fodor's cannot accept responsibility for facts that become outdated or for inadvertent errors or omissions. So **always confirm information when it matters**, especially if you're making a detour to visit a specific place. Your experiences—positive and negative—matter to us. If we have missed or misstated something, **please write to us.** We follow up on all suggestions. Contact the Essential Europe editor at editors@fodors.com or c/o Fodor's at 1745 Broadway, New York, NY 10019.

PRINTED IN THE UNITED STATES OF AMERICA

10 9 8 7 6 5 4 3 2 1

Be a Fodor's Correspondent

Your opinion matters. It matters to us. It matters to your fellow Fodor's travelers, too. And we'd like to hear it. In fact, we need to hear it.

When you share your experiences and opinions, you become an active member of the Fodor's community. That means we'll not only use your feedback to make our books better, but we'll publish your names and comments whenever possible. Throughout our guides, look for "Word of Mouth," excerpts of your unvarnished feedback.

Here's how you can help improve Fodor's for all of us.

Tell us when we're right. We rely on local writers to give you an insider's perspective. But our writers and staff editors—who are the best in the business—depend on you. Your positive feedback is a vote to renew our recommendations for the next edition.

Tell us when we're wrong. We're proud that we update most of our guides every year. But we're not perfect. Things change. Hotels cut services. Museums change hours. Charming cafés lose charm. If our writer didn't quite capture the essence of a place, tell us how you'd do it differently. If any of our descriptions are inaccurate or inadequate, we'll incorporate your changes in the next edition and will correct factual errors at fodors.com immediately.

Tell us what to include. You probably have had fantastic travel experiences that aren't yet in Fodor's. Why not share them with a community of like-minded travelers? Maybe you chanced upon a beach or bistro or B&B that you don't want to keep to yourself. Tell us why we should include it. And share your discoveries and experiences with everyone directly at fodors.com. Your input may lead us to add a new listing or highlight a place we cover with a "Highly Recommended" star or with our highest rating, "Fodor's Choice."

Give us your opinion instantly at our feedback center at www.fodors.com/feedback. You may also e-mail editors@fodors.com with the subject line "Essential Europe Editor." Or send your nominations, comments, and complaints by mail to Essential Europe Editor, Fodor's, 1745 Broadway, New York, NY 10019.

You and travelers like you are the heart of the Fodor's community. Make our community richer by sharing your experiences. Be a Fodor's correspondent.

Bon voyage!

Tim Jarrell, Publisher

CONTENTS

ABOUT THIS BOOK

Our Ratings

Sometimes you find terrific travel experiences and sometimes they just find you. But usually the burden is on you to select the right combination of experiences. That's where our ratings come in.

As travelers we've all discovered a place so wonderful that its worthiness is obvious. And sometimes that place is so experiential that superlatives don't do it justice: you just have to be there to know. These sights, properties, and experiences get our highest rating, **Fodor's Choice** indicated by orange stars throughout this book.

Black stars highlight sights and properties we deem **Highly Recommended** places that our writers, editors, and readers praise again and again for consistency and excellence.

By default, there's another category: any place we include in this book is by definition worth your time, unless we say otherwise. And we will.

Disagree with any of our choices? Care to nominate a place or suggest that we rate one more highly? Visit our feedback center at www.fodors.com/feedback.

Budget Well

Hotel and restaurant price categories from ¢ to $$$$ are defined in the opening pages of each chapter. For attractions, we always give standard adult admission fees; reductions are usually available for children, students, and senior citizens. Want to pay with plastic? **AE, D, DC, MC, V** following restaurant and hotel listings indicate if American Express, Discover, Diners Club, MasterCard, and Visa are accepted.

Restaurants

Unless we state otherwise, restaurants are open for lunch and dinner daily. We mention dress only when there's a specific requirement and reservations only when they're essential or not accepted—it's always best to book ahead.

Hotels

Hotels have private bath, phone, TV, and air-conditioning and operate on the European Plan (aka EP, meaning without meals), unless we specify that they use the Breakfast Plan (BP, with a full breakfast), or Modified American Plan (MAP, with breakfast and dinner daily), or Full American Plan (FAP, with three meals a day). We always list facilities but not whether you'll be charged an extra fee to use them, so when pricing accommodations, find out what's included.

Many Listings

★ Fodor's Choice
★ Highly recommended
⊠ Physical address
✦ Directions
✐ Mailing address
☎ Telephone
🖷 Fax
⊕ On the Web
✎ E-mail
✎ Admission fee
☉ Open/closed times
Ⓜ Metro stations
🚍 Credit cards

Hotels & Restaurants

🏨 Hotel
🛏 Number of rooms
ð Facilities
🍽 Meal plans
✕ Restaurant
🛋 Reservations
↘ Smoking
ﾴ BYOB
✕🏨 Hotel with restaurant that warrants a visit

Outdoors

⛳ Golf
⛺ Camping

Other

☾ Family-friendly
⇨ See also
⊠ Branch address
☞ Take note

Experience Europe

Ia, Santorini, Greece

WORD OF MOUTH

"I always love the moment when the plane is just about to touch down (in Europe!). The trip is planned and the anticipation at maximum level."

—uec1

WHAT'S WHERE

1 Ireland. While isolated at Europe's westernmost extreme, Ireland still holds a powerful allure. Modern **Dublin** has trendy hotels and hipster cafes, but the old stuff is still best—from the ancient pubs to the the Georgian elegance. More classical experiences lies to the south and west, where the **Blarney Stone**, the **Ring of Kerry**, and the **Rock of Cashel** are set in a land of emerald glory. (⇨ Chapter 9.)

2 Great Britain. The island of Great Britain includes three countries—England, Scotland, and Wales—each demonstrating the flexibility of tradition. **London**, one of the world's most exciting cities, is filled with ancient pageantry and contemporary buzz. Many top destinations are within two hours of it, including **Oxford** and **Cambridge**, centuries-old university towns. **Stratford-upon-Avon** is Shakespeare's birthplace; to its south are quintessential villages of the **Cotswolds**. Farther west is **Bath**, rich with Palladian architecture. Four hundred miles north of London, **Edinburgh's** landmarks include a medieval castle and a modern Parliament building. (⇨ Chapter 7.)

3 Scandinavia. The northernmost countries of Europe, collectively known as Scandinavia, share a Viking heritage

and a sturdy disposition. Residents of the main cities are at once urbane and outdoorsy. Given the Viking past, it's no surprise that they have an affinity for water—whether that entails hiking along the Oslofjord south of **Oslo**, guiding a boat through the archipelago of **Stockholm**, or taking a dip from one of **Copenhagen's** quays. (⇨ Chapter 13.)

4 The Netherlands. The Netherlands really is a land of windmills, tulips, and canals, while being a progressive 21st-century nation. The capital, **Amsterdam**, is famous for its waterways and its laid-back atmosphere. **The Hague** is home to the queen and a center for international diplomacy. And **Delft** and **Haarlem** are smaller, character-rich cities. (⇨ Chapter 11.)

5 Belgium. Diminutive Belgium is split between the Flemish-speaking north and French-speaking south. The two most cosmopolitan cities are **Brussels**, the multicultural capital, and **Antwerp**, a bustling port and fashion hotbed. The so-called picture-book towns, **Gent** and **Brugge** haveh a staggering wealth of fine art. (⇨ Chapter 3.)

0	100 mi
0	100 km

Barents Sea

Norwegian Sea

Hammerfest

Zapolyarnyy

Tromsø
Polyarnyy

Harstad

Narvik
Kovdor
Kiruna

Bodø
Kemimärvi

Mo i Rana
Malmberget
Rovaniemi

SWEDEN
Kemi

Pitea
Lulea

Namsos
Skelleftea
Raahe
Oulu

Stenkjaer
Lycksele
FINLAND

Trondheim
Umeå
Kokkola

Kristiansund
Jakobstad

Alesund
Ostersund
Vaasa
Kuopio

NORWAY

SHETLAND
ISLANDS
Sundsvall
Jyvaskyla
Mikkeli

Lerwick
S C A N D I N A V I A
Tampere

Bergen
Gjovik
Bollnäs
Pori
Lappeenranta

3

Haugesund
OSLO
Gavle
Turku
Espoo
HELSINKI

Sauda
Vasteras

Stavanger
Skien
Örebro
TALLINN
Jarve

Aberdeen
Egersund
Arendal
STOCKHOLM
ESTONIA

Mandal
Uddevalla
Linköping
Tartu

Göteborg
Jönköping

North Sea
Thisted
Alborg
Ljungby
LATVIA

DENMARK
RIGA
Balvi

Viborg
Kalmar
Liepaja

Århus
Klaipeda
LITHUANIA

COPENHAGEN
Malmö
Taurage
VILNIUS

Schleswig
Kiel
Gdánsk

NETHERLANDS
4
Rostock
MINSK

THE HAGUE
AMSTERDAM
Hamburg
Szczecin
BELARUS

Dover
Hannover
BERLIN
POLAND

Brugge
Antwerp
Poznań
WARSAW
Brest

Reims
BRUSSELS
GERMANY

BELGIUM
5
Dresden
Wrocław
Lublin
Rivne

LUXEMBOURG
UKRAINE

Metz
LUXEMBOURG
PRAGUE

PARIS
Nancy
Nürnberg
CZECH
Ostrava
Kraków
L'viv

Strasbourg
Stuttgart
Brno
REPUBLIC
SLOVAKIA

WHAT'S WHERE

6 France. A trip to France should include Paris, the City of Light, to see the Eiffel Tower, Notre-Dame, the Louvre, and scores of other treasures. Yet just on the other side of the *Périphérique* is the French countryside, where châteaux—including Versailles—and some of the world's best food and wine await. And thanks to the country's high-speed trains, you can whisk down to Provence or the French Riviera in a little more than three hours. (⇨ *Chapter 5.*)

7 Switzerland. Switzerland packs abundant attractions into a tiny space. Among the cities, Zürich mixes Old World charm with a youthful vibe, while Geneva is wealthy and cosmopolitan, and easy to navigate. But outdoors is where you find Switzerland's scenic masterpieces, such as the lakes, valleys, and peaks of the Berner Oberland region, Matterhorn, and adjacent Zermatt, a fairytale version of an Alpine village. (⇨ *Chapter 15.*)

8 Germany. Bordered by nine countries and two seas, Germany sits at the heart of Europe. Its top cities exemplify the country's diversity: The capital, **Berlin,** is the essence of hip, with cutting-edge art and a "poor but sexy" attitude. In the southeast, **Munich** is famed for its Oktoberfest and beer gardens. To the west are **Frankfurt,** Germany's transportation hub, and **Hamburg,** known for its historic harbor and colorful red-light district. Outside the cities, roads wind past half-timbered towns, hillside vineyards, picturesque castles, and soaring mountains. (⇨ *Chapter 6.*)

9 Austria. It's not a large country, but Austria's landscape is almost as varied as its cultural offerings. To some Austria is synonomous with skiing and hiking in the **Tyrolean Alps.** To others it means the Old World charms of **Vienna**—with its magnificent opera houses, grand art museums, and unmistakable coffee houses. And if you love *The Sound of Music* you won't want to pass up **Salzburg.** (⇨ *Chapter 2.*)

10 The Czech Republic. After years of Communist rule, the Czech Republic is now finishing its second decade beyond the Iron Curtain. The most popular destination is **Prague,** where Gothic splendors, including the Charles Bridge and Prague Castle, are dazzling relics of Europe's past. The castles in southern **Bohemia** and the spa resorts in the west of the region are also rewarding visits. (⇨ *Chapter 4.*)

SCOTLAND

North Sea

Nottingham

LONDON

Dover

Calais

Rouen

PARIS

Orleans

FRANCE 6

Dijon

Lyon

Grenoble

Valence

Nîmes

Avignon

Marseille

Nice

Monte Carlo

MONACO

Mediterranean Sea

CORSICA

Ajaccio

Sassari

Siniscola

Göteborg

Thisted

Jönköping

DENMARK

SWEDEN

Viborg

Arhus

COPENHAGEN

Malmo

Baltic Sea

Schleswig

Kiel

Rostock

Gdánsk

NETHERLANDS

Hamburg

AMSTERDAM

Bremen

Szczecin

THE HAGUE

Hannover

BERLIN

POLAND

Antwerp

GERMANY 8

Poznań

BRUSSELS

Kassel

Łódź

BELGIUM

Liege

Dresden

Wrocław

LUXEMBOURG

LUXEMBOURG

Frankfurt

PRAGUE

Nancy

Nürnberg

CZECH 10

Ostrava

Strasbourg

Stuttgart

REPUBLIC

Rhine

Brno

Munich

Danube

SLOVAKIA

Zurich

LIECHTENSTEIN

Linz

BRATISLAVA

Lausanne

BERN 7

Salzburg

VIENNA

Geneva

SWITZERLAND

Innsbruck

AUSTRIA 9

BUDAPEST

Martigny

Graz

HUNGARY

Novara

ITALY

LJUBLJANA

Turin

Milan

SLOVENIA

ZAGREB

Venice

CROATIA

Genoa

Ravenna

BOSNIA &

Florence

HERZEGOVINA

Pisa

Ancona

SARAJEVO

Perugia

ROME

PODGORICA

0   100 mi

0   100 km

Bari

Meuse

Loire

WHAT'S WHERE

La Baule-Escoublac○ Nantes○ Tours○ Nancy○
La Roche-sur-Yon○ Poitiers○ **FRANCE** Dijon○
A Coruña○ El Ferrol○ La Rochelle○ Limoges○ **BERN**
Bay of Biscay Bordeaux○ Geneva○
Pontevedra○ Oviedo○ Santander○ Bilbao○ Toulouse○ Valence○
Porto○ **ANDORRA** Nîmes○
PORTUGAL Valladolid○ Zaragoza○
Coimbra○ **MONA**
Sintra○ **MADRID** **COR**
LISBON Toledo○ **SPAIN** Barcelona○ Ajac
Badajoz○ Valencia○
Lagos○ Córdoba○ *Mediterranean Sea* SARDINIA
Seville○ Murcia○
Cadiz○ Málaga○ Caglic
GIBRALTAR Tetouan○
RABAT Oran○ **ALGIERS** Annabc
Fez○ Oujda○ Tlemcen○ Skikda○
Meknes○ Sougueur○ M'sila○
Berguent○ Djelfa○ Tebessa○ TU
Kasba Tadla○ Laghouat○
MOROCCO **ALGERIA** TU

11 Portugal. Portugal's long Atlantic coastline means that much of the country's history and culture have been strongly influenced by the sea. The capital, **Lisbon,** is a port city that mixes modernity and mellow age, with graceful old buildings and contemporary high-rises sharing the terrain. A short hop to the northwest is **Sintra,** a town that was a summer home for Portugese royals and aristocrats. The country's second-largest city, **Porto,** is the cultural center of the northern region; it successfully combines a slick commercial hub with a charmingly ramshackle riverfront district. (⇨ *Chapter 12.*)

12 Spain. Spain's largest cities, **Barcelona** and **Madrid,** vie with each other for pre-eminence. Madrid is the lively political and economic capital, with a cosmopolitan surface and a warm Castilian heart, while Barcelona is generally seen as the center of culture and style. Both have fabulous restaurants, famous museums, and their own distinctive charms. Venture farther afield—to postcard lovely **Andalusia,** medieval **Toledo,** or **Bilbao** with its renowned museum—and you'll be struck by how the regions differ, while still sharing the Spanish zest for life. (⇨ *Chapter 14.*)

13 Italy. Italy's distinctive boot shape makes it easy to spot on the map. It's fair to say that no other country in Europe is so packed with cultural and natural treasures. The top draws are three remarkable cities: In the northeast, waterborne **Venice** woos you with its opulent, East-meets-West architecture and its unique canals. Due south, **Florence** is a Renaissance museum come to life, where the works of Michelangelo, Leonardo, and Brunelleschi compete for your attention. Farther south, half-way down the boot, stands **Rome,** one of the world's greatest cities for over 2,000 years. (⇨ *Chapter 13.*)

14 Greece. Framed by the bluer-than-blue Aegean Sea and only about the size of New York State, Greece has a continent's worth of extraordinary sights and timeless landscapes. All roads lead to **Athens,** where the ancient Parthenon stands sentinel over a bustling city. A day-trip away is time-stained **Delphi,** "navel of the world." For a true Grecian escape, however, head to the islands of **Mykonos** and **Santorini**—both were blessed by the gods with natural beauty and the mysteries of forgotten civilizations. (⇨ *Chapter 8.*)

EUROPE PLANNER

When to Go

Most travelers visit Europe in the summer, when school is out and the weather is warm. While summer may be the best time to hit the beach or hike in the mountains, throughout the continent you will be faced with the largest crowds and highest prices of the year.

Summer temperatures can get uncomfortably hot; anywhere south of Scandinavia cities can turn sweltering. On top of that, in August many Europeans go on vacation, meaning that along the Champs Élysées you may encounter more fellow tourists than locals.

Winter provides relative solitude everywhere except at winter resorts, but services may be less readily available, the daylight hours are few in the north, and bad weather can leave you holed up in your hotel, huddling by the radiator or the fire.

If you have the flexibility to choose when you travel, you can't beat late spring and early fall for a happy balance. Crowds and prices are down from the summer highs, and the weather is generally good.

Getting Here by Air

All of the capitals of the countries covered in this guide, and numerous other major cities as well, have daily airline service to and from North America. For details about flying in and out of specific destinations, see the the "Getting Here & Around" sections at the beginning of each country chapter.

If you're planning a trip that will span several countries, consider an "open jaw" flight itinerary, where you arrive in one city and return home from another. For instance, if you want to tour Great Britain, France, and Italy, you could fly into London and depart from Rome. Round-trip fares with major airlines are often comparable to what you'd pay flying in and out of the same airport.

Airport security is generally tighter in Europe than in North America. Upon arrival, you may find the airport patrolled by gun toting security officers and drug-sniffing dogs; on your departure there's a greater chance of being frisked than what you're used to when boarding domestic flights. Despite (or because of) the heightened measures, European airports are very safe.

Getting Around by Air

Flying is often a good option for getting around within Europe, particularly when you want to cover a significant distance (say, for instance, from Madrid to Prague). Discount carriers such as easyJet and Ryan Air have inexpensive one-way fares, but there are a couple of caveats to consider before booking.

First, flights are often to and from secondary airports, which can cause asorted inconveniences. Second, there are usually fees and weight restrictions for baggage—you can end up paying much more for your suitcase than you do for yourself. When booking online, be sure to check the "terms and conditions." Ultimately, flights on major airlines sometimes wind up being comparable in price.

Getting Around by Train

Throughout Europe the primary means of public transportation between cities is the train—the network of railways is much more extensive than what you find in North America. For details about train service in the countries where you're planning to travel, check the "Getting Here & Around" sections at the beginning of each chapter in this book. Here are some general factors to consider when traveling by train:

■ Most trains have two seating classes. The difference between first and second class is often marginal, particularly on short-haul regional trains. In some cases, though, you can only reserve seats in first class, meaning that with a second-class ticket on a full train you may end up standing. The differences in classes are greater on long-haul express trains (such as Eurostars).

■ For longer trips, consider taking an overnight train. A sleeping berth is more expensive than a regular seat, but you save the cost of a night in a hotel.

■ Most national railway systems have discount passes for travelers making multiple trips—see the country chapters for details. Eurail passes, available for travel in all of the countries covered in this book except for Great Britain, can be a good deal if you're planning on lots of train travel. They have to be purchased from home before you travel; for details, see their web site, ⊕www.eurail.com.

Getting Around by Car

Driving conditions and rules of the road vary from country to country, but a good rule of thumb everywhere in Europe is: a car in a city is a liability, whle a car in the countryside is a plus. Because European cities predate automobiles, their streets are usually ill equipped to handle them, resulting in traffic snarls and parking headaches. If you have a car, find a secure parking place for it when you enter a city and leave it there until you depart.

Outside of cities, a car is often the most convenient, and sometimes the only, way to get where you want to go. If you can, plan your itinerary to begin and end with a city, and rent a car only for the period in between.

What to Pack

The oldest advice is still the best: pack light. In summer that means not only keeping your luggage light, but also wearing light clothing, as things can get steamy throughout the continent. But throw in a sweater in case of cool evenings, especially if you're headed for the mountains or the shore. In winter, bring a coat, gloves, hats, scarves, and sturdy shoes. Comfortable walking shoes are important in any season.

As a rule, Europeans dress well. They do not usually wear shorts. Men are seldom required to wear ties or jackets, except in some of the grander hotel dining rooms and top-level restaurants, but are expected to look reasonably sharp—and they do. A certain modesty of dress (no bare shoulders or knees) is expected in many churches, and strictly enforced in some.

If you're traveling with electric appliances (such as laptops or razors), consider making the small investment in a universal adapter, which has several types of plugs. Most laptops and phone chargers are dual voltage (operating equally well on 110 and 220 volts), meaning they require only an adapter, not a converter.

If you have room, consider packing binoculars, which will help you get a good look at painted ceilings and domes. If you're staying in budget hotels, bring your own soap—some places don't provide it.

EUROPE PLANNER

Telephones

Calling from a hotel is almost always the most expensive option; hotels usually add huge surcharges, particularly on international calls. Calling cards usually keep costs to a minimum, and as expensive as mobile phone calls can be, they are still usually a cheaper option than calling from your hotel.

Calling Cards: Prepaid phone cards are available throughout most of Europe. Cards in different denominations are sold at post offices, newsstands, and tobacco shops. There are two types of cards: those for domestic calls made on pay phones; and international cards, which allow you to phone abroad at reasonable rates.

Mobile Phones: A cell phone can be used in Europe if it's triband, quad-band, or GSM. You should ask your cell-phone company if their phone fits in this category, and make sure it is activated for international calling before leaving home. Roaming fees can be steep, however: $1 a minute is considered reasonable. It's almost always cheaper to send a text message than to make a call. If your trip is extensive, you could simply buy a new cell phone in your destination. You can also rent a cell phone from most car-rental agencies.

Keeping Safe

Taking some simple precautions will go a long way toward making sure you have a safe, crime-free trip to Europe. Be alert to the potential of petty theft—purse snatching, pickpocketing, and the like—particularly in larger cities and at major tourist attractions. Use common sense: avoid pulling out a lot of money in public; carry a handbag with long straps that you can wear across your body, with a zippered compartment for your money and passport. Men should keep their wallets up front rather than in a hip pocket.

When withdrawing money from cash machines, be especially aware of your surroundings and anyone standing too close. If you feel uneasy, press the cancel button and walk to an area where you feel more comfortable.

Car break-ins, especially in isolated parking lots, aren't uncommon. Don't leave valuables in your car: take them with you or leave them at your hotel.

Passports

U.S. citizens need only a valid passport to enter Europe for stays of up to six months. Travelers should be prepared to show sufficient funds to support and accommodate themselves (credit cards will usually suffice for this) and to show a return or onward airplane ticket. If you're within six months of your passport's expiration date, renew it before you leave—nearly extinct passports are not strictly banned, but they make immigration officials anxious, and may cause you problems.

Visitor Information

Most countries in Europe have significant tourism resources, and their mission is to serve you. All countries have tourism Web sites and literature they will send you before your trip, but the most valuable resource is usually the Tourist Information Office, which you can find throughout major cities and in most smaller towns. There you can often get maps, tour itineraries, and personalized advice. Look for office addresses and contact information throughout this book.

1

Money Matters

The euro is the accepted currency in the majority of the countries covered in this book. Exceptions are the Czech Republic, Great Britain, Switzerland, and the countries of Scandinavia—for information about money in those places, see the introductions of the corresponding chapters. Euro coins and notes are broken down into denominations similar to U.S. dollars and are easy for North Americans to understand and use. In recent years the value of the euro has fluctuated between $1.25 and $1.65.

It's a good idea to pick up a small amount of your destination's currency before you leave home. Many banks have limited supplies of foreign bills on hand, so you may have to order money a week or so in advance.

ATMs: Once you're in Europe, ATMs are the best way to get cash. Your own bank will probably charge a fee for using ATMs abroad; the foreign bank you use may also charge a fee. Nevertheless, you'll usually get a better rate of exchange at an ATM than you will at a currency-exchange office or even when changing money in a bank. And extracting funds as you need them is a safer option than carrying around a large amount of cash. Make sure before leaving home that your credit and debit cards have been programmed for ATM use abroad—ATMs in Europe usually require PINs of four digits.

Credit Cards: Visa and MasterCard are accepted with about the same prevalence throughout Europe as they are in the United States—some smaller stores, restaurants, and hotels operate only in cash, but they're the exception. American Express is accepted at most larger establishments, but at many smaller ones it's not.

Inform your credit-card company before you travel, especially if you're going abroad and don't travel internationally very often. Otherwise, the credit-card company might put a hold on your card owing to unusual activity. Record all your credit-card numbers in a safe place. There are numbers for both MasterCard (☏636/722-7111) and Visa (☏410/581-9994) you can call (collect if you're abroad) if your card is lost, but you're better off calling the number of your issuing bank, since MasterCard and Visa usually just transfer you to your bank; your bank's number is usually printed on your card.

Note that credit cards usually apply a transaction fee—as much as 3%—for charges made abroad. It can be worth it to shop around for a card with a lower fee.

Breaking the Language Barrier

English has become a second language for many Europeans (except, of course, for those who speak it as a first language). In major cities and significant tourist destinations you won't have a hard time finding locals who speak at least rudimentary English. The farther off the beaten path you travel, the fewer English speakers you'll encounter, but if nothing else someone at your hotel will know a few words.

Learning some common phrases in the native tongue can be useful ("Do you speak English?" being the most important, followed by "Where is the bathroom?"). But keep in mind that if you speak to a German in her native language, you're likely to get a reply back in German—and it will usually be incomprehensible to someone equipped only with a phrase book and good intentions. Hand gestures and simple English phrases (a single word is best) will often achieve your goal. Speaking slowly helps; speaking loudly doesn't.

The barrier can be most frustrating when you're ordering in a restaurant. If you anticipate problems, try asking when you're seated for a waiter who knows English. Another option is to have your waiter suggest what to order. It's an act of faith, but particularly in less touristed areas the waiter is likely to guide you to the whatever the restaurant does best.

TOP EUROPE ATTRACTIONS: LANDMARKS

Schönbrunn Palace, Vienna, Austria
You could spend an entire day here (and still not see all the rooms in the palace), or choose from several shorter tours of one of Austria's premier attractions, the palace built by Empress Maria Theresa. (⇨ *Chapter 2.*)

Grand'Place, Brussels, Belgium
(B) In Brussels's main square the spectacular 15th-century town hall is a stunning example of medieval Flemish architecture, and the surrounding guild houses complement it beautifully. (⇨ *Chapter 3.*)

Eiffel Tower, Paris, France
(A) There's no monument that better symbolizes Paris than Gustav Eiffel's Iron Lady. It's breathtaking whether you see it from afar or take the ride to the top in the glass-bottomed elevator. (⇨ *Chapter 5.*)

Mont-St-Michel, Normandy, France
(F) From its silhouette against the horizon to its magnificent church, you'll never forget this awe-inspiring abbey, the crowning glory of medieval France. (⇨ Chapter 5.)

Neuschwanstein Castle, The Romantic Road, Germany
(H) Walt Disney modeled the castle in *Sleeping Beauty* and later the Disneyland castle itself on Neuschwanstein. "Mad" King Ludwig II's creation is best admired from the heights of the Marienbrücke, a delicate-looking bridge over a deep, narrow gorge. (⇨ *Chapter 6.*)

Tower of London, Great Britain
(G) This extraordinary minicity of 20 towers has been the scene of much blood and gore since the 11th century. The Yeoman Wardens, known as Beefeaters, give magnificent tours. All this, and the Crown Jewels are here, too. (⇨ Chapter 7.)

Acropolis, Athens, Greece

(E) The great emblem of classical Greece has loomed above Athens for 2,500 years. Even from afar, the sight of the Parthenon—the great marble temple that crowns the site—stirs strong feelings about the achievements and failings of Western Civilization. (⇨ *Chapter 8.*)

The Colosseum, Rome, Italy

(D) One of the seven wonders of the world, this mammoth amphitheater was begun by Emperor Vespasian and inaugurated by Titus in the year 80. For "the grandeur that was Rome," it can't be topped. (⇨ *Chapter 10.*)

Duomo, Florence, Italy

The massive dome of Florence's Cathedral of Santa Maria del Fiore (aka the Duomo) is one of the world's great feats of engineering. (⇨ *Chapter 10.*)

La Sagrada Familia, Barcelona, Spain

(C) *The* symbol of Barcelona, Gaudí's extraordinary unfinished cathedral should be included on everyone's must-see list. The pointed spires, with organic shapes that resemble a honeycombed stalagmite, give the whole city a fairy-tale quality. (⇨ *Chapter 14.*)

Alhambra, Granada, Spain

Nothing can prepare you for the Moorish grandeur of Andalusia's greatest monument. The ornamental palace is set around sumptuous courtyards and gardens complete with bubbling fountains, magnificent statues, and brilliantly colored flower beds. (⇨ *Chapter 14.*)

TOP EUROPE ATTRACTIONS: MUSEUMS & ART

Louvre, Paris, France

(F) France's grandest museum was a royal palace until the French Revolution, when it was transformed into the home for the young Republic's art collection. The Big Three—*Mona Lisa, Winged Victory,* and *Venus de Milo*—should not be misssed (⇨ *Chapter 5.*)

Museum Island, Berlin, Germany

(D) Germany's capital has over 150 museums, but this spot should be your first stop. It holds five state museums with world-class collections ranging fromclassical antiquities to 20th century paintings and sculpture. (⇨ *Chapter 6.*)

British Museum, London, Great Britain

(C) The self-appointed protector of treasures from around the globe, this vast museum is packed to bursting with antiquities and alluring objects. Among the greatest hits are the Parthenon Mar-

bles, the Rosetta Stone, and Egyptian mummies. (⇨ *Chapter 7.*)

Book of Kells, Trinity College, Dublin, Ireland

(A) Often called "the most beautiful book in the world," this manuscript dating to the 8th or 9th century is a marvel of intricacy and creativity, executed by monks working with reed pens. (⇨ *Chapter 9.*)

Vatican Museums, Rome, Italy

(B) The lines waiting for entry here can be intimidating, but the reward—a vast collection of masterpieces, highlighted by the Sistine Chapel—makes it well worth the wait. (⇨ *Chapter 10.*)

Galleria degli Uffizi, Florence, Italy

The Uffizi—Renaissance art's hall of fame—contains masterpieces by Leonardo, Michelangelo, Raphael, Botticelli, Caravaggio, and dozens of other luminaries. (⇨ *Chapter 10.*)

Rijksmuseum, Amsterdam, The Netherlands

(H) This is the place to go when you're looking for Dutch masters, including Rembrandt, Vermeer, Hals, and a slew of others. (⇨ *Chapter 11*.)

Museu Calouste Gulbenkian, Lisbon, Portugal

(G) The collection here—one part devoted to Egyptian, Greek, Roman, Islamic, and Asian art, the other to European— isn't large, but the quality is high. Add a stroll through the sculpture garden, and you have a great museum experience. (⇨ *Chapter 12*.)

The Nationalmuseet, Copenhagen, Denmark

Immerse yourself in the Viking exhibits here; one shows how the Vikings could navigate their ships across vast oceans at a time when most people believed the world was flat. (⇨ *Chapter 13*.)

Guggenheim Museum, Bilbao, Spain

(E) All swooping curves and rippling forms, this architecturally innovative museum was built on the site of the city's former shipyards and inspired by the shape of a ship's hull. The collection is pretty good as well, including such masters as Picasso and Miró. (⇨ *Chapter 14*.)

Museo del Prado, Madrid, Spain

Set in a magnificent neoclassical building on one of the capital's most elegant boulevards, the Prado is Spain's answer to the Louvre and a regal home to renowned Spanish masterpieces. Much of the collection dates back to the museum's inauguration in 1819. (⇨ *Chapter 14*.)

TOP EUROPE ATTRACTIONS: PICTURESQUE TOWNS

Brugge, Belgium

(F) Known as the "Venice of the North," Brugge is one of the most beautiful small cities in Europe. Strolling through the maze of winding, cobbled alleys, alongside the winding canals and over the romantic bridges, it's easy to see why UNESCO included the entire medieval city center on its World Heritage list. (⇨ *Chapter 3.*)

Èze, the Riviera, France

(E) The most perfectly perched of the French Riviera's *villages perchés,* Èze has some of the most breathtaking views this side of a NASA space capsule. (⇨ *Chapter 5.*)

Rothenburg-ob-der-Tauber, The Romantic Road, Germany

(D) Germany's classic medieval town seems almost too perfect to be true, with its towers, fountains, half-timber architecture, and explosions of flowers. An economic downturn resulting from the 30 Years' War had the beneficial effect of preserving the town in time. (⇨ *Chapter 6.*)

Bath, Great Britain

(C) Exquisitely preserved but entertaining, this Georgian town still centers around the hot mineral springs that made it *the* fashionable spa for the wealthy in the 18th and early 19th centuries. Streets lined with Palladian buildings made of golden limestone, an ancient abbey, tea shops, boutiques, and ruined Roman baths combine to give Bath real character. (⇨ *Chapter 7.*)

Mykonos Town, Greece

(H) Backbackers and jet-setters alike share the beautiful beaches and the Dionysian nightlife, but the old ways of life continue undisturbed along mazelike streets of Mykonos Town. Not only are the hotels and cafés picture-perfect, the famous windmills actually seem to be posing for your camera. (⇨ *Chapter 8.*)

Lucca, Tuscany, Italy
(B) This laid-back yet elegant town is sur-rounded by tree-bedecked 16th-century ramparts that are now a delightful prom-enade. With limited automobile traffic within the city walls, it's an ideal place for getting around by bike. (⇨ *Chapter 10.*)

Delft, The Netherlands
(A) Holland's most attractive town feels like a tiny Amsterdam, with canals, cob-blestone streets, and the air of a simpler time. You can recognize the quiet atmo-sphere that pervades many of the paintings by Delft's most famous citizen, Johannes Vermeer. (⇨ *Chapter 11.*)

Sintra, Portugal
"A glorious Eden" is how Lord Byron described Sintra, a town west of Lisbon that served as a retreat for Portugese roy-alty. It's a magical place studded with magnificent palaces, gardens, and luxury *quintas* (manor houses). UNESCO has deemed the entire town a Word Heritage Site in recognition of its splendid architec-ture. (⇨ Chapter 12.)

Mürren, Berner Oberland, Switzerland
A Noah's Ark village pasted 5,400 feet up a mountainside, Mürren offers a so-close-you-can-touch-it vista of the Jung-frau and the Eiger. This was the birthplace of downhill and slalom skiing, and it remains a great place to hit the slopes. (⇨ *Chapter 15.*)

TOP EUROPE ATTRACTIONS: GETTING OUTDOORS

Charles Bridge, Prague, The Czech Republic

(F) Prague's greatest landmark is as much a town square as a bridge—people meet and hang out here at all hours. It's also the optimum place for spectacular views of the city, particularly at night, when the foot traffic diminishes and the surrounding monuments are bathed in colored light. (⇨ Chapter 4.)

Jardin du Luxembourg, Paris, France

(E) This is one of Paris's prime leisure spots. Relax in a reclining park chair with a picnic lunch or a book and watch a game of *boules* while the kids enjoy a marionette show. (⇨ Chapter 5.)

Giverny, Ile-de-France, France

(G) Replacing paint and canvas with earth and water, Claude Monet transformed his 5-acre garden into a veritable live-in Impressionist painting. Come to Giverny to see his lily pond—itself a half-acre "Monet"—then peek around his charming home and stroll the time-warped streets to the ultrastylish American Art Museum. (⇨ Chapter 5.)

Hills & Villages of the Cotswolds, Great Britain

(C) Marked by soft rolling hills, vivid green fields, and small limestone cottages with prim flower beds, the Cotswolds, 100 mi west of London, make a peaceful getaway. There's little to do in the idyllic villages except to stroll and pile more clotted cream on your scone, but that's the point. Gardens and stately homes add to the charm. (⇨ Chapter 7.)

Santorini, Greece

One of the world's most picturesque islands cradles the sunken caldera of a volcano that last erupted around 1600 BC. To merely link the phenomenon to the Atlantis myth and the Minoan collapse misses the point—what matters is the ravishing

sight of the multicolor cliffs rising 1,100 feet out of sparkling blue waters, a visual treat that makes the heart skip a beat or two. (⇨ *Chapter 8.*)

Ring of Kerry, Western Ireland

(D) This route around the Iveraugh Peninsula is one of Europe's great drives, with gorgeous views of classic Irish coastline. Get off the main road and you'll find fabulous places to hike, bike, and boat. An excursion out to the Skellig rocks is an unforgettable adventure. (⇨ *Chapter 9.*)

Bulb Fields, Southern Netherlands

(A) In spring the fields stretching from Leiden to Haarlem are awash in color, filled with millions of blooming tulips and other flowers. You can tour the region by car or bike. However you go, you'll want to make a stop in the town of Lisse at Keukenhof, the largest flower garden on earth, with roots—in terms of legacy—that date back to the 15th century. (⇨ *Chapter 11.*)

Tivoli Gardens, Copenhagen, Denmark

(B) Copenhagen's top attraction is an amusement park, and much more. There are gardens with glorious flowers, ponds, concerts, theater, and over 30 restaurants. Visit twice—once during the day, once at night. (⇨ *Chapter 13.*)

The Matterhorn, Switzerland

(H) From the summit station of Gernergrat, this snaggle-toothed mountain steals the thunder from all the surrounding Alpine peaks. In the valley below, Zermatt is one of Switzerland's most appealing resort towns. (⇨ *Chapter 15.*)

TOP EXPERIENCES

With its sophisticated culture, rich history, and abundant beauty (both natural and man-made), Europe offers satisfying experiences for every type of traveler — your greatest challenge is narrowing down your choices from among so many options.

Looking over the categories below can help bring focus to your trip; you can also get a sense of which countries are best for which experiences by reading the "Top Reasons to Go" sections at the beginning of each chapter.

Stepping Back in Time

When you travel to Europe, it can feel as though you're entering a time machine — history stretches back for thousands of years, and its remnants are found everywhere.

For Europeans, 1776 seems like yesterday. They think nothing of living in 500-year-old houses, strolling along thousand-year-old streets, and passing between columns where Aristotle and Julius Caesar once roamed.

Many of Europe's historic structures were built to impress; there's no book learning required to feel a sense of awe when you enter the Alhambra in Granada or St. Peter's Basilica in Rome. Nonetheless, a little knowledge goes a long way. The descriptions found in this book will give you an overview of each sight's essential facts and historical highlights.

The amount of further study you can do is nearly limitless. Some travelers enjoy zeroing in on one particular sight from their itinerary, researching it in depth before they leave home, then dedicating a day (or more) to exploring their chosen destination. If research isn't your thing, you might instead try hiring a tour guide

— a good one can bring a pile of ancient stones to life.

Drinking Up

In much of Europe you'll find wonderful wine: France, Italy, and Spain are top producers, in terms of both quality and quantity. You don't have to be a connoisseur or a big spender to enjoy a good bottle. The first rule of thumb is to drink what's made locally. Whether you're in Chianti or Bordeaux, there's nothing quite like sipping a wine produced from the surrounding vineyards.

It's a fortunate phenomenon that the places in Europe not known for their wine often make great beer. Belgium, Holland, Denmark, England, Ireland, the Czech Republic, and Germany (no slouch in the wine department itself) all turn out exceptional brews, from crisp pilsners to sturdy stouts. Whether it's beer or wine, Europe has set the standard for the rest of the world.

Hiking, Biking & Driving

Europe's greatest treasures aren't all found in museums and palaces. Natural beauty is abundant and diverse, from the soaring peaks of the Swiss Alps to the craggy shores of Ireland's Ring of Kerry. And on the whole, getting out into nature is easier in Europe than anywhere else in the world.

Hiking trails are everywhere, and they're usually maintained with care. Exploring by car curtails your access to a degree, but you can still wind through forests and scale mountains on Europe's excellent network of roads and highways.

Bicycling is a popular way to tour both town and country. You can rent bikes by the hour, the day, or the week, either going

it alone or joining organized excursions. Europeans' enthusiasm for cycling means that bikers' rights are respected — drivers know how to share the road.

Getting Your Caffeine Fix
Having a cup of coffee in Europe can be a cultural adventure. In Viennese coffeehouses, arguably the most renowned on the continent, patrons linger through the afternoon over a whipped-cream-topped cup and a decadent pastry. Parisian cafés are communal living rooms, where customers exchange ideas, share gossip, and people-watch. In Italy most coffee-bar patrons sip their espresso standing at the counter and after a minute or two are on their way.

The English, meanwhile, are legendary tea-drinkers; for some afternoon tea, accompanied by scones, biscuits, cakes, and sandwiches, serves as the fourth meal of the day.

From Greece to Sweden, every country has its own coffee- or tea- drinking rituals that have been refined over centuries. Joining in is easy and (with a few luxe exceptions) inexpensive.

Hitting the Beach
With so much to see and do in the Europe, you stand the risk of running yourself ragged. Scheduling some time at the beach can be a great "vacation from your vacation."

In the height of summer, locals head to stretches of sand all along Europe's coasts (there's even beach-going in Ireland), but for a truly exceptional experience, set your sights on the Greek islands or the French Riviera. The sand and sea are gorgeous, and if you want it you can find glamour

and sophistication unlike any other beach destinations in the world.

Going Slow
The Slow Food movement was initiated in the 1980s to oppose the opening of a McDonald's restaurant in Rome's historic Piazza di Spagna area. Though it failed to prevent the opening—today the McDonald's is one of the busiest in Europe—the movement sparked a flourishing "Slow" phenomenon, with the central goal of preserving tradition and pushing back against the forces of mass-production and cultural homogenization.

Today the organization Slow Food has more than 80,000 members scattered around the world and an increasingly famous logo featuring the stylized image of a snail. It has also sparked a minor mania for all things slow; in your travels you may well encounter Slow Cities, Slow Design, and Slow Companies.

In every case, "slow" is synonymous attention to detail and adherence to tradition, and fortunately it's a concept that's still second nature to many Europeans, regardless of whether they're consciously taking part in a movement. You can encounter it almost anywhere — from a French meal that took hours to prepare, to a medieval cathedral that took centuries to build.

Austria

Opera ball, Vienna

WORD OF MOUTH

"We walked through [Vienna's] Hofburg complex, admiring the architecture, and bought tickets for the Schatzkammer (Imperial Treasury). The visit inside was well worth it. Excellent collection of cloaks and dresses of kings of a bygone era. The jewels were jaw-dropping: a 2680 carat emerald, a 450 carat aquamarine! . . . Then we walked to Hotel Sacher to have their famed Sacher Torte. It looked as beautiful as it tasted. Delicious."

—indiancouple

WHAT'S WHERE

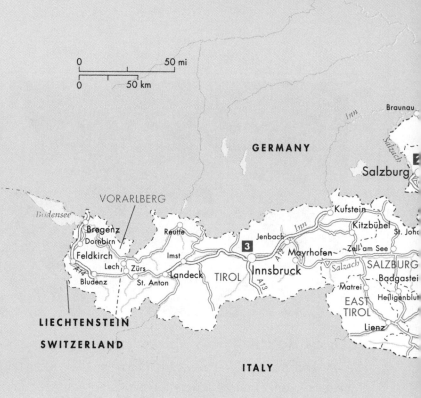

1 Vienna. In the country's northeast corner, Vienna intriguingly mixes Old World charm with elements of a modern metropolis. The city's neighborhoods offer a journey thick with history and architecture, peopled by the spirits of Empress Maria Theresa, Haydn, Beethoven, Mozart, and Klimt—but there is also space and renown for antitraditional structures like Friedensreich Hundertwasser's modernist Hundertwasserhaus. The famous coffeehouses are havens for the age-old coffee-drinking ritual.

2 Salzburg. Depending on who is describing this elegant city filled with gilded salons, palatial mansions, and Italianate churches, Salzburg is alternately known as the "Golden City of the High Baroque," the "Austrian Rome," or, thanks to its position astride the River

CZECH REPUBLIC

SLOVAKIA

Waidhofen

Gmünd

Horn

Zwettl

Poysdorf

LOWER AUSTRIA (NIEDERÖSTERREICH)

Freistadt

Krems

Schärding

Stockerau

Linz

Eferding

Melk

St. Pölten

Vienna

Enns

Danube (Donau)

A1

A21

Danube

Ried

Wels

Mödling

Hainburg

Baden

UPPER AUSTRIA (OBERÖSTERREICH)

Steyr

Scheibbs

Bruck

Neusiedler See

Vöcklabruck

Wiener Neustadt

Gmunden

Mariazell

Neunkirchen

Eisenstadt

St. Wolfgang

Enns

Bad Ischl

Bad Aussee

Enns

Mürzzuschlag

Kapfenberg

BURGENLAND

Bischofshofen

Liezen

Leoben

Bruck a. d. Mur

Radstadt

Hartberg

A10

Knittelfeld

STYRIA (STEIERMARK)

A2

Mur

Judenburg

Graz

Fürstenfeld

Feldbach

CARINTHIA (KÄRNTEN)

A2

Bad Gleichenberg

HUNGARY

Spittal

Bad Radkersburg

Feldkirchen

St. Veit

Drau

A2

Mura

Villach

Klagenfurt

Drava

SLOVENIA

Salzach, the "Florence of the North." What you choose to call this beloved city will depend on what brings you here, whether it be music, museums and architecture, the Trapp family, or simply the old-fashioned cafés, narrow medieval streets, and glorious fountains.

3 Innsbruck. The Tirol province is so different from the rest of Austria that you might think you've crossed a border, and in a way you have. The frontier between Salzburg and Tirol is defined by mountains; four passes routed over them are what make traffic possible. This is also where you'll find the historic city Innsbruck: it's the Tirol's treasure house—historically, culturally, and commercially.

A "BLAST FROM THE PAST" is how one recent visitor described her journey through Austria. It remains, she explained, a place where children laugh at marionette shows in the parks, couples linger for hours over pastries at gilt-ceiling cafés, and Lipizzan stallions dance to Mozart minuets—in other words, Austria is a country that has not forgotten the elegance of a time gone by.

In a way, this is true—but look beyond the postcard clichés of dancing white horses, the Vienna Boys Choir, and *The Sound of Music,* and you'll find a conservative-mannered yet modern country, one of Europe's richest, in which the juxtaposition of old and new often creates excitement. Vienna has its sumptuous palaces, but it is also home to an assemblage of UN organizations housed in a wholly modern complex. Salzburg may be known for its High Baroque architecture, but it also showcases avant-garde art in its Museum de Moderne. By no means is the country frozen in a time warp: rather, it is the contrast between the old and the new that makes Austria such a fascinating place to visit.

Where should you start? There's no question, really. Vienna's spectacular historical and artistic heritage—exemplified by the legacies of Beethoven, Freud, Klimt, and Mahler—remains to lure travelers. A fascinating mélange of Apfelstrudel and psychoanalysis, Schubert and sausages, Vienna possesses a definite Old World charm that natives would be the last to underplay. The sights here are not just the best in Austria, they're some of the most impressive in Europe. The grand Kunsthistorisches Museum holds one of the greatest art collections anywhere. The Staatsoper is one of the continent's finest opera houses. Schönbrunn Palace is indicative of the glories of Imperial Austria.

But as with most countries, the capital is only a small part of what Austria has to offer. A grand tour of the country reveals considerably more faces of Austria than the nine provinces would suggest. And no tour of Austria is complete without a visit to Salzburg, home every summer to one of the world's ritziest music festivals. As far as architecture goes, Salzburg's many fine buildings blend into a harmonious whole. Perhaps nowhere else in the world is there so cohesive a flowering of Baroque splendor. You've seen many of these sights in *The Sound of Music,* but they are even more beautiful in person. Make sure, however, not to miss world-class art collections such as the Salzburg Museum.

As the hub of the Alps, Innsbruck beckons skiers to explore the resorts of Lech, St. Anton, and Kitzbuhel. The charming Old World aspect of Innsbruck has remained virtually intact, and includes ample evidence of its Baroque lineage. The skyline encircling the center suffers somewhat from high-rises, but the heart—the **Altstadt,** or Old City— remains much as it was 400 years ago. The protective vaulted arcades along main thoroughfares, the tiny passageways giving way to noble squares, and the ornate restored houses all contribute to an unforgettable picture.

TOP REASONS TO GO

World of Music. Feel the spirit of 1,300 years of musical history as you listen to the music of Wolfgang Amadeus Mozart, the greatest composer who ever lived, in Salzberg's Mirabell Palace. Or delight your eyes and ears with a night out at Vienna's Staatsoper or Musikverein to experience what secured it the title "heart of the music world."

Ride the Ringstrasse. Hop on streetcar No. 1 or No. 2 and travel full circle along Vienna's best-known avenue. Those monumental buildings along it reflect the imperial splendor of yesteryear.

Kunsthistorisches Museum. In Vienna, enjoy the classic collection of fine art, including the best of Brueghel, Titian, Rembrandt, and Rubens, at Austria's leading museum.

Schönbrunn Palace. Rococo romantics and Habsburg acolytes should step back in time and spend a half day experiencing the Habsburgs' former summer home in Vienna.

An extended coffee break. Savor the true flavor of Vienna at some of its great café landmarks. Every afternoon around 4 the coffee-and-pastry ritual of *Kaffeejause* takes place from one end of the city to the other. For historical overtones, head for the Café Central, the opulent Café Landtmann, or elegant Café Sacher.

The view from Fortress Hohensalzburg: Go up to the fortress on the peak and see what visitors to Salzberg enjoy so much—the soul-stirring combination of gorgeous architecture in a stunning natural location.

Medieval city: After exploring the Salzberg's grand churches and squares, cross the river Salzach to take in the completely different atmosphere of the narrow, 16th-century Steingasse, where working people once lived and shops, galleries, and clubs now beckon.

Inviting Innsbruck. A city that preserves the charm of ancient times, Innsbruck has everything to offer: interesting culture, stellar restaurants, and trendy nightclubs.

WHEN TO GO

Austria has two main tourist times: spring and early fall. The weather usually turns glorious around Easter and holds until about mid-October, sometimes later. Because much of the country remains "undiscovered," you'll usually find crowds only in the major cities and resorts. May and early June, September, and October are the most pleasant months for travel, when there is less demand for restaurant tables, and hotel prices tend to be lower. A foreign invasion takes place between Christmas and New Year's Day and over the long Easter weekend, and hotel rooms in Vienna are then at a premium.

Austria has four distinct seasons, all fairly mild. But because of altitudes and the Alpine divide, temperatures and dampness vary considerably from one part of the country to another; for example, northern Austria's winter is often overcast and dreary, while the southern half of the country basks in sunshine. The eastern part of the country, especially Vienna and the areas near the Czech border, can become bitterly cold in winter. The *Föhn* is a wind that makes the country as a whole go haywire. It comes from the south, is warm, and announces itself by clear air, blue skies, and long wisps of cloud. Whatever the reason, the Alpine people (all the way to Vienna) begin acting up; some become obnoxiously aggressive, others depressive, many people have headaches, and (allegedly) accident rates rise. The Föhn breaks with clouds and rain.

GETTING HERE & AROUND

BY AIR

Austria's major air gateway is Vienna's **Schwechat Airport**. **Salzburg Airport** is Austria's second-largest airport. Two other airports you might consider, depending on where in Austria you intend to travel, are Bratislava's **M.R. Stefanik** international airport in neighboring Slovakia, and **Munich's airport**, not far from Salzburg. Bratislava is about 60 km (36 mi) east of Vienna and is the hub for RyanAir and Sky Europe, two budget carriers with connections to several European cities. Frequent buses take you from Bratislava airport to Vienna in an hour. Consider Munich if your destination is Salzburg or Innsbruck.

BY BUS

Austria has an extensive national network of buses run by the national postal and railroad services. Where Austrian trains don't go, buses do, and you'll find the railroad and post-office buses (bright yellow for easy recognition) in even remote regions carrying passengers as well as mail. You can get tickets on the bus, and in the off-season there is no problem getting a seat; on routes to favored ski areas, though, reservations are essential during holiday periods. Bookings can be handled at the ticket office (there's one in most towns with bus service) or by travel agents. In most communities bus routes begin and end at or near the railroad station, making transfers easy. Increasingly, coordination of bus service with railroads means that many of the discounts and special tickets available for trains apply to buses as well. Buses in Austria run like clockwork, typically departing and arriving on time.

BY CAR

If your plans are to see Vienna and one or two other urban destinations, you're better off saving yourself the hassles and added expense of driving, and take the train. Bear in mind the bumper-to-bumper traffic on most of the roads connecting the major cities and the constant headache of finding a place to park. But if your plan is a more leisurely tour of the country, including back roads and off-the-beaten-track destinations, then car rental is certainly an option. You'll have more freedom and be able to reach places where public transportation is scarce. Roads in Austria are excellent and well maintained—perhaps too well maintained, judging by the frequently encountered construction zones on the autobahns. Secondary roads may be narrow and winding.

BY TRAIN

Austrian train service is excellent: it's fast and, for Western Europe, relatively inexpensive, particularly if you take advantage of discount fares. Austrian Federal Railways trains are identifiable by the letters that precede the train number on the timetables and posters. The IC (InterCity) or EC (EuroCity) trains are fastest. The difference between *erste Klasse* (first class), and *zweite Klasse* (second class) on Austrian trains is mainly a matter of space. Women traveling alone may book special compartments on night trains or long-distance rides (ask for a *Damenabteil*).

ABOUT THE RESTAURANTS

When dining out, you'll get the best value at simpler restaurants. Most post menus with prices outside. If you begin with the *Würstelstand* (sausage vendor) on the street, the next category would be the *Imbiss-Stube,* for simple, quick snacks. Many meat stores serve soups and a daily special at noon; a blackboard menu will be posted outside. A number of cafés also offer lunch, but watch the prices; some can turn out to be more expensive than restaurants. *Gasthäuser* are simple restaurants or country inns. Austrian hotels have some of the best restaurants in the country, often with outstanding chefs. With migration from Turkey and Northern Africa on the rise, thousands of small kebab restaurants have set up shop all over Austria, offering both Middle Eastern fare and sometimes pizza at a reasonable rate.

Austrians are manic about food quality and using agricultural techniques that are in harmony with the environment. The country has the largest number of organic farms in Europe, as well as some of the most stringent food-quality standards. An increasing number of restaurants use food and produce from local farmers, ensuring the freshest ingredients for their guests.

MEALS & MEALTIMES
Besides the normal three meals—*Frühstück* (breakfast), *Mittagessen* (lunch), and *Abendessen* (dinner)—Austrians sometimes throw in a few snacks in between, or forego a meal for a snack. The typical day begins with an early continental breakfast of rolls and coffee. *Gabelfrühstück,* normally served a little later in the morning, is a slightly more substantial breakfast with eggs or cold meat. A main meal is usually served between noon and 2, and an afternoon *Jause* (coffee with cake) is taken at teatime. Unless you are dining out, a light supper ends the day, usually between 6 and 9, but tending toward the later hour. Many restaurant kitchens close in the afternoon, but some post a notice saying *durchgehend warme Küche,* meaning that hot food is available even between regular mealtimes. In Vienna some restaurants go on serving until 1 and 2 AM, a tiny number also through the night. The rest of Austria is more conservative.

WINES, BEER & SPIRITS
Austrian wines range from unpretentious *Heurigen* whites to world-class varietals. Look for the light, fruity white *Grüner Veltliner*, intensely fragrant golden *Traminer*, full-bodied red *Blaufränkisch*, and the lighter red *Zweigelt*. Sparkling wine is called *Sekt*, some of the best coming from the Kamptal region northwest of Vienna. Some of the best sweet

dessert wines in the world (*Spätlesen*) come from Burgenland. Austrian beer rivals that of Germany for quality. Each area has its own brewery and local beer that people are loyal to. A specialty unique to Austria is the dark, sweet Dunkles beer. Look for Kaiser Doppelmalz in Vienna. Schnapps is an after-dinner tradition in Austria; many restaurants offer several varieties to choose from.

WHAT IT COSTS IN EUROS				
¢	$	$$	$$$	$$$$
Restaurants in Vienna & Salzburg	Under €7	€7–€12	€13–€17	€18–€22	over €22
¢	$	$$	$$$	$$$$
Restaurants in Innsbruck	Under €7	€7–€12	€13–€17	€18–€22	over €22

Prices are per person for a main course at dinner.

ABOUT THE HOTELS

You can live like a king in a real castle in Austria or get by on a modest budget. Starting at the lower end, you can find a room in a private house or on a farm, or dormitory space in a youth hostel. Next up the line come the simpler pensions, many of them identified as a *Frühstück-spensionen* (bed-and-breakfasts). Then come *Gasthäuser,* the simpler country inns. Fancier pensions in cities can often cost as much as hotels; the difference lies in the services they offer. Most pensions, for example, do not staff the front desk around the clock. Among the hotels you can find accommodations ranging from the most modest, with a shower and toilet down the hall, to the most elegant, with every possible amenity. Increasingly, more and more hotels in the lower to middle price range include breakfast with the basic room charge, but check when booking. Room rates for hotels in the rural countryside often include breakfast and one other meal (in rare cases, all three meals are included).

Lodgings in Austria are generally rated from one to five stars, depending mainly on the facilities offered and the price of accommodation rather than on more subjective attributes like charm and location. In general, five-star properties are top of the line, with every conceivable amenity, and priced accordingly. The distinctions get blurrier the farther down the rating chain you go. There may be little difference between a two- and three-star property except perhaps the price, so we recommend not relying too heavily on the star system, and always trying to see the hotel and room before you book. That said, lodging standards are generally very good, and even in one- and two-star properties you can usually be guaranteed a clean room and a private bath.

These German words might come in handy when booking a room: air-conditioning (*Klimaanlage*); private bath (*Privatbad*); bathtub (*Badewanne*); shower (*Dusche*); double bed (*Doppelbett*); twin beds (*Einzelbetten*).

WHAT IT COSTS IN EUROS				
¢	$	$$	$$$	$$$$
Hotels in Vienna & Salzburg	Under €80	€80–€120	€120–€170	€170–€270	over €270
¢	$	$$	$$$	$$$$
Hotels in Innsbruck	Under €70	€70–€100	€101–€135	€136–€175	over €175

Prices are for two people in a standard double room in high season, including taxes and service. Assume that hotels operate on the European Plan (EP, with no meals provided) unless we note that they use the Breakfast Plan (BP).

PLANNING YOUR TIME

If you're picking just one place in Austria to visit, there's no question that it should be Vienna. Austria's vibrant capital city has more than enough to captivate you for a week or more, but train service is so good here that you can take quick jaunts to almost anywhere else in the country with ease. On the other hand, if you're just looking to add a taste of Austria to a European adventure, you might find Vienna to be a little out of the way; if you happen to be in southern Germany, Salzburg makes a convenient side trip from Munich. (Many people use that city's airport when they are headed to Salzburg.) From Switzerland and Italy, Innsbruck can be a great excursion.

VIENNA

One of the great capitals of Europe, Vienna was for centuries the main stamping grounds for the Habsburg rulers of the Austro-Hungarian Empire. The empire is long gone, but many reminders of the city's imperial heyday remain, carefully preserved by the tradition-loving Viennese. When it comes to the arts, the glories of the past are particularly evergreen, thanks to the cultural legacy created by the many artistic geniuses nourished here.

PLANNING YOUR TIME

Culturally, high season in Vienna is May, June, and September, when festivals, marathons, concerts, and operas are in full swing. The ball season December to February offers everyone a chance to brush up on his or her footwork, and the many Christmas markets attract crowds from all over the world.

GETTING HERE & AROUND
BY AIR

Vienna's airport is at Schwechat, about 19 km (12 mi) southeast of the city. The fastest way into Vienna from Schwechat Airport is the double-decker City Airport Train. From the airport to the center of the city takes only 16 minutes and costs €8. The cheapest way to get into town from the airport is the S7 train, called the Schnellbahn, which takes about 35 minutes and costs €3.40. Another cheap option is the bus, which whisks you downtown for €6. A taxi to the city center will charge between €33 and €37.

BY BUS

International long-distance bus services arrive either at the Südbahnhof (south railway station) on the Gürtel or at the large Erdbergstrasse bus station. Most postal (local) and railroad buses arrive at either a railway station or the Wien Mitte-Landstrasse Bahnhof located behind the Hotel Hilton on Stadtpark.

BY CAR

On highways from points south or west or from Vienna's airport, ZENTRUM signs clearly mark the route to the center of Vienna. Traffic congestion within Vienna is not as bad as in some places, but driving to in-town destinations generally takes longer than public transportation does. In the city a car is a burden. Public transportation is always the better bet in the city—it's clean, reliable, and easy to use.

BY PUBLIC TRANSIT

Vienna's public transportation system is fast, clean, safe, and easy to use. Five subway (*U-Bahn*) lines, whose stations are prominently marked with blue U signs, crisscross the city. The most famous tram lines are No. 1, which travels the great Ringstrasse avenue clockwise, and No. 2, which travels it counterclockwise; each offers a cheap way to admire the glories of Vienna's 19th-century Ringstrasse monuments. Where streetcars don't run, buses—*Autobusse*—do. Buy single tickets for €2.20 from dispensers on the streetcar or bus; you'll need exact change for the former. The ticket machines (labeled *VOR-Fahrkarten*) at subway stations give change. As with most transport systems in European cities, it is essential to validate your ticket. You'll find the validation machines on all buses, trams, and at the entrance of each U-Bahn station.

BY TRAIN

Trains from Germany, Switzerland, and western Austria arrive at the Westbahnhof (West Station), on Europaplatz, where Mariahilferstrasse crosses the Gürtel. If you're coming from Italy or Hungary, you'll generally arrive at the Südbahnhof (South Station). There are currently two stations for trains to and from Prague and Warsaw: Wien Nord (North Station) and Franz-Josef Bahnhof.

TOURS

When you're pressed for time, a good way to see the highlights of Vienna is via a sightseeing bus tour, which gives you a once-over-lightly of the heart of the city and allows a closer look at Schönbrunn and Belvedere palaces. You can cover almost the same territory on your own by taking either streetcar 1 or 2 around the Ring and then walking through the heart of the city. For tours, there are a couple of reputable firms: Vienna Sightseeing Tours and Cityrama Sightseeing.

ESSENTIALS

Airport Contacts Schwechat Airport (*VIE* ☎ *01/7007-0 for flight information* ⊕ *www.viennaairport.com*).

Bus Contacts **Bus Station** (✉ *Erdbergstrasse 200A*).

Public Transporation Contacts Vorverkaufsstellen der Wiener Linien (☎ *7909/105* ⊕ *www.wienerlinien.at*).

Train Contacts Central train information (☎ *05/1717*).

Visitor & Tour Information Cityrama Sightseeing (✉ *Börsegasse 1* ☎ *01/534–130* ⊕ *www.cityrama.at*). **Vienna City Tourist Office** (✉ *Am Albertinaplatz 1, 1st District* ☎ *01/24–555* ⊠ *01/216–84–92 or 01/24555–666*). **Vienna Sightseeing Tours** (✉ *Weyringergasse 28A* ☎ *01/712–4683–0* ⊕ *www.viennasightseeingtours.com*).

EXPLORING VIENNA

Most of Vienna lies roughly within an arc of a circle with the straight line of the Danube Canal as its chord. The most prestigious address of city's 23 *Bezirke,* or districts, is its heart, the **Innere Stadt** ("Inner City"), or 1st District, bounded by the Ringstrasse (Ring). It's useful to note that the fabled 1st District holds the vast majority of sightseeing attractions and once encompassed the entire city.

The circular 1st District is bordered on its northeastern section by the Danube Canal and 2nd District, and clockwise from there along the Ringstrasse by the 3rd, 4th, 6th, 7th, 8th, and 9th districts. The 3rd District contains the Belvedere Palace. The 7th District has the celebrated Kunsthistorisches Museum and headline-making MuseumsQuartier, as well as the charming Spittelberg quarter. A little father out, the 13th District is home to the fabulous Schönbrunn Palace.

Numbers in the text correspond to numbers in the margin and on the Exploring Vienna map.

⑬ Albertina Museum. This not-to-be-missed collection is home to some of the greatest Old Master drawings in Vienna—including Dürer's iconic *Praying Hands* and beloved *Alpine Hare.* The core collection of nearly 65,000 drawings and almost a million prints was begun by the 18th-century Duke Albert of Saxony-Teschen. All the names are here, from Leonardo da Vinci, Michelangelo, Raphael, and Rembrandt on down. ✉ *Augustinerstrasse 1, 1st District* ☎ *01/534–830* ⊕ *www.albertina.at* 🎟 *€9.50* ⊙ *Daily 10–6, Wed. 10–9* Ⓤ *U3/Herrengasse.*

⑯ Belvedere Palace. One of the most splendid pieces of Baroque architecture anywhere, the Belvedere Palace—actually two imposing palaces separated by a 17th-century French-style garden parterre—is one of the masterpieces of architect Lucas von Hildebrandt. Built outside the city fortifications between 1714 and 1722, the complex originally served as the summer palace of Prince Eugene of Savoy; much later it became the home of Archduke Franz Ferdinand, whose assassination in 1914 precipitated World War I. Though the lower palace is impressive in its own right, it is the much larger upper palace, used for state receptions, banquets, and balls, that is acknowledged as Hildebrandt's masterpiece. ✉ *Prinz-Eugen-Strasse 27, 3rd District/Landstrasse* ☎ *01/795–57–134* ⊕ *www.belvedere.at* 🎟 *€12.50* ⊙ *Daily 10–6; Lower Belvedere and*

Fodor'sChoice
★

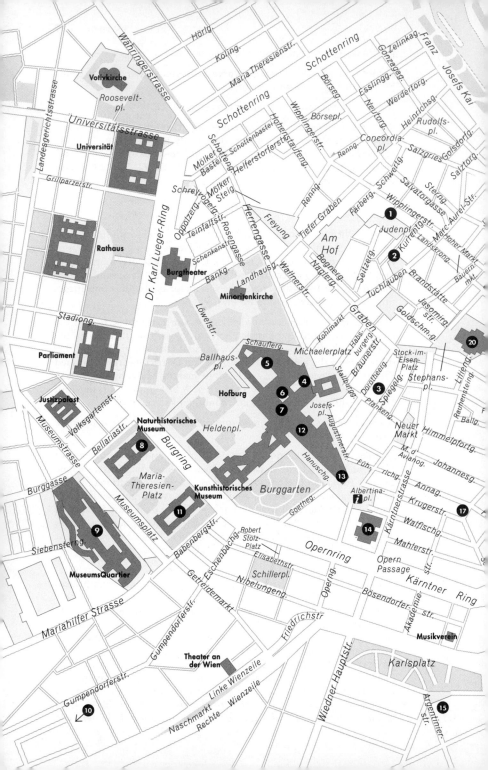

Vienna

0   1/4 mi

0   1/4 km

Stephansdom

Konzerthaus

Stadtpark

Bahnhöf Wien-Mitte

Central Air Terminal

KEY

𝙞 Tourist Information

Orangerie Wed. 10–9 Ⓤ*U1, U2, or U4 Karlsplatz, then Tram D/ Belvederegasse.*

⑰ **Haus der Musik** *(House of Music).* You could spend an entire day at this
Ⓒ ultra-high-tech museum. Pride of place goes to the rooms dedicated to
each of the great Viennese composers—Haydn, Mozart, Beethoven,
Strauss, and Mahler—complete with music samples and manuscripts.
You can even take a turn as conductor of the Vienna Philharmonic—
the conductor's baton is hooked to a computer, which allows you to
have full control over the computer-simulated orchestra. ✉*Seilerstätte
30, 1st District* ☎*01/51648–51* 🎟*€10* 🕐*Daily 10–10* ⚐*Restaurant* Ⓤ*U1, U2, or U4/Karlsplatz, then Tram D/Schwarzenbergplatz.*

⑫ **Hofbibliothek** *(National Library).* This is one of the grandest Baroque
★ libraries in the world, a cathedral of books. Its centerpiece is the spectacular Prunksaal—the Grand Hall of the National Library—which
probably contains more book treasures than any comparable collection outside the Vatican. ✉*Josefsplatz 1, 1st District* ☎*01/534–100*
⊕*www.onb.ac.at* 🎟*€7* 🕐 *Tues., Wed., and Fri.–Sun. 10–6, Thurs.
10–9* Ⓤ*U3/Herrengasse.*

⑦ **Hofburgkapelle** *(Chapel of the Imperial Palace).* Fittingly, this is the
main venue for the beloved Vienna Boys' Choir *(Wiener Sängerkna-
ben)*, since the group has its roots in the Hofmusikkapelle choir founded
by Emperor Maximilian I five centuries ago (Haydn and Schubert were
both participants as young boys). The choir sings mass here at 9:15 on
Sunday from mid-September to June (tickets range from €5 to €29).
✉*Hofburg, Schweizer Hof, 1st District* ☎*01/533–9927* ⊕*www.
hofburgkapelle.at/ or www.wsk.at* Ⓤ*U3/Herrengasse.*

❸ **Jewish Museum.** The former Eskeles Palace, once an elegant private residence, now houses the Jüdisches Museum der Stadt Wien. Permanent
exhibits tell of the momentous role that Vienna-born Jews have played
in realms from music to medicine, art to philosophy, both in Vienna—
until abruptly halted in 1938—and in the world at large. ✉*Dorotheer-
gasse 11, 1st District* ☎*01/535–0431* 🎟*€6.50 combination ticket with
Judenplatz Museum; €10 (includes entry to the medieval synagogue)*
🕐*Sun.–Fri. 10–6* Ⓤ*U1 or U3/Stephansplatz.*

❶ **Judenplatz Museum.** In what was once the old Jewish ghetto, construction workers discovered the remains of a 13th-century synagogue while
digging for a new parking garage. Simon Wiesenthal (a former Vienna
resident) helped to turn it into a museum dedicated to the Austrian
Jews who died in World War II. Marking the outside is a concrete cube
whose faces are casts of library shelves, signifying Jewish love of learning, designed by Rachel Whiteread. Downstairs are three exhibition
rooms devoted to medieval Jewish life and the synagogue excavations.
✉*Judenplatz 8, 1st District* ☎*01/535–0431* ⊕*www.jmw.at* 🎟*€4;
combination ticket with Jewish Museum €10 (includes visit to the medieval synagogue)* 🕐*Sun.– Thurs. 10–6, Fri. 10–2.*

⑮ **Karlskirche.** Dominating the Karlsplatz is one of Vienna's greatest buildings, the Karlskirche, dedicated to St. Charles Borromeo. The giant

Baroque church is framed by enormous freestanding columns, mates to Rome's famous Trajan's Column. The columns may be out of keeping with the building as a whole, but were conceived with at least two functions in mind: to portray scenes from the life of the patron saint; and the to symbolize the Pillars of Hercules, suggesting the right of the Habsburgs to their Spanish dominions. The result is an architectural tour de force. ⊠ *Karlsplatz, 4th District/Wieden* ☎ *01/504–61–87* 🖃 *€6* ☉ *Daily 9–12:30 and 1–6* Ⓤ *U1, U2, or U4 Karlsplatz.*

⓫ **Kunsthistorisches Museum** *(Museum of Fine Art).* However short your

Fodor'sChoice stay in Vienna, you'll want to visit this museum with one of the greatest

★ art collections in the world. It's no dry-as-dust museum illustrating the history of art, as its name implies: its collections of Old Master paintings reveal the royal taste and style of many members of the mighty House of Habsburg, who during the 16th and 17th centuries ruled over the greater part of the Western world. The collection stands in the same class with those of the Louvre, the Prado, and the Vatican. It is most famous for the largest collection of paintings under one roof by the Netherlandish 16th-century master Pieter Brueghel the Elder— many art historians say that seeing his sublime *Hunters in the Snow* is worth a trip to Vienna. ⊠ *Maria-Theresien-Platz, 7th District/Neubau* ☎ *01/525240* ⊕ *www.khm.at* 🖃 *€10* ☉ *Tues.–Sun. 10–6; Thurs. until 9 PM* Ⓤ *U2/MuseumsQuartier, U2, or U3/Volkstheater.*

⓮ **Mozarthaus.** This is Mozart's only still-existing abode in Vienna. Get the excellent audio guide and start on the third floor: you can hear about Mozart's time in Vienna: where he lived and performed, who his friends and supporters were, his relationship to the Freemasons, and his passion for expensive attire and gambling—he spent more money on clothes than most royals at that time. ⊠ *Domgasse 5, 1st District* ☎ *01/512–1791* ⊕ *www.mozarthausvienna.at* 🖃 *€9* ☉ *Daily 10–8* Ⓤ *U1 or U3/Stephansplatz.*

⓲ **Museum für Angewandte Kunst (MAK)** *(Museum of Applied Arts).* This fascinating museum contains a large collection of Austrian furniture, porcelain, art objects, and priceless Oriental carpets. The Jugendstil display devoted to Josef Hoffman and his Secessionist followers at the Wiener Werkstätte is particularly fine. ⊠ *Stubenring 5, 1st District* ☎ *01/711–36–0* ⊕ *www.mak.at* 🖃 *€7.90; free Sat.* ☉ *Tues. 10 AM–midnight; Wed.–Sun. 10–6* Ⓤ *U3/Stubentor.*

⑨ **MuseumsQuartier** *(Museum Quarter).* New and old, past and present,

☼ Baroque and Modernism collide in this headline-making, vast culture center that opened in 2001. Claiming to be among the ten largest of its kind in the world, the MuseumsQuartier—or **MQ** as many now call it—is in what was once the Imperial Court Stables. Where 900 cavalry horses were once housed, now thousands of artistic masterworks of the 20th and 21st centuries are exhibited, in a complex that is itself a subtle blending of historic and cutting-edge architecture. ⊠ *Museumsplatz 1–5, 7th District/Neubau* ☎ *01/523–5881* ⊕ *www.mqw.at* 🖃 *Combination ticket to museums €16–€25, depending on the muse-*

ums/exhibitions included ⊙ *Daily 24 hrs* Ⓤ*U2 MuseumsQuartier/U2 or U3/Volkstheater.*

❽ **Naturhistorisches Museum** *(Natural History Museum).* This is the home of, among other artifacts, the Venus of Willendorf, a tiny statuette (actually a replica; the original is in a vault) thought to be some 20,000 years old; this symbol of the Stone Age was originally unearthed in the Wachau Valley, not far from Melk. The reconstructed dinosaur skeletons draw the most attention. ⊠ *Maria-Theresien-Platz, 7th District/Neubau* ☎ *01/521-77-0* ☜ *€8* ⊙ *Wed. 9–9, Thurs.–Mon. 9–6:30* Ⓤ*U2 or U3/Volkstheater.*

❻ **Schatzkammer** *(Imperial Treasury).* The entrance to the Schatzkammer,
Fodor'sChoice with its 1,000 years of treasures, is tucked away at ground level behind
★ the staircase to the Hofburgkapelle. Here you'll find such marvels as the Holy Lance—reputedly the lance that pierced Jesus's side—the Imperial Crown (a sacred symbol of sovereignty once stolen on Hitler's orders), and the Saber of Charlemagne. Don't miss the Burgundian Treasure, connected with that most romantic of medieval orders of chivalry, the Order of the Golden Fleece. ⊠ *Schweizer Hof, 1st District* ☎ *01/525240* ☜ *€10* ⊙ *Wed.–Mon. 10–6* Ⓤ*U3/Herrengasse.*

❿ **Schönbrunn Palace.** Originally designed by Johann Bernhard Fischer von
Fodor'sChoice Erlach in 1696 and altered considerably for Maria Theresa 40 years
★ later, Schönbrunn Palace, the huge Habsburg summer residence, is amazing. The vast main courtyard is ruled by a formal design of rigorous symmetry: wing nods at wing, facade mirrors facade, and every part stylistically complements every other. The courtyard, however, turns out to be a mere appetizer; the feast lies beyond. The breathtaking view that unfolds on the other side of the palace is one of the finest in all Europe and one of the supreme achievements of Baroque planning. Formal *Allées* (garden promenades) shoot off diagonally, the one on the right toward the zoo, the one on the left toward a rock-mounted obelisk and a fine false Roman ruin. But these, and the woods beyond, are merely a frame for the composition in the center: the sculpted marble fountain; the carefully planted screen of trees behind; and the sudden, almost vertical rise of the grass-covered hill beyond. In the palace, the state salons are up to the splendor of the gardens, but note the contrast between these chambers and the far more modest rooms in which the rulers—particularly Franz Josef—lived and spent most of their time. Of the 1,441 rooms, 40 are open to the public on the regular tour. ⊠ *Schönbrunner-Schloss-Strasse, 13th District/Hietzing* ☎ *01/81113–239* ⊕ *www.schoenbrunn.at* ☜ *Guided grand tour of palace interior (40 rooms) €14. 40, self-guided tour €12.90* ⊙ *Apr.–June, Sept., and Oct., daily 8:30–5; July and Aug., daily 8:30–6; Nov.–Mar., daily 8:30–4:30. Park Apr.–Oct., daily 6 AM–dusk; Nov.–Mar., daily 6:30 AM–dusk* Ⓤ*U4/Schönbrunn.*

❺ **Silberkammer** *(Museum of Court Silver and Tableware).* The large courtyard on the far side of the Michaelertor rotunda is known as In der Burg; here on the west side is the entrance to the sparkling Silberkammer. Highlights include Emperor Franz Josef's vermeil banqueting service, the jardinière given to Empress Elisabeth by Queen Victoria, and gifts from Marie-Antoinette to her brother Josef II. ⊠*Hofburg, Michael-ertrakt, 1st District* ☎*01/533-7570* ☎*€9.90 including Kaiserappar-tements* ⊘*Sept.–June, daily 9–5; July and Aug., daily 9–5:30* Ⓤ*U3/ Herrengasse.*

④ Spanische Reitschule *(Spanish Riding School).* Between Augustinerstrasse and the Josefsplatz is the world-famous Spanish Riding School, a favor-ite for centuries, and no wonder: who can resist the sight of the stark-white Lipizzaner horses going through their masterful paces? For the last 300 years they have been perfecting their *haute école* riding dem-onstrations to the sound of Baroque music in a ballroom that seems to be a crystal-chandeliered stable. ⊠*Michaelerplatz 1, Hofburg, 1st District* ☎*01/533-9031-0* ⊕*www.srs.at* ☎*€35–€110, standing room €22–€28, morning training sessions €12* ⊘*Mar.–June and late Aug.– mid-Dec. Closed tour wks* Ⓤ*U3/Herrengasse.*

⑲ Staatsoper *(State Opera House).* The Vienna Staatsoper on the Ring vies with the cathedral for the honor of emotional heart of the city—it's a focus for Viennese life and one of the chief symbols of resurgence after World War II. The auditorium is plain when compared to the red-and-gold eruptions of London's Covent Garden or some of the Italian opera houses, but it has an elegant individuality that shows to best advantage when the stage and auditorium are turned into a ballroom for the great Opera Ball. ⊠*Opernring 2, 1st District* ☎*01/514-44-2613* ⊕*www. staatsoper.at* ☎*€5* ⊘*Tours year-round when there are no rehearsals, but call for times* Ⓤ*U1, U2, or U4 Karlsplatz.*

⑳ Stephansdom *(St. Stephen's Cathedral).* Vienna's soaring centerpiece, this beloved cathedral enshrines the heart of the city—although when first built in 1144–47 it stood outside the city walls. Vienna can thank a period of hard times for the Catholic Church for the cathedral's dis-tinctive silhouette. Originally the structure was to have had matching 445-foot-high spires, a standard design of the era, but funds ran out, and the north tower to this day remains a happy reminder of what glori-ously is not. The lack of symmetry creates an imbalance that makes the cathedral instantly identifiable from its profile alone. ⊠*Stephansplatz, 1st District* ☎*01/515-5237-67* ☎*Guided tour €4.50; catacombs €4.50; stairs to south tower €3.50; elevator to Pummerin bell €4.50; Sat. tour €10* ⊘*Mon.–Sat. 6 AM–10 PM. Sun. 7 AM–10 PM. Guided tours in English daily Apr.–Oct. at 3:45; catacombs tour (minimum 5 people) Mon.–Sat. every half hr 10–11:30 and 1:30–4:30, Sun. every half hr 1:30–4:30; North Tower elevator to Pummerin bell, Apr.–Oct., daily 8:30–5:30; July and Aug., daily 8:30–6; Nov.–Mar., daily 8:30–5; evening tours June–Sept., Sat. at 7 pm* Ⓤ*U1 or U3/Stephansplatz.*

② Uhrenmuseum *(Clock Museum).* At the far end of Kurrentgasse, which is lined with appealing 18th-century houses, is one of Vienna's most appealing museums: the Uhrenmuseum (enter to the right on the Schul-hof side of the building). The museum's three floors display clocks and watches—more than 3,000 timepieces—dating from the 15th century to the present. The ruckus of bells and chimes pealing forth on any hour is impressive, but for the full cacophony try to be here at noon. ⊠*Schulhof 2, 1st District* ☎*01/533–2265* ⊠*€4, Sun. free* ⊙*Tues.– Sun. 10–6* Ⓤ*U1 or U3/Stephansplatz.*

WHERE TO EAT

$–$$ ✕**Demel.** Vienna's best-known pastry shop, Demel offers a dizzying selection, so if you have a sweet tooth, a visit will be worth every euro. And in a city famous for its tortes, its almond-chocolate Senegaltorte takes the cake. Demel's windows have some of the most mouthwatering and inventive displays in Austria. ⊠*Kohlmarkt 14, 1st District* ☎*01/535–1717–0* ⊕*www.demel.at* Ⓤ*U1 or U3/Stephansplatz.*

$–$$ ✕**Figlmüller.** This Wiener Schnitzel institution is known for breaded veal and pork cutlets so large they overflow the plate, and it's always packed. The cutlet is so large because it's been hammered (you can hear the mallets pounding from a block away). Meat winds up wafer-thin but delicious, because the quality, as well as the size, is unrivaled (a quarter kilo of quality meat for each schnitzel). ⊠*Wollzeile 5, 1st District* ☎*01/512–6177* ▤*AE, DC, MC, V* ⊙*Closed first 2 wks Aug.* Ⓤ*U1 or U3/Stephansplatz.*

$$$–$$$$ ✕**Griechenbeisl.** Mozart, Beethoven, and Schubert all dined here—so how can you resist? Neatly tucked away in a quiet and quaint area of the Old City, this ancient inn goes back half a millennium. You can hear its age in the creaking floorboards when you walk through some of the small, dark-wood panel rooms. Yes, it's touristy, yet the food, including all the classic hearty dishes like goulash soup, Wiener Schnitzel, and *Apfelstrudel,* is as good as in many other Beisln. The Mark Twain room has walls and ceiling covered with signatures of the famed who have been served here. ⊠*Fleischmarkt 11, 1st District* ☎*01/533–1941* ▤*AE, DC, MC, V* Ⓤ*U1 or U4/Schwedenplatz.*

$$$$ ✕**Korso.** In the Bristol Hotel, just across from the Staatsoper, the Korso
Fodor's Choice bei der Oper has always been one of the favorites of Vienna's posh
★ crowd. Chef Reinhard Gerer's specialty is fish, and he's known throughout Austria for his creative touch. Try the delicately fried *Rotbarsch* (rosefish) paired with crispy fried parsley and the smoothest of pureed polenta. Salzkammergut lake trout is grilled and drizzled with a sensational shallot sauce, and *Saibling* (char) caviar is enhanced with organic olive oil. ⊠*Mahlerstrasse 2, 1st District* ☎*01/515–16–546* ⊘*Reservations essential* ▤*AE, DC, MC, V* Ⓤ*U4/Karlsplatz.*

$$$$ ✕**Steirereck.** Possibly the most raved-about restaurant in Austria, Steir-
Fodor's Choice ereck is in the former Milchhauspavilion, a grand Jugendstil-vintage
★ dairy overlooking the Wienfluss promenade in the Stadtpark, the main city park on the Ringstrasse. Winning dishes include delicate smoked catfish, turbot in an avocado crust, or char in white garlic sauce. At the end of the meal, an outstanding selection of more than 60 cheeses from Steirereck's own cheese cellar await. ⊠ *Im Stadtpark; Am Heumarkt 2A, 3rd District/Landstrasse* ☎*01/713–3168* ⊘*Reservations essential* ▤*AE, DC, MC, V* Ⓤ*U4/Stadtpark.*

$$–$$$ ✕**Urania.** This beautifully restored Jugendstil building is one of Vienna's trendiest locations. The interior design is cool, modern, and urban; its

biggest boon besides the great food is the view from the terrace across the water. Chef Norbert Fiedler's creations include fillet of trout on chanterelle risotto and tender duck served with ginger ravioli. ⊠ *Urani-astrasse 1, 1st District* ☎*01/7133066* ⚞ *Reservations essential* ☰ *AE, DC, MC, V* Ⓤ*U1 or U4/Schwedenplatz.*

$$-$$$ ✕ **Vestibül.** Attached to the Burgtheater, this was once the carriage vesti-bule of the emperor's court theater. Today the Marmorsaal dining room with marble Corinthian columns, coffered arcades, and candlelight adds romance, but don't expect high drama: as an example of Ringstrasse architecture, the Burgtheater offers splendor at its most staid. In fact, you might opt instead for a lighter meal in the adjoining bar salon, with its views of the boulevard. ⊠ *Burgtheater/Dr.-Karl-Lueger-Ring 2, 1st District* ☎*01/532–4999* ☰ *AE, DC, MC, V* ☉ *Closed Sun. No lunch Sat.* Ⓤ*Tram: 1 or 2.*

WHERE TO STAY

$$$ 🏨 **Astoria.** Built in 1912 and still retaining the outward charm of that era, the Astoria is one of the grand old Viennese hotels and enjoys a superb location on the Kärnterstrasse, between the Opera and St. Stephen's. The wood-paneled lobby is an essay in Wiener Werkstätte style, and all four floors have a soft contemporary style with pretty fabrics in beige tones, polished dark wood, and Oriental rugs. **Pros:** location hard to beat; some special (cheap) rates available. **Cons:** charge for Internet, no air-conditioning. ⊠ *Kärntnerstrasse 32–34, 1st District* ☎*01/51577* ⊕*www.austria-trend.at/asw* ⤴*118 rooms* ⚹*In-room: no a/c. In-hotel: bar, Internet* ☰ *AE, DC, MC, V* ⏵*BP.*

$$$$ 🏨 **Grand Hotel Wien.** With one of the great locations on the Ringstrasse,
Fodor'sChoice just across from the Musikverein and a minute on foot from the Opera,
★ the Grand Hotel Wien (the first luxury hotel in Vienna) rose to new splendor in the early 1990s. The interior has a palatial feel, thanks to its exquisite fabrics and rare antiques, and the rooms are elegant, with dark-wood walls and pastel accents. **Pros:** great restaurants in-house, good shopping next door. **Cons:** desk staff can be haughty. ⊠ *Kärntnerring 9, 1st District* ☎*01/515–800* ⊕*www.grandhotelwien.com* ⤴*205 rooms* ⚹*In-hotel: restaurant, bar, gym, no-smoking rooms, Wi-Fi* ☰ *AE, DC, MC, V.*

$$$$ 🏨 **Imperial.** One of the landmarks of the Ringstrasse, this hotel has
Fodor'sChoice exemplified the grandeur of imperial Vienna ever since it was built.
★ Adjacent to the Musikverein concert hall, the emphasis here is on Old Vienna elegance and privacy, which accounts for a guest book littered with names like Elizabeth Taylor, José Carreras, and Bruce Springsteen. The main lobby looks as opulent as a Hofburg ballroom. **Pros:** service is top-class. **Cons:** some rooms are on the small side, bathrooms can be tiny. ⊠ *Kärntnerring 16, 1st District* ☎*01/501–10–0* ⊕*www.luxury collection.com/imperial* ⤴*138 rooms* ⚹*In-hotel: restaurant, bar, gym, no-smoking rooms, Internet, Wi-Fi* ☰ *AE, DC, MC, V .*

$-$$ 🏨 **Pension Zipser.** This 1904 house is one the city's better values. It's in the picturesque Josefstadt neighborhood of small cafés, shops, bars, and good restaurants, yet within steps of the J streetcar line to the city center. Rooms are in browns and beiges, with modern furniture. The balconies of some of the back rooms overlook tree-filled neighborhood courtyards. The accommodating staff will help get theater and concert tickets. If available, ask for a room with balcony. **Pros:** friendly staff, quiet area. **Cons:** far from the city center. ⊠ *Langegasse 49, 8th District/ Josefstadt* ☎*01/404–540* ⊕*www.zipser.at* ⤳*47 rooms* ♿*In-room: no a/c. In-hotel: bar, Internetlobby* ⊟*AE, DC, MC, V* ⦿|*BP.*

$$$$ ⊞ **The Ring.** Following the trend toward smaller boutique properties, this new luxury accommodation takes its place alongside some of the Vienna's opulent grand hotels, at a somewhat more reasonable price. The 1860 historic facade remains, as does the old-fashioned wrought-iron elevator, but otherwise the house oozes sumptuous modernity, with a soothing color scheme fitting to the city: *café au lait* with splashes of pistachio throughout. **Pros:** has the best vodka bar in Vienna; you can often find good last-minute deals. **Cons:** trams frequently thunder around the block. ⊠ *Kärntner Ring 8, 1st District* ☎*01/221–22–0* ⊕*www.theringhotel.com* ⤳*68 rooms* ♿*In-hotel: restaurant, bar, gym, Wi-Fi* ⊟*AE, DC, MC, V* .

$$$ ⊞ **Style Hotel Vienna.** Within the hotel's Art Nouveau shell, London
Fodor'sChoice   interior designer Maria Vafiadis has paid tribute to Viennese Art Deco
★   and the result is über-stylish yet comfortable. Smack in the middle of the lobby is an eye-catching glass-enclosed vault; the property used to be a bank and the big bucks were stashed here, though today it serves as a wine cellar and you can enjoy a glass of wine in the elegant marble-and-wood wine bar, which has an enormous open fireplace. Rooms are full of streamlined, sedate furnishings. The location is unbeatable. **Pros:** excellent rates available online, quiet area of old city. **Cons:** small reception area, reception desks oddly too low. ⊠ *Herrengasse 12, 1st District* ☎*01/22–780–0* ⊕*www.stylehotel.at* ⤳*78 rooms* ♿*In-hotel: restaurant, bar, gym, Wi-Fi* ⊟*AE, DC, MC, V* ⦿|*BP.*

$$–$$$ ⊞ **Wandl.** The restored facade identifies this 300-year-old house that has been in family hands as a hotel since 1854. You couldn't find a better location, tucked behind St. Peter's Church, just off the Graben. The hallways are punctuated by bright openings that look out onto a glassed-in inner court, making the whole feel quite airy. The rooms are modern, but some are a bit plain and charmless, despite parquet flooring and red accents. Ask for one of the rooms done in period furniture, with decorated ceilings and gilt mirrors. **Pros:** top location, quiet square, helpful staff. **Cons:** no Wi-Fi, rooms can get stuffy. ⊠ *Petersplatz 9, 1st District* ☎*01/534–55–0* ⊕*www.hotel-wandl.com* ⤳*138 rooms* ♿*In-room: no a/c. In-hotel: bar, Internet* ⊟*AE, DC, MC, V* ⦿|*BP.*

THE ARTS

★   The most important concert halls are in the buildings of the Gesellschaft der Musikfreunde, called the **Musikverein** (⊠*Dumbastrasse 3, ticket office at Karlsplatz 6* ☎*01/505–8190* 🖷*01/505–8190–94* ⊕*www. musikverein.at*). There are six halls in this magnificent theater. The **Konzerthaus** (⊠*Lothringerstrasse 20, 1st District* ☎*01/242002* ⊕*www. konzerthaus.at*), home to the Grosser Konzerthaussaal, Mozartsaal, and Schubertsaal. The first is a room of magnificent size, with red-velvet and gold accents. Here you'll see concerts by the Wiener Philharmoniker and the Wiener Symphoniker.

★ The **Staatsoper** (*State Opera House* ✉*Opernring 2, 1st District* ☎*01/514–440* ⊕*www.wiener-staatsoper.at*), one of the world's great opera houses, has been the scene of countless musical triumphs and a center of unending controversy over how it should be run and by whom. A performance takes place virtually every night September to June, drawing on the vast repertoire of the house, with emphasis on Mozart, Verdi, and Wagner works. Guided tours of the opera house are given year-round.

SHOPPING

The **Kärntnerstrasse, Graben,** and **Kohlmarkt** pedestrian areas in the 1st District claim to have the best shops in Vienna, and for some items, like jewelry, they're probably the some of the best anywhere, but prices are steep. The side streets in this area have developed their own character, with shops selling antiques, art, jewelry, and period furniture. A collection of attractive small boutiques can be found in the **Palais Ferstel** passage at Freyung 2 in the 1st District.

SALZBURG

Art lovers call Salzburg the "Golden City of High Baroque"; historians refer to it as the "Florence of the North" or the "German Rome"; and, of course, music lovers know it as the birthplace of one of the world's most beloved composers, Wolfgang Amadeus Mozart (1756–91).

PLANNING YOUR TIME

The biggest event on the calendar—as it has been since it was first organized by composer Richard Strauss, producer Max Reinhardt, and playwright Hugo von Hofmannsthal in 1920—is the summer **Salzburger Festspiele** (✉*Hofstallgasse 1, Salzburg* ☎*0662/8045–500* ⊕*www.salz burgfestival.at*).

GETTING HERE & AROUND

A tourist map (available from tourist offices in Mozartplatz and the train station) shows all bus routes and stops; there's also a color-coded map of the public transport network, so you should have no problem getting around. Virtually all buses and trolleybuses (O-Bus) run via Mirabellplatz and/or Hanuschplatz. Single bus tickets bought from the driver cost €1.80.

BY AIR

Salzburg Airport, 4 km (2½ mi) west of the city center, is Austria's second-largest international airport. There are direct flights from London and other European cities to Salzburg, but not from the United States. From the United States you can fly to Munich and take the 90-minute train ride to Salzburg. Taxis are the easiest way to get downtown from the Salzburg airport; the ride costs around €13–€14 and takes about 20 minutes. City Bus No. 2, which makes a stop by the airport every

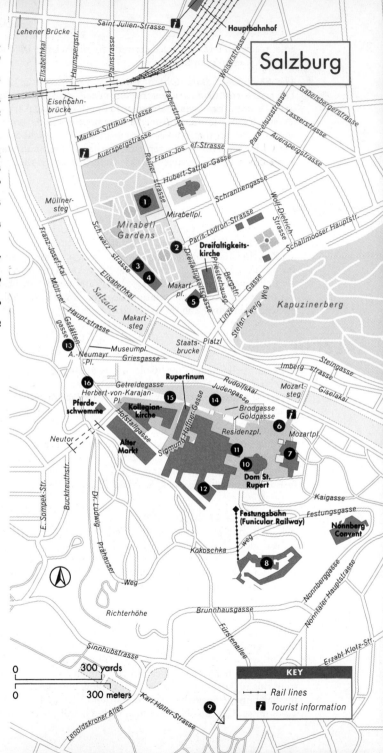

Salzburg

Lehener Brücke

Saint Julien-Strasse

Hauptbahnhof

Eisenbahn-
brücke

Markus-Sittikus-Strasse

Auerspergstrasse

Müllner-
steg

Mirabell
Gardens

Mirabellpl.

Dreifaltigkeits-
kirche

Makart-
pl.

Kapuzinerberg

Makart-
steg

Staats-
brucke

Platzl

Museumpl.

A.-Neumayr
-Pl.

Griesgasse

Rudolfskai

Mozart-
steg

Imberg strasse

Steingasse

Giselakai

Getreidegasse

Rupertinum

Judengasse

Herbert-von-Karajan-
Pl.

Pferde-
schwemme

Kollegian-
kirche

Brodgasse

Goldgasse

Residenzpl.

Mozartpl.

Alter
Markt

Sigmund-Haffner-Gasse

Dom St.
Rupert

Neutor

Festungsbahn
(Funicular Railway)

Kaigasse

Festungsgasse

Nonnberg
Convent

Kokoschka

weg

Richterhöhe

Brunnhausgasse

Sinnhubstrasse

Karl-Höller-Strasse

Leopoldskroner Allee

| 0 | 300 yards |
| 0 | 300 meters |

15 minutes, runs down to Salzburg's train station (about 20 minutes), where you can change to Bus No. 3 or 5 for the city center.

BY CAR
The fastest routes into Salzburg are the autobahns. From Vienna (320 km [198 mi]), take A1; from Munich (150 km [93 mi]), A8 (in Germany it's also E11); from Italy, A10. The only advantage to having a car in Salzburg itself is that you can get out of the city for short excursions. The Old City on both sides of the river is a pedestrian zone, and the rest of the city, with its narrow, one-way streets, is a driver's nightmare

BY TRAIN
You can get to Salzburg by rail from most European cities. Salzburg Hauptbahnhof is a 20-minute walk from the center of town in the direction of Mirabellplatz. The bus station and the suburban railroad station are at the square in front. A taxi to the center of town should take about 10 minutes and cost €9.

TOURS
Several local companies conduct 1½- to 2-hour city tours. The tour will be in a minibus, since large buses can't enter the Old City. Tours briefly cover the major sights in Salzburg, including Mozart's Birthplace, the festival halls, the major squares, the churches, and the palaces at Hellbrunn and Leopoldskron. Bob's Special Tours is well known to American visitors. Salzburg Panorama Tours and Salzburg Sightseeing Tours offer similar tours.

ESSENTIALS
Airport Contacts **Flughafen München (MUC)** (☎ *08997500* ⊕ *www.munich-air port.de*). **Salzburg Airport (SZG)** (✉ *Innsbrucker Bundesstrasse 96* ☎ *0662/8580* ⊕ *www.salzburg-airport.com*).

Bus Contacts **Salzburger Verkehrsverbund (Main ticket office)** (✉ *Schrannengasse 4* ☎ *0662/44801500*).

Train Information **ÖBB** (⊕ *www.oebb.at*) **Salzburg Hauptbahnhof** (✉ *Südtirolerplatz* ☎ *05/1717*).

Tour Info **Bob's Special Tours** (✉ *Rudolfskai 38, Salzburg* ☎ *0662/849511* ⊕ *www. bobstours.com*). **Salzburg Panorama Tours** (✉ *Schrannengasse 2/2, Salzburg* ☎ *0662/883211-0* ⊕ *www.panoramatours.com*). **Salzburg Sightseeing Tours** (✉ *Am Mirabellplatz 2, Salzburg* ☎ *0662/881616* ⊕ *www.welcome-salzburg.at*).

Visitor Info **Salzburg City Tourist Office** (✉ *Auerspergstrasse 6* ☎ *0662/88987-0* ⊕ *www.salzburginfo.at*). **Salzburg-Süd Information** (✉ *Park & Ride-Parkplatz, Alpensiedlung-Süd, Alpenstrasse 67* ☎ *0662/88987-360*).

EXPLORING SALZBURG

Getting to know Salzburg is not too difficult, because most of its sights are within a comparatively small area. The Altstadt (Old City) is a compact area between the jutting outcrop of the Mönchsberg and the Salzach River. The rest of the Old City belonged to the wealthy burghers:

the Getreidegasse, the Alter Markt (old market), the town hall, and the tall, plain burghers' houses (like Mozart's Birthplace).

(14) **Alter Markt** *(Old Market)*. Right in the heart of the Old City is the Alter Markt, the old marketplace and center of secular life in past centuries. The square is lined with 17th-century middle-class houses, colorfully hued in shades of pink, pale blue, and yellow ocher.

> **RIDING IN STYLE**
>
> One of the most delightful ways to tour Salzburg is by horse-drawn carriage. Most of Salzburg's *Fiaker* are stationed in Residenzplatz, and cost €36 for 20 minutes, €72 for 50 minutes. During the Christmas season, large, decorated, horse-drawn carts take people around the Christmas markets.

(10) **Dom** *(Cathedral)*. The cathedral is considered to be the first early Italian Baroque building north of the Alps. Its facade is of marble, its towers reach 250 feet into the air, and it holds 10,000 people. There has been a cathedral on this spot since the 8th century, but the present structure dates from the 17th century. To see remains of the old cathedral, go down the steps from the left-side aisle into the crypt, where the archbishops from 1600 on are buried. Mozart was christened, the day after he was born, at the 14th-century font here, and he later served as organist from 1779 to 1781. ⊠*Domplatz* ☎*0662/844189* ⊕*www.kirchen. net/dommuseum* 🖾*Museum €5* ☉*Early May–late Oct., Mon.–Sat. 10–5, Sun. and holidays 11–6.*

(8) **Fortress Hohensalzburg.** Founded in 1077, the Hohensalzburg is Salz-
♺ burg's acropolis and the largest preserved medieval fortress in Central
★ Europe. Brooding over the city from atop the Festungsberg, it holds the glittering **Golden Room**, the **Burgmuseum**—a collection of medieval art—and the **Rainer's Museum**, with its brutish arms and armor. Don't miss the exquisite late-Gothic **St. George's Chapel**. The 200-pipe organ from the beginning of the 16th century is best heard from a respectful distance, as it is not called "the Bull" without reason. ⊠*Fortress Hohensalzburg, Mönchsberg 34* ☎*0662/620808–400* ⊕*www. salzburgmuseum.at* 🖾*€7* ☉*Jan.–Apr. and Oct. –Dec., daily 9:30–5; May–Sept., daily 9–7.*

(4) **Marionettentheater** *(Marionette Theater)*. The Salzburger Marionetten-
♺ theater is both the world's greatest marionette theater and—surprise!—
★ a sublime theatrical experience. Many critics have noted that viewers quickly forget the strings controlling the puppets, which assume lifelike dimensions and provide a very real dramatic experience. ⊠*Schwarz-strasse 24* ☎*0662/872406–0* ⊕*www.marionetten.at* 🖾*€18–€35* ☉*Box office Mon.–Sat. 9–1 and 2 hrs before performance; Salzburg season May–Sept., Christmas, Mozart Week (Jan.), Easter.*

(2) **Mirabellgarten** *(Mirabell Gardens)*. While there are at least four entrances
♺ to the Mirabell Gardens, you'll want to enter from the Rainerstrasse
Fodor'sChoice and head for the Rosenhügel (Rosebush Hill): you'll arrive at the top of
★ the steps where Julie Andrews and her seven charges showed off their singing ability in *The Sound of Music*. This is also an ideal vantage

point from which to admire the formal gardens and one of the best views of Salzburg.

1 **Mirabell Palace.** The "Taj Mahal of Salzburg," Schloss Mirabell was built in 1606 by the immensely wealthy and powerful Prince-Archbishop Wolf-Dietrich for his mistress, Salomé Alt. A disastrous fire hit in 1818, but happily, three of the most spectacular set-pieces of the palace—the Chapel, the Marble Hall, and the Angel Staircase—survived. The Marble Hall is now used for civil wedding ceremonies, and is regarded as the most beautiful registry office in the world. ⊠ *Off Makartplatz* ☎ *0662/889-87-330* ⌨ *Free* ☾ *Weekdays 8–6.*

5 **Mozart Wohnhaus** *(Mozart Residence).* The Mozart family moved from ⟳ its cramped quarters in Getreidegasse to this house on the Hannibal ★ Platz, as it was then known, in 1773. Mozart composed the "Salzburg Symphonies" here, as well as all five violin concertos, church music and some sonatas, and parts of his early operatic masterpieces, including *Idomeneo.* ⊠ *Makartplatz 8* ☎ *0662/874227* ⊕ *www.mozarteum.at* ⌨ *Mozart residence €6.50, combined ticket for Mozart residence and birthplace €10* ☾ *Sept.–June, daily 9–5:30; July and Aug., daily 9–8.*

3 **Mozarteum.** At the International Foundation Mozarteum is the famous **Zauberflötenhäuschen**—the summerhouse where Mozart composed parts of *The Magic Flute*, with the encouragement of his frantic librettist, Emanuel Schikaneder, who locked the composer inside to force him to complete his work. ⊠ *Schwarzstrasse 26* ☎ *0662/88940-21* ⊕ *www. mozarteum.at* ☾ *Summerhouse: only during Grosser Saal concerts.*

6 **Mozartplatz** *(Mozart Square).* In the center of the square stands the statue of Wolfgang Amadeus Mozart, a work by sculptor Ludwig Schwanthaler unveiled in 1842 in the presence of the composer's two surviving sons. It was the first sign of public recognition the great composer had received from his hometown since his death in Vienna in 1791. The statue, the first for a non-noble person in old Austria, shows a 19th-century stylized view of Mozart, draped in a mantle, holding a page of music and a copybook.

15 **Mozart Geburtshaus** *(Mozart's Birthplace).* Mozart was born in this tall house, then owned by a family friend. The family lived here, when they were not on tour, from 1747 to 1773. As the child prodigy composed many of his first compositions in these rooms, it is fitting and touching to find Mozart's tiny first violin and his viola on display. ⊠ *Getreidegasse 9* ☎ *0662/844313* ⊕ *www.mozarteum.at* ⌨ *€6.50; combined ticket for Mozart residence and birthplace €10* ☾ *Sept.–June, daily 9–5:30; July and Aug., daily 9–8.*

13 **Museum der Moderne.** Enjoying one of Salzburg's most famous scenic spots, the dramatic museum of modern and contemporary art reposes atop the sheer cliff face of the Mönchsberg. The setting was immortalized in *The Sound of Music*—this is where Julie and the kids start warbling "Doe, a deer, a female deer . . ." ⊠ *Mönchsberg 32* ☎ *0662/842220* ⊕ *www.museumdermoderne.at* ⌨ *€8* ☾ *Tues. and Thurs.–Sun. 10–6, Wed. 10–9.*

⑪ **Residenz.** At the heart of Baroque
★ Salzburg, the Residenz overlooks
the spacious Residenzplatz and its
fountain. The palace in its present form was built between 1600
and 1619 as the home of Wolf-
Dietrich, the most powerful of
Salzburg's prince-archbishops. The
Kaisersaal (Imperial Hall) and the
Rittersaal (Knight's Hall), one of
the city's most regal concert halls,
can be seen along with the rest of

> ### GET CARDED
>
> Consider purchasing the Salzburg
> Card. SalzburgKarten are good for
> 24, 48, or 72 hours for €24–€37,
> and allow no-charge entry to
> most museums and sights, use of
> public transporton, and special
> discount offers. Children under
> 15 pay half.

the magnificent **State Rooms** on a self-guided tour. ✉ *Residenzplatz 1*
☎ *0662/8042–2690, 0662/840451 art collection* ⊕ *www.residenzgalerie.
at* 🖼 *€8.20 for both museums; art collection only, €6* ⊗ *March–Jan.,
daily 10–5.*

⑦ **Salzburg Museum** *(Neugebäude).* This building was Prince-Archbishop
Fodor'sChoice Wolf-Dietrich's "overflow" palace (he couldn't fit his entire archiepis-
★ copal court into the main Residenz across the plaza). As such, it features 10 state reception rooms that were among the first attempts at a
stil Renaissance in the North. Highlights of the archaeological collection include Hallstatt Age relics, remains of the town's ancient Roman
ruins, and the famous Celtic bronze flagon found earlier this century
on the Dürrnberg near Hallein (15 km [10 mi] south of Salzburg).
✉ *Mozartplatz 1* ☎ *0662/620808–700* ⊕ *www.salzburgmuseum.at*
🖼 *€7* ⊗ *Tues., Wed., and Fri.–Sun. 9–5, Thurs. 9–8.*

⑨ **Schloss Hellbrunn** *(Hellbrunn Palace).* Just 6½ km (4 mi) south of Salz-
☺ burg, the Lustschloss Hellbrunn was the prince-archbishops' pleasure
Fodor'sChoice palace. The castle has some fascinating rooms, including an octagonal
★ music room and a banquet hall with a trompe-l'oeil ceiling. From the
gardens and tree-lined avenues to the ponds, Hellbrunn Park is often
described as a jewel of landscape architecture. ✉ *Fürstenweg 37, Hellbrunn* ☎ *0662/820372* ⊕ *www.hellbrunn.at* 🖼 *Tour of palace and water
gardens €8.50* ⊗ *Apr. and Oct., daily 9–4:30; May–Sept., daily 9–5:30;
evening tours July and Aug., daily on the hr 6–10.*

⑯ **Spielzeugmuseum** *(Toy Museum).* On a rainy day this is a delightful diver-
☺ sion for both young and old, with a collection of dolls, teddy bears,
and model trains. ✉ *Bürgerspitalplatz 2* ☎ *0662/620808–300* ⊕ *www.
salzburgmuseum.at* 🖼 *€3* ⊗ *Daily 9–5.*

⑫ **Stiftkirche St. Peter** *(Collegiate Church of St. Peter).* The most sumptuous church in Salzburg, St. Peter's is where Mozart's famed *Great
Mass in C Minor* premiered in 1783, with his wife, Constanze, singing the lead soprano role. Wolfgang directed the orchestra and choir
and also played the organ. The front portal of what was originally a
Romanesque basilica dates from 1245. Inside, the low-ceiling aisles
are charmingly painted in Rococo candy-box style. ✉ *St. Peter Bezirk*
☎ *0662/844578–0* 🖼 *Free* ⊗ *Apr.–Sept., daily 6:30 AM–7 PM; Oct.–
Mar., daily 6:30–6.*

WHERE TO EAT

$–$$ ✕**Café Tomaselli.** This inn opened its doors in 1705 as an example of that
Fodor'sChoice new-fangled thing, a "Wiener Kaffeehaus" (Vienna coffeehouse). It was
★ an immediate hit. Feast on the famous "Tomaselliums Café" (mocha,
Mozart liqueur, and whipped cream) and the large selection of excellent
homemade cakes, tarts, and strudels. Inside, the decor is marble, wood,
and walls of 18th-century portraits. In summer the best seats are on
the terrace and at the pretty "Tomaselli-Kiosk" on the square. ⊠*Alter
Markt 9* ☎*0662/844488–0* ⊕*www.tomaselli.at* ⊟*No credit cards.*

$$–$$$ ✕**Mundenhamer.** Chef Ernst Breitschopf knows the repertoire of good
old Upper Austrian dishes inside and out: an *Innviertler* (raw ham with
horseradish, dark bread, and butter); a garlic soup with bread croutons;
a roast pork chop served in a pan with bread dumplings and warm
bacon-cabbage salad; homemade spaetzle with braised white cabbage
and bacon; a Salzburger Schnitzel (scallop of veal filled with minced
mushrooms and ham) with buttered finger dumplings. ⊠*Rainerstrasse
2* ☎*0662/875693* ⊟*AE, DC, MC, V* ☾*Closed Sun.*

$$$$ ✕**Pfefferschiff.** The "Pepper Ship" is one of the most acclaimed restaurants in Salzburg—though it's 3 km (2 mi) northeast of the center. It's
in a pretty, renovated rectory, dated 1640, adjacent to a pink-and-cream
chapel. Klaus Fleishhaker, an award-winning chef, makes you feel pampered in the country-chic atmosphere, adorned with polished wooden
floors, antique hutches, and tabletops laden with fine bone china and
Paloma Picasso silverware. The menu changes seasonally. ⊠*Söllheim
3, Hallwang* ☎*0662/661242* ⚐*Reservations essential* ⊟*AE.*

$$–$$$$ ✕**Stiftskeller St. Peter.** Legends swirl about the famous St. Peter's Beer
Fodor'sChoice Cellar. Locals claim that Mephistopheles met Faust here, others say
★ Charlemagne dined here, and some believe Columbus enjoyed a glass
of its famous Salzburg Stiegl beer just before he set sail for America in
1492. But there is no debating the fact that this place—first mentioned
in a document dating back to 803—is Austria's oldest restaurant. It is
also one of the most dazzling dining experiences in Salzburg. Choose
between the fairly elegant, dark-wood-panel Prälatenzimmer (Prelates'
Room) or one of several less formal banqueting rooms. ⊠*St. Peter
Bezirk 4* ☎*0662/841268–0* ⊕*www.haslauer.at* ⊟*AE, DC, MC, V.*

$ ✕**Zum Fidelen Affen.** The name means "At the Faithful Ape," which
explains the monkey motifs in this popular Gasthaus dominated by
a round copper-topped bar and stone pillars under a vaulted ceil-
ing. Besides the beer on tap, the kitchen offers tasty Austrian dishes,
such as *Schlutzkrapfen,* cheese ravioli with a light topping of chopped
fresh tomatoes, or a big salad with strips of fried chicken. ⊠*Priester-
hausgasse 8* ☎*0662/877361* ⚐*Reservations essential* ⊟*DC, MC, V*
☾*Closed Sun. No lunch.*

WHERE TO STAY

$ ⊞**Am Dom.** Tucked away on a tiny street near Residenzplatz, this small
pension in a 14th-century building offers simply furnished rooms, some
with oak-beam ceilings. Note the beautiful hand-carved Renaissance
reception desk. The selling point here is the great location in the heart

of the Altstadt. **Pros:** rustic atmosphere, well-kept rooms. **Cons:** few amenities. ⊠ *Goldgasse 17,* ☎ *0662/842765* ⊕ *www.amdom.at* 15 *rooms* ⅃ *In-room: no a/c, no TV* ⊟ *AE, DC, MC, V* ⊘ *Closed 2 wks in Feb.* ⊺⊙⎮*BP.*

$$$$
Fodor'sChoice
★
◨ **Goldener Hirsch.** Celebrities from Picasso to Pavarotti have favored the "Golden Stag" for its legendary *Gemütlichkeit,* patrician pampering, and adorable decor. It's near the most popular sites, but double-paned windows ensure that you won't hear a thing once you enter this special, private world. Inside, it's delightfully rustic, with hand-carved wood, peasant-luxe furniture, and some of the lowest ceilings in town; the stag motif is even on lamp shades, which were hand-painted by an Austrian countess. **Pros:** unbeatable location, top-notch dining, charm to spare. **Cons:** noisy neighborhood, now part of a chain. ⊠ *Getreidegasse 37,* ☎ *0662/8084–0* ⊕ *www.goldenerhirsch.com* 64 *rooms, 5 suites* ⅃ *In-room: refrigerator. In-hotel: 2 restaurants, bar, parking (paid), Internet terminal* ⊟ *AE, DC, MC, V.*

$$$$
◨ **Sacher Salzburg.** On the Salzach River, this mammoth hotel has attracted guests from the Beatles and the Rolling Stones to Hillary and Chelsea Clinton. It's owned by the Gürtler family, who make sure that even if you don't have a Vuitton steamer trunk you'll feel welcome. The main atrium is a symphony in marble, while the grand staircase still looks like the Empress Sisi could make a dazzling entrance amidst its ferns. Upstairs, guest rooms are so lovely there is a danger you won't want to leave (especially if you get one with picture-perfect views of the Old City). Each is different, but all are exquisitely decorated. **Pros:** some great views, delicious buffet breakfast, plenty of dining options. **Cons:** gets overcrowded during festival. ⊠ *Schwarzstrasse 5–7,* ☎ *0662/88977* ⊕ *www.sacher.com* 118 *rooms* ⅃ *In-room: refrigerator, Internet. In-hotel: 5 restaurants, bar, gym, parking (paid), no-smoking rooms, Wi-Fi* ⊟ *AE, DC, MC, V* ⊺⊙⎮*BP.*

$$
◨ **Weisse Taube.** In the heart of the pedestrian area of the Altstadt, the centuries-old "White Dove" is around the corner from Mozartplatz, the Salzburg Museum, and the Residenz. Comfortably renovated into a hotel, this 14th-century burgher's house has been traditionally restored, but some time-burnished touches remain: uneven floors, ancient stone archways, and wood-beam ceilings. Guest rooms are simply furnished, with dark-wood accents. **Pros:** excellent location, friendly staff. **Cons:** noisy area at night. ⊠ *Kaigasse 9,* ☎ *0662/842404* ⊕ *www.weisse taube.at* 33 *rooms* ⅃ *In-room: no a/c. In-hotel: bar, parking (paid), no-smoking rooms, Internet terminal* ⊟ *AE, DC, MC, V* ⊘ *Closed 2 wks in Jan.* ⊺⊙⎮*BP.*

THE ARTS

MUSIC

The season at the **Landestheater** (⊠ *Schwarzstrasse 22,* ☎ *0662/871512–21* ⊕ *www.salzburger-landestheater.at*) runs from September to June includes operas like Benjamin Britten's *Death in Venice and Mozart's The Abduction from the Seraglio.* The **Salzburger Schlosskonzerte** (⊠ *Theatergasse 2,* ☎ *0662/848586* ⊕ *www.salzburger.schlosskonzerte.at* €29–€35) presents concerts in the legendary Mirabell Palace. The

Salzburger Festungskonzerte (✉ *Fortress Hohensalzburg,* ☎0662/825858 ⊕*www.mozartfestival.at* ✆*€31–€38*) are presented in the grand Prince's Chamber at Festung Hohensalzburg.

SHOPPING

The most fashionable specialty stores and gift shops are along Getreide-gasse and Judengasse and around Residenzplatz. Linzergasse, across the river, is less crowded and good for more practical items. There are interesting antiques shops in the medieval buildings along Steingasse and Goldgasse.

INNSBRUCK

The charming Old World aspect of Innsbruck has remained virtually intact, and includes ample evidence of its Baroque lineage. The skyline encircling the center suffers somewhat from high-rises, but the heart, the **Altstadt,** or Old City, remains much as it was 400 years ago. The protective vaulted arcades along main thoroughfares, the tiny passage-ways giving way to noble squares, and the ornate restored houses all contribute to an unforgettable picture.

GETTING HERE & AROUND
BY AIR
Innsbruck Flughafen, the airport 3 km (2 mi) west of Innsbruck, is served principally by Austrian Airlines, as well as by many low-cost carriers during the high season. Buses (Line F) to the main train station in Innsbruck take about 20 minutes. Get your ticket (€1.70) from the driver. Taxis should take no more than 10 minutes into town, and the fare is about €10–€12.

BY BUS
In Innsbruck most bus and streetcar routes begin or end at Maria-There-sien-Strasse, nearby Bozner Platz, or the main train station (Hauptbah-nhof). You can get single tickets costing €1.70 on the bus or streetcar. You can transfer to another line with the same ticket as long as you continue in more or less the same direction in a single journey.

BY CAR
If you're driving, remember that the Altstadt (Old City) is a pedestrian zone. Private cars are not allowed on many streets, and parking requires vouchers that you buy from blue coin-operated dispensers found around parking areas. Each half hour normally costs €0.50–€1.

BY TRAIN
Direct trains serve Innsbruck from Munich, Vienna, Rome, and Zürich, and all arrive at the railroad station Innsbruck Hauptbahnhof at Südti-roler Platz. The station is outfitted with restaurants, cafés, a supermar-ket, and even a post office.

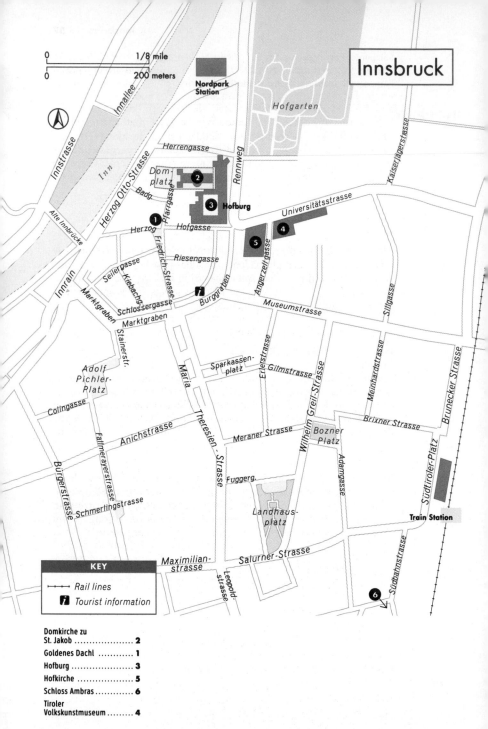

Innsbruck

Nordpark Station

Hofgarten

Herrengasse

Dom-platz ❷

❸ **Hofburg**

Rennweg

Universitätsstrasse

❹

❶ Herzog Hofgasse

❺

Badg.

Herzog Otto-Strasse

Pfarrgasse

Inn

Innstrasse

Alte Innbrücke

Riesengasse

Seilergasse

Kiebachg.

Friedrich-Strasse

Schlossergasse

Marktgraben

Stainerstr.

Innrain

Burggraben

Angerzeilgasse

Museumstrasse

Kaiserjägerstrasse

Sillgasse

Adolf Pichler-Platz

Colingasse

Anichstrasse

Faltmerayerstrasse

Maria Theresien-Strasse

Sparkassen-platz

Erlerstrasse

Gilmstrasse

Wilhelm Greil-Strasse

Meinhardstrasse

Brunecker Strasse

Meraner Strasse

Bozner Platz

Brixner Strasse

Bürgerstrasse

Schmerlingstrasse

Fuggerg.

Landhaus-platz

Adamgasse

Südtiroler-Platz

Train Station

Maximilian-strasse

Leopold-strasse

Salurner-Strasse

Südbahnstrasse

❻

KEY

⊢———⊢ *Rail lines*

🛈 *Tourist information*

0 ———— 1/8 mile
0 ———— 200 meters

TOURS

The red **Sightseer** bus, part of the Innsbruck Tourist Office, is the best way to see the sights of Innsbruck. It has a recorded commentary in several languages, including English. There are two routes, both beginning from Maria-Theresien-Strasse in the Old City, but you can catch the bus from any of the nine marked stops, and jump off and on whenever you like.

ESSENTIALS

Airport Information Innsbruck Flughafen Airport (*INN* ☎ *0512/22525 flight information* ⊕ *www.innsbruck-airport.com*).

Bus Information Postbus AG (☎ *0512/390390 or 0810/222333* ⊕ *www. postbus.at*).

Train Information Innsbruck Hauptbahnhof (⊠ *Südtiroler Platz* ☎ *0512/93000–0*). **Österreichisches Bundesbahn** (☎ *05–1717 information and reservations* ⊕ *www. oebb.at*).

Visitor Information Innsbruck Tourist Office (⊠ *Burggraben 3A-6021* ☎ *0512/59850* ⊕ *www.innsbruck.info*). **Österreichischer Alpenverein** (⊠ *Wilhelm-Greil-Strasse 15* ☎ *0512/59547*). **Tirol Werbung** (⊠ *Maria-Theresien-Strasse 55* ☎ *0512/7272* ⊕ *www.tirol.at*).

EXPLORING INNSBRUCK

② The main attraction of the Baroque **Domkirche zu St. Jakob** is the high-altar painting of the Madonna by Lucas Cranach the Elder, dating from about 1530. The cathedral was built in 1722. In the ornate Baroque interior, look in the north aisle for a 1620 monument honoring Archduke Maximilian III. ⊠ *Domplatz 6* ☎ *0512/5839–02* ☞*Free* ☉ *Nov.–Apr., Mon.–Sat. 7:30–6:30; May–Oct., daily 7:30–7:30 except during worship.*

①
Fodor'sChoice
★
Any walking tour of Innsbruck should start at the **Goldenes Dachl** *(Golden Roof)*, which made famous the late-Gothic mansion whose balcony it covers. The 15th-century house was owned by Maximilian I, who added a balcony in 1501 as a sort of "royal box" for watching street performances in the square below. The Golden Roof building houses the **Maximilianeum,** a small museum which headlines memorabilia and paintings from the life of Emperor Maximilian I. The short video presentation about Maximilian is worth a look. ⊠ *Herzog-Friedrich-Strasse 15* ☎ *0512/5811–11* ☞*€4* ☉ *Oct.–Apr., Tues.–Sun. 10–5; May–Sept., daily 10–5.*

③
★
One of Innsbruck's most historic attractions is the **Hofburg,** or Imperial Palace, which Maximilian I commissioned in the 15th century. Center stage is the **Giant's Hall**—designated a marvel of the 18th century as soon as it was topped off with its magnificent trompe-l'oeil ceiling painted by Franz Anton Maulpertsch in 1775. The Rococo decoration and the portraits of Habsburg ancestors in the ornate white-and-gold great reception hall were added in the 18th century by Maria Theresa; look for the portrait of "Primal" (primrose)—to use the childhood

nickname of the empress's daughter, Marie-Antoinette. The booklet in English available at the ticket office will tell you more interesting tidbits about the palace than the tour guide. ⊠*Rennweg 1* ☎*0512/587186* 🎫*€5.50* ⊘ *Tours daily at 11 and 2.*

❺ Close by the Hofburg is the **Hofkirche** *(Court Church),* built as a mausoleum for Maximilian I (although he is actually buried in Wiener Neustadt, south of Vienna). The emperor's ornate black-marble tomb is surrounded by 24 marble reliefs depicting his accomplishments, as well as 28 larger-than-life-size statues of his ancestors, including the legendary King Arthur of England. ⊠*Universitätsstrasse 2* ☎*0512/59489–511* ⊕*www.hofkirche.at* 🎫*€4, €8 combined ticket with Zeughaus and Ferdinandeum* ⊘ *Mon.–Sat. 9–5, Sun. 12:30–5.*

❻ When Archduke Ferdinand II wanted to marry a commoner, the court grudgingly allowed it, but the couple was forced to live outside the city limits. Ferdinand revamped a 10th-century castle for the bride, Philippine Welser, and when completed in 1556 it was every bit as luxe as what he had been accustomed to in town. Amid acres of gardens and woodland, **Schloss Ambras** is an inviting castle with cheery red-and-white shutters on its many windows, and is, curiously, home to an oddball collection of armaments. ⊠*Schloss Strasse 20* ☎*0152/524745* ⊕*www. khm.at/ambras* 🎫*Prices vary, check Web site* ⊘ *Sept., Oct., and Dec.–July, daily 10–5; Aug., daily 10–7*

❹ The **Tiroler Volkskunstmuseum** *(Tyrolean Folk Art Museum),* in the same complex as the Hofkirche, exhibits Christmas crèches, costumes, and entire rooms from old farmhouses and inns, decorated in styles ranging from Gothic to Rococo. ⊠*Universitätsstrasse 2* ☎*0512/59489-511* ⊕*www.tiroler-volkskunstmuseum.at* 🎫*€5* ⊘ *Mon.–Sat. 9–5, Sun. and holidays 10–5.*

WHERE TO EAT

$$–$$$ ✕**Goldener Adler.** This restaurant is as popular with locals as with travelers. The traditional dining rooms on the arcaded ground floor and the summer-only terrace are both lovely—the former is more romantic and private. Start with a glass of *Sekt* (local sparkling wine) flavored with a dash of blackberry liqueur as you peruse the menu. The kitchen takes a modern approached to traditional dishes: pork medallions are topped with ham and Gorgonzola, and the veal steaks are ladled with a creamy herb sauce. ⊠*Herzog-Friedrich-Strasse 6* ☎*0512/5711* ▭*AE, DC, MC, V.*

$ ✕**Hofgarten.** This is *the* summer gathering place in Innsbruck, perhaps because it is so pleasant to eat and drink outdoors amid the beauty of the city's ancient and splendid park. Whether enjoying a beer and light meal on a sunny afternoon or dropping by after a show at the nearby Landestheater, this is a fine place for having fun. It's popular with students. ⊠*Rennweg 6a* ☎*0512/588871* ▭*AE, DC, MC, V.*

$$ ✕**Ottoburg.** This family-run restaurant offers excellent food and an extraordinary location. This ancient landmark, built in 1180 as a city watchtower, conveys an abundance of historic charm. It's fun just to explore the rabbit warren of paneled rustic rooms named after emperors. Several of the bay-window alcoves in the shuttered house have great views of the main square, while others overlook the river. Try the Tafelspitz, a typical Viennese specialty of boiled beef served with vegetables and horseradish, or the Pfandl, a fillet of pork and a steak served in an old-fashioned pan. ⊠ *Herzog-Friedrich-Strasse 1* ☎ *0512/584338* 🖃 *AE, DC, MC, V* ☉ *Closed Mon.*

2

$$$ ✕ **Pfefferkorn.** A meal at this two-level restaurant is an unforgettable experience. The modern decor—dim lighting, dark wood, and the most comfortable armchairs you're likely to find, make the time pass quickly. The cuisine is remarkable as well, including a variety of seasonal dishes culled from the specialties of the region, such as pepper steak. ⊠ *Seilergasse 8* ☎ *0512/565–444* 🖃 *AE, DC, MC, V* ☉ *Closed Mon.*

$$ ✕ **Weisses Rössl.** In the authentically rustic dining rooms, an array of antlers adds to the charm. This is the right place for solid local standards, like *Tiroler Gröstl,* a tasty hash, and Wiener Schnitzel (veal cutlet), both of which taste even better on the outside terrace in summer. Ask about the specials that don't appear on the menu, such as wild game or freshly picked mushrooms. Because the place hosts regular local gatherings it can get quite lively here, but all you have to do is request a table in one of the smaller parlors. ⊠ *Kiebachgasse 8* ☎ *0512/583057* 🖃 *AE, MC, V* ☉ *Closed Sun., early Nov., and mid-Apr.*

WHERE TO STAY

$$$$ 🏨 **Grand Hotel Europa.** Adjacent to the train station, this elegant hotel has provided lodging to the celebrated and wealthy since it opened in 1869, and it has lost none of its warmth and charm in the ensuing years. Bavarian King Ludwig II is reported to have called it "the most desirable place in Innsbruck to celebrate a festival." Inside, modern Italian interior design meets traditional Tyrolean style. Rooms are richly appointed and comfortable; the staff provides attentive service. **Pros:** spacious rooms, modern lobby, nice bar. **Cons:** few nice views. ⊠ *Südtirolerplatz 2* ☎ *0512/5931* ⊕ *www.grandhoteleuropa.com* ⤶ *120 rooms, 10 suites* ⌂ *In-room: safe, Wi-Fi. In-hotel: restaurant, room service, bar, gym, laundry service, parking (paid), no-smoking rooms* 🖃 *AE, DC, MC, V* ⦿ *BP, MAP.*

$$–$$$ 🏨 **Mondschein.** Among the city's oldest houses stands the pink Moonlight Hotel, a welcoming family-run establishment. Richly furnished rooms facing the Inn River have excellent views of the Old City. There are only four standard rooms on the river side, worth requesting in advance; the others face the less appealing courtyard, but cost the same. Bathrooms are big and elegant compared to the room size. **Pros:** friendly staff, free parking, riverfront location. **Cons:** some rooms can be noisy, courtyard rooms are dark, small parking lot. ⊠ *Mariahilfstrasse 6,* ☎ *0512/22784* ⊕ *www.mondschein.at* ⤶ *34 rooms* ⌂ *In-room: safe (some), Wi-Fi. In-hotel: room service, bar, Internet terminal, parking (free), no-smoking rooms* 🖃 *AE, DC, MC, V* ⦿ *BP.*

$$$$ 🏨 **Schwarzer Adler.** The 500-year-old building now occupied by the Black Eagle was once Emperor Maximilian's stables. It's much more romantic today, and most of the guest rooms are decorated with taste

and creativity. For a bit of the good life, request the Swarovski Dream, a suite with a crystal bathroom. The open-air rooftop terrace offers an eye-popping view of the city and the mountains, making it the ideal spot to enjoy an aperitif. If the weather cooperates, head to the small spa, one of the most intimate in Innsbruck. **Pros:** lovely spa, efficient staff, unique rooms. **Cons:** only one elevator, some rooms face busy street. ✉ *Kaiserjägerstrasse 2,* ☎*0512/587109* ⊕*www.deradler.com* ⇨ *20 rooms, 7 suites* ⚬*In-room: Internet. In-hotel: restaurant, bar, spa, no-smoking rooms* ☰ *AE, DC, MC, V.*

$ 🏨**Weisses Kreuz.** This lovely hotel, set over stone arcades in the heart of the Old City, has quite a long history: the first guesthouse stood on this site in 1465. Rooms are simple but comfortable, with rustic furnishings and lots of pale wood. Service is friendly and accommodating, even though sometimes you might have to wait for a staffer to arrive. Breakfast is served in one of the building's original parlors. **Pros:** good value, family-friendly, charming building. **Cons:** parking is a short walk from the hotel, noisy neighborhood. ✉*Herzog-Friedrich-Strasse 31,* ☎*0512/59479* ⊕*www.weisseskreuz.at* ⇨*40 rooms, 9 rooms without bath* ⚬*In-room: no a/c. In-hotel: Internet, Wi-Fi, parking (paid), no-smoking rooms* ☰*AE, MC, V* ❴❩*BP.*

THE ARTS

The **Festwochen der Alten Musik** (*Festival of Early Music* ✉*Burggraben 3* ☎*0512/5710–32* ⊕*www.altemusik.at*) is a good reason to visit Innsbruck between mid-July and late August, as the annual festival highlights music from the 14th to 18th centuries, performed by many of Europe's finest musicians in such dramatic settings as Innsbruck's beautiful Schloss Ambras and the Hofkirche. In summer there are frequent brass-band (*Musikkapelle*) concerts in the Old Town.

SHOPPING

The best shops are along the arcaded Herzog-Friedrich-Strasse in the heart of the Old City, and along its extension, Maria-Theresien-Strasse, and the adjoining streets Meraner Strasse and Anichstrasse. Innsbruck is the place to buy native Tyrolean clothing, particularly lederhosen and loden.

Belgium

Belgian chocolate

WORD OF MOUTH

"I adore the charming, smaller scale of the Belgian cities and I love the French joie de vivre meets Dutch practicality that Belgium offers. Belgium isn't Rome (or Paris for that matter) but that's precisely why I enjoy it so much."

—global_guy

WHAT'S WHERE

1 Brussels. Brussels is the capital not just of Belgium, but also of the European Union. In many respects, it's a thoroughly modern city, with shining steel-and-glass office blocks jostling Gothic spires and Art Nouveau town houses. It's the only place in the country that really exudes the "big city" feel, and as befits a capital, it's teeming with top-class museums and restaurants.

2 Brugge. Famed as the birthplace of Flemish painting, Brugge has museums displaying some of the finest masterpieces of Jan van Eyck, Memling, and Hieronymus Bosch. Just 60 mi from Brussels, you can contemplate its weathered beauty in the dark mirror of its peaceful canals. The medieval feel of the city center is so perfectly-preserved you may feel you have slipped back in time to another era. The one drawback to this is that its beauty is no well-kept secret, and in the height of summer you will share your experience with hordes of others, creating long queues outside all the major attractions.

3 Antwerp. Vibrant Antwerp is a major port and diamond center 29 mi from Brussels. An unmistakably hip buzz permeates the entire city. While Antwerp is most famous for its diamond trade, these days fashionistas know it as a leader in avant-garde clothing design.

4 Gent. Gent is a living city, not a museum, as is often said of Brugge. While much is also medieval here, every stone has a role in contemporary life. The city has much to recommend it, including museums, canals, and architecture that can rival the best of Brugge, but without the volume of tourists found in its illustrious neighbor.

NETHERLANDS

Westerschelde

Essen
Kalmthout
ANTWERP
Arendonk

Malle
Antwerp
(Antwerpen)
Turnhout
Lommel
Achel

Beveren
Sint-
Niklaas
Herentals
Peer
Bree

EAST FLANDERS
Lier
Geel
KEMPEN

Olen
Westerlo
LIMBURG

Gent
(Ghent)
Dendermonde
Mechelen
Aarschot
Diest

Aalst
Keerbergen
Leuven
Hasselt
Genk

BRUSSELS
BRABANT
Zoutleeuw

Oudenaarde
Gaasbeek
BRUSSELS
(BRUXELLES)
Tienen
Tongeren

Geraards-
bergen
Beersel
Sint
Truiden

Ranse
Halle
Hoegaarden

Enghien
Waterloo
Ronquières

Ath
Soignies
Nivelles
Meuse
Liège

HAINAUT
Namur
Huy
Ourthe
LIÈGE
Spa
Malmedy

Mons
La Louvière
Gosselies
NAMUR
Durbuy
ARDENNES
Houffalize

Binche
Charleroi
Yvoir
La Roche-
en-Ardenne
Wemperhaardt

Sambre
Thuin
Dinant
Rochefort

Beaumont
Anhée
Han-sur-Lesse
Bastogne

Philippeville
LUXEMBOURG

Chimay
Meuse
Neufchâteau
Martelange
Romach
LUXEMBOURG

Notre Dame de
Scourmont
Bouillon
Arlon
Aizette

Florenville
Orval
Virton
Pétange
Luxembourg

Longwy

FRANCE

GERMANY

LUXEMBOURG

BELGIUM IS A CONNOISSEUR'S DELIGHT. Famous for its artistic inspiration, the land of Brueghel and Van Eyck, Rubens and Van Dyck, and Ensor and Magritte is where their best work can still be seen. Belgian culture was and remains that of a bourgeois, mercantile society. Feudal lords may have built Belgium's many castles, and the clergy its splendid churches, but merchants and craftsmen are responsible for the guild houses and sculpture-adorned town halls of Brussels, Antwerp, Gent, and Brugge.

Belgium packs nearly 6 million Flemish-speaking Flemings and just over 4 million French-speaking Walloons into a country the size of Vermont or Wales. The presence of two major language communities enriches its intellectual life but also creates constant political and social tension. The creation in the mid-1990s of three largely self-governing regions—Flanders, Wallonia, and the city of Brussels, which is bilingual—has only emphasized these divisions, and talks between the different factions often plunge the country into constitutional crisis.

Belgium's neutrality was violated during both world wars, when much of its architectural heritage was destroyed and great suffering was inflicted by the occupying forces. This may be why Belgium, home to most of the European Union (EU) institutions, staunchly supports the EU.

Belgium has attractions out of proportion to its diminutive size. The two largest, most cosmopolitan cities are Brussels (Brussel, Bruxelles), the lively capital, and Antwerp (Antwerpen, Anvers), a bustling port and high-fashion hotbed. The so-called picture-book towns, Gent (Ghent, Gand) and Brugge (Bruges), are both medieval gems with a staggering wealth of fine art. Beyond this the countryside contains the sites of some of the bloodiest stalemates of World War I, and—in perfect contrast to these somber memorials—a string of abbeys where brewing beer is the order of the day.

WHEN TO GO

The best times to visit the country are in the late spring—when the northern European days are long and the summer crowds have not yet filled the highways or the museums—and in fall. The stereotype of overcast Belgian skies is not unfounded, and early spring and fall do get quite a bit of rain, but the weather can change dramatically in the space of a few hours, and temperatures above 30°C are also occasionally experienced at this time.

Because Belgians take their vacations in July and August, these months are not ideal for visiting countryside regions, but this is a very good time to be in Brussels, Antwerp, or Gent, as you may be able to get a break on hotel prices; on the other hand, this is also vacation time for some restaurants.

You may want to try to coincide a visit with one of the of Brussels' more spectacular festivals. The **Ommegang** (*02/548–0454, www.ommegang. be*) takes over Brussels's Grand'Place on the first Thursday in July, and also the preceding Tuesday. It's a sumptuous and stately pageant reenacting a procession that honored Emperor Charles V in 1549. Book

TOP REASONS TO GO

An Architectural Dream. The Grand'Place in Brussels is a spectacular fantasy of medieval architecture that will melt your heart and take your breath away.

To Market, To Market. Every day of the week guarantees at least one lively market where stalls sell everything from olives and fruit to antique furniture and dog-eared books.

Walking Back in Time. The planning laws in picture-perfect Brugge have been very strict for many years, meaning there are few new buildings to spoil the illusion that you've waltzed back to another age.

Float on the Canals. The canals that cut though the centers of

Brugge and Gent are among the most beautiful you will find anywhere. Take a boat trip and travel down them at a pace that befits their grandeur.

Belgium in Miniature. If you're looking to experience every cliché about Belgium in one tidy package, Brugge is the place to find it: chocolate, lace, waffles, fries, beer, and Flemish stepped gables. All within steps of one another.

The Cuisine of Gent. Gent boasts some of Belgium's best regional food specialties. Favorites include *waterzooi* (creamy chicken broth) and *paling in't groen* (eel in green sauce). Wash them down with a glass of the local beer, Karmeliet Tripel.

early if you want a room in town. **Belgium's National Day,** July 21, is celebrated in Brussels with a military march, followed by a popular feast in the Parc de Bruxelles and brilliant fireworks.

GETTING HERE & AROUND

BY AIR

The major international airport serving Belgium is Brussels Airport (Zaventem), 14 km (9 mi) northeast of Brussels. The airport has non-stop flights from the United States and Canada, and many destinations within Europe. Ryanair uses the smaller Brussels South Charleroi Airport, 46 km (29 mi) south of Brussels, as a hub. Belgium's national airline, SN Brussels Airlines, has routes to the United States, Africa, and all over Europe.

There are no scheduled domestic flights within Belgium.

Trains run up to four times each hour from Brussels Airport to the city center, taking around 15 minutes. A one-way ticket costs €2.90. Direct services also run from the airport to several other cities. Bus connections to the city leave from level 0. These cost about the same, but take longer. Taxis cost around €35 to the city center.

Autocars l'Elan operates an hourly shuttle-bus service between Brussels South Charleroi Airport and Brussels South railway station. The journey takes 40 minutes and costs €13 one way, €22 return.

Airport Information Brussels Airport *(BRU)* (☎ 02/753–7753 ⊕ *www.brus selsairport.be)*. **Brussels South Charleroi Airport** *(CRL)* (☎ 071/25–12–29

⊕ *www.charleroi-airport.com*). **SN Brussels Airlines** (☎ *516/622–2248 in U.S., 0870/735–2345 in U.K., 02/200–6234 in Belgium* ⊕ *www.brusselsairlines.com*). **Ryanair** (⊕ *www.ryanair.com*).

Contacts Autocars l'Elan (⊕ *www.voyages-lelan.be*). **SNCB/NMBS** (☎ *02/528–2828 or 02/555–2525* ⊕ *www.b-rail.be*).

BY BUS

Belgium has an extensive network of reasonably priced urban and intercity buses. STIB/MIVB covers service around the Brussels region. De Lijn runs buses in Flanders, including Antwerp, Brugge, and Gent. Eurolines has up to three daily express services between Brussels and Amsterdam, Berlin, Frankfurt, Paris, and London, and offers student fares.

Bus Information De Lijn (☎ *070/22-02-00*). **Eurolines** (☎ *02/274–1350* ⊕ *www. eurolines.com*). **STIB/MIVB** (☎ *0900/10–310* ⊕ *www.stib.be*).

BY CAR

Belgium is a small country, and driving distances are not great. Most destinations are not more than two hours from Brussels. There are no tolls, but the major highways can get very congested. Driving within cities can be a nightmare if you're not used to Belgian roads. You may have to compete with trams or taxi drivers with a death wish. Brussels is 204 km (122 mi) from Amsterdam on E19; and 308 km (185 mi) from Paris on E19.

On highways in Belgium the speed limit is 120 KPH (75 MPH). The limit on other rural roads is 90 KPH (55 MPH), and 50 KPH (30 MPH) in urban areas. Use of seatbelts is compulsory, both in front and rear seats. Turning right on a red light is not permitted. Your car must carry a red warning triangle in case of breakdown. All cars rented in Belgium will already have these. Drinking and driving is prohibited.

BY FERRY

Transeuropa Ferries has services between Ramsgate, England, and Oostende, with four daily round-trips. P & O Ferries operates overnight ferry services once daily from Hull, England, to Zeebrugge. You can take your car.

P & O Ferries (☎ *070/70-77-71, 08716/645-645 in U.K.* ⊕ *www.poferries. com*). **Transeuropa Ferries** (☎ *059/34-02-60, 01843/595-522 in U.K.* ⊕ *www. transeuropaferries.com*).

BY TRAIN

The easiest mode of transportation within Belgium is the train. Belgian National Railways (SNCB/NMBS) maintains an extensive network of prompt and frequent services. Intercity trains have rapid connections between the major towns and cities, while local and regional trains stop at all smaller towns in between.

An expanding network of high-speed trains also puts Brussels within commuting distance of many European cities. Most of these services leave from Brussels's Gare du Midi.

Eurostar (☎ *02/528-2828* ⊕ *www.eurostar.com*). **SNCB/NMBS** (☎ *02/528-2828* or *02/555-2525* ⊕ *www.b-rail.be*). **Thalys** (☎ *0900/10-177* ⊕ *www.thalys.be*).

ABOUT THE RESTAURANTS

Belgium's better restaurants are on a par with the most renowned in the world. Prices are similar to those in France and Britain. The Belgian emphasis on high-quality food filters down to more casual options as well, from main-square cafés to the street vendors you'll find in towns large and small.

Most restaurants are open for lunch and dinner only. A set-price, three-course menu for lunch (*déjeuner* in French, *lunch* in Flemish) is offered in many restaurants. Dinner (*dîner* in French, *diner* in Flemish) menus are very similar to lunch menus. You can also order a quick sandwich lunch or a light one-course meal at cafés, pubs, cafeterias, and snack bars. Smoking in Belgian cafés and restaurants is prohibited. However, some bars above a certain size with adequate ventilation have an exemption.

MEALS & MEAL TIMES
Belgian specialties include steamed mussels, served throughout the country. *Waterzooi is* a creamy stew made with chicken or fish. *Carbonnades* or *stoverij is* a beef stew cooked in beer, while *stoemp* is a filling mix of mashed potatoes and vegetables. Eel is served, most notably as *paling in 't groen* (Flemish) or *anguilles au vert* (French), with a green herb sauce. Belgian endive (*chicons* in French, *witloof* in Flemish) is usually cooked with ham, braised, and topped with a cheese gratin. Complete your meal with *frites* or *frieten* (french fries), which Belgians proudly claim to have invented. A favorite snack is the waffle (*gaufres* in French, *wafels* in Flemish), which you can buy at stands in cities. It would also be almost criminal to visit Belgium and not try a generous sampling of the country's world-famous chocolates.

Breakfast is served in hotels from about 7 to 10. Lunch is served noon–2, and dinner 7–9. Pubs and cafés often serve snacks until midnight.

PAYING
Major credit cards are widely accepted, but smaller establishments may not. Tipping 15% is not common practice in Belgium. Nonetheless, it is customary to round off the total.

WINES, BEER & SPIRITS
Belgium is a beer-lover's paradise. Artisanal breweries produce around 800 types. Kriek, a fruit-flavored beer, and Duvel, a very strong blond beer, are favorites. Some Trappist monasteries still produce their own brews, such as Orval, Westmalle, Rochefort, and Chimay. Popular mass-produced brands are Stella Artois, Jupiler, and Maes. Keep in mind that many Belgian beers have a high alcohol content; 8%–9% alcohol per volume is not unusual.

Be sure to try locally produced *genièvre* or *jenever,* a strong, ginlike spirit taken neat. Sometimes its edge is taken off with sweeter fruit flavors like apple, lemon, and red currant.

Belgians tend not to drink their own tap water. It's perfectly safe to do so, but water aficionados don't like the taste. The locally produced Spa mineral water brands are an excellent and reasonably priced alternative.

WHAT IT COSTS IN EUROS				
¢	$	$$	$$$	$$$$
Restaurants under €10	€10–€15	€15–€20	€20–€30	over €30

Restaurant prices are per person for a main course at dinner.

ABOUT THE HOTELS

Belgium offers a range of options, from the major international hotel chains and small, modern local hotels to family-run restored inns and historic houses. Prices in metropolitan areas are significantly higher than those in outlying towns and the countryside.

DISCOUNTS
Most hotels that cater to business travelers will grant substantial weekend rebates. These discounted rates are often available during the week as well as in July and August, when business travelers are thin on the ground. Moreover, you can often qualify for a "corporate rate" when hotel occupancy is low. The moral is, always ask what's the best rate a hotel can offer before you book. No hotelier was ever born who will give a lower rate unless you ask for it.

CLASSIFICATIONS
Hotels in Belgium are rated by the Benelux Hotel Classification System, an independent agency that inspects properties in Belgium, the Netherlands, and Luxembourg. The organization's star system is the accepted norm for these countries; one star indicates the most basic hotel and five stars indicates the most luxurious. Stars are based on detailed criteria— mainly facilities and amenities, such as private baths, specific items of furniture in guest rooms, and so on. Rooms in one-star hotels are likely not to have a telephone or television, and two-star hotels may not have air-conditioning, or elevators. Four- and five-star hotels have conference facilities and offer amenities such as pools, tennis courts, saunas, private parking, dry-cleaning service, and room service. Three-, four-, and five-star hotels are usually equipped with hair dryers and coffeemakers. All hotels listed have private bath unless otherwise noted.

RESERVATIONS
It's wise to reserve your hotel in advance. You may reserve your room by telephoning or writing in English, as all hoteliers and reservations services in Belgium understand the language, and increasingly online via the hotel's own Web site.

WHAT IT COSTS IN EUROS					
	¢	$	$$	$$$	$$$$
Hotels	under €75	€75–€100	€100–€150	€150–€225	over €225

Hotel prices are for two people in a standard double room in high season, excluding tax.

PLANNING YOUR TIME

3

The four cities listed in this chapter represent the essence of modern Belgium. How you divide your time between them depends on how much of it you have and where your main interests lie. But the beauty of this land's diminutive size is that you can comfortably base yourself in one place and trip out to the others. For a one- or two-day visit you would do best to concentrate on the one city that appeals to you most. With a week, you can get a taste of all four places mentioned here. All are worth spending a few nights getting to know if you can.

Brussels is the closest thing Belgium has to a metropolis, with great museums and restaurants and a definite cosmopolitan air. While there is enough to keep you happy here for many days, the noisy traffic-clogged streets may leave you craving somewhere quieter after a while.

If that's the case, consider Brugge or Gent, together known as "The Art Cities of Flanders"—a phrase that immediately conjures up images of proud spires and medieval architecture. In the 15th century these were among the richest cities in Europe, and the aura of that golden age still seems to emanate from their cloth halls, opulent merchants' homes, and cathedrals. Of the two, Brugge is the more thoroughly preserved— visiting there really does feel like stepping into another century—but also the more popular with tourists. Gent provides similar pleasures in a more laidback environment.

Antwerp merits at least a weekend for exploring its outstanding museums, lovely architecture, top fashion shopping, fabulous restaurants, and nonstop nightlife. While the city has grown and modernized apace, it preserves a great deal of yesterday's glories.

BRUSSELS

Brussels's vibrant, cosmopolitan atmosphere and multicultural beat make it much more than simply the administrative hub of Europe. For all its world-class restaurants, architecture, and art, though, the city keeps a relatively low profile, so you'll have the breathing room to relish its landmarks, cobbled streets, and beautiful parks.

Brussels started life as a village toward the end of the 10th century. Over the next eight centuries it grew as a center for trading and crafts, and was alternately ruled by everyone from local counts of Leuven, the Burgundians Philip the Good and Charles V, to the Spanish and later Austrians. Despite its history of occupation, after 1815 the city resisted Dutch attempts to absorb it, and 1830 saw the uprising that finally gained Belgium its independence.

At the end of the 19th century Brussels was one of the liveliest cities in Europe, known for its splendid cafés and graceful Art Nouveau architecture. It later became the European Economic Community's headquarters, a precursor to its hosting of the EU's administrative and political arms. The city is technically bilingual, though French is the dominant language.

PLANNING YOUR TIME

Your first priority in Brussels should be to wander the narrow, cobbled lanes surrounding the main square and visit the graceful, arcaded Galeries St-Hubert, an elegant 19th-century shopping gallery. Head down rue de l'Etuve to see the Manneken Pis, the famed statue. Walk to the place du Grand Sablon to window-shop at its many fine antiques stores and galleries. Have lunch in one of the cafés lining the perimeter, and don't forget to buy chocolates at one of the top chocolatiers on the square. Then head to the Musée d'Art Moderne and the Musée d'Art Ancien. End with dinner on the fashionable rue Antoine Dansaert or have a drink in one of Grand'Place's many cafés.

On your second day, start at the Musée des Instruments de Musique, which houses one of Europe's finest collections of musical instruments. Hop a tram to avenue Louise in Ixelles for a little shopping and lunch. After lunch, visit architect Horta's own house, now the Musée Horta, on rue Américaine. If you crave more art and architecture, go to the Musée David-et-Alice-Van-Buuren. For dinner head to place Ste-Catherine for a feast of Belgian seafood specialties. Later, check out the many cafés and bars around the Bourse.

GETTING HERE & AROUND
BY CAR

Driving in Brussels can be an unnerving experience. Belgians weren't required to have driver's licenses until 1979, and local driving habits are often slapdash, and roads can get very busy around peak hours.

BY PUBLIC TRANSPORTATION

The metro, trams, and buses operate as part of the same system run by the city's transport authority, STIB/MIVB. A single "Jump" ticket, which can be used on all three systems in an hour-long time frame, costs €1.50. The best buy is a 10-trip ticket, which costs €10. Special tourist tickets are also a good value at €3.80 for a one-day unlimited travel card; €9 for three days; and €12 for five days (weekdays only). You can purchase these tickets in any metro station or at newsstands. Single tickets can be purchased on the bus or on the tram. You need to validate your ticket in the orange machines on the bus or tram; in the metro, validate your card at the orange machines in the station. Metro trains, buses, and trams run from around 5:30 AM until 12:30 AM.

BY TAXI

You can catch a taxi at cab stands around town, indicated with yellow signs. All officially registered taxis have a yellow-and-blue sign on their roofs. A cab ride within the city center costs between €6.20 and €12.40. Tips are included in the fare.

ESSENTIALS

Bus Station CCN Gare du Nord (✉ *rue du Progrès 80, St-Josse* ☎ *02/ 203–0707).*

Public Transportation Info STIB/MIVB (☎ *02/515–2000* ⊕ *www.stib.irisnet.be).*

Taxis Taxis Oranges (☎ *02/349–4343).* **Taxis Verts** (☎ *02/349–4949).*

Train Stations Gare Centrale (✉ *carrefour de l'Europe 2, Upper Town* ☎ *02/555–2555).* **Gare du Midi** (✉ *rue de France, Lower Town* ☎ *02/555–2555).* **Gare du Nord** (✉ *rue du Progres 76, St-Josse* ☎ *02/555–2555).*

Visitor Information Tourist Information Brussels (*TIB* ✉ *Hôtel de Ville, Grand' Place, Lower Town* ☎ *02/513–8940* ⊕ *www.brusselsinternational.be* ☺ *Weekdays 9–6).*

EXPLORING BRUSSELS

LOWER TOWN: THE HEART OF BRUSSELS

2 **Cathédrale St-Michel et Ste-Gudule.** The twin Gothic towers and outstanding stained-glass windows of the city's cathedral look down over the city. One namesake, St. Michael, is the recognized patron saint of Brussels. Very little is known about St. Gudule, the daughter of a 7th-century Carolingian nobleman, but her relics have been preserved here for the past 1,000 years. Construction of the cathedral began in 1226 and continued through the 15th century. ✉ *Parvis Ste-Gudule, Upper Town* ☎ *02/217–8345* ☺ *Weekdays 7–7, Sat. 7:30–7, Sun. 8–7.* Ⓜ *Metro: Gare Centrale. Bus: 71, 38, 65.*

1 **Centre Belge de la Bande Dessinée.** It fell to the land of Tintin, a cherished ☾ cartoon character, to create the world's first museum dedicated to the ninth art—comic strips. Despite its primary appeal to children, comic-strip art has been taken seriously in Belgium for decades. Based in an elegant 1903 Victor Horta–designed Art Nouveau building, the museum is long on history but sadly short on kid-friendly interaction. ✉ *rue des Sables 20, Lower Town* ☎ *02/219–1980* ⊕ *www.comicscenter. net* 🎫 *€7.50* ☺ *Tues.–Sun. 10–6* Ⓜ *Metro: Botanique.*

3 **Galeries St-Hubert.** This arcade was built in 1847 as the world's first covered shopping gallery, thanks to new engineering techniques that allowed architects to use iron girders to design soaring constructions of glass. The shops are generally open Monday–Saturday 10–6. ✉ *Access from rue des Bouchers or carrefour de l'Europe, Lower Town* ☎ *02/512–2116* Ⓜ *Metro: Gare Centrale.*

NEED A BREAK? **A la Mort Subite** (✉ *rue Montagne-aux-Herbes-Potagères 7, Lower Town* ☎ *02/513–1318)* **is a Brussels institution named after a card game called Sudden Death. This 1920s café with its high ceilings, wooden tables, and mirrored walls brews its own traditional Brussels beers, Lambic, Gueuze, and Faro.**

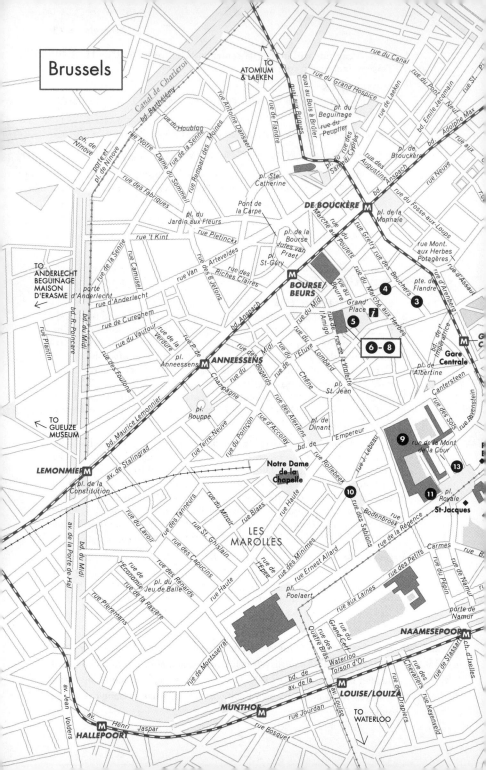

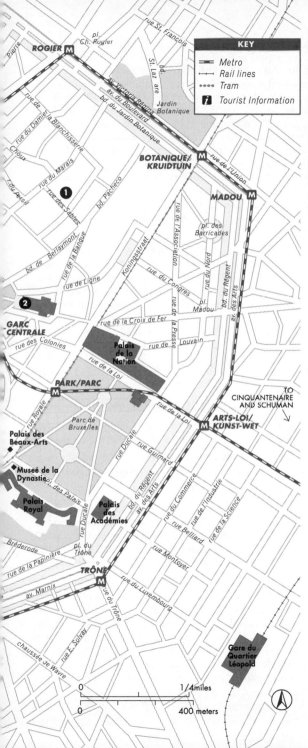

⑤ Grand'Place. This jewel is arguably Europe's most ornate and most the-
Fodor's Choice atrical square. It's a vital part of the city—everyone passes through
★ at some point. At night the flood-lit burnished facades of the guild
houses and their gilded statuary look especially dramatic. Built in ornate
Baroque style soon after 1695, the square's guild houses have a striking
architectural coherence. Among the buildings on the north side of the
square, Nos. 1–2, **Le Roy d'Espagne,** belonged to the bakers' guild. **Le
Sac,** No. 4, commissioned by the guild of joiners and coopers, and No.
6, **Le Cornet,** built for the boatmen, were both designed by Antoon
Pastorana, a gifted furniture maker. **Le Renard,** No. 7, was designed
for the guild of haberdashers and peddlers. **Le Cygne,** No. 9, was formerly a butchers' guild. ⊠ *Intersection of rue des Chapeliers, rue Buls,
rue de la Tête d'Or, rue au Beurre, rue Chair et Pain, rue des Harengs,
and rue de la Colline, Lower Town* Ⓜ *Metro: De Brouckere, Gare
Centrale. Tram: Bourse.*

Hôtel de Ville. The Gothic town hall, which dates from the early 15th century, dominates the Grand'Place. It's nearly 300 years older than the surrounding guild houses, as it survived the devastating fires of 1695. The
left wing was begun in 1402, but was soon found to be too small. An
extension was begun in 1444. Inside are a number of excellent Brussels
and Mechelen tapestries, some of them in the Gothic Hall, where recitals and chamber-music concerts are frequently held. ⊠ *Grand'Place,
Lower Town* ☎ *02/279–4365* 💶 *€3* ☉ *Guided tours only, Tues. and
Wed.: Dutch 1:45, French 2:30, English 3:15. Sun: Dutch 10, English
10:45 and 12:15, French 11:30* Ⓜ *Metro: De Brouckere, Gare Centrale.
Tram: Bourse.*

**NEED A
BREAK?** There are plenty of cafés to choose from on Grand'Place. But **Le Roy
d'Espagne** (⊠ *Grand'Place 1, Lower Town* ☎ *02/513–0807* ⊕ *www.royd
espagne.be*) is by far the most popular. In the summer, sit out on the terrace and soak up the beauty of the square; in winter, snuggle up to the huge
fire. You can expect to pay a few euros more for coffees and beers in the
Grand'Place area, but the view is worth it.

⑧ Maison de la Brasserie. On the same side of the Grand'Place as the Hôtel
de Ville, this was once the brewers' guild. The building houses a modest
brewery museum, appropriate enough in a country that still brews 400
different beers. ⊠ *Grand'Place 10, Lower Town* ☎ *02/511–4987* 💶 *€5*
☉ *Daily 10–5* Ⓜ *Metro: De Brouckere, Gare Centrale. Tram: Bourse.*

⑥ Manneken Pis. This emblem of Brussels has drawn sightseers for centuries—but you may be underwhelmed by this small statue of a pee-
ing boy. The first mention of him dates from 1377, and he's said to
symbolize what Belgians think of the authorities. The present version
was commissioned from sculptor Jerome Duquesnoy in 1619. It is a
copy; the original was seized by French soldiers in 1747. On one or
two days of the year, he spouts wine or beer rather than water. ⊠ *rue
de l'Etuve at rue du Chêne, Lower Town* Ⓜ *Metro: Gare Centrale.
Bus: 34, 48, 95.*

7 **Musée du Costume et de la Dentelle.** The costume and lace museum pays
tribute to Brussels' textile-making past. Housed in four 17th-century houses and a warehouse, the museum is something of a 17th-to 18th-century fashion show. ⊠*rue de la Violette 12, Lower Town* ☎*02/213–4450* ☜*€3* ✆*Mon., Tues., Thurs., and Fri. 10–12:30 and 1:30–5; weekends 2–5.* Ⓜ*Metro: Gare Centrale.*

UPPER TOWN: ROYAL BRUSSELS

11 **Musée d'Art Ancien.** In the first of the interconnected art museums, the
Ancient Art Museum pays special attention to the great, so-called Flemish Primitives of the 15th century, who revolutionized the art of painting with oil. The Spanish and the Austrians pilfered some of the finest works, but there's plenty left by the likes of Rogier van der Weyden and Hieronymus Bosch. The collection of works by Pieter Brueghel the Elder is outstanding. Works by Rubens, Van Dyck, and Jordaans are on the floor above. An underground passage connects this museum to the adjacent Musée d'Art Moderne. ⊠*rue de la Régence 3, Upper Town* ☎*02/508–3211* ⊕*www.fine-arts-museum.be* ☜*€5* ✆*Tues.–Sun. 10–5* Ⓜ*Metro: Louise/Park. Tram: 92, 94.*

9 **Musée d'Art Moderne.** Rather like New York's Guggenheim Museum in
reverse, the Modern Art Museum burrows underground, circling downward eight floors. The collection is strong on Belgian and French art of the past 100 years, including such Belgian artists as the Expressionist James Ensor and the Surrealists Paul Delvaux and René Magritte. ⊠*pl. Royale 1, Upper Town* ☎*02/508–3211* ⊕*www.fine-arts-museum.be* ☜*€5* ✆*Tues.–Sun. 10–5* Ⓜ*Metro: Louise/Park. Tram: 92, 94.*

12 **Musée des Instruments de Musique (MIM).** In addition to seeing the more
than 1,500 instruments on display, you can listen to them via infrared headphones. There's a rich selection of European folk instruments, as well as creations by the amazingly prolific Adolphe Sax. The entrance is in one of the city's most beautiful Art Nouveau buildings—the former Old England department store, designed by architect Paul Saintenoy in 1899. ⊠*rue Montagne de la Cour 2, Upper Town* ☎*02/545–0130* ⊕*www.mim.fgov.be* ☜*€5* ✆*Tues.–Fri. 9:30–5, weekends 10–5* Ⓜ*Metro: Gare Centrale. Tram: 92. 94, Bus: 71.*

10 **Place du Grand Sablon.** "Sand Square" is where the people of Brussels
come to see and be seen. The elegant square is surrounded by restaurants, cafés, and antiques shops. Every weekend morning a lively antiques market takes over the upper end. ⊠*Intersection of rue de Rollebeek, rue Lebeau, rue de la Paille, rue Ste-Anne, rue Boedenbroeck, rue des Sablons, petite rue des Minimes, rue des Minimes, and rue Joseph Stevens, Upper Town* Ⓜ*Metro: Louise. Tram: 92, 94.*

4 **Quartier de l'Îlôt Sacré.** Flimflam artists and jewelry vendors mingle with
the crowds in the narrow rue des Bouchers and even narrower petite rue des Bouchers. While many streets in central Brussels were widened as part of the preparations for the 1958 World's Fair, these tiny routes escaped, and the area was given special protection. As long as you watch out for pickpockets, it's all good-natured fun in the liveliest area in Brussels, where restaurants and cafés stand cheek by jowl, their tables

spilling out onto the sidewalks. The restaurants make strenuous efforts to pull you in with huge displays of seafood. The quality, alas, is a different matter, and there have been arrests in recent years for large-scale credit-card fraud. *(For one outstanding exception, see Where to Eat, below.)* ⊕*www.ilotsacre.be* Ⓜ*Metro: Gare Centrale.*

SCHUMAN

Musées Royaux d'Art et de l'Histoire. For a chronologically and culturally wide-ranging collection of artworks, hit the sprawling Royal Museums of Art and History. The vast numbers of antiquities and ethnographic treasures come from all over the world. Don't miss the colossal Easter Island statue. ✉*Parc du Cinquantenaire 10, Etterbeek* ☎*02/741–7211* ⊕*www.kmkg-mrah.be* 🎟*€5, free 1st Wed. of every month 1–5* ⊙*Tues.–Sun. 10–5* Ⓜ*Metro: Schuman, Merode, Tram: 81.*

IXELLES

Musée Horta. The house where Victor Horta (1861–1947), the creator of Art Nouveau, lived and worked until 1919 is the best place to see his mesmerizing interiors and furniture. Inside, a glazed skylight filters light down the curling banisters, lamps hang like tendrils from the ceilings, and mirrored skylights evoke giant butterflies with multicolor wings of glass and steel. Like Frank Lloyd Wright after him, Horta had a hand in every aspect of his design, from door hinges to wall treatments. ✉*rue Américaine 25, Ixelles* ☎*02/543–0490* ⊕*www.hortamuseum.be* 🎟*€7* ⊙*Tues.–Sun. 2–5:30* Ⓜ*Tram: 92, 81.*

NORTH OF CENTER

🕙 **Atomium.** Built for the 1958 World's Fair, the model of an iron molecule enlarged 165 billion times is one of Brussels' landmarks. It reopened in 2006 after a massive renovation spruced up its exhibition spaces, and put in a new café. Take an express elevator to the top, 400 feet up, for panoramic views of Brussels. ✉*blvd. du Centenaire, Heysel* ☎*02/475–4777* ⊕*www.atomium.be* 🎟*€9* ⊙*Daily 10–7* Ⓜ*Metro: Heysel. Tram: 23, 81.*

Musée Magritte. The Surrealist artist René Magritte (1898–1967) lived in this house with his wife for 24 highly productive years. You can visit his studio and see a collection of original works, documents, personal effects, and photographs. Take tram 49 to the Woeste stop (in Jette commune). ✉*rue Esseghem 135, Jette* ☎*02/428–2626* ⊕*www.magritte museum.be* 🎟*€7* ⊙*Wed.–Sun. 10–6* Ⓜ*Tram: 49.*

WHERE TO EAT

$$–$$$$ ✗**Aux Armes de Bruxelles.** A reliable choice among the many tourist traps of the Ilôt Sacré, this kid-friendly restaurant attracts a largely local clientele with its slightly tarnished middle-class elegance and Belgian classics: turbot waterzooi, a variety of steaks, and mussels prepared every conceivable way. The place is cheerful and light, and service is friendly if frequently overstretched. ✉*rue des Bouchers 13, Lower Town* ☎*02/511–5550* ⊟*AE, DC, MC, V* ⊙*Closed Mon.* Ⓜ*Metro: Gare Centrale.*

$$$–$$$$ ✕**Belga Queen.** Any runs on this former bank are now impelled by the kitchen's modern take on traditional Belgian cuisine. A trendy crowd gathers under the 19th-century stained-glass ceiling, angling for a place at the oyster bars or a dish of *waterzooi* cooked in a wok. Don't be alarmed by the unisex bathroom stalls—the clear-glass doors become opaque once they're locked. ⊠*rue du Fossé-aux-Loups 32, Lower Town* ☎*02/217–2187* ⌿*Reservations essential* ▤*AE, DC, MC, V* Ⓜ*Metro: De Brouckere.*

$$$$ ✕**Comme Chez Soi.** Pierre Wynants, the perfectionist owner-chef of what
Fodor'sChoice   many consider the best restaurant in the country, has decorated his
★   bistro-size restaurant in Art Nouveau style. The superb cuisine, excellent wines, and attentive service complement the warm decor. Wynants is ceaselessly inventive, and earlier creations are quickly relegated to the back page of the menu. Book weeks in advance to be sure of a table. ⊠*pl. Rouppe 23, Lower Town* ☎*02/512–2921* ⌿*Reservations essential Jacket and tie* ▤*AE, DC, MC, V* ⊘*Closed Sun., Mon., July, and Dec. 25–Jan. 1. No lunch Wed.* Ⓜ*Metro: Anneessens.*

$$–$$$ ✕**La Quincaillerie.** The name means "The Hardware Store," and that's precisely what this place used to be. It still looks the part, except now there are tables perched on the narrow balcony and there's an oyster bar downstairs. It attracts a stylish, youngish clientele and offers good deals on business lunches. The menu consists mostly of brasserie standbys, but it's enlivened by such selections as honey-baked Barbary duck with lime and a glorious seafood platter. ⊠*rue du Page 45, Ixelles* ☎*02/538–2553* ▤*AE, DC, MC, V* ⊘*No lunch weekends* Ⓜ*Tram: 81.*

$$–$$$ ✕**L'Idiot du Village.** Don't believe the modest name of this restaurant in the Marolles; its focus on smart, well-crafted food has fostered a loyal clientele. The decor is relaxed and intimate, kitschy rather than trendy. Dishes include bass with lemon confit, and warm escalope of foie gras with pepper and vanilla. ⊠*rue Notre-Seigneur 19, Upper Town* ☎*02/502–5582* ▤*AE, DC, MC, V* ⊘*Closed weekends* Ⓜ*Metro: Gare Centrale. Tram: 92, 94.*

$–$$$ ✕**Taverne du Passage.** This Art Deco brasserie in the famous shopping arcade has been here since 1928 and remains a benchmark of its kind, serving chicken waterzooi, sauerkraut, herring, and lobster from noon to midnight nonstop. Most fun of all, however, are the roasts, which are carved before you. The multilingual waiters are jolly, and the wine list is exceptional—not surprising in a restaurant owned by the president of the Belgian guild of sommeliers. ⊠*Galerie de la Reine 30, Upper Town* ☎*02/512–3731* ▤*AE, DC, MC, V* ⊘*Closed Wed. and Thurs. and June and July* Ⓜ*Metro: Gare Centrale, De Brouckere.*

$–$$ ✕**'t Kelderke.** Head down into this 17th-century vaulted cellar restaurant for traditional Belgian cuisine served at plain wooden tables. Portions are huge, and mussels are the house specialty, but the *stoemp et saucisses* (mashed potatoes and sausages) are equally tasty. It's a popular place with locals, and there are no reservations, so turn up early to be sure of a table. ⊠*Grand'Place 15, Lower Town* ☎*02/513–7344* ▤*AE, DC, MC, V* Ⓜ*Metro: De Brouckere. Tram: Bourse.*

WHERE TO STAY

$$$$ ⊞**Amigo.** A block from the Grand'Place, the Amigo pairs contemporary
★ design with antiques and plush wall hangings. Rooms are decorated
in green, red, or blue, with silk curtains, leather headboards, and a
mix of modern furniture and antiques. Works by Belgian artists hang
on the walls, while Tintin pictures and figurines cheer up the mosaic-
tiled bathrooms. If you'd like a view over the surrounding rooftops,
ask for a room on one of the higher floors (these also have a higher
rate). **Pros:** conveniently located next to many of Brussels' major attractions. **Cons:** location can make it noisy, some rooms are small. ⊠*rue
d'Amigo 1–3, Lower Town* ☎*02/547–4747* ⊕*www.roccofortehotels.
com* ⊲*176 rooms, 18 suites* ⌂*In-room: safe, Internet. In-hotel: restaurant, room service, bar, gym, parking (paid)* ☰*AE, DC, MC, V*
Ⓜ*Metro: De Brouckere, Gare Centrale. Tram: Bourse.*

¢–$ ⊞**George V.** Ivy-covered and quiet, this hotel fills a large house dating
from 1859. Rooms, which accommodate up to four people, are simple
but spacious, bright, and clean. Some have a deep shower tub rather
than a full bath. The homey breakfast room has wicker chairs. Although
centrally located, the hotel's on a calm residential street. **Pros:** family-
run hotel, reasonable prices, close to the Brussels nightlife. **Cons:** some
rooms are small. ⊠*rue t' Kint 23, Lower Town* ☎*02/513–5093* ⊲*16
rooms* ⌂*In-room: Internet, Wi-Fi. In-hotel: room service, bar, parking
(paid)* ☰*AE, MC, V* ⚊|CP Ⓜ*Tram: Bourse.*

$$$$ ⊞**Jolly Grand Sablon.** Part of the Sablon square's lineup of antiques
shops, cafés, and chocolate makers, the Jolly offers discreet luxury
behind an elegant white facade. The reception area is set within a
hushed arcade of private art galleries, and there's a pretty interior cobbled courtyard. Ask for a room at the back, as the square outside is
often clogged with traffic and the weekend antiques market gets going
at 6 AM. **Pros:** good location in the pretty Sablon. **Cons:** staff can be a
bit unfriendly. ⊠*rue Bodenbroeck 2–4, Upper Town* ☎*02/512–8800*
⊲*193 rooms, 6 suites* ⌂*In-room: Internet. In-hotel: restaurant, bar,
parking (paid)* ☰*AE, DC, MC, V* ⚊|BP Ⓜ*Metro: Louise, Park.*

¢–$ ⊞**La Vieille Lanterne.** More bed-and-breakfast than hotel, this tiny, old
place of six rooms is run by the family that owns the gift shops on the
ground floor. All rooms look out onto the street and the crowds that
cluster round the famous Manneken Pis fountain opposite; each has
a bathroom with shower only. The linoleum floors and wood furniture are cheered by pink, green, and yellow stained-glass windows.
Breakfast is served in the rooms. **Pros:** good price for such a central
location. **Cons:** its location near Manneken Pis makes it a noisy, hectic location; no on-site parking. ⊠*rue des Grands Carmes 29, Lower
Town* ☎*02/512–7494* ⊲*6 rooms* ⌂*In hotel: room service, some pets
allowed* ☰*AE, DC, MC, V* ⚊|CP Ⓜ*Metro: Bourse.*

$$$–$$$$ ⊞**Le Dixseptième.** Here you can stay in what was once the residence of
Fodor'sChoice the Spanish ambassador. The stylishly restored 17th-century building
★ lies between the Grand'Place and the Gare Centrale. Rooms surround
a lovely interior courtyard, and suites are up a splendid Louis XVI
staircase. Named after Belgian artists, rooms have whitewashed walls,
plain floorboards, exposed beams, and suede sofas. **Pros:** good central

location, hotel has more charm than chain brands. **Cons:** some reviews complain of unfriendly staff. ✉*rue de la Madeleine 25, Lower Town* ☎*02/502–5744* ⊕*www.ledixseptieme.be* ⤴*22 rooms, 2 suites* ♿*In-room: safe, kitchen (some), Internet, Wi-Fi. In-hotel: bar* ▤*AE, DC, MC, V* Ⓜ*Metro: De Brouckere.*

$$–$$$ ⊞ **Stanhope.** This exclusive hotel was created out of three adjoining
★   town houses and continues to expand. Some rooms have high ceilings, marble bathrooms, and luxurious furniture, while others have a more modern look aimed at business travelers. Larger rooms and suites, indicated by thematic names, have individual looks and canopied beds. **Pros:** friendly staff, nice rooms. **Cons:** slightly farther from historic center than some hotels. ✉*rue du Commerce 9, Upper Town* ☎*02/506–9111* ⊕*www.summithotels.com* ⤴*108 rooms, 7 suites, 2 royal suites* ♿*In-room: safe, Internet. In-hotel: restaurant, bar, gym, parking (paid)* ▤*AE, DC, MC, V* ⏍*CP* Ⓜ*Metro: Trone.*

SHOPPING

There are galleries scattered across Brussels, but low rents have made **boulevard Barthélémy** the "in" place for avant-garde art. On the **place du Grand Sablon** and adjoining streets and alleys you'll find antiques dealers and smart art galleries. The **Galeries St-Hubert** is a rather stately shopping arcade lined with posh shops selling men's and women's clothing, books, and objets d'art. In the trendy **rue Antoine Dansaert** and **place du Nouveau Marché aux Grains,** near the Bourse, are a number of boutiques carrying fashions by young designers and interior design and art shops. **Avenue Louise** and its surrounding streets in Ixelles have a number of chic boutiques offering clothes new and vintage, jewelry, antiques, and housewares.

BRUGGE

Long thought of as a Sleeping Beauty reawakened, Brugge is an ancient village whose heritage has been well preserved. However, the contemporary comparison is sometimes closer to Beauty and the Beast—particularly in summer, when visitors flock here in overwhelming numbers. Still, in the quiet, colder seasons, the city offers a peaceful refuge, and you can feel the rhythm of life centuries ago. Brugge is compact, like a small island amid the winding waterways, and the twists and turns may lead you to unexpected pleasures.

PLANNING YOUR TIME

Must-see spots include the Begijnhof near Minnewater, as well as the great buildings around Burg and Markt squares. Soak up the artwork, including the Groeninge and Memling museums, and Michelangelo's sculpture in the Onze-Lieve-Vrouwekerk. You might take an afternoon canal ride—or, after dinner, when crowds have thinned, wander alongside the water.

GETTING HERE & AROUND

BY BIKE

Considering the flat-as-a-pancake terrain, it's easy to travel on two wheels. You can rent bikes at rental shops or at the train station. A valid train ticket gets you a discounted rate. **Quasimundo Bike Tours** organizes several itineraries, including an introduction to Brugge and a nighttime Brugge ride, for €24 per person.

BY BUS

The **De Lijn** bus company provides bus services in Brugge. Most buses run every five minutes (less often on Sundays). Several lines take you from the station to the city center. Buy your tickets on board (€1.60) or from ticket machines (€1.20) at the terminus.

BY CAR

Brugge is 5 km (3 mi) north of the E40 motorway, which links it to Brussels. It is 126 km (76 mi) from the Le Shuttle terminus at Calais. Access for cars into Brugge's center is severely restricted. The historic streets are narrow and often one-way. There are huge parking lots at the railway station and near the exits from the ring road, plus underground parking at 't Zand.

BY TRAIN

The Belgian national railway, **NMBS/SNCB,** sends two trains each hour to Brugge from Brussels (50 minutes) and three an hour from Gent (25 minutes).

BY BOAT

The waterways in the center of Brugge make for lovely sightseeing. Independent motor launches depart from four jetties along the Dijver and Katelijnestraat and by the Vismarkt as soon as they are reasonably full (every 15 minutes or so) daily March–November and depending on the weather in December and February. The trips take half an hour and cost €5.50.

ESSENTIALS

Bus De Lijn (☎059/56–52–11 West Flanders, www.delijn.be).

Bike Tours Quasimundo Bike Tours (☎050/33–07–75 ⊕www.quasimundo. com).

Bike Rental Bauhaus Bike Rental (✉Langestraat 135 ☎050/34–10–93).

Car Rentals Avis (✉Koningin Astridlaan 97 ☎050/39–44–00 ⊕www.avis.be).

Train Station Brugge (✉Stationsplein ☎050/38–23–82).

Visitor Information Brugge (✉In&Uit Brugge, 't Zand 34 ☎050/44–46–46 ⊕www.brugge.be).

EXPLORING BRUGGE

Brugge has tangled streets, narrow canals, handsome squares, and old gabled buildings that were such a powerful magnet more than a century ago. Although often called Bruges, its French name, the city's official name is indeed Brugge (*bruhg*-guh), and you'll score points with the locals by using the Flemish title. You can buy a €15 combination ticket for entry into five municipal museums: the Museum voor Volkskunde, the Groeningemuseum, the Gruuthusemuseum, the Memling, and the Arentshuis. These tickets are available at all participating museums.

❽ Begijnhof. The 13th-century beguinage is a pretty and serene cluster of small, whitewashed houses, a pigeon tower, and a church surrounding a pleasant green at the edge of a canal. The Begijnhof was founded in 1245 by Margaret, Countess of Constantinople, to bring together the Beguines—girls and widows from all social backgrounds who devoted themselves to charitable work but who were not bound by religious vows. Today the site is occupied by Benedictine nuns. One house has been set aside as a small museum. ✉ *Oude Begijnhof, off Wijngaard-straat* ☏ *050/33–00–11* 🔖 *Free, house visit €2* ◷ *Mar.–Nov., daily 9:30–5; Dec.–Feb., Mon., Tues., Fri. 10–noon, Wed. and Thurs. 2–4* Ⓜ *Bus 12.*

❷ Burg. A popular daytime meeting place and an enchanting, floodlit scene after dark, the Burg is flanked by striking civic buildings. Named for the fortress built by Baldwin of the Iron Arm, the Burg was also the former site of the 10th-century Carolingian Cathedral of St. Donaas, which was destroyed by French Republicans in 1799. ✉ *Hoogstraat and Breidelstraat* Ⓜ *Bus 1 or 12.*

❺ Groeningemuseum. The holdings of this gallery give you a crash course
★ in the Flemish Primitives and their successors. Hugo Van der Goes, Hieronymus Bosch, Pieter Bruegel (both Elder and Younger)—all are represented here. You can see Jan van Eyck's wonderfully realistic *Madonna with Canon Van der Paele,* in which van Eyck achieved texture and depth through multiple layers of oil and varnish. There's also one of Hans Memling's greatest works, the *Moreel Triptych.* ✉ *Dijver 12* ☏ *050/44–87–11* 🔖 *€8, includes an audioguide, combination ticket €15* ◷ *Tues.–Sun. 9:30–5* Ⓜ *Bus 1 or 12.*

❸ Heilig Bloed Basiliek. The Basilica of the Holy Blood manages to include both the austere and the ornate under one roof—not to mention one of Europe's most precious relics. The 12th-century Lower Chapel retains a stern, Romanesque character. From this sober space, an elaborate, external Gothic stairway leads to the stunningly lavish Upper Chapel. The basilica's namesake treasure is a vial thought to contain a few drops of the blood of Christ, brought from Jerusalem to Brugge in 1149 by Derick of Alsace when he returned from the Second Crusade. It is exposed every Friday in the Lower Chapel 8:30–10 and in the Upper Chapel 10–11 and 3–4. On Ascension Day it becomes the centerpiece of the magnificent *De Heilig Bloedprocessie* (Procession of the Holy Blood), a major medieval-style pageant in which it is carried through the streets of Brugge. ✉ *Burg* ☏ *050/33–67–92* ⊕ *www.holyblood.com* 🔖 *Museum: €1.50* ◷ *Apr.–Sept., Thurs.–Tues. 9:30–noon and 2–6, Wed. 9:30–noon; Oct.–Mar., Thurs.–Tues. 9:30–noon and 2–4, Wed. 9:30–noon* Ⓜ *Bus 1 or 12.*

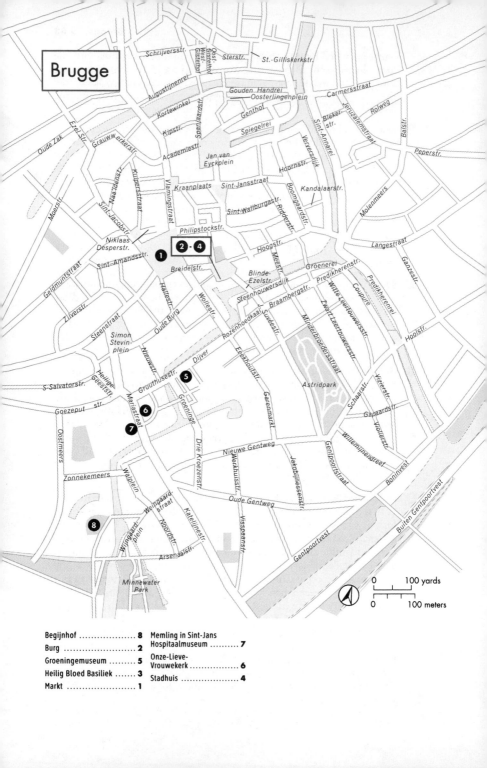

Brugge

0   100 yards

0   100 meters

NEED A BREAK? In an alley off Breidelstraat you'll find the tiny, two-tier, brick-and-beam coffeehouse and pub De Garre (⊠ *De Garre 1* ☎ *050/34–10–29*). The menu lists more than 100 regional beers. A plate of cheese, such as Oude Brugge, is a good match with one of the heartier brews. De Garre is open from noon to midnight. No credit cards.

① **Markt.** Used as a marketplace since AD 958, this square is still one of the liveliest places in Brugge. On the east side stand the provincial government house and the post office, a pastiche of Burgundian Gothic, while old guild houses with step-gabled facades line the west and north sides. The tower of the medieval **Belfort** (Belfry) on the south side dates to the 13th century (its crowning octagonal lantern was added in the 15th century). It rises to a height of 270 feet, commanding the city and the surrounding countryside. You can climb 366 winding steps to the clock mechanism, and enjoy a gorgeous panoramic view. Back down in the square, you may be tempted by the **horse-drawn carriages** that congregate here; a half-hour ride for up to four people costs €30 plus "something for the horse." ⊠ *Intersection of Steenstraat, St-Amandstraat, Vlamingstraat, Philipstockstraat, Breidelstraat, and Wollestraat* ☎ *050/44–87–11* ⊠ *€5* ☉ *Tues.–Sun., 9:30–5. Carillon concerts: Sun. 2:15–3. June 15–July 1 and Aug. 15–Sept., Mon., Wed., and Sat. 9 PM–10 PM. Oct.–June 14, Wed. and Sat. 2:15–3* Ⓜ *Bus 1 or 12.*

Fodor's Choice
★

③ **Memling in Sint-Jans Hospitaalmuseum.** The collection contains just six works, but they are of breathtaking quality and among the greatest of the Flemish Primitive school. In *The Altarpiece of St. John the Baptist and St. John the Evangelist,* two leading personages of the Burgundian court are believed to be portrayed: Mary of Burgundy (buried in the Onze-Lieve-Vrouwekerk) as St. Catherine, and Margaret of York as St. Barbara. The "paintings within the painting" give details of their lives. The miniature paintings that adorn the St. Ursula Shrine are likewise marvels of detail and poignancy. The Memling is housed in **Oud Sint-Janshospitaal,** one of the oldest surviving medieval hospitals in Europe. It was founded in the 12th century and remained in use until the early 20th century. ⊠ *Mariastraat 38* ☎ *050/44–87–11* ⊠ *€8, includes audioguide, combination ticket €15* ☉ *Tues.–Sun. 9:30–5* Ⓜ *Bus 1 or 12.*

★

⑥ **Onze-Lieve-Vrouwekerk.** The towering spire of the plain, Gothic Church of Our Lady, begun about 1220, rivals the Belfry as Brugge's symbol. It is 381 feet high, the tallest brick construction in the world. While brick can be built high, it cannot be sculpted like stone; hence the tower's somewhat severe look. Look for the small *Madonna and Child* statue, an early work by Michelangelo. The great sculptor sold it to a merchant from Brugge when the original client failed to pay. It was stolen by Napoléon, and during World War II by Nazi leader Hermann Göring; now the white-marble figure sits in a black-marble niche behind an altar at the end of the south aisle. ⊠ *Dijver and Mariastraat* ☎ *No phone* ⊠ *€6, includes entry to Gruuthusemuseum* ☉ *Weekdays 9–4:50, Sat. 9–4:40, Sun. 1:30–5* Ⓜ *Bus 1 or 12.*

Reien. The narrow and meandering *reien,* or canals, with their old humpback stone bridges, give Brugge its character, opening up perspective and imposing their calm. The view from the **Meebrug** is especially picturesque. Farther along the Groenerei are the **Godshuizen De Pelikaan,** almshouses dating from the early 18th century. There are several such charitable buildings in the city, tiny houses built by the guilds for the poor, some still serving their original purpose. From the **Rozenhoedkaai** canal the view of the heart of the city includes the pinnacles of the town hall, basilica, and Belfry—the essence of Brugge.

> ### A FAMILY BREW
>
> **De Halve Maan** (⊠ *Walplein, between Wijngaardstraat and Zonnkemeers* ☎ *050/33–26–97* ⊘ *Daily 10–6*) is the only family brewery left in Brugge. Their beers are called Brugse Zot (Fool of Brugge); it owes its name to Maximilian of Austria, who was welcomed to the city by a procession of fools and jesters. Work up a thirst by touring the brewery itself for €5, drink included.

4 **Stadhuis.** White sandstone towers with 48 decorated window recesses define the town hall, a jewel of Gothic architecture that marked the transition of power from the nobility to the city aldermen. Built at the end of the 14th century, it's the oldest town hall in Belgium, and served as the model for the community centers in every Flemish town. Inside, a grand staircase ascends to the Gothic Hall, which has a marvelous, double-vaulted timber roof. ⊠ *Burg 12* ☎ *050/44–81–41* 💰 *€2.50, includes Museum van het Brugse Vrije in the Voormalige Civiele Griffie and audioguide* ⊘ *Daily 9:30–5* Ⓜ *Bus 1 or 12.*

WHERE TO EAT

$$–$$$$ ✕ **Breydel–De Coninc.** In a plum spot along the route from the Markt to the Burg, this no-frills restaurant is well known among locals. The plain furnishings leave the focus on the fresh seafood for which the establishment is famed. Although eel and steak are available, the restaurant's biggest draw is mussels—there's nothing more deliciously Belgian than a huge crock heaped high with shiny, blue-black shells. ⊠ *Breidelstraat 24* ☎ *050/33–97–46* ⊟ *MC, V* ⊘ *Closed Wed.* Ⓜ *Bus 1 or 12.*

$$$–$$$$ ✕ **Chez Olivier.** Set above a quiet canal, with white swans gliding below, this French charmer is purely romantic. Chef Olivier Foucad uses impeccably fresh ingredients for "light food," such as scallops in ginger and herbs, duck in rosemary honey, and lightly marbled Charolais beef. For the best views, request a window seat next to the water. ⊠ *Meestraat 9* ☎ *050/33–36–59* ⊟ *MC, V* ⊘ *Closed Thurs. and Sun. No lunch Sat.* Ⓜ *Bus 1.*

$$$$ ✕ **De Karmeliet.** This stately, 18th-century house with a graceful English
★ garden is a world-renowned culinary landmark. Owner-chef Geert Van Hecke's inventive kitchen changes the menu every two months; you might be offered goose liver with truffled potatoes or cod carpaccio with asparagus. ⊠ *Langestraat 19* ☎ *050/33–82–59* ⊘ *Reservations essential. Jacket required* ⊟ *AE, DC, MC, V* ⊘ *Closed Sun. and Mon.* Ⓜ *Bus 6.*

$$$$ ✕**Den Gouden Harynck.** Few culinary artists have the depth and natural flair of chef Philippe Serruys. In his unpretentious, airy dining room you are treated to beautifully presented, creative French dishes, though the name of the restaurant, "the golden herring," is hardly a French specialty. ✉*Groeninge 25* ☎*050/33–76–37* ▭*AE, DC, MC, V* ⊙*Closed Sun. and Mon. No lunch Sat.* Ⓜ*Bus 1 or 12.*

$$$ ✕**'t Bourgoensch Hof.** Although its weathered timbers and sharp-raked roofs were rebuilt at the turn of the 20th century, this restaurant, 't Bourgoensch Hof, is housed in one of the most medieval-looking buildings in Brugge. It also has one of the city's most romantic, canal-side settings, with the light from the windows shedding kaleidoscopic reflections onto the water. The cuisine is as appealing as the setting, with selections including panfried langoustines with wild mushrooms, and turbot medallions with coriander and caramelized leeks. ✉*Wollestraat 39* ☎*050/33–16–45* ⊕*www.bourgoensch-hof.be* ▭*AE, DC, MC, V* ⊙*Closed Tues. and Wed.* Ⓜ*Bus 1 or 11.*

3

WHERE TO STAY

$–$$ 🏨**Bryghia.** This restored German–Austrian trade center is a handsome 15th-century landmark. Outside, the brick walls are lined with paned windows and flower boxes; inside, the hotel is warmed by pastel floral fabrics and beech cabinets. Bedrooms are simple yet comfortable, and the public rooms include small sitting areas and a beamed, slate-floor breakfast salon. **Pros:** quiet location. **Cons:** a little way from the sights. ✉*Oosterlingenplein 4* ☎*050/33–80–59* ⊕*www.bryghiahotel.be* ↩*18 rooms* ♿*In-room: safe, minibar. In-hotel: bar, parking (paid)* ▭*AE, DC, V* ⦿*BP* Ⓜ*Bus 4 or 14.*

¢–$ 🏨**De Pauw.** From the ivy-covered brick exterior to the fresh flowers and doilies in the breakfast parlor, this is a welcoming little inn, set in a square opposite Sint-Gillis church. Rooms have names rather than numbers to give them a homier feel, and needlepoint cushions and old framed prints add to the warmth. **Pros:** quiet location; good value. **Cons:** limited parking; rooms quite small. ✉*Sint-Gilliskerkhof 8* ☎*050/33–71–18* ⊕*www.hoteldepauw.be* ↩*8 rooms, 6 with bath* ♿*In-hotel: parking (free)* ▭*MC, V* ⦿*BP* Ⓜ*Bus 4 or 14.*

$$$–$$$$ 🏨**De Tuileriëen.** Patrician tastes suffuse this 15th-century mansion. The decor is genteel, with reproduction antique furniture, Venetian glass windows, and weathered marble complemented by mixed-print fabrics and wall coverings in celadon, slate, and cream. Rooms are romantic, with marble-accented bathrooms, although those with canal views receive some traffic noise; courtyard rooms are quieter. The firelit bar is filled with cozy tartan wing chairs. When the weather holds, breakfast is served on the terrace alongside the canal. **Pros:** charming; elegant; historic building. **Cons:** very expensive; on main tourist drag, so can get noisy. ✉*Dijver 7* ☎*050/34–36–91* ⊕*www.hoteltuilerieen.com* ↩*22 rooms, 23 suites* ♿*In-room: safe, Internet. In-hotel: bar, pool, bicycles, laundry service, parking (paid)* ▭*AE, DC, MC, V* ⦿*BP* Ⓜ*Bus 1 or 12.*

$$$ ⊞**Hotel Heritage.** Once a private mansion, this 19th-century building
★ has been converted into a lavish hotel. Guest rooms are in keeping
with the building's heritage—elegant, with chandeliers, reproduc-
tion antique furniture, and warm fabrics in reds and golds. The hotel
is just a few steps from the Markt. There's also a sauna and fitness
room in the vaulted cellar. **Pros:** great location; friendly staff; historic
building. **Cons:** parking somewhat limited. ⊠*Niklaas Desparsstraat
11* ☎*050/44–44–44* ⊕*www.hotel-heritage.be* ⏎*20 rooms, 4 suites*
⟐*In-room: minibar, safe, Internet, Wi-Fi. In-hotel: bar, Wi-Fi* ▤*AE,
DC, MC, V* ⏏○⏐*BP* Ⓜ*Bus 2 or 12.*

$$$–$$$$ ⊞**Relais Bourgondisch Cruyce.** This truly magnificent hotel is situated in
★ one of the most romantic corners of Brugge. Some rooms overlook the
canal, and all of them, whether with classic or modern furnishings, live
up to the highest expectations. Bathrooms are large and well equipped;
all rooms have a large flat-screen TV. **Pros:** great location; historic build-
ing; friendly. **Cons:** limited parking (reserve in advance). ⊠*Wollestraat
41–47* ☎*050/33–79–26* ⊕*www.relaisbourgondischcruyce.be* ⏎*16
rooms* ⟐*In-room: minibar. In-hotel: restaurant, parking (paid)* ▤*AE,
MC, V* Ⓜ*Bus 1 or 11.*

ANTWERP

Antwerp is Europe's second-largest port, and has much of the zest often
associated with a harbor town. But it also has an outsized influence in a
very different realm: that of clothing design. Since the 1980s, Antwerp-
trained fashion designers have become renowned for experimental styles
paired with time-honored workmanship.

In its heyday, Antwerp (Antwerpen in Flemish, Anvers in French) played
second fiddle only to Paris. Thanks to artists such as Rubens, Van Dyck,
and Jordaens, it was one of Europe's leading art centers. Its printing
presses produced missals for the farthest reaches of the Spanish empire.
It became, and has remained, the diamond capital of the world. Its civic
pride was such that the Antwerpen *Sinjoren* (patricians) considered
themselves a cut above just about everybody else. They still do.

PLANNING YOUR TIME

Avoid limiting your visit to a Monday, when the museums are closed.

On your first day, wander the narrow streets of the Oude Stad, window-
shopping and perhaps sampling some local beer along with a lunch of
the ubiquitous mussels and french fries. Then head to Rubenshuis to
see a faithful and rich re-creation of the famous painter's own house
and studio. Afterwards, make a trip to see the Bruegels at the Museum
Mayer Van den Bergh, and the Plantin-Moretus Museum, home and
printing plant of a publishing dynasty that spanned three centuries.

On a second day here, walk along the river Scheldt to appreciate
Antwerp's centuries-long tradition as a major European port. Absorb
a sense of the city's religious history by visiting some of its churches,
including Sint-Pauluskerk and Sint-Jacobskerk, where Rubens is buried.
Indulge your covetous streak with a trip to the Diamantwijk, and take

advantage of Antwerp's ranking as a key European fashion center by window-shopping along the streets radiating off Meir.

GETTING HERE & AROUND
BY CAR
Antwerp is 48 km (29 mi) north of Brussels on the E19; 60 km (36 mi) northeast of Gent on the E17. A car isn't necessary—and is often a burden—when exploring Antwerp's crowded central area. Street parking is rare, but there are several central parking lots, including lots near Grote Markt and Groenplaats.

BY PUBLIC TRANSPORT
De Lijn operates Antwerp's city bus service; it's an easy system to use. Most lines begin outside Centraal Station on Koningin Astridplein. Antwerp's tram and metro public transit system is also extensive and reliable. The most useful subway line links Centraal Station (metro: Diamant) with the left bank (Linkeroever), via the Groenplaats (for the cathedral and Grote Markt). A €1.20 (€1.60 bought on board) ticket is good for one hour on all forms of public transport, including buses; a €5 (€6 on board) pass buys unlimited travel for one day. Tickets are available at De Lijn offices, the tourist office, and at the Diamant, Opera–Frankrijklei, and Groenplaats metro stops. Public transport runs from 6 AM–midnight.

BY TRAM
Touristram operates hour-long tram tours with cassette commentary in the Oude Stad and old harbor area. Tickets are sold on the tram, and tours leave on the hour. Departure is from Groenplaats. From mid-February to mid-March, and November to mid-December, tours run only on weekends 11–4; from mid-March to September they run daily 11–5; in October, daily 1–4.

BY TRAIN
NMBS/SNCB, the national railway, connects Antwerp with all other major Belgian cities. There are four to five trains an hour between Antwerp and Brussels. Trains also run seven times a day between Antwerp and Paris, and hourly to and from Amsterdam.

ESSENTIALS
Bus Station (✉ *Franklin Rooseveltplaats, Meir* ☎ *070/22-02-00*).

Rental Cars **Avis** (✉ *Centraal Station* ☎ *03/218-9496* ⊕ *www.avis.be*).

Taxis **Antwerp Tax** (☎ *03/238-3838* ⊕ *www.antwerp-tax.be*).

Tour Companies **Touristram** (☎ *03/480-9388*).

Train Station **Centraal Station** (✉ *Koningin Astridplein, Meir* ☎ *03/204-2040*).

Visitor Information **Toerisme Antwerpen** (✉ *Grote Markt 13, Oude Stad* ☎ *03/ 232-0103* ⊕ *www.antwerpen.be* ☺ *Mon.–Sat. 9–5:45, Sun. 9–4:45*).

EXPLORING ANTWERP

Diamantwijk. The diamond trade has its own quarter in Antwerp, where the skills of cutting and polishing the gems have been handed down for generations by a tightly knit community. Some 85% of the world's uncut diamonds pass through here. Twenty-five million carats are cut and traded every year, more than anywhere else in the world. A large part of the community is Jewish, so you'll see shop signs in Hebrew and Hasidic men with traditional dark clothing and side curls. ⊠ *Bounded by De Keyserlei, Pelikaanstraat, Lange Herentalsestraat, and Lange Kievitstraat* Ⓜ *Metro 2.*

❶ **Grote Markt.** The heart of the Oude Stad, the Grote Markt is dominated by a huge fountain splashing water onto the paving stones. Atop the fountain stands the figure of the legendary Silvius Brabo, who has been poised to fling the hand of the giant Druon Antigon into the river Scheldt since the 19th century.

The triangular square is lined on two sides by guild houses and on the third by the Renaissance **Stadhuis.** Antwerp's town hall was built in the 1560s during the city's Golden Age, when Paris and Antwerp were the only European cities with more than 100,000 inhabitants. In its facade, the fanciful fretwork of the late-Gothic style has given way to the discipline and order of the Renaissance. ⊠ *Grote Markt, Oude Stad* ☎ *03/220–8020* 🖃 *€0.75* Ⓜ *Metro 2, 3, or 5.*

❺ **Koninklijk Museum voor Schone Kunsten.** A must for the student of Flemish art, the Royal Museum of Fine Arts collection is studded with masterworks from Bruegel to Ensor. Paintings recovered from the French after the fall of Napoléon form the nucleus of a collection of 2,500 works of art. Room H is devoted to Jacob Jordaens; Room I mostly to monumental Rubens; and Room G to Bruegel. ⊠ *Leopold de Waelplaats 2, Het Zuid* ☎ *03/238–7809* ⊕ *museum.antwerpen.be/kmska* 🖃 *€6* 🕙 *Tues.–Sat. 10–5, Sun. 10–6* Ⓜ *Tram 8.*

❻ **Museum Mayer Van den Bergh.** Pieter Bruegel the Elder's arguably great-
★ est and most enigmatic painting, *Dulle Griet,* is the showpiece here (Room 9). Often referred to in English as "Mad Meg," it portrays an irate woman wearing helmet and breastplate striding across a field strewn with the ravages and insanity of war. Some consider it one of the most powerful antiwar statements ever made. The museum also has a set of Bruegel's witty, miniature illustrations of *Twelve Proverbs,* based on popular Flemish sayings. ⊠ *Lange Gasthuisstraat 19, Kruidtuin* ☎ *03/232–4237* ⊕ *museum.antwerpen.be/mayervandenbergh* 🖃 *€4, €6 for combination ticket with Rubenshuis* 🕙 *Tues.–Sun. 10–5* Ⓜ *Tram 8.*

❸ **Onze-Lieve-Vrouwekathedraal.** A miracle of soaring Gothic lightness, the
FodorśChoice Cathedral of Our Lady contains some of Rubens's greatest paintings and
★ is topped by a 404-foot-high north spire—now restored to its original gleaming white and serving as a beacon that can be seen from far away. Work began in 1352, and continued in fits and starts until 1521. The cathedral contains an outstanding collection of 17th-century religious

Antwerp

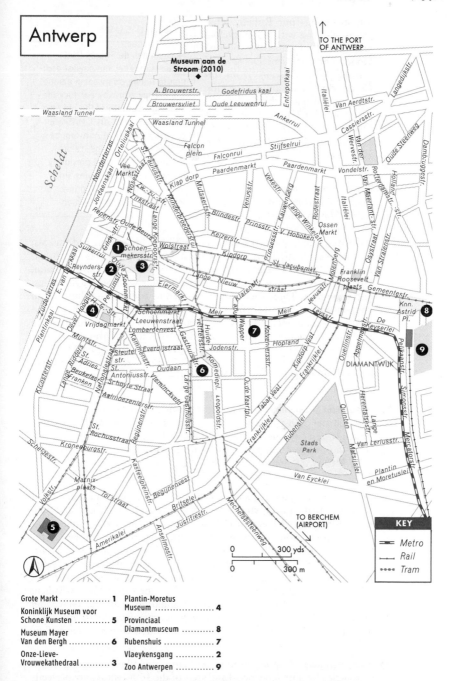

TO THE PORT
OF ANTWERP

Museum aan de
Stroom (2010)

A. Brouwerstr.
Brouwersvliet
Godefridus kaai
Oude Leeuwenrui

Waasland Tunnel

Waasland Tunnel

Scheldt

Falcon plein
Falconrui
Stijfselrui

Vee Markt
Paardenmarkt
Paardenmarkt
Vondelstr.

Klap dorp

Blindestr.
Prinsstr.
V. Hoboken
Ossen Markt

Keizerstr.

Wolstraat
Kipdorp
St. Jacubsmkt.

Schoenmakersstr.
Eiermarkt
Lange Nieuw straat
Franklin Roosevelt plaats
Gemeentestr.

Reyndersstr.
Schoenmarkt
Meir
Meir
Kon. Astrid Pl.

Vrijdagmarkt
Leeuwenstraat
Lombardenvest
Wapper
Hopland
De Keyserlei

Muntstr.
Sleutel str.
Everdijstraat
Jodenstr.
Kipdorp Vest
DIAMANTWIJK

St. Adries
St. Antoniusstr.
Oudaan
Frankrijklei

Beukelaer
Schuyte Straat
Vlemnckveld

Aalmoezenierstr.

St. Rochusstraat

Kronenburgstr.

Stads Park

Van Eycklei

Marnix plaats

Britselei
Justitiestr.

TO BERCHEM
(AIRPORT)

| 0 | 300 yds |
| 0 | 300 m |

KEY
═══ Metro
↦ Rail
•••• Tram

art, including four Rubens altarpieces, glowing with his marvelous red, allegedly fortified by pigeon's blood. The panels of *De Kruisafneming* (*The Descent from the Cross*) triptych are among the most delicate and tender biblical scenes ever painted. ⊠*Handschoenmarkt, Oude Stad* ☎*03/213–9951* ⊕*www.dekathedraal.be* ⊠*€2* ☉ *Weekdays 10–5, Sat. 10–3, Sun. 1–4* Ⓜ*Metro 2, 3, or 5.*

COMING SOON . . .

Museum aan de Stroom (MAS) (⊕ *www.mas.be*), the newest addition to Antwerp's museum parade, will occupy a brand-new dockside building just north of the old town when it opens in 2010. MAS will cover the history of Antwerp, as well as feature art and historical artifacts that were previously housed in other museums. Pride of place will go to the former Maritime Museum's collection.

❹ **Plantin-Moretus Museum.** This was the home and printing plant of an extraordinary publishing dynasty. For three centuries, beginning in 1576, the family printed innumerable bibles, breviaries, and missals; Christophe Plantin's greatest technical achievement was the *Biblia Regia* (in Room 16): eight large volumes containing the Bible in Latin, Greek, Hebrew, Syriac, and Aramaic, complete with notes, glossaries, and grammars. Three rooms are furnished in 16th-century luxury and contain portraits by Rubens. Others remain as they were when occupied by accountants, editors, and proofreaders, while many contain Bibles and religious manuscripts dating back to the 9th century. The workshops are filled with 16 printing presses. ⊠*Vrijdagmarkt 22–23, Sint-Andrieskwartier* ☎*03/221–1450* ⊕*museum.antwerpen.be/plantin_moretus* ⊠*€6, free last Wed. of the month* ☉ *Tues.–Sun. 10–5* Ⓜ*Tram 8.*

❽ **Provinciaal Diamantmuseum.** Enter the world of a "girl's best friend" through the high-tech interactive displays in this diamond museum. Touch-screen computers and amazing exhibits illustrate the entire production process, from mining to gem cutting. ⊠*Koningin Astridplein 19–23, Centraal Station* ☎*03/202–4890* ⊕*www.diamantmuseum.be* ⊠*€6* ☉ *Feb.–Dec., Thurs.–Tues. 10–5:30* Ⓜ*Metro 2, 3, or 5.*

❼ **Rubenshuis.** A fabulous picture of Rubens as painter and patrician is presented here at his own house. Only the elaborate portico and temple, designed by Rubens in Italian Baroque style, are original. Most is a reconstruction (completed in 1946). It represents Rubens at the pinnacle of his fame, a period during which he was appointed court painter to Archduke Albrecht and, with his wife, was sent on a diplomatic mission to Madrid, where he also painted some 40 portraits. The most evocative room is the huge studio, where drawings by Rubens and his pupils help to re-create the original atmosphere. ⊠*Wapper 9, Meir* ☎*03/201–1555* ⊕*museum.antwerpen.be/rubenshuis* ⊠*€6, includes admission to Museum Mayer Van den Bergh* ☉ *Tues.–Sun. 10–5* Ⓜ*Metro 2, 3, or 5.*

❷ **Vlaeykensgang.** A quiet cobblestone lane, the Vlaeykensgang seems untouched by time. The mood and style of the 16th century are perfectly preserved here. The alley ends in Pelgrimsstraat, where there is a great view of the cathedral spire. **Jordaenshuis,** nearby, was the home of Jacob Jordaens (1593–1678), the painter many saw as the successor of Rubens. Unfortunately, it's no longer open to the public, but you can see the exterior. ⊠ *Reyndersstraat 6, Oude Stad* Ⓜ *Metro 2, 3, or 5.*

❾ Zoo Antwerpen. Antwerp's zoo houses its residents in style. Giraffes, ostriches, and African antelopes inhabit an Egyptian temple; a Moorish villa is home to the rhinoceroses; and a thriving okapi family grazes around an Indian temple. In part, this reflects the public's taste when the zoo was created 150 years ago. Today animals are allowed maximum space, and much research is devoted to endangered species. ⊠ *Koningin Astridplein 26, Centraal Station* ☎ *03/202–4540* ⊕ *www.zooantwerpen. be* 💰 *€17.50* ⊙ *Jan., Feb., Nov., and Dec., daily 10–4:45; Mar., Apr., and Oct., daily 10–5:30; May, June, and Sept., daily 10–6; July and Aug., daily 9–6:30* Ⓜ *Metro 2, 3, or 5.*

3

WHERE TO EAT

$$$–$$$$ ✗ **Dome.** Architecture and food aficionados will appreciate the classic French cuisine and somber decor in this splendid Art Nouveau building. This former teahouse, sewing school, and police office maintains its original floor mosaic, and the whitewashed walls and dome-shaped roof parallel its haute cuisine. French chef Julien Burlat and wife Sophie Verbeke set up this restaurant in the upscale Zurenborg neighborhood. The sign by the front door here is so discreet you may well walk straight past without realizing it. ⊠ *Grote Hondstraat 2, Zurenborg* ☎ *03/239–9003* ⊟ *AE, DC, MC, V* ⊙ *Closed Sun. and Mon. No lunch Sat.* Ⓜ *Bus 9.*

$$$$ ✗ **Gin Fish.** In a house on a narrow street, this tiny two-level restaurant serves some of the best, most sophisticated fish dishes in the city. Chef Didier Garnich serves four-course meals in a relaxed environment—in fact, you don't even have to decide between dishes. There's no menu; instead, the daily meal is driven by the morning's market purchases. ⊠ *Haarstraat 9, Oude Stad* ☎ *03/231–3207* ⚐ *Reservations essential* ⊟ *AE, DC, MC, V* ⊙ *Closed Sun., Mon., and June. No lunch* Ⓜ *Metro 2, 3, or 5.*

$–$$ ✗ **Het Hemelse Gerecht.** In this cozy nook behind the cathedral the daily menu is written on a three-panel chalkboard that seems to be bigger than the restaurant itself. Up on the board you'll find an eclectic mix, from tapas to jambalaya to a solid rendition of the classic *waterzooi* (traditional Flemish stew with chicken or seafood). With five tables, this is a small gem. You're wise to phone ahead for a table, as hours of operation are sometimes dictated by the reservation book. ⊠ *Lijnwaadmarkt 3, Oude Stad* ☎ *03/231–2927* ⊟ *No credit cards* ⊙ *Closed Wed.* Ⓜ *Tram 10 or 11.*

$$$–$$$$ ✗ **Het Nieuwe Palinghuis.** The name means the New Eelhouse, and sweetfleshed eel, prepared in a variety of ways, is the house specialty, along with grilled turbot, grilled scallops, and sole in lobster sauce. Fittingly for an Antwerp landmark, the restaurant has dark wood and a comfortable, deep-rooted air. ⊠ *St-Jansvliet 14, Oude Stad* ☎ *03/231–7445* ⊟ *AE, DC, MC, V* ⊙ *Closed Mon., Tues., and June* Ⓜ *Bus 6 or 34.*

$$–$$$ ✗**Horta.** The iron framework of the 18th-century Maison du Peuple, a building designed by the famed Art Nouveau architect Victor Horta, now supports this brasserie. It siphons a hip crowd from trendy Hopland Street and keeps a sunny feel with large mustard-yellow industrial beams and windows all around. The kitchen sends out such tempting contemporary dishes as roasted perch with asparagus, shiitake mushrooms, and artichokes with a warm rouille. ✉*Hopland 2, Oude Stad* ☎*03/232-2815* ▤*AE, DC, MC, V* Ⓜ*Tram 2, 3, or 5, or Bus 9.*

$$–$$$ ✗**In de Schaduw van de Kathedraal.** Cozier and more traditional than the wave of contemporary restaurants dominating the scene, this little place makes good on its name: it has a dining room facing the cathedral square and a terrace where you can take your meal in the cathedral's shadow. Try the delicious North Sea crab gratiné. ✉*Handschoenmarkt 17–21, Oude Stad* ☎*03/232-4014* ▤*AE, DC, MC, V* ⊘*Closed Tues.* Ⓜ*Metro 2, 3, or 5.*

$–$$ ✗**'t Hofke.** It's worth visiting here for the location alone, in the Vlaeykensgang alley, where time seems to have stood still. The cozy dining room has the look and feel of a private home, and the menu includes a large selection of salads and omelets, as well as more substantial fare. Try for a table in the courtyard. ✉*Vlaeykensgang, Oude Koornmarkt 16, Oude Stad* ☎*03/233-8606* ▤*AE, MC, V* Ⓜ*Tram 2, 3, or 5.*

WHERE TO STAY

$$$$ 🏨**Antwerp Hilton.** This five-story complex incorporates the fin-de-siècle facade of what was once the Grand Bazar department store. Mahogany doors open onto spacious guest rooms with duvet-topped beds and flat-screen TVs. The bathroom mirrors are even heated so they won't steam up when you most need them. Afternoon tea is served in the marble-floor lobby. **Pros:** luxurious; large rooms; centrally located. **Cons:** such luxury doesn't come cheap. ✉*Groenplaats, Oude Stad* ☎*03/204-1212* ⊕*www.hilton.com* ⤳*193 rooms, 18 suites* ♿*In-room: safe, Wi-Fi. In-hotel: 2 restaurants, bar, gym, parking (paid), no-smoking rooms, Wi-Fi* ▤*AE, DC, MC, V* Ⓜ*Tram 2 or 15. The hotel has an entrance in the Groenplaats metro station.*

$$$$ 🏨**De Witte Lelie.** Three step-gabled 16th-century houses have been com-
★   bined to make the "White Lily," Antwerp's most exclusive hotel. As soon as you enter the grand lobby, a stylish blend of old and new, it's clear that personal service is the watchword. As the name suggests, the hotel's decor is mostly white, punctuated with colorful carpets and modern art. Elegant salons have grand fireplaces, and breakfasts are served on a loggia that opens onto the inner courtyard. **Pros:** large rooms; friendly, attentive service. **Cons:** some rooms have no elevator access. ✉*Keizerstraat 16–18, Stadswaag* ☎*03/226-1966* ⊕*www.dewittelelie. be* ⤳*4 rooms, 6 suites* ♿*In-room: safe, Wi-Fi. In-hotel: parking (paid)* ▤*AE, MC, V* Ⓜ*Tram 10 or 11.*

$$ 🏨**Hotel Rubens.** A peaked tower marks this small, colorful hotel directly behind the Grote Markt. The tower is said to be the oldest in Antwerp, and was part of the original city walls. The room decor may not be terribly original, but the deep bathtubs make for a good soak at the end of the day. **Pros:** friendly staff; great location; quiet courtyard garden.

Cons: parking limited. ⊠ *Oude Beurs 29, Oude Stad* ☎*03/222–4848* ⊕*www.hotelrubensantwerp.be* ↩*36 rooms* ⚷*In-room: safe, Wi-Fi. In-hotel: bar, parking (paid), Wi-Fi* ⊟*AE, DC, MC, V* ¶◎*CP* Ⓜ*Tram 10 or 11.*

$$ ⊞ **Prinse.** Set well back from the street, this 400-year-old landmark with an interior courtyard was once the home of 16th-century poet Anna Bijns. Now it has a modern look, with black leather chairs, soft blue curtains, and tile bathrooms. Exposed beams give top-floor rooms more character. Soothing music resounds in the lobby. **Pros:** quiet location; friendly staff; historic building. **Cons:** limited parking. ⊠ *Keizerstraat 63, Stadswaag* ☎*03/226–4050* ⊕*www.hotelprinse.be* ↩*35 rooms* ⚷*In-room: Internet (some), minibar* ⊟*AE, DC, MC, V* ¶◎*BP* Ⓜ*Tram 10 or 11.*

$$$ ⊞ **'t Sandt.** A former soap factory is now one of Antwerp's classiest
★   hotels. Each guest room has a unique configuration; simple backdrops of white walls and beamed ceilings set off rich furnishings. Some rooms have antique furnishings. A handful of others have a view of the cathedral. You can also get a cathedral view from the tranquil garden. **Pros:** great location; friendly staff; quiet garden. **Cons:** limited parking. ⊠ *Zand 13–19, Oude Stad* ☎*03/232–9390* ⊕*www.hotel-sandt. be* ↩*30 suites, 6 apartments* ⚷*In-room: safe, Wi-Fi, minibar* ⊟*AE, DC, MC, V* Ⓜ*Metro 2, 3, or 5.*

GENT

Located midway between Brugge and Brussels at the confluence of the rivers Leie and Schelde, Gent (also called Ghent in English) is the capital of the East Flanders Province. The city's early anchors were two 7th-century abbeys, Sint-Pieter (St. Peter) and Sint-Baafs (St. Bavo), and the 9th-century castle of Gravensteen. Baldwin of the Iron Arm, the region's first ruler, built a castle to protect his burgeoning kingdom; thus Gent became the seat of the counts of Flanders. By the 14th century, Gent had attracted more than 5,000 textile workers.

The city has a long history of rebellion. In 1448 the townspeople refused to pay a salt tax imposed by Philip the Good, Duke of Burgundy. For five years their militia stood firm against Philip's troops, and when they were finally overwhelmed, 16,000 had perished. Calvinist iconoclasts proclaimed the city a republic in 1577, only to be overthrown by Spanish forces seven years later. In the 18th century, French armies marched on Gent on four different occasions.

Gent was rescued from oblivion by a daring young merchant named Lieven Bauwens, who at the end of the 18th century smuggled a spinning mule out of Britain. Bauwens's risky exploit provided the foundation for a cotton textile industry that employed 160,000 workers a century later.

Today Gent has transformed its historic center into a commercial area of almost 400,000 residents. The city's prestigious university attracts students from all over the world. This influx of international young people gives Gent an especially vibrant, energetic feel—the city may be historic, but it isn't locked into the past. Its canals, gables, castles, beguinages, medieval lanes, art masterpieces, and settings that recall Breugel paintings beautifully mix with modern facades and street-side fashions.

PLANNING YOUR TIME

For a great day in Gent, arrive as early as possible and begin your tour with a classic view of the city's three towers from St. Michael's Bridge. Divide the rest of your day between the guild houses of the Graslei district, the Gothic cathedral, and the Gravensteen, the ancient castle of the counts of Flanders. After a dinner in the lively Patershol area, take a walk around the illuminated historic district.

GETTING HERE & AROUND

BY BIKE

Bikes can be rented at rental shops or the ticket window at Sint-Pieters railway station. (If you have a valid train ticket, you get a discounted rate.) Both adult (with or without baby seats) and children's bikes are available.

BY BOAT

Several companies can take you on 40- to 90-minute boat rides on the waterways of Gent from around €5.50.

BY BUS & TRAM

De Lijn has one trolley, three trams, and dozens of bus lines. There are stops all over town, and most buses run every 10 to 15 minutes. You can buy a ticket (€1.60) or a day pass (€6) on board, but you will save money if you buy the ticket (€1.20) or pass (€5) in advance from the terminal. If you arrive in Gent by train, take tram 1, 11, or 12 for the city center.

BY CAR

From Brussels, Gent is reached via the E40 highway, which continues to Brugge and the coast; get off at exit 9. From Antwerp, take the E17.

BY TRAIN

The Belgian national railway, NMBS/SNCB, sends two nonstop trains every hour to Gent from Brussels (35 minutes). There's also a frequent direct train connection from Brussels airport to Gent, which takes about an hour. Trains run twice an hour from Antwerp (50 minutes).

ESSENTIALS

Bike Rental Biker (⊠ *Steendam 16* ☎ *09/224–2903*). **Sint-Pieters** (☎ *09/241–2224*).

Boat & Ferry Contacts Boat in Gent (⊠ *Kraanlei* ☎ *0478/63–36–30* ⊕ *www. boatingent.be*). **Minerva Boten** (⊠ *Lindelei 2a* ☎ *09/233–7917* ⊕ *www.miner vaboten.be*).

Train Contacts NMBS/SNCB (☎ *02/555–2525* ⊕ *www.b-rail.be*).

Tram Contacts De Lijn (Oost-Vlaanderen) (☎ *09/210–9311 East Flanders* ⊕ *www.delijn.be*).

Visitor Information Gent (⊠ *Botermarkt 17A, under the Belfry* ☎ *09/266–5660* ⊕ *www.visitgent.be*).

EXPLORING GENT

6 Belfort. Begun in 1314, the 300-foot belfry tower symbolizes the power of the guilds and used to serve as Gent's watchtower. Since 1377 the structure has been crowned with a gilded copper weather vane shaped into a dragon, the city's symbol of freedom. (The current stone spire was added in 1913.) A 53-bell carillon, claimed by experts to be one of the best in the world, is set on the top floor. One of the original bells, the Triumphanta, cast in 1660 and badly cracked in 1914, rests in a garden at the foot of the tower. The view from the tower is one of the city's highlights. ✉ *Sint-Baafsplein, Torenrij* ☎ *09/233-0772* 💰 *€3* ⊙ *Mid-Mar.–mid-Nov., daily 10–6; mid-Nov.–mid-Mar., guided visits on request only.*

3 Graslei. This magnificent row of guild houses in the original port area
★ is best seen from across the river Leie on the **Korenlei** (Corn Quay). The guild house of the **Metselaars** (Masons) is a copy of a house from 1527. The **Eerste Korenmetershuis** (the First Grain Measurers' House), representing the grain weighers' guild, is next. It stands next to the oldest house of the group, the brooding, Romanesque **Koornstapelhuis** (Granary), which was built in the 12th century; this was where grain claimed by the tax collectors was stored. It stands side by side with the narrow Renaissance **Tolhuis** (Toll House). No. 11 is the **Tweede Korenmetershuis** (Second Grain Measurers' House), a late Baroque building from 1698. The **Vrije Schippers** (Free Bargemen), at No. 14, is a late Gothic building from 1531. Almost opposite this, across the water at No. 7 Korenlei, is the **Huis der Onvrije Schippers** (Unfree Bargemen), built in 1740. Every night the Graslei and the other historic monuments are illuminated from sunset to midnight. ✉ *Graslei, Gravensteen/Patershol.*

2 Gravensteen. Surrounded by a moat, the Castle of the Counts of Flanders resembles an enormous battleship steaming down the sedate Lieve Canal. From its windswept battlements there's a splendid view over the rooftops of Old Gent. There has been a fortress on this site for centuries. The Gravensteen was built in 1180 by the Count of Flanders on top of an existing fortress, and has been rebuilt several times since then—most recently in the 19th century. The castle also houses a historical weapons museum, with armor, swords, pikes, and crossbows, as well as torture instruments dating from the times of the Council of Flanders. If weapons aren't your glass of beer, you can at least enjoy the view from the castle tower. ✉ *Sint-Veerleplein, Gravensteen/Patershol* ☎ *09/225-9306* 💰 *€6* ⊙ *Apr.–Sept., daily 9–6; Oct.–Mar., daily 9–5.*

NEED A BREAK? Drop by **Het Groot Vleeshuis** (*Great Meat Hall* ✉ *Groentenmarkt 7, Gravensteen/Patershol* ☎ *09/223-2324*) for coffee or lunch and a spot of toothsome shopping. The wood-beamed hall dates from the early 15th century, and was used as a covered meat market. Today it is used as a covered market for regional products. It is a good place to try the local specialty waterzooi. The hall is open from 10–6 and closed Monday.

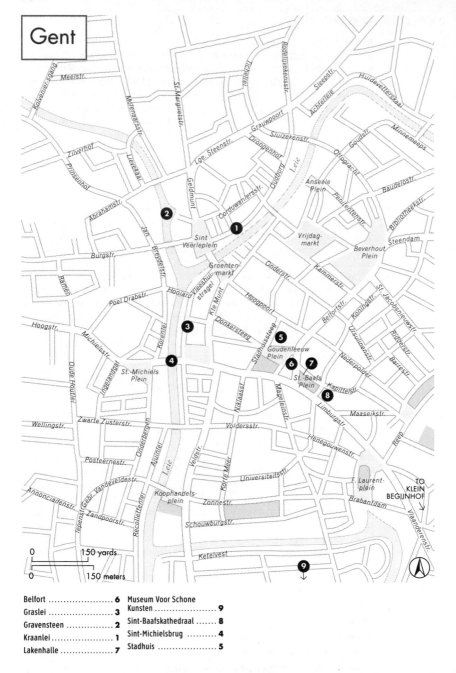

Gent

Klein Begijnhof. Founded in 1234 by Countess Joanna of Constantinople, the Small Beguinage is the best-preserved of Gent's three beguinages. Protected by a wall and portal, the surrounding petite homes with individual yards were built in the 17th and 18th centuries, but are organized in medieval style. ⊠ *Lange Violettestraat 71, Klein Begijnhof.*

3

❶ Kraanlei. At the top of the narrow waterfront, medieval Crane Lane is the guild house of the Kraankinders (men of small stature who worked the cranes to unload the barges). A figure of a flute player crowns No. 55; the house dates from 1669 and has panels representing the five senses. The panels of No. 57 illustrate six acts of mercy; hospitality to travelers was considered the seventh act, as the building was once an inn. ⊠ *Kraanlei at the corner of Rodekoning, Gravensteen/Patershol.*

❼ Lakenhalle. Built as the center for the cloth trade in the 15th century, the Cloth Hall was still unfinished when the trade collapsed. Its vaulted cellar was used as a prison for 150 years; currently it houses the tourist information center and serves as the entrance to the Belfort. From the Lakenhalle you can enter a small adjacent building, formerly the prison warder's lodging. ⊠ *Sint-Baafsplein, Torenrij.*

❾ Museum voor Schone Kunsten. Built in 1902 at the edge of Citadelpark, the neoclassical Museum of Fine Arts is one of Belgium's best. The museum's holdings span from the Middle Ages to the early 20th century, including works by Rubens, Géricault, Corot, Ensor, and Magritte. Its collection of Flemish Primitives is particularly noteworthy, with two paintings by Hieronymus Bosch, *Saint Jerome* and *The Bearing of the Cross.* ⊠ *Fernand Scribedreef 1, Citadelpark* ☎ *09/240–0700* ⊕ *www.mskgent.be* 🏛 *€5* ⊙ *Tues.–Sun. 10–6.*

❽ Sint-Baafskathedraal. St. Bavo's Cathedral, begun in the 13th century but finished in the 16th in the ornate Brabantine Gothic style, dramatically rises from a low, unimposing entryway. It contains one of the greatest treasures in Christendom, Van Eyck's *The Adoration of the Mystic Lamb.*

Fodor's Choice ★

The Order of the Golden Fleece, instituted in Brugge by Philip the Good in 1430, was convened here in 1559 by Philip II of Spain. It is still in existence, currently presided over by King Juan Carlos of Spain. A Rubens masterpiece, *Saint Bavo's Entry into the Monastery,* hangs in one of the chapels. Other treasures include a baroque-style organ built in 1623 and a crypt crammed with tapestries, church paraphernalia, and 15th- and 16th-century frescoes. ⊠ *Sint-Baafsplein 4, Torenrij* 🏛 *Cathedral free, De Villa Chapel €3, audiotape €0.50* ☎ *09/269–2065* ⊕ *www.visitgent. be* ⊙ *Cathedral: Apr.–Oct., Mon.–Sat. 8:30–6, Sun. 1–6; Nov.–Mar., Mon.–Sat. 8:30–5, Sun. 1–5. Chapel: Apr.–Oct., Mon.–Sat. 9:30–4:15,*

Sun. 1–4:15; Nov.–Mar., Mon.–Sat. 10:30–3:15, Sun. 1–3:15 ☞*No visits to cathedral or chapel during services.*

❹ **Sint-Michielsbrug.** The view of Gent from this spot is so perfect it should
★ be patented as the Three Towers from St. Michael's Bridge. You'll see the three medieval towers of Sint-Niklaaskerk, the Belfort, and Sint-Baafskathedraal. ✉*Torenrij.*

❺ **Stadhuis.** The Town Hall is an early example of what raising taxes can do to a city. In 1516 two prominent Antwerp architects were called in to build a town hall that would put all others to shame. However, before the building could be completed, Emperor Charles V imposed new taxes that drained the city's resources. The architecture thus reflects the city's changing fortunes: the side built in 1518–60 facing Hoogpoort is in Flamboyant Gothic style; when work resumed in 1580, the Botermarkt side was completed in a stricter and more economical Renaissance style. ✉*Botermarkt 1, Torenrij* ☎*09/266–5111* 💶*Tour €4* ☉*Tours May–Oct., Mon.–Thurs. at 2:30.*

WHERE TO EAT

$$–$$$ ✕**Belga Queen.** A magnificent restaurant in a magnificent location. The
Fodor's Choice former grain warehouse bordering the Leie has been redesigned by
★ the chef himself, Antoine Pino. The large terrace leads to the ground floor's impressive bar, high tables, and cozy leather seats. The menu has daily fresh suggestions, and a three-course lunch is €16. There's a cigar bar with occasional live jazz on the top floor. ✉*Graslei 10, De Kuip* ☎*09/280–0100* ⚞*Reservations essential* 🍽*AE, DC, MC, V.*

$$$ ✕**De 3 Biggetjes.** The name means "the three little pigs," and you'll definitely be tempted to wolf down the wonderful food at this tiny, step-gabled building set on the cobbled Zeugsteeg, or Sow Lane. Even if you huff and puff a bit to get there, the cooking makes the trip worthwhile. The menu combines Belgian, Vietnamese, and French influences. Sea-food dishes are a highlight. There's also a small garden terrace at the back, open in summer. The set menus are a very good value. ✉*Zeugsteeg 7, Gravensteen/Patershol* ☎*09/224–4648* ⚞*Reservations essential* 🍽*MC, V* ☉*Closed Wed. and Sun. No lunch Sat.*

$$–$$$ ✕**Cassis.** In a tranquil setting combining beamed ceilings, light wood, and wicker chairs, Cassis offers both traditional and modern Belgian specialties, as well as huge, inventive salads (for example, asparagus, shrimp, smoked salmon, and goat cheese) presented as artfully as a Flemish still life. For the best people-watching, sit on the terrace over-looking the Vrijdagmarkt while the market's in swing. ✉*Vrijdagmarkt 5, Vrijdagmarkt* ☎*09/233–8546* 🍽*AE, MC, V.*

$$$–$$$$ ✕**Jan van den Bon.** With room for 30, this distinguished restaurant is a
Fodor's Choice local favorite for French and classic Belgian dishes, particularly seafood
★ and seasonal specialties. White asparagus, for instance, is cooked and sauced to perfection. Sip your aperitif on the terrace overlooking the garden, which supplies the herbs used in the kitchen. ✉*Koning Leopold II Laan 43, Citadelpark* ☎*09/221–9085* ⚞*Reservations essential. Jacket and tie* 🍽*AE, DC, MC, V* ☉*Closed Sun. No lunch Sat.*

$$–$$$ ✕ **'t Buikske Vol.** This cozy, popular, and chic restaurant is well suited to special occasions, as you're virtually guaranteed a sophisticated meal—and one with a dash of the pleasingly unpredictable. While the service and presentation are dependably good, the menu has some adventurous flavors, such as *fillet de biche* (doe steak) and rabbit served with sweetbreads. ⊠ *Kraanlei 17, Gravensteen/Patershol* ☎ *09/225–1880* ⚑ *Reservations essential on weekends* ☰ *AE, MC, V* ⊘ *Closed Wed., Sun., Easter wk, and 1st 2 wks of Aug.*

3

WHERE TO STAY

$$ 🚢 **The Boatel.** Get a different perspective on Gent by staying aboard this 1953 riverboat docked on the Leie since Portus Ganda opened. A roughly 10-minute walk from the city center, the rebuilt vessel shows off sections of the original woodwork. Cabins are large and bright, particularly the two master bedrooms above the sea line. Even though it is tightly roped to the shore, remember that boats tend to rock a bit. **Pros:** friendly staff; your hotel is an actual riverboat. **Cons:** far from the sights. ⊠ *Voorhoutkaai 44, Portus Ganda* ☎ *09/267–1030* ⊕ *www. theboatel.com* ⛵ *7 rooms* ⚏ *In-room: no a/c* ☰ *AE, MC, V.*

$$ 🏠 **Erasmus.** From the flagstone and wood-beam library-lounge to the
★ stone mantels in the individually decorated bedrooms, every inch of this noble 16th-century town house has been scrubbed, polished, and decked with period ornaments. Even the tiny garden has been carefully manicured. Peter Broos, who runs this distinctive hotel near the Korenlei, takes care of everything, from answering the room-service bell pull at night to serving a delicious breakfast in the parlor. **Pros:** central location; friendly staff; personalized service. **Cons:** street noise can be a problem. ⊠ *Poel 25, Torenrij* ☎ *09/224–2195* ⊕ *www.erasmushotel.be* ⛵ *12 rooms* ⚏ *In-room: no a/c. In-hotel: bar* ☰ *AE, MC, V* ⊘ *Closed mid-Dec.–mid-Jan.*

$$–$$$ 🏠 **Gravensteen.** Steps from its namesake, this handsome 19th-century mansion exudes atmosphere—at least from most angles. The public areas are ornate with carved stucco, a marble staircase, and a cupola. Hallways wind to small rooms with a more modern look; some have castle or canal views. Note that some rooms are in a newer, less attractive building at the back and that bathrooms are small, some with showers only. **Pros:** historic old building; close to center; friendly staff. **Cons:** on noisy street. ⊠ *Jan Breydelstraat 35, Gravensteen/Patershol* ☎ *09/225–1150* ⊕ *www.gravensteen.be* ⛵ *49 rooms, 2 suites* ⚏ *In-room: no a/c (some), Wi-Fi. In-hotel: bar, parking (paid)* ☰ *AE, DC, MC, V.*

$–$$ 🏠 **Monasterium PoortAckere.** A complex comprising a former abbey, convent, and beguinage now provides a serene place to stay in a central neighborhood. Some sections date back to the 13th century; most of the buildings, though, are 19th-century Gothic Revival. There are large, comfortable rooms in the Monasterium, the former convent, while in the adjacent convent former cells have been transformed into small guest rooms with a washbasin, shared showers, and toilets. **Pros:** quiet location; beautiful old building. **Cons:** some rooms have shared bathroom; one wing has no elevator. ⊠ *Oude Houtlei 56, Torenrij* ☎ *09/269–2210*

⊕*www.monasterium.be* ➔*56 rooms, 13 without bath* ⟵*In-room: no a/c, no phone, Internet (some). In-hotel: restaurant, bar, parking (paid)* ▭*AE, DC, MC, V* ⦿*IBP.*

$$$$ ⊡ **NH Gent–Belfort.** In the heart of the Old City, this grand hotel mirrors the elegance of the renowned Spanish chain. Warming red with sandy-beige color schemes in the spacious rooms, and chic modern styles throughout, help it stick to a business-friendly look. Great weekend deals are available if you book in advance. **Pros:** great location; friendly staff; all-modern luxuries. **Cons:** it's part of a chain, albeit a very good one. ⊠*Hoogpoort 63, Torenrij* ☎*09/233–3331* ⊕*www.nh-hotels.com* ➔*171 rooms, 3 suites* ⟵*In-room: safe, minibar, Wi-Fi. In-hotel: restaurant, bar, gym, parking (paid), Wi-Fi* ▭*AE, DC, MC, V.*

Czech Republic

The Stavoske divadlo (Estates Theater), Prague

WORD OF MOUTH

"If I had it to do over again, I would have planned at least one more day in Prague. Four days simply were not enough. I think that is a measure of success. As the old showtime axiom goes: Leave 'em wanting more. Prague did just that."

—bob_brown

"Is Cesky Krumlov worth it? YES! Don't miss it and plan on spending at least one night there, two if you can spare the time. You will love it."

—Orlando_Vic

WHAT'S WHERE

1 Prague. Praha, "Golden Prague," the "City of One Hundred Spires," the "Beer Drinking Capital of Europe": the Czech capital goes by many names . . . and has many neighborhoods, each of which boasts a distinct personality: Old Town is Prague's historic heart. This is also "tourist central," jam-packed with people marveling at the architectural mélange while waiting for a 15th-century astronomical clock to strike the hour. There's also the original Jewish Quarter, where the past is still apparent in the tilting headstones of the Old Jewish Cemetery and in the synagogues. The "Lesser Quarter" is filled with winding (and hilly!) cobblestone streets edged with Baroque buildings. The high point of this city—quite literally—is Prague Castle, looming above Prague since the 10th century. Proving that "new" is a relative term in these parts, Prague's "New Town" was laid out in the 14th century. Its focal point is Wenceslas Square: a grand commercial boulevard lined with shops, restaurants, and hotels.

2 Southern Bohemia. Bordering Germany and the former Austro-Hungarian Empire, Southern Bohemia long held a strategically important position that needed to be defended with a series of fortifications—and today that makes it a magnet for castle connoisseurs. If you can see only one, make it Hrad Krumlov. Perched above popular Český Krumlov (a UNESCO World Heritage Site), it comes complete with a tower, moat, and dungeon, and in the Czech Republic it is second only to Pražský Hrad in Prague in terms of size.

3 Western Bohemia. Western Bohemia is spa country, and Karlovy Vary (which was discovered in the 14th century by Charles IV) is its undisputed king. Mariánské Lázně and Františkovy Lázně—two other contenders—have their own allure. But you shouldn't come to any of them expecting hot stones, aromatherapies, and exfoliations with orange rinds. Thermal spas in the Czech Republic take themselves seriously, and concentrate on health and history more than hedonism.

0   60 miles
0   90 km

Görlitz

POLAND

Děčín   Liberec
Ústí   Česká Lípa   Jablonec
Litoměřice

Mladá
Boleslav   Náchod

Hradec Králové

Kladno
☆ PRAGUE   Kolín   Pardubice
Beroun   Chrudim
            Kutná
            Hora   Opava   Ostrava   Karviná
BOHEMIA   Český
                                                 Nový Jičín   Těšín
Příbram   Vlašim   Svitavy   MORAVIA   Frýdek-Místek
                                             Olomouc
Milevsko   Havlíčkův   Prostějov   Přerov
            Tábor   Brod
                    Jihlava   Vsetín
Písek
                    Telč   Otrokovice   Zlín
                                      Brno
            Třeboň
②   Uherské Hradiste
        České
        Budějovice   Znojmo   Mikulov
        Český   Břeclav
        Krumlov
                                                        SLOVAKIA

Donau (Danube)

AUSTRIA   Vienna ✪   ◉ Bratislava

HUNGARY

THE EXPERIENCE OF VISITING THE Czech Republic still involves stepping back in time. Even in Prague, now deluged by tourists two-thirds of the year, the sense of history—stretching back through centuries of wars, empires, and monuments to everyday life—remains uncluttered by the trappings of modernity. The peculiar melancholy of Central Europe still lurks in narrow streets and forgotten corners. Crumbling facades, dilapidated palaces, and treacherous cobbled streets both shock and enchant the visitor used to a world where what remains of history has been spruced up for tourist eyes.

Outside the capital, for those willing to put up with the inconveniences of shabby hotels and mediocre restaurants, the sense of rediscovering a neglected world is even stronger. And the range is startling: from imperial spas, with their graceful colonnades and dilapidated villas, to the many arcaded town squares, modestly displaying the passing of time with each splendid layer of once-contemporary style. Gothic towers, Renaissance facades, Baroque interiors, and aging modern supermarkets merge. Between the man-made sights, you are rewarded with glorious mountain ranges and fertile rolling countryside laced with carp ponds and forests.

WHEN TO GO

Prague is beautiful year-round, but in summer and during the Christmas and Easter holidays the city is overrun with tourists. Spring and fall generally combine good weather with a more bearable level of tourism. In winter you'll encounter fewer tourists and have the opportunity to see Prague breathtakingly covered in snow, but it can get very cold. In much of the rest of Bohemia and Moravia, even in midsummer, the number of visitors is far smaller than in Prague. The Giant Mountains of Bohemia come into their own in winter. January and February generally bring the best skiing—and great difficulty in finding a room. If you're not a skier, try visiting the mountains in late spring (May or June) or fall, when the colors are dazzling and you'll have the hotels and restaurants nearly to yourself. The "off" season keeps shrinking as people discover the pleasures of touring the country in every season. Castles and museums now frequently stay open 9, 10, or even 12 months of the year. In midwinter, however, you may well come across this disappointing notice tacked to the door of a museum or even a hotel: CLOSED FOR TECHNICAL REASONS—which, for those in the proper frame of mind, merely adds to the charm of winter travel.

GETTING HERE & AROUND

BY AIR

Almost all international flights go into Prague, with a few budget flights now landing in Brno. Central Connect flies from Ostrava to Vienna, though it's usually more cost-effective to drive or take a bus or train. Czech Airlines, the main carrier in the country, also flies to Ostrava and Brno.

ČSA (Czech Airlines), the Czech national carrier, offers the only direct flights from New York (JFK) to Prague, with six flights a week most

TOP REASONS TO GO

Karlův Most. Paris has the Eiffel Tower and Prague has this beautiful Gothic bridge. Dotted with statues, both romantic and frightful, the bridge is packed with crowds taking in the riverside views.

Stunning City Skyline. Walking next to the Vltava River, stop to admire the Prague skyline, one of the most striking collections of architecture in Europe.

Castles & Châteaux. More than 2,000 castles, manor houses, and châteaux form a precious and not-to-be-missed part of the country's cultural and historical heritage. Grim ruins glower from craggy hilltops, and fantastical Gothic castles guard ancient trade routes.

Beer. Czechs drink more beer per capita than any other nation on earth; small wonder, as many connoisseurs rank Bohemian lagers among the best in the world. This cool, crisp brew was invented in Plzeň in 1842, although older varieties of Czech beer had been brewed for centuries.

4

times (daily flights during the busiest season). It's also possible to connect through a major European airport and continue to Prague. The flight from New York to Prague takes about 8 hours; from the West Coast, including a stopover, 12 to 16 hours. Go Airways, easyJet and others offer discount flights to Prague from Britain. Another way to save money is either by changing flights in Frankfurt or catching a bus from Frankfurt to Prague.

BY BUS

Several bus companies run direct services between major Western European cities and Prague. The Czech Republic's extremely comprehensive state-run bus service, ČSAD, is usually much quicker than the normal trains and more frequent than express trains, unless you're going to the major cities. Prices are quite low—essentially the same as those for second-class rail tickets. Buy your tickets from the ticket window at the bus station or directly from the driver on the bus. Buses can be full to bursting. On long-distance trips it's a good idea to buy advance tickets when available (indicated by an "R" in a circle on timetables); get them at the local station or at some travel agencies. The only drawback to traveling by bus is figuring out the timetables. They are easy to read, but beware of the small letters denoting exceptions to the times given. If in doubt, inquire at the information window or ask someone for assistance. **ČSAD** (☎222–630–851 *in Prague* ⊕*www.jizdnirady.cz*). **Eurolines** (☎224–218–680 ⊕*www.eurolines.com*).

BY CAR

There are no special requirements for renting a car in the Czech Republic, but be sure to shop around, as prices can differ greatly. A surcharge of 5%–12% applies to rental cars picked up at Prague's Ruzyně Airport.

The Prague city center is mostly a snarl of traffic, one-way streets, and tram lines. If you plan to drive outside the capital, there are few four-lane highways, but most of the roads are in reasonably good shape, and traffic is usually light. Roads can be poorly marked, however, so before you start out, buy one of the inexpensive multilingual auto atlases available at any bookstore.

BY TRAIN

You can take a direct train from Paris via Frankfurt to Prague (daily) or from Berlin via Dresden to Prague (five times a day). Vienna is a good starting point for Prague, Brno, or Bratislava. There are three trains a day from Vienna's Südbahnhof (South Station) to Prague (five hours). Southern Moravia and southern Bohemia are served by trains from Vienna and Linz.

The state-run rail system is called České dráhy (ČD). On longer runs, it's not really worth taking anything less than an express (*rychlík*) train, marked in red on the timetable. Tickets are still very inexpensive. First-class is considerably more spacious and comfortable and well worth the cost (50% more than a standard ticket). A 40 Kč–60 Kč supplement is charged for the excellent international expresses, EuroCity (EC) and InterCity (IC), and for domestic SuperCity (SC) schedules. A 20 Kč supplement applies to reserved seats on domestic journeys. If you haven't bought a ticket in advance at the station (mandatory for seat reservations), you can buy one aboard the train from the conductor. On timetables, departures (*odjezd*) appear on a yellow background; arrivals (*příjezd*) are on white. It is possible to book sleepers (*lůžkový*) or the less roomy couchettes (*lehátkový*) on most overnight trains.

ABOUT THE RESTAURANTS

The quality of restaurant cuisine and service in the Czech Republic has improved dramatically in recent years. In Prague you can expect sophisticated cuisine on the level of that of any other European capital. Outside of Prague dining can be uneven, but delicious meals can be found. You'll still find the traditional dishes—roast pork or duck with dumplings, or broiled meat with sauce—can be quite tasty when well prepared. Grilled trout appears on most menus and is often the best item available. An annoying "cover charge" usually makes its way onto restaurant bills, seemingly to subsidize the salt and pepper shakers. You should discreetly check the bill, since a few unscrupulous proprietors still overcharge foreigners.

Lunch, usually eaten between noon and 2, is the main meal for Czechs

CURRENCY & EXCHANGE

The unit of currency in the Czech Republic is the koruna, or crown (Kč), which is divided into 100 haléřů, or hellers. There are (little-used) coins of 50 hellers; coins of 1, 2, 10, 20, and (rarely) 50 Kč; and notes of 50, 100, 200, 500, 1,000, 2,000, and 5,000 Kč. Notes of 1,000 Kč and up may not always be accepted for small purchases. At this writing, the koruna stood at approximately 22 to the U.S. dollar and 28 to the euro.The euro is sometimes accepted as currency—especially in Prague, —but the country isn't scheduled to switch its currency over officially to the euro until 2015 at the earliest.

and the best deal. Many restaurants put out a special lunch menu (*denní listek*), with more appetizing selections at better prices. Dinner is usually served from 5 until 9 or 10, but don't wait too long to eat. Restaurant cooks frequently leave early on slow nights, and the later you arrive, the more likely it is that the kitchen will be closed. In general, dinner menus do not differ substantially from lunch offerings, with the exception of prices, which are higher.

WHAT IT COSTS IN CZECH KORUNA				
¢	$	$$	$$$	$$$$
Restaurants	Under Kč 100	Kč 100–Kč 150	Kč 150– Kč 300	Kč 300– Kč 500	over Kč 500

Prices are per person for a main course at dinner.

4

ABOUT THE HOTELS

The number of hotels and pensions has increased dramatically throughout the Czech Republic, in step with the influx of tourists. Finding a room should not be a problem, although it is highly recommended that you book ahead during the peak tourist season (nationwide, July and August; in Prague, April through October and the Christmas, New Year, and Easter holidays). Hotel prices, in general, remain high. This is especially true in Prague and in the spa towns of western Bohemia.

Most of the old-fashioned hotels away from the major tourist centers, invariably situated on a town's main square, have been modernized and now provide private bathrooms in most or all rooms and a higher comfort level throughout. Newer hotels, often impersonal concrete boxes, tend to be found on the outskirts of towns; charming, older buildings in the center of town—newly transformed into hotels and pensions—are often the best choice. Bare-bones hostels are a popular means of circumventing Prague's summer lodging crunch; many now stay open all year.

At certain times, such as Easter and during festivals, prices can jump 15%–25%. As a rule, always ask the price before taking a room. Unless otherwise noted, breakfast is included in the rate.

WHAT IT COSTS				
¢	$	$$	$$$	$$$$
Hotels in Koruna	Under Kč 1200	Kč 1200– Kč 2200	Kč 2200– Kč 4000	Kč 400– Kč 6500	over Kč 6500
Hotels in Euros	Under €40	€40–€80	€80–€140	€140–€230	over €230

Prices are for two people in a standard double room in high season, including taxes and service. Assume that hotels operate on the European Plan (EP, with no meals provided) unless we note that they use the Breakfast Plan (BP).

PLANNING YOUR TIME

Many visitors to the Czech Republic concentrate on Prague alone, but that's a pity. It's easy to travel around various parts of the Bohemian countryside, and you'll get a more realistic view of daily life outside the touristy capital. Both the bus system and the train system make traveling from town to town a single-day effort. Some excursions, like Kutná Hora, can even be done as day trips from Prague. Research your options carefully: for locations like Karlovy Vary the train is not recommended, because the route takes twice as long as it would by bus.

PRAGUE

A stunning backdrop of towering churches and centuries-old bridges and alleyways makes this European capital flat-out beautiful. Prague achieved much of its present glory in the 14th century, during the long reign of Charles IV, king of Bohemia and Moravia and Holy Roman Emperor. It was Charles who established a university in the city and laid out the New Town, charting Prague's growth.

Amid Prague's cobblestone streets and gold-tipped spires, new galleries, cafés, and clubs teem with young Czechs and members of the city's colony of "expatriates." New shops and—perhaps most noticeably—scads of new restaurants have opened, expanding the city's culinary reach far beyond the traditional roast pork and dumplings. Many have something to learn in the way of presentation and service, but Praguers still marvel at a variety that was unthinkable not so many years ago.

PLANNING YOUR TIME

Most of Prague's top sights are crowded near one another, and could be connected together in a long one-day stroll. However, just because they're near each other doesn't mean you can comfortably do all these sights in a day. Prague Castle could take a day alone, depending on how much you explore the courtyards and other spaces. If you have a limited amount of time, focus on Old Town and the Castle Area (crossing the Charles Bridge between them) and with more time head South to the Lesser Quarter and New Town. Remember to build in some time for getting lost on the winding side street.

GETTING HERE

Prague's Ruzyně Airport (☎ *220–111–111* ⊕*www.prg.aero*) is 20 km (12 mi) northwest of the downtown area. It's small but easily negotiated. An expanded main terminal has eased traffic flow.

If your visit is restricted to the Czech capital, you'll do better not to rent a car. The capital is congested, and you'll save yourself a lot of hassle if you rely on public transportation. If you are planning to take excursions into the country, then a car will be useful, but don't pick it up until you are ready to depart. If you are arriving by car, you'll find that Prague is well served by major roads and highways from anywhere in the country. On arriving in the city, simply follow the signs to CEN-TRUM (city center).

International trains arrive at and depart from either of two stations: the main station, Hlavní nádraží, is about 500 yards east of Wenceslas Square on Opletalova or Washingtonova street. Then there's the suburban Nádraží Holešovice, about 2 km (1 mi) north of the city center. This is an unending source of confusion—always make certain you know which station your train is using.

GETTING AROUND

Prague's extensive bus and streetcar network (⊕*www.dp-praha.cz*) allows for fast, efficient travel throughout the city. Tickets are the same as those used for the metro, although you validate them at machines inside the bus or tram. Tickets (*jízdenky*) can be bought at hotels, some newsstands, and from dispensing machines in the metro stations.

Prague's subway system, the metro, is clean and reliable; the stations are marked with an inconspicuous M sign. Validate your ticket at an orange machine before descending the escalator.

Though far less common than before, dishonest taxi drivers remain a problem. Luckily, you probably won't need to rely on taxis for trips within the city center (it's usually easier to walk or take the subway). To minimize the chances of getting ripped off, avoid taxi stands in Wenceslas Square, Old Town Square, and other heavily touristed areas. The best alternative is to phone for a taxi in advance. Many radio-taxi firms have English-speaking operators.

VISITOR INFORMATION

The Czech Tourist Authority office (⊠*Staroměstské nám. 6, Staré Město* ☎*227–158–111*) on Old Town Square can provide information on tourism outside Prague, but does not sell tickets or book accommodations. The Prague Information Service has four central offices (*PIS* ⊠*Staroměstská radnice [Old Town Hall], Staré Město* ☎*224–482–562* ⊕*www.pis.cz* ⊠*Na Příkopě 20, Nové Město* ☎*No phone* ⊠*Hlavní nádraží, lower hall, Staré Město* ☎*No phone* ⊠*Malostranská mostecká věž, Malá Strana* ☎*No phone*).

STARÉ MĚSTO (OLD TOWN)

Prague's Old Town was spared from bombing during World War II, leaving it with one of the best-preserved centers of any major city in Europe. On any sunny summer weekend Old Town Square is rush-hour packed with revelers. The 15th-century astronomical clock, which is on the side of the town hall, has a procession of 12 apostles that make their rounds when certain hours strike. From another side, the Church of Our Lady before Týn's Gothic spires and the solid gold effigy of the Virgin Mary keep watch over onlookers. You will find the streets most subdued on early weekday mornings.

EXPLORING STARÉ MĚSTO

❼ Franz Kafka Exposition. Kafka came into the world on July 3, 1883, in a house next to the Kostel svatého Mikuláše (Church of St. Nicholas). For years the writer was only grudgingly acknowledged by the Communist cultural bureaucrats, reflecting the traditionally ambiguous attitude

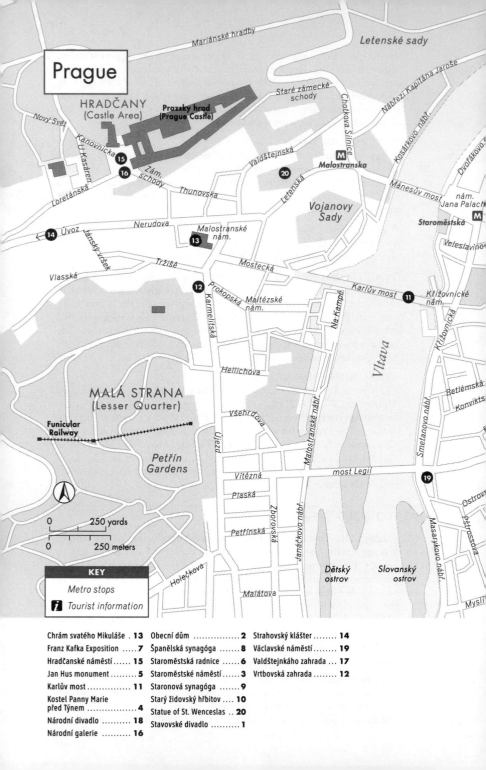

Chrám svatého Mikuláše . **13**
Franz Kafka Exposition **7**
Hradčanské náměstí **15**
Jan Hus monument **5**
Karlův most **11**
Kostel Panny Marie
před Týnem **4**
Národní divadlo **18**
Národní galerie **16**

Obecní dům **2**
Španělská synagóga **8**
Staroměstská radnice **6**
Staroměstské náměstí **3**
Staronová synagóga **9**
Starý židovský hřbitov **10**
Statue of St. Wenceslas .. **20**
Stavovské divadlo **1**

Strahovský klášter **14**
Václavské náměstí **19**
Valdštejnského zahrada ... **17**
Vrtbovská zahrada **12**

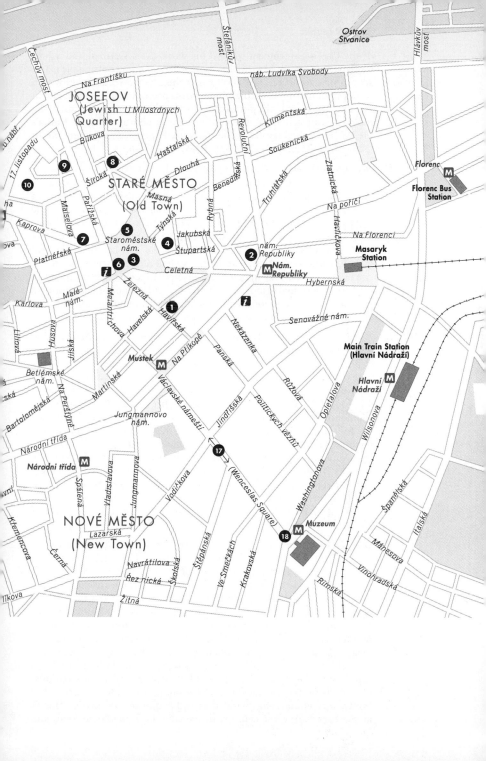

of the Czech government toward his work. As a German and a Jew, moreover, Kafka could easily be dismissed as standing outside the mainstream of Czech literature. Following the 1989 revolution, however, Kafka's popularity soared, and his works are now widely available in Czech. Though only the portal of the original house remains, inside the building is a fascinating little exhibit (mostly photographs) on Kafka's life, with commentary in English. ⊠ *Nám. Franze Kafky 3, Staré Město* ▧ *50 Kč* ⊙ *Tues.–Fri. 10–6, Sat. 10–5, Sun. 10–6.*

⑤ Jan Hus monument. Few memorials have elicited as much controversy as this one, which was dedicated in July 1915, exactly 500 years after Hus was burned at the stake in Constance, Germany. Some maintain that the monument's Secessionist style (the inscription seems to come right from turn-of-the-20th-century Vienna) clashes with the Gothic and Baroque of the square. Others dispute the romantic depiction of Hus, who appears here in flowing garb as tall and bearded. The real Hus, historians maintain, was short and had a baby face. Still, no one can take issue with the influence of this fiery preacher, whose ability to transform doctrinal disputes, both literally and metaphorically, into the language of the common man made him into a religious and national symbol for the Czechs. ⊠ *Staroměstské nám., Staré Město.*

④ Kostel Panny Marie před Týnem *(Church of the Virgin Mary Before Týn).* The exterior of the church is one of the best examples of Prague Gothic and is in part the work of Peter Parler, architect of the Charles Bridge and Chrám svatého Víta (St. Vitus's Cathedral). Construction of its twin black-spire towers was begun later, by King Jiří of Poděbrad in 1461, during the heyday of the Hussites. Jiří had a gilded chalice, the symbol of the Hussites, proudly displayed on the front gable between the two towers. Following the defeat of the Czech Protestants by the Catholic Habsburgs, the chalice was removed and eventually replaced by a Madonna. As a final blow, the chalice was melted down and made into the Madonna's glimmering halo (you still can see it by walking into the center of the square and looking up between the spires). The entrance to the church is through the arcades on Old Town Square, under the house at No. 604. *Staroměstské nám., between Celetná and Týnská, Staré Město.*

② Obecní dům *(Municipal House).* The city's Art Nouveau showpiece still fills the role it had when it was completed in 1911: it's a center for concerts, rotating art exhibits, and café society. The mature Art Nouveau style recalls the lengths the Czech middle classes went to at the turn of the 20th century to imitate Paris, then the epitome of style and glamour. Much of the interior bears the work of Art Nouveau master Alfons Mucha, Max Švabinský, and other leading Czech artists. Mucha decorated the Hall of the Lord Mayor upstairs with impressive, magical frescoes depicting Czech history; unfortunately it's not open to the public. The beautiful **Smetanova síň** (Smetana Hall), which hosts concerts by the Prague Symphony Orchestra as well as international players, is on the second floor. The ground-floor café is touristy but lovely, with glimmering chandeliers and exquisite woodwork. There's also a beer hall in the cellar with passable beer, mediocre food, and superbly executed ceramic murals on the walls. ⊠*Nám. Republiky 5, Staré Město* ☎*222–002–101* ⊕*www.obecnidum.cz* ⊙*Information center and box office daily 10–7.*

⑥ Staroměstská radnice *(Old Town Hall).* This is one of Prague's magnets: ★ hundreds of people gravitate to it to see the hour struck by the mechanical figures of the **astronomical clock.** Just before the hour, look to the upper part of the clock, where a skeleton begins by tolling a death knell and turning an hourglass upside down. The Twelve Apostles parade momentarily, and then a cockerel flaps its wings and crows, piercing the air as the hour finally strikes. To the right of the skeleton, the dreaded Turk nods his head, seemingly hinting at another invasion like those of the 16th and 17th centuries. This small spectacle doesn't clue viewers in to the way this 15th-century marvel indicates the time—by the season, the zodiac sign, and the positions of the sun and moon. The calendar under the clock dates from the mid-19th century.

The Old Town Hall served as the center of administration for the Old Town beginning in 1338, when King John of Luxembourg first granted the city council the right to a permanent location. The impressive 200-foot **Town Hall Tower,** where the clock is mounted, was first built in the 14th century and given its current late-Gothic appearance around 1500 by the master Matyáš Rejsek. For a rare view of the Old Town and its maze of crooked streets and alleyways, climb the ramp or ride the elevator to the top of the tower.

If you walk around the hall to the left, you'll see it's actually a series of houses jutting into the square; they were purchased over the years and successively added to the complex. On the other side, jagged stonework reveals where a large, neo-Gothic wing once adjoined the tower until it was destroyed during fighting between townspeople and Nazi troops in May 1945.

Guided tours (most guides speak English, and English texts are on hand) of the Old Town Hall depart from the main desk inside. Previously unseen parts of the tower were opened to the public in 2002, and you can now see the inside of the famous clock. ⊠*Staroměstské nám., Staré Město* ⊙*Apr.–Oct., Tues.–Sun. 9–6, Mon. 11–6; Nov.–Mar., Tues.– Sun. 9–5, Mon. 11–5* ☒*Tower 60 Kč, tours 60 Kč.*

③ Staroměstské náměstí *(Old Town Square).* There are places that, on first **Fodor's**Choice glimpse, stop you dead in your tracks in sheer wonder. Old Town Square ★ is one such place. Long the heart of the Old Town, the square grew to its present proportions when the city's original marketplace was moved away from the river in the 12th century. Its shape and appearance have changed little over the years. During the day the square is festive, as musicians vie for the favor of onlookers and artists display renditions of Prague street scenes. At night the gaudily lighted towers of the Church of the Virgin Mary Before Týn rise ominously over the glowing baroque facades. The crowds thin out, and the ghosts of the square's stormy past return.

During the 15th century the square was the focal point of conflict between Czech Hussites and German Catholics. In 1422 the radical Hussite preacher Jan Želivský was executed here for his part in storming the New Town's town hall three years earlier. In the 1419 uprising, three Catholic consuls and seven German citizens were thrown out the window—the first of Prague's many famous defenestrations. Within a few years the Hussites had taken over the town, expelled the Germans, and set up their own administration.

Twenty-seven white crosses set flat in the paving stones in the square, at the Old Town Hall's base, mark the spot where 27 Bohemian noblemen were killed by the Habsburgs in 1621 during the dark days following the defeat of the Czechs at the Battle of White Mountain. The grotesque spectacle, designed to quash any further national or religious opposition, took some five hours to complete, as the men were put to the sword or hanged one by one.

One of the most interesting houses on the Old Town Square juts out into the small extension leading into Malé náměstí. The house, called **U Minuty** (⊠3 Staroměstské nám., Staré Město), with its 16th-century Renaissance sgraffiti of biblical and classical motifs, was the home of the young Franz Kafka in the 1890s.

❶ **Stavovské divadlo** (Estates Theater). Built in the 1780s in the classical style, this handsome theater was for many years a beacon of Czech-language culture in a city long dominated by the German variety. It is probably best known as the site of the world premiere of Mozart's opera Don Giovanni in October 1787, with the composer himself conducting. Prague audiences were quick to acknowledge Mozart's genius: the opera was an instant hit here, though it flopped nearly everywhere else in Europe. Mozart wrote most of the opera's second act in Prague at the Villa Bertramka, where he was a frequent guest. You must attend a performance here to see inside. ⊠Ovocný tř. 1, Staré Město ☎224–902–322 box office ⊕www.narodni-divadlo.cz.

JOSEFOV (JEWISH QUARTER)

Prague's Jews survived centuries of discrimination, but two unrelated events of modern times have left their historic ghetto little more than a collection of museums. Around 1900, city officials decided for hygienic purposes to raze the minuscule neighborhood—at this time the majority of its residents were actually poor Gentiles—and pave over its crooked streets. Only some of the synagogues, the town hall, and the cemetery survived this early attempt at urban renewal. The second event was the Holocaust. Under Nazi occupation, a staggering percentage of the city's Jews were deported or murdered in concentration camps. Of the 35,000 Jews living in Prague before World War II, only about 1,200 returned to resettle the city after the war.

EXPLORING JOSEFOV

⑧ Španělská synagóga *(Spanish Synagogue)*. A domed Moorish-style synagogue was built in 1868 on the site of the Altschul, the city's oldest synagogue. Here, the historical exposition that begins in the Maisel Synagogue continues, taking the story up to the post–World War II period. The displays are not that compelling, but the building's painstakingly restored interior definitely is. ✉ *Vězeňská 1, Josefov* ☏ *224–819–456* ⊕ *www.jewishmuseum.cz* 🎟 *Combined ticket to museums and Old-New Synagogue 480 Kč; museums only, 300 Kč* ⊗ *Apr.–Oct., Sun.–Fri. 9–6; Nov.–Mar., Sun.–Fri. 9–4:30.*

⑨ Staronová synagóga *(Old-New Synagogue, or Altneuschul)*. Dating from the mid-13th century, this is one of the most important early-Gothic works in Prague. The odd name recalls the legend that the synagogue was built on the site of an ancient Jewish temple, and that stones from the temple were used to build the present structure. The oldest part of the synagogue is the entrance, with its vault supported by two pillars. The synagogue has not only survived fires and the razing of the ghetto at the end of the last century, but also emerged from the Nazi occupation intact; it is still in active use. As the oldest synagogue in Europe that still serves its original function, it is a living storehouse of Bohemian Jewish life. Note that men are required to cover their heads inside, and that during services men and women sit apart. ✉ *Červená 2, Josefov* ☏ *224–819–456* ⊕ *www.jewishmuseum.cz* 🎟 *Combined ticket to Old-New Synagogue and museums 480 Kč; Old-New Synagogue only, 200 Kč* ⊗ *Apr.–Oct., Sun.–Fri. 9–6; Nov.–Mar., Sun.–Fri. 9–4:30.*

⑩ ★ Starý židovský hřbitov *(Old Jewish Cemetery)*. This unforgettably melancholy sight not far from the busy city was, from the 15th century to 1787, the final resting place for all Jews living in Prague. The confined space forced graves to be piled one on top of the other. Tilted at crazy angles, the 12,000 visible tombstones are but a fraction of countless thousands more buried below. Walk the path amid the gravestones; the relief symbols you see represent the names and professions of the deceased. The oldest marked grave belongs to the poet Avigdor Kara, who died in 1439; the grave is not accessible from the pathway, but the original tombstone can be seen in the Maisel Synagogue. The best-known marker is that of Jehuda ben Bezalel, the famed Rabbi Loew (died 1609), a chief rabbi of Prague and profound scholar who is credited with creating the mythical Golem. Even today, small scraps of paper bearing wishes are stuffed into the cracks of the rabbi's tomb in the hope that he will grant them. Loew's grave lies near the exit. ✉ *Široká 3 (enter through Pinkasova synagóga), Josefov* ☏ *224–819–456* ⊕ *www. jewishmuseum.cz* 🎟 *Combined ticket to museums and Old-New Synagogue 480 Kč; museums only, 300 Kč* ⊗ *Apr.–Oct., Sun.–Fri. 9–6; Nov.–Mar., Sun.–Fri. 9–4:30.*

KARLŮV MOST (CHARLES BRIDGE) & MALÁ STRANA (LESSER QUARTER)

One of Prague's most exquisite neighborhoods, the Lesser Quarter (or Little Town) was established in 1257 and for years was where the merchants and craftsmen who served the royal court lived. The Lesser Quarter is not for the methodical traveler. Its charm lies in the tiny lanes, the sudden blasts of bombastic architecture, and the soul-stirring views that emerge for a second before disappearing behind the sloping roofs.

EXPLORING KARLŮV MOST & MALÁ STRANA

⑬ **Chrám svatého Mikuláše** *(Church of St. Nicholas).* With its dynamic curves, this church is one of the purest and most ambitious examples of High Baroque. The celebrated architect Christoph Dientzenhofer began the Jesuit church in 1704 on the site of one of the more active Hussite churches of 15th-century Prague. Work on the building was taken over by his son Kilian Ignaz Dientzenhofer, who built the dome and presbytery. Anselmo Lurago completed the whole in 1755 by adding the bell tower. The juxtaposition of the broad, full-bodied dome with the slender bell tower is one of the many striking architectural contrasts that mark the Prague skyline. Inside, the vast pink-and-green space is impossible to take in with a single glance. Every corner bristles with movement, guiding the eye first to the dramatic statues, then to the hectic frescoes, and on to the shining faux-marble pillars. Many of the statues are the work of Ignaz Platzer, and in fact they constitute his last blaze of success. Platzer's workshop was forced to declare bankruptcy when the centralizing and secularizing reforms of Joseph II toward the end of the 18th century brought an end to the flamboyant Baroque era. The tower, with an entrance on the side of the church, is open in summer. ⊠ *Malostranské nám., Malá Strana* 🖅 *50 Kč* 🕑 *Daily 9–4:30 for sightseeing, 8:30–9 AM for prayer only (no admission charge).*

⑪ **Karlův most** *(Charles Bridge).* Break out the camera—the view from the foot of the bridge on the Old Town side is nothing short of breathtaking, encompassing the towers and domes of the Lesser Quarter and the soaring spires of St. Vitus's Cathedral. This heavenly vision changes subtly in perspective as you walk across the bridge, attended by the host of Baroque saints that decorate the bridge's peaceful Gothic stones. At night its drama is spellbinding: St. Vitus's Cathedral lighted in a ghostly green, the castle in monumental yellow, and the Church of St. Nicholas in a voluptuous pink, all viewed through the menacing silhouettes of the bowed statues and the Gothic towers. If you do nothing else in Prague, you must visit the Charles Bridge at night.

Fodor's Choice
★

Charles IV appointed the 27-year-old German Peter Parler, the architect of St. Vitus's Cathedral, to build a proper bridge here in 1357. After 1620, following the defeat of Czech Protestants by Catholic Habsburgs at the Battle of White Mountain, the bridge became a symbol of the Counter-Reformation's vigorous re-Catholicization efforts. The many Baroque statues that began to appear in the late 17th century, commissioned by Catholics, eventually came to symbolize the totality of the

Austrian (hence Catholic) triumph. The religious conflict is less obvious nowadays, leaving only the artistic tension between Baroque and Gothic that gives the bridge its allure. Eighth on the right, the statue of St. John of Nepomuk, designed by Johann Brokoff in 1683, begins the Baroque lineup of saints. On the left-hand side, sticking out from the bridge between the 9th and 10th statues (the latter has a wonderfully expressive vanquished Satan), stands a Roland (Bruncvík) statue. This knightly figure, bearing the coat of arms of the Old Town, was once a reminder that this part of the bridge belonged to the Old Town before Prague became a unified city in 1784.

In the eyes of most art historians, the most valuable statue is the 12th on the left, near the Lesser Quarter end. Mathias Braun's statue of St. Luitgarde depicts the blind saint kissing Christ's wounds. The most compelling grouping, however, is the second from the end on the left, a work of Ferdinand Maxmilian Brokoff (son of Johann) from 1714. Here the saints are incidental; the main attraction is the Turk, his face expressing extreme boredom at guarding the Christians imprisoned in the cage at his side. When the statue was erected, just 31 years after the second Turkish siege of Vienna, it scandalized the Prague public.

Staroměstská mostecká věž (Old Town Bridge Tower), at the bridge entrance on the Old Town side, is where Peter Parler, the architect of the Charles Bridge, began his bridge building. The carved facades he designed for the sides of the tower were destroyed by Swedish soldiers in 1648, at the end of the Thirty Years' War. The sculptures facing the Old Town, however, are still intact (although some are recent copies); they depict an old and gout-ridden Charles IV with his son, who later became Wenceslas IV. Above them are two of Bohemia's patron saints, Adalbert of Prague and Sigismund. The top of the tower offers a spectacular view of the city for 60 Kč; it's open daily 10–5 (until 10 in the summer).

⑫ **Vrtbovská zahrada** *(Vrtba Garden).* An unobtrusive door on noisy Karmelitská hides the entranceway to a fascinating oasis that also has one of the best views of the Lesser Quarter. The street door opens onto the intimate courtyard of the Vrtbovský palác (Vrtba Palace), which is now private housing. Two Renaissance wings flank the courtyard; the left one was built in 1575, the right one in 1591. The owner of the latter house was one of the 27 Bohemian nobles executed by the Habsburgs in 1621 before the Old Town Hall. The house was given as confiscated property to Count Sezima of Vrtba, who bought the neighboring property and turned the buildings into a late-Renaissance palace. The Vrtba Garden, created a century later, reopened in summer 1998 after an excruciatingly long renovation. This is the most elegant of the Lesser Quarter's public gardens, built in five levels rising behind the courtyard in a wave of statuary-bedecked staircases and formal terraces leading up to a seashell-decorated pavilion at the top. (The fenced-off garden immediately behind and above belongs to the U.S. Embassy.) The powerful stone figure of Atlas that caps the entranceway in the courtyard and most of the other classically derived statues are from the workshop of Mathias Braun, perhaps the best of the Czech Baroque sculptors. ⊠*Karmelitská 25, Malá Strana* 🖾*40 Kč* ⊙*Apr.–Oct., daily 10–6.*

⑰ Valdštejnskáho zahrada *(Wallenstein Gardens).* Albrecht von Wallenstein, onetime owner of the house and gardens, began a meteoric military career in 1622, when the Austrian emperor Ferdinand II retained him to save the empire from the Swedes and Protestants during the Thirty Years' War. Wallenstein, wealthy by marriage, offered to raise 20,000 men at his own cost and lead them personally. Ferdinand II accepted and showered Wallenstein with confiscated land and titles. Wallenstein's first acquisition was this enormous area. Having knocked down 23 houses, a brick factory, and three gardens, in 1623 he began to build his magnificent palace with its idiosyncratic high-walled gardens and superb, vaulted Renaissance *sala terrena* (room opening onto a garden). Walking around the formal paths, you'll come across numerous statues, an unusual fountain with a woman spouting water from her breasts, and a lava-stone grotto along the wall. Most of the palace itself now serves the Czech Senate as a meeting chamber and offices. The palace's cavernous former *Jízdárna,* or riding school, now hosts occasional art exhibitions. ⊠*Letenská 10, Malá Strana* 🖾*Free* ⊙*Apr. 1–Oct. 31, daily 10–6.*

HRADČANY (CASTLE AREA)

To the west of Prague Castle is the residential Hradčany (Castle Area), the town that during the early 14th century emerged out of a collection of monasteries and churches. The concentration of history packed into Prague Castle and Hradčany challenges those not versed in the ups and downs of Bohemian kings, religious uprisings, wars, and oppression. The picturesque area surrounding Prague Castle, with its breathtaking vistas of the Old Town and the Lesser Quarter, is ideal for just wandering. But the castle itself, with its convoluted history and architecture, is difficult to appreciate fully without investing a little more time.

EXPLORING HRADČANY

⑮ Hradčanské náměstí *(Hradčany Square).* With its fabulous mixture of Baroque and Renaissance housing, topped by the castle itself, the square had a prominent role (disguised, ironically, as Vienna) in the film *Amadeus,* directed by the then-exiled Czech director Miloš Forman. The house at No. 7 was the set for Mozart's residence, where the composer was haunted by the masked figure he thought was his father. Forman used the flamboyant rococo Arcibiskupský palác (Archbishop's Palace), on the left as you face the castle, as the Viennese archbishop's palace. The plush interior, shown off in the film, is open to the public only on Maundy Thursday (the Thursday before Easter). No. 11 was home for a brief time after World War II to a little girl named Marie Jana Korbelová, who would grow up to be Madeleine Albright.

⑯ Národní galerie *(National Gallery).* Housed in the 18th-century Šternberský palác (Sternberg Palace), this collection, though impressive, is limited compared with German and Austrian holdings. During the time when Berlin, Dresden, and Vienna were building up superlative Old Master galleries, Prague languished, neglected by her Viennese rulers. Works by Rubens and Rembrandt are on display; other key pieces wait in the wings. Other branches of the National Gallery are scattered around town. ⊠ *Hradčanské nám. 15, Hradčany* ☎ *233–090–570* ⊕ *www.ngprague.cz* ⊠ *130 Kč* ☉ *Tues.–Sun. 10–6.*

⑭ Strahovský klášter *(Strahov Monastery).* Founded by the Premonstratensian order in 1140, the monastery remained in its hands until 1952, when the Communists suppressed all religious orders and turned the entire complex into the **Památník národního písemnictví** (Museum of National Literature). The major building of interest is the **Strahov Library,** with its collection of early Czech manuscripts, the 10th-century Strahov New Testament, and the collected works of famed Danish astronomer Tycho Brahe. Also of note is the late-18th-century **Philosophical Hall.** Spread across its ceiling is a startling sky-blue fresco that depicts an unusual cast of characters, including Socrates' nagging wife Xanthippe; Greek astronomer Thales, with his trusty telescope; and a collection of Greek philosophers mingling with Descartes, Diderot, and Voltaire. Also on the premises is the order's small art gallery, highlighted by late-Gothic altars and paintings from Rudolf II's time. ⊠ *Strahovské nádvoří 1/132, Hradčany* ☎ *233–107–718* ⊠ *80 Kč* ☉ *Gallery Tues.– Sun. 9–noon and 12:30–5; library daily 9–noon and 1–5.*

PRAŽSKÝ HRAD (PRAGUE CASTLE)

Despite its monolithic presence, the Prague Castle is not a single structure but rather a collection of buildings dating from the 10th to the 20th century, all linked by internal courtyards. The most important structures are **Chrám svatého Víta,** clearly visible soaring above the castle walls, and the **Královský palác,** the official residence of kings and presidents and still the center of political power in the Czech Republic. The castle is compact and easy to navigate.

EXPLORING PRAŽSKÝ HRAD

Bazilika svatého Jiří *(St. George's Basilica).* This church was originally built in the 10th century by Prince Vratislav I, the father of Prince (and St.) Wenceslas. It was dedicated to St. George (of dragon fame), who it was believed would be more agreeable to the still largely pagan people. The outside was remodeled during early Baroque times, although the striking rusty-red color is in keeping with the look of the Romanesque edifice. The interior looks more or less as it did in the 12th century, and is the best-preserved Romanesque relic in the country. The effect is at once barnlike and peaceful, the warm golden yellow of the stone walls and the small arched windows exuding a sense of enduring harmony. The house-shaped painted tomb at the front of the church holds the remains of the founder, Vratislav I. Up the steps, in a chapel to the right, is the tomb Peter Parler designed for St. Ludmila, the grandmother of St. Wenceslas. ⊠ *Nám. U sv. Jiří, Hradčany* ☎ *224–373–368 Castle Information* ⊕ *www.prague-info.cz* ⊠ *50 Kč. Requires castle ticket for 250 Kč or 350 Kč* ☉ *Apr.–Oct., daily 9–5; Nov.–Mar., daily 9–4.*

★ **Chrám svatého Víta** *(St. Vitus's Cathedral).* With its graceful, soaring towers, this Gothic cathedral—among the most beautiful in Europe—is the spiritual heart not only of Prague Castle but of the entire country. It has a long and complicated history, beginning in the 10th century and continuing to its completion in 1929. If you want to hear its history in depth, English-speaking guided tours of the cathedral and the Královský palác can be arranged at the information office across from the cathedral entrance.

Once you enter the cathedral, pause to take in the vast but delicate beauty of the Gothic and neo-Gothic interior glowing in the colorful light that filters through the startlingly brilliant stained-glass windows. This western third of the structure, including the facade and the two towers you can see from outside, was not completed until 1929, following the initiative of the Union for the Completion of the Cathedral, set up in the last days of the 19th century.

If you walk halfway up the right-hand aisle, you will find the **Svatováclavská kaple** (Chapel of St. Wenceslas). With a tomb holding the saint's remains, walls covered in semiprecious stones, and paintings depicting the life of Wenceslas, this square chapel is the ancient heart of the cathedral.

A little beyond the Chapel of St. Wenceslas on the same side, stairs lead down to the underground **royal crypt,** interesting primarily for the information it provides about the cathedral's history.

The cathedral's **Kralovské oratorium** (Royal Oratory) was used by the kings and their families when attending mass. Built in 1493, the work is a perfect example of the late-Gothic style, laced on the outside with a stone network of gnarled branches very similar in pattern to the ceiling vaulting in the Královský palác.

A few more steps toward the east end, you can't fail to catch sight of the ornate silver **sarcophagus of St. John of Nepomuk.** According to legend, when Nepomuk's body was exhumed in 1721 to be reinterred, the tongue was found to be still intact and pumping with blood. This strange tale served a highly political purpose. The Catholic Church and the Habsburgs were seeking a new folk hero to replace the Protestant forerunner Jan Hus, whom they despised.

The eight chapels around the back of the cathedral are the work of the original architect, Mathias d'Arras. Opposite the wooden relief, depicting the looting of the cathedral by Protestants in 1619, is the **Valdštejnská kaple** (Wallenstein Chapel). Since the 19th century, the chapel has housed the Gothic tombstones of its two architects, d'Arras and Peter Parler, who died in 1352 and 1399, respectively. If you look up to the balcony, you can just make out the busts of these two men, designed by Parler's workshop. The other busts around the triforium depict royalty and other VIPs of the time. *St. Vitus's Cathedral, Pražský Hrad* ☎224–373–368 *Castle Information* ⊕*www.katedralapraha.cz* ✉*Western section free; chapels, crypt, and tower require 2-day castle ticket for 350 Kč* ⊙*Mar.–Oct., Mon.–Sat. 9–5, Sun. noon–5; Nov.–Feb., Mon.–Sat. 9–4, Sun. noon–4.*

Druhé nádvoří *(Second Courtyard).* Empress Maria Theresa's court architect, Nicolò Pacassi, received the imperial approval to remake the castle in the 1760s, as it was badly damaged by Prussian shelling during the Seven Years' War in 1757. The Second Courtyard was the main victim of Pacassi's attempts at imparting classical grandeur to what had been a picturesque collection of Gothic and Renaissance styles. Except for the view of the spires of St. Vitus's Cathedral, the exterior courtyard offers little for the eye to feast upon. This courtyard also houses the rather gaudy **Kaple svatého Kříže** (Chapel of the Holy Cross), with decorations from the 18th and 19th centuries, which now serves as a souvenir and ticket stand.

Artworks that survived the turmoil of the Thirty Years' War are displayed in the **Obrazárna** *(Picture Gallery* ⊡*100 Kč* ⊘*Daily 10–6),* on the left side of the courtyard as you face St. Vitus's. In rooms elegantly redecorated by the official castle architect, Bořek Šípek, there are good Renaissance, Mannerist, and Baroque paintings that hint at the luxurious tastes of Rudolf's court. Across the passageway by the gallery entrance is the **Císařská konírna** (Imperial Stable), where temporary exhibitions are held. The passageway at the northern end of the courtyard forms the northern entrance to the castle and leads out over a luxurious ravine known as the **Jelení příkop** (Stag Moat), which can be entered (from April through October) either here or at the lower end via the metal catwalk off Chotkova ulice, when it isn't closed for sporadic renovations. ⊠*Obrazárna: Second Courtyard, Hradčany* ☎*224–373–368 Castle Information* ⊕*www.prague-info.cz* ⊡*Courtyard free; Picture Gallery 150 Kč* ⊘*Apr.–Oct., daily 9–6; Nov.–Mar., daily 9–4.*

Informační středisko *(Castle Information Office).* This is the place to come for entrance tickets, guided tours, headphones for listening to recorded tours in English, tickets to cultural events held at the castle, and money changing. Tickets are valid for one day and allow admission to the older parts of St. Vitus's Cathedral (the 20th-century sections are free), Královský palác, St. George's Basilica (but not the adjacent National Gallery exhibition, which has an additional entry fee), and a medieval bastion called Mihulka with an exhibition on alchemy. Other castle sights—including Golden Lane—require separate tickets, and you purchase these at the door. If you just want to walk through the castle grounds, note that the gates close at midnight April–October and at 11 PM the rest of the year, although the gardens are open April–October only. ⊠*Třetí nádvoří, across from entrance to St. Vitus's Cathedral, Pražský Hrad* ☎*224–373–368* ⊕*www.prague-info.cz* ⊡*Castle tickets 250 Kč (short) or 350 Kč (long); Golden Lane 50 Kč; St. George's Basilica 50 Kč; English-language guided tours 400 Kč for up to 4 people, 100 Kč per additional person, advance booking recommended; grounds and gardens free* ⊘*Apr.–Oct., daily 9–5; Nov.–Mar., daily 9–4.*

Klášter svatého Jiří *(St. George's Convent).* The first convent in Bohemia was founded here in 973 next to the even older St. George's Basilica. The National Gallery collections of Czech Mannerist and Baroque art are housed here. The highlights include the voluptuous work of Rudolf

II's court painters, giant Baroque religious statuary, and some fine paintings by Karel Škréta and Petr Brandl. Although inside Prague Castle, the museum has a separate admission. ⊠ *Nám. U sv. Jiří, Hradčany* ☎257–320–536 ⊕*www.ngprague.cz* 🎟️*130 Kč* ☉*Daily 10–6.*

Královská zahrada *(Royal Garden).* This peaceful swath of greenery affords an unusually lovely view of St. Vitus's Cathedral and the castle's walls and bastions. Originally laid out in the 16th century, it endured devastation in war, neglect in times of peace, and many redesigns, reaching its present parklike form early in the 20th century. Luckily, its Renaissance treasures survive. One of these is the long, narrow **Míčovna** (Ball Game Hall), built by Bonifaz Wohlmut in 1568, its garden front completely covered by a dense tangle of allegorical sgraffiti.

The **Královský letohrádek** (Royal Summer Palace, also known as the Belvedere), at the garden's eastern end, deserves its usual description as one of the most beautiful Renaissance structures north of the Alps. Italian architects began it; Wohlmut finished it off in the 1560s with a copper roof like an upturned boat's keel riding above the graceful arcades of the ground floor. ⊠ *U Prašného mostu ul. and Mariánské hradby ul. near Chotkovy Park, Hradčany* ☎224–373–368 *Castle Information* ⊕*www.prague-info.cz* 🎟️*Free* ☉*Mar.–June and Sept.–Oct., daily 10–7; July–Aug., daily 10–8.*

Královský palác *(Royal Palace).* The palace is an accumulation of the styles and add-ons of many centuries. The best way to grasp its size is from within the **Vladislavský sál** (Vladislav Hall), the largest secular Gothic interior space in Central Europe. The enormous hall was completed in 1493 by Benedikt Ried, who was to late-Bohemian Gothic what Peter Parler was to its earlier version. The room imparts a sense of space and light, softened by the sensuous lines of the vaulted ceilings and brought to a dignified close by the simple oblong form of the early Renaissance windows.

From the front of the hall, turn right into the rooms of the **Česká kancelář** (Bohemian Chancellery). This wing was built by the same Benedikt Ried only 10 years after the hall was completed, but it shows a much stronger Renaissance influence.

At the back of the Vladislav Hall, a staircase leads up to a gallery of the **Kaple všech svatých** (All Saints' Chapel). Little remains of Peter Parler's original work, but the church contains some fine works of art. The large room to the left of the staircase is the **Stará sněmovna** (council chamber), where the Bohemian nobles met with the king in a kind of prototype parliament. The descent from Vladislav Hall toward what remains of the **Romanský palác** (Romanesque Palace) is by way of a wide, shallow set of steps. This **Jezdecké schody** (Riders' Staircase) was the entranceway for knights who came for the jousting tournaments. ⊠ *Royal Palace, Třetí nádvoří, Pražský Hrad* ☎224–373–368 *Castle Information* ⊕*www.prague-info.cz* 🎟️*140 Kč or part of 2-day castle ticket, 250 Kč or 350 Kč* ☉*Apr.–Oct., daily 9–5; Nov.–Mar., daily 9–4.*

Lobkovický palác *(Lobkowicz Palace).* From the beginning of the 17th century until the 1940s, this building was the residence of the powerful Catholic Lobkowicz family. During the 1970s the building was restored to its early Baroque appearance and now is used for the National Museum's temporary exhibitions and concerts. If you want to get a chronological understanding of Czech history from the beginnings of the Great Moravian Empire in the 9th century to the Czech national uprising in 1848, this is the place. Copies of the crown jewels are on display here, but it is the rich collection of illuminated Bibles, old musical instruments, coins, weapons, royal decrees, paintings, and statues that makes the museum well worth visiting. Detailed information on the exhibits is available in English. Although inside Prague Castle, this museum has a separate admission. ✉ *Jiřská ul., Hradčany* ⊕ *www.nm.cz* 🖃 *20 Kč* ⊙ *Tues.–Sun. 10:30–6.*

4

Třetí nádvoří *(Third Courtyard).* The contrast between the cool, dark interior of St. Vitus's Cathedral and the brightly colored Pacassi facades of the Third Courtyard just outside is startling. The courtyard's clean lines are the work of Slovenian architect Josip Plečnik in the 1930s, but the modern look is a deception. Plečnik's paving was intended to cover an underground world of house foundations, streets, and walls dating from the 9th through 12th century and rediscovered when the cathedral was completed. (You can see a few archways through a grating in a wall of the cathedral.)

🖙 **Zlatá ulička** *(Golden Lane).* An enchanting collection of tiny, ancient, brightly colored houses crouches under the fortification wall and looks remarkably like a set for *Snow White and the Seven Dwarfs.* Legend has it that these were the lodgings of the international group of alchemists whom Rudolf II brought to the court to produce gold. The truth is a little less romantic: the houses were built during the 16th century for the castle guards, who supplemented their income by practicing various crafts. By the early 20th century Golden Lane had become the home of poor artists and writers. Franz Kafka, who lived at No. 22 in 1916 and 1917, described the house on first sight as "so small, so dirty, impossible to live in and lacking everything necessary." But he soon came to love the place. As he wrote to his fiancée: "Life here is something special . . . to close out the world not just by shutting the door to a room or apartment but to the whole house, to step out into the snow of the silent lane." The lane now houses tiny stores selling books, music, and crafts.

Within the walls above Golden Lane, a timber-roof **corridor** (enter between Nos. 23 and 24) is lined with replica suits of armor and weapons (some of it for sale), mock torture chambers, and the like. A shooting range allows you to fire five bolts from a crossbow for 50 Kč. ✉ *Pražský Hrad* ☎ *224–373–368* ⊕ *www.prague-info.cz* 🖃 *Included in combination 2-day castle tickets for 250 Kč or 350 Kč; free after 6 PM.*

NOVÉ MĚSTO (NEW TOWN)

To this day, Charles IV's most extensive scheme, the New Town, is still such a lively, vibrant area you may hardly realize that its streets, Gothic churches, and squares were planned as far back as 1348. With Prague fast outstripping its Old Town parameters, Charles IV extended the city's fortifications. A high wall surrounded the newly developed 2½ square km (1½ square mi) area south and east of the Old Town, tripling the walled territory on the Vltava's right bank. The wall extended south to link with the fortifications of the citadel called Vyšehrad. In the mid-19th century, new building in the New Town boomed in a welter of Romantic and neo-Renaissance styles, particularly on Wenceslas Square and avenues such as Vodičkova, Na Poříčí, and Spálená. One of the most important structures was the Národní divadlo (National Theater), meant to symbolize in stone the revival of the Czechs' history, language, and sense of national pride.

EXPLORING NOVÉ MĚSTO

⑱ Národní divadlo *(National Theater)*. The idea for a Czech national theater began during the revolutionary decade of the 1840s. In a telling display of national pride, donations to fund the plan poured in from all over the country, from people of every socioeconomic stratum. The cornerstone was laid in 1868, and the "National Theater generation" who built the neo-Renaissance structure became the architectural and artistic establishment for decades to come. Its designer, Josef Zítek (1832–1909), was the leading neo-Renaissance architect in Bohemia. The nearly finished interior was gutted by a fire in 1881, and Zítek's onetime student Josef Schulz (1840–1917) saw the reconstruction through to completion two years later. Statues representing Drama and Opera rise above the riverfront side entrances; two gigantic chariots flank figures of Apollo and the nine Muses above the main facade. The performance space itself is filled with gilding, voluptuous plaster figures, and plush upholstery. Next door is the modern (1970s–80s) Nová scéna (New Stage), where the popular Magic Lantern black-light shows are staged. The Národní divadlo is one of the best places to see a performance; ticket prices start as low as 30 Kč, and you'll have to buy a ticket if you want to see inside because there are no public tours. ⊠ *Národní tř. 2, Nové Město* ☎ *224–901–448 box office* ⊕ *www.narodni-divadlo.cz.*

⑳ Statue of St. Wenceslas. Josef Václav Myslbek's huge equestrian grouping of St. Wenceslas with other Czech patron saints around him is a traditional meeting place at times of great national peril or rejoicing. In 1939, Praguers gathered to oppose Hitler's takeover of Bohemia and Moravia. It was here also, in 1969, that the student Jan Palach set himself on fire to protest the bloody invasion of his country by the Soviet Union and other Warsaw Pact countries in August of the previous year. The invasion ended the "Prague Spring," a cultural and political movement emphasizing free expression, which was supported by Alexander Dubček, the popular leader at the time. Although Dubček never intended to dismantle Communist authority completely, his political and economic reforms proved too daring for fellow comrades in the rest of Eastern Europe. In the months following the invasion, conservatives loyal to the Soviet Union were installed in all influential positions. The subsequent two decades were a period of cultural stagnation. Hundreds of thousands of Czechs and Slovaks left the country, a few became dissidents, and many more resigned themselves to lives of minimal expectations and small pleasures. ⊠ *Václavské nám., Nové Město.*

⑲ **Václavské náměstí** *(Wenceslas Square).* You may recognize this spot, for it was here that some 500,000 students and citizens gathered in the heady days of November 1989 to protest the policies of the former Communist regime. The government capitulated after a week of demonstrations, without a shot fired or the loss of a single life, bringing to power the first democratic government in 40 years (under playwright-president Václav Havel). Today this peaceful transfer of power is half ironically referred to as the "Velvet" or "Gentle" Revolution *(něžná revoluce).* It was only fitting that the 1989 revolution should take place on Wenceslas Square: throughout much of Czech history, the square has served as the focal point for popular discontent. The long "square," which is more like a broad, divided boulevard, was first laid out by Charles IV in 1348 as a horse market at the center of the New Town.

WHERE TO EAT

STARÉ MĚSTO (OLD TOWN)

$$$$
Fodor'sChoice
★
✕ **Allegro.** Andrea Accordi, arguably the city's most heralded chef, serves luscious, seasonal dishes from around Italy like duo of sea scallops and spaghetti with scorpionfish, all in a snazzy, almost nautical dining room. To say the chef and the restaurant have raised the bar for Prague dining is an understatement, though the kitchen is apt to go on flights of fancy at times (think foams). Regularly recognized as one of the best Italian kitchens in Central Europe, Allegro is a treat for those who indulge in the top of the line. ⊠ *Four Seasons Prague, Veleslavinova 21, Staré Město 110 00* ☎*221–427–000* ♨*Reservations essential* ⊟*AE, DC, MC, V* Ⓜ*Line A: Staroměstská.*

$$$
✕ **Angel.** Huddled into a touristy part of Old Town, this restaurant is easy to miss, but keep your eyes peeled: from the golden bird's-nest chandelier hanging above the intimate dining room to the explosive flavors bolstering each seasonal dish, Angel is one of Prague's best restaurants, period. Here the perennial Czech favorite duck becomes a tangy, summery salad, with basil and green papaya; pushing farther abroad, there's Borneo-style sea bass and Cambodian curry. Desserts, the weak spot in many an Asian menu, are recommended, especially the tamarind-ripple ice cream. ⊠ *V kolkovně 7, Staré Město* ☎*773–222–422* ⊟*AE, DC, MC, V* Ⓜ*Line A: Staroměstská* ⊘*Closed Sun.*

$–$$
Fodor'sChoice
★
✕ **Kavárna Slavia.** Easily the city's best-known café, Slavia serves good coffee, drinks, and light snacks, as well as the standards of Czech cuisine: roast duck with potato dumplings and sauerkraut, beef goulash, and roast smoked pork with white cabbage and potato pancakes. Sandwiches and quotidian pasta plates offer lighter, less-expensive options, though aesthetes can make a full meal out of the rich views of the National Theater, the Vltava, and Prague Castle. This spectacular location has a historic air that winds from the days of Viktor Oliva's painting

The Absinthe Drinker (which hangs in the main room), through the era of the playwright and regular patron Václav Havel, and continues into the modern day. ✉*Smetanovo nábř. 1012/2, Staré Město 110 00* ☎*224–218–493* ▤*AE, MC, V* Ⓜ*Line B: Národní Třida.*

$$–$$$ ✕**Kolkovna.** For Czechs and expatriates living in Prague, this is one
★ of the most popular spots to take visitors for a taste of local cuisine. The wood-and-copper decor gives off an appropriate air of a brewery taproom, and you can wash down traditional meals—such as *svíčkova* (beef tenderloin in cream sauce), roast duck, and fried pork cutlets, or upgrades of traditional food, such as turkey steak with Roquefort sauce and walnuts—with a mug of unpasteurized Pilsner Urquell. ✉*V Kolkovně, Staré Město 110 00* ☎*224–818–701* ▤*AE, MC, V* Ⓜ*Line A: Staroměstská.*

MALÁ STRANA (LESSER QUARTER)

$–$$$ ✕**Café Savoy.** Stellar service and elegant meals of high quality at moderate prices are de rigueur here. Oh, and killer sweets. This restored café, a onetime favorite of the city's fin-de-siècle Jewish community, serves everything from meal-sized split-pea and cream of spinach soups to Wiener schnitzel, with huge salads complemented by fresh breads from the in-house bakery. The house cake, topped with marzipan, makes a properly sweet finish. If you're looking for eggs, Savoy's breakfasts are without question some of Prague's best. ✉*Vitězná 1, Smíchov 150 00* ☎*257–311–562* ▤*AE, DC, MC, V* Ⓜ*Line A: Malostranská.*

$$$–$$$$ ✕**Kampa Park.** The zenith of riverside dining is offered at this legendary
Fodor'sChoice restaurant just off Charles Bridge, known almost as much for its chic
★ decor and celebrity guests as it is for elegant continental cuisine and great wines—it's the kind of place where European royals and heads of state mingle with their head-of-studio counterparts from Hollywood. But the real star power arrives on the plate, courtesy of chef Marek Raditsch, whose sophisticated cooking blends seasonal ingredients with worldly culinary technique: halibut with black truffles and crispy bacon, seared turbot with pumpkin puree, venison with veal tongue in cardamom sauce. Incredible foods, incredible views. ✉*Na Kampě 8/b, Malá Strana 118 00* ☎*257–532–685* ▤*AE, DC, MC, V* Ⓜ*Line A: Malostranská.*

$$$–$$$$ ✕**Pálffy Palác.** Tucked inside an establishment that's literally palatial,
★ age-old elegance and artful continental cuisine combine on the second story of a Baroque palazzo just below Prague Castle. A favorite for special occasions, magical evenings, and affairs to remember, Pálffy is one of the few ancient locations in Prague to maintain a feel for the past without seeming stuffy, kitschy, or fake. Instead, it's all high ceilings, candlelight, and haute cuisine: baked yellowfin with fennel puree, young bull steak with veggie sauce, and ostrich carpaccio. The overall effect is elegant, yet lighthearted. ✉*Valdštejnská 14, Malá Strana 118 00* ☎*257–530–522* ▤*AE, MC, V* Ⓜ*Line A: Malostranská.*

NOVÉ MĚSTO (NEW TOWN) & VYŠEHRAD

$$–$$$$ ✕**Brasserie M.** When chef Jean-Paul Manzac left the Prague Marriott to open his own shiny bistro, he changed the very definition of local French food. Since then, Brasserie M. has toned down the excess, but the

spacious restaurant still has all the classics, from coquilles St. Jacques, passing by way of hearty coq au vin and rabbit fricassee and ending on a traditional chocolate mousse (the recipe was passed down from the chef's father). It's all excellent, and generally about half the price of fancier French places around town. ⊠ *Vladislavova 17, Nové Město 110 00* ☎*224–054–070* ⊟*AE, MC, V* Ⓜ*Line B: Národní Třída.*

$$$–$$$$
Fodor's Choice
★

✕**CzecHouse.** This favorite spot of convention-goers staying at the Hilton upgraded its kitchen by adding Belgian Peter De Smedt as a new chef. Spying on his work through the window in the kitchen, diners can watch him add haute flair to Czech classics like *svíčkova* (marinated beef with cream sauce) or experiment with dishes like headcheese and melon. Czech wines are similarly of a higher standard, though beer goes very well with most recipes. De Smedt is also a whiz with the restaurant's wide selection of U.S. beef. Excellent service provides another reason to make the trip to metro station Florenc. ⊠*Pobřezní 1, Karlín 186 00* ☎*224–842–125* ⊟*AE, DC, MC, V* Ⓜ*Line B or C: Florenc.*

$–$$$

✕**Don Pedro.** Right on the riverfront, yet overlooked by most tourists, this Latin bistro serves authentic dishes from Bogotá, courtesy of the Colombian-Czech couple that owns the place. In large part that means beef: clear beef broth with stewed beef rib known as *caldo de costilla*; white-corn empanadas stuffed with ground beef and rice; and *arepas*, thick corn pancakes filled with gooey white cheese. Both the 300-gram (10-ounce) steak and the grilled beef liver are excellent meals for hearty appetites. ⊠*Masarykovo nábř. 2, Nové Město 120 00* ☎*224–923–505* ⊟*No credit cards* Ⓜ*Line B: Národní Třída.*

WHERE TO STAY

STARÉ MĚSTO (OLD TOWN)

$$$$

🏨 **Four Seasons Prague.** If you love hotels with every small luxury— morning newspapers with your breakfast, in-room massages, and twice-daily maid service—the expense of the rooms will be easier to justify. Sean Connery and Owen Wilson could only agree, having stayed here while they worked in Prague. A Baroque house from 1737 and a renovated neoclassical former factory from 1846 are joined together through a contemporary building to form this large luxury hotel with an unbeatable riverside location. And in 2007 designer Pierre-Yves Rochon sprinkled his sophisticated French charm in a redesign of the rooms. Rooms 234 and 701 both represent the proverbial "room with a view," offering a sweeping vista of the Charles Bridge and Prague Castle, respectively. Service is consistently excellent, and the friendliness and patience of the staff are unbeatable. The in-house restaurant could serve the best meal of your trip—or possibly of your entire life. **Pros:** One of the most prized restaurants in the city; enviable address near the Charles Bridge. **Cons:** Some Four Seasons aficionados say the lobby is cumbersome; with two computers in the business center, there can be a wait to check those e-mails. ⊠*Veleslavinova 2a, Staré Město 110 00* ☎*221–427–000* ⊕*www.fourseasons.com* ➥*141 rooms, 20 suites* ♿*In-room: safe, Internet. In-hotel: restaurant, bar, gym, concierge, parking (fee), no-smoking rooms, some pets allowed (fee)* ⊟*AE, DC, MC, V* ⦿*EP* Ⓜ*Line A: Staroměstská.*

MALÁ STRANA (LESSER QUARTER)

$$$$
Fodor'sChoice
★

🖫 **Alchymist Grand Hotel Spa.** When picturing Prague hotels, the Alchymist is the type of establishment that comes to mind. Both the front of the hotel (which is UNESCO protected) and the squished lobby disguise how large this building actually is. It brings together four Renaissance and Baroque houses from the late 15th century. Owned by an Italian and possessed of that signature Italian flair, this hotel not only features a 500-year-old staircase, but the imported tiki wood creates a bridge (over a fish-filled pond) that brings together the massage rooms and the sushi bar in the basement. It's truly an embarrassment of riches. **Pros:** Gorgeous spa, with an extensive menu for relaxation. **Cons:** Can be a little overdone for some; for those wanting to hit the nightlife, the other side of the bridge might be more appropriate. ⊠ *Tržiště 19, Malá Strana* ☎*257–286–011-016* ⊕*www.alchymisthotelresidence.com* ↝*26 rooms, 20 suites* ♿*In-room: safe, DVD, dial-up. In-hotel: restaurant, gym, spa, laundry service* ⊟*AE, DC, MC, V* ¶◎¶*BP* Ⓜ*Line A: Malostranská.*

$$$$
Fodor'sChoice
★

🖫 **Mandarin Oriental Prague.** The picture of understated taste, this outpost of the Mandarin Oriental opened in late 2006. Built in a former monastery, it features vaulted ceilings and original 14th century staircases, offering a luxurious serenity to guests. Contemporary Asian touches work into a harmonious blend of beige, red, black, and navy. Silk tassels in red or gold indicate to the staff "do not disturb" or "please make up my room." An underground passageway leads to the spa, where a glass floor displays the ruins of a Gothic church uncovered during construction. Here you can receive a Czech specialty, the Linden Blossom scrub, using blossoms long believed to be medicinal in Czech culture, or opt for a stellar stone massage. The restaurant serves seasonal dishes that could easily be your best meal in Prague. And parents take note: children are given a toy on arrival, as well as special toiletries (including a rubber ducky). **Pros:** Heavenly spa services; fantastic restaurant. **Cons:** Some guests feel that some of the rooms are on the small side; the restaurant's wine list can be seen as overpriced; the hotel offers continental, English, and Japanese breakfast, but none is included in the room price. ⊠*Nebovidská 459, Malá Strana 118 00* ☎*233–088–888* ⊕*www.mandarin oriental.com* ↝*99 rooms, 22 suites* ♿*In-room: safe, DVD, Internet. In-hotel: restaurant, bars, gym, spa, laundry service, parking (fee), Wi-Fi* ⊟*AE, DC, MC, V* ¶◎¶*EP* Ⓜ*Line A: Malostranská.*

$$

🖫 **U Tří Pštrosů.** This inviting inn has taken a couple of licks—first it was flooded, then burned to the ground, and then rebuilt, only to be taken by the Communists. Now it's been restituted to the family owners. But there is beauty in triumph, and the location is so close to the Charles Bridge that you could barter with one of the street vendors from your window. The rooms are spacious and feature beautifully ornate ceilings. Sadly, there is no air-conditioning, but the rooms do have Wi-Fi, so it's behind the times in some ways and ahead in others. **Pros:** Location, location, location. **Cons:** Top-floor rooms are smaller than those on the other floors; though it's a small house, stairs are stairs, and the lack of an elevator can be tiring. ⊠*Dražického nám. 12, Malá Strana 118 00* ☎*257–288–888* ⊕*www.utripstrosu.cz* ↝*14 rooms, 4 suites*

⟡ *In-room: no a/c, Wi-Fi. In-hotel: restaurant, laundry service* ☰AE, DC, MC, V ⑩BP Ⓜ *Line A: Malostranská.*

HRADČANY

$$$$ 🎞 **Savoy.** A modest yellow Jugendstil façade conceals one of the city's most luxurious small hotels. Once a budget hotel, the building was gutted and lavishly refurbished in the mid-1990s. A harmonious maroon-and-mahogany color scheme carries through the public spaces; some rooms are furnished in a purely modern style, and others have a 19th-century period look. A tram stop is practically at the front door, making trips into the center quick and easy. Pros: Away from the chaos of the city, it's a quiet choice in Prague; the interior can be a bit stuffy for some. Cons: For an up-all-night vacation, the hotel is far from the central hub; staff can be less than helpful. ✉ *Keplerova 6, Hradčany 118 00* ☎ *224–302–430* ⊕ *www.hotel-savoy.cz* ⇘ *55 rooms, 6 suites* ⟡ *In-room: safe, DVD, Wi-Fi. In-hotel: restaurant, gym, concierge, no-smoking rooms, some pets allowed (fee)* ☰AE, DC, MC, V ⑩BP.

4

NIGHTLIFE & THE ARTS

THE ARTS

Classical concerts are held all over the city throughout the year. In addition to Prague's two major professional orchestras, classical ensembles are the most common finds, and the standard of performance ranges from adequate to superb, though the programs tend to take few risks. Serious fans of Baroque music may have the opportunity to hear works of little-known Bohemian composers at these concerts. Some of the best chamber ensembles are the Martinů Ensemble, the Prague Chamber Philharmonic (also known as the Prague Philharmonia), the Wihan Quartet, the Czech Trio, and the Agon contemporary music group.

Performances are held regularly at many of the city's palaces and churches, including the Garden on the Ramparts below Prague Castle (where the music comes with a view); both Churches of St. Nicholas; the Church of Sts. Simon and Jude on Dušní in the Old Town; the Church of St. James on Malá Štupartská, near Old Town Square; the Zrcadlová kaple (Mirror Chapel) in the Klementinum on Mariánské náměstí in the Old Town; and the Lobkowicz Palace at Prague Castle. If you're an organ-music buff, you'll most likely have your pick of recitals held in Prague's historic halls and churches. Popular programs are offered at the Church of St. Nicholas in the Lesser Quarter and the Church of St. James, where the organ plays amid a complement of Baroque statuary.

Dvořák Hall (✉ *Rudolfinum, nám. Jana Palacha, Staré Město* ☎ *224–893–111* ⊕ *www.czechphilharmonic.cz*) is home to one of Central Europe's best orchestras, the Czech Philharmonic. Frequent guest conductor Sir Charles Mackerras is a leading proponent of modern Czech music. One of the best orchestral venues is the resplendent Art Nouveau **Smetana Hall** (✉ *Obecní dům, nám. Republiky 5, Staré Město* ☎ *222–002–100* ⊕ *www.obecnidum.cz*), home of the excellent Prague Symphony Orchestra and major venue for the annual Prague Spring music festival. Concerts at the **Villa Bertramka** (✉ *Mozartova 169,*

Smíchov ☎*257–318–461* ⊕*www.bertramka.cz*) emphasize the music of Mozart and his contemporaries.

NIGHTLIFE
For details of cultural and nightlife events, look for the English-language newspaper the *Prague Post* or one of the multilingual monthly guides available at hotels, tourist offices, and newsstands.

Most social life of the drinking variety takes place in pubs (*pivnice* or *hospody*), which are liberally sprinkled throughout the city's neighborhoods. Tourists are welcome to join in the evening ritual of sitting around large tables and talking, smoking, and drinking beer. Before venturing in, however, it's best to familiarize yourself with a few points of pub etiquette: always ask if a chair is free before sitting down (*Je tu volno?*). To order a beer (*pivo*), do not wave the waiter down or shout across the room; he will usually assume you want beer—most pubs serve one brand—and bring it over to you without asking. He will also bring subsequent rounds to the table without asking. To refuse, just shake your head or say no thanks (*ne, děkuju*).

SHOPPING

Bohemian crystal and porcelain deservedly enjoy a worldwide reputation for quality, and plenty of shops offer excellent bargains. The local market for antiques and art is still relatively undeveloped, although dozens of antiquarian bookstores harbor some excellent finds, particularly German and Czech books and graphics.

SHOPPING DISTRICTS
The major shopping areas are **Na Příkopě**, which runs from the foot of Wenceslas Square to náměstí Republiky (Republic Square), and the area around **Old Town Square**. The Old Town **Pařížská ulice** and **Karlova ulice** are streets dotted with boutiques and antiques shops. In the Lesser Quarter, try **Nerudova ulice,** the street that runs up to Hradčany. An artistically designed modern glass shopping mall, **Nový Smíchov** (✉ *Corner of Plzeňská and Nádražní, Smíchov* ⊕*www.novysmichovoc.cz* Ⓜ*Anděl*), covers an entire city block. It opened in 2001 and includes a multiplex cinema and bowling alley plus clothing, perfume, electronics, and book stores.

SOUTHERN BOHEMIA

With Prague at its heart and Germany and the former Austro-Hungarian Empire on its mountainous borders, the kingdom of Bohemia was for centuries buffeted by religious and national conflicts, invasions, and wars. But its position also meant that Bohemia benefited from the cultural wealth and diversity of Central Europe. The result is a glorious array of history-laden castles, walled cities, and spa towns set in a gentle, rolling landscape.

Southern Bohemia (separate sections on the northern and western areas follow) is particularly famous for its involvement in the Hussite religious

Southern
Bohemia

GERMANY

AUSTRIA

wars of the 15th century. But the area also has more than its fair share of well-preserved and stunning walled towns, built up by generations of noble families, who left behind layers of Gothic, Renaissance, and Baroque architecture (particularly notable in Český Krumlov). Farther north and an easy drive east of Prague is the old silver-mining town of Kutná Hora, once a rival to Prague for the royal residence.

Český Krumlov (along with the spas of western Bohemia) offers some of the best accommodations in the Czech Republic outside the capital.

PLANNING YOUR TIME
Kutná Hora is often seen as a day trip from Prague. Try to hit the "Bone Church" before coming into town and focus on seeing St. Barbara's Cathedral first. Český Krumlov, on the other hand, is a longer trip, and mainly centered on Krumlov Castle. It makes for a relaxing excursion from the more bustling city.

GETTING HERE & AROUND
All the major destinations in the region are reachable from Prague and České Budějovice on the ČSAD bus network.

Car travel affords the greatest ease and flexibility in this region. The main artery through the region, the two-lane E55 from Prague south to

Tábor and České Budějovice, though often crowded, is in relatively good shape. If you are driving from Vienna, take the E49 toward Gmünd.

Benešov (Konopiště), Tábor, and České Budějovice lie along the major southern line in the direction of Linz, and train service to these cities from Prague is frequent and comfortable. Most Vienna–Prague trains travel through Moravia, but a few stop at Třeboň and Tábor (with a change at Gmünd).

KUTNÁ HORA

The approach to Kutná Hora looks much as it has for centuries. The town owes its illustrious past to silver, discovered here during the 12th century. For some 400 years the mines were worked with consummate efficiency. As the silver began to run out during the 16th and 17th centuries, however, Kutná Hora's importance faded. Since the early 1990s the town has beautified itself to a degree, but despite a significant tourist industry, modern Kutná Hora is dwarfed by the splendors of the Middle Ages. The city became a UNESCO World Heritage Site in 1995.

GETTING HERE
You can either take the train or bus to Kutná Hora and each trip takes about an hour. The train actually stops in the neighboring town of Sedlec, which gives you a chance to see the "Bone Church," but means a long walk of over a mile into town. By car, Highway 333 goes all the way to Kutná Hora.

VISITOR INFORMATION
Kutná Hora Tourist Information (⊠ *Palackého nám. 377* ☎ *327–512–378* ⊕ *www.kutnahora.cz*).

EXPLORING KUTNÁ HORA
★ Approaching the **Chrám svaté Barbory** *(St. Barbara's Cathedral)*, overlooking the river, you pass through a magnificent landscape. The 10-minute stroll from the main Palackého náměstí along Barborská ulice is lined with Baroque statues in front of a vast former Jesuit college as you near St. Barbara's. From a distance, the three-peak roof of the church gives the impression of a large, magnificently peaked tent more than a religious center. St. Barbara's is undoubtedly Kutná Hora's masterpiece and a high point of the Gothic style in Bohemia. Begun in the 1380s, it drew on the talents of the Peter Parler workshop as well as two luminaries of the late Gothic of the late 15th century, Matyáš Rejsek and Benedikt Ried. The soaring roof was added as late as 1558, replaced in the 18th century, and finally restored in the late 1800s; the western facade also dates from the end of the 19th century. From here you can see the romantic view over the town, marked by the visibly tilting 260-foot-tower of St. James's Church.

St. Barbara is the patron saint of miners, and silver-mining themes dominate the interior of the church. Gothic frescoes depict angels carrying shields with mining symbols. The town's other major industry, minting, can be seen in frescoes in the **Mintner's Chapel.** A statue of a miner, donning the characteristic smock, stands proudly in the nave and dates from 1700. But the main attraction of the interior is the vaulting itself, which carries the eye effortlessly upward. ⊠*Barborská ul.* ☎*327–515–797* ⌷*40 Kč* ☉*Apr.–Oct., Tues.–Sun. 9–5:30, Mon. 10–4:30; Nov.–Mar., Tues.–Sun. 10–4:30.*

The **České Muzeum Stříbra** *(Czech Museum of Silver),* housed in the Hrádek (Little Castle) that was once part of the town's fortifications, is a museum of mining and coin production. In the 16th century Kutná Hora boasted the deepest mines in the world, some going down as far as 1,650 feet. It's somewhat fitting, then, that the highlight of the Hrádek—and the focal point of the longer museum tours—is a hike down into a claustrophobic medieval mine tunnel. The small trek (you're inside for about 30 minutes) is more titillating than scary, though you may be happy you weren't a medieval miner. The cheapest tour, which doesn't include the mine, is dull, unless you're a fan of ore samples and archaeology. If it's available, go for the 1½-hour tour, which includes a portion of the displays from the museum proper, plus the mine. ⊠*Barborská ul. 28* ☎*327–512–159* ⊕*www.cms-kh.cz* ⌷*60 Kč–110 Kč* ☉*Apr. and Oct., Tues.–Sun. 9–5; May, June, and Sept., Tues.–Sun. 9–6; July and Aug., Tues.–Sun. 10–6.*

Coins were first minted at the **Vlašský dvůr** *(Italian Court)* in 1300, made by Italian artisans brought in from Florence—hence the mint's odd name. It was here that the Prague groschen, one of the most widely circulated coins of the Middle Ages, was minted until 1726. There's a **coin museum,** where you can see the small, silvery groschen being struck and buy replicas. ⊠*Havlíčkovo nám.* ☎*327–512–873* ⌷*80 Kč* ☉*Apr.–Sept., daily 9–6; Oct. and Mar., daily 10–5; Nov.–Feb., daily 10–4.*

No trip to Kutná Hora is complete without a visit to the nearby suburb of Sedlec (about 2 km [1 mi] from the center of the city), where you can find one of Europe's most chilling sights: a chapel decorated with the bones of some 40,000 people. The Kaple všech svatých (All Saints' ★ Chapel), commonly known as the **Kostnice** *(ossuary* or "Bone Church"), is just up the road from the former Sedlec Monastery. The church came into being in the 16th century, when development forced the clearing of a nearby graveyard. Monks of the Cistercian order came up with the bright idea of using the bones to decorate the chapel; the most recent creations date from the end of the 19th century. The run-down **Church of the Assumption of the Virgin** at the former Sedlec monastery exemplifies the work of Giovanni Santini (1667–1723). A master of expressive line and delicate proportion, this one-of-a-kind architect fathered a bravura hybrid of Gothic and Baroque. ⊠*Zámecka 127, Sedlec* ☎*728–125–488* ⊕*www.kostnice.cz* ⌷*40 Kč* ☉*Apr.–Sept., daily 8–6; Oct. and Mar., daily 9–noon and 1–5; Nov.–Feb., daily 9–noon and 1–4. Church closed Sun. and Mon.*

ČESKÝ KRUMLOV

Fodor's Choice Český Krumlov, the official residence of the Rosenbergs for some 300
★ years, is an eye-opener. None of the surrounding towns or villages, with their open squares and mixtures of old and new buildings, will prepare

you for the beauty of the Old Town. Here the Vltava works its wonders as nowhere else but in Prague itself, swirling in a nearly complete circle around the town. Across the river stands the proud castle, rivaling any in the country in size and splendor.

For the moment, Český Krumlov's beauty is still intact, even though the dilapidated buildings that lend the town its unique atmosphere are slowly metamorphosing into boutiques and pensions. Visitor facilities are improving, but can become overburdened during peak months. Overlook any minor inconveniences, however, and enjoy a rare, unspoiled trip in time back to the Bohemian Renaissance. Greenways lead to and from the town; for details, contact the tourist office.

GETTING HERE
A direct bus connects Prague to Český Krumlov. The trip takes about three hours. There is no direct train, but you can reach the town by connecting trains. By car, follow signs for České Budějovice and then continue following signs for Český Krumlov.

VISITOR INFORMATION
Český Krumlov Tourist Information ⊠Nám. Svornosti 1 ☎380–711–183 ⊕www.ckrumlov.cz)

EXPLORING ČESKÝ KRUMLOV
The town's main square, **náměstí Svornosti** (*Unity Square*), is home base for an exploration of the Old Town. Tiny alleys fan out in all directions—there's no point in trying to plan an orderly walk. Simply choose a direction and go. Each turn seems to bring a new drop-dead gorgeous vista of the castle or a charming café or shop that begs for a stop. On the main square itself, the **town hall,** at No. 1, built in 1580, is memorable for its Renaissance friezes and Gothic arcades. You'll also find the main tourist information office here.

The tower of the Gothic **Kostel svatého Víta** (*St. Vitus's Church*), built in the early 1400s, offsets the castle's larger, older tower across the river. Within the church, a marble-column baldachin shelters an elaborate baptismal font. At one time it covered the tomb of Vilém von Rozmberk (1535–92), who was one of his line's most august heads and a great patron of the town. ⊠*Kostelní ul.*

To get to **Hrad Krumlov** (*Krumlov Castle*), cross the Vltava on the main street, Radniční, and enter via the staircase leading up from Latrán Street, or continue a little farther up the street to the massive main gateway on the left (walking away from the main square). The oldest and most striking part of the castle is the round, 13th-century **tower,** renovated in the 16th century to look something like a minaret, with its delicately arcaded Renaissance balcony. Part of the old border fortifications, the tower guarded Bohemian frontiers from the threat of Austrian incursion.

Vilém von Rožmberk oversaw a major refurbishment of the castle, adding buildings, heightening the tower, and adding rich decorations—generally making the place suitable for one of the grandest Bohemians of the day. The castle passed out of the Rožmberks' hands, however, when Vilém's brother and last of the line, the dissolute Petr Vok, sold both castle and town to Emperor Rudolf II in 1602 to pay off his debts. Under the succeeding Eggenberg and Schwarzenberg dynasties, the castle continued to transform into an opulent palace. The Eggenbergs' prime addition was a **theater,** which was begun in the 1680s and completed in 1766 by Josef Adam of Schwarzenberg. Much of the theater and its accoutrements—sets, props, costumes, stage machinery— survives intact as a rare working display of period stagecraft.

As you enter the castle area, look into the old moats, where two playful brown bears now reside. In season, the castle rooms are open to the public. Be sure to ask at the ticket office about newly accessible areas of this enormous monument, as renovations and additional openings are ongoing. One sightseeing tour focuses on the Renaissance, Baroque, and rococo rooms, taking in the delightful **Maškarní Sál** (Masquerade Hall), with its richly detailed 18th-century frescoes. A second tour highlights the seigneurial apartments of the Schwarzenbergs, who owned the castle until the Gestapo seized it in 1940. (The castle became state property in 1947.) The courtyards and passageways of the castle are open to the public year-round. *Český Krumlov* ☎*380–711–687* 🎟*Garden free, castle tours 160 Kč, tower 35 Kč, theater tours 180 Kč* 🕐*Garden Apr. and Oct., Tues.–Sun. 9–5:30; May–Sept., Tues.–Sun. 9–7. Castle interior Apr. and Oct., Tues.–Sun. 9–5:30; May and June, Tues.–Sun. 9–6; July and Aug., daily 9–6; Sept., Tues.–Sun. 9–5:30. Tower May–Sept., Tues.–Sun. 9–7; Apr. and Oct., Tues.–Sun. 9–4:30. Theater May–Oct., Tues.–Sun. 10–4.*

The **Egon Schiele Center** exhibits the work of Schiele and other 20th-century and contemporary European and Czech artists in a rambling Renaissance building near the river. The museum closes occasionally during the winter season. ⊠*Široká 70–72* ☎*380–704–011* ⊕*www. schieleartcentrum.cz* 🎟*120 Kč* 🕐*Daily 10–6.*

WHERE TO STAY

$$$–$$$$ 🏨 **Hotel Růže.** Converted from a Renaissance monastery, this excellent hotel is only a two-minute walk from the main square. The decor is Ye Olde Bohemian but tastefully done, even extending to, ahem, the bathroom "thrones." The rooms are spacious, and a few have drop-dead views of the castle, so ask to see several before choosing. Note that some double rooms have two narrow single beds, whereas some singles have beds large enough for two. **Pros:** Central location; great views; quality restaurant. **Cons:** Inconsistent bed layouts; Baroque decorations are a bit overdone; pricey. ⊠*Horní 154* ☎*380–772–100* ⊕*www.hotelruze.cz* 🛏*71 rooms* 🛎*In-room: no a/c. In-hotel: 2 restaurants, pool, gym, bicycles, laundry service, some pets allowed (fee)* 🟰*AE, MC, V* 🍴*BP.*

WESTERN BOHEMIA

Until World War II, western Bohemia was the playground of Central Europe's rich and famous. Its three well-known spas, Karlovy Vary, Mariánské Lázně, and Františkovy Lázně (better known by their German names, Karlsbad, Marienbad, and Franzensbad, respectively), were

the annual haunts of everybody who was anybody: Johann Wolfgang von Goethe, Ludwig van Beethoven, Karl Marx, and England's King Edward VII, to name but a few. Although strictly "proletarianized" in the Communist era, the spas still exude a nostalgic aura of a more elegant past and, unlike most of Bohemia, offer a basic tourist infrastructure that makes dining and lodging a pleasure.

PLANNING YOUR TIME

All of Western Bohemia's spa towns are grouped closely together. Karlovy Vary has the most sights to explore, so focus your time there. Many visitors make camp in Karlovy Vary and take day trips to neighboring spa towns, sometimes crossing the border into Germany.

Most major towns are easily reachable by bus service. Smaller towns, though, might have only one bus a day or even fewer. Be sure to know when the next bus comes so you won't be stranded. Frequent bus service between Prague and Karlovy Vary makes the journey only about two hours each way. Many places such as Plzeň are reachable by both bus and train. Both the price and time differences can be great.

If you're driving, you can take the E48 directly from Prague to Karlovy Vary. Roads in the area tend to be in good condition, though they can sometimes be quite narrow.

Good, if slow, train service links all the major towns west of Prague. The Prague–Karlovy Vary run takes far longer than it should—more than three hours by the shortest route.

KARLOVY VARY

★ Karlovy Vary, better known outside the Czech Republic by its German name, Karlsbad, is the most famous Bohemian spa. It is named for Emperor Charles IV, who allegedly happened upon the springs in 1358 while on a hunting expedition. The spa reached its heyday in the 19th century, when royalty came here from all over Europe for treatment. The long list of those who "took the cure" includes Peter the Great, Goethe, Schiller, Beethoven, and Chopin. Even Karl Marx, when he wasn't decrying wealth and privilege, spent time at the resort; he wrote some of *Das Kapital* here between 1874 and 1876.

GETTING HERE
Bus service from Prague to Karlovy Vary is about two hours each way. Avoid the train, which takes much longer and is more expensive. By car, take E48 directly from Prague to Karlovy Vary.

Karlovy Vary Tourist Information (Kur-Info ⊠ *Vřídelní kolonáda [Vřídlo Colonnade], Karlovy Vary* ☎.353–322–4097 ⊕*www.karlovy vary.cz* ⊠*Nám. Dr. M. Horákové 18 [near bus station], Karlovy Vary* ☎*353–222–833*).

EXPLORING KARLOVY VARY
Shooting its scalding water to a height of some 40 feet, the Vřídlo is indeed the Karlovy Vary's hottest and most dramatic gusher, and built around it is the jarringly modern **Vřídelní kolonáda** *Vřídlo Colonnade).* Walk inside the arcade to watch hundreds of patients take the famed Karlsbad drinking cure. They shuffle somnambulistically up and down, eyes glazed, clutching drinking glasses filled periodically at one of the five "sources." The waters, which range from -1°C to 22°C (30°F to 72°F), are said to be especially effective against diseases of the digestive and urinary tracts. They're also good for gout (which probably explains the spa's former popularity with royals). If you want to join the crowds and take a sip, you can buy your own spouted cup from vendors within the colonnade. ⊠ *Vřídelní ul., near Kosterní nám.*

To the right of the Vřídlo Colonnade, steps lead up to the white **Kostel Maří Magdaleny** *(Church of Mary Magdalene).* Designed by Kilian Ignaz Dientzenhofer (architect of the two churches of St. Nicholas in Prague), this is the best of the few Baroque buildings still standing in Karlovy Vary. ⊠*Moravská ul.* ☎*No phone* ☉*Daily 9–6.*

The neo-Renaissance pillared hall **Mlýnská kolonáda** *(Mill Colonnade),* along the river, is the town's centerpiece. Built from 1871 to 1881, it has four springs: Rusalka, Libussa, Prince Wenceslas, and Millpond. ⊠*Mlýnské nábřeží.*

Delicately elegant, the **Sadová kolonáda** *(Park Colonnade)* is laced with white wrought iron. It was built in 1882 by the Viennese architectural duo Fellner and Helmer, who sprinkled the Austro-Hungarian Empire with many such edifices during the late 19th century. They also designed the town's theater, the quaint wooden Tržní kolonáda (Market Colonnade) next to the Vřídlo Colonnade, and one of the old bathhouses. ✉ *Zahradní.*

From Kostel svatého Lukáše, take a sharp right uphill on a redbrick road, then turn left onto a footpath through the woods, following signs to **Jelení skok** *(Stag's Leap)*. After a while steps lead up to a bronze statue of a deer looking over the cliffs, the symbol of Karlovy Vary. From here a winding path threads toward a little red gazebo opening onto a mythical panorama. ✉ *Sovava trail in Petrova Výšina park.*

WHERE TO STAY

$$$–$$$$ 🏨 **Grandhotel Pupp.** This is one of Central Europe's most famous resorts. Under the Communists, when the hotel was called "Moskva-Pupp," standards and service slipped, but the highly professional management has more than made up for the decades of neglect. So much so that it was the stand-in for the Montenegro casino in the Bond flick *Casino Royale.* The Baroque-style rooms are quite large, and come well furnished with a big tub and a flat-screen TV. Be warned, though, that extras (like Internet access) don't come cheap. The adjacent Parkhotel Pupp, under the same management, is a more affordable alternative. **Pros:** Large rooms; living history; a sleek casino. **Cons:** Costly extras; rooms are opulent but not that modern. ✉ *Mírové nám. 2* ☎ *353–109–630* ⊕ *www.pupp.cz* ⤷ *75 rooms, 34 suites* ⚿ *In-room: no a/c (some), safe, Internet, Wi-Fi (some). In-hotel: 4 restaurants, bar, gym, spa, some pets allowed (fee)* ▤ *AE, DC, MC, V* ☯ *BP.*

MARIÁNSKÉ LÁZNĚ

Your expectations of what a spa resort should be may come nearest to fulfillment here. The sanatoriums, most built during the 19th century in a confident, outrageous mixture of "neo" styles, fan out impressively around a finely groomed oblong park. Cure takers and curiosity seekers alike parade through the Empire-style Cross Spring pavilion and the long colonnade near the top of the park. Buy a spouted drinking cup (available at the colonnades) and join the rest of the sippers taking the drinking cure. Be forewarned, though: the waters from the Rudolph, Ambrose, and Caroline springs, though harmless, all have a noticeable diuretic effect.

For information on spa treatments, inquire at the main **spa offices** (✉ *Masarykova 22* ☎ *354–655–501* ⊕ *www.marienbad.cz*). Walk-in treatments can be arranged at the **Nové Lázně** (*New Spa* ✉ *Reitenbergerova 53* ☎ *354–644–111*).

France

Provence

WORD OF MOUTH

"This is where the legend begins—great wine, great architecture and great chefs who know exactly where they fit it in the order of the universe: first. And even if the servers see your order coming last, the French experience is unmatchable for any connoisseur."

—Carlos

WHAT'S WHERE

1 Paris. A quay-side vista that takes in the Seine, a passing boat, Notre-Dame, the Eiffel Tower, and mansard roofs all in one generous sweep is enough to convince you that Paris is indeed the most beautiful city on Earth.

2 Ile-de-France. Appearing like all France in miniature, the Ile-de-France region is the nation's heartland. Here Louis XIV built vainglorious Versailles, Chartres brings the faithful to their knees, and Monet's Giverny enchants all.

3 Loire Valley. Chenonceaux, Chambord, and Saumur—the parade of royal and near-royal châteaux magnificently captures France's golden age of monarchy in an idyllic region threaded by the Loire River.

4 Normandy. Sculpted with cliff-lined coasts, Normandy has been home to saints and sculptors, with a dramatic past marked by Mont-St-Michel's majestic abbey, Rouen's towering cathedral, and the D-Day beaches.

5 Burgundy. Hallowed ground for wine lovers, Burgundy hardly needs to be beautiful—but it is. Around the gastronomic hub of Dijon, the region is famed for its verdant vineyards and Romanesque churches.

6 Lyon & the Alps. Local chefs rival their Parisian counterparts in treasure-filled Lyon, heart of a diverse region where you ski down Mont Blanc or take a heady trip along the Beaujolais Wine Road.

7 Provence. Famed for its Lavender Route, the honey-gold hill towns of the Luberon, and vibrant cities like Aix and Marseilles, this region was dazzlingly abstracted into geometric daubs of paint by Van Gogh and Cézanne.

8 French Riviera. From glamorous St-Tropez through beauteous Antibes to sophisticated Nice, this sprawl of pebble beaches and zillion-dollar houses has always captivated sun lovers and socialites.

CALAIS

Boulogne

NORTH
Lille

BELGIUM

Arras

Dieppe

PICARDY
Amiens

Cambrai

LUXEMBOURG

Cherbourg

St. Quentin

Le Havre

Beauvais

Rouen

CHAMPAGNE
ARDENNES

Caen

2 ÎLE-DE-
FRANCE

Reims

Metz

LORRAINE

NORMANDY **4**

1 PARIS

Châlons-en-
Champagne

Nancy

Strasbourg

Chartres

Sens

Troyes

Colmar

Le Mans

Orléans

Mulhouse

ALSACE

Angers

Tours

Blois

Auxerre

Dijon

Belfort

PAYS-DE-
LOIRE

LOIRE
VALLEY **3**

Bourges

Beaune

Besançon

Poitiers

Nevers

5

FRANCHE-
COMTÉ

Niort

BURGUNDY

POITOU-
CHARENTES

Vichy

Mâcon

Bourg-en-
Bresse

SWITZERLAND

Saintes

Limoges

Angoulême

LIMOUSIN

Clermont-
Ferrand

Lyon

ALPES

Périgueux

Brive-la-
Gaillarde

AUVERGNE

6

Chambéry

Bordeaux

Aurillac

Le Puy

Grenoble

ITALY

Langon

Dordogne

Cahors

Rodez

RHÔNE
VALLEY

AQUITAINE

Montauban

Millau

Montélimar

Gap

Pau

Albi

PROVENCE

Sisteron

FRENCH
RIVIERA

Tarbes

MIDI-
PYRÉNÉES

Toulouse

LANGUEDOC
ROUSSILLON

Nîmes

7

Avignon

Aix-en-
Provence

Nice

8

Monte Carlo

Carcassonne

Montpellier

Cannes

Narbonne

Marseille

ANDORRA

Perpignan

Mediterranean
Sea

Toulon

IT IS A FABLED LAND of unmatched food and delicious wine that has inspired many to gasp in satisfied contentment—"We all have two countries—our own, and France!". But it is not just a country for those who worship at the altar of gastronomy. The sheer beauty of the rose-colored rooftops, the immaculately restored farm houses, architecture, cultivated scenery, and historic hearts give justice to the sentiment. Not to mention those glorious hidden landscapes that only those lucky few in the know ever discover.

Who can resist the allure of Paris? Even the grumpy waiters have a certain charm. Especially if you can try a little bit of French—a simple "bonjour" or "parlez-vous anglais?" will take you a long way and you'll find out how quickly a surly waiter will melt if you say hello.

But if you want to visit France at its most French, and have already visited Paris—at least for the first time—head to the Loire Valley and the Ile de France, just south and north of Paris. Here, at the heart of the country, you'll find French culture at its most elegant, pure and refined—even the language here is fabled for its refined beauty and grace. Farther afield this "Frenchiness" becomes mixed (delightfully so) with other cultures.

If you go west to solidly Norse Normandy, you'll find D-Day landings, with the dramatic Mont St. Michel overlooking La Manche (the English Channel). In Provence and Cote d'Azur you'll learn the most important thing in France—to slow down—and you can easily linger over a bottle of wonderful local vintage and watch the sun go down over the magnificent bay and make your visit all the more authentic and satisfying.

WHEN TO GO

Summer is the most popular (and expensive) season. July in Paris is crowded and hot, although the Paris Plage, the "beach" on the banks of the Seine, is a very popular with locals and tourists alike. The Riviera sparkles in August—but the notorious *embouteillages* (traffic jams) on the drive south can make you'd wish you stayed home. Famously fickle weather means you never know what to expect in Normandy and Brittany, where picture-postcard villages and languorous sandy beaches are never jam-packed.

GETTING HERE & AROUND

BY AIR

There are two major gateway airports to France just outside the capital: Orly, 16 km (10 mi) south of Paris, and Charles de Gaulle, 26 km (16 mi) northeast of the city. At Charles de Gaulle, also known as Roissy, there's a TGV (*train à grande vitesse*) station at Terminal 2, where you can connect to high-speed trains going all over the country.

TOP REASONS TO GO

Ahh, Paris, Paris. There is no other town like it in the world. Trip the light *fantastic* at the Eiffel Tower's nightly show, or shine your best half-smile on Mona in the Louvre, and then, when you are ready for some serious fun, paint the town *rouge* at Au Lapin Agile, Picasso's hangout.

Chartres Cathedrale: This 13th-century masterpiece is the pinnacle of Gothic achievement, with peerless stained glass and a hilltop silhouette visible for miles around.

Monet's Waterlilies: Come to Giverny to see his lily pond—a half-acre "Monet"—then peek around his charming home and stroll the time-warped streets to the ultra-stylish American Art Museum.

Romantic Chenonceau: Half bridge, half pleasure palace, this epitome of picturesque France extends across the Cher River, so why not row a boat under its arches?

Mont-St-Michel: The spire-topped silhouette of this mighty offshore mound, dubbed the Marvel of the Occident, is one of the greatest sights in Europe. Get there at high tide, when the water races across the endless sands.

Le Beaujolais Nouveau est arrivé!: The third Thursday of November is a party like no other in France, when wine celebrations in honor of the new Beaujolais harvest go around the clock.

Wine Is a Wonderful Thing: Burgundy vineyards are among the world's best, so take the time to stroll through Clos de Vougeot and really get a feel for the "terroir."

Aix's extraordinary Cours Mirabeau: It's considered to be the Champs-Élysees of Provence: a tree-lined boulevard laced with cafes in which a lengthy roster of famous literati have lounged about.

Nice, queen of the Riviera: With its candy-striped palaces, crystal-blue Bay of Angels and timeless (and time-stained) Old Town, this is one of France's most colorful cities.

BY TRAIN

Once in France, the best way to travel is by train, either high-speed TGV or regional train. A France Rail Pass allows three days of unlimited train travel in a one-month period. With train service efficient and enjoyable, long-distance bus service is rarely used, though there are some regional buses that cover areas where train service is spotty.

BY CAR

If you're traveling by car, there are excellent links between Paris and most French cities, but poor ones between the provinces. For the fastest route between two points, look for roads marked A for *autoroute*. A *péage* (toll) must be paid on most expressways: the rate varies, but can be steep. Note that gas prices are also steep, upward of €1.40 a liter, or about $6 a gallon.

Although renting a car is about twice as expensive as in the United States, it's the best way to see remote corners of the lovely French countryside. To get the best rate, book a rental car at home, and well in advance if you're planning a trip in summer and early fall. If you want automatic transmission, which is more expensive, be sure to ask for it when you reserve. If you are traveling from Paris but ending your trip in, say, Nice, be sure to use a larger rental company like Avis or Hertz, so that you can pick up at one location and drop off at another.

Another good tip: If you're traveling from Paris, a practical option is to take the TGV to another large city, such as Avignon or Nice, and rent a car there.

ABOUT THE RESTAURANTS

Forget the Louvre—the real reason for a visit to France is to dine at its famous temples of gastronomy. Once you dive into Taillevent's lobster soufflé, you'll quickly realize that food in France is far more than fuel. The French regard gastronomy as essential to the art of living, so don't feel guilty if your meal at Paris's Grand Véfour takes as long as your visit to the Musée d'Orsay: two hours for a three-course menu is par, and you may, after relaxing into the routine, feel pressured at less than three.

MEALS AND MEAL TIMES
Restaurants follow French mealtimes, serving lunch from noon to 2 or 2:30 and dinner from 7:30 or 8 on. Some cafés in larger cities serve food all day long.

RESERVATIONS
Always reserve a table for dinner, as top restaurants book up months in advance. You must ask for the check (it's considered rude to bring it unbidden) except in cafés, where a register slip often comes with your order.

MONEY-SAVING TIPS
To save money on food, take advantage of France's wonderful outdoor markets and chain supermarkets. Just about every town has its own market once or a couple of times a week. For supermarkets, the largest chain is Monoprix. Some of the bigger stores have cafés where you can sit down and eat whatever you buy.

WHAT IT COSTS IN EUROS				
¢	$	$$	$$$	$$$$
Restaurants	Under €11	€11–€17	€17–€23	€23–€30	Over €30

Restaurant prices are per person for a main course at dinner, including tax.

ABOUT THE HOTELS

If your France fantasy involves staying in a historic hotel with the smell of fresh-baked croissants gently rousing you in the morning, here's some good news: you need not be Ritz-rich to realize it. Throughout the country, you'll find stylish lodging options—from charming hotels and intimate bed-and-breakfasts to regal apartments and grand country houses—in all price ranges.

B&BS

In the countryside, seek out chambres d'hôtes (bed-and-breakfasts), which can mean anything from a modest room in a host's home to a grand suite in a Norman château or Provençal farmhouse. Or rent a gîte rural, a furnished apartment, often on a farm or a larger property.

HOTELS

Rates are always by room, not per person. Sometimes a hotel in a certain price category will have a few less expensive rooms; it's worth asking about. In the off-season—usually November to Easter (except for southern France)—tariffs may be lower. Always inquire about promotional specials and weekend deals. Rates must be posted in all rooms, with extra charges clearly indicated.

APARTMENT & HOUSE RENTALS

If you want more spacious accommodations with cooking facilities, consider a furnished rental. These can save you money, especially if you're traveling with a group. Renting a gîte rural—furnished house in the country—for a week or month can also save you money. Gîtes are nearly always maintained by on-site owners, who greet you on your arrival and provide information on groceries, doctors, and nearby attractions.

WHAT IT COSTS IN EUROS				
¢	$	$$	$$$	$$$$
Hotels	Under €50	€50–€80	€80–€120	€120–€190	Over €190

Prices are for a standard double room in high season.

PLANNING YOUR TIME

Every trip to France should start in Paris. It is one of the most magical cities in the world, and the easiest to travel to and from, It is *très facile* to spend your whole trip here—the city alone would take months to explore properly—but let's assume at least that you've seen Paris, and you're ready to venture into the countryside. Here are some ideas to help you plan your time exploring France to maximum effect, no matter where your interests lie.

Base yourself in the market town of Beaune in historic Burgundy and visit its famous Hospices and surrounding vineyards. For more vineyards, follow the Côte d'Or from Beaune to Dijon. From here it's a two-hour drive to Lyon, where you can feast on this city's famous earthy cuisine. Another three hours' push takes you deep into the heart of Provence. Arles is the atmospheric, sun-drenched southern town that inspired Van Gogh and Gauguin. Make a day trip into grand old Avignon, home to the 14th-century rebel popes, to view their imposing palace. And make a pilgrimage to the Pont du Gard, the famous triple-tiered Roman aqueduct west of Avignon. From here, two hours' drive will bring you to the glittering Côte d'Azur.

PARIS

If there's a problem with a trip to Paris, it's the embarrassment of riches that faces you. No matter which aspect of Paris you choose—touristy, historic, fashion-conscious, pretentious-bourgeois, thrifty, or the legendary bohemian arty Paris of undying attraction—one thing is certain: you will carve out your own Paris, one that is vivid, exciting, ultimately unforgettable.

Veterans know that Paris is a city of vast, noble perspectives and intimate, ramshackle streets, of formal *espaces vertes* (green open spaces) and quiet squares. This combination of the pompous and the private is one of the secrets of its perennial pull. Another is its size: Paris is relatively small as capitals go, with distances between many of its major sights and museums invariably walkable.

For the first-timer there will always be several must-dos at the top of the list, but getting to know Paris will never be quite as simple as a quick look at Notre-Dame, the Louvre, and the Eiffel Tower. You'll discover that around every corner, down every *ruelle* (little street) lies a resonance-in-waiting. If this is your first trip, you may want to take a guided tour of the city—a good introduction that will help you get your bearings and provide you with a general impression before you return to explore the sights that particularly interest you.

PLANNING YOUR TIME

Paris is one of the world's most-visited cities—with crowds to prove it, so it pays to be prepared. Buy tickets online when you can. Investigate alternate entrances at popular sites (there are three at the Louvre) and check when rates are reduced, often during once-a-week late openings. Also, most major museums—including the Louvre and the Musée d'Orsay—are free the first Sunday of each month. Museums are also closed one day a week, usually Tuesday, and most stay open late at least one night each week, which is also the least crowded time to visit.

A Paris Museum Pass can save you money if you're planning serious sightseeing, but better yet, it allows you to bypass the lines. It's sold at the destinations it covers and at airports, major métro stations, and the tourism office in the Carrousel du Louvre (2-, 4- or 6-day passes are €30, €45, and €60, respectively; www.parismuseumpass.com).

If you plan to take public transport everywhere, consider getting a one-day Mobilus ticket (€5.60) or a multi-day Paris-Visite, which also gives discounts at some museums (€8.50 for one day up to €27.20 for five days.).

Generally, restaurants are open from noon to about 2:30 and from 7:30 or 8 to 10 or 10:30. It's best to make reservations. July and August are the most common months for annual closings, although Paris in August is no longer the wasteland it once was.

Store hours are generally 10 AM to 7:30 PM, though smaller shops may not open until 11 am, only to close for several hours during the afternoon. Some retailers are still barred by law from doing business on

Sunday, but exceptions include the shops along the Champs-Élysées, the Carrousel du Louvre, and around the Marais, where most boutiques open at 2 PM.

GETTING HERE & AROUND

Paris is served by two international airports, Orly and Charles de Gaulle (also called Roissy). Orly has two terminals: Orly Ouest (domestic flights) and Orly Sud (international, regular, and charter flights).

RER trains travel between Paris and the suburbs. When they go through Paris, they act as a sort of supersonic métro—they connect with the métro network at several points—and can be great time-savers. From Charles de Gaulle, take the RER-B into Paris; the journey takes 30 minutes. Additionally, the Roissybus runs directly between Roissy and rue Scribe by the Opéra. The RER-C line goes into Paris from Orly Airport; the train journey takes about 35 minutes. There's also the Orlybus between Orly and the Denfert-Rochereau métro station. In addition, Paris has five international train stations: Gare du Nord; Gare St-Lazare; Gare de l'Est; Gare de Lyon; and Gare d'Austerlitz.

If you're driving into Paris, which is not advisable, the major ring road encircling the city is called the *périférique,* with the *périférique intérieur* going counterclockwise around the city, and the *périférique extérieur,* or the outside ring, going clockwise. Up to five lanes wide, the périférique is a major highway from which *portes* (gates) connect Paris to the major highways of France.

Paris is divided into 20 *arrondissements* (or neighborhoods) spiraling out from the center of the city. The numbers reveal the neighborhood's location, and its age, the 1st arrondissement at the city's heart being the oldest. The *arrondissements* in central Paris—the 1st to 8th—are the most-visited.

The *métro* (subway) goes just about everywhere you're going for €1.50 a ride (a *carnet,* or "pack" of 10 tickets is €11.10); tickets are good for buses and trams, too.

ESSENTIALS

Air contacts Charles de Gaulle/Roissy (☎ *01–48–62–22–80 in English* ⊕ *www. adp.fr),* **Orly** (☎ *01–49–75–15–15* ⊕ *www.adp.fr),* **RATP (Paris Transit Authority: including Roissybus, Orlybus, Orlyval)** (☎ *08–92–68–77–14* *€0.35 per min* ⊕ *www.ratp.com).*

Train Contacts SNCF/Transilien (☎ *08–91–36–20–20* ⊕ *www.sncf.fr).* **RER/RATP** (☎ *08–92–68–77–14* ⊕ *www.ratp.fr).*

Visitor Information Espace du Tourisme d'Ile-de-France (✉ *Carrousel du Louvre, 99 rue de Rivoli* ☎ *08–92–68–30–00* ⊕ *www.pidf.com* Ⓜ *Palais-Royal Musée du Louvre).*

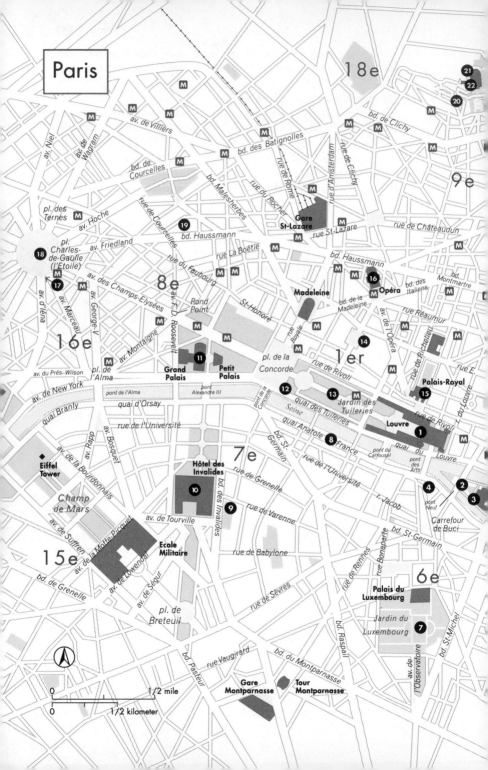

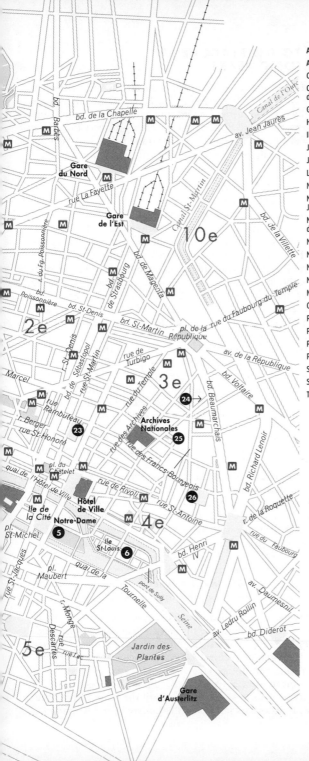

FROM NOTRE-DAME TO THE PLACE DE LA CONCORDE: THE HISTORIC HEART

In the center of Paris, nestled in the River Seine are the two celebrated islands, the Ile de la Cité, where you'll find Notre-Dame, and the Ile St-Louis. Nearby is the immense Louvre, and beyond it lie the graceful Tuileries Gardens, the grand Place de la Concorde—the very hub of the city—and the Belle Époque splendor of the Grand Palais and the Pont Alexandre III. All in all, this area comprises some of the most historic and beautiful sights to see in Paris.

EXPLORING NOTRE DAME TO THE PLACE DE LA CONCORDE

⑪ Grand Palais *(Grand Palace).* With its curved glass roof, the Grand Palais is unmistakable when approached from either the Seine or the Champs-Élysées, and forms a turn-of-the-20th-century Beaux-Arts showpiece with the **Petit Palais** on the other side of Avenue Winston-Churchill. Today the Grand Palais plays host to major exhibitions (some of blockbuster status, so book tickets in advance). Its smaller counterpart, the Petit Palais, set just off the Champs-Élysées, presents a permanent collection of French painting and furniture, with splendid canvases by Courbet and Bouguereau. Along with temporary exhibitions and antiques fairs, the building itself is a real draw, a 1902 cream puff of marble and gilt, with huge windows overlooking the Seine. ⊠ *Av. Winston-Churchill, Champs-Élysées* ☎ *01–44–13–17–30 Grand Palais, 01–42–65–12–73 Petit Palais* ⊕ *www.grandpalais.fr* ☒ *Grand Palais: €11.10 with reservation; €10 no reservation. Petit Palais: free, temporary exhibit entry fees vary* ⊙ *Grand Palais: hrs vary. Petit Palais: Tues.–Sun. 10–6* Ⓜ *Champs-Élysées–Clemenceau.*

⑬ Jardin des Tuileries *(Tuileries Gardens).* Monet and Renoir captured this
ℭ gracious garden (really more of a long park) with paint and brush, Left Bank songstresses warble about its beauty, and all Parisians know it as a charming place to stroll and survey the surrounding cityscape. A palace once stood here on the site of a clay pit that supplied material for many of the city's tile roofs. (Hence the name *tuileries,* or tile works.) During the Revolution, Louis XVI and his family were kept in the Tuileries under house arrest. Now the Tuileries is a typically French garden: formal and neatly patterned, with statues, rows of trees, fountains with gaping fish, and gravel paths. No wonder the Impressionists liked it here—note how the gray, austere light of Paris makes green trees look even greener. ⊠ *Bordered by Quai des Tuileries, Pl. de la Concorde, Rue de Rivoli, and the Louvre, Louvre/Tuileries* Ⓜ *Tuileries.*

❶ Louvre. Leonardo da Vinci's *Mona Lisa* and *Virgin and St. Anne,* Vero-
Fodor's Choice nese's *Marriage at Cana,* Giorgione's *Concert Champêtre,* Delacroix's
★ *Liberty Guiding the People,* Whistler's *Mother (Arrangement in Black and White)* . . . you get the picture. After two decades of renovations, the Louvre is a coherent, unified structure, and search parties no longer need to be sent in to bring you out. Begun by Philippe-Auguste in the 13th century as a fortress, it was not until the reign of pleasure-loving François I, 300 years later, that the Louvre of today gradually

began to take shape. Through the years Henri IV (1589–1610), Louis XIII (1610–43), Louis XIV (1643–1715), Napoléon I (1804–14), and Napoléon III (1852–70) all contributed to its construction.

The number one attraction is the "Most Famous Painting in the World": Leonardo da Vinci's enigmatic *Mona Lisa* (*La Joconde*, to the French), painted in 1503–06 and now the cynosure of all eyes in the museum's Salle des États, where it was ensconced in its own special alcove in 2005. The Louvre is packed with legendary collections, which are divided into eight curatorial departments: Near Eastern Antiquities; Egyptian Antiquities; Greek, Etruscan, and Roman Antiquities; Islamic Art; Sculptures; Decorative Arts; Paintings; and Prints and Drawings. Don't try to see it all at once; try, instead, to make repeat visits. Some other highlights of the painting collection are Jan van Eyck's magnificent *The Madonna and Chancellor Rolin,* painted in the early 15th century; *The Lacemaker,* by Jan Vermeer (1632–75); *The Embarkation for Cythera,* by Antoine Watteau (1684–1721); *The Oath of the Horatii,* by Jacques-Louis David (1748–1825); *The Raft of the Medusa,* by Théodore Géricault (1791–1824); and *La Grande Odalisque,* by Jean-Auguste-Dominique Ingres (1780–1867).

5

The French crown jewels (in the Gallerie d'Apollon—a newly renovated 17th-century extravaganza) include the mind-boggling 186-carat Regent diamond. Atop the marble Escalier Daru is the Nike, or *Winged Victory of Samothrace,* which seems poised for flight over the stairs. Among other much-loved pieces of sculpture are Michelangelo's two *Slaves,* intended for the tomb of Pope Julius II. These can be admired in the Denon Wing, where a medieval and Renaissance sculpture section is housed partly in the former imperial stables. The Richelieu Wing is the new home of the famous *Venus de Milo.* If you're a fan of the Napoléon III style—the apotheosis of 19th-century, red-and-gilt opulence—be sure to see the galleries that once housed the Ministry of Finance.

To get into the Louvre, you may have to wait in two long lines: one outside the Pyramide entrance portal and another downstairs at the ticket booths. You can avoid the first by entering through the Carrousel du Louvre and buying a ticket at the machines. Your ticket (be sure to hold on to it) will get you into any and all of the wings as many times as you like during one day—and once you have your ticket you can skip the entry line. Once inside, you should stop by the information desk to pick up a free color-coded map and check which rooms are closed for the day. Remember that the Louvre is closed on Tuesday. ⊠ *Palais du Louvre, Louvre/Tuileries* ☎ *01–40–20–53–17 information* ⊕ *www. louvre.fr* 💳 *€9, €6 after 6 PM Wed. and Fri. Free 1st Sun. of month; €9.50 for Napoléon Hall exhibitions* ⊘ *Mon., Thurs., and weekends 9–6, Wed. and Fri. 9 AM–10 PM* Ⓜ *Palais-Royal.*

⑫ **Musée de l'Orangerie.** The most beautiful Claude Monet paintings in the world—eight vast mural-size *Nymphéas* (Water Lilies)—can be found at this newly removed museum, which also includes a collection of early-20th-century paintings, with works by Renoir, Paul Cézanne, Henri Matisse, and Marie Laurencin, among other masters. The museum's name, by the way, isn't misleading; the building was originally used to store the Tuileries' citrus trees over the winter. ☒*Pl. de la Concorde, Louvre/Tuileries* ☎*01-44-77-80-07* ⊕*www.musee-orangerie. fr/* ☜*€7.50* ⊙ *Wed.–Thurs., and Sat.-Mon. 12:30–7, Fri. 12:30–9* Ⓜ*Concorde.*

⑤ Notre-Dame. Looming above the large, pedestrian Place du Parvis is la
★ cathédrale de Notre-Dame, the most enduring symbol of Paris. Begun in 1163, completed in 1345, badly damaged during the Revolution, and restored by Viollet-le-Duc in the 19th century, Notre-Dame may not be France's oldest or largest cathedral, but in terms of beauty and architectural harmony, it has few peers—as you can see by studying the facade from the open square. The facade divides neatly into three levels. At the first-floor level are the three main entrances, or portals: the Portal of the Virgin, on the left; the Portal of the Last Judgment, in the center; and the Portal of St. Anne, on the right. All three are surmounted by magnificent carvings—most of them 19th-century copies of the originals—of figures, foliage, and biblical scenes. Above these are the restored statues of the kings of Israel, the Galerie des Rois. Above the gallery is the great rose window and, above that, the Grande Galerie, at the base of the twin towers. The south tower houses the great bell of Notre-Dame, as tolled by Quasimodo, Victor Hugo's fictional hunchback. The 387-step climb to the top of the towers is worth the effort for a close-up of the famous gargoyles—most added in the 19th century by Viollet-le-Duc—as they frame an expansive view of the city. If some find both towers a bit top heavy, that's because they were designed to be topped by two needlelike spires, which were never built. The spectacular cathedral interior, with its vast proportions, soaring nave, and soft multicolor light dimly filtering through the stained-glass windows, inspires awe—visit early in the morning, when the cathedral is at its lightest and least crowded.

If your interest in the cathedral is not yet sated, duck into the **Musée de Notre-Dame** (☒*10 rue du Cloître-Notre-Dame, Ile de la Cité*), across the street from the North Door. The museum's paintings, engravings, medallions, and other objects and documents chart the history of the cathedral. When it comes to views of Notre-Dame, no visit is complete without a riverside walk past the cathedral through **Square Jean-XXIII.** It offers a breathtaking sight of the east end of the cathedral, ringed by flying buttresses and surmounted by the spire. To put the cathedral in its proper medieval context, explore the super-charming **Ancien Cloître Quarter,** set just to the north of the cathedral. ☒*Pl. du Parvis, Ile de la Cité* ☎*01–53–10–07–00* ⊕*www.monum.fr* ☜*Cathedral free, towers €7.50, crypt €3.30, treasury €3, museum €2.50* ⊙ *Cathedral daily 8–7. Towers Apr.–June and Sept., daily 10-6:30 PM; July and Aug., weekends 10 AM–11 PM; Oct.–Mar., daily 10–5:30. Note Towers close early when overcrowded. Treasury Mon.–Sat. 9:30–6:30, Sunday1:30–6:30. Crypt Tues.–Sun. 10–6. Museum Wed. and weekends 2:30–6* Ⓜ*Cité.*

❸ Sainte-Chapelle *(Holy Chapel).* Not to be missed and one of the most magical sights in European medieval art, this Gothic chapel was built by Louis IX (1226–70; later canonized as St. Louis) in the 1240s to house what he believed to be Christ's Crown of Thorns, purchased from Emperor Baldwin of Constantinople. The Sainte-Chapelle is essentially an enormous magic lantern illuminating 1,130 figures from the Bible, to create—as one writer poetically put it—"the most marvelous colored and moving air ever held within four walls." Originally, the king's holy relics were displayed in the raised apse and shown to the faithful on Good Friday. Today the magic of the chapel comes alive during the regular concerts held here; call to check the schedule. ⊠4 bd. du Palais, Ile de la Cité ☎01–53–40–60–97 ⊕www.monum.fr ☜€7.50, joint ticket with Conciergerie €10.50 ☉Mar.-Oct., daily 9:30–6, Nov.–Feb., daily 9–5 Ⓜ Cité.

❷ **Pont Neuf** *(New Bridge).* Crossing the Ile de la Cité, just behind Square du Vert-Galant, is the oldest bridge in Paris, confusingly called the New Bridge—the name was given when it was completed in 1607, and it stuck. It was the first bridge in the city to be built without houses lining either side, allegedly because Henri IV wanted a clear view of Notre-Dame from his windows at the Louvre. ⊠*Ile de la Cité* Ⓜ*Pont-Neuf.*

5

FROM THE EIFFEL TOWER TO THE ARC DE TRIOMPHE: MONUMENTS & MARVELS

The Eiffel Tower (or Tour Eiffel, to use the French) lords over southwest Paris, and from nearly wherever you are on this walk you can see its jutting needle. Water is the second highlight in this area: fountains playing beneath Place du Trocadéro and boat tours along the Seine on a Bateau Mouche. Museums are the third; the area around Trocadéro is full of them. Style is the fourth, and not just because the buildings here are overwhelmingly elegant—but because this is also the center of haute couture, with the top names in fashion all congregated around Avenue Montaigne, only a brief walk from the Champs-Élysées, to the north.

EXPLORING THE EIFFEL TOWER TO THE ARC DE TRIOMPHE

❶❽ ★ **Arc de Triomphe.** Set on Place Charles-de-Gaulle—known to Parisians as L'Étoile, or the Star (a reference to the streets that fan out from it)—the colossal, 164-foot Arc de Triomphe arch was planned by Napoléon but not finished until 1836, 20 years after the end of his rule. It's decorated with some magnificent sculptures by François Rude, such as the *Departure of the Volunteers,* better known as *La Marseillaise,* to the right of the arch when viewed from the Champs-Élysées. A small museum halfway up the arch is devoted to its history. France's Unknown Soldier is buried beneath the archway; the flame is rekindled every evening at 6:30. ⊠*Pl. Charles-de-Gaulle, Champs-Élysées* ☎01–55–37–73–77 ⊕www.monum.fr ☜€8, free under 18 ☉Apr.–Sept., daily 10 AM–11 PM; Oct.–Mar., daily 10 AM–10:30 PM Ⓜ*Métro or RER: Étoile.*

☾ **Bateaux Mouches.** If you want to view Paris in slow motion, hop on one of these famous motorboats, which set off on their hour-long tours of the city waters regularly (every half-hour in summer) from Place de l'Alma. Their route heads east to the Ile St-Louis and then back west, past the Tour Eiffel, as far as the Allée des Cygnes and its miniature version of

Continued on page 158

la TOUR EIFFEL

New York has the Statue of Liberty, London has Big Ben—and Paris has the Eiffel Tower. This symbol of Paris, recognized the world over, did not, however, begin life as the beloved icon it is today. Engineer Gustave Eiffel's iron creation for the 1889 World's Fair was greeted with disgust by Parisians, who dubbed it the Giant Asparagus. French author Guy de Maupassant supposedly hated the tower so much that he often ate lunch there, explaining that it was the only place in the city where he could avoid seeing it. Parisians eventually warmed to the tower, an inescapable part of the landscape that has captured the minds and hearts of generations.

5

Total height: 1,063 feet

■ The 200 millionth visitor went to the top of the Eiffel Tower in 2002.

■ If you're in good shape, you can take the stairs to the 2nd level. If you want to go to the top you have to take the elevator.

■ To get to the first viewing platform, Gustave Eiffel originally used avant-garde hydraulic cable elevators designed by American Elisha Otis for two of the curved base legs of the tower. French elevators with a chain-drive system were used in the other two legs. During the 1989 renovation, all the elevators were rebuilt by the Otis company.

■ Every 7 years the tower is repainted. The job takes 15 months and uses 60 tons of "Tour Eiffel Brown" paint in three shades—lightest on top, darkest at the bottom.

Jules Verne

The Eiffel Tower contains 12,000 pieces of metal and 2,500,000 rivets.

■ An expensive way to beat the queue is to reserve a table at **Le Jules Verne**, the restaurant on the 2nd level, which has a private elevator. Taken over by star chef Alain Ducasse, count on a dinner bill of €450 for 2 with wine, though there's an €85 prix-fine menu at lunch (without wine). ⊕ www.lejulesverne-paris. com ☎01–45–55–61–44.

■ The tower nearly became a giant heap of scrap in 1909, when its concession expired, but its use as a radio antenna saved the day.

■ The tower is most breathtaking at night, when the girders are illuminated. The light show, conceived to celebrate the turn of the millennium, was so popular that the 20,000 lights were reinstalled for permanent use in 2003. It does its electric shimmy for 5 minutes every hour on the hour (cut from 10 to save energy) until 1 AM.

The base formed by the tower's feet is 410 by 410 feet.

☎01–44–11–23–23

⊕ www.tour-eiffel.fr

✉ By elevator: 1st level, €4.80 (€2.50 kids 11 and under), 2nd level, €7.80 (€4.30 kids), top, €12 (€6.70 kids) By stairs: 1st and 2nd levels only, €4 (€3.10 under 25)

🕙 June 13–Aug. 31, daily 9 AM–11 PM; Sept. 1–Dec. 31, 9:30 AM–10:30 PM; Jan. 1–June 12, 9:30–11 PM (10:30 for summit); Stairs: June 13–Aug. 31, 9 AM–midnight; Sept 1–June 12, 9:30 AM–6 PM

Ⓜ Bir-Hakeim, Trocadéro, Ecole Militaire; RER Champ de Mars

■ TIP→ A **Museums and Monuments Pass** will let you skip long lines but might not be worth the investment.

NEED A BITE?

Attitude 95, the restaurant on the first level, is under renovation and scheduled to reopen in mid-2009 with a new look and a new name.

Le Café Branly, in the nearby Musée du Quai Branly, 27 Quai Branly, Trocadéro/Tour Eiffel, 01–47–53–68–01 is a good choice for lunch or a late-afternoon snack.

the Statue of Liberty. Note that some travelers prefer to take this Seine cruise on the smaller Vedettes du Pont Neuf, which depart from Square du Vert-Galant on the Ile de la Cité, as the Vedettes have a guide giving commentary in French and English, while the Bateaux Mouches have a loud recorded spiel in several languages. For the quietest journey, take the city-run Batobus, which has no commentary and allows you to get on and off at its various quayside stops. ⊠ *Pl. de l'Alma, Trocadéro/Tour Eiffel* ☎ *01-42-25-96-10* ⊕ *www.bateaux-mouches.fr* ⊠ *€10* Ⓜ *Alma-Marceau.*

Champs-Élysées. Marcel Proust lovingly described the elegance of the world's most famous avenue, the Champs-Élysées, during its Belle Époque heyday, when its cobblestones resounded to the clatter of horses and carriages. Today, despite the constant surge of cars up and down the "Champs" (as Parisians casually call the boulevard) and the influx of chain stores, there's still a certain *je ne sais quoi* about strolling up the avenue, especially at dusk as the refurbished street lamps are just coming on. The bustle means that the café tables are always good for people-watching, and the cinemas, nightclubs, and late-hour shopping ensure that the parade continues well into the night. Ⓜ *Champs-Élysées–Clemenceau, Franklin-D.-Roosevelt, George V, Etoile.*

⓱ Tour Eiffel *(Eiffel Tower). See highlighted listing in this chapter.*

THE FAUBOURG ST-HONORÉ: LE STYLE, C'EST PARIS

Fashions change, but the Faubourg St-Honoré, just north of the Champs-Élysées and the Tuileries, has been unfailingly chic since the early 1700s. The streets of this walk include some of the oldest in Paris. The centerpiece of the area is the stately Place Vendôme; on this ritzy square, famous boutiques sit side by side with famous banks—but then elegance and finance have never been an unusual combination.

EXPLORING THE FAUBOURG ST-HONORÉ

⓯ **Palais-Royal** *(Royal Palace).* One of the most Parisian sights in all of
★ Paris, the Palais-Royal is especially loved for its gardens, where children play, lovers whisper, and senior citizens crumble bread for the sparrows, seemingly oblivious to the ghosts of history that haunt this place. The buildings of this former palace—royal only in that all-powerful Cardinal Richelieu (1585–1642) magnanimously bequeathed them to Louis XIII—date from the 1630s. In front of one of its shop fronts Camille Desmoulins gave the first speech calling for the French Revolution in 1789. Today the Palais-Royal is occupied by the French Ministry of Culture and private apartments (Colette and Cocteau were two lucky former owners), and its buildings are not open to the public. You can, however, visit its colonnaded courtyard—the setting where Audrey Hepburn had to choose between Cary Grant and Walter Matthau at the climax of Stanley Donen's *Charade*—and classical gardens, a tranquil oasis prized by Parisians. Around the exterior of the complex are famous arcades—notably the Galerie Valois—whose elegant shops have been attracting customers since the days when Thomas Jefferson used

to come here for some retail therapy. ✉*Pl. du Palais-Royal, Louvre/ Tuileries* Ⓜ*Palais-Royal.*

⓮ **Place Vendôme.** Snobbish and self-important, this famous square is also gorgeous; property laws have kept away cafés and other such banal establishments, leaving the plaza stately and refined, the perfect home for the rich and famous (Chopin lived and died at No. 12; today's celebs camp out at the **Hôtel Ritz,** while a lucky few, including the family of the Sultan of Brunei, actually own houses here). Mansart's rhythmic, perfectly proportioned example of 17th-century urban architecture still shines in all its golden-stone splendor. Napoléon had the square's central column made from the melted bronze of 1,200 cannons captured at the Battle of Austerlitz in 1805. There he is, perched vigilantly at the top. If you're feeling properly soigné, repair to Hemingway's Bar at the Hôtel Ritz and raise a glass to "Papa" (see the Close-Up box "Hemingway's Paris"). Ⓜ*Opéra.*

THE GRANDS BOULEVARDS: URBAN KALEIDOSCOPE

The makeup of the neighborhoods along the Grand Boulevards changes steadily as you head east from the posh 8e arrondissement toward working-class east Paris. The *grands magasins* (department stores) epitomize upscale Paris shopping and stand on Boulevard Haussmann. The opulent Opéra Garnier, just past the grands magasins, is the architectural showpiece of the period.

EXPLORING THE GRANDS BOULEVARDS

㉔ **Cimetière du Père-Lachaise** *(Père-Lachaise Cemetery).* As far as cemeteries go, this one is a powerhouse, forming a veritable necropolis with cobbled avenues and tombs competing in pomposity and originality. Named after the Jesuit father—Louis XIV's confessor—who led the reconstruction of the Jesuit Rest House in 1682, the cemetery houses the tombs of the famed medieval lovers Héloïse and Abélard; composer Chopin; artists Ingres and Georges Seurat; playwright Molière; writers Balzac, Proust, Colette, Wilde (usually covered in lipstick kisses), and (buried in the same grave) Gertrude Stein and Alice B. Toklas; popular French actress Simone Signoret and her husband, singer–actor Yves Montand; singer Edith Piaf; and rock-star Jim Morrison of the Doors. Make sure to get a map at the entrance (it's easy to get lost!) and track them down. ✉*Entrances on Rue des Rondeaux, Bd. de Ménilmontant, Rue de la Réunion, Père Lachaise* ⊕*www.pere-lachaise.com* ☉*Easter– Sept., daily 8–6; Oct.–Easter, daily 8–5* Ⓜ*Gambetta, Philippe-Auguste, Père-Lachaise.*

⓳ **Musée Jacquemart-André.** Often compared to New York City's Frick Collection, this was one of the grandest private residences of 19th-century Paris. Built between 1869 and 1875, it found Hollywood fame when used as Gaston Lachaille's mansion in the 1958 musical *Gigi,* as a great stand-in for the floridly opulent home of a sugar millionaire played by Louis Jourdan. Edouard André and his painter-wife, Nélie Jacquemart, the house's actual owners, were rich and cultured, so art from the Italian Renaissance and 18th-century France compete for attention here. Note the freshly restored Tiepolo frescoes in the staircase and on the dining-room ceiling, while salons done in the fashionable "Louis XVI–Empress" style (favored by Empress Eugénie) are hung with great paintings, including Rembrandt's *Pilgrims of Emmaus.* You can tour the house with the free English audio guide. The Tiepolo salon is home to a lovely café with a terrace open in warm weather. ✉*158 bd. Haussmann, Parc Monceau* ☎*01–45–62–11–59* ⊕*www.musee-jacquemart-andre.com/jandre/* 🎟*€9.50* ⊙*Daily 10–6* Ⓜ*St-Philippe-du-Roule or Miromesnil.*

⑯ **Opéra Garnier.** Haunt of the *Phantom of the Opera,* setting for Degas's famous ballet paintings, and still the most opulent theater in the world, the Paris Opéra was begun in 1862 by Charles Garnier at the behest of Napoléon III. But it was not completed until 1875, five years after the emperor's abdication. Awash with Algerian colored marbles and gilt putti, it's said to typify Second Empire architecture: a pompous hodgepodge of styles with about as much subtlety as a Wagnerian cymbal crash. The composer Debussy famously compared it to a Turkish bathhouse, but lovers of pomp and splendor will adore it. If you're one of those who decide to opt for one of the cheaper *sans-visibilité* (without a view of the stage) seats, at least you'll have images from Chagall's favorite operas and ballets to stare at on the ceiling. Or skip a performance and pay the €8 entry fee, which allows access to the auditorium and grand foyer. Or take a guided tour in English. Today the Opéra is the home of the Paris Ballet. (Most operas are performed at the Opéra de la Bastille). ✉*Pl. de l'Opéra, Opéra/Grands Boulevards* ☎*08–92–89–90–90* ⊕*www.opera-de-paris.fr* 🎟*€8 for solo visit; €12 for guided visit Daily 10–4:30* Ⓜ*Opéra.*

THE MARAIS & THE BASTILLE: C'EST SUPER COOL

The Marais is one of the city's most historic and sought-after residential districts. Except for the architecturally whimsical Pompidou Center, the tone here is set by the gracious architecture of the 17th and 18th centuries. Many hôtels particuliers have been restored; many are now museums, including the noted Musée Picasso and Musée Carnavalet. There are hyper-trendy boutiques and cafés among the kosher shops in what used to be a predominantly Jewish neighborhood around Rue des Rosiers. Also here is the gorgeous Place des Vosges, a definite don't-miss.

EXPLORING THE MARAIS & THE BASTILLE

㉓ **Centre Georges Pompidou.** Known as the Beaubourg (for the neighborhood), this modern art museum and performance center is named for French president Georges Pompidou (1911–74), although the project was actually initiated by his art-loving wife. Designed by then-unknowns Renzo Piano and Richard Rogers, the Centre was unveiled in 1977, three years after Pompidou's death. Its radical purpose-coded colors and spaceship appearance scandalized Parisians, but they've learned to love the futuristic apparition. The **Musée National d'Art Moderne** (Modern Art Museum, entrance on Level 4) has doubled in size to occupy most of the center's top two stories: one devoted to modern art—including major works by Matisse, the Surrealists, Modigliani, Duchamp, and Picasso—the other to contemporary art from the 1960s onward, including video installations. ✉*Pl. Georges-Pompidou, Beaubourg/Les Halles* ☎*01–44–78–12–33* ⊕*www.cnac-gp.fr* ⊠*€10–€12; free 1st Sun. of month* ⊙*Wed.–Mon. 11–10* Ⓜ*Rambuteau.*

㉕ Musée Picasso. Housed in the 17th-century Hôtel Salé, this museum has the largest collection of Picassos in the world—and these are "Picasso's Picassos," not necessarily his most famous works but rather the paintings and sculptures the artist valued most. Arranged chronologically, the museum gives you a great snapshot (with English info panels) of the painter's life. There are also works by Cézanne, Miró, Renoir, Braque, Degas, and Matisse. The building is showing some of the wear and tear that goes with being one of the city's most popular museums; on peak summer afternoons this place is more congested than the Gare du Lyon. ✉*5 rue de Thorigny, Le Marais* ☎*01–42–71–25–21* ⊕*www. musee-picasso.fr* ⊠*€6.50; free 1st Sun. of month* ⊙*Wed.–Mon. 9:30–5:30* Ⓜ*St-Sébastien.*

㉖ Place des Vosges. The oldest monumental square in Paris—and probably
★ still its most nobly proportioned—the Place des Vosges was laid out by Henri IV at the start of the 17th century. Originally known as Place Royale, it has kept its Renaissance beauty nearly intact, although its buildings have been softened by time, their pale pink brick crumbling slightly in the harsh Parisian air and the darker stone facings pitted with age. It was always a highly desirable address, reaching a peak of glamour in the early years of Louis XIV's reign, when the nobility were falling over themselves for the privilege of living here. The two larger buildings on either side of the square were originally the king's and queen's pavilions. The statue in the center is of Louis XIII. It's not the original; that was melted down in the Revolution, the same period when the square's name was changed in honor of the French département of the Vosges, the first in the country to pay the new revolutionary taxes. With its arcades, symmetrical pink-brick town houses, and trim green garden, bisected in the center by gravel paths and edged with plane trees, the square achieves harmony and balance: it's a pleasant place to tarry on a sultry summer afternoon. Better yet, grab an arcade table at one of the many cafés lining the square—even a simple cheese crêpe becomes a feast in this setting. To get inside one of the imposing town houses, visit the Maison de Victor Hugo, at No. 6, on the southeast corner of the square. ✉*Chemin Vert or St-Paul.*

THE ILE ST-LOUIS & THE LATIN QUARTER: ACROSS THE SEINE

Set behind the Ile de la Cité is one of the most romantic spots in Paris, tiny Ile St-Louis. Of the two islands in the Seine—the Ile de la Cité is just to the west—the St-Louis best retains the romance and loveliness of *le Paris traditionnel.* South of the Ile St-Louis on the Left Bank of the Seine is the bohemian Quartier Latin (Latin Quarter), with its warren of steep, sloping streets, populated largely by Sorbonne students and academics.

EXPLORING THE ILE ST-LOUIS & THE LATIN QUARTER

❻ Ile St-Louis. ★ One of the more fabled addresses in Paris, this tiny island has long harbored the rich and famous, including Chopin, Daumier, Helena Rubinstein, Chagall, and the Rothschild family, who still occupy the island's grandest house. In fact, the entire island displays striking architectural unity, stemming from the efforts of a group of early-17th-century property speculators led by Christophe Marie. The group commissioned leading Baroque architect Louis Le Vau (1612–70) to erect a series of imposing town houses. Other than some elegant facades and the island's highly picturesque quays along the Seine, there are no major sights here—just follow your nose and soak in the atmosphere. Study the plaques on the facades of houses describing who lived where when. An especially somber reminder adorns 19 quai de Bourbon: "Here lived Camille Claudel, sculptor, from 1899 to 1913. Then ended her brave career as an artist and began her long night of internment." Rodin's muse, she was committed by her family to an insane asylum, where she was forbidden to practice her art. In your tour of the St-Louis, don't miss the views of Notre-Dame from the Quai d'Orleans, the historic Hôtel Lauzun museum, or, *bien sûr*, the Grand-Marnier ice cream or Pamplemousse Rose sorbet at Berthillon, found on the center street of the island. Ⓜ *Pont-Marie.*

NEED A BREAK? Cafés all over town sell Berthillon, the haute couture of ice cream, but the Berthillon (✉ *31 rue St-Louis-en-l'Ile, Ile St-Louis* ☎ *01–43–54–31–61*) shop itself is the place to go. More than 30 flavors are served; expect to wait in line. The shop is open Wednesday—Sunday 10–8 PM, but closes during the peak summer season, from July 15–Sept. 1. Down the street at No. 47, up-and-comer Amorino serves up tasty Italian gelato every day, noon-midnight.

❹ Musée National du Moyen-Age *(National Museum of the Middle Ages).* Rivaling New York City's Cloisters as the greatest museum of medieval art in the world, the Musée Cluny—a name that is more popularly used—is housed in the 15th-century Hôtel de Cluny, erstwhile residence of the abbots of Cluny (the famous—but now largely destroyed—abbey in Burgundy). A stunning selection of tapestries, including the exquisite *Dame à la Licorne* (*Lady and the Unicorn*) series, headlines its exhibition of medieval decorative arts. Alongside the mansion are the city's Roman baths and the *Boatmen's Pillar,* Paris's oldest sculpture. ✉ *6 pl. Paul-Painlevé, Quartier Latin* ☎ *01–53–73–78–00* ⊕ *www.musee-moyenage.fr* 🖃 *€7.50, free 1st Sun. of month, otherwise €4 on Sun.* ☉ *Wed.–Mon. 9:15–5:45* Ⓜ *Cluny–La Sorbonne.*

FROM ORSAY TO ST-GERMAIN-DES-PRÉS: TOUJOURS LA POLITESSE

This area covers the Left Bank, from the Musée d'Orsay in the stately 7e arrondissement to the chic and colorful area around St-Germain-des-Prés in the 6e. To the east, away from the splendor of the 7e, the Boulevard St-Michel slices the Left Bank in two: on one side, the Latin Quarter; on the other, the Faubourg St-Germain, named for St-Germain-des-Prés, the oldest church in Paris. In the southern part of this district is the city's most colorful park, the Jardin du Luxembourg.

EXPLORING ORSAY TO ST-GERMAIN-DES-PRÉS

⑩ Hôtel des Invalides. Famed as the final resting place of Napoléon, Les Invalides, as it is known, is probably the world's grandest rest home. The sprawling building was designed by Libéral Bruand in the 1670s at the behest of Louis XIV's finance minister, Colbert, to house wounded soldiers. Although no more than a handful of old-timers live here these days, the army link remains in the form of the **Musée de l'Armée**, one of the world's foremost military museums. The showpiece here beneath the massive dome is that grandiose monument to glory and hubris, **Napoléon's Tomb.** The dome itself, over the impressive **Église du Dôme,** is the second-tallest building in Paris, after the Eiffel Tower. For the 200th anniversary of the French revolution in 1989, the dome was regilded using more than half a million gold leaves, or more than 20 pounds of gold. ⊠*Pl. des Invalides, Trocadéro/Tour Eiffel* ☎*01–44–42–37–72 Army and Model museums* ⊕*www.invalides. org* ⊠€7 ⊗*Église du Dôme and museums Apr.–Sept., daily 10–6; Oct.–Mar., daily 10–5. Closed 1st Mon. of every month* Ⓜ*La Tour-Maubourg.*

⑦ Jardin du Luxembourg *(Luxembourg Gardens).* Immortalized in count-less paintings, the Luxembourg Gardens possess all that is unique and befuddling about Parisian parks: swarms of pigeons, cookie-cutter trees, ironed-and-pressed dirt walkways, and immaculate lawns meant for admiring, not touching. The tree- and bench-lined paths offer a reprieve from the incessant bustle of the Quartier Latin, as well as an opportunity to discover the dotty old women and smooching university students who once found their way into Doisneau photographs. The park's northern boundary is dominated by the Palais du Luxembourg, surrounded by a handful of well-armed guards; they're protecting the senators who have been deliberating in the palace since 1958. Although the garden may seem purely French, the original 17th-century planning took its inspiration from Italy. When Maria de' Medici, widow of Henri IV, acquired the estate of the deceased Duke of Luxembourg in 1612, she decided to turn his mansion into a version of the Florentine Medici home, the Palazzo Pitti. The **Musée du Luxembourg,** (☎*01–44–32–18–00* ⊕*www.museeduluxembourg.fr*), which is part of the palace, plays host to prestigious (and crowded) temporary exhibitions. ⊠*Bordered by Bd. St-Michel and Rues de Vaugirard, de Médicis, Guynemer, and Auguste-Comte, St-Germain-des-Prés* Ⓜ*Free; Open daily until sunset Odéon; RER: Luxembourg.*

5

8 Musée d'Orsay. In a spectacularly converted Belle Époque train station, the Orsay Museum—devoted to the arts (mainly French) spanning the period 1848–1914—is one of the city's most popular, thanks to the presence of the world's greatest collection of Impressionist and Postimpressionist paintings. Here you can find Manet's *Déjeuner sur l'Herbe* (*Lunch on the Grass*), the painting that scandalized Paris in 1863 when it was shown at the Salon des Refusés, an exhibit organized by artists refused permission to show their work at the Academy's official annual salon, as well as the artist's provocative nude *Olympia*. There's a dazzling rainbow of masterpieces by Renoir (including his beloved *Le Moulin de la Galette*), Sisley, Pissarro, and Monet. The Postimpressionists—Cézanne, van Gogh, Gauguin, and Toulouse-Lautrec—are on the top floor. On the ground floor you can find the work of Manet, the powerful realism of Courbet, and the delicate nuances of Degas. If you prefer more academic paintings, look for Puvis de Chavannes's larger-than-life classical canvases. And if you're excited by more modern developments, look for the early-20th-century Fauves (meaning "wild beasts," the name given them by an outraged critic in 1905)—particularly Matisse, Derain, and Vlaminck.

The museum is arranged on three floors. Once past the ticket booths (get your tickets in advance through the Web site to avoid the lines), you can pick up an English-language audio guide along with a free color-coded map of the museum. Then step down the stairs into the sculpture hall. Here the vastness of the space complements a ravishing collection of French sculpture from 1840 to 1875. ⊠*1 rue de la Légion d'Honneur, St-Germain-des-Prés* ☎*01–40–49–48–14* ⊕*www. musee-orsay.fr* ⊠*€8, €5.50 after 4:15 except Thurs. after 6; free 1st Sun. of every month* ⊙*Tues.-Sun., 9:30–6, Thurs. 9:30 am–9:45 pm* Ⓜ*Solférino; RER: Musée d'Orsay.*

9 Musée Rodin. The exquisitely palatial 18th-century Hôtel Biron makes a gracious stage for the sculpture of Auguste Rodin (1840–1917). You'll doubtless recognize the seated *Le Penseur* (*The Thinker*), with his elbow resting on his knee, and the passionate *Le Baiser* (*The Kiss*). From the upper rooms, which contain some fine if murky paintings by Rodin's friend Eugène Carrière (1849–1906), there are some lovely views of the gardens. Elsewhere are fine sculptures by Rodin's mistress, Camille Claudel (1864–1943), a remarkable artist in her own right. Her torturous relationship with Rodin drove her out of his studio—and out of her mind. In 1913 she was packed off to an asylum, where she remained, barred from any artistic activities, until her death. For much more soothing scenarios, repair to the mansion garden: it's exceptional not only for its rosebushes and sculpture, but also its view of the Invalides dome with the Eiffel Tower behind, and its superb cafeteria. ⊠*77 rue de Varenne, Invalides/Eiffel Tower* ☎*01–44–18–61–10* ⊠*www.musee-rodin.fr* ⊠*€6, gardens only €1* ⊙*Apr.–Oct., Tues.–Sun. 9:30–5:45; Nov.–Mar., Tues.–Sun. 9:30–4:45* Ⓜ*Varenne.*

MONTMARTRE: THE CITADEL OF PARIS

On a dramatic rise above the city is Montmartre, site of the Sacré-Coeur Basilica and home to a once-thriving artist community. This was the quartier that Toulouse-Lautrec and Renoir immortalized with a flash of their brush and a tube of their paint. Although the great painters have long departed, and the fabled nightlife of Old Montmartre has fizzled down to some glitzy nightclubs and skin shows, Montmartre still exudes history and Gallic charm.

EXPLORING MONTMARTRE

㉑ Au Lapin Agile. One of the most picturesque spots in Paris, this legendary bar-cabaret (sorry—open nights only) is a miraculous survivor from the 19th century. It got its curious name—the Nimble Rabbit—when the owner, André Gill, hung up a sign (now in the Musée du Vieux Montmartre) of a laughing rabbit jumping out of a saucepan clutching a bottle of wine. Founded in 1860, this adorable maison-cottage was a favorite subject of painter Maurice Utrillo. Once owned by Aristide Bruant (immortalized in many Toulouse-Lautrec posters), it became the home-away-from-home for Braque, Modigliani, Apollinaire, and Vlaminck. The most famous habitué, however, was Picasso, who once paid for a meal with one of his paintings, then promptly went out and painted another, which he named after this place (it now hangs in New York's Metropolitan Museum, which purchased it for $50 million). ⊠*22 rue des Saules, Montmartre* ☎*01–46–06–85–87* ⊕*www.au-lapin-agile.com* ⊠*€24 (includes first drink)* ☉*Tues.–Sun. 9* PM*–2* AM Ⓜ*Lamarck-Caulaincourt.*

⓴ Moulin Rouge *(Red Windmill).* This world-famous cabaret was built in 1885 as a windmill, then transformed into a dance hall in 1900. Those wild, early days were immortalized by Toulouse-Lautrec in his posters and paintings. It still trades shamelessly on the notion of Paris as a city of sin: if you fancy a gaudy Vegas-style night out—sorry, admirers of the Baz Luhrmann film won't find any of its charm here—this is the place to go. The cancan, by the way—still a regular sight here—was considerably raunchier when Toulouse-Lautrec was around. ⊠*82 bd. de Clichy, Montmartre* ☎*01–53–09–82–82* ⊕*www.moulin-rouge.com* ⊠*€89–€175* ☉*Shows nightly at 9 and 11* Ⓜ*Blanche.*

㉒ Sacré-Coeur. Often compared to a "sculpted cloud" atop Montmartre, ★ the Sacred Heart Basilica was erected as a sort of national guilt offering in expiation for the blood shed during the Paris Commune and Franco-Prussian War in 1870–71, and was largely financed by French Catholics fearful of an anticlerical backlash under the new republican regime. The basilica was not consecrated until 1919. Stylistically, the Sacré-Coeur borrows elements from Romanesque and Byzantine models. The gloomy, cavernous interior is worth visiting for its golden mosaics; climb to the top of the dome for the view of Paris. Try to visit at sunrise or long after sunset, as otherwise this area is crammed with bus groups, young lovers, postcard sellers, guitar-wielding Christians, and sticky-finger types; be extra cautious with your valuables. ⊠*Pl. du Parvis-du-Sacré-Coeur, Montmartre* ☎*01–53–41–89–00* ⊠*Free, dome*

€4.50 ◷ *Basilica daily 6* AM–*10:30* PM; *dome and crypt Oct.–Mar., daily 9–6; Apr.–Sept., daily 10–5* Ⓜ *Anvers plus funicular.*

WHERE TO EAT

A new wave of culinary confidence is running through one of the world's great food cities and spilling over both banks of the Seine. Whether cooking up *grand-mère's* roast chicken and *riz au lait* or placing a whimsical hat of cotton candy atop wild-strawberry-and-rose ice cream, Paris chefs are breaking free from the tyranny of tradition and following their passions.

But self-expression is not the only driving force behind the changes. A traditional high-end restaurant can be prohibitively expensive to operate. As a result, more casual bistros and cafés have become attractive businesses for even top chefs, making the cooking of geniuses such as Joël Robuchon and Pierre Gagnaire more accessible to all (even if these star chefs rarely cook in their lower-priced restaurants).

RESTAURANTS (IN ALPHABETICAL ORDER)

$$$–$$$$
FRENCH FUSION
Invalides, 7ᵉ

Le 144 Petrossian. Promising young chef Rougui Dia has injected her cosmopolitan style into this contemporary French restaurant with a czarist spin. In a conscious decision to opt out of the "star chase," the restaurant is changing its menu less often and has put an end to the haute-cuisine flourish of serving "drinkable perfumes" before dessert. This means that regulars will always find favorite dishes such as *agneau Yagouline*, lamb cooked until spoon-tender and served with a Moroccan-style fruit tagine (part of the set menu for €35 at lunch and €45 at dinner), and *oeuf Petrossian*, a breaded and fried soft-boiled egg topped with caviar. The à la carte selection is peppered with luxury ingredients like caviar and smoked salmon, and the indecisive can choose a sampler of three or five desserts. ✉ *144 rue de l'Université* ☎ *01–44–11–32–32* ▭ *AE, DC, MC, V* ◷ *Closed Sun., Mon., last wk in July, and 3 wks in Aug.* Ⓜ *La Tour–Maubourg, Invalides.*

$$
BISTRO
Louvre/Tuileries,
1ᵉʳ

L'Ardoise. This minuscule storefront, decorated with enlargements of old sepia postcards of Paris, is a model of the kind of contemporary bistros making waves in Paris. Chef Pierre Jay's first-rate three-course dinner menu for €32 tempts with such original dishes as mushroom and foie gras ravioli with smoked duck; farmer's pork with porcini mushrooms; and red mullet with creole sauce (you can also order à la carte, but it's less of a bargain). Just as enticing are the desserts, such as a superb *feuillantine au citron*—caramelized pastry leaves filled with lemon cream and lemon slices—and a boozy baba au rhum. With friendly waiters and a small but well-chosen wine list, L'Ardoise would be perfect if it weren't often crowded and noisy. ✉ *28 rue du Mont Thabor* ☎ *01–42–96–28–18* ▭ *MC, V* ◷ *Closed Mon. and Aug. No lunch Sun.* Ⓜ *Concorde.*

¢–$

ISRAELI

Le Marais, 4ᵉ

☺

L'As du Fallafel. Look no further than the fantastic falafel stands on the newly pedestrian Rue de Rosiers for some of the cheapest and tastiest meals in Paris. L'As (the Ace) is widely considered the best of the bunch, which accounts for the lunchtime line that extends into the street. A falafel sandwich costs €5 to go, €7 in the dining room, and comes heaped with grilled eggplant, cabbage, hummus, tahini, and hot sauce. The *shawarma* (grilled, skewered meat) sandwich, made with chicken or lamb, is also one of the finest in town. Though takeout is popular, it can be more fun (and not as messy) to eat off a plastic plate in one of the two frenzied dining rooms. Fresh lemonade is the falafel's best match. ✉*34 rue des Rosiers* ☎*01–48–87–63–60* ☐*MC, V* ☽*Closed Sat. No dinner Fri.* Ⓜ*St-Paul.*

$$$–$$$$

MODERN FRENCH

St-Germain, 7ᵉ

L'Atelier de Joël Robuchon. Famed chef Joël Robuchon retired from the restaurant business for several years before opening this red-and-black-lacquered space with a bento-box-meets-tapas aesthetic. High seats surround two U-shape bars, and this novel plan encourages neighbors to share recommendations and opinions. Robuchon's devoted kitchen staff whip up "small plates" for grazing (€10–€25) as well as full portions, which turn out to be the better bargain. Highlights from the oft-changing menu have included an intense tomato jelly topped with avocado purée and thin-crusted mackerel tart, although his inauthentic (but who's complaining?) take on carbonara with cream and Alsatian bacon, and the *merlan* Colbert (fried herb butter) remain signature dishes. Bookings are taken for the 11:30 AM and 6:30 PM sittings only. ✉*5 rue Montalembert* ☎*01–42–22–56–56* ☐*MC, V* Ⓜ*Rue du Bac.*

$$–$$$

BISTRO

Opéra/Grands
Boulevards, 2ᵉ

Aux Lyonnais. With a passion for the old-fashioned bistro, Alain Ducasse has resurrected this 1890s gem by appointing a terrific young chef to oversee the short, frequently changing, and reliably delicious menu of Lyonnais specialties. Dandelion salad with crisp potatoes, bacon, and silky poached egg; watercress soup poured over parsleyed frogs' legs; and fluffy quenelles de brochet (pike-perch dumplings) show he is no bistro dilettante. The decor hews to tradition, too, with a zinc bar, an antique coffee machine, and original turn-of-the-20th-century woodwork. There is a no-choice lunch menu for €28, but the temptation is strong to splurge on the more luxurious à la carte dishes. ✉*32 rue St-Marc* ☎*01–42–96–65–04* ☐*AE, MC, V* ☽*No lunch Sat. Closed Sun. and Mon., 1 wk in July, and 3 wks in Aug.* Ⓜ*Bourse.*

$$$–$$$$

BISTRO

Le Marais, 4ᵉ

☺

Benoît. If you loved Benoît before it became the property of Alain Ducasse and Thierry de la Brosse—the pair that revived Aux Lyonnais—chances are you'll adore it now. Without changing the vintage 1912 setting, which needed nothing more than a minor dusting, the illustrious new owners have subtly improved the menu with dishes such as marinated salmon, frogs' legs in a morel-mushroom cream sauce, and an outstanding cassoulet served in a cast-iron pot. Hardworking young chef David Rathgeber, formerly of Aux Lyonnais, keeps the kitchen running smoothly, and the waiters are charm incarnate. It's a splurge to be here, so go all the way and top off your meal with tarte tatin that's caramelized to the core or a rum-doused baba. ✉*20 rue St-Martin* ☎*01–42–72–25–76* ☐*AE, MC, V* ☽*Closed Aug.* Ⓜ*Châtelet.*

5

$$–$$$
BISTRO
Quartier Latin,
5ᵉ

Chez René. Run by the same family for 50 years, Chez René changed owners in 2007. The new team has wisely preserved the bistro's traditional spirit while brightening the decor and adding chic touches such as valet parking. The menu still consists mainly of Lyonnais classics, but you'll now find some of these grouped into color-themed menus such as "red" (beet salad, coq au vin, and Quincy wine) or "yellow" (Swiss chard gratin, pike-perch in beurre blanc sauce with steamed potatoes, and Mâcon wine). The best sign of the new regime's success is that the old regulars keep coming back, including the former owners, who live upstairs. ⊠*14 bd. St-Germain* ☏*01–43–54–30–23* ⊟*AE, MC, VC* ⊘*Closed Sun., Mon., Christmas wk, and Aug. No lunch Sat.* Ⓜ*Maubert-Mutualité.*

$$–$$$
BISTRO
Champs-Elysées,
8ᵉ

Chez Savy. Just off the glitzy Avenue Montaigne, Chez Savy occupies its own circa-1930s dimension, oblivious to the area's fashionization. The Art Deco cream-and-burgundy interior looks blissfully intact (avoid the back room unless you're in a large group), and the waiters show not a trace of attitude. Fill up on rib-sticking specialties from the Auvergne in central France—lentil salad with bacon, foie gras (prepared on the premises), perfectly charred lamb with feather-light shoestring frites, and pedigreed Charolais beef. Order a celebratory bottle of Mercurey with your meal and feel smug that you've found this place. ⊠*23 rue Bayard* ☏*01–47–23–46–98* ⊟*MC, V* ⊘*Closed weekends and Aug.* Ⓜ*Franklin-D.-Roosevelt.*

$–$$
BISTRO
Montmartre, 18ᵉ

Chez Toinette. Between the red lights of Pigalle and the Butte Montmartre, this cozy bistro with red walls and candlelight hits the romance nail on the head. In autumn and winter, game comes into play in long-simmered French dishes—choose from *marcassin* (young wild boar), venison, and pheasant. Regulars can't resist the crème brûlée and the raspberry tart. With friendly, professional waiters and reasonable prices, Chez Toinette is a rare find for this neighborhood. ⊠*20 rue Germain Pilon* ☏*01–42–54–44–36* ⊕ ⊟*MC, V* ⊘*Closed Sun. and Aug. No lunch* Ⓜ*Pigalle.*

$$$
BISTRO
St-Germain, 6ᵉ

Le Comptoir du Relais Saint-Germain. Run by legendary bistro chef Yves Camdeborde, this tiny Art Deco hotel restaurant is booked up several months in advance for the single dinner sitting that comprises a five-course, €48 set menu of haute-cuisine-quality food. On weekends and before 6 PM during the week a brasserie menu is served and reservations are not accepted, resulting in long lineups and brisk service. Start with charcuterie or pâté, then choose from open-faced sandwiches, salads, and a handful of hot dishes such as braised beef cheek, roast tuna, and Camdeborde's famed deboned and breaded pig's trotter. Sidewalk tables make for prime people-watching in summer, and Le Comptoir also runs a down-to-earth snack shop next door that serves crêpes and sandwiches. ⊠*9 carrefour de l'Odéon* ☏*01–44–27–07–50* ⊟*AE, DC, MC, V* Ⓜ*Odéon.*

$$–$$$
MODERN FRENCH
Beaubourg/Les
Halles, 3ᵉ

Le Georges. One of those rooftop showstopping venues so popular in Paris, Le Georges preens atop the Centre Georges Pompidou. The staff is as streamlined and angular as the furniture, and at night the terrace has distinct snob appeal. Come snappily dressed or you may be relegated to something resembling a dentist's waiting room. Part of the Costes brothers' empire, the establishment trots out fashionable dishes such as sesame-crusted tuna and coriander-spiced beef fillet flambéed with cognac. It's all considerably less dazzling than the view, except for the suitably decadent desserts (indulge in the Cracker's cheesecake with yogurt sorbet). ⊠ *Centre Pompidou, 6th fl., 19 rue Rambuteau* ☎ *01–44–78–47–99* ▤ *AE, DC, MC, V* ⊘ *Closed Tues.* Ⓜ *Rambuteau.*

$$$$ **Le Grand Véfour.** Victor Hugo could stride in and still recognize this
HAUTE FRENCH place—in his day, as now, a contender for the title of most beautiful
Louvre/Tuileries, restaurant in Paris. Originally built in 1784, it has welcomed everyone
1ᵉʳ from Napoléon to Colette to Jean Cocteau. The mirrored ceiling and early-19th-century glass paintings of goddesses and muses create an air of restrained seduction. Foodies as well as the fashionable gather here to enjoy chef Guy Martin's unique blend of sophistication and rusticity, as seen in dishes such as frogs' legs with sorrel sauce, and oxtail parmentier (a kind of shepherd's pie) with truffles. The outstanding cheese trolley pays tribute to his native Savoie. For dessert, try the house specialty, *palet aux noisettes* (meringue cake with milk-chocolate mousse, hazelnuts, and salted caramel ice cream). Prices are as extravagant as the decor, but there is an €88 lunch menu. ⊠ *17 rue de Beaujolais* ☎ *01–42–96–56–27* ♣ *Reservations essential. Jacket and tie* ▤ *AE, DC, MC, V* ⊘ *Closed weekends, Aug., 1 wk in Apr., 1 wk at Christmas. No dinner Fri.* Ⓜ *Palais-Royal.*

$$$$ **Hélène Darroze.** The eponymous chef here has won many followers with
HAUTE FRENCH her refined take on southwestern French cooking from the lands around
St-Germain, 6ᵉ Albi and Toulouse. You know it's not going to be *la même chanson*— the same old song—as soon as you see the contemporary tableware, and Darroze's intriguingly modern touch comes through in such dishes as a sublime duck foie gras confit served with an exotic-fruit chutney or a blowout of roast wild duck stuffed with foie gras and truffles. Expect to spend a hefty €350 for two à la carte (with drinks) upstairs. For a more affordable taste of her style, try the relatively casual Salon d'Hélène downstairs; the sultry Boudoir, which specializes in chic finger food; or her new Latin Quarter bistro Toustem. ⊠ *4 rue d'Assas* ☎ *01–42–22–00–11* ▤ *AE, DC, MC, V* ⊘ *Closed Sun., Mon., and Aug.* Ⓜ *Sèvres Babylone.*

$$$$ **Il Vino.** It might seem audacious to present hungry diners with nothing
FRENCH FUSION more than a wine list, but the gamble is paying off for Enrico Bernardo
Invalides, 7ᵉ at his newly opened restaurant with a branch in Courcheval. Winner of the world's best sommelier award in 2005, this charismatic Italian has left the George V to oversee a dining room where food plays second fiddle (in status, not quality). The hip decor—plum banquettes, body-hugging white chairs, a few high tables—has attracted a mostly young clientele that's happy to play the game by ordering one of the blind, multicourse tasting menus for €75 or €100. This might bring you a white Mâcon with saffron risotto, crisp Malvasia with crabmeat and black radish, a full-bodied red from Puglia with Provençal-style

5

lamb, sherrylike *vin jaune* d'Arbois with aged Comté cheese, and sweet Jurançon with berry crumble. You can also order individual wine-food combinations à la carte or pick a bottle straight from the cellar and ask for a meal to match. ⊠ *13 bd. de la Tour-Maubourg* ⓂInvalides ☎01–44–11–72–00 ═AE, DC, MC, V

$$$$
HAUTE FRENCH
Tour Eiffel, 7ᵉ

Jules Verne. Alain Ducasse doesn't set his sights low, so it was no real surprise when he took over this prestigious dining room on the second floor of the Eiffel Tower. During months of renovations he did away with the dated black decor, replacing it with designer Patrick Jouin's neo-futuristic look in shades of brown. Sauces and pastries are prepared in a kitchen below the Champ de Mars before being whisked up the elevator to the kitchen, which is overseen by young chef Pascal Féraud. Most accessible is the €75 lunch menu (weekdays only), which brings you à la carte dishes in slightly smaller portions. Spend more (about €150–€200 per person) and you'll be entitled to more lavish dishes such as lobster with celery root and black truffle, and fricassee of Bresse chicken with crayfish. For dessert the kitchen reinterprets French classics, as in an unsinkable pink grapefruit soufflé with grapefruit sorbet. Book months ahead or try your luck at the last minute. ⊠ *Tour Eiffel, south pillar, Av. Gustave Eiffel* ☎01–45–55–61–44 ⚛Reservations essential Jacket required ═AE, DC, MC, V ⓂBir-Hakeim

$
MODERN FRENCH
Quartier Latin,
5ᵉ

Le Pré Verre. Chef Philippe Delacourcelle knows his cassia bark from his cinnamon, thanks to a long stint in Asia, and he opened this lively bistro, with its purple-gray walls and photos of jazz musicians, to showcase his unique culinary style, rejuvenating archetypal French dishes with Asian and Mediterranean spices. So popular has it proved, especially with Japanese visitors, that the restaurant opened a branch in Tokyo in late 2007. His bargain prix-fixe menus (€13 at lunch for a main dish, glass of wine, and coffee; €26.50 for three courses at dinner) change constantly, but his trademark spiced suckling pig with crisp cabbage is a winner, as is his rhubarb compote with gingered white-chocolate mousse. Ask for advice in selecting wine from a list that highlights small producers. ⊠*8 rue Thénard* ☎01–43–54–59–47 ═MC, V ⊙Closed Sun., Mon., and 3 wks in Aug. ⓂMaubert-Mutualité.

$$$
BISTRO
Louvre/Tuileries,
1ᵉʳ

Restaurant du Palais-Royal. This stylish modern bistro decorated in jewel tones serves food to match its stunning location under the arcades of the Palais-Royal, facing its magnificent gardens. Sole, scallops, and risotto—including a dramatic black squid-ink and lobster or an all-green vegetarian version—are beautifully prepared, but juicy beef fillet with *pommes Pont Neuf* (thick-cut frites) is also a favorite of expense-account lunchers. Finish with an airy mille-feuille that changes with the seasons—berries in summer, chestnuts in winter—or a decadent baba doused with rum from Guadeloupe. Book in advance, especially in summer, when the terrace tables are hotly sought after. ⊠*Jardins du Palais-Royal, 110 Galerie Valois* ☎01–40–20–00–27 ═AE, DC, MC, V ⊙Closed Sun. ⓂPalais-Royal.

$$$$
HAUTE FRENCH
Champs-Elysées,
8^e

Taillevent. Perhaps the most traditional—for many diners this is only high praise—of all Paris luxury restaurants, this *grande dame* basks in renewed freshness under brilliant chef Alain Solivérès, who draws inspiration from the Basque country, Bordeaux, and Languedoc for his daily-changing menu. Traditional dishes such as scallops meunière (with butter and lemon) are matched with contemporary choices such as a splendid spelt risotto with truffles and frogs' legs or panfried duck liver with caramelized fruits and vegetables. One of the 19th-century paneled salons has been turned into a winter garden, and contemporary paintings adorn the walls. The service is flawless, and the exceptional wine list is well priced. All in all, a meal here comes as close to the classic haute-cuisine experience as you can find in Paris. You must reserve dinner tables a month in advance. ⊠*15 rue Lamennais* ☎*01–44–95–15–01* ⚑*Reservations essential Jacket and tie* ▭*AE, DC, MC, V* ☉*Closed weekends and Aug.* Ⓜ*Charles-de-Gaulle–Etoile.*

$$$–$$$$
HAUTE FRENCH
Invalides, 7^e
Fodor's Choice
★

Le Violon d'Ingres. Following in the footsteps of Joël Robuchon and Alain Senderens, Christian Constant has given up the star chase in favor of more accessible prices and a packed dining room (book at least a week ahead). In 2006 Constant began offering a single €48 set menu (with several choices for each course), and put Stéphane Schmidt in charge of the kitchen so he could dash between his four restaurants in this street, making sure the hordes are happy. And why wouldn't they be? The food is sophisticated and the atmosphere is lively; you can even find signature dishes such as the almond-crusted sea bass with rémoulade sauce (a buttery caper sauce), alongside game and scallops (in season), and comforting desserts like *pots de crème* and chocolate tart. The food is still heavy on the butter, but with wines starting at around €20 this is a wonderful place for a classic yet informal French meal. ⊠*135 rue St-Dominique* ☎*01–45–55–15–05* ⚑*Reservations essential* ▭*AE, DC, MC, V* ☉*Closed Sun. and Mon.* Ⓜ*Ecole Militaire.*

$–$$
MODERN FRENCH
Louvre/Tuileries,
1er

Willi's Wine Bar. More a restaurant than a wine bar, this British-owned spot is a stylish haunt for Parisian and visiting gourmands who might stop in for a glass of wine at the oak bar or settle into the wood-beamed dining room. The selection of reinvented classic dishes changes daily and might include roast cod with artichokes and asparagus in spring, venison in wine sauce with roast pears and celery-root chips in fall, and mango candied with orange and served with vanilla cream in winter. The restaurant is prix-fixe only; you can have appetizers at the bar. The list of about 250 wines reflects co-owner Mark Williamson's passion for the Rhône Valley and Spanish sherries. ⊠*13 rue des Petits-Champs* ☎*01–42–61–05–09* ▭*MC, V* ☉*Closed Sun.* Ⓜ*Bourse.*

CAFÉS & SALONS DE THÉ

Along with air, water, and wine (Parisians eat fewer and fewer three-course meals), the café remains one of the basic necessities of life in Paris; following is a small selection of cafés and *salons de thé* (tearooms) to whet your appetite.

Les Editeurs (⊠*4 carrefour de l'Odéon, St-Germain-des-Prés, 6e* ☎*01–43–26–67–76* Ⓜ*St-Germain-des-Prés*), strategically placed near prestigious Rive Gauche publishing houses, attracts passersby with red velour seats and glossy books on display. The terrace just off the Boulevard St-Germain is great for people-watching, but not ideal for catching a waiter's eye. **La Charlotte en l'Ile** (✉ *24 rue St-Louis-en-l'Ile, Ile St-Louis, 4ᵉ* ☎ *01–43–54–25–83* Ⓜ *Pont-Marie*) would be fancied by the witch who baked gingerbread children in *Hansel and Gretel*—set with fairy lights, carnival masques, and decoupaged detritus, it's a tiny, storybook spot that offers more than 30 varieties of tea along with a sinfully good hot chocolate. **Ladurée** (✉ *16 rue Royale, Opéra/Grands Boulevards, 8ᵉ* ☎ *01–42–60–21–79* ⊕ *www.laduree.fr* Ⓜ *Madeleine* ✉ *75 avenue des Champs-Élysées, Champs-Élysées, 8ᵉ* ☎ *01–40–75–08–75* Ⓜ *Georges V*) is pretty enough to bring a tear to Proust's eye—these salons de thé have barely changed since 1862 (there's another outpost on the Left Bank at 21 rue Bonaparte). For sheer Traviata opulence, the one on the Champs-Élysées can't be beat: wait until you see the pâtisserie counter or the super-sumptuous Salon Paéva. You can dote on the signature lemon-and-caramel macaroons, or try them in a dazzling array of other flavors including hazelnut praline, rose petal, pistachio, blackcurrant violet, or salted butter caramel. Oooooh! **Mariage Frères** (✉ *30 rue du Bourg-Tibourg, Le Marais, 4ᵉ* ☎ *01–42–72–28–11* Ⓜ *Hôtel-de-Ville*) is an outstanding tea shop serving 500 kinds of tea, along with delicious tarts.

Le Vieux Colombier (✉ *65 rue de Rennes, St-Germain-des-Prés, 7ᵉ* ☎ *01–45–48–53–81* Ⓜ *St-Sulpice*) is just around the corner from St-Sulpice and the Vieux Colombier Theater.

WHERE TO STAY

Winding staircases, flower-filled window boxes, concierges who seem to have stepped out of a 19th-century novel—all of these can still be found in Paris hotels, and despite the scales' being tipped in favor of the well-heeled, overall there's good news for travelers of all budgets. Increased competition means that the bar for service and amenities has been raised everywhere. Now it's not uncommon for mid-range hotels to have a no-smoking floor, for inexpensive hotels to offer air-conditioning and buffet breakfast service, and even for budget places to have wireless Internet or an Internet terminal in their little lobbies. So, whatever price you're looking for, compared to most other cities Paris is a paradise for the weary traveler tired of dreary, out-of-date, or cookie-cutter rooms.

1ᴱᴿ ARRONDISSEMENT (LOUVRE/LES HALLES)

$ Ⓣ **Hôtel Henri IV.** Princes once made the regal Ile de la Cité their home, but even paupers can call it home, thanks to one of Paris's most beloved (and popular) rock-bottom sleeps. Set in a 400-year-old building that once housed Henri IV's printing presses, it has a drab lobby and narrow staircase (five flights, no elevator) but guest rooms wear their age with pride. Nothing beats the top location, set on gorgeous Place Dauphine and just a short stroll to the Louvre and Notre-Dame. Bathrooms are in the hallway; pay a little extra and get a room with a private shower, or reserve room No. 16, the only one with a tub. **Pros:** very quiet, central location; good value. **Cons:** steep stairs and no elevator; no services or amenities; no e-mail or online reservations. ✉*25 pl. Dauphine, Ile de la Cité* ☎*01–43–54–44–53* ☞*20 rooms, 7 with shower/bath* ⚇*In-room: no a/c, no phone, no TV* ⊟*MC, V* Ⓜ*Cité, St-Michel, Pont Neuf.*

$$ 🏨**Hôtel Londres St-Honoré.** An appealing combination of character and comfort distinguishes this small, inexpensive hotel, which is a five-minute walk from the Louvre. Exposed oak beams, statues in niches, and rustic stone walls give this place an old-fashioned air. Though rooms have floral bedspreads and standard hotel furniture, they are pleasant, and the price is right. Note that the elevator only starts on the second floor. **Pros:** within walking distance of major sites; good value for the neighborhood. **Cons:** small elevator that doesn't go to ground floor; small beds; upper rooms can get very hot in summer (fans are available). ✉*13 rue St-Roch, Louvre/Tuileries* ☎*01–42–60–15–62* ⊕*www. hotellondresthonore-paris.com* ☞*21 rooms, 4 suites* ⚇*In-room: no a/c (some), safe, Wi-Fi. In-hotel: public Internet, no-smoking rooms, some pets allowed, minibar* ⊟*AE, DC, MC, V* Ⓜ*Pyramides.*

$$$$ 🏨**Hôtel Meurice.** With millions lavished on this famous hotel in recent years by its owner, the Sultan of Brunei, the Meurice sparkles as never before—and that's saying something, since it has welcomed royalty and celebrity since 1835. The restaurant—a fabled extravaganza of cream boiseries and glittering chandeliers—and the elaborately gilded 18th-century Rococo salons cast a spell as they have always done, and who can resist afternoon tea under the Winter Garden's stunning stained-glass ceiling and palm trees. Guest rooms are aswim in Persian carpets, marble mantelpieces, and ormolu clocks, and are in either a gilded Louis XVI or Napoleonic-Empire style. Most have a Tuileries/Louvre or Sacré-Coeur view, but the massive Royal Suite takes in a 360-degree panorama (reportedly Paris's only). Baths are marble, with two sinks and deep, spacious tubs. The health club includes grape seed–based Caudalíe treatments, such as "cabernet sauvignon" massages, while children are pampered with their own Meurice teddy bear and tot-sized slippers and bathrobe. **Pros:** views over the gardens; trendy public spaces; free high-speed Internet in rooms. **Cons:** on a noisy street; popularity makes the public areas not very discreet. ✉*228 rue de Rivoli, Louvre/Tuileries* ☎*01–44–58–10–10* 🖷*01–44–58–10–15* ⊕*www. meuricehotel.com* ☞*160 rooms, 36 suites* ⚇*In-room: safe, dial-up. In-hotel: 2 restaurants, room service, bar, gym, concierge, public Internet, no-smoking rooms, some pets allowed, minibar* ⊟*AE, DC, MC, V* Ⓜ*Tuileries, Concorde.*

$$$$ 🏨**Hôtel Ritz.** Festooned with Napoleonic gilt, sparkling crystal chandeliers, and *qualité de Louvre* antiques, this majestic and legendary hotel was founded back in 1896 by Cesar Ritz. Yes, the glamour quotient declines precipitously in the back wing, but even if you get one of the humbler chambers, you could easily spend days without venturing past the main gates, thanks to the hotel's dazzling shops, bars, clubs, and restaurants. There's the luxe Espadon restaurant, which overlooks the prettiest dining courtyard in Paris; the famed Ritz Escoffier cooking; the newly reopened Ritz Bar and the famous Hemingway Bar;

5

not to mention the basement health club. Kids get their own bathrobe and slippers, and can participate in swimming or cooking lessons with bilingual babysitters. **Pros:** spacious swimming pool; selection of bars and restaurants; top-notch service. **Cons:** can feel stuffy and old-fashioned; easy to get "lost" in the vast hotel; paparazzi magnet. ✉ *15 pl. Vendôme, Louvre/Tuileries* ☎ *01–43–16–30–30* ⊕ *www.ritzparis.com* ⤴ *106 rooms, 56 suites* ⌖ *In-room: safe, Ethernet, Wi-Fi. In-hotel: 3 restaurants, room service, bars, pool, gym, spa, children's programs (ages 6–12), parking (fee), minibar* ⊟ *AE, DC, MC, V* Ⓜ *Opéra.*

3ᴱ ARRONDISSEMENT (BEAUBOURG/MARAIS)

$$$$ ⊡ **Pavillon de la Reine.** This enchanting countrylike château is hidden off the regal Place des Vosges behind a stunning garden courtyard. Gigantic beams, chunky stone pillars, original oils, and a weathered fireplace speak to the building's 1612 origins. The hotel has large doubles, duplexes, and suites decorated in either contemporary or 18th-century-style wall fabrics. Many rooms look out on the entry court or an interior Japanese-inspired garden. **Pros:** beautiful garden courtyard; typically Parisian historic character; proximity to the Place des Vosges without the noise. **Cons:** expensive for the Marais and the size of the rooms; the nearest métro is a few long blocks away. ✉ *28 pl. des Vosges, Le Marais* ☎ *01–40–29–19–19, 800/447–7462 in U.S.* ⊕ *www.pavillon-de-la-reine. com* ⤴ *30 rooms, 26 suites* ⌖ *In-room: safe, Wi-Fi. In-hotel: room service, bar, concierge, laundry service, parking (no fee), some pets allowed* ⊟ *AE, DC, MC, V* Ⓜ *Bastille, St-Paul.*

4ᴱ ARRONDISSEMENT (MARAIS/ILE ST-LOUIS)

$ ⊡ **Grand Hôtel Jeanne-d'Arc.** You can get your money's worth at this hotel in an unbeatable location off the tranquil Place du Marché Ste-Catherine, one of the city's lesser-known pedestrian squares. The 17th-century building has been a hotel for more than a century, and although rooms are on the spartan side they're well maintained, with spotless tiled bathrooms and cheery, if somewhat mismatched, colors (back rooms are dimmer). The welcoming staff is informal and happy to recount the history of this former market quartier. **Pros:** charming street close to major sites; good value for the Marais; lots of drinking and dining options nearby. **Cons:** late-night revelers on the square can be noisy after midnight; minimal amenities; rooms have varying quality and size. ✉ *3 rue de Jarente, Le Marais* ☎ *01–48–87–62–11* 🖷 *01–48–87–37–31* ⊕ *www.hoteljeannedarc.com* ⤴ *36 rooms* ⌖ *In-room: no a/c. In-hotel: some pets allowed, Wi-Fi.* ⊟ *MC, V* Ⓜ *St-Paul.*

$$–$$$ ⊡ **Hôtel Caron de Beaumarchais.** The theme of this intimate hotel is the work of former next-door neighbor Pierre-Augustin Caron de Beaumarchais, supplier of military aid to American revolutionaries and author of *The Marriage of Figaro.* First-edition copies of his books adorn the public spaces, and the salons faithfully reflect the taste of 18th-century French nobility, right down to the wallpaper and 1792 pianoforte. Richly decorated with floral fabrics and white wooden period furnishings, the rooms have original wooden beams, hand-painted bathroom tiles, and gilded mirrors. All rooms have flat-screen TVs and wireless Internet access. **Pros:** cozy, historic Parisian decor; central location within easy walking distance to major monuments. **Cons:** small rooms; busy street of bars and cafés can be noisy. ⊠*12 rue Vieille-du-Temple, Le Marais* ☎*01–42–72–34–12* ⊕*www.carondebeaumarchais.com* ◄*19 rooms* ⑆*In-room: safe, dial-up, Wi-Fi, laundry service, minibar* ☰*AE, DC, MC, V* Ⓜ*Hôtel de Ville.*

$$–$$$ 🗓**Hôtel Saint-Louis Marais.** Once an annex to a local convent, this 18th-century hotel has retained its stone walls and beams while adding red-clay tile floors and antiques. A wooden-banistered stair leads to the small but proper rooms, decorated with basic red carpet and green bedspreads. (Those with heavy luggage, beware: no elevator.) One room is equipped with a kitchenette. The hotel's in Village St-Paul, a little tangle of medieval lanes just south of the well-traveled Marais that has an excellent English-language bookstore and is not yet overrun by tourists. **Pros:** quiet area of the Marais within walking distance of the islands and Bastille; historic Parisian character; Wi-Fi. **Cons:** no elevator; small rooms with outdated decor. ⊠*1 rue Charles V, Le Marais* ☎*01–48–87–87–04* 🖥 ⊕*www.saintlouismarais.com* ◄*19 rooms* ⑆*In-room: no a/c, safe, Wi-Fi. In-hotel: public Internet, some pets allowed* ☰*DC, MC, V* Ⓜ*Sully Morland, Bastille.*

5ᴱ ARRONDISSEMENT (LATIN QUARTER)

$$ 🗓**Hôtel des Jardins du Luxembourg.** Blessed with a personable staff and a smart, stylish look, this hotel, on an unbelievably calm cul-de-sac just a block from the Luxembourg Gardens, is an oasis for contemplation. A cheery hardwood-floored lobby with fireplace leads to smallish rooms furnished with wrought-iron beds, puffy duvets, and contemporary bathrooms. Ask for one with a balcony, or request one of the larger ground-floor rooms with private entrance directly onto the street. **Pros:** quiet spot close to gardens; nice decor; hot buffet breakfast; Close to RER station to airport or Eurostar. **Cons:** extra charge to use Wi-Fi; some very small rooms; weak air-conditioning. ⊠*5 impasse Royer-Collard, Quartier Latin* ☎*01–40–46–08–88* 🖥*www.les-jardins-du-luxembourg. com* ◄*26 rooms* ⑆*In-room: safe, Wi-Fi, minibar* ☰*AE, DC, MC, V* Ⓜ*RER: Luxembourg.*

$ 🗓**Hôtel Marignan.** Paul Keniger, the energetic third-generation owner, ⏰ has cultivated a convivial atmosphere here for independent international travelers. The Marignan lies squarely between no-star and youth hostel (no TVs or elevator) and offers lots of communal conveniences—a fully stocked and accessible kitchen, free laundry machines, and copious tourist information. Rooms are modest (some sleeping four or five) but have firm mattresses and clean bathrooms. **Pros:** great value for the location; kitchen and laundry open to guests; Wi-Fi. **Cons:** no elevator; room phones only take incoming calls; youth-hostel atmosphere ⊠*13 rue du Sommerard, Quartier Latin* ☎*01–43–54–63–81 www.hotel-marignan. com* ◄*30 rooms, 12 with bath* ⑆*In-room: no a/c, kitchen, no TV. In-hotel: laundry facilities* ☰*MC, V* Ⓜ*Maubert Mutualité.*

$$ 🗓**Hôtel Saint-Jacques.** Nearly every wall in this bargain hotel is bedecked with faux-marble and trompe-l'oeil murals. As in many old and independent Paris hotels, each room is unique, but a general 19th-century theme of Empire furnishings and paintings dominates, with a Montmartre cabaret theme in the new breakfast room that includes a player piano.

Wireless Internet is available in the lounge bar. About half the rooms have tiny step-out balconies that give a glimpse of Notre-Dame and the Panthéon. Room 25 has a round-the-corner balcony; room 16 is popular for its historic ceiling fresco and moldings. Repeat guests get souvenir knickknacks or T-shirts. **Pros:** unique Parisian decor; friendly service; close to Latin Quarter sights. **Cons:** no air-conditioning; too noisy to open windows in summer; thin walls between rooms. ⊠*35 rue des Écoles, Quartier Latin* ☎*01–44–07–45–45* ⊕*www.hotel-saintjacques. com* 📠*38 rooms* ⑂*In-room: no a/c, safe, Wi-Fi. In-hotel: public Internet* ⊟*AE, DC, MC, V* Ⓜ*Maubert Mutualité.*

6ᴱ ARRONDISSEMENT (ST-GERMAIN)

$ 🏨 **Hôtel de Nesle.** This one-of-a-kind budget hotel is like a quirky and enchanting dollhouse. Services are bare-bones—no elevator, phones, TVs, or breakfast—but the payoff is in the snug rooms cleverly decorated by theme. Sleep in Notre-Dame de Paris, lounge in an Asian-style boudoir, spend the night with writer Molière, or steam it up in Le Hammam. Decorations include colorful murals, canopy beds, and custom lamps. Most rooms overlook an interior garden. **Pros:** fun decor; good value for chic location; quiet; small garden. **Cons:** no amenities or services; no air-conditioning; reservations by phone only. ⊠*7 rue de Nesle, St-Germain-des-Prés* ☎*01–43–54–62–41* 📠 ⊕*www.hotelde nesleparis.com* 📠*20 rooms, 9 with bath* ⑂ *In-hotel: some pets allowed* ⊟*MC, V* Ⓜ*Odéon.*

$$$ 🏨 **Hôtel Relais Saint-Sulpice.** A savvy clientele with discerning taste frequents this fashionable little hotel sandwiched between Place St-Sulpice and the Luxembourg Gardens. Eclectically selected art objects and furnishings, some with an Asian theme, oddly pull off a unified look. The rooms themselves, set around an ivy-clad courtyard, are understated, with Provençal fabrics, duvet bedding, carved wooden furnishings, and sisal carpeting. **Pros:** chic location, sauna, close to two métro stations; bright breakfast room and courtyard, good value. **Cons:** smallish rooms in the lower category; noise from the street on weekend evenings. ⊠*3 rue Garancière, St-Germain-des-Prés* ☎*01–46–33–99–00* 📠*01–46–33–00–10* ⊕*www.relais-saint-sulpice.com* 📠*26 rooms* ⑂*In-room: safe, Wi-Fi In-hotel: laundry service* ⊟*AE, DC, MC, V* Ⓜ*St-Germain-des-Prés, St-Sulpice.*

$$$$ 🏨 **Le Relais Christine.** This exquisite property was once a 13th-century abbey, but don't expect monkish quarters. You enter from the impressive stone courtyard into a lobby and fireside honor bar done up in rich fabrics, stone, wood paneling, and antiques. The cavernous breakfast room and adjacent fitness center flaunt their vaulted medieval stonework. The spacious, high-ceilinged rooms (many spanned by massive beams) offer a variety of classical and contemporary styles: Asian-theme wall fabrics or plain stripes, rich aubergine paints or regal scarlet-and-gold. Split-level lofts house up to five people, and several ground-level rooms open onto a lush garden with private patios and heaters. **Pros:** quiet location while still close to the action; historic character; luxuriously appointed rooms. **Cons:** some guests report noise from doors on the street; no Wi-Fi; no on-site restaurant. ⊠*3 rue Christine, St-Germain-des-Prés* ☎*01–40–51–60–80, 800/525–4800 in U.S* ⊕*www.relais-christine.com*

≈33 rooms, 18 suites ♿ In-room: safe, DVD (some), dial-up. In-hotel: room service, parking (no fee), no-smoking rooms, some pets allowedr ⊟AE, DC, MC, V Ⓜ Odéon.

7ᴱ ARRONDISSEMENT (TOUR EIFFEL/INVALIDES)

$$$$ ⊡ **Le Bellechasse.** French designer Christian Lacroix helped decorate all 34 rooms of Le Bellechasse, which is just around the corner from the popular Musée d'Orsay. Guests enter a refreshingly bright lobby of black slate floors, white walls, and mismatched velour and leather armchairs. Floor-to-ceiling windows overlook the elegant patio courtyard. Each room design is unique, but all have an eclectic mix of fabrics, textures, and colors, as well as Lacroix's whimsical characters screened on the walls and ceilings. Most guest rooms have an open-concept bathroom, with the bathtub and sink in a corner and a separate toilet. Four rooms have doors leading to the patio courtyard. **Pros:** central location near top Paris museums; unique style; spacious and bright; Anne Semonin toiletries. **Cons:** street-facing rooms can be a bit noisy. ✉ 8 rue de Bellechasse, Invalides ☎ 01—45–50–22–31 ⊕ www.lebel lechasse.com ≈34 rooms ♿ In-room: safe, Wi-Fi, Ethernet. In-hotel: room service, bar, laundry service ⊟AE, DC, V.

$$$ ⊡ **Hôtel Le Tourville.** Here is a rare find: a cozy upscale hotel that doesn't cost a fortune. Each room has crisp, milk-white damask upholstery set against pastel or ocher walls, a smattering of antique bureaus and lamps, original artwork, and fabulous old mirrors. The junior suites have hot tubs, whereas the Superior room has its own private garden terrace. The staff couldn't be more helpful. **Pros:** close to the Eiffel Tower and Invalides; attentive service; soundproofed windows. **Cons:** no shower curtains for the bathtubs; air-conditioning only in summer. ✉ 16 av. de Tourville, Invalides ☎ 01–47–05–62–62 🖷 01–47–05–43–90 ⊕ www. hoteltourville.com ≈27 rooms, 3 suites ♿ In-room: safe (some), dial-up. In-hotel: room service, bar, no-smoking rooms, some pets allowed, Internet ⊟AE, DC, MC, V Ⓜ École Militaire.

8ᴱ ARRONDISSEMENT (CHAMPS-ÉLYSÉES)

$$$$ ⊡ **Four Seasons Hôtel George V Paris.** The George V is as poised and
Fodor'sChoice polished as the day it opened in 1928: the original Art Deco detailing
★ and 17th-century tapestries have been restored, the bas-reliefs regilded, the marble-floor mosaics rebuilt tile by tile. Rooms are decked in fabrics and Louis XVI trimmings but have homey touches like selections of CDs and French books. Le Cinq restaurant is one of Paris's hottest tables, and the business center has six working stations with computers and printers. The low-lighted spa and fitness center pampers guests with 11 treatment rooms, walls covered in toile de Jouy fabrics, and an indoor swimming pool evoking Marie-Antoinette's Versailles. A relaxation room is available for guests who arrive before their rooms are ready. Even children get the four-star treatment with personalized T-shirts and portable DVD players to distract them at dinnertime. **Pros:** in the couture shopping district; courtyard dining in the summer; guest-only indoor swimming pool. **Cons:** several blocks from the nearest métro; lacks the intimacy of smaller boutique hotels. ✉ 31 av. George V, Champs-Élysées ☎ 01–49–52–70–00, 800/332–3442 in

U.S. ☎01–49–52–70–10 ⊕*www.fourseasons.com/paris* ⌑*184 rooms, 61 suites* ⚕*In-room: safe, kitchen (some), DVD, Ethernet, Wi-Fi. In-hotel: 2 restaurants, room service, bar, pool, gym, spa, concierge, children's programs (ages 1–12), laundry service, airport shuttle, some pets allowed* ⊟*AE, DC, MC, V* Ⓜ*George V.*

$$$$ ⛭**Hôtel Plaza-Athenée.** Prime-time stardom as Carrie Bradshaw's Parisian pied-à-terre in the final episodes of *Sex and the City* boosted the street cred of this 1911 palace hotel. Its revival as the city's lap of luxury, however, owes more to the meticulous attention of the renowned chef Alain Ducasse, who oversees everything from the hotel's flagship restaurant and restored 1930s Relais Plaza brasserie to the quality of the breakfast croissants. Rooms have been redone in Regency, Louis XVI, or Art Deco style, with remote-control air-conditioning, mini hi-fi/CD players, and even a pillow menu. The trendy bar has as its centerpiece an impressive Bombay glass comptoir glowing like an iceberg. **Pros:** on a luxury shopping street; stylish clientele and locals at the bar and restaurants; special attention to children. **Cons:** vast difference in style of rooms; easy to feel anonymous in such a large hotel. ✉*25 av. Montaigne, Champs-Élysées* ☎*01–53–67–66–65, 866/732–1106 in U.S.* ⊕*www.plaza-athenee-paris.com* ⌑*145 rooms, 43 suites* ⚕*In-room: safe, DVD, Ethernet. In-hotel: 3 restaurants, room service, bar, concierge, laundry service, some pets allowed* ⊟*AE, DC, MC, V* Ⓜ*Alma-Marceau.*

9ᴱ ARRONDISSEMENT (OPÉRA)

$$ ⛭**Hôtel Amour.** The hipster team behind this designer boutique hotel just off the trendy Rue des Martyrs already counts among its fiefdoms some of the hottest hotels, bars, and nightclubs in Paris. But despite the cool factor and the funky rooms individually decorated by Parisian avant-garde artists, the prices remain democratically bohemian. Of course, there are few amenities, but there is a 24-hour retro brasserie and garden terrace in the back where locals come to hang out in warmer weather. It's best to take the kids elsewhere; vintage nudie magazines decorate, and the sex shops of Pigalle are blocks away. **Pros:** hip clientele and locals at the brasserie; close to Montmartre; garden dining in summer. **Cons:** few amenities; a few blocks from the nearest métro; close to red-light district. ✉*8 rue Navarin, Montmartre* ☎*01–48–78–31–80* ⊕*www.hotelamour.com* ⌑*20 rooms* ⚕*In-room: no a/c, no phone, no TV. In-hotel: restaurant, bar, public Wi-Fi, room service, laundry service, some pets allowed* ⊟*AE, DC, MC, V* Ⓜ*Pigalle.*

$$$ ⛭**Hôtel George Sand.** This family-run boutique hotel where the 19th-
★   century writer George Sand once lived is fresh and modern, while preserving some original architectural details. Rooms have tea/coffee-making trays and high-tech comforts such as complimentary high-speed Internet and cordless phones. Bathrooms are decked out in yacht-inspired wood flooring, with Etro toiletries. **Pros:** next door to two department stores; historic atmosphere; free Internet. **Cons:** noisy street; some rooms are quite small. ✉*26 rue des Mathurins, Opéra/Grands Boulevards* ☎*01–47–42–63–47* ⊕*www.hotelgeorgesand.com* ⌑*20 rooms* ⚕*In-room: safe, Ethernet, Wi-Fi. In-hotel: room service, laundry service* ⊟*AE, MC, V* Ⓜ*Havre Caumartin.*

NIGHTLIFE & THE ARTS

Detailed entertainment listings can be found in the weekly magazines *Pariscope* (⊕*www.pariscope.fr*) and *L'Officiel des Spectacles*. Also look for the online *Paris Voice* (⊕*www.parisvoice.com*), and *Aden* and *Figaroscope*, the Wednesday supplements to the newspapers *Le Monde* and *Le Figaro*, respectively. The 24-hour hotline and the Web site of the **Paris Tourist Office** (☎*08–92–68–30–00 in English [€0.34min]* ⊕*www.parisinfo.com*) are other good sources of information.

NIGHTLIFE

For those who prefer clinking glasses with the A-list set, check out the Champs-Élysées area, where the posh surroundings are met with expensive drinks and surly bouncers. More laid-back, bohemian-chic revelers can be found in the northeastern districts like Canal St. Martin and Belleville. Students tend to infiltrate the Bastille and Latin Quarter, and fun-loving types can find a wild party nearly every night in the Marais. the Grands Boulevards and Rue Montorgueil, just north of Les Halles, are quickly turning into party central for young professionals and the fashion crowd, and the Pigalle/Montmartre area is increasingly lively with plenty of theaters, cabarets, bars, and concert venues. In warm weather, head to the Seine, where floating clubs and bars are moored from Bercy to the Eiffel Tower.

BARS & CLUBS

American Bar at La Closerie des Lilas (⊠*171 bd. du Montparnasse, Montparnasse, 6ᵉ* ☎*01–40–51–34–50* Ⓜ*Montparnasse*) lets you drink in the swirling action of the adjacent restaurant and do it at a bar hallowed by plaques honoring such former habitués as Man Ray, Jean-Paul Sartre, and Samuel Beckett. Happily, many Parisians still call this watering hole their home away from home. A cherished relic from the days of Picasso and Modigliani, **Au Lapin Agile** (⊠*22 rue des Saules, Montmartre, 18ᵉ* ☎*01–46–06–85–87* Ⓜ*Lamarck-Caulaincourt*), the fabled artists' hangout in Montmartre, is a miraculous survivor from the early 20th century. This is an authentic French cabaret of songs, poetry, and humor in a publike setting . The namesake of **Buddha Bar** (⊠*8 rue Boissy d'Anglas, Champs-Élysées, 8ᵉ* ☎*01–53–05–90–00* Ⓜ*Concorde*), a towering gold-painted Buddha, contemplates enough Dragon Empress screens and colorful chinoiserie for five MGM movies. Although quite past its prime as a Parisian hot spot, it manages to remain packed in the evening with an eclectic crowd.

Café Charbon (⊠*109 rue Oberkampf, Oberkampf, 11ᵉ* ☎*01–43–57–55–13* Ⓜ*St-Maur, Parmentier*) is a beautifully restored 19th-century café with a trendsetting crowd that has made this place one of the mainstays of trendy Okerkampf.

★ **De la Ville Café** (⊠*34 bd. Bonne Nouvelle, 10ᵉ, Opéra/Grands Boulevards* ☎*01–48–24–48–09* Ⓜ*Bonne Nouvelle, Grands Boulevards*) is a funky, industrial-baroque place, with its huge, heated sidewalk terrace, mosaic-tile bar, and swish lounge. As the anchor of the slowly reawakening Grands Boulevards scene, it requires that you arrive early on weekends for a seat.

Harry's New York Bar (✉ *5 rue Daunou, Opéra/Grands Boulevards, 2ᵉ* ☎*01–42–61–71–14* Ⓜ*Opéra*), a cozy, wood-paneled hangout decorated with dusty college pennants and popular with expatriates, is haunted by the ghosts of Ernest Hemingway and F. Scott Fitzgerald. This place claims to have invented the Bloody Mary, and one way or another, the bartenders here do mix a mean one. Don't miss the piano bar downstairs, where Gershwin composed *An American in Paris.*

SHOPPING

Window shopping is one of this city's greatest spectator sports; the French call it *lèche-vitrine*—literally, "licking the windows"—which is fitting because many of the displays look good enough to eat. The capital of style, Paris has an endless panoply of delights to tempt shop-'til-you-droppers, from grand couturiers like Dior to the funkiest flea markets. Most stores—excepting department stores and flea markets—stay open until 6 or 7 PM, but many take a lunch break sometime between noon and 2 PM. Many shops traditionally close on Sunday.

SHOPPING BY NEIGHBORHOOD
AVENUE MONTAIGNE
Shopping doesn't come much more chic than on Avenue Montaigne, with its graceful town mansions housing some of the top names in international fashion: **Chanel, Dior, Céline, Valentino, Krizia, Ungaro, Prada, Dolce & Gabbana,** and many more. Neighboring Rue François 1ᵉʳ and Avenue George-V are also lined with many designer boutiques: **Versace, Fendi, Givenchy,** and **Balenciaga.**

CHAMPS-ÉLYSÉES
Cafés and movie theaters keep the once-chic Champs-Élysées active 24 hours a day, but the invasion of exchange banks, car showrooms, and fast-food chains has lowered the tone. Four glitzy 20th-century arcade malls—**Galerie du Lido, Le Rond-Point, Le Claridge,** and **Élysées 26**—capture most of the retail action, not to mention the **Gap** and the **Disney Store.** Some of the big luxe chain stores—also found in cities around the globe—are here: **Sephora** has reintroduced a touch of elegance, and the mothership **Louis Vuitton** (on the Champs-Élysées proper) has kept the cool factor soaring.

THE FAUBOURG ST-HONORÉ
This chic shopping and residential area is also quite a political hub. It's home to the Élysée Palace as well as the official residences of the American and British ambassadors. The Paris branches of **Sotheby's** and **Christie's** and renowned antiques galleries such as **Didier Aaron** add artistic flavor. Boutiques include **Hermès, Lanvin, Gucci, Chloé,** and **Christian Lacroix.**

LEFT BANK
For an array of bedazzling boutiques with hyper-picturesque goods—antique toy theaters, books on gardening—and the most fascinating antiques stores in town, be sure to head to the area around Rue Jacob, nearly lined with *antiquaires,* and the streets around super-posh Place

Furstenberg. After decades of clustering on the Right Bank's venerable shopping avenues, the high-fashion houses have stormed the Rive Gauche. The first to arrive were **Sonia Rykiel** and **Yves St-Laurent** in the late '60s. Some of the more recent arrivals include **Christian Dior, Giorgio Armani,** and **Louis Vuitton.** Rue des St-Pères and Rue de Grenelle are lined with designer names.

LOUVRE–PALAIS ROYAL
The elegant and eclectic shops clustered in the 18th-century arcades of the Palais-Royal sell such items as antiques, toy soldiers, music boxes, cosmetics, jewelry, and some of the world's most exclusive vintage designer dresses

LE MARAIS
The Marais is a mixture of many moods and many influences; its lovely, impossibly narrow cobblestone streets are filled with some of the most original, small name, nonglobal goods to be had—a true haven for the original gift—including the outposts of **Jamin Puech, The Red Wheelbarrow,** and **Sentou Galerie.** Avant-garde designers **Azzedine Alaïa** and Tsumori Chistato have boutiques within a few blocks of stately Place des Vosges and the Picasso and Carnavalet museums. The Marais is also one of the few neighborhoods that has a lively Sunday-afternoon (usually from 2 PM) shopping scene.

OPÉRA TO LA MADELEINE
Two major department stores—**Printemps** and **Galeries Lafayette**—dominate Boulevard Haussmann, behind Paris's ornate 19th-century Opéra Garnier. Place de la Madeleine tempts many with its two luxurious food stores, **Fauchon** and **Hédiard.**

PLACE VENDÔME & RUE DE LA PAIX
The magnificent 17th-century Place Vendôme, home of the Ritz Hotel, and Rue de la Paix, leading north from Vendôme, are where you can find the world's most elegant jewelers: **Cartier, Boucheron, Bulgari,** and **Van Cleef and Arpels.** The most exclusive, however, is the discreet **Jar's.**

PLACE DES VICTOIRES & RUE ÉTIENNE MARCEL
The graceful, circular Place des Victoires, near the Palais-Royal, is the playground of fashion icons such as **Kenzo,** while **Comme des Garçons** and **Yohji Yamamoto** line Rue Étienne Marcel. In the nearby oh-so-charming Galerie Vivienne shopping arcade, **Jean-Paul Gaultier** has a shop that has been renovated by Philippe Starck, and is definitely worth a stop.

RUE ST-HONORÉ
A fashionable set makes its way to Rue St-Honoré to shop at Paris's trendiest boutique, **Colette.** The street is lined with numerous designer names, while on nearby Rue Cambon you can find the wonderfully elegant **Maria Luisa** and the main **Chanel** boutique.

ILE-DE-FRANCE

Paris may be small as capital cities go, with just under 2 million inhabitants, but Ile-de-France, the region around Paris, contains more than 10 million people—a sixth of France's entire population. That's why on closer inspection the once rustic villages of Ile-de-France reveal cosseted gardens, stylishly gentrified cottages, and extraordinary country restaurants no peasant farmer could afford to frequent.

Ile-de-France offers a rich and varied minisampling of everything you expect from France—cathedrals, painters' villages, lavish palaces, along with the bubblegum-pink turrets of Disneyland Paris—and all delightfully set within easy day trips from Paris.

PLANNING YOUR TIME

With so many legendary sights in the Ile-de-France—many of which are gratifying human experiences rather than just guidebook necessities—you could spend weeks visiting the region. For a stimulating mix of pomp, nature, and spirituality, we suggest your three priorities should be Versailles, Giverny, and Chartres. You definitely need a day for Versailles, the world's grandest palace. For that sublime treat of medieval art and architecture, the cathedral of Chartres, you need at least half a day. Ditto for Monet's ravishing home and garden at Giverny. You can easily see Fontainbleau and Vaux-le-Vicomte in a day. As for Disneyland Paris, it all depends on your priorities.

GETTING HERE & AROUND

A comprehensive rail network ensures that most towns in Ile-de-France can make comfortable day trips from Paris, but make sure you know the right station to head out from (Gare de Lyon for Fontainebleau and Gare Montparnasse for Chartres). RER (commuter) trains tunnel through central Paris en route to Versailles and Disneyland.

A handful of venues need other means of access. To reach Giverny, rail it to Vernon, then take a taxi or local bus (or bike). To reach Vaux-le-Vicomte, head first for Melun, then take a taxi or local bus (in summer a shuttle service). Note that Fontainebleau station is in neighboring Avon, and getting to the château means a 10-minute bus ride.

A13 links Paris (from the Porte d'Auteuil) to Versailles. You can get to Chartres on A10 from Paris (Porte d'Orléans). For Fontainebleau, take A6 from Paris (Porte d'Orléans), or for a more attractive, although slower route through the Forest of Sénart and the northern part of the Forest of Fontainebleau, take N6 from Paris (Porte de Charenton) via Melun. A4 runs from Paris (Porte de Bercy) to Disneyland. Although a comprehensive rail network ensures that most towns in Ile-de-France can make comfortable day trips from Paris, the only way to crisscross the region without returning to the capital is by car. There's no shortage of expressways or fast highways, but be prepared for delays close to Paris and during the morning and evening rush hours.

ESSENTIALS

Train Contacts Gare SNCF Fontainbleau (⊠ *1 pl. François-Mitterrand* ☎ *03–80–43–16–34).* **Gare SNCF Versailles** (⊠ *Cour de la Gare* ☎ *03–80–43–16–34).* **SNCF** (☎ *08–91–36–20–20 €0.23 per min* ⊕ *www.tran silien.com).*

Visitor Information Espace du Tourisme d'Ile-de-France (⊠ *Carrousel du Louvre, 99 rue de Rivoli, Paris* ☎ *08–26–16–66–66).* **Disneyland Paris reservations office** (⊡ *B.P. 100, cedex 4, 77777 Marne-la-Vallée* ☎ *01–60–30–60–30, 407/824–4321 in U.S.).* **Chartres** (⊠ *Pl. de la Cathédrale* ☎ *02–37–18–26–26* ⊕ *www.chartres-tourisme. com).* **Versailles** (⊠ *2 bis, av. de Paris* ☎ *01–39–24–88–88* ⊕ *www.versailles-tourisme. com)*

VERSAILLES

16 km (10 mi) west of Paris via A13.

GETTING HERE

Versailles has three train stations, all reached from different stations in Paris (journey time 25–40 mins). The handiest is Versailles Rive Gauche, reached by the RER-C5 line (main stations at Paris's Gare d'Austerlitz, St-Michel, Invalides, and Champ-de-Mars). The round-trip fare is €6. There are also regional SNCF trains from Gare Montparnasse to Versailles Chantiers, and from Gare St-Lazare to Versailles Rive Droite. Versailles Chantiers (about a 20-min walk from Versailles's front gates, although a municipal bus runs between the two) connects Versailles with several other towns in the Ile-de-France, notably Chartres (with about three trains every two hours for the 50-min trip). The other two stations in Versailles are about a 10-minute walk from the château, although the municipal Bus B or a summertime shuttle service (use métro ticket or pay small fee in coins) can also deposit you at the front gates.

EXPLORING

Fodor'sChoice It's hard to tell which is larger at **Château de Versailles**—the world-famous ★ château that housed Louis XIV and 20,000 of his courtiers or the mass of tour buses and visitors standing in front of it. The grandest palace in France remains one of the marvels of the world. Itwas not just home to the Sun King, it was to be the new headquarters of the French government capital (from 1682 to 1789 and again from 1871 to 1879). To accompany the palace, a new city—in fact, a new capital—had to be built from scratch. Tough-thinking town planners took no prisoners, dreaming up vast mansions and avenues broader than the Champs-Élysées. If you have any energy left after exploring Louis XIV's palace and park, a tour of Versailles—a textbook 18th-century town—offers a telling contrast between the majestic and the domestic.

WHERE TO STAY & EAT

$–$$ 🏨 **Le Cheval Rouge.** This unpretentious old hotel, built in 1676, is in a corner of the town market square, close to the château and strongly recommended if you plan to explore the town on foot. Some rooms around the old stable courtyard have their original wood beams. Several were

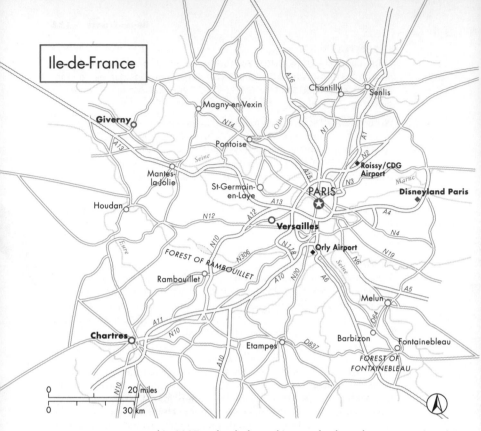

renovated in 2007 and upholstered in pastel colors; the most spacious is Room 108, one of the few rooms with a bath rather than just a shower. **Pros:** great setting in town center; good value for Versailles. **Cons:** bland public areas; some rooms need renovating. ⊠ *18 rue André-Chénier* ☎ *01–39–50–03–03* ⊕ *www.chevalrouge.fr.st* ⤵ *38 rooms* ♻ *In-room: no a/c, WiFi. In-hotel: room service, bar, some pets allowed (fee), no elevator, parking (free)* ⊟ *AE, DC, MC, V.*

$$$$
Fodor$Choice
★
🏨 **Trianon Palace.** A modern-day Versailles, this deluxe hotel is in a turn-of-the-20th-century, creamy white creation of imposing size, filled with soaring rooms (including the historic Salle Clemenceau, site of the 1919 Versailles Peace Conference), palatial columns, and with a huge garden close to the château park. Once faded, the hotel, now part of the Westin chain, is aglitter once again with a health club (the pool idles beneath a glass pyramid) and a refurbished lobby glammed up with Murano chandeliers and high-back, green-leather armchairs. The hotel headliner these days is famed, foul-mouthed superchef Gordon Ramsay,who has remade the luxury restaurant here (along with a more casual eaterie) with a big splash. As for the guest rooms, try to avoid the newer annex, the Pavillon Trianon, and insist on the full treatment in the main building (ask for one of the even-numbered rooms, which look out over the woods near the Trianons; odd-numbered rooms overlook the modern annex). **Pros:** palatial glamor; wonderful setting right by château park;

Gordon Ramsay. **Cons:** lack of a personal touch after recent changes of ownership. ⊠*1 bd. de la Reine* ☎*01–30–84–51–20* ⊕*www.trianon palace.fr* ⤳*165 rooms, 27 suites* ⚓*In-room: safe, refrigerator, Wi-Fi. In-hotel: 2 restaurants, room service, bar, pool, gym, public Wi-Fi, parking (free), pets allowed (free)* ⊟*AE, DC, MC, V* ⦿*BP.*

CHARTRES

39 km (24 mi) southwest of Rambouillet via N10 and A11, 88 km (55 mi) southwest of Paris.

All the descriptive prose and poetry that have been lavished on this supreme cathedral can only begin to suggest the glory of its 12th- and 13th-century statuary and stained glass, somehow suffused with burning mysticism and a strange sense of the numinous. Chartres is more than a church—it's a nondenominational spiritual experience. If you arrive in summer from Maintenon across the edge of the Beauce, the richest agrarian plain in France, you can see Chartres's spires rising up from oceans of wheat. The whole town—with its old houses and picturesque streets—is worth a leisurely exploration.

GETTING HERE

Both regional and main-line (Le Mans–bound) trains leave Paris's Gare Montparnasse for Chartres (50–70 mins); ticket price is around €25 round-trip. Chartres's train station on Place Pierre-Sémard puts you within walking distance of the cathedral.

★ Worship on the site of the **Cathédrale Notre-Dame,** better known as Chartres Cathedral, goes back to before the Gallo-Roman period; the crypt contains a well that was the focus of druid ceremonies. In the late 9th century Charles II (known as the Bald) presented Chartres with what was believed to be the tunic of the Virgin Mary, a precious relic that went on to attract hordes of pilgrims. The current cathedral, the sixth church on the spot, dates mainly from the 12th and 13th centuries, and was erected after the previous building, dating from the 11th century, burned down in 1194. A well-chronicled outburst of religious fervor followed the discovery that the Virgin Mary's relic had miraculously survived unsinged. Princes and paupers, barons and bourgeois gave their money and their labor to build the new cathedral. Ladies of the manor came to help monks and peasants on the scaffolding in a tremendous resurgence of religious faith that followed the Second Crusade. Just 25 years were needed for Chartres Cathedral to rise again, and it has remained substantially unchanged since.

⊠*16 cloître Notre-Dame* ☎*02–37–21–75–02* ⊕*www.chartres-tourisme. com* ⌛*Crypt €3* ☉*Cathedral 8:30–7:30, guided tours of crypt Easter–Oct., daily at 11, 2:15, 3:30, and 4:30; Nov.–Easter, daily at 11 and 4:15.*

WHERE TO STAY & EAT

$$–$$$ ✕**Moulin de Ponceau.** Ask for a table with a view of the River Eure, with the cathedral looming behind, at this 16th-century converted water mill. Better still, on sunny days you can eat outside, beneath a parasol on the

stone terrace by the water's edge—an idyllic setting. Choose from a regularly changing menu of French stalwarts such as rabbit terrine, trout with almonds, and tarte tatin, or splurge on "la trilogie" of scallops, foie gras, and langoustine. ⊠*21 rue de la Tannerie* ☎*02–37–35–30–05* ⊕*www.moulindeponceau.fr* ▭*AE, MC, V* ⊙*Closed 2 wks in Feb. No dinner Sun.*

$$–$$$ ⛴**Le Grand Monarque.** Set on Chartres's main town square not far from the cathedral, this is a delightful option with decor that remains seductively and warmly redolent of the 19th century. Built originally as a coaching inn (and today part of the Best Western chain), the hotel has numerous rooms, many attractively outfitted with brick walls, wood antiques, lush drapes, and modern bathrooms; the best are in a separate turn-of-the-20th-century building overlooking a garden, while the most atmospheric are tucked away in the attic. Downstairs, the stylishly decorated Georges restaurant serves such delicacies as pheasant pie and scallops with lentils and has prix-fixe menus starting at €29.50. It's closed Monday and there's no dinner Sunday, but the hotel's Madrigal brasserie is open daily. **Pros:** old-fashioned charm; good restaurant. **Cons:** best rooms are in an annex; stiff uphill walk to cathedral. ⊠*22 pl. des Épars* ☎*02–37–18–15–15* ⊕*www.bw-grand-monarque.com* ⏗*55 rooms* ⌂*In-room: no a/c (some), refrigerator, Wi-Fi. In-hotel: restaurant, bar, public Wi-Fi, parking (fee), some pets allowed (fee)* ▭*AE, DC, MC, V* ⏳|*BP.*

GIVERNY

8 km (5 mi) west of La Roche-Guyon on D5, 45 km (27 mi) northwest of Thoiry via D11 and D147, 70 km (44 mi) northwest of Paris.

The small village of Giverny (pronounced jee-vair-knee), just beyond the Epte River, which marks the boundary of Ile-de-France, has become a place of pilgrimage for art lovers. It was here that Claude Monet lived for 43 years, until his death at the age of 86 in 1926. Although his house is now prized by connoisseurs of 19th-century interior decoration, it's his garden, with its Japanese-inspired water-lily pond and its bridge, that remains the high point for many—a 5-acre, three-dimensional Impressionist painting you can stroll around at leisure.

GETTING HERE

Take a main-line train (departures every couple of hours) from Paris's Gare St-Lazare to Vernon (50 mins) on the Rouen–Le Havre line, then a taxi, bus, or bike (which you can hire at the café opposite Vernon station—head down to the river and take the cycle path once you've crossed the Seine) to Giverny, 6 mi away. Buses, which run April through October only, meet the trains daily and whisk you away to Giverny for €4 more.

EXPLORING

Fodor's Choice   The **Maison et Jardin Claude-Monet** *(Monet's House and Garden)* has
★   been lovingly restored. Monet was brought up in Normandy and, like many of the Impressionists, was captivated by the soft light of the Seine Valley. After several years in Argenteuil, just north of Paris, he moved

downriver to Giverny in 1883 along with his two sons, his mistress, Alice Hoschedé (whom he later married), and her six children. By 1890 a prospering Monet was able to buy the house outright. With its pretty pink walls and green shutters, the house has a warm feeling that may come as a welcome change after the stateliness of the French châteaux. Rooms have been restored to Monet's original designs: the kitchen with its blue tiles, the buttercup-yellow dining room, and Monet's bedroom on the second floor. The house was fully and glamorously restored only in the 1970s, thanks to the millions contributed by fans and patrons (who were often Americans). Reproductions of his works, and some of the Japanese prints he avidly collected, crowd its walls. During this era, French culture had come under the spell of Orientalism, and these framed prints were often gifts from visiting Japanese diplomats, whom Monet had befriended in Paris.

Three years after buying his house and cultivating its garden—which the family called the "Clos Normand"—the prospering Monet purchased another plot of land across the lane to continue his gardening experiments. The garden is a place of wonder, filled with butterflies, roosters, nearly 100,000 plants bedded every year, and more than 100,000 perennials. No matter that nearly 500,000 visitors troop through it each year; they fade into the background thanks to all the beautiful roses, purple carnations, lady's slipper, aubrieta, tulips, bearded irises, hollyhocks, poppies, daises, lambs' ears, larkspur, and azaleas, to mention just a few of the blooms (note that the water lilies flower during the latter part of July and the first two weeks of August). Even so, during the height of spring, when the gardens are particularly popular, try to visit during midweek. If you want to pay your respects, Monet is buried in the family vault in Giverny's village church. ⊠*84 rue Claude-Monet* ☎*02–32–51–28–21* ⊕*www.fondation-monet.com* ✉*Gardens and home €5.50, gardens only €4* ⊙*Apr.–Oct., Tues.–Sun. 10–6.*

WHERE TO STAY & EAT

$$ 🍴**Le Clos Fleuri.** Giverny's dire shortage of hotels is made up for by several enticing, stylish, and affordable B&Bs set up in village homes; among the best is Le Clos Fleuri, the domaine of Danielle and Claude Fouche, a charming couple (she speaks English thanks to years spent in Australia). Set in a large garden, with Giverny's picturesque church steeple looming in the background, and just 600 yards from Monet's estate and a bit farther from the Musée Américain, Le Clos beckons enticingly. Inside, three sweet and tranquil accommodations (all with their own entrance) welcome weary travelers: the "Poppies" and "Waterlilies" rooms have Louis Philippe–style beamed ceilings and both overlook the house gardens, while "Clematis" has a very dramatic cathedral ceiling. The couple adore gardening and are fonts of information about touring the immediate area. Needless to say, book in advance. **Pros:** colorful oasis in the heart of the village, gardening is in the air. **Cons:** no a/c; no pets. ⊠*5 rue de la Dîme* ☎*02–32—21—36—51* ⊕*www.giverny.org/ hotels/fouche/* 🛏*3 rooms* ⚴*In-room: no a/c, no room TV, no pets.* ▭*MC, V* ⊙*Closed Nov.–Mar.* 🍴❙*BP.*

DISNEYLAND PARIS

☾ *68 km (40 mi) southwest of Pierrefonds via D335, D136, N330, and*
Fodor's Choice *A4, 38 km (24 mi) east of Paris via A4.*
★

GETTING HERE

Take the RER from central Paris (stations at Étoile, Auber, Les Halles, Gare de Lyon, and Nation) to Marne-la-Vallée–Chessy, 100 yards from the Disneyland entrance. Journey time is around 40 minutes, and trains operate every 10–30 minutes, depending on the time of day. Note that a TGV (Train à Grande Vitesse) station links Disneyland to Lille, Lyon, Brussels, and London (via Lille and the Channel Tunnel). Disneyland's hotel complex offers a shuttle-bus service to Orly and Charles de Gaulle airports for €21.

EXPLORING

Disneyland Paris (originally called Euro Disney) is probably not what you've traveled to France to experience. But if you have a child in tow, the promise of a day here may get you through an afternoon at Versailles or Fontainebleau. If you're a dyed-in-the-wool Disney fan, you'll want to make a beeline for the park to see how it has been molded to appeal to the tastes of Europeans (Disney's "Imagineers" call it their most lovingly detailed park). And if you've never experienced this particular form of Disney showmanship, you may want to put in an appearance if only to see what all the fuss is about. When it opened, few turned up to do so; today the place is jammed with crowds, and Disneyland Paris is here to stay—and grow, with **Walt Disney Studios** opened alongside it in 2002.

Disneyland Park, as the original theme park is styled, consists of five "lands": Main Street U.S.A., Frontierland, Adventureland, Fantasyland, and Discoveryland. The central theme of each land is relentlessly echoed in every detail, from attractions to restaurant menus to souvenirs. The park is circled by a railroad, which stops three times along the perimeter. **Main Street U.S.A.** goes under the railroad and past shops and restaurants toward the main plaza; Disney parades are held here every afternoon and, during holiday periods, every evening.

Top attractions at **Frontierland** are the chilling Phantom Manor, haunted by holographic spooks, and the thrilling runaway mine train of Big Thunder Mountain, a roller coaster that plunges wildly through floods and avalanches in a setting meant to evoke Utah's Monument Valley. Whiffs of Arabia, Africa, and the West Indies give **Adventureland** its exotic cachet; the spicy meals and snacks served here rank among the best food in the park. Don't miss the Pirates of the Caribbean, an exciting mise-en-scène populated by eerily humanlike, computer-driven figures, or Indiana Jones and the Temple of Doom, a breathtaking ride that re-creates some of this luckless hero's most exciting moments.

Fantasyland charms the youngest parkgoers with familiar cartoon characters from such classic Disney films as *Snow White, Pinocchio, Dumbo,* and *Peter Pan.* The focal point of Fantasyland, and indeed Disneyland Paris, is Le Château de la Belle au Bois Dormant (Sleeping

Beauty's Castle), a 140-foot, bubblegum-pink structure topped with 16 blue- and gold-tipped turrets. Its design was allegedly inspired by illustrations from a medieval *Book of Hours*—if so, it was by way of Beverly Hills. The castle's dungeon conceals a 2-ton scaly green dragon that rumbles in its sleep and occasionally rouses to roar—an impressive feat of engineering, producing an answering chorus of shrieks from younger children. **Discoveryland** is a futuristic eye-knocker for high-tech Disney entertainment. Robots on roller skates welcome you on your way to Star Tours, a pitching, plunging, sense-confounding ride based on the *Star Wars* films. In Le Visionarium, a simulated space journey is presented by 9-Eye, a staggeringly realistic robot. One of the park's newest attractions, the Jules Verne–inspired **Space Mountain Mission 2**, pretends to catapult *exploronauts* on a rocket-boosted, comet-battered journey through the Milky Way.

Disneyland Paris is peppered with places to eat, ranging from snack bars and fast-food joints to five full-service restaurants—all with a distinguishing theme. In addition, Walt Disney Studios, Disney Village, and Disney Hotels have restaurants open to the public. But since these are outside the park, it's not recommended that you waste time traveling to them for lunch. Disneyland Paris has relaxed its no-alcohol policy and now serves wine and beer in the park's sit-down restaurants, as well as in the hotels and restaurants outside the park.

Walt Disney Studios opened next to the Disneyland Park in 2002. The theme park is divided into four "production zones." Beneath imposing entrance gates and a 100-foot water tower inspired by the one erected in 1939 at Disney Studios in Burbank, California, **Front Lot** contains shops, a restaurant, and a studio re-creating the atmosphere of Sunset Boulevard. In **Animation Courtyard,** Disney artists demonstrate the various phases of character animation; Animagique brings to life scenes from *Pinocchio* and *The Lion King*; while the Genie from *Aladdin* pilots Flying Carpets over Agrabah. **Production Courtyard** hosts the Walt Disney Television Studios; Cinémagique, a special-effects tribute to U.S. and European cinema; and a behind-the-scenes Studio Tram tour of location sites, movie props, studio decor, and costuming, ending with a visit to Catastrophe Canyon in the heart of a film shoot. **Back Lot** majors in stunts. At Armageddon Special Effects you can confront a flaming meteor shower aboard the Mir space station, then complete your visit at the giant outdoor arena with a Stunt Show Spectacular involving cars, motorbikes, and Jet Skis. ☎*01–60–30–60–30* ⊕*www. disneylandparis.com* ✉*€46, €120 for 3-day Passport; includes admission to all individual attractions within Disneyland or Walt Disney Studios, but not meals; tickets for Walt Disney Studios are also valid for admission to Disneyland during last 3 opening hrs of same day* ☉*Disneyland mid-June–mid-Sept., daily 9 am–10 pm; mid-Sept.–mid-June, weekdays 10–8, weekends 9–8; Dec. 20–Jan. 4, daily 9–8; Walt Disney Studios daily 10–6* ▭*AE, DC, MC, V.*

WHERE TO STAY

$$$–$$$$ ⊡ **Sequoia Lodge.** Ranging from superluxe to still-a-pretty-penny, Disneyland Paris has 5,000 rooms in five hotels (plus the not-so-rustic Camp Davy Crockett). Perhaps your best mid-range bet is the Sequoia Lodge—although it's just a few minutes' walk from the theme park, the mood here is quite different from the other, glitzier big hotels at the resort. Surrounded by already towering evergreens, this hotel conjures up the ambience of an American mountain lodge; in fact, you're greeted when you arrive by an open fire crackling on a giant stone hearth in the "Redwood Bar." Guest rooms have natural wooden furniture, meant to evoke log cabins; it's best to try for one in the main Montana building, with a view of Lake Disney, rather than find yourself in one of the smaller annexes ("lodges"). Facilities include indoor and outdoor pools, a whirlpool, sauna, and fitness room. For youngsters there's a children's corner, outdoor play area, and video-game room. For food, the choice is between the family-oriented, buffet-service Hunter's Grill and the more upscale Beaver Creek Tavern offering international cuisine. Free transportation to the park is available at every hotel. Packages including Disneyland lodging, entertainment, and admission are available through travel agents in Europe. Note that room prices can fluctuate strongly depending on season and school vacation period—keep hunting to find lower-priced days. **Pros:** package deals include room prices and admission to theme park; cozy, secluded feel; great pools. **Cons:** restaurants a bit ho-hum, many rooms do not have lake view. ⌖ *Centre de Réservations, B.P. 100, cedex 4, 77777 Marne-la-Vallée* ☎ *01–60–30–60–30, 407/934–7639 in U.S.* ⌖ *In-room: refrigerator. In-hotel: 3 restaurants, café, indoor pool, outdoor pool, health club, sauna, childrens' programs (3-12), bar, Wi-Fi* ⊟ *AE, DC, MC, V* ⦿ *FAP.*

THE LOIRE VALLEY

The Loire Valley, which pretty much splits France in two, has been much traversed down the ages, once by Santiago pilgrims, now by Bordeaux-bound TGV trains. It retains a backwater feel that mirrors the river's sluggish, meandering waters, although trade along the river gave rise to major towns along its banks, such as Saumur and Blois. But Tours remains the gateway to the region, not only for its central position but because the TGV links it with Paris in little more than an hour.

To the west of Tours, breathtaking châteaux dot the Indre Valley. This is the most glamorous part of the Val de Loire, and the beauty pageant begins with the fabled gardens of the Château de Villandry. Continue on to the fairy-tale châteaux of Azay-le-Rideaux, and Ussé. Farther on, no one will want to miss Saumur or Saché—perhaps the Loire's prettiest village.

PLANNING YOUR TIME

More than a region in the usual sense, the Loire Valley is just that: a valley. Although most of the sites are close to the meandering river, it's a long way—140 mi—from east to west. We suggest you divide the Valley into three segments and choose the base(s) as your time and tastes

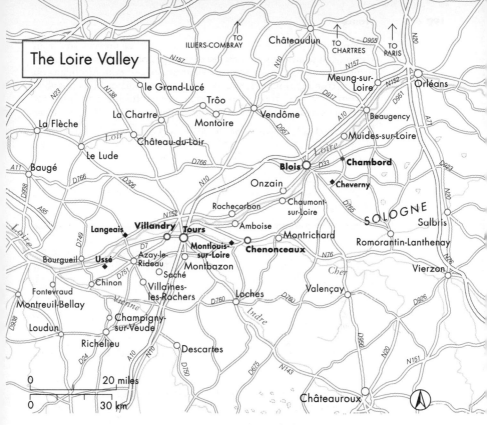

The Loire Valley

dictate. To cover the eastern Loire, including Chambord, base yourself in or near Blois. For the central Loire (Amboise, Chenonceaux, Villandry, Azay-le-Rideau), base yourself in or around Tours. For the western Loire, including Ussé, opt for pretty Saumur.

GETTING HERE & AROUND

The Loire Valley is an easy drive from Paris. A10 runs from Paris to Orléans—a distance of around 125 km (80 mi)—and on to Tours, with exits at Meung, Blois, and Amboise. After Tours, A10 veers south toward Poitiers and Bordeaux. A11 links Paris to Angers and Saumur via Le Mans. Slower but more scenic routes run from the Channel ports down through Normandy into the Loire region.

The "easiest" way to visit the Loire châteaux is by car; N152 hugs the riverbank and is excellent for sightseeing. But note that signage can be few and far between once you get off the main road, and many a traveler has horror stories about a 15-minute trip lasting two hours ("Next time, by bus and train . . ."). You can rent a car in all the large towns in the region, or at train stations in Orléans, Blois, Tours, or Angers, or in Paris.

If you chose not to drive, Tours is the gateway to the entire region because the TGV high-speed train can deposit you there from Paris in little more than an hour. Don't let the lack of a car prevent you from visiting and overnighting in the lovely villages of the region, because a surprising number can be accessed via train, bus, or taxi. Although you may be rushing around to see as many famous châteaux as possible, make time to walk through the poppy-covered hills, picnic along the riverbanks, and sample the famous local wines.

The regional rail line along the riverbank will get you to the main towns (Saumur, Tours, and Blois), while some other châteaux are served by branch lines (Chenonceau and Azay) or SNCF bus.

ESSENTIALS

Train Contacts SNCF (☎ *36–35, €0.34 per min* ⊕ *www.voyages-sncf.com*). **TGV** (⊕ *www.tgv.com*).

Visitor Information Amboise (⊠ *Quai du Général-de-Gaulle* ☎ *02–47–57–09–28* ⊕ *www.amboise-valdeloire.com*). **Blois** (⊠ *3 av. du Dr-Jean-Laigret* ☎ *02–54–90–41–41* ⊕ *www.loiredeschateaux.com*). **Saumur** (⊠ *Pl. de la Bilange* ☎ *02–41–40–20–60* ⊕ *www.ot-saumur.fr*). **Tours** (⊠ *78 rue Bernard-Palissy* ☎ *02–47–70–37–37* ⊕ *www.ligeris.com*).

TOURS

240 km (150 mi) southwest of Paris.

Little remains of Tours's own château—one of France's finest cathedrals more than compensates—but the city serves as the transportation hub for the Loire Valley. The town has mushroomed into a city of a quarter of a million inhabitants, with an ugly modern sprawl of factories, high-rise blocks, and overhead expressway junctions cluttering up the outskirts. But the timber-frame houses in **Le Vieux Tours** (Old Tours) and the attractive medieval center around place Plumereau were smartly restored after extensive damage in World War II.

GETTING HERE

The handful of direct TGV trains from Paris (Gare Montparnasse) to Tours each day cover the 150 mi in 70 minutes; fare is €39.10–€53.60 depending on time of day. Some trains involve a change in suburban St-Pierre-des-Corps. A cheaper, slower alternative is the twice-daily traditional (non-TGV) service from Gare d'Austerlitz that takes around 2 hours, 30 minutes but costs only €28.70.

The **Cathédrale St-Gatien,** built between 1239 and 1484, reveals a mixture of architectural styles. The richly sculpted stonework of its majestic, soaring, two-tower facade betrays the Renaissance influence on local château-trained craftsmen. The stained glass dates from the 13th century (if you have binoculars, bring them). Also take a look at the little tomb with kneeling angels built in memory of Charles VIII and Anne of Brittany's two children; and the **Cloître de La Psalette** (cloister), on the south side of the cathedral. ⊠ *Rue Lavoisier* ☎ *02–47–47–05–19* ⊙ *Daily 8–noon and 2–6.*

WHERE TO STAY & EAT

$$ ✕**Les Tuffeaux.** This friendly restaurant, between the cathedral and the Loire, is the city's best value. Chef Gildas Marsollier wins customers with delicious fennel-perfumed salmon, oysters in an egg sauce seasoned with Roquefort; various takes on regional chicken; and remarkable desserts. Wine is served by the glass, a great way to try some of the local *appellations*. Gentle lighting and the 17th-century wood beams and stone walls provide a soothing background. ✉*19 rue Lavoisier* ☎*02–47–47–19–89* ▤*AE, DC, MC, V* ⊘*Closed Sun. No lunch Wed.*

$$$–$$$$ ⊞**Les Hautes Roches.** *Extraordinaire* is the word for some of the dozen luxe-troglodyte rooms at this famous hotel, set 5 km (3 mi) to the east of Tours in elegant Rochecorbon (a favored country residence for rich Parisians). Studding a towering cliff-face, these amazing accommodations come replete with elegant sash windows, gas-lantern lamps, and finished marble steps. Don't expect furnishings à la Fred Flintstone: half the guest-room walls are Ice Age, but stylish fabrics, Louis Treize seating, and carved fireplaces are the main allurements. Some prefer rooms in the regular house—no cave-dwelling drama, but exquisitely comfortable and air-conditioned. The restaurant (closed Monday, no lunch Wednesday, no dinner Sunday) has an extremely staid decor, so most everyone repairs to the enchanting terrace to feast on a panoply of foie gras, fish and duck dishes, and architectonic desserts—one of the best kitchens in the Loire (don't forget to order a selection from the gigantic cheese tray). To top it all off, a small pool tempts all during the Loire's stifling summer. Rochecorbon is a treat (once you get off the main traffic road), thanks to its pretty town center, acres of vineyards, and the only "Bateaux Promenade" (boat-ride) on the Loire. **Pros:** unique troglodyte setting; river views. **Cons:** apprentice-style service; busy road nearby. ✉*86 quai de la Loire, Rochecorbon* ☎*02–47–52–88–88* ⊕*www.leshautesroches.com* ↩*15 rooms* ⚅*In-room: no a/c (some), refrigerator, Wi-Fi. In-hotel: restaurant, pool, some pets allowed (fee)* ▤*AE, DC, MC, V* ⊘*Closed mid-Jan.–mid-Mar.* ⨁*MAP.*

CHENONCEAUX

12 km (8 mi) southeast of Amboise via D81, 32 km (20 mi) east of Tours.

GETTING HERE

Three to five trains run daily between Tours and Chenonceaux (30 mins, €6.30), one of the main destinations on one of the extensive branch lines of the Loire rail system. The station is especially convenient, a minute's walk from the front gates of the château; across the tracks is the one-road town.

EXPLORING

Fodor'sChoice ★ Achingly beautiful, the **Château de Chenonceau** was built in 1520 by Thomas Bohier, a wealthy tax collector, for his wife, Catherine Briçonnet. When he went bankrupt, it passed to François I. Later, Henri II gave it to his mistress, Diane de Poitiers. After his death, Henri's not-so-understanding widow, Catherine de' Medici, expelled Diane to nearby Chaumont and took back the château. Before this time, Diane's five-arched bridge over the River Cher was simply meant as a grand ceremonial entryway leading to a gigantic château, a building never constructed. It was to Catherine, and her architect, Philibert de l'Orme, that historians owe the audacious plan to transform the bridge itself into the most unusual château in France. Two stories were constructed over the river, including an enormous gallery that runs from one end of the château to the other. This design might seem the height of originality but, in fact, was inspired by Florence's covered Ponte Vecchio bridge, commissioned by a Medici queen homesick for her native town.

July and August are the peak months at Chenonceau: only then can you escape the madding crowds by exiting at the far end of the gallery to walk along the opposite bank (weekends only), rent a rowboat to spend an hour just drifting in the river (where Diane used to enjoy her morning dips), and enjoy the **Promenade Nocturne**, an evocative son et lumière performed in the illuminated château gardens.

Before you go inside, pick up an English-language leaflet at the gate. Then walk around to the right of the main building to see the harmonious, delicate architecture beyond the formal garden—the southern part belonged to Diane de Poitiers, the northern was Catherine's—with the river gliding under the arches (providing superb "air-conditioning" to the rooms above). Inside the château are splendid ceilings, colossal fireplaces, scattered furnishings, and paintings by Rubens, del Sarto, and Correggio. The curatorial staff have delightfully dispensed with velvet ropes and adorned some of the rooms with bouquets designed in 17th-century style. As you tour the salons, be sure to pay your respects to former owner Madame Dupin, tellingly captured in Nattier's charming portrait: thanks to the affection she inspired among her proletarian neighbors, the château and its treasures survived the Revolution intact (her grave is enshrined near the northern embankment). The château's history is illustrated with wax figures in the **Musée des Cires** (Waxwork Museum) in one of the château's outbuildings. A cafeteria, tearoom, and the ambitious Orangerie restaurant handle the crowds' varied appetites. ☎02–47–23–90–07 ⊕*www.chenonceau.com* ≌*Château €10; including Musée des Cires, €11.50; night visit of gardens €5* ⊘*Mid-Mar.– mid-Sept., daily 9–7; mid-Feb.–mid-Mar. and mid-Sept.–mid-Oct., daily 9–6; mid-Oct.–mid-Feb., daily 9–5.*

WHERE TO STAY & EAT

$$–$$$ ⊞ **Le Bon Laboureur.** In 1882 this ivy-covered inn won Henry James's praise, and the author might be even more impressed today. Thanks to four generations of the Jeudi family, this remains one of the Loire's most stylish auberges. Charm is in abundance—many guest rooms are enchantingly accented in toile de Jouy fabrics, rustic wainscotting, tiny lamps, and Redouté pink-and-blue pastels. Those in the main house are comfortably sized (a few overlook the main street—avoid these if you are a light sleeper), those in the former stables are larger (some overlook a pert vegetable garden) and more renovated, but our favorites are the quaint rooms in the separate patio house near the terrace. Don't lose any time bagging a table in the "old" dining room (book this room, not the more modern ones), whose wood-beamed ceiling, glazed terra-cotta

walls, and Louis XVI chairs are almost as elegant as chef Jean-Marie Burnet's turbot with red pepper and fennel. And that is saying something: meals here are marvels. **Pros:** charming decor; outstanding food. **Cons:** small bathrooms; some rooms overlook busy road. ⊠*6 rue du Dr-Bretonneau* ☎*02–47–23–90–02* ⊕*www.amboise.com/laboureur* ⇨*25 rooms* ⊘*In-room: refrigerator, safe dial-up. In-hotel: restaurant, bar, pool, bicycles, some pets allowed (fee), no elevator* ⊟*AE, MC, V* ⊘*Closed Jan.–mid-Feb. and mid-Nov.–mid-Dec.* ⏸*MAP.*

$–$$ ⊞**La Roseraie.** The Bon Laboureur may be Chenonceaux's most famous hostelry, but this runs close for charm, thanks in part to the joyful welcome of its English-speaking hosts, Laurent and Sophie Fiorito. But let's not forget the guest rooms, many of which are designed with florals, checks, and lace, or the copious meals served in the wood-beamed dining room (where foie gras, duck with fruit and honey, and apple tart are among the specialties), or the pretty pool. Try to get a garden-side room, even if too many pink tablecloths and white chairs make the patio less than restful. If car traffic bothers you, be sure to avoid the rooms overlooking the main street. **Pros:** wonderful welcome; verdant setting. **Cons:** some rooms in separate block; garish patio-pool area. ⊠*7 rue du Dr-Bretonneau* ☎*02–47–23–90–09* ⊕*www.charmingroseraie. com* ⇨*18 rooms* ⊘*In-room: Wi-Fi. In-hotel: restaurant, bar, pool, no elevator, room service, some pets accepted (fee)* ⊟*AE, MC, V* ⊘*Closed mid-Nov.–mid-Mar.* ⏸*BP.*

CHAMBORD

★ *13 km (21 mi) northeast of Chaumont-sur-Loire via D33, 19 km (12 mi) east of Blois, 45 km (28 mi) southwest of Orléans.*

GETTING HERE

There is surprisingly little public transportation to Chambord. There are no trains, but Transports du Loir et Cher (⊕*tlcinfo.net*) offers a bus route from Blois (departures 9 AM and 1 PM) only from June 15 to September 15.

EXPLORING

The "Versailles" of the 16th century and the largest of the Loire châteaux, the **Château de Chambord** is set in the middle of a royal game forest, with just a cluster of buildings—barely a village—across the road. With a facade that is 420 feet long, 440 rooms, and 365 chimneys, a wall 32 km (20 mi) long to enclose a 13,000-acre forest (you can wander through 3,000 acres of it; the rest is reserved for wild boar and other game), this is one of the greatest buildings in France. Under François I, building began in 1519, a job that took 12 years. Later kings also used Chambord as an occasional retreat, and Louis XIV, the Sun King, had Molière perform here. In the 18th century Louis XV gave the château to the Maréchal de Saxe as a reward for his victory over the English and Dutch at Fontenoy (southern Belgium) in 1745. Now, after long neglect—all the original furnishings vanished during the French Revolution—Chambord belongs to the state.

There's plenty to see inside. You can wander freely through the vast rooms, filled with exhibits (including a hunting museum)—not all concerned with Chambord, but interesting nonetheless—and lots of Ancien Régime furnishings. The high point here is the spectacular chimney-scape—the roof terrace whose forest of Italianate towers, turrets, cupolas, gables, and chimneys has been compared to everything from the minarets of Constantinople to a bizarre chessboard. The most eye-popping time to see this roof is at night, when the château is spectacularly illuminated with slide projections; the presentation, called "Les Claires de Lune," is free and held nightly during July and August from 10 PM to midnight. During the year there's a packed calendar of activities on tap, from 90-minute tours of the park in a 4x4 vehicle (€15) to guided tours on bike or horseback. A soaring three-story-tall hall has been fitted out to offer lunches and dinners. ☎02–54–50–40–00 ⊕www.chambord. org ⊠€9.50 ⊙Apr.–Sept., daily 9–6:15; Oct.–Mar., daily 9–5:15.

WHERE TO STAY & EAT

$$$$ ✕**Relais de Bracieux.** Masterminded by chef Bernard Robin, this is one of the Loire's top restaurants. Out of the gleaming kitchens comes sumptuous nouvelle cuisine: lobster with dried tomatoes or shepherd's pie with oxtail and truffles. Connoisseurs also savor Robin's simpler fare: carp, game in season, and salmon with beef marrow. Others delight in his opulent details—accompanying your dessert you may find a fairy-tale forest of mushrooms and elves spun in sugar. The four-course menu costs €60, and there's a three-course weekday lunch menu at €30. The dining room is traditional-modern, with cane-back chairs, and the best tables are by the large windows overlooking the garden. ⊠1 av. de Chambord, 8 km (5 mi) south of Chambord, 9 km (6 mi) northeast of Cour-Cheverny on road to Chambord, Bracieux ☎02–54–46–41–22 ⊕www.relaisdebracieux.com ⩔Reservations essential, jacket and tie ⊟AE, DC, MC, V ⊙Closed mid-Dec.–end Jan., Tues. and Wed.

$–$$ ⊞**Grand St-Michel.** The village of Chambord is as tiny as its château is massive. Its leading landmark is this historic hotel, a revamped hunting lodge set across the lawn from the château. Guest rooms once boasted fabled views of the palace, but towering oak trees now block the view from all but two—room No. 5 has the best view. No matter—this is a most enjoyable hotel, with a cozy lobby, solidly bourgeois guest rooms, and a 19th-century-flavored restaurant. Adorned with mounted deer heads, majolica serving platters, and thick curtains, this room is straight out of a Flaubert novel. The fare is local, hearty (including deer pâté, pumpkin soup, and game in fall), attractively priced (especially the €21 menu), and there's a delightfully leafy terrace café facing the château. **Pros:** wondrous location opposite Chambord; impressive, good-value restaurant. **Cons:** little village has some garish tourist shops; creeky hallways, lugubrious lobby. ⊠Pl. St-Louis ☎02–54–20–31–31 ⊕www. saintmichel-chambord.com ⌨40 rooms ⎙In-room: no a/c. In-hotel: restaurant, tennis court, some pets allowed (fee), public Internet, no elevator ⊟MC, V ⊙Closed mid-Nov.–mid-Dec. ⍣BP.

BLOIS

54 km (34 mi) southwest of Orléans, 58 km (36 mi) northeast of Tours.

GETTING HERE

Trains from Paris (Gare d'Austerlitz) leave for Blois every 1 or 2 hours; the 115-mi trip (€23.50) takes between 1 hour, 30 minutes and 1 hour, 55 minutes, according to service. There are trains every two hours or so from Blois to Tours (30–40 mins, €10.40) and Orléans (25–40 mins, €9.50).

EXPLORING

Perched on a steep hillside overlooking the Loire, site of one of France's most historic châteaux, and birthplace of those delicious Poulain chocolates and gâteaux (check out the bakeries along Rue Denis-Papin and tour the nearby Poulain factory), the bustling big town of Blois is a convenient base, well served by train and highway. A signposted route leads you on a walking tour of the **Vieille Ville** (Old Town)—a romantic honeycomb of twisting alleys, cobblestone streets, and half-timber houses—but it's best explored with the help of a map available from the tourist office. The historic highlight is Place St-Louis, where you can find the Maison des Acrobats (note the timbers carved with *jongleurs,* or jugglers), Cathédrale St-Louis, and Hôtel de Villebresme, but unexpected Renaissance-era galleries and staircases also lurk in tucked-away courtyards, such as the one in the Hôtel d'Alluye, built by Florimond Robertet, finance minister to three kings and the last patron to commission a painting from Leonardo da Vinci. The best view of the town, with its château and numerous church spires rising sharply above the river, can be had from across the Loire.

The massive **Château de Blois** spans several architectural periods and is among the valley's finest. Your ticket entitles you to a guided tour—given in English when there are enough visitors who don't understand French—but you're more than welcome to roam around without a guide if you visit between mid-March and August. Before you enter, stand in the courtyard to admire examples of four centuries of architecture. On one side stand the 13th-century hall and tower, the latter offering a stunning view of the town and countryside. The Renaissance begins to flower in the Louis XII wing (built between 1498 and 1503), through which you enter, and comes to full bloom in the François I wing (1515–24). The masterpiece here is the openwork spiral staircase, painstakingly restored. The fourth side consists of the Classical Gaston d'Orléans wing (1635–38). Upstairs in the François I wing is a series of enormous rooms with tremendous fireplaces decorated with the gilded porcupine, emblem of Louis XII, the ermine of Anne of Brittany, and, of course, François I's salamander, breathing fire and surrounded by flickering flames. Many rooms have intricate ceilings and carved, gilt paneling; there's even a sad little picture of Mary, Queen of Scots. In the council room the Duke of Guise was murdered by order of Henri III in 1588. In the **Musée des Beaux-Arts** (Fine Arts Museum), in the Louis XII wing, you can find royal portraits, including Rubens's puffy portrayal of Maria de' Medici as France Personified. Every evening mid-April through mid-September, **son-et-lumière** shows are staged (in English on Wednesday). Call 02–54–90–33–33 for details; tickets cost €7 (joint ticket with château €11.50). *☎02–54–90–33–33 ☒€7.50 ⊘Apr.–Sept., daily 9–6:30; Oct.–Mar., daily 9–12:30 and 1:30–5:30.*

WHERE TO STAY & EAT

$$$$ ✗**Au Rendez-Vous des Pêcheurs.** This friendly restaurant in an old gro-
★   cery near the Loire has simple decor but impressively creative cook-
ing. Chef Christophe Cosme was an apprentice with Burgundy's late Bernard Loiseau, and his inventive dishes range from fish and seafood specialties (try the crayfish-and-parsley flan) to succulent baby pigeon on a bed of cabbage. *⊠27 rue du Foix ☎02–54–74–67–48 ⊕www. rendezvousdespecheurs.com ⌂Reservations essential ⊟AE, MC, V ⊘Closed Sun., 2 wks Aug. No lunch Mon.*

$$ ▦**Le Médicis.** Rooms at this smart little hotel 1 km (½ mi) from the château de Blois are comfortable, air-conditioned, and soundproof; all share a joyous color scheme but are individually decorated. Room No. 211 is the largest. The restaurant alone—done Renaissance-style with a coffered ceiling—makes a stay here worthwhile. Chef-owner Damien Garanger turns his innovative classic dishes into a presenta-tion—*coquilles St-Jacques* (scallops) with bitter *roquette* lettuce, roast pigeon, and thin slices of roast hare with a black-currant sauce. For des-sert, try the raspberry sorbet with brioche and chocolate sauce. The staff is cheerful, and there are 250 wines to choose from (the restaurant does not serve Sunday dinner October–March). **Pros:** soundproof rooms; excellent restaurant. **Cons:** no views; not in town center. *⊠2 allée François-Ier ☎02–54–43–94–04 ⊕www.le-medicis.com ➴10 rooms ⌂In-room: refrigerator, Wi-Fi. In-hotel: restaurant, no elevator, some pets allowed ⊟AE, DC, MC, V ⊘Closed 3 wks in Jan. ⏐◯⏐MAP.*

VILLANDRY

18 km (11 mi) west of Tours via D7, 48 km (30 mi) northwest of Loches.

Green-thumbers get weak in the knees at the mere mention of the **Château de Villandry,** a grand estate near the Cher River, thanks to its painstakingly relaid 16th-century **gardens,** now the finest example of Renaissance garden design in France. These were originally planted in 1906 by Dr. Joachim Carvallo and Anne Coleman, his American wife, whose passion resulted in two terraces planted in styles that combine the French monastic garden with Italianate models depicted in historic Du Cerceau etchings. Seen from Villandry's cliff-side walkway, the garden terraces look like flowered chessboards blown up to the nth power—a breathtaking sight.

Beyond the water garden and an ornamental garden depicting symbols of chivalric love is the famous *potager,* or vegetable garden, which stretches on for bed after bed—the pumpkins here are *les pièces de résistance.* Flower lovers will rejoice in the main *jardin à la française* (French-style garden): framed by a canal, it's a vast carpet of rare and colorful blooms planted *en broderie* ("like embroidery"), set into patterns by box hedges and paths. The aromatic and medicinal garden, its plots neatly labeled in three languages, is especially appealing. Below an avenue of 1,500 precisely pruned lime trees lies an ornamental lake that is home to two swans: not a ripple is out of place. The château interior was restored in the mid-19th century; of particular note are the painted and gilt Moorish ceiling from Toledo and the collection of Spanish pictures. Note that the quietest time to visit is usually during the two-hour French lunch break, while the most photogenic is during the **Nuits des Mille Feux** (Nights of a Thousand Lights, usually held in early July), when paths and pergolas are illuminated with myriad lanterns and a dance troupe offers a tableau vivant. There are also a Baroque music festival in late August and a gardening weekend held in early September. There is no train station at Villandry, so train to nearby Savonnières and taxi the 4-km (2½-mi) distance. ☎ *02–47–50–02–09* ⊕ *www.chateauvillandry.com* ✉ *Château and gardens €9, gardens only €6* ☉ *Château Apr.–Oct., daily 9–6; mid-Feb., Mar., and 1st half Nov., daily 9–5. Gardens Apr.–Sept., daily 9–7; Oct.–mid-Nov., daily 9–5.*

WHERE TO STAY & EAT

$$$ ⌕ **Auberge du XII***e* **Siècle.** You half expect Balzac himself to come strolling
★   in the door of this half-timber, delightfully historic auberge, so little has it changed since the 19th century. Still sporting a time-stained painted sign and its original exterior staircase, and nearly opposite the great author's country retreat, this inn retains its centuries-old dining room, now warmed by a fireplace, bouquets, and rich wood tables. Beyond this room is a modern extension—all airy glass and white walls, but not exactly what you're looking for in such historic surrounds. Balzac's ample girth attested to his great love of food, and he would no doubt enjoy the sautéed lobster or the nouvelle spins on his classic *géline* chicken favorites served here today, or the *aiguillettes de canard rosées en réduction de Chinon* (slices of duck flavored in Chinon wine). Dessert is excellent, and so is the coffee, a refreshment Balzac drank incessantly (little wonder he created more than 2,000 characters). ✉ *1 rue du Château* ☎ *02–47–26–88–77* ☐ *MC, V* ☉ *Closed 2 wks in Jan., 1 wk in June, 1 wk in Sept., 1 wk in Nov., and Mon. No dinner Sun., no lunch Tues.*

$ ⌕ **Le Cheval Rouge.** A half-minute walk from the great château of Villandry, this is a fine, comfortable, and casual hotel-restaurant. Since it's set on a major traffic route, book one of the quieter rooms at the back. The restaurant is popular with locals, who come for the surprisingly good and classic food and wine; menus start at €18.50. Best bets are the terrine of foie gras, the calf sweetbreads, and the wood-fired-grill fare. **Pros:** only hotel in town; fine dining spot. **Cons:** lackluster decor; some rooms a bit noisy. ✉ *9 rue Principale* ☎ *02–47–50–02–07* ⊕ *www.lecheval-rouge.com* ⌂ *41 rooms* ☐ *In-room: Ethernet. In-hotel: restaurant, some pets allowed (fee), no elevator* ☐ *MC, V* ☉ *Closed Jan.* ⧉ *BP.*

5

Normandy

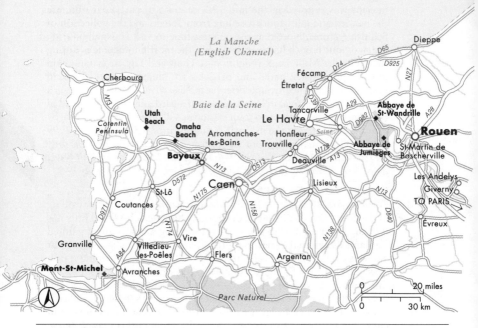

La Manche
(English Channel)

Dieppe

Cherbourg

Fécamp
Étretat

Baie de la Seine

Utah
Beach

Cotentin
Peninsula

Omaha
Beach

Arromanches-
les-Bains

Tancarville

Le Havre

Honfleur

Trouville

Abbaye de
St-Wandrille

Rouen

Abbaye de
Jumièges

St-Martin de
Boscherville

Bayeux

Deauville

St-Lô

Caen

Lisieux

Les Andelys

Giverny

TO PARIS

Coutances

Évreux

Granville

Villedieu-
les-Poêles

Vire

Flers

Argentan

Mont-St-Michel

Avranches

Parc Naturel

0   20 miles

0   30 km

NORMANDY

For generations England and Normandy vacillated and blurred, merged,
and diverged. Today you can still feel the strong flow of English culture over the Channel, from the Deauville horse races frequented by
high-born ladies in gloves, to silver spoons mounded high with teatime
cream; from the bowfront, slope-roof shops along the harbor at Honfleur to the black-and-white row houses of Rouen, which would seem
just as much at home in the setting of *David Copperfield* as they are
in *Madame Bovary*.

And just as in the British Isles, no matter how you concentrate on history and culture, sooner or later you'll find yourself beguiled by the
countryside, by Normandy's rolling green hills dotted with dairy cows
and half-timber farmhouses. Like the locals, you'll be tempted by seafood fresh off the boat, by sauces rich with crème fraîche, by cheeses
redolent of farm and pasture. And perhaps with cheeks pink from the
apple-scented country air, you'll eventually succumb to the local anti-
dote to northern damp and chill: a mug of tangy hard cider sipped by
a crackling fire, and the bracing tonic of Normandy's famous apple
brandy, Calvados.

PLANNING YOUR TIME

You won't want to miss medieval Rouen, seaside Honfleur, or magnificent Mont-St-Michel. But if you get away from these popular spots you can lose yourself along the cliff-lined coast and in the green spaces inland, where the closest thing to a crowd is a farmer with his herd of brown-and-white cows. From Rouen to the coast—the area known as Upper Normandy—medieval castles and abbeys stand guard above rolling countryside, while resort and fishing towns line the white cliffs of the Côte d'Alabâtre. Popular seaside resorts and the D-Day landing sites occupy the sandy beaches along the Côte Fleurie; apple orchards and dairy farms sprinkle the countryside of the area known as Lower Normandy. The Cotentin Peninsula to the west juts out into the English Channel. Central Normandy encompasses the peaceful, hilly region of La Suisse Normande, along the scenic Orne River.

GETTING HERE & AROUND

If driving, the A13 expressway is the gateway from Paris, running northwest to Rouen and then to Caen. From there the A84 takes you almost all the way to Mont-St-Michel.

Although this is one of the few areas of France with no high-speed rail service—perhaps because it's so close to Paris, or because it's not on a lucrative route to a neighboring country—Normandy's regional rail network is surprisingly good, meaning that most towns can be reached by train. Rouen is the hub for Upper Normandy, Caen for Lower Normandy. For Mont-St-Michel, a combination of train and bus is required. To visit the D-Day beaches, a guided minibus tour, leaving from Caen is your best bet.

ESSENTIALS

Train Contacts Gare SNCF Rouen (⊠ *Rue Jeanne d'Arc* ☎ *08-36-35-35-39*). **SNCF** (☎ *08-36-35-35-35* ⊕ *www.ter-sncf.com/uk/basse-normandie*).

Visitor Information Caen (⊠ *Pl. du Canada* ☎ *02-31-27-90-30* 🖷 *02-31-27-90-35*). **Honfleur** (⊠ *9 rue de la Ville* ☎ *02-31-89-23-30*). **Mont-St-Michel** (⊠ *Corps de Garde* ☎ *02-33-60-14-30* ⊕ *www.ot-montsaintmichel. com*). **Rouen** (⊠ *25 pl. de la Cathédrale* ☎ *02-32-08-32-40* 🖷 *02-32-08-32-44* ⊕ *www.rouentourisme.com*).

ROUEN

32 km (20 mi) north of Louviers, 130 km (80 mi) northwest of Paris, 86 km (53 mi) east of Le Havre.

"O Rouen, art thou then to be my final abode!" was the agonized cry of Joan of Arc as the English dragged her out to be burned alive on May 30, 1431. The exact spot of the pyre is marked by a concrete-and-metal cross in front of the Église Jeanne-d'Arc, an eye-catching modern church on Place du Vieux-Marché, just one of the many landmarks that make Rouen a fascinating destination. Although much of the city was destroyed during World War II, a wealth of medieval half-timber houses still lines the cobblestone streets, many of which are pedestrian-only—most famously Rue du Gros-Horloge between Place du Vieux-

Marché and the cathedral, suitably embellished halfway along with a giant Renaissance clock. Rouen is also a busy port—the fifth-largest in France.

GETTING HERE

Trains from Paris (Gare St-Lazare) leave for Rouen every two hours or so (€19.50); the 85-mi trip takes 70 minutes. Change in Rouen for Dieppe (2 hrs from Paris, €26). Several trains daily link Rouen to Caen (90 mins, €22) and Fécamp (90 mins, €12.50), sometimes requiring a change to a bus at Bréauté-Beuzeville.

Rouen is known as the City of a Hundred Spires, because many of its important edifices are churches. Lording it over them all is the highest spire in France, erected in 1876, a cast-iron tour-de-force rising 490 feet above the crossing of the **Cathédrale Notre-Dame.** The original 12th-century construction was replaced after a devastating fire in 1200; only the left-hand spire, the **Tour St-Romain** (St. Romanus Tower), survived the flames. Construction on the imposing 250-foot steeple on the right, known as the **Tour de Beurre** (Butter Tower), was begun in the 15th century and completed in the 17th, when a group of wealthy citizens donated large sums of money for the privilege of continuing to eat butter during Lent. Interior highlights include the 13th-century choir, with its pointed arcades; vibrant stained glass depicting the crucified Christ (restored after heavy damage during World War II); and massive stone columns topped by some intriguing carved faces. The first flight of the famous **Escalier de la Librairie** (Library Stairway), attributed to Guillaume Pontifs (also responsible for most of the 15th-century work seen in the cathedral), rises from a tiny balcony just to the left of the transept. ⊠*Pl. de la Cathédrale, St-Maclou* ☎*02–32–08–32–40* ☉*Daily 8–6.*

A stupendous example of high Gothic architecture is the **Abbaye St-Ouen** next to the imposing neoclassical City Hall. The abbey's stained-glass windows, dating from the 14th to the 16th century, are the most spectacular grace notes of the spare interior, along with the 19th-century pipe organ, among the finest in France. ⊠*Pl. du Général-de-Gaulle, Hôtel de Ville* ☎*02–32–08–13–90* ☉*Mid-Mar.–Oct., Wed.–Mon. 8–12:30 and 2–6; Nov.–mid-Dec. and mid-Jan.–mid-Mar., Wed. and weekends 10–12:30 and 2–4:30.*

One of Rouen's cultural mainstays is the **Musée des Beaux-Arts** *(Fine Arts Museum)*, which has a scintillating collection of paintings and sculptures from the 16th to the 20th century, including works by native son Géricault as well as by David, Rubens, Caravaggio, Velásquez, Poussin, Delacroix, Chassériau, Degas, and Modigliani, not to mention the impressive Impressionist gallery, with Monet, Renoir, and Sisley, and the Postimpressionist School of Rouen headed by Albert Lebourg and Gustave Loiseau. ⊠*Square Verdrel, Gare* ☎*02–35–71–28–40* ⊕*www. rouen-musees.com* 🎫*€3, €5.35 includes Musée Le Secq des Tournelles and Musée de la Céramique* ☉*Wed.–Mon. 10–6.*

The **Musée Le Secq des Tournelles** *(Wrought-Iron Museum)*, near the Musée des Beaux-Arts, claims to have the world's finest collection of wrought iron, with exhibits spanning from the 4th through the 19th century. The displays, imaginatively housed in a converted medieval church, include the professional instruments of surgeons, barbers, carpenters, clockmakers, and gardeners. ✉*2 rue Jacques-Villon, Gare* ☎*02–35–88–42–92* 💶*€2.30, €5.35 includes Musée des Beaux-Arts and Musée de la Céramique* 🕓 *Wed.–Mon. 10–1 and 2–6.*

Dedicated to Joan of Arc, the **Église Jeanne d'Arc** *(Joan of Arc Church)* was built in the 1970s on the spot where she was burned to death in 1431. The aesthetic merit of its odd cement-and-wood design is debatable—the shape of the roof is *supposed* to evoke the flames of Joan's fire. Not all is new, however: the church showcases some remarkable 16th-century stained-glass windows taken from the former Église St-Vincent, bombed out in 1944. The adjacent **Musée Jeanne-d'Arc** evokes Joan's history with waxworks and documents. ✉*33 pl. du Vieux-Marché, Vieux-Marché* ☎*02–35–88–02–70* ⊕*www.jeanne-darc. com* 🏛*museum €4* 🕓 *Museum: mid-Apr.–mid-Sept., daily 9:30–1 and 1:30–7; mid-Sept.–mid-Apr., daily 10–noon and 2–6:30.*

WHERE TO STAY & EAT

$$ ✗**Dufour.** Opened in 1906 on an old street near the cathedral, this wood-beamed, stone-walled restaurant is a local institution. Character is here aplenty—model ships sway overhead, a variety of quirky brass lamps bedeck the walls, the city's steepest, narrowest staircase leads up to the restrooms, and overdressed bourgeois arrive early to claim the best tables (in the corner beneath the large, pastel-paned windows). But it's Michelle Dufour's cuisine that keeps them coming back. Duckling à la rouennaise (cooked in blood) and fish are specialties—try the grilled sole or brill in cider nicely lubricated by some startlingly tasty Quincy (a white wine from south of the Loire). Among the welter of fixed-price menus, the choice extends from plump green asparagus, in lightly whisked butter sauce, to a sagging platter of Normandy cheeses, followed by a copious helping of homemade apple tart or chocolate profiteroles. ✉*67 bis, rue St-Nicolas, St-Maclou* ☎*02–35–71–90–62* ⊕*www.restaurant-dufour. com* 🚪*AE, MC, V* 🕓*Closed Mon. No dinner Sun.*

$$ ✗**La Toque d'Or.** Overlooking the Église Jeanne d'Arc, this large, bustling restaurant has been renowned since time immemorial for Normandy classics such as veal with Camembert flamed in Calvados, breast of duck glazed in cider, or spicy braised turbot. Try the excellent house-smoked salmon (they'll give you a tour of the smokehouse if you wish) and the Norman apple *tarte soufflée*. Cheaper meals are available in the *grill* upstairs. ✉*11 pl. du Vieux-Marché, Vieux-Marché* ☎*02–35–71–46–29* 🚪*AE, MC, V.*

$–$$ 🏨**Cathédrale.** There are enough half-timbered walls and beams here to fill a super-luxe hotel, but the happy news is that this a budget option—even better, it is found on a narrow pedestrian street just behind the cathedral. Ensconced in a 17th-century building, the pretty Normand decor begins in the lobby, extends to the large dining room—fitted out with grand 17th-century-style chairs and a historic fireplace—and crescendos in the flower-laden patio, a green oasis oh-so-picturesquely framed with walls of timber and stucco. Done largely in pastel patterns, guest rooms are petite but neat and comfortable; No. 7 is the largest.

Breakfast is served in the beamed tearoom. **Pros:** storybook decor; can't-be-beat location. **Cons:** small rooms; no car access. ✉ *12 rue St-Romain, St-Maclou* ☎*02–35–71–57–95* ⊕*www.hotel-de-la-cathedrale.fr* ⟿ *26 rooms* ♿ *In-room: no a/c, Wi-Fi. In-hotel: bar, no elevator, parking (fee), some pets allowed (fee)* ▭ *AE, DC, MC, V.*

\$\$\$\$ 🍽 **La Couronne.** If P.T. Barnum, Florenz Ziegfeld, and Cecil B. DeMille had put together a spot distilling all the charm and glamour of Normandy, this would be it. Behind a half-timber facade gushing geraniums, the "oldest inn in France," dating from 1345, is a sometimes-ersatz extravaganza crammed with stained leaded glass, sculpted wood beams, marble Norman chimneys, leather-upholstered chairs, and damasked curtains. The Salon Jeanne d'Arc is the largest room and has a wonderful wall-wide sash window and quaint paintings, but the only place to sit is the adorably cozy, wood-lined Salon des Rôtisseurs, an antiquarian's delight. The star attractions on Vincent Taillefer's €29 menu—lobster soufflé, sheeps' feet, duck in blood sauce—make few modern concessions. Dine at La Couronne and you'll be adding your name to a list that includes Sophia Loren, John Wayne, Jean-Paul Sartre, Salvador Dalí, and Princess Grace of Monaco. ✉ *31 pl. du Vieux-Marché, Vieux-Marché* ☎*02–35–71–40–90* ⊕*www.lacouronne.com.fr* ▭ *AE, DC, MC, V.*

BAYEUX

28 km (17 mi) northwest of Caen.

Bayeux, the first town to be liberated during the Battle of Normandy, was already steeped in history—as home to a Norman Gothic cathedral and the world's most celebrated piece of needlework: the Bayeux Tapestry. Bayeux's medieval backcloth makes it a popular base, especially among British travelers, for day trips to other towns in Normandy. Since Bayeux had nothing strategically useful like factories or military bases, it was never bombed by either side, leaving its beautiful cathedral and Old Town intact. The Old World mood is at its most boisterous during the Fêtes Médiévales, a market-cum-carnival held in the streets around the cathedral on the first weekend of July. A more traditional market is held every Saturday morning. The town is a good starting point for visits to the World War II sites; there are many custom-tour guides, but Taxis du Bessin (02–31–92–92–40) is one of the best.

Really a 225-foot-long embroidered scroll stitched in 1067, the **Bayeux Tapestry** *(Tapestry Museum)*, known in French as the *Tapisserie de la Reine Mathilde* (Queen Matilda's Tapestry), depicts, in 58 comic strip–type scenes, the epic story of William of Normandy's conquest of England in 1066, narrating Will's trials and victory over his cousin Harold, culminating in the Battle of Hastings on October 14, 1066. The tapestry was probably commissioned from Saxon embroiderers by the count of Kent—who was also the bishop of Bayeux—to be displayed in his newly built cathedral, the Cathédrale Notre-Dame. Despite its age, the tapestry is in remarkably good condition; the extremely detailed, often homey scenes provide an unequaled record of the clothes, weapons, ships, and lifestyles of the day. It's showcased in the **Musée de la**

Tapisserie; free headphones let you to listen to an English commentary about the tapestry. ⊠ *Centre Guillaume-le-Conquérant, 13 bis, rue de Nesmond* ☎*02–31–51–25–50* ⊕*www.tapisserie-bayeux.fr* ✆*€7.70, includes Musée Baron-Gérard* ☉ *May–Aug., daily 9–7; Sept.–Apr., daily 9:30–12:30 and 2–6.*

Bayeux's mightiest edifice, the **Cathédrale Notre-Dame,** is a harmonious mixture of Norman and Gothic architecture. Note the portal on the south side of the transept that depicts the assassination of English arch-bishop Thomas à Becket in Canterbury Cathedral in 1170, following his courageous opposition to King Henry II's attempts to control the church. ⊠ *Rue du Bienvenu* ☎*02–31–92–01–85* ☉ *Daily 8:30–6.*

About 16 km (10 mi) southwest of Bayeux stands the **Château de Balleroy.** A connoisseur's favorite, it was begun by architect François Mansart in 1626 and took a decade to complete. The *cour d'honneur* is marked by two stylish side pavilions—an architectural grace note adapted from Italian Renaissance models—which beautifully frame the small, but very seignorial, central mass of the house. Inside, the *salon d'honneur* is the very picture of Louis XIV decoration, while other rooms were recast in chic 19th-century style by Malcolm Forbes, who bought the château in 1970. A gallery houses the fascinating **Musée des Ballons** (Balloon Museum). The companion village to the château was designed by Mansart in one of the first examples of town planning in France. Note that the château itself is closed mid-October to mid-March, but the museum remains open. ⊠ *Balleroy* ☎*02–31–21–60–61* ⊕*www. chateau-balleroy.com* ✆*€8* ☉ *Château and museum: mid-Mar.–mid-Oct., Wed.–Mon. 10–6; museum also open mid-Oct.–mid-Mar., week-days 10–noon and 1:30–5.*

WHERE TO STAY & EAT

$$$ 🏨 **Château d'Audrieu.** This family-owned château with an elegant 18th-century facade fulfills a Hollywood notion of a palatial prop-erty: princely opulence, overstuffed chairs, wall sconces, and antiques. Guest rooms 50 and 51 have peaked ceilings with exposed-wood beams. The enchanting restaurant (closed Monday except for guests; no lunch weekdays)—all white wainscotting, crystal chandeliers, gilt accents—has an extensive wine list. Chef Cyril Haberland explores an exotic repertoire of dishes, like scallops with chestnuts and cranberry juice. **Pros:** grandiose building; magnificent gardens. **Cons:** out of the way; bland decor in some rooms, food too nouvelle-ish. ⊠ *13 km (8 mi) southeast of Bayeux off N13, Audrieu* ☎*02–31–80–21–52* ⊕*www. chateaudaudrieu.com* ⇄*28 rooms, 1 suite* ⚹ *In-room: refrigerator, safe. In-hotel: restaurant, bar, pool, no elevator, public Internet, some pets allowed* ⊟*AE, MC, V* ☉ *Closed Dec. and Jan.* ⦿*MAP.*

$$$–$$$$ 🏨 **Manoir du Carel.** The narrow slits serving as windows on the tower recall the origins of the 17th-century Manoir du Carel, set nicely half-way between Bayeux and the sea, and built as a fortified manor during the Hundred Years' War. Owner Jacques Aumond enjoys welcoming guests to his comfortable rooms with modern furnishings. The cottage on the grounds, ideal for families, has a kitchen plus a fireplace that masks a brick oven where villagers once had their bread baked. Pets are not allowed. **Pros:** delightful old building; English-speaking own-ers, wonderful breakfasts. **Cons:** no pets. ⊠*5 km (3 mi) northwest of Bayeux, Maisons* ☎*02–31–22–37–00* ⊕*www.bienvenue-au-chateau. com* ✍*2 rooms, 1 cottage* ⟁*In-room: no a/c. In-hotel: tennis court, no elevator* ⊟*DC, MC, V* ⫶⦿⫶*BP.*

$–$$ ⫶⫶**Grand Hôtel du Luxembourg.** The Luxembourg has small but adequate guest rooms, fully renovated with bland modern furniture but with chic color schemes; all but two face a courtyard garden. Happily, it has one of the town's best restaurants, Les Quatre Saisons (closed January), set in a bright-red salon, with a seasonal menu and regular favorites like sole with vanilla and regional tripe. Depending on the time of year, choose the honey-roasted ham with melted apples, or braised turbot with sage. **Pros:** quiet; central, fine restaurant. **Cons:** unprepossessing lobby; some rooms are on the dark side. ⊠*25 rue des Bouchers* ☎*02–31–92–00–04, 800/528–1234 for U.S. reservations* ☎*02–31–92–54–26* ⊕*www.adeauville.com/henri/hotelbayeux* ✍*25 rooms, 3 suites* ⟁*In-room: no a/c, Wi-Fi. In-hotel: restaurant, bar, some pets allowed (fee)* ⊟*AE, MC, V* ⫶⦿⫶*MAP.*

MONT-ST-MICHEL

Fodor's Choice
★   *44 km (27 mi) south of Granville via D973, N175, and D43; 123 km (77 mi) southwest of Caen; 67 km (42 mi) north of Rennes; 325 km (202 mi) west of Paris.*

That marvel of French architecture, Mont-St-Michel, is the most-visited sight in France after the Eiffel Tower and the Louvre. This beached mass of granite, rising some 400 feet, was begun in 709 and is crowned with the "Marvel," or great monastery, that was built during the 13th century. Fortifications were added 200 years later to withstand attacks from the English.

GETTING HERE
There are two routes to Mont-St-Michel, depending on whether you arrive from Caen or from Paris. From Caen you can take either an early-morning or an afternoon train to Pontorson (2 hrs, €22.80), the nearest station; then it's another 15 minutes to the foot of the abbey by bus or taxi. (Both leave from in front of the station.) From Paris, take the TGV from Gare Montparnasse to Rennes, then take a Courriers Bretons bus (☎02–99–19–70–80). The total journey takes 3 hours, 20 minutes (€40 if booked in advance). There are three trains daily, but the only one that allows you a full day on the Mont leaves at 6:35 AM and arrives at 9:55 AM. The other options are 11:05 (arriving 3:13 PM) and 1:05 PM (arriving 5:04).

EXPLORING
Wrought by nature and centuries of tireless human toil, this sea-sur-rounded mass of granite adorned with the soul-lifting silhouette of the **Abbaye du Mont-St-Michel** may well be your most lasting image of Nor-mandy. The abbey is perched on a 264-foot-high rock a few hundred yards off the coast: it's surrounded by water during the year's highest tides and by desolate sand flats the rest of the time. Be warned: tides

in the bay are dangerously unpredictable. The sea can rise up to 45 feet at high tide and rushes in at incredible speed—more than a few ill-prepared tourists over the years have drowned. Also, be warned that there are patches of dangerous quicksand. A causeway—to be replaced in time by a bridge, allowing the bay waters to circulate freely—links Mont-St-Michel to the mainland. Leave your car in the parking lot (€4) along the causeway, outside the main gate. Just inside you can find the tourist office, to the left, and a pair of old cannons (with cannonballs) to the right. If you're staying the night on Mont-St-Michel, take what you need in a small suitcase; you cannot gain access to your hotel by car and the parking lot is unguarded at night. The Mont's tourist office is in the Corps de Garde des Bourgeois, just to the left of the island gates.

Legend has it that the Archangel Michael appeared in 709 to Aubert, Bishop of Avranches, inspiring him to build an oratory on what was then called Mont Tombe. The rock and its shrine were soon the goal of pilgrimages. The original church was completed in 1144, but further buildings were added in the 13th century to accommodate monks as well as the hordes of pilgrims who flocked here even during the Hundred Years' War, when the region was in English hands. During the period when much of western France was subjected to English rule, the abbey remained a symbol, both physical and emotional, of French independence. Because of its legendary origins and the sheer exploit of its centuries-long construction, the abbey became known as the *"Merveille de l'Occident"* (Wonder of the Western World). The granite used to build it was transported from the nearby Isles of Chausey and hauled up to the site. The abbey's construction took more than 500 years, from 1017 to 1521. The abbey's monastic independence was undermined during the 17th century, when the monks began to flout the strict rules and discipline of their order, drifting into a state of decadence that culminated in their dispersal and the abbey's conversion into a prison, well before the French Revolution. In 1874 the former abbey was handed over to a governmental agency responsible for the preservation of historic monuments. Emmanuel Frémiet's great gilt statue of St. Michael was added to the spire in 1897. Monks now live and work here again, as in medieval times: you can join them for daily mass at 12:15.

All year long, the hour-long guided tour in English (two a day and night in high season) and French (up to two an hour) takes you through the impressive Romanesque and Gothic abbey and the spectacular **Église Abbatiale,** the abbey church, which crowns the rock, as well as the **Merveille,** a 13th-century, three-story collection of rooms and passageways. La Merveille was built by King Philippe Auguste around and on top of the monastery; on its second floor is the Mont's grandest chamber, the **Salle des Chevaliers.** Another tour, which also includes the celebrated **Escalier de Dentelle** (Lace Staircase), and the pre-Roman and exquisitely evocative **Notre-Dame-sous-Terre** is longer, has a higher ticket price, and is only given in French. Invest in at least one tour while you are here—some of them get you on top of or into things you can't see alone. If you do go it alone, stop halfway up Grande-Rue at the medieval parish church of St-Pierre to admire the richly carved side chapel with its dramatic statue of St. Michael slaying the dragon. The **Grand Degré**, a steep, narrow staircase, leads to the abbey entrance, from which a wider flight of stone steps climbs to the **Saut Gautier Terrace** (named after a prisoner who jumped to his death from it) outside the sober, dignified church. After visiting the arcaded cloisters alongside, which offer vertiginous views of the bay, you can wander at leisure, and probably get lost, among the maze of rooms, staircases, and vaulted halls. Scattered throughout the mount are four mini-museums (closed January), which cost €8 individually or €16 together. The **Logis Tiphaine** (☎02–33–60–23–34) was the home that Bertrand Duguesclin, a general fierce in his allegiance to the cause of French independence, built for his wife Tiphaine in 1365. The **Musée Historique** (⊠*Chemin de la Ronde* ☎02–33–60–07–01) traces the 1,000-year history of the Mont in one of its former prisons. The **Musée Maritime** (⊠*Grande Rue* ☎02–33–60–14–09) explores the science of the Mont's tidal bay and has a vast collection of model ships. The **Archéoscope** (⊠*Chemin de la Ronde* ☎02–33–60–14–09) explores the myths and legends of the Mont through a sound and light show. Some exhibits use wax figures fitted out in the most glamorous threads and costumes of the 15th century. If you have time for just one museum, this one makes the best introduction to the area.

The island village, with its steep, narrow streets, is best visited out of season, from September to June. In summer the hordes of tourists and souvenir sellers can be stifling. Give yourself at least half a day here, and follow your nose. The mount is full of nooks, crannies, little gardens, and echoing views from the ramparts. The Mont is spectacularly illuminated every night from dusk to midnight. ☎02–33–89–80–00 ⊕*mont-saint-michel.monuments-nationaux.fr* ≈*€8.50, €12.50 with audio guide* ⊗*May–Aug., daily 9–7; Sept.–Apr., daily 9:30–5.*

PROVENCE

As you approach Provence there's a magical moment when you finally leave the north behind: cypresses and red-tile roofs appear; you hear the screech of cicadas and breathe the scent of wild thyme and lavender. Along the highway, oleanders bloom on the center strip against a backdrop of austere, sun-filled landscapes, the very same that inspired the Postimpressionists.

This is Provence, a disarming culture of *pastis* (an anise-based aperitif), *pétanque* (lawn bowling), and shady plane trees, where dawdling is a way of life. You may seat yourself at a sidewalk café, wander aimlessly down narrow cobbled alleyways, heft melons in the morning marketplace and, after a three-hour lunch, take an afternoon snooze in the cool shade of a 500-year-old olive tree.

Plus, there are plenty of sights to see: some of the finest Roman ruins in Europe, from the Pont du Gard to the arenas at Arles and Nîmes; the pristine Romanesque abbeys of Senanque and de Montmajour; bijou chapels and weathered mas; the monolithic Papal Palace in old

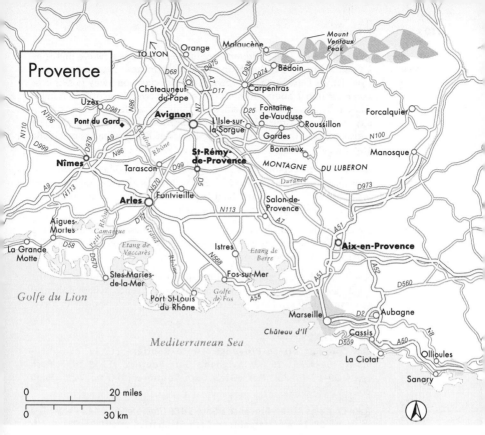

Provence

Avignon; and everywhere vineyards, pleasure ports, and sophisticated city museums. Between sights, allow yourself time to feel the rhythm of modern Provençal life, to listen to the pulsing *breet* of the insects, smell the *parfum* of a tiny country path, and feel the air of a summer night on your skin . . ..

PLANNING YOUR TIME

Provence is about lazy afternoons and spending "just one more day," and Avignon is a good place to have a practice run: it's cosmopolitan enough to keep the most energetic visitor occupied, while old and wise enough to teach the value of time. From here you can access every part of Provence easily, either by train, by bus, or by car.

You'll eat late in the south, rarely before 1 for lunch, usually after 9 at night. In summer, shops and museums may shut down until 3 or 4, as much to accommodate lazy lunches as for the crowds taking sun on the beach.

GETTING HERE & AROUND

Public transport is well organized in Provence, with most towns accessible by train or by bus. It's best to plan on combining the two—often smaller Provençal towns won't have their own train station, but a local bus connection to the train station at the nearest town over.

The high-speed TGV *Méditerranée* line ushered in a new era in Trains à Grande Vitesse travel in France; the route means that you can travel from Paris's Gare de Lyon to Avignon (first class, one-way tickets cost about €90) in 2 hours, 40 minutes, with a mere 3-hour trip to Nîmes, Aix-en-Provence, and Marseille. Not only is the idea of Provence as a day trip now possible (though, of course, not advisable), you can even whisk yourself there directly upon arrival at Paris's Charles de Gaulle airport.

If you plan to explore Provence by bus, Avignon, Marseille, Aix-en-Provence, and Arles are good bases. Avignon is also the starting point for excursion-bus tours and boat trips down the Rhône. In most cases, you can buy bus tickets on the bus itself.

Driving is also a good option, although for the first-time visitor driving on the highways in Provence can be a scary experience. It is fast . . . regardless of the speed limit.

A6–A7 (a toll road) from Paris, known as the Autoroute du Soleil—the Highway of the Sun—takes you straight to Provence, where it divides at Orange, 659 km (412 mi) from Paris; the trip can be done in a fast five or so hours.

ESSENTIALS

Bus Contacts Aix-en-Provence's Gare Routière (✉ *Av. de la Europe* ☎ *04–42–91–26–80*). **Avignon's Gare Routière** (✉ *58 bd. St-Roch* ☎ *04–90–82–07–35*). **Marseille's Gare Routière** (✉ *3 pl. Victor-Hugo* ☎ *04–91–08–16–40*).

Train Contacts Aix-en-Provence's Gare SNCF (*Train station,* ✉ *Av. Victor Hugo* ☎ *04–91–08–16–40*). **Marseilles's Gare St-Charles** (☎ *04–91–08–16–40*). **SNCF** (☎ *08–92–68–82–66, €0.34 per min* ⊕ *www.voyages-sncf.com*). **TGV** (☎ *877/284–8633* ⊕ *www.tgv.com*). **www.beyond.fr** (⊕ *www.beyond.fr*).

Visitor Information Comité Regional du Tourisme de Provence-Alpes-Côte d'Azur (✉ *12 pl. Joliette, Marseille* ☎ *04–91–56–47–00* 🖷 *04–91–56–47–01* ⊕ *www.crt-paca.fr/fre/accueil_flash.jsp*).

ARLES

If you were obliged to choose just one city to visit in Provence, lovely little Arles would give Avignon and Aix a run for their money. It's too chic to become museumlike, yet has a wealth of classical antiquities and Romanesque stonework, quarried-stone edifices and shuttered town houses, and graceful, shady Vieille Ville streets and squares. Throughout the year there are pageantry, festivals, and cutting-edge arts events. Its panoply of restaurants and small hotels makes it the ideal headquarters for forays into the Alpilles and the Camargue.

The remains of this golden age are reason enough to visit Arles today, yet its character nowadays is as gracious and low-key as it once was cutting-edge. Seated in the shade of the plane trees on Place du Forum or strolling the rampart walkway along the sparkling Rhône, you can see what enchanted Gauguin and drove Van Gogh frantic with inspiration.

If you plan to visit many of the monuments and museums in Arles, buy a *visite generale* ticket for €13.50 This covers the entry fee to the Musée de l'Arles et de la Provence Antiques and any and all of the other museums and monuments (except the independent Museon Arlaten, which charges €4). The ticket is good for the length of your stay.

36 km (22 mi) southwest of Avignon, 31 km (19 mi) east of Nîmes, 92 km (57 mi) northwest of Marseille, 720 km (430 mi) south of Paris.

GETTING HERE

If you're arriving by plane, note that Arles is roughly 20 km (12 mi) from the Nîmes-Arles-Camargue airport (☎04–66–70–49–49). The easiest way from the landing strip to Arles is by taxi (about €30). Buses run between Nîmes and Arles three times daily on weekdays and twice on Saturday (not at all on Sunday), and four buses weekdays between Arles and Stes-Maries-de-la-Mer, through Cars de Camargue (☎04–90–96–36–25). The SNCF (☎08–92–35–35–35) runs three buses Monday–Saturday from Avignon to Arles, and Cartreize (☎08–00–19–94–13 ⊕www.lepilote.com) runs a service between Marseille and Arles. Arles is along the main coastal train route, and you can take the TGV (Trains à Grands Vitesses) to Avignon from Paris and jump on the local connection to Arles. For all train information, check out www.voyages-sncf.com, or call.

EXPLORING

Église St-Trophime. Classed as a world treasure by UNESCO, this extraordinary Romanesque church alone would justify a visit to Arles, though it's continually upstaged by the antiquities around it. Its transepts date from the 11th century and its nave from the 12th; the church's austere symmetry and ancient artworks (including a stunning Roman-style 4th-century sarcophagus) are fascinating in themselves. But it's the church's superbly preserved Romanesque sculpture on the 12th-century **portal**— its entry facade—that earns international respect. Particularly remarkable is the frieze of the Last Judgment, with souls being dragged off to Hell in chains or, on the contrary, being lovingly delivered into the hands of the saints. ✉*Pl. de la République.*

Musée de l'Arles et de la Provence Antiques. (*Museum of Ancient Arles and Provence*). Though it's a hike from the center, this state-of-the-art museum is a good place to set the tone and context for your exploration of Arles. The bold, modern triangular structure (designed by Henri Ciriani) lies on the site of an enormous Roman *cirque* (chariot-racing stadium). The permanent collection includes jewelry, mosaics, town plans, and 4th-century carved sacophagi from Les Alyscamps. You can learn all about Arles in its heyday, from the development of its monuments to details of daily life in Roman times. Ask for the English-language guidebook. ✉*Presqu'île du Cirque Romain* ☎04–90–18–88–88 ⊕*www.arles-antique.cg13.fr* ✎€5.50, free 1st Sun. of every month ☺*Apr.–Oct., daily 9–7; Nov.–Apr., daily 10–5.*

WHERE TO STAY & EAT

$$ ✕ **Brasserie Nord-Pinus.** With its tile-and-ironwork interior, tastefully framed black-and-white photos, crisp white tablecloths, and its terrace packed with all the right people, this cozy-chic retro brasserie showcases light and unpretentious cooking: zucchini-flower risotto with fresh goat cheese, oven-cooked bass, or wild king prawns sautéed with pepper and cognac are some signature dishes. ⊠ *Pl. du Forum* ☎ *04–90–93–02–03* ⊟ AE, DC, MC, V ⊗ *Closed mid–Jan.–mid–Mar. Closed Tues. No lunch Wed.*

$$$ ✕ **La Chassagnette.** Sophisticated yet down-home comfortable, this restaurant is the fashionable address in the area (14 km [8 mi] south of Arles). Reputedly the only registered "organic" restaurant in Provence, this spot is fetchingly designed and has a dining area that extends outdoors, where large family-style picnic tables can be found under a wooden slate canopy overlooking the extensive gardens. The menu is based on Camarguais "tapas"—you might hit as many as 30 tapas tastes in one meal. Using ingredients that are certified organic and grown right on the property, innovative master chef Luc Rabanel also serves up open-rotisserie-style prix-fixe menus that are a refreshing mix of modern and classic French-country cuisine. ⊠ *Rte. du Sambuc, 14 km (8 mi) south of Arles on D36* ☎ *04–90–97–26–96* ⊕ *www.avignon-et-provence. com.* ⩜ *Reservations essential* ⊟ *MC, V* ⊗ *Closed Tues. and Nov.–mid-Dec. No lunch Wed.*

$$$$ ⛻ **L'Hôtel Particulier.** Once owned by the Baron of Chartrouse, this extraordinary 18th-century *hôtel particulier* (mansion) is delightfully intimate and carefully discreet behind a wrought-iron gate. Decor is sophisticated yet charmingly simple: stunning gold-framed mirrors, white-brocaded chairs, marble writing desks, artfully hung curtains, and hand-painted wallpaper. Rooms look out onto a beautifully landscaped garden; even if you take the five-minute walk into the center of town you can come back, stretch out by the pool, and listen to the birds chirp. **Pros:** off the beaten track, quiet and secluded, this hotel is a charming retreat into a modernized past – all the history with modern high-tech conveniences. **Cons:** the pool is small, which can be difficult in the middle of summer when you and every other guest want to be in the water, and no, there isn't any room service. ⊠ *4 rue de la Monnaie* ☎ *04–90–52–51–40* ⊕ *www.hotel-particulier.com* ⇜ *8 rooms* ⩜ *In-room: dial-up. In-hotel: pool, some pets allowed (fee), parking (fee)* ⊟ *AE, DC, MC, V.*

$ ⛻ **Muette.** With 12th-century exposed stone walls, a 15th-century spiral staircase, weathered wood, and an Old Town setting, a hotelier wouldn't have to try very hard to please. But the couple that owns this place does: hand-stripped doors, antiques, sparkling blue-and-white-tile baths, hair dryers, good mattresses, Provençal prints, and fresh sunflowers in every room show they care. **Pros:** the authentic, enthusiastic welcome translates to a down-home country-kitchen feel which can be a refreshing change for travellers. **Cons:** like many of the hotels near tourist attractions, the hotel has some rooms that can be very noisy, especially in the summer. ⊠ *15 rue des Suisses* ☎ *04–90–96–15–39*

⊕*www.hotel-muette.com* 📠*18 rooms* ♿*In-hotel: parking (fee), some pets allowed, Ethernet* ☰*AE, MC, V* ⊘*Closed last 2 wks in Feb.*

$$$ 🏨**Nord-Pinus.** Picasso felt right at home at this eclectic and quintessentially Mediterranean hotel on Place du Forum. The salon is dramatic with angular wrought iron, heavy furniture, colorful ceramics, and a standing collection of Peter Beard's black-and-white photographs. Rooms are individually decorated: wood or tiled floors, large bathrooms, handwoven rugs, and tasteful (if somewhat exotic) artwork are cleverly set off to stylish art director–chic advantage. Although it's hard to beat the low-key and accommodating service, this hotel may not be for everyone: traditionalists should head for the more mainstream luxuries of the Jules César. As the hotel fronts the busy Place du Forum, ask for a room in the back if noise bothers you. **Pros:** the unique atmosphere in this hotel transports you to a time less complicated, when bull-fighting was not part of the political arena, and people still dressed for dinner. **Cons:** rooms can be noisy at the front of the hotel, especially in summer, and the decor is not to everyone's taste. ⊠*Pl. du Forum* ☎*04–90–93–44–44* ⊕*www.nord-pinus.com* 📠*26 rooms* ♿*In-room: Wi-Fi, refrigerator (some). In-hotel: bar, parking (fee), some pets allowed* ☰*AE, DC, MC, V.*

NÎMES

35 km (20 mi) north of Aigues-Mortes, 43 km (26 mi) south of Avignon, 121 km (74 mi) west of Marseille.

If you've come to the south seeking Roman treasures, you need look no farther than Nîmes (pronounced *neem*): the Arènes and Maison Carrée are among continental Europe's best-preserved antiquities. But if you've come in search of a more modern mythology—of lazy, graceful Provence—give Nîmes a wide berth. It's a feisty, run-down rat race of a town, with jalopies and Vespas roaring irreverently around the ancient temple. Its medieval Vieille Ville has none of the gentrified grace of those in Arles or St-Rémy. Yet its rumpled and rebellious ways trace directly back to its Roman incarnation, when its population swelled with newly victorious soldiers flaunting arrogant behavior after their conquest of Egypt in 31 BC.

Already anchoring a fiefdom of pre-Roman *oppida* (elevated fortresses) before ceding to the empire in the 1st century BC, this ancient city grew to formidable proportions under the Pax Romana. Its next golden age bloomed under the Protestants, who established an anti-Catholic stronghold here and wreaked havoc on iconic architectural treasures—not to mention the papist minority. Their massacre of some 200 Catholic citizens in 1567 is remembered as the Michelade; many of those murdered were priests sheltered in the *évêché* (bishop's house), now the Museum of Old Nîmes.

GETTING HERE
On the Paris-Avignon-Montpellier train line, Nîmes has a direct rail link to and from Paris (about a three-hour ride). For TGV and train information go to: www.voyages-sncf.com, or call 08–36–35–35–35. The

Nîmes gare routière (bus station) is just behind the train station. Cars de Camargue (04–90–96–36–25) runs several buses to and from Arles (four daily Mon.–Sat., two Sun.). STD Gard (04–66–29–27–29) has several buses (daily except Sun.) between Avignon and Nîmes and Uzès and Nîmes. Some Uzès buses stop at Remoulins for the Pont du Gard and a few continue on to St-Quentin-la-Poterie. Note that although all the sites in Nîmes are walkable, the useful La Citadine bus (TNC 04–66–38–15–40) runs a good loop from the station and passes by many of the principal sites along the way €1.30.

EXPLORING

★ **Arènes** *(Arena)*. This arena is considered the best-preserved Roman amphitheater in the world. A miniature of the Colosseum in Rome (note the small carvings of Romulus and Remus—the wrestling gladiators— on the exterior and the intricate bulls' heads etched into the stone over the entrance on the north side), it stands more than 520 feet long and 330 feet wide, and has a seating capacity of 24,000. Bloody gladiator battles and theatrical wild-boar chases drew crowds to its bleachers. Nowadays its most colorful use is the **corrida,** the bullfight that transforms the arena (and all of Nîmes) into a sangria-flushed homage to Spain. Concerts are held year-round thanks to a new high-tech glass-and-steel structure that covers the arena for winter use. ⊠*Bd. Victor-Hugo* ☎04–66–76–72–95, 04–66–02–80–80 feria box office ⊕*www. arenesdenimes.com* ⊠€7.70; joint ticket to Arènes, Tour Magne, and Maison Carée €9.50 ☉Apr., May, and Sept., daily 9–6; Oct. and Nov., daily 9–5:30; Dec.–Mar., daily 9–4:30.

Temple de Diane *(Temple of Diana)*. This shattered Roman ruin dates from the 2nd century BC. The temple's function is unknown, though it's thought to have been part of a larger Roman complex that is still unexcavated. In the Middle Ages Benedictine nuns occupied the building before it was converted into a church. Destruction came during the Wars of Religion.

Tour Magne *(Magne Tower)*. At the far end of the Jardin de la Fontaine, you'll find the remains of a tower the emperor Augustus had built on Gallic foundations; it was probably used as a lookout post. Despite a loss of 30 feet in height over the course of time, it still provides fine views of Nîmes for anyone energetic enough to climb the 140 steps. ⊠*Quai de la Fontaine* ☎04–66–67–65–56 ⊠*Tour Magne €2.70, joint ticket to Arènes, Maison Carrée, €9.50* ☉Apr., May, and Sept., daily 9–6; June–Aug., daily 9–7; Oct. and Nov., daily 9–5:30; Dec.–Mar., daily 9–4:30.

WHERE TO STAY & EAT

$$$ ✕**Alexandre.** Rising star chef Michel Kayser adds a personal touch to local specialties at this *à la mode* modern restaurant. Wild Camargue rice soufflé with shellfish, lemon pulp, and local olive oil, or rich bull steak roasted in its own juice served with panfried mashed potatoes and anchovy *beignets* are headliners, but the menu changes by the season and by the chef's creative whimsy. Decor is elegantly spare, with a bent for luscious purples, burnt siennas, stone walls, and large bay windows.

The gardens are extensive, and often stray apricots and peaches plucked from the overhanging branches will appear on your plate, magically transformed into some delicious goody. ✉*2 rue Xavier Tronc, rte. de l'Aeroport* ☎*04–66–70–08–99* ⊕*www.michelkayser.com* 🚗*Reservations essential* ▭*AE, DC, MC, V* ⊘*Closed Mon., and no lunch Wed. and Sun. in Sept.–June. Closed Sun. and Mon. in July and Aug.*

$$ ✗**Le Jardin d'Hadrien.** This chic enclave, with its quarried white stone, ancient plank-and-beam ceiling, and open fireplace, would be a culinary haven even without its lovely hidden garden, a shady retreat for summer meals. Fresh cod crisped in salt and olive oil, zucchini flowers filled with *brandade* (the creamy, light paste of salt cod and olive oil), and a frozen parfait perfumed with licorice all show chef Alain Vinouze's subtle skills. Prix-fixe menus are €18 and €28. ✉*11 rue Enclos Rey* ☎*04–66–22–07–01* 🚗*Reservations essential* ▭*AE, MC, V* ⊘*Closed Wed. No dinner Tues. Closed Sun. and no lunch Mon. in July and Aug.*

$$$ ▦**La Maison de Sophie.** Far from the hustle of town and yet just five minutes from the Arena, this luxurious *hôtel particulier* has all the charm that the city itself often lacks. Rooms are elegant, large and airy, with a sense of tranquillity rarely found in Nîmes. The drifting scents of jasmine lead you out to the garden, where colorful bougainvilleas gently mix with the deep blue of the pool. Drift back to the lovely sitting room in the early-evening for a cup of tea or a glass of wine, and curl up with one of the many good books thoughtfully provided by your hosts. **Pros:** big-city elegance mixes nicely with country charm and quiet nights. The warm welcome of the owners makes guests feel right at home. **Cons:** it is often fully booked a long time in advance, and the pool is quite small. ✉*31 av. Carnot* ☎*04–66–70–96–10* ⊕*www.hotel-lamaisondesophie. com* 🛏*5 suites* ₫*In room: Wi-Fi. In hotel: parking (fee), some pets allowed (fee), pool* ▭*MC, V*

ST-RÉMY-DE-PROVENCE

★ *8 km (5 mi) north of Les Baux, 24 km (15 mi) northeast of Arles, 19 km (12 mi) south of Avignon.*

There are other towns as pretty as St-Rémy-de-Provence, and others in more dramatic or picturesque settings. Ruins can be found throughout the south, and so can authentic village life. Yet something felicitous has happened in this market town in the heart of the Alpilles—a steady infusion of style, of art, of imagination—all brought by people with a respect for local traditions and a love of Provençal ways. Here, more than anywhere, you can meditate quietly on antiquity, browse redolent markets with basket in hand, peer down the very row of plane trees you remember from a Van Gogh, and also enjoy urbane galleries, cosmopolitan shops, and specialty food boutiques. An abundance of chic choices in restaurants, mas, and even châteaux awaits you; the almond and olive groves conceal dozens of stone-and-terra-cotta gîtes, many with pools. In short, St-Rémy has been gentrified through and through, and is now a sort of arid, southern Martha's Vineyard or, perhaps, the Hamptons of Provence.

Before crossing into town, you'll be confronted with two of the most miraculously preserved classical monuments in France, simply called **Les Antiques.** Dating from 30 BC, the **Mausolée** (mausoleum), a wedding-cake stack of arches and columns, lacks nothing but its finial on top, yet it's dedicated to a Julian (as in Julius Caesar), probably Caesar Augustus. A few yards away stands another marvel: the **Arc Triomphal,** dating from AD 20.

Across the street from Les Antiques and set back from D5, a slick visitor center prepares you for entry into the ancient village of **Glanum** with scale models of the site in its various heydays. A good map and an English brochure guide you stone by stone through the maze of foundations, walls, towers, and columns that spread across a broad field; helpfully, Greek sites are noted by numbers, Roman ones by letters. ⊠ *Off D5, direction Les Baux* ☎ *04–90–92–23–79* 🖃 *€6.10; €7.50 includes entry to Hôtel de Sade* ☉ *Apr.–Sept., daily 9–7; Oct.–Mar., daily 10:30–noon and 2–5.*

WHERE TO STAY & EAT

$$$$ ✕ **Bistrot d'Eygalières.** Belgian chef Wout Bru's understated restaurant in nearby Eygalières has gained a reputation (and stars) for its elegant, light, and subtly balanced cuisine, like sole with goat cheese, lobster salad with candied tomatoes, and foie-gras carpaccio with summer truffles. The wine list is both eclectic and thorough, though prices are a bit on the high side. Guest rooms are very chic, very comfortable; Wout's wife, Suzy, has a wonderful eye and a welcoming disposition. Book well ahead. **Pros:** an elegant stay in the country is the best way to describe spending the night here, with lovely decor and a very good menu. **Cons:** some visitors have found the reception a little cool, and the wine list a little short. ⊠ *Rue de la République, 10 km (6 mi) southeast of St-Rémy-de-Provence on D99 then D24,Eygalières* ☎ *04–90–90–60–34* ⊕ *www.chezbru.com* ⌲ *Reservations essential* 🖙 *2 rooms, 2 suites* ⏦ *In-room: Wi-Fi, refrigerator. In-hotel: restaurant, some pets allowed, no elevator* ▤ *AE, MC, V* ☉ *Closed mid-Nov.–mid-Mar. Restaurant closed Mon. No dinner Sun. in Oct. and Nov. No lunch Tues. in May–Sept.*

$$ ✕ **La Gousse d'Ail.** It may have moved to larger premises around the corner, but thankfully, this intimate, indoor Vieille Ville hideaway and family-run bistro remains fundamentally the same. It continues to live up to its name (the Garlic Clove), serving robust, highly flavored southern dishes in hearty portions. Try the house specialties: grilled bull steak with creamed garlic or a powerful garlic-almond pesto. Aim for Wednesday night, when there's Gypsy music and jazz. ⊠ *6 bd. Marceau* ☎ *04–90–92–16–87* ▤ *AE, DC, MC, V* ☉ *Closed mid-Nov.–mid-Mar. No lunch Thurs. and Sat.*

$$$–$$$$ ⊡ **Mas de Cornud.** An American stewards the wine cellar and an Egyptian runs the kitchen, but the attitude is pure Provence: David and Nito Carpita have turned their fairly severe, stone, black-shuttered farmhouse just outside St-Rémy into a B&B filled with French country furniture and objects from around the world. The welcome is so sincere you'll feel like one of the family in no time. Table d'hôte dinners, cooking classes, and tours can be arranged. Breakfast is included, and

the minimum stay is two nights. **Pros:** the international feel makes for a convivial atmosphere around the dinner table, and the days are filled with interesting activities. **Cons:** the mas is often full, you need to book a long time in advance. ✉ *Rte. de Mas-Blanc* ☎*04–90–92–39–32* 📠*04–90–92–55–99* ⊕*www.mascornud.com* ◻*5 rooms, 1 suite* ◬*In-room: no a/c, dial-up. In-hotel: restaurant, pool, parking (no fee), some pets allowed (fee), no elevator* ⊟*No credit cards* ⊘*Closed Jan. and Feb.* ❍|*BP, MAP.*

AVIGNON

82 km (51 mi) northwest of Aix-en-Provence, 95 km (59 mi) northwest of Marseille, 224 km (140 mi) south of Lyon.

Avignon is anything but a museum; it surges with modern ideas and energy and thrives within its ramparts as it did in the heyday of the popes—and, like those radical church lords, it's sensual, cultivated, and cosmopolitan, with a taste for worldly pleasures. Avignon remained papal property until 1791, and elegant mansions bear witness to the town's 18th-century prosperity. From its famous Palais des Papes (Papal Palace), where seven exiled popes camped between 1309 and 1377 after fleeing from the corruption and civil strife of Rome, to the long, low bridge of childhood-song fame stretching over the river, you can beam yourself briefly into 14th-century Avignon, so complete is the context, so evocative the setting. Note that the free Avignon-Villeneuve PASSion (available at the tourist office) gives 20% to 50% reductions on most museums and sights after you buy the first ticket.

GETTING HERE

Taxi Radio Avignonnais (✉Pl. Pie ☎04–90–82–20–20) is the easiest way to get into town. The main bus station is on Avenue Monteclar (☎04–90–82–07–35) next to the train station. Town buses and services to the TGV station are run by TCRA (☎04–32–74–18–32 ⊕www.tcra.fr). Avignon is at the junction of the Paris–Marseille and Paris–Montpellier lines. The Gare Centre Ville has frequent links to Arles, Nîmes, Orange, Toulon, and Carcassonne. The Gare TGV (☎08–92–35–35–35 ⊕ *www.tgv.com*) is 4 km (2½ mi) south of Avignon. Train information can be found at www.voyages-sncf.com, or call 08–36–35–35–35. A bus service leaves from the station at the arrival of each train and takes passengers to the Centre Ville station, and leaves from the Centre Ville station to the TGV station every 15 minutes.

EXPLORING

★ **Palais des Papes.** This colossal palace creates a disconcertingly fortress-like impression, underlined by the austerity of its interior. Most of the original furnishings were returned to Rome with the papacy, others were lost during the French Revolution. Some imagination is required to picture its earlier medieval splendor, awash with color and with worldly clerics enjoying what the 14th-century Italian poet Petrarch called "licentious banquets." On close inspection, two different styles of building emerge at the palace: the severe **Palais Vieux** (Old Palace), built between 1334 and 1342 by Pope Benedict XII, a member of the

Cistercian order, which frowned on frivolity, and the more decorative **Palais Nouveau** (New Palace), built in the following decade by the artsy, lavish-living Pope Clement VI. The Great Court, entryway to the complex, links the two.

The main rooms of the Palais Vieux are the **Consistory** (Council Hall), decorated with some excellent 14th-century frescoes by Simone Martini; the **Chapelle St-Jean** (original frescoes by Matteo Giovanetti); the **Grand Tinel,** or Salle des Festins (Feast Hall), with a majestic vaulted roof and a series of 18th-century Gobelin tapestries; the **Chapelle St-Martial** (more Giovanetti frescoes); and the **Chambre du Cerf,** with a richly decorated ceiling, murals featuring a stag hunt, and a delightful view of Avignon. The principal attractions of the Palais Nouveau are the **Grande Audience,** a magnificent two-nave hall on the ground floor, and, upstairs, the **Chapelle Clémentine,** where the college of cardinals once gathered to elect the new pope. ☒ *Pl. du Palais* ☎ *04–90–27–50–00* ⊕ *www.palais-des-papes.com* ✉ *€9.50 entry includes choice of guided tour or individual audio guide; €11.50 includes audio-guided tour to pont St-Bénézet* ☉ *Oct.–Mar., daily 9:30–5:45; Apr.–Nov., daily 9–7; July, during theater festival until end of Aug., daily 9–9.*

Pont St-Bénézet *(St. Bénézet Bridge). This bridge* is the subject of the famous children's song: "*Sur le pont d'Avignon on y danse, on y danse . . .*" ("On the bridge of Avignon one dances, one dances . . ."). Unlike London Bridge, this one still stretches its arches across the river, but only partway: half was washed away in the 17th century. Its first stones allegedly laid with the miraculous strength granted St-Bénézet in the 12th century, it once reached all the way to Villeneuve. ☒ *Port du Rochre* ⊕ *www.avignon-tourisme.com* ✉ *€4* ☉ *Apr.–Oct., daily 9–8; Nov.–Mar., daily 9–5:45.*

★   **Rocher des Doms** *(Rock of the Domes).* Walk from the entrance to the Pont St-Bénézet along the ramparts to a spiral staircase leading to these hilltop gardens. Set with grand Mediterranean pines, this park on a bluff above town offers extraordinary views of the palace, the rooftops of Old Avignon, the Pont St-Bénézet, and formidable Villeneuve across the Rhône. On the horizon loom Mont Ventoux, the Luberon, and Les Alpilles. Often called the "cradle of Avignon," the rock's grottoes were among the first human habitations in the area. Today, the park also has a fake lake, home to some swans. ☒ *Montée du Moulin off pl. du Palais* ⊕ *www.avignon-et-provence.com.*

Petit Palais. The was the former residence of bishops and cardinals before Pope Benedict built his majestic palace—and it has a large collection of Old Master paintings. The majority are Italian works from the early-Renaissance schools of Siena, Florence, and Venice—styles with which the Avignon popes would have been familiar. Later key works to seek out include Sandro Botticelli's *Virgin and Child* and Venetian paintings by Vittore Carpaccio and Giovanni Bellini. ☒ *Pl. du Palais* ☎ *04–90–86–44–58* ⊕ *www.petit-palais.org* ✉ *€6* ☉ *Oct.–May, Wed.–Mon. 9:30–1 and 2–5:30; June–Sept., Wed.–Mon. 10–1 and 2–6.*

WHERE TO STAY & EAT

$$$ ✕ **Brunel.** Stylishly decorated in a hip, retro-bistro style with urbane shades of gray (look for the Philippe Starck chairs), this Avignon favorite entices with the passionate Provençal cooking of Avignon-born and -bred chef Roger Brunel. This is down-home bistro fare based on a sophisticated larder: parchment-wrapped mullet with eggplant, peppers, and tomatoes; pigeon roasted with basil; and caramelized apples in tender pastry. The prix-fixe menu is €38. ⊠ *46 rue de la Balance* ☎ *04–90–85–24–83* ⩐ *Reservations essential* ▤ *MC, V* ⊘ *Closed Sun. and Mon.*

$$–$$$ ✕ **Le Grand Café.** Behind the Papal Palace and set in a massive former army supply depot—note the carefully preserved industrial decay—this urban-chic entertainment complex combines an international cinema, a bar, and this popular bistro. Gigantic 18th-century mirrors and dance-festival posters hang against crumbling plaster and brick, and votive candles half-light the raw metal framework—an inspiring environment for intense film talk and a late supper of apricot lamb on a bed of semoule, goat cheese, or marinated artichokes. The prix-fixe dinner menu is €30. ⊠ *La Manutention, Cours Maria Casares* ☎ *04–90–86–86–77* ⊕ *www.legrandcafe.com* ▤ *AE, MC, V* ⊘ *Closed Jan. and Sun. and Mon.*

$$$$ ▥ **Hôtel de la Mirande.** A designer's dream of a hotel, this *petit palais* permits you to step into 18th-century Avignon, thanks to painted coffered ceilings, sumptuous antiques, and other superb *grand siècle* touches (those rough sisal mats on the floors were the height of chic back in the Baroque era). The central lounge is a skylighted and jazz-warmed haven. Upstairs, guest rooms are both gorgeous and comfy, with extraordinary baths and even more extraordinary handmade wall coverings. The costume-drama dining room is the perfect setting for the restaurant's sophisticated cuisine, one of the best in Avignon under chef Sébastien Aminot. Look for friendly Tuesday- and Wednesday-night cooking classes (€85) from guest chefs in the massive downstairs "country" kitchen. **Pros:** the convivial atmosphere of the cooking classes and the spectacular setting of the hotel, with the backdrop of the beautiful rooms, makes a heady combination. **Cons:** the service can be slow, with a touch of snobbery, and some rooms are small. ⊠ *Pl. de la Mirande* ☎ *04–90–14–20–20* *www.la-mirande.fr* ⥲ *19 rooms, 1 suite* ⩜ *In-room: Wi-Fi, refrigerator. In-hotel: restaurant, bar, parking (fee), some pets allowed (fee)* ▤ *AE, DC, MC, V.*

$$–$$$ ▥ **La Banasterie.** Hidden away on a side street by the Palais des Papes, this new upmarket B&B offers up one of the most warmly elegant welcomes in Avignon. The Parisian couple who own it ask for little more than to share their passion: *chocolat*. The handful of warmly and luxuriously decorated bedrooms all bear the names of different kinds of chocolate; the gracious hosts offer you a hot cup of sinfully rich cocoa before bed, and the most scrumptious chocolates appear nightly on your pillow. **Pros:** with its location on a quiet side street in the center of town, the warm welcome of the proud owners and the very comfortable rooms, this is a hard to beat place. **Cons:** if you are unfamiliar with Avignon, it can be hard to find, and the neighborhood is

5

a little louche. ⊠*11 rue de la Banasterie* ☎*04–32–76–30–78* ⊕*www. labanasterie.com* ⇄*2 rooms, 3 suites* ⚹*In-room: Wi-Fi, refrigerator. In-hotel: no parking* ⊟*MC, V.*

AIX-EN-PROVENCE

★ *48 km (29 mi) southeast of Bonnieux, 82 km (51 mi) southeast of Avignon, 176 km (109 mi) west of Nice, 759 km (474 mi) south of Paris.*

Gracious, posh, cultivated, and made all the more cosmopolitan by the presence of some 30,000 international university students, the lovely old town of Aix (pronounced *ex*) was once the capital of Provence. The vestiges of that influence and power—fine art, noble architecture, and graceful urban design—remain beautifully preserved today. That and its thriving market, vibrant café life, and world-class music festival make Aix vie with Arles and Avignon as one of the towns in Provence that shouldn't be missed.

Romans were first drawn here by mild thermal baths, naming the town Aquae Sextiae (Waters of Sextius) in honor of the consul who founded a camp near the source in 123 BC. Just 20 years later some 200,000 Germanic invaders besieged Aix, but the great Roman general Marius pinned them against the mountain known ever since as Ste-Victoire. Marius remains a popular local first name to this day. Under the wise and generous guidance of Roi René (King René) in the 15th century, Aix became a center of Renaissance arts and letters. At the height of its political, judicial, and ecclesiastic power in the 17th and 18th centuries, Aix profited from a surge of private building, each grand *hôtel particulier* (mansion) vying to outdo its neighbor. Its signature *cours* (courtyards) and *places* (squares), punctuated by grand fountains and intriguing passageways, date from this time.

GETTING HERE

The center of Aix is best explored on foot, but there's a municipal bus service that serves the entire town and the outlying suburbs. Most leave from La Rotonde in front of the tourism office (☎04–42–16–11–61 ⊕www.aixenprovencetourism.com), where you can also buy tickets (€1.30 one-way) and ask for a bus route map. The Aix TGV station is 10 km (6 mi) west of the city and is served by regular shuttle buses. The old Aix station is on the slow Marseille–to–Sisteron line, with trains arriving roughly every hour from Marseille St-Charles

EXPLORING

Atelier Cézanne *(Cézanne Studio).* Just north of the Vieille Ville loop you'll find this painting master's studio. After the death of his mother forced the sale of the painter's beloved country retreat, known as Jas de Bouffan, he had this studio built just above the town center. In the upstairs work space Cézanne created some of his finest paintings, including *Les Grandes Baigneuses* (*The Large Bathers*). But what is most striking is its collection of simple objects that once featured prominently in the portraits and still-lifes he created—redingote, bowler hat, ginger jar—all displayed as if awaiting his return. ⊠*9 av. Paul-Cézanne*

☎04–42–21–06–53 ⊕*www.atelier-cezanne.com* 🎫€5.50 ⊙*Apr.–*
*June., daily 10–noon and 2–6; July–Sept., daily 10–6; Oct.–Mar., daily
10–noon and 2–5.*

Cathédrale St-Sauveur. This cathedral juxtaposes so many eras of architectural history, all clearly delineated and preserved, it's like a survey
course in itself. It has a double nave—Romanesque and Gothic side by
side—and a Merovingian (5th-century) **baptistery,** its colonnade mostly
recovered from Roman temples built to honor pagan deities. Shutters
hide the ornate 16th-century carvings on the **portals,** opened by a guide
on request. The guide can also lead you into the tranquil Romanesque
cloister next door, so that you can admire its carved pillars and slender
columns. As if these treasures weren't enough, the cathedral also has
an extraordinary 15th-century triptych painted by Nicolas Froment in
the heat of inspiration following his travels in Italy and Flanders. Called
the *Triptyque du Buisson Ardent* (*Burning Bush Triptych*), it depicts the
generous art patrons King René and Queen Jeanne kneeling on either
side of the Virgin, who is poised above a burning bush. These days, to
avoid light damage, it's only opened for viewing on Tuesday from 3 to
4. (✉ *Place des Martyrs de la Resistance* ☎*04–42–23–45–65* ⊕*www.
cathedrale-aix.net*).

★ **Pavillon de Vendôme.** This extravagant Baroque villa was first built in
1665 as a "country" house for the Duke of Vendome; its position just
outside the city's inner circle allowed the duke to commute discreetly
from his official home on the Cours Mirabeau to this love nest, where
his mistress, La Belle du Canet, was comfortably installed. Though
never officially inhabited, it was expanded and heightened in the 18th
century to draw attention to the classical orders—Ionic, Doric, and
Corinthian—in its parade of neo-Grecian columns. Inside its cool, broad
chambers you can find a collection of Provençal furniture and artwork.
Note the curious two giant Atlantes that hold up the interior balcony.
✉*34 rue Celony* ☎*04–42–21–05–78* 🎫*€2* ⊙*Mar.–mid-Sept., Wed.–
Mon. 10–6; mid-Sept.–Dec. and Feb., Wed.–Mon. 1:30–5.*

WHERE TO STAY & EAT

$$$$ ✕**Le Clos de la Violette.** Whether you dine under the chestnut trees or in
the airy, pastel dining room, you can get to experience the cuisine of one
of the south's top chefs, Jean-Marc Banzo. He spins tradition into gold,
from poached crab set atop a humble white-bean-and-shrimp salad to
grilled red mullet with squid-stuffed cabbage. The restaurant isn't far
from the Atelier Cézanne, outside the Vieille Ville ring. Some feel that
the service can be erratic, but the welcome is warm. ✉*10 av. de la Violette* ☎*04–42–23–30–71* ⊕*www.closdelaviolette.fr* ⌂*Reservations
essential; jacket required* 🍴*AE, MC, V* ⊙*Closed Sun. and Mon.*

$$$ ✕**Le Passage.** This is an edgy, urban brasserie from chef Franck Dumond,
who has created a wildly popular setting in which to eat good, afford-
able food. In a sleekly converted former candy factory in the center
of town, the complex also has a bookstore, cooking workshop, and
a small wine store and épicerie all arranged around a sunny atrium.
Its New York vibe runs from the Andy Warhol reproductions in the
main dining room to the menu: roasted beef fillet with thick-cut fries

and a terrific raspberry crème brûlée with fig chutney. ⊠ *10 rue Villars* ☎*04–42–37–09–00* ⊕*www.le-passage.fr* ⚥*Reservations essential* ⊟*AE, MC, V.*

$$$$ ⚏ **Le Pigonnet.** Cézanne painted Ste-Victoire from what is now the large flower-filled garden terrace of this enchanting abode, and the likes of Princess Caroline, Iggy Pop, and Clint Eastwood have spent a few nights under the luxurious roof of the family-owned, Old World, country-style hotel. Spacious and filled with light, each room is a marvel of decoration: baby-soft plush rugs, beautifully preserved antique furniture, rich colors of burnt reds, autumn yellows, and delicate oranges. The restaurant's terrace spills out onto a sculpted green, but the inside dining salon is equally pleasant on a rainy day, thanks to its softly draped yellow curtains and large picture windows. For sheerest Provençal luxe, this place can't be beat. **Pros:** this is a hotel with a unique garden setting in the center of Aix. The welcome is friendly, the decor soft and elegant, and the rooms all have large French windows. **Cons:** the reception area has been called stuffy and old-fashioned, and some of the antiques are a little threadbare. ⊠ *5 av. du Pigonnet* ☎*04–42–59–02–90* ☎*04–42–59–47–77* ⊕*www.hotelpigonnet.com* ⚐*52 rooms, 1 apartment* ⚒*In-room: Wi-Fi, refrigerator. In-hotel: restaurant, pool, parking* ⊟*AE, MC, V.*

$$ ⚏ **Quatre Dauphins.** In the quiet Mazarin quarter, this modest but impeccable lodging inhabits a noble *hôtel particulier*. Its pretty, comfortable little rooms have been spruced up with *boutis* (Provençal quilts), Les Olivades fabrics, quarry tiles, jute carpets, and hand-painted furniture. The house-proud but unassuming owner-host bends over backward to please. **Pros:** a great favorite among regular visitors, this hotel oozes charm and friendly service. **Cons:** it is often fully booked, so reserve early. ⊠ *55 rue Roux-Alphéran* ☎*04–42–38–16–39* ☎*04–42–38–60–19* ⚐*13 rooms* ⚒*In-room: dial-up. In-hotel: some pets allowed (fee)* ⊟*MC, V.*

THE FRENCH RIVIERA

Veterans of the area know that the beauty of the French Riviera coastline is only skin deep, a thin veneer of coddled glamour that hugs the water and hides a more ascetic region up in the hills. These low-lying mountains and deep gorges are known as the arriére-pays (backcountry) for good cause: they are as aloof and isolated as the waterfront resorts are in the swim. Medieval stone villages cap rocky hills and play out scenes of Provençal life—the game of boules, the slowly savored pastis (the anise-and-licorice-flavored spirit mixed slowly with water), the farmers' market—as if the ocean were a hundred miles away. Some of them—Èze, St-Paul, Vence—have become virtual Provençal theme parks, catering to busloads of tourists day-tripping from the coast. But just behind them, dozens of hill towns stand virtually untouched, and you can lose yourself in a cobblestone maze.

The Riviera
(Côte d'Azur)

ITALY

Menton
Èze   Monte Carlo
Vence   Monaco
St-Paul-de-Vence
Nice
Grasse   Cagnes-sur-Mer
Mougins   Baie des
Anges
Antibes
Juan-les-Pins
Cannes
Iles des Lérins
Mt. Vinaigre ▲   Golfe de la
St-Raphaël   Napoule
Fréjus
Agay

Mediterranean Sea

Ste-Maxime
St-Tropez
Port-Grimaud
Gassin   Ramatuelle

20 miles

30 km

PLANNING YOUR TIME

If you're settling into one town and making day trips, it's best to divide
your time by visiting west and then east of Nice. Parallel roads along
the Corniches allow for access into towns with different personalities.
The A8 main *autoroute* (keep spare change at the ready, as it costs
€2.40 to use this road between Cannes and Nice), as well as the coastal
train, makes zipping up and down from Monaco to Fréjus-St-Raphaël
a breeze.

Visit different resort towns, but make sure you tear yourself away from
the coastal *plages* (beaches) to visit the perched villages that the region is
famed for. Venturing farther north to reach these villages, east or west,
either by the Route Napoléon (RN 98), the D995, or on the Corniche
roads, plan on at least one overnight.

And unless you enjoy jacked-up prices, traffic jams, and sardine-style
beach crowds, avoid the coast like the plague in July and August. Many
of the better restaurants simply shut down to avoid the coconut-oil
crowd, and the Estérel is closed to hikers during this flash-fire season.
Cannes books up early for the film festival in May, so aim for another
month (April, June, September, or October). Between Cannes and Menton, the Côte d'Azur's gentle microclimate usually provides moderate

winters; it's protected by the Estérel from the mistral wind that razors through places like Fréjus and St-Raphaël.

GETTING HERE & AROUND

The less budget-conscious can consider jetting around by helicopter (heliports in Monaco, Nice, Cannes, St-Tropez, and some of the hill towns) or speedboat (access to all resort towns), but affordable public transport along the Riviera boils down to the train, the bus, or renting a car. The train accesses all major coastal towns, and most of the *gares* (train stations) are in town centers. Note that only a handful of hill towns have train stations. The bus network between towns is fantastic. Renting a car is a good option, and the network of roads here is well marked and divided nicely into slow and very curvy (Bord de Mer Coast Road), faster and curvy (Route National 98), and fast and almost straight (Autoroute A8). Make sure you leave extra time if you're driving or taking the bus, as traffic is always heavy.

ESSENTIALS

Train Contacts Gare Cannes Ville (*Train station*, ✉ *Rue Jean Jaurès*). **Gare Nice Ville** (✉ *Av. Thiers* ☎ *08-36-35-35-35*). **SNCF** (☎ *08-92-68-82-66, €0.34 per min* ⊕ *www.voyages-sncf.com*). **TGV** (☎ *877/2848633* ⊕ *www.tgv.com*). **www. beyond.fr** (⊕ *www.beyond.fr*)

Visitor Information Comité Régional du Tourisme Riviera Côte d'Azur (✉ *55 promenade des Anglais, B.P. 1602, Cedex 1 Nice* ☎ *04-93-37-78-78* ⊕ *www. crt-riviera.fr*).

CANNES

6 km (4 mi) east of Mandelieu-La Napoule, 73 km (45 mi) northeast of St-Tropez, 33 km (20 mi) southwest of Nice.

A tasteful and expensive breeding ground for the upscale, Cannes is a sybaritic heaven for those who believe that life is short and sin has something to do with the absence of a tan. Backed by gentle hills and flanked to the southwest by the Estérel, warmed by dependable sun but kept bearable in summer by the cool Mediterranean breeze, Cannes is pampered with the luxurious climate that has made it one of the most popular and glamorous resorts in Europe. The cynosure of sun worshippers since the 1860s, it has been further glamorized by the modern success of its film festival.

Its bay served as nothing more than a fishing port until 1834, when an English aristocrat, Lord Brougham, fell in love with the site during an emergency stopover with a sick daughter. He had a home built here and returned every winter for a sun cure—a ritual quickly picked up by his peers. With the democratization of modern travel, Cannes has become a tourist and convention town; there are now 20 compact Twingos for every Rolls-Royce. But glamour—and the perception of glamour—is self-perpetuating, and as long as Cannes enjoys its ravishing climate and setting, it will maintain its incomparable panache. If you're a culture-lover of art of the noncelluloid type, however, you should look elsewhere—there are only two museums here: one is devoted to history, the other to a collection of dolls. Still, as his lordship instantly understood, this is a great place to pass the winter.

GETTING HERE

Cannes has one central train station, the Gare SNCF (⊠ *Rue Jean Jaures* ⊕ *www.voyages-sncf.com*). All major trains pass through here—check out the SNCF Web site for times and prices—but many of the trains run the St-Raphaël-Ventimiglia route. You can also take the TGV directly from Paris (6½ hrs). Cannes's main bus station, which is on Place de l'Hôtel-de-Ville by the port, serves all coastal destinations. Rapides Côtes d'Azur runs most of the routes out of the central bus station on Place Bernard Gentille, including Nice (1½ hrs, €6), Mougins (20 mins, €2), Grasse (45 mins, €4), and Vallauris (30 mins, €3). Within Cannes, Bus Azur runs the routes, with a ticket costing €1.30 (a weekly ticket is available). The bus line RCA (☎ *04–93–85–64–44* ⊕ *www.rca.tm.fr*) goes to Nice along the coast road, stopping in all villages along the way, and to the Nice airport, every 30 minutes, Monday–Saturday, for a maximum ticket price of €13.70 round-trip. From the Gare SNCF, RCA goes to Grasse every 30 minutes Monday–Saturday and every hour Sunday, via Mougins. The other option is any of the Transport Alpes Maritimes (TAM) buses (☎ *08–10–06–10–06* ⊕ *www.ligneda zur.com*), which service the same destinations and are now cheaper thanks to a government initiative toward communal transport and are a bargain-basement €1.30 to all destinations along the coast (but, be patient, you may not get a seat). For the big spender, Cannes also has a heliport, with a free shuttle to the center of town. Heli Air Monaco helicopters (⊕ *www.heliairmonaco.com*) leave from the airport in Nice, the ride takes about 20 minutes, and costs around €80 depending on the season.

EXPLORING

Climb up Rue St-Antoine into the picturesque Vieille Ville neighborhood known as **Le Suquet**, on the site of the original Roman *castrum.* Shops proffer Provençal goods, and the atmospheric cafés give you a chance to catch your breath; the pretty pastel shutters, Gothic stonework, and narrow passageways are lovely distractions.

The hill is crowned by the 11th-century château, housing the **Musée de la Castre,** and the imposing four-sided **Tour du Suquet** (Suquet Tower), built in 1385 as a lookout against Saracen-led invasions. ⊠ *Pl. de la Castre, Le Suquet* ☎ *04–93–38–55–26* ⊠ *€3* ⊙ *Apr.–June, Tues.–Sun. 10–1 and 2–6; July and Aug., daily 10–7; Sept., Tues.–Sun. 10–1 and 2–6.*

WHERE TO STAY & EAT

$$$ ✕**Astoux et Brun.** Deserving of its reputation for impeccably fresh *fruits de mer,* this restaurant is a beacon to all fish lovers. Well-trained staffnegotiate cramped quarters to lay down heaping seafood platters, shrimp casseroles, or piles of oysters shucked to order. Astoux is noisy, cheerful, and always busy, so arrive early to get a table and avoid the line. ⊠ *27 rue Felix Faure, La Croisette* ☎ *04–93–39–21–87* ⊟ *AE, MC, V.*

$$ ✕**Pastis.** With its sleek milk-bar decor and reasonable prices, this busy lunch hot spot is a must in Cannes. Just off the Croisette, the service

is remarkably friendly and the food good. There are nice American touches—the grilled-chicken Caesar salad, the club sandwich and home-cut fries, pizza—which can make for a comfortable day off from your gourmet voyage through Provençal cuisine. ⊠*288 rue Commandant André, Croisette* ☎ *04–92–98–95–40* ⊟ *AE, DC, MC, V.*

$$$$ ⟦⟧ **Le Cavendish Boutique Hotel.** Lovingly restored by friendly owners Christine and Guy Welter, this giddily opulent former residence of English Lord Cavendish is a true delight. Rooms—designed by Christopher Tollemar of JoJo Bistro in New York fame—are done in bright swaths of color ("wintergarden" greens, "incensed" reds) that play up both contemporary decor and 19th-century elegance. Beauty, conviviality, even smells—sheets are scented with lavender water, and fresh flowers line the entryway—all work together in genuine harmony. The downstairs bar is cozy for a nightcap, and the copious buffet breakfast is simply excellent. **Pros:** the genuine welcome at this out of the way hotel is a refreshing change from the notoriously frosty reception at other Cannes palace hotels. The obliging owners bend over backward to make your stay as stress-free as possible. **Cons:** even though the rooms all have double-paned windows, the hotel is located on the busiest street in Cannes, which means an inevitable amount of noise. It is also a 15 minute walk from the beach. ⊠*11 bd. Carnot, St-Nicolas* ☎*04–97–06–26–00* 🖷*04–97–06–26–01* ⊕*www.cavendish-cannes. com* ⟿*34 rooms* ☖*In-room: refrigerator, Wi-Fi. In-hotel: bar, parking (fee), some pets allowed (fee)* ⊟*AE, MC, V.*

$$–$$$ ⟦⟧ **Molière.** Plush, intimate, and low-key, this hotel, a short stroll from the Croisette, has pretty tile baths and small rooms in cool shades of peach, indigo, and white-waxed oak. Nearly all overlook the vast, enclosed front garden, where palms and cypresses shade terrace tables, and where breakfast, included in the price, is served most of the year. **Pros:** the charm of paying a low price for excellent service never wears thin. And when the beach becomes tiresome, the lovely garden is a real refuge. **Cons:** high season brings a lot of party vacationers, who see the garden as a perfect place to have one last nightcap. This can mean a pretty noisy night, unless you feel like going down to join in. ⊠*5 rue Molière, La Croisette* ☎*04–93–38–16–16* 🖷*04–93–68–29–57* ⊕*www.hotel-moliere.com* ⟿*24 rooms* ☖*In-room: Wi-Fi. In-hotel: bar, some pets allowed (fee)* ⊟*AE, MC, V* ⊘*Closed mid-Nov.–late Dec.* ⏻*BP.*

ST-PAUL-DE-VENCE

★ *4 km (2½ mi) south of Vence, 18 km (11 mi) northwest of Nice.*

The famous medieval village of St-Paul-de-Vence can be seen from afar, standing out like its companion, Vence, against the skyline. In the Middle Ages St-Paul was basically a city-state, and it controlled its own political destiny for centuries. But by the early 20th century St-Paul had faded to oblivion, overshadowed by the growth of Vence and Cagnes—until it was rediscovered in the 1920s when a few penniless artists began paying for their drinks at the local auberge with paintings. Those artists turned out to be Signac, Modigliani, and Bonnard, who met at the Auberge de la Colombe d'Or, now a sumptuous inn, where the walls are still covered with their ink sketches and daubs. Nowadays art of a sort still dominates in the myriad tourist traps that take your eyes off the beauty of St-Paul's old stone houses and its rampart views. The most commercially developed of Provence's hilltop villages, St-Paul is nonetheless a magical place when the tourist crowds thin. Artists are still drawn to St-Paul's light, its pure air, its wraparound views, and its honey-color stone walls, soothingly cool on a hot Provençal afternoon. Film stars continue to love its lazy yet genteel ways, lingering on the garden-bower terrace of the Colombe d'Or and challenging the locals to a game of pétanque under the shade of the plane trees. Even so, you have to work hard to find the timeless aura of St-Paul; get here early in the day to get a jump on the cars and tour buses, which can clog the main D36 highway here by noon, or plan on a stay-over. Either way, do consider a luncheon or dinner beneath the Picassos at the Colombe d'Or, even if the menu prices seem almost as fabulous as the collection.

★ Many people come to St-Paul just to visit the **Fondation Maeght,** founded in 1964 by art dealer Aimé Maeght and set on a wooded cliff top high above the medieval town. It's not just a small modern art museum but an extraordinary marriage of the arc-and-plane architecture of José Sert; the looming sculptures of Miró, Moore, and Giacometti; and a humbling hilltop perch of pines, vines, and flowing planes of water. On display is an intriguing and ever-varying parade of the work of modern masters, including the wise and funny late-life masterwork *La Vie (Life),* by Chagall. On the extensive grounds, the fountains and impressive vistas help to beguile even those who aren't into modern art. ☎04–93–32–81–63 ⊕*www.fondation-maeght.com* ☜€11 ⊙*July–Sept., daily 10–7; Oct.–June, daily 10–12:30 and 2:30–6.*

WHERE TO STAY & EAT

$$$$
Fodor's Choice
★

🖫 **La Colombe d'Or.** Considered by many to be the most beautiful inn in France, "the golden dove" occupies a lovely, rose-stone Renaissance mansion set just outside the walls of St-Paul. Walk into the dining room and you'll do a double take—yes, those are real Mirós, Bonnards, and Légers on the walls, given in payment in hungrier days when this inn was known as the heart of St-Paul's artistic revival. Back then, it was the cherished retreat of Picasso and Chagall, Maeterlinck and Kipling, Yves Montand and Simone Signoret (who met and married here). Today, a ceramic Léger mural still lords it over the famous fig-tree luncheon terrace, a Calder stabile soaks in the giant pool, and there's even a Braque in the bar. The food is yumptious if not as four-star as the crowd (this is one of the very few places where movie stars enjoy being recognized). Upstairs, the guest rooms are bewitching, replete with Louis XIII armoires, medieval four-posters, wood beams, Provençal borders, and painted murals (even rooms in the two annexes are flawless in taste). Henri Matisse once called La Colombe "a small paradise," and who are we to argue? Simply put: if you haven't visited La Colombe, you really haven't been to the French Riviera. **Pros:** where else can you have the apéritif under a real Picasso? Where else can you wander in the garden, glass of wine in hand, and stare at a real Rodin? **Cons:** the menu is give or take: sometimes there are moments of brilliance but often menu items are outshone by the art. As well, service is quite slow, which can be a good thing if you have the time to sit back and enjoy the atmosphere. ⊠*Pl. Général-de-Gaulle* ☎*04–93–32–80–02* 🖷*04–93–32–77–78* ⊕*www.la-colombe-dor.com* ☜*16 rooms, 10 suites* ♿*In-room: no a/c (some), refrigerator. In-hotel: restaurant, bar, pool, some pets allowed, public Wi-Fi, no elevator* ☐*AE, DC, MC, V* ☉*Closed Nov.–mid-Dec. and 2 wks in Jan.* ❩❙*MAP.*

$$ ⊡ **Hostellerie les Remparts.** With original stone walls, coved ceilings, light-color fabrics, a warm welcome, and perfect location in the center of the Vieille Ville, this small medieval hotel is an uncut gem. Its restaurant serves good regional specialties. In summer expect to book at least two months in advance, and at least 10 days in advance for a table. **Pros:** this is an inexpensive and friendly hotel with a lot of charm. Rooms are airy and big, and the location in the center of the old town is ideal. **Cons:** they are usually full, so you need to book way in advance. Often, even if you reserve, there is a longish wait for a table in the restaurant, especially in the summertime. ⊠*72 rue Grande* ☎*04–93–32–09–88* 🖷*04–93–32–09–88* ☜*9 rooms* ♿*In-room: no a/c, no TV, refrigerator. In-hotel: restaurant, some pets allowed, no elevator* ☐*AE, MC, V.*

NICE

As the fifth-largest city in France, this distended urban tangle is sometimes avoided, but that decision is one to be rued: Nice's waterfront, paralleled by the famous Promenade des Anglais and lined by grand hotels, is one of the noblest in France. It's capped by a dramatic hilltop château, below which the slopes plunge almost into the sea and at whose base a bewitching warren of ancient Mediterranean streets unfolds.

It was in this old quarter, now Vieux Nice, that the Greeks established a market-port in the 4th century BC and named it Nikaia. After falling to the Saracen invasions, Nice regained power and developed into an important port in the early Middle Ages. In 1388, under Louis d'Anjou, Nice, along with the hill towns behind, effectively seceded from the county of Provence and allied itself with Savoie as the Comté de Nice (Nice County). It was a relationship that lasted some 500 years, and added rich Italian flavor to the city's culture, architecture, and dialect.

Nowadays Nice strikes an engaging balance between historic Provençal grace, port-town exotica, urban energy, whimsy, and high culture. You could easily spend your vacation here, attuned to Nice's quirks, its rhythms, its very multicultural population, and its Mediterranean tides. The high point of the year falls in mid-February, when the city hosts one of the most spectacular Carnival celebrations in France (⊕www. nicecarnaval.com).

GETTING HERE

Nice is the main point of entry into the French Riviera region. It's home to the second-largest airport in France, which sits on a peninsula between Antibes and Nice, the Aéroport Nice-Côte d'Azur (☎08–20–42–33–33 ⊕www.nice.aeroport.fr)), which is 7 km (4 mi) south of the city. From the airport, you can take a bus to almost anywhere. There are a few options: RCA (☎04–93–85–64–44 ⊕www.rca. tm.fr), which is more comfortable and more expensive (☎€6) to Nice or the Transport Alpes Maritimes (TAM) buses (☎08–10–06–10–06 ⊕www.lignedazur.com), which service the same destinations and are cheaper (☎€1.30). If you plan on heading on via train, take the No. 99 bus from the airport (☎€1.30), which will take you to the main Gare SNCF train station (✉Av. Thiers ☎04–92–14–80–80). From here you can access all coastal major cities by train.

EXPLORING

Cathédrale Ste-Réparate. An ensemble of columns, cupolas, and symmetrical ornaments dominates the Vieille Ville, flanked by its own 18th-century bell tower and capped by its glossy ceramic-tile dome. The cathedral's interior, restored to a bright palette of ocher, golds, and rusts, has elaborate plasterwork and decorative frescoes on every surface. ✉Rue Ste-Réparate, Vieux Nice.

Cours Saleya. This long pedestrian thoroughfare, half street, half square, is the nerve center of Old Nice, the heart of the Vieille Ville and the stage-set for the daily dramas of marketplace and café life. Framed with 18th-century houses and shaded by plane trees, the long, narrow square bursts into a fireworks-show of color Tuesday through Sunday, when flower-market vendors roll armloads of mimosas, irises, roses, and orange blossoms into *cornets* (paper cones) and thrust them into the arms of shoppers. Cafés and restaurants, all more or less touristy, fill outdoor tables with onlookers who bask in the sun. At the far-east end, antiques and *brocantes* (collectibles) draw avid junk-hounds every Monday morning. At this end you can also find Place Félix. Little wonder the great painter Matisse lived (from 1921 to 1938) in the imposing yellow stone building that looms over the square. Indeed, you don't need to visit the city's famous Musée Matisse to understand this great artist: simply stand in the doorway of his former apartment (at 1 Place Charles Félix) and study the Place de l'Ancien Senat 10 feet away—it's a golden Matisse pumped up to the nth power.

Musée des Beaux-Arts Jules-Chéret *(Jules-Chéret Fine Arts Museum).* Although the collection here is impressive, it's the 19th-century Italianate mansion that houses it that remains the showstopper. Originally built for a member of Nice's Old Russian community, the Princess Kotschoubey, this was a Belle Époque wedding cake, replete with one of the grandest staircases on the coast, salons decorated with Neo-Pompéienne frescoes, an English-style garden, and white columns and balustrades by the dozen. After the *richissime* American James Thompson took over and the last glittering ball was held here, the villa was bought by the municipality as a museum in the 1920s. Unfortunately, much of the period decor was sold but, in its place, now hang paintings

5

by Degas, Boudin, Monet, Sisley, Dufy, and Jules Chéret, whose posters of winking *damselles* distill all the *joie* of the Belle Époque. From the Negresco Hotel area the museum is about a 15-minute walk up a gentle hill. ⊠ *33 av. des Baumettes, Centre Ville* ☏ *04–92–15–28–25* ⊕ *www. musee-beaux-arts-nice.org* 🖅 *€4* ⊘ *Tues.–Sun. 10–6.*

Palais Masséna *(Masséna Palace).* This spectacular Belle Époque building, housing the **Musée d'Art et d'Histoire** (Museum of Art and History), has recently undergone a thorough renovation. Visit the free palace gardens; set with towering palm trees, a marble bust of the handsome General Masséna, and backdropped by the wedding-cake trim of the Hotel Negresco, this is one of Nice's most imposing oases. ⊠ *Entrance at 65 rue de France, Centre Ville* ☏ *04–93–88–11–34.*

ÈZE

Fodor'sChoice ★ *2 km (1 mi) east of Beaulieu, 12 km (7 mi) east of Nice, 7 km (4½ mi) west of Monte Carlo.*

Towering like an eagle's nest above the coast and crowned with ramparts and the ruins of a medieval château, preposterously beautiful Èze (pronounced *ehz*) is unfortunately the most accessible of all the perched villages—this means crowds, many of whom head here to shop in the boutique-lined staircase-streets (happily most shops here are quite stylish, and there's a nice preponderance of bric-a-brac and vintage fabric dealers). But most come here to drink in the views, for no one can deny that this is the most spectacularly sited of all coastal promontories; if you can manage to shake the crowds and duck off to a quiet overlook, the village commands splendid views up and down the coast, one of the draws that once lured fabled visitors—lots of crowned heads, Georges Sand, Friedrich Nietzsche—and residents: Consuelo Vanderbilt, when she was tired of being duchess of Marlborough, traded in Blenheim Palace for a custom-built house here.

GETTING HERE

Èze is one of the most-visited perched villages in France, and is fairly easy to access via public transporation. Take the train from Nice's Gare SNCF (⊠ *Av. Thiers* ☏ *04–92–14–80–80* ⊕ *www.voyages-sncf.com*) to the village by the sea, Èze-bord-de-Mer. From the station there take bus No. 83 run by Lignes d'Azur bus (☏ *08–10–06–10–06* ⊕ *www.lignedazur.com*) for a shuttle (frequent departures) between the station and the sky-high village of Èze, which runs about every hour year-round and costs €1.30. Note that if you're rushing to make a train connection this shuttle trip has many switchbacks up the steep mountainside and takes a full 15 minutes. If you want to avoid the train entirely and are traveling on a budget, from the Nice Gare Routière (⊠ *5 bd. Jean Jaures* ⊕ *www. rca.tm.fr*) you can take the Transport Alpes Maritimes's 100 TAM bus (☏ *04–93–85–61–81* ⊕ *www.cg06.fr/transport/transports-tam. html*), which costs €1.30 and will take you directly to Èze-bord-de-Mer along the lower Corniche, where you can then transfer to the No. 83 shuttle listed above. Otherwise, you can take the RCA bus No. 112 at Nice's Gare Routière, which goes from Nice to Beausoleil and stops at Èze Village. By car, you should arrive using the Moyenne Corniche, which deposits you near the gateway to Èze Village; buses (from Nice and Monaco) also use this highway.

EXPLORING

From the crest-top **Jardin Exotique** *(Tropical Garden),* full of rare succulents, you can pan your videocam all the way around the hills and waterfront. But if you want a prayer of a chance of enjoying the magnificence of the village's arched passages, stone alleyways, and ancient fountains, come at dawn or after sunset—or (if you have the means) stay the night—but spend the midday elsewhere. The church of **Notre-Dame,** consecrated in 1772, glitters inside with Baroque retables and altarpieces. Èze's tourist office, on Place du Général-de-Gaulle, can direct you to the numerous footpaths—the most famous being the **Sentier Friedrich Nietzsche**—that thread Èze with the coast's three corniche highways. Note that Èze Village is the famous hilltop destination, but Èze extends down to the coastal beach and the township of Èze-sur-Mer.

5

WHERE TO STAY & EAT

$$$ 🖬 **La Bastide aux Camelias.** There are only four bedrooms in this lovely B&B, each individually decorated with softly draped fabrics and polished antiques. Close to Èze Village, set in the nearby Grande Corniche Park, it offers up the usual run of breathtaking views, but also has inviting, less precipitous ones of garden greenery. Have the complimentary breakfast on the picture-perfect veranda, indulge in a cooling drink by the gorgeous pool, or stretch out on the manicured lawn. There's even a spa, hamman, and Jacuzzi included in the price. It's gentle hospitality that's much in demand, however, so reserve well in advance. **Pros:** the heart-warming welcome is down-home country genuine, and the breakfast is scrumptious. **Cons:** its distance from the village is significant, and there are few options for restaurants that do not require a car. ⊠*Rte. de l'Adret* 🕿*04–93–41–13–68* 🖷*04–93–41–13–68* ⊕*www. bastideauxcamelias.com* ⇝*4 rooms* ⌂*In-room: refrigerator. In-hotel: pool, parking (no fee), some pets allowed (fee), public Internet, no elevator* ❙⊙❙*BP.*

$$$$ 🖬 **Château de la Chèvre d'Or.** Giving substance to Riviera fairy tales, this
Fodor'sChoice extraordinary Xanadu seems to sit just below cloud level like a Hilton
★ penthouse, medieval-style. The "château of the Golden Goat" is actually an entire stretch of the village, streets and all, bordered by gardens that hang to the mountainside in nearly Babylonian style. The fanciest guest rooms come replete with stone boulder walls, peasant-luxe fireplaces, faux 15th-century panel paintings, and chandeliered rock-grotto bathrooms, but nearly all have exposed stone and exposed beams (even the cheapest have views over Èze's charming tile roofs). No fewer than three restaurants, ranging from the nicely affordable grill to the *haute gastronomique* grand dining room with its panoramic view, spoil you for choice. Children are just plain spoiled with the hotel's fabulous Chicken in Coca-Cola sauce (€30). The swimming pool alone, clinging like a swallow's nest to the hillside, may justify the investment, as do the liveried footmen who greet you at the village entrance to wave you, VIP-style, past the cattle drive of tourists, or the breakfast on the spectacular

terrace, which seems to levitate over the bay. **Pros:** the spectacular setting is unique along the coast, with eagle nest views out to the sea and an infinity pool dropping off the cliff. **Cons:** service can be cool, and attention is certainly paid to the type of car you drive and the label on your clothes. ✉ *Rue du Barri* ☎ *04–92–10–66–66* 🖷 *04–93–41–06–72* ⊕ *www.chevredor.com* ↩ *23 rooms, 9 suites* ⚫ *In-room: refrigerator, Wi-Fi. In-hotel: 3 restaurants, bar, tennis court, pool, some pets allowed* ▤ *AE, DC, MC, V* ⊗ *Closed Dec.–Feb.*

Germany

Octoberfest, Munich

WORD OF MOUTH

"I think München is one of the most beautiful European cities, beautifully preserved architecture, lovely residential quarters and friendly people."

—AndrewDavid

"If you are interested in modern architecture, ancient and modern art collections, a vibrant city scene and music, Berlin is the place to go."

—JudyC

WHAT'S WHERE

1 Munich. If Germany has a second capital, it must be Munich. Munich boasts wonderful opera, theater, museums, and churches, but the main appeal is its laid-back attitude, appreciated best in its parks, cafés, and beer gardens.

2 The Bavarian Alps. Majestic peaks, lush green pastures, and frescoed houses brightened by flowers make for Germany's most photogenic region. Quaint villages like Garmisch-Partenkirchen and Berchtesgaden have preserved their charming historic architecture, but nature is the prime attraction here.

3 The Romantic Road. The Romantische Strasse is more than 355 km (220 mi) of soaring castles, medieval villages, half-timber houses, and imposing churches, all set against a pastoral backdrop. It features such top destinations as Rothenburg-ob-der-Tauber and Schloss Neuschwanstein, King Ludwig II's fantastical castle.

4 Heidelberg. This medieval town is quintessential Germany, full of cobblestone alleys, half-timber houses, vineyards, castles, wine pubs, and Germany's oldest university—all of which attract crowds of camera-carrying vacationers. Still, if you're looking for a fairy-tale town, Heidelberg is it.

5 Frankfurt. Nicknamed "Mainhattan" because of its many skyscrapers, Frankfurt is Germany's financial center and transportation hub.

6 The Rhineland. The "castle and vineyard" banks of the Rhine, between Wiesbaden and Bonn, gave rise to the expression "Rhine Romance." And the Mosel, the Rhine's most important tributary, is said to be one of the most hauntingly beautiful river valleys in the world.

7 Hamburg. Hamburg loves to be snobbish, and the Hanseaten can be a little stiff, but the city, dominated by lakes, canals, the river Elbe, and Germany's biggest harbor, is undeniably beautiful. World-class museums of modern art, the Reeperbahn, and a new warehouse quarter make Hamburg worth the visit.

8 Berlin. No trip to Germany is complete without a visit to Berlin—Europe's hippest city. Dirty, noisy, and overcrowded, it has an intensity that makes it a unique laboratory for new trends and ideas. Check out the cutting-edge art exhibits, stage dramas, musicals, rock bands, and two cities' worth of world-class museums and historical sights.

GERMANY IS A LAND OF half-timbered towns, of pastoral landscapes with castles, churches, and hillside vineyards. It is filled with a strong sense of cultural heritage, where men still don lederhosen and women dirndls. There is beer by the stein under the shade of old chestnut trees. No matter what part of Germany you visit, there are thick layers of history: from Roman relics to medieval castles and from Baroque palaces to communist-era apartment blocks.

But, for all the tradition, Germany is a modern country. High speed autobahns and clean, comfortable trains link its cities. It's a leader in avant-garde fashion, culture, and art, which is reflected in its many museums and the vibrant Berlin art scene.

Germans take their leisure seriously. The great outdoors has always been an important escape, with great beaches in the north, Alpine skiing in the south, and world-class hiking almost anywhere. Big-city party neighborhoods like Frankfurt's apple wine district, Sachsenhausen, and Hamburg's seedy Reeperbahn help shake things up.

Each season has its own festivities: Fasching (Carnival) heralds the end of winter, and beer gardens open up with the first warm rays of sunshine, fall is celebrated with the Munich Oktoberfest, and Advent brings the colorful Christmas markets.

WHEN TO GO

The tourist season in most of Germany runs from May through October, when the weather is at its best. Prices are generally higher in summer, so consider visiting during the off-season to save money (but be aware that the weather is often cold and some attractions are closed or have shorter hours in winter). Munich's Oktoberfest comes late in the tourist season, in late September and early October. The Christmas markets, held in just about every city during the month leading up to Christmas, are another off-season draw. The riotous Fasching season takes place during the weeks before Ash Wednesday in February or March.

It's wise to avoid cities at times of major trade fairs, when attendees commandeer all hotel rooms and prices soar. You can check trade-fair schedules with the German National Tourist Office.

GETTING HERE & AROUND

BY AIR

Most flights into Germany arrive at Frankfurt's Flughafen Frankfurt Main (FRA) or Munich's Flughafen München (MUC). Flying time to Frankfurt is 1½ hours from London, and 7½ hours from New York.

Domestic air travel can be cheaper than the train. Air Berlin, German-Wings, and Lufthansa offer very low fares on inter-German routes, and a number of airlines, notably Ryanair, offer cheap flights into Germany from secondary European airports.

TOP REASONS TO GO

Munich's Oktoberfest: For 12 days at the end of September and into early October, Munich hosts the world's largest beer bonanza, one that now welcomes over 6 million visitors and serves more than 5 million liters of beer.

Herrenchiemsee Castle: Take the old steam-driven ferry to the island in Chiemsee in the Bavarian Alps to visit the last and most glorious castle of Mad King Ludwig.

An Overnight in a Medieval Town: Dodge the daytrippers by spending the night in Rothenburg-ob-der-Tauber. Patrol the city walls with the night watchman, explore the streets in the morning light (perfect for photos), then get out of town before the tour buses begin to arrive.

Neuschwanstein castle: Look familiar? Walt Disney modeled the castle in *Sleeping Beauty* and later the Disneyland castle itself on Neuschwanstein. Its position at the end of the Romantic Road only adds to its fairy-tale quality.

Heidelberg Castle: The architectural highlight of the region's most beautiful castle is the Renaissance courtyard—harmonious, graceful, and ornate.

Sachsenhausen: Frankfurt's "South Bank"—with acres of gourmet restaurants, fast-food joints, live music establishments, and bars—is one big outdoor party in summer.

Rhine in Flames: These massive fireworks displays take place in the towns along the Rhine from May to September.

Harbor Cruises: Take a bumpy harbor tour through Hamburg's Freihafen, absorb the grand scenery of the city, and gaze at the seafaring steel hulks ready to ply the oceans of the world.

Museum Island: The architectural monuments and art treasures here will take you from an ancient Greek altar to a Roman market town to 18th-century Berlin and back in a day.

Christmas Markets: You can catch the spirit of the season throughout December when just about every German city sets up its outdoor Christmas market.

BY BOAT

The American-owned Viking River Cruises company tours the Rhine, Main, Elbe, and Danube rivers, with four- to eight-day itineraries. Köln–Düsseldorfer Deutsche Rheinschiffahrt (KD Rhine Line) offers trips of one day or less on the Rhine and Mosel.

BY BUS

Deutsche Touring, a subsidiary of the Deutsche Bahn (German Railroad), travels from Germany to other European countries, and offers one-day tours along the Castle Road and the Romantic Road. Towns of every size have local buses, which often link up with trams (streetcars) and electric railway (S-bahn) and subway (U-bahn) services. Fares sometimes vary according to distance, but a ticket usually allows you to transfer freely between the various forms of transportation. Most cities issue day tickets at special rates

BY CAR

Entry formalities for motorists are few: all you need is proof of insurance, an international car-registration document, and a U.S., Canadian, Australian, or New Zealand driver's license. All major car-rental companies are represented in Germany. Gasoline is very expensive (about $8.50 per gallon), and parking in major cities can be difficult. Nevertheless, a car gives you the flexibility to explore on your own. The marvelous autobahn network enables you to get wherever you want to go in a hurry. ■TIP➔**Most cars in Germany have manual transmission, and more and more cities are banning environmentally unfriendly cars from their city centers.**

BY TRAIN

Travel by train is the most relaxing and often fastest way to go. The super-fast InterCity Express (ICE) trains of the Deutsche Bahn (DB–German Railroad) are frequent, fast, and comfortable. They serve all the large cities, and there are plenty of local trains to get you to small towns as well. Tickets are always less expensive online or from ticket machines than from ticket agents, and tickets with flexible schedules cost more. The DB's Web site will tell you everything you want to know, in English, about trains, departures, connections, and prices.

There are a number of ways the savvy traveler can save. Ask about the "Sparpreis 50" and "Sparpreis 25" tickets, which get you, respectively, half or a fourth off the ticket price under certain conditions. There's also the "Happy Weekend Ticket" providing unlimited travel for up to five persons on local trains. Eurail and German Rail passes get you unlimited train travel, but you must order them before you leave for Europe.

ESSENTIALS

Airport Information Berlin: **Schönefeld** (*SXF* ☎ *01805/000–186 €0.12 per minute* ⊕ *www.berlin-airport.de*). **Tegel** (*TXL* ☎ *01805/000–186 €0.12 per minute* ⊕ *www. berlin-airport.de*). Frankfurt: **Flughafen Frankfurt Main** (*FRA* ☎ *01805/372–4636, 069/6900 from outside Germany* ⊕ *www.airportcity-frankfur.de*)Hamburg: **Hamburg International Airport** (*HAM* ☎ *040/50750* ⊕ *www.ham.airport.de*). Munich: **Flughafen München** (*MUC* ☎ *089/97500* ⊕ *www.munich-airport.de*).

Boat Contacts **KD Rhine Line** (☎ *0221/208–8318* ⊕ *www.k-d.com*). **Viking River Cruises** (☎ *1-800-304-9616* ⊕ *www.vikingrivercruises.com*).

Bus Contacts **Deutsche Touring** (☎ *069/790–350* ⊕ *www.deutsche-touring. de*).

Train Contacts **Deutsche Bahn** (*German Rail* ☎ *0800/150–7090 for automated schedule information, 11861 for 24-hr hotline €0.39 per minute, 491805/996–633 from outside Germany €0.12 per minute* ⊕ *www.bahn.de*). **Eurail** (⊕ *www.eurail. com*).

Visitor & Tour Information **German National Tourist Board** (☎ 069/974640 ⊕ www.germany-tourism.de).

ABOUT THE RESTAURANTS

BUDGET EATING TIPS

Imbiss (snack) stands can be found in almost every busy shopping street, in parking lots, train stations, and near markets. It's acceptable to bring sandwich fixings to a beer garden so long as you order a beer there. Butcher shops, known as *Metzgereien*, often serve warm snacks or very good sandwiches, and restaurants in department stores are especially recommended for appetizing and inexpensive lunches.

MEALS & MEAL TIMES

In most restaurants it is not customary to wait to be seated. Simply walk in and take any unreserved space. When in doubt, ask. German restaurants do not automatically serve water. If you order water, you will be served mineral water and be expected to pay for it.

Most hotels serve a buffet-style breakfast (*Frühstück*), which is often included in the price of a room. By American standards, a cup (*Tasse*) of coffee in Germany is very petite. Order a pot or *Kännchen* if you want a larger portion. For lunch (*Mittagessen*) many fine restaurants have special, affordable lunch menus. Dinner (*Abendessen*) is usually accompanied by a potato or spätzle side dish. A salad sometimes comes with the main dish.

Gaststätten (restaurants) normally serve hot meals from 11:30 AM to 9 PM; many places stop serving hot meals between 2 PM and 6 PM, although you can still order cold dishes. Once most restaurants have closed, your options are limited. Take-out pizza parlors and Turkish eateries often stay open later. Failing that, your best option is a train station or a gas station with a convenience store. Many bars serve snacks.

PAYING

German waitstaff are more than happy to split the check so that everyone can pay individually. Credit cards are generally accepted only in moderate to expensive restaurants, so check before sitting down. You will need to ask for the bill (*die Rechnung*), and when you get it pay the waiter directly rather than leaving any money or tip on the table.

RESERVATIONS & DRESS

It's a good idea to make reservations ahead of time. Very few restaurants nowadays require gentlemen to wear a jacket and tie, but even when Germans dress casually, their look is generally crisp and neat.

TIPPING

When you get the check, round up to the next even euro. Add a euro if the total is more than €20. For larger amounts, rounding up and adding 5% is appropriate. Don't leave a tip on the table.

WINE, BEER & SPIRITS

The German Wine Academy (⊕ *www.germanwineusa.org*) promotes the country's wines and can supply you with information on wine festivals and visitor-friendly wineries. It also arranges six-day guided winery tours in spring and fall.

6

Germany holds its brewers to a "purity law" that dates back to 1516. Bavaria is not the only place to try beer. Beer connoisseurs will want to travel to places further north like Bamberg, Erfurt, Cologne, or Görlitz, where smaller breweries produce top-notch brews.

WHAT IT COSTS IN EUROS					
	¢	$	$$	$$$	$$$$
RESTAURANT	under €9	€9–€15	€16–€20	€21–€25	over €25

Restaurant prices are per person for a main course at dinner.

ABOUT THE HOTELS

The standards of German hotels are very high. You can nearly always expect courteous and polite service and clean and comfortable rooms. Most hotels in Germany do not have air-conditioning, nor do they need it.

BED AND BREAKFASTS
Bed and Breakfasts remain one of the most popular options. They are often inexpensive, although the price depends on the amenities. For breakfast, expect some muesli, cheese, cold cuts, jam, butter, and hard-boiled eggs at the very least. Some B&Bs also supply lunch baskets if you intend to go hiking, or arrange an evening meal for a very affordable price.

BOOKING
Tourist offices will help you make bookings for a nominal fee, but they may have difficulty doing so after 4 PM in high season and on weekends. Most hotels and other lodgings require you to give your credit-card details before they will confirm your reservation. Get confirmation in writing and have a copy of your confirmation handy when you check in. Most hotels allow children under a certain age to stay in their parents' room at no extra charge, but others charge for them as extra adults; find out the cutoff age ahead of time.

BUDGET STAYS
The *Gasthöfe* (country inns that serve food and also have rooms) offer a great value. An alternative to hotels are *Fremdenzimmer,* meaning simply "rooms," normally in private houses. Look for the sign reading ZIMMER FREI (room available) or ZU VERMIETEN (to rent) on a green background; a red sign reading BESETZT means there are no vacancies. The country's hundreds of *Jugendherbergen* (youth hostels) are among the most efficient and up-to-date in Europe.

Prices are generally higher in summer, so consider visiting during the off-season (but be aware that some attractions are closed or have shorter hours in winter). Most resorts offer between-season (*Zwischensaison*) and edge-of-season (*Nebensaison*) rates, and tourist offices can provide lists of hotels that offer low-price weekly packages (*Pauschal-angebote*).

Room rates are by no means inflexible and depend very much on supply and demand. Many expensive city hotels cut their prices dramatically on weekends and when business is quiet, but major events like Munich's Oktoberfest and the Frankfurt Book Fair will drive prices through the ceiling.

WHAT IT COSTS IN EUROS					
	¢	$	$$	$$$	$$$$
HOTEL	under €50	€50–€100	€101–€175	€176–€225	over €225

Hotel prices are for two people in a standard double room, including tax and service.

PLANNING YOUR TIME

Frankfurt, the transportation hub for most travelers to Germany, is a good place to begin both as a destination in itself and with its proximity to the celebrated parts of the Rhine, Heidelberg, and the beginning of the Romantic Road.

If the romance of castles, cobblestone streets, half-timber houses, and quaint towns entices, head to the Romantic Road, Heidelberg, or the Bavarian Alps. Must-sees include two of King Ludwig's castles, Neuschwanstein and Schloss Herrenchiemsee. It's a good idea to get an early start at major attractions like Heidelberg's castle, Rothenburg-ob-der-Tauber, and Neuschwanstein.

If fashion, culture, and art are your dish, head to one of the four big cities: Munich, Hamburg, Frankfurt, or Berlin. Check out the museums by day, like the Kunsthalle and the Deichtorhallen in Hamburg or Museum Island in Berlin. Then indulge in the rich nightlife of Hamburg's titillating Reeperbahn, Frankfurt's Sachsenhausen, Munich's beer gardens, or Berlin's hip bar scene.

MUNICH

Munich represents what the rest of the world sees as "typical Germany," embodied in the world-famous Oktoberfest, traditional *lederhosen* (leather pants), busty Bavarian waitresses in *dirndls* (traditional dresses), beer steins, and sausages. There are myriad local brews to say *Prost* (cheers) with, either in one of the cavernous beer halls or a smaller *Kneipe,* a bar where all types get together to eat and drink. When the first rays of spring sun begin warming the air, follow the locals to their beloved beer gardens, shaded by massive chestnut trees.

Respect for the fine arts is another Munich hallmark. The city's appreciation of the arts began under the kings and dukes of the Wittelsbach Dynasty, which ruled Bavaria for more than 750 years until 1918. The Wittelsbach legacy is alive and well in the city's fabulous museums, the Opera House, the Philharmonic, and of course, the Residenz, the city's royal palace.

PLANNING YOUR TIME

Set aside at least a whole day for the Old Town, hitting Marienplatz when the glockenspiel plays at 11 AM or noon before a crowd of spectators. The pedestrian zone can get maddeningly full between noon and 2, when everyone in town seems to be taking a quick shopping break. If you've already seen the glockenspiel, try to avoid the area at that time. Avoid the museum crowds in Schwabing and Maxvorstadt by visiting as early in the day as possible. All Munich seems to discover an interest in art on Sunday, when most municipal and state-funded museums are free; you might want to take this day off from culture and have a late breakfast or brunch at the Elisabethmarkt. Some beer gardens and taverns have Sunday-morning jazz concerts. Many Schwabing bars have happy hours between 6 and 8—a relaxing way to end your day.

GETTING HERE & AROUND

BY AIR

Munich's International Airport is 28 km (17 mi) northeast of the city center and has excellent air service from all corners of the world. An excellent train service links the airport with downtown. The bus service is slower than the S-bahn link and more expensive. A taxi from the airport costs around €50.

BY BUS

Touring Eurolines buses arrive at and depart from Arnulfstrasse, north of the main train station in the adjoining Starnberger Bahnhof. Check their excellent Web site for trips to Neuschwanstein and the Romantic Road.

BY CAR

From the north (Nürnberg or Frankfurt), leave the autobahn at the Schwabing exit. From Stuttgart and the west, the autobahn ends at Obermenzing, Munich's most westerly suburb. The autobahns from Salzburg and the east, Garmisch and the south, and Lindau and the southwest all join the Mittlerer Ring (city beltway). When leaving any autobahn, follow the signs reading STADTMITTE for downtown Munich.

BY PUBLIC TRANSIT

Munich has an efficient and well-integrated public-transportation system, consisting of the U-bahn (subway), the S-bahn (suburban railway), the Strassenbahn (streetcars), and buses. Marienplatz forms the heart of the U-bahn and S-bahn network.

BY TAXI

Munich's cream-color taxis are numerous. Hail them in the street or phone for one. A novel way of seeing the city is to hop on one of the bike-rickshaws. The bike-powered two-seater cabs operate between Marienplatz and the Chinesischer Turm in the Englischer Garten.

BY TRAIN

All long-distance rail services arrive at and depart from the Hauptbahnhof. For travel information at the main train station, go to the DB counter at the center of the main departures hall. With more complex questions, go to the EurAide office, which serves English-speaking train travelers.

ESSENTIALS

Air Contacts Flughafen München (*MUC* ☎ *089/97500* ⊕ *www.munich-airport. de*).

Bus Contacts Touring Eurolines (Administrative offices ✉ *Hirtenstr. 14, Leopoldvorstadt* ☎ *089/ 8898–9513* ⊕ *www.touring.de*).

Taxi Contacts Taxi (☎ *089/21610 or 089/19410*).

Visitor Information Hauptbahnhof (✉ *Bahnhofpl. 2, Leopoldvorstadt* ⊕ *www. munich-tourist.de*). **Info-Service** (✉ *Marienpl., City Center* ☎ *089/2332–8242*). **Tourismusverband München-Oberbayern** (*Upper Bavarian Regional Tourist Office* ✉ *Radolfzeller 15* ☎ *089/829–2180*).

EXPLORING MUNICH

Munich is a wealthy city—and it shows. At times this affluence may come across as conservatism. But what makes Munich so unique is that it's a new city superimposed on the old. Hip neighborhoods are riddeld with traditional locales, and flashy materialism thrives together with a love of the outdoors.

CITY CENTER

❹ Deutsches Museum *(German Museum)*. Aircraft, vehicles, locomotives,

Fodor's Choice and machinery fill a monumental building on an island in the Isar River.

★ The immense collection is spread out over 19 km (12 mi) of corridors,

Ⓒ six floors of exhibits, and 30 departments. Children now have their own area, the **Kinderreich,** where they can learn about modern technology and science through numerous interactive displays (parents must accompany their child). The most technically advanced planetarium in Europe has up to six shows daily and includes a Laser Magic display. The Internet café on the third floor is open daily 9–3. ■ **TIP→ To arrange for a two-hour tour in English, call at least two weeks in advance.** The Verkehrszentrum (Center for Transportation), on the former trade fair grounds at the Theresienhöhe (where Oktoberfest is held), has been completely renovated and houses an amazing collection of the museum's transportation exhibits. It is open until 8 PM on Thursday. ✉ *Museumsinsel 1, City Center* ☎ *089/21791, 089/217–9252 for tour* ⊕ *www.deutsches-museum.de* 🖾 *Museum €8.50, Center for Transportation €2.50 (€10 with museum plus shuttle)* ⊙ *Daily 9–5* Ⓜ *Isartor (S-bahn)*.

❶ Frauenkirche *(Church of Our Lady)*. Munich's *Dom* (cathedral) is a distinctive late-Gothic brick structure with two towers. Each is more than 300 feet high, and both are capped by onion-shape domes. The towers are an indelible feature of the skyline and a Munich trademark—some say because they look like overflowing beer mugs.

The main body of the cathedral was completed in 20 years (1468–88)—a record time in those days. The onion domes on the towers were added, almost as an afterthought, in 1524–25. Jörg von Halspach, the Frauenkirche's original architect, apparently dropped dead after laying

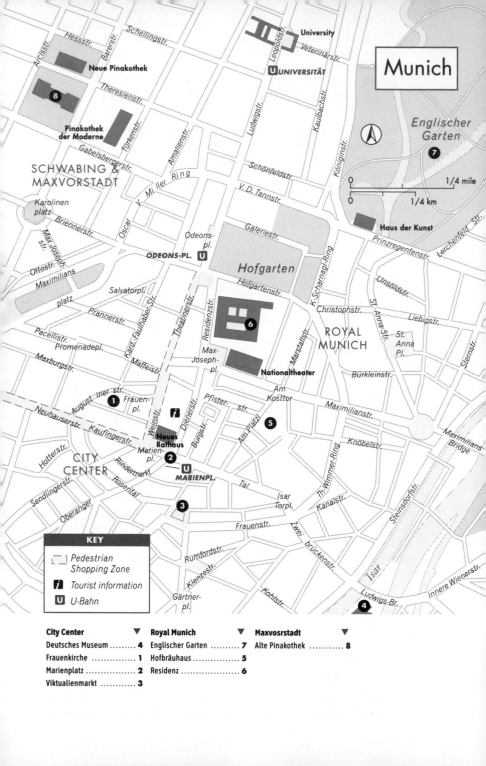

Munich

Englischer Garten

ROYAL MUNICH

SCHWABING & MAXVORSTADT

CITY CENTER

Neue Pinakothek

Pinakothek der Moderne

Karolinen platz

Haus der Kunst

Hofgarten

Nationaltheater

Neues Rathaus

MARIENPL.

Frauen-pl.

KEY

⌐⌐⌐ Pedestrian Shopping Zone

🄳 Tourist information

Ⓤ U-Bahn

City Center ▼	Royal Munich ▼	Maxvosrstadt ▼
Deutsches Museum 4	Englischer Garten 7	Alte Pinakothek 8
Frauenkirche 1	Hofbräuhaus 5	
Marienplatz 2	Residenz 6	
Viktualienmarkt 3		

the last brick and is buried here. The building suffered severe damage during Allied bombing and was restored between 1947 and 1957. Inside, the church combines most of von Halspach's original features with a stark, clean modernity and simplicity of line, emphasized by slender, white octagonal pillars that sweep up through the nave to the tracery ceiling. As you enter the church, look on the stone floor for the dark imprint of a large foot—the *Teufelstritt* (Devil's Footprint). According to lore, the devil challenged von Halspach to build a nave without windows. The architect accepted the challenge. When he completed the job, he led the devil to the one spot in the bright church from which the 66-foot-high windows could not be seen. The devil stomped his foot in rage and left the Teufelstritt. The cathedral houses an elaborate 15th-century black-marble tomb guarded by four 16th-century armored knights. It's the final resting place of Duke Ludwig IV (1302–47), who became Holy Roman Emperor Ludwig the Bavarian in 1328. The Frauenkirche's great treasure, however, is the collection of 24 wooden busts of the apostles, saints, and prophets above the choir, carved by the 15th-century Munich sculptor Erasmus Grasser.

The observation platform high up in one of the towers offers a splendid view of the city. But beware—you must climb 86 steps to reach the tower elevator. ⊠ *Frauenpl., City Center* ☎ *089/290–0820* ⊠ *Cathedral free, tower €3* ◷ *Tower elevator Apr.–Oct., Mon.–Sat. 10–5* Ⓜ *Marienplatz (U-bahn and S-bahn).*

❷ Marienplatz. Bordered by the Neues Rathaus, shops, and cafés, this square is named after the gilded statue of the Virgin Mary that has watched over it for more than three centuries. It was erected in 1638 at the behest of Elector Maximilian I as an act of thanksgiving for the city's survival of the Thirty Years' War, the cataclysmic religious struggle that devastated vast regions of Germany. When the statue was taken down from its marble column for cleaning in 1960, workmen found a small casket in the base containing a splinter of wood said to be from the cross of Christ. ■TIP➜ **On the fifth floor of a building facing the Neues Rathaus is the Café Glockenspiel. It overlooks the entire Platz and provides a perfect view of the glockenspiel from the front and St. Peter's Church from the back terrace. Entrance is around the back.** ⊠ *Bounded by Kaufingerstr., Rosenstr., Weinstr., and Dienerstr., City Center* Ⓜ *Marienplatz (U-bahn and S-bahn).*

❸ Viktualienmarkt *(Victuals Market).* The city's open-air market really is the beating heart of downtown Munich. It has just about every fresh fruit or vegetable you can imagine, as well as German and international specialties. All kinds of people come here for a quick bite, from well-heeled businesspeople and casual tourists to mortar- and paint-covered workers. It's also the realm of the garrulous, sturdy market women who run the stalls with dictatorial authority. ■TIP➜ **Whether here, or at a bakery, *do not* try to select your pickings by hand. Ask for it first and let it be served to you.** Try Poseidon's for quality fish treats, Mercado Latino on the south side of the market for an empanada and fine wines from South America, or Freisinger for Mediterranean delights. There's also a great beer garden (open pretty much whenever the sun is shining), where you can enjoy your snacks with some cold local beer. A sign above the counter tells you which beer is on tap. The choice rotates throughout the year among the six major Munich breweries, which are displayed on the May Pole. These are also the only six breweries officially allowed to serve their wares at the Oktoberfest, because they all brew within the city limits. Ⓜ*Marienplatz (U-bahn and S-bahn).*

ROYAL MUNICH

❼ Englischer Garten *(English Garden).* This endless park, which melds into
★ the open countryside at Munich's northern city limits, was designed for the Bavarian prince Karl Theodor by Benjamin Thompson, later Count Rumford, from Massachusetts, who fled America after having taken the wrong side during the War of Independence. Practically speaking, it's 5 km (3 mi) long and 1½ km (about 1 mi) wide, making it Germany's largest city park. The open, informal landscaping—reminiscent of the rolling parklands with which English aristocrats of the 18th century liked to surround their country homes—gave the park its name. It has a boating lake, four beer gardens, and a series of curious decorative and monumental constructions, including the Monopteros, a Greek temple designed by Leo von Klenze for King Ludwig I and built on an artificial hill in the southern section of the park. There are great sunset views of Munich from the Monopteros hill. In the center of the park's most popular beer garden is a Chinese pagoda erected in 1789. It was destroyed during the war and then reconstructed. ■TIP→ **The Chinese Tower beer garden is world famous, but the park has prettier places for sipping a beer: the Aumeister, for example, along the northern perimeter. The Aumeister's restaurant is in an early-19th-century hunting lodge.** At the Seehaus, on the shore of the Kleinhesseloher*see* (lake), choose between a smart restaurant or a cozy *Bierstube* (beer tavern) in addition to the beer garden right on the lake.

The Englischer Garten is a paradise for joggers, cyclists, musicians, soccer players, sunbathers, dog owners, and, in winter, cross-country skiers. The park has designated areas for nude sunbathing—the Germans have a positively pagan attitude toward the sun—so don't be surprised to see naked bodies bordering the flower beds and paths. ✉*Main entrances at Prinzregentenstr. and Königinstr., Schwabing, and Lehel.*

❺ Hofbräuhaus. Duke Wilhelm V founded Munich's most famous brewery in 1589. *Hofbräu* means "court brewery," and the golden beer is poured in pitcher-sized liter mugs. If the cavernous ground-floor hall is too noisy for you, there is a quieter restaurant upstairs. In this legendary establishment Americans, Australians, and Italians far outnumber Germans, and the brass band that performs here most days adds modern pop and American folk music to the traditional German numbers. ✉*Am Platzl 9, City Center* ☎*089/290–1360* ⊗*Daily 11–11* Ⓜ*Marienplatz (U-bahn and S-bahn).*

❻ Residenz *(Royal Palace).* One of the city's true treasures, Munich's royal palace began as a small castle in the 14th century. The Wittelsbach dukes moved here when the tenements of an expanding Munich encroached upon their Alter Hof. In succeeding centuries the royal residence developed according to the importance, requirements, and interests of its occupants. It came to include the Königsbau (on Max-Joseph-Platz) and then (clockwise) the Alte Residenz; the Festsaal (Banquet Hall); the newly renovated Altes Residenztheater/Cuvilliés-Theater; the Allerheiligenhofkirche (All Saints' Church), a venue for cultural events; the Residenztheater; and the Nationaltheater.

Building began in 1385 with the **Neuveste** (New Fortress), which comprised the northeast section. Most of it burned to the ground in 1750, but one of its finest rooms survived: the 16th-century **Antiquarium,** which was built for Duke Albrecht V's collection of antique statues (today it's used chiefly for state receptions). The throne room of King Ludwig I, the **Neuer Herkulessaal,** is now a concert hall. The accumulated Wittelsbach treasures are on view in several palace museums. The **Schatzkammer** (*Treasury* ✉€6, *combined ticket with Residenzmuseum* €9 ⊙*Apr.–Oct. 15, daily 9–6; Oct. 16–Mar., daily 10–4*) has a rather rich centerpiece—a small Renaissance statue of St. George studded with 2,291 diamonds, 209 pearls, and 406 rubies. Paintings, tapestries, furniture, and porcelain are housed in the **Residenzmuseum** (✉€6 ⊙*Apr.–Oct. 15, daily 9–6; Oct. 16–Mar., daily 10–4*). Antique coins glint in the **Staatliche Münzsammlung** (✉€2, *free Sun.* ⊙ *Wed.–Sun. 10–5*). Egyptian works of art make up the **Staatliche Sammlung Ägyptischer Kunst** (⊠*Hofgarten entrance* ☎*089/298–546* ✉€5, *Sun.* €1 ⊙*Tues. 9–5 and 7–9 PM, Wed.–Fri. 9–5, weekends 10–5*). ■TIP➡ **All the different halls and galleries of the Residenz can be visited with a combination ticket that costs €9.** In summer, chamber-music concerts take place in the inner courtyard. Also in the center of the complex is the small, rococo **Altes Residenztheater/Cuvilliés-Theater** (⊠*Residenzstr.* ✉€3 ⊙ *Closed during rehearsals*). It was built by François Cuvilliés between 1751 and 1755, and performances are still held here. The French-born Cuvilliés was a dwarf who was admitted to the Bavarian court as a decorative "bauble." Prince Max Emanuel recognized his innate artistic ability and had him trained as an architect. The prince's eye for talent gave Germany some of its richest rococo treasures. ⊠*Max-Joseph-Pl. 3, entrance through archway at Residenzstr. 1, City Center* ☎*089/290–671* ⊙*Closed a few days in early Jan.* Ⓜ*Odeonsplatz (U-bahn).*

MAXVORSTADT & OUTER MUNICH

❽ Fodor'sChoice ★ **Alte Pinakothek** *(Old Picture Gallery).* The long, massive brick Alte Pinakothek was constructed by Leo von Klenze between 1826 and 1836 to exhibit the collection of Old Masters begun by Duke Wilhelm IV in the 16th century. By all accounts it is one of the world's great picture galleries. Among the European masterpieces here from the 14th to the 18th centuries are paintings by Dürer, Titian, Rembrandt, Rubens (the museum has one of the world's largest collections of works by Rubens), and two celebrated Murillos. Not to be missed. ⊠*Barerstr. 27, Maxvorstadt* ☎*089/2380–5216* ⊕*www.alte-pinakothek.de* ✉€5.50, €1 *Sun.* ⊙*Tues.–Sun. 10–6* Ⓜ*Königsplatz (U-bahn).*

Schloss Nymphenburg. This glorious Baroque and rococo palace is the largest of its kind in Germany, stretching more than 1 km (½ mi) from one wing to the other. The palace grew in size and scope over a period

OKTOBERFEST

Not even the wildest Bavarians can be held wholly responsible for the staggering consumption of beer and food at the annual Oktoberfest, which starts at the end of September and ends in early October. On average, around 1,183,000 gallons of beer along with 750,000 roasted chickens and 650,000 sausages are put away by revelers from around the world. To partake, book lodging by April, and if you're traveling with a group, also reserve bench space within one of the 14 tents.

See Munich's Web site, ⊕ *www. muenchen-tourist.de,* for beer-tent contacts. The best time to arrive at the grounds is lunchtime, when it's easier to find a seat—by 4 PM it's packed and they'll close the doors. Take advantage of an hour or two of sobriety to tour the fairground rides, which are an integral part of Oktoberfest. Under no circumstances attempt any rides—all of which claim to be the world's most dangerous—after a couple of beers.

of more than 200 years, beginning as a summer residence built on land given by Prince Ferdinand Maria to his beloved wife, Henriette Adelaide, on the occasion of the birth of their son and heir, Max Emanuel, in 1663. The princess hired the Italian architect Agostino Barelli to build both the Theatinerkirche and the palace, which was completed in 1675 by his successor, Enrico Zuccalli. Within the original building, now the central axis of the palace complex, is a magnificent hall, the **Steinerner Saal,** extending over two floors and richly decorated with stucco and grandiose frescoes. In summer, chamber-music concerts are given here. One of the surrounding royal chambers houses the famous **Schönheitsgalerie** (Gallery of Beauties). The walls are hung from floor to ceiling with portraits of women who caught the roving eye of Ludwig I, among them a butcher's daughter and an English duchess. The most famous portrait is of Lola Montez, a sultry beauty and high-class courtesan who, after a time as the mistress of Franz Liszt and later Alexandre Dumas, so enchanted King Ludwig I that he almost bankrupted the state for her sake and was ultimately forced to abdicate.

The palace is in a park laid out in formal French style, with low hedges and gravel walks extending into woodland. Among the ancient tree stands are three fascinating structures. The **Amalienburg** hunting lodge is a rococo gem built by François Cuvilliés. The silver-and-blue stucco of the little Amalienburg creates an atmosphere of courtly high life, making clear that the pleasures of the chase did not always take place outdoors. Of the lodges, only Amalienburg is open in winter. In the lavishly appointed kennels you'll see that even the dogs lived in luxury. The **Pagodenburg** was built for royal tea parties. Its elegant French exterior disguises a suitably Asian interior in which exotic teas from India and China were served. Swimming parties were held in the **Badenburg,** Europe's first post-Roman heated pool.

Nymphenburg contains so much of interest that a day hardly provides enough time. Don't leave without visiting the former royal stables, now ℭ the **Marstallmuseum** (*Museum of Royal Carriages* 🖃€2.50). It houses a fleet of vehicles, including an elaborately decorated sleigh in which King Ludwig II once glided through the Bavarian twilight, postilion torches lighting the way. On the walls hang portraits of the royal horses. Also exhibited are examples of Nymphenburg porcelain, produced here between 1747 and the 1920s. A popular museum in the north wing of the palace has nothing to do with the Wittelsbachs but is one of Nymphenburg's major attractions. The **Museum Mensch und Natur** (*Museum of Man and Nature* ☎*089/179–5890* 🖃*€2.50, €1 Sun.* ⊙*Tues.–Fri. 9–5, weekends 10–6*) concentrates on three areas of interest: the variety of life on Earth, the history of humankind, and our place in the environment. Main exhibits include a huge representation of the human brain and a chunk of Alpine crystal weighing half a ton. Take Tram 17 or Bus 41 from the city center to the Schloss Nymphenburg stop. ✉*Notburgastr. at bridge crossing Nymphenburg Canal, Nymphenburg* ☎*089/179–080* ⊕*www.schloesser.bayern.de* 🖃*Schloss Nymphenburg complex, combined ticket including Marstallmuseum but not Museum Mensch und Natur, €10, €8 in winter, when parts of complex are closed* ⊙*Apr.–Oct. 15, daily 9–6; Oct. 16–Mar., daily 10–4.*

WHERE TO EAT

CITY CENTER

$ ✕ **Bier-und Oktoberfest Museum.** In one of the oldest buildings in Munich, dating to 1327, the museum takes an imaginative look at the history of this popular elixir, the monasteries that produced it, the purity laws that govern it, and Munich's own long tradition with it. A restaurant consisting of a few heavy wooden tables opens along with the museum at 1 PM and serves hot meals from 6 PM. ■**TIP➔You can visit the restaurant without paying the museum's admission fee and try beer from one of Munich's oldest breweries, the Augustiner Bräu.** ✉*Sterneckstr. 2, City Center* ☎*089/2423–1607* ⊕*www.bier-und-oktoberfestmuseum.de* 🖃*€4* ⊙*Tues.–Sat. 1–5* Ⓜ*Isartor (U-bahn and S-bahn).*

$$$–$$$$ ✕ **Königshof.** As you cross the threshold of its unremarkable building, you step into a different world. From a window table in this elegant and luxurious restaurant in one of Munich's grand hotels, you can watch the hustle and bustle of Munich's busiest square below. You'll forget the outside world, however, when you taste the outstanding French- and Japanese-influenced dishes created by chef Martin Fauster, former sous-chef at Tantris. Ingredients are fresh and menus change often, but you might see lobster with fennel and candied ginger, lamb with sweetbreads, venison with goose liver and celery, and for dessert, flambéed peach with champagne ice cream. Service is expert and personal; let the sommelier help you choose from the fantastic wine selection. ✉*Karlspl. 25, City Center* ☎*089/5513–6142* ⊕ *www.koenigshof-hotel.de* ⚕*Reservations essential. Jacket and tie* ▤*AE, DC, MC, V* ⊙*Closed 1st week in Jan., Aug., Sun. and Mon.* Ⓜ*Karlsplatz (U-bahn and S-bahn).*

$$ ✕ **Nürnberger Bratwurst Glöckl am Dom.** Munich's most original beer tavern is dedicated to the delicious *Nürnberger Bratwürste* (finger-size sausages), a specialty from the rival city of Nürnberg. They're served

by a busy team of friendly waitresses dressed in Bavarian dirndls who flit between the crowded tables with remarkable agility. There are other options available as well. In summer, tables are placed outside under a large awning and in the shade of the nearby Frauenkirche. In winter the mellow dark-panel dining rooms provide relief from the cold. ■ TIP➔ For a quick beer you can check the side door where, just inside, there is a little window serving fresh Augustiner from a wooden barrel. You can stand there with some of the regulars or enjoy the small courtyard if the weather is nice. ⊠ *Frauenpl. 9, City Center* ☎ *089/220–385* ⊟ *DC, MC, V* Ⓜ *Marienplatz (U-bahn and S-bahn).*

$$ ✕ **Oskar Maria.** A mixed crowd frequents this stylish gallery, bistro, and restaurant in the Literaturhaus, a converted city mansion. The vaulted high ceiling and plate-glass windows make for a light and spacious atmosphere. Fare includes German nouvelle cuisine and Mediterranean flavors, but there's a strong Gallic touch with dishes such as veal marengo and leg of venison. ⊠ *Salvatorpl. 1, City Center* ☎ *089/2919–6029* ⊟ *AE, DC, MC, V* Ⓜ *Odeonsplatz (U-bahn).*

LEOPOLDVORSTADT & SCHWABING

¢–$ ✕ **Augustiner Keller.** This 19th-century establishment is the flagship beer restaurant of one of Munich's oldest breweries. It is also the location of the absolutely unbeatable Augustiner beer garden, which you have to experience once in your life. The menu changes daily and offers Bavarian specialties, but try to order their "top seller" —¼ duck with a good slab of roast suckling pig, dumpling, and blue cabbage. Follow that with a *Dampfnudel* (yeast dumpling served with custard), and you probably won't feel hungry again for quite a while. ⊠ *Arnulfstr. 52, Leopoldvorstadt* ☎ *089/594–393* ⊟ *AE, MC* Ⓜ *Hauptbahnhof (U-bahn and S-bahn).*

$$$$ ✕ **Tantris.** Despite the unappealing exterior, this restaurant will spoil
Fodor's Choice you for other food for days. Select the menu of the day and accept the
★ suggestions of the charming and competent sommelier or choose from the à la carte options and you'll be treated to a feast that may include langostino with curry bok choy, mushrooms, and spicy coconut cream, a lightly smoked pigeon breast with goose liver, turbot with artichoke stock, and carré of lamb. No wonder Chef Hans Haas has kept his restaurant at the top of the critics' charts in Munich. When the last course of dessert arrives, you'll hesitate to disturb the inventive creation put before you. But not for long. ⊠ *Johann-Fichte-Str. 7, Schwabing* ☎ *089/361–9590* ⌂ *Reservations essential. Jacket and tie* ⊟ *AE, DC, MC, V* ☉ *Closed Sun. and Mon.* Ⓜ *Münchener Freiheit (U-bahn).*

WHERE TO STAY

CITY CENTER

$$$$ 🏨 **Bayerischer Hof.** This is *the* address for luxury in Munich, as it has
Fodor's Choice been since 1841, when His Majesty Ludwig I of Bavaria came twice a
★ month to take a "royal bath," as his own residence lacked a bathtub. He probably never imagined that 167 years later guests would enjoy a magnificent view over Munich while swimming in a rooftop pool. Today the guest rooms have everything from fireplaces and whirlpool

tubs to antique furniture and flat-screen TVs; huge windows frame the fabulous view, and some suites have kitchens. In addition to the excellent Bavarian restaurant Palais Keller, there are four very different restaurants to choose from in-house. When meeting someone at "the bar," specify which one: there are five, as well as a nightclub. **Pros:** posh public rooms with valuable oil paintings, the roof-garden restaurant has an impressive view of the Frauenkirche just two blocks away, impressive amenities and views. **Cons:** expensive. ⊠ *Promenadepl. 2–6, City Center,* ☎ *089/21200* ⊕ *www.bayerischerhof.de* ⤳ *313 rooms, 60 suites* ♿ *In-room: safe, Ethernet, Wi-Fi. In-hotel: 4 restaurants, room service, 6 bars, laundry service, concierge, executive floor, pool, spa, public Internet, public Wi-Fi, parking (fee), no-smoking rooms, some pets allowed (fee)* ⊟ *AE, DC, MC, V* ⊺⊚⊺ *BP* Ⓜ *Karlsplatz (U-bahn and S-bahn) or Marienplatz (U-bahn and S-bahn).*

$$ ⊡ **Hotel am Markt.** You can literally stumble out the door of this hotel onto the Viktualienmarkt. Perfect location, fair prices, and simple rooms are what you get here. Small meals are served in the café connected with the hotel. Wi-Fi Internet access is available for free in the hotel's public spaces. **Pros:** excellent location, very friendly helpful service, free Wi-Fi. **Cons:** rooms are simple, some spots could use fresh paint. ⊠ *Heiliggeiststr. 6, City Center* ☎ *089/225–014* ⊕ *www.hotel-am-markt.eu* ⤳ *22 rooms* ♿ *In-room: no a/c. In-hotel: public Wi-Fi* ⊟ *No credit cards* ⊺⊚⊺ *CP* Ⓜ *Marienplatz (U-bahn and S-bahn).*

$$–$$$ ⊡ **Platzl.** The privately owned Platzl has won awards and wide recognition for its ecologically aware management, which uses heat recyclers in the kitchen, environmentally friendly detergents, recyclable materials, waste separation, and other ecofriendly practices. It stands in the historic heart of Munich, near the famous Hofbräuhaus beer hall and a couple of minutes' walk from Marienplatz and many other landmarks. Its Pfistermühle restaurant, with 16th-century vaulting, is one of the area's oldest and most historic establishments. **Pros:** good restaurant, around the corner from the Hofbräuhaus. **Cons:** rooms facing the Hofbräuhaus get more noise, some rooms are on the small side. ⊠ *Sparkassenstr. 10, City Center* ☎ *089/237–030, 800/448–8355 in U.S.* ⊕ *www.platzl.de* ⤳ *167 rooms* ♿ *In-room: no a/c (some), Ethernet, Wi-Fi (some). In-hotel: restaurant, bar, gym, parking (fee), nosmoking rooms, some pets allowed (fee)* ⊟ *AE, DC, MC, V* ⊺⊚⊺ *BP* Ⓜ *Marienplatz (U-bahn and S-bahn).*

HAUPTBANHOF & ISARVORSTADT

$$$ ⊡ **Admiral.** The small, privately owned Admiral enjoys a quiet sidestreet location and its own garden, close to the Isar River and Deutsches Museum. A very comfortable bar with comfortable easy chairs is right behind the lobby. Many of the nicely furnished and warmly decorated bedrooms have a balcony overlooking the quiet, secluded garden. The breakfast buffet is a dream, complete with homemade jams, fresh bread, and Italian and French delicacies; two tables are set out in the garden. The use of the minibar is included in the room price, and Wi-Fi Internet access is free. **Pros:** quality prints on the wall, attention to detail, excellent service. **Cons:** no restaurant, small lobby. ⊠ *Kohlstr. 9, Isarvorstadt* ☎ *089/216–350* ⊕ *www.hotel-admiral.de* ⤳ *33 rooms* ♿ *In-room: no*

6

a/c, Ethernet, Wi-Fi. In-hotel: bar, public Internet, public Wi-Fi, parking (fee), no-smoking rooms, some pets allowed ⊟*AE, DC, MC, V* ⦿❘*BP* Ⓜ*Isartor (S-bahn).*

$–$$ 🏨**Hotel Mirabell.** This family-run hotel is used to American tourists who appreciate the friendly service, central location (between the main railway station and the Oktoberfest fairgrounds), and reasonable room rates. Three apartments are for small groups or families. Rooms are furnished in modern light woods and bright prints. Breakfast buffet is included. **Pros:** top location, family run, personalized service. **Cons:** no restaurant, streets outside the hotel are seedy. ✉*Landwehrstr. 42, entrance on Goethestr., Hauptbahnhof* ☎*089/549–1740* ⊕*www. hotelmirabell.de* 🛏*65 rooms, 3 apartments* ♿*In-room: no a/c, Wi-Fi. In-hotel: bar, public Wi-Fi, no-smoking rooms, some pets allowed (fee)* ⊟*AE, DC, MC, V* ⦿❘*BP* Ⓜ*Hauptbahnhof (U-bahn and S-bahn).*

BOGENHAUSEN & LUDWIGVORSTADT

$–$$ 🏨**Hotel Uhland.** This stately villa is a landmark building and is addition-
★ ally special in that the owner and host was born here and will make you feel at home, too. She and her staff welcome all questions and seem to love answering them. The spacious, inviting breakfast room filled with light and the excellent food will get you ready for the day ahead. Some of the pleasant rooms are quite large and can accommodate three people. **Pros:** a real family atmosphere, care is given to details. **Cons:** no restaurant or bar. ✉*Uhlandstr. 1, Ludwigvorstadt* ☎*089/543–350* ⊕*www.hotel-uhland.de* 🛏*27 rooms* ♿*In-room: no a/c, Wi-Fi (some). In-hotel: public Internet, public Wi-Fi, some pets allowed* ⊟*AE, DC, MC, V*

$$$–$$$$ 🏨**The Westin Grand München Arabellapark.** The building itself with its 22 floors may raise a few eyebrows. It stands on a slight elevation and is not the shapeliest of the Munich skyline. What goes on inside, however, is sheer five-star luxury. Guests of the four top floors, the Tower Rooms and Suites, are greeted with a glass of champagne; snacks, drinks, and a fantastic view of the city and the Bavarian Alps are available in the Tow-ers Lounge. Room service is available around the clock. The excellent restaurant Ente vom Lehel is here as well. And if you'd like to add a spe-cial Bavarian flavor to your stay, book one of the 60 "Bavarian rooms" on the 15th and the 16th floors, with antique wood furniture and a country feel. **Pros:** luxurious lobby and restaurant, rooms facing west toward the city have a fabulous view. **Cons:** it's not possible to reserve west-facing rooms, hotel is difficult to reach via public transportation. ✉*Arabellastr. 5, Bogenhausen* ☎*089/92640* ⊕*www.arabellasheraton. de* 🛏*629 rooms, 28 suites* ♿*In-room: dial-up, Wi-Fi (some). In-hotel: 2 restaurants, room service, bars, pool, laundry service, concierge, pub-lic Internet, public Wi-Fi, parking (fee), no-smoking rooms, some pets allowed (fee)* ⊟*AE, DC, MC, V* ⦿❘*BP* Ⓜ*Arabellapark (U-bahn).*

NIGHTLIFE

Munich has a lively nocturnal scene ranging from beer halls to bars to chic, see-and-be-seen clubs. The fun neighborhoods for a night out are City Center, Isarvorstadt (around Gärtnerplatz), and Schwabing around

Schellingstrasse and Münchener Freiheit. Regardless of their size or style, many bars, especially around Gärtnerplatz, have DJs spinning either mellow background sounds or funky beats. The city's eclectic taste in music is quite commendable.

BARS

CITY CENTER   Around the corner from the Hofbräuhaus, **Bar Centrale** (⊠*Ledererstr. 23, City Center* ☎*089/223–762*) is very Italian—the waiters don't seem to speak any other language. The coffee is excellent; small fine meals are served as well. They have a retro-looking back room with leather sofas. Also near the Hofbräuhaus is the **Atomic Café** (⊠*Neutrumstr. 5, City Center* ☎*089/2283–053*). This club/lounge has excellent DJs nightly, playing everything from '60s Brit pop to '60s/'70s funk and soul. Atomic also has great live acts on a regular basis. Cover charge is typically €7. Just behind the Frauenkirche, **Kilian's Irish Pub and Ned Kelly's Australian Bar** (⊠*Frauenpl. 11, City Center* ☎*089/2421–9899*) offers an escape from the German tavern scene. Naturally, they have Guinness and Foster's, but they also serve Munich's lager, Augustiner, and regularly televise international soccer, rugby, and sports in general.

At **Schumann's** (⊠*Odeonspl. 6–7, City Center* ☎*089/229–060*) the bartenders are busy shaking cocktails after the curtain comes down at the nearby opera house. Exotic cocktails are the specialty at **Trader Vic's** (⊠*Promenadenpl. 4, City Center* ☎*089/226–192*), a smart cellar bar in the Hotel Bayerischer Hof that's popular among out-of-town visitors. The Bayerischer Hof's **Night Club** (⊠*Promenadepl. 2–6, City Center* ☎*089/212–00*) has live music, from jazz to reggae to hip-hop; a small dance floor; and a very lively bar.

Eisbach (⊠*Marstallplatz 3, City Center* ☎*089/2280–1680*) occupies a corner of the Max Planck Institute building opposite the Bavarian Parliament. The bar is among Munich's biggest, and is overlooked by a mezzanine restaurant area where you can choose from a limited but ambitious menu. Outdoor tables nestle in the expansive shade of huge parasols. The nearby Eisbach brook, which gives the bar its name, tinkles away like ice in a glass.

The **Kempinski Vier Jahreszeiten** (⊠*Maximilianstr. 17, City Center* ☎*089/21250*) offers piano music until 9 PM and then dancing to recorded music or a small combo. At the English, nautical-style **Pusser's New York Bar** (⊠*Falkenturmstr. 9, City Center* ☎*089/220–500*) great cocktails and Irish-German black and tans (Guinness and strong German beer) are made to the sounds of live jazz. Try the "Pain Killer," a specialty of the house. The pricey sandwiches are about the only "New York" in Pusser's.

SCHWABING   Media types drink Guinness and Kilkenny at the square bar at **Alter Simpl** (⊠*Türkenstr. 57, Schwabing* ☎*089/272–3083*). More than 100 years old, this establishment serves German pub food until 2 AM. Across the street is the **Türkenhof** (⊠*Türkenstr. 78, Schwabing* ☎*089/ 2800–235*), another solid local joint that serves Augustiner and good food. Up on Schellingstrasse is **Schall und Rauch** (⊠*Schellingstr. 22, Schwabing* ☎*089/2880–9577*). This legendary student hangout, whose name literally means "Noise and Smoke," has great music and food. Another absolute cornerstone in the neighborhood is the **Schelling Salon** (⊠*Schellingstr. 54, Schwabing* ☎*089/2720–788*). On the corner of Barerstrasse, the bar has several pool tables and even a secret Ping-Pong room in the basement with an intercom for placing beer orders. It's closed on Tuesday and Wednesday.

BEER GARDENS

CITY CENTER The only true beer garden in the city center, and therefore the easiest to find, is the one at the **Viktualienmarkt** (☎*089/2916–5993*). The beer on tap rotates every six weeks among the six Munich breweries to keep everyone happy throughout the year. The rest of the beer gardens are a bit farther afield and can be reached handily by bike or S- and U-bahn.

AROUND TOWN The famous **Biergarten am Chinesischen Turm** (⊠*Englischer Garten 3* ☎*089/383–8730*) is at the five-story Chinese Tower in the Englischer Garten. Enjoy your beer to the strains of oompah music played by traditionally dressed musicians. The Englischer Garten's smaller beer garden, **Hirschau** (⊠*Gysslingstr. 15* ☎*089/322–1080*), is about 10 minutes north of the Kleinhesselohersee. The **Seehaus im Englischen Garten** (⊠*Kleinhesselohe 3*) is on the banks of the artificial lake Kleinhesselohersee, where all of Munich converges on hot summer days (bus line 44, exit at Osterwaldstrasse; you can't miss it).

The **Augustiner Beer Garden** (⊠*Arnulfstr. 52, Hauptbahnhof* ☎*089/594–393*) is one of the more authentic of the beer gardens, with excellent food, beautiful chestnut shade trees, a mixed local crowd, and Munich Augustiner beer. From the north exit of the main train station, go left on Arnulfstrasse and walk about 10 minutes. It's on the right.

A SIDE TRIP FROM MUNICH: DACHAU

20 km (12 mi) northwest of Munich.

Dachau is infamous worldwide as the site of the first Nazi concentration camp, which was built just outside it. Dachau preserves the memory of the camp and the horrors perpetrated there with deep contrition while trying to signal that the town has other points of interest.

GETTING HERE & AROUND

By public transport take the S-2 from Marienplatz or Hauptbahnhof in the direction of Petershausen, and get off at Dachau. From there, take the clearly marked bus from right outside the Dachau S-bahn station (it leaves about every 20 minutes). If you are driving from Munich, take the autobahn toward Stuttgart, get off at Dachau, and follow the signs.

ESSENTIALS

Visitor Information Tourist Information Dachau (⊠*Konrad-Adenauer-Str. 1* ☎*08131/75286* ⊕*www.dachau.info*).

EXPLORING DACHAU

The site of the infamous camp, now the **KZ-Gedenkstätte Dachau** *(Dachau Concentration Camp Memorial)*, is just outside town. Photographs, contemporary documents, the few remaining cell blocks, and the grim crematorium create a somber and moving picture of the camp, where more than 30,000 of the 200,000-plus prisoners lost their lives. A documentary film in English is shown daily at 11:30 and 3:30. The former camp has become more than just a grisly memorial: it's now a place where people of all nations meet to reflect upon the past and on the present. Several religious shrines and memorials have been built to honor the dead, who came from Germany and all occupied nations. ✉ *Alte Römerstr. 75* ☎ *08131/669–970* ⊕ *www.kz-gedenkstaette-dachau.de* 💶 *Free, 2-hr guided tour €3* ⊙ *Tues.–Sun. 9–5. Tours May–Oct., Tues.–Fri. at 1:30, weekends at noon and 1:30; Nov.–Apr., Thurs. and weekends at 1:30.*

THE BAVARIAN ALPS

Fir-clad mountains, rocky peaks, lederhosen, and geranium-covered houses make for Germany's most photogenic region. Quaint towns full of frescoed half-timber houses covered in snow pop up among the mountain peaks and shimmering hidden lakes, as do the creations of "Mad" King Ludwig II. The entire area has sporting opportunities galore, regardless of the season, including the country's finest skiing in Garmisch-Partenkirchen.

6

Each region of the Bavarian Alps has its die-hard fans. The constants, however, are the incredible scenery, clean air, and a sense of Bavarian *Gemütlichkeit* (coziness) omnipresent in every Hütte, Gasthof, and beer garden. The focus here is on the outdoors; the area almost completely lacks the high-culture institutions that dominate German urban life.

PLANNING YOUR TIME

The Alps are spread along Germany's southern border, but are fairly compact and easy to explore. Chose a central base and fan out from there. Garmisch-Partenkirchen and Berchtesgaden are the largest towns with the most convenient transportation connections. Smaller destinations like Ettal are quieter and make for pleasant overnight stays.

GETTING HERE & AROUND
BY CAR

The Bavarian Alps are well connected to Munich by train, and an extensive network of buses links even the most remote villages. But the best way to visit the area is by car. Three autobahns reach into the Bavarian Alps: A-7, A-95, and A-8. It is a good idea to pick a town like Garmisch-Partenkirchen as a base and explore the area from there.

BY TRAIN

Most Alpine resorts are connected with Munich by regular express and slower service trains. With some careful planning—see ⊕ *www. bahn.de* for schedules and to buy tickets—you can visit this region without a car.

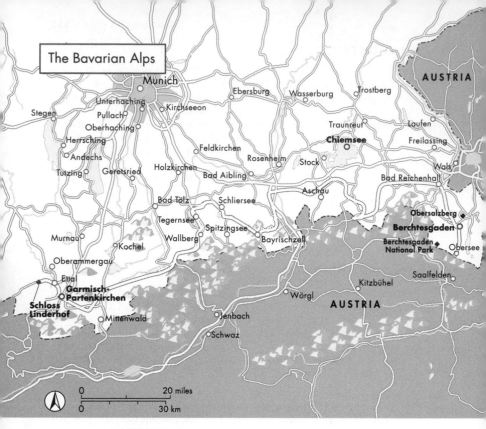

The Bavarian Alps

AUSTRIA

Munich

Ebersburg Wasserburg Trostberg

Stegen Unterhaching Kirchseeon Traunreut Laufen
Pullach Freilassing
Oberhaching Chiemsee
Herrsching Feldkirchen Wals
Andechs Rosenheim Stock
Tutzing Geretsried Holzkirchen Bad Aibling Bad Reichenhall
Bad Tölz Schliersee Aschau
Tegernsee Obersalzberg
Murnau Spitzingsee Berchtesgaden
Wallberg Bayrischzell Berchtesgaden
Kochel National Park Obersee
Oberammergau Saalfelden
Ettal Kitzbühel
Garmisch- Wörgl
Partenkirchen AUSTRIA
Schloss
Linderhof Mittenwald Jenbach
Schwaz

0   20 miles
0   30 km

ESSENTIALS

Visitor Information **Tourismusverband München Oberbayern** (✉ *Bodenseestr. 113 Munich* ☎ *089/829–2180* ⊕ *www.oberbayern-tourismus.de*).

GARMISCH-PARTENKIRCHEN

90 km (55 mi) southwest of Munich.

Garmisch, as it's more commonly known, is a bustling, year-round resort and spa town and is the undisputed capital of Alpine Bavaria. Winter sports rank high on the agenda here. There are more than 99 km (62 mi) of downhill ski runs, 40 ski lifts and cable cars, and 180 km (112 mi) of *Loipen* (cross-country ski trails). You can usually count on good skiing from December through April (and into May on the Zugspitze).

GETTING HERE & AROUND

Garmisch-Partenkirchen is the cultural and transportation hub of the Werdenfelser Land. The autobahn A–95 links Garmisch directly to Munich. Regional German Rail trains head directly to Munich (90 minutes). Garmisch is a walkable city, and you probably won't need to use its frequent city-bus services.

The Garmisch mountain railway company, the Bayerische Zugspitz-bahn, offers special excursions to the top of the Zugspitze, Germany's highest mountain, by cog rail and cable car.

ESSENTIALS
Railway Tour Bayerische Zugspitzbahn (☎ *08821/7970).*

Visitor Information Garmisch-Partenkirchen (⊠ *Verkehrsamt der Kurverwaltung, Richard-Strauss-Pl. 2* ☎ *08821/180–420* ⊕ *www.garmisch-partenkirchen.de).*

EXPLORING
The number one attraction in Garmisch is the **Zugspitze,** the highest mountain (9,731 feet) in Germany. There are two ways up the mountain: a leisurely 75-minute ride on a cog railway from the train station in the town center, combined with a cable-car ride up the last stretch; or a 10-minute hoist by cable car, which begins its giddy ascent from the Eibsee, 10 km (6 mi) outside town on the road to Austria. There are two restaurants with sunny terraces at the summit and another at the top of the cog railway.

Garmisch-Partenkirchen isn't all sports, however. In Garmisch beautiful examples of Upper Bavarian houses line Frühlingstrasse, and a pedestrian zone begins at Richard-Strauss-Platz. Off Marienplatz, at one end of the car-free zone, is the 18th-century parish church of **St. Martin.** It contains some significant stuccowork by the Wessobrunn artists Schmutzer, Schmidt, and Bader. The chancel is by another fine 18th-century artist from Austria, Franz Hosp.

Objects and exhibitions on the region's history can be found in the excellent **Werdenfelser Museum,** which is itself housed in a building dating back to around 1200. The museum is spread over five floors, and explores every aspect of life in the Werdenfels region, which was an independent county for more than 700 years (until 1802). ⊠ *Ludwigstr. 47, Partenkirchen* ☎ *08821/2134* ☒ *€2.50* ☉ *Tues.–Sun. 10–5.*

On the eastern edge of Garmisch, at the end of Zöppritzstrasse, stands the **villa of composer Richard Strauss,** who lived here until his death in 1949. It's the center of activity during the *Richard-Strauss-Tage,* an annual music festival held in mid-June that features concerts and lectures on the town's most famous son. Displays are audiovisual, and each day at 10, 12, 2, and 4 samples of Strauss's works are played in the concert hall.

WHERE TO STAY & EAT
$–$$ ✕ **See-Hotel Riessersee.** On the shore of a small, green, tranquil lake—a 3-km (2-mi) walk from town—this café-restaurant is an ideal spot for lunch or afternoon tea (on summer weekends there's live zither music from 3 to 5). House specialties are fresh trout and local game (which fetches the higher prices on the menu). ⊠ *Riess 6* ☎ *08821/95440* ☐ *AE, MC, V* ☉ *Closed Mon. and Dec. 1–15.*

$$–$$$ ⊞ **Reindl's Partenkirchner Hof.** Owner Karl Reindl ranks among the
★   world's top hoteliers. His award-winning hotel is a real family affair; his daughter cooks up excellent Bavarian and international dishes, from roasted suckling pig to coq au vin. The light-filled bistro annex ($–$$)

serves meals, coffee, and cake in an atmosphere that contrasts sharply with the heavier wood-and-velvet main building. Each guest room has pinewood furniture and a balcony or patio. Some of the double rooms are huge. An infra-red sauna and whirlpools soothe tired muscles. If you're planning to stay for several days, ask about specials. **Pros:** ample-size rooms, great views. **Cons:** front rooms are on a busy street. ✉ *Bahnhofstr. 15* ☎ *08821/943–870* ⊕ *www.reindls.de* ➳ *35 rooms, 17 suites* ⌂ *In-room: no a/c (some), Wi-Fi (some). In-hotel: restaurant, bar, pool, gym, spa, bicycles, no-smoking rooms* ☐ *AE, DC, MC, V* ⎮⚪⎮ *BP.*

> ## WORD OF MOUTH
>
> "Hiking the 'klamms' (gorges near Mittenwald or Garmisch) is often fun for kids, or hiking from one alpine 'Sennhütte' to another. These 'huts' often cater food and drinks, and/or sell their own cheese and milk."
>
> —Cowboy1968

SPORTS & THE OUTDOORS

HIKING & WALKING There are innumerable spectacular walks on 300 km (186 mi) of marked trails through the lower slopes' pinewoods and upland meadows. If you have the time and good walking shoes, try one of the two trails that lead to striking gorges (called *Klammen*). The **Höllentalklamm** route starts at the **Zugspitze Mountain railway terminal** (✉ *Olympiastr. 27*) in town and ends at the mountaintop (you'll want to turn back before reaching the summit unless you have mountaineering experience). The **Partnachklamm** route is quite challenging, and takes you through a spectacular, tunneled water gorge (entrance fee), past a pretty little mountain lake, and far up the Zugspitze; to do all of it, you'll have to stay overnight in one of the huts along the way. Ride part of the way up in the **Eckbauer cable car** (€8 one-way, €11 round-trip), which sets out from the Skistadion off Mittenwalderstrasse. The second cable car, the **Graseckbahn**, takes you right over the dramatic gorges (€3.50 one-way, €6 round-trip). There's a handy inn at the top, where you can gather strength for the hour-long walk back down to the Graseckbahn station. Horse-drawn carriages also cover the first section of the route in summer; in winter you can skim along it in a sleigh. The carriages wait near the Skistadion. Or you can call the local coaching society, the **Lohnkutschevereinigung** (☎ *08821/942–920*), for information.

Contact Deutscher Alpenverein (*German Alpine Association* ✉ *Von-Kahr-Str. 2–4 Munich* ☎ *089/140–030* ⊕ *www.alpenverein.de*) for details on hiking and on staying in mountain huts.

SKIING & SNOW-BOARDING Garmisch-Partenkirchen was the site of the 1936 Winter Olympics, and remains Germany's premier winter-sports resort. The upper slopes of the Zugspitze and surrounding mountains challenge the best ski buffs and snowboarders, and there are also plenty of runs for interme-diate skiers and families. The area is divided into two basic regions. The **Riffelriss** with the **Zugspitzplatt** is Germany's highest skiing area, with snow guaranteed from November to May. Access is via the **Zug-spitzbahn** funicular. Cost for a day pass is €34.50, for a 2½-day pass €75 (valid from noon on the first day). The **CLASSIC-Gebiet,** or classical area, has 17 lifts in the **Alpspitz, Kreuzeck,** and **Hausberg** region. Day passes cost €29.50, a two-day pass €53. The town has a number of ski schools and tour organizers. Skiers looking for instruction can try the **Skischule Alpin** (✉ *Reintalstr. 8, Garmisch* ☎ *08821/945–676*). Cross-country skiers should check with the **Erste Skilanglaufschule Garmisch-Partenkirchen** (☎ *08821/1516*) at the eastern entrance of the Olympic stadium in Garmisch. For snowboarders, there's the **Snowboardschule Erwin Gruber** (✉ *Mittenwalderstr. 47d, Garmisch* ☎ *08821/76490*). Telemark skiing is also popular in these rugged mountains. For information, contact the **Telemark Schule Leismüller** (✉ *Waldeckstr. 7, Garmisch* ☎ *08821/752–696*).

The best place for information for all your snow-sports needs is the Alpine office at the tourist information office, **Alpine Auskunftstelle** (✉ *Richard-Strauss-Pl. 2, Garmisch* ☎ *08821/180–744* ⊘ *Mon.– Thurs. 4–6*).

SCHLOSS LINDERHOF

★ *95 km (59 mi) south of Munich.*

Built between 1870 and 1879 on the spectacular grounds of his father's hunting lodge, Schloss Linderhof was the only one of Ludwig II's royal residences to have been completed during the monarch's short life. It was the smallest of this ill-fated king's castles, but his favorite country retreat among the various palaces at his disposal. Set in sylvan seclusion, between a reflecting pool and the green slopes of a gentle mountain, the charming, French-style, rococo confection is said to have been inspired by the Petit Trianon at Versailles. From an architectural standpoint it's a whimsical combination of conflicting styles, lavish on the outside, somewhat overly decorated on the inside. But the main inspiration came from the Sun King of France, Louis XIV, who is referred to in numerous bas-reliefs, mosaics, paintings, and stucco pieces. Ludwig's bedroom is filled with brilliantly colored and gilded ornaments, the Hall of Mirrors is a shimmering dream world, and the dining room has a clever piece of 19th-century engineering—a table that rises from and descends to the kitchens below.

The formal gardens contain still more whimsical touches. There's a Moorish pavilion—bought wholesale from the 1867 Paris Universal Exposition—and a huge artificial grotto in which Ludwig had scenes from Wagner operas performed, with full lighting effects. It took the BASF chemical company much research to develop the proper glass for the blue lighting Ludwig desired. The gilded Neptune in front of the castle spouts a 100-foot water jet. According to hearsay, while staying at Linderhof the eccentric king would dress up as the legendary knight Lohengrin to be rowed in a swan boat on the grotto pond; in winter he took off on midnight sleigh rides behind six plumed horses and a platoon of outriders holding flaring torches. ⚠ **In winter be prepared for an approach road as snowbound as in Ludwig's day—drive carefully.** ☎ *08822/92030* ⊕ *www.schlosslinderhof.de* 🎫 *Summer €7, winter €6; palace grounds only in summer €3* ⊘ *Apr.–Sept., daily 9–6; Oct.–Mar., daily 10–4; pavilion and grotto closed in winter.*

CHIEMSEE

80 km (50 mi) southeast of Munich, 120 km (75 mi) northeast of Garmisch-Partenkirchen.

Chiemsee is north of the Deutsche Alpenstrasse, but it demands a detour, if only to visit King Ludwig's huge palace on one of its idyllic islands. It's the largest Bavarian lake, and although it's surrounded by reedy flatlands, the nearby mountains provide a majestic backdrop. The town of **Prien** is the lake's principal resort. ■ TIP→ **The tourist offices of Prien and Aschau offer a €19 transportation package covering a boat trip, a round-trip rail ticket between the two resorts, and a round-trip ride by cable car to the top of Kampen Mountain, above Aschau.**

GETTING HERE & AROUND

Prien is the jumping-off point for exploring the Chiemsee. Frequent trains connect Prien with Munich and Salzburg. The only way to reach the Herreninsel is by boat.

ESSENTIALS

Visitor Information Chiemsee (⊠ *Kur- und Tourismusbüro Chiemsee, Alte Rathausstr. 11, Prien* ☎ *08051/69050* ⊕ *www.chiemsee.de*).

EXPLORING

Fodor'sChoice   Despite its distance from Munich, the beautiful Chiemsee drew Bavarian
★   royalty to its shores. Its dreamlike, melancholy air caught the imagination of King Ludwig II, and it was on one of the lake's three islands that he built his third and last castle, sumptuous **Schloss Herrenchiemsee.** The palace was modeled after Louis XIV's Versailles, but this was due to more than simple admiration: Ludwig, whose name was the German equivalent of Louis, was keen to establish that he, too, possessed the absolute authority of his namesake, the Sun King. As with most of Ludwig's projects, the building was never completed, and Ludwig spent only nine days in the castle. Moreover, Herrenchiemsee broke the state coffers and Ludwig's private ones as well. The gold leaf that seems to cover more than half of the rooms is especially thin. Nonetheless, what remains is impressive—and ostentatious. Regular ferries out to the island depart from Stock, Prien's harbor. If you want to make the journey in style, board the original 1887 steam train from Prien to Stock to pick up the ferry. A horse-drawn carriage (€3) takes you to the palace itself.

Most spectacular is the Hall of Mirrors, a dazzling gallery where candle-lighted concerts are held in summer. Also of interest are the ornate bedrooms Ludwig planned, the "self-rising" table that ascended from the kitchen quarters, the elaborately painted bathroom with a small pool for a tub, and the formal gardens. The south wing houses a **museum** containing Ludwig's christening robe and death mask, as well as other artifacts of his life. While the palace was being built, Ludwig stayed in a royal suite of apartments in a former monastery building on the island, the Altes Schloss. Germany's postwar constitution was drawn up here in 1948, and this episode of the country's history is the center-piece of the museum housed in the ancient building, the **Museum im Alten Schloss.** ☎ *08051/68870 palace* ⊕ *www.herren-chiemsee.de* ✉ *Palace,* *including Museum im Alten Schloss €7* ⊙ *Mid-Mar.–late Oct., daily 9–6; late Oct.–mid-Mar., daily 10–4:15; English-language palace tours daily; once per hr.*

WHERE TO STAY & EAT

$$ ✕**Wirth von Amerang.** Theme restaurants are an up-and-coming business in Bavaria, and the Wirth is the spearhead. The interior design comes very close to medieval, with brick stoves of handmade bricks, dripping candles, and a floor resembling packed clay. The food is definitely Bavarian, with *Knödel* (dumplings) and pork roast, hocks, and a top-notch potato soup. Reservations are recommended. You may want to purchase the pumpkinseed oil or a homemade schnapps. ⊠*Postweg 4, Amerang* ☎*08075/185–918* ⊕*www.wirth-von-amerang.de* ⊟*No credit cards* ⊙*No lunch Nov.–Mar.*

$–$$ ⊞**Hotel Luitpold am See.** Boats to the Chiemsee islands tie up right outside your window at this handsome old Prien hotel, which organizes shipboard disco evenings as part of its entertainment program. Rooms have either traditional pinewood furniture, including carved cupboards and bedsteads, or are modern and sleek (in the new annex). Fish from the lake is served at the pleasant restaurant ($–$$). **Pros:** directly on the lake. **Cons:** near a busy boat dock. ⊠*Seestr. 110, Prien am Chiemsee* ☎*08051/609-100* ⊕*www.luitpold-am-see.de* ⌨*79 rooms* ♿*In-room: no a/c. In-hotel: 2 restaurants, public Internet, some pets allowed, no elevator, no-smoking rooms* ⊟*AE, DC, MC, V* ⎟⎝*BP.*

BERCHTESGADEN

20 km (12 mi) south of Salzburg.

Berchtesgaden's reputation is unjustly rooted in its brief association with Adolf Hitler, who dreamed of his "1,000-year Reich" from the mountaintop where millions of tourists before and after him drank in only the superb beauty of the Alpine panorama. The historic old market town and mountain resort has great charm. In winter it's a fine place for skiing and snowboarding; in summer it becomes one of the region's most popular (and crowded) resorts. An ornate palace and working salt mine make up some of the diversions in this heavenly setting.

GETTING HERE & AROUND

The easiest way to reach Berchtesgaden is with the hourly train connection via Bad Reichenhall from Salzburg Hbf. Trains to Munich require a change in Freilassing. Hamburg and Dortmund are both served with one direct train per day. Frequent local bus service makes it easy to explore the town and to reach the Königssee. The Schwaiger bus company runs tours of the area and across the Austrian border as far as Salzburg. An American couple runs Berchtesgaden Mini-bus Tours out of the local tourist office, opposite the railroad station.

ESSENTIALS

Visitor & Tour Information Berchtesgaden (⊠*Kurdirektion* ☎*08652/9670* ⊕ *www.berchtesgadener-land.com*). **Berchtesgaden Mini-bus Tours** (☎*08652/64971*). **Schwaiger** (☎*08652/2525*).

EXPLORING

The **Salzbergwerk** *(salt mine)* is one of the chief attractions of the region. In the days when the mine was owned by Berchtesgaden's princely rulers, only select guests were allowed to see how the source of the city's wealth was extracted from the earth. Today, during a 90-minute tour, you can sit astride a miniature train that transports you nearly 1 km (½ mi) into the mountain to an enormous chamber where the salt is mined. Included in the tour are rides down the wooden chutes used by miners to get from one level to another and a boat ride on an underground saline lake the size of a football field. Although the tours take about an hour, plan an extra 45–60 minutes for purchasing the tickets and changing into and out of miners clothing. You may wish to partake of the special four-hour **brine dinners** down in the mines (€75). These are very popular, so be sure to book early ⊠ *2 km (1 mi) from center of Berchtesgaden on B–305 Salzburg Rd.* ☎ *08652/600–220* ⊕ *www.salzzeitreise.de.de* ⌨ *€14, combined ticket with Bad Reichenhall's saline museum €17.50* ⊙ *May–mid-Oct., daily 9–5; mid-Oct.–Apr., Mon.–Sat. 11:30–3.*

> ## WORD OF MOUTH
>
> "There are so many trails in Berchtesgaden you could just go to heaven. Trails are clean, well marked, well scored for difficulty and offer fantastic views of the Alps. If you remember the opening scene of *The Sound of Music*, it is a good example of the scenery of these great hiking areas."
>
> —EmilyC

The **Obersalzberg,** site of Hitler's luxurious mountain retreat, is part of the north slope of the Hoher Goll, high above Berchtesgaden. It was a remote mountain community of farmers and foresters before Hitler's deputy, Martin Bormann, selected the site for a complex of Alpine homes for top Nazi leaders. Hitler's chalet, the Berghof, and all the others were destroyed in 1945, with the exception of a hotel that had been taken over by the Nazis, the Hotel zum Türken. Beneath the hotel is a section of the labyrinth of tunnels built as a last retreat for Hitler and his cronies; the macabre, murky **bunkers** (⌨ *€3* ⊙ *May–Oct., Tues.–Sun. 9–5; Nov.–Apr., daily 10–3*) can be visited. Nearby, the **Dokumentation Obersalzberg** (⊠ *Salzbergstr. 41* ☎ *08652/947–960* ⊕ *www.obersalzberg.de* ⌨ *€3* ⊙ *Apr.–Oct., Tues.–Sun. 9–5; Nov.–Mar., Tues.–Sun. 10–3*) documents the Third Reich's history by specific themes with rare archival material. Beyond Obersalzberg, the hairpin bends of Germany's highest road come to the base of the 6,000-foot peak on which sits the **Kehlsteinhaus** (☎ *08652/2969* ⊕ *www.kehlsteinhaus.de*), also known as the Adlerhorst (Eagle's Nest), Hitler's personal retreat and his official guesthouse. It was Martin Bormann's gift to the Führer on Hitler's 50th birthday. The road leading to it, built in 1937–39, climbs more than 2,000 dizzying feet in less than 6 km (4 mi). A tunnel in the mountain will bring you to an elevator that whisks you up to what appears to be the top of the world (you can walk up in about half an hour). There are refreshment rooms and a restaurant. The round-trip from Berchtesgaden's post office by bus and elevator costs €15 per person. The bus runs mid-May through September, daily from 9 to 4:50. By car you can travel only as far as the Obersalzberg bus station. From there the round-trip fare is €14.50. The full round-trip takes one hour. ∎**TIP→To get the most out of your visit to the Kehlsteinhaus, consider taking one of the informative tours offered by David Harper.** Reserve in advance at ☎*08652/ 64971* or ⊕*www.eagles-nest-tours.com.* Tours meet across from the train station and cost €45.

WHERE TO STAY

$$ ☶**Hotel zum Türken.** The view alone is worth the 10-minute journey from Berchtesgaden to this hotel. Confiscated during World War II by the Nazis, the hotel is at the foot of the road to Hitler's mountaintop retreat. Beneath it are remains of Nazi wartime bunkers. The decor, though fittingly rustic, is a bit dated. There's no restaurant, although evening meals can be ordered in advance. **Pros:** location, sense of history, Frau Schafenberg can cook! **Cons:** not all rooms have attached bathrooms, and some are far away. ⊠*Hintereck 2, Obersalzberg-Berchtesgaden* ☎*08652/2428* ⊕*www.hotel-zum-tuerken.de* ⇗*17 rooms, 12 with bath or shower* ☖*In-room: no a/c, no phone (some). In-hotel: no elevator, some pets allowed, no-smoking rooms,* ☰*AE, DC, MC, V* ☺*Closed Nov.–Dec. 20* ☷*BP.*

THE ROMANTIC ROAD

Of all the tourist routes that crisscross Germany, none rivals the aptly named Romantische Strasse, or Romantic Road. The route is memorable for the medieval towns like Rothenburg-ob-der-Tauber, Dinkelsbühl and Nördlingen. The final stop and highlight of the route is the "Mad King" Ludwig II's fantastical castle, Neuschwanstein.

The Romantic Road concept developed as West Germany rebuilt its tourist industry after World War II. A public-relations wizard coined the catchy title for a historic passage through Bavaria and Baden-Württemberg that could be advertised as a unit. In 1950 the Romantic Road was born. The name itself isn't meant to attract lovebirds, but rather uses the word "romantic" as meaning wonderful, fabulous, and imaginative. And, of course, the Romantic Road started as a road on which the Romans traveled.

PLANNING YOUR TIME

At the two best-known and therefore most visited places, Rothenburg-ob-der-Tauber and Neuschwanstein, it pays to arrive by night in order to get up early to tour the next morning. You can follow the night watchman in Rothenburg as he makes his rounds, and then see the town in the early morning. For Neuschwanstein an early start is even more important to beat the crowds.

GETTING HERE & AROUND
BY AIR
The major international airports serving the Romantic Road are Frankfurt and Munich. Regional airports include Nürnberg and Augsburg.

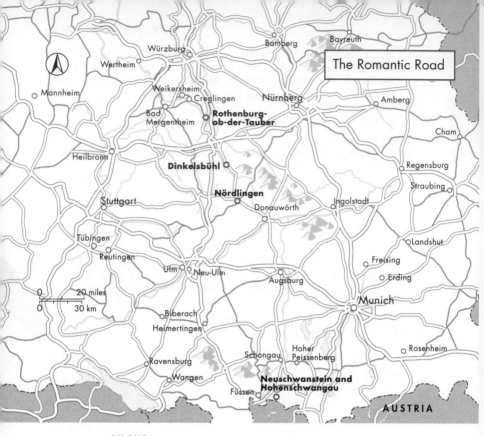

BY BUS

Daily bus service covers the northern stretch of the Romantic Road, between Frankfurt and Munich, from April through October. A second bus covers the section of the route between Dinkelsbühl and Füssen. Deutsche Touring also operates six more extensive tours along the Romantic Road for which reservations are essential.

BY CAR

The Romantic Road is most easily traveled by car, starting from Würzburg, the northernmost city, If you're coming up from the south and using Munich as a gateway, Augsburg is 60 km (37 mi) away.

BY TRAIN

Infrequent trains link most major towns of the Romantic Road, but both Würzburg and Augsburg are on the InterCity and high-speed Inter-City Express routes.

ESSENTIALS

Airport Contacts Airport Nürnberg (⊠ *Flughafenstr. 100D–90411* ☎ *0911/93700* ⊕ *www.airport-nuernberg.de*). **Augsburg Airport** (⊠ *Flughafenstr. 1D–86169* ☎ *0821/270–8111* ⊕ *www.augsburg-airport.de*).

Bus Contacts Deutsche Touring (⊠ *Am Römerhof 17D–60486 Frankfurt am Main* ☎ *069/790–3501* ⊕ *www.touring-germany.com*).

Visitor Information Touristik-Arbeitsgemeinschaft Romantische Strasse (*Central Tourist Information Romantic Road* ✉ *Segringerstr. 19, Dinkelsbühl* ☎ *09851/551–387* ⊕ *www.romantischestrasse.de*).

ROTHENBURG-OB-DER-TAUBER

Fodor'sChoice ★ *75 km (47 mi) west of Nürnberg.*

Rothenburg-ob-der-Tauber is the kind of medieval town that even Walt Disney might have thought too picturesque to be true, with half-timber architecture galore and a wealth of fountains and flowers against a backdrop of towers and turrets. It's undoubtedly something of a tourist trap, but genuine enough for all the hype. Don't miss Käthe Wohlfahrt's Christmas store, probably the most charming retail establishment in Germany.

> ### WORD OF MOUTH
>
> "We stayed two nights in Rothenburg. We enjoyed the town thoroughly. It is crowded during the day but we hiked along the wall and outside the wall to a small town nearby and missed the crowds. We listened to an organ concert in a church there, ate with the English Club, took the Night Watchman's Tour, saw the Crime Museum, shopped, etc."
>
> —kkukura

GETTING HERE & AROUND

The easiest way to get here is by car. You can also come by the Romantic Road bus from Frankfurt via Würzburg. By local train it takes about an hour from Würzburg— change trains at Steinach. The costumed night watchman conducts a nightly tour of the town, leading the way with a lantern.

ESSENTIALS

Visitor Information Rothenburg-ob-der-Tauber (✉ *Tourist-Information, Rathaus, Marktpl. 2* ☎ *09861/404800* ⊕ *www.rothenburg.de*).

EXPLORING

Mittelalterliches Kriminalmuseum *(Medieval Criminal Museum)*. The gruesome medieval implements of torture on display here are not for the fainthearted. The museum, the largest of its kind in Europe, also soberly documents the history of German legal processes in the Middle Ages. ✉ *Burgg. 3* ☎ *09861/5359* ⊕ *www.kriminalmuseum.rothenburg.de* 🎟 *€4* ⊙ *Apr.–Oct., daily 9:30–6; Nov., Jan., and Feb., daily 2–4; Dec. and Mar., daily 10–4.*

Stadtmauer *(City Wall)*. Rothenburg's city walls are more than 2 km (1 mi) long and provide an excellent way to circle the town from above. The walls' wooden walkway is covered by eaves. Stairs every 200 or 300 yards provide ready access. There are superb views of the tangle of pointed and tiled red roofs and of the rolling country beyond.

WHERE TO STAY

$–$$ ★ 🏨 **Burg-Hotel.** This exquisite little hotel abuts the town wall and was once part of a Rothenburg monastery. Most rooms have a view of the Tauber Valley. All have plush furnishings, with antiques or fine reproductions. The Steinway Cellar holds a grand piano. Breakfast is served in good weather on the terrace on top of the town wall, with an even more stunning wide-angle view into the Tauber Valley and the hills beyond. The owner and staff are gracious hosts. **Pros:** no crowds, terrific view from most rooms, nice touches throughout. **Cons:** parking is difficult for late-comers, no restaurant, too quiet for kids. ⊠*Klosterg. 1–3* ☎*09861/94890* ⊕*www.burghotel.rothenburg.de* ⤶*17 rooms* &*In-room: no a/c, Wi-Fi. In-hotel: spa, laundry service, public Wi-Fi, no-smoking rooms* ⊟*AE, DC, MC, V* ❡❮*CP.*

$$–$$$ ☷**Hotel Eisenhut.** It's fitting that the prettiest small town in Germany should have one of the prettiest small hotels. Every one of the 79 rooms is different—each with its own charming color scheme, most with antique furniture. ■**TIP**➔ **Try for one on the top floor toward the back, overlooking the old town and the Tauber River valley.** The restaurant ($$–$$$), one of the region's best, offers impeccable service along with delicious food and a lovely view of the garden. In summer you'll want to eat on the terrace, surrounded by flowers. **Pros:** spacious, elegant lobby, exceptional service, very good food. **Cons:** expensive, caters to elderly guests, nothing for teenage kids. ⊠*Herrng. 3–5* ☎*09861/7050* ⊕*www.eisenhut.com* ⤶*77 rooms, 2 suites* &*In-room: no a/c, Wi-Fi. In-hotel: restaurant, room service, bar, laundry service, public Wi-Fi, parking (fee), no-smoking rooms* ⊟*AE, DC, MC, V*

$$ ☷**Romantik-Hotel Markusturm.** The Markusturm began as a 13th-century customs house, an integral part of the city defense wall, and has since developed over the centuries into an inn and staging post and finally into a luxurious small hotel. Some rooms are beamed, others have Laura Ashley decor or gaily painted bedsteads, and some have valuable antiques from the Middle Ages. Try to book a reservation for dinner when you arrive, as the beamed, elegant restaurant ($–$$) may fill up. The fish is excellent—you may want to try it as part of their Romantic Gourmet dinner. Besides well-selected wines, you can order three kinds of home-brewed beer. In summer head for the patio. **Pros:** very tastefully decorated hotel and rooms, elegant atmosphere, excellent food, responsive owner. **Cons:** difficult to reach during the day because of the crowds. ⊠*Röderg. 1* ☎*09861/94280* ⊕*www.markusturm.de* ⤶*23 rooms, 2 suites* &*In-room: no a/c, Wi-Fi. In-hotel: restaurant, public Wi-Fi, parking (fee), no-smoking rooms* ⊟*AE, DC, MC, V* ❡❮*CP.*

FESTIVALS

The highlight of Rothenburg's annual calendar is the **Meistertrunk Festival,** over the Whitsun weekend, celebrating the famous wager said to have saved the town from destruction in the Thirty Years' War. It's a spectacular festival, when thousands of townspeople and local horsemen reenact the event in period costume.

SHOPPING

Käthe Wohlfahrt (⊠*Herrng. 1* ☎*09861/4090*) carries children's toys and seasonal decorations. The Christmas Village part of the store is a wonderland of mostly German-made toys and decorations. **Teddyland** (⊠*Herrng. 10* ⊕*www.teddyland.de* ☎*09861/8904*) has Germany's largest teddy-bear population. More than 5,000 of them pack this extraordinary store. ■**TIP**➔ **Children adore the place, but be prepared: these are pedigree teddies, and they don't come cheap. Check out the**

guided tour on their Web site for photos of bears taking in Rothenburg's sights.

DINKELSBÜHL

26 km (16 mi) south of Schillingsfürst.

Within the walls of Dinkelsbühl, a beautifully preserved medieval town, the rush of traffic seems a lifetime away. There's less to see here than in Rothenburg, and the mood is much less tourist-oriented. Like Rothenburg, Dinkelsbühl was caught up in the Thirty Years' War, and it also preserves a fanciful episode from those bloody times. An annual open-air-theater festival takes place from mid-June until mid-August.

LOCAL LEGEND

When Dinkelsbühl was under siege by Swedish forces and in imminent danger of destruction, a young girl led the children of the town to the enemy commander and implored him in their name for mercy. The commander of the Swedish army is said to have been so moved by the plea that he spared the town. Whether or not it's true, the story is retold every year during the Kinderzech Festival, a pageant by the children of Dinkelsbühl during a 10-day festival in July.

GETTING HERE & AROUND

In Dinkelsbühl you can patrol the illuminated old town with the night watchman at 9 PM free of charge, starting from the Münster St. Georg.

ESSENTIALS

Visitor Information Touristik-Arbeitsgemeinschaft Romantische Strasse (Central Tourist Information Romantic Road) (⊠ *Segringerstr. 19 Dinkelsbühl* ☎ *09851/551–387* ⊕ *www.romantischestrasse.de).* **Dinkelsbühl** (⊠ *Tourist-Information, Marktpl.* ☎ *09851/90240* ⊕ *www.dinkelsbuehl.de).*

EXPLORING

The **Münster St. Georg** *(Minster St. George)* is the standout sight in town. At 235 feet in length it's large enough to be a cathedral, and it's among the best examples in Bavaria of the late-Gothic style. Note the complex fan vaulting that spreads sinuously across the ceiling. If you can face the climb, head up the 200-foot tower for amazing views over the jumble of rooftops. ⊠ *Marktpl.* ☎ *09851/2245* ⌨ *Tower €1.50* ☉ *Church daily 9–noon and 2–5; tower May–Sept., weekends 2–6.*

WHERE TO STAY

$$ 🏨 **Hotel Deutsches Haus.** This medieval inn, with a facade of half-timber gables and flower boxes, has many rooms fitted with antique furniture. One of them has a romantic four-poster bed. Dine beneath heavy oak beams in the restaurant ($–$$), where you can try the local specialty, a type of grain called Dinkel. It's very nutritious and often served roasted with potatoes and salmon. **Pros:** genuine antique hotel, modern touches like free Wi-Fi. **Cons:** some rooms noisy, quite expensive. ⊠ *Weinmarkt 3* ☎ *09851/6058* ⊕ *www.deutsches-haus-dkb.de* ⤴ *16 rooms, 2 suites* ⚶ *In-room: no a/c, dial-up (some). In-hotel: restaurant, bar, parking*

(fee), no-smoking rooms ☰*AE, DC, MC, V* ⊘*Closed Jan. and Feb.* ⊙|*CP.*

$–$$ ⊞**Goldene Rose.** Since 1450 the inhabitants of Dinkelsbühl and their guests—among them Queen Victoria in 1891—have enjoyed good food and refreshing drinks in this half-timber house. Dark paneling in the restaurant ($–$$) creates the cozy atmosphere in which you can enjoy good regional cuisine, especially fish and game. Many of the comfortably furnished rooms have half-timber walls. **Pros:** family-friendly atmosphere, good food, hotel has a parking lot. **Cons:** some rooms need renovating, rooms at the front are noisy. ✉*Marktpl. 4* ☎*09851/57750* ⊕*www.hotel-goldene-rose.com* ⊅*31 rooms* ♿*In-room: no a/c, Wi-Fi. In-hotel: restaurant, bar, public Wi-Fi, parking (fee), some pets allowed* ☰*DC, MC, V* ⊙|*CP.*

SHOPPING

Deleika (✉*Waldeck 33* ☎*09857/97990*) makes barrel organs to order, although it won't deliver the monkey! The firm also has a museum of barrel organs and other mechanical instruments. It's just outside Dinkelsbühl. Call ahead. At **Dinkelsbüler Kunst-Stuben** (✉*Segringerstr. 52* ☎*09851/6750*), the owner, Mr. Appelberg, sells his own drawings, paintings, and etchings of the town.

NÖRDLINGEN

32 km (20 mi) southeast of Dinkelsbühl, 70 km (43 mi) northwest of Augsburg.

In Nördlingen the cry *"So G'sell so"*—*"All's well"*—still rings out every night across the ancient walls and turrets.

ESSENTIALS

Visitor Information Nördlingen (✉*Tourist-Information, Marktpl. 2* ☎*09081/84116* ⊕*www.noerdlingen.de*).

EXPLORING

Sentries sound out the traditional *"So G'sell so"* message from the 300-foot tower of the central parish church of **St. Georg** at half-hour intervals between 10 PM and midnight. The tradition goes back to an incident during the Thirty Years' War, when an enemy attempted to slip into the town and was detected by a resident. You can climb the 365 steps up the tower—known locally as the Daniel—for an unsurpassed view of the town and countryside, including, on clear days, 99 villages. The ground plan of the town is two concentric circles. The inner circle of streets, whose central point is St. Georg, marks the earliest medieval boundary. A few hundred yards beyond it is the outer boundary, a wall built to accommodate expansion. Fortified with 11 towers and punctuated by five massive gates, it's one of the best-preserved town walls in Germany. ✉*Marktpl.* ☎*Tower €1.50* ⊙*Daily 9–dusk.*

Nördlingen lies in the center of a huge, basinlike depression, the **Ries,** that until the beginning of this century was believed to be the remains of an extinct volcano. In 1960 it was proven by two Americans that the 24-km-wide (15-mi-wide) crater was caused by a meteorite at least

1 km (½ mi) in diameter. ■ **TIP**→ The compressed rock, or *Suevit,* formed by the explosive impact of the meteorite was used to construct many of the town's buildings, including St. Georg's tower.

WHERE TO STAY

$ 🏨 **Hotel Goldene Rose.** This small, modern hotel is just inside the town wall and is ideal for those who wish to explore Nördlingen on foot. The in-house restaurant serves wholesome, inexpensive dishes. **Pros:** new, small, family-run. **Cons:** front rooms noisy, restaurant closed on Sunday. ✉ *Baldingerstr. 42* 🕿 *09081/86019* ⊕ *www.goldene-rose-noerdlingen. de* 🛏 *17 rooms, 1 apartment* ♿ *In-room: no a/c. In-hotel: restaurant, parking (no fee), no-smoking rooms* ▭ *MC, V* 🍽 *CP.*

$–$$ 🏨 **Kaiserhof-Hotel-Sonne.** The great German poet Goethe stayed here, only one in a long line of distinguished guests starting with Emperor Friedrich III in 1487. The vaulted-cellar wine tavern is a reminder of those days. The three honeymoon suites are furnished in 18th-century style, with hand-painted four-poster beds. The property is right in the center of the city, in the shadow of the big church tower. **Pros:** historic hotel, in the center of town. **Cons:** hotel needs renovating, no Web site. ✉ *Marktpl. 3* 🕿 *09081/5067* 🖷 *09081/29290* 🛏 *40 rooms* ♿ *In-room: no a/c, Wi-Fi (some). In-hotel: restaurant, bar, parking (no fee), public Wi-Fi, some pets allowed, no-smoking rooms* ▭ *AE, MC, V* ⊘ *Closed Nov. Restaurant closed Jan. and Feb., Sun. dinner, and Wed.* 🍽 *CP.*

NEUSCHWANSTEIN & HOHENSCHWANGAU

93 km (60 mi) south of Augsburg, 105 km (65 mi) southwest of Munich.

These two famous castles belonging to the Wittelbachs, one historic and the other nearly "make-believe," are 1 km (½ mi) across a valley from each other, near the town of Schwangau. Bavaria's King Ludwig II (1845–86) spent much of his youth at Schloss Hohenschwangau (Hohenschwangau Castle). It's said that its neo-Gothic atmosphere provided the primary influences that shaped his wildly romantic Schloss Neuschwanstein (Neuschwanstein Castle), the fairy-tale castle he built after he became king, which has since become one of Germany's most recognized sights.

GETTING HERE & AROUND

From Schwangau (5 km [3 mi] north of Füssen, 91 km [59 mi] south of Augsburg, 103 km [64 mi] southwest of Munich), follow the road signs marked KÖNIGSCHLÖSSER (Royal Castles). After 3 km (2 mi) you come to Hohenschwangau, a small village consisting of a few houses, some good hotels, and five spacious parking lots (parking €4.50). You have to park in one of them and then walk to the ticket center serving both castles. The main street of the small village Hohenschwangau is lined with restaurants and quick eateries of all categories.

ESSENTIALS

Tickets Ticket Center (✉ *Alpseestr. 12 Hohenschwangau* 🕿 *08362/930–830* ⊕ *www.hohenschwangau.de*).

EXPLORING

Fodor's Choice ★ **Neuschwanstein.** This castle was conceived by a set designer instead of an architect, thanks to King Ludwig II's deep love of the theater. The castle soars from its mountainside like a stage creation—it should hardly come as a surprise that Walt Disney took it as the model for his castle in the movie *Sleeping Beauty* and later for the Disneyland castle itself.

The life of this spectacular castle's king reads like one of the great Gothic mysteries of the 19th century, and the castle symbolizes that life. Yet during the 17 years from the start of Schloss Neuschwanstein's construction until King Ludwig's death, the king spent less than six months in the country residence, and the interior was never finished. The Byzantine-style throne room is without a throne; Ludwig died before one could be installed. However, the walls of the rooms leading to Ludwig's bedroom are painted with murals depicting characters from Wagner's operas—Siegfried and the Nibelungen, Lohengrin, Tristan, and others. Ludwig's bed and its canopy are made of intricately carved oak. A small corridor behind the bedroom was styled as a ghostly grotto, reminiscent of Wagner's *Tannhäuser*. **Castle concerts** (☎08362/81980) are held in September in the gaily decorated minstrels' hall—one room, at least, that was completed as Ludwig conceived it. On the walls outside the castle's gift shop are plans and photos of the castle's construction. There are some spectacular walks around the castle. The delicate **Marienbrücke** (Mary's Bridge) is spun like a medieval maiden's hair across a deep, narrow gorge. From this vantage point there are giddy views of the castle and the great Upper Bavarian Plain beyond.

To reach Neuschwanstein from the ticket center below, take one of the clearly marked paths (about a 40-minute uphill walk) or one of the horse-drawn carriages that leave from Hotel Müller (uphill €5, downhill €2.50). A shuttle bus leaves from the Hotel Lisl (uphill €1.80, downhill €1) and takes you halfway up the hill past an outlook called Aussichtspunkt Jugend to a spot just above the castle. ⚠ **From there it's a steep 10-minute downhill walk to the castle, which is not recommended for the physically handicapped, or a 5-minute uphill walk to the Marienbrücke.** ✉ *Neuschwansteinstr. 20* ☎*08362/930–830* ⊕*www.neuschwanstein. de* 🎫*€9, including guided tour; ticket for both castles €17* ☉*Apr.–Sept., daily 8–5; Oct.–Mar., daily 9–3.*

Hohenschwangau. Built by the knights of Schwangau in the 12th century, this castle was remodeled later by King Ludwig II's father, the Bavarian crown prince (and later king) Maximilian, between 1832 and 1836. Unlike Ludwig's more famous castle across the valley, Neuschwanstein, the somewhat garishly yellow Schloss Hohenschwangau has the feeling of a noble home, where comforts would be valued as much as outward splendor. It was here that the young Ludwig met the composer Richard Wagner. Their friendship shaped and deepened the future king's interest in theater, music, and German mythology—the mythology Wagner drew upon for his *Ring* cycle of operas.

After obtaining your ticket at the ticket center in the village, you can take a 25-minute walk up either of two clearly marked paths to the castle,

The Fairy-Tale King

King Ludwig II (1845–86), the enigmatic presence indelibly associated with Bavaria, was one of the last rulers of the Wittelsbach dynasty, which ruled Bavaria from 1180 to 1918. Though his family had created grandiose architecture in Munich, Ludwig II disliked the city and preferred isolation in the countryside, where he constructed monumental edifices born of fanciful imagination, and spent most of the royal purse on his endeavors. Although he was also a great lover of literature, theater, and opera (he was Richard Wagner's great patron), it is his fairy-tale-like castles that are his legacy.

Ludwig II reigned from 1864 to 1886, all the while avoiding political duties

whenever possible. By 1878 he had completed his Schloss Linderhof retreat and immediately began Schloss Herrenchiemsee, a tribute to Versailles and Louis XIV. The grandest of his extravagant projects is Neuschwanstein, one of Germany's top attractions and concrete proof of the king's eccentricity. In 1886, before Neuschwanstein was finished, members of the government became convinced that Ludwig had taken leave of his senses. A medical commission declared the king insane and forced him to abdicate. Within two days of incarceration in the Berg Castle, on Starnbergersee, Ludwig and his doctor were found drowned in the lake's shallow waters. Their deaths are still a mystery.

or board one of the horse-drawn carriages that leave from Hotel Müller (uphill €3.50, downhill €1.50). *€9, including guided tour; ticket for both castles €17* ☎ *08362/930–830* ⊕ *www.hohenschwangau.de* ⊙ *Apr.–Sept., daily 8–5; Oct.–Mar., daily 9–3.*

WHERE TO STAY

$$ ☷ **Hotel Müller.** Between the two Schwangau castles, the Müller fits beautifully into the stunning landscape, its creamy Bavarian Baroque facade complemented by the green mountain forest. Inside, the Baroque influence is everywhere, from the finely furnished bedrooms to the chandelier-hung public rooms and restaurant ($–$$). The mahogany-paneled, glazed veranda (with open fireplace) provides a magnificent view of Hohenschwangau Castle. Round out your day with a local specialty such as the *Allgäuer Lendentopf* (sirloin) served with spaetzle. **Pros:** view of the castles, personalized service, variety of rooms. **Cons:** during the day crowds in and around the hotel, expensive in season. ⊠ *Alpseestr. 16 Hohenschwangau* ☎ *08362/81990* ⊕ *www.hotel-mueller.de* ☎ *39 rooms, 4 suites* ⅙ *In-room: no a/c. In-hotel: 2 restaurants, bar, public Wi-Fi, parking (no fee), some pets allowed, no-smoking rooms* ▭ *AE, DC, MC, V* ⊙ *Closed mid–Feb.–late Mar.* ℉ *CP.*

HEIDELBERG

The natural beauty of Heidelberg is created by the embrace of mountains, forests, vineyards, and the Neckar River—all crowned by the famous ruined castle. If any city in Germany encapsulates the spirit of the country, it is Heidelberg. Scores of poets and composers—virtually the entire 19th-century German Romantic movement—have sung its praises. Goethe and Mark Twain both fell in love here: the German writer with a beautiful young woman, the American author with the city itself. Sigmund Romberg set his operetta *The Student Prince* in the city; Carl Maria von Weber wrote his lushly Romantic opera *Der Freischütz* here. Composer Robert Schumann was a student at the university. The campaign these artists waged on behalf of the town has been astoundingly successful. Heidelberg's fame is out of all proportion to its size (population 140,000); more than 3½ million visitors crowd its streets every year.

Above all, Heidelberg is a university town, with students making up a large part of its population. And a youthful spirit is felt in the lively restaurants and pubs of the Altstadt. Modern Heidelberg has changed as U.S. army barracks and industrial development stretched into the suburbs, but the old heart of the city remains intact, exuding the spirit of romantic Germany.

PLANNING YOUR TIME
To fully appreciate Heidelberg, try to be up and about before the tour buses arrive. After the day-trippers have gone and most shops have closed, the good restaurants and the nightspots open up. Walking the length of Heidelberg's Hauptstrasse (main street) will take an hour— longer if you are easily sidetracked by the shopping opportunities. Strolling through the Old Town and across the bridge to look at the castle will take you at least another half-hour, not counting the time you spend visiting the sites.

GETTING HERE & AROUND
BY TRAIN
Heidelberg is 15 minutes away from Mannheim, where four ICE-trains and five Autobahn routes meet. Everything in town may be reached on foot. A funicular takes you up to the castle and Heidelberg's Königstuhl mountain, and a streetcar takes you from the center of the city to the main station.

ESSENTIALS
Bus Information Lufthansa Airport Bus (☎ *0180/583–8426 in Heidelberg* ⊕ *www.lufthansa-airportbus.com*).**TLS** (☎ *06221/770–077* ⊕ *www.tls-heidelberg. de*).

Visitor Information Heidelberger Convention and Visitors Bureau (✉ *Ziegelhäuser, Landstr. 3* ☎ *06221/142–223* ⊕ *www.heidelberg-marketing. de*). **Heidelberg** (✉ *Tourist-Information am Hauptbahnhof, Willy-Brandt-Pl. 1* ☎ *06221/19433* ⊕ *www.cvb-heidelberg.de*).

EXPLORING HEIDELBERG

⑤ Alte Brücke *(Old Bridge)*. Framed by two *Spitzhelm* towers (so called for their resemblance to old German helmets), this bridge was part of medieval Heidelberg's fortifications. In the west tower are three dank dungeons that once held common criminals. Above the portcullis you'll see a memorial plaque that pays warm tribute to the Austrian forces who helped Heidelberg beat back a French attempt to capture the bridge in 1799. The bridge itself is one of many to be built on this spot; ice floes and floods destroyed its predecessors. The elector Carl Theodor, who built it in 1786–88, must have been confident that this one would last: he had a statue of himself erected on it, upon a plinth decorated with river gods and goddesses (symbolic of the Neckar, Rhine, Danube, and Mosel rivers). As you enter the bridge from the Old Town, you'll also notice a statue of an animal that appears somewhat catlike. It's actually a monkey holding a mirror. Legend has it that the statue was erected to symbolize the need for both city-dwellers and those who live on the other side of the bridge to take a look over their shoulders as they cross—that neither group is more elite than the other.

4 **Alte Universität** *(Old University).* The three-story Baroque structure, officially named Ruprecht-Karl-University, was built between 1712 and 1718 at the behest of the elector Johann Wilhelm. It houses the University Museum, with exhibits that chronicle the history of Germany's oldest university. The present-day Universitätsplatz (University Square) was built over the remains of an Augustinian monastery that was destroyed by the French in 1693. ⊠*Grabeng. 1–3* ☎*06221/542–152* 🏷*€3* ☉*Apr.–Oct., Tues.–Sun. 10–6; Nov.–Mar., Tues.–Sat. 10–4.*

3 **Königstuhl** *(King's Throne).* The second-highest hill in the Odenwald range—1,700 feet above Heidelberg—is only a hop, skip, and funicular ride from Heidelberg. On a clear day you can see as far as the Black Forest to the south and west to the Vosges Mountains of France. The hill is at the center of a close-knit network of hiking trails. Signs and colored arrows from the top lead hikers through the woods of the Odenwald.

1 **Königstuhl Bergbahn** *(funicular).* The funicular hoists visitors to the summit of the Königstuhl in 17 minutes. On the way it stops at the ruined Heidelberg Schloss and Molkenkur. The funicular usually leaves every 10 minutes in summer and every 20 minutes in winter. ⊠*Kornmarkt* ⊕*www.bergbahn-heidelberg.de* 🏷*Round-trip to Schloss, Molkenkur, or Königstuhl €3.50.*

2 **Schloss** *(Castle).* What's most striking is the architectural variety of
Fodor'sChoice this great complex. The oldest parts still standing date from the 15th
★ century, though most of the castle was built in the Renaissance and Baroque styles of the 16th and 17th centuries, when the castle was the seat of the Palatinate electors. There's even an "English wing," built in 1612 by the elector Friedrich V for his teenage Scottish bride, Elizabeth Stuart; its plain, square-window facade is positively foreign compared to the castle's more opulent styles. (The enamored Friedrich also had a charming garden laid out for his young bride; its imposing arched entryway, the Elisabethentor, was put up overnight as a surprise for her 19th birthday.) The architectural highlight remains the Renaissance courtyard—harmonious, graceful, and ornate.

The castle includes the **Deutsches Apotheken–Museum** *(German Apothecary Museum* ☎*06221/25880* ☉ *Daily 10–5:30).* This museum, on the lower floor of the Ottheinrichsbau (Otto Heinrich Building), is filled with ancient flagons and receptacles (each with a carefully painted

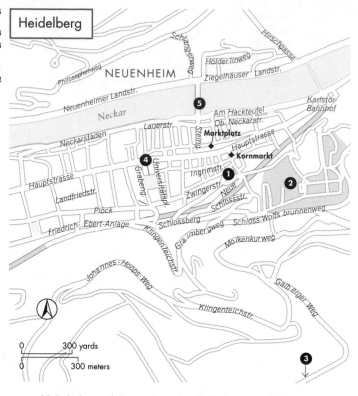

enamel label), beautifully made scales, little drawers, shelves, a marvelous reconstruction of an 18th-century apothecary shop, dried beetles
and toads, and a mummy with a full head of hair. Even if you have to
wait, you should make a point of seeing the *Grosses Fass* (Great Cask),
an enormous wine barrel in the cellar, made from 130 oak trees and
capable of holding 58,500 gallons. It was used to hold wines paid as
taxes by wine growers in the Palatinate.

In summer there are fireworks displays from the castle terrace (on the
first Saturday in June and September and the second Saturday in July).
In July and August the castle hosts a theater festival. Performances of
The Student Prince often figure prominently. The castle may be reached
by taking the Königstuhl Bergbahn. Generations of earlier visitors hiked
up to it on the Burgweg, a winding road. ☎06221/538–431 ⊕*www.
heidelberg-schloss.de* ⊠€3; audio tours an additional €4 ۩ Mar.–Nov.,
daily 9:30–6; Dec.–Feb., daily 10–5; tours in English daily from 11,
when demand is sufficient.

WHERE TO EAT

$$$$ ✕**Schlossweinstube.** This spacious Baroque dining room specializes in
★ *Ente von Heidelberg* (roast duck), but there's always something new on
the seasonal menu. Whatever you order, pair it with a bottle from the
extensive selection of international wines. Adjacent to the dining room
is the Bistro Backhaus (¢–$), which has rustic furnishings and a nearly
50-foot-high *Backkamin* (baking oven). Light fare as well as coffee and
cake are served indoors and on the shaded terrace. You can sample rare
wines (Eiswein, Beerenauslese) by the glass in the shared wine cellar, or
pick up a bottle with a designer label depicting Heidelberg. Reservations are essential for terrace seating in the summer. ⊠*Schlosshof, on
castle grounds* ☎*06221/97970* ═*AE, DC, MC, V* ☉*Schlossweinstube
closed late-Dec.–Jan. and Wed. No lunch.*

$$$$ ✕**Schwarz Das Restaurant.** Sleek, contemporary furnishings, soft lighting, stunning panoramic views, and Manfred Schwarz's creative
cuisine make for unforgettable dining in this 12th-floor restaurant,
complete with an apéritif bar and cigar lounge. The five- to seven-
course gourmet menu of the month varies from Asiatic to Mediterranean to French. On the menu you may find sautéed goose liver on
truffled polenta with raspberry vinegar sauce or gratinéed scallops
with chive sauce and caviar. ⊠*Kurfürsten-Anlage 60, opposite train
station* ☎*06221/757–030* ═*AE, DC, MC, V* ☉*Closed Sun., Mon.,
and 1st 2 wks of Jan. No lunch.*

$$–$$$ ✕**Simplicissimus.** Olive oil and herbs of Provence accentuate many of
★ chef Johann Lummer's culinary delights. Saddle of lamb and sautéed
liver in honey-pepper sauce are specialties; the *Dessertteller,* a sweet
sampler, is a crowning finish to any meal. The wine list focuses on
Old World estates, particularly clarets. The elegant Art Nouveau interior is done in shades of red with dark-wood accents. ⊠*Ingrimstr. 16*
☎*06221/183–336* ═ *MC, V* ☉*Closed Mon., Feb., and 2 wks in Aug.
and Sept. No lunch.*

$–$$ ✕**Zur Herrenmühle.** A 17th-century grain mill has been transformed
into this romantic restaurant. The old beams add to the warm atmosphere. In summer, try to arrive early to get a table in the idyllic courtyard. Fish, lamb, and homemade pasta are specialties. The prix-fixe
menu offers an especially good value. ⊠*Hauptstr. 239, near Karlstor*
☎*06221/602–909* ═*AE, MC, V* ☉*Closed Sun. No lunch.*

¢–$ ✕**Zum Roten Ochsen.** Many of the rough-hewn oak tables here have
initials carved into them, a legacy of the thousands who have visited
Heidelberg's most famous old tavern. Mark Twain, Marilyn Monroe,
and John Wayne may have left their mark—they all ate here. You can
wash down simple fare, such as goulash soup and bratwurst, or heartier
dishes, such as *Tellerfleisch* (boiled beef) and sauerbraten, with German
wines or Heidelberg beer. The "Red Ox" has been run by the Spengel
family for 165 years. Come early to get a good seat. ⊠*Hauptstr. 217*
☎*06221/20977* ═*MC, V* ☉*Closed Sun. dinner and mid-Dec.–mid-
Jan. No lunch Nov.–Mar.*

6

WHERE TO STAY

$$$–$$$$
Fodor'sChoice
★

Der Europäische Hof–Hotel Europa. The most luxurious of Heidelberg's hotels is located on secluded grounds next to the Old Town. Its many public parlors are outfitted with stunning turn-of-the-last-century furnishings, and bedrooms are spacious and tasteful; all suites have whirlpool tubs. In the elegant restaurant, the Kurfürstenstube ($$$–$$$$), rich shades of yellow and blue are offset by the original woodwork of 1865. In summer, meals are served on the fountain-lined terrace. There are great views of the castle from the two-story, glass-lined fitness and wellness centers. **Pros:** pure luxury and perfection, warm welcome. **Cons:** Kurfürstenstube closed in summer, expensive. ⊠ *Friedrich-Ebert-Anlage 1* ☎ *06221/5150* ⊕ *www.europaeischerhof.com* ⚓ *100 rooms, 15 suites, 3 apartments* ♿ *In-room: no a/c (some), Wi-Fi. In-hotel: 2 restaurants, bar, pool, gym, laundry service, public Internet, public Wi-Fi, parking (fee), some pets allowed, no-smoking rooms* ⊟ *AE, DC, MC, V* ⎢◎⎥*BP.*

$$$$

Hotel Die Hirschgasse. A stunning castle view marks this historic inn (1472), located across the river opposite Karlstor (15-minute walk to Old Town). Convivial Ernest Kraft and his British wife Allison serve upscale regional specialties (and wines from the vineyard next door) in the Mensurstube ($$–$$$), once a tavern where university students indulged in fencing duels, as mentioned in Mark Twain's *A Tramp Abroad.* Beamed ceilings, stone walls, and deep red fabrics make for romantic dining in elegant Le Gourmet ($$$–$$$$). The hotel's decor is also romantic, filled with floral prints, artwork, and deep shades of red. The suites are quite large, comfortable, and elegantly appointed. **Pros:** terrific view, very elegant suites, very good food in both restaurants, only no-smoking rooms. **Cons:** only no-smoking rooms, sometimes not enough parking, expensive. ⊠ *Hirschg. 3* ☎ *06221/4540* ⊕ *www.hirschgasse.de* ⚓ *20 suites* ♿ *In-room: no a/c, Wi-Fi. In-hotel: 2 restaurants, bar, laundry service, public Wi-Fi, parking, some pets allowed, no-smoking rooms* ⊟ *AE, DC, MC, V* ◎ *Le Gourmet closed 2 wks in early Jan., 2 wks in early Aug., and Sun. and Mon.; Mensurstube closed Sun. No lunch at either restaurant.*

$–$$
★

Nh Heidelberg. The glass-covered entrance hall is very spacious—not surprising, as it was the courtyard of a former brewery. The hotel is within reasonable walking distance of Heidelberg's major sites, about 1 km (½ mi) from Old Town. You can dine at one of three on-site restaurants, including the Raustubert, which specializes in regional German fare. Rooms are colorful and cozy. As it is mainly a business hotel, you get very good room rates in summer, especially in August. **Pros:** incredibly spacious yet welcoming lobby, good food in two restaurants, good room rates in summer, as it is a business hotel. **Cons:** business hotel, lacks charm, not in center of town. ⊠ *Bergheimerstr. 91* ☎ *06221/13270* ⊕ *www.nh-hotels.com* ⚓ *174 rooms* ♿ *In-room: Wi-Fi. In-hotel: 2 restaurants, room service, bar, gym, laundry service, public Wi-Fi, parking (fee), no smoking rooms* ⊟ *AE, DC, MC, V.*

$$$–$$$$

Romantik Hotel zum Ritter St. Georg. If this is your first visit to Germany, try to stay here. It's the only Renaissance building in Heidelberg (1592) and has a top location opposite the market square in the heart of Old Town. The staff is exceptionally helpful and friendly. Some rooms are more modern and spacious than others, but all are comfortable. You can enjoy German and international favorites in the restaurants Belier ($–$$$) and Ritterstube ($–$$). Both are wood paneled and have Old World charm. **Pros:** charm and elegance, fabulous food and terrific service, top location in center of town, nice

> ### WORD OF MOUTH
>
> "I would recommend Heidelberg because it is a quaint student town/city with a lot of nightlife. Plenty of traditional German atmosphere but very youthful and perhaps even rowdy."
>
> —DAX

views, spacious rooms. **Cons:** expensive, parking garage 5 minutes away on foot. ⊠*Hauptstr. 178* ☎*06221/1350* ⊕*www.ritter-heidelberg.de* ↘*37 rooms, 1 suite* &*In-room: no a/c, Wi-Fi. In-hotel: 2 restaurants, laundry service, public Internet, public Wi-Fi, some pets allowed, no-smoking rooms* ⊟*AE, DC, MC, V.*

NIGHTLIFE

Heidelberg nightlife is concentrated in the area around the Heiliggeist-kirche (Church of the Holy Ghost), in the Old Town. Don't miss a visit to one of the old student taverns that have been in business for ages.

Mark Twain rubbed elbows with students at **Zum Roten Ochsen** (⊠*Hauptstr. 217* ☎*06221/20977*). **Zum Sepp'l** (⊠*Hauptstr. 213* ☎*06221/23085*) is another traditional, always-packed pub. **Schnookeloch** (⊠*Haspelg. 8* ☎*06221/138–080*) has long been patronized by dueling frats.

Today's students, however, are more likely to hang out in one of the dozen or more bars on **Untere Strasse,** which runs parallel to and between Hauptstrasse and the Neckar River, starting from the market square. **Destille** (⊠*Unterestr. 16* ☎*06221/22808*) has a tree in the middle of the room that is always decorated according to season. The young crowd that packs the place is always having a good time.

FRANKFURT

Although modest in size (fifth among German cities, with a population of 667,000), Frankfurt is Germany's financial powerhouse. Not only is the German Central Bank (Bundesbank) here, but also the European Central Bank (ECB), which manages the euro. Some 300 credit institutions (more than half of them foreign banks) have offices in Frankfurt, including the headquarters of five of Germany's largest banks. You can see how the city acquired its other nickname, "Bankfurt am Main."

Legend has it that the Frankish Emperor Charlemagne was chasing a deer on the Main's south bank when the animal plunged into the river and, to the emperor's amazement, crossed it with its head always above water. A stone ridge had made the river shallow at that point. That supposedly was the origin of Frankfurt (literally "Frankish Ford") as an important river crossing. Commerce flourished from then on.

PLANNING YOUR TIME

The weather in Frankfurt is moderate throughout the year, though rather wet. Summers are mild with the occasional hot day, and it rarely gets very cold in winter and hardly ever snows. The mild temperatures make visiting in the off-season a great idea, but watch out for trade fairs, which also occur at this time of year. Winter or summer, days can be spent visiting the museums or shopping on the Zeil. In the evening, head across the river to the apple wine district of Sachsenhausen for dinner and drinks.

GETTING HERE & AROUND
BY AIR

There are two airports with the name "Frankfurt": Flughafen Frankfurt Main (FRA), which receives direct flights from many U.S. cities and from all major European cities, and Frankfurt-Hahn (HHN), which is a former U.S. air base 70 mi west of Frankfurt and handles some super-cheap flights, mainly to and from secondary European airports.

BY BUS & SUBWAY

Frankfurt's smooth-running, well-integrated public transportation system (called RMV) consists of the U-bahn (subway), S-bahn (suburban railway), Strassenbahn (streetcars), and buses. Fares for the entire system, which includes a very extensive surrounding area, are uniform, though they are based on a complex zone system. Within the time that your ticket is valid (one hour for most inner-city destinations), you can transfer from one part of the system to another.

Tickets may be purchased from automatic vending machines, which are at all U-bahn and S-bahn stations. If you're caught without a ticket, there's a fine of €40.

BY CAR

Frankfurt is the meeting point of a number of major autobahns. The most important are A–3, running south from Köln and then on east to Würzburg and Nürnberg, and A–5, running south from Giessen and then on toward Heidelberg and Basel.

In Frankfurt speeders are caught with hidden cameras, and tow trucks cruise the streets in search of illegal parkers. There are many reasonably priced parking garages around the downtown area and a well-developed "park and ride" system with the suburban train lines. The transit map shows nearly a hundred outlying stations with a "P" symbol beside them, meaning there is convenient parking there.

BY TAXI

Cabs are not always easy to hail from the sidewalk; some stop, whereas others will pick up only from the city's numerous taxi stands or outside hotels or the train station. You can always order a cab. Fares start at €2 (€2.50 in the evening) and increase by a per-kilometer (½ mi) charge of €1.60 for the first 3, €1.38 thereafter.

BY TRAIN

EuroCity, InterCity, and InterCity Express trains connect Frankfurt with all German cities and many major European ones. The InterCity Express line links Frankfurt with Berlin, Hamburg, Munich, and a number of other major hubs. All long-distance trains arrive at and depart from the Hauptbahnhof, and many also stop at the long-distance train station at the airport.

ESSENTIALS

Airport Contacts Flughafen Frankfurt (☎ *01805/372–4636* ⊕ *www.airport city-frankfurt.de*). **Flughafen Hahn** (☎ *06543/509–113* ⊕ *www.hahn-airport.de*).

Bus Contacts Bohr Busreisen (☎ *06543/50–190* ⊕ *www.bohr-omnibusse.de*). **Deutsche Touring** (✉ *Mannheimerstr. 15, City Center* ☎ *069/230–735* ⊕ *www. touring.de*). **Verkehrsgesellschaft Frankfurt am Main** (*City Transit Authority* ☎ *069/2132–2425* ⊕ *www.vgf-ffm.de* or *www.ebbelwei-express.com*).

Taxi Contacts Taxis (☎ *069/250–001, 069/230–001, 069/230–033,* or *069/792–020*). **Velotaxi** (☎ *0700/8356-8294*).

Train Contacts Deutsche Bahn (German Railways ☎ *11861* ⊕ *www.bahn.de*).

Visitor Information Tourismus und Congress GmbH Frankfurt/Main (✉ *Römerberg 27, Altstadt* ☎ *069/2123–8800* ⊕ *www.frankfurt-tourismus.de*).

EXPLORING FRANKFURT

The Hauptbahnhof (main train station) area and adjoining Westend district are mostly devoted to business, as evidenced by the banks towering overhead. You'll find the department stores of the Hauptwache and Zeil a half-mile east of the station, and you'll want to avoid the drug-ridden red-light district southwest of the station. The city's past can be found in the Old Town's restored medieval quarter and in Sachsenhausen, across the river, where pubs and museums greatly outnumber banks.

CITY CENTER & WESTEND

⑥ Alte Oper *(Old Opera House).* Kaiser Wilhelm I traveled from Berlin for the gala opening of the opera house in 1880. Gutted in World War II, the house remained a hollow shell for 40 years while controversy raged over its reconstruction. The exterior and lobby are faithful to the original, though the remainder of the building is more like a modern multipurpose hall. ✉ *Opernpl., City Center* ☎ *069/134–0400* ⊕ *www. alte-oper-frankfurt.de* Ⓜ *Alte Oper (U-bahn).*

⑤ Fressgasse *("Pig-Out Alley").* Grosse Bockenheimer Strasse is the proper name of this pedestrian street, which Frankfurters have given this sobriquet because of its amazing choice of delicatessens, wine merchants, cafés, and restaurants, offering everything from crumbly cheeses and smoked fish to vintage wines and chocolate creams. Ⓜ *Hauptwache (U-bahn and S-bahn), Alte Oper (U-bahn).*

⑧ Goethehaus und Goethemuseum *(Goethe's House and Museum).* The house
★ where Germany's most famous poet was born in 1749 is furnished with many original pieces that belonged to his family, including manuscripts

in his own hand. The original house was destroyed by Allied bombing and has been carefully rebuilt and restored in every detail.

Johann Wolfgang von Goethe studied law and became a member of the bar in Frankfurt. He was quickly drawn to writing, however, and in this house he eventually wrote the first version of his masterpiece, *Faust.* The adjoining museum contains works of art that inspired Goethe (he was an amateur painter) and works associated with his literary contemporaries. ⊠ *Grosser Hirschgraben 23–25, Altstadt* ☎ *069/138–800* ⊕ *www.goethehaus-frankfurt.de* 🎟️ *€5* ⊙ *Mon.–Sat. 10–6, Sun. 10–5:30* Ⓜ *Hauptwache (U-bahn and S-bahn)*.

❾ Jüdisches Museum *(Jewish Museum)*. The story of Frankfurt's Jewish quarter is told in the former Rothschild Palais. Prior to the Holocaust, the community was the second-largest in Germany. The museum contains a library of 5,000 books, a large photographic collection, and a documentation center. *Untermainkai 14–15, Altstadt* ☎ *069/2123–5000* ⊕ *www.juedischesmuseum.de* 🎟️ *€4* ⊙ *Tues. and Thurs.–Sun. 10–5, Wed. 10–8* Ⓜ *Willy-Brandt-Platz (U-bahn)*.

A branch of the Jewish museum, **Museum Judengasse** (⊠ *Kurt-Schu-macher-Str. 10, City Center* ☎ *069/297–7419* 🎟️ *€2* ⊙ *Tues. and Thurs.–Sun. 10–5, Wed. 10–8* Ⓜ *Konstablerwache [U-bahn]*), is built around the foundations of mostly 18th-century buildings, which once made up the Jewish quarter. The branch is also near the Alter Jüdischer Friedhof.

❷ Kaiserdom. Because the Holy Roman emperors were chosen and crowned here from the 16th to the 18th century, the church is known as the Kaiserdom (Imperial Cathedral), even though it isn't the seat of a bishop. Officially the Church of St. Bartholomew, it was built largely between the 13th and 15th centuries and survived World War II with most of its treasures intact. The most impressive exterior feature is the tall, red sandstone tower (almost 300 feet high), which was added between 1415 and 1514. It is anticipated that the public can climb the tower in 2009. The **Dommuseum** (Cathedral Museum) occupies the former Gothic cloister. ⊠ *Dompl. 1, Altstadt* ☎ *069/1337–6184* ⊕ *www.dom-frank furt.de* 🎟️ *Dommuseum €3* ⊙ *Church Mon.–Thurs. and Sat. 9–noon and 2:30–6, Fri. and Sun. 2:30–6. Dommuseum Tues.–Fri. 10–5, weekends 11–5* Ⓜ *Römer (U-bahn)*.

❼ Palmengarten und Botanischer Garten *(Tropical Garden and Botanical* ꜱ *Gardens)*. A splendid cluster of tropical and semitropical greenhouses contains a wide variety of flora, including cacti, orchids, and palms. The surrounding park, which can be surveyed from a miniature train, has many recreational facilities, including a small lake where you can rent rowboats, a play area for children, and a wading pool. ■ TIP→ In summer there's an extensive concert program that takes place in an outdoor pavilion. ⊠ *Siesmayerstr. 61, Westend* ☎ *069/2123–3939* ⊕ *www. palmengarten-frankfurt.de* 🎟️ *€5* ⊙ *Daily 9–6* Ⓜ *Westend (U-bahn)*.

❶ Römerberg. This square north of the Main River, lovingly restored after wartime bomb damage, is the historical focal point of the city. The

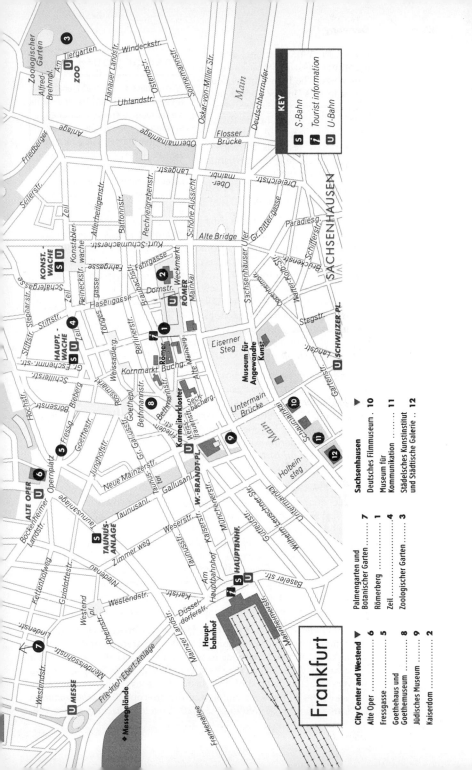

Frankfurt

City Center and Westend ▼

KEY

S S-Bahn
i Tourist information
U U-Bahn

Römer, the Nikolaikirche, and the half-timber Ostzeile houses are all found here. The 16th-century Fountain of Justitia (Justice), which flows with wine on special occasions, stands in the center of the Römerberg. The square is also the site of many public festivals throughout the year, including the Christmas markets in December. ⊠ *Between Braubachstr. and Main River, Altstadt* Ⓜ *Römer (U-bahn).*

❹ **Zeil.** The heart of Frankfurt's shopping district is this bustling pedestrian street running east from Hauptwache Square. With mass consumerism in mind, it's lined with department stores, a few smaller boutiques, drugstores, cellphone franchises, electronics shops, fast-food eateries, restaurants, and more, and there is an outdoor farmers' market every Thursday and Saturday. Ⓜ *Hauptwache, Konstablerwache (U-bahn and S-bahn).*

❸ **Zoologischer Garten** *(Zoo).* Founded in 1858, this is one of the most important and attractive zoos in Europe. Its remarkable collection includes some 4,500 animals of 500 different species, an exotarium (aquarium plus reptiles), a new large ape house, and an aviary, reputedly the largest in Europe. Nocturnal creatures move about in a special section. ⊠ *Bernhard-Grzimek-Allee 1, Ostend* ☎ *069/2123–3735* ⊕ *www.zoo-frankfurt.de* 🎫 *€8* ⊗ *Nov.–Mar., daily 9–5; Apr.–Oct., daily 9–7* Ⓜ *Zoo (U-bahn).*

SACHSENHAUSEN

Fodor'sChoice
★
The old quarter of Sachsenhausen, on the south bank of the Main River, has been sensitively preserved, and its cobblestone streets, half-timber houses, and beer gardens make it a very popular area to stroll. Sachsenhausen has two big attractions. One is the famous *Apfelwein* (apple-wine or -cider) taverns around the Rittergasse pedestrian area. You can eat well in these small establishments. The other is the **Museumufer** (Museum Riverbank), which has seven museums almost next door to one another. They exhibit motion pictures, communication, art, architecture, world culture, applied art, and sculpture.

❿ **Deutsches Filmmuseum** *(German Film Museum).* Germany's first museum of cinematography has everything from demonstrations of the methods for making animated cartoons to a virtual ride over the city aboard a flying carpet. A theater in the basement has regular evening screenings of every imaginable type of film, historical to avant-garde. There are also showings of films for children in the afternoon. ⊠ *Schaumainkai 41, Sachsenhausen* ☎ *069/9612–20220* ⊕ *www.deutschesfilmmuseum.*

de 🔲*€2.50* ⊙ *Tues., Thurs., and Fri. 10–5, Sun. and Wed. 10–7, Sat. 2–7* Ⓜ *SchweizerPlatz (U-bahn).*

◾ **NEED A BREAK?** Two of Sachsenhausen's liveliest Apfelwein taverns are well removed from the Rittergasse and handy to the Museumufer. You'll find them adjacent to one another if you turn south down Schweizer Strasse, next to the Deutsches Filmmuseum, and walk five minutes. **Zum Gemalten Haus** (⊠ *Schweizerstr. 67, Sachsenhausen* ☎ *069/614–559*) will provide all the hard cider and *Gemütlichkeit* you could want. **Zum Wagner** (⊠ *Schweizerstr. 71, Sachsenhausen* ☎ *069/612–565*) reeks so with "Old Sachsenhausen" schmaltz that it's downright corny.

⓫ **Museum für Kommunikation** *(Museum for Communication).* This is the place for talking on picture telephones and learning about glass-fiber technology. Exhibitions on historic communication methods include mail coaches, a vast collection of stamps from many countries and eras, and ancient dial telephones with their clunky switching equipment. ⊠ *Schaumainkai 53, Sachsenhausen* ☎ *069/60600* ⊕ *www.museumss tiftung.de* 🔲*€2.50* ⊙ *Tues.–Fri. 9–6, weekends 11–7* Ⓜ *SchweizerPlatz (U-bahn).*

⓬ **Städelsches Kunstinstitut und Städtische Galerie** *(Städel Art Institute and Municipal Gallery).* You'll find one of Germany's most important art collections at this newly renovated museum, with paintings by Dürer, Vermeer, Rembrandt, Rubens, Monet, Renoir, and other masters. ◾ **TIP➜ The section on German expressionism is particularly strong, with representative works by Frankfurt artist Max Beckmann.** ⊠ *Schaumainkai 63, Sachsenhausen* ☎ *069/605–0980* ⊕ *www.staedelmuseum.de* 🔲*€10* ⊙ *Tues. and Fri.–Sun. 10–6, Wed. and Thurs. 10–9* Ⓜ *Schweizer Platz (U-bahn).*

6

WHERE TO EAT

CITY CENTER

$ ✕ **Maintower.** Atop the skyscraper that houses the Hessischer Landesbank, this popular cocktail bar and gourmet restaurant captures an
★ unbeatable view. Through 25-foot floor-to-ceiling windows, you can take in all of "Mainhattan." The cuisine is part global, part regional. It's hard to get a table for supper, though it's less of a problem for afternoon coffee or an evening at the bar. ◾ **TIP➜ Prices are surprisingly reasonable, though you will have to pay €4.60 per person just to take the elevator up and down.** ⊠ *Neue Mainzerstr. 52–58, City Center* ☎ *069/3650–4770* ⌂ *Reservations essential* 🍴*AE, MC, V* Ⓜ *Alte Oper (U-bahn).*

$ ✕ **Metropol.** Breakfast is the main attraction at this café near the Römerberg and Dom. The dining room is large, and in the warmer months it's extended to include seating on a garden patio. In addition to the daily selection of tantalizing cakes and pastries, the menu features salads, pastas, and a few traditional German dishes. If you're up late, remember that Metropol is open until 1 AM. ⊠ *Weckmarkt 13–15, City Center* ☎ *069/288–287* ⊙ *Closed Mon.* 🍴*No credit cards* Ⓜ *Römer (U-bahn).*

WESTEND

$ ✕ **Cafe Siesmayer.** Frankfurt's Palmengarten at last has dining facilities worthy of the beloved botanical garden. Cafe Siesmayer, accessible either from the garden or from the street, has a terrace where you can enjoy your coffee and cake with a splendid garden view. A full range of main courses is also available, and it is open for breakfast. ✉ *Siesmayerstr. 59, Westend* ☎ *069/90029–200* 🖃 *AE, DC, MC, V* Ⓜ *Westend (U-bahn).*

$$$$ ✕ **Erno's Bistro.** This tiny, unpretentious place in a quiet Westend neighborhood seems an unlikely candidate for the best restaurant in Germany. Yet that's what one French critic called it. The bistro's specialty, fish, is often flown in from France. It's closed weekends, during the Christmas and Easter seasons, and during much of the summer—in other words, when its patrons, well-heeled business executives, are unlikely to be in town. ✉ *Liebigstr. 15, Westend* ☎ *069/721–997* ⚐ *Reservations essential* 🖃 *AE, MC, V* ⊘ *Closed weekends and July–early Aug.* Ⓜ *Westend (U-bahn).*

$$$$ ✕ **Gargantua.** One of Frankfurt's most creative chefs, Klaus Trebes, who
Fodor's Choice   doubles as a food columnist, serves up modern versions of German
★   classics and French-accented dishes. His specialties include angel codfish served with cabbage and a champagne-mustard butter, and stuffed oxtail with mushrooms, onions, and a potato-celery puree. ■ **TIP→** One corner of the restaurant is reserved for those who only want to sample the outstanding wine list. ✉ *Liebigstr. 47, Westend* ☎ *069/720–718* 🖃 *AE, MC, V* ⊘ *Closed Sun. No lunch Sat.* Ⓜ *Westend (U-bahn).*

SACHSENHAUSEN

$$–$$$ ✕ **Maingau Stuben.** Chef Jörg Döpfner greets you himself and lights your candle at this excellent restaurant. A polished clientele is drawn by the linen tablecloths, subdued lighting, and such nearly forgotten practices as carving the meat at your table. The menu includes asparagus salad with homemade wild-boar ham and braised veal cheek with wild-garlic risotto. The place also has a cellar full of rare German wines. ✉ *Schifferstr. 38–40, Sachsenhausen* ☎ *069/610–752* 🖃 *AE, DC, MC, V* ⊘ *Closed Mon. No lunch Sat., no dinner Sun.* Ⓜ *Schweizer Platz (U-bahn).*

$ ✕ **Zum Wagner.** The kitchen produces the same hearty German dishes as
★   other apple-cider taverns, only better. Try the schnitzel or the *Tafelspitz mit Frankfurter Grüner Sosse* (stewed beef with a sauce of green herbs), or come on Friday for fresh fish. Cider is served in large quantity in the noisy, crowded dining room. This Sachsenhausen classic, with sepia-tone murals of merrymaking, succeeds in being touristy and traditional all at once. Warning: it serves no beer! ✉ *Schweizerstr. 71, Sachsenhausen* ☎ *069/612–565* 🖃 *AE, MC, V* Ⓜ *SchweizerPlatz (U-bahn).*

WHERE TO STAY

CITY CENTER

$$ 🏨 **Hotel Nizza.** This beautiful Victorian building, only a five-minute walk from the main train station, is filled with antiques. The proprietor has added a modern touch in some bathrooms with her own hand-

painted murals. **Pros:** antique furnishings, roof garden with shrubbery and a view of the skyline. **Cons:** right in the unattractive Bahnhof district. ⊠*Elbestr. 10, City Center* ☎*069/242–5380* ⊕*www.hotelnizza. de* ⤙*25 rooms* ♿*In-room: no a/c, Wi-Fi (some). In-hotel: bar, some pets allowed, no-smoking rooms* ⊟*MC, V* ⍩*CP* Ⓜ*Willy-Brandt-Platz (U-bahn and S-bahn).*

$ 🖳 **InterCity Hotel.** If there ever was a hotel at the vortex of arrivals and departures, it's this centrally located hostelry in an elegant Old World building across the street from the main train station. InterCity hotels were set up by the Steigenberger chain with the business traveler in mind. The station's underground garage is at your disposal. **Pros:** guests get a pass for unlimited local transportation. **Cons:** overlooks a cargo facility. ⊠*Poststr. 8, Bahnhof* ☎*069/273–910* ⊕*www.intercityhotel. com* ⤙*384 rooms, 3 suites* ♿*In-room: dial-up, Wi-Fi (some). In-hotel: restaurant, bar, gym, public Internet, some pets allowed, no-smoking rooms* ⊟*AE, DC, MC, V* ⍩*BP* Ⓜ*Hauptbahnhof (U-bahn and S-bahn).*

$$$$
Fodor's Choice
★
🖳 **Steigenberger Hotel Frankfurter Hof.** The neo-Gothic, five-star "Frankfurter Hof" is the "first lady" of Frankfurt hotellerie, the first choice of visiting heads of state and business and finance moguls. It fronts on a grand courtyard, and there's little that such guests desire that isn't available: 24-hour room service; suites up to a thousand square feet in dark woods and brass with air conditioning (rare in Germany); marble baths with Jacuzzis, slippers; mirrored, walk-in closets. It's one of the city's oldest hotels, but its modern services earn it kudos. **Pros:** an atmosphere of old-fashioned, formal elegance, with burnished wood floors, fresh flowers, and thick carpeting. **Cons:** expensive. ⊠*Kaiserpl., City Center* ☎*069/21502* ⊕*www.frankfurter-hof.steigenberger.de* ⤙ *360 rooms, 41 suites* ♿*In-room: no a/c (some), refrigerator, dial-up, Wi-Fi. In-hotel: 5 restaurants, room service, bar, concierge, public Internet, parking (fee), some pets allowed* ⊟*AE, DC, MC, V* Ⓜ*Willy-Brandt-Platz (U-bahn).*

SACHSENHAUSEN

$ 🖳 **Maingau.** You'll find this pleasant hotel-restaurant in the middle of the lively Sachsenhausen quarter. Rooms are modest but spotless, comfortable, and equipped with TVs; the room rate includes a substantial breakfast buffet. The restaurant, Maingau-Stuben, is one of Frankfurt's best. **Caution: Though the hotel is inexpensive, the restaurant is anything but! Pros:** handy to Sachsenhausen nightlife, fantastic restaurant. **Cons:** on a busy street. ⊠*Schifferstr. 38–40, Sachsenhausen* ☎*069/609–140* ⊕*www.maingau.de* ⤙*80 rooms* ♿*In-room: no a/c, refrigerator. In-hotel: restaurant, some pets allowed* ⊟*AE, DC, MC, V* ⍩*BP* Ⓜ*Schweizer Platz (U-bahn).*

6

THE RHINELAND

The banks of the Rhine are crowned by magnificent castle after castle and by breathtaking, vine-terraced hills that provide the livelihood for many of the villages hugging the shores. The vineyards, a legacy of the

Romans, are an inherent part of the Rhine landscape from Wiesbaden to Bonn. The Rhine tempers the climate sufficiently for grapes to ripen this far north, and the world's finest Rieslings come from the Rheingau and from the Rhine's most important tributary, the Mosel. The river is steeped in legend and myth. The Loreley, a jutting sheer slate cliff, was once believed to be the home of a beautiful and bewitching maiden who lured boatmen to a watery end in the swift currents.

The Mosel is one of the most hauntingly beautiful river valleys on earth. Here, as in the Rhine Valley, forests and vines carpet steep hillsides; castles and church spires dot the landscape; and the river's countless bends and loops slow its pace and lend the region a special charm.

PLANNING YOUR TIME
Those seeking "Rhine romance" should visit the Rhine Gorge, the river's most spectacular stretch with its castles, vineyards, and the Loreley. The Mosel landscape is no less majestic, but it's less narrow and more peaceful than that of the Rhine Gorge.

GETTING HERE & AROUND
BY AIR
The Rhineland is served by three international airports: Frankfurt, Düsseldorf, and Köln-Bonn. Bus and rail lines connect each airport with its respective downtown area and provide rapid access to the rest of the region. The Luxembourg Findel International Airport is close to the upper Mosel River valley.

BY TRAIN
InterCity and EuroCity trains between Frankfurt and Bonn serve the Rhine Gorge en route. Local trains from Koblenz serve the Mosel Valley.

ESSENTIALS
Airport Contacts Flughafen Düsseldorf (☎ *0211/4210* ⊕ *www.duesseldorf-international.de*). **Flughafen Frankfurt** (☎ *01805/372–4636* ⊕ *www.airportcity-frankfurt.de*). **Flughafen Köln/Bonn** (✉ *Köln* ☎ *02203/404-001* ⊕ *www.koeln-bonn-airport.de*). **Luxembourg Findel International Airport** (☎ *00352/2464–1* ⊕ *www.luxairport.lu*).

Train Contacts Deutsche Bahn (☎ *11861* ⊕ *www.bahn.de*). **Kölner Verkehrs-Betriebe** (*KVB* ☎ *0221/547-3333*).

Visitor Information Rheingau–Taunus Kultur & Tourismus (✉ *An der Basilika 11a, Oestrich–Winkel* ☎ *06723/99550* ⊕ *www.rheingau-taunus-info.de*).

ELTVILLE

14 km (9 mi) west of Wiesbaden via A–66 and B–42.

The former Cistercian monastery **Kloster Eberbach** is idyllically set in a secluded forest clearing 3 km (2 mi) west of Kiedrich. ■TIP➔ Its **Romanesque and Gothic buildings (12th–14th centuries) look untouched by time—one reason why the film of Umberto Eco's medieval murder mystery *The Name of the Rose,* starring Sean Connery, was filmed here.**

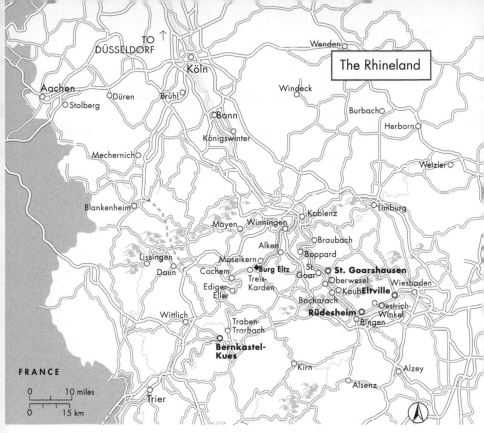

The monastery's impressive collection of old winepresses bears witness to a viticultural tradition that spans nearly nine centuries. The wines can be sampled year-round in the **vinothek** or restaurant on the grounds. The church, with its excellent acoustics, and the large medieval dormitories are the settings for concerts, wine auctions, and festive wine events. ⊠ *Stiftung Kloster Eberbach* ☎ *06723/91780* ⊕ *www.klostereberbach.de* ✉ *€3.50* ⊙ *Apr.–Oct., daily 10–6; Nov.–Mar., daily 11–5.*

WHERE TO EAT

$$$$ ✕**Kronenschlösschen.** The atmosphere of this stylish Art Nouveau house (1894) is intimate. Chef Patrik Kimpel, vice-president of the German Young Restaurateurs, oversees both the gourmet restaurant Kronenschlösschen and the more casual Bistro. Fish is a house specialty (try the halibut with a lemon-lime crust and a carrot-ginger sauce). You can also dine in the parklike garden. The wine list focuses on the finest Rheingau estates for whites and Old and New World estates for reds. ⊠ *Rheinallee Eltville-Hattenheim* ☎ *06723/640* ⊟ *AE, MC, V.*

RÜDESHEIM

30 km (19 mi) west of Wiesbaden.

Tourism and wine are the heart and soul of Rüdesheim.

ESSENTIALS

Visitor Information Rüdesheim (✉ *Tourist-Information, Geisenheimer Str. 22* ☎ *06722/19433* ⊕ *www.ruedesheim.de*).

EXPLORING

Less than 500 feet long, **Drosselgasse** *(Thrush Alley),* is a narrow, pub-lined lane, which is abuzz with music and merrymaking from noon until well past midnight every day from Easter through October.

Since 1892 the **Asbach Weinbrennerei** has produced one of Germany's most popular brands of *Weinbrand* (wine brandy, the equivalent of cognac). It's a key ingredient in brandy-filled *Pralinen* (chocolates) and in the local version of Irish coffee, Rüdesheimer Kaffee. You can tour the plant and shop for the goodies it produces. ✉ *Asbach Besucher Center, Ingelheimer Str. 4, on eastern edge of town* ☎ *06722/497–345* ⊕ *www.asbach.de* ⊙ *Mar.–Dec., Tues.–Sat. 9–5.*

High above Rüdesheim and visible for miles stands *Germania,* a colossal female statue crowning the **Niederwald-Denkmal** *(Niederwald Monument).* This tribute to German nationalism was built between 1877 and 1883 to commemorate the rebirth of the German Empire after the Franco-Prussian War (1870–71). Germania faces across the Rhine toward the eternal enemy, France. At her base are the words to a stirring patriotic song: "Dear Fatherland rest peacefully! Fast and true stands the watch, the watch on the Rhine!" There are splendid panoramic views from the monument and from other vantage points on the edge of the forested plateau. You can reach the monument on foot, by car (via Grabenstrasse), or over the vineyards in the *Seilbahn* (cable car). There's also a *Sessellift* (chairlift) to and from Assmannshausen, a red-wine enclave, on the other side of the hill. ✉ *Oberstr. 37* ☎ *06722/2402* ⊕ *www.seilbahn-ruedesheim.de* 🎫 *One way €4.50, round-trip or combined ticket for cable car and chairlift €6.50* ⊙ *Mid-Mar.–Apr. and Oct., daily 9:30–5; May–Sept., daily 9:30–6.*

WHERE TO STAY

$$ 🏨 **Breuer's Rüdesheimer Schloss.** Guests at this stylish, historic hotel (note: it was never a castle) are welcomed with a drink from the family's Rheingau wine estate. Marissa Breuer, daughter of gracious hosts Susanne and Heinrich Breuer, was named Rheingau Wine Queen. Most rooms offer a vineyard view. Cellar or vineyard tours and wine tastings can be arranged. If you stay a week you pay only for six days. **Pros:** right off the Drosselgasse. **Cons:** noisy touristic area. ✉ *Steing. 10* ☎ *06722/90500* ⊕ *www.ruedesheimer-schloss.com* 🛏 *23 rooms, 3 suites* ♿ *In-room: no a/c, refrigerator, dial-up, Wi-Fi. In-hotel: restaurant, bar, bicycles, laundry service, some pets allowed, no-smoking rooms* ⊟ *AE, DC, MC, V* ⊙ *Closed Christmas–early Jan.* ❤️*BP.*

$$ 🏨 **Hotel Krone Assmannshausen.** From its humble beginnings in 1541 as an inn for sailors and ferrymen, the Krone evolved into an elegant,

antiques-filled hotel. Rooms at the back face on busy railroad tracks, but thick glass provides good soundproofing. Two of the suites have their own sauna. The restaurant ($$$$) offers first-class service and fine wining and dining. Classic cuisine prepared by chef Jens Kottke and a superb collection of wines, including the famed Spätburgunder red wines of Assmannshausen, make for very memorable meals indoors or on the terrace overlooking the Rhine. **Pros:** charming views of vineyards and the Rhine. **Cons:** right on a main rail line. ⊠ *Rheinuferstr. 10, Rüdesheim-Assmannshausen* ☎*06722/4030* ⊕*www.hotel-krone. com* ⇨*52 rooms, 13 suites, 1 apartment* ⚘*In-room: no a/c, dial-up, Wi-Fi. In-hotel: restaurant, bar, pool, laundry service, no-smoking rooms* ⊟*AE, MC, V*

ST. GOARSHAUSEN

29 km (18 mi) north of Rüdesheim, ferry from St. Goar.

One of the Rhineland's main attractions lies 4 km (2½ mi) south of St. Goarshausen: the steep (430-foot-high) slate cliff named after the beautiful blond nymph **Loreley.** Here she supposedly sat, singing songs so lovely that sailors and fishermen were lured to the treacherous rapids—and their demise. The rapids really were once treacherous. The Rhine is at its narrowest here, and the current the swiftest. Contrary to popular belief, the Loreley nymph doesn't stem from legend. She was invented in 1812 by author Clemens Brentano, who drew his inspiration from the sirens of Greek legend. Her tale was retold as a ballad by Heinrich Heine and set to music by Friedrich Silcher at the height of Rhine Romanticism in the 19th century. The haunting melody is played on the PA systems of the Rhine boats whenever the Loreley is approached.

EN ROUTE **Burg Eltz** *(Eltz Castle)* is one of Germany's most picturesque, genuinely medieval castles (12th–16th centuries), and merits as much attention as King Ludwig's trio of castles in Bavaria. The 40-minute English-language tour, given when enough English-speakers gather, guides you through the period rooms and massive kitchen. There is also a popular treasure vault filled with gold and silver. To get here, exit B–416 at Hatzenport (opposite and southwest of Alken), proceed to Münstermaifeld, and follow signs to the parking lot near the Antoniuskapelle. From here it's a 15-minute walk, or take the shuttle bus (€1.50). Hikers can reach the castle from Moselkern in 40 minutes. ⊠ *Burg Eltz/ Münstermaifeld* ☎*02672/950–500* ⊕*www.burg-eltz.de* 🖾*Tour and treasure vault €8* ⊙*Apr.–Oct., daily 9:30–5:30.*

BERNKASTEL-KUES

100 km (62 mi) southwest of Koblenz on B–53.

Bernkastel and Kues straddle the Mosel, on the east and west banks, respectively.

ESSENTIALS

Visitor Information Bernkastel-Kues (⊠ *Tourist-Information, Gestade 6* ☎ *06531/4023* ⊟ *06531/7953* ⊕ *www.bernkastel.de*).

EXPLORING

Elaborately carved half-timber houses (16th–17th centuries) and a Renaissance town hall (1608) frame St. Michael's Fountain (1606) on Bernkastel's photogenic **market square.** In early September the square and riverbank are lined with wine stands for one of the region's largest wine festivals, the Weinfest der Mittelmosel.

From the hilltop ruins of the 13th-century castle, **Burg Landshut,** there are splendid views. It was here that Trier's Archbishop Boemund II is said to have recovered from an illness after drinking the local wine. This legendary vineyard, still known as "the Doctor," soars up from Hinterm Graben street near the town gate, Graacher Tor. You can purchase these exquisite wines from Weingut J. Lauerburg at the estate's tasteful wineshop. ⊠ *Am Markt 10* ☎ *06531/3898* ⊗ *Apr.–Oct., weekdays 1–5, Sat. 11–4.*

WHERE TO STAY & EAT

$$$$
Fodor'sChoice
★

✕ **Waldhotel Sonnora.** At their elegant country inn set in the forested Eifel Hills, Helmut and Ulrike Thieltges offer guests one of Germany's absolute finest dining experiences. Helmut is an extraordinary chef, renowned for transforming truffles, foie gras, and Persian caviar into culinary masterpieces. Challans duck in an orange-ginger sauce is his specialty. The wine list is equally superb. The dining room, with gilded and white-wood furnishings and plush red carpets, has a Parisian look. Pretty gardens add to a memorable visit. ⊠ *Auf dem Eichelfeld, 8 km (5 mi) southwest of Wittlich, which is 18 km (11 mi) west of Kues via B–50; from A–1, exit Salmtal Dreis* ☎ *06578/98220* ♙ *Reservations essential* ⊟ *AE, MC, V* ⊗ *Closed Mon. and Tues., Jan. and 1st 2 wks in July.*

$

⌂ **Gästehaus Erika Prüm.** The traditional wine estate S. A. Prüm has state-of-the-art cellars, a tastefully designed vinothek, and a beautiful guesthouse with an idyllic patio facing the Mosel. The spacious rooms and baths are individually decorated in a winning mixture of contemporary and antique furnishings. Erika Prüm is a charming host, and her husband, Raimund (the redhead), is an excellent winemaker who offers tastings and cellar tours. **Pros:** spacious rooms and baths. **Cons:** no elevator. ⊠ *Uferallee 25, north of Kues Bernkastel-Wehlen* ☎ *06531/3110* ⊕ *www.sapruem.com* ➟ *8 rooms* ♿ *In-room: no a/c, dial-up. In-hotel: no elevator, some pets allowed* ⊟ *AE, MC, V* ⊗ *Closed mid-Dec.–Feb.* ⦿ *BP.*

HAMBURG

Water—in the form of the Alster Lakes and the Elbe River—is Hamburg's defining feature and the key to the city's success. A harbor city with an international appeal, Hamburg is one of the most open-minded of German cities. But for most Europeans the port city invariably triggers thoughts of the gaudy Reeperbahn underworld, that sleazy strip of clip joints, sex shows, and wholesale prostitution that helped earn

Hamburg its reputation as "Sin City." Today the infamous red-light district is just as much a hip meeting place for young Hamburgers and tourist crowds, who flirt with the bright lights and chic haunts of the not-so-sinful Reeperbahn, especially on warm summer nights.

The distinguishing feature of downtown Hamburg is the artificial lake known as the Alster. It's lined with stately hotels, department stores, fine shops, and cafés and by parks and gardens against a backdrop of private mansions. The city is at the mouth of the Elbe, one of Europe's great rivers and the 97-km (60-mi) umbilical cord that ties the harbor to the North Sea.

> **WORD OF MOUTH**
>
> "I would have to say that Berkastel might have been my favorite town in the entire region. It was large enough to have lots to explore, but laid out so that exploration on foot was very possible and rewarding."
>
> —phieaglefan

PLANNING YOUR TIME

The downtown area features most of Hamburg's must-see attractions, such as the grand, historic churches and most museums. Take a stroll along the two major boulevards in the area, the Jungfernstieg along the Alster and the Mönckebergstrasse, and venture out to the many side streets and canal-side walks. Any visit to Hamburg should include a walk along the Reeperbahn in St. Pauli, as well as a closer inspection of the Altstadt with its 19th century warehouses and cobblestone alleys. Boat tours of the massive harbor and the cosmopolitan Alster Lake are very good ways to get to know the city.

GETTING HERE & AROUND

BY AIR

Hamburg's international airport, Fuhlsbüttel, is 11 km (7 mi) northwest of the city. The Airport-City-Bus runs nonstop between the airport and Hamburg's main train station daily at 15- to 30-minute intervals.

BY BUS & SUBWAY

Hamburg's bus station, the Zentral-Omnibus-Bahnhof, is directly behind the main train station. The HVV, Hamburg's public transportation system, includes the U-bahn (subway), the S-bahn (suburban train), and buses. Tickets are available on all buses and at automatic machines in all stations and at most bus stops. You must validate your ticket at a machine at the start of your journey. If you are found without a validated ticket, the fine is €40.

BY CAR

Hamburg is easier to handle by car than many other German cities, and traffic is relatively uncongested. During rush hour, however, there can be gridlock. Several autobahns (A–1, A–7, A–23, A–24, and A–250) connect with Hamburg's three beltways, which then easily take you to the downtown area.

BY TAXI

Taxi meters start at €2.40, then add €1.68 per km thereafter. You can hail taxis on the street or at stands, or order one by phone.

BY TRAIN

There are two principal stations: the central Hauptbahnhof (Main Train Station) and Hamburg-Altona, west of the downtown area. EuroCity and InterCity trains connect Hamburg with all German cities and many major European ones. InterCity Express "supertrain" lines link Hamburg with Berlin, Frankfurt, and Munich

ESSENTIALS

Airport Information **Fuhlsbüttel** (☎040/50750 ⊕ www.ham.airport.de).

Bus Information **Hamburg Passenger Transport Board** (Hamburger Verkehrsverbund ⊠ Steindamm 94, Altstadt ☎040/325-7750 ⊕ www.hvv.de ☉ Daily). **Zentral-Omnibus-Bahnhof** (ZOB ⊠ Adenauerallee 78, St. Georg ☎040/247-576).

Taxi Information **Taxi** (☎040/441-011, 040/686-868, or 040/666-666).

Train Information **Hauptbahnhof** (⊠ Steintorpl., Altstadt ☎11861).

Visitor Information **Hamburg-Hotline** (☎040/3005-1300 ⊕ www.hamburg-tourism.de). **Hamburg Tourismus GmbH** (⊠ Hauptbahnhof, Altstadt ☎040/3005-1300 ⊠ St. Pauli Landungsbrücken, St. Pauli ☎040/3005-1200 or 040/3005-1203 ⊠ Steinstr. 7, Altstadt ☎040/3005-1144 ⊕ www.hamburg-tourism.de). **Stade Tourismus GmbH** (⊠ Hansestr. 16Stade ☎04141/40910 ⊟04141/409-150 ⊕ www.stade.de).

EXPLORING HAMBURG

Hamburg's most important attractions stretch between the Alster Lakes to the north and the harbor and Elbe River to the south. This area consists of four distinct quarters. St. Georg is the business district around the Hauptbahnhof (Main Train station). The historic Altstadt (Old City) clusters near the harbor and surrounds the Rathaus (Town Hall). West of the Altstadt is Neustadt (New City). The shabby but thrilling district of St. Pauli includes the Reeperbahn, a strip of sex clubs and bars.

DOWNTOWN

❸ **Hagenbecks Tierpark** *(Hagenbecks Zoo).* One of the country's oldest and
ⓒ most popular zoos is family owned. Founded in 1848, it was the world's first city park to let wild animals such as lions, elephants, chimpanzees, and others roam freely in vast, open-air corrals. Weather permitting, you can ride one of the elephants. In the Troparium, an artificial habitat creates a rain forest, an African desert, and a tropical sea. ⊠ *Lokstedter Str. at Hamburg-Stellingen, Niendorf* ☎040/540–0010 ⊕ *www.hagenbeck.de* ☎€15 ☉ *Mar.–June, daily 9–6; July and Aug., daily 9–7; Sept. and Oct., daily 9–6; Nov.–Feb., daily 9–4:30; last admission at 3:30* Ⓜ *Hagenbecks Tierpark (U-bahn).*

❶ **Jungfernstieg.** This wide promenade looking out over the Alster Lakes is the city's premier shopping boulevard. Laid out in 1665, it used to be part of a muddy millrace that channeled water into the Elbe. Hidden from view behind the sedate facade of Jungfernstieg is a network of nine covered arcades that together account for almost a mile of shops selling everything from souvenirs to haute couture. Many of these air-conditioned passages have sprung up in the past two decades, but some have been here since the 19th century; the first glass-covered arcade, called Sillem's Bazaar, was built in 1845. ⊠*Neustadt* Ⓜ*Jungfernstieg (U-bahn)*.

❷ **Rathaus** *(Town Hall)*. To most Hamburgers this large building is the
★ symbolic heart of the city. As a city-state—an independent city and simultaneously one of the 16 federal states of Germany—Hamburg has a city council and a state government, both of which have their administrative headquarters in the Rathaus. A pompous neo-Renaissance affair, the building dictates political decorum in the city. To this day, the mayor of Hamburg never welcomes VIPs at the foot of its staircase, but always awaits them at the very top—whether it's a president or the queen of England.

Both the Rathaus and the **Rathausmarkt** (Town Hall Market) lie on marshy land, a fact vividly brought to mind in 1962, when the entire area was severely flooded. The large square, with its surrounding arcades, was laid out after Hamburg's Great Fire of 1842. The architects set out to create a square with the grandeur of Venice's Piazza San Marco. The Rathaus was begun in 1866, when 4,000 piles were sunk into the moist soil to support the structure. It was completed in 1892, the year a cholera epidemic claimed the lives of 8,605 people in 71 days. A fountain and monument to that unhappy chapter in Hamburg's history are in a rear courtyard of the Rathaus.

The immense building, with its 647 rooms (6 more than Buckingham Palace) and imposing central clock tower, is not the most graceful structure in the city, but the sheer opulence of its interior is astonishing. A 45-minute tour begins in the ground-floor Rathausdiele, a vast pillared hall. Although you can only view the state rooms, their tapestries, huge staircases, glittering chandeliers, coffered ceilings, and grand portraits give you a sense of the city's great wealth in the 19th century and its understandable civic pride. ⊠*Rathausmarkt, Altstadt* ☎*040/428–310* ⊕*www.hamburg.de* ✉*English-language tour €3* ⊙*Tours Mon.–Thurs., hourly 10:15–3:15, Fri., hourly 10:15–1:15, Sat., hourly 10:15–5:15, Sun., hourly 10:15–4:15* Ⓜ*Mönckebergstr. (U-bahn)*.

THE HARBOR & HISTORIC HAMBURG

❺ **Freihafen Hamburg.** Hamburg's Free Port, the city's major attraction,
Fodor's Choice dates to the 12th century, when the city was granted special privileges
★ by Holy Roman Emperor Frederick I (Barbarossa). One of these was
Ⓒ freedom from paying duties on goods transported on the Elbe River. The original Free Port was where the Alster meets the Elbe, near Deichstrasse, but it was moved farther south as Hamburg's trade expanded. When Hamburg joined the German Empire's Customs Union in the late 1800s, the Free Port underwent major restructuring to make way for additional storage facilities. An entire residential area was torn down

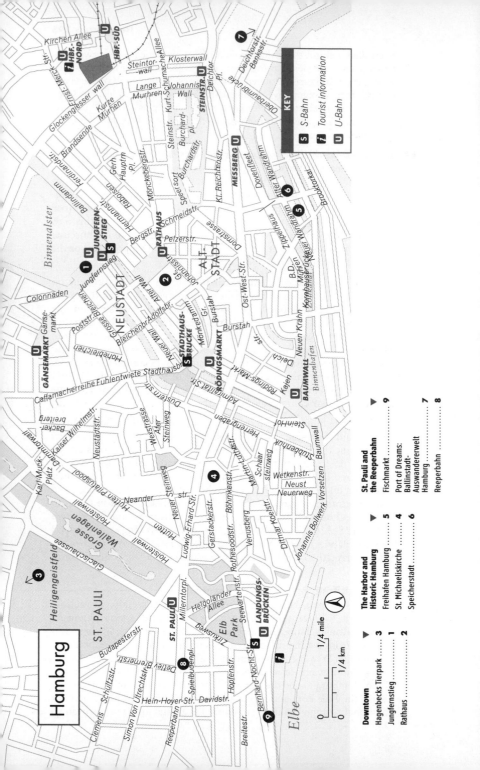

Hamburg

Downtown ▶

Hagenbecks Tierpark 3
Jungfernstieg 1
Rathaus 2

The Harbor and Historic Hamburg ▶

Freihafen Hamburg 5
St. Michaeliskirche 4
Speicherstadt 6

St. Pauli and the Reeperbahn ▶

Fischmarkt 9
Port of Dreams: Ballinstadt-Auswandererwelt Hamburg 7
Reeperbahn 8

KEY

S S-Bahn
i Tourist information
U U-Bahn

0 ___ 1/4 mile
0 ___ 1/4 km

ST. PAULI

NEUSTADT

ALTSTADT

Binnenalster

Elbe

Heiligengeistfeld

GÄNSEMARKT U

JUNGFERNSTIEG U S

RATHAUS U

STADTHAUSBRÜCKE S

RÖDINGSMARKT U

STEINSTR. U

MESSBERG U

HBF.-NORD

HBF.-SÜD

ST. PAULI U

LANDUNGSBRÜCKEN U S

(including many Renaissance and Baroque buildings), and the Speicherstadt warehouses, the world's largest block of continuous storage space, came into being between 1885 and 1927. Ⓜ*St. Pauli Landungsbrücken (U-bahn)*.

WORD OF MOUTH

"I was in Hamburg last week—our first foray into northern Germany. Loved the city, and the harbor tour was fantastic—an absolute must-see."

—hausfrau

❹ **St. Michaeliskirche** *(St. Michael's Church)*. The Michel, as it's called locally, is Hamburg's principal church and northern Germany's finest Baroque-style ecclesiastical building. Constructed between 1649 and 1661 (the tower followed in 1669), it was razed after lightning struck almost a century later. It was rebuilt between 1750 and 1786 in the decorative Nordic Baroque style, but was gutted by a terrible fire in 1906. The replica, completed in 1912, was demolished during World War II. The present church is a reconstruction.

The distinctive 433-foot brick-and-iron tower bears the largest tower clock in Germany, 26 feet in diameter. Just above the clock is a viewing platform (accessible by elevator or stairs) that affords a magnificent panorama of the city, the Elbe River, and the Alster Lakes. ∎TIP➜ **Twice a day, at 10 AM and 9 PM (Sunday at noon), a watchman plays a trumpet solo from the tower platform, and during festivals an entire wind ensemble crowds onto the platform to perform.** The Multivisionsshow (slide and audio show), located one floor beneath the viewing platform, recounts Hamburg's history on a 16-foot screen. ⊠*St. Michaeliskirche, Altstadt* ☎*040/376–780* ⊕*www.st-michaelis.de* ▱*Tower €2.50; crypt €1.25; tower and show €4; crypt and show €2.75; show, tower, and crypt €4.50* ⊙*May–Oct., Mon.–Sat. 9–8, Sun. 12:30–8; Nov.–Apr., Mon.–Sat. 10–6, Sun. 12:30–6; multimedia screening daily on the half hr, 12:30–3:30* Ⓜ*Landungsbrücken, Rödingsmarkt (U-bahn)*.

❻ **Speicherstadt** *(Warehouse District)*. These imposing warehouses in the Freihafen Hamburg reveal yet another aspect of Hamburg's extraordinary architectural diversity. A Gothic influence is apparent here, with a rich overlay of gables, turrets, and decorative outlines. These massive rust-brown buildings are still used to store and process every conceivable commodity, from coffee and spices to raw silks and hand-woven Oriental carpets.

Although you won't be able to enter the buildings, the nonstop comings and goings will give you a good sense of a port at work. If you want to learn about the history and architecture of the old warehouses, detour to the **Speicherstadtmuseum.** ⊠*St. Annenufer 2, Block R, Speicherstadt* ☎*040/321–191* ⊕*www.speicherstadtmuseum.de* ▱*€3* ⊙*Apr.–Oct., Tues.–Fri. 10–5, weekends 10–6; Nov.–Mar., Tues.–Sun., 10–5* Ⓜ*Messberg (U-bahn)*.

Opposite the historic Speicherstadt sits one of Europe's largest urban-development projects, the **HafenCity.** This new district will have both business and residential areas spread over 387 acres. Once completed,

6

the HafenCity will include a cruise-ship terminal, a high-tech symphony hall (the Elbphilmarmonie), a maritime art museum, and a science center with an aquarium. You can see a model of the project, slated for completion in 2025, in the visitor center in Speicherstadt's old power plant. Take a closer look at the ongoing construction at a bright red observation platform on Strandkai—the first buildings along the Marco-Polo Terrassen are finally complete. It's a nice place to watch passing ships. ⊠*Am Sandtorkai 30, Speicherstadt* ☎*040/3690–1799* ⊕*www.hafen city.com* 🖾*Free* ☉ *Visitor Center: Tues.–Sun. 10–6; May–Sept., Tues.– Wed., Fri.–Sun. 10–6, Thurs. 10–8* Ⓜ*Messberg (U-bahn).*

ST. PAULI & THE REEPERBAHN

❾ **Fischmarkt** *(Fish Market).* A trip to the open-air Altona Fischmarkt is
☾ worth getting out of bed early for—or staying up all night. The pitch of fervent deal making is unmatched in Germany. Offering real bargains, the market's barkers are famous for their sometimes rude but usually successful bids to shoppers. Sunday fish markets became a tradition in the 18th century, when fishermen sold their catch before church services. Today freshly caught fish are only a part of the scene. You can find almost anything here—from live parrots and palm trees to armloads of flowers and bananas, valuable antiques, and fourth-hand junk. ⊠*Between Grosse Elbestr. and St. Pauli Landungsbrücken, St. Pauli* ☉*Apr.–Sept., Sun. 5 AM–9:30 AM; Oct.–Mar., Sun., 7–9:30* Ⓜ*Land-ungsbrücken (U-bahn).*

❼ **Port of Dreams: BallinStadt–Auswandererwelt Hamburg** *(Hamburg–City of Emigrants).* This new museum and family research center tells the fascinating story of German emigration to the United States and elsewhere and invites visitors to research their own ancestors' migration history. The museum is located on a peninsula where in the late 19th century the HAPAG shipping line—named for the HAPAG General Director of the time, Albert Ballin—began construction of a departure "city" ("Stadt" in German). Completed in 1907, the city served as a holding and quarantine area for emigrants leaving Europe; 5 million Germans made their way to the New World from BallinStadt between 1850 and 1934. The museum includes the historic remains of BallinStadt and provides a thrilling look at living conditions in the holding facility as it was 100 years ago. A permanent exhibit focuses on the lives of emigrants, their decision to leave Germany, their often arduous journeys, and their lives in America. As compelling as the exhibits are, the main draw is the research booths, where you can search the complete passenger lists of all ships that left the harbor. ■TIP➔**Research assistants are available to help locate and track your ancestors.** From St. Pauli, the museum can be reached by U-bahn or boat at Landungsbrücke No. 10. ⊠*Veddeler Bogen 2, Veddel* ☎*040/3197–9160* ⊕*www.ballinstadt.de* 🖾*€9.80* ☉ *Daily 10–6* Ⓜ*Veddel (U-bahn).*

❽ **Reeperbahn.** The hottest spots in town are concentrated in the St. Pauli
★ Harbor area on the Reeperbahn thoroughfare and on a little side street known as the Grosse Freiheit (Great Liberty—and that's putting it mildly). In the early '60s a then obscure band called the Beatles had their first live acts at the now demolished Star Club. The striptease

shows are expensive and explicit, but a walk through this area is an experience in itself and costs nothing. Saturday night finds St. Pauli pulsating with people determined to have a good time. ■TIP➔ It's *not* advisable, however, to venture into the darker side streets alone in the wee hours of the morning.

Although some of the sex clubs are relatively tame, a good many others are extremely racy. They all get going around 10 PM, and will accommodate you until the early hours. ■TIP➔ Order your own drinks rather than letting the hostess do it, and pay for them as soon as they arrive, double-checking the price list again before handing over the money.

Among the attractions in the St. Pauli area are theaters, clubs, music pubs, discos, and all kinds of bizarre shops. Ⓜ*St. Pauli (U-bahn).*

WHERE TO EAT

DOWNTOWN & HISTORIC HAMBURG

$$$ ✕**Die Bank.** In an ironic nod to Wall Street, this restored, late-19th-century bank—complete with steel vault doors—is abuzz with businesspeople and the "it" crowd. Award-winning chef Fritz Schilling dishes out lean, quick international cuisine with a touch of the French brasserie, including fresh oysters. Well-cooked fish, salads, and light meat dishes are the staples, and service is friendly. The bar, under high ceilings, is a great place to "invest" some time. ✉*Hohe Bleichen 17, Neustadt* ☎*040/238–0030* ▤*AE, V* ☉*Closed Sun.* Ⓜ*Gänsemarkt (U-bahn).*

$$$ ✕**Fillet of Soul.** The art of fine dining is celebrated in the open show kitchen of this hip yet casual restaurant right next to the modern art shows of the Deichtorhallen. Chefs Patrick Gebhardt and Florian Pabst prepare straightforward, light German nouvelle cuisine with an emphasis on fresh fish. The minimalist dining room, highlighted only by a bright-red wall, might not be to everyone's liking, but the buzzing atmosphere, artsy clientele, fragrant food, and great personal attention from the waitstaff make this the top choice. ✉*Deichtorstr. 2, Speicherstadt* ☎*040/7070–5800* ▤*No credit cards* ☉*Closed Mon.* Ⓜ*Steinstrasse (U-bahn).*

ST. PAULI

$ ✕**Mess.** This is one of the most popular restaurants in the hip and
FodorŝChoice upcoming Karolinenviertel (called "Karo-Viertel" by Hamburgers).
★ True to its worldly, young patrons, it dares to offer a wild mixture of old German standards like *Königsberger Klopse* (meatballs in a thick butter-and-caper sauce served with potatoes) along with more exotic fare such as ostrich steak. For lunch, order the three-course menu (€19) or the daily pasta special for just €6. ■TIP➔ In summer, try to get a table in the small garden under the pergola and sample vintages from the restaurant's own specialty wine store. ✉*Turnerstr. 9, St. Pauli* ☎*040/4325–0152* ▤*AE* ☉*No lunch weekends* Ⓜ*Messehallen (U-bahn).*

$-$$ ✕**River-Kasematten.** There is no other restaurant in town that better
★ embodies Hamburg's international spirit and its lust for style, entertainment, and good seafood. Once a legendary jazz club with performances by Ella Fitzgerald and the like, it now hosts a fascinating mix of hip

guests. Sushi, spiced-up regional fish dishes, and exotic soups are the order of the day. The lunch buffet (weekdays noon–3) for just €9.90 is a steal; it's even better on the outside terrace. Nighthawks love the late-night menu (midnight–4 AM). The ambience—black oak floors, leather seats, and redbrick walls—is elegant yet casual. ⊠ *Fischmarkt 28–32, St. Pauli* ☎ *040/892–760* ⚑ *Reservations essential* ⊟ *AE, DC, MC, V* Ⓜ *Reeperbahn or Landungsbrücken (U-bahn).*

UHLENHORST

$–$$ ✕ **Phuket.** Though it has an unimaginative name and dull facade, Phuket is by far the best Thai, or Asian for that matter, restaurant in town. The place is often jammed with locals who come to sample the truly hot fish dishes or the famous chicken in red-wine sauce. ⊠ *Adolph-Schönfelder-Str. 33–35, Uhlenhorst* ☎ *040/2982–3380* ⊟ *AE, V* Ⓜ *Hamburger Strasse (U-bahn).*

WHERE TO STAY

DOWNTOWN & HISTORIC HAMBURG

$$$$ 🏨 **Fairmont Vier Jahreszeiten.** Some claim that this 19th-century town
Fodor's Choice   house on the edge of the Binnenalster is the best hotel in Germany.
★   Antiques—the hotel has a set of near-priceless Gobelin tapestries—fill the public rooms and accentuate the stylish bedrooms; fresh flowers overflow from massive vases; rare oil paintings adorn the walls; and all rooms are individually decorated with superb taste. ■ **TIP→ One of the three restaurants, the Jahreszeiten-Grill, has been restored to its 1920s Art Deco look with dark woods, making it worth a visit.** Pros: luxury hotel with great view of Alster lakes, close to shopping on Jungfernstieg, charming, large rooms. Cons: formal service, high prices even in off-season, far away from nightlife and new city quarters like Schanzen- and Katharinenviertel. ⊠ *Neuer Jungfernstieg 9–14, Neustadt* ☎ *040/34940* ⊕ *www.hvj.de* ⚑ *156 rooms, 32 suites* ⚐ *In-room: safe, refrigerator, Ethernet, dial-up, Wi-Fi. In-hotel: 3 restaurants, room service, bar, gym, concierge, laundry service, public Wi-Fi, parking (fee), no-smoking rooms* ⊟ *AE, DC, MC, V* Ⓜ *Jungfernstieg (U-bahn).*

$ 🏨 **Hotel Village.** Once a thriving brothel nearby the central train station, this hotel still exudes the hot breath of lasciviousness. Red-and-black carpets and glossy wallpaper in the rooms are a nod to the hotel's past; some rooms even have their old large beds, replete with canopy and revolving mirror. Pros: in the heart of downtown, cozy, individually designed rooms, affordable eateries nearby. Cons: sometimes casual service, seedy neighborhood not suited for families, some rooms are worn. ⊠ *Steindamm 4, Altstadt* ☎ *040/480–6490* ⊕ *www.hotel-village.de* ⚑ *20 rooms* ⚐ *In-room: no a/c, Wi-Fi. In-hotel: no elevator, parking (fee), some pets allowed* ⊟ *AE, MC, V* ⦿|*CP* Ⓜ *Hauptbahnhof (U-bahn and S-bahn).*

🏨 **Side.** Deeming itself to be "the luxury hotel of the 21st century," this ultrahip hotel is one of the most architecturally sophisticated places to stay in Germany. Premier Milanese designer Matteo Thun served as the driving force behind the five-star resort in the heart of the city. His vision provided for the stunning lighting arrangement as well as the interior design. Whether soothed by the eggshell-white accents in your room or wowed by the lobby's soaring and stark atrium, you won't ever want to leave. **Pros:** very clean and well-kept hotel, convenient downtown location yet quiet. **Cons:** somewhat sterile, many business travelers, small rooms. ⊠*Drehbahn 49, Altstadt* ☎*040/309–990* ⊕*www. side-hamburg.de* ⇌*178 rooms, 10 suites* ⟡*In-room: safe, refrigerator, Ethernet, Wi-Fi. In-hotel: restaurant, room service, bar, gym, spa, laundry service, public Wi-Fi, parking (fee), no-smoking rooms, some pets allowed* ☐*AE, DC, MC, V* Ⓜ*Gänsemarkt (U-bahn).*

ALTONA & ELSEWHERE

$$ 🏨 **Gastwerk Hotel Hamburg.** Proudly dubbing itself Hamburg's first design hotel, the Gastwerk, in a century-old gas plant, is certainly the most stylish accommodation in town. The simple but incredibly chic furnishings reflect the building's industrial design, but are warmed by the use of natural materials, various woods, and thick carpets. ■ **TIP→ The loft rooms with large windows, bare walls, and a lot of space are the most exciting accommodations in Hamburg.** **Pros:** large rooms, stunning interior design, large and well-equipped health club. **Cons:** far away from downtown area and any sightseeing, few restaurants nearby, public spaces like breakfast room and bar can get crowded. ⊠*Beim alten Gaswerk 3, at Daimlerstr. 67, Altona* ☎*040/890–620* ⊕*www.gastwerk.com* ⇌*128 rooms, 13 suites* ⟡*In-room: safe, Wi-Fi. In-hotel: restaurant, room service, bar, gym, laundry service, public Wi-Fi, parking (no fee), no-smoking rooms, some pets allowed* ☐*AE, DC, MC, V* Ⓜ*Bahrenfeld (S-bahn).*

$–$$ 🏨 **Yoho.** Centrally located between the hip Schanzenviertel and the downtown area, the upscale Yoho is the youth hostel of the 21st century. Housed in a historic, imposing villa with contemporary interior design, it offers simple yet elegant rooms with modern amenities otherwise not found in a hostel. Guests under 27 receive a special rate of €65 for a single or €85 for a double room, including breakfast. Everybody else has to pay €115—still a fair deal considering the great location. **Pros:** located close to hip, artsy neighborhoods, historic flair, very good furnishings at budget prices. **Cons:** limited breakfast, sometimes noisy due to young travelers, away from all major sightseeing. ⊠*Moorkamp 5, Eimsbüttel* ☎*040/284–1910* ⊕*www.yoho-hamburg. de* ⇌*30 rooms* ⟡*In-room: no a/c, dial-up. In-hotel: restaurant, no elevator, parking (no fee), some pets allowed* ☐*AE, DC, MC, V* �ⓄⅠCP Ⓜ*Schlump (U-bahn).*

NIGHTLIFE

THE REEPERBAHN

Whether you think it sordid or sexy, the Reeperbahn, in the St. Pauli District, is as central to the Hamburg scene as the classy shops along Jungfernstieg. A walk down **Herbertstrasse** (men only, no women or children permitted), just two blocks south of the Reeperbahn, can be quite an eye-opener. Here prostitutes sit displayed in windows as they await customers—nevertheless, it's the women choosing their clients, as these are the highest-paid prostitutes in the city. On nearby **Grosse Freiheit** you'll find a number of the better-known sex-show or table-dance clubs: **Colibri,** at No. 34; **Safari,** at No. 24; and **Dollhouse,** at No. 11. They cater to the package-tour trade as well as those on the prowl by themselves. Prices are high. Not much happens here before 10 PM.

The quirky **Schmidts Tivoli** (⊠ *Spielbudenpl. 24–28, St. Pauli* ☎ *040/3177–8899*) has become Germany's most popular variety theater, presenting a classy repertoire of live music, vaudeville, chansons, and cabaret.

BARS
The Hansestadt has a buzzing and upscale bar scene, with many spots that feature live music or DJs and dancing. A nightlife institution still going strong is the fashionable but cozy **Bar Hamburg** (⊠ *Rautenbergstr. 6–8, St. Georg* ☎ *040/2805–4880*). The new **Mandalay** (⊠ *Neuer Pferdemarkt 13, St. Pauli* ☎ *040/4321–4922*) is typical of the new upscale, sleek bars for thirtysomethings in rough St. Pauli. **Christiansen's** (⊠ *Pinnasberg 60, St. Pauli* ☎ *040/317–2863*), near the Fischmarkt, is said to mix the best cocktails in town.

BERLIN

Since the fall of the Iron Curtain, no city in Europe has seen more development and change than Berlin. In the scar of barren borderland between the two parts of the city sprang up government and commercial centers that have become the glossy spreads of travel guides and architecture journals. The city's particular charm lies in its spaciousness, its trees and greenery, and its anything-goes atmosphere. The city embraces its future as an international center for avant-garde fashion, culture, art, and media, with a zeal rarely found in other cities. The really stunning parts of the prewar capital are in the historic eastern part of town, which has grand avenues, monumental architecture, and museums that house world treasures.

Berlin began prospering in the 1300s, thanks to its location at the intersection of important trade routes. Later, Frederick the Great (1712–86) made Berlin and nearby Potsdam his glorious centers of the enlightened yet autocratic Prussian monarchy. In 1871 Prussia, ruled by the "Iron Chancellor" Count Otto von Bismarck, unified the many independent German states into the German Empire and made Berlin the capital. World War I ended the German monarchy. But it also brought an end to Prussian autocracy, resulting in Berlin's golden years during the Roaring '20s. The city, the energetic, modern, and sinful counterpart to Paris, became a center for the cultural avant-garde.

The golden era came to an end with the Depression and the rise of Hitler, who also made Berlin his capital. By World War II's end, 70% of the city lay in ruins. Berlin was partitioned and finally divided by the Berlin Wall, with Soviet-controlled East Berlin as the capital of its new communist puppet state, the German Democratic Republic (GDR), and West Berlin an outpost of western democracy.

PLANNING YOUR TIME

As one of Europe's biggest cities and certainly one of the world's top capitals, with very distinctive individual neighborhoods and sights, Berlin is difficult to tackle in just one or two days. Any visit should include a walk on the Kurfürstendamm, the city's premier shopping boulevard. For culture buffs, great antique, medieval, Renaissance, and modern art can be found at the Kulturforum in the Tiergarten, and on Museum Island in Mitte—both cultural centers are a must, and either will occupy at least a half-day. Most of the historic sights of German and Prussian history line the city's other grand boulevard, Unter den Linden, in eastern Berlin, which can be strolled in a leisurely two hours, with stops. Avail yourself of the efficient transportation options, and you'll see more. Note that shops are closed on Sunday.

GETTING HERE & AROUND

BY AIR

Major airlines will continue to serve western Berlin's Tegel Airport (TXL) after a first stop at a major European hub (such as Frankfurt) until 2011, when eastern Berlin's Schönefeld Airport, about 24 km (15 mi) outside the center, will have been expanded into BBI, the international airport of the capital region. Schönefeld is now used principally by charter and low-budget airlines. Massive Tempelhof Airport closed in late 2008. The two Berlin airports share a central phone number.

BY BUS

BerlinLinien Bus is the only intra-Germany company serving Berlin. Gullivers Reisen serves foreign destinations. Make reservations at ZOB-Reisebüro, or buy your ticket at its office at the central bus terminal, the Omnibusbahnhof.

BY CAR

Rush hour is relatively mild in Berlin, but the public transit system is so efficient here that it's best to leave your car at the hotel altogether. As of 2008 cars entering downtown Berlin inside the S-Bahn ring need to have an environmental certificate. Daily parking fees at hotels can run up to €18 per day. Vending machines in the city center dispense timed tickets to display on your dashboard. Thirty minutes cost €0.50.

BY PUBLIC TRANSIT

The city has one of the most efficient public-transportation systems in Europe, a smoothly integrated network of subway (U-bahn) and suburban (S-bahn) train lines, buses, and trams (in eastern Berlin only). Get a map from any information booth.

Most visitor destinations are in the broad reach of the fare zones A and B. Tickets are available from vending machines at U-bahn and S-bahn stations. After you purchase a ticket, you are responsible for validating it when you board the train or bus. If you're caught without a ticket or with an unvalidated one, the fine is €60. .

BY TAXI

The base rate is €3, after which prices vary according to a complex tariff system. Figure on paying around €8 for a ride the length of the

Ku'damm. You can hail cabs on the street, get them at taxi stands or order them by calling.

BY TRAIN

All long-distance trains stop at the huge and modern central station, Hauptbahnhof–Lehrter Bahnhof, which lies at the north edge of the government district in former West Berlin. Regional trains also stop at the two former "main" stations of the past years: Bahnhof Zoo (in the West) and Ostbahnhof (in the East). Regional trains also stop at the central eastern stations Friedrichstrasse and Alexanderplatz.

ESSENTIALS

Airport Information Central airport service (☎ *0180/500–0186* ⊕ *www. berlin-airport.de*).

Bus Information ZOB-Reisebüro (✉ *Zentrale Omnibusbahnhof, Masurenallee 4–6, at Messedamm, Charlottenburg* ☎ *030/301–0380 for reservations* ⊕ *www. berlinlinienbus.de* ⊙ *Weekdays 6* AM*–9* PM*, weekends 6* AM*–3* PM).

Public Transit Information Berliner Verkehrsbetriebe (☎ *030/19449* ⊕ *www. bvg.de*). **S-Bahn Berlin GmbH** (☎ *030/2974–3333* ⊕ *www.s-bahn-berlin.de*). **VBB** (✉ *Hardenbergpl. 2, Western Downtown* ☎ *030/2541–4141 or 030/2541–4145* ⊕ *www.vbbonline.de*).

Visitor Information Berlin Infostore (✉ *Kurfürstendamm 21, Neues Kranzler Eck, Western Downtown* ☎ *030/250–025* ⊙ *Mon.–Thurs. 9:30–8, Fri. and Sat. 9:30–9, Sun. 9:30–6* ⊕ *www.berlin-tourist-information.de*). **MD Infoline** (☎ *030/2474–9888* ⊙ *Weekdays 9–4, weekends 9–1*).

Taxi Information Taxis (☎ *030/210–101, 030/210–202, 030/443–322, or 030/260–26*).

EXPLORING BERLIN

Berlin is a large city with several downtown centers that evolved during the 30 years of separation. Of Berlin's 12 boroughs, the most interesting are Charlottenburg-Wilmersdorf in the west; Tiergarten (a district of the Mitte borough) and Kreuzberg-Friedrichhain in the center; Mitte, the historic core of the city in the eastern part of town; and Prenzlauer Berg in the northeast. Southwest Berlin has lovely escapes in the secluded forests and lakes of the Grunewald area.

KURFÜRSTENDAMM & WESTERN DOWNTOWN

❷ **Kaiser-Wilhelm-Gedächtnis-Kirche** *(Kaiser Wilhelm Memorial Church)*. A dramatic reminder of World War II's destruction, the ruined bell tower is all that remains of the once massive church, which was completed in 1895 and dedicated to the emperor, Kaiser Wilhelm I. The Hohenzollern dynasty is depicted inside in a gilded mosaic, whose damage, like that of the building, will not be repaired. The exhibition revisits World War II's devastation throughout Europe. On the hour, the tower chimes out a melody composed by the last emperor's great-grandson, the late Prince Louis Ferdinand von Hohenzollern.

In stark contrast to the old bell tower (dubbed the "Hollow Tooth"), which is in sore need of a restoration now, are the adjoining Memorial Church and Tower, designed by the noted German architect Egon Eiermann in 1959–61. These ultramodern octagonal structures, with their myriad honeycomb windows, have nicknames as well: "the Lipstick" and the "Powder Box." Brilliant, blue stained glass from Chartres dominates the interiors. Church music and organ concerts are presented in the church regularly. ✉ *Breitscheidpl., Western Downtown* ☎ *030/218-5023* ✆ *www.gedaechtniskirche.de* ✆ *Free* 🕙 *Old Tower Mon.–Sat. 10–6:30, Memorial Church daily 9–7* Ⓜ *Zoologischer Garten (U-bahn and S-bahn).*

❶ **Kurfürstendamm.** This busy thoroughfare began as a riding path in the 16th century. The elector Joachim II of Brandenburg used it to travel between his palace on the Spree River and his hunting lodge in the Grunewald. The Kurfürstendamm (Elector's Causeway) was transformed into a major route in the late 19th century, thanks to the initiative of Bismarck, Prussia's Iron Chancellor.

Even in the 1920s, the Ku'damm was still relatively new and by no means elegant; it was fairly far removed from the old heart of the city, which was Unter den Linden in Mitte. The Ku'damm's prewar fame was due mainly to its rowdy bars and dance halls, as well as the cafés where the cultural avant-garde of Europe gathered. Almost half of its 245 late-19th-century buildings were completely destroyed in the 1940s, and the remaining buildings were damaged in varying degrees. As in most of western Berlin, what you see today is either restored or newly constructed. Many of the 1950s buildings have been replaced by high-rises, in particular at the corner of Kurfürstendamm and Joachimstaler Strasse.

TIERGARTEN & THE GOVERNMENT DISTRICT

❸ **Brandenburger Tor** *(Brandenburg Gate).* Once the pride of Prussian Berlin and the city's premier landmark, the Brandenburger Tor was left in a desolate no-man's-land when the Wall was built. Since the Wall's dismantling, the sandstone gateway has become the scene of the city's Unification Day and New Year's Eve parties. This is the sole remaining gate of 14 built by Carl Langhans in 1788–91, designed as a triumphal arch for King Frederick Wilhelm II. Its virile classical style pays tribute to Athens's Acropolis. The quadriga, a chariot drawn by four horses and driven by the Goddess of Victory, was added in 1794. Troops paraded through the gate after successful campaigns—the last time in 1945, when victorious Red Army troops took Berlin. The upper part of the gate, together with its chariot and Goddess of Victory, was destroyed in the war. In 1957 the original molds were discovered in West Berlin, and a new quadriga was cast in copper and presented as a gift to the people of East Berlin. A tourist-information center is in the south part of the gate.

The gate faces one of Europe's most famous historic squares, **Pariser Platz,** a classicist piazza with bank headquarters, the ultramodern French embassy, as well as offices of the federal parliament. On the

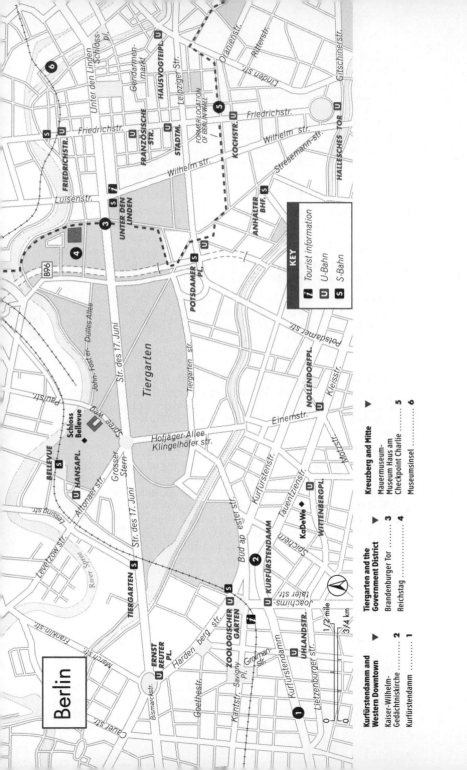

Berlin

KEY

🛈 Tourist information
Ⓤ U-Bahn
Ⓢ S-Bahn

Kurfürstendamm and Western Downtown ▶

Kaiser-Wilhelm-
Gedächtniskirche 2
Kurfürstendamm 1

Tiergarten and the Government District ▶

Brandenburger Tor 3
Reichstag 4

Kreuzberg and Mitte ▶

Mauermuseum-
Museum Haus am
Checkpoint Charlie 5
Museumsinsel 6

0 ⊢⊢⊢⊢⊢ 1/2 mile
0 ⊢⊢⊢⊢⊢ 3/4 km

southern side, Berlin's sleek Academy of Arts, integrating the ruins of its historic predecessor, and the DZ Bank, designed by star architect Frank Gehry, are cheek-by-jowl with the new American embassy, opened on July 4, 2008, built on its prewar location. ✉ *Pariser Pl., Mitte* Ⓜ *Unter den Linden (S-bahn).*

❹ **Reichstag** *(Parliament Building).* After last meeting here in 1933, the Bundestag, Germany's federal parliament, returned to its traditional seat in the spring of 1999. British architect Sir Norman Foster lightened up the gray monolith with a glass dome, which quickly became one of the city's main attractions: you can circle up a gently rising ramp while taking in the rooftops of Berlin and the parliamentary chamber below. At the base of the dome is an exhibit on the Reichstag's history, in German and English. ■**TIP➔The best way to visit the Reichstag dome without waiting in line is to arrive at 8 AM, or to make a reservation for the pricey rooftop Käfer restaurant (☎030/2262–9933). Those with reservations can use the doorway to the right of the Reichstag's main staircase.** Completed in 1894, the Reichstag housed the imperial German parliament and later served a similar function during the ill-fated Weimar Republic. On the night of February 27, 1933, the Reichstag burned down in an act of arson, a pivotal event in Third Reich history. The fire led to state protection laws that gave the Nazis a pretext to arrest their political opponents. The Reichstag was rebuilt but again badly damaged in 1945. The graffiti of the victorious Russian soldiers can still be seen on some of the walls in the hallways. Tours of the interior are only given to groups who have applied in advance by letter or fax. The building is surrounded by ultramodern new federal government offices, such as the boxy, concrete **Bundeskanzleramt** (German Federal Chancellery). Built by Axel Schultes, it's one of the few new buildings in the government district by a Berlin architect. Participating in a guided tour of the Chancellery is possible if you apply in writing several weeks prior to a visit. A riverwalk with great views of the government buildings begins behind the Reichstag. ✉ *Pl. der Republik 1, Tiergarten* ☎*030/2273–2152, 030/2273–5908 Reichstag* ☎*030/2273–0027 Reichstag, 030/4000–1881 Bundeskanzleramt* ⊕*www.bundestag.de* ✆*Free* ⊙*Daily 8 AM–midnight; last admission 10 PM. Reichstag dome closes for 1 wk 4 times a yr* Ⓜ *Unter den Linden (S-bahn).*

KREUZBERG & MITTE

❺ **Mauermuseum-Museum Haus am Checkpoint Charlie.** Just steps from the ★ famous crossing point between the two Berlins, the Wall Museum— House at Checkpoint Charlie tells the story of the Wall and, even more riveting, the stories of those who escaped through, under, and over it. The homespun museum reviews the events leading up to the Wall's construction and, with original tools and devices, plus recordings and

6

photographs, shows how East Germans escaped to the West (one of the most ingenious contraptions was a miniature submarine). Exhibits about human rights and paintings interpreting the Wall round out the experience. ■TIP➡ Come early or late in the day to avoid the multitudes dropped off by tour buses. Monday can be particularly crowded. ⊠*Friedrichstr. 43–45, Kreuzberg* ☎*030/253–7250* ⊕*www.mauermuseum.com* 🖃*€9.50* ⊙*Daily 9* AM*–10* PM Ⓜ*Kochstrasse (U-bahn).*

❻ **Museumsinsel** *(Museum Island).* On the site of one of Berlin's two origi-
Fodor's Choice nal settlements, this unique complex of four state museums, a UNESCO
★ World Heritage Site, is an absolute must.

The **Alte Nationalgalerie** (Old National Gallery, entrance on Bodestrasse) houses an outstanding collection of 18th-, 19th-, and early-20th-century paintings and sculptures. Works by Cézanne, Rodin, Degas, and one of Germany's most famous portrait artists, Max Liebermann, are part of the permanent exhibition. Its Galerie der Romantik (Gallery of Romantik) collection has masterpieces from such 19th-century German painters as Karl Friedrich Schinkel and Caspar David Friedrich, the leading members of the German Romantic school. The **Altes Museum** (Old Museum), a red-marble, neoclassical building abutting the green Lustgarten, was Prussia's first building purpose-built to serve as a museum. Designed by Karl Friedrich Schinkel, it was completed in 1830. Until fall 2009, when the collection relocated to the then completely restored Neues Museum, it served as home to the Egyptian collection, which traces Egypt's history from 4000 BC and whose prize piece is the exquisite 3,300-year-old bust of Queen Nefertiti. The permanent collection of the Altes Museum consists of everyday utensils from ancient Greece as well as vases and sculptures from the 6th to 4th centuries BC. Etruscan art is its highlight, and there are a few examples of Roman art. Antique sculptures, clay figurines, and bronze art of the Antikensammlung (Antiquities Collection) are also housed here; the other part of the collection is in the Pergamonmuseum. At the northern tip of Museum Island is the **Bode-Museum,** a somber-looking gray edifice graced with elegant columns. Reopened in 2006, it now presents the state museums' stunning collection of German and Italian sculptures since the Middle Ages, the Museum of Byzantine Art, and a huge coin collection. Even if you think you aren't interested in the ancient world, make an exception for the **Pergamonmuseum** (entrance on Am Kupfergraben), one of the world's greatest museums. The museum's name is derived from its principal display, the Pergamon Altar, a monumental Greek temple discovered in what is now Turkey and dating from 180 BC. The altar was shipped to Berlin in the late 19th century. Equally impressive are the gateway to the Roman town of Miletus and the Babylonian processional way. Art and culture buffs who want to enjoy as many Berlin museums as possible should consider the three-day pass for €19, which allows unlimited access to all of Berlin's state museums. If you get tired of antiques and paintings, drop by any of the museums' cafés. ⊠*Entrance to Museumsinsel: Am Kupfergraben, Mitte* ☎*030/–2661 or 030/2090–5577* ⊕*www.smb.museum* 🖃*All Museum Island museums €8, but may be higher during special exhibits.* ⊙*Pergamonmuseum*

Fri.–Wed. 10–6, Thurs. 10–10. Alte Nationalgalerie Tues., Wed., and Fri.–Sun. 10–6, Thurs. 10–10. Altes Museum Fri.–Wed. 10–6, Thurs. 10–10. Bode-Museum Fri.–Wed. 10–6, Thurs. 10–10 Ⓜ*Hackescher Markt (S-bahn).*

WHERE TO EAT

WESTERN DOWNTOWN

$ ✕**Kuchi.** Japanese sushi, sashimi, yakitori, and dunburi dishes along
JAPANESE with some Thai, Chinese, and Korean recipes are served in this groovy landmark restaurant, one of the finest sushi places in town. Chefs work with an almost religious devotion to quality and imagination (they even wear shirts saying SUSHI WARRIOR), and the knowledgeable Asian-German staff makes you feel at home. The spicy, fresh, and healthy ingredients and the laid-back vibe pack the restaurant in the evening, so reservations are a must. ■**TIP➔ Try to get a seat at the sushi bar or at one of the three more private tables at the window.** ⊠*Kantstr. 30, Western Downtown* ☎*030/3150–7815* ⌕*Reservations essential* ▭*AE, MC, V* Ⓜ*Zoologischer Garten (U-bahn and S-bahn).*

$–$$ ✕**Lubitsch.** One of the few traditional, artsy restaurants left in bohemian
GERMAN Charlottenburg, the Lubitsch—named after the famous Berlin film direc-
★ tor Ernst Lubitsch and exuding a similar air of faded elegance—serves hearty Berlin and German food hard to find these days. Reminiscent of good old home cooking, dishes like Königsberger Klopse (cooked dumplings in a creamy caper sauce) or Kasseler Nacken mit Sauerkraut (salted, boiled pork knuckle) are devoured mostly by locals, who don't mind the dingy seating or good-humored, but sometimes cheeky service. In summer the outdoor tables make for some great people-watching in one of Berlin's most beautiful streets. Enjoy a three-course lunch for just €10 or €12. ⊠*Bleibtreustr. 47, Western Downtown* ☎*030/882–3756* ▭*AE, MC, V* Ⓜ*Savignypl. (S-Bahn).*

MITTE

$$$–$$$$ ✕**Borchardt.** The menu changes daily at this fashionable celebrity
FRENCH meeting place. The high ceiling, plush maroon benches, Art Nouveau mosaic (discovered during renovations), and marble columns create the impression of a 1920s café. The cuisine is high-quality French-German, including several dishes with fresh fish, veal, and some of Berlin's best (and most tender) beef classics. ⊠*Französische Str. 47, Mitte* ☎*030/8188–6262* ⌕*Reservations essential* ▭*AE, MC, V* Ⓜ*Französische Strasse (U-bahn).*

$$–$$$ ✕**Lutter & Wegner.** One of the city's oldest vintners (*Sekt,* German
AUSTRIAN champagne, was first conceived here in 1811 by actor Ludwig Devrient), Lutter & Wegner has returned to its historic location across from the Konzerthaus and Gendarmenmarkt. The dark wood-panel walls, parquet floor, and multitude of rooms take you back to 19th-century Vienna. The cuisine is mostly Austrian, with superb game dishes in winter and, of course, a Wiener schnitzel with lukewarm potato salad. The sauerbraten (marinated pot roast) with red cabbage has been a national prizewinner. ■**TIP➔ In the Weinstube, meat and cheese plates are served**

6

until 3 A.M. ⊠ *Charlottenstr. 56, Mitte* ☎ *030/2029–5417* ▤ *AE, MC, V* Ⓜ *Französische Strasse and Stadtmitte (U-Bahn).*

TIERGARTEN

$$$$ ✕ **Facil.** One of Germany's top restaurants, Facil is also the most afford-
FRENCH able and relaxed one of its class. The elegant, minimalist setting—com-
Fodor's Choice plete with green marble walls, exquisite wall panels, and a Giallo Reale
★ patinato floor, all set under a glass roof (opened in summer, yet no view
of the city)—and the impeccable, personal service make the six-course
dinners a highlight in any gourmet's life. The food is a careful combination of French and regionally inspired first-class cuisine. Don't hesitate
to ask sommelier Felix Voges for advice, as he certainly ranks among
the most knowledgeable in his art. ⊠ *Potsdamer Str. 3, at the Mandala
Hotel, Tiergarten* ☎ *030/5900–51234* ▤ *AE, DC, MC, V* ⊘ *Closed
weekends* Ⓜ *Potsdamer Platz (U-bahn and S-bahn).*

WHERE TO STAY

CHARLOTTENBURG

$$ 🖼 **Art Nouveau Hotel.** The owners' discerning taste in antiques, color
combinations, and even televisions (designed by Philippe Starck) makes
this B&B-like pension a pleasure to live in. Each room has a prize piece,
such as a hand-carved 18th-century Chinese dresser or a chandelier
from the Komische Oper's set of *Don Carlos.* Several rooms are hung
with a large black-and-white photo by Sabine Kačunko. The apart-
ment building shows its age only in the antique wood elevator, high
stucco ceilings, and an occasionally creaky floor. You can serve yourself
tea or coffee in the breakfast room throughout the day and mix your
own drinks at the honor bar. Your English-speaking hosts are Mr. and
Mrs. Schlenzka. **Pros:** stylish ambience, friendly and personal service,
great B&B feeling, despite being a hotel. **Cons:** can be noisy due to
heavy traffic on Leibnizstrasse, few amenties for a hotel of this price
category, downtown location, yet longer walks to all major sights in
the area. ⊠ *Leibnizstr. 59, Charlottenburg* ☎ *030/327–7440* ⊕ *www.
hotelartnouveau.de* ⇆ *19 rooms, 3 suites* ⟐ *In-room: no a/c, Wi-Fi.
In-hotel: bar, laundry service, no-smoking rooms* ▤ *AE, MC, V* ⎮◎⎮*CP*
Ⓜ *Adenauerplatz (U-bahn).*

WESTERN DOWNTOWN

$–$$ 🖼 **Hotel-Pension Dittberner.** For traditional Berlin accommodations, this
★ third-floor pension (with wooden elevator) run by Frau Lange since
1958 is the place to go. Close to Olivaer Platz and next to Ku'damm,
the turn-of-the-20th-century house shows its age, but the huge rooms
are wonderfully furnished with antiques, plush stuffed sofas, and artwork selected by Frau Lange's husband, a gallery owner. The high ceilings have stuccowork, and some rooms have balconies. Wi-Fi Internet
access is available in the foyer. **Pros:** personal touch and feel of a B&B,
unusually large rooms, good location on quiet Ku'damm side street.
Cons: disappointing breakfast, some rooms and furniture in need
of update, staff sometimes not up to task. ⊠ *Wielandstr. 26, Western Downtown* ☎ *030/884–6950* ⊕ *www.hotel-dittberner.de* ⇆ *21*

rooms, 1 suite &*In-room: no a/c. In-hotel: concierge, laundry service, some pets allowed, public Wi-Fi* ⊟*AE, MC, V* ⓘⓞⓘ*CP* Ⓜ*Adenauer-platz (U-bahn).*

MITTE

$$ ⊡**Arte Luise Kunsthotel.** This hotel's name suggests a bohemian commune, but all the residents are paying guests. The Luise is one of Berlin's most original boutique hotels, with each fantastically creative room in the 1825 house or new wing—facing the Reichstag—styled by a different artist. Memorable furnishings range from a suspended bed and airplane seats to a gigantic sleigh bed and a freestanding, podlike shower with multiple nozzles. A lavish breakfast buffet in the neighboring restaurant costs €9. The hotel is a stretch from the Friedrichstrasse train station, but a convenient bus line stops just outside. **Pros:** quiet location, historic flair, individually designed rooms. **Cons:** simple rooms with limited amenities and hotel facilities, some rooms with no noise reduction but still next to railways tracks, no elevator. ✉*Luisenstr. 19, Mitte* ☎*030/284–480* ⊕*www.luise-berlin.com* ✏*50 rooms, 40 with bath; 3 apartments* &*In-room: no a/c (some), no TV (some), Wi-Fi. In-hotel: restaurant, laundry service, no-smoking rooms, some pets allowed, no elevator in historic part* ⊟*MC, V* Ⓜ*Friedrichstrasse (U-bahn and S-bahn).*

$$$$ ⊡**Hotel Adlon Berlin.** Aside from its prime setting on Pariser Platz, the allure of the government's unofficial guesthouse is its almost mythical predecessor. Until its destruction during the war, the Hotel Adlon was considered Europe's ultimate luxury resort. Rebuilt in 1997, the hotel's elegant rooms are furnished in 1920s style with cherrywood trim, myrtle-wood furnishings, and brocade silk bedspreads. The large bathrooms are done in black marble. Book a suite for a Brandenburger Tor view. Sipping coffee in the lobby of creamy marble and limestone makes for good people-watching. The new Adlon spa made a huge splash in the city, as did the annex of fine restaurants, under the supervision of Germany's top chef, Tim Rause. **Pros:** top-notch luxury hotel, surprisingly large rooms, excellent in-house restaurants. **Cons:** sometimes stiff service with an attitude, rooms off the Linden are noisy with the windows open, inviting lobby often crowded. ✉*Unter den Linden 77, Mitte* ☎*030/22610* ⊕*www.hotel-adlon.de* ✏*304 rooms, 78 suites* &*In-room: safe, Wi-Fi. In-hotel: 3 restaurants, room service, bar, pool, gym, spa, concierge, laundry service, parking (fee), no-smoking rooms, some pets allowed* ⊟*AE, DC, MC, V* Ⓜ*Unter den Linden (S-bahn).*

$$ ⊡**Lux Eleven.** This hidden gem of a designer apartment hotel is coveted
★ for its discreet service and great minimalist design in white. Among the devoted fans of Lux Eleven are Hollywood celebrities wishing to remain anonymous and young, international, design-oriented travelers. All apartments come with a fully equipped kitchenette, satellite TV with DVD players, and even a washer and dryer in the bathroom. Rooms seem to be taken directly from a Miami Beach hotel and are decorated either in off-white or subdued browns. The "in" restaurant Shiro i Shiro, a stylish Ulf Haines designer fashion store, and a hair salon are also on the premises. **Pros:** great location in northern Mitte, extremely stylish yet comfortable rooms, friendly, knowledgeable service. **Cons:**

6

immediate neighborhood may be noisy, not suitable for families. ✉ *Rosa-Luxemburg-Str. 9–13, Mitte* ☎ *030/936–2800* ⊕ *www.lux-eleven.com* ↩ *72 apartments* ⌂ *In-room: no a/c (some), Wi-Fi. In-hotel: restaurant, laundry service, no-smoking rooms* ▤ *AE, DC, MC, V* Ⓜ *Rosa-Luxemburg-Pl. (U-bahn.*

NIGHTLIFE

Today's Berlin has a tough time living up to the reputation it gained from the film *Cabaret*. Political gaffes are now the prime comic material for Berlin's cabarets, so your German will have to be up to snuff to understand them. Berlin's nightspots are open to the wee hours of the morning. Clubs often switch the music they play nightly, so their crowds and popularity can vary widely. Clubs and bars in downtown western Berlin as well as in Mitte tend to be dressier and more conservative; the scene in Kreuzberg, Prenzlauer Berg, the Scheunenviertel, and Friedrichshain is laid-back, alternative, and grungy. Dance clubs don't get going until about 12:30 AM, but parties labeled "after-work" start as early as 8 PM for professionals looking to socialize during the week.

BARS & LOUNGES

In Germany the term *Kneipen* is used for down-to-earth bars that are comparable to English pubs. These places are pretty simple and laidback; you probably shouldn't try to order a three-ingredient cocktail at one unless you spot a lengthy drink menu.

The most elegant bars and lounges are in western downtown Berlin, and though not frequented by Berliners, Berlin's five-star hotels provide stylish, seductive settings. The cocktail menu is the size of a small guidebook at **Bar am Lützowplatz** (✉ *Am Lützowpl. 7, Tiergarten* ☎ *030/262–6807*), where an attractive, professional crowd lines the long blond-wood bar. The subdued and elegant **Victoria Bar** (✉ *Potsdamer Str. 102, Tiergarten* ☎ *030/2575—9977*) is an ironic homage to the '60s and '70s jet-set age, and ultimately stylish. It usually attracts a middle-age, affluent, and artsy crowd. Old World **E. & M. Leydicke** (✉ *Mansteinstr. 4, Schöneberg* ☎ *030/216–2973*) is a must for out-of-towners. The proprietors operate their own distillery and have a superb selection of sweet wines and liqueurs. Shabby **Kumpelnest 3000** (✉ *Lützowstr. 23, Tiergarten* ☎ *030/261–6918*) has a reputation as wild as its carpeted walls. It's the traditional last stop of the evening.

A mature crowd that wants to concentrate on conversing and appreciating outstanding cocktails heads to **Green Door** (✉ *Winterfeldstr. 50, Schöneberg* ☎ *030/215–2515*), a Schöneberg classic with touches of 1960s retro style that lighten the mood. Now the oldest posh bar in Mitte, marble-lined **Newton** (✉ *Charlottenstr. 57, Mitte* ☎ *030/2029–5421*) flaunts Helmut Newton's larger-than-life photos of nude women across its walls. The laid-back, loungelike **Solar** (✉ *Stresemannstr. 76, Kreuzberg*) is the playground for the city's younger party crowd.

Groups of friends fill the tables, battle at foosball tables, and dance in the small back room at **August Fengler** (✉ *Lychner Str. 11, Prenzlauer*

CLOSE UP

Berlin's Art Scene

Berlin has always been a liberal city, embracing new art movements and young talent. During the Cold War, West Berlin evolved as a laboratory for art, music, and literature. At the same time, the tough Socialist regime in East Berlin pushed artists underground where they created important political art. Today Berlin is attracting artists and gallery owners from around the world—thanks to its inexpensive rents, ample space, and cultural subsidizing programs for young newcomers.

More than 400 galleries showcase works by artists who seem to account for half the entries of world-class art shows such as the documenta in Kassel or the Biennale in Venice. In addition, Berlin's own art fair, the **Art Forum Berlin** (⊕ *www.art-forum-berlin. de)*, is staged annually in October. Longtime galleries present classic modern German and European art along Kurfürstendamm's side streets, between Leibnizstrasse and Uhlandstrasse. Equally established institutions are in Tiergarten (Lützowplatz) and Schöneberg, while Kreuzberg plays host to galleries whose alternative days are behind them.

The real buzz is happening in Mitte, specifically in the Scheunenviertel,

where Auguststrasse has emerged as an informal art alley. Typical for Berlin, new galleries and shops open and close all the time; makeshift, temporary locations are a thrill to discover. Berlin is also known for its large-scale sound and art installations and shows in old, empty houses.

Attracting international jet-setters are the top collections in the city, such as the **Flick Collection** at the Hamburger Bahnhof (⊕ *www.friedrich christianflick-collection.com)*, the body of modern works owned by Daimler and presented in the **Weinhaus Huth** (⊕ *www.sammlung.daimlerchrysler. com)*, or the shows at the **Deutsche Guggenheim** (⊕ *www.deutsche-guggenheim.de)* on Unter den Linden. Privately owned spaces such as **KW Institute for Contemporary Art** (⊕ *www.kw-berlin.de)*, located in an abandoned margarine factory in Mitte, or the **Sammlung Hoffmann** (⊕ *www.sammlung-hoffmann.de)* add special appeal. As hard as it is to keep track of a scene constantly on the move, various resources like the city magazines *tip Berlin* (⊕ *www. tip-berlin.de)* and *zitty Berlin* (⊕ *www. zitty.de)*, as well as the gallery guide *artery Berlin* (⊕ *www.artery-berlin.de)*, will help you find your very own piece of Berlin art.

6

Berg ☎*030/4435–6640)*. On weekends the place is packed. ■**TIP→ If there's no room, head farther up the street to the bars around Helmholtz-platz.** Sitting canal-side on a deck chair at **Freischwimmer** (⊠ *Vor dem Schlesischen Tor 2a, Kreuzberg* ☎*030/6107–4309)* is perfect for warm nights, but heat lamps and an enclosed section make a cozy setting on cool ones, too. To get here, walk five minutes south of the Schlesisches Tor subway station and turn left down a path after the 1920s gas station.

Great Britain

Tea at Claridge's Hotel, London

WORD OF MOUTH

"The key to London's extraordinary museums and art galleries is that they're mostly free. So popping into several not only costs no money, but there are no ticket queues. And they'll still be there in a hundred years' time. Don't treat them like shrines: treat them like a city center park, that you just slip into for a couple of minutes. Above all, in London, be spontaneous."

—flanneruk

WHAT'S
WHERE

1 London. Britain's capital city is an ancient metropolis energized with contemporary cool. Lovers of palaces and pageantry will delight in Buckingham Palace and, outside town, Hampton Court Palace and Windsor Castle. Besides its renowned monuments and museums, London retains intriguing villagelike neighborhoods that you can explore on its iconic double-decker buses.

2 Oxford. This university town is wonderfully walkable, with one golden-stone building after another to discover. Beyond the tidy quadrangles and graceful spires, Oxford has a lively selection of pubs and restaurants. An easy excursion is to the vast, ornate, extraordinary Blenheim Palace.

3 Stratford-upon-Avon & the Cotswolds. One hundred mi northwest of London, Stratford is the place to see Shakespeare's birthplace and watch his plays. Close by is noble Warwick Castle, while to the south, the Cotswold Hills are rural England at its best, the sheep-strewn slopes separated by picture-postcard towns and villages.

4 Bath. The Georgian town of Bath is one of England's most harmonious cities, adorned with graceful 18th- and 19th-century architecture. At its heart is a complex of beautifully preserved Roman baths, built around the country's only hot spring. Today you can relax at the modern Thermae Bath Spa, with its rooftop pool. You can also make a side trip to Stonehenge, the world's most famous prehistoric stone circle.

5 Cambridge. The home of the famous university is perfect for ambling around the ancient colleges and museums. Don't miss the entrancing King's College Chapel, a Gothic masterpiece, and be sure stop in the outstanding Fitzwilliam Museum. The best views of the university's colleges and immaculate lawns (and some famous bridges) are from a punt on the River Cam.

6 Edinburgh. Scotland's capital captivates many people at first sight, with a skyline dominated by Edinburgh Castle and an array of Georgian and Victorian architecture. The Scottish Parliament is a new addition. Far from being locked in the past, this is a modern, cosmopolitan city, its ancient Old Town and 18th-century New Town enlivened by first-class restaurants and bars.

FROM SOARING MEDIEVAL CATHEDRALS TO the latest postmodern structures, from prehistoric Stonehenge to Regency Bath, from one-pub Cotswold villages to Edinburgh's buzzing eateries, Great Britain is a spectacular tribute to the strength—and flexibility—of tradition. Alongside the grand country mansions and grim fortified castles, you'll find cutting-edge art, stylistic innovation, and up-to-the-minute shopping.

Nowhere is this meeting of heritage and contemporary flair more evident than in the nation's capital, London, where the city's turn-of-the-millennium building frenzy produced a slew of goodies, including the gigantic Tate Modern art gallery and the British Museum's sparkling glass-roofed Great Court. Consequently, don't be surprised to find glass-and-steel tower blocks marching two abreast the length of the River Thames, or, riding high and white over the city skyline, the stately dome of St. Paul's Cathedral being nudged by glittering skyscrapers.

With all London's cosmopolitan pizzazz, you're more likely to find Britain's more traditional character outside the metropolis. Anyone wishing to penetrate the mystique of the British monarchy should visit Windsor, the Thameside town that is home to the medieval and massive Windsor Castle. Centuries-old customs collide with a lively student vibe amid the scholarly quadrangles and graceful spires of Oxford and Cambridge. Conducive to relaxed strolling and long coffee breaks, these are arguably the world's most attractive university towns. To the west, exquisitely Georgian Bath still centers around the hot mineral springs that made it the fashionable spa for the wealthy in the 18th and early 19th centuries. Here, you'll find streets lined with Palladian buildings made of golden limestone, an ancient abbey, ruined Roman baths, tea shops, and boutiques.

Northwest of Bath extend the rolling Cotswold Hills, the quintessence of rural England, as immortalized in countless books, paintings, and films. The Cotswolds can hardly claim to be undiscovered, but, happily, the area's poetic appeal has survived the tour buses and antiques shops. Just north of the Cotswolds, the continuity of past into present can be experienced in Stratford-upon-Avon, celebrated as the birthplace of Shakespeare and the best place in the world to view one of his plays, which are often given inventively modern interpretations.

Finally, it is important to remember that Great Britain consists of three nations—England, Scotland, and Wales—and that 400 miles north of London lies the capital city of Edinburgh, whose streets and monuments bear witness to the often turbulent and momentous history of the Scottish people. Edinburgh Castle and the Palace of Holyroodhouse are key sights, but there's more to the city than its past. Check out the modern Parliament building, the artistic treasures of the National Museum of Scotland and the National Gallery of Scotland, and the vibrant restaurant scene—as well as the city's famous arts festivals, including the Edinburgh International Festival.

TOP REASONS TO GO

Houses of Parliament & Big Ben: One of the world's most famous sights, the gold-tipped towers of Parliament and the famous clock tower stand at the center of British power, and at the heart of London.

Westminster Abbey: Steeped in history, this church is the final resting place of the men and women who built Britain. Its great Gothic hall has hosted nearly every coronation since 1308.

British Museum: The self-appointed protector of treasures from around the globe, this vast and varied museum in London is packed to bursting with antiquities and alluring objects. Among the greatest hits are the Parthenon Marbles, the Rosetta Stone, and Egyptian mummies.

Windsor Castle: The mystique of eight successive royal houses of the British monarchy permeates Windsor, where a fraction of the current Queen's vast wealth is displayed in heraldic splendor.

Roman Baths, Bath: Take a break from the town's Georgian elegance and return to its Roman days on a fascinating tour around this beautifully preserved bath complex, built around the country's only hot spring.

Christ Church, Oxford: Nothing encapsulates the special atmosphere of this "city of dreaming spires" better than Christ Church, home of Oxford's largest quadrangle and the must-see Christ Church Picture Gallery.

Perfect Cotswold Villages: With their golden stone cottages, Cotswold villages tend to be improbably picturesque; Broadway, Chipping Campden, and Stow-on-the-Wold are among the most seductive.

King's College Chapel, Cambridge: The famous university town is perfect for aimless ambling, but prepare to be awestruck by King's College Chapel, one of England's greatest monuments.

Royal Mile, Edinburgh: Take a trip north of the border and stroll along this famous thoroughfare, overlooked by the mighty profile of Edinburgh Castle.

7

WHEN TO GO

Generally, the climate in England is mild. Summer temperatures can reach the 90s, with high humidity. Scotland is usually three or four degrees cooler than southern England. In winter there can be heavy frost, thin snow, thick fog, and rain, rain, rain.

The British tourist season peaks from mid-April to mid-October, and many historic houses outside London and other major cities close from October to Easter. During July and August, accommodations in popular resorts and areas are in high demand and at their most expensive. The winter cultural season in London and Edinburgh is lively. Hotel rates are lower then, too. Spring and fall can be good alternatives, as prices are still below high-season rates, and the crowds are thinner.

Festivals in Britain are often worth planning your schedule around. For a full list of events see VisitBritain's Web site, ⊕*www.visitbritain. com*—the ones mentioned here are among the highlights. In London, the Head of the River Boat Race in late March offers the spectacle of up to 420 eight-man crews slicing through the Thames, followed a few days later by the Oxford versus Cambridge University Boat Race. The Queen's Birthday earns a showy 41-gun salute in London's Hyde Park on April 21, and in June Elizabeth II's ceremonial birthday is celebrated by Trooping the Colour at Horse Guards Parade. The massive Edinburgh Festival in August is absolutely thrilling—the highlight of many a trip. Finally, Guy Fawkes Night on November 5 commemorates a foiled 1605 attempt to blow up Parliament and features fireworks and bonfires all over the country.

GETTING HERE & AROUND

BY AIR
Most international flights arrive at either London's Heathrow Airport (LHR), 15 mi west of London, or at Gatwick Airport (LGW), 27 mi south of the capital. A third, much smaller airport, Stansted (STN), 35 mi northeast of the city, handles mainly European and domestic traffic, as does Luton Airport (LLA).

London has excellent bus and train connections between its airports and downtown. From Heathrow, for example, you can take the less expensive Underground (50 minutes); National Express buses take over an hour, and the Heathrow Express trains take 15 minutes but cost £15 one way. Taxis are pricey (£35 to £50 from Heathrow); your hotel may be able to recommend a car service if this is your preference.

Airport Contacts Gatwick Airport (☎ *0870/000–2468* ⊕ *www.gatwickairport. com*). **Heathrow Airport** (☎ *0870/000–0123* ⊕ *www.heathrowairport.com*). **Luton Airport** (☎ *01582/405100* ⊕ *www.london-luton.co.uk*). **Stansted Airport** (☎ *0870/850–2825* ⊕ *www.stanstedairport.com*).

BY BOAT
There are regular crossings between Britain and France, Spain, Ireland, and Scandinavia, operated by a number of companies. Sailings can be rough. For fares and schedules, contact the companies directly.

Boat Contacts DFDS Seaways (☎ *01255/240240 or 0870/533–3000* ⊕ *www. dfdsseaways.co.uk*). **Ferry Cheap** (⊕ *www.ferrycheap.com*). **Hoverspeed** (☎ *0870/240–8070* ⊕ *www.hoverspeed.com*). **P&O Irish Sea** (☎ *0870/242–4777* ⊕ *www.poirishsea.com*). **P&O North Sea** (☎ *0870/129–6002* ⊕ *www.ponsf.com*). **P&O Portsmouth** (☎ *0870/242–4999* ⊕ *www.poportsmouth.com*). **P&O Stena Line** (☎ *0870/600–0600* ⊕ *www.posl.com*). **Seaview** (⊕ *www.seaview.co.uk*). **Stena Line** (☎ *0870/570–7070* ⊕ *www.stenaline.co.uk*).

BY BUS
Britain has a comprehensive bus (short-haul) and coach (the British term for long-distance buses) network. National Express is the major coach operator, and Victoria Coach Station, near Victoria Station in central London, is the hub of the National Express network. Megabus is a discount service between major cities; book tickets online. Coach tickets can be as low as half the price of a train ticket, but many services take twice as long as trains.

Bus Contacts **Megabus**
(☎ *0900/160–0900* ⊕ *www.megabus.
com*), 60p per minute for calls from
landlines in U.K. **National Express**
(☎ *0870/580–8080* ⊕ *www.nationalex
press.com*). **Victoria Coach Station**
(✉ *164 Buckingham Palace Rd., London SW1* ☎ *020/7730–3466 for station,
020/7730–3499 for booking* ⊕ *www.tfl.
gov.uk/vcs*).

BY CAR

With a road system designed in
part for horse-drawn carriages and
in which people drive on the left
side of the road, Britain can be a
challenging place in which to drive.
There's no reason to rent a car for a
stay in desperately congested London or for traveling between the
main centers, since there is adequate
public transportation in both cases.

MONEY & EXCHANGE

The unit of currency in Great
Britain is the pound sterling (£),
divided into 100 pence (p). The
bills (called notes in Britain) are
50, 20, 10, and 5 pounds. Coins
are £2, £1, 50p, 20p, 10p, 5p,
2p, and 1p. Scotland has its own
bills, which are accepted in the
rest of Britain. At the time of this
writing, the exchange rate was
about U.S. $1.42 to £1. Make sure
your credit and debit cards have
been programmed for ATM use
abroad—ATMs in Britain accept
PINs of four or fewer digits. Most
keypads in Britain show numbers
only, not letters.

For the Cotswold Hills, however, a car can be very handy. Rental rates
are generally reasonable, and insurance costs are relatively low.

BY TRAIN

Eurostar operates a fast and efficient rail service through the Channel
Tunnel. Travel time is 35 minutes between Folkestone and Calais, 2
hours and 15 minutes between London's St. Pancras Station and Paris's
Gare du Nord, and 2 hours between St. Pancras and Brussels.

With all major cities and many small towns in Britain served by trains,
rail travel is the most pleasant way to cover long distances, though fares
can be high. For trips of less than 200 mi, trains are usually cheaper and
quicker than planes. Buying tickets in advance can save you a substantial amount. Call National Rail Enquiries for information on all services
as well as regional rail passes. BritRail passes, purchased before your
trip, can save you money; Eurail passes cannot be used in Britain.

Train Contacts Eurostar (☎ *0870/518–6186 in the U.K.* ⊕ *www.eurostar.co.uk*). **National Rail Enquiries** (☎ *0845/748–4950, 020/7278–5240 outside Britain* ⊕ *www.
nationalrail.co.uk*).**Rail Europe** (☎ *888/382–7245 in the U.S., 0870/584–8848 in
the U.K. inquiries and credit-card bookings* ⊕ *www.raileurope.com*).

ABOUT THE RESTAURANTS

MEALS & MEALTIMES

Outside London almost every accommodation option in Britain
includes breakfast in the bill. Usually, this will mean a "full English
breakfast," consisting of eggs, bacon, grilled tomato, and tea or coffee;
there may be a lighter, "continental breakfast" option—rolls, croissants, or pastries.

DISCOUNTS & DEALS

All national collections (such as the Natural History Museum, Science Museum, and the Victoria & Albert Museum, all in London) are free, a real bargain for museum-goers.

If you plan to visit castles, gardens, and historic houses during your stay, look into discount passes or organization memberships. Match what the pass or membership offers against your itinerary to see if it's worthwhile. VisitBritain's Great British Heritage Pass is £30 for 4 days, £44 for one week, and £59 for 15 days, and includes more than 500 properties belonging to English Heritage and the National Trust. (Those organizations each have their own passes, too.) The pass is sold online and at major tourist information centers in Britain. Family passes are available. Annual membership in the National Trust (through the Royal Oak Foundation, the U.S. affiliate) is $55 a year, versus £46 if you join in Britain.

Information English Heritage (☎ *0870/333–1181* ⊕ *www. english-heritage.org.uk*). **Great British Heritage Pass** (⊕ *www.british heritagepass.com*). **National Trust** (☎ *0844/800–1895* ⊕ *www.national trust.org.uk*). **Royal Oak Foundation** (☎ *212/480–2889 or 800/913–6565* ⊕ *www.royal-oak.org*).

At lunch you can grab a sandwich between sights, pop into the local pub, or sit down in a restaurant. Note that most pubs do not have any waitstaff and that you are expected to go to the bar, order a beverage and your meal, and inform them of your table number.

Breakfast is generally served between 7:30 and 9, lunch between noon and 2, dinner or supper between 7:30 and 9:30, sometimes earlier, seldom later except in large cities. Tea shops are often open all day in touristy areas, offering drinks and snacks. Many pubs do not serve lunch after 2 or 3 PM, or dinner after 9 PM. Since 2007, smoking has been banned in pubs, clubs, and restaurants throughout Britain.

WINE, BEER & SPIRITS

Among the hundreds of British beers, the traditional brew is known as bitter and is not carbonated; it's usually served at room temperature. Locally-brewed "real ales" are worth seeking out. Chilled, fizzy American-style beer is called lager. Stouts like Guinness and Murphy's are thick, pitch-black brews you'll either love or hate; ciders, made from apples (or sometimes pears), are an alcoholic drink in Britain; shandies are a low-alcohol mix of beer and lemon soda. The legal drinking age is 18. Most pubs tend to be child-friendly, but others have restricted hours for children. If you're in doubt, ask the bartender.

PAYING

Be sure that you don't double-pay a service charge. Some restaurants exclude service charges from the printed menu, then add 10% to 15% to the check. Others will stamp SERVICE NOT INCLUDED along the bottom of the bill, in which case you should add 10% to 15%. Credit cards are widely accepted in restaurants, but many pubs still require cash.

RESERVATIONS & DRESS

We mention reservations only when these are essential or when they are not accepted. For popular restaurants, book as far ahead as you can (often 30 days); large parties should always call ahead. We mention dress only if men are required to wear a jacket or a jacket and tie.

CUTTING COSTS

Eating out in Britain can be expensive, but you can also do it cheaply. Try local cafés, where heaped plates of comfort food (bacon sandwiches and stuffed baked potatoes, for example) are served. Britain has the big names in fast food, as well as smaller places selling sandwiches, fish-and-chips, burgers, and the like. Among restaurants, Indian curry houses often have the lowest prices. Marks & Spencer, Sainsbury, and Waitrose chain supermarkets offer good-quality fare for groceries, pre-made sandwiches, and picnic fixings. In the evening, pre- or post-theater fixed-price menus are generally a good value.

WHAT IT COSTS IN POUNDS				
¢	$	$$	$$$	$$$$
Restaurants in London	Under £10	£10–£16	£17–£23	£24–£32	over £32
Restaurants elsewhere	Under £10	£10–£14	£15–£19	£20–£25	Over £25

Restaurant prices are per person for a main course at dinner.

ABOUT THE HOTELS

Britain has everything from luxurious retreats in converted country houses to budget chain hotels and bed-and-breakfasts. In many towns and cities you will find former coaching inns from the stagecoach era. Some older hotels can be old-fashioned, but they're usually cheaper. B&Bs are popular with British travelers and can be a great way to meet locals. Some B&Bs are gorgeous, and many are in handy locations; others are neither, so be careful.

Hotels, guesthouses, inns, and B&Bs in the United Kingdom are all graded from one to five stars by the tourism board, VisitBritain. Basically, the more stars a property has, the more facilities it has, and the facilities will be of a higher standard.

Especially in London, rooms and bathrooms may be smaller than what you find in the United States. Most places offer "en suite" (attached) bathrooms, although some older ones may have only washbasins in the rooms; in this case, showers and bathtubs (and toilets) are usually just down the hall. A "private bathroom" is one for your exclusive use, but not attached. When you book a room in the mid-to-lower price categories, it's best to confirm your request for a room with en-suite or private facilities.

Hotel rates in major cities tend to be cheapest on weekends, while rural hotels are cheapest on weeknights. Early December and most of January have the lowest occupancy rates, so hotels offer cheaper rooms at these times. Chains such as Premier Travel Inn offer low rates and reliable rooms, and are usually close to major sights and cities. Lastminute.com offers deals on hotel rooms all over the United Kingdom.

In some cities and towns, universities offer their residence halls to paying vacationers between terms. The facilities are usually compact single sleeping units that share bath facilities, and they can be rented on a nightly basis. Check with local tourist boards for information.

Britain is a popular vacation destination, so be sure to reserve hotel rooms weeks (months for London) in advance. During festivals especially, prices will increase and availability diminish. Tourist Information Centres will reserve rooms, usually for a small fee.

Unless otherwise noted, all lodgings listed have an elevator, a private bathroom, air-conditioning, a room phone, and a television.■ TIP➜ Assume that hotels operate on the European Plan (EP, no meals) unless we specify that they use the Breakfast Plan (BP, with full breakfast), Continental Plan (CP, continental breakfast), or Modified American Plan (MAP, breakfast and dinner).

WHAT IT COSTS IN POUNDS				
¢	$	$$	$$$	$$$$
Hotels in London	Under £80	£80–£140	£141–£200	£201–£300	over £300
Hotels elsewhere	Under £70	£70–£120	£121–£160	£161–£220	over £220

Hotel prices are for two people in a standard double room in high season, including V.A.T.

PLANNING YOUR TIME

For many, London is the main priority of any visit to Britain, and with good reason. The capital has a concentration of everything that most visitors associate with the country: colorful pageantry, time-burnished monuments, and some of the world's greatest museums, not to mention cutting-edge art, fashion, and nightlife. The city's charms could easily swallow up an entire holiday without exhausting its marvels.

However, there are good reasons for limiting your time here and moving outside the metropolis. London is one of the most expensive spots on the planet, for a start. Secondly, the chances are getting properly acquainted with the country and its population are slim—in fact, there are some places where locals may seem pretty thin on the ground. But the best reason of all to venture beyond the confines of London is to sample the diverse attractions that Britain has to offer away from the noise and crowds of the capital. You can immerse yourself in the rarefied, history-soaked atmosphere of Oxford and Cambridge, or dip into the elegance and vivacity of Bath. For a once-in-a-lifetime play-going experience, there is no substitute for seeing an authentic slice of Shakespeare in his home town of Stratford-upon-Avon. Each of these places is comparatively close to London (1.5–2.5 hours driving) and could be visited on a day excursion, though a stay of a night or two would allow a deeper appreciation.

For England's rural charms, you couldn't do better than mosey around the time-defying churches, sleepy hamlets, and ancient farmsteads that make up the Cotswold Hills, about 2 hours northwest of London. For this mellow region, a leisurely tour of a day or more would be ideal, for which you could base yourself in either Bath or Stratford.

With more time, you could detach yourself entirely from London's ambit to experience another side of Britain, in Edinburgh. A surprise awaits those for whom these northern reaches conjure images of a harsh and bleak country. There is plenty of dramatic splendor in Edinburgh Castle, as well as rousing spirit at events such as the Edinburgh Festival. Scotland offers a genuine friendliness that sometimes seems lacking in fast-moving London. A couple of days would be sufficient to appreciate Edinburgh's individual character. However, you would have to factor in the travel time required to reach it.

LONDON

London is an ancient city whose history greets you at every turn; it's also one of the coolest cities in the world. To gain a sense of its continuity, stand on Waterloo Bridge at sunset. To the east, the great globe of St. Paul's Cathedral glows golden in the fading sunlight as it has since the 17th century, still majestic amid the modern glass towers. To the west stand the mock-medieval ramparts of Westminster, home to the "Mother of Parliaments." Past them both snakes the swift, dark Thames, which flowed past the Roman settlement of Londinium nearly 2,000 years ago. If London contained only its famous landmarks—the Tower of London, Big Ben, Westminster Abbey, Buckingham Palace—it would still rank as one of the world's top cities. But London is so much more.

The capital beckons with great museums, royal pageantry, and history-steeped houses. There's no other place like it in its medley of styles, in its mixture of the green loveliness of parks and the modern gleam of neon. Modern-day London largely reflects its medieval layout, a willfully difficult tangle of streets. Even Londoners, most of whom own a dog-eared copy of an indispensable A–Z street finder, get lost in their own city. But the bewildering street patterns will be a plus for anyone who likes to walk and get lost in atmosphere.

Today the city's art, style, fashion, and dining scenes make headlines around the world. London's chefs have become superstars. Its fashion designers have conquered Paris, avant-garde artists have caused waves at the august Royal Academy of Arts, the raging after-hours scene is packed with music mavens ready to catch the Next Big Thing, and the theater continues its tradition of radical, shocking productions. And the city is now looking forward to hosting the 2012 Olympics.

7

PLANNING YOUR TIME

London is large, so you might focus a day's efforts in adjacent areas. It's easy, for example, to spend a day or more in the dense concentration of sights around Westminster and Royal London. If you're heading east to see St. Paul's Cathedral in the City, you might visit the Tower of London, which is nearby. You can make a day out of the major museums, but take a break in one of London's beloved parks. To get the most out of London, set aside time for random wandering. Walk in the city's backstreets and mews, around Park Lane and Kensington. Pass up Buckingham Palace for Kensington Palace, and abandon the city's standard-issue chain stores for its wonderful markets.

GETTING HERE & AROUND

BY AIR

For information about flying to London, see the Great Britain Planner, above.

BY BUS

Buses, or "coaches," as long-distance services are known here, operate mainly from London's Victoria Coach Station to more than 1,200 major towns and cities.

In central London, buses are traditionally bright red double- and single-deckers. You must purchase tickets from machines at bus stops along the routes before you board. Bus stops are clearly indicated. When the word REQUEST is written across the sign, you must flag the bus down. Buses are a good way to see the town, but don't take one if you're in a hurry.

A flat-rate fare of £2 applies for all bus fares. You can get an Oystercard, an electronic smart card that you load with money, which is then deducted each time you use the card on buses or the tube: a single fare is £1 or £1.50. A One-Day Bus Pass for zones one through four is £3.50 (a seven-day pass is £13) but must be bought before boarding from one of the machines at bus stops, most newsagents, or underground stations.

If you're traveling on the tube (subway) as well as the bus, consider an off-peak one-day Travelcard (£5.60), which allows unrestricted travel on buses *and* tubes after 9:30 AM and all day on weekends and national holidays. "Peak" travelcards—those for use before 9:30 AM—are more expensive (£7.40). Children under 11 travel free on the tube and buses after 9:30 AM, while children ages 11–15 travel free on buses as long as they order an Oystercard at least four weeks before they travel.

BY CAR

The major approach roads to London are six-lane motorways. Motorways (from Heathrow, M4; from Gatwick, M23 to M25, then M3; Stansted, M11) are usually the faster option for getting in and out of town, although rush-hour traffic is horrendous.

The simple advice about driving in London is: don't. If you must drive in London, remember to drive on the left and stick to the speed limit (30 mph on most city streets). An £8 "congestion charge" is levied on all vehicles entering central London (bounded by the Inner Ring Road;

street signs and "C" road markings note the area) on weekdays from 7 AM to 6:30 PM, excluding bank holidays. Pay in advance (by phone, mail, or Internet) or on that day until 10 PM if you're entering the central zone. There are no tollbooths; cameras monitor the area. For current information, check ⊕*www.cclondon.com.*

BY TAXI

Taxis are expensive, but if you're with several people they can be practical. Hotels and main tourist areas have taxi ranks; you can also hail taxis on the street. If the yellow FOR HIRE sign is lighted on top, the taxi is available. Drivers often cruise at night with their signs unlighted, so if you see an unlighted cab, keep your hand up. Generally fares start at £2.20 and increase according to distance. Tips are extra, usually 10% to 15% per ride. The average cost for a journey within central London is £8. To go into the surrounding area—Islington or Knightsbridge, for example—expect to pay approximately £12.

BY TRAIN

London has 8 major train stations, each serving a different area of the country, all accessible by Underground or bus. Trains are operated by a number of private companies, but National Rail Enquiries acts as a central rail information number.

BY TUBE

London's extensive Underground (tube) system has color-coded routes, clear signs, and extensive connections. Trains run out into the suburbs, and all stations are marked with the London Underground circular symbol. (In Britain, the word "subway" means "pedestrian underpass.") Some lines have branches (Central, District, Northern, Metropolitan, and Piccadilly), so be sure to note which branch is needed for your destination. Electronic platform signs tell you the final stop and route of the next train and how many minutes until it arrives.

London is divided into six concentric zones. The more zones your trip crosses, the higher the fare. Most tourist sights are within zone 1. If you inadvertently travel into a zone for which you do not have the right ticket, you can purchase an "extension" to your own ticket at the ticket office by the barriers. This usually costs a pound, and merely equalizes your fare. Buy an Oystercard (⇨ *see By Bus, above*) for fare reductions; it can be a huge money-saver.

The tube begins running just after 5 AM Monday through Saturday; the last services leave central London between midnight and 12:30 AM. On Sunday, trains start two hours later and finish about an hour earlier.

TOURS

Year-round, but more frequently from April to October, boats cruise the Thames, offering a different view of the London skyline. Most leave from Westminster Pier, Charing Cross Pier, and Tower Pier.

Guided sightseeing tours from the top of double-decker buses, which are open-top in summer, are a good introduction to the city, as they cover all the main central sights. Numerous companies run daily bus tours that depart from central points. You may board or alight at any of the numerous stops to view the sights, and reboard on the next bus. Tickets can be bought from the driver and are good all day. The typical price is £20.

Green Line, Evan Evans, and National Express offer day excursions by bus to places within easy reach of London, such as Hampton Court, Oxford, Stratford, and Bath.

ESSENTIALS

Boat Tour Contacts Thames Cruises (☎ *020/7930-3373 www.thamescruises. com*). **Westminster Passenger Services** (☎ *020/7930-4097*). **Westminster Passenger Service (Upriver)** (☎ *020/7930-2062* ⊕ *www.wpsa.co.uk*).

Bus Tour Contacts Big Bus Company (☎ *020/7233-9533* ⊕ *www.big bustours.com*). **Evan Evans** (☎ *020/7950-1777* ⊕ *www.evanevans.co.uk*). **Green Line** (☎ *0870/608-7261* ⊕ *www.greenline.co.uk*). **National Express** (☎ *0870/580-8080* ⊕ *www.nationalexpress.com*). **Original London Sightseeing Tour** (☎ *020/8877-1722* ⊕ *www.theoriginaltour.com*).

Transportation Contacts National Rail Enquiries (☎ *0845/748-4950* ⊕ *www. nationalrail.co.uk*). **Transport for London** (☎ *020/7222-1234* ⊕ *www.tfl.gov.uk*).

Visitor Information Britain and London Visitor Centre (✉ *1 Regent St., Piccadilly Circus, St. James's* ☎ *No phone* ⊕ *www.visitbritain.com*). **London Tourist Information Centre** (✉ *Victoria Station Forecourt, Victoria* ☎ *No phone*). **Visit-London** (⊕ *www.visitlondon.com*).

EXPLORING LONDON

Westminster and the City contain many of the grand buildings that have played a central role in British history: Westminster Abbey and the Houses of Parliament, Buckingham Palace and the older royal palace of St. James's, and the Tower of London and St. Paul's Cathedral.

Within a few minutes' walk of Buckingham Palace lie St. James's and Mayfair, neighboring quarters of elegant town houses built for the nobility during the 17th and early 18th centuries and now notable for shopping opportunities. Hyde Park and Kensington Gardens, preserved by past kings and queens for their own hunting and relaxation, create a swath of parkland across the city center. A walk across Kensington Gardens brings you to the museum district of South Kensington, with the Natural History Museum, the Science Museum, and the Victoria & Albert Museum. The South Bank has many cultural highlights: the theaters of the South Bank Centre, the Tate Modern, and the reconstruction of Shakespeare's Globe theater. The London Eye observation wheel here gives stunning city views.

WESTMINSTER & ROYAL LONDON

If you have time to visit only one part of London, this is it. Westminster and Royal London might be called "London for Beginners." If you went no farther than these few acres, you would have seen many of the famous sights, from the Houses of Parliament, Big Ben, Westminster Abbey, and Buckingham Palace, to two of the world's greatest art collections, in the National and Tate Britain galleries. You can truly call this area Royal London, since it is bounded by the triangle of streets that make up the route that the Queen usually takes when journeying from Buckingham Palace to Westminster Abbey or to the Houses of Parliament on state occasions. The three points on this royal triangle are Trafalgar Square, Westminster, and Buckingham Palace.

GETTING HERE   Trafalgar Square—easy to access and smack dab in the center of the action—is a good place to start. Take the Tube to Embankment (District and Circle lines) and walk north until you cross the Strand, or alight at Charing Cross (Bakerloo, Jubilee, and Northern lines), where the Northumberland Avenue exit deposits you on the southeast corner of the Square.

1 **Buckingham Palace.** Supreme among the symbols of London—indeed of Britain generally and of the Royal Family in particular—Buckingham Palace tops many must-see lists, although the building itself is no masterpiece and has housed the monarch only since Victoria (1819–1901) moved here from Kensington Palace on her accession in 1837. Its great gray bulk sums up the imperious splendor of so much of the city: stately, magnificent, and ponderous. In 1824 the palace was substantially rebuilt by John Nash, that tireless architect, for George IV, that tireless spendthrift. The palace contains some 600 rooms, including the Ballroom and the Throne Room. The state rooms are open to the public while the Royal Family is away during the summer. The **Changing of the Guard**—which, with all the pomp and ceremony monarchists and children adore, remains one of London's best free shows—culminates in front of the palace. Marching to live music, the guards proceed up the Mall from St. James's Palace to Buckingham Palace. Shortly afterward, the replacement guard approaches from Wellington Barracks via Birdcage Walk. Once the old and new guards are in the forecourt, the old guard symbolically hands over the keys to the palace. ■ **TIP**➡ **Get there by 10:30** AM **to grab a spot in the best viewing section at the gate facing the palace, since most of the hoopla takes place behind the railings in the forecourt.** ✉ *Buckingham Palace Rd., St. James's* ☎ *020/7766–7300* ⊕ *www.royalcollection.org.uk* 💷 *£15.50, includes audio tour, credit-card reservations subject to booking charge* ⊘ *Late July–late Sept., daily 9:45–6, last admission 3:45; confirm dates, which are subject to Queen's mandate. Changing of the Guard Apr.–July, daily 11:30* AM*; Aug.–Mar., alternating days only 11:30* AM ⊟ *AE, MC, V* Ⓤ *Victoria, St. James's Park.*

4 **Houses of Parliament.** Seat of Great Britain's government, the Houses of
FodorsChoice   Parliament are, arguably, the city's most famous and photogenic sight.
★   The most romantic view of the complex is from the opposite, south side of the river, a vista especially dramatic at night when the spires, pinnacles, and towers of the great building are floodlighted green and gold. After a catastrophic fire in 1834, these buildings arose, designed in glorious, mock-medieval style by two Victorian-era architects, Sir Charles Barry and Augustus Pugin. The Palace of Westminster, as the complex is still properly called, was established by Edward the Confessor in the 11th century. It has served as the seat of English administrative power, on and off, ever since. Now virtually the symbol of London, the 1858

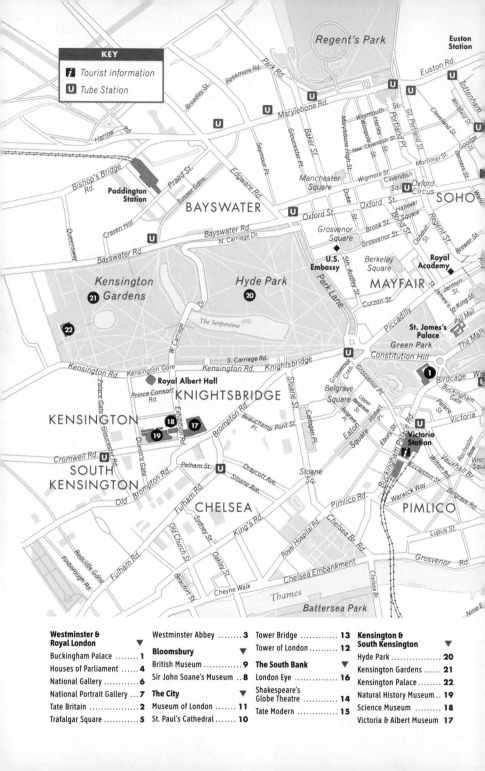

KEY

🅸 *Tourist information*
🆄 *Tube Station*

Regent's Park

Euston Station

BAYSWATER

Paddington Station

SOHO

Kensington Gardens

㉑

㉒

Hyde Park

⑳

MAYFAIR

U.S. Embassy

Royal Academy

St. James's Palace

Green Park

①

Royal Albert Hall

KNIGHTSBRIDGE

KENSINGTON

⑱ ⑰
⑲

Belgrave Square

Victoria Station
🅸

SOUTH KENSINGTON

CHELSEA

PIMLICO

Battersea Park

Thames

BLOOMSBURY

⑨

Coram's
Fields

Judd St.
Torrington Pl.
Bernard St.
Russell Square
Guilford St.
Gr. Ormond St.
John St.
Gower St.
Southampton Row
Gray's Inn Rd.
Theobalds Rd.
Jockey's Fields
Red Lion St.

Farringdon Rd.
Roseberry Ave.
Clerkenwell Rd.
Hatton Gdns.
Leather La.

Goswell Rd.

Beech St.

Cowcross St.
Charterhouse St.
W. Smithfield
W. Long La.

Barbican Center
London Wall
⑪

Liverpool St. Station

Broad St. Station

Bank Of England

THE CITY

⑧
New Oxford St.
High Holborn
Lincoln's Inn Fields
Drury La.
Kingsway
Covent Garden

Holborn Viaduct
St. Andrew St.
Shoe La.
Fetter La.
Carey St.

Old Bailey ◆
Newgate St.

Moorgate

Bishopsgate

Cheapside
Cornhill
Leadenhall St.
Fenchurch St.

⑨

Soho Square
Charing Cross Rd.
Shaftesbury Ave.
Bedford St.

Law Courts

Strand
Aldwych
Temple Pl.

Fleet St.
New Bridge St.
Ludgate Hill
⑩

Queen Victoria St.
⑩

Cannon St.

Piccadilly Circus
⑥ ⑦
⑤

Regent St.
Haymarket
Northumberland Ave.
Whitehall

Charing Cross Stn.
U
Hungerford Br.
Waterloo Br.

Victoria Embankment

Blackfriars Station

Blackfriars Br.

Great Suffolk St.
Bankside
Park St.
Summer St.
⑭
⑮

Cannon St. Station

London Br.

Southwark Br.

Lower Thames St.

Thames

⑫

⑬

South Bank Centre
⑯

Stamford St.
The Cut

York Rd.
Waterloo Rd.

Southwark St.
Union St.

Blackfriars Rd.

Bridge Rd.

Borough High St.

Tooley St.
St. Thomas St.

London Bridge Station

St. James's Park

Walk

③
④

Westminster Br.

Millbank

Waterloo Station

Westminster Br. Rd.

SOUTH BANK

Borough Rd.

London Rd.

U

Newington Causeway
Harper Rd.

Tower Bridge Rd.

VICTORIA

Great Peter St.
Horseferry Rd.
Marsham St.
Regency St.
Vincent Square

Lambeth Palace Rd.
Lambeth Br.
Lambeth Rd.

Albert Embankment

Brook Dr.

Imperial War Museum

St. George's Rd.

Elephant Rd.
New
Kent Rd.

Old Kent Rd.

Rd.

②

Vauxhall Br.

Kennington La.

Kennington Rd.

Kennington Park Rd.

Walworth Rd.

Vauxhall Station

Kennington Oval

U

London

Clock Tower designed by Pugin contains the bell known as **Big Ben** that chimes the hour (and the quarters). There are two houses, the Lords and the Commons. You can see democracy in action in the Visitors' Galleries—if, that is, you're patient enough to wait in line for hours (the Lords line is shorter) or have applied in advance for the special "line of route" tour for overseas visitors in summer (late July through August and mid-September through early October). Tickets can be prebooked by phone or on the Web site; alternatively, you can take a chance and buy same-day tickets from the ticket office opposite the Houses of Parliament. Be sure to have your name placed in advance on the waiting list for the twice-weekly tours of the **Lord Chancellor's Residence,** a popular attraction since its renovation. ✉ *St. Stephen's Entrance, St. Margaret St., Westminster* ☎ *020/7219–4272 Commons information, 020/7219–3107 Lords information, 020/7219–2184 Lord Chancellor's Residence, 0870/906–3773 summer tours* ⊕ *www.parliament.uk* 🎫 *Free, £12 summer tours* ☉ *Commons Mon. and Tues. 2:30–10:30, Wed. 3–10, Thurs. 11:30–7:30; Lords Mon.–Thurs. 2:30–10; Lord Chancellor's Residence Tues. and Thurs. 10:30–12:30. Closed Easter wk, late July–early Sept., 3 wks for party conference recess mid-Sept.– early Oct., and 3 wks at Christmas* Ⓤ *Westminster.*

❻ ★ National Gallery. Jan Van Eyck's *Arnolfini Marriage,* Leonardo da Vinci's *Virgin and Child,* Diego Velázquez's *Rokeby Venus,* John Constable's *Hay Wain . . .* you get the picture. There are approximately 2,200 other paintings in this museum, many of them among the most treasured works of art anywhere. The museum's low, gray, colonnaded, neoclassical facade fills the north side of Trafalgar Square. The gallery's east wing in sleek black and white marble has cafés and improved visitor information, such as boards with a color code for different eras of paintings. The National's collection includes paintings of the early Renaissance— in the modern Sainsbury Wing—the Flemish and Dutch masters, the Spanish school, and the English tradition (notably William Hogarth, Thomas Gainsborough, George Stubbs, and Constable).

A good place to begin is one of the computer terminals in the "Art Start" multimedia room in the Sainsbury Wing or the Espresso Bar in the East Wing. The interactive screens give you access to information on all of the museum's holdings; you can print out a free personal tour map. The museum is too overwhelming to absorb in a single viewing, but the free admission encourages repeat visits. The ultracool National Gallery Café in the East Wing makes a fun stop even if you're not visiting the gallery. ✉ *Trafalgar Sq., Westminster* ☎ *020/7747–2885* ⊕ *www.nationalgallery.org.uk* 🎫 *Free, charge for special exhibitions* ☉ *Daily 10–6, Wed. until 9; 1-hr free guided tour starts at Sainsbury Wing daily at 11:30 and 2:30, and additionally Wed. 6 and 6:30, Sat. 12:30 and 3:30* Ⓤ *Charing Cross, Leicester Sq.*

❼ National Portrait Gallery. A suitably idiosyncratic collection that presents a potted history of Britain through its people, past and present, this museum is an essential stop for all history and literature buffs. Some of the faces are obscure and will be just as unknown to you if you're English, because the portraits outlasted their sitters' fame—not so surprising when the portraitists are such greats as Reynolds, Gainsborough, Lawrence, and Romney. But the annotation is comprehensive, the layout is easy to negotiate—chronological, with the oldest at the top—and there's a separate research center for those who get hooked on particular personages. At the summit, a sleek restaurant, open beyond gallery hours, will satiate skyline droolers. ⊠ *St. Martin's Pl., Covent Garden* ☎ *020/7312–2463 recorded information* ⊕ *www.npg.org.uk* ▦ *Free, charge for special exhibitions* ⊙ *Mon.–Wed., weekends 10–6, Thurs. and Fri. 10–9* Ⓤ *Charing Cross, Leicester Sq.*

❷ **Tate Britain.** Although the building is not quite as awe-inspiring as its younger sister the Tate Modern, on the south bank of the Thames, Tate Britain's lovely, bright galleries hold only a fraction of the Modern's crowds, making it a pleasant, hands-on place to explore great British art from 1500 to the present. Each room has a theme and displays key works by major British artists: Van Dyck, Hogarth, and Reynolds rub shoulders with Rossetti, Sickert, Hockney, and Bacon. Not to be missed are the extensive collection of works by J.M.W. Turner and the generous selection of Constable landscapes. ⊠ *Millbank, Westminster* ☎ *020/7887–8888, 020/7887–8008 recorded information* ⊕ *www.tate.org.uk/britain* ▦ *Free, exhibitions £3–£10* ⊙ *Daily 10–5:50, last entry at 5* Ⓤ *Pimlico (signposted 5-min walk).*

❺ **Trafalgar Square.** This is literally the center of London: a plaque on the corner of the Strand and Charing Cross Road marks the spot from which distances on U.K. signposts are measured. It's the home of the **National Gallery** on its north side, and **Nelson's Column** at the heart of the square. Great events, such as the Christmas Tree lighting ceremony, New Year's Eve, royal weddings, political protests, and sporting triumphs always see the crowds gathering in the city's most famous square. ⊠ *Trafalgar Sq., Westminster* Ⓤ *Charing Cross.*

❸ **Westminster Abbey.**

Fodor's Choice
★ *See the illustrated feature in this chapter.*

BLOOMSBURY

The hub of intellectual London, Bloomsbury is anchored by the British Museum and the University of London. As a result, the streets and cafés around Bloomsbury's Russell Square are often crawling with students and professors engaged in heated conversation, while literary agents and academics surf the shelves of the antiquarian bookstores nearby. The leafy squares are fun to explore, and the neighborhood is adjacent to the restaurants and pubs of Soho.

GETTING HERE Tottenham Court Road on the Northern and Central lines or Russell Square (Piccadilly Line) are best for the British Museum.

❾ **British Museum.** With a facade like a great temple, this celebrated treasure house, filled with plunder of incalculable value and beauty from around the globe, occupies a ponderous Greco-Victorian building that makes a suitably grand impression. Inside are some of the greatest relics of humankind: the **Parthenon Marbles**, the **Rosetta Stone**, the **Mausoleum of Halikarnassos**, the Anglo-Saxon **Sutton Hoo Treasure**,

Fodor's Choice
★

7

and a fine selection of Egyptian mummies—almost everything, it seems, but the Ark of the Covenant. The focal point is the **Great Court,** a brilliant techno-classical design with a vast glass roof that highlights and reveals the museum's best-kept secret—an inner courtyard. The revered **Reading Room** has a blue-and-gold dome, ancient tomes, and computer screens. If you want to navigate the highlights of the almost 100 galleries, join one of the free **Eyeopener** 50-minute tours by museum guides (details at the information desk). ⊠ *Great Russell St., Bloomsbury* ☎ *020/7323–8000* ⊕ *www.thebritishmuseum.ac.uk* ✍ *Free, donation suggested; tickets for special exhibitions vary in price* ⊙ *Museum Sat.–Wed. 10–5:30, Thurs. and Fri. 10–8:30. Great Court Sun.–Wed. 9–6, Thurs.–Sat. 9* AM*–11* PM Ⓤ *Holborn, Russell Sq., Tottenham Court Rd.*

⑧ Sir John Soane's Museum. Sir John (1753–1837), architect of the Bank of England, bequeathed his house to the nation on condition that nothing be changed. He obviously had enormous fun with his home: in the Picture Room, for instance, two of Hogarth's *Rake's Progress* series are among the paintings on panels that swing away to reveal secret gallery pockets with more paintings. Everywhere mirrors and colors play tricks with light and space, and split-level floors worthy of a fairground fun house disorient you. Due to the small size of the museum, limited numbers are allowed entry at any one time, so you may have a short wait outside. ⊠ *13 Lincoln's Inn Fields, Bloomsbury* ☎ *020/7440–4263* ⊕ *www.soane.org* ✍ *Free, Sat. tour £5* ⊙ *Tues.–Sat. 10–5; also 6–9 on 1st Tues. of month* Ⓤ *Holborn.*

THE CITY

The City, as opposed to the city, is the capital's fast-beating financial heart. Behind a host of imposing neoclassical facades lie the banks and exchanges whose frantic trade determines the fortunes that underpin London—and the country. But the "Square Mile" is much more than London's Wall Street—the capital's economic engine room also has currency as a religious and political center. St. Paul's Cathedral has looked after Londoners' souls since the seventh century, and the Tower of London—that moat-surrounded royal fortress, prison, and jewel house—has taken care of beheading them.

The pedestrian-only Millennium Bridge connects the area with the South Bank; it's well worth the walk.

GETTING HERE   The City is well served by Underground stops: St Paul's and Bank, on the Central Line; and Mansion House, Cannon Street, and Monument, on the District and Circle lines.

⑪ Museum of London. If there's one place to get the history of London
ⓒ sorted out, right from 450,000 BC to the present day, it's here—although there's a great deal to sort out: Oliver Cromwell's death mask, Queen Victoria's crinolined gowns, Selfridges' Art Deco elevators, and the Lord Mayor's coach are just some of the goodies. The museum is currently undergoing modernization work so sections may be off-limits to visitors until spring 2010. ⊠ *London Wall, The City* ☎ *0870/444–3851*

Continued on page 338

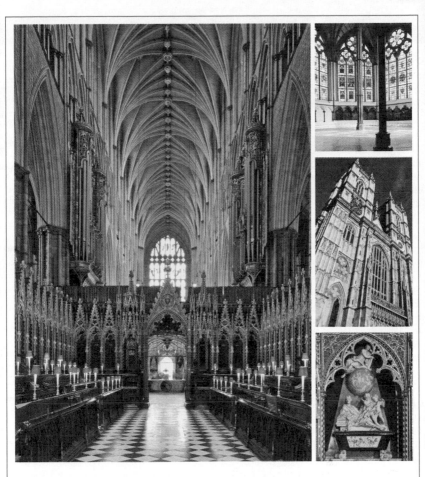

WESTMINSTER ABBEY

A monument to the rich—and often bloody and scandalous— history of Great Britain, Westminster Abbey rises on the Thames skyline as one of the most iconic sites in London.

The mysterious gloom of the lofty medieval interior is home to more than 600 monuments and memorial statues. About 3,300 people, from kings to composers to wordsmiths, are buried in the abbey. It has been the scene of 14 royal weddings and no less than 38 coronations—the first in 1066, when William the Conqueror was made king here.

TOURING THE ABBEY

There's only one way around the abbey, and as there will almost certainly be a long stream of shuffling tourists at your heels, you'll need to be alert to catch the highlights. Enter by the north door.

When you enter the church, turn around and look up to see the ❶ **painted-glass rose window,** the largest of its kind.

The ❷ **Coronation Chair,** at the foot of the Henry VII Chapel, has been briefly graced by nearly every regal posterior since Edward I ordered it in 1301. Look for the graffiti on the back of the Coronation chair. It's the work of 18th- and 19th-century visitors and Westminster schoolboys who carved their names there.

The ❸ **Henry VII's Lady Chapel** contains the tombs of Henry VII and his queen, Elizabeth of York. Close by are monuments to the young daughters of James I, and an urn purported to hold the remains of the so-called Princes in the Tower—Edward V and Richard. Interestingly, arch enemies Elizabeth I and her half-sister Mary Tudor share a tomb here. An inscription reads: "Partners both in throne and grave, here rest two sisters, Elizabeth and Mary, in the hope of the Resurrection."

In front of the ❹ **High Altar,** which was used for the funerals of Princess Diana and the Queen Mother, is a black-and-white marble pavement

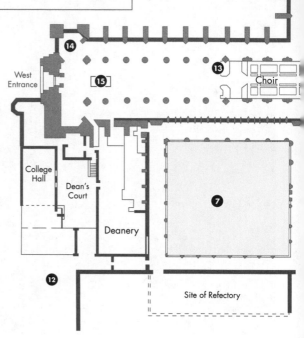

West Entrance

College Hall

Dean's Court

Deanery

Choir

Site of Refectory

laid in 1268. The intricate Italian Cosmati work contains three Latin inscriptions, one of which states that the world will last for 19,683 years.

The ❺ **Shrine of St. Edward the Confessor** contains the shrine to the pre-Norman king. Because of its great age, you must join a tour with the verger to be admitted to the chapel. (Details are available at the admission desk; there is a small extra charge.)

Geoffrey Chaucer was the first poet to be buried in ❻ **Poets' Corner** in 1400. Other memorials include: William Shakespeare, William Blake, John Milton, Jane Austen, Samuel Taylor Coleridge, William Wordsworth, and Charles Dickens.

A door from the south transept and south choir aisle leads to the calm of the ❼ **Great Cloisters.**

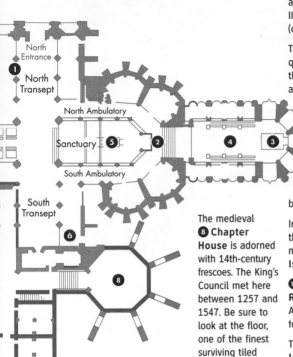

North Entrance
1
North Transept
North Ambulatory
Sanctuary **5**
2
4
3
South Ambulatory
South Transept
6
8
9
10
11

and actual clothing of Charles II and Admiral Lord Nelson (complete with eye patch).

The **10** **Little Cloister** is a quiet haven, and just beyond, the **11** **College Garden** is a delightful diversion. Filled with medicinal herbs, it has been tended by monks for more than 900 years.

The **12** **Dean's Yard** is the best spot for a fine view of the massive flying buttresses above.

The medieval **8** **Chapter House** is adorned with 14th-century frescoes. The King's Council met here between 1257 and 1547. Be sure to look at the floor, one of the finest surviving tiled floors in the country.

The **9** **Abbey Museum** includes a collection of deliciously macabre effigies made from the death masks

In the choir screen, north of the entrance to the choir, is a marble **13** **monument to Sir Isaac Newton.**

14 **A plaque to Franklin D. Roosevelt** is one of the Abbey's very few tributes to a foreigner.

The **15** **Grave of the Unknown Warrior,** in memory of the soldiers who lost their lives in both world wars, is near the exit of the abbey.

7

IN FOCUS WESTMINSTER ABBEY

QUIRKY LONDON

Near the Henry VII chapel, keep an eye open for St. Wilgefortis, who was so concerned to protect her chastity that she prayed to God for help and woke up one morning with a full growth of beard.

A BRIEF HISTORY

960 AD Benedictine monastery founded on the site by King Edward and King Dunstan.

1045–65 King Edward the Confessor enlarges the original monastery, erecting a stone church in honor of St. Paul the Apostle. Named "west minster" to distinguish from "east minster" (St. Paul's Cathedral).

1065 The church is consecrated on December 28. Edward doesn't live to see the ceremony.

1161 Following Edward's canonization, his body is moved by Henry III to a more elaborate resting place behind the High Altar. Other medieval kings are later buried around his tomb.

1245–54 Henry III pulls down the abbey and starts again with a new Gothic style influenced by his travels in France. Master mason Henry de Reyns ("of Rheims") constructs the transepts, north front, and rose windows, as well as part of the cloisters and Chapter House.

1269 The new abbey is consecrated and the choir is completed.

1350s Richard II resumes Henry III's plan to rebuild the monastery. Henry V and Henry VII continue as benefactors.

1503 The Lady Chapel is demolished and the foundation stone of Henry VII's Chapel is laid on the site.

1540 The abbey ceases to be used as a monastery.

1560 Elizabeth I refounds the abbey as a Collegiate Church. From this point on it is a "Royal Peculiar," exempt from the jurisdiction of bishops.

1745 The western towers, left unfinished from medieval times, are finally completed, based on a design by Sir Christopher Wren.

1995 Following a 25-year restoration program, saints and allegorical figures are added to the niches on the western towers and around the Great West Door.

PLANNING YOUR DAY

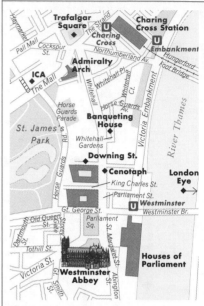

GETTING HERE: The closest Tube stop is Westminster. When you exit the station, walk west along Great George Street, away from the river. Turn left on St. Margaret Street.

CONTACT INFO: ⊠ Broad Sanctuary, Westminster SW1 P3PA ☎ 020/7222–5152 ⊕ www.westminster-abbey.org.

ADMISSION: Adults: Abbey and museum £12. **Family ticket** (2 adults and 2 children): £28. **Children under 11:** free.

HOURS: The abbey is a house of worship. Services may cause changes to the visiting hours on any given day, so be sure to call ahead.
Abbey: Weekdays 9:30–3:30, Wed. until 6, Sat. 9:30–1:30; closes 1 hr after last admission.
Museum: Daily 10:30–4.
Cloisters: Daily 8–6.
College Garden: Apr.–Sept., Tues.–Thurs., 10–6.
Chapter House: Daily 10:30–4.

WHAT'S NEARBY: To make the most of your day, arrive at the abbey early (doors open at 9:30), then make an afternoon visit to the Parliament buildings and finish with a sunset ride on the **London Eye.** Post-flight, take a walk along the fairy-lit South Bank and have dinner (or a drink in the bar) with a view, at the **Oxo Tower Restaurant** (☎ 020/7803–3888)or the Royal Festival Hall's **Strylon Restaurant** (☎020/7654–7800).

Please note that overseas visitors can no longer visit the **Houses of Parliament** during session. However, tours of the buildings are available in August and September. For more information and booking call ☎ 0870/90–3773. Also, it's advisable to prebook tickets for the London Eye. Do this online at www.londoneye.com, or call 0870/990–8883.

IN A HURRY?

If you're pressed for time, concentrate on the following four highlights: the Coronation Chair; Chapter House; Poets' Corner; and Grave of the Unknown Warrior.

THINGS TO KNOW

■ Photography and filming are not permitted anywhere in the abbey.

■ In winter the interior of the abbey can get quite cold; dress accordingly.

■ For an animated history of the museum, join one of the tours that depart from the information desk, tour times vary.

■ Touring the abbey can take half a day, especially in summer, when lines are long.

■ To avoid the crowds, make sure you arrive early. If you're first in line you can enjoy parts of the abbey in relative calm before the mad rush descends.

■ If you want to study up before you go, visit www.westminster-abbey.org, which includes an in-depth history and self-guided tour of the abbey. Otherwise pick up a free leaflet from the information desk.

■ On Sundays the abbey is not open to visitors. Join a service instead. Check the Web site for service times, as well as details of concerts, organ recitals, and special events.

7

IN FOCUS WESTMINSTER ABBEY

⊕ *www.museumoflondon.org.uk* 🎟️*Free* ⊙ *Mon.–Sat. 10–5:50, Sun. noon–5:50; last admission 5:30* Ⓤ *Barbican, St Paul's.*

⑩ St. Paul's Cathedral. The symbolic heart of London, St. Paul's may take
★ your breath away, even more so now that it's been spruced up for its 300th anniversary. The dome—the world's third largest—peeps through the skyline from many an angle around London. The structure is Sir Christopher Wren's masterpiece, completed in 1710 after 35 years of building. Beneath the lantern is Wren's famous epitaph, which his son composed and had set into the pavement, and which reads succinctly: LECTOR, SI MONUMENTUM REQUIRIS, CIRCUMSPICE—"Reader, if you seek his monument, look around you." The epitaph also appears on Wren's memorial in the Crypt. If you're in shape, you can walk up 280 feet from ground level to a gallery around the dome that has a spectacular panorama of London.

The remains of the poet John Donne, who was dean of St. Paul's for his final 10 years (he died in 1631), are in the south choir aisle. The vivacious choir-stall carvings nearby are the work of Grinling Gibbons, as are those on the organ, which Wren designed and Handel played. Among the famous whose remains lie in the **Crypt** are the duke of Wellington and Admiral Lord Nelson. ✉️*St. Paul's Churchyard, The City* ☎️*020/7236–4128* ⊕*www.stpauls.co.uk* 🎟️*£10, audio tour £3.50, guided tour £3* ⊙*Cathedral Mon.–Sat. 8:30–4:30; last admission at 4; closed occasionally for special services. Shop and Crypt Café also open Sun. 10:30–5* Ⓤ *St. Paul's.*

⑬ Tower Bridge. Despite its medieval, fairy-tale appearance, this is a Vic-
🐾 torian youngster. Constructed of steel, then clothed in Portland stone, the Horace Jones masterpiece was deliberately styled in the Gothic persuasion to complement the Tower next door. The **Tower Bridge Experience** exhibition is a fun tour inside the structure to discover how one of the world's most famous bridges actually works. One highlight is the glorious view from up high on the covered walkway between the turrets. ☎️*020/7403–3761* ⊕*www.towerbridge.org.uk* 🎟️*£6* ⊙*Daily 9:30–5:30; last entry at 5* Ⓤ *Tower Hill.*

⑫ Tower of London. Nowhere else does London's history come to life so
🐾 vividly as in this minicity of 20 towers filled with heraldry and trea-
Fodor'sChoice sure, the intimate details of lords and dukes and princes and sovereigns
★ etched in the walls (literally, in some places), and quite a few pints of royal blood spilled on the stones. ■TIP→ **This is one of Britain's most popular sights—the Crown Jewels are here—and you can avoid lines by buying a ticket in advance on the Web site, by phone, at any tube station, or at an on-site kiosk; arriving before 11 can also help at busy times.** The visitor center provides an introduction to the Tower. Allow at least three hours for exploring, and take time to stroll along the battlements for a wonderful overview.

A person was mighty privileged to be beheaded in the peace and seclusion of **Tower Green** instead of before the mob at Tower Hill. In fact, only seven people were ever important enough—among them Anne Boleyn and Catherine Howard, wives two and five of Henry VIII's six;

Elizabeth I's friend Robert Devereux, earl of Essex; and the nine-day queen, Lady Jane Grey, age 17.

Free tours depart every half hour or so from the Middle Tower. They are conducted by the 39 Yeoman Warders, better known as Beefeaters—ex-servicemen dressed in resplendent navy-and-red (scarlet-and-gold on special occasions) Tudor outfits. Beefeaters have been guarding the Tower since Henry VII appointed them in 1485. One of them, the Yeoman Ravenmaster, is responsible for the Tower ravens.

In prime position stands the oldest part of the Tower and the most conspicuous of its buildings, the **White Tower;** the other towers were built in the next few centuries. This central keep was begun in 1078 by William the Conqueror; Henry III (1207–72) had it whitewashed, which is where the name comes from. The spiral staircase is the only way up, and here are the **Royal Armouries,** with a collection of arms and armor. Most of the interior of the White Tower has been altered over the centuries, but the **Chapel of St. John the Evangelist,** downstairs from the armories, is a pure example of 11th-century Norman style—very rare, very simple, and very beautiful. Across the moat, **Traitors' Gate** lies to the right. Opposite Traitors' Gate is the former Garden Tower, better known since about 1570 as the **Bloody Tower.** Its name comes from one of the most famous unsolved murders in history, the saga of the "little princes in the Tower." In 1483 the uncrowned boy king, Edward V, and his brother Richard were left here by their uncle, Richard of Gloucester, after the death of their father, Edward IV. They were never seen again, Gloucester was crowned Richard III, and in 1674 two little skeletons were found under the stairs to the White Tower.

The most famous exhibits are the **Crown Jewels,** in the Jewel House, Waterloo Block. Moving walkways on either side of the jewels hasten progress at the busiest times. You get so close to the fabled gems you feel you could polish them (there are, however, wafers of bulletproof glass).

Evocative **Beauchamp Tower** was built west of Tower Green by Edward I (1272–1307). It was soon designated as a jail for the higher class of miscreant, including Lady Jane Grey, who is thought to have added her Latin graffiti to the many inscriptions carved by prisoners here.

⊠ *H. M. Tower of London, Tower Hill, The City* ☎ *0844/482–7799 recorded information and advance booking* ⊕ *www.hrp.org.uk* ⊠ *£16* ⊙ *Mar.–Oct., Tues.–Sat. 9–6, Sun. and Mon. 10–6; Nov.–Feb., Tues.–Sat. 9–5, Sun. and Mon. 10–5. Last admission 1 hr before closing time; and all internal bldgs. close 30 mins after last admission. Free Yeoman Warder guided tours leave daily from Middle Tower (subject to weather and availability) about every 30 mins until 3:30 Mar.–Oct., 2:30 Nov.–Feb.* Ⓤ *Tower Hill.*

THE SOUTH BANK

There's an old North London quip about needing a passport to cross the Thames, but times have changed dramatically—culture, history, sights: the South Bank has it all. The Tate Modern is the star attraction, installed in a 1930s power station, with the eye-catching Millennium Bridge linking its main door across the river to the City. Near the theaters of the South Bank Centre, the London Eye observation wheel gives you a flight over the city.

It's fitting that so much of London's artistic life should once again be centered on the South Bank—in the past, Southwark was the location of theaters, taverns, and cockfighting arenas. The Globe Theatre, in which Shakespeare acted and held shares, was one of several here.

GETTING HERE   For the South Bank use Westminster station on the Jubilee or Northern line, from where you can walk across Westminster Bridge; Embankment on District, Circle, Northern, and Bakerloo lines, where you can walk across Hungerford Bridge; or Waterloo on the Jubilee, Northern, and Bakerloo lines, where it's a five-minute walk to the Royal Festival Hall.

⑯ **London Eye.** The London Eye is the largest observation wheel ever built, and in the top 10 tallest structures in London. The 25-minute slow-motion ride inside one of the enclosed passenger capsules is so smooth you'd hardly know you were suspended over the Thames, moving slowly round. On a clear day you can take in a range of up to 25 mi. ⊠*Jubilee Gardens, South Bank* ☎*0870/990–8883* ⊕*www.londoneye. com* ☑*£15* ⊙*June and Sept., daily 10–9; July and Aug., daily 10–9:30; Oct.–May, daily 10–8* Ⓤ*Waterloo.*

⑭ **Shakespeare's Globe Theatre.** A spectacular theater, this is a replica of Shakespeare's open-roof, wood-and-thatch Globe Playhouse (built in 1599 and burned down in 1613), where most of the Bard's great plays premiered. For several decades, American actor and director Sam Wanamaker worked ceaselessly to raise funds for the theater's reconstruction, 200 yards from its original site, with authentic materials and techniques; his dream was realized in 1996. The "pit," or orchestra level, can take 500 standees—or "groundlings," to use the historical term—in front of the high stage, and 1,000 can sit in the covered wooden bays. A repertory season of three or four plays is presented in summer, in daylight—and sometimes rain. Throughout the year you can tour the theater as part of the **Shakespeare's Globe Exhibition,** an adjacent museum that provides background material on the Elizabethan theater and the construction of the modern-day Globe. ⊠*21 New Globe Walk, Bankside, South Bank* ☎*020/7401–9919 box office, 020/7902–1400 New Shakespeare's Globe Exhibition* ⊕*www.shakespeares-globe.org* ☑*£9 for exhibition and tour* ⊙*Exhibition daily 10–5, plays May–early Oct.; call for schedule* Ⓤ*Mansion House, then walk across Southwark Bridge; Blackfriars, then walk across Blackfriars Bridge; or Southwark, then walk down to river.*

⑮ **Tate Modern.** This former power station has glowered on the banks on the Thames since the 1930s, and after a dazzling renovation by Herzog & de Meuron, provides a grand space for a massive collection of international modern art. The vast Turbine Hall is a dramatic entrance point. On permanent display in the galleries are classic works from 1900 to the present day, by Matisse, Picasso, Dalí, Francis Bacon, Andy Warhol, and the most-talked-about upstarts. They are arranged in themes that mix the historic with the contemporary—Landscape, Still Life, and the Nude—on different levels, reached by a moving staircase. This is a good museum for kids, who respond to the unusual space as well as the art; there are kids' programs, too. The changing exhibitions, for which there are often long lines, are always the talking point of Londoners who have their fingers on the pulse. ⊠ *Bankside, South Bank* ☎ *020/7887–8888* ⊕ *www.tate.org.uk* ⊡ *Free* ⊙ *Sun.–Thurs. 10–6, Fri. and Sat. 10–10* Ⓤ *Blackfriars, Southwark.*

KENSINGTON & SOUTH KENSINGTON

Splendid houses with pillared porches, as well as fascinating museums, stylish squares, and glittering antiques shops, line the streets of the Royal Borough of Kensington. Also here is Kensington Palace (the former home of both Diana, Princess of Wales, and Queen Victoria), which put the district literally on the map back in the 17th century. To Kensington's east is one of the highest concentrations of important artifacts anywhere, the "museum mile" of South Kensington, with the rest of Kensington offering peaceful strolls and a noisy main street.

GETTING HERE   South Kensington and Gloucester Road on the District, Circle, and Piccadilly lines are convenient stops for the South Kensington museums.

20 **Hyde Park.** Along with the smaller St. James's and Green parks to the east, Hyde Park started as Henry VIII's hunting grounds. Along its south side runs **Rotten Row,** once Henry's royal path to the hunt—the name is a corruption of *route du roi* (route of the king). It's still used by the Household Cavalry, who live at the **Knightsbridge Barracks**—a high-rise and a low, ugly, red block to the left. This brigade mounts the guard at the palace, and you can see them leave to perform this duty, in full regalia, at about 10:30, or await the return of the ex-guard about noon. Hyde Park is wonderful for strolling, watching the locals, or just relaxing by the **Serpentine,** the long body of water near its southern border. On Sunday, **Speakers' Corner,** in the park near Marble Arch, is an unmissable spectacle of vehement, sometimes comical, and always entertaining orators. ☎ *020/7298–2100* ⊕ *www.royalparks. gov.uk* ⊙ *Daily 5* AM–*midnight* Ⓤ *Hyde Park Corner, Lancaster Gate, Marble Arch.*

21 **Kensington Gardens.** More formal than neighboring Hyde Park, Kensington Gardens was first laid out as palace grounds. The paved Italian garden at the top of the Long Water, the **Fountains,** is a reminder of this, although **Kensington Palace** itself is the main clue to its royal status, with the early-19th-century Sunken Garden north of it. Nearby is George Frampton's beloved 1912 *Peter Pan,* a bronze of the boy who lived on an island in the Serpentine and never grew up, and whose creator, J. M. Barrie, lived at 100 Bayswater Road, not 500 yards from here. The **Round Pond** is a magnet for model-boat enthusiasts and duck feeders. The fabulous **Princess Diana Memorial Playground** has specially designed structures and areas on the theme of Barrie's Neverland. ☎ *020/7298–2100* ⊕ *www.royalparks.gov.uk* ⊙ *Daily 6* AM–*dusk* Ⓤ *Lancaster Gate, Queensway.*

7

㉒ Kensington Palace. Not as splendid as Buckingham Palace, or as famous as Hampton Court, Kensington Palace is the most intimate of London's great royal residences. Originally a more modest dwelling called Nottingham House, it was bought in 1689 by King William III, whose acute asthma made it necessary for him to live outside the city (Kensington was, in those days, a small countryside village). He commissioned Wren and Hawksmoor to turn the building into a palace, and royals have been living here in grand style ever since.

The **Royal Ceremonial Dress Collection** displays garments dating to the 18th century. State and occasional dresses, hats, shoes, and gloves from the present Queen's wardrobe are showcased, as are some incredible evening gowns worn by that most fashionable of royal icons, Princess Diana. Other displays interpret the symbolism of ceremonial court dress and also show the labor that went into producing this attire. The **State Apartments,** especially the King's Apartments, are an imposing statement of regal power.

But despite all this splendor, it is perhaps the gardens that are the true natural gem of this palace. The **Orangery,** built for Queen Anne, was the scene of many a royal family party; you can take a cup of tea here, before admiring the Sunken Garden with its fountains and Tudor design that echoes Hampton Court. ⊠ *The Broad Walk, Kensington Gardens, Kensington* ☎ *0844/482–7799 advance booking, 0844/482–7777 information* ⊕ *www.hrp.org.uk* ✍ *£12.00; discounted joint tickets for one other palace, specified at time of purchase, are available* ۞ *Mar.–Oct., daily 10–6; Nov.–Feb., daily 10–5; last admission 1 hr before closing* Ⓤ *Queensway.*

⑲ Natural History Museum. When you want to heed the call of the wild,
Ⓒ explore this fun place. Don't be surprised when the dinos notice you—the fierce, animatronic Tyrannosaurus Rex senses when human prey is near and "responds" in character. Don't miss the ambitious Earth Galleries or the Creepy Crawlies Gallery, which includes a nightmarish, super-enlarged scorpion. In the basement, hands-on activities can be experienced in Investigate, which allows you to do just that, with actual objects, from old bones to bugs. The Darwin Centre showcases the museum's entire collection—all 22 million creatures—from a tiny Seychellian frog to the Komodo dragon lizard. Daily Explore tours leave from the museum's main information desk. ⊠ *Cromwell Rd., South Kensington* ☎ *020/7942–5000* ⊕ *www.nhm.ac.uk* ✍ *Free* ۞ *Daily 10–5:50, last admission 5:30* Ⓤ *South Kensington.*

⑱ Science Museum. Hands-on exhibits include the Launch Pad gallery,
Ⓒ which demonstrates basic scientific principles (try the plasma ball, where your hands attract "lightning"—if you can get them on it); *Puffing Billy,* the oldest steam locomotive in the world; and the actual *Apollo 10* capsule. The six floors are devoted to subjects as diverse as the history of flight, space exploration, steam power, medicine, and a sublime exhibition on science in the 18th century. ⊠ *Exhibition Rd., South Kensington* ☎ *0870/870–4868* ⊕ *www.sciencemuseum.org.uk* ✍ *Free, charge for the cinema shows and special exhibitions* ۞ *Daily 10–6* Ⓤ *South Kensington.*

⑰ Victoria & Albert Museum. Recognizable by the copy of Victoria's Imperial Crown on the lantern above the central cupola, this huge museum showcases the decorative arts of all disciplines, periods, nationalities, and tastes. The collections of the V&A, as it's always called, are *so* all-encompassing that confusion is a hazard; select a few galleries to

focus on. The British Galleries provide a social context for British art and design from 1500 to 1900. Free one-hour tours whirl you by some of the museum's prized treasures. The shop is the museum in microcosm, and quite the best place to buy Art Nouveau or arts-and-crafts gifts. ⊠ *Cromwell Rd., South Kensington* ☎ *020/7942–2000* ⊕ *www. vam.ac.uk* ⊠ *Free* ⊙ *Thurs.–Wed. 10–5:45, Fri. 10–10; free tours daily at 10:30, 11:30, 1:30, and 3:30* ⓤ *South Kensington.*

EXCURSIONS ALONG THE THAMES

Upstream, the royal palaces and grand houses that dot the area were built not as town houses but as country residences with easy access to London by river; Hampton Court Palace and Windsor Castle are the best and biggest of all.

HAMPTON COURT PALACE
★ *20 mi southwest of central London.*

On a loop of the Thames lies Hampton Court, one of London's oldest royal palaces and more like a small town in size; you need a day to do it justice. It's actually two palaces in one—a Tudor residence and a late-17th-century Baroque one—as well as a renowned garden. The magnificent Tudor brick house, with its cobbled courtyards and cavernous kitchens, was begun in 1514 by Cardinal Wolsey, the ambitious lord chancellor (roughly, prime minister) of England and archbishop of York. He wanted it to be the best palace in the land, and succeeded so well that Henry VIII grew envious, whereupon Wolsey gave Hampton Court to the king. Henry moved in during 1525, added a great hall and chapel, and proceeded to live much of his astonishing life here. Later, during the reign of William and Mary, Christopher Wren expanded the palace substantially, adding the graceful Baroque south and east fronts that are highlights of the palace. Six themed routes, including Henry VIII's State Apartments and the King William III's Apartments, help you plan your visit; special guides in period costume add to the fun.

The idyllic 60 acres of ornamental gardens, lakes, and ponds include almost half a mile of paths in a fiendish maze planted in 1714. ⊠ *East Molesey on A308* ☎ *0870/752–7777* ⊕ *www.hrp.org.uk* ⊠ *Palace, gardens, and maze £13.00, gardens only £4.50, maze only £3.50, park grounds free* ⊙ *State apartments Apr.–Oct., daily 10–6; last admission at 5; Nov.–Mar., daily 10–4:30; grounds daily 7–dusk* ⓤ *Richmond, then Bus R68; National Rail, South West: Hampton Court Station, 35 min from Waterloo.*

7

WINDSOR CASTLE

12 mi west of London.

The imposing turrets and towers of Windsor Castle are visible for miles. From William the Conqueror to Queen Victoria, the kings and queens of England added towers and wings to the brooding structure, and it's now the largest inhabited castle in the world. Despite the multiplicity of hands involved in its design, the palace manages to have a unity of style and character.

Fast Green Line buses arrive from London's Victoria Station every half hour. National Express buses arrive every hour or so from London's Victoria Coach Station and Heathrow Airport's Terminal 5. The journey takes about 2 hours. South West Trains travel from London Waterloo every 30 minutes, or you can catch a more frequent train from Paddington and change at Slough. The trip takes less than an hour. If you're driving, take the M4 from London and park in one of the public lots near the edge of the town center.

William the Conqueror began work on the castle in the 11th century, and Edward III modified and extended it in the mid-1300s. One of Edward's largest contributions was the enormous and distinctive **Round Tower.** Finally, between 1824 and 1837, George IV transformed the still essentially medieval castle into the fortified royal palace you see today. It is the only royal residence in continuous use by the royal family since the Middle Ages. Admission includes an audio guide and, if you wish, a guided tour of the castle precincts.

As you enter the castle, **Henry VIII's gateway** leads uphill into the wide castle precincts, where you are free to wander. Across from the entrance is the exquisite **St. George's Chapel** (closed Sunday). Here lie 10 of the kings of England, including Henry VI, Charles I, and Henry VIII (Jane Seymour is the only one of his six wives buried here). One of the noblest buildings in England, the chapel was built in the Perpendicular style popular in the 15th and 16th centuries, with elegant stained-glass windows, a high, vaulted ceiling, and intricately carved choir stalls.

From the North Terrace, you enter the **State Apartments,** which are open to the public when the Queen is not in residence (call in advance to see if they're open). Queen Elizabeth uses the castle far more than any of her predecessors did, as a sort of country weekend home. ■ TIP→ To see the castle come magnificently alive, check out the Changing of the Guard, which takes place at 11 AM Monday to Saturday from April through July and on odd-numbered weekdays and Saturday from August through March. Because the dates are changeable, confirm the exact schedule.

Although a fire in 1992 gutted some of the State Apartments, hardly any works of art were lost. Phenomenal repair work restored the **Grand Reception Room,** the **Green and Crimson Drawing Rooms,** and the **State and Octagonal dining rooms.** A green oak hammer-beam (a short horizontal roof beam that projects from the tops of walls for support) roof looms magnificently over the 600-year-old **St. George's Hall,** where the Queen gives state banquets. The tour's high points are the **Throne Room** and the **Waterloo Chamber.**

☺ **Queen Mary's Doll's House,** on display to the left of the entrance to the State Apartments, is a perfect miniature Georgian palace-within-a-palace, created in 1923. ☎*020/7766–7304 tickets, 01753/831118 recorded information* ⊕*www.royalresidences.com* ✉*£15 for Precincts, State Apartments, Gallery, St. George's Chapel, Albert Memorial Chapel, and Doll's House; £8.50 when State Apartments are closed* ⊙*Mar.–Oct., daily 9:45–5:15, last admission at 4; Nov.–Feb., daily 9:45–4:15, last admission at 3.*

WHERE TO EAT

Swinging London rivals New York and Tokyo as one of the best places to eat in the world right now. The sheer diversity of restaurants here is unparalleled. Among the city's 6,700 restaurants are see-and-be-seen hot spots, casual ethnic eateries, innovative gastro-pubs, and temples to haute cuisine.

Two caveats: first, an outright ban on smoking in public places—such as restaurants—was enacted in 2007. Second, beware of Sunday. Many restaurants are closed, especially in the evening; likewise public holidays. Over the Christmas period, London virtually shuts down—it seems only hotels are prepared to feed travelers. When in doubt, call ahead. It's a good idea to book a table at all times.

London is not an inexpensive city. A modest meal for two can cost £40 (about $80) and the £100-a-head meal is not so taboo. Damage-control strategies include making lunch your main meal—the top places have bargain lunch menus, halving the price of evening à la carte—and ordering a second appetizer instead of an entrée, to which few places object. Note that an appetizer, usually known as a "starter" or "first course," is sometimes called an "entrée," as it is in France, and an entrée in England is dubbed the "main course" or simply "mains." Seek out fixed-price menus, and watch for hidden extras on the check: cover, bread, or vegetables charged separately, and service.

BLOOMSBURY

£££   **Galvin Bistrot de Luxe.** The Galvin brothers successfully blaze a trail
BISTRO   for the bistro de luxe concept on Baker Street. Feted chefs Chris and Jeff forsake Michelin stars and cut loose under the brasserie banner. An older crowd enjoys impeccable service in a handsome mahogany-paneled salon. There's no finer crab lasagna around, and mains punch above their weight: rabbit and polenta, rump of lamb, sea trout with samphire. The £15.50 set lunch is worth noting. ✉*66 Baker St., Bloomsbury* ☎*020/7935–4007* ▭*AE, MC, V* Ⓤ*Baker St.*

££   **North Sea Fish Restaurant.** Come here and nowhere else for the British
SEAFOOD   national dish of fish-and-chips—battered cod, thick fries with salt and vinegar, and a dollop of fresh tartar sauce. Note that it's tricky to find: head three blocks south of St. Pancras station and the British Library, then down Judd Street. It has net curtains and worn carpet, and it's filled with academics from the Library. They serve only freshly caught fish, which you can order grilled—but that would defeat the purpose. ✉*7–8*

Leigh St., Bloomsbury ☎*020/7387–5892* ▤*AE, MC, V* ⊘*Closed Sun.* Ⓤ*Russell Sq.*

CHELSEA

£££££   **Gordon Ramsay at Royal Hospital Road.** The infamous Mr. Ramsay—of
FRENCH   *Hell's Kitchen* fame—whips up a heavenly storm of white beans, lobster, foie gras, and shaved truffles at this acclaimed restaurant. He's one of Britain's finest and most notorious chefs, and wins the highest accolades here, where tables are booked months in advance. For £110, splurge on seven courses; for £85, dance through a three-course dinner; or breeze through a £40 three-course lunch. ✉*69 Royal Hospital Rd., Chelsea* ☎*020/7352–4441* ⌓*Reservations essential* ▤*AE, DC, MC, V* ⊘*Closed weekends* Ⓤ*Sloane Sq.*

££   **PJ's Bar & Grill.** Enter PJ's and assume the Polo Joe lifestyle: wooden
AMERICAN   floors and stained glass, a slowly revolving propeller from a 1911 Vickers Vimy flying boat, and vintage polo gear galore. The place is packed, relaxed, and efficient, and the menu, which includes all-American staples like steaks, salads, and brownies, pleases all except vegetarians. PJ's opens late, and the bartenders are pros. Weekend brunch is *de rigueur* with the wealthy Chelsea set. ✉*52 Fulham Rd., Chelsea* ☎*020/7581–0025* ▤*AE, MC, V* Ⓤ*South Kensington.*

THE CITY

££   **Canteen.** It's posh pies and trendy British classics at this well-lit, ultra-
BRITISH   modern, diner-style canteen in Spitalfield's finance district. With booths and communal oak tables, a mainly City lunch crowd wolfs down Coronation chicken and savory pies (chicken-and-mushroom and steak-and-kidney are favorites), with mashed potatoes, greens, or mushy peas. Finish with treacle tart or Eton Mess (strawberries, meringue, and cream). Everything tastes good and is reasonably priced. ✉*2 Crispin Place, The City* ☎*0845/686–1122* ▤*AE, MC, V* Ⓤ*Liverpool St.*

COVENT GARDEN

£   **Food for Thought.** It may only be a '70s-style subterranean, unfussy veg-
VEGETARIAN   etarian café with no liquor license, but be prepared to queue down the stairs here in the heart of Covent Garden. It has communal tables and a crunchy daily menu of soups, quiches, stir-fries, bakes, and casseroles. Wheat-free, gluten-free, genetically unmodified, and vegan options are available, but note that it often closes early. ✉*31 Neal St., Covent Garden* ☎*020/7836–9072* ⌓*Reservations not accepted* ▤*No credit cards* Ⓤ*Covent Garden.*

£££££   **L'Atelier de Joël Robuchon.** A-listers sit side by side at the counter and
FRENCH   graze tapas-style at French legend Joël Robuchon's super-seductive London outpost. Decked out in plush red and black, counter seating frames the ground-floor open kitchen, creating a spectacle that is pure culinary theater. Navigate exquisite French tapas—from frogs' legs and pig's trotter to veal rib and quail with truffle mash. The £80 six-course tasting menu is a neat way to experience multiple flavors. There's also a cocktail bar, and a sit-down restaurant, La Cuisine, on the first floor. ✉*13–15 West St., Covent Garden* ☎*020/7010–8600* ▤*AE, DC, MC, V* Ⓤ*Leicester Square.*

WHERE TO REFUEL AROUND TOWN

When you're on the go or don't have time for a leisurely meal—and Starbucks simply won't cut it—you might want to try a good local chain restaurant or sandwich bar.

Café Rouge: A classic 30-strong French bistro chain that's been around for eons—so "uncool" that it's now almost fashionable. ⊕ www.caferouge.co.uk

Carluccio's Caffé: Affable TV chef Antonio Carluccio's chain of 12 all-day traditional Italian café/bar/food shops are freshly sourced and make brilliant stops on a shopping spree. ⊕ www.carluccios.com

Gourmet Burger Kitchen (aka GBK): Peter Gordon's line of burger joints is wholesome and handy, with Aberdeen Angus beef, lamb, or venison burgers. ⊕ www.gbkinfo.co.uk

Pizza Express: Serving tasty but utterly predictable pizzas, Pizza Express seems to be everywhere (there are 95 in London). Soho's branch has a cool live jazz program. ⊕ www.pizzaexpress.com

Pret a Manger: London's take-out supremo isn't just for sandwiches: there are wraps, noodles, sushi, salads, and tea cakes as well. ⊕ www.pretamanger.com

Strada: Stop here for authentic pizzas baked over a wood fire, plus simple pastas and risottos. It's stylish, cheap, and packed. ⊕ www.strada.co.uk

Wagamama: Londoners drain endless bowls of noodles at this chain of high-tech, high-turnover, high-volume Japanese canteens. ⊕ www.wagamama.com

KNIGHTSBRIDGE

££££££   **The Capital.** The French haute cuisine is sublime at this legendary club-
FRENCH   like hotel dining room that retains a grown-up atmosphere and formal service. Chef Eric Chavot serves impeccable dishes in chic surroundings. Go for exquisite smoked-haddock carpaccio with quail eggs, roasted scallops with black pudding, or halibut and Provençal tian. Desserts like mint parfait or almond mousse and lemon sorbet are sensational, too. The £29.50 set lunch is a bargain. ✉ 22–24 Basil St., Knightsbridge ☎ 020/7589–5171 ⚐ Reservations essential ▤ AE, DC, MC, V Ⓤ Knightsbridge.

££££   **Rasoi Vineet Bhatia.** Chef-proprietor Vineet Bhatia showcases the fin-
INDIAN   est new Indian cuisine in London at this tony town-house venue off
Fodor'sChoice   the King's Road. Super seductive and decked with Indian prints, silks,
★   and ornaments, Bhatia pushes the boundaries with signatures like wild mushroom rice with tomato ice cream or grilled lobster with cocoa and sour spices. Don't leave without sampling the chocolate samosas. ✉ 10 Lincoln St., Knightsbridge ☎ 020/7225–1881 ▤ AE, DC, MC, V Ⓤ Sloane Sq.

MAYFAIR

£££   **Cecconi's.** Enjoy all-day buzz at this fashionable Italian brasserie
ITALIAN   opposite the Royal Academy on Burlington Gardens. Just off Savile Row and New Bond Street, the glam brigade pitch up for breakfast, brunch, and Italian tapas (cicchetti) at the bar, and return for something more formal later on. Ilse Crawford's green-and-brown interior

7

is a stylish background for classics like veal Milanese, beef carpaccio, zucchini fritti, Venetian calves' liver, and tiramisu. Note: it's a great pit stop during a shopping spree. ⊠*5A Burlington Gardens, Mayfair* ☎*020/7434–1500* ⚑*Reservations essential* ▤*AE, DC, MC, V* Ⓤ*Green Park, Piccadilly Circus.*

££££ **Le Gavroche.** Michel Roux Jr. thrives at this clubby basement haven,
FRENCH which some critics rate the best formal dining in London. With silver
Fodor'sChoice domes and unpriced ladies' menus, Roux's mastery of classic French cui-
★ sine dazzles with signatures like foie gras with cinnamon-scented crispy duck pancake, grilled turbot with cauliflower and lemon, or saddle of rabbit with Parmesan cheese. Desserts, like the pear and puff pastry, also astound. The set lunch is a relatively affordable treat at £48—with water, a half bottle of wine, and coffee. In fact, it may be the best way to eat here if you don't have an expense account, which most patrons clearly do. ⊠*43 Upper Brook St., Mayfair* ☎*020/7408–0881* ⚑*Reservations essential* ▤*AE, DC, MC, V* ⊘*Closed 10 days at Christmas. No lunch weekends* Ⓤ*Marble Arch.*

NOTTING HILL

£ **Churchill Thai Kitchen.** There's a cult appeal to this super-value Thai
THAI kitchen attached to an English pub swamped in horse tack, bedpans, and Sir Winston Churchill memorabilia. With big portions of all dishes priced around £6, it's a bargain for this section of town, and hence is full most nights. The *pad thai* noodles are a sure bet, as are the prawn and chicken dishes and red or green curries. ⊠*Churchill Arms, 119 Kensington Church St., Notting Hill* ☎*020/7792–1246* ▤*MC, V* Ⓤ*Notting Hill Gate, High Street Kensington.*

££££ **The Ledbury.** Notting Hill's private equity partners have created a "strong
FRENCH buy" with this fantastic neighborhood fine-dining restaurant housed in a handsome high-ceiling dining room. The £60 tasting menu is a tour de force that weaves from roast zander to pigeon with girolles to foie gras with pear. Finish with the standout Sauternes custard with apricots and vanilla. Excellent service and a confident sommelier round out this winning proposition. ⊠*127 Ledbury Rd., Notting Hill* ☎*0207/7792–9090* ▤*AE, MC, V* Ⓤ*Westbourne Park.*

ST. JAMES'S

£££ **St. Alban.** Well located for Theaterland and with a stylish retro-Modern
MEDITERRANEAN aesthetic, St. Alban is one of the most fashionable places to dine in town. The '60s-style interior—gray slate walls, turquoise-and-cerise banquettes, carpets, light wells, and Michael Craig-Martin murals—is a winning backdrop for the Mediterranean-inspired menu. Try paella, wood-fired pizza, wild boar pappardelle, or Sardinian fish stew. ⊠*4–12 Regent St., St. James's* ☎*020/7499–8588* ⚑*Reservations essential* ▤*AE, DC, MC, V* Ⓤ*Piccadilly.*

£££ **The Wolseley.** *Le tout* London enjoys Belle-Époque elegance at this
AUSTRIAN Viennese-style grand café on Piccadilly, run by Messrs. Corbin and
Fodor'sChoice King, the city's top restaurateurs. Framed with black lacquerware, the
★ brasserie begins its long, decadent days with breakfast at 7 AM and is open until midnight. Linger for fare like scrambled eggs and brioche, Wiener Holstein (with fried egg and anchovies), or Matjes herrings with

pumpernickel. For dessert, go for apple strudel and *Kaiserschmarren,* a pancake with stewed fruit. It's also great for sinful pastries and afternoon tea. ⊠*160 Piccadilly, St. James's* ☏*020/7499–6996* ▤*AE, DC, MC, V* Ⓤ *Green Park.*

SOUTH BANK

££–£££
MODERN BRITISH

Anchor & Hope. Great things at friendly prices come from the open kitchen at this permanently packed, no-reservations, leading gastro-pub on the Cut: pot-roast duck and cod with red pepper are two standouts. It's cramped, informal, and highly original, and there are great dishes for groups, like leg of lamb. Expect to share a table, too. ⊠*36 The Cut, South Bank* ☏*020/7928–9898* ⌂*Reservations not accepted* ▤*MC, V* Ⓤ *Waterloo, Southwark.*

£££
MODERN
EUROPEAN

Skylon. Located in the Royal Festival Hall, Skylon is South Bank's destination restaurant/bar/grill. Spacious, attractive, and with huge picture windows framing spectacular views of the Thames, Skylon guarantees a classy meal before or after a performance in the Festival Hall. Concertgoers can sip lush cocktails at the central bar and dine on venison sausages at the grill, or on smoked haddock, lamb with polenta, or scallops with cranberries in the restaurant. The food is highly accomplished, and the setting impressive. ⊠*Royal Festival Hall, Belvedere Rd., South Bank* ☏*020/7654–7800* ⌂*Reservations essential* ▤ *MC, V* Ⓤ *Waterloo.*

PUBS & AFTERNOON TEA

PUBS

The list below offers a few pubs selected for central location, historical interest, a pleasant garden, music, or good food, but you might just as happily adopt your own temporary local.

✕**Black Friar.** A step from Blackfriars Tube stop, this spectacular pub has an arts-and-crafts interior that is entertainingly, satirically ecclesiastical, with inlaid mother-of-pearl, wood carvings, stained glass, and marble pillars all over the place. In spite of the finely lettered temperance tracts on view just below the reliefs of monks, fairies, and friars, there is a nice group of beers on tap from independent brewers. ⊠*174 Queen Victoria St., The City* ☏*020/7236–5474* Ⓤ*Blackfriars.*

✕**Museum Tavern.** Across the street from the British Museum, this Victorian pub makes an ideal resting place after the rigors of the culture trail. This heavily restored hostelry once helped Karl Marx unwind after a hard day in the Library. He could have spent his *Kapital* on any of six beers available on tap. ⊠*49 Great Russell St., Bloomsbury* ☏*020/7242–8987* Ⓤ*Tottenham Court Rd.*

✕**Prospect of Whitby.** Named after a ship, this is London's oldest riverside pub, dating from 1520. Once upon a time it was called the Devil's Tavern because of the lowlife criminals—thieves and smugglers—who congregated here. Ornamented with pewter ware and nautical objects, this much-loved boozer is often pointed out from boat trips up the Thames. ⊠*57 Wapping Wall, East End* ☏*020/7481–1095* Ⓤ*Wapping.*

✕**White Hart.** The drinking destination of the theater community, this elegant, family-owned pub on Drury Lane is one of the best places to mix with cast and crew of the stage. A female-friendly environment, a cheery skylight above the lounge area, and well-above-average pub fare make the White Hart one of the most sociable pubs in London. ⊠*191 Drury La., Covent Garden* ☎*020/7242–2317* Ⓤ*Holborn.*

AFTERNOON TEA

✕**Fortnum & Mason.** Upstairs at the Queen's grocers, three set teas are ceremoniously served: standard afternoon tea (sandwiches, scones, and cakes: £28), old-fashioned high tea (the traditional nursery meal, adding something more robust and savory: £32), and champagne tea (£42). ⊠*St. James's Restaurant, 4th fl., 181 Piccadilly, St. James's* ☎*020/7734–8040 Ext. 2241* ⊟*AE, DC, MC, V* ⊗*Tea Mon.–Sat. 3–5:30* Ⓤ*Green Park.*

✕**Patisserie Valerie at Sagne.** Scoff decadent patisseries with afternoon tea at this ever-reliable, reasonably priced, and stylish café. It's a perfect Marylebone High Street resting point, and you'll adore the towering cakes, chandelier, and murals on the walls. ⊠*105 Marylebone High St., Marylebone* ☎*020/7935–6240* ⊟*AE, MC, V* ⊗*Weekdays 7:30 AM–7 PM, Sat. 8 AM–7 PM, Sun. 9 AM–6 PM* Ⓤ*Marylebone.*

> ### WORD OF MOUTH
>
> "My favorite pub in London is the Black Friar. The beer's good and the pub is an absolutely gorgeous Art Nouveau masterpiece. It is a cathedral of drink, no joke. Crowded immediately after work, not at other times." —fnarf999

WHERE TO STAY

It's hard to get a bargain on a London hotel. If money is no object, though, you can have the most indulgent luxury imaginable: when it comes to pampering, few do it better than the British.

WHICH NEIGHBORHOOD?

Where you stay can affect your experience. Hotels in Mayfair and St. James's are central and yet distant in both mileage and sensibility from funky, youthful neighborhoods such as Notting Hill and from major tourist sights. On the edges of the West End, Soho and Covent Garden are crammed with eateries and entertainment options. South Kensington, Kensington, Chelsea, and Knightsbridge are patrician and peaceful. From Bloomsbury it's a stroll to the shops and restaurants of Covent Garden, to Theatreland, and to the British Museum; Hampstead and Islington are close enough to explore easily, too. Bayswater is an affordable haven north of Hyde Park. The South Bank, with all its cultural attractions, is an affordable option.

RESERVATIONS

Wherever you decide to stay, do reserve in advance. The **VisitLondon Accommodation Booking Service** (☎*020/7932–2020* ⊕*www.visitlondon.com*) is open weekdays 9 to 6, Saturday 10 to 2; it offers a best-price guarantee.

PRICES & MONEY-SAVING OPTIONS

Finding a cheap but tolerable double room is a real coup. Look around Russell Square in Bloomsbury, around Victoria and King's Cross stations, on the South Bank, in Bayswater or Earl's Court, or farther out in Shepherd's Bush. Your cheapest option is a B&B or a dorm bed in a hostel; apartments are an increasing popular choice.

University residence halls offer a cheap alternative during university vacation periods. Whatever the price, *don't* expect a room that's large by American standards. **City University Hall of Residence: Walter Sickert Hall** (⊠ *Graham St.* ☎*020/7040–8822* 🖷*020/7040–8825* ⊕*www.city. ac.uk/ems*) costs £60 for a double year-round and includes continental breakfast. **London School of Economics Vacations** (☎*020/7955–7575* 🖷*0207/955–7676* ⊕*www.lsevacations.co.uk*) charges £50 for a double without a toilet to £62 for a double with a toilet. You can choose from a variety of rooms in their five halls of residence around London. **University College London** (⊠ *Residence Manager, Campbell House, 5–10 Taviton St.* ☎*020/7679–1479* 🖷*020/7388–0060*) charges £35–£40 for a double and is open from mid-June to mid-September.

In any event, you should confirm *exactly* what your room costs before checking in. British hotels are obliged by law to display a price chart at the reception desk; study it carefully. In January and February you can often find reduced rates, and large hotels with a business clientele have frequent weekend packages. The usual practice these days in all but the cheaper hotels is for quoted prices to cover room alone; breakfast, whether continental or "full English," costs extra. V.A.T. (Value Added Tax—sales tax) follows the same rule, with the most expensive hotels excluding a hefty 17.5%; middle-of-the-range and budget places include it in the initial quote.

BAYSWATER & NOTTING HILL

£££ ⛭ **Guesthouse West.** The goal of this hip hotel is to offer high-class chic at moderate prices. They almost get it right. The minimalist decor and technology—cool black-and-white photos and flat-screen TVs—are stylish. Rooms, however, are truly tiny, and there's no room service. The restaurant is child-friendly and packed with locals, and the bar is a beautiful homage to the 1930s. The hotel's relationship with a local spa and restaurant provides guests with discounts. **Pros:** sophisticated decor, lots of gadgets. **Cons:** a bit out of the way, tiny rooms, no room service. ⊠*163–165 Westbourne Grove, Notting Hill* ☎*020/7792–9800* 🖷*020/7792–9797* ⊕*www.guesthousewest.com* 🛏*20 rooms* ⚙*In-room: DVD, Wi-Fi. In-hotel: restaurant, bar, parking (fee), no-smoking rooms* ▤*AE, MC, V* Ⓤ*Notting Hill Gate.*

££ ⛭ **The Pavilion Hotel.** This eccentric Victorian town house calls itself the Pavilion *Fashion Rock 'n' Roll* Hotel, and that should give you an idea that this is a trendy address for fashionistas, actors, and musicians. Often used for fashion shoots, the kitsch bedrooms veer wildly from Moroccan fantasy (the "Casablanca Nights" room) to acres of plaid ("Highland Fling") and satin ("Enter the Dragon"). Triples and family rooms are ideal for groups looking for space *and* style. **Pros:** small and friendly, great for arty types. **Cons:** few guest services, neighborhood's not very handy. ⊠*34–36 Sussex Gardens, Bayswater* ☎*020/7262–0905* 🖷*020/7262–1324* ⊕*www.pavilionhoteluk.com* 🛏*30 rooms* ⚙*In-room: no a/c, DVD (some), dial-up. In-hotel: room* *service, bar, laundry service, parking (fee), no-smoking rooms, no elevator* ⊟*AE, D, MC, V* ⟦◯⟧*CP* ⟦U⟧*Paddington, Edgware Rd.*

BLOOMSBURY & HOLBORN

£ ⟦📷⟧**The Generator.** This is where the young, enthusiastic traveler comes to find fellow partyers. It's also the cleverest youth hostel in town. Set in a former police barracks, its rooms are in the old prison cells, and the decor makes the most of the bunk beds and dim lighting. The Internet café provides handy maps and leaflets. The Generator Bar has cheap drinks and a rowdy crowd, and the Fuel Stop cafeteria provides inexpensive meals. Prices run from £20 per person for a bed in a 12-bed dorm room to £35 per person for a double room. **Pros:** funky, youthful attitude, great location. **Cons:** bar is crowded and noisy, party atmosphere is not for everyone. ⊠*MacNaghten House, Compton Pl. off 37 Tavistock Pl., Bloomsbury* ☎*020/7388–7666* 🖷*020/7388–7644* ⊕*www. generatorhostels.com* ↩*215 beds* ঌ*In-room: no a/c, no phone, no TV. In-hotel: restaurant, bars, concierge, airport shuttle, parking (fee), no-smoking rooms, public Internet* ⊟*MC, V* ⟦◯⟧*CP* ⟦U⟧*Russell Sq.*

£££–££££ ⟦📷⟧**Zetter Rooms.** By day, nothing but business suits buzz through the area between Holborn and Clerkenwell. By night, though, the ties are loosened and it's all oh-so-trendy. One of London's latest "it" hotels, Zetter reflects both personalities. The dizzying five-story atrium, Art Deco staircase, and slick European restaurant are your first indications of what to expect at this converted warehouse: a breath of fresh air (and a little space) in London's mostly Victorian hotel scene. Rooms are smoothly done up in soft dove-gray and vanilla fabrics, and the views of the city from the higher floors are wonderful. **Pros:** big rooms, lots of gadgets. **Cons:** prices rise during the week. ⊠*86–88 Clerkenwell Rd., Holborn* ☎*020/7324–4444* 🖷*020/7324–4445* ⊕*www.thezetter.com* ↩*59 rooms* ঌ*In-room: safe, DVD, Ethernet, refrigerator. In-hotel: restaurant, room service, bar, concierge, laundry service, no-smoking rooms* ⊟*AE, MC, V* ⟦U⟧*Farringdon.*

COVENT GARDEN

£££££ ⟦📷⟧**One Aldwych.** An understated blend of contemporary and classic results in pure, modern luxury here. Flawlessly designed inside an Edwardian building, One Aldwych is coolly eclectic, with an artsy lobby, feather duvets, Italian linen sheets, and quirky touches (a TV in every bathroom, all-natural toiletries). It's the ultimate in 21st-century style, from the free, hotel-wide Wi-Fi down to the gorgeous swimming pool in the awesome health club. Suites have amenities such as a private gym, a kitchen, and a terrace. Breakfast is made with organic ingredients. The pool at One Aldwych has underwater speakers that play music you can hear only when you dive in. **Pros:** understated (and underwater) luxury. **Cons:** all this luxury doesn't come cheap. ⊠*1 Aldwych, Covent Garden* ☎*020/7300–1000* 🖷*020/7300–1001* ⊕*www.onealdwych. co.uk* ↩*93 rooms, 12 suites* ঌ*In-room: safe, kitchen (some), refrigerator, Wi-Fi. In-hotel: 2 restaurants, room service, bars, pool, gym, spa, concierge, laundry service, parking (fee), no-smoking rooms* ⊟*AE, MC, V* ⟦U⟧*Charing Cross, Covent Garden.*

KENSINGTON & SOUTH KENSINGTON

£ 🖥️**easyHotel.** This budget hotel opened in 2005 as London's first "pod hotel." Crammed into a big white townhouse are 34 tiny rooms, all with a double bed, private bathroom, and little else. Each is brightly decorated in the trademark orange-and-white of the easyGroup (which includes the cruise-line company easyCruise, and the budget airline easyJet). The idea behind the hotel is to provide quality basics (bed, sink, shower, and toilet) for little money. The small reception desk can't offer much in terms of service, and if you want your room cleaned while you stay, it's £10 a day. The concept continues to be a huge hit—easyHotel is fully booked months in advance and has opened near Victoria Station and elsewhere in Kensington, which are sometimes easier to reserve. **Pros:** amazing price, safe and pleasant space. **Cons:** everything costs extra, from a TV in your room to fresh towels. ✉️*14 Lexham Gardens, Kensington* ☎️*020/7216–1717* 🌐*www.easyhotel.com* 🛏️*34 rooms* ⚙️*In-room: no a/c, no phone. In-hotel: no-smoking rooms, no elevator* 🚇*MC, V* Ⓤ*Gloucester Rd.*

£££–££££
Fodor's Choice
★
🖥️**Number Sixteen.** In a white-portico row of Victorian houses, close to the South Kensington Tube and a short walk from the Victoria & Albert Museum, Number Sixteen is a lovely luxury B&B. Rooms are spacious and have marble- and oak-clad bathrooms. The style is not so much interior-designed as understated—new furniture and modern prints are juxtaposed with weighty oil paintings and antiques. The staff is friendly, so lingering in the drawing rooms is a pleasure, and drinks are served in the garden in summer. **Pros:** just the right level of helpful service; decor is gorgeous. **Cons:** there's no restaurant; very small elevator. ✉️*16 Sumner Pl., South Kensington* ☎️*020/7589–5232, 800/553–6674 in U.S.* 🖨️*020/7584–8615* 🌐*www.firmdale.com* 🛏️*42 rooms* ⚙️*In-room: no a/c (some), safe, refrigerator, Wi-Fi. In-hotel: room service, bar, concierge, laundry service* 🚇*AE, MC, V* 🍽️*CP* Ⓤ*South Kensington.*

KNIGHTSBRIDGE & CHELSEA

£££££ 🖥️**Mandarin Oriental Hyde Park.** Stay here, and the three greats of Knightsbridge—Hyde Park, Harrods, and Harvey Nichols—are on your doorstep. Built in 1880, the Mandarin Oriental is one of London's most elegant hotels. Bedrooms are Victorian but with hidden high-tech gadgets and luxurious touches like Frette-linen duvets, fresh orchids, and delicate chocolates. Miles of marble were used to fill the grand entrance. The Park restaurant, glittering Foliage, and quirky Mandarin Bar all attract Europe's jet-setters. The service here is legendary and there's a butler on every floor. **Pros:** amazing views of Hyde Park. **Cons:** nothing here comes cheap. ✉️*66 Knightsbridge, Knightsbridge* ☎️*020/7235–2000* 🖨️*020/7235–2001* 🌐*www.mandarinoriental.com* 🛏️*177 rooms, 23 suites* ⚙️*In-room: safe, DVD (some), Wi-Fi, refrigerator. In-hotel: 2 restaurants, room service, bar, gym, spa, concierge, laundry service, airport shuttle, parking (fee), no-smoking rooms* 🚇*AE, DC, MC, V* Ⓤ*Knightsbridge.*

£££–££££ 🖥️**myhotel chelsea.** This small, chic hotel tucked away down a Chelsea side street is a charmer. Rooms are bijou small but sophisticated, with mauve satin throws atop crisp white down comforters. Tiny bathrooms are made cheery with pale-pink granite countertops. Flat-screen TVs,

DVD players, and Wi-Fi keep you digital. The beauty is in the details here—there's no restaurant, but the fire-warmed bar serves light meals and tea. The guest library loans DVDs and books, and is a quiet place to relax. Best of all, you can get a good deal if you book in advance via the Web site. **Pros:** it claims to use feng shui principles in its design—good luck will be yours! **Cons:** tiny rooms. ⌧ *35 Ixworth Pl., Chelsea* ☎ *020/7225–7500* 🖶 *020/7225–7555* ⊕ *www.myhotels.com* 🛏 *45 rooms, 9 suites* ⚘ *In-room: safe, refrigerator, DVD, Wi-Fi. In-hotel: room service, bar, gym, spa, laundry service, no-smoking rooms, some pets allowed* ☰ *AE, D, MC, V* Ⓤ *South Kensington.*

MAYFAIR & ST. JAMES'S

££ 🏨 **22 York Street.** This Georgian town house has a cozy, family feel with pine floors and plenty of quilts and antiques. Pride of place goes to the central, communal dining table where guests share a varied continental breakfast. A living room with tea/coffeemaker is at your disposal as well. The homey bedrooms are individually furnished. Triples and family rooms for four are available. **Pros:** handy guesthouse in a great location for shoppers. **Cons:** price is a bit steep for what is, in the end, a glorified B&B. ⌧ *22 York St., Mayfair* ☎ *020/7224–2990* 🖶 *020/7224–1990* ⊕ *www.22yorkstreet.co.uk* 🛏 *10 rooms* ⚘ *In-room: no a/c. In-hotel: bar, no-smoking rooms, no elevator* ☰ *AE, MC, V* ⧆ *CP* Ⓤ *Baker St.*

££££–£££££ 🏨 **Claridge's.** Stay here, and you're staying at a hotel legend (founded in
Fodor's Choice 1812), with one of the world's classiest guest lists. The friendly, liveried
★ staff is not in the least condescending, and the rooms are never less than luxurious. Enjoy a cup of tea in the lounge, or retreat to the stylish bar for cocktails—or, better, to Gordon Ramsay's inimitable restaurant. The bathrooms are spacious (with enormous showerheads), as are the bedrooms (Victorian or Art Deco). The grand staircase and magnificent elevator complete with sofa and driver are equally glamorous. **Pros:** serious luxury everywhere—this is an old-money hotel. **Cons:** it's a bit pretentious—the guests in the hotel bar can be almost cartoonishly snobbish. ⌧ *Brook St., St. James's* ☎ *020/7629–8860, 800/637–2869 in U.S.* 🖶 *020/7499–2210* ⊕ *www.claridges.co.uk* 🛏 *203 rooms* ⚘ *In-room: safe, DVD, Wi-Fi, refrigerator. In-hotel: restaurant, bar, gym, spa, concierge, laundry service, airport shuttle, parking (fee), no-smoking rooms* ☰ *AE, DC, MC, V* Ⓤ *Bond St.*

SOUTH BANK

££ 🏨 **Premier Travel Inn Southwark.** This excellent branch of the Premier Travel
☾ Inn chain is a bit out of the way on the South Bank, but it sits on a quiet cobbled lane, and is ideally located for visiting the Tate Modern or the Globe Theatre. Rooms are simply decorated, and all have the chain's signature 6-foot-wide beds (really two 3-foot-wide beds zipped together). Ask for a room away from the elevators, which can be a little noisy. **Pros:** great location for the South Bank, quiet street. **Cons:** small rooms, limited customer services. ⌧ *34 Park St., South Bank* ☎ *020/7089–2580 or 0870/990–6402* 🖶 *0870/990–6403* ⊕ *www.premiertravelinn.com* 🛏 *56 rooms* ⚘ *In-room: dial-up. In-hotel: parking (fee), no-smoking rooms* ☰ *AE, DC, MC, V* Ⓤ *London Bridge.*

WESTMINSTER & VICTORIA

££–£££ ⊡**Jolly Hotel St. Ermin's.** The hotel is just a short stroll from Westminster Abbey, Buckingham Palace, and the Houses of Parliament. An Edwardian anomaly in the shadow of modern skyscrapers, it's set on a tiny cul-de-sac courtyard. The lobby is an extravaganza of Victorian stylings like cake-frosting stuccowork in shades of baby blue and creamy white, and guest rooms are tastefully decorated. The hotel's Cloisters restaurant is an ornately carved 19th-century Jacobean-style salon, and one of the most magnificent rooms in which to dine in London. **Pros:** amazing lobby, great location near Buckingham Palace. **Cons:** rooms are a bit small. ⊠ *2 Caxton St., Westminster* ☎*020/7222–7888* 🖷*020/7222–6914* ⊕*www.jollyhotels.it* ⊷*277 rooms, 8 suites* ♿*In-room: safe (some), dial-up, refrigerator. In-hotel: restaurant, room service, bar, laundry service, parking (fee), no-smoking rooms* ⊟*AE, DC, MC, V* Ⓤ*St. James's Park.*

££ ⊡**New England Hotel.** This family-run B&B in a 19th-century town house is cheap(ish) and cheerful. The power showers, comfortable beds, and electronic key cards are pluses, but there's nothing fancy about the interior. View this as a fall-back option if other, better budget places are booked up. **Pros:** handy location, friendly owners. **Cons:** a bit battered, prices a little high for what you get. ⊠ *20 Saint George's Dr., Victoria* ☎*020/7834–8351* 🖷*020/7834–9000* ⊕*www.newenglandhotel.com* ⊷*25 rooms* ♿*In-room: no a/c, dial-up. In-hotel: parking (fee), no-smoking rooms, no elevator* ⊟*AE, DC, MC, V* Ⓞⵏ*BP* Ⓤ*Victoria.*

NIGHTLIFE & THE ARTS

London is a veritable utopia for excitement junkies and culture fiends. Whether you prefer a romantic evening at the opera, rhythm and blues with fine French food, the gritty guitar riffs of east London, a pint and gourmet pizza at a local gastro-pub, or swanky cocktails and sushi at London's sexiest lair, the U.K. capital is sure to feed your fancy.

One of the special experiences the city has to offer is great theater. London's theater scene consists, broadly, of the state-subsidized companies, the Royal National Theatre and the Royal Shakespeare Company; the commercial West End, equivalent to Broadway; and the Fringe—small, experimental companies. Most of the West End theaters are in the neighborhood nicknamed Theatreland, around the Strand and Shaftesbury Avenue.

Theater-going isn't cheap. Tickets under £10 are a rarity; in the West End you should expect to pay from £15 for a seat in the upper balcony to at least £25 for a good one in the stalls (orchestra) or dress circle (mezzanine). However, as the vast majority of theaters have some tickets (returns and house seats) available on the night of performance, you may find some good deals. Tickets may be booked through ticket agents, at individual theater box offices, or over the phone by credit card. Be sure to inquire about any extra fees. Be *very* careful of scalpers (known locally as "ticket touts") and unscrupulous ticket agents outside theaters and in the line at TKTS.

Ticketmaster (☎*0870/060–0800* ⊕*www.ticketmaster.co.uk*) sells tickets to a number of different theaters, although they charge a booking fee. You can book tickets in the United States through **Keith Prowse** (✉*234 W. 44th St., Suite 1000, New York, NY* ☎*800/669–8687* ⊕*www.keithprowse.com*). For discount tickets, **Society of London Theatre** (☎*020/7557–6700*) operates TKTS, a half-price ticket booth (☎*No phone*) on the southwest corner of Leicester Square, and sells the best available seats to performances at about 25 theaters. It's open Monday–Saturday 10 AM–7 PM, Sunday noon–3 PM; there's a £2 service charge. Major credit cards are accepted. There's now also a TKTS booth at Canary Wharf station in Docklands, open Monday–Saturday 10 AM–3:30 PM.

To find out what's showing on the cultural scene, check the weekly magazine *Time Out*. The *Evening Standard* also carries listings, especially in the Thursday supplement "Metro Life," as do London's free newspapers, many Sunday papers, and the Saturday *Independent, Guardian,* and *Times*.

BARS & VENUES

★ **Barfly Club.** At one of the finest small clubs in the capital, punk, indie guitar bands, and new metal rock attract a nonmainstream crowd. Weekend club nights upstairs host DJs who rock the decks. ✉*49 Chalk Farm Rd., Camden Town* ☎*020/7691–4244* ⊕*www.barflyclub.com* 🎫*£5–£8* ⊙*Mon.–Thurs. 7:30 PM–midnight, Fri. and Sat. 8 PM–3 AM, Sun. 7:30 PM–11 PM* Ⓤ*Camden Town, Chalk Farm.*

Cargo. Housed under a series of old railway arches, this vast brick-wall bar, restaurant, dance floor, and live music venue pulls an international crowd with its hip vibe and diverse music. Long tables bring people together, as does the food, which draws on global influences and is served tapas-style. ✉*83 Rivington St., Shoreditch* ☎*0871/075–1741* ⊕*www.cargo-london.com* ⊙*Mon.–Thurs. noon–1 AM, Fri. noon–3, Sat. 6 PM–3 AM, Sun. 1 PM–midnight* Ⓤ*Old St.*

FodorsChoice **Claridge's Bar.** This elegant Mayfair meeting place remains unpretentious ★ even when it brims with beautiful people. A library of rare champagnes and brandies as well as a delicious choice of traditional and exotic cocktails—try the Black Pearl—will occupy your taste buds. ✉*55 Brook St., Mayfair* ☎*020/7629–8860* ⊙*Mon.–Sat. 11 PM–1 AM, Sun. 4 PM–midnight* Ⓤ*Bond St.*

Jazz Café. A palace of high-tech cool in bohemian Camden—it remains an essential hangout for fans of both the mainstream end of the repertoire and hip-hop, funk, rap, and Latin fusion. Book ahead if you want a prime table overlooking the stage, in the balcony restaurant. ✉*5 Pkwy., Camden Town* ☎*020/7916–6060 restaurant reservations, 0870/150–0044 standing tickets* ⊕*www.jazzcafe.co.uk* 🎫*£10–£25* ⊙*Daily 7 PM–2 AM* Ⓤ*Camden Town.*

CLASSICAL MUSIC

Royal Albert Hall. Built in 1871, this splendid iron-and-glass–dome auditorium hosts a varied music program, including Europe's most democratic music festival, the Henry Wood Promenade Concerts—the Proms, running for eight weeks from July to September (⊕*www.bbc.co.uk/*

proms). The Hall is also open for daily daytime guided tours (£6). ✉*Kensington Gore, Kensington* ☎*020/7589–8212* ⊕*www.royalalbert hall.com* Ⓤ*South Kensington.*

St. Martin-in-the-Fields. Popular lunchtime concerts (£3.50 donation suggested) are held in this lovely 1726 church, as are regular evening concerts. ■**TIP→ Stop for a snack at the Café in the Crypt.** ✉*Trafalgar Sq., Covent Garden* ☎*020/7839–8362* ⊕*www.smitf.org* Ⓤ*Charing Cross.*

Wigmore Hall. Hear chamber-music and song recitals in this charming hall with near-perfect acoustics. Don't miss the mid-morning Sunday concerts. ✉*36 Wigmore St., Marylebone* ☎*020/7935–2141* ⊕*www. wigmore-hall.org.uk* Ⓤ *Bond St.*

THEATER

Below are some theaters known for excellent or innovative work.

Almeida Theatre. This Off–West End venue premieres excellent new plays and exciting twists on the classics. Hollywood stars often perform here. ✉*Almeida St., Islington* ☎*020/7359–4404* ⊕*www.almeida.co.uk* Ⓤ*Angel, Highbury & Islington.*

★ **Donmar Warehouse.** Hollywood stars often perform here in diverse and daring new works, bold interpretations of the classics, and small-scale musicals. ✉*41 Earlham St., Covent Garden* ☎*0870/060–6624* ⊕*www.donmar-warehouse.com* Ⓤ*Covent Garden.*

National Theatre. Opened in 1976, the National Theatre has three venues: the 1,120-seat Olivier, the 890-seat Lyttelton, and the 300-seat Cottesloe. Musicals, classics, and new plays are in repertoire. ■**TIP→ An adventurous ticketing scheme means some performances can be seen for as little as £10.** It's closed Sunday. ✉*South Bank Arts Centre, Belvedere Rd., South Bank* ☎*020/7452–3000* ⊕*www.nationaltheatre.org. uk* Ⓤ*Waterloo.*

Open Air Theatre. On a warm summer evening, classical theater in the pastoral and royal Regent's Park is hard to beat for magical adventure. Enjoy supper before the performance or during intermission on the picnic lawn, and drinks in the spacious bar. ✉*Inner Circle, Regent's Park* ☎*0870/060–1811* ⊕*www.openairtheatre.org* Ⓤ*Baker St., Regent's Park.*

Royal Court Theatre. Britain's undisputed epicenter of new writing, the RCT has produced gritty British and international drama since the middle of the 20th century, much of which gets produced in the West End. ■**TIP→ Don't miss the best deal in town—£10 tickets on Monday.** ✉*Sloane Sq., Chelsea* ☎*020/7565–5000* ⊕*www.royalcourttheatre. com* Ⓤ*Sloane Sq.*

Fodor'sChoice ★ **Shakespeare's Globe Theatre.** This faithful reconstruction of the open-air playhouse where Shakespeare worked and wrote many of his greatest plays re-creates the 16th-century theater-going experience. Standing room costs £5. The season runs May through September. ✉*New Globe Walk, Bankside, South Bank* ☎*020/7401–9919* ⊕*www.shake speares-globe.org* Ⓤ*Southwark, Mansion House, walk across Southwark Bridge; Blackfriars, walk across Blackfriars Bridge.*

7

SHOPPING

Napoléon was being scornful when he called Britain a nation of shopkeepers, but Londoners have had the last laugh. The finest emporiums are in London, still. Apart from bankrupting yourself, the only problem you may encounter is exhaustion in traveling between the many far-flung shopping areas. If you have limited time, zoom in on one of the city's specialty shops or grand department stores, or browse through one of the markets.

Apart from bankrupting yourself, the only problem you may encounter is exhaustion. London is a town of many far-flung shopping areas.
■ TIP➜ Real shophounds plan their excursions with military precision, taking in only one or two shopping districts in a day, with fortifying stops for lunch, tea, and a pint or glass of wine in the pub.

COVENT GARDEN
This neighborhood has chain clothing stores and top designers, stalls selling crafts, and shops selling gifts of every type—bikes, kites, tea, herbs, beads, hats—you name it.

KENSINGTON
Kensington's main drag, Kensington High Street, houses some small, classy shops, with a few larger stores at the eastern end. Try Kensington Church Street for expensive antiques, plus a little fashion.

KNIGHTSBRIDGE
Knightsbridge, east of Kensington, has Harrods but also Harvey Nichols, the top clothes stop, and many expensive designers' boutiques along Sloane Street, Walton Street, and Beauchamp Place.

MAYFAIR
In Mayfair are the two Bond streets, Old and New, with desirable dress designers, jewelers, and fine art. South Molton Street has high-price, high-style fashion, and the tailors of Savile Row have worldwide reputations.

NOTTING HILL
Go westward from the Portobello Road market and explore the Ledbury Road–Westbourne Grove axis, Clarendon Cross, and Kensington Park Road for a mix of antiques and up-to-the-minute must-haves for body and lifestyle.

REGENT STREET
At right angles to Oxford Street is Regent Street, with possibly London's most pleasant department store, Liberty, plus Hamleys, the capital's favorite toy store. Shops around once-famous Carnaby Street stock designer youth paraphernalia and 57 varieties of the T-shirt.

ST. JAMES'S
Here the English gentleman buys everything but the suit (which is from Savile Row): handmade hats, shirts and shoes, silver shaving kits, and hip flasks. Nothing in this neighborhood is cheap, in any sense.

DEPARTMENT STORES

Fodor's Choice
★
Harrods (⊠ *87–135 Brompton Rd., Knightsbridge* ☎ *020/7730–1234* Ⓤ *Knightsbridge*), one of the world's most famous department stores, can be forgiven its immodest motto, *Omnia, omnibus, ubique* ("everything, for everyone, everywhere"), because it has more than 300 well-stocked departments. The food halls are stunning—so are the crowds, especially during the sales that usually run during the last three weeks of January.

Harvey Nichols (⊠*109–125 Knightsbridge, Knightsbridge* ☎*020/7235–5000* Ⓤ*Knightsbridge*) is famed for five floors of ultimate fashion; every label any chic, well-bred London lady covets is here, as well as a home-furnishings department. It's also known for the restaurant, Fifth Floor.

★ **Selfridges** (⊠*400 Oxford St., Oxford Street* ☎*0870/837–7377* Ⓤ*Bond St.*), huge and hip, is giving Harvey Nicks a run as London's leading fashion department store. It's packed with high-profile, popular designer clothes for everyone in the family. There's a globe-spanning Food Hall on the ground floor, and a theater ticket counter and a British Airways travel shop in the basement.

STREET MARKETS

Bermondsey is the market the dealers frequent for small antiques, which gives you an idea of its scope. The real bargains start going at 4 AM, but there'll be a few left if you arrive later. Take Bus 15 or 25 to Aldgate, then Bus 42 over Tower Bridge to Bermondsey Square; or take the tube to London Bridge and walk. ⊠*Long La. and Bermondsey Sq., South Bank* ☉*Fri. 5 AM–noon* Ⓤ*London Bridge.*

Covent Garden has craft stalls, jewelry designers, clothes makers, potters, and other artisans who congregate in the covered central area known as the Apple Market. The Jubilee Market, toward Southampton Street, is less classy (printed T-shirts and the like), but on Monday the selection of vintage collectibles is worthwhile. This is more of a tourist magnet than other markets, and prices may reflect this. ⊠*The Piazza, Covent Garden* ☉*Daily 9–5* Ⓤ*Covent Garden.*

FodorsChoice ★ **Portobello Market,** London's most famous market, still wins the prize for the all-round best. There are 1,500 antiques dealers here, so bargains are still possible. Nearer Notting Hill Gate, prices and quality are highest; the middle is where locals buy fruit and vegetables and hang out in trendy restaurants. Under the Westway elevated highway is a great flea market, and more bric-a-brac and bargains appear as you walk toward Golborne Road. Take Bus 52 or the tube here. ⊠*Portobello Rd., Notting Hill* ☉*Fruit and vegetables Mon.–Wed. and Fri. 8–5, Thurs. 8–1; antiques Fri. 8–3; food market and antiques Sat. 6–4:30* Ⓤ*Ladbroke Grove, Notting Hill Gate.*

Spitalfields, an old 3-acre indoor fruit market near Petticoat Lane, has turned into Trendsville, with crafts and design shops. It also has food and clothes stalls, cafés, and performance areas. On Sunday the place comes alive, with stalls selling antique clothing, handmade rugs, and cookware. The resident stores have lovely things for body and home. For refreshment, you can eat anything from tapas to Thai. ⊠*Brushfield St., East End* ☉*General market weekdays 10–4, Sun. 10–5* Ⓤ*Liverpool St., Aldgate, Aldgate East.*

OXFORD

With arguably the most famous university in the world, Oxford has been a center of learning since 1167; only the Sorbonne is older. Alumni of Oxford University include 47 Nobel Prize winners, 25 British Prime

Ministers, and 28 foreign presidents, along with poets, authors, and artists. Victorian writer Matthew Arnold described Oxford's "dreaming spires," a phrase that has become famous. Students rush past you on the sidewalks on the way to their exams, clad with marvelous antiquarian style in their requisite mortar caps, flowing dark gowns, stiff collars, and crisp white bow ties.

The university is not one easily identifiable campus but a sprawling mixture of more than 39 colleges scattered around the city center, each with its own distinctive identity and focus. Oxford students live and study at their own college, and also use the centralized resources of the over-arching university. Most of the grounds and magnificent dining halls and chapels of the individual colleges are open to visitors, though the opening times (displayed at the entrance gates) vary greatly.

Oxford is 55 mi northwest of London, at the junction of the Thames and Cherwell rivers. The city is more cosmopolitan than Cambridge, and also bigger, though the interest is all at the center, where the Old Town curls around the grand stone buildings, good restaurants, and historic pubs. Eight miles northwest of Oxford, Blenheim Palace, one of the grandest houses in England, is well worth a side trip.

PLANNING YOUR TIME
You can explore major sights in town in a day or so, but you'll need more than a day to spend an hour in all of the key museums and absorb the scene at the colleges. Some colleges are open only in the afternoon during university terms; when the undergraduates are in residence, access is often restricted to the chapels, dining rooms, and libraries, too. All are closed certain days during exams, usually from mid-April to late June.

GETTING HERE & AROUND
Megabus, Oxford Bus Company, and Oxford Tube all have buses traveling from London 24 hours a day. In London, Megabus departs from Victoria Coach Station, and Oxford Bus Company and Oxford Tube have pick-up points near Victoria Station and Baker Street and Marble Arch Underground stations. Most of the companies have multiple stops in Oxford, the final stop being the most convenient for most travelers.

Trains to Oxford depart from London's Paddington station. Oxford Station is just at the edge of the historic town center on Botley Road. By car, the M40 heads northwest from London. It's an hour's drive, except during rush hour, when it can take twice as long. St. Clement's parking lot before the roundabout that leads to Magdalen Bridge is the best option for public parking.

Bordered by High Street, St. Giles Street, and Long Wall Road, the town center is quite compact and walkable, with most of Oxford University's most famous buildings within this area. The public bus route No. 20 runs (usually every half hour) between Oxford and Woodstock (for Blenheim Palace).

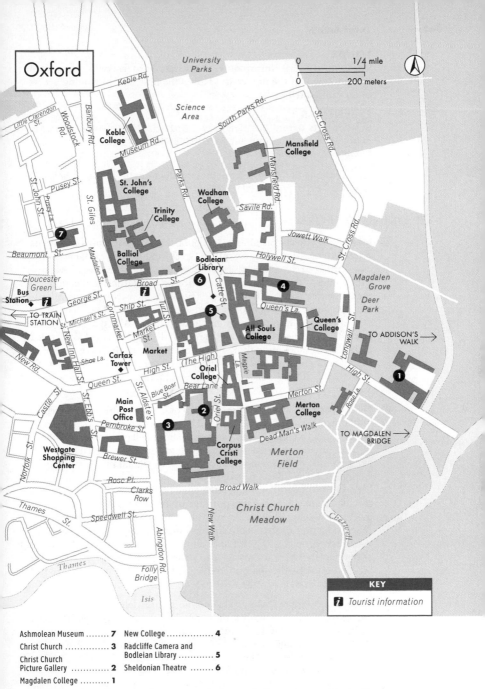

Oxford

University Parks

Keble Rd.

Science Area

South Parks Rd.

St. Cross Rd.

0 —— 1/4 mile
0 —— 200 meters

Little Clarendon St.

Woodstock Rd.

Banbury Rd.

Keble College

Museum Rd.

Mansfield College

Mansfield Rd.

Pusey St.

St. John St.

St. Giles

Parks Rd.

St. John's College

Wadham College

Savile Rd.

Jowett Walk

Trinity College

Beaumont St.

Magdalen St.

Balliol College

Bodleian Library

Holywell St.

Magdalen Grove

Deer Park

Gloucester Green

Bus Station

George St.

Broad St.

Catte St.

New College

TO ADDISON'S WALK

TO TRAIN STATION

St. Michael's St.

Cornmarket

Ship St.

Market St.

Queen's La.

Queen's College

Longwall St.

New Inn Hall St.

Shoe La.

Carfax Tower

Market

High St.

All Souls College

High St.

Magpie La.

Castle St.

New Rd.

Queen St.

St. Aldate's

Blue Boar St.

Oriel College

Bear Lane

Oriel St.

Merton St.

Merton College

Rose La.

TO MAGDALEN BRIDGE

Norfolk St.

St. Ebb's St.

Main Post Office

Pembroke St.

Corpus Cristi College

Dead Man's Walk

Merton Field

Westgate Shopping Center

Brewer St.

Rose Pl.

Clarks Row

Broad Walk

New Walk

Christ Church Meadow

Cherwell

Thames St.

Speedwell St.

Thames

Folly Bridge

Isis

Abingdon Rd.

KEY

i Tourist information

TOURS

The Oxford Tourist Information Centre has up to five two-hour guided walking tours of the university. This is the best way of gaining access to the collegiate buildings.

ESSENTIALS

Bus Contacts Oxford Bus Company (☎ *01865/785400* ⊕ *www.oxfordbus. co.uk*). **Stagecoach Oxford Tube** (☎ *01865/772250* ⊕ *www.stagecoachbus. com/oxfordshire*).

Visitor Information Oxford Tourist Information Centre (⊠ *15/16 Broad St.* ☎ *01865/726871* ⊕ *www.visitoxford.org*)

EXPLORING OXFORD

❼ **Ashmolean Museum.** Britain's oldest public museum contains among its priceless collections many Egyptian, Greek, and Roman artifacts uncovered during archaeological expeditions conducted by the university. Michelangelo drawings and an extraordinary statuary collection are highlights, as is the Alfred Jewel. This ancient piece features a large semiprecious stone set in gold carved with the words AELFRED MEC HEHT GEWYRCAN, which translates from old English as "Alfred ordered me to be made." The piece dates from the reign of King Alfred the Great (ruled 871–899). A renovation that will double the size of the museum means that the museum will be closed until November 2009. ⊠ *Beaumont St.* ☎ *01865/278000* ⊕ *www.ashmolean.org* 🎫 *Free* ☉ *Tues.–Sat. 10–5, Sun. noon–5; call to check opening hours.*

❸ **Christ Church.** Built in 1546, the college of Christ Church is referred to

Fodor'sChoice   by its members as "The House." This is the site of Oxford's largest

★   quadrangle, Tom Quad, named after the huge bell (6¼ tons) that hangs in the Christopher Wren–designed gate tower and rings 101 times at five past nine every evening in honor of the original number of Christ Church scholars. The vaulted, 800-year-old chapel in one corner has been Oxford's cathedral since the time of Henry VIII. The college's medieval dining hall contains portraits of many famous alumni, including John Wesley, William Penn, and 13 of Britain's prime ministers. A reproduction of this room appears in the banquet scenes at Hogwarts School in the *Harry Potter* films. Lewis Carroll was a teacher of mathematics here for many years; a shop opposite the meadows on St. Aldate's sells Alice paraphernalia. ⊠ *St. Aldate's* ☎ *01865/276150* ⊕ *www.chch.ox.ac.uk* 🎫 *£4.90* ☉ *Mon.–Sat. 9–5, Sun. 1–5.*

❷ **Christ Church Picture Gallery.** This connoisseur's delight in Canterbury Quadrangle exhibits works by the Italian masters as well as Hals, Rubens, and Van Dyck. Drawings in the 2,000-strong collection are shown on a changing basis. ⊠ *Oriel Sq.* ☎ *01865/276172* ⊕ *www. chch.ox.ac.uk* 🎫 *£2* ☉ *May.–Sept., Mon.–Sat. 10:30–5, Sun. 2–5; Oct.– Apr., Mon.–Sat., 10:30–1 and 2–4:30, Sun. 2–4:30.*

❶ **Magdalen College.** Founded in 1458, with a handsome main quadrangle

★   and a supremely monastic air, Magdalen (pronounced "*maud*-lin") is one of the most impressive of Oxford's colleges and attracts its most artistic students. Alumni include such diverse people as Cardinal Wolsey, P.G. Wodehouse, Edward Gibbon, Oscar Wilde, Dudley Moore, and U.S. Supreme Court Justice David Souter. The school's large, square tower is a famous local landmark. A stroll around the Deer Park and along Addison's Walk is a good way to appreciate the place. ✉ *High St.* ☎ *01865/276000* ⊕ *www.magd.ox.ac.uk* 🎟 *£3.50* ☺ *July–Sept., daily noon–6; Oct.–June, daily 1–6.*

❹ **New College.** One of the university's best-known and oldest colleges (dating to 1379), New College stands alongside New College Lane, known for its Italianate Bridge of Sighs. Its grounds are big and enticing, with acres of soft green grass and pristinely maintained gardens. The college buildings, in ivory stone, are partly enclosed by the medieval city wall, and feature one of the city's best displays of Gothic gargoyles. ✉ *Holywell St.* ☎ *01865/279555* ⊕ *www.new.ox.ac.uk* 🎟 *Easter–Sept. £2, Oct.–Easter free* ☺ *Easter–Sept., daily 11–5; Oct.–Easter, daily 2–5.*

❺ **Radcliffe Camera and Bodleian Library.** A vast library, the round, domed Radcliffe Camera is Oxford's most spectacular building, built in 1737–49 by James Gibbs in Italian Baroque style. The Camera contains part of the Bodleian Library's enormous collection, which was begun in 1602 and has grown to more than 6 million volumes. Much like the Library of Congress in the United States, the Bodleian contains a copy of every book printed in Great Britain. The Bodleian, parts of which you can tour, is made up of multiple buildings connected by underground tunnels; the old buildings are magnificent and hold lovely art and ancient tomes. Most of the library's books are in underground spaces beneath the square in which the Camera sits. Another lovely part of the Bodleian, the Divinity School, is worth visiting. This superbly vaulted room dates to 1462. In the *Harry Potter* films, some interior scenes at Hogwarts School take place in the Bodleian, including the Divinity School. There's a self-guided audio tour. ✉ *Broad St.* ☎ *01865/277224 for information on tour* ⊕ *www.bodley.ox.ac.uk* 🎟 *Audio tour £2.50; guided tour £6, extended tour £12* ☺ *Bodleian weekdays 9–4:15, Sat. 9–3:30. Divinity School weekdays 9–4:45, Sat. 9–4:30.*

❻ **Sheldonian Theatre.** This fabulously ornate theater is where Oxford's impressive graduation ceremonies are held, conducted almost entirely in Latin. Dating to 1663, it was the first building designed by Sir Christopher Wren when he served as professor of astronomy. The D-shape theater has pillars, balconies, and an elaborately painted ceiling. The stone pillars outside are topped by 18 massive stone heads, sculpted in the 1970s to replace originals destroyed by air pollution. ✉ *Broad St.* ☎ *01865/277299* ⊕ *www.sheldon.ox.ac.uk* 🎟 *£2* ☺ *Mon.–Sat. 10–12:30 and 2–4:30; mid-Nov.–Feb., closes at 3:30. Closed for 10 days at Christmas and Easter and for degree ceremonies and events.*

WHERE TO EAT

££ ✗ **Brasserie Blanc.** Raymond Blanc's sophisticated brasserie, a hipper
★ cousin of Le Manoir aux Quat' Saisons in Great Milton, is the finest place to eat in Oxford. The changing menu always lists innovative,

visually stunning adaptations of bourgeois French fare, sometimes with Mediterranean or Asian influences. Try the steamed Loch Fyne mussels in a white-wine and cream sauce. The fixed-price menus (which start at £12 for lunch) are a good value. ⊠*71–72 Walton St.* ☎*01865/510999* ⊟*AE, DC, V.*

££   ✗**Fishers.** Everything is remarkably fresh at what is widely viewed as the city's best seafood restaurant. Seafood is prepared with a European touch in such dishes as baked salmon with roasted fennels and peppers and lemon sole with ham and leek beurre blanc. Oysters are served baked, fried, or resting comfortably on the half-shell. The interior has a casual nautical theme that borders on the kitschy, with wooden floors and tables, porthole windows, and fishing nets. Bustling but relaxed, this place is often fully booked. ⊠*36–37 St. Clements St.* ☎*01865/243003* ◬*Reservations essential* ⊟*MC, V.*

£   ✗**Grand Café.** Golden-hue tiles, towering columns, and antique marble tables make this café both architecturally impressive and an excellent spot for a light meal or leisurely drink. It's touristy and service can be slow, but it's still a pretty spot for afternoon tea. At night it transforms into a popular cocktail bar. ⊠*84 High St.* ☎*01865/204463* ⊟*AE, DC, MC, V.*

WHERE TO STAY

Oxford is pricey; for the cheapest lodging, contact the tourist information office for B&Bs in locals' homes.

£   ▥**Newton House.** A handsome Victorian mansion just a five-minute walk from all of Oxford's action, the Newton is a sprawling, friendly place. Decent-size rooms are brightly decorated with lemony walls and red curtains; some have original Victorian features. The breakfast menu is more varied than that of some guesthouses, with cereals and croissants along with the usual eggs and bacon. This is one of the best deals in the city center, so book early. **Pros:** great breakfasts, comfortable rooms. **Cons:** decor is a bit too bright, bathrooms are tiny. ⊠*82 Abingdon Rd.* ☎*01865/240561* ⊠*01865/244647* ✐*newton.house@ btinternet.com* ⊲*11 rooms* ♿*In room: dial-up, no a/c. In hotel: no elevator* ⊟*MC, V* ⵏⵔ*BP.*

£££–££££   ▥**Old Parsonage.** A 17th-century gabled stone house in a small garden next to St. Giles Church, this hotel provides a dignified escape from the surrounding city center. Dark-wood paneling and a crackling wood fire make the lobby a relaxing retreat. The fresh guest rooms are done in crisp white shades with bright splashes of color; bathrooms are marble. Memorable meals by the fire (or in the walled garden terrace in summer) keep people coming back. Afternoon teas with scones and clotted cream are excellent. **Pros:** interesting building, quiet location, great afternoon tea. **Cons:** pricey given what's on offer, bathrooms are small. ⊠*1 Banbury Rd.* ☎*01865/310210* ⊕*www.oldparsonage-hotel.co.uk* ⊲*26 rooms, 4 suites* ♿*In-room: no a/c, safe, Ethernet. In-hotel: restaurant, room service, bar, laundry service, parking (no fee), no-smoking rooms, no elevator* ⊟*AE, DC, MC, V.*

SIDE TRIP TO BLENHEIM PALACE

Fodor's Choice
★
So grandiose is Blenheim's masonry and so breathtaking are its articulations of splendor that it was named a World Heritage Site, the only historic house in Britain to receive the honor. Built by Sir John Vanbrugh in the early 1700s, Blenheim was given by Queen Anne and the nation to General John Churchill, first duke of Marlborough, in gratitude for his military victories against the French in 1704. The exterior is mind-boggling, with its huge columns, enormous pediments and obelisks, all exemplars of English Baroque. In most of the opulent rooms great family portraits look down at sumptuous furniture, tapestries illustrating important battles, and immense pieces of silver. For some visitors, however, the most memorable room is the small, low-ceiling chamber where Winston Churchill (his father was the younger brother of the then-duke) was born in 1874; he is buried in nearby Bladon. The 2,000 acres of grounds, the work of Capability Brown, 18th-century England's most gifted landscape gardener, are arguably the best example of the "cunningly natural" park in the country, and the formal gardens include notable water terraces. ⊠ *Woodstock* ☎ *0870/060–2080* ⊕ *www.blenheim palace.com* ▣ *Palace, park, and gardens: Nov.–mid-Mar. £9.50; mid-Mar.–Oct. £16.50. Park and gardens only: £7.50 Nov.–mid-Mar., £9.50 mid-Mar.–Oct.* ☉ *Palace mid-Feb.–mid-Dec., daily 10:30–4:45; park daily 9–4:45.*

7

STRATFORD-UPON-AVON & THE COTSWOLDS

Even under the weight of busloads of visitors coming to see the Shakespeare sights or plays at the Royal Shakespeare Theatre, Stratford, on the banks of the slow-flowing River Avon, has somehow hung on to much of its ancient character. It can, on a good day, still feel like an English market town. Outside Stratford, a detour to the huge fortress of Warwick Castle provides a glimpse into Britain's turbulent history, while, some 15 miles south, the rolling uplands of the Cotswold Hills represent the quintessence of rural England. In this blissfully unspoiled region, deservedly popular with visitors, you can taste the glories of the old English village—its stone slate roofs, low-ceiling rooms, and gardens; its atmosphere is as thick as honey, and equally as sweet.

PLANNING YOUR TIME

If you have only a day in Stratford-upon-Avon, arrive early and confine your visit to two or three Shakespeare Birthplace Trust properties, a few other town sights, a pub lunch, and a walk along the river, capped off by a stroll to the cottage of Anne Hathaway. Avoid visiting on weekends and school holidays, and take in the main Shakespeare shrines in the early morning to see them at their least frenetic. One high point of Stratford's calendar is the Shakespeare Birthday Celebrations, usually on the weekend nearest to April 23. You would do well to avoid weekends in the busier areas of the Cotswolds, but during the week, even in summer, you may hardly see a soul in the more remote spots.

GETTING HERE & AROUND

First Great Western Link and Virgin trains serve the area from London; service to Stratford is good, but it's very limited in the Cotswolds.

A car is the best way to tour the Cotswold region, given the limitations of public transportation. From Stratford, follow B4623 south to Chipping Campden or Broadway. From London you can either follow M4 and A429 northwest to southern Gloucestershire (about a two-hour drive), or M40, from which a network of minor roads link the villages.

By bus, National Express buses head to Cheltenham, on the edge of the Cotswolds in about three hours from London's Victoria Coach Station. Stagecoach, Castleways, Swanbrook, and Pulhams operate within the region, though services can be extremely limited. Traveline has full schedules.

Ask at Stratford's tourist office about bus tours to Warwick and through the Cotswolds.

ESSENTIALS

Bus Contacts Castleways (☎ 01242/602949). **First** (☎ 0845/606–4446 ⊕ www.firstbadgerline.co.uk). **National Express** (☎ 0870/580–8080 ⊕ www.nationalexpress.com). **Pulhams** (☎ 01451/820369 ⊕ www.pulhamscoaches.com). **Stagecoach** (☎ 01242/224853 ⊕ www.stagecoachbus.com). **Swanbrook** (☎ 01452/712386 ⊕ www.swanbrook.co.uk). **Traveline** (☎ 0871/200–2233 ⊕ www.traveline.org.uk).

Train Contacts National Rail Enquiries (☎ 0845/748–4950 ⊕ www.national rail.co.uk).

Visitor Information Heart of England Tourism (✉ Larkhill Rd., Worcester ☎ 01905/761100 ⊕ www.visitheartofengland.com).

STRATFORD-UPON-AVON

100 mi northwest of London, 37 mi southeast of Birmingham.

It doesn't take long to figure out who's the center of attention here. Born in a half-timber, early-16th-century building in the center of Stratford on April 23, 1564, William Shakespeare died on April 23, 1616, his 52nd birthday, in a more imposing house at New Place. Although he spent much of his life in London, the world still associates him with "Shakespeare's Avon." You can see his whole life here, from his birthplace on Henley Street to his burial place in Holy Trinity Church.

Most sights cluster around Henley Street, High Street, and Waterside, which skirts the public gardens through which the River Avon flows. Bridge Street and Sheep Street (parallel to Bridge) are Stratford's main thoroughfares and the site of most banks, shops, and eating places. The town's tourist office lies at Bridgefoot, next to Clopton Bridge.

GETTING HERE

Stratford's train station is at the edge of the town center on Alcester Road. There are usually taxis to pick up arriving passengers—alternatively it's an easy walk into town. You can travel by train *and* bus using the Shakespeare Connection Road & Rail Link from London's Euston Station, taking around two hours. There's a train to London after theatre performances. Call National Rail Enquiries for information.

VISITOR INFORMATION

Stratford-upon-Avon (⊠*Bridgefoot* ☎*0870/160–7930* ⊕*www.strat ford-upon-avon.co.uk*)

EXPLORING

The **Shakespeare Birthplace Trust** runs the main places of Shakespearean interest: Anne Hathaway's Cottage, Hall's Croft, Mary Arden's House, Nash's House and New Place, and Shakespeare's Birthplace. They have similar opening times. ■TIP➔You can buy a money-saving combination ticket to the three in-town properties or to all five properties, or pay separate entry fees if you're visiting only one or two. Family tickets are an option too. You can check out special events at the properties, from talks about Tudor life to performances of Shakespeare's plays. ☎*01789/204016* ⊕*www.shakespeare.org.uk* ⊠*Joint ticket to 5 properties £15; joint ticket to Shakespeare's Birthplace, Hall's Croft, and Nash's House– New Place £11.*

★ **Anne Hathaway's Cottage.** The most picturesque of the Shakespeare Trust properties, on the western outskirts of Stratford, was the family home of the woman Shakespeare married in 1582. The "cottage," actually a substantial Tudor farmhouse, has latticed windows and a grand thatch roof. Inside is period furniture including a rare carved Elizabethan bed; outside is a garden planted in lush Victorian style with herbs and flowers. In a nearby field the **Shakespeare Tree Garden** has 40 trees mentioned in the playwright's works, a yew maze, and sculptures with Shakespearean themes. ■TIP➔ The best way to get here is to walk, especially in late spring when the apple trees are in blossom. There are two main footpaths, one via Greenhill Street by the railroad bridge, the other leaving from Holy Trinity Church up Old Town and Chestnut Walk. ⊠*Cottage La., Shottery* ☎*01789/204016* ⊕*www.shakespeare. org.uk* ⊠*£6, Shakespeare Trust 5-property ticket £15* ☉*Apr., May, Sept., and Oct., Mon.–Sat. 9:30–5, Sun. 10–5; June–Aug., Mon.–Sat. 9–5, Sun. 9:30–5; Nov.–Mar., Mon.–Sat. 10–4, Sun. 10:30–4; last entry 30 mins before closing.*

Holy Trinity Church. The burial place of William Shakespeare, this 13th-century church sits on the banks of the Avon, with a graceful avenue of lime trees framing its entrance. Shakespeare's final resting place is in the chancel, rebuilt in 1465–91 in the late Perpendicular style. He was buried here not because he was a famed poet but because he was a lay rector of Stratford, owning a portion of the township tithes. On the north wall of the sanctuary, over the altar steps, is the famous marble bust created by Gerard Jansen in 1623, and thought to be a true likeness of Shakespeare. The bust offers a more human, even humorous, perspective when viewed from the side. Also in the chancel are the graves of Shakespeare's wife, Anne; his daughter Susanna; his son-in-law, John Hall; and his granddaughter's husband, Thomas Nash. Nearby, the

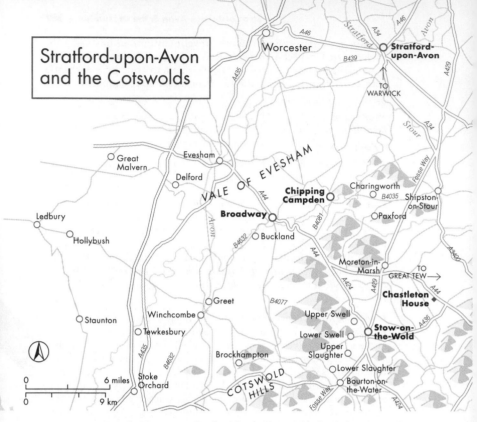

Stratford-upon-Avon
and the Cotswolds

Parish Register is displayed, containing both Shakespeare's baptismal entry (1564) and his burial notice (1616). ⊠ *Trinity St.* 🎫*£3 for chancel* ⊙ *Mar., Mon.–Sat. 9–5, Sun. 12:30–5; Apr.–Oct., Mon.–Sat. 8:30–6, Sun. 12:30–5; Nov.–Feb., Mon.–Sat. 9–4, Sun. 12:30–5; last admission 20 mins before closing.*

Shakespeare's Birthplace. A half-timber house typical of its time, the playwright's birthplace is a much-visited shrine that has been altered and restored since he lived here. You enter through the somewhat over-the-top **Shakespeare Centre,** where the exhibits consist mostly of poster-size Shakespeare quotations, with written information about the age in which he lived. It's mainly geared to the groups of school children who often fill the place, so don't feel bad about hustling on to the house itself, which is across the garden from the large, modern center. The few furnishings in the actual house reflect comfortable middle-class Elizabethan domestic life. Shakespeare's father, John, a glove maker and wool dealer, purchased the house; a reconstructed workshop shows the tools of the glover's trade. An auction notice describes the property as it was when it was offered for sale in 1847. You can also see the signatures of earlier pilgrims including Mark Twain and Charles Dickens, who according to the Shakespeare Trust, scratched with their diamond rings into Shakespeare's windowpanes. ⊠ *Henley St.* ☎ *01789/204016*

⊕*www.shakespeare.org.uk* ✉*£8, Shakespeare Trust ticket for 3 in-town properties £11, 5-property ticket £15* ⊗*Nov.–Mar., Mon.–Sat. 10–4, Sun. 10:30–4; Apr. and May, Mon.–Sat. 10–5, Sun. 10:30–5; June–Aug., Mon.–Sat. 9–5, Sun. 9:30–5; Sept. and Oct., Mon.–Sat. 10–5, Sun. 10:30–5; last entry 30 mins before closing.*

WHERE TO EAT & STAY

£ ✕**Black Swan.** Known locally as the Dirty Duck, one of Stratford's most celebrated pubs has attracted actors since Garrick's days. Its little veranda overlooks the theaters and the river. You can sample English grill specialties as well as bar meals such as mussels and fries. Few people come here for the food, which is mediocre: the real attractions are the ambience and the other customers. ✉*Southern La.* ☎*01789/297312* ▭*AE, MC, V* ⊗*No dinner Sun.*

££ ✕**Russons.** A 16th-century building holds a quaint dining room that's popular with theatergoers. The fare, though reasonably priced, doesn't skimp on quality. On the daily-changing menu, chalked on a blackboard, are English specialties such as roast lamb and guinea fowl. ✉*8 Church St.* ☎*01789/268822* ⚄*Reservations essential* ▭*AE, MC, V* ⊗*Closed Mon.*

£££–££££ 🛏**Shakespeare Hotel.** Built in the 1400s, this Elizabethan town house in the heart of town is a vision right out of *The Merry Wives of Windsor*, with its five gables and long, stunning, black-and-white half-timber facade. The restaurant, bar, and lounge have blackened beams and a pleasantly aged look. The intelligently modernized interiors have a touch of luxury; Shakespeareana and old playbills decorate the public areas. Hewn timbers carved with rose-and-thistle patterns decorate some rooms; all have new beds and a clean, neutral decor. There are good deals on room rates in the off-season. **Pros:** historic building, great lounge to relax in. **Cons:** prices are high for what's on offer, some small bedrooms. ✉*Chapel St.* ☎*0870/400–8182* ⊕*www.mercure.com* ⇌*64 rooms, 6 suites* ⚅*In-room: no a/c, dial-up. In-hotel: restaurant, room service, bar, laundry service, parking (fee), no-smoking rooms, some pets allowed (fee), no elevator* ▭*AE, DC, MC, V.*

££ 🛏**White Swan.** Exposed beams, low ceilings, and winding corridors
★ make this cozy hotel a delight for those who like a little authenticity. It claims to be the oldest building in Stratford, and the look of the exterior (circa 1450) reinforces that boast. Each room is individually decorated, and although fabrics are not luxurious, admirable effort has been made to avoid traditional chintz. Heavy antiques mix with reproductions; some rooms have fireplaces, and some have four-poster beds. Bathrooms are tucked into what little space is available. ∎**TIP➜The popular pub, a traditional English boozer with ancient beams, attracts visitors and locals. Pros:** great for those who like ancient buildings, unique decor. **Cons:** some rooms are small, most bathrooms are even tinier. ✉*Rother St.* ☎*01789/297022* ⊕*www.pebblehotels.com* ⇌*41 rooms* ⚅*In-room: no a/c (some), dial-up (some). In-hotel: restaurant, room service, parking (no fee), no elevator* ▭*MC, V* ❖*BP.*

7

NIGHTLIFE & THE ARTS

Fodor'sChoice   The **Royal Shakespeare Company** (⊠ *Waterside, Stratford-upon-Avon*
★   ☎ *0844/800–1110 ticket hotline, 01789/296655 general information*
⊕*www.rsc.org.uk*) performs Shakespeare plays year-round in Stratford,
as well as in other venues around Britain. Stratford's Royal Shakespeare
Theatre is the home of the RSC, one of the finest repertory troupes in the
world and long the backbone of the country's theatrical life. Although
the company's main stage is closed until 2010, performances will take
place at theaters throughout town, including the temporary 1,000-seat
Courtyard Theatre on Southern Lane. The Swan Theatre, behind the
Royal Shakespeare Theatre, stages plays by Shakespeare and contemporaries such as Christopher Marlowe and Ben Jonson. Prices usually
are £7 to £45. ■TIP➔Book ahead through the RSC, as seats go fast, but
day of performance (two per person to personal callers only) and returned
tickets are often available. You can book tickets from London with **Ticketmaster** (☎ *0870/534–4444* ⊕*www.ticketmaster.co.uk*), operating 24
hours a day. You can book tickets in the United States (a 20% surcharge
applies) with **Keith Prowse** (☎ *212/398–1430 or 800/669–8687* ⊕*www.
keithprowse.com*).

WARWICK

9 mi northeast of Stratford-upon-Avon.

Most famous for Warwick Castle—that vision out of the feudal ages—
the town of Warwick is an interesting architectural mixture of Georgian
redbrick and Elizabethan half-timbering.

GETTING HERE

To get to Warwick, catch a National Express bus from Stratford-
upon-Avon's riverside bus station to Warwick's Castle Hill. It's a
20-minute trip.

VISITOR INFORMATION

Warwick (⊠ *Court House, Jury St.* ☎ *01926/492212* ⊕ www.warwick-uk.co.uk).

EXPLORING

★   The vast bulk of medieval **Warwick Castle** rests on a cliff overlooking
⟲   the Avon—"the fairest monument of ancient and chivalrous splendor
which yet remains uninjured by time," to use the words of Sir Walter
Scott. Today the castle is owned by the people who run the Madame
Tussauds wax museums, and the exhibits and diversions can occupy a
full day; it's a great castle experience for kids, though it's pricey (there
are family prices). Warwick's two soaring towers can be seen for miles:
the 147-foot-high Caesar's Tower, built in 1356, and the 128-foot-high
Guy's Tower, built in 1380. The castle's most powerful commander was
Richard Neville, earl of Warwick, known during the 15th-century Wars
of the Roses as the Kingmaker. Warwick Castle's monumental walls
enclose an impressive armory of medieval weapons, as well as state
rooms with historic furnishings and paintings by Peter Paul Rubens,
Anthony Van Dyck, and other old masters. Twelve rooms are devoted
to an imaginative wax exhibition, "A Royal Weekend Party—1898."

Another exhibit displays the sights and sounds of a great medieval household as it prepares for an important battle. Below the castle, along the Avon, strutting peacocks patrol 60 acres of grounds elegantly landscaped by Capability Brown in the 18th century. ■TIP→The castle is popular; arrive early to beat the crowds. If you book online, you can save on ticket prices. Lavish medieval banquets (extra charge) and

special events, including festivals, jousting tournaments, and a Christmas market, take place throughout the year, and plenty of food stalls serve lunches. ⊠ *Castle La. off Mill St., Warwick* ☎ *01926/495421, 08704/422000 24-hr information line* ⊕ *www.warwick-castle.co.uk* 🖃 *Jan.–Mar. £15.95, Apr.–mid-July, mid-Sept.–Oct. £16.95, mid-July–Sept. £18.95* ☉ *Nov.–Jan., Apr.–Sept., daily 10–6; Oct.–Dec., Jan.–Mar., daily 10–5.*

BROADWAY

10 mi south of Stratford-upon-Avon.

The Cotswold town to end all Cotswold towns, Broadway has become a favorite of day-trippers. William Morris first discovered the delights of this village, and J. M. Barrie, Vaughan Williams, and Edward Elgar soon followed. Today you may want to avoid Broadway in summer, when it's clogged with cars and buses. Named for its handsome, wide main street (well worth a stroll), the village includes the renowned Lygon Arms hotel and numerous antiques shops, tea parlors, and boutiques. Step off onto Broadway's back roads and alleys and you can discover any number of honey-color houses and colorful gardens.

GETTING HERE

Take B4632 southwest from Stratford, then A44 southeast.

VISITOR INFORMATION

Broadway (⊠ *Russell Sq.* ☎ *01386/852937*).

EXPLORING

Among the attractions of **Broadway Tower Country Park,** on the outskirts of town, is its tower, an 18th-century "folly" built by the sixth earl of Coventry. Exhibits describe the tower's past, and the view from the top takes in three counties. (The tower normally stays open longer than the advertised times in fine weather.) Peaceful countryside surrounds you on the nature trails and picnic grounds. ⊠ *Off A44* ☎ *01386/852390* 🖃 *Park free, tower £4* ☉ *Tower Apr.–Oct., daily 10:30–5; Nov.–Mar., weekends 10:30–3.*

WHERE TO EAT & STAY

£££ ✕**Russell's.** With a courtyard at the back and a patio at the front, this chic "restaurant with rooms" is perfect for a light lunch at midday or a full meal in the evening. The restaurant, in a furniture factory once belonging to local designer George Russell, is modern and plush. The à la carte and fixed-price menus concentrate on modern British dishes, with such temptations as grilled sardines, roast partridge with braised red cabbage, and grilled Scotch rump steak with truffle mash. The boutique-style rooms upstairs (£££–££££) are very sleek. ⊠*20 High St.* ☎*01386/853555* ⭥ ☰*AE, MC, V* ⊗*No dinner Sun.*

£££–££££ 🏨**Lygon Arms.** Modern luxury, epitomized in the luxurious spa and health club, combines in perfect symbiosis with old-fashioned charm right in the heart of Broadway. In business since 1532, the inn (pronounced "Liggon") has a gabled roof and mullioned windows dating to 1620. Inside, look for antiques-bedecked parlors, baronial fireplaces, rich paneling, and rooms that once sheltered Charles I and Oliver Cromwell. Behind the house are more modern (and less expensive) bedrooms and 3 acres of formal gardens. One restaurant, the Great Hall (££££–£££££), complete with a minstrel's gallery, focuses on creative adaptations of traditional dishes. A good and cheaper option is Goblets Bistro. **Pros:** historic main building, refurbished rooms, great spa facilities. **Cons:** annex lacks character, disappointing breakfast, service sometimes sloppy. ⊠*High St.* ☎*01386/852255* ⊕*www.paramount-hotels.co.uk* ⭥*60 rooms, 2 suites* ♿*In-room: no a/c (some), Ethernet. In-hotel: 2 restaurants, bar, public Wi-Fi, tennis court, pool, spa, some pets allowed (fee), no elevator* ☰*AE, DC, MC, V* ◉*BP.*

CHIPPING CAMPDEN

4 mi east of Broadway.

Undoubtedly one of the most beautiful towns in the area, Chipping Campden, with its population of about 2,500, is the Cotswolds in a microcosm. It has St. James, the region's most impressive church; frozen-in-time streets; a silk mill that was once the center of the Guild of Handicrafts; and pleasant, un-touristy shops. A seductive setting unfolds before you as you travel on B4081 through sublime English countryside and happen upon the town, tucked in a slight valley.

GETTING HERE

Take minor roads to reach Chipping Campden, 4 miles east of Broadway, or else—a slightly longer route—follow A44 southeast, then B4081 north.

VISITOR INFORMATION

Chipping Campden (⊠ *The Old Police Station, High St.* ☎*01386/841206* ⊕*www. visitchippingcampden.com*).

EXPLORING

The soaring pinnacled tower of **St. James,** a prime example of a Cotswold wool church (rebuilt in the 15th century with money from wool merchants), announces the town from a distance; it's worth stepping inside to see the lofty nave. It recalls the old saying, which became popular because of the vast numbers of houses of worship in the Cotswolds, "As sure as God's in Gloucestershire." ✉*Church St.* ☎*01386/841927* ⊕*www.stjameschurchcampden.co.uk* ✉£1 *donation suggested* ☉*Apr.–Oct., weekdays 10–5, Sat. 11–5, Sun. 2–5:45; Nov.–Mar., weekdays 11–3, Sat. 11–4, Sun. 2–4.*

In 1902 the Guild of Handicrafts took over the **Silk Mill,** and Arts and Crafts evangelist Charles Robert Ashbee (1863–1942) brought 150 acolytes here from London, including 50 guildsmen, to revive and practice such skills as cabinetmaking and bookbinding. The operation folded in 1920, but the refurbished building houses an exhibition and workshops, including those of a silversmith, jeweler, and stone carver. ✉*Sheep St.* ☎ *No phone* ✉*Free* ☉ *Weekdays 9–5, Sat. 9–1.*

WHERE TO EAT & STAY

££   ✕**Churchill Arms.** In this small country pub just outside Chipping Campden, plain wooden tables and benches, a flagstone floor, and a roaring fire provide the backdrop for excellent food. Daily specials—steamed lemon sole filled with salmon and chive mousse, and pot-roasted partridge with parsnips and red wine—appear on the blackboard. If you feel like staying overnight, upstairs are four antiques-furnished bedrooms. ✉*Off B4035, Paxford* ☎*01386/594000* ▤*MC, V.*

££   ▦**Badgers Hall.** Expect a friendly welcome at this antique B&B above a tearoom just across from the Market Hall. The spacious, spotless rooms have low, beamed ceilings and exposed stonework. Guests are greeted with a cream tea on arrival, and the excellent breakfast will set you up for the day. Two nights is the minimum stay. **Pros:** atmospheric building, spacious rooms. **Cons:** low ceilings, entrance is through tea shop. ✉*High St.* ☎*01386/840839* ⊕*www.badgershall.com* ⌨*3 rooms* &*In-hotel: public Wi-Fi, no kids under 10, no-smoking rooms, no elevator* ▤*MC, V* ⦿*BP.*

STOW-ON-THE-WOLD

10 mi southeast of Chipping Campden.

At an elevation of 800 feet, Stow is the highest town in the Cotswolds— "Stow-on-the-Wold, where the wind blows cold" is the age-old saying. Built around a wide square, the imposing golden stone houses have been discreetly converted into a good number of high-quality antiques stores. Stow is the leading center for antiques in the Cotswolds, with more than 40 dealers centered around the Square, Sheep Street, and Church Street.

Also here are St. Edward's Church and the Kings Arms Old Posting House, its wide entrance still seeming to wait for the stagecoaches that used to stop here on their way to Cheltenham.

GETTING HERE
Stow is about 10 miles southeast of Broadway via A44 and A424; from Chipping Campden, take B4081 to A44 and A424.

VISITOR INFORMATION
Stow-on-the-Wold (⊠ *Hollis House, The Square* ☎ *01451/831082* ⊕ *www. cotswold.gov.uk*).

EXPLORING

The **Square,** as it is known, has a fascinating history. In the 18th century Daniel Defoe wrote that more than 20,000 sheep could be sold here on a busy day; such was the press of livestock that sheep runs, known as "tures," were used to control the sheep, and these narrow streets still run off the main square. Today pubs and cafés fill the area.

Chastleton House, one of the most complete Jacobean properties in Britain, opts for a beguilingly lived-in appearance, taking advantage of almost 400 years' worth of furniture and trappings accumulated by many generations of the single family that owned it until 1991. The house was built between 1605 and 1612 for William Jones, a wealthy wool merchant, and has an appealing authenticity: cobwebs and bric-a-brac are strewn around, wood and pewter are unpolished, upholstery uncleaned. ■ **TIP➡ Admission is by timed ticket, so it's a good idea to call ahead to reserve.** Chastleton is 6 mi northeast of Stow, signposted off A436 between Stow and A44. ⊠ *Off A436, Moreton-in-Marsh* ☎ *01608/674355, 01494/755560 for recorded information* ⊕ *www. nationaltrust.org.uk* ⊠ *£7* ☉ *Mid-Mar.–Sept., Wed.–Sat. 1–5; Oct., Wed.–Sat. 1–4.*

WHERE TO STAY

£–££   🖫 **Number Nine.** Beyond the traditional stone and creeper exterior of this former coaching inn are unfussy, spacious bedrooms done in soothing white and pale colors. The inglenook fireplace is a draw in winter, and wholesome breakfasts include poached fruits and specialty breads. **Pros:** very friendly staff, excellent breakfasts, attention to detail. **Cons:** not all bathrooms have showers, many steps to climb. ⊠ *9 Park St.* ☎ *01451/870333* ⊕ *www.number-nine.info* ⇆ *3 rooms* ⅍ *In-room: no a/c, no phone, Wi-Fi. In-hotel: no-smoking rooms, public Internet, no elevator* ⊟ *MC, V* �ⓘ *BP.*

BATH

"I really believe I shall always be talking of Bath . . . Oh! who can ever be tired of Bath," enthused Catherine Morland in Jane Austen's *Northanger Abbey,* and today plenty of people agree with these sentiments. In Bath you are surrounded by magnificent 18th-century architecture, a lasting reminder of the vanished world described by Austen.

Bath is no museum, though: it's lively, with good dining and shopping, excellent art galleries and museums, the remarkable excavated Roman baths, and theater, music, and other performances all year. Many people rush through Bath in a day, but there's enough to do to merit an overnight stay—or more.

The Romans put Bath on the map in the 1st century, when they built a temple here, in honor of the goddess Minerva, and a sophisticated network of baths to make full use of the mineral springs that gush from the

earth at a constant temperature of 116°F (46.5°C). ■TIP→ Don't miss
the remains of these baths, one of the city's glories. Visits by Queen Anne
in 1702 and 1703 brought attention to the town, and soon 18th-century
"people of quality" took it to heart. Bath became the most fashionable
spa in Britain. The architects John Wood and John Wood the Younger
created a harmonious city, building graceful terraces (row houses),
crescents (curving rows of houses), and villas of the same golden local
limestone used by the Romans.

PLANNING YOUR TIME

Schedule a visit to Bath during the week, as weekends see an influx of
visitors. The city gets similarly crowded during its various festivals,
though the added conviviality and cultural activity during these events
are big draws in themselves. Early morning and late afternoon are the
best times to view nearby Stonehenge at its least populated.

GETTING HERE & AROUND

Bath lies 115 mi west of London and 13 mi southeast of Bristol. Frequent trains from Paddington and National Express buses from Victoria connect Bath with London. The bus and train stations are close to
each other south of the center. From Bath numerous private companies
operate tours to Stonehenge.

By car, M4 is the main route west from London to Bath; expect about a
two-hour drive. From Exit 18, take A46 south to Bath. Public parking
lots in the historic area fill up early, but the Park and Ride lots on the
outskirts provide inexpensive shuttle service into the center, which is
pleasant to stroll around. Drivers from Bath to Stonehenge should take
A36/A303, and from London to Stonehenge, M3/A303.

TOURS

City Sightseeing runs 50-minute guided tours of Bath on open-top buses
year-round, leaving three or four times an hour from High Street, near
the Abbey. Mad Max Tours runs full-day tours to Stonehenge.

ESSENTIALS

Visitor & Tour Information Bath (⊠ Abbey Chambers, Abbey Churchyard
☎ 0906/711–2000 [calls cost 50p per minute] ⊕ www.visitbath.co.uk). City
Sightseeing (☎ 01225/330444 in Bath ⊕ www.city-sightseeing.com). Mad Max
Tours (☎ 01225/464323 or 0799/050–5970 ⊕ www.madmax.abel.co.uk). Mayor
of Bath's Honorary Tours (☎ 01225/477411).

EXPLORING BATH

❷ **Bath Abbey.** Dominating Bath's center, this 15th-century edifice of
golden, glowing stone has a splendid west front, with carved figures of
angels ascending ladders on either side. Notice, too, the miter, olive tree,
and crown motif, a play on the name of the current building's founder,
Bishop Oliver King. More than 50 stained-glass windows fill about
80% of the building's wall space, giving the interior an impression of
lightness. The abbey was built in the Perpendicular (English late-Gothic)
style on the site of a Saxon abbey, and the nave and side aisles contain
superb fan-vaulted ceilings. There are six services on Sunday. ⊠ Abbey

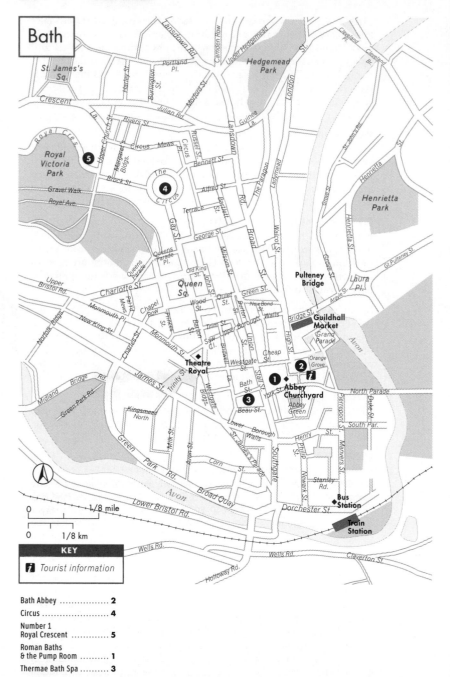

Bath

St. James's Sq.

Crescent

Portland Pl.

Hedgemead Park

Royal Victoria Park

Royal Cres.

Gravel Walk

Royal Ave.

Henrietta Park

The Circus **4**

5

Pulteney Bridge

Laura Pl.

Queen Sq.

Charlotte St.

Upper Bristol Rd.

Chapel Row

Monmouth Pl.

New King St.

Norfolk Bridge

Guildhall Market

Grand Parade

Theatre Royal

James St.

Midland Bridge Rd.

Green Park Rd.

Kingsmead North

Theatre Royal

Westgate Bldgs.

3

Beau St.

1

Abbey Churchyard

Abbey Green

2

Orange Grove

i

North Parade

South Par.

Lower Borough Walls

Henry Philip St.

Stanley Rd.

Newark St.

Dorchester St.

Bus Station

Train Station

Corn St.

Broad Quay

Avon

Lower Bristol Rd.

Wells Rd.

Wells Rd.

Holloway Rd.

Claverton St.

0 —— 1/8 mile

0 —— 1/8 km

Churchyard ☎*01225/422462* ⊕*www.bathabbey.org* ✉*Abbey £2.50 donation, Heritage Vaults free* ☉*Abbey Apr.–Oct., Mon.–Sat. 9–6, Sun. 1–2:30 and 4:30–5:30; Nov.–Mar., Mon.–Sat. 9–4:30, Sun. 1–2:30 and 4:30–5:30. Heritage Vaults Mon.–Sat. 10–4.*

4 ★ **Circus.** John Wood designed the masterful Circus, a circle of curving, perfectly proportioned Georgian houses interrupted just three times for intersecting streets. Wood died shortly after work on the Circus began; his son, the younger John Wood, completed the project. Notice the carved acorns atop the houses: Wood nurtured the myth that Prince Bladud founded Bath, ostensibly with the help of an errant pig rooting for acorns (this is one of a number of variations of Bladud's story), and the architect adopted the acorn motif in a number of places. A garden fills the center of the Circus. The painter Thomas Gainsborough (1727–88) lived at No. 17 from 1760 to 1774.

5 **Number 1 Royal Crescent.** The majestic arc of the Royal Crescent, much used as a film location, is the crowning glory of Palladian architecture in Bath; Number 1 offers you a glimpse inside this splendor. The work of John Wood the Younger, the 30 houses fronted by 114 columns were laid out between 1767 and 1774. A house in the center is now the Royal Crescent Hotel. On the corner of Brock Street and the Royal Crescent, Number 1 Royal Crescent has been turned into a museum and furnished as it might have been at the turn of the 19th century. The museum crystallizes a view of the English class system—upstairs all is elegance, and downstairs is a kitchen display. ☎*01225/428126* ⊕*www.bath-preservation-trust.org.uk* ✉*£5* ☉*Mid-Feb.–Oct., Tues.– Sun. and national holidays 10:30–5; Nov., Tues.–Sun. 10:30–4; last admission 30 mins before closing.*

1 Fodor'sChoice ★ **Roman Baths & the Pump Room.** The hot springs have drawn people here since prehistoric times, so it's quite appropriate to begin an exploration of Bath at this excellent museum on the site of the ancient city's temple complex and primary "watering hole." Here Roman patricians would gather to immerse themselves, drink the mineral waters, and socialize. With the departure of the Romans, the baths fell into disuse and were partially covered. When bathing again became fashionable, the site was reopened; the magnificent Georgian building now standing was erected at the end of the 18th century. During the 19th century almost the entire Roman bath complex was rediscovered and excavated, and the museum displays relics of the temple once dedicated to Sulis Minerva. Exhibits include a mustachioed, Celtic-influenced Gorgon's head, fragments of colorful curses invoked by the Romans against some of their neighbors, and information about Roman bathing practices. The **Great Bath** is now roofless, and the statuary and pillars belong to the 19th century, but much remains from the original complex, and the steaming, somewhat murky waters are undeniably evocative. ■**TIP→There are free hourly tours of the baths, and in August you can take torch-lighted tours at night.**

Adjacent to the Roman bath complex is the famed **Pump Room**, built in 1792–96, a rendezvous for members of 18th-century and 19th-century Bath society, who liked to check on the new arrivals to the city. Today you can take in the elegant space—or you can simply, for a small fee, taste the fairly vile mineral water. Charles Dickens described it as tasting like warm flatirons. ⊠*Abbey Churchyard* ☎*01225/477785* ⊕*www. romanbaths.co.uk* ⊠*Pump Room free, Roman Baths £10.50, £11 in July and Aug. with audio guide; combined ticket with Fashion Museum and Assembly Rooms (valid 7 days) £14* ☉*Mar.–June, Sept., and Oct., daily 9–6; July and Aug., daily 9* AM*–10* PM*; Nov.–Feb., daily 9:30–5:30; last admission 1 hr before closing.*

❸ Thermae Bath Spa. Now you can take the waters, 21st-century-style, in this historic spa town. The only place in Britain where you can bathe in natural hot-spring water, and in an open-air rooftop location as well, this striking complex designed by Nicholas Grimshaw consists of a Bath-stone building surrounded by a glass curtain wall. ∎**TIP➔ It's recommended to book spa treatments ahead.** Towels, robes, and slippers are available for rent. Weekdays are the quietest time to visit. ⊠*Hot Bath St.* ☎*01225/331234* ⊕*www.thermaebathspa.com* ⊠*£22 for 2 hrs, £32 for 4 hrs, £50 all day; extra charges for treatments* ☉*Daily 9* AM*–10* PM*; last entry at 7:30* PM.

WHERE TO EAT

£££ ✕**Olive Tree.** This sleek space in the basement of the Queensberry Hotel
★ makes a calm, contemporary setting for top-notch English and Mediterranean dishes. The range of seductive choices includes chicken and wild mushrooms for starters and such main courses as pork belly with mashed celeriac. Some dessert picks are poached figs in mulled wine and baked vanilla cheesecake. Fixed-price menus are available at lunchtime. ⊠*Russel St.* ☎*01225/447928* ⊟*AE, MC, V* ☉*No lunch Mon.*

££ ✕**Pump Room.** The 18th-century Pump Room, next to the Roman Baths, serves morning coffee, lunches of chicken and lamb dishes, and afternoon tea, often to music by a pianist or string trio. Its stately setting is the selling point rather than the food, but do sample the English cheese board and homemade Bath biscuits. The Terrace Restaurant has views over the Baths and is also open occasionally for fixed-price dinners (reservations are essential). Be prepared to wait in line for a table during the day. ⊠*Abbey Churchyard* ☎*01225/444477* ⊟*AE, DC, MC, V* ☉*No dinner except during July, Aug., Dec., and festivals.*

££ ✕**Sally Lunn's.** Small and slightly twee, this tourist magnet near Bath Abbey occupies the oldest house in Bath, dating to 1482. It's famous for the Sally Lunn bun, actually a semisweet bread served here since 1680. You can choose from more than 40 sweet and savory toppings to accompany your bun, or turn it into a meal with such dishes as trencher pork with sherry and tarragon sauce. There's also an economical early-bird two-course evening menu. Daytime diners can view the small kitchen museum in the cellar (30p for nondining visitors). ⊠*4 N. Parade Passage* ☎*01225/461634* ⊟*MC, V.*

WHERE TO STAY

££   ⌂**Albany Guest House.** Homey and friendly, this Edwardian house close to the Royal Crescent has contemporary, simply furnished rooms. Most are decorated with neutral, beige, and cream colors. The attic room is the largest and best. Vegetarian and other dietary preferences are accommodated at breakfast, which may include tasty homemade vegetarian sausages. **Pros:** spotless rooms, excellent breakfasts. **Cons:** some rooms are very small, limited parking. ⊠*24 Crescent Gardens* ☎*01225/313339* ⊕*www.albanybath.co.uk* ✑*5 rooms* ⌕*In-room: no a/c, no phone, Wi-Fi. In-hotel: parking (no fee), public Wi-Fi, no-smoking rooms, no elevator* ⊟*AE, MC, V* ⦿*BP.*

£££–££££   ⌂**Queensberry Hotel.** Intimate and elegant, this boutique hotel in a residential street near the Circus occupies three 1772 town houses built by John Wood the Younger for the marquis of Queensberry. Guests will find here a perfect marriage of chic sophistication, homey comforts, and attentive service. Renovations have preserved the Regency stucco ceilings and cornices and marble tile on the fireplaces, and each room is individually decorated in contemporary style. Four secluded, terraced gardens invite a summer aperitif, and downstairs is the excellent semiformal, understated Olive Tree restaurant. **Pros:** efficient service, good location, comfortable accommodations. **Cons:** some street noise. ⊠*Russel St.* ☎*01225/447928* ⊕*www.thequeensberry.co.uk* ✑*26 rooms, 3 suites* ⌕*In-room: no a/c, dial-up. In-hotel: restaurant, bar, public Wi-Fi, parking (no fee)* ⊟*AE, MC, V.*

££–£££   ⌂**Three Abbey Green.** Just steps away from Bath Abbey, a majestic sycamore tree dominates the gorgeous square that is home to this welcoming B&B. Parts of the building date from 1689, but contemporary design lightens the spacious, pastel-hue rooms. The Lord Nelson room is extra big, with a four-poster, separate sitting area, and handsome fireplace; there are also family rooms. The only downsides are Bath's perennial shortage of parking space—though parking lots are nearby—and the occasional noise at night. The hosts are ready with tips for visiting the city and beyond. Self-catering apartments are also available. **Pros:** superb location, airy rooms. **Cons:** some noise from pub-goers, only one suite has a bathtub, no parking. ⊠*3 Abbey Green* ☎*01225/428558* ⊕*www.threeabbeygreen.com* ✑*7 rooms* ⌕*In-room: no a/c, Wi-Fi. In-hotel: no-smoking rooms, public Internet, no elevator* ⊟*MC, V* ⦿*BP.*

SIDE TRIP FROM BATH

STONEHENGE

★ *35 mi southeast of Bath, 8 mi north of Salisbury.*

Mysterious and ancient, Stonehenge has baffled archaeologists for centuries. One of England's most-visited monuments, the circle of giant stones that sits in lonely isolation on the wide sweep of Salisbury Plain still has the capacity to fascinate and move those who view it. Visitors are kept on a path a short distance away from the stones, so that you can no longer walk among them or see up close the prehistoric carvings, some of which show axes and daggers. But if you visit in the early morning, when the crowds have not yet arrived, or in the evening, when the sky is heavy with scudding clouds, you can experience Stonehenge as it once was: a mystical, awe-inspiring place.

Stonehenge was begun about 3000 BC, enlarged between 2100 and 1900 BC, and altered yet again by 150 BC. It has been excavated and rearranged several times over the centuries. Many of the huge stones that ringed the center were brought here from great distances, but it is not certain by what ancient form of transportation they were moved. The original 80 bluestones (dolerite), which made up the two internal circles, originated in the Preseli mountains, on the Atlantic coast of Wales. The labor involved in quarrying, transporting, and carving these stones is astonishing.

Although some of the mysteries concerning the site have been solved, the reason Stonehenge was built remains unknown. It is fairly certain that it was a religious site, and that worship here involved the cycles of the sun; the alignment of the stones to point to sunrise at midsummer and sunset in midwinter makes this clear. Recent finds have shown Stonehenge not to be an isolated monument, but part of a much larger complex of ceremonial structures.

Drivers will find the monument near the junction of A303 with A344. Organized excursions are available from Bath, and there is a bus service from Salisbury. ⊠*Junction of A303 and A344/A360, near Amesbury* ☎*0870/333–1181, 01722/343834 for information about private access outside regular hrs* ⊕*www.english-heritage.org.uk* ⊠*£6.50* ⊗*Mid-Mar.–May and Sept.–mid-Oct., daily 9:30–6; June–Aug., daily 9–7; mid-Oct.–mid-Mar., daily 9:30–4.*

CAMBRIDGE

With the spires of its university buildings framed by towering trees and expansive meadows, its medieval streets and passages enhanced by gardens and riverbanks, the city of Cambridge is among the loveliest in England. The city predates the Roman occupation of Britain, but there's confusion about when the university was founded. One story attributes its founding to impoverished students from Oxford, who came in search of eels—a cheap source of nourishment.

Cambridge embodies a certain genteel, intellectual, and sometimes anachronistically idealized image of Englishness. The exquisite King's College choir defines the traditional English Christmas, when the Festival of Nine Lessons and Carols is broadcast live on Christmas Eve. Filled with tiny gardens, ancient courtyards, imposing classic buildings, alleyways that lead past medieval churches, and wisteria-hung facades, the city remains an extraordinary center of learning and research where innovation and discovery still happen behind its ancient walls.

Keep in mind that there is no recognizable campus: the scattered colleges *are* the university. Each of the 25 oldest colleges is built around a series of courts, or quadrangles, whose velvety lawns are the envy of many a gardener. Since students and fellows (faculty) live and work in these courts, access is restricted. Visitors are not normally allowed into college buildings other than chapels, dining halls, and some libraries; some colleges charge admission for certain buildings. Public visiting hours vary from college to college, and it's best to call, check with the city tourist office or consult the university's Web site, ⊕ *www.cam. ac.uk.*

■ **TIP→ When the colleges are open, the best way to gain access is to join a walking tour led by an official Blue Badge guide—many areas are off-limits unless you do.** The two-hour tours (£9–£10) leave up to four times daily from the city tourist office.

Perhaps the best views are from the Backs, the green parkland that extends along the River Cam behind several colleges. This broad, sweeping openness, a result of the larger size of the colleges and from the lack of industrialization in the city center, is just what distinguishes Cambridge from Oxford. The other traditional view of the colleges is gained from a punt—the boats propelled by pole on the River Cam.

PLANNING YOUR TIME

Colleges close to visitors during the main exam time, late May to mid-June. Term time (when classes are in session) means roughly October to December, January to March, and April to June. During the summer vacation (July to September) and over the Easter and Christmas holidays, Cambridge is devoid of students, its heart and soul. Summer, however, is enlivened by festivals, notably the Strawberry Fair (June) and the Folk Festival and Arts Festival (both July). The May Bumps, intercollegiate boat races, are, confusingly, held the first week of June in Cambridge.

GETTING HERE & AROUND

Good bus (2 hours) and train (1 to 1½ hours) services connect London and Cambridge. The train station is a mile or so southeast of the center and is connected by city bus service 3 to Emmanuel Street, which is just around the corner from the long-distance bus terminus on Drummer Street. If you're driving, don't attempt to venture very far into the center—parking is scarce and pricey. The center is amenable to explorations on foot, or you could join the throng by renting a bicycle.

Stagecoach sells Dayrider (£3) tickets for all-day bus travel within Cambridge, and Megarider tickets (£10) for seven days of travel within the city.

TOURS

City Sightseeing operates open-top bus tours of Cambridge (£10), which can be joined at marked bus stops in the city. Also ask the tourist office about walking tours.

ESSENTIALS

Bus Contacts First (☎ *0845/602–0121* ⊕ *www.firstgroup.com*). **Stagecoach** (☎ *01223/423578* ⊕ *www.stagecoachbus.com/cambridge*).

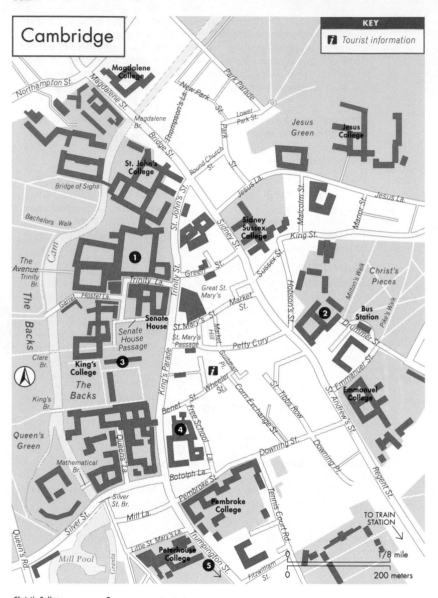

Cambridge

Magdalene College

Northampton St.

Magdalene St.

Magdalene Br.

Bridge St.

Thompson's La.

New Park St.

Park Parade

Lower Park St.

Park St.

Jesus Green

Jesus College

St. John's College

Round Church St.

Jesus La.

Jesus La.

Bridge of Sighs

St. John's St.

Sidney St.

Jesus La.

Malcolm St.

Manor St.

Bachelors Walk

Sidney Sussex College

King St.

The Avenue

Trinity Br.

The Cam

①

Trinity La.

Trinity St.

Green St.

Sussex St.

Hobson's St.

Christ's Pieces

Milton's Walk

Pike's Walk

The Backs

Garret Hostel La.

Great St. Mary's

Market St.

②

Bus Station

Drummer St.

Clare Br.

Senate House Passage

Senate House

St. Mary's St.

Market Hill

St. Mary's Passage

Petty Cury

Market St.

Emmanuel St.

King's Br.

King's College

③

King's Parade

Guildhall Pl.

ℹ

Wheeler St.

St. Tibbs Row

Corn Exchange St.

St. Andrew's St.

Emmanuel College

Queen's Green

The Backs

Queen's La.

Benet St.

Free School La.

④

Downing St.

Downing Pl.

Regent St.

Mathematical Br.

Silver St. Br.

Botolph La.

Pembroke St.

Tennis Court Rd.

Silver St.

Mill La.

Pembroke College

Queen's Rd.

Little St. Mary's La.

Trumpington St.

Peterhouse College

⑤

Fitzwilliam St.

TO TRAIN STATION

Mill Pool

Granta

0 — 1/8 mile
0 — 200 meters

Visitor & Tour Information Cambridge (⊠ Wheeler St. 📞 0871/226–8006, 44/1223464732 from abroad ⊕ www.visitcambridge.org). **Cambridge University** (⊕ www.cam.ac.uk).**City Sightseeing** (⊠ Cambridge train station 📞 01708/866000 ⊕ www.city-sightseeing.com).

EXPLORING CAMBRIDGE

② Christ's College. To see the way a college has grown over the centuries you could not do better than visit here. The main gateway bears the enormous coat of arms of its patroness, Lady Margaret Beaufort, mother of Henry VII, who established the institution in 1505. It leads into a fine courtyard, with the chapel framed by an ancient magnolia. In the dining hall hang portraits of John Milton and Charles Darwin, two of the college's more famous students. You next walk past a fellows' building credited to Inigo Jones, to the spacious garden (once the haunt of Milton), and finally to a modern zigguratlike confection. ⊠ St. Andrew's St. 📞 01223/334900 ⊕ www.christs.cam.ac.uk ☻ Term time, except exam period, daily 9:30–dusk; out of term, daily 9:30–noon.

④ Corpus Christi College. If you visit only one quadrangle, make it the beautiful, serene, 14th-century Old Court here. Founded in 1352, it's the longest continuously inhabited college quadrangle in Cambridge. ⊠ King's Parade 📞 01223/338000 ⊕ www.corpus.cam.ac.uk ☝ Free ☻ Daily dawn–dusk.

⑤ Fitzwilliam Museum. In a Classical Revival building renowned for its grand Corinthian portico, the Fitzwilliam, founded by the seventh viscount Fitzwilliam of Merrion in 1816, has one of Britain's most outstanding collections of art and antiquities. Highlights also include two large Titians, an extensive collection of French Impressionist painting, and many paintings by Matisse and Picasso. The opulent interior displays its treasures to marvelous effect, from Egyptian pieces such as inch-high figurines and painted coffins to sculptures from the Chinese Han dynasty of the 3rd century BC. ⊠ Trumpington St. 📞 01223/332900 ⊕ www. fitzmuseum.cam.ac.uk ☝ Free ☻ Tues.–Sat. 10–5, Sun. noon–5.

③ King's College Chapel. Based on Sainte Chapelle, the 13th-century royal chapel in Paris, this house of worship is the final, perhaps most glorious flowering of Perpendicular Gothic in Britain. Henry VI, the king after whom the college is named, oversaw the work. This was the last period before the classical architecture of the ancient Greeks and Romans, then being rediscovered by the Italians, began to make its influence felt in northern Europe. From the outside, the most prominent features are the expanses of glass, the massive flying buttresses, and the fingerlike spires that line the length of the building. Inside,

Fodor's Choice ★

WORD OF MOUTH
"King's College Chapel in Cambridge is amazing, beautifully ornate. It's all you get to see besides the quad, but the chapel's worth it. Another Cambridge college well worth a visit is Trinity—it has a nice central fountain and central quad, and a pleasant chapel. Christopher Wren's library is a highlight."   –bachslunch

7

384 < **Great Britain**

the most obvious impression is of great space—the chapel has been described as "the noblest barn in Europe"—and of light flooding in from its huge windows. Behind the altar is *The Adoration of the Magi*, an enormous painting by Peter Paul Rubens. Every Christmas Eve a festival of carols sung by the chapel's famous choir is broadcast worldwide from here. ⊠ *King's Parade* ☎ *01223/331155* ⊕ *www.kings.cam.ac.uk* 🎫 *£5, includes college and grounds* ⊙ *Term-time, weekdays 9:30–3:30, Sat. 9:30–3:15, Sun. 1:15–2:30; out of term, Mon.–Sat. 9:30–4:30, Sun. 10–5; hrs vary, so call ahead.*

❶ **Trinity College.** Founded in 1546 by Henry VIII, Trinity replaced a 14th-century educational foundation and is the largest college in either Cambridge or Oxford, with nearly 700 undergraduates. Many of the buildings match its size, not least its 17th-century "great court." Here the massive gatehouse holds "Great Tom," a giant clock that strikes each hour with high and low notes. The college's greatest masterpiece is Christopher Wren's **library**, colonnaded and seemingly constructed with as much light as stone. Alongside the books, you can also see A. A. Milne's handwritten manuscript of *The House at Pooh Corner*. ⊠ *St. John's St.* ☎ *01223/338400* ⊕ *www.trin.cam.ac.uk* 🎫 *£2.20, free Oct.–mid-Mar.* ⊙ *College mid-Mar.–Oct., daily 10–5, except exam period; library weekdays noon–2, Sat. in term time 10:30–12:30; hall and chapel hrs vary.*

WHERE TO EAT

£££££ ✕ **Midsummer House.** An elegant restaurant beside the River Cam on the edge of Midsummer Common, the gray-brick Midsummer House has a comfortable conservatory and a handful of tables in a lush secluded garden under fruit trees. Fixed-price menus for lunch and dinner offer innovative French and Mediterranean dishes. Choices might include braised turbot, smoked eel salad, or grilled pigeon. ⊠ *Midsummer Common* ☎ *01223/369299* 🕭 *Reservations essential* ▤ *AE, MC, V* ⊙ *Closed Sun. and Mon. No lunch Tues.*

££ ✕ **River Bar & Kitchen.** Fashionable and stylish, this waterfront eatery designed by Terence Conran focuses on contemporary food with the occasional Eastern influence, such as spicy lamb samosas with mint and cucumber dip and Moroccan tagine. Light lunches are served between noon and 3 and cocktails are the flavor of the evening. Dinner service begins at 6:30. ⊠ *Quayside, off Bridge St.* ☎ *01223/307030* 🕭 *Reservations essential* ▤ *AE, MC, V* ⊙ *Closed Mon. No dinner Sun.*

£££ ✕ **Three Horseshoes.** This early-19th-century pub-restaurant in a thatched ★ cottage has an elegant dining space in the conservatory, and more informal tables in the airy bar area. The tempting, beautifully presented, and carefully sourced dishes are modern Italian with a British slant. Appetizers include risotto with slow-cooked beef shin, while among the main courses is grilled scallops and monkfish. The bar menu of two- and three-course meals (£12 to £17) is an especially good value. It's 5 mi west of Cambridge, about a 10-minute taxi ride. ⊠ *High St., Madingley* ☎ *01954/210221* ▤ *MC, V.*

WHERE TO STAY

£   ⊡**Cityroomz.** A good budget option, this low-key hostelry outside the train station has small bedrooms with wood floors, white walls, and futon beds. Most double rooms have bunk beds. The sparsely furnished spaces are for those who want a cheap, clean place to sleep. **Pros:** tidy and clean, handy for train station. **Cons:** minuscule rooms, can be noisy. ✉*Station Rd.* ☎*01223/304050* ⊕*www.cityroomz.com* ⇆*25 rooms* ♿*In-room: no a/c, no phone. In-hotel: parking (no fee), no-smoking rooms, no elevator* ⊟*MC, V* ⦿*CP.*

££–£££   ⊡**De Vere University Arms Hotel.** The 19th-century De Vere is well placed in the city center, with comfortable, traditionally furnished guest rooms. Many rooms have views of Parker's Piece, the green backing the hotel, although you pay slightly more for these; Parker's Bar also overlooks the green. The lounge serves afternoon tea by the fireplace. Guests can use a nearby swimming pool and a health club 2 mi away. **Pros:** friendly staff, good location, tasty food. **Cons:** small rooms, faded decor. ✉*Regent St.* ☎*01223/351241* ⊕*www.devere-hotels.com* ⇆*117 rooms, 2 suites* ♿*In-room: safe, Ethernet. In-hotel: restaurant, room service, bars, public Wi-Fi, parking (fee), some pets allowed (fee)* ⊟*AE, DC, MC, V.*

££–£££   ⊡**Regent Hotel.** A rare smaller hotel in Cambridge's city center, this handsome Georgian town house looks across Parker's Piece, a tree-lined park, through wooden sash windows. The cozy licensed bar has an open fire; bedrooms are a little more anonymous but are decorated in pale modern tones and all have bathtubs. **Pros:** good view from top rooms, close to bars and restaurants. **Cons:** no parking, a tad scruffy, disappointing breakfasts. ✉*41 Regent St.* ☎*01223/351470* ⊕*www. regenthotel.co.uk* ⇆*22 rooms* ♿*In-room: Wi-Fi. In-hotel: lounge, bar, no-smoking rooms* ⊟*AE, DC, MC, V.*

EDINBURGH

Although Scotland and England have been united in a single kingdom since 1603, Scotland retains its own marked political and social character, with separate legal and educational systems quite distinct from those of England and, since 1999, a Parliament of its own. The nation's proud capital is one of the world's stateliest cities, and is built—like Rome—on seven hills. Its spectacular buildings, with Doric, Ionic, and Corinthian pillars, add touches of neoclassical grandeur to the largely Presbyterian backdrop. Named UNESCO's first City of Literature, Edinburgh is known worldwide for its International Festival, which attracts lovers of all the arts in August and September.

Take time to explore the streets—peopled by the spirits of Mary, Queen of Scots, Sir Walter Scott, and Robert Louis Stevenson—and pay your respects to the world's best-loved terrier, Greyfriars Bobby. In the evening you can enjoy a pub or a folk *ceilidh* (a traditional Scottish dance with music [pronounced *kay*-lee]), though you should remember that you haven't earned your porridge until you've climbed Arthur's Seat.

PLANNING YOUR TIME

If you have just two days here, don't miss the four key sights of Edinburgh Castle, the Palace of Holyroodhouse, the National Museum of Scotland, and the National Gallery of Scotland for the quintessential Edinburgh experience. But for those who have more time, make sure you see both halves of the city, the Old Town and the New Town. You need a good part of a day to weave through the Old Town and down the Royal Mile, the city's historic thoroughfare. Beyond Princes Street, the spacious New Town also needs a day.

GETTING HERE AND AROUND

BY AIR

Edinburgh Airport, 7 mi west of the city center, offers only a few transatlantic flights. It does, however, have air connections to London's Gatwick and Heathrow airports and other UK and European destinations. Glasgow Airport, 50 mi west of Edinburgh, serves as the major point of entry into Scotland for transatlantic flights.

The airport is connected by the Airport bus link to Waverley Station via Haymarket; the trip takes 25-50 minutes. A single-fare tickets cost £3, a return £5. Taxis are readily available outside the terminal. The trip takes 25 to 35 minutes to the city center. The fare is roughly £20.

BY BUS

Megabus (book online) and National Express provides bus service to and from London and other major towns and cities. The main terminal, St. Andrew Square bus station, is a couple of minutes (on foot) north of Waverley station. Long-distance coaches must be booked in advance. Edinburgh is approximately ten hours by bus from London.

Lothian Buses is the main operator within Edinburgh. You can buy tickets on the bus. The Day Ticket (£2.50), allowing unlimited one-day travel on the city's buses.

BY CAR

Metered parking in the city center is scarce and expensive, and the local traffic wardens are a feisty bunch. Illegally parked cars are routinely towed away, and getting your car back will be expensive. After 6 PM the parking situation improves considerably.

BY TAXI

The following taxi stands are the most convenient: the west end of Princes Street; South St. David Street, and North St. Andrew Street (both just off St. Andrew Square); Princes Mall; Waterloo Place; and Lauriston Place. Alternatively, hail any taxi displaying an illuminated FOR HIRE sign.

BY TRAIN

Edinburgh's main train hub is Waverley Station. Travel time from Edinburgh to London by train is as little as 4½ hours for the fastest service. Edinburgh's other main station is Haymarket, about four minutes (by rail) beyond the west end of Princes Street. All Glasgow and other western and northern services stop here.

TOURS

City Sightseeing and the vintage bus MacTours are both open-top tours and cost £9 including multilingual commentary. All tours take you to the main attractions. Tickets are sold on board and, departing from Waverley Bridge, the tours are hop on/hop off services.

ESSENTIALS

Air Contacts Edinburgh Airport (☎ *0870/040-0007* ⊕ *www.baa.com*). **Glasgow Airport** (☎ *0870/040-0008* ⊕ *www.baa.com*).

Bus Contacts Lothian Buses (⊠ *Waverley Bridge, Old Town* ☎ *0131/555-6363* ⊕ *www.lothianbuses.co.uk*). **Megabus** (⊕ *www.megabus.com*). **National Express** (☎ *08705/808080* ⊕ *www.nationalexpress.co.uk*).

Tour Contacts Lothian Buses (☎ *0131/555-6363* ⊕ *www.edinburghtour.com*).

Train Contacts First ScotRail (☎ *0845/601-5929* ⊕ *www.firstgroup.com/scotrail*). **National Rail Enquiries** (☎ *08457/495051* ⊕ *www.nationalrail.co.uk*).

Visitor Information Edinburgh and Scotland Information Centre (⊠ *3 Princes St., East End* ☎ *0845/225-511* ⊕ *www.edinburgh.org*).

EXPLORING EDINBURGH

The key to understanding Edinburgh is to make the distinction between the Old and New Towns. Until the 18th century the city was confined to the rocky crag on which its castle stands, straggling between the fortress at one end and the royal residence, the Palace of Holyroodhouse, at the other. In the 18th century, during a time of expansion known as the Scottish Enlightenment, the city fathers fostered the construction of another Edinburgh, one a little to the north, the elegant New Town. Apart from the Old and New Towns in central Edinburgh, some outlying neighborhoods are also worth a visit. Leith, Edinburgh's port, throbs with chic bars and restaurants, while Dean Village is home to the Scottish National Gallery of Modern Art. ■**TIP**➔ **Don't forget that some attractions have special hours during the Edinburgh International Festival: check the hours ahead of time.**

OLD TOWN

East of Edinburgh Castle, the historic castle esplanade becomes the street known as the Royal Mile. It leads from the castle down through Old Town to the Palace of Holyroodhouse and is made up of one thoroughfare that bears, in consecutive sequence, different names—Castlehill, Lawnmarket, Parliament Square, High Street, and Canongate. Before the 18th century expansions to the south and north, everybody lived here; the richer folk on the lower floors of houses, with less well-to-do families on the middle floors—the higher up, the poorer. Time and progress (of a sort) have swept away some of the narrow closes and tall tenements of the Old Town, but enough survive for you to be able to imagine the original profile of Scotland's capital.

❶ Edinburgh Castle. The crowning glory of the Scottish capital also has
ⓒ breathtaking views of the city and beyond from its battlements: allow
Fodor'sChoice at least three hours here to do the site justice. You enter across the
★ **Esplanade,** the huge forecourt built in the 18th century as a parade
ground that comes alive with color and music each August when it's
used for the Military Tattoo, a festival of magnificently outfitted marching bands and regiments. Heading over the drawbridge and through
the gatehouse, past the guards, you can find the rough stone walls of
the **Half-Moon Battery,** where the one-o'clock gun is fired every day in
an impressively anachronistic ceremony; these curving ramparts give
Edinburgh Castle its distinctive appearance from miles away. Climb
up through a second gateway and you come to the oldest surviving
building in the complex, the tiny 11th-century **St. Margaret's Chapel,**
named in honor of Saxon queen Margaret (1046–93), wife of King Malcolm III (circa 1031–93). The **Crown Room** contains the "Honours of
Scotland"—the crown, scepter, and sword that once graced the Scottish
monarch. Upon the **Stone of Scone,** also in the Crown Room, Scottish
monarchs once sat to be crowned. In the section now called **Queen
Mary's Apartments,** Mary, Queen of Scots, gave birth to James VI of
Scotland. The **Great Hall** displays arms and armor under an impressive vaulted, beamed ceiling. Military features of interest include the
Scottish National War Memorial, the **Scottish United Services Museum,**
and the famous 15th-century Belgian-made cannon *Mons Meg.* ⊠ *Off
Castle Esplanade and Castlehill, Old Town* ☎ *0131/225–9846 Edinburgh Castle, 0131/226–7393 War Memorial* ⊕ *www.edinburghcastle.
gov.uk* 🎟 *£10* ⊙ *Apr.–Oct., daily 9:30–6; Nov.–Mar., daily 9:30–5; last
entry 45 min before closing.*

❸ High Street (Royal Mile). Some of Old Town's most impressive buildings
and sights are on High Street, one of the five streets making up the
Royal Mile. Parliament House was the seat of Scottish government until
1707, when the governments of Scotland and England were united; it
now houses the Supreme Law Courts of Scotland. The High Kirk of St.
Giles dominates Parliament Square. There has been a church here since
AD 854, although most of the present structure dates from either 1120
or 1829, when the church was restored. The most elaborate feature is
the **Chapel of the Order of the Thistle,** built onto the southeast corner
of the church in 1911 for the exclusive use of Scotland's only chivalric
order, the Most Ancient and Noble Order of the Thistle.

Just outside Parliament House is the **Mercat Cross** (*mercat* means "market"), a great landmark of Old Town life. It was an old mercantile
center, where in the early days executions were held, and where royal
proclamations were read. Across High Street from the High Kirk of St.
Giles stands the **City Chambers,** now the seat of local government. Note
how the building drops 11 stories to Cockburn Street on its north side.
⊠ *Between Lawnmarket and Canongate, Old Town.*

❺ Kirk of the Greyfriars. Greyfriars Church, built circa 1620 on the site of
a medieval monastery, was where the National Covenant, declaring
that the Presbyterian Church in Scotland was independent of the monarch, was signed in 1638. The covenant plunged Scotland into decades

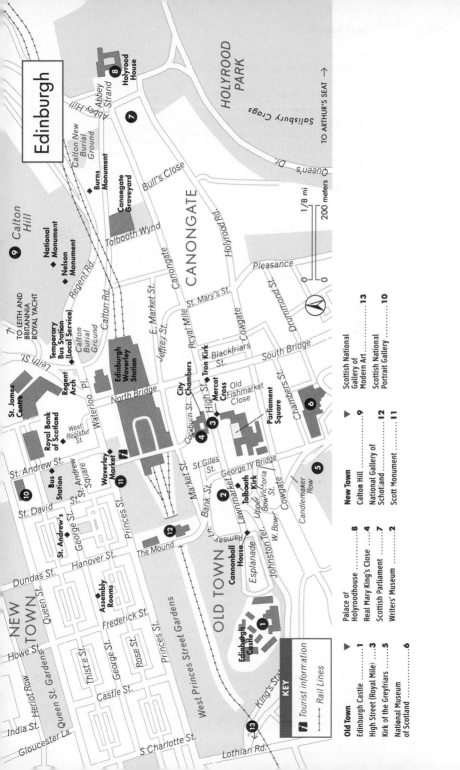

Edinburgh

Calton Hill 9

Calton Hill 9

National Monument ◆

Nelson Monument ◆

HOLYROOD PARK

Salisbury Crags

TO ARTHUR'S SEAT →

Queen's Dr.

Holyrood House 8

Abbey Strand

Abbey Hill

Calton New Burial Ground

Burns Monument

Canongate Graveyard

Bull's Close

CANONGATE

Tolbooth Wynd

Holyrood Rd.

Pleasance

Canongate

Royal Mile

St. Mary's St.

Cowgate

Drummond St.

1/8 mi

200 meters

TO LEITH AND BRITANNIA ROYAL YACHT ↗

Leith St.

St. James Centre

Royal Bank of Scotland

Temporary Bus Station (Local Service)

Regent Arch

Regent Rd.

Calton Rd.

Calton Burial Ground

West Register St.

Waterloo Pl.

North Bridge

Edinburgh Waverley Station

E. Market St.

Jeffrey St.

High St.

Tron Kirk

Mercat Cross

Blackfriars St.

South Bridge

Chambers St.

Cowgate

St. Andrew St.

Bus Station

St. Andrew Square

St. David's

St. Andrew's

Hanover St.

Waverley Market

City Chambers

Cockburn St.

Market St.

Bank St.

St. Giles St.

George IV Bridge

Old Fishmarket Close

Parliament Square

Candlemaker Row

6

5

St. James Centre

10

11

i

Assembly Rooms

The Mound

Lawnmarket

Tolbooth Kirk

Upper Bow

Victoria St.

W. Bow

Cowgate

NEW TOWN

Howe St.

Dundas St.

Queen St.

Queen St. Gardens

Frederick St.

Hanover St.

George St.

Thistle St.

Rose St.

Princes St.

West Princes Street Gardens

Heriot Row

India St.

Gloucester La.

Castle St.

S Charlotte St.

Lothian Rd.

King's Sta.

OLD TOWN

Edinburgh Castle 1

Esplanade

Cannonball House

Ramsay Ln.

Johnston Ter.

13

2

12

3

4

Scottish National Gallery of Modern Art 13

Scottish National Portrait Gallery 10

KEY

i Tourist Information

◀◀◀ Rail Lines

Old Town

Edinburgh Castle **1**
High Street (Royal Mile) **3**
Kirk of the Greyfriars **5**
National Museum
of Scotland **6**
Palace of
Holyroodhouse **8**
Real Mary King's Close **4**
Scottish Parliament **7**
Writers' Museum **2**

New Town

Calton Hill **9**
National Gallery of
Scotland **12**
Scott Monument **11**
Scottish National
Gallery of
Modern Art **13**
Scottish National
Portrait Gallery **10**

of civil war. Informative panels tell the story, and there's a visitor center on-site. Be sure to search out the graveyard—one of the most evocative in Europe. Nearby, at the corner of George IV Bridge and Candlemaker Row, stands one of the most-photographed sites in Scotland, the Greyfriars Bobby statue. ⌧ *Greyfriars Pl., Old Town* ☎ *0131/225–1900* ⊕ *www.grey friarskirk.com* ⌧ *Free* ⊙ *Easter– Oct., weekdays 10:30–4:30, Sat. 10:30–2:30; Nov.–Easter, Thurs. 1:30–3:30.*

> ### SAVE ON SIGHTS
>
> The money-saving **Edinburgh Pass** (☎ *0131/473-3600* ⊕ *www.edinburghpass.org*) gives you city bus transport (including a return ticket on the airport bus), access to more than 30 attractions, and other exclusive offers. A one-day pass costs £24; two-day pass £36, and three-day pass £48. Passes are available from the tourist information centers in Princes Street, at Edinburgh Airport, or online.

❻ ★ ♻ National Museum of Scotland. In an imposing Victorian building on Chambers Street, the National Museum houses an internationally renowned collection of art and artifacts relating to natural, scientific, and industrial history. Its treasures include the Lewis Chessmen, 11 intricately carved ivory chessmen found on one of the Western Isles in the 19th century. The museum's main hall, with its soaring roof and birdcage design, is architecturally interesting in its own right. The striking, contemporary annex exhibits playful models, complex reconstructions, and paraphernalia ranging from ancient Pictish articles to 21st-century cultural artifacts. ⌧ *Chambers St., Old Town* ☎ *0131/225-7534* ⊕ *www.nms.ac.uk* ⌧ *Free* ⊙ *Daily 10–5.*

❽ ★ Palace of Holyroodhouse. Once the setting for high drama—including at least one notorious murder, several major fires, and centuries of the colorful lifestyles of larger-than-life, power-hungry personalities—this is now Queen Elizabeth's official residence in Scotland. When the queen or royal family is not in residence, you can take a guided tour. Many monarchs, including Charles II, Queen Victoria, and George V, have left their mark on its rooms, but it's Mary, Queen of Scots, whose spirit looms largest. For some visitors the most memorable room here is the little chamber in which David Rizzio (1533–66), secretary to Mary, Queen of Scots, met an unhappy end in 1566. Mary's second husband, Lord Darnley (Henry Stewart, 1545–65), burst into the queen's rooms with his henchmen, dragged Rizzio into an antechamber, and stabbed him more than 50 times; a bronze plaque marks the spot. Darnley himself was murdered the next year to make way for the queen's marriage to her lover, Bothwell.

The **King James Tower** is the oldest surviving section, containing the rooms of Mary, Queen of Scots, on the 2nd floor, and Lord Darnley's rooms below. Though much has been altered, there are fine fireplaces, paneling, plasterwork, tapestries, and 18th- and 19th-century furnishings throughout. At the south end of the palace front you can find the **Royal Dining Room,** and along the south side are the **Throne Room** and other drawing rooms now used for social and ceremonial occasions.

At the back of the palace is the **King's Bedchamber.** The 150-foot-long **Great Picture Gallery,** on the north side, displays the portraits of 110 Scottish monarchs. The **Queen's Gallery** holds rotating exhibits from the Royal Collection.

Holyroodhouse has its origins in an Augustinian monastery founded by David I (1084–1153) in 1128. In the 15th and 16th centuries, Scottish royalty, preferring the comforts of the abbey to the drafty rooms of Edinburgh Castle, settled into Holyroodhouse, expanding and altering the buildings until the palace eventually eclipsed the monastery. In 1660 Holyrood was rebuilt in the architectural style of Louis XIV (1638–1715), and this is the style you see today. Looming over the palace are Arthur's Seat and the Salisbury Crags. To reach the tops of these, follow Queen's Drive around the park until you're at the back of the hill where you'll find Dunsapie Loch. There's a the paved stairway which will take you up to the best views in the city. ⊠ *Abbey Strand, Holyrood, Old Town* ☎ *0131/556–1096* 🖷 *0131/557–5256* ⊕ *www. royal.gov.uk* ✍ *£9.80;* £13 including the Queen's Gallery ⊙ *Apr.–Oct., daily 9:30–6; Nov.–Mar., daily 9:30–4:30; last admission 1 hr before closing. Closed during royal visits.*

❹ Real Mary King's Close. Hidden beneath the City Chambers, this narrow, cobbled *close,* or lane, named after a former landowner, is said to be one of Edinburgh's most haunted sites. In 1645 victims of the bubonic plague were quarantined here. After the plague passed, the bodies were removed and buried, and the street was reopened. A few people returned, but they soon reported ghostly goings-on and departed, leaving the close empty for decades. In 1753 city authorities again sealed it off and built the Royal Exchange (later the City Chambers) directly over the close. Today you can walk among the remains of the close's shops and houses. ■ TIP➡ **Although kids like the spookiness of this attraction, it's not for the youngest ones. In fact, children under 5 are not admitted.** ⊠ *Writers' Court, Old Town* ☎ *0870/243–0160* ⊕ *www.realmarykings close.com* ✍ *£10* ⊙ *Apr.–July, Sept., and Oct., daily 10–9; Aug., daily 9–9; Nov.–Mar., daily 10–4.*

❼ Scottish Parliament. Scotland's somewhat controversial Parliament building, completed in 2004, is dramatically modern, with irregular curves and angles that mirror the twisting shapes of the surrounding landscape. The structure's artistry is most apparent when you step inside, where the gentle slopes, oak, polished concrete and granite, walls of glass, and water features create an understated magnificence appropriate to the modest but proud Scots. It's worth taking the 45-minute tour (book in advance) to see some key areas. ⊠ *Horse Wynd, Old Town* ☎ *0131/348–5200* ⊕ *www.scottish.parliament.uk* ✍ *Free; £5.85 for tour* ⊙ *Tours Nov.–Mar., daily 10–4; Apr.–Oct., daily 10–6; no tours when Parliament is sitting, generally Tues.–Thurs.*

❷ Writers' Museum. Down a close off Lawnmarket is Lady Stair's House, built in 1622 and a good example of 17th-century urban architecture. Inside, the Writer's Museum evokes Scotland's literary past with such exhibits as the letters, possessions, and original manuscripts of

Sir Walter Scott, Robert Louis Stevenson, and Robert Burns. ⊠*Off Lawnmarket, Old Town* ☎*0131/529–4901* ⊕*www.cac.org.uk* ⊠*Free* ⊘*Mon.–Sat. 10–5, last admission 4:45, Sun. during festival noon–5.*

NEW TOWN

It was not until the Scottish Enlightenment, a civilizing time of expansion in the 1700s, that the city fathers decided to break away from the Royal Mile's rocky slope and create a new Edinburgh below the castle, a little to the north. This was to become the New Town, with elegant squares, classical facades, wide streets, and harmonious proportions. The plan of architect James Craig (1744–95) called for a grid of three main east–west streets, balanced at either end by two grand squares. These streets survive today, though some of the buildings that line them have been altered by later development.

Save time by riding the free galleries bus, which connects the National Gallery of Scotland, Scottish National Portrait Gallery, Scottish National Gallery of Modern Art, and Dean Gallery daily from 11 to 5. You can board or leave the bus at any of the galleries.

OFF THE BEATEN PATH

Britannia. Moored on the waterfront at Leith, Edinburgh's port north of the city center, is the former Royal Yacht *Britannia,* launched in Scotland in 1953 and now retired to her home country. The Royal Apartments and the more functional engine room, bridge, galleys, and captain's cabin are all open to view. The land-based visitor center within the huge Ocean Terminal shopping mall has exhibits and photographs about the yacht's history. ⊠*Ocean Terminal, Leith* ☎*0131/555–5566* ⊕*www. royalyachtbritannia.co.uk* ⊠*£9.50* ⊘*Mar.–Oct., daily 9:30–4:30; Nov.–Feb., daily 10–3:30.*

❾ **Calton Hill.** Robert Louis Stevenson's favorite view of his beloved city was from the top of this hill. The architectural styles represented by the extraordinary collection of monuments here include mock Gothic—the Old Observatory, for example—and neoclassical. The so-called **National Monument,** with a columned façade, is a never-completed monument for the dead of the Napoleonic Wars. The tallest monument on Calton Hill is the 100-foot-high **Nelson Monument,** completed in 1815 in honor of Britain's naval hero Horatio Nelson (1758–1805); you can climb its 143 steps for sweeping city views. The **Burns Monument** is the circular Corinthian temple below Regent Road. ⊠*Bounded by Leith St. to the west and Regent Rd. to the south, Calton* ☎*0131/556–2716* ⊕*www.cac.org.uk* ⊠*£3 Nelson Monument* ⊘*Nelson Monument Apr.–Sept., Mon. 1–6, Tues.–Sat. 10–6; Oct.–Mar., Mon.–Sat. 10–3.*

⓬ ★ **National Gallery of Scotland.** Opened to the public in 1859, the National Gallery presents a wide selection of paintings from the Renaissance to the postimpressionist period within a grand neoclassical building designed by William Playfair. All the great names are here; works by Velázquez, El Greco, Rembrandt, Goya, Poussin, Turner, Degas, Monet, and Van Gogh, among others, complement a fine collection of Scottish art. The Weston Link connects the National Gallery of Scotland to the **Royal Scottish Academy,** which hosts temporary art exhibitions. It provides expanded gallery space as well as a restaurant, bar, café, information center, and shop. The free galleries bus stops here daily on the hour from 11 to 4. ✉*The Mound, Old Town* ☎*0131/624–6200 general inquiries, 0131/332–2266 recorded information* ⊕*www.nationalgaller ies.org* ✉*Free* ⊘*Fri.–Wed. 10–5, Thurs. 10–7. Print Room, week-days 10–12:30 and 2–4:30 by appointment.*

⓫ **Scott Monument.** What appears to be a Gothic cathedral spire chopped off and planted in the east end of the Princes Street Gardens is the nation's tribute to Sir Walter—a 200-foot-high monument looming over Princes Street. Built in 1844 in honor of Scotland's most famous

> ## LEITH, EDINBURGH'S SEAPORT
>
> Just north of the city, Leith sits on the south shore of the Firth of Forth and was a separate town until it merged with the city in 1920. After World War II and up until the 1980s, the declining seaport had a reputation for poverty and crime. In recent years, however, it has been revitalized with the restoration of commercial buildings as well as the construction of new luxury housing, bringing a buzz of trendiness.

author, Sir Walter Scott, the author of *Ivanhoe, Waverley,* and many other novels and poems, it's centered on a marble statue of Scott and his favorite dog, Maida. In the gardens is the famous **monument to David Livingstone,** whose African meeting with H. M. Stanley is part of Scot-American history. ✉*Princes St., New Town* ☎*0131/529–4068* ⊕*www.cac.org.uk* ✉*£3* ⊘*Apr.–Sept., Mon.–Sat. 9–6, Sun. 10–6; Oct.–Mar., Mon.–Sat. 9–3, Sun. 10–3.*

⓭ **Scottish National Gallery of Modern Art.** This handsome former school building on Belford Road, close to the New Town, displays paintings and sculpture, including works by Pablo Picasso, Georges Braque, Henri Matisse, and André Derain. The gallery also has an excellent restaurant in the basement. The free galleries bus stops here on the half hour. Across the street is the **Dean Gallery,** also part of the National Galleries of Scotland. It showcases modern art and changing exhibitions. ✉*Belford Rd., Dean Village* ☎*0131/556–8921* ⊕*www.nationalgalleries.org* ✉*Free* ⊘*Daily 10–5; extended hrs during festival.*

⓾ **Scottish National Portrait Gallery.** A magnificent red-sandstone Gothic building dating from 1889 on Queen Street houses this must-visit institution. The gallery contains a superb Thomas Gainsborough painting and portraits by the Scottish artists Allan Ramsay (1713–84) and Sir Henry Raeburn (1756–1823), among many others. You can see portraits of classic literary figures such as Robert Burns and Sir Walter Scott, and modern portraits depict actors, sports stars, and living members of the royal family. The free galleries bus stops here every day from 11:15 to 4:15. ✉*1 Queen St., New Town* ☎*0131/624–6200* ⊕*www. nationalgalleries.org* ✉*Free; charge for special exhibitions* ⊘*Fri.–Wed. 10–5, Thurs. 10–7; extended hrs during festival.*

WHERE TO EAT

££ ✕**David Bann.** In the heart of the Old Town, this ultrahip vegetarian and
★ vegan favorite attracts young locals with its light, airy, modern dining
room and creative menu. Tap water comes with mint and strawberries;
dishes are sizable and extremely colorful. The food is so flavorful that
carnivores may forget they're eating vegetarian. Try the spinach and
smoked cheese strudel and the malt-whisky pannacotta. ✉ *56–58 St.
Mary's St., Old Town* ☎ *0131/556–5888* ☰ *AE, DC, MC, V.*

££ ✕**Doric Tavern.** Beyond the bar's grand entrance staircase is a languid
bistro environment enhanced by the stripped wood floor, plain wood
tables, and color scheme in subdued orange and terra-cotta. The menu
lists a selection of fresh fish, meat, and vegetarian dishes, plus a daily
special such as honey-baked salmon with oatcakes. Prix-fixe lunch (£10)
and dinner (£18) are an excellent value. ✉ *15/16 Market St., Old Town*
☎ *0131/225–1084* ⚐ *Reservations essential* ☰ *AE, MC, V.*

£ ✕**Henderson's.** This was Edinburgh's original vegetarian restaurant long
before it was fashionable to serve healthful, meatless creations. The
salad bar has more than a dozen different salads each day, and a massive plateful costs less than £7. The £10 fixed-price dinner is a great
value. Tasty hot options include Moroccan stew with couscous and
moussaka. Live mellow music plays six nights a week (seven during
the festival). Around the corner on Thistle Street is the Bistro, from
the same proprietors; it serves snacks, meals, and decadent desserts
such as chocolate fondue. There's also an impressive organic wine list.
✉ *94 Hanover St., New Town* ☎ *0131/225–2605* ☰ *AE, DC, MC, V*
☾ *Closed Sun. except during festival.*

££ ✕**La Rusticana.** Hanover Street exists to delight lovers of Italian food;
some of the best pasta and pizza restaurants compete here, but this one
usually wins the day. Stronger on pasta than pizza, La Rusticana remains
a good value, only marginally above average in price. Along with a sister restaurant in the Old Town, it's a fundamental part of Edinburgh's
food culture, a favorite for business meetings, and a generous patron of
charity events. ✉ *90 Hanover St., New Town* ☎ *0131/225–2227* ✉ *25
Cockburn St., Old Town* ☎ *0131/225–2832* ☰ *AE, DC, MC, V.*

£££££ ✕**Martin Wishart.** Slightly out of town but worth every penny of the taxi
fare, this rising culinary star woos diners with an impeccable and varied
menu of beautifully presented, French-influenced dishes. Terrine of foie
gras, compote of Agen prunes, and sole Murat (glazed fillet of sole with
baby onions, artichoke, parsley, and lemon) with *pommes en cocotte*
(potatoes cooked in a casserole) typify the cuisine. There are prix-fixe
tasting, lunch, and à la carte options. Reservations are essential. ✉ *54
The Shore, Leith* ☎ *0131/553–3557* ☰ *AE, MC, V* ☾ *Closed Sun. and
Mon. No lunch Sat.*

£££ ✕**Skippers Bistro.** This superb seafood restaurant has a traditional, snug,
cluttered interior with dark wood, shining brass, and lots of pictures
and seafaring ephemera. For a starter, try the fragrant Cullen skink.
Main dishes change daily but might include Finnan haddie, halibut,
salmon, or monkfish in delicious sauces. Reservations are essential on
weekends. ✉ *1A Dock Pl., Leith* ☎ *0131/554–1018* ☰ *AE, MC, V.*

££££
Fodor's Choice
★
✕**Witchery by the Castle.** The hundreds of "witches" who were executed on Castlehill, just yards from where you'll be seated, are the inspiration for this outstanding and atmospheric restaurant. The cavernous interior, complete with flickering candlelight, is festooned with cabalistic insignia and tarot-card characters. Gilded and painted ceilings reflect the close links between France and Scotland, as does the menu, which includes roasted quail with braised endive and scallops with spiced pork belly and carrot puree. Pre- and post-theater two-course specials are excellent value. (The restaurant also offers lodging in seven sumptuous suites.) ⊠ *Castlehill, Royal Mile, Old Town* ☎ *0131/225–5613* ⊟ *AE, DC, MC, V.*

WHERE TO STAY

Rooms are harder to find in August and September, when the festivals take place, so reserve at least three months in advance.

£££££
Fodor's Choice
★
⊡**Balmoral Hotel.** The attention to detail in the elegant rooms—colors were picked to echo the country's heathers and moors—and the sheer élan that has re-created the Edwardian splendor of this grand, former railroad hotel make staying at the Balmoral a special introduction to Edinburgh. Here, below the landmark clock tower marking the east end of Princes Street, the lively buzz makes you feel as if you're at the center of city life. The hotel's main restaurant is the plush and stylish Number One, serving excellent Scottish seafood and game. If you overindulge, recuperate at the luxurious spa. **Pros:** big and beautiful building, top-hatted doorman, lovely touches in the rooms. **Cons:** pool is small, spa books up fast, the restaurants can be very busy. ⊠ *1 Princes St., New Town* ☎ *0131/556–2414* ⊕ *www.thebalmoralhotel.com* ⇦ *188 rooms, 20 suites* ♿ *In-room: Ethernet. In-hotel: 2 restaurants, bar, pool, gym, spa, public Internet, parking (fee)* ⊟ *AE, DC, MC, V* ⦿ *BP*

££££
⊡**The Bonham.** This hotel in the elegant West End carries out a successful, sophisticated flirtation with modernity that makes it stand out from its neighbors. Bold colors and contemporary Scottish art set off its late-19th-century architecture and classic furniture. The good-size rooms are typical of an Edinburgh town house but offer peace and quiet without the noise often associated with this type of hotel. **Pros:** thorough yet unobtrusive service, excellent restaurant. **Cons:** not many common areas, can have a business-hotel feel. ⊠ *35 Drumsheugh Gardens, West End* ☎ *0131/226–6050* ⊕ *www.thebonham.com* ⇦ *48 rooms, 3 suites* ♿ *In-room: no a/c, Ethernet. In-hotel: restaurant, parking (no fee)* ⊟ *AE, DC, MC, V* ⦿ *BP.*

£££
⊡**Gerald's Place.** Although he is not a native of the city, Gerald Della-Porta is one of those B&B owners to whom Edinburgh owes so much. Forget the clichés—you really are welcomed into his home and treated like a most welcome guest. The rooms are furnished in classic style, with huge beds, fresh flowers, and original artwork (much of it for sale). A block beyond Queen Street, this lodging has a fairly central location. **Pros:** the advice and thoughtfulness of the owner, spacious rooms. **Cons:** the stairs are difficult to manage, it's an uphill walk to the city center. ⊠ *21B Abercromby Pl.* ☎ *0131/558–7017* ⊕ *www.geraldsplace.com*

7

⤴2 *rooms* ⚷*In-room: no a/c, Wi-Fi. In-hotel: no elevator* ▤*MC, V* ⑂⃝*BP.*

£££ ⌗**Knight Residence.** Ten minutes from the Grassmarket, the Knights is made up of 19 different apartments. You are greeted by a concierge who will show you to your unit, which will be pleasingly furnished and filled with the things you need for a perfect stay, including a washer-dryer and a DVD library. Breakfast can be found in the fridge. **Pros:** comfortable apartments, secure location, kitted out to a high standard. **Cons:** lack of staff won't suit everyone, better for stays of two or more nights. ✉*12 Lauriston St., Old Town* ☎*0131/622–8120* ⊕*www.theknight residence.co.uk* ⤴*19 apartments* ⚷*In-room: no a/c, Wi-Fi. In-hotel: parking (no fee)* ⑂⃝*CP.*

£££££ ⌗**The Scotsman.** This magnificent turn-of-the-20th-century, gray-sandstone building, with a marble staircase and a fascinating history—it was once the headquarters of the *Scotsman* newspaper—now houses a modern, luxurious hotel. Dark wood, earthy colors, tweeds, and contemporary furnishings decorate the rooms and public spaces. North Bridge, the casual-chic brasserie, serves shellfish and grill food, whereas the formal Vermilion concocts beautiful presentations of Scottish-French dishes. **Pros:** gorgeous surroundings, personalized service. **Cons:** no air-conditioning, spa is a bit noisy. ✉*20 N. Bridge, Old Town* ☎*0131/556–5565* ⊕*www.thescotsmanhotel.co.uk* ⤴*56 rooms, 12 suites* ⚷*In-room: no a/c, dial-up, Wi-Fi. In-hotel: 2 restaurants, bar, pool, gym, spa* ▤*AE, DC, MC, V* ⑂⃝*BP.*

££ ⌗**Victorian Town House.** In a leafy crescent, this house once belonged to David Alan Stevenson, cousin of Robert Louis Stevenson. The writer would doubtless be happy to lay his head in this lovingly preserved home away from home. The bright yet calming rooms have beds that are piled with plump duvets. **Pros:** serene surroundings, gracious staff. **Cons:** no parking nearby. ✉*14 Eglinton Terr., Haymarket* ☎*0131/337–7088* ⊕*www.thevictoriantownhouse.co.uk* ⤴*3 rooms* ⚷*In-room: no a/c. In-hotel: no elevator* ▤*No credit cards* ⑂⃝*BP.*

NIGHTLIFE & THE ARTS

The List, a publication available from city-center bookstores and newsstands, has information about all types of events.

THE ARTS
FESTIVALS
The **Edinburgh Festival Fringe** (✉*Edinburgh Festival Fringe Office, 180 High St., Old Town* ☎*0131/226–0026* ⊕*www.edfringe.com*) presents many theatrical, musical and comedy events each August, some by amateur groups (you have been warned), and is more of a grab bag than the official festival. Many events are free, but some do require tickets; prices start at £2 and go up to £15.

Fodor'sChoice The **Edinburgh International Festival** (✉*The Hub, Edinburgh Festi-*
★ *val Centre, Castlehill, Old Town* ☎*0131/473–2009 information, 0131/473–2000 tickets* ⊕*www.eif.co.uk*), the flagship arts event held in August each year, attracts performing artists of international caliber

to a celebration of music, dance, drama, and visual art. Tickets range from £7 to £60, depending on the event; plan well ahead if you want to attend.

★ The **Edinburgh Military Tattoo** (⊠ *Edinburgh Military Tattoo Office, 32 Market St., Old Town* ☎*0131/225–1188 or 08707/555–1188* ⊕*www. edintattoo.co.uk*) may not be art, but it is certainly Scottish culture. This August celebration of martial music and skills with bands, gymnastics, and stunt motorcycle teams is on the castle esplanade. Dress warmly for late-evening performances.

NIGHTLIFE
BARS & PUBS
Café Royal (⊠*17 W. Register St., New Town* ☎*0131/557–4792*), immediately west of Register House, serves good Scottish lagers and ales, and simple lunch items like stovies and, of course, oysters. The 18th-century building has plenty of character.

Cloisters (⊠*26 Brougham St., Tollcross* ☎*0131/221–9997*) prides itself on the absence of modern pub gimmicks; it specializes instead in real ales, malt whiskies, and good food, all at reasonable prices.

Milne's Bar (⊠*35 Hanover St., New Town* ☎*0131/225–6738*) is known as the poets' pub because of its popularity with the Edinburgh literati. Victorian advertisements give the place an old-time feel.

SHOPPING

Despite its renown, **Princes Street** may disappoint some visitors with its average chain stores. One block north of Princes Street, **Rose Street** has many smaller specialty shops. **George Street** shops are fairly upscale, with names such as Jaegar and Penhaligons.

The streets crossing George Street—Hanover, Frederick, and Castle—are also worth exploring. **Dundas Street,** the northern extension of Hanover Street, beyond Queen Street Gardens, has several antiques shops. **Thistle Street** has several boutiques and more antiques shops. **Stockbridge is** an oddball shopping area of some charm, particularly on St. Stephen Street.

Many shops along the **Royal Mile** sell what may be politely or euphemistically described as tourist-ware—whiskies, tartans, and tweeds.

7

Greece

8

WORD OF MOUTH

"Hello to the Fodorites who patiently helped and answered my questions about Santorini and Mykonos (travelerjan, Heimdall, Brotherleelove). Well, my husband and I got back two weeks ago and we loved Greece! What a great country! The people were friendly, the country was beautiful and clean, and the food delicious. We spent one week on the islands and another week on the mainland. We will most definitely return!!"

—nilady

WHAT'S WHERE

1 Athens. The capital is greeting the new millennium with new swaths of parkland, a sleek subway, and other spiffy and long-overdue municipal makeovers. But for five million Athenians and their 15 million annual visitors, it's still the tried and true pleasures that put the spin on urban life here: sitting in an endless parade of cafés, strolling the streets of the Plaka and other old neighborhoods, and most of all, admiring the glorious remnants of one the greatest civilizations the West ever produced, such as the Acropolis, the Agora, and the Theater of Herod Atticus.

2 Delphi & the Apollo Coast. Attica, the southeastern tip of Central Greece, is much more than the home of Athens—it is also a fertile land, with sandy beaches to the south, serene mountains like Parnassus to the north, and beautiful Byzantine monasteries in between. Amazing archaeology abounds. Just a few hours from Athens lies Delphi, the center of the universe for the ancients. Southward along the coast lies the spectacular Temple of Poseidon. Hovering between sea and sky atop its cliff, it is the hero of a 1,001 travel posters.

3 The Cyclades: Santorini & Mykonos. These islands compose a quintessential Mediterranean archipelago, with ancient sites, droves of vineyards and olive trees, and stark whitewashed cubist houses, all seemingly crystallized in a backdrop of lapis lazuli. The two major stars in this island constellation in the central Aegean Sea are Santorini and Mykonos. Volcanic, spectacular Santorini is possibly the last remnant of the "lost continent" of Atlantis—the living here is as high as the towns' cliff-top perches. There's no shortage of worldly pleasures on this most southerly of the islands, from shopping to yachting, but pastimes need be no more fancy than climbing up a snakelike staircase to the top of the 1,000-foot cliffs encircling the famed flooded caldera or simply gazing out to sea across the blindingly white cubes of Cycladic architecture. As for lively, liberated Mykonos, the rich arrive by plane, the middle class by plane, the backpackers by boat—but everyone is out to enjoy the golden sands and Dionysian nightlife. Happily, the old ways of life continue in fishing ports and along mazelike town streets.

FORMER
YUGOSLAV
REPUBLIC OF
MACEDONIA

ALBANIA

Florina
Kastoria
Kozani
Konitsa
Grevena
Delvinakio
Metsovo
Meteora
Corfu
Kalambaka
Corfu
Igoumenitsa
Trikala
Paramythia
Parga
Arta
Aliki
Preveza
Karpenissi
Lefkas
Vassiliki
Agrinio
Kephalonia
Ithaki
Natpaktl
Messolongi
Lixouri
Sami
Patras
Killini
Loutra
Zakynthos
Amalias
Zakynthos
Pyrgos
Olymp
Kaïafas
PELOPC
Kyparissia
Messir
Ionian Sea
Gargaliani
Pilos
Methoni
Koro

Mediterranea

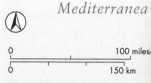

0   100 miles
0   150 km

THE SIGHT GREETS YOU TIME and again in Greece—a line of solid, sun-bleached masonry silhouetted against a clear blue sky. If you're lucky, a cypress waves gently to one side. What makes the scene all the more fulfilling is the realization that a kindred spirit looked up and saw the same temple or theater some 2,000 or more years ago. Temples, theaters, statues, a stray Doric column or two, the fragment of a Corinthian capital: these traces of the ancients are thick on the ground in Greece. Perhaps this is one reason why it can be disorienting—especially for visitors conditioned by textbooks, college Greek, and Keats' Grecian Urn—to arrive in Athens and find the natives roaring around in sports cars and talking about the latest nouvelle restaurant. Shouldn't they look like the truncated statues in the British Museum and have brows habitually crowned with wild olive? Incongruous as it may seem, most Greeks have two arms and two legs attached to the torso in the normal places. And these days a goodly number of them are talking about the hottest new nightspot.

From its recently opened museums to its hipsterious island hangouts, Greece is more than ever a dazzling paradox—the word is Greek—of old and new, ancient and modern. The country is now alive with vibrant trends and styles, especially after the mammoth 2004 Olympic Games were held in Athens and succeeded in catapulting the country into the 21st century. These days everything old—even 25 centuries old—is new again: the post-Olympic "European" Greece dazzles with boutique hotels, chic eateries, and elegant resorts that dramatically challenge the old Zorba-era conceptions of the Spartan Aegean.

Thankfully, Greece still remains an agelessly impressive land. Western poetry, music, architecture, politics, medicine, law—all had their birth centuries ago here. The Greek countryside itself remains a stunning presence, dotted with cypress groves, vineyards, and olive trees; carved into gentle bays or dramatic coves bordered with startling white sand; or articulated into rolling hills and rugged mountain ranges that plunge into the sea. In Greece, indeed, you cannot travel far across the land without encountering the sea, or far across the sea without encountering one of its roughly 2,000 islands. Approximately equal in size to New York State and roughly the size of England, Greece has 15,019 km (9,312 mi) of coastline, more than any other country of its size. The sea is everywhere, not on three sides only but at every turn, reaching into the shoreline like a probing hand.

Wherever you head, you should explore this fascinating country with open eyes. Chances are you'll enjoy it in all its forms: its slumbering cafés and buzzing tavernas, its elaborate religious rituals, and its stark, bright beauty. As the lucky traveler soon learns, although their countryside may be bleached and stony, the Greeks themselves provide the vibrant color that has long since vanished from classical monuments once saturated with blue, gold, and vermilion pigment under the eye-searing Aegean sun.

TOP REASONS TO GO

Athens's Acropolis: The great emblem of Classical Greece has loomed above Athens (whose harbor of Piraeus is gateway to all the Greek Islands) for 2,500 years. Even from afar, the sight of the Parthenon—the great marble temple that the 5th century BC statesmen Pericles conceived to crown the site—stirs strong feelings about the achievements and failings of Western Civilization.

Delphi: Set in a spectacular vale, this was the ancient site of the most venerated and consulted Greek oracle. The site is breathtaking, and the remnant artworks, such as the fabled Charioteer, even more so.

Mykonos: Backpackers and jet-setters alike share the beautiful beaches and the Dionysian nightlife—this island is not called the St-Tropez of the Aegean without reason—but the old ways of life continue undisturbed in fishing ports and along mazelike town streets. Not only are the hotels and cafés picture-perfect, the famous windmills actually seem to be posing for your camera.

Delos: Just a short boat ride away from sybaritic, this-worldly Mykonos is ruin-strewn Delos, a proudly other-wordly and sacred island. Windswept and uninhabited, this islet was revered as the sacred birthplace of Apollo. Ponder the evidence of past glory: the sprawling site was once the religious and commercial center of the entire eastern Mediterranean.

Santorini: One of the world's most picturesque islands cradles the sunken caldera of a volcano that last erupted in 1650 BC. To merely link the phenomenon to the Atlantis myth and the Minoan collapse misses the point—what matters is the ravishing sight of the multicolored cliffs rising 1,100 feet out of sparkling blue waters, a visual treat that makes the heart miss a beat or two. The main town of Ia is a white Cubist stage set for sunsets that make the knees go weak.

8

WHEN TO GO

The best times to visit Greece are late spring and early fall. In May and June the days are warm, even hot, but dry, and the seawater has been warmed by the sun. For sightseeing or hitting the beach, this is the time. Greece is relatively tourist-free in spring, so if beaches and swimming don't top your agenda, April and early May are good; the local wildflowers are at their loveliest, too. Carnival, usually in February just before Lent, and Greek Easter are seasonal highlights. July and August (most locals vacation in August) are always busy—especially on the islands. If you visit during this peak, plan well ahead and be prepared to fight the crowds. September and October are a good alternative to spring and early summer, especially in the cities where bars and cultural institutions stay open. Elsewhere, things begin to shut down in November. Transportation to the islands is limited in winter, and many hotels outside large cities are closed until April.

GETTING HERE & AROUND

BY BOAT

Ferries, catamarans, and hydrofoils make up an essential part of the national transport system of Greece. With so many private companies operating, so many islands to choose from, and complicated timetables with departures changing not just by season but also by day of the week, the most sensible way to arrange island hopping is to select the islands you would like to see, then visit a travel agent to ask how your journey can be put together. Greece's largest and busiest port is Piraeus, which lies 10 km (6 mi) south of downtown Athens. Athens's second port is Rafina, with regular daily ferry crossings to the Cycladic islands of Mykonos and Santorini. You can also travel to Greece's ports of Igoumenitsa and Patras by boat directly from Italy, and from Turkey to various Aegean islands.

BY BUS

Organized bus tours can be booked together with hotel reservations by your travel agent. Many tour operators have offices in and around Syntagma and Omonia squares in central Athens. It is easy to get around Greece on buses, and it is the preferred mode of arriving at Delphi, the great ancient site in Attica. The price of public transportation in Greece has risen steeply since the 2004 Olympic year, but it is still cheaper than in other western European cities. Greece has an extensive and reliable regional bus system (KTEL) made up of local operators—buses often reach even the most far-flung villages.

BY CAR

Road conditions in Greece have improved significantly in the last decade, yet driving in Greece still presents certain challenges. If you are traveling quite a bit by boat, taking along a car increases ticket costs substantially and limits your ease in hopping on any ferry. International driving permits (IDPs) are required for drivers who are not citizens of an EU country. These international permits, valid only in conjunction with your regular driver's license, are universally recognized; having one may save you a problem with local authorities.

BY PLANE

There are direct flights to Athens from most major cities in the world. The frequency of flights varies according to the time of year (with an increase between Greek Easter and November), and it is essential to book well in advance for summer or for festivals and holidays, especially on three-day weekends. Domestic flights are a good deal for many destinations. There are flights most days to and from Santorini and Mykonos. The option of flying to them is a good choice, especially if you're on a tight schedule: unlike boats, flights are rarely affected by the weather.

BY TRAIN

Greece is one of 18 countries in which you can use Eurail passes, which provide unlimited first-class rail travel in all of the participating countries for the duration of the pass. If you plan to rack up the miles in several countries, get a standard pass. Among those passes you might want to consider: the Greece Pass, which allows first-class rail travel throughout Greece; the Greece-Italy Pass, which gives you 4 days' travel time over a span of two months; and the Balkan Flexipass. Greece is not particularly geared to rail travel; traveling around Greece by train can be laborious, since the trains are sluggish and often late. There is only one line connecting the north of Greece down to the south in the Peloponnese. There are no trains on the islands.

ABOUT THE RESTAURANTS

Restaurants in Greece range from the classic taverna—where the chef is often a grandma who's following her grandma's recipes—to luxurious nouvelle temples of gastronomy that have made Athens into a culinary hot spot. There are many kinds of eateries here. You'll often find fine tablecloths, carefully placed silverware, candles, and multipage menus at an *estiatorio,* or restaurant. Now enjoying a retro resurgence, the simple *oinomageirio* is often packed with blue-collar workers filling up on casseroles and listening to *rembetika,* Greece's version of the blues. A taverna is vintage Greece—a family-style eatery noted for great spreads of grilled meat "tis oras" (of the hour), all shared around a big table. A *psarotaverna* is every bit like a regular taverna, except the star of the menu is fresh fish (remember that fish usually comes whole; if you want it filleted, ask "Mporo na exo fileto?"). *Mezedopoleia* are the Greek version of tapas bars, where you can graze on a limited menu of dips, salads, and hot and cold mezedes. An *ouzeri* serves up the potent liquor known as Ouzo, along with plates of mezedes. Coffee rules at the *kafeneio* (café), along with light menus of food. Finish up a dinner at a *zacharoplasteio* (patisserie).

8

HOURS
Breakfast is available from 7 to 10 at most hotels and until early afternoon in relaxed beach resorts. Lunch is between 1:30 and 4:00, and dinner is served from about 8:30 to midnight, later in the big cities and resort islands. Most Greeks dine late, around 10 or 11 PM. In the early evening, they can often be found sipping frappé in a busy café, preparing for the long night ahead. Tips are included in restaurant bills, but most people add more money if service was good.

MEALS & FAVORITE DISHES
Greeks eat their main meal at either lunch or dinner, and this can be a traditional dish like "ladero" or oil-based home-cooked style foods such as meat with potatoes or rice, vegetables, pulses, or short pasta. Simpler, faster options include cheese, spinach, or other pies from chainstores such as Everest or Grigoris, where the customer can compose the perfect sandwich from a broad variety of ingredients, or fast-food chains such as Goodys. Appetizers at tavernas include bread accompaniments such as *taramosalata* (made from fish roe), *melitzanosalata* (made from smoked eggplant, lemon, oil, and garlic), *tyrokafteri* (spicy feta cheese), and the well-known yogurt, cucumber, and garlic tzatziki as well as, of course, the classic *horiatiki* or Greek salad, made with tomato, feta cheese, cucumber, onion, olives, and oregano. In most

places, the menu is broken down into appetizers (*orektika*) and main course (*kiria piata*)—mainly grilled meats—with additional headings for salads (this includes dips like tzatziki) and vegetable side plates. Often the food arrives all at the same time, or as soon as it's prepared. Locals prefer the cheaper yet sometimes highly qualitative hima wine, served in jugs and often drunk with a small splash of soda water or ice for extra zing.

WHAT IT COSTS IN EUROS					
	¢	$	$$	$$$	$$$$
Restaurants	under €8	€8–€15	€15–€22	€22–€28	over €28

Restaurant prices are per person for a main course at dinner.

ABOUT THE HOTELS

In this era of the post-Zorba European Greece, the days of the bare cottage, the creaky apartment, and the shabby motel have come and gone. So accommodations now vary from super-luxurious island xanadus bedecked with latest in-room high-tech amenities to simple yet charming traditional settlements incorporating local style to inexpensive basic rented rooms peddled at the harbor. Apartments with kitchens are available as well in most resort areas. Most areas have pensions—usually clean, bright, and recently built. On islands in summer owners wait for tourists at the harbor, and signs in English throughout villages indicate available "rooms to rent." Look for the words *Dhomatia* (rooms) or *Pansiyons* (pensions). The quality of these rooms has improved a great deal in recent years, with many featuring air-conditioning, a TV set, and a refrigerator. One rule remains: look before you commit.

PRICES & MAKING RESERVATIONS

Often you can reduce the price by eliminating breakfast, by bargaining when it's off-season, or by going through a local travel agency for the larger hotels on major islands and in Athens. An 8% government tax (6% outside the major cities) and 2% municipality tax are added to all hotel bills, though usually the rate quoted includes the tax; be sure to ask. If your room rate covers meals, another 2% tax may be added. It is probably wise to book at least one month in advance for the months of June, July, and September, and ideally even two to three months in advance for the high season, from late July to the end of August, especially in high-profile destinations like Mykonos and Santorini.

WHAT IT COSTS IN EUROS					
	¢	$	$$	$$$	$$$$
Hotels	under €70	€70–€125	€125–€180	€180–€220	over €220

Hotel prices are for two people in a standard double room in high season, excluding tax.

PLANNING YOUR TIME

Greece offers two main experiences, the mainland and the islands. Both have wooed and wowed travelers for many centuries. Since the easiest route to most of the islands is from the port of Piraeus (although many have airports as well), which is located in a suburb of Athens, it is often recommended to first visit the big-city capital when you arrive in Greece. *Don't.* Instead, the first leg of the journey should be the islands. Only when you've enjoyed several idyllic days on Mykonos and Santorini will you be well rested enough to enjoy the mighty bustle and sophistication of Athens. So, hard as it may be, arrive at Athens's airport only to use it as a transfer point to a flight (or opt for a boat) heading to the islands. The most admired are Santorini (5–8 hours from Piraeus depending on type of boat) and Mykonos (2–6 hours). Take note that ferry schedules change frequently, and it can be tricky to coordinate island-hopping excursions in advance, so if tight on time it is best to fly—both islands have airports. If that is the case, remember to book well in advance.

Indulge yourself with three full days on spectacular Santorini, the southernmost island of the Cycladic group, which has an other-worldly quality because of the eruption of its volcano around 1500 BC. Then island-hop to magical Mykonos and enjoy some of Greece's most glamorous and busy beaches, restaurants, shops—as well as a beautifully characteristic main town—for two days. After a restful island interlude, head back to Athens. Base yourself in the center of town, for easy access to the Acropolis, most other archaeological sites, as well as major museums. After two to three days in the capital, take a "vacation from your vacation"—two great day trips via excursion bus from Athens. The first is to "the belly button of the Earth": Delphi, home to the Oracle of Apollo and Greece's most sacred ancient site. The second is to the Temple of Poseidon at Sounion. The venerated temple, prized especially for its breathtaking views, is perched on a cliff overlooking the sparkling Aegean—a fitting grand finale for any trip to Greece.

ATHENS

It's no wonder that all roads lead to the fascinating and maddening metropolis of Athens. Lift your eyes 200 feet above the city to the Parthenon, its honey-color marble columns rising from a massive limestone base, and you behold architectural perfection that has not been surpassed in 2,500 years. But today this shrine of classical form, this symbol of Western civilization and political thought, dominates a 21st-century boomtown. Athens is now home to 4.4 million souls, many of whom spend the day discussing the city's faults: the murky pollution cloud known as the *nefos*, the overcrowding, the traffic jams with their hellish din, and the characterless cement apartment blocks. Romantic travelers, nurtured on the truth and beauty of Keats's Grecian Urn, are dismayed to find that much of Athens has succumbed to that red tubular glare that owes only its name, neon, to the Greeks.

To experience Athens—Athìna in Greek—fully is to understand the essence of Greece: ancient monuments surviving in a sea of cement, startling beauty amid the squalor, tradition juxtaposed with modernity—a smartly dressed lawyer chatting on her cell phone as she maneuvers around a priest in flowing robes heading for the ultramodern metro. Locals depend upon humor and flexibility to deal with the chaos; you should do the same. The rewards are immense if you take the time to catch the purple glow of sundown on Mt. Hymettus, light a candle in a Byzantine church beside black-shrouded grandmas while teens outside argue vociferously about soccer, or breathe in the tangy sea air while sipping a Greek coffee after a night at the coastal clubs.

WHEN TO GO

Athens has a typical Mediterranean climate: hot, dry summers and cool, wet winters. Snow is not uncommon in Athens, and many places are not well heated. Spring and fall are the best time to go, with warm days and balmy evenings. In midsummer, the hot winds from Africa make over-heated (and over-polluted) Athens a hellish challenge, so try to head here in the "shoulder seasons."

GETTING HERE AND AROUND

BY BUS

Athens and its suburbs are covered by a good network of buses and trams, with express buses running between central Athens and major neighborhoods, including nearby beaches. During the day buses tend to run every 15–30 minutes, with reduced service at night and on weekends. Buses run from about 5 AM to midnight. Main bus stations are at Akadimias and Sina and at Kaningos Square. Bus tickets cost €0.80 and can be used for all public transport transfers for 90 minutes. A tram link between downtown Athens and the coastal suburbs features two main lines. Line A runs from Syntagma to Glyfada; Line B traces the shoreline from Glyfada to the Peace & Friendship Stadium on the outskirts of Piraeus.

BY METRO

The best magic carpet ride in town is the metro. Cars are not worth the stress and road rage and, happily, the metro is fast, cheap, and convenient; its three lines go to all the major spots in Athens. Line 1, or the Green Line, of the city's metro (subway) system, is often called the *elektrikos*, or the electrical train and runs from Piraeus to the northern suburb of Kifissia, with several downtown stops. Downtown stations on Line 1 most handy to tourists include Victorias Square, near the National Archaeological Museum; Omonia Square; Monastiraki, in the old Turkish bazaar; and Thission, near the ancient Agora and the nightlife districts of Psirri and Thission. Line 2, or the Red Line, starts from Syntagma Square and includes stops at Panepistimiou (near Numismatic Museum), Omonia Square, Stathmos Larissis (next to train station), and the Acropolis. Line 3, or the Blue Line, heads to Gazi and Monastiraki districts. Tickets are €0.70 (Line 1) or €0.80 (2 and 3). Validate all tickets in machines before you board.

BY PLANE

The best way to get to the sleek Eleftherios Venizelos International Airport from downtown Athens is by metro or light rail. Single tickets cost €6 and include transfers (don't forget to validate the ticket again) to bus, trolley, or tram. Also, in Athens three reliable express buses connect the airport with the metro (Ethniki Amyna station), Syntagma Square, and Piraeus. Bus E95 will take you to Syntagma Square (Amalias avenue); E94 goes to the bus terminus at the Ethniki Amyna metro stop (Line 3), which will get you into Syntagma within 10 minutes. Bus E96 takes the Vari–Koropi road inland and links with the coastal road, passing through Voula, Glyfada, and Alimo; it then goes on to the great ship harbor at Piraeus (opposite Karaiskaki Square). Bus tickets to and from the airport cost €2.90. Taxis are readily available at the airport; they cost an average of €22 to get to the city.

BY TAXI

Most drivers in Athens speak basic English. Although you can find an empty taxi on the street, it's often faster to call out your destination to one carrying passengers; if the taxi is going in that direction, the driver will pick you up. Likewise, don't be alarmed if your driver picks up other passengers (although he should ask your permission first, and he will never pick up another fare if you are a woman traveling alone at night). Each passenger pays full fare for the distance he or she has traveled. Neither tipping nor bargaining is generally practiced; if your driver has gone out of the way for you, a small gratuity (10% or less) is appreciated. The leading taxi companies are Athina I, Ermis, Hellas, and Parthenon—ask your hotel concierge for contact information.

DISCOUNTS & DEALS

Athens's best deal is the €12 ticket that allows one week's admission to all the sites and corresponding museums along the Unification of Archaeological Sites walkway. You can buy the ticket at any of the sites, which include the Acropolis, ancient Agora, and Temple of Olympian Zeus. Admission to almost all museums and archaeological sites is free on Sunday from mid-November through March.

TOUR OPTIONS

The "Athens Sightseeing Public Bus Line," or Bus 400, stops at all the city's main sights: buses run every 30 minutes, from 7:30 AM to 9 PM and tickets cost €5. The full journey takes 90 minutes, but you can hop on and off as you please. Bus 400 stops are marked by bright blue waist-high pillars. There are also full-day (and nighttime) tours by bus, often including a guided tour of the Acropolis and National Archaeological Museum (when open) and includes lunch in a Plaka taverna. Morning tours usually begin around 8:45. Reservations can be made through most hotels. The tours run daily, year-round, and cost around €50. Two top tour-bus companies are CHAT Tours and Key Tours.

VISITOR INFORMATION

The main office of the Greek National Tourism Organization (GNTO; EOT in Greece) is on Tsochas Street, in the Ambelokipi district, just by the National Gardens, not far from central Syntagma Square in the heart of Athens. Their offices generally close around 2 PM. The Web site

Leoforos Alexandras

Notara
Palpouta
Sp. Trikoupi
Loustinianou
Pouli horias
Kountouriotou

LOFOS
STREFI

Irinis
Athinaias
Voulgaroktonou
Valtetsi
Mavromichali
Ippokrato

Tsamadou
Oikonomou
Emm.
Benaki
Komninon

Eresou
Zoodhochou Pigis
Iseuron
Arianiou

Derveniou
Tsamiski
Smolensky
Nikiforou Ouranou

Aracho
Valtetsiou
Zoodhochou Pigis
Kalidhromiou
Mathonis

A. Metaxa
Charilaou Trikoupi
Mavromichali

Asklipiou
Dafnomyli
Doxapatri
Sarantapichou

NEAPOLIS

12

Ippokratous
Didotou
Asklipiou
Solonos

Ayios
Georgios ◆

Massalias

Funicular

Municipal
Cultural
Center ◆

Sina
Statha Gianni
Navarinou

Omirou
Lykavittou
Dinokritou

Aristippou
Kleomenous
Deinokratous

Loukianou
Spefsippou
Ploutarchou

Lykavittou
Akadimias
Voukourestiou
Pindarou
Iraklettou

Patriarchou Ioakim
Irodotou
Karneadou

13

Kanari

Ypsilantou

M
Syntagma

10

11

Vasilissis Sofias

9

◆ Parliament

Tomb of the
Unknown Soldier ◆

Stisichorou
Rigillis

Irodou Attikou

Presidential
◆ Palace

Vasiliseos Konstantinou

Zappion
Hall

Isiodou

KEY

M Metro lines
Rail Road

Vasilissis Olgas

of the city of Athens (⊕ *www.cityofathens.gr*) has a small but growing section in English.

ESSENTIALS

Bus Tour Contacts CHAT Tours (✉ *4 Stadiou.* ☎ *210/322-3137* ⊕ *www.chatours. gr*). **Key Tours** (✉ *4 Kallirois* ☎ *210/923-3166* ⊕ *www.keytours.gr*).

Bus & Tram Contacts City Trams (⊕ *www.tramsa.gr*). **KTEL Buses** (☎ *210/821-0872* ⊕ *www.ktel.org*).

Metro Contact Athens Metro (⊕ *www.ametro.gr*).

Visitor Information Greek National Tourism Organization (EOT) (✉ *Tsochas 7, near Syntagma Square,* ☎ *210/870-7000* ⊕ *www.greektourism.com*).

EXPLORING ATHENS

Although Athens covers a huge area, the major landmarks of the ancient Greek, Roman, and Byzantine periods are close to the modern city center. The center of the city is small, stretching from the Acropolis in the southwest to Mt. Lycabettus in the northeast. The layout is simple: three parallel streets—Stadiou, Eleftheriou Venizelou (familiarly known as Panepistimiou), and Akadimias—link two main squares, Syntagma (Constitution) and Omonia (Concord). As you explore, you will discover that Athens may seem like one huge city but it is really a conglomeration of neighborhoods with distinctive characters. The Eastern influences that prevailed during the 400-year rule of the Ottoman Empire are still evident in Monastiraki, the bazaar area near the foot of the Acropolis. On the northern slope of the Acropolis, stroll through Plaka, an area of tranquil streets lined with renovated mansions, to get the flavor of the 19th-century's gracious lifestyle. The narrow lanes of Anafiotika, a section of Plaka, thread past tiny churches and small, color-washed houses with wooden upper stories, recalling a Cycladic island village.

Formerly run-down old quarters, such as Thission, Gazi, and Psirri, popular nightlife areas filled with bars and *mezedopoleia* (similar to tapas bars), are now in the process of gentrification, although they still retain much of their original charm. The area around Syntagma Square, the tourist hub, and Omonia Square, the commercial heart of the city about 1 km (½ mi) northwest, is distinctly European, having been designed by the court architects of King Otho, a Bavarian, in the 19th century. To the east, the chic shops and bistros of ritzy Kolonaki nestle at the foot of Mt. Lycabettus, Athens's highest hill (909 feet), and the best place for a bird's-eye view of all Athens.

WEST ATHENS: THE ACROPOLIS, PLAKA, ANAFIOTIKA & MONASTIRAKI

(ΑΚΡΟΠΟΛΗ, ΠΛΑΚΑ, ΑΝΑΦΙΩΤΙΚΑ, & ΜΟΝΑΣΤΗΡΑΚΙ)
Towering over the modern metropolis of four million as it once stood over the ancient capital of 50,000, the ancient Acropolis has remained Athens's most spectacular attraction ever since its first settlement around 5000 BC. After viewing the Parthenon all will at first seem to

be an anticlimax. But there is still much that is well worth seeing on the citadel's periphery, including the neoclassic buildings lining its main street, Dionyssiou Areopagitou, and the great centuries-old Odeon of Herodes Atticus.

Fanning north from the slopes of the Acropolis, the relentlessly picturesque Plaka is the last corner of 19th-century Athens. Set with Byzantine accents provided by churches, the "Old Town" district extends north to Ermou street and eastward to the Leofóros Amalias. At night merrymakers crowd the old tavernas, which feature traditional music and dancing; many have rooftops facing the Acropolis. If you keep off the main tourist shopping streets of Kidathineon and Adrianou, you will be amazed at how peaceful the area can be, even in summer. Above Plaka is Anafiotika, built on winding lanes that climb up the slopes of the Acropolis, its upper reaches resembling a tranquil village.

To the west of Anafiotika lies Athens's fabled ancient Agora, once the focal point of urban life and site of the Hephaistion, the best-preserved Doric temple in Greece. Just to the north of the Agora, you can still experience the sights and sounds of the marketplace in Monastiraki, the former Turkish bazaar area, which retains vestiges of the 400-year period when Greece was subject to the Ottoman Empire. On the opposite side of the Agora is another meeting place of sorts: Thission, one of the most sought-after residential neighborhoods since about 1990 and a vibrant nightlife district.

① **Acropolis.** Towering over a modern city of 4 million much as it stood

FodorśChoice over the ancient capital of 50,000, the Acropolis (literally "high

★ city") continues to be Athens's most spectacular, photogenic, and visited attraction despite hundreds of years of renovations, bombings, and artistic lootings. The buildings, constructed under the direction of Pericles during the city's Golden Age in the 5th century BC, were designed to be as visually harmonious as they were enormous, and they stand today in a perfect balance of stubborn immortality and elegant fragmentation. For an in-depth look at this emblem of the glories of classical Greek civilization, see our photo-feature, "The Acropolis: Ascent to Glory" in this chapter.

⑤ **Anafiotika.** Set in the shadow of the Acropolis, this is the closest thing

☾ you'll find in Athens to the whitewashed villages of the Cycladic islands

FodorśChoice featured on travel posters of Greece. It is populated by many descen-

★ dants of the Anafi stonemasons who arrived from that small island in the 19th century to work in the expanding capital. Anafiotika is an enchanting area of simple stone houses, many nestled right into the bedrock, most little changed over the years, others stunningly restored. Cascades of bougainvillea and pots of geraniums and marigolds enliven the balconies and rooftops, and the prevailing serenity is in blissful contrast to the cacophony of modern Athens. Perched on the bedrock of the Acropolis is **Ayios Georgios tou Vrachou** (St. George of the Rock), which marks the southeast edge of the district. One of the most beautiful

8

Continued on page 422

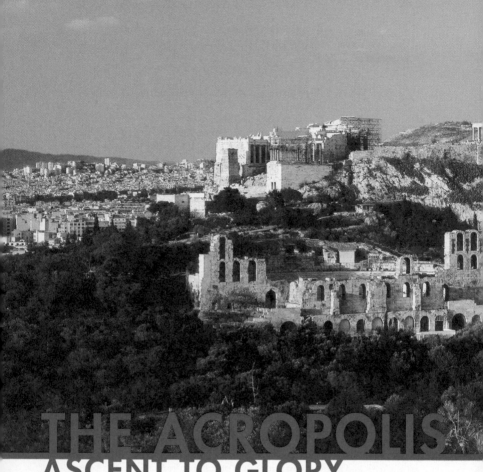

THE ACROPOLIS
ASCENT TO GLORY

One of the wonders of the world, the Acropolis symbolizes Greece's Golden Age. Its stunning centerpiece, the Parthenon, was commissioned in the 5th century BC by the great Athenian leader Pericles as part of an elaborate building program designed to epitomize the apex of an iconic culture. Thousands of years later, the Acropolis pulls the patriotic heartstrings of modern Greeks and lulls millions of annual visitors back to an ancient time.

You don't have to look far in Athens to encounter perfection. Towering above all—both physically and spiritually—is the Acropolis, the ancient city of upper Athens and womb of Western civilization. Raising your eyes to the crest of this *ieros vrachos* (sacred rock), the sight of the Parthenon will stop you in your tracks. The term Akropolis (to use the Greek spelling) means "High City" and today's traveler who climbs this table-like hill is paying tribute to the prime source of civilization as we know it.

A TITANIC TEMPLE
Described by the 19th-century French poet Alphonse de Lamartine as "the most perfect poem in stone," the Acropolis is a true testament to the Golden Age of Greece. While archaeological evidence has shown that the flat-top limestone outcrop, 512 feet high, attracted settlers as early as Neolithic times, most of its most imposing structures were built from 461 to 429 BC, when the intellectual and artistic life of Athens flowered under the influence of the Athenian statesman, Pericles. Even

in its bleached and silent state, the Parthenon—the Panathenaic temple that crowns the rise—has the power to stir the heart as few other ancient relics do.

PERICLES TO POLLUTION
Since the Periclean Age, the buildings of the Acropolis have been inflicted with the damages of war, as well as unscrupulous transformations into, at various times, a Florentine palace, an Islamic mosque, a Turkish harem, and a World War II sentry. Since then, a more insidious enemy—pollution—has emerged. The site is presently undergoing conservation measures as part of an ambitious rescue plan. Today, the Erechtheion temple has been completely restored, and work on the Parthenon, Temple of Athena Nike, and the Propylaea is due for completion by the end of 2010. A final phase, involving massive landscaping works, will last through 2020. Despite the ongoing restoration work, a visit to the Acropolis today can evoke the spirit of the ancient heroes and gods who were once worshiped here.

THE PARTHENON
PINNACLE OF THE PERICLEAN AGE

DEDICATED TO ATHENA

At the loftiest point of the Acropolis stands the Parthenon, the architectural masterpiece conceived by Pericles and executed between 447 and 438 BC by the brilliant sculptor Pheidias, who supervised the architects Iktinos and Kallikrates in its construction. It not only raised the bar in terms of sheer size, but also in the perfection of its proportions.

Dedicated to the goddess Athena (the name Parthenon comes from the Athena Parthenos, or the virgin Athena) and inaugurated at the Panathenaic Festival of 438 BC, the Parthenon served primarily as the treasury of the Delian League, an ancient alliance of cities formed to defeat the Persian incursion.In fact, the Parthenon was built as much to honor the city's power as to venerate Athena. Its foundations, laid after the victory at Marathon in 490 BC, were destroyed by the Persian army in 480–79 BC. In turn, the city-state of Athens banded together with Sparta to rout the Persians by 449 BC.

To proclaim its hegemony over all Greece, Athens envisioned a grand new Acropolis. After a 30-year building moratorium, the titanic-scale project of reconstructing the temple was initiated by Pericles around 448 BC.

490 BC
Foundation for Acropolis laid

447-438 BC
The Parthenon is constructed

420 BC
Temple of Athena Nike is completed

TIMELINE

EDIFICE REX: PERICLES

His name means "surrounded by glory." Some scholars consider this extraordinary, enigmatic Athenian general to be the architect of the destiny of Greece at its height, while others consider him a megalomaniac who bankrupted the coffers of an empire, and an elitist who catered to the privileged few at the expense of the masses.

Indeed, Pericles (460–429 BC) plundered the treasury of the Athenian alliance for the Acropolis building program. One academic has even called the Periclean building program the largest embezzlement in human history.

MYTH IN MARBLE

But Pericles' masterstroke becomes more comprehensible when studied against the conundrum that was Athenian democracy. In truth an aristocracy that was the watchdog of private property and public order, this political system financed athletic games and drama festivals; it constructed exquisite buildings. Its motto was not only to live, but to live well. Surrounded by barbarians, the Age of Pericles was the more striking for its high level of civilization, its qualities of proportion, reason, clarity, and harmony, all of which are epitomized nowhere else as beautifully as in the Parthenon. To their credit, the Athenians rallied around Pericles' vision: the respect for the individualistic character of men and women could be revealed through art and architecture.

Even jaded Athenians, when overwhelmed by the city, feel renewed when they lift their eyes to this great monument.

TRICK OF THE TRADE

One of the Parthenon's features, or "refinements," is the way it uses meiosis (tapering of columns) and entasis (a slight swelling so that the column can hold the weight of the entablature), deviations from strict mathematics that breathed movement into the rigid marble. Architects knew that a straight line looks curved, and vice versa, so they cleverly built the temple with all the horizontal lines somewhat curved. The columns, it has been calculated, lean toward the center of the temple; if they were to continue into space, they would eventually converge to create a huge pyramid.

1456
Converted to mosque by occupying Turks

September 26, 1687
The Parthenon, used for gunpowder storage, explodes after being hit by a mortar shell

The Acropolis in Pericles' Time

RAISING A HUE

"Just by color—beige!" So proclaimed Elsie de Wolfe, celebrated decorator to J. Pierpont Morgan, when she first saw the Parthenon. As it turns out, the original Parthenon was anything but beige. Especially ornate, it had been covered with a tile roof, decorated with statuary and marble friezes, adorned with gilded wooden doors and ceilings, and walls and columns so brightly hued that the people protested, "We are adorning our city like a wanton woman" (Plutarch). The finishing touch was provided by the legendary sculptor Pheidias, who created some of the sculpted friezes—these were also brightly hued.

THE ERECHTHEION

PARTHENON

ATHENA PROMACHOS
Pheidias's colossal bronze statue of Athena Promachos, one of the largest of antiquity at 30' (9m) high, could be seen from the sea. It was destroyed after being moved to Constantinople in 1203.

THE PROPYLAEA

TOURING THE ACROPOLIS

Most people take the metro to the Acropolis station, where the New Acropolis Museum is to open in 2008. They then follow the pedestrianized street Dionyssiou Aerogapitou, which traces the foothill of the Acropolis to its entrance at the Beulé Gate. Another entrance is along the rock's northern face via the Peripatos, a paved path from the Plaka district.

THE BEULÉ GATE

You enter the Acropolis complex through this late-Roman structure named for the French archaeologist Ernest Beulé, who discovered the gate in 1852. Made of marble fragments from the destroyed monument of Nikias on the south slope of the Acropolis, it has an inscription above the lintel dated 320 BC, dedicated by "Nikias son of Nikodemos of Xypete." Before Roman times, the entrance to the Acropolis was a steep processional ramp below the Temple of Athena Nike. This Sacred Way was used every fourth year for the Panathenaic procession, a spectacle that honored Athena's remarkable birth (she sprang from the head of her father, Zeus).

THE PROPYLAEA

This imposing structure was designed to instill the proper reverence in worshipers as they crossed from the temporal world into the spiritual world of the sanctuary, for this was the main function of the Acropolis. Conceived by Pericles, the Propylaea was the masterwork of the architect Mnesicles. Conceived to be the same size as the Parthenon, it was to have been the grandest secular building in Greece. Construction was suspended during the

Peloponnesian War, and it was never finished. The structure shows the first use of both Doric and Ionic columns together, a style that can be called Attic. Six of the sturdier fluted Doric columns, made from Pendelic marble, correspond with the gateways of the portal. Processions with priests, chariots, and sacrificial animals entered via a marble ramp in the center (now protected by a wooden stairway), while ordinary visitors on foot entered via the side doors. The slender Ionic columns had elegant capitals, some of which have been restored along with a section of the famed paneled ceiling, originally decorated with gold eight-pointed stars on a blue background. Adjacent to the Pinakotheke, or art gallery (with paintings of scenes from Homer's epics and mythological tableaux), the south wing is a decorative portico. The view from the inner porch of the Propylaea is stunning: the Parthenon is suddenly revealed in its full glory, framed by the columns.

THE TEMPLE OF ATHENA NIKE

The 2nd-century traveler Pausanias referred to this fabled temple as the Temple of Nike Apteros, or Wingless Victory, for "in Athens they believe Victory will stay forever because she has no wings." Designed by Kallikrates, the mini-temple was built in 427–424 BC to celebrate peace with Persia. The bas-reliefs on the surrounding parapet depicting the Victories leading heifers to be sacrificed must have been of exceptional quality, judging from the section called "Nike Unfastening Her Sandal" in the Acropolis Museum. In 1998, Greek archaeologists began dismantling the entire temple for conservation. After laser-cleaning the marble, to remove generations of soot, the team will reconstruct the temple on its original site.

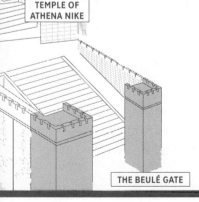

TEMPLE OF
ATHENA NIKE

THE BEULÉ GATE

THE ERECHTHEION

If the Parthenon is the masterpiece of Doric architecture, the Erechtheion is undoubtedly the prime exemplar of the more graceful Ionic order. A considerably smaller structure than the Parthenon, it outmatches, for sheer refinement of design and execution, all other buildings of the Greco-Roman world. For the populace, the much smaller temple—*not* the Parthenon—remained Athena's holiest shrine: legend has it that on this spot Poseidon plunged his trident into the rock, dramatically producing a spring of water, whereas Athena created a simple olive tree, whose produce remains a main staple of Greek society. A panel of judges declared her the winner, and the city was named Athena. A gnarled olive tree still grows outside the Erechtheion's west wall, where Athena's once grew, and marks said to be from Poseidon's trident can be seen on a rock wedged in a hole near the north porch. Completed in 406 BC, the Erechtheion was divided into two Ionic sanctuaries. The most delightful feature is the Caryatid Porch, supported on the heads of six strapping but shapely maidens (caryatids) wearing delicately draped Ionian garments, their folds perfectly aligned to resemble flutes on columns.

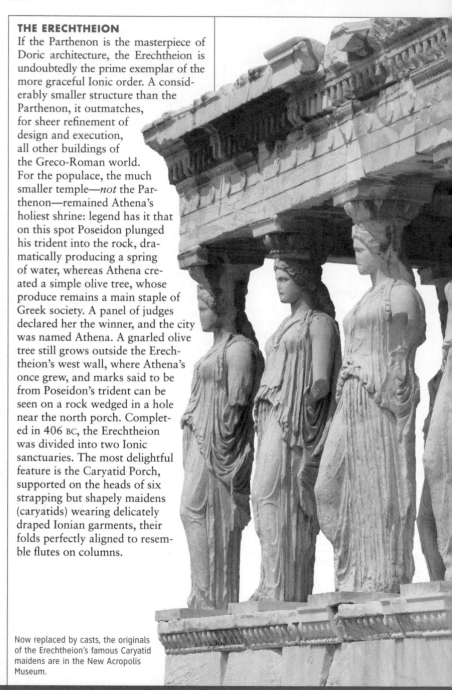

Now replaced by casts, the originals of the Erechtheion's famous Caryatid maidens are in the New Acropolis Museum.

PLANNING YOUR VISIT

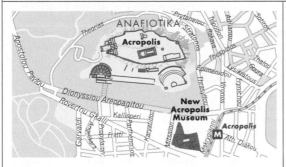

Sooner or later, you will climb the Acropolis hill to witness, close up, its mighty marble monuments whose beauty and grace have not been surpassed in two millennia. When you do, keep these pointers in mind.

What Are the Best Times to Go? Such is the beauty of the Acropolis and the grandeur of the setting that a visit in all seasons and at all hours is rewarding. In general, the earlier you start out the better. In summer, by noon the heat is blistering and the reflection of the light thrown back by the rock and the marble ruins is almost blinding. An alternative, in summer, is to visit after 5 PM, when the light is best for taking photographs. In any season the ideal time might be the two hours before sunset, when occasionally the fabled violet light spreads from the crest of Mt. Hymettus (which the ancients called "violet-crowned") and gradually embraces the Acropolis. After dark the hill is spectacularly floodlighted, creating a scene visible from many parts of the capital. A moonlight visit—sometimes scheduled by the authorities during full moons in summer—is highly evocative. In winter, if there are clouds trailing across the mountains, and shafts of sun lighting up the marble columns, the setting takes on an even more dramatic quality.

How Long Does a Visit Usually Run? Depending on the crowds, the walk takes about four hours, including one spent in the Acropolis Museum.

Are Tour Guides Available? The Union of Official Guides (Apollonos 9A, Syntagma, 210/322-9705, 210/322-0090) offers licensed guides for tours of archaeological sites within Athens. Another option is Amphitrion Holidays (Syngrou 7, Koukaki, 210/900-6000), which offers walking tours of the Acropolis. Guides will also help kids understand the site better.

What's the Handiest Place to Refuel? The Tourist Pavilion (Filoppapou Hill, 210/923-1665), a landscaped, tree-shaded spot soundtracked by chirping birds. It serves drinks, snacks, and a few hot dishes.

Dionysiou Areopagitou, Acropolis

☏ 210/321-4172 or 210/321-0219

✎ www.culture.gr

🎫 Joint ticket for all Unification of Archaeological Sites €12. Good for five days—and for free admission—to the Ancient Agora, Theatre of Dionysus, Kerameikos cemetery, Temple of Olympian Zeus, and the Roman Forum.

🕑 Apr.–Oct., daily 8–sunset; Nov.–Mar., daily 8–2:30

DON'T FORGET:

■ If it's hot, remember to bring water, sunscreen, and a hat to protect yourself from the sun.

■ Get a free bilingual pamphlet guide (in English and Greek) at the entrance gate. It is packed with information, but staffers usually don't bother to give it out unless asked.

■ An elevator now ascends to the summit of the Acropolis, once inaccessible to people with disabilities.

■ All large bags, backpacks, and shopping bags will have to be checked in the site cloakroom.

churches of Athens, it is still in use today. **Ayios Simeon,** a neoclassical church built in 1847 by the settlers, marks the western boundary and contains a copy of a famous miracle-working icon from Anafi, Our Lady of the Reeds. The **Church of the Metamorphosis Sotiros** (Transfiguration), a high-dome 14th-century stone chapel, has a rear grotto carved right into the Acropolis. ✉ *On northeast slope of Acropolis rock, Plaka* Ⓜ*Acropolis.*

❼ **Ancient Agora (Archaia Agora).** The commercial hub of ancient Athens,
★ the Agora was once lined with statues and expensive shops, the favorite strolling ground of fashionable Athenians as well as a mecca for merchants and students. The long colonnades offered shade in summer and protection from rain in winter to the throng of people who transacted the day-to-day business of the city, and, under their arches Socrates discussed matters with Plato and Zeno expounded the philosophy of the Stoics (whose name comes from the six *stoa,* or colonnades of the Agora).

The Agora's showpiece was the **Stoa of Attalos II,** where Socrates once lectured and incited the youth of Athens to adopt his progressive ideas on mortality and morality. Today the Museum of Agora Excavations, this two-story building was first designed as a retail complex and erected in the 2nd century BC by Attalos, a king of Pergamum. The reconstruction in 1953–56 used Pendelic marble and creamy limestone from the original structure. The most notable sculptures, of historical and mythological figures from the 3rd and 4th centuries BC, are at ground level outside the museum.

On the low hill called Kolonos Agoraios in the Agora's northwest corner stands the best-preserved Doric temple in all Greece, the **Hephaistion,** sometimes called the Thission because of its friezes showing the exploits of Theseus. A little older than the Parthenon, it is surrounded by 34 columns and is 104 feet in length, and was once filled with sculptures. The Hephaistion was originally dedicated to Hephaistos, god of metalworkers, and it is interesting to note that metal workshops still exist in this area near Ifestou. Behind the temple, paths cross the northwest slope past archaeological ruins half hidden in deep undergrowth. Here you can sit on a bench and contemplate the same scene that Englishman Edward Dodwell saw in the early 19th century, when he came to sketch antiquities. ✉ *3 entrances: from Monastiraki on Adrianou; from Thission on Apostolou Pavlou; and descending from Acropolis on Ayios Apostoloi, Monastiraki* ☎*210/321–0185* ⊕*www. culture.gr* 🎟*€4; €12 joint ticket for all Unification of Archaeological Sites* ⊙*May–Oct., daily 8–7; Nov.–Apr., daily 8–5; museum closes ½ hr before site* Ⓜ*Thiseio.*

❽ **Greek Folk Art Museum.** Run by the Ministry of Culture, the museum focuses on folk art from 1650 to the present, with especially interesting embroideries, stone and wood carvings, Carnival costumes, and *Karaghiozis* (shadow player figures). Everyday tools—stamps for communion bread, spinning shuttles, raki flasks—attest to the imagination with which Greeks have traditionally embellished the most utilitarian objects. ✉*Kidathineon 17, Plaka* ☎*210/321–3018* ⊕*www.culture.gr* 🎟*€3* ⊙*Tues.–Sun. 10–2.*

❸ New Acropolis Museum. After languishing for years in a small museum,
Fodor'sChoice the treasures of the Parthenon and other temples are now ensconced in
★ a striking new showcase set at the foot of the Acropolis. Built by the
Greek government, this postmodern addition to ancient Greece was
designed by Swiss architect Bernard Tschumi. With more than twice the
space of the old museum, the new museum is centered around a glassed-
in rooftop room built with the exact proportions of the Parthenon,
with views of the temple itself and showcasing the sublime Parthenon
sculptures that Greece still owns (more than half remain in London's
British Museum). Other great treasures here include the famed Caryatid
statues (from the Erechtheion), the charismatic *Calf-Bearer*, and *Nike
Unfastening Her Sandal*. Linking the three floors of the museum is a
striking ramp; on ground level, glass panels in the floor allow views
of the ancient Cycladic village that once occupied the museum's site.
✉ *Dionyssiou Areopagitou and Makriyianni* ☎ *Phone number not set
at press time* ⊕ *www.newacropolismuseum.gr* ⌨ *Admission not set at
press time* ⊙ *Fri.—Wed., 10—6, Thurs., 10–10* Ⓜ *Acropolis*

❷ Odeon of Herodes Atticus. Hauntingly beautiful, this ancient theater was
built in AD 160 by the affluent Herodes Atticus in memory of his wife,
Regilla. Known as the Irodion by Athenians, it is nestled Greek-style
into the hillside, but with typically Roman arches in its three-story stage
building and barrel-vaulted entrances. The circular orchestra has now
become a semicircle, and the long-vanished cedar roof probably covered
only the stage and dressing rooms, not the 34 rows of seats. The theater,
which holds 5,000, was restored and reopened in 1955 for the Elliniko
Festival, or Hellenic Festival. To enter you must hold a ticket to one
of the summer performances. Contact the Elliniko Festival (Hellenic
Festival) box office for ticket information. ✉ *Dionyssiou Areopagitou
near intersection with Propylaion, Acropolis* ☎ *210/323–2771* ⊙ *Open
only during performances* Ⓜ *Acropolis*.

❻ Tower of the Winds (Aerides). Surrounded by a cluster of old houses on
★ the western slope of the Acropolis and adjacent to the ancient Roman
Agora, the world-famous **Tower of the Winds (Aerides)** is the most
appealing and well preserved of the Roman monuments of Athens.
Keeping time since the 1st century BC, it was originally a sundial, water
clock, and weather vane topped by a bronze Triton with a metal rod in
his hand, which followed the direction of the wind. Its eight sides face
the direction of the eight winds into which the compass was divided;
expressive reliefs around the tower personify these eight winds, called *I
Aerides* (the Windy Ones) by Athenians. Note the north wind, Boreas,
blowing on a conch, and the beneficent west wind, Zephyros, scattering
blossoms. ✉ *Pelopidas and Aiolou, Plaka* ☎ *210/324–5220* ⊕ *www.
culture.gr* ⌨ *€2; €12 joint ticket for all Unification of Archaeological
Sites* ⊙ *May–Oct., daily 8–7; Nov.–Apr., daily 8–3* Ⓜ *Monastiraki*.

**NEED A
BREAK?**
Vyzantino (✉ *Kidathineon 18, Plaka* ☎ *210/322-7368*) is directly on Plaka's
main square—great for people-watching and a good, reasonably priced bite
to eat. Try the fish soup, roast potatoes, or baked chicken. **Glikis** (✉ *Aggelou
Geronta 2, Plaka* ☎ *210/322-3925*) and its shady courtyard are perfect for a

Greek coffee or ouzo and a *mikri pikilia* (a small plate of appetizers, including cheese, sausage, olives, and dips).

FROM CENTRAL ATHENS TO NATIONAL ARCHAEOLOGICAL MUSEUM
ΑΘΗΝΑ (ΚΕΝΤΡΟ) ΤΟ ΕΘΝΙΚΟ ΑΡΧΑΙΟΛΟΓΙΚΟ ΜΟΥΣΕΙΟ

Sooner or later, everyone passes through the heart of modern Athens: spacious Syntagma Square (Constitution Square), which is surrounded by sights that span Athens's history from the days of the Roman emperors to King Otho's reign after the 1821 War of Independence, whose former palace is now the national Parliament. It is here, on this square, that the Evzone guards, dressed in their *foustanella* (pleated skirts), stand on duty at the Tomb of the Unknown Soldier. In many places in downtown Athens, the grand rubs elbows with the squalid. The cavernous, chaotic Central Market sits cheek-by-jowl with incense-scented, 12th-century Byzantine churches; they, in turn, are shadowed by hideous 1970s apartment blocks. The mix has become more heady as artists and fashionistas move to the neighborhoods of Psirri and Gazi and transform long-neglected warehouses into galleries, nightclubs, and ultrachic restaurants.

Head a good ten blocks directly north of the Old University complex to find the glorious National Archaeological Museum. One of the most exciting collections of Greek antiquities in the world, this is a must-do for any travelers to Athens, nay, Greece. Here are the sensational finds made by Heinrich Schliemann, discoverer of Troy and father of modern archaeology, in the course of his excavations of the royal tombs on the Homeric site of Mycenae in the 1870s. Here, too, are world-famous bronzes such as the *Jockey of Artemision* and a bronze of Poseidon throwing a trident—or is it Zeus hurling a thunderbolt? Neighboring Kolonaki—the chic shopping district and one of the most fashionable residential areas—occupies the lower slopes of Mt. Lycabettus. Take the funicular ride to the top of the peak, three times the height of the Acropolis, as the view—pollution permitting—reveals that this center-city sector is packed with marvels and wonders.

⑩
Fodor's Choice
★

Benaki Museum. Greece's oldest private museum, established in 1926 by an illustrious Athenian family, the Benaki was one of the first to place emphasis on Greece's later heritage at a time when many archaeologists were destroying Byzantine artifacts to access ancient objects. The collection moves chronologically from the ground floor upward, from prehistory to the formation of the modern Greek state and you might see anything from a 5,000-year-old hammered gold bowl to Lord Byron's pistols, all contrasted against the marble and crystal-chandelier grandeur of the Benaki home. The Benaki's gift shop, a destination in itself, tempts with exquisitely reproduced ceramics and jewelry. The second-floor café serves coffee and snacks, with a few daily specials, on a veranda overlooking the National Garden. ⊠*Koumbari 1, Kolonaki* ☎*210/367–1000* ⊕*www.benaki.gr* 💶*€6, free Thurs.* ☉*Mon., Wed., Fri., and Sat. 9–5, Thurs. 9 AM–midnight, Sun. 9–3* Ⓜ*Syntagma or Evangelismos.*

⑫ **Mount Lycabettus.** Myth claims that Athens's highest hill came into exis-
Ⓢ tence when Athena removed a piece of Mt. Pendeli, intending to boost
the height of her temple on the Acropolis. While she was en route, a
crone brought her bad tidings, and the flustered goddess dropped the
rock in the middle of the city. Kids love the ride up the steeply inclined
teleferique (funicular) to the summit, crowned by whitewashed **Ayios
Georgios** chapel with a bell tower donated by Queen Olga. From Mt.
Lycabettus you can watch the sun set and then turn about to watch
the moon rise over "violet-crowned" Hymettus as the lights of Athens
blink on all over the city. ⊠ *Base: 15-min walk northeast of Syntagma
Sq.; funicular every 10 mins from corner of Ploutarchou and Aristippou
(take Minibus 060 from Kanari or Kolonaki Sq., except Sun.), Kolonaki*
☎ *210/722–7065* 🎫 *Funicular €4* ⊙ *Funicular daily 9 AM–3 AM.*

⑪ **Museum of Cycladic Art.** Also known as the Nicholas P. Goulandris Foundation, and funded by one of Greece's richest families, this museum
has an outstanding collection of 350 Cycladic artifacts dating from
the Bronze Age, including many of the enigmatic marble figurines
whose slender shapes fascinated such artists as Picasso, Modigliani,
and Brancusi. Other collections focus on Greek art from the Bronze
Age through the 6th century AD. A glass corridor connects the main
building to the gorgeous adjacent Stathatos Mansion, where temporary
exhibits are mounted. There's also a lovely café in a courtyard centered
around a Cycladic-inspired fountain. ⊠ *Neofitou Douka 4, Kolonaki*
☎ *210/722–8321 through 210/722–8323* ⊕ *www.cycladic.gr* 🎫 *€3.50*
⊙ *Mon. and Wed.–Fri. 10–4, Sat. 10–3* Ⓜ *Evangelismos.*

⑭ **National Archaeological Museum.** The classic culture which was the gran-
Fodor's Choice deur of the Greek world no longer exists. It died, for civilizations are
★ mortal, but it left indelible markers in all domains, most particularly in
art—and many of its greatest achievements in sculpture and painting
are housed here in the most important museum in Greece. Artistic highlights from every period of ancient Greek civilization, from Neolithic
to Roman times, make this a treasure trove beyond compare. With a
massive renovation completed in 2008, the panoply of ancient Greek
art appears more spectacular than ever.

The museum's most celebrated display is the **Mycenaean Antiquities.**
Here are the stunning gold treasures from Heinrich Schliemann's 1876
excavations of Mycenae's royal tombs: the funeral mask of a bearded
king, once thought to be the image of Agamemnon but now believed
to be much older, from about the 15th century BC; a splendid silver
bull's-head libation cup; and the 15th-century BC Vaphio Goblets, masterworks in embossed gold. Withheld from the public since they were
damaged in the 1999 earthquakes, but not to be missed, are the beautifully restored **frescoes from Santorini,** delightful murals depicting daily
life in Minoan Santorini. The collection of classical art (5th to 3rd century BC) contains some of the most renowned surviving ancient statues:
the bareback *Jockey of Artemision,* a 2nd-century BC Hellenistic bronze
salvaged from the sea; from the same excavation, the bronze *Artemision Poseidon* (some say Zeus), poised and ready to fling a trident; and
the *Varvakios Athena,* a half-size marble version of the gigantic gold-

8

and-ivory cult statue that Pheidias erected in the Parthenon. Light refreshments are served in a lower ground-floor café. ⊠*28 Oktovriou (Patission) 44, Exarchia* 🕾*210/821–7717* ⊕*www.culture.gr* ⌨*€6* ⏱*Apr. 15–Oct. 15, Mon. 1–7:30, Tues.–Sun. 8–7:30; Oct. 16–Apr. 14, Mon. 1–7:30, Tues.–Fri. 8:30–7:30, weekends 8:30–3. Closed Jan. 1, Mar. 25, May 1, Easter Sun., Dec. 25–26; open reduced hrs other holidays* Ⓜ*Victorias, then 10-min walk.*

⓭ **Numismatic Museum Iliou Melathron.** Even those uninterested in coins might want to visit this museum for a glimpse of the former home of Heinrich Schliemann, who excavated Troy and Mycenae in the 19th century. In this exquisite neoclassical mansion, seemingly haunted

Fodor's Choice
★

> ## FULL FRONTAL FASHION
>
> Near the Parliament, you can watch the **changing of the Evzone guards** at the Tomb of the Unknown Soldier—in front of Parliament on a lower level— which takes place at intervals throughout the day. On Sunday the honor guard of tall young men dons a dress costume—a short white *foustanella* (kilt) with 400 neat pleats, one for each year of the Ottoman occupation, and red shoes with pompons—and still manage to look brawny rather than silly. A band accompanies them: they all arrive by 11:15 AM in front of Parliament.

by the spirit of the great historian, you can see more than 600,000 coins; displays range from the archaeologist's own coin collection to 4th-century BC measures employed against forgers to coins grouped according to what they depict—animals, plants, myths, and famous buildings like the Lighthouse of Alexandria. The house was designed and decorated by Ernst Ziller, who called it the "Palace of Troy." Note the Pompeiian aesthetic in the ocher, terra-cotta, and blue touches; the mosaic floors inspired by Mycenae; and the dining-room ceiling painted with food scenes, under which Schliemann would recite the *Iliad* to guests. ⊠*Panepistimiou 12, Syntagma Sq.* 🕾*210/361–2190 or 210/364–3774* ⊕*www.nma.gr* ⌨*€3* ⏱*Tues.–Sun., 8:30 AM–3 PM* Ⓜ*Syntagma or Panepistimiou.*

⑨ **Syntagma (Constitution) Square.** At the top of the city's main square stands **Parliament,** formerly King Otho's royal palace, completed in 1838 for the new monarchy. It seems a bit austere and heavy for a southern landscape, but it was proof of progress, the symbol of the new ruling power. The building's saving grace is the stone's magical change of color from off-white to gold to rosy mauve as the day progresses. Here you can watch the **changing of the Evzone guards** at the **Tomb of the Unknown Soldier**—in front of Parliament on a lower level—which takes place at intervals throughout the day. On a wall behind the Tomb of the Unknown Soldier, the bas-relief of a dying soldier is modeled after a sculpture on the Temple of Aphaia in Aegina; the text is from the funeral oration said to have been given by Pericles. Pop into the gleaming **Syntagma metro station** (⊠*Upper end of Syntagma Sq.* ⏱*Daily 5 AM–midnight*) to examine artfully displayed ancient artifacts uncovered during subway excavations in a floor-to-ceiling cross section of earth. ⊠ *Vasilissis Amalias and Vasilissis Sofias, Syntagma Sq.* Ⓜ *Syntagma.*

NEED A BREAK? Lovely cafés like **Ethnikon** (⊠ *Syntagma Sq.* ☎ *210/331–0676*) have opened as a result of the city's 2004 Olympics remodeling. This café is shady, atmospheric, and has an excellent selection of desserts, including chocolate cake and homemade spoon sweets, or *glykia tou koutaliou.*

❹ **Temple of Olympian Zeus.** Begun in the 6th century BC, the temple was completed in AD 132 by Hadrian, who also commissioned a huge gold-and-ivory statue of Zeus for the inner chamber and another, only slightly smaller, of himself. Only 15 of the original Corinthian columns remain, but standing next to them may inspire a sense of awe at their bulk, which is softened by the graceful carving on the acanthus-leaf capitals. The site is floodlighted on summer evenings, creating a majestic scene when you round the bend from Syngrou. ⊠ *Vasilissis Olgas 1, National Garden* ☎ *210/922–6330* ☜ *€2; €12 joint ticket for all Unification of Archaeological Sites* ⊙ *Tues.–Sun. 8:30–3* Ⓜ *Acropolis.*

WHERE TO EAT

Whether you sample octopus and ouzo in a 100-year-old taverna or cutting-edge cuisine in a trendy restaurant, dining in the city is just as relaxing as it is elsewhere in Greece. Athens's dining scene is experiencing a renaissance, with a particular focus on the intense flavors of regional Greek cooking. International options such as classic Italian and French still abound—and a recent Greek fascination with all things Japanese means that sushi is served in every happening bar in town—but today traditional and nouvelle Greek are the leading contenders for the Athenian palate. Traditional restaurants serve cuisine a little closer to what a Greek grandmother would make. Just follow your nose to find the classic authentic Athenian taverna—the one where wicker chairs inevitably pinch your bottom, checkered tablecloths are covered with butcher paper, wobbly tables need coins under one leg, and wine is drawn from the barrel.

8

$$$$ ECLECTIC ✕ **Balthazar.** With its airy neoclassic courtyard—paved with original painted tiles, canopied by huge date palms, and illuminated by colored lanterns—Balthazar truly feels like an oasis in the middle of Athens. The crowd is hip, moneyed, and beautiful, so you might wish to come for dinner, then stay to mingle as the DJ picks up the beat. Talented young chef Yiorgos Tsiktsiras keeps the quality and flavor high on the up-to-the-minute menu, with prices to match. Try any of the creative salads, the East-meets-West fish dishes, and the homemade desserts, especially the grape sorbet. ⊠ *Tsoha 27, at Soutsou, Ambelokipi* ☎ *210/644–1215* ⟐ *Reservations essential* ▭ *AE, MC, V* ⊙ *Closed Sun. No lunch.*

$$$$ ECLECTIC ★ ✕ **Cibus.** The lush Zappion Gardens have always been a tranquil green oasis for stressed-out Athenians, who head here to gaze at the distant views of the Parthenon and Temple of Olympian Zeus, or catch an open-air cinema showing, or chill out at the landmark café. Now, the

café is gone and a chic new restaurant is luring both fashionables and families. The food has an Italian touch, thanks to chef Mauro Peressini, and it's expensive but fantastic (reservations are essential for dinner). Try the ravioli with red radicchio and almonds, with a fondue of Montasio cheese and truffles, or one of several outstanding risotto dishes, including one with crayfish and tomatoes. After dinner, have a drink and listen to the latest grooves with the beautiful people at the neighboring Lallabai club. ⊠*Zappion Gardens, National Garden* 🕿*210/336–9364* ☰*AE, DC, MC, V. Closed Sunday nights.*

¢–$
GREEK
✗**Diporto.** Through the years, everyone in Omonia has come here for lunch—butchers from the Central Market, suit-clad brokers from the nearby stock exchange, artists, migrants, and even bejeweled ladies who lunch; they're often sitting at the same tables when it gets crowded. Owner-chef Barba Mitsos keeps everyone happy with his handful of simple, delicious, and dirt-cheap dishes. There's always an exceptional *horiatiki* (Greek salad), sometimes studded with fiery-hot green pepperoncini; other favorites are his buttery *gigantes* (large, buttery white beans cooked in tomato sauce), *vrasto* (boiled goat, pork, or beef with vegetables), warming chickpea soup, and fried finger-size fish. ⊠*Theatrou and Sofokleous, Central Market* 🕿*No phone* ☰*No credit cards* 🕓*No dinner.*

$$–$$$
GREEK
✗**I Palia Taverna tou Psarra.** Founded way back in 1898, this is one of the few remaining Plaka tavernas serving reliably good food as well as having the obligatory mulberry-shaded terrace. The owners claim to have served Brigitte Bardot and Laurence Olivier, but it's the number of Greeks who come here that testifies to Psarra's appeal. Oil-oregano octopus and marinated *gavros* (a small fish) are good appetizers. Simple, tasty entrées include rooster in wine, *arnaki pilino* (lamb baked in clay pots), and pork chops with ouzo. Can't make up your mind? Try the *ouzokatastasi* ("ouzo situation"), a plate of tidbits to nibble while you decide. ⊠*Erechtheos 16, at Erotokritou, Plaka* 🕿*210/321–8733* ☰*AE, MC, V.*

$–$$
GREEK
Fodor'sChoice
★
✗**O Platanos.** Set on a picturesque corner, this is one of the oldest tavernas in Plaka, and it's a welcome sight compared with the many overpriced tourist traps in the area. A district landmark—it is set midway between the Tower of the Winds and the Museum of Greek Popular Musical Instruments—it warms the eye with its pink-hue house, nicely color-coordinated with the bougainvillea-covered courtyard. Although the rooms here are cozily adorned with old paintings and photos, most of the crowd opts to relax under the courtyard's plane trees (which give the place its name). Platanos is packed with locals, who flock here because the food is good Greek home cooking and the waiters fast and polite. ⊠*Diogenous 4, Plaka* 🕿*210/322–0666* ☰*No credit cards* 🕓*Closed Sun.*

$$$–$$$$
CONTEMPORARY
✗**Orizontes.** Have a seat on the terrace atop Mt. Lycabettus: the Acropolis glitters below, and, beyond, Athens unfolds like a map out to the Saronic Gulf. It's tough to compete with such a view and, at times, the food and the service (or both) fail to match it. But best bets include the black sea bream with silver beet, mussels, grated tomato, and sea-urchin roe, or the beef paillard with yogurt risotto and glazed tomato.

CLOSE UP

Greek Fast Food

The *souvlaki* is the original Greek fast food: spit-roasted or grilled meat, tomatoes, onions, and garlicky *tzatziki* wrapped in a pita to go. Greeks on the go have always eaten street food such as the endless variations of cheese pie, *koulouri* (sesame-covered bread rings), roasted chestnuts or ears of corn, and palm-size paper bags of nuts. But modern lifestyles and the arrival of foreign pizza and burger chains have cultivated a taste for fast food—and spawned several local brands definitely worth checking out. Goody's serves burgers and spaghetti as well as some salads and sandwiches. Items like baguettes with grilled vegetables or seafood salads are seasonal additions to the menu. At I Pitta tou Pappou you can sample

several takes on the souvlaki: grilled chicken breast or pork-and-lamb patties, each served with a special sauce. Everest is tops when it comes to "tost"–oval-shape sandwich buns with any combination of fillings, from omelets and smoked turkey breast to fries, roasted red peppers, and various spreads. It also sells sweet and savory pies, ice cream, and desserts. Its main rival is Grigoris, a chain of sandwich and pie shops that also runs the City Espresso Bars. If you want to sit down while you eat your fast food, look for a Flocafe Espresso Bar. Along with espresso, frappé, *filtro* (drip), and cappuccino, they also serve a selection of pastries and sandwiches, including brioche with mozzarella and pesto.

No road goes this high: the restaurant is reached by cable car. ⌂*Mt. Lycabettus, Kolonaki* ☎*210/721–0701 or 210/722–7065* ⌂*Reservations essential* ☐*AE, DC, MC, V.*

8

$-$$ ✕**Strofi.** Walls lined with autographed photos of actors from the nearby
GREEK Odeon of Herodes Atticus attest to Strofi's success with the after-theater crowd. Despite the many tourists, the dramatic rooftop garden views of the Acropolis still attract locals who have been coming here for decades. Start with a tangy *taramosalata* (fish roe dip) or velvety tzatziki, which perfectly complements the thinly sliced fried zucchini. Another good appetizer is *fava*, a puree of yellow split peas. For the main coarse, choose roast lamb with *hilopites* (thin egg noodles cut into small squares), rabbit *stifado* (a stew of meat, white wine, garlic, cinnamon, and spices), veal with eggplant, or kid goat prepared with oil and oregano. ⌂*Rovertou Galli 25, Makriyianni* ☎*210/921–4130 or 210/922–3787* ☐*DC, MC, V* ☾*Closed Sun. No lunch.*

$-$$ ✕**Taverna Filipou.** This unassuming taverna is hardly the sort of place
GREEK you'd expect to find in chic Kolonaki, yet its devotees include cabinet ministers, diplomats, actresses, and film directors. The appeal is simple, well-prepared Greek classics, mostly *ladera* (vegetable or meat casseroles cooked in an olive-oil–and–tomato sauce), roast chicken, or fish baked in the oven with tomatoes, onions, and parsley. In summer and on balmy spring or autumn evenings, choose a table on the pavement; in winter, seating is in a cozy dining room a few steps below street level. ⌂*Xenokratous 19, Kolonaki* ☎*210/721–6390* ☐*No credit cards* ☾*Closed Sat night and Sundays as well as national holidays.*

$$$–$$$$ ✕**To Varoulko.** Not one to rest on his Michelin star, acclaimed chef
SEAFOOD   Lefteris Lazarou is constantly trying to outdo himself, with magnificent
Fodor'sChoice   results. Rather than use the menu, give him an idea of what you like
★   and let him create your dish from what he found that day at the market.
Among his most fabulous compilations are octopus simmered in sweet
red *mavrodafni* wine and served with mousse made from a sourdough
pasta called *trahana*, crayfish dolmas wrapped in sorrel leaves, and
red snapper with black truffle and eggplant mousse. Some dishes fuse
traditional peasant fare like the Cretan *gamopilafo* ("wedding rice"
flavored with boiled goat) with unusual flavors like bitter chocolate.
The multilevel premises stand next to the Eridanus Hotel; in summer,
dinner is served on a rooftop terrace with a wonderful Acropolis view.
✉ *Pireos 80, Gazi* ☎ *210/522–8400* ⚜ *Reservations essential* ☰ *AE,
DC, V* ☉ *Closed Sun. No lunch.*

WHERE TO STAY

Along with higher quality have come higher hotel prices: room rates in
Athens are not much less than in many European cities. Still, there are
bargains to be had. Paradoxically, you may get up to a 20% discount
if you book the hotel through a local travel agent; it's also a good
idea to bargain in person at smaller hotels, especially off-season. When
negotiating a rate, bear in mind that the longer the stay, the lower the
nightly rate.

$$$–$$$$ ⊞ **Electra Palace.** If you want simple elegance, excellent service, and a
great location in Plaka, this is the hotel for you. Located on an attrac-
tive street close to area museums, its guest rooms are comfortable and
beautifully decorated, with ample storage space. Rooms from the fifth
floor up have a view of the Acropolis–which you can also enjoy from
the rooftop garden bar. Before setting out in the morning, fill up with
one of the city's best buffet breakfasts—sausage, pancakes, and home
fries. In the evening, relax in a steam bath in the hotel spa. **Pros:** excel-
lent service, great breakfast. **Cons:** could have more amenities for the
money; pricey. ✉ *Nikodimou 18–20, Plaka, 10557* ☎ *210/337–0000*
⊕ *www.electrahotels.gr* ⮑ *131 rooms, 19 suites* ⚭ *In-room: refrigera-
tor, Wi-Fi, safe, TV, AC. In-hotel: two restaurants, two pools* ☰ *AE,
DC, MC, V* ⏀ *BP.*

$$$ ⊞ **Eridanus.** Dazzling modern art, a sparkling staircase, luscious beds,
top-line bath products—this lovely hotel on the edge of the rising-star
neighborhood of Gazi has it all. The building has a neoclassic vibe but
the interiors are cool/hot 21st century, thanks to a dramatic, white mini-
malistic lobby, bedrooms that are designed for the *Wallpaper* crowd,
and some high-style marble bathrooms. You can see the Acropolis from
seven of the rooms, especially from the gorgeous rooftop suite. The in-
house restaurant, Parea, is a great place for meat-lovers (note: the city's
best seafood is right next door at the Michelin-starred To Varoulko).
Pros: top restaurant on site; high style. **Cons:** set in Gazi, a transition-
ing neighborhood that looks a bit pockmarked in places. ✉ *Pireos 78,
Kerameikos 10435* ☎ *210/520–5360* ⊕ *www.eridanus.gr* ⮑ *38 rooms,*

3 suites ⟨⟩ *In-room: refrigerator, safe, TV, AC. In-hotel: restaurant, bar, gym, Wi-Fi.* ☰ *AE, DC, MC, V.*

$$$$ 🏨 **Grande Bretagne.** Rest on custom-made silk ottomans in the lobby; drink tea from gold-leafed porcelain in the atrium; call your personal butler 24 hours a day from your room—the landmark Grande Bretagne, built in 1842, remains the most exclusive hotel in Athens. The guest list includes more than a century's worth of royals, rock stars, and heads of state. An all-out-luxury renovation, completed in 2003, recaptured the original grandeur, restoring 19th-century oil paintings, antiques, and hand-carved details as they were a century earlier. There's also a lovely spa where you can pamper yourself with indulgences such as ouzo-oil massages. **Pros:** super-sumptuous restaurant; rooftop eatery has to-die-for vista of the Acropolis. **Cons:** not the most elegant of addresses; lobby and cheaper rooms have a luxe generic look. ⊠ *Vasileos Georgiou A' 1, Syntagma Sq. 10564* ☎ *210/333–0000* ⊕ *www.grandebretagne.gr* ⟨⟩ *290 rooms, 37 suites* ⟨⟩ *In-room: refrigerator, Ethernet, safe, TV, ac. In-hotel: 2 restaurants, 2 bars 1 cafe, 2 pools, gym, spa* ☰ *AE, DC, MC, V.*

$–$$ 🏨 **Jason Inn.** The cool marble lobby leads up to guest rooms furnished in warm peaches and pinks. All have mini-refrigerators, good-size closets, and safes. A buffet breakfast is included in the price, and the rooftop garden restaurant has an intriguing panorama spreading from the Acropolis to the ancient Kerameikos Cemetery to the modern-day warehouse district of Gazi. This hotel is steps away from the buzzing nightlife districts of Psirri and Thission, not to mention the ancient Agora. **Pros:** cinerama view from roof; good deal for the money. **Cons:** set on a somewhat run-down, seemingly out-of-the-way little corner. ⊠ *Ayion Assomaton 12, Thission 10553* ☎ *210/325–1106* ⊕ *www.douros-hotels.com* ⟨⟩ *54 rooms* ⟨⟩ *In-room: refrigerator, safe, ac, TV, Wi-Fi. In-hotel: restaurant, bar* ☰ *AE, MC, V* 🍽️ *BP.*

$$$$ 🏨 **King George II Palace.** A spacious lobby done in marble, mahogany,
Fodor's Choice velvet, leather, and gold trim lures you into a world where antique
★ crystal lamps and frosted-glass shower stalls with mother-of-pearl tiles raise standards of luxury to dizzying heights. Each room is individually furnished with one-of-a-kind handcrafted furniture, antique desks, and raw-silk upholstery. Heavy brocade curtains are no more than a decorative flourish: the rooms are soundproofed, and their lighting calibrated to the natural light. At the Tudor Hall restaurant, savor Mediterranean delicacies and a view of the city skyline stretching from the Panathenaic Stadium to the Parthenon. **Pros:** probably best hotel in Athens; flawless taste in decor; outstanding food. **Cons:** boutique-hotel distinctiveness marred a bit by conventions and meetings. ⊠ *Vasileos Georgiou A' 2, Syntagma Sq. 10564* ☎ *210/322–2210* ⊕ *www.classicalhotels.com* ⟨⟩ *77 rooms, 25 suites* ⟨⟩ *In-room: minibar, Ethernet, free Wi-Fi, safe, a/c, TV, satellite. In-hotel: 1 restaurant, 1 bar-restaurant, spa, gym* ☰ *AE, DC, MC, V.*

$$–$$$ 🏨 **Periscope.** This sleek concept hotel combines minimalist urban-chic design, amenity-filled rooms, and exceptional service for a truly relaxing experience. Business travelers and urbane globe-trotters love the efficient staff. Guest rooms are a bit small with disappointing views

but no one will complain about the flat-screen TVs. Many of the city's best restaurants and cafés are here, and it's only a short walk to the metro. **Pros:** located in old-money neighborhood of Kolonaki; spotless rooms. **Cons:** decor is mod minimalism—cool and cold. ⊠*Haritos 22, Kolonaki 10675* ☎*210/729–7200* ⊕*www.periscope.gr* ⚲*16 rooms, 4 junior suites, 1 penthouse suite* ⚑*In-room: refrigerator, free Wi-Fi, safe. In-hotel: bar, Wi-Fi, laptop loan* ⊟*AE, DC, MC, V.*

$$–$$$ ⛄**Plaka Hotel.** Tastefully decorated, with deep-blue velvet curtains that
Fodor'sChoice   match the upholstery on the wood-arm easy chairs, the guest rooms in
★   this charming hotel are a comfortable place to rest while in the heart of old Athens. This hotel flourishes in its location; some rooms have views of the Acropolis, which you can also enjoy from the roof garden. The staff is helpful, the rooms small but well kept, and breakfast is served in a glassed-in, taverna-style space overlooking the shopping thoroughfare of Ermou, Syntagma, and the Monastiraki metro. **Pros:** excellent location, diligent staff, good breakfast and lounge areas. **Cons:** small and sometimes stuffy rooms. ⊠*Kapnikareas 7, Plaka 10556* ☎*210/322–2706* ⊕*www.plakahotel.gr* ⚲*67 rooms* ⚑*In-room: refrigerator, TV, AC, safe, Wi-Fi.* ⊟*AE, DC, MC, V* ⏹*BP.*

¢–$ ⛄**Student and Travellers' Inn.** Not only is it cheap, this place is in the
★   pricey Plaka! Wood floors, regular spruce-ups, and large windows make this spotless hostel cheerful and homey. The renovated house on an attractive and bustling street in Plaka has private rooms and shared dorm bedrooms. You pay extra for a private bathroom, but all rooms have a sink and mirror. Breakfast costs 3–5 euros. The inn does not accept credit cards for payment, but a credit-card number is required to make a reservation. **Pros:** it's cheap! And it's in Plaka!. **Cons:** noisy; shared bathrooms; minimal privacy; no visitors. ⊠*Kidathineon 16, Plaka 10658* ☎*210/324–4808* ⊕*www.studenttravellersinn.com* ⚲*35 rooms, 14 with bath* ⚑*In-room: a/c, reception phone, no TV. In-hotel: free Wi-Fi, TV room* ⊟*No credit cards.*

NIGHTLIFE & THE ARTS

From ancient Greek tragedies in quarried amphitheaters to the chicest disco clubs, Athens rocks at night. Several of the former industrial districts are enjoying a renaissance, most notably Gazi, a neighborhood surrounding Technopolis, a former 19th-century foundry-turned-arts complex (located at Pireos 100, 210/346–0981, metro stop: Thiseio). Today Gazi is synonymous with the hippest restaurants, edgiest galleries, and trendiest nightclubs in town, providing one-stop shopping for an evening's entertainment.

For all listings, consult the Greek pocket-sized weekly *Athinorama* for current performances, gallery openings, and films, along with the weekly English-language newspapers *Athens News,* published Friday, and daily *Kathimerini,* inserted in the *International Herald Tribune,* available Monday through Saturday, or its newest addition every Friday, *Athens Plus.*

NIGHTLIFE

Athens's heady nightlife starts late. Most bars and clubs don't get hopping until midnight, and they stay open at the very least until 3 AM. Often there is a cover charge on weekends at the most popular clubs, which also have bouncers. In summer many major downtown bars and clubs close their in-town location and move to the seaside. Ask your hotel for recommendations and summer closings. Few clubs take credit cards for drinks.

BARS

Soul Garden. Popular Soul Garden is unquestionably hip but also friendly. Relax with a cocktail and snacks in the plant-filled, lantern-lighted courtyard; after 1 AM the dance floor inside picks up pace. ⊠*Evripidou 65, Psirri* ☎*210/331–0907.*

Stavlos. All ages feel comfortable at the bar in what used to be the Royal Stables. Sit in the courtyard or in the brick-wall restaurant for a snack like Cretan *kalitsounia* (similar to a calzone), or dance in the long bar. Stavlos often hosts art exhibits, film screenings, miniconcerts, and other happenings, as the Greeks call them, throughout the week. ⊠*Iraklidon 10, Thission* ☎*210/345–2502 or 210/346–7206.*

BOUZOUKIA

Many tourists think Greek social life centers on large clubs where live bouzouki music plays while patrons smash up the plates. Plate-smashing is now prohibited, but plates of flowers are sold for scattering over the performer or your companions when they take to the dance floor. Be aware that bouzoukia food is overpriced and often second-rate. There is a per-person minimum (€30) or a prix-fixe menu. For those who choose to stand at the bar, a drink runs about €15 to €20 at a good bouzoukia place.

Fever. One of Athens's most popular bouzoukia clubs showcases the most popular singers of the day, including the ageless Anna Vissi, Greece's own answer to Madonna. It's open Wednesday through Sunday. ⊠*Syngrou 259, Neos Kosmos* ☎*210/942–7580 through 210/942–7583.*

Rex. Over-the-top is the way to describe a performance at Rex—it's a laser-light show, multi–costume-change extravaganza, with headlining pop and bouzouki stars. ⊠*Panepistimiou 48, Central Athens* ☎*210/381–4591.*

REMBETIKA

The Greek equivalent of the urban blues, rembetika is rooted in the traditions of Asia Minor and was brought to Greece by refugees from Smyrna in the 1920s and still enthralls clubgoers today. At these thriving clubs you can even join the dances. The two most common dances are the *zeimbekikos,* in which the man improvises in circular movements that become ever more complicated, and the belly-dance-like *tsifteteli.* Most of the clubs are closed in summer; call in advance. Food is often expensive and unexceptional; it's wisest to order a fruit platter or a bottle of wine.

★ **Stoa ton Athanaton.** "Arcade of the Immortals" has been around since 1930, housed in a converted warehouse in the meat-market area. Not much has changed since then. The music is enhanced by an infectious, devil-may-care mood and the enthusiastic participation of the audience, especially during the best-of-rembetika afternoons (3:30–7:30). Food here is delicious and reasonably priced, but liquor is expensive. Make reservations for evening performances, when the orchestra is led by old-time rembetis greats. The club is closed Sunday. ⊠*Sofokleous 19, Central Market* ☎*210/321–4362 or 210/321–0342.*

Taximi. At one time or other, most of Greece's greatest rembetika musicians have played at this old-time bar; many of their black-and-white pictures are on the smoke-stained walls. ⊠*Isavron 29, at Harilaou Trikoupi, Exarchia* ☎*210/363–9919.*

TAVERNAS WITH MUSIC
Stamatopoulou Palia Plakiotiki Taverna. Enjoy good food and an acoustic band with three guitars and bouzouki playing old Athenian songs in an 1822 house. In summer the show moves to the garden. Greeks will often get up and dance, beckoning you to join them, so don't be shy. ⊠*Lysiou 26, Plaka* ☎*210/322–8722 or 210/321–8549.*

Kapnikarea. The ideal lunchtime spot in town to stop at after a long stroll along the city's main shopping boulevard, Ermou St, Kapnikarea is named after the sunken Byzantine church that it's located beside, near Monastiraki station. Here you can enjoy the live afternoon performance of rembetika musicians as you sip ouzo and savour traditional specialties as well as dishes inspired from owner Dimitris' world travels. ⊠ *Hristopoulou 2 & Ermou 57.* ☎ *210/322-7394*

THE ARTS
CONCERTS, DANCE & OPERA
Dora Stratou Troupe. The country's leading folk dance company performs Greek folk dances from all regions, as well as from Cyprus, in eye-catching authentic costumes. The programs change every two weeks. Performances are held Tuesday through Sunday from the end of May through September at 9:30 PM and Sunday at 8:15 PM at the Dora Stratou Theater. Tickets cost €13 and can be purchased at the box office before the show. ⊠*Arakinthou and Voutie, Filopappou* ☎*210/921–4650 theater, 210/324–4395 troupe's office* ☎*210/324–6921* ⊕*www.grdance.org.*

Megaron Mousikis/Athens Concert Hall. World-class Greek and international artists take the stage at the Megaron Mousikis to perform in concerts and opera from September through June. Information and tickets are available weekdays 10–6 and Saturday 10–4. Prices range from €18 to €90; there's a substantial discount for students and those 8 to 18 years old. Tickets go on sale a few weeks in advance, and many events sell out within hours. On the first day of sales, tickets can be purchased by cash or credit card only in person at the Athens Concert Hall. From the second day on, remaining tickets may be purchased by phone, in person from the downtown box office (weekdays 10–4), and online. ⊠*Vasilissis Sofias and Kokkali, Ilisia* ☎*210/728-2333*

🖷210/728–2300 ⊕www.megaron.gr Downtown box office ✉Omirou 8, Central Athens ☎No phone.

FESTIVALS

★ **Hellenic Festival.** The city's primary artistic event, the Hellenic Festival (formerly known as the Athens Festival), runs from June through September at the Odeon of Herodes Atticus. The festival has showcased performers such as Norah Jones, Dame Kiri Te Kanawa, Luciano Pavarotti, and Diana Ross; symphony orchestras; and local groups performing ancient Greek drama. The Odeon theater makes a delightful backdrop, with the floodlighted Acropolis looming behind the audience and the Roman arches behind the performers. The upper-level seats have no cushions, so bring something to sit on, and wear low shoes, since the marble steps are steep. For viewing most performances the Gamma zone is the best seat choice. Tickets go on sale two weeks before performances but sell out quickly for popular shows; they are available from the festival box office. *Odeon of Herodes Atticus ✉Dionyssiou Areopagitou, Acropolis ☎210/323–2771, 210/323–5582 box office ⊕www.greekfestival.gr Festival box office ✉Panepistimiou 39, Syntagma Sq. ☎210/322–1459.*

SHOPPING

For serious retail therapy, most natives head to the shopping streets that branch off central Syntagma and Kolonaki squares. Syntagma is the starting point for popular Ermou, a pedestrian zone where large, international brands like Espirit and Marks & Spencer's have edged out small, independent retailers. You'll find local shops on streets parallel and perpendicular to Ermou: Mitropoleos, Voulis, Nikis, Perikleous, and Praxitelous among them. Much ritzier is the Kolonaki quarter, with boutiques and designer shops on fashionable streets like Anagnostopoulou, Tsakalof, Skoufa, Solonos, and Kanari.

8

SPECIALTY SHOPS

★ **Afternoon.** Prices are lower than what you'll find abroad at this shop with an excellent collection of fashions by Greece's best new designers, including Sophia Kokosalaki, whose work has often graced the pages of *Vogue.* Look for labels from up-and-comers like Deux Hommes, Vasso Consola, and Pavlos Kyriakides. ✉*Deinokratous 1, Kolonaki* ☎*210/722–5380.*

★ **Center of Hellenic Tradition.** The Center is an outlet for quality handicrafts—ceramics, weavings, sheep bells, and old paintings. Take a break from shopping in the center's Oraia Ellada café, in clear view of the Parthenon. ✉*Mitropoleos 59 and Pandrossou 36, Monastiraki* ☎*210/321–3023, 210/321–3842 café.*

Lalaounis. A world-famous Greek jeweler experiments with his designs, taking ideas from nature, biology, and ancient Greek pieces—the last are sometimes so close to the original that they're mistaken for museum artifacts. ✉*Panepistimiou 6, Syntagma Sq.* ☎*210/361–1371* ✉*Athens Tower, Sinopis 2, Ambelokipi* ☎*210/770–0000.*

Martinos. Serious antiques collectors should head here to look for items such as exquisite dowry chests, old swords, and Venetian glass. ⊠*Pandrossou 5, Monastiraki* ☎*210/321–3110* ⊠*Pindarou 24, Kolonaki* ☎*210/360–9449.*

Oikotechnia. Craftspeople throughout Greece provide folk crafts for sale here by the National Welfare Organization: stunning handwoven carpets, flat-weave kilims, and tapestries from original designs. Hand-embroidered tablecloths and wall decorations make handsome presents; flokati rugs are also for sale. ⊠*Filellinon 14, Syntagma Sq.* ☎*210/325–0240.*

Stavros Melissinos. A legendary poet and gentle soul, as well as shoemaker, Stavros outfits many tourists with his handmade sandals. The Beatles and many other celebs have visited his shop. ⊠*Ayias Theklas 2, Monastiraki* ☎*210/321–9247.*

DELPHI & THE APOLLO COAST ΔΕΛΦΟΙ

Athens is set between two of the most magnificent ancient sites in Greece. Masses of Athenians engulf the Apollo Coast—the stretch of shoreline that runs about 40 miles southeast of the city—to commune with the sea, frolic at lavish resorts like Glyfada, and visit the fabled Temple of Poseidon. Perched atop a cliff at Sounion, this is a coastal site where thousands of travelers have come to ooh and ahh (including Lord Byron, who in a fit of ego, carved his name on one of the temple's columns). Heading westward from Athens for about 120 miles brings you to spectacular Delphi, the center of the universe for the ancients and one of the most beautiful and revered sites for lovers of antiquity. Heading out from Athens, bus excursion companies specialize in ferrying travelers to these sights, two great trophies for any sightseer to bag on their trip to Greece.

PLANNING YOUR TIME

The trip out to Sounion is the most famous day-trip of all from Athens, but if you want to overnight there is a wide array of hotels here. Below the temple is one of Greece's most famous beaches, so allot some hours for sun-worshipping if you so desire. As for Delphi, stunning mountain scenery, a world-famous archaeological site, and an excellent museum can easily add up to two full days. If you day-trip it, get an early start from Athens, as the trip can last as long as four hours by car. Numerous bus companies run day-trip excursions to the site, but to truly savor the spectacle opt for an overnight.

GETTING HERE

Orange KTEL buses (2 hour trip) leave for Sounion from the Mavromateon station (28 Oktovriou, at Platía Aigyptou) and Platía Klafthmonos (on Odos Stadiou, between Syntagma and Omonia squares). Take a *paraliakó* (coastal) rather than a *mesoyiakó* (inland) bus, as they're faster and more scenic. Other than the private bus excursion companies offering day trips to Delphi—CHAT and Key Tours are among the most popular—take a KTEL bus (3 hours, about €13), which serves western Attica from Terminal B in Athens (to get to Terminal B from downtown Athens, catch Bus 24 on Amalias in front of the National Garden; tickets for these buses are sold only at this terminal, so book seats well in advance during high season). The bus stops at the site, but if you want to ensure a seat on the bus, walk the 2 km (1 mi) back from the ruins to the "bus station" (a table in a taverna) on the far side of modern Delphi.

TOURS

CHAT and Key Tours have the best service and guides, plus comfortable air-conditioned buses. Taking a half-day trip to the breathtaking Temple of Poseidon at Sounion (€36) avoids the hassle of dealing with the crowded public buses or paying a great deal more for a taxi. A one-day tour to Delphi with lunch costs €93, but the two-day tour (€135) gives you more time to explore this wonder.

ESSENTIALS

Bus Contacts **Athens Terminal B** (⊠ *Liossion 260, Athens* ☎ *210/831–7179).* **KTEL Delphi** (☎ *210/831–7096 or 210/831–7173).* **KTEL Sounion** (☎ *210/880–8080).*

Tour Contacts **CHAT** (⊠ *Xenofontos 9, Syntagma, Athens* ☎ *210/322–2886 or 210/323–0827* ⊕ *www.chatours.gr).* **KEY TOURS** (⊠ *Kallirois 4, Syntagma, Athens* ☎ *210/923–3166 or 210/923–3266* ⊕ *www.keytours.gr).*

DELPHI ΔΕΛΦΟΙ

10 km (6 mi) west of Arachova, 189 km (118 mi) northwest of Athens.

Nestled in the mountain cliffs, modern Delphi is perched dramatically on the edge of a grove leading to the sea, west of an extraordinary ancient site. Ancient Delphi, the home of a famous oracle in antiquity, can be seen from the town's hotels or terraced village houses. It's easily reached from almost any point in the central town, at most a 5- to 10-minute walk. When the archaeological site is first seen from the road, it would appear that there is hardly anything left to attest to the existence of the ancient religious city. Only the Treasury of the Athenians and a few other columns are left standing, but once you are within the precincts, the plan becomes clearer and the layout is revealed in such detail that it is not impossible to conjure up a vision of what the scene must have once been when Delphi was the holiest place in all Greece.

According to Plutarch, who was a priest of Apollo at Delphi, the famous oracle was discovered by chance, when a shepherd noticed that his flock went into a frenzy when it came near a certain chasm in the rock. When he approached, he also came under a spell and began to utter prophecies, as did his fellow villagers. Eventually a *Pythia,* an anointed woman over 50 who lived in seclusion, was the one who sat on the three-footed stool and interpreted the prophecy. During the 8th and 7th centuries BC, the oracle's advice played a significant role in the colonization of southern Italy and Sicily (Magna Graecia) by Greece's Amphictyonic League. Increasingly an international center,

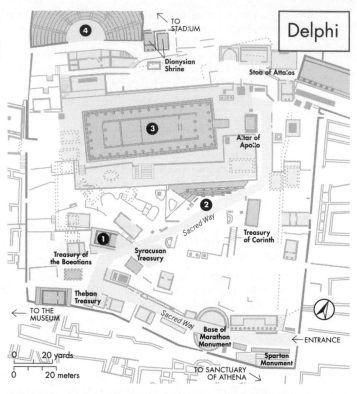

Delphi attracted supplicants from beyond the Greek mainland, including such valued clients as King Midas and King Croesus, both hailing from Asia Minor. During this period of prosperity many cities built treasure houses at Delphi.

Start your tour of the old Delphi in the same way the ancients did, with a visit to the **Sanctuary of Athena.** Pilgrims who arrived on the shores of the Bay of Itea proceeded up to the sanctuary, where they paused before going on to the Ancient Delphi site. The most notable among the numerous remains on this terrace is the **Tholos** (Round Building), a graceful 4th-century BC ruin of Pendelic marble, the purpose and dedication of which are unknown, although round templelike buildings were almost always dedicated to a goddess. By the 2nd millennium BC the site was already a place of worship of the earth goddess Gaia and her daughter Themis, one of the Titans. The Tholos remains one of the purest and most exquisite monuments of antiquity. Theodoros, its architect, wrote a treatise on his work: an indication in itself of the exceptional architectural quality of the monument. Beneath the Phaedriades, in the cleft between the rocks, a path leads to the **Castalian Fountain,** a spring where pilgrims bathed to purify themselves before continuing. On the main road, beyond the Castalian Fountain, is the modern entrance to the sanctuary. ⊠*Below road to Arachova, before Phaedriades* ⬛€6 *for* *all Delphi sites, €9 for Delphi sites and Delphi museum ⊘ Apr.–Oct., daily 7:30–7; Nov.–Mar., daily 8:30–2:45.*

Fodor's Choice
★
After a square surrounded by late-Roman porticoes, pass through the main gate to **Ancient Delphi** and continue on to the **Sacred Way,** the approach to the Altar of Apollo. Walk between building foundations and bases for votive dedications, stripped now of ornament and statue, mere scraps of what was one of the richest collections of art and treasures in antiquity. Thanks to the 2nd-century AD writings of Pausanias, archaeologists have identified treasuries built by the Thebans, the Corinthians, the Syracusans, and others. The **Treasury of the Athenians,** on your left as you turn right, was built with money from the victory over the Persians at Marathon. The **Temple of Apollo** visible today is from the 4th century BC. Although ancient sources speak of a chasm within, there is no trace of that opening in the earth from which emanated trance-inducing vapors. Above the temple is the well-preserved **theater,** which seated 5,000. It was built in the 4th century BC, restored in about 160 BC, and later was restored again by the Romans. From a sun-warmed seat on the last tier you see a panoramic bird's-eye view of the sanctuary and the convulsed landscape that encloses it. Also worth the climb is the view from the **stadium** still farther up the mountain, at the highest point of the ancient town. Built and restored in various periods and cut partially from the living rock, the stadium underwent a final transformation under Herodes Atticus, the Athenian benefactor of the 2nd century AD. ⊠ *Road to Arachova, immediately east of modern Delphi* ☏22650/82312 ⊕*www.culture.gr* ⊠€6 ⊘ *Apr.–Oct., daily 7:30–7; Nov.–Mar., daily 8:30–2:45.*

8

★
The **Delphi Museum** contains a wonderful collection of art and architectural sculpture, principally from the Sanctuaries of Apollo and Athena Pronoia. Visiting the museum is essential to understanding the site and sanctuary's importance to the ancient Greek world, which considered Delphi its center. (Look for the copy of the *omphalos,* or Earth's navel, a sacred stone from the adytum of Apollo's temple.) Thanks to renovations in 2004, you can now view all the world-famous pediments from Apollo's temple together.

One of the greatest surviving ancient bronzes on display commands a prime position in a spacious hall: the *Delphi Charioteer* is a sculpture so delicate in size (but said to be scaled to life) it is surprising when you see it in person for the first time. Created in about 470 BC, the human figure is believed to have stood on a terrace wall above the Temple of Apollo, near which it was found in 1896. Scholars do not agree on who executed the work, although Pythagoras of Samos is sometimes mentioned as a possibility. The donor is supposed to have been a well-known patron of chariot racing, Polyzalos, the Tyrant of Gela in Sicily. Historians now believe that a sculpted likeness of Polyzalos was originally standing next to the charioteer figure. Note the eyes, inlaid with a white substance resembling enamel, the pupils consisting of two concentric onyx rings of different colors. Elsewhere, the museum's recent expansion also allowed curators to give more space to the famous *metopes,* marble sculptures depicting the feats of Greece's two greatest heroes, Heracles and Theseus, from the Treasury of the Athenians. ✉ *East of Ancient Delphi* ☎ *22650/82312* ⊕ *www.culture. gr* 🖳 *€6; Ancient Delphi and museum €9* ⊙ *Apr.–Nov., Tues.–Sun. 7:30* AM–*7:30* PM, *Mon. noon–6:30* PM; *Dec.–Mar., daily 8:30–3* PM.

WHERE TO EAT & STAY

$–$$
★
✕**Taverna Vakchos.** Owner Andreas Theorodakis, his wife, and their two sons keep a watchful eye on the kitchen and on the happiness of their customers. Choose to eat in the spacious dining room or out on the large sheltered veranda with vines growing across the balcony rail, a Bacchus-themed wall painting, and a stunning valley view. The menu is heavy on meat dishes, either grilled, boiled, or simmered in the oven, but vegetarians can put together a small feast from boiled greens and other homemade meatless Greek classics. ✉ *Apollonos 31* ☎ *22650/83186* ▤ *MC, V.*

$$$
Fodor'sChoice
★
🛏**Amalia.** Clean-cut retro chic predominates at this 1965 landmark built by architect Nikos Valsamakis. Thirty-five acres of gardens spread down the mountainside, helping the low-lying Amalia blend seamlessly with the olive groves and pines of surrounding Delphi. An open, central hearth in the lobby sitting area is complemented by modern furnishings and a multihue blue-gray slate floor blocked off in large, varied squares. Comfortable, renovated contemporary rooms have light-color wood furniture, olive-green cupboards, and balconies. **Pros:** breathtaking views of Itea port seen from various public verandas, the rooms, and poolside bar; relaxing gardens. **Cons:** dated decor. ✉ *Apollonos 1 33054* ☎ *2260/82101* ⊕ *www.amalia.gr* ⤴ *184 rooms* ⌂ *In-hotel: restaurant, bar, pool* ▤ *AE, DC, MC, V* ⍿ *BP.*

$
★
🛏**Fedriades.** This hotel in the center of Delphi was purchased by the family that runs Epikouros and Acropole. Their 2008 renovation has created a look accented by warm colors and a touch of Greek mountain style. The basic amenities and cleanliness offered for a reasonable price make it a good choice. **Pros:** avoids "ancient kitsch" of other nearby hotels; good value for money. **Cons:** decor—simple and functional says it all. ✉ *Karamanlis (formerly Friderikis) 46, at Vas. Pavlou* ☎ *22650/82370* ⊕ *www.fedriades.com* ⤴ *23 rooms* ⌂ *In-room: refrigerator, satellite TV, safe, ac, Wi-Fi.* ▤ *AE, DC, MC, V* ⍿ *BP.*

SOUNION ΣΟΥΝΙΟ

70 km (44 mi) southeast of Athens.

Poised at the edge of a rugged 195-foot cliff, the Temple of Poseidon hovers between sea and sky, its "marble steep, where nothing save the waves and I may hear mutual murmurs sweep" unchanged in the centuries since Lord Byron penned these lines. Today the archaeological site at Sounion is one of the most photographed in Greece. There is a tourist café-restaurant by the temple, and a few minimarts are on the road, but no village proper. Arrange your visit so that you enjoy the panorama of sea and islands from this airy platform either early in the morning, before the summer haze clouds visibility and the tour groups arrive, or at dusk, when the promontory has one of the most spectacular sunset vantage points in Attica. The Cape of Sounion was called the "sacred headland" by Homer. From here Aegeus, legendary king of Athens, threw himself off the cliff when he saw his son's ship approaching flying a black flag. Theseus, in fact, had forgotten to change his ship's sails from black to white—the signal that his mission had succeeded. To honor Aegeus, the Greeks named their sea, the Aegean, after him.

Fodor's Choice Although the columns at the **Temple of Poseidon** appear to be gleaming
★ white from a distance in the full sun, when you get closer you can see that they are made of gray-veined marble, and have 16 flutings rather than the usual 20. Climb the rocky path that roughly follows the ancient route, and beyond the scanty remains of an ancient *propylon* (gateway) you enter the temple compound. On your left is the *temenos* (precinct) of Poseidon, on your right, a *stoa* (arcade) and rooms. The temple itself (now roped off) was commissioned by Pericles, the famous leader of Greece's golden age. It was probably designed by Ictinus, the same architect who helped design the Temple of Hephaistos in the ancient Agora of Athens, and was built between 444 and 440 BC. The 15 Doric columns that remain stand sentinel over the Aegean, visible from miles away. Lord Byron had a penchant for carving his name on ancient monuments, and you can see it and other graffiti on the right corner pillar of the portico. The view from the summit is breathtaking—have your Nikon handy. ⊠ *Cape of Sounion* ☎ *22920/39363* ⊕ *www.culture.gr* ☜ *€4* ☉ *Daily 9.30* AM–*dusk.*

THE CYCLADES: MYKONOS ΜΥΚΟΝΟΣ

The magical words "Greek Islands" conjure up beguiling images. If for **8** you they suggest blazing sun and sea, bare rock and mountains, olive trees and vineyards, white rustic architecture and ancient ruins, fresh fish and fruity oils, the Cyclades are isles of quintessential plenty, the ultimate Mediterranean archipelago. "The islands with their drinkable blue volcanoes," wrote Odysseus Elytis, winner of the Nobel Prize for poetry, musing on Santorini. That Homer—who loved these islands—is buried here is unverifiable but spiritually true.

Set in the heart of the Grecian Mediterranean, the nearly 2,000 islands and islets are scattered like a ring (Cyclades is the Greek word for "circling ones") around the sacred isle of Delos, birthplace of the god Apollo. Gateways to this Aegean archipelago include the airports on Mykonos and Santorini, the two most famous and beloved Greek islands. In a magnificent fusion of sunlight, stone, and sparkling aqua sea, these both offer both culture and hedonism: ancient sites, Byzantine castles and museums, lively nightlife, shopping, dining, and beaches plain and fancy. Many people start off their island adventure in the famed town of Mykonos, where whitewashed houses huddle together against the meltemi winds and backpackers rub elbows with millionaires in the glorious mazelike white-marble streets.

PLANNING YOUR TIME

The experience of Mykonos and other Cycladic islands (like Santorini) is radically different summer and winter. In summer all services are operating on overload, the beaches are crowded, the clubs noisy, the restaurants packed, and the scene swinging. Walkers, nature lovers, and devotees of classical and Byzantine Greece would do better to come in spring and fall, ideally in late April-June or September-October, when temperatures are lower and tourists are fewer. But off-season travel means less frequent boat service; in winter many shops, hotels, and restaurants are closed, and the open cafés are full of locals recuperating from summer's intensities. While it is true that feverish partying can overwhelm the young in summer, other seasons allow for temptations that are fewer, gentler, and more profound.

GETTING HERE & AROUND

Olympic Airways has six flights daily to Mykonos (10 daily during peak tourist season). The Olympic Airways offices in Mykonos are at the port and at the airport. Aegean Airlines also has five daily flights to Mykonos, but their schedules are often subject to change. In summer there are two to three ferries daily to Mykonos from Athens's Piraeus port. There are daily departures via ferry to Santorini. Check which dock they leave from, as there are both new and old docks. For complete information, consult travel agencies in town and in Athens. For traveling by bus on Mykonos itself, the main station is at Ayios Loukas in the Fabrica quarter at the south end of town.

TOURS

Windmills Travel takes a group every morning for a day tour of the sacred isle of Delos (€35). The company also has half-day guided tours of the Mykonos beach towns, with a stop in Ano Mera for the Panayia Tourliani Monastery (€20). Windmills arranges private tours of Delos and Mykonos and off-road jeep trips (€50).

ESSENTIALS

Bus Contacts Mykonos Buses (☎ 22890/23360).

Air Information Aegean Airlines (☎ 210/626–1000 ⊕ www.aegeanair.com). **Olympic Airways** (✉ Port, Mykonos town ☎ 22890/22490 or 22890/22495 ⊕ www.olympicair.com). **Mykonos Airport** (4 km [2½ mi] southeast of Mykonos town ☎ 22890/22327).

Visitor Information Mykonos Tourist Police (✉ Mykonos town harbor, near departure point for Delos ☎ 22890/22716 ⊕ mykonos-accommodation.com).

Windmills Travel (✉ Fabrica ☎ 22890/26555 or 22890/23877 ⊕ www.windmillstravel.com).

MYKONOS TOWN ΜΥΚΟΝΟΣ (ΧΩΡΑ)

Put firmly on the map by Jackie O in the 1960s, Mykonos town—called Hora by the locals—remains the Saint-Tropez of the Greek islands. The scenery is memorable, with its whitewashed streets, Little Venice, the Kato Myli ridge of windmills, and Kastro, the town's medieval

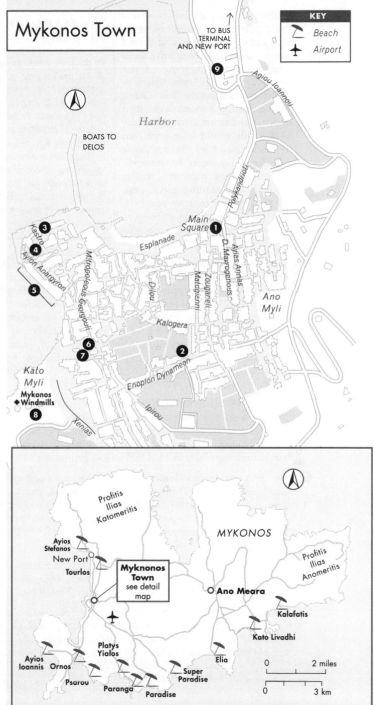

Mykonos Town

KEY

🏖 *Beach*

✈ *Airport*

TO BUS
TERMINAL
AND NEW PORT

9

Agiou Ioannou

Harbor

BOATS TO
DELOS

3 Kastro

4 Ayion Anargyron

5

Mitropoleos Georgouli

Esplanade

*Main
Square* **1**

Ayies Annas

D. Mavrogenous

Polykandrioti

*Ano
Myli*

Diiou

Kalogera

Zouganeli

Matogianni

*Kato
Myli*

6
7

Enoplon Dynameon

2

Ipirou

**Mykonos
◆ Windmills**

8

Xenias

---

*Profitis
Ilias
Katomeritis*

MYKONOS

*Profitis
Ilias
Anomeritis*

Ayios
Stefanos

New Port

Tourlos

**Myknonos
Town**
*see detail
map*

○ **Ano Meara**

🏖 Kalafatis

Kato Livadhi

Ayios
Ioannis   Ornos

Platys
Yialos

🏖 Elia

Psarou

Paranga

Paradise

**Super
Paradise**

0		2 miles

0		3 km

quarter. Its cubical two- or three-story houses and churches, with their red or blue doors and domes and wooden balconies, have been long celebrated as some of the best examples of classic Cycladic architecture. Luckily, the Greek Archaeological Service decided to preserve the town, even when the Mykonians would have preferred to rebuild, and so the authentic Old Town has been impressively preserved. Pink oleander, scarlet hibiscus, and trailing green pepper trees form a contrast amid the dazzling whiteness, whose frequent renewal with whitewash is required by law.

> ## THE PRANCE OF THE PELICAN
>
> By the time morning's open-air fish market picks up steam in Mykonos town, Petros the Pelican—the town mascot—preens and cadges eats. In the 1950s a group of migrating pelicans passed over Mykonos, leaving behind a single exhausted bird; Vassilis the fisherman nursed it back to health, and locals say that the pelican in the harbor is the original Petros (though there are several).

1 Start a tour of Mykonos town (Hora) on the main square, **Mando Mavrogenous Square** (sometimes called Taxi Square). Pride of place goes to a bust of Mando Mavrogenous, the island heroine, standing on a pedestal. In the 1821 War of Independence the Mykonians, known for their seafaring skills, volunteered an armada of 24 ships, and in 1822, when the Ottomans landed a force on the island, Mando and her soldiers forced them back to their ships. After independence, a scandalous love affair caused the heroine's exile to Paros, where she died. An aristocratic beauty who becomes a great revolutionary war leader and then dies for love may seem unbelievably Hollywoodish, but it is true.

The main shopping street, **Metoyanni** (⊠ *Perpendicular to harbor*), is lined with jewelry stores, clothing boutiques, chic cafés, and candy shops. Owing to the many cruise ships that disgorge thousands of shoppers daily in season, the rents here rival Fifth Avenue's, and the more interesting shops have skedaddled to less-prominent side streets.

2 The charming **Aegean Maritime Museum** contains a collection of model ships, navigational instruments, old maps, prints, coins, and nautical memorabilia. The backyard garden displays some old anchors and ship's wheels and a reconstructed 1890 lighthouse, once lighted by oil. ⊠ *Enoplon Dynameon* ☎ *22890/22700* 💶 *€3* ⊙ *Daily 10:30–1 and 6:30–9.*

Take a peek into **Lena's House,** an accurate restoration of a middle-class Mykonos house from the 19th century. ⊠ *Enoplon Dynameon* ☎ *22890/22591* 💶 *Free* ⊙ *Apr.–Oct., daily 7 PM–9 PM.*

3 The **Folk Museum,** housed in an 18th-century house, exhibits a bedroom furnished and decorated in the fashion of that period. On display are looms and lace-making devices, Cycladic costumes, old photographs, and Mykoniot musical instruments that are still played at festivals. ⊠ *South of boat dock* ☎ *22890/22591 or 22890/22748* 💶 *Free* ⊙ *Mon.–Sat. 4–8, Sun. 5:30–8.*

❹ Mykonians claim that exactly 365 churches and chapels dot their land-
★ scape, one for each day of the year. The most famous of these is the
Church of Paraportiani (*Our Lady of the Postern Gate* ✉ *Ayion Anargyron, near folk museum*). The sloping, whitewashed conglomeration of
four chapels, mixing Byzantine and vernacular idioms, looks fantastic;
it is solid and ultimately sober, and its position on a promontory facing
the sea sets off the unique architecture.

❺ Many of the early ship's captains built distinguished houses directly on
★ the sea here, with wooden balconies overlooking the water. Today this
neighborhood, at the southwest end of the port, is called **Little Venice**
(✉ *Mitropoleos Georgouli*). This area, architecturally unique and one
of the most attractive in all the islands, is so called because its handsome
houses, which once belonged to shipowners and aristocrats, rise from
the edge of the sea, and their elaborate buttressed wooden balconies
hang over the water—there are no Venetian marble palazzi reflected
in still canals. Many of these fine old houses are now elegant bars
specializing in sunset drinks, or cabarets, or shops, and crowds head
to the cafés and clubs, many found a block inland from Little Venice.
These are usually soundproofed (Mykonians are still sad that a rent
fight closed Pierro's, the Mediterranean's most famous gay bar, though
maybe residents who lived nearby aren't).

❻ The **Greek Orthodox Cathedral of Mykonos** (✉ *On square that meets both
Ayion Anargyron and Odos Mitropolis*) has a number of old icons of
the post-Byzantine period.

❼ Next to the Greek Orthodox Cathedral is the **Roman Catholic Cathedral**
(✉ *On square that meets both Ayion Anargyron and Odos Mitropolis*) from the Venetian period. The name and coat of arms of the
Ghisi family, which took over Mykonos in 1207, are inscribed in the
entrance hall.

8

❽ Across the water from Little Venice, set on a high hill, are the famous
Mykonos windmills, echoes of a time when wind power was used to grind
the island's grain. The area from Little Venice to the windmills is called
Alefkandra, which means "whitening": women once hung their laundry here. A little farther toward the windmills the bars chockablock on
shoreside decks are barely above sea level, and when the north wind is
up (often) surf splashes the tables. Farther on, the shore spreads into an
unprepossessing beach, and tables are placed on sand or pebbles. After
dinner (there are plenty of little tavernas here), the bars turn up their
music, and knowing that the beat thumps into the night, older tourists
seek solace elsewhere.

❾ Before setting out on the mandatory boat excursion to the isle of Delos,
check out the **Archaeological Museum,** set at the northern edge of town.
It affords insight into the intriguing history of its ancient shrines. The
museum houses Delian funerary sculptures, many with scenes of mourn-
ing; most were moved to Rhenea when the Athenians cleansed Delos
in the 6th century, during the sixth year of the Peloponnesian war,
and, under instruction from the Delphic Oracle, the entire island was
purged of all dead bodies. The most significant work from Mykonos

is a 7th-century BC *pithos* (storage jar), showing the Greeks in the Trojan horse and the sack of the city. ⊠*Ayios Stefanos, between boat dock and town* ☎22890/22325 ⌨€3 ۞ *Wed.–Mon. 8:30–2:30.*

Fodor's Choice Thirty minutes by caïque from
★ Mykonos, legendary **Delos** was the islands' ancient religious center, sacred to Apollo and Artemis. Its Exedra ton Leonton (Terrace of the Lions), a weathered row of nine Naxian marble sculptures from the 7th century BC (now copies), over-

looks the dried-up sacred lake. Other highlights are a group of houses of the Hellenistic and Roman periods, with their fine floor mosaics in situ, and the avenue of enormous stone phalli at the entrance to the Sanctuary of Dionysus. Museum, theater, houses—this vast site is one of the most fabled of antiquity. Tuesday through Sunday, boats leave Mykonos from 8:30 to 9:30 and return from 12:30 to 1:30, depending on the winds. Find the excursion boats on Mykonos harbor.

BEACHES

There is a beach for every taste in Mykonos. Beaches near Mykonos town, within walking distance, are **Tourlos** and **Ayios Ioannis. Ayios Stefanos,** about a 45-minute walk from Mykonos town, has a mini-golf course, water sports, restaurants, and umbrellas and lounge chairs for rent. The south coast's **Psarou,** protected from wind by hills and surrounded by restaurants, offers a wide selection of water sports and is often called the finest beach. Nearby **Platys Yialos,** popular with families, is also lined with restaurants and dotted with umbrellas for rent. **Ornos** is also perfect for families; boats leave from here for more distant beaches, and there is lively nightlife patronized by locals as well as visitors. **Paranga, Paradise, Super Paradise,** and **Elia** are all on the southern coast of the island, and are famously nude, though getting less so; one corner of Elia is gay. **Super Paradise** is half gay, half straight, and swings at night. The scene at Paradise's bars throbs till dawn. All have tavernas on the beach.

WHERE TO EAT

$$$$ ✕**La Maison de Catherine.** This hidden restaurant's Greek and French
Fodor's Choice cuisine and hospitality—Katerina is still in charge—are worth the search
★ through the Dilou quarter of Mykonos. The splendid air-conditioned interior mixes Cycladic arches and whitewash with a French feeling and a faded 16th-century tapestry from Constantinople. Candles and classical music set the tone for baby squid stuffed with rice and Greek mountain spices, or soufflé, puffed to perfection and loaded with cheese, mussels, and prawns. ⊠*Ayios Gerasimos, Dilou 84600* ☎22890/22169 fax:22890/26946 ⌨*Reservations essential* ☰*AE, DC, MC, V.*

$$$ ✕**Sea Satin Market–Caprice.** If the wind is up, the waves sing at this
★ magical spot, set on a far tip of land below the famous windmills of

Mykonos. The preferred place for Greek shipowners, Sea Satin Market sprawls out onto a seaside terrace and even onto the sand of the beach bordering Little Venice. When it comes to fish, prices vary according to weight. Shellfish is a specialty, and everything is beautifully presented. In summer, live music and dancing add to the liveliness. ✉ *On seaside under windmills* ☎ *22890/24676* 🖃 *AE, MC, V.*

WHERE TO STAY

$$$$
Fodor'sChoice
★
🖵 **Belvedere.** You may not have to go to Greece once you view the "movie" presentation on this hotel's Web site—it is almost as relaxing, blue-and-white, and high style as this hotel (but not quite). Favored by the hip, replete with Matsuhita Mykonos—an outpost of famed sushi chef Nobu—and designed in the best dreamy manner, the Beledevere has a club-like atmosphere, convenient location, and view over Mykonos town and harbor that ensures this hotel's popularity. Slip off your Tods in the dramatically decorated guest rooms, white-on-white sanctums with sailcloth drapes, rope accents, and a beautifully laid-back touch. **Pros:** the Mykonos dream made real; magical views from various guest rooms. **Cons:** very pricey; too hip for its own good? ✉ *School of Fine Arts district 84600* ☎ *22890/25122* ⊕ *www.belvederehotel.com* ⇗ *42 rooms, 6 suites* ⚭ *In-room: refrigerator. In-hotel: restaurant, bar, pool, spa, public Internet* 🖃 *AE, MC, V* ⊘ *Closed Nov.–Mar.* ⍟*BP.*

$
🖵 **Philippi.** Of the inexpensive hotels scattered throughout town, this is the most attractive. The rooms have balconies that overlook the garden If you want to get away from it all, go elsewhere. **Pros:** location is in the center of things; owner Christos Kontizas is a passionate gardener. **Cons:** you can't get here by vehicle. ✉ *Kalogera 25 84600* ☎ *22890/22294* ⊕ *www.philippi-hotel.com* ⇗ *13 rooms* ⚭ *In-room: refrigerator, ac. TV, Wi-Fi. In hotel: no elevator* 🖃 *AE, MC, V* ⊘ *Closed Nov.–Mar.*

NIGHTLIFE & THE ARTS

Whether it's bouzouki music, break beat, or techno, Mykonos's nightlife beats to an obsessive rhythm until undetermined hours—little wonder Europe's gilded youth comes here *just* to enjoy the night scene. After midnight, they often head to the techno bars along the Paradise and Super Paradise beaches. Some of Little Venice's nightclubs become gay in more than one sense of the word, while in the Kastro, convivial bars welcome all for tequila-*sambukas* at sunset. What is "the" place of the moment? The scene is ever-changing—so you'll need to track the buzz once you arrive.

BARS &
DISCOS
Little Venice is a good place to begin an evening, and Damianos Griparis's **Galleraki** (✉ *Little Venice* ☎ *22890/27118*) is one of the best cocktail bars in town; it's so close to the water you may get wet when a boat passes. Upstairs in the old mansion (Delos's first archaeologists lived here), you'll find an art gallery—a handy sanctum for drinks on windy nights. Kostas Karatzas's long-standing **Kastro Bar** (✉ *Behind Paraportiani* ☎ *22890/23072* ⊕ *www.kastrobar.com*), with heavy beamed ceilings and island furnishings, creates an intimate environment for enjoying the evening sunset over the bay; classical music sets the tone. **Montparnasse** (✉ *Agion Anargyron 24, Little Venice* ☎ *22890/23719*

8

⊕*www.thepianobar.com*) hangs paintings by local artists; its superb sunset view precedes nights of live cabaret and musicals.**El Pecado–Remezzo** (⊠*North of waterfront*) is a high-tech, wild dance club.

SHOPPING

FASHION   Yiannis **Galatis** (⊠*Mando Mavrogenous Square, opposite Lalaounis* ☎*22890/22255*) has outfitted such famous women as Elizabeth Taylor, Ingrid Bergman, and Jackie Onassis. Yiannis will probably greet you personally and show you some of his coats and costumes, hostess gowns, and long dresses. He also has men's clothes. His memoirs capture the old days on Mykonos, when Jackie O was a customer.

FINE &   Soula Papadakou's **Venetia** (⊠*Ayion Anargyron 16, Little Venice*
DECORATIVE   ☎*22890/24464*) carries authentic copies of traditional handmade
ART   embroideries in clothing, tablecloths, curtains, and such, all in white; the women who work for her come from all over Greece, including a nunnery in Ioannina. Mykonos used to be a weaver's island, where 500 looms clacked away. Two shops remain.

THE CYCLADES: SANTORINI (THIRA) ΣΑΝΤΟΡΙΝΗ (ΘΗΡΑ)

Undoubtedly the most extraordinary island in the Aegean, crescent-shape Santorini remains a mandatory stop on the Cycladic tourist route—even if it's necessary to enjoy the sensational sunsets from Ia, the fascinating excavations, and the dazzling white towns with a million other travelers. Called Kállisti (the "Loveliest") when first settled, the island has now reverted to its subsequent name of Thira, after the 9th-century BC Dorian colonizer Thiras. The place is better known, however, these days—outside Greece, that is—as Santorini, a name derived from its patroness, St. Irene of Thessaloniki, the Byzantine empress who restored icons to Orthodoxy and died in 802.

Fly to Santorini if you must, but a boat trip around the caldera is a must—a spectacular, almost mandatory introduction to the unforgettable volcanic crater, one of the world's truly breathtaking sights: a demilune of cliffs rising 1,100 feet, with the white clusters of the white-on-white towns of Thera and Ia perched along the top. Santorini and its four neighboring islets are the fragmentary remains of a larger landmass that exploded about 1600 BC: the volcano's core blew sky high, and the sea rushed into the abyss to create the great bay. There has been much speculation about the identification of Santorini with the mythical Atlantis, and if the island is known as the "Greek Pompeii," it is because of the archaeological site of **ancient Akrotiri**, near the tip of the southern horn of the island. In July and August, of course, the masses arrive and you will have a pushy time walking down Thera's main street. Still and all, there's plenty of unforgettable Greek splendor if you know where to look for it.

ESSENTIALS

Air Information **Aegean Airlines**
(☎ *210/626–1000* ⊕ *www.aegeanair.
com*). **Olympic Airways** (⊠ *Port, Mykonos town* ☎ *22890/22490* ⊕ *www.olym
picair.com*).**Santorini Airport** (⊠ *On east
coast, 8 km [5 mi] from Fira, Monolithos*
☎ *22860/31525*).

**Tour and Visitor Information Nomikos
Travel** (⊠ *Fira* ☎ *22860/23660* ⊕ *www.
nomikosvillas.gr*). **Pelican Travel** (⊠ *Fira*
☎ *22860/22220* ✍ *info@pelican.gr*
⊕ *www.pelican.gr*).

WALK ON BY

Tourist touts still like to promote
mules as a mode of transport to
take you up the zigzag cliff path
to the island capital of Thera.
But animal rights groups would
prefer you didn't. And you should
be aware of another reason: the
mules on Santorini are piously
believed to contain souls of the
dead, who are thus doing their
purgatory. It is an arduous ascent.

FIRA ΦHPA

10 km (6 mi) west of the airport, 14 km (8½ mi) southeast of Ia.

To experience life here as it was until only a couple of decades ago,
walk down the much-photographed, winding **staircase** that descends
from town to the water's edge—walk or take the cable car back up,
avoiding the drivers who will try to plant you on the sagging back of
one of their bedraggled-looking donkeys.

The modern Greek Orthodox cathedral of **Panayia Ypapantis** (⊠ *Southern part of town*) is a major landmark; the local priests, with somber
faces, long beards, and black robes, look strangely out of place in summertime Thera.

Along **Eikostis Pemptis Martiou** (*25th of March street* ⊠ *East of Panayia
Ypapantis*) you'll find inexpensive restaurants and accommodations.

The blocked-off Ypapantis street (west of Panayia Ypapantis) leads
to **Kato Thera** (*Lower Thera*), built into the cliff side overlooking the
caldera, where prices are higher and the vista wonderful. For centuries
the people of the island have been digging themselves rooms-with-a-
view right in the cliff face—many bars and hotel rooms now occupy
the caves.

★ The **Museum of Prehistoric Thera** displays pots and frescoes from the famed
excavations at Akrotiri. Note the fresco fragments with the painted
swallows (who flocked here because they loved the cliffs) and the
women in Minoan dresses. The swallows, which still come in spring,
remain the island's favorite design motif. The fossilized olive leaves from
60,000 BC prove the olive to be indigenous. ⊠ *Mitropoleos, behind big
church* ☎ *22860/23217* ⊕ *www.culture.gr* ✆ *€5 including Archaeological Museum; €8 including Archeological Museum and Akrotiri*
⊙ *Tues.–Sun. 8:30–3.*

The **Archaeological Museum** displays pottery, statues, and grave artifacts
found at excavations mostly from ancient Thira and Akrotiri, from
the Minoan through the Byzantine periods. ⊠ *Stavrou and Nomikos,*

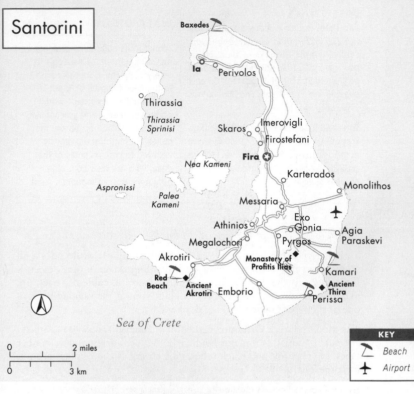

Santorini

Baxedes

Ia
Perivolos

Thirassia

Thirassia
Sprinisi

Skaros
Imerovigli
Firostefani

Fira

Nea Kameni

Karterados
Monolithos

Aspronissi

Palea
Kameni

Messaria

Athinios
Exo
Gonia

Agia
Paraskevi

Megalochori
Pyrgos

Akrotiri

Monastery of
Profitis Ilias

Red
Beach
Ancient
Akrotiri
Emborio

Kamari

Ancient
Thira
Perissa

Sea of Crete

0   2 miles
0   3 km

KEY

🏖   *Beach*

✈   *Airport*

8

PLANNING YOUR TIME

Crowds in Fira and Ia towns resemble the running of the bulls in Pamplona in the peak season months of July and August, so try to visit in May, June, or September instead. And slow down to savor it all: if you move too fast, you will see little, and the beauty here is in the general impression of sea, sky, mountain, and village,

GETTING HERE & AROUND

Olympic has six daily flights to Santorini Airport from Athens in peak season. Aegean Airlines has four daily flights to Santorini in summer, but their schedules are often subject to change. On Santorini buses leave from the main station in central Fira (Deorgala) for Ia and other villages.

TOURS

Pelican Travel runs coach tours, wine tastings, and visits to Ia; it also has daily boat trips to the volcano and Thirassia (half day €12, full day €25). Nomikos Travel—also a top place for tourist information—has tours to the same sights and to the island's wineries and the Monastery of Profitis Ilias. This is the place to sign up for a caldera submarine trip (€60).

Mitropoleos, behind big church ☎22860/22217 ☒€5 *including Museum of Prehistoric Thera* ☉ *Tues.–Sun. 8:30–3.*

WHERE TO EAT

$ ✕ **Nicholas.** This is Santorini's oldest taverna, where you'll find the natives camped out in winter. Island dishes are prepared well and served in a simple, attractive room. Try the local fava bean puree, an island specialty, and the lamb fricassee with an egg-lemon sauce. ☒ *2 streets in from cliff side on Erythrou Stavrou* ☎ *No phone* ▭ *No credit cards.*

$$$$ ✕ **Sphinx.** When Thera locals want more than a taverna, they come to
★ this pretty vaulted room, which glows with spotlighted Cycladic sculptures and blush-pink walls. As lush as this is, however, few can resist an outdoor terrace table, thanks to the striking caldera views in one direction and a vista of the giant cathedral in the other. Owner George Psichas is his own chef, and winners include the fresh grouper with grape and grappa sauce or the steak fillet with mushrooms, truffle oil, arugula, and Parmesan flakes. ☒ *Cliff-side walkway in front of Panayia Ypapantis* ☎22860/23823 ⊕ *www.sphinx.com* ⚏ *Reservations essential in summer* ▭ *AE, MC, V.*

WHERE TO STAY

$$$$ 🏨 **Aigialos.** For a taste of old aristocratic Santorini, venture to Aigialos
Fodor'sChoice ("seashore"), a cluster of buildings from the 18th and 19th centuries.
★ The most comfortable and discreetly luxurious place to stay in Thera, it comprises an array of one- and two-bedroom villas. Outside, various abodes are built in traditional volcanic stone, lime-washed in heavenly pastels. Inside, you'll find marble floors, magnificently beautiful antique furniture, and walls festooned with 19th-century engravings. Nearly all guest rooms have sublime terraces or balconies overlooking the caldera—no need to venture out at sunset. The restaurant serves its Mediterranean cuisine only to residents, and you can eat on your private terrace. **Pros:** gorgeous decor; great caldera vistas; private restaurant. **Cons:** a lot of steps, even for Santorini. ☒ *South end of cliff-side walkway 84700* ☎22860/25191 ⊕ *www.aigialos.gr* 🛏 *17 villas* ⚏ *In-room: refrigerator. In-hotel: bar, pool, spa, no elevator, public Internet* ▭ *AE, DC, MC, V* ☉ *Closed Nov.–Mar.* ⦿ *BP.*

$$ 🏨 **Costa Marina Villas.** Set in the tranquil Costa Marina neighborhood,
★ surrounded by a garden, and vaulted and shimmering-white in archetypal Cycladic fashion, this is a nifty option (built in 2002). Although just a block or so from the main square, the immediate precinct is a quiet, domestic neighborhood. Most guest rooms have a tiny balcony overlooking the garden or with an eastern sea view; "family" rooms (which anyone can book) are most spacious, thanks to their impressive double-height loft ceilings. **Pros:** great value for the money. **Cons:** Costa Marina may be a hike from the caldera, but it is romantic all the same. ☒ *Along road leading to camping grounds 84700* ☎22860/28923 ⊕ *www.santorini.org/hotels/costamarina-hotel* 🛏 *21 rooms* ⚏ *In-room: refrigerator, kitchen (some). In-hotel: no elevator* ▭ *MC, V* ⦿ *BP.*

8

NIGHTLIFE & THE ARTS

DANCING The **Koo Club** (⊠ *North end of cliff-side walkway* ☎ *22860/22025*) is Thera's most popular outdoor disco by far. **Santorinia** (⊠ *Next to Nomikos Conference Center* ☎ *22860/23777*) is the place for live Greek music and dancing. Nothing happens before midnight.

> ### A "PRIVATE" BALCONY?
>
> Remember that many of Santorini's hotel cliffside balconies elbow each other out of the way for the best view and, with footpaths often running above and aside them, privacy is often hard to come by.

MUSIC The popular **Franco's Bar** (⊠ *Below cliff-side walkway* ☎ *22860/24428* ⊕ *www.francos.gr*) plays classical music and serves champagne cocktails. It has a caldera view.

SHOPPING

EMBROIDERY **Costas Dimitrokalis** and Matthew Dimitrokalis sell locally made embroideries of Greek linen and Egyptian cotton, rugs, pillowcases in hand-crocheted wool with local designs, and more. Purchases can be mailed anywhere. ⊠ *1 block from cable car* ☎ *22860/22957* ⊟ *AE, D, MC, V.*

GALLERIES **Phenomenon.** Christoforos Asimis studied painting at Athens University, and has had many exhibitions there and abroad. The nearby cathedral's murals are his. His paintings specialize in the light and landscape of his home island. His wife Eleni, who also studied in Athens, shows sculptures, ceramics, and jewelry; her jewelry, in elegant designs both classic and modern, is executed with the highest craftsmanship. Few of Thera's proliferating jewelry shops have work to compare with this. ⊠ *Ypapantis walkway, Palia Fabrika* ☎ *22860/23041* ⊕ *www.santorini. info/paliafabrika/index.html.*

IA OIA

Fodor'sChoice
★

14 km (8½ mi) northwest of Thera.

At the tip of the northern horn of the island sits Ia (or Oia), Santorini's second-largest town and the Aegean's most photographed village. Ia is more tasteful than Thera (for one thing, no establishment here is allowed to play music that can be heard on the street), and the town's cubical white houses (some vaulted against earthquakes) stand out against the green-, brown-, and rust-color layers of rock, earth, and solid volcanic ash that rise from the sea. Every summer evening, travelers from all over the world congregate at the caldera's rim—sitting on whitewashed fences, staircases, beneath the town's windmill, on the old **kastro**—each looking out to sea in anticipation of the performance: the Ia sunset. The three-hour rim-edge walk from Ia to Thera at this hour is magnificent.

Although Thera, also damaged in the 1956 earthquake, rebuilt rapidly, Ia proceeded slowly, sticking to the traditional architectural style. The perfect example of that style is the Restaurant 1800, a renovated ship-captain's villa. Ia is set up like the other three towns—Thera, Firostefani, and Imerovigli—that adorn the caldera's sinuous rim. There is a car road, which is new, and a cliff-side walkway (Nikolaos Nomikou), which is old. Shops and restaurants are all on the walkway, and hotel entrances mostly descend from it—something to check carefully if you cannot negotiate stairs easily. Although it is not as crowded as Thera, where the tour boats deposit their thousands of hasty shoppers, relentless publicity about Ia's beauty and tastefulness, accurate enough, are making it impassable in August. The sunset in Ia may not really be much more spectacular than in Thera, but there is something tribally satisfying at the sight of so many people gathering in one spot to celebrate pure beauty.

WHERE TO EAT

$$$$

Fodor's Choice

★

✕**1800.** Clearly, some of Santorini's old sea captains lived graciously, as you'll note when dining at one of Santorini's most famous restaurants, 1800 (the name refers to the date when the house was built). Owner, architect, and restaurateur John Zagelidis has lovingly restored this magnificent old captain's house with original colors (white, olive-green, and gray) and furnishings, including antique sofas, wooden travel chests, and a hand-painted Venetian bed. To top it all off, a superlative roof terrace was constructed, with a vista framed by Ia's most-spectacular church cupolas—a perfect perch on hot nights for taking in the famous Ia sunset. Maître d' Eleni Economou is efficient, knowledgeable, and charming, while the chef, Thansis Sfougkaris—winner of Greece's prestigious Golden Toque award in 2004—does full honor to the beautiful surroundings. A top choice is the baked lamb cutlets with fennel, young peas, and porcini sauce. ⊠*Main street 84702* ☏*22860/71485* ⊕*www. oia-1800.com* ☐*AE, DC, MC, V.*

$-$$

★

✕**Kastro.** Spyros Dimitroulis's restaurant is primarily patronized for its view of the famous Ia sunset, and at the magical hour it is always filled. Happily, the food makes a fitting accompaniment. A good starter is olives stuffed with cream cheese dipped in beer dough and fried, served on arugula with a balsamic sauce. For a main dish try lamb scallops in wine and rosemary sauce, or pappardelle with asparagus and a sauce of dried tomato and garlic. Lunch is popular. ⊠*Near Venetian castle* ☏*22860/71045* ☐*AE, MC, V.*

WHERE TO STAY

$

🏠**Leandros Village.** If you want to momentarily indulge yourself in the fantasy that you live in a delightfully cozy and elegant little house with some of Ia's most stunning, sprawling views, this is the place for you. Warm, welcoming, and creative Leandros is from one of the oldest families in Santorini. The lovingly maintained four suites, each named after one of his sea-captain grandparents and decorated with traditional and family art, are built into the cave and have spacious living rooms, fully equipped kitchens, and modern bathrooms, but the best part is that every window you glance out of looks on to an endlessly glorious view of the caldera and the sea. **Pros:** open all year round; huge terraces around the suites. **Cons:** wildly popular, so book far in advance. ⊠ *Near Aghios Giorgos Church, on the cliff-side of Ia 84700* ☏*22860/71832* ⊕*www. leandrosvipsuites.com* ⇥*21 rooms* ♿*In-room: refrigerator, fully equipped kitchen, safe, a/c, dial-up connection. In-hotel: no elevator* ☐*MC, V* ⦿*BP.*

8

Ireland

On the road, Ireland

WORD OF MOUTH

"I decided to take one of Dublin's hop-on/hop-off tours to get my bearings, riding through the close-packed streets, seeing modern buildings next to Georgian townhouses, ivy and glass becoming roommates. I waved at a truck driver and he smiled and waved back; Amid the noisy motorcycles, the shush of buses, and the singing of brave birds, I found the magic of Dublin. Oh, and for those who doubt it, there really IS a pub on every corner!"

—Green Dragon

WHAT'S WHERE

1 Dublin. A transformed city since the days of O'Casey and Joyce, Ireland's capital may have replaced its legendary tenements with modern highrises but its essential spirit remains intact. For the past ten years one of Europe's biggest boomtowns, Dublin is a colossally entertaining city, all the more astonishing considering its intimate size. It has art, culture, Georgian architecture, an army of booksellers, and, of course, hundreds of pubs where conversation and vocal dexterity continue to flourish within its increasingly multicultural mix. Get spirited (pun intended) at the Guinness Brewery, "Rock n' Stroll" your way through hip Temple Bar, and be illuminated by the Book of Kells at Trinity College's great library.

2 Cashel to Cork. Heading south from Dublin you enter the Southeast, Ireland's sunniest corner (with almost double the national average), where blue skies will hopefully be shining over the medieval, magical, and magnificent Rock of Cashel (buses directly connect the town of Cashel with Dublin). As you explore Ireland's most impressive medieval monument—once fabled home to the Kings of Munster—you'll be following in the footsteps of St. Patrick himself. Continue southwest

to County Cork, where Cork city is a Venice-like port city of canals and bridges, a bustling mercantile center that remains one of Ireland's liveliest. Nearby, don't forget to kiss the Blarney Stone.

3 The Ring of Kerry. Ever since Killarney and the Ring of Kerry were discovered by travelers in the late 18th-century, visitors have come away searching for superlatives to describe the vistas afforded by its heather-clad sandstone mountains, deep blue island-studded lakes, long sandy beaches, wild rocky headlands, and sheltered wooded coves. Combining mountainous splendour with a spectacularly varied coastline, the Ring of Kerry is a 176-km (110-mi) drive that can be accessed at a number of places, although most people start out from the town of Killarney. If you don't mind sharing the road with half of Ireland—this is one of the country's most popular tourist destinations—you can glory in Ireland's most beautiful rugged countryside.

ATLANTIC OCEAN

Achill Island
Clare Island
Inishturk
Inishbofin

Oileáin Árainn
(Aran Islands)

Mouth of
the Shann

Córca Dhuibne
(Dingle Peninsula
Blasket
Islands   Dingle Bay
KERR
Iveragh
Skellig   Peninsula
Rocks   Bear
Kenmare Bay Penins
Bantry
Mizen Head

Malin Head

Toraigh
(Tory Island)

Rathlin Island

Portrush

SCOTLAND
(UNITED KINGDOM)

Ariann Mhor
(Aranmore Island)

Letterkenny

Derry City

Coleraine

Lough Foyle

North Channel

Gweebarra
Bay

DONEGAL

DERRY

Ballymena

Larne

Strabane

NORTHERN

Donegal
Town

IRELAND

Island Magee

ANTRIM

(UNITED KINGDOM)

Donegal
Bay

Omagh

Cookstown

Lough
Neagh

BELFAST

Belfast Lough

Ballyshannon

Lower
Lough Erne

TYRONE

Dungannon

DOWN

Newtownards

Sligo

FERMANACH

Armagh City

Killala
Bay

Upper
Lough Erne

Monaghan
City

ARMAGH

Newcastle

Sligo Town

LEITRIM

Ballina

MAYO

SLIGO

Newry

Cavan

MONAGHAN

Lough
Conn

Castlebar

ROSCOMMON

CAVAN

Dundalk

Dundalk Bay

Knock

Longford

LOUTH

Lough
Mask

LONGFORD

MEATH

Drogheda

Lough
Corrib

GALWAY

WESTMEATH

Mullingar

DUBLIN

Athlone

Galway
City

Ballinasloe

OFFALY

Naas

DUBLIN

Dún Laoghaire

Galway Bay

Birr

KILDARE

Bray

Irish Sea

Portlaoise

REPUBLIC OF IRELAND

LAOIS

Athy

WICKLOW

Wicklow

Ennis

Nenagh

Roscrea

Arklow

CLARE

Shannon

TIPPERARY

Kilkenny
City

CARLOW

Kilrush

Limerick City

Thurles

Gorey

LIMERICK

KILKENNY

Newcastle
West

Tipperary
Town

Cashel

WEXFORD

Listowel

Clonmel

Carrick-on-Suir

Wexford Town

Tralee

Farahy

WATERFORD

Waterford

Killarney

Mallow

Youghal

CORK

Midleton

St. George's Channel

Cork City

Cobh

Kinsale

0   50 mi

Skibbereen

0   50 km

IF YOU FLY INTO IRELAND, your descent will probably be shrouded by gray clouds. As your plane breaks through the mists, you'll see the land for which the Emerald Isle was named: a lovely patchwork of rolling green fields speckled with farmhouses, cows, and sheep. Shimmering lakes, meandering rivers, narrow roads, and stone walls add to the impression that rolled out before you is a luxurious welcome carpet, one knit of the legendary "forty shades of green." This age-old view of misty Ireland may be exactly what you imagined. But don't expect to still find Eire the land of leprechauns, shillelaghs, shamrocks, and mist. The only known specimens of leprechauns or shillelaghs these days are those in souvenir shop windows; shamrock only blooms on St. Patrick's Day or around the borders of Irish linen handkerchiefs and tablecloths; and the mists—in reality a soft, apologetic rain—can envelop the entire country, in a matter of minutes.

Today's Ireland is two-faced, like the Janus stones and sheela-na-gigs of its pre-Christian past. It's a complex place where the mystic lyricism of the great poet W. B. Yeats, the hard Rabelaisian passions of James Joyce, and the spare, aloof dissections of Samuel Beckett grew not only from a rich and ancient culture but also from 20th-century upheavals, few of which have been as dramatic as the transformation that has changed Ireland since the 1990s. Until it hit a recent speed-bump, Ireland's economy—christened the "Celtic Tiger"—was one of the fastest-growing in the industrialized world. In the last decade, galleries, art-house cinemas, elegant shops, and a stunning variety of restaurants have transformed Dublin from a provincial capital that once suffocated Joyce into a city almost as cosmopolitan as the Paris to which he fled. Irish culture, also, has boomed, thanks to Bono and U2, Daniel Day-Lewis, *Riverdance* (18 million people and more than $1 billion in box office receipts at last count), and *Angela's Ashes*.

Thankfully, the pace of life outside Dublin is more relaxed. Indeed, the farther you travel from the metropolis, the more you'll be inclined to linger. And once you take a deep breath of some of the best air in the western world and look around, you'll find some dazzling sights: the fabled Rock of Cashel, the fun and foodie-friendly hub of Cork city, and the spectacularly majestic Ring of Kerry. In one of the little villages on this peninsula of Ireland's extreme southwest, you'll hopefully be able to venture down a backroad, find an old pub, and savor the *craic*, the Irish term for a rousing good time. Undoubtedly, you'll be on first-name terms in no time.

WHEN TO GO

In summer the weather is pleasant, the days are long (daylight lasts until after 10 in late June and July), and the countryside is green. But there are crowds in popular holiday spots, and prices for accommodations are at their peak. As British and Irish school vacations overlap from late June to mid-September, vacationers descend on popular coastal resorts in the south, west, and east. Unless you're determined to enjoy the short (July and August) swimming season, it's best to visit Ireland outside peak travel months. Fall and spring are good times to travel

TOP REASONS TO GO

Dublin's Book of Kells: If you visit only one attraction in Dublin, let it be this extraordinary creation housed in Trinity College. Often called "the most beautiful book in the world," the manuscript dates to the eighth or ninth century and remains a marvel of intricacy and creativity, thanks to its elaborate interlaces, abstractions, and "carpet-pages."

Blarney Stone: One of the country's most enduring, and some would say ludicrous, myths, wherein kissing a stone high upon the battlements of a ruined Cork castle bestows a magical eloquence on the visitor. Grasped by the ankles and hanging perilously upside down to pucker upon ancient rock, you'll certainly have a tall tale to tell the folks back home.

Rock of Cashel: The center of tribal and religious power for over a thousand years, this medieval and mountainous settlement became the seat of the Munster kings in the 5th century. Handed over to the early Christian Church in 1101, the medieval abbey perched on a limestone mount in Tipperary contains rare Romanesque carvings celebrating St. Patrick's visit there in 450.

Cork City: Long called "The Rebel County," Cork is a Venice-like port city of canals and bridges. It was once home to writers Sean O'Faolain and Frank O'Connor, and is famed for its hip university, its fabulous food markets, and its passion for hurling, that fast and furious ancient game that makes soccer look like kick-the-can.

Ballymaloe House: The breeding ground for the new Irish gastronomy, this old Georgian farm estate was where Myrtle Allen created her everything-old-is-new-again-but-better take on Irish cookery. Long before organic became a buzzword, she made freshness her mantra. Today Darina Allen—the Martha Stewart of Ireland—runs the place.

Ring of Kerry: Just to the north of Cork, travelers have been thrilling to the Ring of Kerry's natural beauty for centuries, as they've gazed down from the heights of Killarney or been awed by spectacular natural wonders like the shoreline's Skellig Islands. Diverse and brazenly scenic, this is Ireland's most celebrated coastal drive.

9

(late September can be dry and warm, although the weather can be unpredictable). Seasonal hotels and restaurants close from early or mid-November until mid-March or Easter. During this off-season, prices are lower than in summer, but your selection is limited, and many minor attractions close. St. Patrick's Week gives a focal point to a spring visit, but some Americans may find the saint's-day celebrations a little less enthusiastic than the ones back home.

GETTING HERE & AROUND

You can arrive in Ireland by plane, train, or boat. Trains and buses take it from there and conveniently connect major Irish cities and towns.

BY BOAT

The ferry is a convenient way to travel between Ireland and elsewhere in Europe, particularly the United Kingdom. There are six main ferry ports to Ireland; three in the republic at Dublin Port, Dun Laoghaire, and Rosslare. Irish Ferries operates the *Ulysses*, the world's largest car ferry, on its Dublin to Holyhead, Wales, route (3 hrs, 15 min); there's also an express service (1 hr, 50 min) between these two ports. Stena Line sails several times a day between Dublin and Holyhead (3 hrs, 15 min). Norfolk Line sails from Dublin to Liverpool service, while P&O Irish Sea vessels run between Larne and Troon, Scotland. Bear in mind, too, that flying can be cheaper, so look into all types of transportation before booking.

BY BUS

In the Republic of Ireland, long-distance bus services are operated by Bus Éireann, which also provides local service in Cork, Galway, Limerick, and Waterford. Outside of the peak season, schedules can be limited. There's often only one trip a day on express routes, and one a week to some remote villages. To ensure that a bus journey is feasible, buy a copy of Bus Éireann's timetable—€6 from any bus terminal—or check online. Many of the destination indicators are in Irish (Gaelic), so make sure you get on the right bus. Check with the bus office to see if reservations are accepted for your route; if not, show up early to get a seat. A round-trip from Dublin to Cork costs €18.

BY CAR

The Irish, like the British, drive on the left-hand side of the road. Safety belts must be worn by the driver and all passengers, and children under 12 must travel in the back unless riding in a car seat. Despite the relatively light traffic, parking in towns can be a problem. Signs with the letter *P* indicate that parking is permitted; a stroke through the *P* warns you to stay away or you'll be liable for a fine of €20–€65; if your car gets towed away, the fine is around €180. Note that Ireland has the highest auto-accident fatality rate in Europe. Road signs in the republic are generally in both Irish (Gaelic) and English. U.S. driver's licenses are recognized in Ireland. On the new green signposts distances are in kilometers; on the old white signposts they're in miles. Speed limits are generally 95 to 100 kph (roughly 60 to 70 mph) on the motorways, 80 kph (50 mph) on other roads, and 50 kph (30 mph) in towns. Roads are classified as *M, N,* or *R:* those designated with an *M* for "motorway" are double-lane divided highways with paved shoulders; *N,* or national, routes are generally undivided highways with shoulders; and *R,* or regional, roads tend to be narrow and twisty.

BY PLANE

Flying time to Ireland is 6½ hours from New York, 7½ hours from Chicago, 10 hours from Los Angeles, and 1 hour from London. The major gateways to Ireland are Dublin Airport (DUB) on the east coast, 10 km (6 mi) north of the city center, and Shannon Airport (SNN) on the west coast, 25 km (16 mi) west of Limerick.

BY TRAIN

The republic's Irish Rail trains are generally reliable, reasonably priced, and comfortable. You can easily reach all the principal towns from Dublin, though services between provincial cities are roundabout. To get to Cork City from Wexford, for example, you have to go via Limerick Junction. It's often quicker, though perhaps less comfortable, to take a bus! Most mainline trains have one standard class. Round-trip tickets are usually cheapest. You should plan to be at the train station at least 30 minutes before your train departs to ensure you'll get a seat. It's not uncommon on busier routes to find that you have to stand, since all seats have been sold and taken. Train schedules are easy to obtain and available in a variety of formats, including Web, by Irish Rail. Sample fare? A round-trip ticket from Dublin to Cork will cost around €60.

ABOUT THE RESTAURANTS

Restaurants range from inexpensive ethnic eateries to luxurious outposts of Cuisine Irelandaise (Irish food accented with a French touch), from classic "carveries" to traditional pubs. In fact, the next time you wander into a pub bent on downing a platter of steak, bland potatoes, and mushy peas, don't be surprised if you end up with a meal of skewered John Dory in Clonmel Cider Sauce and a finale of Cooleeney Camembert ganache with Lavender Jelly. Begorrah—you've encountered the much-vaunted Irish Food revolution! Since the mid-1990s, the New Irish Cuisine has remade the old beige, boiled, and boring menu of yore. Today haute-hungry foodies packing chubby wallets are all abuzz over discovering emerging culinary wizards; artisanal producers of farmhouse cheeses; organic beef and smoked fish; and some of the best farmers' markets and provisioners around.

FAVORITE DISHES

The abundant high-quality produce the country is famous for is finally receiving the care and attention of world-class chefs in the capital city's restaurants, so don't be surprised to find your Irish stew is spiced and topped with a tangy avocado salsa. Even the humble potato is being shaped and transformed into *boxty* (potato-and-flour pancake) and *colcannon*—a traditional Irish dish with bacon and cabbage—is getting a nouvelle spin. Besides excellent Irish beef, pork, ham, and lamb, look for the rich seafood harvests of fresh and smoked salmon, oysters, mussels, and shellfish in many guises. Ireland is famed for its excellent dairy products, so leave room for the mature cheddars and luscious blue cheeses, the slightly sweet Dubliner, St. Tola goat's cheese from Clare, and Carrigburne Brie from Wexford. Indulge at least once in the traditional Irish breakfast, which is often served all day. It includes rashers (bacon), sausages, black-and-white pudding (types of sausage), mushrooms, tomatoes, and a fried egg—with lots of traditional homemade brown and soda breads and the famous Irish creamery butter. This "breakfast" is often the biggest meal of the day. But portions in Ireland can be huge for any meal, and this can happily mean shared dishes—another way to beat the euro!

9

HOURS

The Irish dine later than Americans. They stay up later, too, and reservations are usually not booked before 6:30 or 7 PM (watch for those "Early Bird" specials) and up to around 10 PM. Lunch is generally served from 12:30 to 2:30. Pubs often serve food through the day-until 8:30 or 9 PM. Most pubs are family-friendly and welcome children until 7 PM.

WHAT IT COSTS IN EUROS					
	¢	$	$$	$$$	$$$$
Restaurants	under €12	€12–€18	€18–€24	€24–€32	over €32

Restaurant prices are for a main course at dinner.

ABOUT THE HOTELS

Dublin is famous for its elegant boutique hotels that occupy former Georgian town houses on both sides of the Liffey, but there are plenty of new, full-scale luxury options also available. Thankfully, the city also has a decent selection of inexpensive accommodations, including many moderately priced hotels with basic but agreeable rooms. Outside Dublín, manors and castles offer a unique combination of luxury and history. Less impressive, but equally charming, are the provincial inns and country hotels with simple but adequate facilities. B&Bs are classified by Faílte Ireland as either town homes, country homes, or farmhouses.

PRICES & MAKING RESERVATIONS

Thanks to the booming Celtic Tiger economy, hotel choices and quality have expanded exponentially, but so have prices. So it's more important than ever to get the best deal for your dollar. Most hotels and other lodgings require you to give your credit-card details before they will confirm your reservation. If you don't feel comfortable e-mailing this information, ask if you can fax it (some places even prefer faxes).

WHAT IT COSTS IN EUROS					
	¢	$	$$	$$$	$$$$
Hotels	under €110	€110–€140	€140–€200	€200–€280	over €280

Hotel prices are for a standard double room in high season.

PLANNING YOUR TIME

There are two contrasting aspects to Ireland: its go-ahead, cosmopolitan capital city, still glowing with energy and confidence from years of economic boom, and the quieter, timeless charm of its unspoilt countryside. Any first-time, week-long tour of Ireland should focus on these two sides of the coin: the friendly people found in Dublin and Cork and the beautiful rural landscape, often gloriously framed by Ireland's time-burnished villages and medieval sites. This chapter concentrates on the geographic swathe that runs from Dublin to Cork, and presumes you'll arrive in the capital city and then fly back out from Shannon (on the West coast).

Your hotels in Dublin and Cork can be home bases from which to spider out and explore the surrounding regions—but also opt for some hours spent in smaller towns and villages, where you'll have a better chance of encountering the "real" Ireland down an unknown *bohereen* (lane). The time of year you go will be important, as traveling in the summer months could give you an extra two hours of sightseeing time over touring during the darker, shorter days of fall and winter. Rain is a constant, so prepare for "soft" weather.

Plan on using a mix of cars, buses, and trains. Opt for public transportation on the longer hauls (Dublin/Cork), then rent cars from where you're based (or research if bus lines can get you around: start with www.irishrail.ie and www.buseireann.ie). Remember that Irish roads can be twisty and signage non-existent, while public transportation allows you to plan the next destination, not spend a white-knuckled day dodging speeding traffic.

DUBLIN

Although it has hit a speed-bump recently, Europe's most intimate capital became a full-fledged boomtown during the past decade. Dublin, famously, has been riding the back of its powerhouse "Celtic Tiger" economy ever since the early 1990s. Although there are fewer construction cranes hovering over both shiny new hotels and old Georgian houses, the city is still in the throes of what may be the nation's most dramatic period of transformation since the 18th-century Georgian period. Indeed, if the town's most famous homeboy—the noted 20th-century author James Joyce—were to return to his once genteel town today and take a quasi-Homeric odyssey through the city (as he so famously does in *Ulysses*), would he even recognize Dublin as his "Dear Dirty Dumpling, foostherfather of fingalls and dotthergills"?

For instance, what would he make of Temple Bar—the city's erstwhile down-at-the-heels neighborhood, now crammed with restaurants and trendy hotels and suffused with a nonstop, international-party atmosphere? Or the old market area of Smithfield, whose Cinderella transformation has changed it into an impressive plaza and winter ice-skating venue? The truth is that local skeptics await the outcome of "Dublin: The Sequel." Can the "new Dublin" get beyond the rage stage without losing its very essence? Their greatest fear is the possibility that the tattered old lady on the Liffey is becoming like everywhere else. Oh ye of little faith: the rare aul' gem that is Dublin is far from buried. The fundamentals—the Georgian elegance of Merrion Square, the Norman drama of Christ Church Cathedral, the foamy pint at an atmospheric pub—are still on hand to gratify and enchant.

PLANNING YOUR TIME

Dublin is delightfully compact—nearly all main sights are within walking distance of the entrance to famed Trinity College. That noted, attempting to explore the city will require the wisdom of Solomon, as the Liffey River neatly splits Dublin into the Southside and the Northside. The Southside is the logical place to begin: many of the top sights are there, set among graceful squares and terraces dating from the city's elegant Georgian heyday. Head out from O'Connell Bridge—the closest thing Dublin has to a central landmark—down Westmoreland Street to vibrant Grafton Street and stop into Bewley's Oriental Café, still redolent of the Victorian 19th century. Venture down College Green to the genteel campus of Trinity College, where your priority should be the Old Library's Long Room and Book of Kells. From there, Grafton Street—Dublin's busiest shopping avenue—brings you to lovely St. Stephen's Green, where, on the northeast corner, you'll find, standing side by side, the National Museum of Archaeology and History, the National Gallery of Ireland, and the National Library.

From these museums, head northeast to famed Merrion Square, another Georgian-era extravaganza, or head north to explore the happening Temple Bar district along the Liffey's banks, and, farther west, St. Patrick's Cathedral and the Guinness Brewery. Cross the river to experience the grittier (though gentrifying) side of central Dublin. This area, called the Northside, is still the place to soak up the pure, adulterated city. It's here that Dublin's literary heart beats strongest—the Dublin Writers Museum is a highlight, and the area is filled with landmarks from events in Irish literary history, both real and imagined. How long will this highlights tour take? If you're moving at speedreader's pace, a frantic day, but you'll want to slow down and pace yourself over two days—even three—to truly savor the Irish Oz.

GETTING AROUND

Central Dublin is compact, so walking is the first choice for getting around. Main thoroughfares can become crowded with pedestrians, especially at rush hour, so plan routes along side streets with less bustle. When your feet need a break, turn to public transit. There's an extensive network of buses, most of which are green double-deckers. Some bus services run on cross-city routes, including the smaller "Imp" buses, but most buses start in the city center. Another regular bus route connects the two main provincial railway stations, Connolly and Heuston. If the destination board indicates AN LÁR, that means that the bus is going to the city center. In the city, fares begin at €1.05 and are paid to the driver, who will accept inexact fares, but you'll have to go to the central office in Dublin to pick up your change as marked on your ticket. The pleasant LUAS tram system also has two lines running through the city center. There are taxi stands beside the central bus station, and at train stations, O'Connell Bridge, St. Stephen's Green, College Green, and near major hotels; the Dublin telephone directory has a complete list. The initial charge is €3.80, with an additional charge of about €1 per kilometer thereafter. Navigating the city on your own in a rental car is an expensive headache.

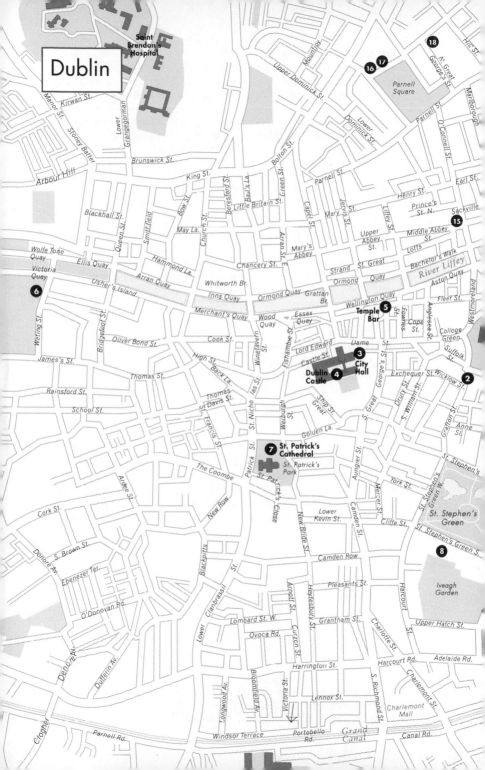

DISCOUNTS & DEALS

Like many tourist capitals around the world, Dublin now features a special pass to help travelers save on admission prices. In conjunction with Dublin Tourism, the **Dublin Pass** is issued for one, two, three, or six days, and allows free (or, rather, reduced, since the cards do cost something) admission to 30 sights, including the Guinness Brewery, the Dublin Zoo, the Dublin Writers Museum, and Christ Church Cathedral. Prices are €31 for one day; €49 for two days; €59 for three days; and €89 for six days; children's prices are much lower. You can buy your card online and have it waiting for you at one of Dublin's tourist information offices when you arrive.

TOUR OPTIONS

Dublin Bus has three- and four-hour "City Tours" of the city center that include Trinity College, the Royal Hospital Kilmainham, and Phoenix Park. The one-hour City Tour, with hourly departures, allows you to hop on and off at any of the main sights. Tickets are available from the driver or Dublin Bus. There's also a continuous guided open-top bus tour (€14), run by Dublin Bus, which allows you to hop on and off the bus as often as you wish and visit some 15 sights along its route. Gray Line Tours runs city-center tours that cover the same sights as the Dublin Bus itineraries.

VISITOR INFORMATION

Fáilte Ireland (aka Bord Fáilte), the Irish Tourist Board, has its own visitor information offices in the entrance hall of its headquarters at Baggot Street Bridge; it's open weekdays 9:15–5:15. The main Dublin Tourism center is in the former (and still spectacular) St. Andrew's Church on Suffolk Street and is open July–September, Monday–Saturday 8:30–6, Sunday 11–5:30, and October–June, daily 9–6.

ESSENTIALS

Dublin Bus (☎ 01/873–4222 ⊕ www.dublinbus.ie). **Dublin Tourism** (✉ Suffolk St., off Grafton St., Southside ☎ 1850/230–330 ⊕ www.visitdublin.com). **Fáilte Ireland** (✉ Baggot St. Bridge, Southside ☎ 01/602–4000 in Dublin, 1850/230–330 in rest of Ireland ⊕ www.discoverireland.com). **Gray Line Tours** (☎ 01/670–8822 ⊕ www.grayline.com). **Heuston Station** (✉ End of Victoria Quay, Dublin West). **Irish Rail–Iarnod Éireann** (⊕ www.irishrail.ie).

DUBLIN'S SOUTHSIDE

The River Liffey provides a useful aid of orientation, flowing as it does through the direct middle of Dublin. If you ask a native Dubliner for directions—from under an umbrella, as it will probably be raining in the approved Irish manner—he or she will most likely reply in terms of "up" or "down," up meaning away from the river, and down toward it. Until recently, Dublin's center of gravity was O'Connell Bridge. But Dublin's heart now beats loudest southward across the Liffey, due in part to a large-scale refurbishment and pedestrianization of Grafton Street, which made this already upscale shopping address the main street on which to shop, stop, and be seen. At the foot of Grafton Street is the city's most famous and recognizable landmark, Trinity College; at

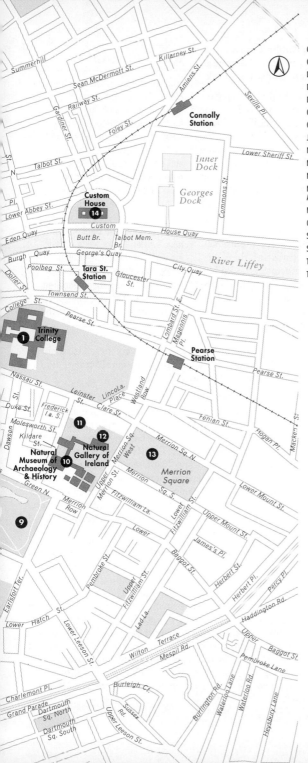

the top of it is Dublin's most popular strolling retreat, St. Stephen's Green, a 27-acre landscaped park.

Eastward lies Dublin's elegant Georgian quarter. If there's one travel poster that signifies "Dublin" more than any other, it's the one that depicts 50 or so Georgian doorways—door after colorful door, all graced with lovely fanlights upheld by columns. A building boom began in Dublin in the early 18th century as the Protestant Ascendancy constructed terraced town houses for themselves, and civic structures for their city, in the style that came to be known as Georgian, after the four successive British Georges who ruled from 1714 through 1830. But Georgian splendor is just the icing on the cake hereabouts, for there are also three of the most fascinating museums in Ireland, conveniently sitting cheek by jowl: the National Gallery of Ireland, the National Library, and the National Museum of Archaeology and History.

> ## WORD OF MOUTH
>
> "One thing to remember in Ireland is that the public transport system is not as good as it should be for a country undergoing an economic boom and so be prepared for late departures and arrivals and delays (especially on some train lines) and no proper timetable or evidence of one existing (Dublin Bus). I am speaking after having lived in Dublin for several years. People have been known to have written books while waiting for some of the elusive Dublin buses. There are some routes whose buses have been declared endangered species, as they are rarely sighted."   — Cathy

EXPLORING THE SOUTHSIDE

③ City Hall. Facing the Liffey from Cork Hill at the top of Parliament Street, this grand Georgian municipal building (1769–79) marks the southwest corner of Temple Bar. Today it's the seat of the Dublin Corporation, the elected body that governs the city. Thomas Cooley designed the building with 12 columns that encircle the domed central rotunda, which has a fine mosaic floor and 12 frescoes depicting Dublin legends and ancient Irish historical scenes. Today, the building houses a multimedia exhibition tracing the evolution of Ireland's 1,000-year-old capital. ⊠ *Dame St., Dublin West* ☎ *01/222-2204* ⊕ *www.dublincity.ie/recreationand culture* ⊠ *€4* ⊗ *Mon.–Sat. 10–5:15, Sun. 2–5.*

④ Dublin Castle. Neil Jordan's film *Michael Collins* captured Dublin Castle's near indomitable status well: seat and symbol of the British rule of Ireland for more than seven centuries, the castle figured largely in Ireland's turbulent history early in the 20th century. The main showpiece is the suite of 18th-century State Apartments, lavishly furnished with rich Donegal carpets and illuminated by Waterford glass chandeliers. One-hour guided tours of the castle are available every half-hour, but the rooms are closed when in official use, so call ahead. The easiest way into the castle is through the Cork Hill Gate, just west of City Hall. ⊠ *Castle St., Dublin West* ☎ *01/645-8813* ⊕ *www.dublincastle. ie* ⊠ *State Apartments €4.50 including tour* ⊗ *Weekdays 10–4:45, weekends 2–4:45.*

② **Grafton Street.** It's no more than 200 yards long and about 20 feet wide, but brick-lined Grafton Street, open only to pedestrians, can claim to be the most humming street in the city, if not in all of Ireland. It's one of Dublin's vital spines: the most direct route between the front door of Trinity College and St. Stephen's Green, and the city's premier shopping street, with Dublin's most distinguished department store, Brown Thomas, as well as tried and trusted Marks & Spencer. Grafton Street and the smaller alleyways that radiate off it offer dozens of independent stores, a dozen or so colorful flower sellers, and some of the Southside's most popular watering holes. In summer, buskers from all over the world line both sides of the street, pouring out the sounds of drum, whistle, pipe, and string.

NEED A BREAK? The granddaddy of the capital's cafés, **Bewley's Oriental Café** (✉ *78 Grafton St., Southside* ☎ *01/677–6761*) recently restored its old grandeur—note the exotic picture wallpaper and trademark stained-glass windows, designed by the distinguished early-20th-century artist Harry Clarke.

⑥ **Guinness Brewery and Storehouse.** Ireland's all-dominating brewery—**Fodor's** Choice ★ founded by Arthur Guinness in 1759 and at one time the largest stout-producing brewery in the world—spans a 60-acre spread west of Christ Church Cathedral. Not surprisingly, it's the most popular tourist destination in town—after all, the Irish national drink is Guinness stout, a dark brew made with roasted malt. The brewery itself is closed to the public, but the Guinness Storehouse is a spectacular attraction, designed to woo you with the wonders of the "dark stuff." In a 1904 cast-iron-and-brick warehouse, the museum display covers six floors built around a huge, central glass atrium. The exhibition elucidates the brewing process and its history. You might think it's all a bit much (it's only a drink, after all)—readers complain about the numerous ads and promos for the brew at nearly every turn. The star attraction is undoubtedly the top-floor **Gravity Bar,** with 360-degree floor-to-ceiling glass walls that offer a nonpareil view out over the city at sunset while you sip your free pint. ✉*St. James' Gate, Dublin West* ☎*01/408–4800* ⊕*www.guinness-storehouse.com* ▱*€14* ☾*July and Aug., daily 9:30–7; Sept.–June, daily 9:30–5.*

Fodor's Choice ★ **⑧** **Newman House.** One of the greatest glories of Georgian Dublin, Newman House is actually two imposing town houses joined together. The earlier of the two, No. 85 St. Stephen's Green (1738), was originally known as Clanwilliam House. Designed by Richard Castle, favored architect of Dublin's rich and famous, it has two landmarks of Irish Georgian style: the Apollo Room, decorated with stuccowork depicting the sun god and his muses; and the magnificent Saloon, "the supreme example of Dublin Baroque," according to scholar Desmond Guinness. The Saloon is crowned with an exuberant ceiling aswirl with cupids and gods, created by the Brothers Lafranchini, the finest *stuccadores* (plaster-workers) of 18th-century Dublin. Next door at No. 86 (1765), the staircase, set against pastel walls, is one of the city's most beautiful Rococo examples. To explore the houses you must join a guided tour. At the back of Newman House lies Iveagh Gardens, a delightful

9

hideaway with statues and sunken gardens that remains one of Dublin's best-kept secrets (you can enter via Earlsfort Terrace and Harcourt Street). ✉*85–86 St. Stephen's Green, Southside* ☎*01/716-7422* ⊕*www.visitdublin.com* ✉*House and garden €5* ⊗*Tours June–Aug., Tues.–Fri. at 2, 3, and 4.*

❾ **St. Stephen's Green.** Dubliners call it simply Stephen's Green, and green it is (year-round)—a verdant, 27-acre Southside square. Flower gardens, formal lawns, a Victorian bandstand, and an ornamental lake with lots of waterfowl are all within the park's borders. Among the park's many statues are a memorial to W. B. Yeats and another to Joyce by Henry Moore. ✉ *Southside* ✉*Free* ⊗*Daily sunrise–sunset.*

❶ **Trinity College.** Founded in 1592 by Queen Elizabeth I to "civilize" (Her
Fodor's Choice Majesty's word) Dublin, Trinity is Ireland's oldest and most famous
★ college. The memorably atmospheric campus is a must; here you can track the shadows of some of the noted alumni, such as Jonathan Swift (1667–1745), Oscar Wilde (1854–1900), Bram Stoker (1847–1912), and Samuel Beckett (1906–89). For centuries Trinity was the preserve of the Protestant Church; a free education was offered to Catholics—provided that they accepted the Protestant faith.

Trinity's grounds cover 40 acres. Most of its buildings were constructed in the 18th and early 19th centuries. The extensive **West Front,** with a classical pedimented portico in the Corinthian style, faces College Green and is directly across from the Bank of Ireland; it was built between 1755 and 1759. The most famous building here, however, is the **Old Library,** which houses Ireland's largest collection of books and manuscripts; its principal treasure is the Book of Kells, generally considered to be the most striking manuscript ever produced in the Anglo-Saxon world and one of the great masterpieces of early Christian art. The book, which dates to the 9th century, is a splendidly illuminated version of the Gospels. In the 20th century, scholars decided instead that the book originated on the island of Iona off Scotland's coast. The 680-page work was re-bound in four volumes in 1953, two of which are usually displayed at a time, so you typically see no more than four original pages. (Some wags have taken to calling it the "Page of Kells.") However, such is the incredible workmanship of the Book of Kells that one folio alone is worth the entirety of many other painted manuscripts. Because of the fame and beauty of the Book of Kells—now the centerpiece of an exhibition called "Turning Darkness into Light"—it's all too easy to overlook the other treasures in the library, including the legendary Book of Durrow, a 7th-century Gospel book from County Offaly.

The main library room, also known as the **Long Room,** is one of Dublin's most staggering sights. At 213 feet long and 42 feet wide, it contains in its 21 alcoves approximately 200,000 of the 3 million volumes in Trinity's collection. Of note are the carved Royal Arms of Queen Elizabeth I above the library entrance—the only surviving relic of the original college buildings—and, lining the Long Room, a grand series of marble busts, of which the most famous is Roubiliac's depiction of Jonathan

Swift. The Trinity College Library Shop sells books, clothing, jewelry, and postcards. ⊠*Front Sq., Southside* 🕾*01/896–2320* ⊕*www.tcd.ie/ library* 🎫*€8* ⊙*May–Sept., Mon.–Sat. 9:30–5, Sun. 9:30–4:30; Oct.– Apr., Mon.–Sat. 9:30–5, Sun. noon–4:30.*

In the college's Thomas Davis Theatre in the arts building, the **"Dublin Experience,"** a 45-minute audiovisual presentation, explains the history of the city over the last 1,000 years. ⊠*Nassau St., Southside* 🕾*01/608–1688* 🎫*€5* ⊙*Mid-May–early Oct., daily 10–5; shows every hr on the hr.*

⑬ **Merrion Square.** Created between 1762 and 1764, this tranquil square
★ a few blocks east of St. Stephen's Green is lined on three sides by some of Dublin's best-preserved Georgian town houses, many of which have brightly painted front doors crowned by intricate fanlights. Leinster House, the National Museum of Natural History, and the National Gallery line the west side of the square. It's on the other sides, however, that the Georgian terrace streetscape comes into its own—the finest houses are on the north border. Several distinguished Dubliners have lived on the square, including Oscar Wilde's parents, Sir William and "Speranza" Wilde (No. 1); Irish national leader Daniel O'Connell (No. 58); and authors W. B. Yeats (Nos. 52 and 82) and Sheridan LeFanu (No. 70). ⊠*Southeast Dublin* ⊙*Daily sunrise–sunset.*

⑫ **National Gallery of Ireland.** Caravaggio's *The Taking of Christ* (1602),
Fodor'sChoice Van Gogh's *Rooftops of Paris* (1886), Vermeer's *Lady Writing a Letter*
★ *with Her Maid* (circa 1670) . . . you get the picture. The National Gallery of Ireland is one of Europe's finer smaller art museums—"smaller" being a relative term: the collection holds more than 2,500 paintings and some 10,000 other works. But unlike Europe's largest art museums, the National Gallery can be thoroughly covered in a morning or afternoon without inducing exhaustion. Other than the great Old Master painting collection, a highlight of the museum is the major group of paintings by Irish artists from the 17th through 20th centuries, including works by Jack B. Yeats (1871–1957), the brother of writer W. B. Yeats, by far the best-known Irish painter of the 20th century. ⊠*Merrion Sq. W, Southeast Dublin* 🕾*01/661–5133* ⊕*www.nationalgallery. ie* 🎫*Free; special exhibits €10* ⊙*Mon.–Wed., Fri., and Sat. 9:30–5:30, Thurs. 9:30–8:30, Sun. noon–5:30.*

NEED A BREAK? **Fitzer's** (⊠*Merrion Sq. W, Southside* 🕾*01/661–4496*), the National Gallery's self-service restaurant, is a find—one of the city's best spots for an inexpensive, top-rate lunch. The 16 to 20 daily menu items are prepared with an up-to-date take on European cuisine. It's open Monday–Saturday 10–5:30 (lunch is served noon–2:30) and Sunday 2–5.

⑪ **National Library.** Happily, Ireland is one of the few countries in the world where you can admit to being a writer. And few countries as geographically diminutive as Ireland have garnered as many recipients of the Nobel Prize for Literature. Along with works by W. B. Yeats (1923), George Bernard Shaw (1925), Samuel Beckett (1969), and Seamus Heaney (1995), the National Library contains first editions of every

9

major Irish writer, including books by Jonathan Swift, Oliver Gold-smith, and James Joyce (who used the library as the scene of the great literary debate in *Ulysses*). The main Reading Room, opened in 1890 to house the collections of the Royal Dublin Society, has a dramatic domed ceiling. The library has a free genealogical consultancy service that can advise you on how to trace your Irish ancestors. ⊠ *Kildare St., Southeast Dublin* ☎ *01/603–0200* ⊕ *www.nli.ie* ☞ *Free* ⊙ *Mon.–Wed. 9:30–9, Thurs. and Fri. 9:30–5, Sat. 9:30–1.*

⑩ **National Museum of Archaeology and History.** Just south of Leinster House,
★ this fabled collection of Irish artifacts ranges from 7000 BC to the pres-ent. It has the largest collection of Celtic antiquities in the world. Among the priceless relics on display are the late Bronze Age gold collar known as the Gleninsheen Gorget; the bronze-coated iron St. Patrick's Bell, the oldest surviving example (5th–8th century) of Irish metalwork; the 8th-century Tara Brooch, an intricately decorated piece made of white bronze, amber, and glass; and the 12th-century bejeweled oak Cross of Cong, covered with silver and bronze panels. ⊠ *Kildare St. Annex, 7–9 Merrion Row, Southeast Dublin* ☎ *01/677–7444* ⊕ *www.museum. ie* ☞ *Free* ⊙ *Tues.–Sat. 10–5, Sun. 2–5.*

❺ **Temple Bar.** Locals sometimes say the place has the feel of a "Dublin Theme Park," but a visit to modern Dublin wouldn't be complete with-out spending some time in the city's most vibrant area. The area, which takes its name from one of the streets of its central spine, took off in the 1990s as Dublin's version of New York's SoHo, Paris's Bastille, or London's Notting Hill—a thriving mix of high and alternative culture. Dotting the area's narrow cobblestone streets and pedestrian alleyways are new apartment buildings, vintage-clothing stores, postage-stamp-size boutiques selling €250 sunglasses and other expensive gewgaws, art galleries, the Clarence (a hotel resuscitated by U2), hip restaurants, pubs, clubs, European-style cafés, a Wall of Fame (devoted to Irish rockers), and a smattering of cultural venues, including the Irish Film Institute. ⊠ *Bordered by Dame Street to the south, the Liffey to the north, Fishamble Street to the west, and Westmoreland Street to the east, Temple Bar*

❷ **St. Patrick's Cathedral.** The largest cathedral in Dublin, this is also the
Fodor's Choice national cathedral of the Church of Ireland. On this site, legend says,
★ St. Patrick baptized many converts at a well in the 5th century. At 305 feet, this is the longest church in the country, a fact Oliver Cromwell's troops—no friends to the Irish—found useful as they made the church's nave into their stable in the 17th century. They left the building in a ter-rible state, with major restoration work begin in 1860. Don't miss the gloriously heraldic Choir of St. Patrick's, hung with colorful medieval banners, and find the tomb of the most famous of St. Patrick's many illustrious deans, Jonathan Swift, immortal author of *Gulliver's Trav-els,* who held office from 1713 to 1745. Swift's tomb is in the south aisle, not far from that of his beloved "Stella," Mrs. Esther Johnson. If you're a music lover, you're in for a treat; matins (9:40 AM) and even-song (5:45 PM) are still sung on many days. ⊠ *Patrick St., Dublin West* ☎ *01/453–9472* ⊕ *www.stpatrickscathedral.ie* ☞ *€5.50* ⊙ *Mar.–Oct.,*

*Mon.–Sat. 9–6, Sun. 9–11, 12:45–3, and 4:15–6; Nov.–Feb. weekdays
9–6, Sat. 9–5, Sun. 10–11 and 12:45–3.*

ACROSS THE LIFFEY: EXPLORING THE NORTHSIDE

Faded stereotypes about the Northside being Dublin's poorer and
more deprived half have been washed away by the economic boom
of Celtic Tiger development. Locals and visitors alike are discovering
the no-nonsense, laid-back charm of the Northside's revamped Georgian wonders, understated cultural gems, high-quality restaurants, and
buzzing ethnic diversity. Here you can begin a pilgrimage into James
Joyce country, along the way savoring the captivating sights of Dublin's
Northside, a mix of densely thronged shopping streets and genteelly
refurbished homes. Once-derelict swaths of houses, especially on and
near the Liffey, have been rehabilitated, and large shopping centers
have opened on Mary and Jervis streets. The high-rise Docklands area,
east of the Custom House, is the new hot place to live, and the Abbey
Theatre is going to move here in a few years. O'Connell Street itself has
been partially pedestrianized, and most impressive of all is the Spire,
the street's new 395-foot-high stainless-steel monument.

EXPLORING THE NORTHSIDE

⑭ Custom House. Seen at its best when reflected in the waters of the Liffey
during the short interval when the high tide is on the turn, the Custom
House is the city's most spectacular Georgian building. Extending 375
feet on the north side of the river, this is the work of James Gandon, an
English architect who arrived in Ireland in 1781, when the building's
construction commenced (it continued for 10 years). A visitor center
traces the building's history and significance, and the life of Gandon.
⊠*Custom House Quay, Northside* ☎*01/888–2538* ⊕*www.visitdublin.
com* ⊠*€1.30* ☼*Mid-Mar.–Oct., weekdays 10–12:30, weekends 2–5;
Nov.–mid-Mar., Wed.–Fri. 10–12:30, Sun. 2–5.*

⑯ Dublin City Gallery, The Hugh Lane. Built as a town house for the Earl of
★ Charlemont in 1762, this residence was so grand its Parnell Square
street was nicknamed "Palace Row" in its honor. Sir William Chambers designed the structure in the best Palladian manner. Charlemont
was one of the cultural locomotives of 18th-century Dublin—his walls
were hung with Titians and Hogarths, and he frequently dined with
Oliver Goldsmith and Sir Joshua Reynolds—so he would undoubtedly be delighted that his home is now a gallery, named after Sir Hugh
Lane, a nephew of Lady Gregory (W.B. Yeats's aristocratic patron).
Lane collected both Impressionist paintings and 19th-century Irish
and Anglo-Irish works. Highlights include Renoir's *Les Paraplu-
ies* and the collection of Irish paintings. ⊠*Parnell Sq. N, Northside*
☎*01/222–5550* ⊕*www.hughlane.ie* ⊠*Free* ☼*Tues.–Thurs. 10–6, Fri.
and Sat. 10–5, Sun. 11–5.*

⑰ Dublin Writers Museum. "If you would know Ireland—body and soul—you
★ must read its poems and stories," wrote Yeats in 1891. Further investiga-
tion into the Irish way with words can be found at this unique museum,
in a magnificently restored 18th-century town house on the north side of

9

Parnell Square. The mansion, once the home of John Jameson, of the Irish whiskey family, centers on the Gallery of Writers, an enormous drawing room gorgeously decorated with paintings, Adamesque plasterwork, and a deep Edwardian lincrusta frieze. Rare manuscripts, diaries, posters, letters, limited and first editions, photographs, and other mementos commemorate the lives and works of the nation's greatest writers, including Joyce, Shaw, J.M. Synge, Lady Gregory, Yeats, Beckett, and others. If you lose track of time and stay until the closing hour, you might want to dine at Chapter One, a highly regarded restaurant in the basement, which would have had Joyce ecstatic over its currant-sprinkled scones. ✉ *18 Parnell Sq. N, Northside* ☎ *01/872-2077* ⊕ *www.writersmuseum. com* 🎫 *€7* ⊙ *June–Aug., weekdays 10–6, Sat. 10–5, Sun. 11–5; Sept.– May, Mon.–Sat. 10–5, Sun. 11–5.*

⑱ **James Joyce Centre.** Few may have read him, but everyone in Ireland has at least heard of James Joyce (1882–1941)—especially since owning a copy of his censored and suppressed *Ulysses* was one of the top status symbols of the early 20th century. Joyce is of course now acknowledged as one of the greatest modern authors, and his *Dubliners, Finnegan's Wake,* and *A Portrait of the Artist as a Young Man* can even be read as quirky "travel guides" to Dublin. Open to the public, this restored 18th-century Georgian town house is a center for Joycean studies, with library, exhibition rooms, a bookstore, and a café. The center is the main organizer of "Bloomstime," which marks the week leading up to the Bloomsday celebrations. (Bloomsday, June 16, is the single day *Ulysses* chronicles, as Leopold Bloom winds his way around Dublin in 1904.) ✉ *35 N. Great George's St., Northside* ☎ *01/878–8547* ⊕ *www. jamesjoyce.ie* 🎫 *€5, guided tour €10* ⊙ *Tues.–Sat. 10–5.*

⑮ **O'Connell Street.** Dublin's most famous thoroughfare, which is 150 feet wide, was previously known as Sackville Street, but its name was changed in 1924, two years after the founding of the Irish Free State. After the devastation of the 1916 Easter Uprising, the Northside street had to be almost entirely reconstructed, a task that took until the end of the 1920s. At one time the main attraction of the street was Nelson's Pillar, a Doric column towering over the city center and a marvelous vantage point, but it was blown up in 1966, on the 50th anniversary of the Easter Uprising. A major cleanup and repaving have returned the street to some of its old glory. The 395-foot-high Spire was built in Nelson's Pillar's place in 2003, and today this gigantic, stainless-steel monument dominates the street.

WHERE TO EAT

$$$$ ✗ **Chapter One.** This wonderful, culture-vulture favorite gets its name
Fodor's Choice   from its location, downstairs in the vaulted, stone-wall basement of the
★   Dublin Writers Museum; the natural stone-and-wood setting makes it cozily cavelike. The contemporary French eatery is currently the culinary king of the Northside, thanks to chef-proprietor Ross Lewis's way with such dishes as pigeon with a white-truffle, honey, and mustard glaze served with cassoulet of white beans and chorizo. Yeats

himself would have loved the hake and langoustine with roast fennel and braised squid, all in a tomato-and-shellfish sauce. ✉*18–19 Parnell Sq., Northside* ☎*01/873–2266* ⊕*www.chapteronerestaurant.com* ⌨*Reservations essential* ☱*AE, DC, MC, V* ⊗*Closed Sun. and Mon. No lunch Sat.*

$$$ ✕**Dax.** When is a wine bar not a wine bar? When it's one of the city's
★ most talked-about restaurants. Opened as a basement wine bar by Olivier Meisonnave, the former sommelier at stellar Thornton's, Dax is quickly becoming the dining spot of choice for Dubliners who care about food. You can choose to drink or dine (tapas-style) at the bar, in the lush armchairs of the open-plan lounge, or in the more formal, restrained-modern dining room. The ballotine of ham hock with herbs is a standout starter, while the veal shin with sweetbreads and butternut squash gnocchi is one of the more daring main courses. ✉*23 Pembroke St., Southeast Dublin* ☎*01/676–1494* ⊕*www.dax.ie* ⌨*Reservations essential* ☱*AE, DC, MC, V* ⊗*Closed Sun. and Mon. No lunch Sat.*

$ ✕**Dunne and Crescenzi.** Nothing succeeds like success. So popular is this
Fodor'sChoice classy little Italian joint just off Nassau Street that they've expanded into
★ the premises two doors down. The menu couldn't be simpler: panini (sandwiches), antipasti, a single pasta special, and desserts. But the all-Italian kitchen staff work wonders with high-quality imported ingredients. A couple of long tables make it perfect for a group, and the hundreds of bottles of wine on shelves cover every inch of the walls. ✉*14 S. Fredrick St., Southside* ☎*01/677–3815* ⊕*www.dunneand crescenzi.com* ☱*AE, MC, V.*

$$ ✕**Eden.** Perennially one of Dublin's hippest places, Eden is where arty and media types are likely to gather to talk about, well, themselves. It has an open kitchen and a high wall of glass through which you can observe one of Temple Bar's main squares. Patio-style doors lead to an outdoor eating area—a major plus in a city with relatively few alfresco dining spots. On weekend nights in summer you can enjoy an outdoor movie in Meeting House Square while you eat. Seasonal menus are in vogue here, but a standout dish is the Castletownebere scallops with minted pea risotto, sugar snap peas, and crispy pancetta. ✉*Meeting House Sq., Temple Bar* ☎*01/670–5372* ⊕*www.edenrestaurant.ie* ⌨*Reservations essential* ☱*AE, DC, MC, V.*

$ ✕**Kilkenny Kitchen.** Take a break from shopping and sightseeing at this big self-service restaurant on the upper floor of the Kilkenny Shop. Homemade soup, casseroles, cold meats, and salads are arranged on a long buffet, along with lots of tasty breads and cakes. Slow-roasted pork with fennel and tomatoes is among the hot lunch choices. Try to get a table by the window overlooking the playing fields of Trinity College. ✉*5–6 Nassau St., Southside* ☎*01/677–7075* ⊕*www.kilkennyshop. com* ☱*AE, DC, MC, V.*

$$$$ ✕**Patrick Guilbaud.** The words "Dublin's finest restaurant" often share
Fodor'sChoice the same breath as the name of this do-be-impressed place on the ground
★ floor of the Merrion Hotel. The menu is described as French, but chef Guillaume Lebrun's genius lies in his occasional daring use of traditional Irish ingredients—so often abused and taken for granted—to create the unexpected. The best dishes are simple and flawless: wild sea bass and

9

asparagus, veal sweetbreads and licorice, and Connemara lobster ravioli. The ambience is just as delicious—if you're into lofty, minimalist dining rooms and Irish modern art. ⊠ *21 Upper Merrion St., Southeast Dublin* ☎*01/676–4192* ⊕*www.restaurantpatrickguilbaud.ie* ⚲*Reservations essential* ☰*AE, DC, MC, V* ☿*Closed Sun. and Mon.*

$$$$ ╳**The Tea Room.** In the Clarence Hotel, you can sit around all day and hope that Bono and the boys of U2—they own the joint, after all—might turn up for a quick snack. Minimalistically hued in golden oak, eggshell white, and light yellows, the high-ceiling room is a perfect stage for off-duty celebs. You can opt for either adventurous specials—spatchcock quail with pea puree, truffled wild mushroom, and pistachio vinaigrette, anyone?—or such consistently good, typically mouthwatering delights as the panfried foie gras with caramelized onion tatin, "wicked apple" cider with muscat raisins, or the artichoke tortellini. ⊠*Clarence Hotel, 6–8 Wellington Quay, Temple Bar* ☎*01/407–0813* ⊕*www.theclarence.ie* ⚲*Reservations essential* ☰*AE, DC, MC, V* ☿ *No lunch Sat.*

$$ ╳**The Winding Stair.** A dark cloud hung over Dublin when one of its
★   favorite secondhand bookshop-cafés, The Winding Stair, was set to close. But the silver lining appeared in the form of this atmospheric, buzzing little restaurant, which reemerged in the old space, replete with a downstairs bookshop and the well-worn name. Upstairs, former habitués will enjoy seeing the old bookcases around the walls (some of which are now stacked with wine). To get the real feel for the place try to get a table looking out over the Ha'penny Bridge and the slow-flowing river beneath. Traditional Irish food re-created with an adventurous twist best describes the terrific, locally sourced menu. ⊠*40 Lower Ormond Quay, Northside* ☎*01/872–7320* ⊕*www.winding-stair.com* ☰*AE, DC, MC, V.*

WHERE TO STAY

$$ ▦**Central Hotel.** Every modern city needs its little oasis, and the Cen-
★   tral's book-and-armchair-filled Library Bar—warmed by a Victorian fireplace—nicely fits the bill. Established in 1887, this grand, old-style redbrick spot is in the heart of the city center, steps from Grafton Street, Temple Bar, and Dublin Castle. Rooms are snug and pretty simple, with flocked bedspreads, racing paintings, and 19th-century bric-a-brac. The stately hotel dining room delights with its pastel-green walls, bookcases, and gilt-frame pictures. **Pros:** delightful Library Bar; original 1887 facade; old-fashioned feel. **Cons:** rooms a bit snug; street noise in some rooms; service can be a bit haphazard. ⊠*1–5 Exchequer St., Southside* ☎*01/679–7302* ⊕*www.centralhotel.ie* ⤱*67 rooms, 3 suites* ⚘*In-room: Wi-Fi. In-hotel: restaurant, bar* ☰*AE, DC, MC, V* ⦿|*BP.*

$$$–$$$$ ▦**The Clarence.** If coolness is contagious you definitely want a room at Temple Bar's most prestigious hotel. You might well bump into celebrity friends of co-owners Bono and the Edge of U2. Dating to 1852, the grand old hotel was given a total, no-expense-spared overhaul by its new owners in the early 1990s. The unique shapes and Arts-and-Crafts style of the old hotel were maintained in the Octagon Bar and the sleekly fabulous Tea Room restaurant. Guest rooms, with Shaker-

style furniture, are decorated in a mishmash of earth tones accented with deep purple, gold, cardinal-red, and royal blue. The laissez-faire service seems to take its cue from the minimalist style, so if you like to be pampered, stay elsewhere. **Pros:** stylish Octagon Bar; the owners might be on-premises; Tea Room restaurant. **Cons:** service not the best in town; paying a premium for "cool." ⊠*6–8 Wellington Quay, Temple Bar* ☎*01/407–0800* ⊕*www.theclarence.ie* ⤳*43 rooms, 84 suites* ⚷*In-room: refrigerator, DVD, Ethernet, Wi-Fi. In-hotel: restaurant, bar, gym, public Wi-Fi, parking (fee)* ▭*AE, DC, MC, V.*

$ **Grafton House.** A stone's throw from the famous shopping street that gave the hotel its name, these two unattached Victorian Gothic–style buildings have been tastefully transformed into one of central Dublin's coolest little hotels, and one of its best bargains. The rooms vary in size, but not price, so be bold and ask for a bigger one. They have a clever, unfinished-but-very-finished look, with original wood floors, and quirky, individual touches like exposed beams. Downstairs you'll find Hogans Bar and L'Gueuleton restaurant, both favorites of discerning locals. **Pros:** best value in city center; classy, underplayed design; cool cocktail bar. **Cons:** some rooms are cramped; located over a busy bar and restaurant; somewhat new and untested. ⊠*1 Fade St., Southside* ☎*01/679–2041* ⊕*www.graftonguesthouse.com* ⤳*36 rooms* ⚷*In-room: no a/c, Wi-Fi. In-hotel: restaurant, bar, no elevator, public Wi-Fi* ▭*AE, MC, V* ⦿*BP.*

$$ **Kilronan House.** A good guesthouse should cheer you up when you come home at the end of a long day's touring. This large, mid-19th-century terraced house with a glorious, elegant white facade will bring a smile to your face every time. The ground-floor sitting room is a real cozy winter treat when a big fire is on. Some of the rooms are quite basic, in cream and beige, but they are all airy and bright, and the richly patterned wallpaper and carpets and orthopedic beds give them a touch of class. The guesthouse is a five-minute walk from St. Stephen's Green. **Pros:** great price for location; beautiful, calming facade; cozy sitting room. **Cons:** public areas a bit worn; uncreative room furnishings; no Internet in rooms. ⊠*70 Adelaide Rd., Southeast Dublin* ☎*01/475–5266* ⊕*www.kilronanhousehotel.com* ⤳*12 rooms* ⚷*In-room: no a/c. In-hotel: no elevator, public Wi-Fi, parking (no fee)* ▭*MC, V.*

¢–$ **Marian Guest House.** A veritable Everest of fine Irish meats, the Marian's mighty full Irish breakfast, with black pudding and smoked bacon, is reason enough to stay at this family-run redbrick guesthouse just off beautiful Mountjoy Square (the whole family can speak Irish, by the way). The place has only six rooms, so you get lots of attention and pampering. Rooms are fairly basic, but clean, bright, and pleasant. **Pros:** heart-stoppingly good breakfast; family-owned and -run; small. **Cons:** located in slightly run-down part of city; gets some street noise; fairly basic rooms. ⊠*21 Upper Gardiner St., Northside* ☎*01/874–4129* ⊕*www.marianguesthouse.ie* ⤳*6 rooms* ⚷*In-room: no a/c. In-hotel: no elevator* ▭*MC, V* ⦿*BP.*

$$$$ **Merrion.** Arthur Wellesley, the Duke of Wellington and hero of Water-
Fodor's Choice loo, once famously commented when queried about his Irish birth:
★ "Just because a man is born in a stable doesn't make him a horse."

9

His "stable," directly across from Government Buildings between Stephen's Green and Merrion Square, is one of the four exactingly restored Georgian town houses that make up this luxurious hotel. Some of the stately guest rooms are appointed in classic Georgian style—from the crisp linen sheets to the Carrara-marble bathrooms. Some are vaulted with delicate Adamesque plasterwork ceilings, and others are graced with magnificent, original marble fireplaces. Still, the decor is almost too spiffy, so to fully enjoy the historic patina, opt for one of the more authentic rooms in the Main House at the front. Leading Dublin restaurateur Patrick Guilbaud has moved his eponymous and fabulous restaurant here. **Pros:** infinity pool; city-center location; attentive staff. **Cons:** you'll pay extra for a room in the original house; overly attentive staff. ⊠ *Upper Merrion St., Southeast Dublin* ☎ *01/603–0600* ⊕ *www. merrionhotel.com* ⇆ *122 rooms, 20 suites* ⚫ *In-room: safe, DVD, Ethernet, Wi-Fi. In-hotel: 2 restaurants, bars, pool, gym, spa, public Wi-Fi, parking (fee)* ⊟ *AE, DC, MC, V.*

$$$–$$$$ ⚟ **Number 31.** Arguably the most unique and authentic Georgian accom-
★ modation Dublin has to offer is in the old home of Sam Stephenson, Dublin's most famous and highly controversial modernist architect. He strikingly renovated two Georgian mews in the early 1960s as a private home. They are now connected via a small but beautiful garden to the grand house they once served. Together they form a one-in-a-million guesthouse a short walk from St. Stephen's Green, which gives you a choice of bedroom styles: sublime Georgian elegance or serene cool modern. **Pros:** the king and queen of guesthouse hosts; serene decor and art; best breakfast in the city. **Cons:** a few rooms can be a little noisy; no elevator; tricky to find. ⊠ *31 Leeson Close, Southeast Dublin* ☎ *01/676–5011* ⊕ *www.number31.ie* ⇆ *18 rooms* ⚫ *In-room: no a/c, DVD, Wi-Fi. In-hotel: no elevator, parking (no fee)* ⊟ *AE, MC, V.*

$$$$ ⚟ **Shelbourne.** Paris has the Ritz, New York has the Pierre, and Dublin
Fodor's Choice has the Shelbourne. Resplendent in its broad, ornamented, pink-and-
★ white, mid-Victorian facade, this grande dame of Stephen's Green has reopened after a no-expense-spared, head-to-toe, two-year renovation. The Constitution of the Irish Free State was framed within its venerable walls, and almost as venerable a tradition was to take tea in the Lord Mayor's Lounge, just off the towering, marble-floor, cream-and-crystal lobby with its gilded pillars and brass candelabras. Recently, however, the Shelbourne transformed its public spaces with original, daring furniture, textiles, and colors—too bad some of the patina was rubbed away. The shock of the new begins in the lobby, where the Irish Chippendale chairs have given way to contempo Irish art. Happily, the guest rooms are almost as luxurious as the lobby; those in front overlook the Green, while those in back are quieter. **Pros:** afternoon tea in Lord Mayor's Lounge; Irish art worth gazing at; all-around luxury. **Cons:** some noise in front rooms; pricey; feels stuffy at times. ⊠ *27 St. Stephen's Green, Southside* ☎ *01/663–4500, 800/543–4300 in U.S.* ⊕ *www.marriott. com* ⇆ *246 rooms, 19 suites* ⚫ *In-room: refrigerator, Wi-Fi. In-hotel: restaurant, bars* ⊟ *AE, DC, MC, V.*

NIGHTLIFE & THE ARTS

Check the following newspapers for informative listings: the *Irish Times* publishes a daily guide to what's happening in Dublin and the rest of the country, and has complete film and theater schedules. The *Evening Herald* lists theaters, cinemas, and pubs with live entertainment. The *Big Issue* is a weekly guide to film, theater, and musical events around the city. The *Event Guide,* a weekly free paper that lists music, cinema, theater, art shows, and dance clubs, is available in pubs and cafés around the city.

NIGHTLIFE
IRISH CABARET, MUSIC & DANCING

★ **Bewley's Cafe Theatre** (⊠ *Grafton St., Southside* ☎086/878–4001), with its "Live at The Oriental Room" nights, has become the atmospheric cabaret hot spot in Dublin.

NIGHTCLUBS

NORTHSIDE **The Academy** (⊠ *57 Middle Abbey St., Northside* ☎01/877–9999) is a brand new music mecca with four floors of entertainment of every kind anchored by big-name local and international DJs. It attracts a young, dance-crazy crowd who like to party until the wee hours.

SOUTHSIDE **Lillie's Bordello** (⊠ *Grafton St., Southside* ☎01/679–9204) is a popular spot for a trendy professional crowd, as well as for rock and film stars.

The Pod (⊠ *Harcourt St., Southside* ☎01/478–0166), also known as the "Place of Dance," qualifies as Dublin's most renowned dance club, especially among the younger set. Whether you get in depends as much on what you're wearing as on your age.

★ **Tripod** (⊠ *Old Harcourt St. Station, Harcourt St., Southside* ☎01/478–0166), adjacent to the Pod and the Crawdaddy music venue, can pack in more than 1,300 people and surround them with state-of-the-art sound and light. It regularly hosts Irish and international rock acts, and celebrity DJs from Europe and the United States. It has full bar facilities.

TEMPLE BAR **Button Factory** (⊠ *Curved St., Temple Bar* ☎01/670–9202), a recently revamped music venue, mixes top DJs and up-and-coming live acts.

Viper Room (⊠ *5 Aston Quay, Temple Bar* ☎01/672–5566), decorated in rich reds and purples, is a delightfully decadent late-night club that plays funk, chart, and rhythm and blues. Downstairs there's live jazz and salsa.

PUBS

Some wag once asked if it was possible to cross Dublin without passing a single pub along the way. The answer was "Yes, but only if you go into every one." For the complete scoop, see our special photo-feature, "A Trip to the Pub."

NORTHSIDE **The Flowing Tide** (⊠ *Lower Abbey St., Northside* ☎01/874–0842), directly across from the Abbey Theatre, draws a lively pre- and post-theater crowd. No TVs, quality pub talk, and a great pint of Guinness make it a worthwhile visit.

SOUTHSIDE & SOUTHEAST DUBLIN

Davy Byrne's (✉ *21 Duke St., Southside* ☎ *01/671–1298*) is a pilgrimage stop for Joyceans. In *Ulysses,* Leopold Bloom stops in here for a glass of Burgundy and a Gorgonzola-cheese sandwich. He then leaves the pub and walks to Dawson Street, where he helps a blind man cross the road. Unfortunately, the decor is greatly changed from Joyce's day, but it still serves some fine pub grub.

Fodor'sChoice ★

Grogans (✉ *15 S. William St., Southside* ☎ *01/677–9320*), also known as the Castle Lounge, is a small place packed with creative folk. Owner Tommy Grogan is known as a patron of local artists, and his walls are covered with their work.

★ **Horseshoe Bar** (✉ *Shelbourne, 27 St. Stephen's Green, Southside* ☎ *01/676–6471*) was recently given a massive face-lift along with the rest of the Shelbourne hotel and is now the hottest ticket in town. Long a popular meeting place for Dublin's businesspeople and politicians, there's comparatively little space for drinkers around the famous semicircular bar—but this does wonders for making friends quickly.

Long Hall Pub (✉ *51 S. Great George's St., Southside* ☎ *01/475–1590*), one of Dublin's most ornate traditional taverns, has Victorian lamps, a mahogany bar, mirrors, chandeliers, and plasterwork ceilings, all more than 100 years old. The pub serves sandwiches and an excellent pint of Guinness.

Neary's (✉ *1 Chatham St., Southside* ☎ *01/677–7371*), with an exotic, Victorian-style interior, was once the haunt of music-hall artists and a certain literary set, including Brendan Behan. Join the actors from the adjacent Gaiety Theatre for a good pub lunch.

Fodor'sChoice ★

Stag's Head (✉ *1 Dame Ct., Southside* ☎ *01/679–3701*) dates from 1770 and was rebuilt in 1895. Theater people from the nearby Olympia, journalists, and Trinity students gather around the unusual Connemara red-marble bar. The interior is a Victorian beaut.

Toner's (✉ *139 Lower Baggot St., Southside* ☎ *01/676–3090*), though billed as a Victorian bar, actually goes back 200 years, with an original flagstone floor to prove its antiquity, as well as wooden drawers running up to the ceiling—a relic of the days when bars doubled as grocery shops. Oliver St. John Gogarty, who was the model for Buck Mulligan in James Joyce's *Ulysses,* accompanied W. B. Yeats here, in what was purportedly the latter's only visit to a pub.

TEMPLE BAR

Oliver St. John Gogarty (✉ *57 Fleet St., Temple Bar* ☎ *01/671–1822*) is a lively bar that attracts all ages and nationalities; it overflows with patrons in summer. On most nights there's traditional Irish music upstairs.

Turks Head (✉ *Parliament St., Temple Bar* ☎ *01/679–2606*), a very non-traditional Irish bar, is known for its extravagant mosaics and vibrant, late-night DJ-driven sounds.

Continued on page 486

A TRIP TO THE PUB

For any visitor to Ireland who wants to see the natives in their bare element—to witness them at full pace, no-holds-barred—a trip to a busy pub is a must. Luckily for you, the pub is above all a welcoming place, where a visitor is seen as a source of new, exotic stories and, more importantly, as an unsullied audience for the locals and their tall tales.

WELCOME TO IRELAND'S LIVING ROOM...

The term "pub" is shorthand for "public house," which is an apt name for one of Ireland's great institutions. Stepping into a pub (and there seems to be one on every corner) is the easiest way to transport yourself into the thick of Irish life.

A pub, of course, is a drinking establishment, and for better or worse the Irish have a deep, abiding relationship with drink—particularly their beloved black stout. The point, however, isn't what you drink, but where: in the warmth of the public house, in company. It's the place to tell stories, most of them true, and to hear music. It's where locals go to mark the key stages of their lives: to wet a new baby's head; to celebrate a graduation; to announce an engagement; and finally to wake a corpse.

HOW TO CHOOSE A PUB

Not all pubs are created equal. Throughout this book we recommend some of the finest, but here are a few ways to distinguish the real gold from the sparkling pyrite:

- Qualified, experienced bar staff—not grubby students dreaming of the round-the-world trip they are working to save up for. A uniform of white shirt and black trousers is often a good sign.

- At least one man over sixty (preferably with a cap of some description) drinking at the bar (not at a table). He should know the good bars by now, right?

- No TV. Or, if there is a TV it should be hidden away in a corner, only to be used for horse racing and other major sporting events.

- No recorded music. A pub is a place to talk and listen. Occasional live music is okay, especially a traditional session.

- Bathrooms are clean but not *too* clean. They are purely functional, not polished chambers for hanging out and chatting with friends about your new Blackberry.

THE QUEST FOR THE CRAIC

Pub-going at its best has a touch of magic to it: conversation flows, spirits rise, and inhibitions evaporate. There's a word in Gaelic for this happy condition: the *craic*, which roughly translates as "lively talk and good times." The craic is the sort of thing that's difficult to find only when you're looking too hard for it. Large crowds, loud music, and one pint too many can also make the craic elusive. When your companions all seem clever and handsome, and you can't imagine better company in the world, that's when you know you've found it.

PUB ETIQUETTE

Some things to keep in mind if you want to get the most out of your trip to the pub:

■ First, if you want to meet people and get into the craic, belly up to the bar counter and pass up a seat at a table.

■ Always place your drink order at the bar and don't heckle the barkeepers to get their attention. They're professionals—they'll see you soon enough.

■ If you do take a table, bring your dirty glasses back to the bar before you leave, or when you order another round.

■ In present-day Ireland, male and female pubgoers usually get equal treatment. At the most traditional places, though, it's still customary in mixed company for the man to order drinks at the bar while the woman takes a table seat.

■ Don't tip the barkeepers, except at Christmas, when you can offer to buy them a drink.

■ Never sip from your Guinness until it has fully settled. You'll know this from the deep black color and perfectly defined white head.

■ Don't smoke in the bar; it's against the law. But feel free to gather outside in the rain and chat with the other unfortunates. It's a great spot to start a romance.

■ You have to be at least 18 years old to *drink* in a pub, but kids are welcome during the day, and nondrinking minors as young as 14 are often tolerated at night.

MAKING THE ROUNDS

You may get caught up in the "rounds" system, in which each pub mate takes turns to "shout" an order. Your new friends may forget to tell you when it's your round, but any failure to "put your hand in your pocket" may lead to a reputation that will follow you to the grave. To miss your "shout" is to become known for "short arms and long pockets" and to be shunned by decent people.

LAST CALL

Technically, pubs have to stop serving at 11:30 Mon.–Thurs., 12:30 Fri.–Sat., and 11 Sun. At the end of the night, ignore the first five calls of "Time please, ladies and gentlemen!" from the barman. You'll know he's getting serious by the roar of his voice.

THE "BLACK STUFF"

Stout, a dark beer made using roasted malts or barley, originated in Ireland, and it's the country's national drink, consumed in pubs with unflagging allegiance.

— Rich, creamy head.

— Nearly black in color, with a very slight coffee-like aftertaste.

— As you drink, the head will leave "rings of pleasure" down the side of the glass.

THE POUR

The storage and pouring of a pint of stout is almost as important as the brewing. The best quality is usually found in older bars that sell a lot of pints—meaning the beer you get hasn't been sitting in the keg too long and the pipes are well coated.

Pouring a pint consists of two stages: The glass is filled three-quarters full, then allowed to sit. After the head settles, the glass is filled to the top (stage two).

Why the painstaking ritual? Because the barkeeper knows you don't want your first sip to be a mouthful of foam. And because the flavor's that much sweeter for the waiting.

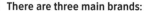

There are three main brands:

GUINNESS For most Irish, the name Guinness is synonymous with stout. With massive breweries in Africa and the Americas, it really is a world brand, but the "true" pint still flows from the original brewery at St. James Gate in Dublin. While some old-timers still drink the more malty bottled version, draught Guinness is now the standard. A deep, creamy texture and slightly bitter first taste is followed by a milder, more "toasty" aftertaste.

MURPHY'S The Murphy Brewery was founded by James Murphy in 1856 in Cork City. Murphy's is very much a Cork drink, and often suffers from "second city" complex in relation to its giant rival Guinness. Corkonians say Murphy's is a less bitter, more nutty flavor than the "Dublin stout."

BEAMISH Another Cork drink, a little sweeter and less dry than either Guinness or Murphy's, and so a little easier on the novice palate. Beamish and Crawford Brewery began making beer in 1792, after purchasing an existing brewery in the heart of Cork's medieval center that dates back to at least 1650 (and possibly 1500).

FOOD, SONG, AND ADDITIONAL DRINK

IN FOCUS A TRIP TO THE PUB

9

Although the majority of your companions will be drinking stout, you do have other options.

- A lager is always available—Heiniken and Carlsberg are the most popular brands.

- If you're thirsting for something stronger, take a nip of Irish whiskey, which tends to be less smoky and intensely flavored than its Scotch cousin. Jameson and Bushmills, both smooth blends, are the standard varieties, and you can usually find a single-malt as well.

- On the other hand, if the booze isn't your thing, you can always choose tea, soda, or a bottle of water. (Ballygowan is the Irish Evian.) It's fine to order nonalcoholic drinks—many people who drive do so.

- Pub food is a lunchtime thing; the prices are reasonable, and the quality can be quite good. Ask for a menu at the bar. If you're near a coast, look for seafood specialties, from oysters and mussels to smoked salmon. With beef-and-Guinness stew, you can drink your stout and eat it too.

"TRAD" MUSIC IN ITS NATURAL DOMAIN

The pub is an ideal place to hear traditional Irish music. Performances can have a spontaneous air to them, but they don't start up just anywhere. Pubs that accommodate live sessions have signs saying so; and they're more common outside Dublin than in the city. To learn more about Irish music, see "Gael Force" in chapter 7.

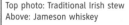

Top photo: Traditional Irish stew
Above: Jameson whiskey

DUBLIN WEST **Brazen Head** (⊠*Bridge St., Dublin West* ☎*01/677–9549*), Dublin's oldest pub (the site has been licensed since 1198), has stone walls and open fireplaces—it has hardly changed over the years. The pub is renowned for traditional-music performances and lively sing-along sessions on Sunday evenings. On the south side of the Liffey quays, it's a little difficult to find—turn down Lower Bridge Street and make a right onto the old lane.

★ **Ryan's Pub** (⊠*28 Parkgate St., Dublin West* ☎*01/677–6097*) is one of Dublin's last genuine, late-Victorian-era pubs, and has changed little since its last (1896) remodeling.

THE ARTS
CLASSICAL MUSIC & OPERA

SOUTHEAST **National Concert Hall** (⊠*Earlsfort*
DUBLIN *Terr., Southeast Dublin* ☎*01/475–1666* ⊕*www.nch.ie*), just off St. Stephen's Green, is Dublin's main theater for classical music of all kinds, from symphonies to chamber groups. The slightly austere neoclassical building was transformed in 1981 into one of Europe's finest medium-size concert halls. It houses the cream of Irish classical musicians, the National Symphony Orchestra of Ireland. The concert year picks up speed in mid-September and sails through to June; July and August also get many dazzling troupes. The smaller, more intimate John Field and Carolan rooms are perfect for chamber music.

FILM

NORTHSIDE **Cineworld** (⊠*Parnell Center, Parnell St., Northside* ☎*01/872–8400*), a 17-screen theater just off O'Connell Street, is the city center's only multiplex movie house; it shows the latest commercial features.

ROCK & CONTEMPORARY MUSIC

NORTHSIDE **The Point** (⊠*Eastlink Br., Northside* ☎*01/836–3633* ⊕*www.thepoint. ie*), a 6,000-capacity arena about 1 km (½ mi) east of the Custom House on the Liffey, is Dublin's premier venue for internationally renowned acts. Call or send a self-addressed envelope to receive a list of upcoming shows; tickets can be difficult to obtain, so book early.

SOUTHSIDE **Crawdaddy** (⊠*Old Harcourt Station., Harcourt St., Southside*
★ ☎*01/478–0166*) is an intimate venue at the center of the hot Pod nightclub complex. A predecessor to *Rolling Stone, Crawdaddy* was the very first rock magazine in the United States. The place is an homage to that bygone era of sweat, three chords, and the truth.

THEATER

NORTHSIDE **Abbey Theatre** (⊠ *Lower Abbey St., Northside* ☎ *01/878–7222* ⊕ *www. abbeytheatre.ie*) is the fabled home of Ireland's national theater company. In 1904 W. B. Yeats and his patron, Lady Gregory, opened the theater, which became a major center for the Irish literary renaissance—the place that first staged works by J. M. Synge and Sean O'Casey, among many others. Plays by recent Irish drama heavyweights like Brian Friel, Tom Murphy, Hugh Leonard, and John B. Keane have all premiered here, and memorable productions of international greats like Mamet, Ibsen, and Shakespeare have also been performed. You should not, however, arrive expecting 19th-century grandeur: the original structure burned down in 1951. Unfortunately, an ugly concrete boxlike auditorium was built in its place—but what it may lack in visuals it makes up for in space and acoustics. Some say the repertoire is overly reverential and mainstream, but such chestnuts as Dion Boucicault's *The Shaughran* wind up being applauded by many. Happily, the Abbey's sister theater at the same address, the Peacock, offers more experimental drama. But the Abbey will always be relevant, since much of the theatergoing public still looks to it as a barometer of Irish culture.

Gate Theatre (⊠ *Cavendish Row, Parnell Sq., Northside* ☎ *01/874–4045* ⊕ *www.gate-theatre.ie*), an intimate 371-seat theater in a jewel-like Georgian assembly hall, produces the classics and contemporary plays by leading Irish writers, including Beckett, Wilde (the production of *Salome* was a worldwide hit), Shaw, and the younger generation of dramatists, such as Conor McPherson.

SHOPPING

Dublin has a tremendous variety of stores, many of which are quite sophisticated—as a walk through Dublin's central shopping area, from O'Connell to Grafton Street, will prove. Most large shops and department stores are open Monday to Saturday 9 to 6, with late hours on Thursday until 9.

SHOPPING STREETS

O'Connell Street, the city's main thoroughfare, is more downscale than Southside city streets (such as Grafton Street), but it is still worth a walk. One of Dublin's largest department stores, Clery's, is here, across from the GPO. On the same side of the street as the post office is Eason's, a large book, magazine, and stationery store.

Grafton Street, Dublin's bustling pedestrian-only main shopping street, has two department stores: down-to-earth Marks & Spencer and *trés* chic Brown Thomas. The rest of the street is taken up by shops, many of them branches of international chains, such as the Body Shop and Bally, and many British chains. This is also the spot to buy fresh flowers, available at reasonable prices from outdoor stands. On the smaller streets off Grafton Street—especially Duke Street, South Anne Street, and Chatham Street—are worthwhile crafts, clothing, and designer housewares shops.

Temple Bar, Dublin's hippest neighborhood, is dotted with small, precious boutiques—mainly intimate, quirky shops that traffic in a small selection of trendy goods, from vintage clothes to some of the most avant-garde Irish garb anywhere in the city.

SHOPPING CENTERS

Powerscourt Townhouse Centre (⊠ *59 S. William St., Southside*), the former town home of Lord Powerscourt, built in 1771, has an interior courtyard that has been refurbished and roofed over; a pianist often plays on the dais at ground-floor level. Coffee shops and restaurants share space with a mix of stores selling antiques and crafts. You can also buy original Irish fashions here by young designers.

St. Stephen's Green Centre (⊠ *Northwest corner of St. Stephen's Green, Southside* ☎ *01/478–0888*), Dublin's largest and most ambitious shopping complex, resembles a giant greenhouse, with Victorian-style ironwork. On three floors overlooked by a giant clock, the 100 mostly small shops sell crafts, fashions, and household goods.

SPECIALTY SHOPS

BOOKS   **Hodges Figgis** (⊠ *56–58 Dawson St., Southeast Dublin* ☎ *01/677–4754*), Dublin's leading independent bookstore, stocks 1½ million books on three floors. There's a pleasant café on the first floor.

Stokes (⊠ *George's Street Arcade, Southside* ☎ *01/671–3584*) is a gem of an antique bookstore with a great used-book section.

CHINA,   **Blarney Woollen Mills** (⊠ *21–23 Nassau St., Southside* ☎ *01/671–0068*)
CRYSTAL,   is one of the best places for Belleek china, Waterford and Galway crys-
CERAMICS &   tal, and Irish linen.
JEWELRY
Kilkenny Shop (⊠ *5–6 Nassau St., Southside* ☎ *01/677–7066*) specializes in contemporary Irish-made ceramics, pottery, and silver jewelry, and regularly holds exhibits of exciting new work by Irish craftspeople.

Trinity Crafts(⊠ *3 Upper O'Connell St., Northside* ☎ *01/874–4961*) is your one-stop shop for everything cheesy Irish, including "The leprechauns make me do it" mugs and Guinness-logo underwear.

Weir & Sons (⊠ *96 Grafton St., Southside* ☎ *01/677–9678*), Dublin's most prestigious jeweler, sells not only jewelry and watches, but also china, glass, lamps, silver, and leather.

CLOTHING   **Costume** (⊠ *10 Castel Market, Southside* ☎ *01/679–4188*) is a classy
STORES   boutique where Dubliners with fashion sense and money like to shop for colorful, stylish clothes. Local designers include Leigh, Helen James, and Antonia Campbell-Hughes; Temperley and Preen are among the international designers featured.

Scarlet Row (⊠ *5 Scarlet Row, Temple Bar* ☎ *01/672–9534*), opened by an ex–Donna Karan shoe designer and a Dublin art curator, is a high-concept shoe store, fashion outlet, and gallery—great for browsing and buying alike.

MUSIC **Gael Linn** (✉26 Merrion Sq., Southside ☎01/676–7283) specializes in traditional Irish music and Irish-language recordings; it's where the aficionados go.

HMV (✉65 Grafton St., Southside ☎01/679–5334 ✉18 Henry St., Northside ☎01/872–2095) is one of the larger record shops in town.

SWEATERS **Avoca Handweavers** (✉11–13 Suffolk St., Southside ☎01/677–4215) is
& TWEEDS a beautiful store with an eclectic collection of knitwear from contemporary Irish designers. The children's wear section on the second floor is a real joy. They also stock original ceramics.

Blarney Woollen Mills (✉21–23 Nassau St., Southside ☎01/451–6111) stocks a good selection of tweed, linen, and wool sweaters from their mills in County Cork, in all price ranges.

HEADING SOUTH: CASHEL TO CORK

Nobody ever came twice to Ireland looking for a tan. But if they did, they would head to the country's Southeast region, which has the mildest, sunniest, and also driest weather in Ireland. Other than the cities of Kilkenny and Waterford, the leading sight of the region is the spectacular Rock of Cashel, one of Ireland's greatest medieval sites and a must-see for many. A further 160 km (100 mi) southwest lies Cork City, Ireland's second-biggest city and one of its most vibrant. A great base for touring the countryside, it's not too far from the Blarney Stone, where you can supposedly get "the gift of the gab" at beautiful Blarney Castle.

PLANNING YOUR TIME
Providing you catch a morning bus from Dublin, you'll be able to enjoy a full afternoon at the Rock of Cashel. However, an overnight is suggested in the town of Cashel (especially if you don't want to hand over your luggage to the attendants at the Rock for storage—unfortunately, they don't have an official cloakroom); note that while Cashel has few hotels it does have many guesthouses—inquire at the tourist office. Or you can opt to forge on that day and catch a bus around sunset heading to Cork. A full day is needed for this large city, plus an extra day for the excursion west to Blarney Castle.

GETTING HERE
The only public transportation that goes directly to the Rock of Cashel is the Dublin-Cork bus, run by Bus Éireann; departures are usually every two hours and the bus ride lasts about 2 ½ hours. Aircoach is a private line that also runs between Dublin and Cork and passes through Cashel. Alternatively, there are trains from Dublin to Thurles, a village 15 minutes away from Cashel (connect via tax or infrequent buses). Bus Éireann's Dublin-Cork bus then connects Cashel with Cork. By car, Cashel is on the big N8 highway connecting north and south. There are numerous trains every day from Dublin to Cork (3 hours). To get to Blarney Castle from Cork, catch buses from the Parnell Place station.

9

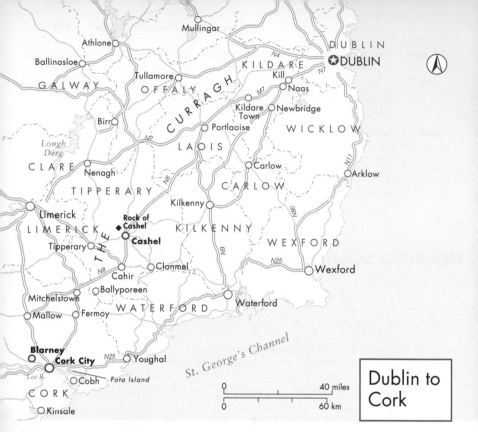

Dublin to Cork

0 _____ 40 miles
0 _____ 60 km

TOURS

Bus Éireann offers a range of daylong and half-day guided tours of the region around Cork from June to September. A full-day tour costs about €30, half-day €15. Bus Éireann also offers open-top bus tours of Cork City on Tuesday and Saturday in July and August for €6.

ESSENTIALS

Bus Contacts Bus Éireann (☎ *01/836–6111 in Dublin* ⊕ *www.buseireann.ie*).
Aircoach (☎ *01/844-7118* ⊕ *www.aircoach.ie*).

Train Contacts Irish Rail (☎ *01/836–6222 in Dublin* ⊕ *www.irishrail.ie.*).

Tour Information Bus Éireann (☎ *01/836–6111 in Dublin* ⊕ *www.buseireann.ie*).

ROCK OF CASHEL

Fodor'sChoice *160 km (100 mi) southwest of Dublin on the N8.*
★

Ireland's "rock of ages," the Rock of Cashel is famed as the haunt of St. Patrick and a place where history, culture, and legend collide in one of Ireland's most stupendous medieval sites. The market town is set on the busy Cork–Dublin road, with a lengthy history as a center of royal and religious power. From roughly AD 370 until 1101, it was the seat of the kings of Munster, and it was probably at one time a center of Druidic worship. Here, according to legend, St. Patrick arrived in about AD 432 and baptized King Aengus, who became Ireland's first Christian ruler. One of the many legends associated with this event is that St. Patrick plucked a shamrock to explain the mystery of the Trinity, thus giving a new emblem to Christian Ireland.

The awe-inspiring, oft-mist-shrouded Rock of Cashel, a short walk north of town, rises as a giant, circular mound 200 feet above the surrounding plain; it's crowned by a tall cluster of gray monastic remains. Legend has it that the devil, flying over Ireland in a hurry, took a bite out of the Slieve Bloom Mountains to clear his path (the gap, known as the Devil's Bit, can be seen to the north of the rock) and spat it out in the Golden Vale. The shell of **St. Patrick's Cathedral** is the largest structure on the summit. The original 13th-century cathedral, built in a flamboyant variation on Romanesque style, was destroyed by fire in 1495. A series of sculptures in the north transept represents the apostles, other saints, and the beasts of the Apocalypse. The entrance to **Cormac's Chapel**, the best-preserved building on top of the Rock, is behind the south transept of the cathedral. The chapel was built in 1127 by Cormac Macarthy, king of Desmond and bishop of Cashel. Note the high corbeled roof, modeled on the traditional covering of early saints' cells (as at Glendalough and Dingle); the typically Romanesque, twisted columns around the altar; and the unique carvings around the south entrance. The **Museum** across from the entrance to the Rock provides a 15-minute audiovisual display, as well as enthusiastic young guides. The best approach to the rock is along the Bishop's Walk, a 5-minute stroll that begins outside the drawing room of the Cashel Palace hotel on Main Street. ⊠ *Rock of Cashel* ☎ *062/61437* ⊕ *www.cashel.ie* ⊠ *€5.30* ◉ *Mid-Mar.–mid-June, daily 9:30–5:30; mid-June–mid-Sept., daily 9–7; mid-Sept.–mid-Oct., daily 9–5:30; mid-Oct.–mid-Mar., daily 9–4:30*

In the same building as the town TIO, the **Cashel of the Kings Heritage Center** explains the historic relationship between the town and the Rock and includes a scale model of Cashel as it looked during the 1600s. ⊠ *City Hall, Main St.* ☎ *062/62511* ⊕ *www.heritagetowns.com/cashel. html* ⊠ *Free* ◉ *Daily 9:30–5:50.*

WHERE TO STAY

$$$$
Fodor's Choice
★

🏨 **Cashel Palace.** Built in 1730 for archbishop Theophilus Bolton, this grand house truly is a palace in every sense. It was designed by Sir Edward Lovett Pearce, who also created the Old Parliament House in Dublin, and is gorgeously offset by parkland replete with fountains and centuries-old trees. Inside, red-pine paneling, barley-sugar staircases, Corinthian columns, and a surfeit of cosseting antiques all create an air of Georgian *volupté.* The Bishop's Buttery restaurant relies on game in season, local lamb and beef, and fresh fish creatively prepared. Don't miss the lovely gardens at the rear of the house. **Pros:** glorious period main house; good restaurant. **Cons:** expensive for this region; popular for weddings; few in-room facilities. ⊠ *Main St., Co. Tipperary* ☎ *062/62707* ⊕ *www.cashel-palace.ie* 🛏 *23 rooms* ⚙ *In-room: no a/c. In-hotel: restaurant, bar, public Wi-Fi* ⊟ *AE, DC, MC, V* ⏚BP.

9

CORK CITY

77 km (48 mi) west of Cashel, 254 km (158 mi) south of Dublin.

The major metropolis of the south, Cork is Ireland's second-largest city—but you have to put this in perspective. It actually runs a distant second, with a population of 123,000, roughly one-tenth the size of Dublin. Cork is a spirited place, with a formidable pub culture, a lively traditional-music scene, a respected and progressive university, attractive art galleries, and offbeat cafés. The city's major sights are spread out a bit, but still the best way to see the city is on foot. Patrick Street is the city center's main thoroughfare. You can tour the center of the city in a morning or an afternoon, depending on how much you plan to shop along the way. To really see everything, however, allow a full day, with a break for lunch at the Farmgate Café in the English Market. Also note that the Crawford Gallery and the English Market are closed on Sunday.

❶ Cork Vision Centre. Located in the renovated St. Peter's Church, an 18th-century building in what was once the bustling heart of medieval Cork, this historical society provides an excellent introduction to the city's history and geography. The highlight is a detailed 1:500 scale model of the city, showing how it has changed over the ages. ✉ *Washington St., Washington Village* ☎ *021/427-2706* 🎟 *Free* ⊙ *Weekdays 9–5.*

❺ Crawford Art Gallery. The large redbrick building was built in 1724 as
★ the customs house and is now home to Ireland's leading provincial art gallery. An imaginative expansion has added an extra 10,000 square feet of gallery space for visiting exhibitions and adventurous shows of modern Irish artists. The permanent collection includes landscape paintings depicting Cork in the 18th and 19th centuries. Take special note of works by Irish painters William Leech (1881–1968), Daniel Maclise (1806–70), James Barry (1741–1806), and Nathaniel Grogan (1740–1807). The café, run by the Allen family of Ballymaloe, is a good place for a light lunch or a homemade sweet. ✉ *Emmet Pl., City Center South* ☎ *021/490-7855* ⊕ *www.crawfordartgallery.com* 🎟 *Free* ⊙ *Mon.–Sat. 9–5.*

❷ English Market. Food lovers: head for one of the misleadingly small
★ entrances to this large market in an elaborate, brick-and-cast-iron Victorian building. (Its official name is the Princes Street Market, and it's also known locally as the Covered Market.) Among the 140 stalls, keep an eye out for the Alternative Bread Co., which produces more than 40 varieties of handmade bread every day. Iago, Sean Calder-Potts's deli, has fresh pasta, lots of cheeses, and charcuterie. The Olive Stall sells olive oil, olive-oil soap, and olives from Greece, Spain, France, and Italy. Kay O'Connell's Fish Stall, in the legendary fresh-fish alley, purveys local smoked salmon. O'Reilly's Tripe and Drisheen is the last existing retailer of a Cork specialty, tripe (cow's stomach), and *drisheen* (blood sausage). Upstairs is the Farmgate, an excellent café. ✉ *Entrances on Grand Parade and Princes St., City Center South* ⊕ *www.corkcity.ie* ⊙ *Mon.–Sat. 9–5:30.*

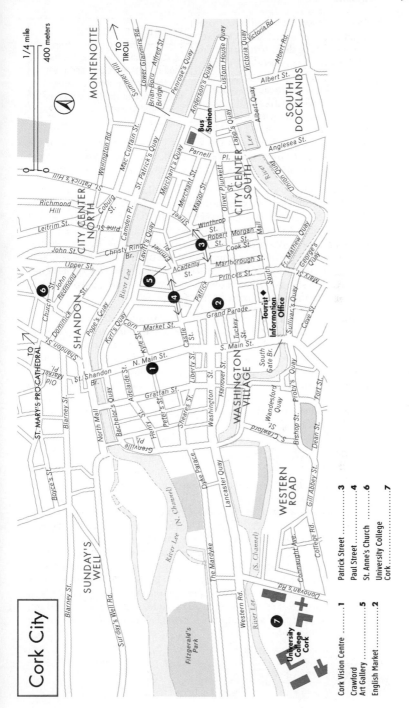

Cork City

1/4 mile
400 meters

MONTENOTTE

TO TIVOLI

SOUTH DOCKLANDS

CITY CENTER NORTH

CITY CENTER SOUTH

SHANDON

WASHINGTON VILLAGE

SUNDAY'S WELL

WESTERN ROAD

TO ST. MARY'S PROCATHEDRAL

Bus Station

Tourist Information Office

University College Cork

Fitzgerald's Park

Richmond Hill

Leitrim St.
John St.
Upper St.
John Redmond St.
Church St.
Dominick St.
Blarney St.
Boyce's St.
Sunday's Well Rd.
Sur'day's Well Rd.

River Lee (N. Channel)
The Mardyke
Dyke Parade
Lancaster Quay
Western Rd.
College Rd.
Connaught Ave.
Donovan's Rd.
Gill Abbey St.
Crawford St.
Bishop St.
Dean St.

Wellington Rd.
Mac Curtain St.
Summer Hill
St. Patrick's Hill
Coburg St.
Bruce Pine St.
Camden Pl.
Christy Ring Br.
Lavitt's Quay
Emmet Pl.
Pope's Quay
Kyrl's Quay
Corn Market St.
N. Main St.
Shandon St.
Market Pl.
P.O.
St. Shandon Br.
Adelaide St.
Bachelor's Quay
North Mall
Grenville Pl.
Henry St.
Peter's St.
Sheares St.
Liberty St.
Hanover St.
Washington St.
Grattan St.
Kyle St.
Castle St.
S. Main St.
S. Crawford St.
Wandesford Quay
Proby's Quay
Fort St.

St. Patrick's Quay
Merchant's Quay
Merchant St.
Mayor St.
St. Patrick's Street
Winthrop St.
Robert St.
Academy St.
Marlborough St.
Princes St.
Patrick
Grand Parade
Tuckey St.
South Main St.
South Gate Br.

Penrose's Quay
Brian Boru Bridge
Lower Glanmire Rd.
Alfred St.
Parnell Pl.
Anderson's Quay
Oliver Plunkett St.
Morgan St.
Cook St.
Robert St.
Mall
George's Quay
Fr. Mathew Quay
Sullivan's Quay
Union Quay
Mark St.
South
Cove St.

Custom House Quay
Lapp's Quay
Albert Quay
Victoria Quay
Victoria Rd.
Albert Rd.
Albert St.
Anglesea St.

River Lee

1
5
2
3
4
6
7

❸ Patrick Street. Extending from Grand Parade in the south to Patrick's Bridge in the north, Panna (as it's known locally) is Cork's main shopping thoroughfare. It has been designed as a pedestrian-priority area with wide walks and special streetlights. A mainstream mix of department stores, boutiques, pharmacies, and bookshops lines the way. If you look above some of the plate-glass storefronts, you can see examples of the bowfront Georgian windows that are emblematic of Old Cork. ⊠ *City Center South.*

> ## WORD OF MOUTH
>
> "Cork's English Market is the best food market in Ireland and great fun to visit. Buy some cheeses, have a look at the fish stalls, and enjoy the banter."   —ter2000

❹ Paul Street. A narrow street between the River Lee and Patrick Street and parallel to both, Paul Street is the backbone of the trendy shopping area that now occupies Cork's old French Quarter. The area was first settled by Huguenots fleeing religious persecution in France. Musicians and other street performers often entertain passersby in the Rory Gallagher Piazza, named for the rock guitarist (of the band Taste), whose family was from Cork. The shops here offer the best in modern Irish design—from local fashions to handblown glass—and antiques, particularly in the alley north of the piazza. ⊠ *City Center South.*

❻ St. Anne's Church. The church's pepper-pot Shandon steeple, which has a four-sided clock and is topped with a golden, salmon-shape weather vane, is visible from throughout the city and is the chief reason why St. Anne's is so frequently visited. The Bells of Shandon were immortalized in an atrocious but popular 19th-century ballad of that name. Your reward for climbing the 120-foot-tall tower is the chance to ring the bells, with the assistance of sheet tune cards, out over Cork. Adjacent is the Shandon Craft Market. ⊠ *Church St., Shandon* ⊕ *www.corkcity. ie* ☜ *€1.50 church, €2 church and bell tower* ☉ *May–Oct., Mon.–Sat. 9:30–4:30; Nov.–Apr., Mon.–Sat. 10–3:30.*

❼ University College Cork. The Doric, porticoed gates of UCC stand about ★ 2 km (1 mi) from the center of the city. The college, which has a student body of roughly 10,000, is a constituent of the National University of Ireland. The main quadrangle is a fine example of 19th-century university architecture in the Tudor-Gothic style, reminiscent of many Oxford and Cambridge colleges. The Honan Collegiate Chapel, east of the quadrangle, was built in 1916 and modeled on the 12th-century, Hiberno-Romanesque style, best exemplified by the remains of Cormac's Chapel at Cashel. Check out the contemporary Irish art on view in the Lewis Glucksman Gallery, opened in late 2004. ⊠ *Western Road* ☎ *021/490–1876* ⊕ *www.ucc.ie* ☜ *Free; Guided tours €4* ☉ *Weekdays, Visitor Centre 9–5; Guided tours May, June, Sept., and Oct., Mon., Wed., Fri., and Sat. at 3* PM; *call for hrs Easter wk, July, Aug., and mid-Dec.–mid-Jan.*

WHERE TO STAY & EAT

$ ✕**Farmgate Café.** One of the best—and busiest—informal lunch spots in town is on a terraced gallery above the fountain at the Princes Street entrance to the atmospheric 19th-century English Market. One side of the gallery opens onto the market and is self-service; the other side is glassed in and has table service (reservations advised). Tripe and drisheen (blood sausage) is one dish that is always on the menu; daily specials include less challenging but no less traditional dishes, such as corned beef with colcannon (potatoes and cabbage mashed with butter and seasonings). ✉*English Market, City Center South* ☎*021/427–8134* ☐*DC, MC, V* ⊘*Closed Sun. No dinner.*

$$ ✕**Greenes.** Tucked away on a cobbled patio accessible only on foot, this
Fodor'sChoice surprising haven is part of a Victorian warehouse conversion. The stone and redbrick walls are the backdrop for a minimalist modern interior with tall-backed green rattan chairs and small tables with linen place mats. The French chef, Frederic Desormeaux, has created a menu featuring both classic continental fare—a best bet is the beef fillet served with horseradish mash, crispy onion rings, and Bordelaise sauce. ✉ *48 MacCurtain St., City Center North* ☎ *021/450–0011* ☐*AE, MC, V* ⊘*No lunch.*

$$$$ ✕**Ivory Tower.** Seamus O'Connell, the adventurous owner-chef here, is
★ famous in Ireland for his television series *Soul Food.* He describes his approach as "trans-ethnic fusion." He has cooked in Mexico and Japan, so his accomplished menu has such brilliantly eclectic dishes as wild duck with vanilla, sherry, and jalapeños; pheasant tamale. Imaginative presentation, including a surprise taster to set the mood, compensates for the bare wooden floors and somewhat stark decor. ✉*35 Princes St., Washington Village* ☎*021/427–4665* ☐*AE, DC, MC, V* ⊘*Closed Sun. and Mon. No lunch.*

$$$ ▥**Clarion.** Black-clad receptionists standing behind simple wooden desks at the far end of the vast, marble-floor lobby are the first indication that this place aspires to boutique-hotel chic. Occupying a corner block beside the River Lee, the Clarion is the first arrival of a huge docklands development. It's kitty-corner across the river from City Hall, and a short walk from shopping and dining. Rooms are built around a central, top-lighted atrium; decor is stylish pale-wood trim complemented by curtains and flooring in a khaki-olive theme. **Pros:** new (2005) and funky; high-luxe rooms. **Cons:** limited car parking; neighborhood deserted after dark; some rooms overlook internal atrium/staircase. ✉*Lapp's Quay, City Center South, Co. Cork* ☎*021/422–4900* ⊕*www.clarionhotelcorkcity.com* ⇆*191 rooms* ⚠*In-room: Ethernet, Wi-Fi (some). In-hotel: restaurant, bar, pool, gym, public Wi-Fi* ☐*AE, DC, MC, V* ⦿*BP.*

$ ▦**Garnish House.** Owner-manager Johanna Lucey will be offering you
★ tea and homemade chocolate cake before you have even crossed the threshold of her home. Johanna provides the kind of old-fashioned hospitality that is fast disappearing in modern Ireland. A pair of large Victorian town houses near the university, and a short walk from the town center, contain impeccably clean, well-aired rooms. **Pros:** a friendly welcome; a genuine Irish experience. **Cons:** seriously unhip;

9

located on a busy main road; rooms book up well in advance. ✉ *Western Road, Washington Village, Co. Cork* ☎*021/427–5111* ⊕*www.garnish.ie* 🛏*14 rooms* ♿*In room: no a/c, Wi-Fi. In hotel: parking (no fee)* ▤*AE, MC, V* ⋈*BP.*

NIGHTLIFE & THE ARTS

See the *Examiner* or the *Evening Echo* for details about movies, theater, and live music performances.

WORD OF MOUTH

"Although I was a teeny bit scared of the height, it was completely amazing to kiss the Blarney Stone. Truly, now I have the gift of gab. Aside from the castle, there's the Blarney woolen mills, and various tiny shops for souvenirs and such."   —Rachael

PERFORMING ARTS

Cork Opera House (✉*Lavitt's Quay, City Center South* ☎*021/427–0022* ⊕*www.corkoperahouse.ie*) is the city's major hall for touring productions and variety acts.

PUBS & NIGHTCLUBS

Traditional music sessions can happen anytime at **An Bodhrán** (✉*42 Oliver Plunkett St., City Center South* ☎*021/437–1392*). **The Bierhaus** (✉*Pope's Quay, Shandon* ☎*021/455–1648*) attracts a hip young crowd, and has over 30 beers to choose from, poker on Tuesday, and a DJ every Friday. **The Savoy** (✉*Patrick Street, City Center South* ☎*021/425–4296* ⊕ *www.savoycork.com*) is the major venue for night owls, operating Wednesday to Saturday from 11 until late. Live acts from Ireland and elsewhere are on offer in the main room, and in the foyer there are comedy acts and DJ sets, which can vary from the Electric Dream 80s Club to Detroit techno.

SIDE TRIP FROM CORK CITY: BLARNEY CASTLE

8 km (5 mi) northwest of Cork City on R617.

On Galway sands they kiss your hands, they kiss your lips at Carney, but by the Lee they drink strong tea, and kiss the stone at Blarney. This famous rhyme celebrates one of Ireland's most noted icons—the Blarney Stone, which is the main reason most people journey to this small community built around a village green.

★ In the center of Blarney is **Blarney Castle,** or what remains of it: the ruined central keep is all that's left of this mid-15th-century stronghold. The castle contains the famed Blarney Stone; kissing the stone, it's said, endows the kisser with the fabled "gift of gab." It's 127 steep steps to the battlements. To kiss the stone, you must lie down on the battlements, hold on to a guardrail, and lean your head way back. It's good fun and not at all dangerous. Expect a line from mid-June to early September; while you wait, you can admire the views of the wooded River Lee valley and chuckle over how the word "blarney" came to mean what it does. As the story goes, Queen Elizabeth I wanted Cormac MacCarthy, Lord of Blarney, to will his castle to the crown, but he refused her requests with eloquent excuses and soothing compliments. Exhausted by his comments, the queen reportedly exclaimed, "This is all Blarney. What he says he rarely means." You can take pleasant walks around the castle grounds; Rock Close contains oddly shaped limestone rocks landscaped in the 18th century and a grove of ancient yew trees that is said to have been a site of Druid worship. In early March there's a wonderful display of naturalized daffodils. ☎021/438-5252 ⊕www.blarneycastle.ie ☜€10 ⊙May and Sept., Mon.–Sat. 9–6:30, Sun. 9–5:30; June–Aug., Mon.–Sat. 9–7, Sun. 9–5:30; Oct.–Apr., Mon.–Sat. 9–sundown, Sun. 9–5:30.

THE RING OF KERRY

If writers like Sir Walter Scott and William Thackeray had to struggle finding the superlatives to describe the lakes of Killarney and mountains framing the Ring of Kerry, it is not surprising that they remain among the most celebrated attractions in Ireland. As well as among the most popular: on a sunny day, it seems like half the nation's visitors are traveling along this two-lane road. The Ring of Kerry, which follows the shoreline of the Iveragh Peninsula, offers incredibly stunning mountain and coastal views—replete with sandy beaches, stone villages, and rocky coves—around almost every turn. The road is narrow and curvy, and the local sheep think nothing of using it for a nap; take it slowly. And because rain blocks views across the water to the Beara Peninsula in the east and the Dingle Peninsula in the west, hope for sunshine. It makes all the difference. Gateway to the Ring of Kerry is the famous town of Killarney, where all tour buses depart.

PLANNING YOUR TIME
Arrive in Killarney from Cork via train. Overrun with touristy hotels, the town will just be a place to place to park yourself at night in order to spend the next unforgettable day touring the Ring of Kerry. Opt for renting a car, biking or hiking, or going with the most popular option, escorted bus tours. Bear in mind that most of these buses leave Killarney between 9 and 10 AM. The trip covers 176 km (110 mi) on N70 (and briefly R562) if you start and finish in Killarney; the journey will be 40 km (25 mi) shorter if you only venture between Kenmare and Killorglin.

GETTING HERE
Take the daily Irish Rail train from Cork to the Killarney Railway Station. Head out to tour the Ring of Kerry using the regular public Bus Éireann service between mid-June and mid-September; note there are only two buses a day, leaving Killarney at 8:45 AM or 1:45 PM. The trip takes more than four hours. As for escorted bus tours of the Ring, they usually tend to start in Killarney and ply the Ring counterclockwise (to get the best views). On your last morning, connect by train from Killarney to Limerick and then transfer to a bus to get to Shannon Airport.

TOURS
Dero's Tours and Corcoran's Tours organize full-day and half-day trips by coach or taxi around Killarney and the Ring of Kerry. Bus Éireann also offers a range of daylong and half-day guided tours of the region.

ESSENTIALS

Bus Contacts Bus Éireann (☎ *01/836–6111 in Dublin* 🌐 *www.buseireann.ie*).

Corcoran's Tours (✉ *10 College St., Killarney* ☎ *064/663–6666*). Dero's Tours (✉ *22 Main St., Killarney* ☎ *064/663–1251* 🌐 *www.derostours.com*).

Train Contacts Irish Rail (☎ *01/836–6222 in Dublin* 🌐 *www.irishrail.ie.*).

Tour Information Bus Éireann (☎ *01/836–6111 in Dublin* 🌐 *www.buseireann.ie*).

KILLARNEY

102 km (65 mi) west of Cork City.

You may want to limit time spent in Killarney itself if discos, Irish cabarets, and singing pubs aren't your thing. But the surrounding countryside is glorious and everybody catches the Ring of Kerry tour buses in this town. **Aghadoe** (✉ *5 km [3 mi] west of Killarney on R562 Beaufort–Killorglin Rd.*) is an outstanding place to get a feel for what Killarney's region is all about: lake and mountain scenery. Stand beside Aghadoe's 12th-century ruined church and round tower, and watch the shadows creep gloriously across Lower Lake, with Innisfallen Island in the distance and the Gap of Dunloe to the west.

★ **Muckross House,** the famous 19th-century, Elizabethan-style manor, now houses the Kerry Folklife Centre, where bookbinders, potters, and weavers demonstrate their crafts. Upstairs, elegantly furnished rooms portray the lifestyle of the landed gentry in the 1800s; downstairs in the basement you can experience the conditions of servants employed in the house. Next door you'll find the Killarney National Park Visitor Centre. The informal grounds are noted for their rhododendrons and azaleas, the water garden, and the outstanding limestone rock garden. In the park beside the house, the Muckross Traditional Farms comprise reconstructed farm buildings. ✉ *Killarney National Park, Muckross Demesne, Muckross Rd. (N71), 6½ km (4 mi) south of Killarney* ☎ *064/663–1440* 🌐 *www.heritageireland.ie* 🎫 *Visitor center free, farms or house €5.75, farms and house €10* ⏲ *House and Visitor Centre: Nov.–mid-Mar., daily 9–5:30; mid-Mar.–June, Sept., and Oct., daily 9–6; July and Aug., daily 9–7. Farms mid-Mar.–Apr., weekends 1–6; May, daily 1–6; June–Sept., daily 10–7; Oct., daily 2–6.*

WHERE TO STAY & EAT

$$–$$$ ✕ **Mentons@The Plaza.** The first-floor restaurant is reached by a wide flight of stone steps, and overlooks a green space where the traditional ponies and traps take their breaks between rides around Muckross Park. This prime location, just around the corner from the commercial bustle of the town's high street, is one of the attractions of Mentons. Another is its spacious, uncluttered interior, armchairs and low tables lighted, at lunchtime, by natural light from large, wood-framed windows. Finally, there is the French-inspired menu. ✉ *Killarney Plaza Hotel, Kenmare Place* ☎ *064/662–1150* 💳 *MC, V* ⏲ *Closed last 3 wks Jan.*

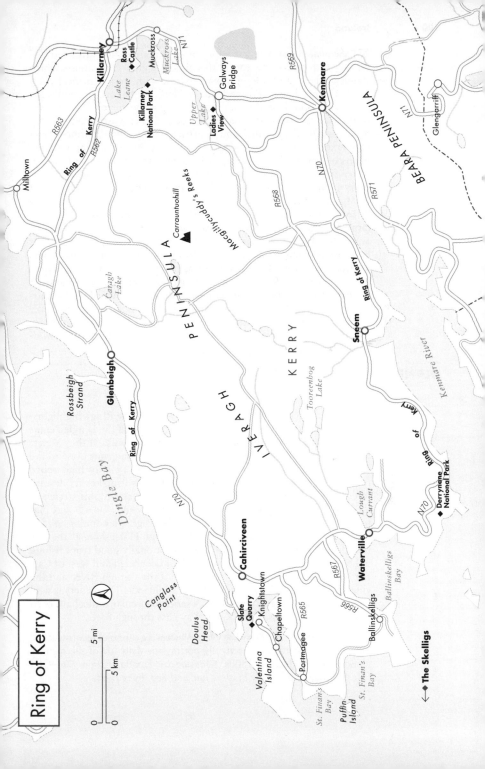

$$$ ⌂**Cahernane House.** Get a glimpse of the Killarney that attracted dis-
Fodor's Choice cerning 19th-century visitors at this imposing gray-stone house, which
★   stands at the end of a long private avenue with trees that meet over-
head to form a tunnel. Formerly the residence of the earls of Pembroke,
the estate borders on the national park, and the current house dates
from 1877. It oozes baronial grandeur and it is worth paying extra
for a room in the original house. **Pros:** great Old World atmosphere;
very luxe; fantastic views. **Cons:** standard rooms are disappointingly
plain compared with more expensive superiors. ⊠*Muckross Rd., Co.
Kerry* ☎*064/663-1895* ⊕*www.cahernane.com* ⇝*36 rooms, 2 suites*
⚷*In-room: no a/c, Ethernet. In-hotel: no-smoking rooms, tennis court*
⊟*MC, V* ⦿*BP.*

$$ ⌂**Earls Court House.** In a quiet suburb within walking distance of Killarney's center, this spacious guesthouse is furnished with interesting
antiques collected by Emer Moynihan, who likes to greet her guests
by offering home-baked goods in front of the open fire. Bedrooms
are spacious, with large bathrooms, a mix of antique and reproduction Victorian furniture. **Pros:** quiet location; plenty of parking;
warm welcome. **Cons:** long walk or taxi ride to town; bland suburban location. ⊠*Woodlawn Junction, Muckross Rd., N71, Co. Kerry*
☎*064/663–4009* ⊕*www.killarney-earlscourt.ie* ⇝*30 rooms* ⚷*In-
room: no a/c, Ethernet. In-hotel: public Wi-Fi* ⊟*MC, V* ⊙*Closed mid-
Nov.–mid-Feb.* ⦿*BP.*

GLENBEIGH

27 km (17 mi) northeast of Cahirciveen on N70.

The road from Glenbeigh to Cahirciveen is one of the Ring's highlights.
To the north are Dingle Bay and the jagged peaks of the Dingle Peninsula, which will, in all probability, be shrouded in mist. If they aren't,
the gods have indeed blessed your journey. The road runs close to the
water here, and around the small village of Kells it climbs high above
the bay, hugging the steep side of Drung Hill as it makes its descent
to Glenbeigh. Note how different the stark character of this stretch of
the Ring is from the gentle, woody Kenmare Bay side. On a boggy plateau by the sea, the block-long town of Glenbeigh is a popular holiday
base—there's excellent hiking in the Glenbeigh Horseshoe, as the surrounding mountains are known, and exceptionally good trout fishing
in Lough Coomasaharn. The area south of Glenbeigh and west of Car-
rantouhill Mountain, around the shores of the Caragh River and the
village of Glencar, is known as the Kerry Highlands. The scenery is wild
and rough but strangely appealing. A series of circular walks have been
signposted, and parts of the Kerry Way pass through here.

☾   Worth a quick look, the **Kerry Bog Village Museum** is a cluster of reconstructed,
fully furnished cottages that vividly portray the daily life of the region's
working class in the early 1800s. ⊠*Beside Red Fox Bar* ☎*066/976–9184*
⊠*€4* ⊙*Mar.–Nov., daily 8:30–7; Jan. and Feb. by request.*

A signpost to the right outside Glenbeigh points to **Caragh Lake,** a tempting excursion south to a beautiful expanse of water set among gorse- and heather-covered hills and majestic mountains. The road hugs the shoreline much of the way.

WHERE TO STAY

$$

Fodor'sChoice

★

Carrig Country House. A rambling two-story Victorian house covered in flowering creepers, and set on 4 acres of lush gardens running down to a secluded lakeshore—this comes pretty close to most people's dream rural retreat. The atmosphere is more grand country house than hotel, with turf fires in the reception rooms encouraging guests to linger in an armchair with a book. Guest rooms are lavishly decorated with period antiques ranging from cozy cottage-style to ornate Victoriana. **Pros:** lovely secluded location; real country-house atmosphere; affable owner-managers. **Cons:** tricky drive from Killorglin (see Web site for directions). ⊠ *Caragh Lake, Killorglin, Co. Kerry* ☎ *066/976–9100* ⊕ *www.carrighouse.com* ⇆ *17 rooms* ⚷ *In-room: no a/c, no TV. In-hotel: restaurant, bar, no elevator, public Internet* ⊟ *MC, V* ☉ *Closed Dec.–Feb.* ◉ *BP.*

CAHIRCIVEEN

18 km (11 mi) north of Waterville on N70.

Cahirciveen (pronounced cah-her-sigh-*veen*), at the foot of Bentee Mountain, is the gateway to the eastern side of the Ring of Kerry and the main market town for southern Kerry. Following the tradition in this part of the world, the modest, terraced houses are each painted in different colors (sometimes two or three)—the brighter the better.

The **O'Connell Memorial Church,** a large, elaborate, neo-Gothic structure that dominates the main street, was built in 1888 of Newry granite and black limestone to honor the local hero Daniel O'Connell. It's the only church in Ireland named after a layman.

The **Cahirciveen Heritage Centre** is in the converted former barracks of the Royal Irish Constabulary, an imposing, castlelike structure built after the Fenian Rising of 1867 to suppress further revolts. The center has well-designed displays depicting scenes from times of famine, the life of Daniel O'Connell, and the restoration of this fine building from a blackened ruin. ⊠ *Barracks* ☎ *066/947-2777* ⌑ *€3.50* ☉ *June–Sept., Mon.–Sat. 10–6, Sun. 2–6; Mar.–May and Oct., weekdays 9:30–5:30.*

9

THE SKELLIGS

Fodor'sChoice

★

21 km (13 mi) northwest of Waterville.

In the far northwestern corner of the Ring of Kerry, across Portmagee Channel, lies Valentia Island, which is reachable by a bridge erected in 1971. Visible from Valentia, and on a clear day from other points along the coast, are the **Skelligs,** one of the most spectacular sights in Ireland. Sculpted as if by the hand of God, the islands of Little Skellig, Great Skellig, and the Washerwoman's Rock are distinctively cone-shape, surrounded by blue swirling seas. The largest island, the Great Skellig, or Skellig Michael, distinguished by its twin peaks, rises 700 feet from the Atlantic. It has the remains of a settlement of early Christian monks, reached by climbing 600 increasingly precipitous steps. In spite of a thousand years of battering by Atlantic storms, the church, oratory, and beehive-shape living cells are surprisingly well preserved.

To visit the Skelligs, you can take a half-day trip in an open boat—perfect for adventurers who pack plenty of Dramamine. The entire visit takes three to four hours, with 1½ hours on the Skellig Michael, where visitors are supervised by resident guides, and the remaining time in transit (the duration varies depending on the weather and tides). During the journey you'll pass Little Skellig, the breeding ground of more than 22,000 pairs of gannets, but the masterpiece is the phenomenal Skellig Michael, home to that amazing 7th–12th-century village of monastic beehive dwellings, and offering vertigo-inducing views. Note that the waters are choppy at the best of times, and trips are made when the weather permits. Even in fine weather it can be a rough, white-knuckle ride as you cross the swell of the open sea, lasting at least 45 minutes, and it's not suitable for small children. One worthy outfitter is **Pat Joe Murphy** (⊠ *Portmagee* ☎ *066/947–7156* 🖃 *€30* ⊙ *Cruises May–Aug., daily at 10 AM, weather permitting*).

Where the bridge joins Valentia Island, **Skellig Experience** (⊠ *Valentia Island* ☎ *066/947–6306* ⊕ *www.skelligexperience.com* 🖃 *€5* ⊙ *Apr.– June and Sept., daily 9:30–5; July and Aug., daily 9:30–7; Oct. and Nov., daily 10–6*) offers an alternative for the less adventurous traveler. This center contains exhibits on local birdlife, the history of the lighthouse and keepers, and the life and work of the early Christian monks. There's also a 15-minute audiovisual show that allows you to "tour" the Skelligs without leaving dry land. But if you're up for it, don't miss the boat ride out to the rocks; Skellig Michael is something you won't soon forget.

WHERE TO STAY

¢
★

🏨 **Shealane Country House.** Cows graze in the adjoining field, and the breakfast room at this easily reached island retreat overlooks the ocean and the mainland hills. The large, modern detached house is on Valentia Island, beside the bridge to the mainland. The Skellig Experience Visitor Centre is across the road, and a brisk five-minute walk across the bridge leads you to Port Magee and should sharpen your appetite for hearty bar food. **Pros:** friendly welcome from local family; quiet rural location. **Cons:** outside the village; rooms book far in advance for July and August. ⊠ *Corha-Mor, Valentia Island* ☎ *066/947–6354* ⊕ *www. valentiaskelligs.com* 🛏 *5 rooms* ♿ *In-room: no a/c, no phone, no TV. In-hotel: no elevator, public Internet* ⊙ *Closed Nov.–Feb.* ¶⊙¶*BP.*

SNEEM

27 km (17 mi) southwest of Kenmare on N70.

The pretty village of Sneem (from the Irish for "knot") is settled around an English-style green on the Ardsheelaun River estuary, and its streets are filled with houses washed in different colors. The effect has been somewhat diminished by a cluster of developments on the southern approach. Beside the parish church are the "pyramids," as they're known locally. These 12-foot-tall, traditional stone structures with stained-glass insets look as though they've been here forever. In fact, the sculpture park was completed in 1990 to the design of the Kerry-born artist James Scanlon, who has won international awards for his work in stained glass.

The approximately 2,500-year-old, stone **Staigue Fort,** signposted 4 km (2 mi) inland at Castlecove, is almost circular and about 75 feet in diameter with a single south-side entrance. From the Iron Age (from 500 BC to the 5th century AD) and early Christian times (6th century AD), such "forts" were, in fact, the fortified homesteads for several families of one clan and their cattle. The walls at Staigue Fort are almost 13 feet wide at the base and 7 feet wide at the top; they still stand 18 feet high on the north and west sides. Within them, stairs lead to narrow platforms on which the lookouts stood. (Private land must be crossed to reach the fort, and a "compensation for trespass" of €1 is often requested by the landowner.)

WHERE TO STAY

$$$$ ⚙ Fodor'sChoice ★ **Parknasilla Resort.** For over a century Parknasilla, a towering, gray stone mansion set on a stunningly beautiful, sheltered inlet of the Kenmare estuary has been synonymous with old-style resort luxury. Everyone from George Bernard Shaw to Princess Grace to Charles de Gaulle favored it as a summer hideaway. Under dynamic new ownership, the grand old house has undergone a thorough refit to bring it into the 21st century while retaining its Old World charm. Public rooms are done in an endearingly homey mix-and-match style, untouched by decorators' latest whims. The large (superior) bedrooms in the main house, however, are beautifully coordinated with fabulous inlaid antique furniture. **Pros:** excellent sports facilities and spa; sheltered coastal location; great family destination. **Cons:** grounds and hotel big enough to get lost in; hugely popular with Irish families in July and August. ⌧ *Co. Kerry* ☎ *064/664–5122* ⊕ *www.parknasillahotel.ie* ⌸ *92 rooms* ⌂ *In-room: refrigerator (some), Ethernet, Wi-Fi (some), room service, no a/c. In-hotel: restaurant, bar, golf course, tennis court, pool, gym, spa* ▤ *AE, DC, MC, V* ⊗ *Closed Jan. and Feb.* ⊙ *BP.*

KENMARE

21 km (13 mi) north of Glengarriff on N71, 34 km (21 mi) south of Killarney.

A lively touring base, this market town is set at the head of the sheltered Kenmare River estuary. It's currently a matter of lively debate as to whether Kenmare has displaced Kinsale as the culinary capital of Ireland. Kenmare offers an amazing number of stylish little restaurants for a town its size. The town was founded in 1670 by Sir William Petty (Oliver Cromwell's surveyor general, a multitasking entrepreneur), and most of its buildings date from the 19th century, when it was part of the enormous Lansdowne Estate—itself assembled by Petty.

The **Kenmare Heritage Centre** explains the town's history and can outline a walking route to Kenmare's places of interest. ⊠ *The Square* ☎ *064/664–1233* ⬚ *Free* ⊙ *Easter–Sept., Mon.–Sat. 9:30–5:30.*

WHERE TO EAT & STAY

$$ ✕ **Packies.** For many returning visitors a meal at this busy little restaurant is a quintessential Kenmare experience. Chef Martin Hallissey has leased it from his mentor—and original owner—Maura Foley, who jump-started the Kenmare restaurant scene back in the 1980s. Stone floors and rough-plastered walls are warmed by colorful local paintings and the buzz of expectation among the closely packed diners. The fresh-tasting, strongly flavored food rises far above the rustic setting. The contemporary Irish menu may feature crab cakes with tartar sauce, roast lobster with garlic butter, or rack of lamb with rosemary-and-garlic gravy. ⊠ *Henry St.* ☎ *064/664–1508* ⬚ *MC, V* ⊙ *Closed Sun. and mid-Jan.–Feb. No lunch.*

$ ⌂ **Sea Shore Farm.** Mary Patricia O'Sullivan offers a warm but professional welcome to her spacious farmhouse on Kenmare Bay. In fair weather there are views across the sea to the hills on the Beara Peninsula, and although the place is very close to Kenmare, you can walk across her farmland to the deserted seashore and view its plentiful wildlife. Rooms are furnished with ornate heirlooms and have good-size bathrooms and placid views. **Pros:** quiet rural spot with views of calm estuary; personal attention from owner-manager. **Cons:** on a working cattle farm; a mile out of town; no bar or restaurant. ⊠ *Tubrid, Co. Kerry* ☎ *064/664–1270* ⊕ *www.seashorekenmare.com* ⤳ *6 rooms* ⌂ *In-room: Ethernet, no a/c. In-hotel: no-smoking rooms, no elevator* ⬚ *MC, V* ⊙ *Closed Nov.–Feb.* ⦿ *BP.*

SPORTS & THE OUTDOORS

☽ **Seafari** (⊠ *Kenmare Pier* ☎ *064/664–2059* ⊕ *www.seafariireland.com*) has fun two-hour ecotours and seal-watching cruises, with complimentary tea and coffee for adults and lollipops for the kids. Cruises cost €20 per adult, with special family rates. Reservations are essential.

Italy

A gondola in Venice

WORD OF MOUTH

"My best advice after traveling to Rome, Florence, and Venice would be to take it slow and enjoy the sights and sounds. Don't kill yourself to get everywhere in one day; your feet will hurt and you will get cranky and worst of all, Italy will be but a blur. Eat a lot of gelato. . . ."

—elcon

10

WHAT'S WHERE

1 **Rome.** Italy's capital is one of the great cities of Europe. It's a large, busy metropolis that lives in the here and now, yet there's no other place on earth where you'll encounter such powerful evocations of a long and spectacular past, from the Colosseum to the dome of St. Peter's. For 2,500 years, emperors, popes, and common citizens have left their mark on the city.

2 **Florence.** It's hard to think of a place that's more closely linked to one specific historical period than Florence. In the 15th century the city was at the center of an artistic revolution, later labeled the Renaissance, that changed the way people see the world. Five hundred years later the Renaissance remains the reason people see Florence—the abundance of treasures is mind-boggling. Present-day Florentines pride themselves on living well, and that means you'll find exceptional restaurants and first-rate shopping to go with all that amazing art.

3 **Tuscany.** Nature outdid herself in Tuscany, the central Italian region that has Florence as its principal city. The hills, draped with woods, vineyards, and olive groves, may not have the drama of mountain peaks or waves crashing on the shore, yet there's an

undeniable magic about them. Aside from Florence, Tuscany has several midsize cities that are well worth visiting, but the greatest appeal lies in the smaller towns, often perched on hilltops and not significantly altered since the Middle Ages.

4 **Milan.** Italy's leading city of commerce is also one of the world's fashion capitals. It feels less Italian and more like the rest of Europe than Italy's other great cities, but there are cultural treasures here that rival those of Florence and Rome.

5 **Venice.** One of the world's most novel cities, Venice has canals where the streets should be and an atmosphere of faded splendor that practically defines the word decadent. It was once one of the world's great sea-trading powers, which explains its rich history and its exotic, East-meets-West architecture.

SWITZERLAND

MT.
BLANC
Aosta
VALLE
D'AOSTA
Turin
Po
Pavia
Asti
PIEDMONT
LIGURIA
Genoa
Lugano
Lake
Maggiore
Milan

FRANCE

San
Remo
RIVIERA

MONACO

Ligurian Sea

CORSICA

Sassari
SARDINIA
SARDINIA
Cagliari

Mediterranean

ALGERIA

AUSTRIA

HUNGARY

TRENTINO-ALTO-ADIGE
Bolzano
FRIULI-VENEZIA GIULIA
Trento
SLOVENIA
Lake Garda
THE DOLOMITES
VENETO
Udine
Bergamo
Vicenza
Treviso
Trieste
Verona
Padua
Venice
CROATIA
LOMBARDY
5
Ferrara
Gulf of Venice
Parma
Modena
Bologna
EMILIA-ROMAGNA
Ravenna
La Spezia
Rimini
BOSNIA AND HERZEGOVINA
Lucca
Pistoia
SAN MARINO
Pisa
Florence
SAN MARINO
Livorno
2
Arezzo
Ancona
THE MARCHES
Siena
Assisi
TUSCANY
Perugia
UMBRIA
3
ELBA
Orvieto
Terni
Pescara
MONTENEGRO
ROME
Tivoli
ABRUZZO
1
LATIUM
MOLISE
Foggia
CAMPANIA
Bari
Naples
VESUVIUS
PUGLIA
Brindisi
ISCHIA
Amalfi
Potenza
CAPRI
BASILICATA
Lecce
Paestum
Taranto
Tyrrhenian Sea
Gulf of Taranto
Olbia
Cosenza
Catanzaro
AEOLIAN ISLANDS
CALABRIA
Ionian Sea
EGADI ISLANDS
Palermo
Messina
Reggio
SICILY
ETNA
Catania
TUNISIA
Agrigento
Siracusa
TUNIS
PANTELLERIA
SICILY

Adriatic Sea

Sea

0   100 miles
0   150 km

WHERE ELSE IN EUROPE CAN you find the blend of great art, delicious food and wine, and human warmth and welcome that awaits you in Italy? This Mediterranean country has made a profound contribution to Western civilization, producing some of the world's greatest thinkers, writers, politicians, saints, and artists. Impressive traces of their lives and works can still be seen in Italy's great buildings and enchanting countryside.

The whole of Italy is one vast attraction, but the triangle of its most-visited cities—Rome (Roma), Florence (Firenze), and Venice (Venezia)—represents the great variety found here. In Rome, especially, you can feel the uninterrupted flow of the ages, from the classical era of the ancient Romans to the bustle and throb of contemporary life being lived in centuries-old settings. Florence is the jewel of the Italian Renaissance, which is evident in the formal grandeur of its palaces and piazzas and the sumptuous villas in the surrounding countryside. Venice, by contrast, seems suspended in time, the same today as it was when it held sway over the eastern Mediterranean. Each of these cities reveals a different aspect of the Italian character: the Baroque exuberance of Rome, Florence's Renaissance harmony, and the dreamy sensuality of Venice.

WHEN TO GO

The main tourist season runs from April to mid-October. The so-called low season from fall to early spring may be cooler and rainier, but it has its rewards: less time waiting in line and more time for unhurried views of what you want to see.

Tourists crowd the major art cities at Easter, when Italians flock to resorts and to the country. From March through May, busloads of schoolchildren take cities of artistic and historical interest by storm.

The best months for sightseeing are April, May, June, September, and October, when the weather is mild. The hottest months, July and August, can be unpleasant. Winters are relatively mild in most places on the main tourist circuit but always include some rainy spells.

GETTING HERE & AROUND

BY AIR

The major gateways to Italy are Rome's Aeroporto Leonardo da Vinci (FCO), better known as Fiumicino, and Milan's Aeroporto Malpensa (MAL). There are some direct flights to Venice and Pisa, but to fly into most other Italian cities you need to make connections at Fiumicino and Malpensa or another European airport. You can also take the FS airport train to Rome's Termini station or a bus to Milan's central train station (Centrale) and catch a train to any other location in Italy. It will take about one hour to get from either Fiumicino or Malpensa to the appropriate train station.

Italy's major airports are not known for being new, fun, or efficient. Airports in Italy have been ramping up security measures, which include

TOP REASONS TO GO

The Vatican. The home of the Catholic Church, a tiny independent state tucked within central Rome, holds some of the city's most spectacular sights, including St. Peter's Basilica, the Vatican Museums, and Michelangelo's Sistine ceiling.

Ancient Rome. The Colosseum and the Roman Forum are remarkable ruins from Rome's ancient past. Sitting above it all is the Campidoglio, with a piazza designed by Michelangelo and museums containing Rome's finest collection of ancient art.

Fashion and Style in Milan. Italian clothing and furniture design are world famous, and the center of the Italian design industry is Milan. The best way to see what's happening in the world of fashion is to browse the boutiques of the fabled *quadrilatero della moda,* along and around Via Montenapoleone.

Venice's Grand Canal. A trip down Venice's "Main Street," whether by water bus or gondola, is a signature Italian experience.

Venice's Piazza San Marco. The centerpiece of the piazza is the Basilica di San Marco, arguably the most beautiful Byzantine church in the West, and right next door is the Venetian Gothic Palazzo Ducale, which was so beloved by the Venetians that when it burnt down in the 16th century, they had it rebuilt *come era, dove era*—exactly how and where it was.

Galleria degli Uffizi, Florence. The Uffizi—Renaissance art's hall of fame—contains masterpieces by Leonardo, Michelangelo, Raphael, Botticelli, Caravaggio, and dozens of other luminaries.

Duomo, Florence. The massive dome of Florence's Cathedral of Santa Maria del Fiore (aka the Duomo) is one of the world's great feats of engineering.

Piazza del Campo, Siena. Siena is Tuscany's classic medieval hill town, and its heart is the Piazza del Campo, the beautiful, one-of-a-kind town square.

random baggage inspection and bomb-detection dogs. All of the airports have restaurants and snack bars, and there is Internet access. Each airport has at least one nearby hotel. In the case of Florence and Pisa, the city centers are only a 15-minute taxi ride away—so if you encounter a long delay, spend it in town.

BY BUS

Italy's regional bus network, much of it operated by private companies, is extensive, but buses are usually not as attractive an option as comparatively cheap, convenient train travel. Schedules are often drawn up with commuters and students in mind and may be sketchy on weekends. Occasionally, though, buses can be faster and more direct than local trains, so it's a good idea to compare bus and train schedules. **SITA** (✉ *Via Santa Caterina da Siena 17/r, Florence* ☎ *055/214721* ⊕ *www.sitabus.it*) operates throughout Italy; **Lazzi Eurolines** (✉ *Via Mercadante 2, Florence* ☎ *055/363041* ⊕ *www.lazzi.it*) operates in Tuscany and central Italy.

Most of the major cities in Italy have urban bus services. These buses are inexpensive, but they can become jammed, particularly at rush hours.

BY CAR

Italy has an extensive network of autostrade (toll highways), complemented by equally well-maintained but free *superstrade* (expressways). Save the ticket you are issued at an autostrada entrance, as you need it to exit; on some shorter autostrade you pay the toll when you enter. Viacards, on sale for €25 at many autostrada locations, allow you to pay for tolls in advance. At special lanes you simply slip the card into a designated slot.

An *uscita* is an "exit." A *raccordo* is a ring road surrounding a city. *Strade regionale* and *strade provinciale* (regional and provincial highways, denoted by *S, SS, SR,* or *SP* numbers) may be two-lane roads, as are all secondary roads; directions and turnoffs aren't always clearly marked.

BY TRAIN

In Italy traveling by train is simple and efficient. Service between major cities is frequent, and trains usually arrive on schedule.

Trains are operated by the Ferrovie dello Stato (FS; ☎ *892021 in Italy* ⊕ *www.trenitalia.com*), the Italian State Railways. The fastest are the Eurostar trains that run between major cities. Seat reservations are mandatory on the Eurostar trains. The next-fastest trains are the *Intercity* (IC) trains. Reservations, required for some IC trains, are always advisable. *Diretto* and *Interregionale* trains make more stops and are a little slower. *Regionale* and *locale* trains are the slowest; many serve commuters.

Most Italian trains have first and second classes. On local trains a first-class fare gets you little more than a clean doily on your headrest, but on long-distance trains you get wider seats, more legroom, and better ventilation and lighting.

Some cities—Milan, Florence, and Rome included—have more than one train station, **so be sure you get off at the right place.** Always purchase tickets before boarding the train, as you cannot purchase one from a conductor. You must validate your ticket before boarding the train by punching it at a yellow box located in the waiting area of smaller train stations or at the end of the track in larger stations.

ABOUT THE RESTAURANTS

Italian cuisine is still largely regional. Ask what the local specialties are: by all means, have spaghetti *alla carbonara* (with bacon and egg) in Rome, *bistecca alla fiorentina* (steak) in Florence, *chingale* (wild boar) in Tuscany, and risotto *alla milanese* in Milan. Although most restaurants in Italy serve traditional local cuisine, you can find Asian and Middle Eastern alternatives in Rome, Venice, and other cities.

DINING CUSTOMS

A meal in Italy has traditionally consisted of five courses, and every menu you encounter will still be organized along this five-course plan:

First up is the antipasto (appetizer), often consisting of cured meats or marinated vegetables. Next to appear is the primo, usually pasta or soup, and after that the secondo, a meat or fish course with, perhaps, a contorno (vegetable dish) on the side. A simple dolce (dessert) rounds out the meal.

This, you've probably noticed, is a lot of food. Italians have noticed as well—a full, five-course meal is an indulgence usually reserved for special occasions. Instead, restaurant meals are a mix-and-match affair: you might order a primo and a secondo, or an antipasto and a primo, or a secondo and a contorno.

The crucial rule of restaurant dining is that you should order at least two courses. It's a common mistake for tourists to order only a secondo, thinking they're getting a "main course" complete with side dishes. What they wind up with is one lonely piece of meat.

WHAT IT COSTS IN EUROS					
	¢	$	$$	$$$	$$$$
Restaurants	under €15	€15–€25	€25 –€35	€35–€45	over €45

Prices are for a first course, second course, and a dessert at dinner.

ABOUT THE HOTELS

Italy has a varied and abundant number of hotels, bed-and-breakfasts, *agriturismi (farm stays)*, and rental properties. Throughout the cities and the countryside you can find very sophisticated, luxurious palaces and villas as well as rustic farmhouses and small hotels. Six-hundred-year-old palazzi and converted monasteries have been restored as luxurious hotels, while retaining the original atmosphere. At the other end of the spectrum, boutique hotels inhabit historic buildings using chic Italian design for the interiors. Increasingly, the famed Italian wineries are creating rooms and apartments for three-day to weeklong stays.

10

Hotels in Italy are usually well maintained (especially if they've earned our recommendation in this book), but in some respects they won't match what you find at comparably priced U.S. lodgings. Keep the following points in mind as you set your expectations, and you're likely to have a good experience:

First and foremost, rooms are usually smaller, particularly in cities. If you're truly cramped, ask for another room, but don't expect things to be spacious.

A "double bed" is commonly two singles pushed together. In the bathroom, tubs are not a given—request one if it's essential. In budget places, showers sometimes use a drain in the middle of the bathroom floor. And washcloths are a rarity.

Most hotels have satellite TV, but there are fewer channels than in the United States, and only one or two will be in English. Don't expect wall-to-wall carpeting. Particularly outside the cities, tile floors are the norm.

WHAT IT COSTS IN EUROS				
¢	$	$$	$$$	$$$$
Hotels	under €80	€80–€140	€140–€210	€210–€290	over €290

Hotel prices are for two people in a standard double room in high season, excluding tax.

PLANNING YOUR TIME

It is not difficult to see two or three diverse parts of Italy in a one-week visit because of the ease of travel by car on the fast freeway system, via the comprehensive railway with the speedy Eurostar trains, and lastly, by air from the two major airports in Milan and Rome to the smaller airports serving Venice, Florence, and Pisa. On the other hand, while you are planning your itinerary, remember that Italy is a long, narrow country and that you don't want to spend your entire vacation in transit. When traveling by car along the smaller country roads or by train on local lines that stop at every station, it will probably take you longer than you think to get from place to place.

Trying to soak up Italy's rich artistic heritage poses a challenge. The country's many museums and churches draw hordes of visitors, all wanting to see the same thing at the same time. From May through September the Sistine Chapel, Michelangelo's *David,* Piazza San Marco, and other key sights are more often than not swamped by tourists. Try to see the highlights at off-peak times. If they are open during lunch, this is often a good time. Seeing some attractions—such as the gleaming facades of Rome's glorious Baroque churches and fountains—does not require waiting in long lines.

Making the most of your time in Italy doesn't mean rushing through it. To gain a rich appreciation for the country, don't try to see everything at once. Practice the Italian-perfected *il dolce far niente*—the sweet art of idleness. Skip a museum to sit at a table in a pretty café and enjoy the sunshine and a cappuccino. Art—and life—is to be enjoyed, and the Italians can show you how.

ROME

The timeless city to which all roads lead, Rome enthralls visitors today as she has since time immemorial. More than Florence, more than Venice, this is Italy's treasure storehouse. Here, the ancient Romans made us heirs-in-law to what we call Western Civilization; where centuries later Michelangelo painted in the Sistine Chapel; where Gian Lorenzo Bernini's Baroque nymphs and naiads still dance in their marble fountains; and where, at Cinecittà Studios, Fellini filmed *La Dolce Vita* and 8½. Today the city remains a veritable Grand Canyon of culture: Ancient Rome rubs shoulders with the medieval, the modern runs into the Renaissance, and the result is like nothing so much as an open-air museum.

PLANNING YOUR TIME

Roma, non basta una vita ("Rome, a lifetime is not enough"): this famous saying should be stamped on the passport of every first-time visitor to the Eternal City. On the other hand, it's a warning: Rome is so packed with sights that it is impossible to take them all in; it's easy to run yourself ragged trying to check off the items on your "must see" list. At the same time, the saying is a celebration of the city's abundance. There's so much here, you're bound to make discoveries you hadn't anticipated. To conquer Rome, strike a balance between visits to major sights and leisurely neighborhood strolls.

In the first category, the Vatican and the remains of ancient Rome loom the largest. Both require at least half a day; a good strategy is to devote your first morning to one and your second to the other. Leave the afternoons for exploring the neighborhoods that comprise "Baroque Rome" and the shopping district around the Spanish Steps and Via Condotti. If you have more days at your disposal, continue with the same approach. Among the sights, Galleria Borghese and the multilayered church of San Clemente are particularly worthwhile, and the neighborhoods of Trastevere and the Ghetto make for great roaming.

Since there's a lot of ground to cover in Rome, it's wise to plan your busy sightseeing schedule with possible savings in mind, and purchasing the Roma Pass (⊕www.romapass.it) allows you to do just that. The three-day pass costs €20 and is good for unlimited use of buses, trams and the metro. It includes free admission to two of more than 40 participating museums or archaeological sites, including the Colosseum (and bumps you to the head of the long line there, to boot), the Ara Pacis museum, the Musei Capitolini, and Galleria Borghese, plus discounted tickets to many other museums. The Roma Pass can be purchased at tourist information booths across the city, at Termini Station, or at Terminal C of the International Arrivals section of Fiumicino Airport.

10

GETTING HERE

Rome's principal airport is Leonardo da Vinci Airport/Fiumicino (☎06/65951 ⊕www.adr.it), commonly known by the name of its location, Fiumicino (FCO). It's 30 km (19 mi) southwest of the city but has a direct train link with downtown Rome. Rome's other airport, with no direct train link, is Ciampino (☎06/794941 ⊕ www.adr.it) or CIA, 15 km (9 mi) south of downtown and used mostly by low-cost airlines.

By car, the main access routes from the north are A1 (Autostrada del Sole) from Milan and Florence and the A12-E80 highway from Genoa. All highways connect with the Grande Raccordo Anulare Ring Road (GRA), which channels traffic into the city center. For driving directions, check out ⊕www.tuttocitta.it. Note: Parking in Rome can be a nightmare—private cars are not allowed access to the entire historic center during the day (weekdays 8–6; Saturday 2 pm–6 pm), except for residents.

The main train stations in Rome are Termini, Tiburtina, Ostiense, and Trastevere. On long-distance routes (to Florence and Venice, for instance), you can either travel by the cheap, but slow, diretto trains, or the fast, but more expensive Intercity or the Eurostar.

GETTING AROUND

Rome's integrated transportation system, ATAC (☎06/46952027 or 800/431784 ⊕www.atac.roma.it), includes the Metropolitana subway, city buses, and trams. A ticket (BIT) valid for 75 minutes on any combination of buses and trams and one entrance to the metro costs €1. Day passes can be purchased for €4, and weekly passes for €16. Tickets (singly or in quantity—it's a good idea to have a few extra tickets handy) are sold at tobacconists, newsstands, some coffee bars, automatic ticket machines in metro stations, some bus stops, and ATAC and COTRAL ticket booths. Time-stamp tickets at metro turnstiles and in little yellow machines on buses and trams when boarding the first vehicle and stamp it again when boarding for the last time within 75 minutes.

Taxis in Rome do not normally cruise, but if free they will stop if you flag them down. They wait at stands and can also be called by phone (☎06/6645, 06/3570, 06/4994, 06/5551, or 06/4157). Always ask for a receipt (*ricevuta*) to make sure the driver charges you the correct amount. Use only licensed cabs with a plaque next to the license plate reading "Servizio Pubblico."

VISITOR INFORMATION

Rome's main APT (Azienda Per Turismo) Tourist Information Office is at Via Parigi 5–11 (☎ 06/488991 ⊕www.romaturismo.it), near the main Termini rail station. In addition, green APT information kiosks with multilingual personnel are near the most important sights and squares, as well as at Termini Station and Leonardo da Vinci Airport.

ANCIENT ROME

If you ever wanted to feel like the Caesars—with all of ancient Rome (literally) at your feet—simply head to Michelangelo's famed Piazza del Campidoglio. There, make a beeline for the terrace flanking the side of the center building, the Palazzo Senatorio, Rome's ceremonial city hall.

From this balcony atop the Capitoline Hill (or from the Tabularium arcade, situated right below in the Musei Capitolini complex) you can take in a panorama that seems like a remnant of a Cecil B. DeMille movie spectacular. For looming before you is the entire Roman Forum, the *"caput mundi"*—the center of the known world for centuries.

Before the Christian era, before the emperors, before the powerful Republic that ruled the ancient seas, Rome was founded on seven hills, and two of them—the Capitoline and the Palatine—surround the Roman Forum, where the Romans of the later Republic and Imperial ages worshipped deities, debated politics, and wheeled and dealed. It's all history now, but this remains one of the world's most striking and significant concentrations of ancient remains—an emphatic reminder of the genius and power that made Rome the fountainhead of the Western world.

EXPLORING ANCIENT ROME

8 Campidoglio. Spectacularly transformed by Michelangelo's late-Renaissance designs, the Campidoglio was once the epicenter of the Roman empire, the place where the city's first shrines stood, including its most sacred, the Temple of Jupiter. Originally, the Capitoline Hill consisted of two peaks: the Capitolium and the Arx (where Santa Maria in Aracoeli now stands). The hollow between them was known as the Asylum: here prospective settlers once came to seek the protection of Romulus, legendary first king of Rome—hence the term "asylum." Later, during the Republic, in 78 BC, the Tabularium, or Hall of Records, was erected here.

By the Middle Ages the Capitoline had become an unkempt hill strewn with ancient rubble. In preparation for the impending visit of Charles V in 1536, triumphant after the empire's victory over the Moors, his host, Pope Paul III Farnese, decided that the Holy Roman Emperor should follow the route of the emperors, climaxing at the Campidoglio. But the pope was embarrassed by the decrepit goat pasture the hill had become and commanded Michelangelo to restore the site to glory; he added a third palace along with Renaissance-style facades and a grand paved piazza. Newly excavated ancient sculptures, designed to impress the visiting emperor, were installed in the palaces, and the piazza was ornamented with the giant stone figures of the Discouri and the ancient Roman equestrian statue of Emperor Marcus Aurelius (original now in Musei Capitolini)—the latter a visual reference to the corresponding glory of Charles V and the ancient emperor.

⓫ Colle Palatino. Just beyond the Arch of Titus lies the Clivus Palatinus, which rises up a slight incline to the heights of the Colle Palatino (Palatine Hill), the oldest inhabited site in Rome. Despite its location overlooking the Forum's traffic and attendant noise, the Palatine was the most coveted address for ancient Rome's rich and famous. More than a few of the Twelve Caesars called the Palatine home, including Caligula, who was murdered in the still-standing and unnerving (even today) tunnel, the Cryptoporticus. The palace of Tiberius was the first to be built here; others followed, notably the gigantic extravaganza constructed for Emperor Domitian. But perhaps the most famous lodging goes back to Rome's very beginning. Once upon a time, skeptics thought Romulus was a myth. Then about a century ago, Rome's greatest archaeologist, Rodolfo Lanciani, excavated a site on the hill and uncovered the remains of an Iron Age settlement dating back to the 9th century BC, supporting the belief that Romulus, founder of Rome, lived here.

During the Republican era the Palatino became the "Beverly Hills" of ancient Rome—an exclusive residential area for wealthy families. Hortensius, Cicero, Catiline, Crassus, and Agrippa all had homes here. Augustus was born on the hill, and as he rose in power he bought up surrounding estates and transformed them into private libraries, halls, and a temple to the god Apollo; the House of Livia, reserved for Augustus's wife, is today the best-preserved structure. To visit the Palatine's ruins in a roughly chronological order, start from the southeast area facing the Aventine. ⊠ *Entrances at Piazza del Colosseo and Via di San*

10

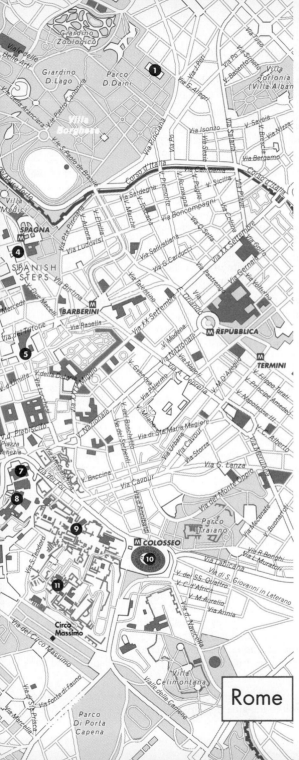

Gregorio 30, Roman Forum ☎*06/39967700* ⊕*www.pierreci.it* ☐*€12 (combined ticket with the Colosseum, Roman Forum, and Imperial Forums, if used within two days), audio guide €4* ⊙*Daily 8:30 –1 hr before sunset* Ⓜ*Colosseo.*

⑩ **Colosseo.** The most spectacular extant edifice of ancient Rome, the Colosseo has a history that is half-gore, half-glory. Here, before 50,000 spectators, gladiators would salute the emperor and cry *Ave, imperator, morituri te salutant* ("Hail, emperor, men soon to die salute thee").

Designed by order of the Flavian emperor Vespasian in ad 72, the Colosseum was inaugurated by Titus eight years later with a program of games lasting 100 days. The arena has a circumference of 573 yards and was faced with stone from nearby Tivoli. Its construction was a remarkable feat of engineering, for it stands on marshy terrain reclaimed by draining an artificial lake on the grounds of Nero's Domus Aurea. Originally known as the Flavian amphitheater, it came to be called the Colosseo because it stood on the site of the Colossus of Nero, a 115-foot-tall gilded bronze statue of the emperor that once towered here.

Inside, senators sat on the marble seating arrangements up front, along with the Vestal Virgins taking the ringside position while the plebs sat in wooden tiers at the back, then the masses above on the top tier. Over all was the amazing velarium, an ingenious system of sail-like awnings rigged on ropes and maneuvered by sailors from the imperial fleet, who would unfurl them to protect the arena's occupants from sun or rain.

Once inside, you can take the wooden walkway across the arena floor for a gladiator's-eye view, then explore the upper level to study a scale model of the Colosseum as it was (sheathed with marble, with statues ornamenting arcades of arches decorated with Doric, Ionic, and Corinthian pillars; one arch near the metro station still has traces of stucco decoration). From the upper tier study the so-called *ipogei*, the subterranean passageways that were the architectural engine rooms that made the events above proceed like clockwork. ⊠*Piazza del Colosseo* ☎*06/39967700* ⊕*www.museicapitolini.org* ☐ *€12 (combined ticket with Roman Forum, Palatine Hill, and Imperial Forums* ⊙*Daily 8:30–1 hr before sunset.*

⑨ **Foro Romano.** From the main entrance on Via dei Fori Imperali, descend into the extraordinary archaeologial complex that is the Foro Romano *(Roman Forum).* This was once the heart of Republican Rome, the austere enclave that preceded the hedonistic society of the emperors and the pleasure-crazed citizens of imperial Rome from the 1st to the 4th century AD. It began life as a marshy valley between the Capitoline and Palatine hills—a valley crossed by a mud track and used as a cemetery by Iron Age settlers. Over the years a market center and some huts were established here, and after the land was drained in the 6th century BC, the site eventually became a political, religious, and commercial center—namely, the Forum.

Hundreds of years of plunder reduced the Forum to its current desolate state. It's difficult to imagine that this enormous area was once Rome's pulsating heart, filled with stately and extravagant temples, palaces, and shops, and crowded with people from all corners of the empire. Adding to the confusion is the fact that the Forum developed over many centuries; what you see today are not the ruins from just one period but from a span of almost 900 years, from about 500 BC to AD 400. Nonetheless, the enduring romance of the place, with its lonely columns and great broken fragments of sculpted marble and stone, makes for a quintessential Roman experience. ✉*Entrances at Via dei Fori Imperiali and Piazza del Colosseo, Roman Forum* ☎*06/39967700* ⊕*www.pierreci.it* 🎫*€12 (combined ticket with the Colosseum, Palatine Hill, and Imperial Forums, if used within two days), guided tour €3.50, audio guide €4* ⊙*Daily 8:30 –1 hr before sunset* Ⓜ*Colosseo.*

❽ **Musei Capitolini.** Surpassed in sheer size and richness only by the Musei Vaticani, this immense collection was the first public museum in the world. A greatest-hits collection of Roman art through the ages, from the ancients to the Baroque, it is housed in the twin Museo Capitolino and Palazzo dei Conservatori that bookend Michelangelo's famous piazza. Here, you'll find some of antiquity's most famous sculptures, such as the poignant *Dying Gaul,* the regal *Capitoline Venus,* the *Esquiline Venus* (identified as another Mediterranean beauty, Cleopatra herself), and the *Lupa Capitolina,* the very symbol of Rome itself. Although some pieces in the collection—first assembled by Sixtus IV (1414–84), one of the earliest of the Renaissance popes—may excite only archaeologists and art historians, others are unforgettable, including the original bronze statue of Marcus Aurelius whose copy sits in the piazza. ✉*Piazza del Campidoglio, Campidoglio* ☎*06/39967800* ⊕*www.museicapitolini.org* 🎫 *€ 6.50 €* ⊙*Tues.–Sun. 9–8.*

NAVONA & CAMPO: BAROQUE ROME

Long called Vecchia Roma ("Old Rome"), this time-burnished district is the city's most beautiful neighborhood. Set between the Corso and the Tiber bend, it is filled with narrow streets bearing curious names, airy piazzas, and half-hidden courtyards. Some of Rome's most coveted residential addresses are nestled here. So, too, are the ancient Pantheon and the medieval square of Campo de' Fiori, but the spectacular, over-the-top Baroque monuments of the 16th and 17th centuries predominate.

10

The hub of the district is the queen of squares, Piazza Navona—a cityscape adorned with the most eye-knocking fountain by Gian Lorenzo Bernini, father of the Baroque. Streets running off the square lead to many historic must-sees, including noble churches by Borromini and Caravaggio's greatest paintings at San Luigi dei Francesi. This district has been an integral part of the city since ancient times, and its position between the Vatican and Lateran palaces, both seats of papal rule, put it in the mainstream of Rome's development from the Middle Ages onward. Craftsmen, shopkeepers, and famed artists toiled in the shadow of the huge palaces built to consolidate the power of leading figures in the papal court. Artisans and artists still live here, but their numbers are diminishing as the district becomes increasingly posh and—so critics say—"Disneyfied." But three of the liveliest piazzas in Rome, Piazza Navona, Piazza del Pantheon, and the Campo de' Fiori, are lodestars in a constellation of some of Rome's most authentic cafés, stores, and wine bars.

EXPLORING NAVONA & CAMPO

⓮ **Campo de' Fiori.** Home to Rome's oldest (since 1490) daily outdoor produce market, this bustling square was originally used for pub-

> **WORD OF MOUTH**
>
> "My 'magic moment' had to be rounding the corner and coming upon the Pantheon without know-ing it was coming up. I can't even describe it. This spot ended up becoming my favorite even after a month in Italy. The building just simply strikes me speechless."
>
> –reedpaints

lic executions, making its name—"Field of Flowers"—a bit sardonic. In fact, the central statue commemorates the philosopher Giordano Bruno, who was burned at the stake here in 1600 by the Inquisition. Today he frowns down upon food vendors galore, who, by early after-noon, are all gone, giving way to the square's caffès and bars which attract throngs of Rome's hip, young professionals as the hours lenghten toward evening.

⓯ **Pantheon.** One of Rome's most impressive and best-preserved ancient monuments, the Pantheon is particularly close to the hearts of Romans. The emperor Hadrian designed it around AD 120 and had it built on the site of an earlier temple that had been damaged by fire. Although the sheer size of the Pantheon is impressive (until 1960 the dome was the largest ever built), what's most striking is its tangible sense of har-mony. In large part this feeling is the result of the building's symmetrical design: the height of the dome is equal to the diameter of the circular interior. The oculus, or opening in the dome, is meant to symbolize the all-seeing "Eye of Heaven"; in practice, it illuminates the building and lightens the heavy stone ceiling. The original bronze doors have survived more than 1,800 years, centuries longer than the interior's rich gold ornamentation, which was plundered by popes and emperors. Art lovers can pay homage to the tomb of Raphael, who is buried in an ancient sarcophagus under the altar of Madonna del Sasso. ⊠ *Piazza della Rotonda, Navona* ☎06/68300230 ☞*Free* ☉*Mon.–Sat. 8:30–7:30, Sun. 9–5:30.*

⓱ **Piazza Navona.** With its carefree air of the days when it was the scene of Roman circus games, medieval jousts, and 17th-century carnivals, the beautiful Piazza Navona today often attracts fashion photogra-phers on shoots and Romans out for their *passeggiata* (evening stroll). Bernini's splashing **Fontana dei Quattro Fiumi** (Fountain of the Four Rivers), with an enormous rock squared off by statues representing the four corners of the world, makes a fitting centerpiece. Behind the fountain is the church of **Sant'Agnese in Agone,** an outstanding example of Baroque architecture built by the Pamphilj Pope Innocent X. The facade—a wonderfully rich mélange of bell towers, concave spaces, and dovetailed stone and marble—is by Borromini, a contemporary and rival of Bernini, and by Carlo Rainaldi (1611–91). One story has

Going Baroque

Flagrantly emotional, heavily expressive, and visually sensuous, the 17th-century artistic movement known as the Baroque was born in Rome. It was the creation of three geniuses: the sculptor and architect Gianlorenzo Bernini (1598–1680), the painter and architect Pietro da Cortona (1596–1669), and the architect and sculptor Francesco Borromini (1599–1667). From the drama found in the artists' paintings to the jewel-laden, gold-on-gold detail of 17th-century Roman palaces, Baroque style was intended both to shock and delight by upsetting the placid, "correct" rules of proportion and scale in the Renaissance. If a building looks theatrical—like a stage or a theater, especially with curtains being drawn back—it is usually Baroque. Look for over-the-top, curvaceous marble work, trompe l'oeil, allusions to other art, and high drama to identify the style. Baroque's appeal to the emotions made it a powerful weapon in the hands of the Counter-Reformation.

it that the Bernini statue nearest the church, which represents the River Plate, has its hand up before its eye because it can't bear the sight of the Borromini facade. Though often repeated, the story is fiction: the facade was built after the fountain. From early December through January 6 a Christmas market fills the square with games, Nativity scenes (some well crafted, many not), and multiple versions of the Befana, the ugly but good witch who brings candy and toys to Italian children on Epiphany. (Her name is a corruption of the Italian word for "epiphany," *Epifania.*) ⊠*Junction of Via della Cuccagna, Corsia Agonale, Via di Sant'Agnese, and Via Agonale, Navona*

⑯ San Luigi dei Francesi. A pilgrimage spot for art lovers everywhere, San Luigi is home to the Cerasi Chapel, adorned with three stunningly dramatic works by Caravaggio (1571–1610), the Baroque master of the heightened approach to light and dark. Set in the Chapel of St. Matthew (at the altar end of the left nave), they were commissioned for San Luigi, the official church of Rome's French colony. The inevitable coin machine will light up his *Calling of St. Matthew, Matthew and the Angel,* and *Matthew's Martyrdom,* seen from left to right, and Caravaggio's mastery of light takes it from there. When painted, they caused considerable consternation to the clergy of San Luigi, who thought the artist's dramatically realistic approach was scandalously disrespectful. But these paintings did to 17th-century art what Picasso's *Demoiselles d'Avignon* did to the 20th century. ⊠*Piazza San Luigi dei Francesi, Navona* ☎*06/688271* ☉*Fri.–Wed. 7–12:30 and 3:30–7.*

10

PIAZZA VENEZIA TO THE SPANISH STEPS

In spirit, and in fact, this section of the city is its most grandiose. The overblown Vittoriano monument, the labyrinthine treasure-chest palaces of Rome's surviving aristocracy, even the diamond-draped denizens of Via Condotti's shops—all embody the exuberant ego of a city at the center of its own universe. Here's where you'll see ladies in furs gobbling pastries at caffè tables, and walk through a thousand snapshots as you climb the famous Spanish Steps, admired by generations from Byron to Versace. Cultural treasures abound around here: gilded 17th-century churches, glittering palaces, and the greatest example of portraiture in Rome: Velázquez's incomparable *Innocent X* at the Galleria Doria Pamphilj. Have your camera ready—along with a coin or two—for that most beloved of Rome's landmarks, the Trevi Fountain.

EXPLORING PIAZZA VENEZIA TO THE SPANISH STEPS

⑤ Fontana di Trevi *(Trevi Fountain).* The huge fountain designed by Nicola Salvi (1697–1751) is a whimsical rendition of mythical sea creatures amid cascades of splashing water. The fountain is the world's most spectacular wishing well: legend has it that you can ensure your return to Rome by tossing a coin into the fountain. It was featured in the 1954 film *Three Coins in the Fountain* and was the scene of Anita Ekberg's aquatic frolic in Fellini's *La Dolce Vita.* By day this is one of the most crowded sites in town; at night the spotlighted piazza feels especially festive. ⊠*Piazza di Trevi, off Via del Tritone, Corso.*

⑦ Monumento a Vittorio Emanuele II. Known as the Vittoriano, this vast marble monument was erected in the late 19th century to honor Italy's first king, Vittorio Emanuele II (1820–78), and the unification of Italy. Aesthetically minded Romans have derided the oversize structure, visible from many parts of the city, calling it "the typewriter," "the wedding cake," and "the eighth hill of Rome." Whatever you think of its design, the views from the top are memorable. ⊠*Entrance at Piazza Ara Coeli, near Piazza Venezia, Corso* ☎*06/6991718* ⊕*www.ambienterm. arti.beniculturali.it/vittoriano/index.html* 🎫*Monument free, museum free, elevator €7* ☉ *Tues.–Sun. 10–4.*

⑥ Palazzo Doria Pamphilj. This bona fide patrician palace is still home to a princely family, which rents out many of its 1,000 rooms. You can visit the remarkably well-preserved **Galleria Doria Pamphilj** (pronounced pam-*fee*-lee), a picture-and-sculpture gallery that gives you a sense of the sumptuous living quarters. Numbered paintings (the bookshop's museum catalog comes in handy) are packed onto every available inch of wall space. The first large salon is nearly wallpapered with paintings, and not just any paintings: on one wall you'll find no fewer than three pictures by Caravaggio, including his *Magdalen* and his breathtaking early *Rest on the Flight to Egypt.* Off the gilded **Galleria degli Specchi** (Gallery of Mirrors)—reminiscent of Versailles—are the famous Velázquez portrait and the Bernini bust of the Pamphiji pope Innocent X. The audio guide by Jonathan Doria Pamphilj, the current heir, provides an intimate family history well worth listening to. ⊠*Piazza del Collegio Romano 2, near Piazza Venezia, Corso* ☎*06/6797323* ⊕*www.doriapamphilj.it* 🎫 *€8* ☉ *Fri.–Wed. 10–5.*

④ Spanish Steps. That icon of postcard Rome, the Spanish Steps—called the Scalinatella di Spagna in Italian—and the Piazza di Spagna from which they ascend both get their names from the Spanish Embassy to the Vatican on the piazza, opposite the American Express office—in spite of the fact that the staircase was built with French funds in

1723. In an allusion to the church of Trinità dei Monti at the top of the hill, the staircase is divided by three landings (beautifully banked with azaleas from mid-April to mid-May). For centuries, the Scalinatella ("staircase," as natives refer to the Spanish Steps) has always welcomed tourists: 18th-century dukes and duchesses on their Grand Tour, 19th-century artists and writers in search of inspiration—among them Stendhal, Honoré de Balzac, William Makepeace Thackeray, and Byron—and today's enthusiastic hordes. The **Fontana della Barcaccia** (Fountain of the Old Boat) at the base of the steps is by Pietro Bernini, father of the famous Gianlorenzo. ⊠*Piazza di Spagna, at head of Via Condotti Spagna*

VILLA BORGHESE & PIAZZA DEL POPOLO

Touring Rome's artistic masterpieces while staying clear of its hustle and bustle can be, quite literally, a walk in the park. Some of the city's finest sights are tucked away in or next to green lawns and pedestrian piazzas, offering a breath of fresh air for weary sightseers, especially in the Villa Borghese park. One of Rome's largest, this park can alleviate gallery gout by offering an oasis in which to cool off under the ilex, oak, and umbrella pine trees. If you feel like a picnic, have an *alimentare* (food shop) make you some *panini* (sandwiches) before you go; food carts within the park are overpriced.

EXPLORING VILLA BORGHESE & PIAZZA DEL POPOLO

3 **Ara Pacis Augustae** *(Altar of Augustan Peace)*. This magnificent classical monument, with an exquisitely detailed frieze, was erected in 13 BC to celebrate Emperor Augustus's triumphant return from military conflicts in Gaul and Spain. It's housed in one of Rome's newest landmarks, a glass-and-travertine structure designed by American architect Richard Meier. The building was opened in 2006 after 10 years of delays and heated controversy concerning the altar's relocation. Overlooking the Tiber on one side and the ruins of the marble-clad Mausoleo di Augusto (Mausoleum of Augustus) on the other, the result is a luminous oasis in the center of Rome. ⊠*Lungotevere in Augusta, near Piazza di Popolo* ☎*06/82059127* ⊕*www.arapacis.it* ⊠*€6.50* ☉*Tues.–Sun. 9–6.*

10

1 **Galleria Borghese.** It's a real toss-up which is more magnificent—the villa built for Cardinal Scipione Borghese in 1615 or the collection of 17th- and 18th-century art that lies within. The luxury-loving cardinal built Rome's most splendiferous palace as a showcase for his fabulous antiquities collection. The interiors are a monument to 18th-century Roman interior decoration at its most luxurious, dripping with porphyry and alabaster, and they are a fitting showcase for the statues of various deities, including one officially known as *Venus Victrix*. There has never been any doubt, however, as to the statue's

> ### WORD OF MOUTH
>
> "The Borghese Gallery is one of the most precious places I have ever had the good fortune to visit—twice. The Bernini Statues bring tears to my eyes. The building is gorgeous. Just a little jewel box of a museum." —bugswife1

real subject: Pauline Bonaparte, Napoléon's sister, who married Prince Camillo Borghese in one of the storied matches of the 19th century. Sculpted by Canova (1757–1822), the princess reclines on a chaise, bare-breasted, her hips swathed in classical drapery, the very model of haughty detachment and sly come-hither. Other rooms hold important sculptures by Bernini, including *David* and the breathtaking *Apollo and Daphne*. The picture collection has splendid works by Titian, Caravaggio, and Raphael, among others. Entrance is every two hours, and reservations are required. Make sure to book online or by phone at least a few days in advance. ⊠ *Piazza Scipione Borghese 5, off Via Pinciana, Villa Borghese* ☎ *06/8413979 information, 06/32810 reservations* ⊕ *www.galleriaborghese.it* ⊠ *€10.50, including €2 reservation fee; audio guide or English tour €5* ⊙ *Tues.–Sun. 9–7, with sessions on hr every 2 hrs*

❷ Piazza del Popolo. Designed by neoclassical architect Giuseppe Valadier (1762–1839) in the early 1800s, this piazza is one of the largest in Rome, and it has a 3,000-year-old obelisk in the middle. A favorite spot for café-sitting and people-watching, the pedestrian-only piazza is landmarked by its two bookend Baroque churches, **Santa Maria dei Miracoli** and **Santa Maria in Montesanto**. On the piazza's eastern side, stairs lead uphill to Villa Borghese's **Pincio**, a formal garden that was highly fashionable in 19th-century Rome. At the north end of the piazza is the 400-year-old **Porta del Popolo**, Rome's northern city gate, and next to it the church of Santa Maria del Popolo. The city gate was designed by Bernini to welcome the Catholic convert Queen Christina of Sweden to Rome in 1605. ⊠ *At head of Corso, near Villa Borghese.*

THE VATICAN: ROME OF THE POPES

Capital of the Catholic Church, this tiny walled city-state is a place where some people go to find a work of art—Michelangelo's frescoes, rare ancient Roman marbles, or Bernini's statues. Others go to find their soul. Whatever the reason, thanks to being the seat of world Catholicism and also address to the most overwhelming architectural achievement of the Renaissance—St. Peter's Basilica—the Vatican attracts millions of travelers every year. In addition, the Vatican Museums are famed for magnificent rooms decorated by Raphael, sculptures such as the *Apollo Belvedere* and the *Laocoön*, frescoes by Fra Angelico, paintings by Giotto and Leonardo, and the celebrated ceiling of the Sistine Chapel. The Church power that emerged as the Rome of the emperors declined gave impetus to a profusion of artistic expression and shaped the destiny of the city for a thousand years. Allow yourself an hour to see the St. Peter's Basilica, two hours for the museums, an hour for Castel Sant'Angelo, and an hour to climb to the top of the dome. Note that ushers at the entrance of St. Peter's Basilica and the Vatican Museums bar entry to people with "inappropriate" clothing—which means no bare knees or shoulders.

EXPLORING THE VATICAN

㉓ Basilica di San Pietro. The largest church of Christendom, St. Peter's Basilica covers about 18,100 square yards, extends 212 yards in length, and carries a dome that rises 435 feet and measures 138 feet across its base. Its history is equally impressive: No less than five of Italy's greatest artists—Bramante, Raphael, Peruzzi, Antonio Sangallo the Younger, and Michelangelo—died while striving to erect this "new" St. Peter's. In fact, the church's history dates back to the year AD 319, when the emperor Constantine built a basilica over the site of the tomb of St. Peter (died AD 64). This early church stood for more than 1,000 years, undergoing a number of restorations, until it was on the verge of collapse.

In 1506 Pope Julius II (1443–1513) commissioned the architect Bramante to build a new and greater basilica, but construction would take more than 170 years. In 1546 Michelangelo was persuaded to take over the job, but the magnificent cupola was finally completed by Giacomo della Porta (circa 1537–1602) and Domenico Fontana (1543–1607). The new church wasn't dedicated until 1626; by that time Renaissance had given way to Baroque, and many of the plan's original elements had gone the way of their designers. At the entrance, the 15th-century bronze doors by Filarete (circa 1400–69) fill the central portal. Off the entry portico, architect and sculptor Gianlorenzo Bernini's famous *Scala Regia,* the ceremonial entry to the Vatican Palace, is one of the most magnificent staircases in the world and is graced with Bernini's dramatic statue of Constantine the Great.

Over an altar in a side chapel near the entrance is Michelangelo's *Pietà,* a sculpture of Mary holding her son Jesus's body after crucifixion—the star attraction here other than the basilica itself. Legend has it that the artist, only 22 at the time the work was completed, overheard passersby expressing skepticism that such a young man could have executed such a sophisticated and moving piece. It's said that his offense at the implication was why he crept back that night and signed the piece—in big letters, on a ribbon falling from the Virgin's left shoulder across her breast.

10

Inlaid in the gorgeous marble pavement of the nave's central aisles are the names of the world's great cathedrals organized by church size—the message is clear, St. Peter's has them all beat. At the crossing of the aisles four massive piers support the dome, and the mighty Bernini **baldacchino** (canopy) rises high above the papal altar, where the pope celebrates Mass. Free one-hour English-language tours of the basilica depart Monday–Saturday at 10 and 3, Sunday at 2:30 (sign up at the little desk under the portico). St. Peter's is closed during ceremonies in the piazza. ✉*Piazza di San Pietro, Vatican* 🕐*Apr.–Sept., daily 7–7; Oct.–Mar., daily 7–6.*

The **roof** of St. Peter's Basilica, reached by elevator or stairs, provides a view among a landscape of domes and towers. An interior staircase (170 steps) leads to the base of the dome for a dove's-eye look at the interior of St. Peter's. Only if you are stout of heart and sound of lung should you attempt the taxing and claustrophobic climb up the remaining 330 steps to the balcony of the lantern, where the view embraces the Vatican Gardens and all of Rome. The up and down staircases are one way; once you commit to climbing, there's no turning back. ☎06/69883462 🖃*Elevator €7, stairs €4* ◷*Daily 8–5 (11:30–5 on Wed. if pope has audience in Piazza San Pietro).*

🐾 ⑱ **Castel Sant'Angelo.** For hundreds of years this fortress guarded the Vatican, to which it is linked by the **Passetto,** an arcaded passageway. According to legend, Castel Sant'Angelo got its name during the plague of 590, when Pope Gregory the Great (circa 540–604), passing by in a religious procession, had a vision of an angel sheathing its sword atop the stone ramparts. Though it may look like a stronghold, Castel Sant'Angelo was in fact built as a tomb for the emperor Hadrian (76–138) in AD 135. By the 6th century it had been transformed into a fortress, and it remained a refuge for the popes for almost 1,000 years. It has dungeons, battlements, cannon and cannonballs, and a collection of antique weaponry and armor. The lower levels formed the base of Hadrian's mausoleum; ancient ramps and narrow staircases climb through the castle's core to courtyards and frescoed halls, where temporary exhibits are held. Off the loggia is a café.

The upper terrace, with the massive angel statue commemorating Gregory's vision, evokes memories of Tosca, Puccini's poignant heroine in the opera of the same name, who threw herself off these ramparts with the cry, *"Scarpia, avanti a Dio!"* ("Scarpia, we meet before God!"). On summer evenings a book fair with musical events and food stalls surrounds the castle. One of Rome's most beautiful pedestrian bridges, **Ponte Sant'Angelo** spans the Tiber in front of the fortress and is studded with graceful angels designed by Bernini. ⊠*Lungotevere Castello 50, near Vatican* ☎06/39967600 ⊕*www.pierreci.it* 🖃*€5* ◷*Tues.–Sun. 9–7:30.*

㉑ **Musei Vaticani** *(Vatican Museums).* The building on your left as you exit St. Peter's Basilica is the Vatican Palace, the papal residence since 1377, with an estimated 1,400 rooms, chapels, and galleries. Other than the pope and his court, the occupant is the Musei Vaticani (Vatican Museums), containing some of art's greatest masterpieces. The Sistine Chapel is the headliner here, but in your haste to get there, don't overlook the Museo Egizio, with its fine Egyptian collection; the famed classical sculptures of the Chiaramonti and the Museo Pio Clementino; and the Stanze di Raffaello (Raphael Rooms), a suite of halls covered floor-to-ceiling in some of the master's greatest works.

Fodor'sChoice ★

On a first visit to the Vatican Museums, you may just want to see the highlights—even that will take several hours and a good, long walk. In peak tourist season, be prepared for at least an hour's wait to get into the museums and large crowds once inside. The best time to avoid lines and crowds is not first thing in the morning but during lunch hour and the Wednesday papal audiences.

The collection is divided among different galleries, halls, and wings connected end to end. Pick up a leaflet at the main entrance to the museums to see the overall layout. The Sistine Chapel is at the far end of the complex, and the leaflet charts two abbreviated itineraries through other collections to reach it. An audio guide (€5.50, about 90 minutes) for the Sistine Chapel, the Stanze di Raffaello, and 350 other works and locations is worth the added expense. Phone or e-mail at least a week in advance (a month for peak season) to book a guided tour (€21.50) through the Guided Visit to Vatican Museums.

WORD OF MOUTH
"At the Vatican Museums, we did the audio tour, and took our time looking at the Map Room, the tapestries, trompe l'oeil ceilings, the stunning Borgia Papal Apartments, and the Raphael Rooms. Finally, we got to the Sistine Chapel. Wow! We just sat on the benches along the wall for 30 minutes, looking at the Old and New Testament frescoes." —Bardo

The main entrance to the museums, on Viale Vaticano, is a long walk from Piazza San Pietro along a busy thoroughfare. Some city buses stop near the main entrance: Bus 49 from Piazza Cavour stops right in front; buses 81 and 492 and Tram 19 stop at Piazza Risorgimento, halfway between St. Peter's and the museums. The Ottaviano–S. Pietro and the Cipro–Musei Vaticani stops on Metro A also are in the vicinity. Entry is free the first Sunday of the month, and the museum is closed on Catholic holidays, of which there are many. Last admission is an hour before closing. ⊠*Main museum entrance, Viale Vaticano; guided visit office, Piazza San Pietro* ☎06/69883332 ⊕*www.vatican.va* ⊠€ 14 ۞*Mon.–Sat. 8:30–6, last entrance at 4; closed Sun., except for last Sun. of month, when admission is free* ☞*Note: ushers at entrance of St. Peter's and Vatican Museums will bar entry to people with bare knees or bare shoulders* Ⓜ*Cipro-Musei Vaticani.*

⑲ **Piazza San Pietro.** As you enter St. Peter's Square you are officially entering Vatican territory. The piazza is one of Bernini's most spectacular masterpieces. It was completed in 1667 after 11 years' work, a relatively short time, considering the vastness of the task. The piazza can hold 400,000 people—as it did in the days following the death of Pope John Paul II. Bernini had a grand visual effect in mind when he designed the square: the surprise of stepping into an immense, airy space after approaching it through a neighborhood of narrow, shadowy streets. The contrast was intended to evoke the metaphor of moving from darkness to light. But in the 1930s Mussolini spoiled the effect. To celebrate the "conciliation" between the Vatican and the Italian government under the Lateran Pact of 1929, he conceived of the Via della Conciliazione, the broad avenue that now forms the main approach to St. Peter's.

10

Remember to look for the Swiss Guards in their colorful uniforms; they've been standing at the Vatican entrances for the past 500 years. ⊠ *At head of Via delle Conciliazione*

THE GHETTO, TIBERINA ISLAND & TRASTEVERE

Each staunchly resisting the tides of change, these three areas are hard to beat for the authentic atmosphere of Old Rome. You begin in the old Ghetto, a warren of twisting, narrow streets, where Rome's Jewish community was once confined, then deported, and now, barely, persists. Ancient bridges, the Ponte Fabricio and Ponte Cestio, link the Ghetto to Tiberina Island, the tiny island that is one of Rome's most picturesque sights. On the opposite side of the Tiber lies Trastevere—"across the Tiber"—long cherished as Rome's Greenwich Village and now subject to rampant gentrification. In spite of this, Trastevere remains about the most tightly knit community in the city, the Trasteverini proudly proclaiming their descent from the ancient Romans. This area is Rome's enchanting, medieval heart.

EXPLORING THE GHETTO, TIBERINA ISLAND & TRASTEVERE

🔞 **Jewish Ghetto.** Rome has had a Jewish community since the 1st century BC, and from that time until the present its living conditions have varied widely according to its relations with the city's rulers. In 1555 Pope Paul II established Rome's Ghetto Ebraico in the neighborhood marked off by the Portico d'Ottavia, the Tiber, and Via Arenula. The area quickly became Rome's most densely populated. The laws were rescinded around the time of the Italian unifications in the 1870s but German troops tragically occupied Rome during World War II and in 1943 wrought havoc here. Today there are a few Judaica shops and kosher groceries, bakeries, and restaurants (especially on Via di Portico d'Ottavia) but the neighborhood mansions are now being renovated and much coveted by the rich and stylish. **Tours of the Ghetto** (€8, about two hours) that explore Rome's Jewish history can be booked through the SIDIC historical society. ✉ *SIDIC Office, Via Garibaldi 28, Ghetto* ☎ *06/67015555* ⊕ *www.sidic.org.*

🔞 **Santa Maria in Trastevere.** Shimmering at night thanks to its medieval facade mosaics, this is one of Rome's most magnificent and oldest churches, first built in the 4th century and then greatly enlarged in the 12th century. Inside, the nave framed by a grand processional of two rows of columns taken from ancient Roman temples often produced involuntary gasps from unsuspecting visitors—this is probably as close as we can get to the imperial splendor of an ancient Roman basilica. A shining burst of Byzantine color and light is added by the celebrated 12th-century mosaics in the apse; also note the Cosmati work, a mosaic style from the 12th and 13th centuries in which tiny squares and triangles were laid with larger stones to form geometric patterns, in the church floors. Outside, the **Piazza di Santa Maria in Trastevere** is a very popular spot for afternoon coffee and evening cocktails at its outdoor cafés. The 13th-century mosaics on Santa Maria's facade—which add light and color to the piazza, especially at night when they are in spotlight—are believed to represent the Wise and Foolish Virgins. In August, processions honoring the Virgin Mary gather at the church as part of Trastevere's famous traditional feast, called *Festa de Noantri*

(Our Own Feast). ⊠ *Piazza di Santa Maria, Trastevere* ☎ *06/5814802* ⊙ *Daily 7:30–1 and 4–7.*

WHERE TO EAT

Rome has been known since ancient times for its great feasts and banquets, and though the days of the triclinium and the Saturnalia are long past, dining out is still the Romans' favorite pastime. The city is distinguished more by its good attitude toward eating out than by a multitude of world-class restaurants; simple, traditional cuisine reigns, although things are slowly changing as talented young chefs explore new culinary frontiers. Many of the city's restaurants cater to a clientele of regulars, and atmosphere and attitude are usually friendly and informal. The flip side is that in Rome the customer is not always right—the chef and waiters are in charge, and no one will beg forgiveness if you wanted *skim* milk in that cappuccino. Be flexible and you're sure to *mangiar bene* (eat well). Lunch is served from approximately 12:30 to 2:30 and dinner from 7:30 or 8 until about 11, though some restaurants stay open later, especially in summer, when patrons linger at sidewalk tables to enjoy the parade of people and the *ponentino* (evening breeze).

PANTHEON, NAVONA, TREVI & QUIRINALE

$
WINE BAR

✕ **Cul de Sac.** This popular wine bar near Piazza Navona is among the city's oldest enoteche and offers a book-length selection of wines from Italy, France, the Americas, and elsewhere. Food is eclectic, ranging from a huge assortment of Italian meats and cheeses (try the delicious *lonza,* cured pork loin, or *speck,* a northern Italian smoked prosciutto) to various Mediterranean dishes, including delicious baba ghanoush, a tasty Greek salad, and a spectacular wild boar pâté. Outside tables get crowded fast, so arrive early, or come late, as they serve until about 1 AM. ⊠ *Piazza Pasquino 73, Navona* ☎ *06/68801094* ⊟ *AE, MC, V* ⊙ *Closed 2 wks in Aug.*

$
PIZZA

✕ **Da Baffetto.** Down a cobblestone street not far from Piazza Navona, this is Rome's most popular pizzeria and a summer favorite for streetside dining. The plain interior is mostly given over to the ovens, but there's another room with more paper-covered tables. Outdoor tables (enclosed and heated in winter) provide much-needed additional seating. Turnover is fast, and lingering is not encouraged. ⊠ *Via del Governo Vecchio 114, Navona* ☎ *06/6861617* ⊟ *No credit cards* ⊙ *Closed Aug. No lunch.*

10

$$$$
MODERN ITALIAN
Fodor's Choice
★

✕ **Il Convivio.** In a tiny, nondescript vicolo north of Piazza Navona, the three Troiani brothers—Angelo in the kitchen, and brothers Giuseppe and Massimo presiding over the dining room and wine cellar—have quietly been redefining the experience of Italian eclectic *alta cucina* for many years. Antipasti include a "roast beef" of tuna fillet lacquered with chestnut honey, rosemary, red peppercorns, and ginger served with a green apple salad, while a squid ink risotto with baby cuttlefish, sea asparagus, lemongrass, and basil sates the appetites of those with dreams of *fantasia.* Main courses include a fabulous version of a cold-weather pigeon dish for which Il Convivio is famous. Service is attentive without being overbearing, and the wine list is exceptional. A splurge spot. ✉ *Vicolo dei Soldati 31, Navona* ☎*06/6869432* ⚓*Reservations essential* ▤*AE, DC, MC, V* ⊘*Closed Sun., 1 wk in Jan., and 2 wks in Aug. No lunch.*

$$ ✗**Ōbikā.** If you've ever wanted to take in a "mozzarella bar," here's
ITALIAN your chance. Mozzarella is featured here much like sushi bars show-case fresh fish—even the decor is modern Japanese minimalism–meets–ancient Roman grandeur. The cheese, in all its varieties, is the focus of the dishes: there's the familiar cow's milk, the delectable water buffalo milk varieties from the Campagna region, and the sinfully rich *burrata* from Puglia (a fresh cow's milk mozzarella encasing a creamy center of unspun mozzarella curds and fresh cream). They're all served with various accompanying cured meats, vegetables, sauces, and breads. An outdoor deck is a great plus for dining alfresco. ✉ *Piazza di Firenze 26, Navona* ☎*06/6832630* ▤*AE, DC, MC, V*

CAMPO DE' FIORI & GHETTO

$ ✗**Brasia.** This spacious trattoria on a back street off of the Campo de'
ITALIAN Fiori is a welcome, inexpensive addition to an area filled with tourist-riddled pizzerias and overpriced restaurants. The place itself is a huge space, but remains cozy because of brick walls and arched ceilings (the space actually harks back to the 17th century, and the name of the street it's on means "street of caves"). There's a wood-burning oven for homemade pizzas, and grilled meats are the other house specialty, here less expensive than in most spots. All typical Roman menu staples are found here as well: bruschette, mixed salumi and antipasti, and a variety of pasta standards. ✉ *Vicolo delle Grotte 17, Campo de' Fiori* ☎*06/97277119.*

$$ ✗**Da Sergio.** Every neighborhood has at least one "old-school" Roman
ROMAN trattoria, and for the Campo de' Fiori area, Da Sergio is it. Once you're seated (there's usually a wait), the red-and-white-check paper table-covering, bright lights, '50s kitsch, and the stuffed boar's head on the wall remind you that you're smack in the middle of the genuine article. Go for the delicious version of pasta *all'amatriciana*, or the generous helping of gnocchi with a tomato sauce and lots of Parmesan cheese, served, as tradition dictates, on Thursday. ✉ *Vicolo delle Grotte 27, Campo de' Fiori* ☎*06/6864293* ▤*DC, MC, V* ⊘*Closed Sun. and 2 wks in Aug.*

$$$ ✗**Evangelista.** This restaurant seems to be so tucked away, even the
ITALIAN locals have difficulty stumbling upon it. Everybody, however, seems to know and love its *carciofi al mattone* (roasted artichokes pressed flat between two hot bricks); this fame is well deserved, as the artichoke comes out crispy and delicious, looking almost like a perfectly seared vegetable carpaccio. Pastas are excellent, including the home-made potato gnocchi, light and fluffy and unadorned in a vegetable ragoût with a touch of saffron. Then feast on roast pork loin with juniper berries in winter, swordfish with Marsala, mint, and pistachio in summer. The arched white ceilings and decorating details lend an air of comfortable elegance. ✉ *Via delle Zoccolette 11/a, Campo de' Fiori* ☎*06/6875810* ▤*AE, MC, V* ⊘*Closed Sun. and Aug. No lunch.*

¢ ✗**Filetti di Baccalà.** For years, Filetti di Baccalà has been serving just
SEAFOOD that—battered, deep-fried fillets of salt cod—and not much else. You'll

find no-frills starters such as *bruschette al pomodoro* (garlic-rubbed toast topped with fresh tomatoes and olive oil), sautéed zucchini, and, in winter months, the cod is served alongside *puntarelle*, chicory stems topped with a delicious anchovy-garlic-lemon vinaigrette. The location, down the street from Campo de' Fiori in a little piazza in front of the beautiful Santa Barbara church, begs you to eat at one of the outdoor tables, weather-permitting. Long operating hours allow those still on U.S. time to eat as early (how gauche!) as 6 PM. ⊠ *Largo dei Librari 88, Campo de' Fiori* ☎ *06/6864018* ⊟ *No credit cards* ⊗ *Closed Sun. and Aug. No lunch.*

TERMINI & SAN LORENZO

$$$$

MODERN ITALIAN

✗ **Agata e Romeo.** For the perfect marriage of fine dining, creative cuisine, and rustic Roman tradition, the husband-and-wife team of Agata Parisella and Romeo Caraccio is the top. Romeo presides over the dining room and delights in the selection of wine-food pairings. And Chef Agata was perhaps the first in the capital city to put a gourmet spin on Roman ingredients and preparations, elevating dishes of the common folk to new levels, wherein familiar staples like *coda alla vaccinara* are transformed into a rich oxtail ragoût with celery root, both as a puree and as shoestring fries. From antipasti to desserts, many dishes are the best versions of classics you can get. The prices here are steep, but for those who appreciate extremely high-quality ingredients, an incredible wine cellar, and warm service, dining here is a real treat. ⊠ *Via Carlo Alberto 45, Termini* ☎ *06/4466115* ⊟ *AE, DC, MC, V* ⊗ *Closed weekends, 2 wks in July, and 2 wks in Aug.*

$$

ITALIAN

✗ **Tram Tram.** This bustling trattoria is usually snugly packed with hungry Romans. The name refers to its proximity to the tram tracks, but could also describe its size, as it's narrow-narrow and often stuffed to the rafters-rafters. In warmer weather, there's a "side car" of tables enclosed along the sidewalk. The focus of the food is the cook's hometown region of Puglia. You'll find an emphasis on seafood and vegetables—maybe prawns with saffron-kissed sautéed vegetables—as well as pastas of very particular shapes. Fish is a good bet here; try the homemade *orecchiette,* ear-shaped pasta, made here with clams and broccoli. ⊠ *Via dei Reti 44/46, San Lorenzo* ☎ *06/490416* ⊟ *AE, DC, MC, V* ⊗ *Closed Mon. and 1 wk in mid-Aug.*

$$

ITALIAN

✗ **Trattoria Monti.** Not far from Santa Maria Maggiore and one of the most dependable, moderately priced trattorias in the city, Monti favors the cuisine of the Marches, an area to the northeast of Rome. There are surprisingly few places specializing in this humble fare considering there are more *marchegiani* in Rome than in the whole region of Le Marche. The fare served up by the Camerucci family is hearty and simple, represented by various roasted meats and game and a selection of generally vegetarian timbales and soufflés that change seasonally. The region's rabbit dishes are much loved, and here the *timballo di coniglio con patate* (rabbit casserole with potatoes) is no exception. ⊠ *Via di San Vito 13, Monti* ☎ *06/4466573* ⊟ *AE, DC, MC, V* ⊗ *Closed Aug., 2 wks at Easter, and 10 days at Christmas.*

10

VATICAN

$$$ ✕ **Taverna Angelica.** The area sur-
ITALIAN   rounding St. Peter's Basilica isn't
known for culinary excellence,
but Taverna Angelica is an excep-
tion. Its tiny size allows the chef
to concentrate on each individual
dish, and the menu is creative with-
out being pretentious. Dishes such
as warm octopus salad on a bed
of warm mashed potatoes with a

basil-parsley pesto drizzle are more about taste than presentation. The
lentil soup with pigeon breast brought hunter's cuisine to a new level.
And the breast of duck in balsamic vinegar was exquisitely executed.
It may be difficult to find, on a section of the street that's set back and
almost subterranean, but it's worth searching out. ⊠ *Piazza A. Capponi
6, Borgo* ☎ *06/6874514* ⚠ *Reservations essential* ☰ *AE, V.*

TRASTEVERE

$$ ✕ **Alle Fratte di Trastevere.** Here you can find staple Roman trattoria fare
ROMAN   as well as dishes with a southern slant. This means that *spaghetti alla
carbonara* (with pancetta, eggs, and cheese) shares the menu with the
likes of penne *alla Sorrentina* (with tomato, basil, and fresh mozarella).
For starters, the bruschette here are exemplary, as is the pressed octopus carpaccio on a bed of arugula. As for secondi, you can again look
south and to the sea for a mixed seafood pasta or a grilled sea bass with
oven-roasted potatoes, or go for the meat with a fillet *al pepe verde*
(green peppercorns in a brandy cream sauce). Service is always with a
smile, as the owners and their trusted waitstaff make you feel at home.
⊠ *Via delle Fratte di Trastevere 49/50* ☎ *06/5835775* ☰ *AE, DC, MC,
V* ☺ *Closed Wed. and 2 wks in Aug.*

$ ✕ **Dar Poeta.** Romans drive across town for great pizza from this neigh-
PIZZA   borhood institution on a small street in Trastevere. Maybe it's the
dough—it's made from a secret blend of flours that's reputed to be
easier to digest than the competition. They offer both thin-crust pizza
and a thick-crust (*"alta"*) Neapolitan-style pizza with any of the given
toppings. For dessert, there's a ridiculously good calzone with Nutella
chocolate-hazelnut spread and ricotta cheese, so save some room. Service from the owners and friendly waitstaff is smile-inducing. ⊠ *Vicolo
del Bologna 45, Trastevere* ☎ *06/5880516* ☰ *AE, MC, V.*

WHERE TO STAY

When planning your Roman Holiday, you may be surprised to learn
that you really will have to *do* as the Romans do, meaning that unless
you're coveting a luxury suite at the Eden, you'll probably find yourself
in a tiny room. The air-conditioning may be weak and the customer
service will likely be indifferent. Naturally, there are exceptions, but the
Eternal City simply doesn't offer the cushy standards that most Americans are accustomed to, though standards in general are improving.

If you're looking for luxury, you're most likely to find it around Via Veneto and the Spanish Steps area. On the contrary, many of the city's cheapest accommodations are located near Stazione Termini. But for the most authentic Roman experience, stay in or near the *centro storico* (the historic center).

PANTHEON

$$$ **Albergo Santa Chiara.** With its white shutters and pretty canteloupe-hue stone, this hotel is comprised of three historic buildings set behind the Pantheon. It's been in the same family for 200 years, and the personal attention shows in meticulously decorated and maintained lounges and rooms. The lobby is *alla Romana*—an all white affair; it's elegantly accented with a Venetian chandelier, a stucco statue, a gilded Baroque mirror, and a walnut concierge desk. Upstairs, the pricier rooms are most fetching, with stylish yet comfortable furniture. Each room has built-in oak headboards, a marble-top desk, and a travertine bath. Double-glaze windows make a difference in those rooms that look out over the Piazza della Minerva. There are also three apartments, for two to five people, with full kitchens. **Pros:** great location in the historic center behind the Pantheon; most of the rooms are spacious; the staff is both polite and helpful. **Cons:** layout is mazelike (you must take two elevators to some of the rooms); rooms don't get a lot of light; no Internet access at the hotel. ⊠ *Via Santa Chiara 21, Pantheon* ☎*06/6872979* 🖷*06/6873144* ⊕*www.albergosantachiara.com* ⋙*96 rooms, 3 suites, 3 apartments* ⚬*In-room: safe, kitchen (some), refrigerator. In-hotel: room service, bar, laundry service, concierge, airport shuttle (fee)* ⊟*AE, DC, MC, V* ⦿*CP.*

$$$–$$$$ **Pantheon.** The Pantheon is a superb place to stay right next door to the grand monument of the same name. The lobby is the very epitome of a Roman hotel lobby—a warm, cozy, yet opulent setting that comes replete with Stil Liberty stained glass, sumptuous wood paneling, a Renaissance beamed ceiling, and a massive and glorious chandelier. A print of one of Rome's obelisks on the door welcomes you to your room, where you'll find antique walnut furniture, fresh flowers, and more wood-beam ceilings. **Pros:** proximity to the Pantheon; big, clean bathrooms; friendly staff. **Cons:** rooms are in need of some upgrading; the lighting is low and the carpets are worn; the breakfast lacks variety. ⊠*Via dei Pastini 131, Pantheon* ☎*06/6787746* 🖷*06/6787755* ⊕*www.hotelpantheon.com* ⋙*13 rooms, 1 suite* ⚬*In-room: safe, refrigerator, Wi-Fi. In-hotel: bar, room service, laundry service, public Wi-Fi, no-smoking rooms* ⊟*AE, DC, MC, V* ⦿*CP.*

CAMPO DE' FIORI & GHETTO

$$ **Arenula.** Standing on an age-worn byway off central Via Arenula, this hotel is a superb bargain by Rome standards. With an imposingly elegant stone exterior, this hotel welcomes you with a luminous and cheerful all-white interior. Guest rooms are simple in decor but have pale-wood furnishings and gleaming bathrooms, as well as double-glaze windows and air-conditioning (in summer only; ask when you reserve). Two of the rooms accommodate four beds. Of course, you can't have everything, so that the graceful oval staircase of white marble

10

and wrought iron in the lobby cues you that there is no elevator. Those guests with rooms on the fourth floor had better be in good shape! **Pros:** it's a real bargain; conveniently located in the Ghetto (close to Campo de' Fiori and Trastevere), and it's spotless. **Cons:** totally no-frills accommodations; four floors and no elevator; traffic and tram noise can be heard throughout the night despite the double-glazing. ⊠ *Via Santa Maria dei Calderari 47, off Via Arenula, Ghetto* ☎06/6879454 🖷06/6896188 ⊕*www.hotelarenula.com* 🖫*50 rooms* ♿*In-room: no a/c (some). In-hotel: no elevator* ▭*AE, DC, MC, V* ⦿*CP.*

$$–$$$ 🖪**Hotel Campo de' Fiori.** Frescoes, exposed brickwork, and picturesque effects throughout this little hotel could well be the work of a set designer, but a recent renovation attributes the charming ambience to interior designer Dario di Blasi. Each room is entirely unique in its colors, furniture, and refined feel. The hotel underwent a complete renovation in 2006, retaining its Old World charm, but modernizing with soundproofing, air-conditioning, flat-screen TVs, pay-per-view movies, DSL, and Wi-Fi in all the rooms. There is also a marvelous view from the roof terrace. If you desire more extensive accommodations, Hotel Campo de' Fiori offers an additional selection of 15 different apartments in the area that can accommodate two to five guests. **Pros:** newly renovated; superb location; modern amenities that many Roman hotels haven't caught up with yet; rooftop terrace. **Cons:** some of the rooms are very small; breakfast works on a voucher system with a nearby caffè; the staff doesn't necessarily go out of their way to help you settle in. ⊠ *Via del Biscione 6, Campo de' Fiori* ☎06/68806865 🖷06/6876003 ⊕*www.hotelcampodefiori.it* 🖫*28 rooms* ♿*In-room: safe, refrigerator, high-speed Internet, Wi-Fi. In-hotel: no-smoking rooms* ▭*MC, V* ⦿*CP.*

VENETO, BORGHESE & SPAGNA

$$$$ 🖪**Eden.** Once the preferred haunt of Hemingway, Bergman, and Fellini, this superlative hotel combines dashing elegance and stunning vistas of Rome with the warmth of Italian hospitality. Set atop a hill near the Villa Borghese (and a bit out of the historic center for serious sightseers), this hotel was opened in the late 19th century and quickly became famous for its balcony views and Roman splendor. You'll now dive deep here into the whoosh of luxury, with antiques, sumptuous Italian fabrics, linen sheets, and marble baths competing for your attention. Banquette window seats, rich mahogany furniture, soaring ceilings, Napoléon-Trois sofas are just some of the allurements here. **Pros:** gorgeous panoramic view from roof terrace; you could be rubbing elbows with the stars; 24-hour room service. **Cons:** expensive (unless money is no object for you); no Wi-Fi in the rooms; some say the staff can be hit-or-miss. ⊠ *Via Ludovisi 49, Veneto* ☎06/478121 🖷06/4821584 ⊕*www.lemeridien.com/eden* 🖫*121 rooms, 13 suites* ♿*In-room: safe, refrigerator, DVD (some), high-speed Internet. In-hotel: restaurant, room service, 2 bars, gym, concierge, laundry service, public Internet, Wi-Fi, airport shuttle (fee), parking (fee), no-smoking rooms, some pets allowed* ▭*AE, DC, MC, V* ⦿*EP.*

$$$$ 🖪**Hassler.** Here, in villas atop the Pincian Hill, Poussin, Piranesi, Ingres, and Berlioz once enjoyed having all of Rome at their feet. Today movie

stars and millionaires do the same by staying at this hotel, which sits just to the right of the church atop the Spanish Steps. The guest rooms here are among the world's most beautiful and opulent. If you're not willing to pay V.I.P prices, you'll get more standard-issue rooms at the rear of the hotel, but many are soigné and some come with views of the Villa Medici park. Better, the hotel has several elegant bars, restaurants, and retreats. The Rooftop Restaurant is world-famous for its view if not for its food; the Palm Court Garden, which becomes the

hotel bar in summer, is overflowing with flowers. **Pros:** charming Old World feel; prime location and panoramic views at the top of the Spanish Steps; just "steps" away from some of the best shopping in the world. **Cons:** V.I.P. prices; many think the staff are too standoffish; some say the cuisine at the rooftop restaurant isn't worth the gourmet price tag. ⊠*Piazza Trinità dei Monti 6, Spagna,* ☎*06/699340* ☎*06/6789991* ⊕*www.lhw.com* ⤴*85 rooms, 13 suites* ♿*In-room: safe, refrigerator, high-speed Internet. In-hotel: restaurant, room service, bar, gym, spa, concierge, laundry service, public Wi-Fi, parking (fee), no-smoking rooms* ⊟*AE, DC, MC, V* ⦿*EP.*

$$$ 🏨**San Carlo.** Marble accents are everywhere at this renovated 17th-century mansion, and there's an overall effect that's refined and decidedly classical. Rooms are bright and comfortable; some have their own terraces with rooftop views. A top-floor terrace is ideal for having breakfast or taking in the sun throughout the day. The rooms also feature flat-screen TVs and free Wi-Fi. **Pros:** rooms with terraces and views of historic Rome; rooftop garden; attentive staff. **Cons:** there are a lot of stairs and no elevator; breakfast is basic Italian fare (great coffee but otherwise just cornetti, cereal, and yogurt); the rooms can be noisy. ⊠*Via delle Carrozze 92–93, Spagna* ☎*06/6784548* ☎*06/69941197* ⊕*www.hotelsancarloroma.com* ⤴*50 rooms, 2 suites* ♿*In-room: refrigerator, Wi-Fi. In-hotel: bar, no elevator, laundry service, public Wi-Fi, no-smoking rooms* ⊟*AE, DC, MC, V* ⦿*CP.*

REPUBBLICA & SAN LORENZO

$ 🏨**The Beehive.** Rome meets the best of Southern California at the Beehive. Started by a Los Angeles couple following their dream, the Beehive might be the most distinctive budget hotel in Rome—although, it's not just a hotel; it's more of an ecologically minded little empire that also offers hostel accommodations, a vegetarian café, a yoga space, and an art gallery with a garden, a reading lounge, and a few off-site apartments. It offers a respite from Rome's chaos, but is conveniently located only a few blocks from Termini. The design is contemporary and hip and the vibe is mellow. All of the rooms come with shared bathrooms. There is a lovely garden with fruit trees, herbs, and flowers. The Beehive

10

offers free Wi-Fi, but no TVs or air-conditioning (rooms do have ceiling fans). **Pros:** yoga, massage, and other therapies offered on-site; free Wi-Fi and Beehive's own guidebook. **Cons:** no TV, a/c, baggage storage, or private bathroom; breakfast is not included in the room rate. ✉ *Via Marghera 8, Repubblica* ☎*06/44704553* ⊕*www.the-beehive.com* ⇨*8 rooms, 1 dormitory, 3 apartments* ⌂*In-room: no a/c, kitchen (some), no TV, Wi-Fi. In-hotel: no elevator, public Wi-Fi, no-smoking rooms* ⊟*MC, V* �̄O⍨*EP.*

$ ⊞ **Italia.** It looks and feels like a classic pensione: low-budget with a lot of heart. A block off the very trafficky Via Nazionale, this friendly, family-run hotel offers inexpensive rooms with big windows, desks, parquet floors, and baths with faux-marble tiles, but the rooms aren't really the point. The price is, and it's made all the more tempting by a generous buffet breakfast and thoughtful touches like an ice machine and free wireless Internet access. Ask for even lower midsummer rates. **Pros:** free Wi-Fi and Internet access in the lobby; great price; individual attention and personal care. **Cons:** no Internet access in the rooms; it's sometimes noisy; a/c is an extra €10. ✉ *Via Venezia 18, Monti* ☎*06/4828355* 🖷*06/4745550* ⊕*www.hotelitaliaroma.com* ⇨*31 rooms, 1 apartment* ⌂*In-room: no a/c (some), safe. In-hotel: bar, concierge, public Internet, public Wi-Fi, airport shuttle (fee), parking (fee), no-smoking rooms* ⊟*AE, MC, V* ⍄O⍨*CP.*

$$ ⊞ **Yes Hotel.** A newcomer to the Rome budget hotel scene, Yes was opened in April of 2007 by the same folks who own Hotel Des Artistes. It's centrally located near Stazione Termini, and thus close to many restaurants and transportation options. One of the nicest things about Yes is that, even though it's a budget hotel, the rooms have a flair for style with a contemporary feel. Yes also offers the kind of amenities that are usually found in more expensive hotels, like flat-screen TVs and air-conditioning. Unfortunately, there is no Internet access at the hotel, but they do have a special deal with a nearby Internet Point shop that allows guests free access for 15 minutes a day. **Pros:** it doesn't feel like a budget hotel, but it is; discount if you pay cash; great value. **Cons:** rooms are small; no individual climate control or refrigerators in the rooms; no Internet in the hotel. ✉ *Via Magenta 15, San Lorenzo* ☎*06/44363836* 🖷*06/44363829* ⊕*www.yeshotelrome.com* ⇨*29 rooms, 1 suite* ⌂*In-room: safe. In-hotel: parking (fee), no-smoking rooms* ⊟*MC, V* ⍄O⍨*CP.*

VATICAN

$$$ ⊞ **Alimandi.** On a side street a block from the Vatican Museums, this family-operated hotel offers excellent value in a neighborhood with moderately priced shops and restaurants. A spiffy lobby, spacious lounges, a tavern, terraces, and roof gardens are some of the perks, as is an exercise room equipped with step machines and a treadmill. Rooms are spacious and well-furnished; many can accommodate extra beds. Needless to say, the location here is quite far away from Rome's historic center. **Pros:** nice family-owned hotel with a friendly staff, a terrace, a tavern, and a gym. **Cons:** breakfast is a good spread but it goes quickly; rooms are small; not close to much of interest other than the Vatican. ✉ *Via Tunisi 8, Vatican* ☎*06/39723948* 🖷*06/39723943*

⊕*www.alimandi.it* ⇆*35 rooms* &*In-room: safe, refrigerator (some), Wi-Fi. In-hotel: bar, gym, public Internet, airport shuttle (fee), parking (no fee), no-smoking rooms* ☰*AE, DC, MC, V* ⁑⊙⁑*BP.*

¢–$ 🔲**Hotel San Pietrino.** It may seem like a miracle, but the San Pietrino is a well-appointed, stylish hotel with bargain prices near the Vatican. It's on the third floor of a 19th-century palazzo that's only a five-minute walk from St. Peter's Square. In addition to clean, simple rooms, San Pietrino offers air-conditioning, TVs with DVD players, and high-speed Internet to guests. There is no breakfast included and no bar in the hotel, but not to worry—with all the local caffès and bars, you won't have any trouble finding yourself a *cornetto* and cappuccino in the morning or a prosecco for aperitivo in the evening. **Pros:** heavenly prices near the Vatican; TVs with DVD players; high-speed Internet. **Cons:** a couple of metro stops away from the center of Rome; no breakfast; no bar. ✉*Via Giovanni Bettolo 43, Prati* ☎*06/3700132* 📠*06/3701809* ⊕*www.sanpietrino. it* ⇆*12 rooms* &*In-room: DVD (some), high-speed Internet, Wi-Fi. In-hotel: public Internet, public Wi-Fi, airport shuttle (fee)* ☰*MC, V* ⁑⊙⁑*EP.*

TRASTEVERE

$$$ 🔲**Hotel Santa Maria.** A Trastevere treasure, this hotel has a pedigree going back four centuries. This ivy-covered, mansard-roofed, rosy-brick-red, erstwhile Renaissance-era convent has been transformed by Paolo and Valentina Vetere into a true charmer. Surrounded by towering tenements, the complex is centered around a monastic porticoed courtyard, lined with orange trees—a lovely place for breakfast. The guest rooms are sweet and simple: a mix of brick walls, "cotto" tile floors, modern oak furniture, and stylishly floral bedspreads and curtains. Best of all, the location is *buonissimo*—just a few blocks from the Tiber and its *isola*. **Pros:** a quaint and pretty oasis in a chaotic city; relaxing courtyard; stocked wine bar. **Cons:** it might be tricky to find; some of the showers drain slowly; it's not always easy finding a cab in Trastevere. ✉*Vicolo del Piede 2, Trastevere* ☎*06/5894626* 📠*06/5894815* ⊕*www.htlsantamaria.com* ⇆*18 rooms, 2 suites* &*In-room: safe, refrigerator. In-hotel: bar, bicycles, laundry service, concierge, public Internet, airport shuttle (fee), no-smoking rooms* ☰*AE, DC, MC, V* ⁑⊙⁑*BP.*

$ 🔲**Hotel Trastevere.** This tiny hotel captures the villagelike charm of the Trastevere district. The entrance hall features a mural of the famous Piazza di Santa Maria, a block away, and hand-painted Art Nouveau wall designs add a touch of graciousness throughout. Open medieval brickwork and a few antiques here and there complete the mood. Most rooms face Piazza San Cosimato, where there's an outdoor food market every morning except Sunday. **Pros:** cheap with a good location; convenient to transportation; friendly staff. **Cons:** no frills; few amenities; no Internet access. ✉*Via Luciano Manara 24–25, Trastevere* ☎*06/5814713* 📠*06/5881016* ⊕*www.hoteltrastevere.net* ⇆*19 rooms, 3 apartments* &*In-room: safe (some), refrigerator (some), kitchen (some). In-hotel: no-smoking rooms* ☰*AE, DC, MC, V* ⁑⊙⁑*CP.*

10

NIGHTLIFE & THE ARTS

THE ARTS

Cultural events are publicized well in advance through the city's Web site ⊕ *www.comune.roma.it.* Weekly events listings can be found in the Cronaca and Cultura sections of Italian newspapers, as well in *Metro* (the free newspaper). The most comprehensive listings are in the weekly *roma c'è* booklet, which comes out every Wednesday. It has a brief yet very detailed English-language section at the back. On the Web, check out www.inromenow.com, an events site written exclusively for the English-speaking community and updated monthly, as well as the site for *Time Out Roma* (⊕ *www.timeout.com/travel/rome*). Two monthly English-language periodicals (with accompanying Web sites), *Wanted in Rome* (⊕ *www.wantedinrome.com*), and *The American* (⊕ *www. theamericanmag.com*), available at many newsstands, have good coverage of arts events. Events and concert listings can also be found in both English and Italian at www.musicguide.it.

NIGHTLIFE

Rome's nightlife is decidedly more happening for locals and insiders who know whose palms to grease and when to go where. The "flavor of the month" factor is at work here, and many places fade into oblivion after their 15 minutes of fame. Smoking has been banned in all public areas in Italy (that's right, it actually happened); Roman aversion to clean air has meant a decrease in crowds at bars and clubs. The best sources for an up-to-date list of nightspots are the *roma c'è* and *Time Out Roma* magazines. Trastevere and the area around Piazza Navona are both filled with bars, restaurants, and, after dark, people. In summer, discos and many bars close to beat the heat (although some simply relocate to the beach, where many Romans spend their summer nights). The city-sponsored Estate Romana (Rome Summer) festival takes over, lighting up hot city nights with open-air concerts, bars, and discos. Pick up the event guide at newsstands.

First and foremost among the bar scene is the wine bar, found (often with outdoor seating) in almost every piazza and on side streets throughout the city. These *enoteche* are mostly small in size, offering a smattering of antipasti to accompany a variety of wines.

SHOPPING

They say when in Rome to do as the Romans do—and the Romans love to shop. Stores are generally open from 9 or 9:30 to 1 and from 3:30 or 4 to 7 or 7:30. There's a tendency for shops in central districts to stay open all day, and hours are becoming more flexible throughout the city. Many places close Sunday, though this is changing, too, especially in the city center. With the exception of food stores, many stores also close Monday morning from September to mid-June and Saturday afternoon from mid-June through August. Stores selling food are usually closed Thursday afternoon.

You can stretch your euros by taking advantage of the Tax-Free for Tourists V.A.T. tax refunds, available at most large stores for purchases over €155. Or hit Rome in January and early February or in late July, when stores clean house with the justly famous biannual sales. There are so many hole-in-the-wall boutiques selling top-quality merchandise in Rome's center that even just wandering you're sure to find something that catches your eye.

SHOPPING DISTRICTS

The city's most famous shopping district, **Piazza di Spagna,** is conveniently compact, fanning out at the foot of the Spanish Steps in a galaxy of boutiques selling gorgeous wares with glamorous labels. Here you can ricochet from Gucci to Prada to Valentino to Versace with less effort than it takes to pull out your credit card. If your budget is designed for lower altitudes, you also can find great clothes and accessories at less extravagant prices. But here buying is not necessarily the point—window displays can be works of art, and dreaming may be satisfaction enough. Via Condotti is the neighborhood's central axis, but there are shops on every street in the area bordered by Piazza di Spagna on the east, Via del Corso on the west, between Piazza San Silvestro and Via della Croce, and extending along Via del Babuino to Piazza del Popolo. Shops along **Via Campo Marzio,** and adjoining Piazza San Lorenzo in Lucina, stock eclectic, high-quality clothes and accessories—both big names (Bottega Veneta, Louis Vuitton) and unknowns—at slightly lower prices. Running from Piazza Venezia to Piazza del Popolo lies **Via del Corso,** a main shopping avenue that has more than a mile of clothing, shoes, leather goods, and home furnishings from classic to cutting-edge. Running west from Piazza Navona, **Via del Governo Vecchio** has numerous women's boutiques and secondhand-clothing stores. **Via Cola di Rienzo,** across the Tiber from Piazza del Popolo, is block after block of boutiques, shoe stores, department stores, and mid-level chain shops, as well as street stalls and upscale food shops. **Via dei Coronari,** across the Tiber from Castel Sant'Angelo, has quirky antiques and home furnishings. Via Giulia and other surrounding streets are good bets for decorative arts. The **Termini** train station has become a good one-stop place for many shopping needs. Its 60-plus shops are open until 10 PM and include a Nike store, the Body Shop, Sephora, Mango (women's clothes), a UPIM department store, and a grocery store.

10

FLORENCE

Florence, the city of the lily, gave birth to the Renaissance and changed the way we see the world. For centuries it has captured the imagination of travelers, who have come seeking rooms with views and phenomenal art. Florence's is a subtle beauty—its staid, unprepossessing palaces built in local stone are not showy. They take on a certain magnificence when day breaks and when the sun sets; their muted colors glow in this light. A walk along the Arno offers views that don't quit and haven't much changed in 700 years; navigating Piazza Signoria, almost always packed with tourists and locals alike, requires patience. There's a reason why everyone seems to be here, however. It's the heart of the city, and home to the Uffizi—arguably the world's finest repository of Renaissance art.

Florence was "discovered" in the 1700s by upper-class northerners making the grand tour. It became a mecca for travelers, particularly the Romantics, who were inspired by the elegance of its palazzi and its artistic wealth. Today millions of modern visitors follow in their footsteps. When the sun sets over the Arno and, as Mark Twain described it, "overwhelms Florence with tides of color that make all the sharp lines dim and faint and turn the solid city to a city of dreams," it's hard not to fall under the city's spell.

PLANNING YOUR TIME

With some planning you can see Florence's most famous sights in a couple of days. Start at the city's most awe-inspiring work of architecture, the **Duomo**, climbing to the top of the dome if you have the stamina. On the same piazza, check out Ghiberti's bronze doors at the **Battistero**. (They're actually high-quality copies; the Museo dell'Opera del Duomo has the originals.) Set aside the afternoon for the **Galleria degli Uffizi**, making sure to reserve tickets in advance.

On Day 2, visit Michelangelo's David in the **Galleria dell'Accademia**—reserve tickets here, too. Linger in the **Piazza della Signoria**, Florence's central square, where a copy of David stands in the spot the original occupied for centuries, then head east a couple of blocks to **Santa Croce**, the city's most artistically rich church. Double back and walk across Florence's landmark bridge, the **Ponte Vecchio**.

Do all that, and you'll have seen some great art, but you've just scratched the surface. If you have more time, put the **Bargello**, the **Museo di San Marco**, and the **Cappelle Medicee** at the top of your list. When you're ready for an art break, stroll through the **Boboli Gardens** or explore Florence's lively shopping scene, from the food stalls of the **Mercato Centrale** to the chic boutiques of the **Via Tornabuoni**.

GETTING HERE

Florence's small **Aeroporto A. Vespucci** (✛ *10 km [6 mi] northwest of Florence* ☎*055/373498* ⊕*www.aeroporto.firenze.it*), commonly called **Peretola**, is just outside of town and receives flights from Milan, Rome, London, and Paris. To get into the city center from the airport by car, take the autostrada A11. Tickets for the local bus service into Florence are sold at the airport's second-floor bar—Bus 62 runs once an hour directly to the train station at Santa Maria Novella. The airport's bus shelter is beyond the parking lot.

Pisa's **Aeroporto Galileo Galilei** (✛ *12 km [7 mi] south of Pisa and 80 km [50 mi] west of Florence* ☎*050/849300* ⊕*www.pisa-airport.com*) is the closest landing point with significant international service, including (at this writing) a few direct flights from the United States each week on Delta. It's a straight shot down SS67 to Florence. A train service connects Pisa's airport station with Santa Maria Novella, roughly a 1½-hour trip. Trains start running about 7 AM from the airport, 6 AM from Florence, and continue service every hour until about 7 PM from the airport, 4 PM from Florence.

Florence is on the principal Italian train route between most European capitals and Rome, and within Italy it is served frequently from Milan, Venice, and Rome by Intercity (IC) and nonstop Eurostar trains. **Stazione Centrale di Santa Maria Novella** (☎ *892021* ⊕ *www.trenitalia.com*) is the main station and is in the center of town. Avoid trains that stop only at the Campo di Marte or Rifredi stations, which are not convenient to the city center.

Florence is connected to the north and south of Italy by the Autostrada del Sole (A1). It takes about 1½ hours of driving on scenic roads to get to Bologna (although heavy truck traffic over the Apennines often makes for slower going), about 3 hours to Rome, and 3 to 3½ hours to Milan. The Tyrrhenian Coast is an hour west on the A11.

GETTING AROUND

Florence's flat, compact city center is made for walking, but when your feet get weary, you can use the efficient bus system, which includes small electric buses making the rounds in the center. Buses also climb to Piazzale Michelangelo and San Miniato south of the Arno.

Maps and timetables for local bus service are available for a small fee at the ATAF (Azienda Trasporti Area Fiorentina) booth next to the train station, or for free at visitor information offices. Tickets must be bought in advance from tobacco shops, newsstands, automatic ticket machines near main stops, or ATAF booths. The ticket must be canceled in the small validation machine immediately upon boarding.

Taxis usually wait at stands throughout the city (in front of the train station and in Piazza della Repubblica, for example), or you can call for one (☎ *055/4390 or 055/4798*). The meter starts at €2.30, with a €3.60 minimum and extra charges at night, on Sunday, and for radio dispatch.

An automobile in Florence is a major liability. If your itinerary includes parts of Italy where you'll want a car (such as Tuscany), pick the vehicle up on your way out of town.

10

VISITOR INFORMATION

The Florence tourist office, known as the APT (☎ *055/290832* ⊕ *www.comune.firenze.it*), has locations next to the Palazzo Medici-Riccardi, in the main train station, and around the corner from the Basilica di Santa Croce. The offices are generally open from 9 in the morning until 7 in the evening. The multilingual staff will give you directions (but usually not free maps) and the latest on happenings in the city. It's particularly worth a stop if you're interested in finding out about performing-arts events. The APT Web site is in Italian only.

THE DUOMO TO THE PONTE VECCHIO

The heart of Florence, stretching from the Piazza del Duomo south to the Arno, is as dense with artistic treasures as anyplace in the world. The churches, medieval towers, Renaissance palaces, and world-class museums and galleries contain some of the most outstanding aesthetic achievements of Western history.

Much of the *centro storico* (historic center) is closed to automobile traffic, but you still must dodge mopeds, cyclists, and masses of fellow tourists as you walk the narrow streets, especially in the area bounded by the Duomo, Piazza della Signoria, Galleria degli Uffizi, and Ponte Vecchio.

EXPLORING THE DUOMO AND THE PONTE VECCHIO

8 **Bargello.** During the Renaissance, this building was headquarters for the
★ chief of police. It also was used as a prison, and the exterior served as a "most wanted" billboard: effigies of notorious criminals and Medici enemies were painted on its walls. Today it houses the **Museo Nazionale,** home to what is probably the finest collection of Renaissance sculpture in Italy. The concentration of masterworks by Michelangelo (1475–1564), Donatello (circa 1386–1466), and Benvenuto Cellini (1500–71) is remarkable; the works are distributed among an eclectic collection of arms, ceramics, and miniature bronzes, among other things. For Renaissance-art lovers, the Bargello is to sculpture what the Uffizi is to painting.

In 1401 Filippo Brunelleschi (1377–1446) and Lorenzo Ghiberti (circa 1378–1455) competed to earn the most prestigious commission of the day: the decoration of the north doors of the Baptistery in Piazza del Duomo. For the contest, each designed a bronze bas-relief panel depicting the sacrifice of Isaac; the panels are displayed together in the room devoted to the sculpture of Donatello, on the upper floor. The judges chose Ghiberti for the commission; see if you agree with their choice. ⊠ *Via del Proconsolo 4, Bargello* ☎ *055/294883* ⊕ *www.polomuseale. firenze.it* 🎟 *€4* ⊙ *Daily 8:15–1:50; closed 2nd and 4th Mon. of month and 1st, 3rd, and 5th Sun. of month.*

6 **Battistero** *(Baptistery).* The octagonal Baptistery is one of the supreme monuments of the Italian Romanesque style and one of Florence's oldest structures. Local legend has it that it was once a Roman temple dedicated to Mars; modern excavations, however, suggest that its foundations date from the fourth to fifth and the eighth to ninth centuries AD, well after the collapse of the Roman Empire. The round Romanesque arches on the exterior probably date from the 11th century. The interior dome mosaics from the beginning of the 14th century are justly renowned, but—glittering beauties though they are—they could never outshine the building's famed bronze Renaissance doors decorated with panels crafted by Lorenzo Ghiberti. The doors—or at least copies of them— on which Ghiberti worked most of his adult life (1403–52) are on the north and east sides of the Baptistery, and the Gothic panels on the south door were designed by Andrea Pisano (circa 1290–1348) in 1330. The original Ghiberti doors were removed to protect them from the effects of pollution and acid rain and have been beautifully restored; they are now on display in the Museo dell'Opera del Duomo. ⊠*Piazza del Duomo* ☎*055/2302885* ⊕*www. operaduomo.firenze.it* 🎫*€3* ☉*Mon.–Sat. noon–7, Sun. 8:30–2; 1st Sat. of month 8:30–2.*

WORD OF MOUTH

"I think the Bargello might be the most underrated museum in Florence, if not Italy." —Jess

❼ Duomo *(Cattedrale di Santa Maria*

Fodor's Choice *del Fiore).* In 1296 Arnolfo di

★ Cambio (circa 1245–circa 1310) was commissioned to build "the loftiest, most sumptuous edifice human invention could devise" in the Romanesque style on the site of the old church of Santa Reparata. The immense Duomo was not completed until 1436, the year it was consecrated. The imposing facade dates only from the 19th century; its neo-Gothic style complements Giotto's genuine Gothic 14th-century campanile. The real glory of the Duomo, however, is Filippo Brunelleschi's dome, presiding over the cathedral with a dignity and grace that few domes to this day can match.

Brunelleschi's **cupola** was an ingenious engineering feat. The space to be enclosed by the dome was so large and so high above the ground that traditional methods of dome construction—wooden centering and scaffolding—were of no use whatsoever. So Brunelleschi developed entirely new building methods, which he implemented with equipment of his own design (including a novel scaffolding method). The result was one of the great engineering breakthroughs of all time: most of Europe's later domes, including that of St. Peter's in Rome, were built employing Brunelleschi's methods, and today the Duomo has come to symbolize Florence in the same way that the Eiffel Tower symbolizes Paris.

The interior is a fine example of Florentine Gothic, but much of the cathedral's best-known art has been moved to the nearby Museo dell'Opera del Duomo. You can explore the upper and lower reaches of the cathedral. The remains of a Roman wall and an 11th-century cemetery have been excavated beneath the nave; the way down is near the first pier on the right. The **climb to the top of the dome** (463 steps) is not for the faint of heart, but the view is superb. ⊠*Piazza del Duomo* ☎*055/2302885* ⊕*www.operaduomo.firenze.it* 🎫*Church free, crypt €3, cupola €6* ☉*Crypt: Mon.–Wed., Fri, Sun. 10–5, Thurs. 10–4:30, Sat. 10–5:45, 1st Sat. of month 10–3:30. Cupola: Weekdays 8:30–7, Sat. 8:30–5:40, 1st Sat. of month 8:30–4. Duomo: Mon.–Wed. and Fri. 10–5, Thurs. 10–4:30, Sat., 10–4:45, Sun. 1:30–4:45, 1st Sat. of month 10–3:30.*

10

⓫ Galleria degli Uffizi. The venerable Uffizi Gallery occupies the top floor

Fodor's Choice of the U-shaped **Palazzo degli Uffizi** fronting on the Arno, designed

★ by Giorgio Vasari (1511–74) in 1560 to hold the *uffizi* (administrative offices) of the Medici grand duke Cosimo I (1519–74). Later, the Medici installed their art collections here, creating what was Europe's first modern museum, open to the public (at first only by request) since 1591. Hard-core museum aficionados can pick up a complete guide to the collections at bookshops and newsstands.

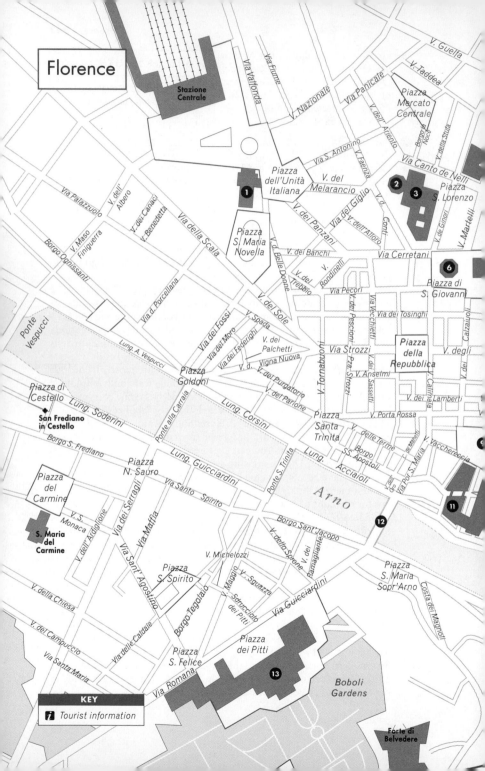

Santissima Annunziata

Piazza SS. Annunziata

Palazzo Medici-Riccardi

Piazza del Duomo

Piazza San Pier Maggiore

Piazza Salvemini

Speziali

Borgo degli Albizi

Piazza della Signoria

Palazzo Vecchio

Borgo dei Greci

Piazza S. Firenze

Piazza Santa Croce

Borgo S. Croce

Ponte Vecchio

Piazza dei Mozzi

V.S. Gallo

V. Cavour

V. Ricasoli

V. Gino Capponi

V. Laura

V. Colonna

V. degli Alfani

V. dei Servi

V. del Castellaccio

Via de' Pucci

Via Bufalini

V. della Pergola

V. Nuova dei Caccini

V. S. Egidio

V. dell'Oriuolo

Borgo Pinti

V. di Mezzo

V. Fiesolana

V. p. Studio

Proconsolo

V. D. Alighieri

V. dei Pandolfini

V. Matteo Palmieri

V. San Pier Maggiore

V. dell'Ulivo

V. dei Cimatori

V. Ghibellina

V. della Vigna Vecchia

V. dell'Agnolo

V. della Condotta

V. d. Acqua

V. d. Burella

Via Torta

V. Ghibellina

V. Verrazzano

V. della Pietrapiana

V. San Cristofori

V. Leoni

Via d. Corno

V. di S. Giuseppe

Via Vinegia

Via Pandectco

Via d. Magalotti

Via d. Rustici

V. de' Pepi

V. Antonio Magliabechi

V. dei Neri

Borgo dei Greci

Via d. Vagelli

Via Y. Malenchini

Corso Tintori

Lung. Diaz

Lung. d. Grazie

V. Tripoli

Lung. Torrigiani

Ponte alle Grazie

V. dei Bardi

Lung. Serristori

V. dei Renai

Via V. di S. Niccolò

Via S. Miniato

0   1/4 mile

0   400 meters

Among the highlights are the *Birth of Venus* and *Primavera* by Sandro Botticelli (1445–1510); the portraits of the Renaissance duke Federico da Montefeltro and his wife, Battista Sforza, by Piero della Francesca (circa 1420–92); the *Madonna of the Goldfinch* by Raphael (1483–1520); a *Self-Portrait as an Old Man* by Rembrandt (1606–69); the *Venus of Urbino* by Titian (circa 1488/90–1576); and the splendid *Bacchus* by Caravaggio (circa 1571/72–1610).

Late in the afternoon is the least crowded time to visit. For a €3 fee, advance tickets can be reserved by phone or, once in Florence, at the Uffizi reservation booth at least one day in advance of your visit. At this writing, an online reservation option has also been launched at ⊕*www. polomuseale.firenze.it*. If you book by phone, remember to keep the confirmation number and take it with you to the door at the museum marked "Reservations." Usually you're ushered in almost immediately. Come with cash, because credit cards are not accepted (though you can use a credit card when booking on-line). When there's a special exhibit on, which is often, the base ticket price goes up to €10. ⊠*Piazzale degli Uffizi 6, Piazza della Signoria* ☎*055/23885 advance tickets* ⊠*Consorzio ITA, Piazza Pitti 1* ☎*055/294883* ⊕*www.uffizi.firenze. it; reservations www.polomuseale.firenze.it* ⌧*€6.50, reservation fee €3* ⊙*Tues.–Sun. 8:15–6:50.*

❾ Piazza della Signoria. This is by far the most striking square in Florence. It was here, in 1497, that the famous "bonfire of the vanities" took place, when the fanatical friar Savonarola induced his followers to hurl their worldly goods into the flames; it was also here, a year later, that he was hanged as a heretic and, ironically, burned. A bronze plaque in the piazza pavement marks the exact spot of his execution.

In the square, the Neptune Fountain, created between 1550 and 1575, takes something of a booby prize. It was created by Bartolomeo Ammannati, who considered it a failure himself. The Florentines call it Il Biancone, which may be translated as "the big white man" or "the big white lump." Giambologna's equestrian statue, to the left of the fountain, pays tribute to Grand Duke Cosimo I. Occupying the steps of the Palazzo Vecchio are a copy of Donatello's proud heraldic lion of Florence, the *Marzocco* (the original is now in the Bargello); a copy of Donatello's *Judith and Holofernes* (the original is in the Palazzo Vecchio); a copy of Michelangelo's *David* (the original is in the Galleria dell'Accademia); and Baccio Bandinelli's *Hercules* (1534).

⓬ Ponte Vecchio *(Old Bridge).* This charmingly simple bridge is to Florence what the Tower Bridge is to London. It was built in 1345 to replace an earlier bridge that was swept away by flood, and its shops housed first butchers, then grocers, blacksmiths, and other merchants. But in 1593 the Medici grand duke Ferdinand I (1549–1609), whose private corridor linking the Medici palace (Palazzo Pitti) with the Medici offices (the Uffizi) crossed the bridge atop the shops, decided that all this plebeian commerce under his feet was unseemly. So he threw out the butchers and blacksmiths and installed 41 goldsmiths and eight jewelers. The bridge has been devoted solely to these two trades ever since.

SAN LORENZO TO THE ACCADEMIA

A sculptor, painter, architect, and even a poet, Florentine native son Michelangelo was a consummate genius, and some of his finest creations remain in his hometown. The Biblioteca Medicea Laurenziana is perhaps his most fanciful work of architecture. A key to understanding Michelangelo's genius can be found in the magnificent Cappelle Medicee, where both his sculptural and architectural prowess can be clearly seen. Planned frescoes were never completed, sadly, for they would have shown in one space the artistic triple threat that he certainly was. The towering yet graceful *David,* his most famous work, resides in the Galleria dell'Accademia.

After visiting San Lorenzo, resist the temptation to explore the market that surrounds the church. You can always come back later, after the churches and museums have closed; the market is open until 7 PM. Note that the Museo di San Marco closes at 1:50 on weekdays.

EXPLORING SAN LORENZO TO THE ACCADEMIA

❷ **Cappelle Medicee** *(Medici Chapels).* This magnificent complex includes the **Cappella dei Principi,** the Medici chapel and mausoleum that was begun in 1605 and kept marble workers busy for several hundred years, and the **Sagrestia Nuova** (New Sacristy), designed by Michelangelo and so called to distinguish it from Brunelleschi's Sagrestia Vecchia (Old Sacristy) in San Lorenzo.

Michelangelo received the commission for the New Sacristy in 1520 from Cardinal Giulio de' Medici (1478–1534), who later became Pope Clement VII and who wanted a new burial chapel for his cousins Giuliano (1478–1534) and Lorenzo (1492–1519). The result was a tour de force of architecture and sculpture. Architecturally, Michelangelo was as original and inventive here as ever, but it is, quite properly, the powerful sculptural compositions of the sidewall tombs that dominate the room. ✉ *Piazza di Madonna degli Aldobrandini, San Lorenzo* ☎ *055/294883 reservations* 💶 *€6* 🕐 *Daily 8:15–4:50. Closed 1st, 3rd, and 5th Mon. and 2nd and 4th Sun. of month.*

10

❺ **Galleria dell'Accademia** *(Accademia Gallery).* The collection of Florentine paintings, dating from the 13th to the 18th centuries, is largely
★ unremarkable, but the sculptures by Michelangelo are worth the price of admission. The unfinished *Slaves,* fighting their way out of their marble prisons, were meant for the tomb of Michelangelo's overly demanding patron Pope Julius II (1443–1513). But the focal point is the original *David,* moved here from Piazza della Signoria in 1873. *David* was commissioned in 1501 by the Opera del Duomo (Cathedral

Works Committee), which gave the 26-year-old sculptor a leftover block of marble that had been ruined by another artist. Michelangelo's success with the block was so dramatic that the city showered him with honors, and the Opera del Duomo voted to build him a house and a studio in which to live and work.

> **WORD OF MOUTH**
>
> "Seeing *David* is a must. It is one of those magical moments in life."
> —JandaO

Today *David* is beset not by Goliath but by tourists, and seeing the statue at all—much less really studying it—can be a trial. Save yourself a long and tiresome wait in line by reserving tickets in advance. ⊠ *Via Ricasoli 60, San Marco* ☎ *055/294883 reservations, 055/2388609 gallery* 🖩 *€6.50, reservation fee €3* ⊙ *Tues.–Sun. 8:15–6:50.*

❹ Museo di San Marco. A former Dominican convent adjacent to the church of San Marco now houses this museum, which contains many stunning works by Fra Angelico (circa 1400–55), the Dominican friar famous for his piety as well as for his painting. When the friars' cells were restructured between 1439 and 1444, he decorated many of them with frescoes meant to spur religious contemplation. His unostentatious and direct paintings exalt the simple beauties of the contemplative life. Fra Angelico's works are everywhere, from the friars' cells to the superb panel paintings on view in the museum. ⊠ *Piazza San Marco 1* ☎ *055/2388608* 🖩 *€4* ⊙ *Weekdays 8:15–1:50, weekends 8:15–6:50. Closed 1st, 3rd, and 5th Sun., and 2nd and 4th Mon. of month.*

❸ San Lorenzo. Filippo Brunelleschi designed this basilica, as well as that of Santo Spirito in the Oltrarno, in the early 15th century. He never lived to see either finished. The two interiors are similar in design and effect and proclaim with ringing clarity the beginning of the Renaissance in architecture. San Lorenzo, however, has a grid of dark, inlaid marble lines on the floor, which considerably heightens the dramatic effect. ⊠ *Piazza San Lorenzo* ☎ *055/2645144* 🖩 *€2.50* ⊙ *Mon.–Sat. 10–5; Mar.–Oct., Sun. 1:30–5. Closed Sun. Nov.–Feb.*

SANTA MARIA NOVELLA TO THE ARNO

Piazza Santa Maria Novella, near the train station, suffers a degree of squalor, especially at night. Nevertheless, the streets in and around the piazza have their share of architectural treasures, including some of Florence's most tasteful palaces. Between Santa Maria Novella and the Arno is Via Tornabuoni, Florence's finest shopping street.

EXPLORING SANTA MARIA NOVELLA TO THE ARNO

❶ Santa Maria Novella. The facade of this church looks distinctly clumsy by later Renaissance standards, and with good reason: it is an architectural hybrid. The lower half was completed mostly in the 14th century; its pointed-arch niches and decorative marble patterns reflect the Gothic style of the day. About 100 years later (around 1456), architect Leon Battista Alberti was called in to complete the job. The marble decoration

Continued on page 555

WHO'S WHO IN RENAISSANCE ART

Michelangelo. Leonardo da Vinci. Raphael. This heady triumvirate of the Italian Renaissance is synonymous with artistic genius. Yet they are only three of the remarkable cast of characters whose work defines the Renaissance, that extraordinary flourishing of art and culture in Italy, especially in Florence, as the Middle Ages drew to a close. The artists were visionaries, who redefined painting, sculpture, architecture, and even what it means to be an artist.

THE PIONEER. In the mid-14th century, a few artists began to move away the flat, two-dimensional painting of the Middle Ages. **Giotto**, who painted seemingly three-dimensional figures who show emotion, had a major impact on the artists of the next century.

THE GROUNDBREAKERS. The generations of **Brunelleschi** and **Botticelli** took center stage in the 15th century. **Ghiberti, Masaccio, Donatello, Uccello, Fra Angelico,** and **Filippo Lippi** were other major players. Part of the Renaissance (or "re-birth") was a renewed interest in classical sources—the texts, monuments, and sculpture of Ancient Greece and Rome. Perspective and the illusion of three-dimensional space in painting was another discovery of this era, known as the Early Renaissance. Suddenly the art appearing on the walls looked real, or more realistic than it used to.

Roman ruins were not the only thing to inspire these artists. There was an incredible exchange of ideas going on. In Santa Maria del Carmine, Filippo Lippi was inspired by the work of Masaccio, who in turn was a friend of Brunelleschi. Young artists also learned from the masters via the apprentice system. Ghiberti's workshop (*bottega* in Italian) included, at one time or another, Donatello, Masaccio, and Uccello. Botticelli was apprenticed to Filippo Lippi.

THE BIG THREE. The mathematical rationality and precision of 15th-century art gave way to what is known as the High Renaissance. **Leonardo, Michelangelo,** and **Raphael** were much more concerned with portraying the body in all its glory and with achieving harmony and grandeur in their work. Oil paint, used infrequently up until this time, became more widely employed: as a result, Leonardo's colors are deeper, more sensual, more alive. For one brief period, all three were in Florence at the same time. Michelangelo and Leonardo surely knew one another, as they were simultaneously working on frescoes (never completed) inside Palazzo Vecchio.

When Michelangelo left Florence for Rome in 1508, he began the slow drain of artistic exodus from Florence, which never really recovered her previous glory.

 10

A RENAISSANCE TIMELINE

IN THE WORLD

Black Death in Europe kills one third of the population, 1347-50.

Joan of Arc burned at the stake, 1431.

IN FLORENCE

Founding of the Medici bank, 1397.

Medici family made official papal bankers.

1434, Cosimo il Vecchio becomes de facto ruler of Florence. The Medici family will dominate the city until 1494.

Dante, a native of Florence, writes *The Divine Comedy*, 1302-21.

1300

1400

IN ART

EARLY RENAISSANCE

Masaccio and Masolino fresco Santa Maria del Carmine, 1424-28.

GIOTTO (ca. 1267-1337)

BRUNELLESCHI (1377-1446)

LORENZO GHIBERTI (ca. 1381-1455)

DONATELLO (ca. 1386-1466)

PAOLO UCCELLO (1397-1475)

FRA ANGELICO (ca. 1400-1455)

MASACCIO (1401-1428)

FILIPPO LIPPI (ca. 1406-1469)

Giotto fresoes in Santa Croce, 1320-25.

1334, 67-year-old Giotto is appointed chief architect of Santa Maria del Fiore, Florence's Duomo (below). He begins to work on the Campanile, which will be completed in 1359, after his death.

Donatello sculpts his bronze *David*, ca. 1440.

Fra Angelico frescoes friars' cells in San Marco, ca. 1438-45.

Ghiberti wins the competition for the Baptistery doors (above) in Florence, 1401.

Uccello's *Sir John Hawkwood*, ca. 1436.

Brunelleschi wins the competition for the Duomo's cupola (right), 1418.

Gutenberg Bible
is printed, 1455.

Columbus discovers
America, 1492.

▼ Martin Luther posts his 95 theses on
the door at Wittenberg, kicking off the
Protestant Reformation, 1517.

Constantinople falls
to the Turks, 1453.

Machiavelli's *Prince*
appears, 1513.

▼ Copernicus proves that
the earth is not the center
of the universe, 1530-43.

Lorenzo "il Magnifico"
(right), the Medici
patron of the arts, rules
in Florence, 1449-92.

Two Medici popes Leo X
(1513-21) and Clement
VII (1523-34) in Rome.

Catherine de'Medici
becomes Queen of
France, 1547.

1450   **1500**   **1550**

HIGH RENAISSANCE   MANNERISM

Fra Filippo Lippi's
*Madonna and
Child*, ca. 1452.

1508, Raphael begins
work on the chambers
in the Vatican, Rome.

▼ 1504, Michelangelo's
David is put on
display in Piazza
della Signoria,
where it remains
until 1873.

Giorgio
Vasari
publishes
his first
edition of
*Lives of
the Artists,*
1550.

Botticelli paints the
Birth of Venus, ca.
1482.

Michelangelo
begins to fresco
the Sistine Chapel
ceiling, 1508.

BOTTICELLI (ca. 1444-1510)

LEONARDO DA VINCI (1452-1519)

RAPHAEL (1483-1520)

MICHELANGELO (1475-1564)

Leonardo paints *The Last Supper* in Milan,
1495-98.

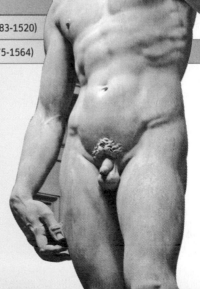

Giotto's *Nativity*

Donatello's *St. John the Baptist*

Ghiberti's *Gates of Paradise*

GIOTTO (CA. 1267-1337)
Painter/architect from a small town north of Florence.

He unequivocally set Italian painting on the course that led to the triumphs of the Renaissance masters. Unlike the rather flat, two-dimensional forms found in then prevailing Byzantine art, Giotto's figures have a fresh, life-like quality. The people in his paintings have bulk, and they show emotion, which you can see on their faces and in their gestures. This was something new in the late Middle Ages. Without Giotto, there wouldn't have been a Raphael.

In Florence: **Santa Croce; Uffizi; Campanile; Santa Maria Novella**

Elsewhere in Italy: **Scrovegni Chapel, Padua; Vatican Museums, Rome**

FILIPPO BRUNELLESCHI (1377-1446)
Architect/engineer from Florence.

If Brunelleschi had beaten Ghiberti in the Baptistery doors competition in Florence, the city's Duomo most likely would not have the striking appearance and authority that it has today. After his loss, he sulked off to Rome, where he studied the ancient Roman structures first-hand. Brunelleschi figured out how to vault the Duomo's dome, a structure unprecedented in its colossal size and great height. His Ospedale degli Innocenti employs classical elements in the creation of a stunning, new architectural statement; it is the first truly Renaissance structure.

In Florence: **Duomo; Ospedale degli Innocenti; San Lorenzo; Santo Spirito; Baptistery Doors Competition Entry, Bargello; Santa Croce**

LORENZO GHIBERTI (CA. 1381-1455)
Sculptor from Florence.

Ghiberti won a competition—besting his chief rival, Brunelleschi—to cast the gilded bronze North Doors of the Baptistery in Florence. These doors, and the East Doors that he subsequently executed, took up the next 50 years of his life. He created intricately worked figures that are more true-to-life than any since antiquity, and he was one of the first Renaissance sculptors to work in bronze. Ghiberti taught the next generation of artists; Donatello, Uccello, and Masaccio all passed through his studio.

In Florence: **Door Copies, Baptistery; Original Doors, Museo dell'Opera del Duomo; Baptistry Door Competition Entry, Bargello; Orsanmichele**

DONATELLO (CA. 1386-1466)
Sculptor from Florence.

Donatello was an innovator who, like his good friend Brunelleschi, spent most of his long life in Florence. Consumed with the science of optics, he used light and shadow to create the effects of nearness and distance. He made an essentially flat slab look like a three- dimensional scene. His bronze *David* is probably the first free-standing male nude since antiquity. Not only technically brilliant, his work is also emotionally resonant; few sculptors are as expressive.

In Florence: ***David*, Bargello; *St. Mark*, Orsanmichele; Palazzo Vecchio; Museo dell'Opera del Duomo; San Lorenzo; Santa Croce**

Elsewhere in Italy: **Padua; Prato; Venice**

Fra Angelico's *The Deposition*   Masaccio's *Trinity*   Filippo Lippi's *Madonna and Child*

PAOLO UCCELLO (1397-1475)
Painter from Florence.
Renaissance chronicler Vasari once observed that had Uccello not been so obsessed with the mathematical problems posed by perspective, he would have been a very good painter. The struggle to master single-point perspective and to render motion in two dimensions is nowhere more apparent than in his battle scenes. His first major commission in Florence was the gargantuan fresco of the English mercenary Sir John Hawkwood (the Italians called him Giovanni Acuto) in Florence's Duomo.
In Florence: *Sir John Hawkwood*, Duomo; *Battle of San Romano*, Uffizi; Santa Maria Novella
Elsewhere in Italy: **Urbino**

FRA ANGELICO (CA. 1400-1455)
Painter from a small town north of Florence.
A Dominican friar, who eventually made his way to the convent of San Marco, Fra Angelico and his assistants painted frescoes for aid in prayer and meditation. He was known for his piety; Vasari wrote that Fra Angelico could never paint a crucifix without a tear running down his face. Perhaps no other painter so successfully translated the mysteries of faith and the sacred into painting. And yet his figures emote, his command of perspective is superb, and his use of color startles even today.
In Florence: **Museo di San Marco; Uffizi**
Elsewhere in Italy: **Vatican Museums, Rome; Fiesole; Cortona; Perugia; Orvieto**

MASACCIO (1401-1428)
Painter from San Giovanni Valdarno, southeast of Florence.
Masaccio and Masolino, a frequent collaborator, worked most famously together at Santa Maria del Carmine. Their frescoes of the life of St. Peter use light to mold figures in the painting by imitating the way light falls on figures in real life. Masaccio also pioneered the use of single-point perspective, masterfully rendered in his *Trinity*. His friend Brunelleschi probably introduced him to the technique, yet another step forward in rendering things the way the eye sees them. Masaccio died young and under mysterious circumstances.
In Florence: **Santa Maria del Carmine; *Trinity*, Santa Maria Novella**

FILIPPO LIPPI (CA. 1406-1469)
Painter from Prato.
At a young age, Filippo Lippi entered the friary of Santa Maria del Carmine, where he was highly influenced by Masaccio and Masolino's frescoes. His religious vows appear to have made less of an impact; his affair with a young nun produced a son, Filippino (Little Philip, who later apprenticed with Botticelli), and a daughter. His religious paintings often have a playful, humorous note; some of his angels are downright impish and look directly out at the viewer. Lippi links the earlier painters of the 15th century with those who follow; Botticelli apprenticed with him.
In Florence: **Uffizi; Palazzo Medici Riccardi; San Lorenzo; Palazzo Pitti**
Elsewhere in Italy: **Prato**

Botticelli's *Primavera*

Leonardo's *Portrait of a Young Woman*

Raphael's *Madonna on the Meadow*

BOTTICELLI (CA. 1444-1510)
Painter from Florence.

Botticelli's work is characterized by stunning, elongated blondes, cherubic angels (something he undoubtedly learned from his time with Filippo Lippi), and tender Christs. Though he did many religious paintings, he also painted monumental, nonreligious panels—his *Birth of Venus* and *Primavera* being the two most famous of these. A brief sojourn took him to Rome, where he and a number of other artists frescoed the Sistine Chapel walls.

In Florence: ***Birth of Venus, Primavera,*** **Uffizi; Palazzo Pitti**

Elsewhere in Italy: **Vatican Museums, Rome**

LEONARDO DA VINCI (1452-1519)
Painter/sculptor/engineer from Anchiano, a small town outside Vinci.

Leonardo never lingered long in any place; his restless nature and his international reputation led to commissions throughout Italy, and took him to Milan, Vigevano, Pavia, Rome, and, ultimately, France. Though he is most famous for his mysterious *Mona Lisa* (at the Louvre in Paris), he painted other penetrating, psychological portraits in addition to his scientific experiments: his design for a flying machine (never built) predates Kitty Hawk by nearly 500 years. The greatest collection of Leonardo's work in Italy can be seen on one wall in the Uffizi.

In Florence: ***Adoration of the Magi,*** **Uffizi**

Elsewhere in Italy: ***Last Supper,*** **Santa Maria delle Grazie, Milan**

RAPHAEL (1483-1520)
Painter/architect from Urbino.

Raphael spent only four highly productive years of his short life in Florence, where he turned out made-to-order paintings of the Madonna and Child for a hungry public; he also executed a number of portraits of Florentine aristocrats. Perhaps no other artist had such a fine command of line and color, and could render it, seemingly effortlessly, in paint. His painting acquired new authority after he came up against Michelangelo toiling away on the Sistine ceiling. Raphael worked nearly next door in the Vatican, where his figures take on an epic, Michelangelesque scale.

In Florence: **Uffizi; Palazzo Pitti**

Elsewhere in Italy: **Vatican Museums, Rome**

MICHELANGELO (1475-1564)
Painter/sculptor/architect from Caprese.

Although Florentine and proud of it (he famously signed his St. Peter's *Pietà* to avoid confusion about where he was from), he spent most of his 90 years outside his native city. He painted and sculpted the male body on an epic scale and glorified it while doing so. Though he complained throughout the proceedings that he was really a sculptor, Michelangelo's Sistine Chapel ceiling is arguably the greatest fresco cycle ever painted (and the massive figures owe no small debt to Giotto).

In Florence: ***David,*** **Galleria dell'Accademia; Uffizi; Casa Buonarroti; Bargello**

Elsewhere in Italy: **St. Peter's Basilica, Vatican Museums, and Piazza del Campidoglio in Rome** of his upper story clearly defers to the already existing work below, but the architectural motifs he added evince an entirely different style. The central doorway, the four ground-floor half-columns with Corinthian capitals, the triangular pediment atop the second story, the inscribed frieze immediately below the pediment—these are borrowings from antiquity, and they reflect the new Renaissance style in architecture.

Inside, of special interest for its great historical importance and beauty is Masaccio's *Trinity,* on the left-hand wall, almost halfway down the nave. Painted around 1426–27 (at the same time he was working on his frescoes in Santa Maria del Carmine), it unequivocally announced the arrival of the Renaissance. The realism of the figure of Christ was revolutionary in itself, but what was probably even more startling to contemporary Florentines was the barrel vault in the background. The mathematical rules for employing perspective in painting had just been discovered (probably by Brunelleschi), and this was one of the first works of art to employ them with utterly convincing success.

In the cloisters of the **Museo di Santa Maria Novella** (⊠ *Piazza Santa Maria Novella 19* 🕾 *055/282187* 🎫 *€2.70* ⊗ *Mon.–Thurs. and Sat. 9–5, Sun. 9–2*), to the left of Santa Maria Novella, is a faded fresco cycle by Paolo Uccello depicting tales from Genesis, with a dramatic vision of the Deluge. Earlier and better-preserved frescoes painted in 1348–55 by Andrea da Firenze are in the chapter house, or the **Cappellone degli Spagnoli** (Spanish Chapel), off the cloister. 🕾 *055/210113* 🎫 *€2.50 for both museum and chapel* ⊗ *Mon.–Thurs. and Sat. 9–5, Sun. 9–2.*

SANTA CROCE

The Santa Croce quarter, on the southeast fringe of the historic center, was built up in the Middle Ages outside the second set of medieval city walls. The centerpiece of the neighborhood was the basilica of Santa Croce, which could hold great numbers of worshippers; the vast piazza could accommodate any overflow and also served as a fairground and, allegedly since the middle of the 16th century, as a playing field for no-holds-barred soccer games. A center of leatherworking since the Middle Ages, the neighborhood is still packed with leatherworkers and leather shops.

EXPLORING SANTA CROCE

⑩ Santa Croce. Like the Duomo, this church is Gothic, but, also like the
★ Duomo, its facade dates from the 19th century. As a burial place, the church probably contains more skeletons of Renaissance celebrities than any other in Italy. The tomb of Michelangelo is on the right at the front of the basilica; he is said to have chosen this spot so that the first thing he would see on Judgment Day, when the graves of the dead fly open, would be Brunelleschi's dome through Santa Croce's open doors. The tomb of Galileo Galilei (1564–1642) is on the left wall; he was not granted a Christian burial until 100 years after his death because of his controversial contention that Earth is not the center of the universe.

The collection of art within the complex is by far the most important of any church in Florence. The most famous works are probably the Giotto frescoes in the two chapels immediately to the right of the high altar. They illustrate scenes from the lives of St. John the Evangelist and St. John the Baptist (in the right-hand chapel) and scenes from the life of St. Francis (in the left-hand chapel). Time has not been kind to these frescoes; through the centuries, wall tombs were placed in the middle of them, they were whitewashed and plastered over, and in the 19th century they suffered a clumsy restoration. But the reality that Giotto introduced into painting can still be seen. He did not paint beautifully stylized religious icons, as the Byzantine style that preceded him prescribed; he instead painted drama—St. Francis surrounded by grieving friars at the very moment of his death. This was a radical shift in emphasis: before Giotto, painting's role was to symbolize the attributes of God; after him, it was to imitate life. ⊠ *Piazza Santa Croce 16* ☎ *055/2466105* 🖃 *€5 combined admission to church and museum* 🕙 *Mon.–Sat. 9:30–5:30, Sun. 1–5.*

THE OLTRARNO

A walk through the Oltrarno (literally "the other side of the Arno") takes in two very different aspects of Florence: the splendor of the Medici, manifest in the riches of the mammoth Palazzo Pitti and the gracious Giardino di Boboli; and the charm of the Oltrarno, a slightly gentrified but still fiercely proud working-class neighborhood with artisans' and antiques shops.

Farther east across the Arno, a series of ramps and stairs climbs to Piazzale Michelangelo, where the city lies before you in all its glory (skip this trip if it's a hazy day). More stairs (behind La Loggia restaurant) lead to the church of San Miniato al Monte. You can avoid the long walk by taking Bus 12 or 13 at the west end of Ponte alle Grazie and getting off at Piazzale Michelangelo; you still have to climb the monumental stairs to and from San Miniato, but you can then take the bus from Piazzale Michelangelo back to the center of town. If you decide to take a bus, remember to buy your ticket before you board.

EXPLORING THE OLTRARNO

🔟 **Palazzo Pitti.** This enormous palace is one of Florence's largest architectural set pieces. The original palazzo, built for the Pitti family around 1460, comprised only the main entrance and the three windows on either side. In 1549 the property was sold to the Medici, and Bartolomeo Ammannati was called in to make substantial additions. Although he apparently operated on the principle that more is better, he succeeded only in producing proof that more is just that: more.

Today the palace houses several museums: The **Museo degli Argenti** displays a vast collection of Medici household treasures. The **Galleria del Costume** showcases fashions from the past 300 years. The **Galleria d'Arte Moderna** holds a collection of 19th- and 20th-century paintings, mostly Tuscan. Most famous of the Pitti galleries is the **Galleria Palatina,** which contains a broad collection of paintings from the 15th to 17th centuries. The rooms of the Galleria Palatina remain much as the Medici left them. ⊠ *Piazza Pitti* ☎ *055/210323* ☒ *Galleria Palatina and Galleria d'Arte Moderna, combined ticket €8.50; Galleria del Costume, Giardino Bardini, Giardino di Boboli, Museo degli Argenti, and Museo Porcelleane, combined ticket €6* ۞ *Tues.–Sun. 8:15–6:50.*

WHERE TO EAT

Florence's popularity with tourists means that, unfortunately, there's a higher percentage of mediocre restaurants here than you'll find in most Italian towns. Some restaurant owners cut corners and let standards slip, knowing that a customer today is unlikely to return tomorrow, regardless of the quality of the meal. So, if you're looking to eat well, it pays to do some research, starting with the recommendations here—we promise there's not a tourist trap in the bunch.

Dining hours start at around 1 for lunch and 8 for dinner. Many of Florence's restaurants are small, so reservations are a must. You can sample such specialties as creamy *fegatini* (a chicken-liver spread) and *ribollita* (minestrone thickened with bread and beans and swirled with extra-virgin olive oil) in a bustling, convivial trattoria, where you share long wooden tables set with paper place mats, or in an upscale *ristorante* with linen tablecloths and napkins.

THE DUOMO TO THE PONTE VECCHIO

$–$$ ✕ **Frescobaldi Wine Bar.** This swanky establishment serves both lunch and dinner. The food is typically Tuscan with some flights of fancy, including *acciughe marinate* (marinated anchovies) and *affettati misti* (a selection of sliced, cured meats). There's a separate wine bar within the restaurant called Frescobaldino. ⊠ *Via de' Magazzini 2–4/r, Piazza della Signoria* ☎ *055/284724* ▭ *MC, V* ۞ *Closed Sun. No lunch Mon.*

SAN LORENZO

$ ✕ **Mario.** Florentines flock to this narrow family-run trattoria near San
★   Lorenzo to feast on Tuscan favorites served at simple tables under a wooden ceiling dating from 1536. A distinct cafeteria feel and genuine Florentine hospitality prevail: you'll be seated wherever there's room, which often means with strangers. Yes, there's a bit of extra oil in most dishes, which imparts calories as well as taste, but aren't you on vacation in Italy? Worth the splurge is *riso al ragù* (rice with ground beef and tomatoes). ⊠ *Via Rosina 2/r, corner of Piazza del Mercato Centrale, San Lorenzo* ☎ *055/218550* ⌕ *Reservations not accepted* ▭ *No credit cards* ۞ *Closed Sun. and Aug. No dinner.*

$$$–$$$$ ✕ **Taverna del Bronzino.** Want to have a sophisticated meal in a 16th-
Fodor's Choice   century Renaissance artist's studio? The former studio of Santi di Tito,
★   a student of Bronzino's, has a simple, formal decor, with white tablecloths and place settings. The classic, dramatically presented Tuscan food is superb, and the solid, afforable wine list rounds out the menu. The service is outstanding. Reservations are advised, especially for eating at the wine cellar's only table. ⊠ *Via delle Ruote 25/r, San Marco* ☎ *055/495220* ▭ *AE, DC, MC, V* ۞ *Closed Sun. and 3 wks in Aug.*

10

SANTA MARIA NOVELLA TO THE ARNO

$$$ ✕ Il Latini. It may be the noisiest, most crowded trattoria in Florence, but it's also one of the most fun. The genial host, Torello ("little bull") Latini, presides over his four big dining rooms, and somehow it feels as if you're dining in his home. Ample portions of *ribollita* prepare the palate for the hearty meat dishes that follow. Both Florentines and tourists alike tuck into the *agnello fritto* (fried lamb) with aplomb. Though reservations are advised, there's always a wait anyway. ⊠ *Via dei Palchetti 6/r, Santa Maria Novella* ☎*055/210916* ⊟*AE, DC, MC, V* ⊘ *Closed Mon. and 15 days at Christmas.*

SANTA CROCE

¢   ✕ All'Antico Vinaio. Florentines like to grab a quick bite to eat at this narrow little sandwich shop near the Uffizi. A handful of stools offer a place to perch while chowing down on one of their very fine sandwiches; most folks, however, simply grab a sandwich, pour themselves a glass of inexpensive wine in a paper cup (more serious wines can be poured into glasses) and mingle on the pedestrians-only street in front. If *porchetta* (a very rich, deliciously fatty roasted pork) is on offer, don't miss it. They also offer first-rate primi, which change daily. ⊠ *Via de' Neri 65, Santa Croce* ☎*No phone* ⊟*No credit cards* ⊘ *Closed Sun.*

$$ ✕ Baldovino. David and Catherine Gardner, expat Scots, have created this lively, brightly colored restaurant down the street from the church of Santa Croce. From its humble beginnings as a pizzeria, it has evolved into something more. It's a happy thing that pizza is still on the menu, but now it shares billing with sophisticated primi and secondi. The menu changes monthly and has such treats as *filetto di manzo alla Bernaise* (filet mignon with light béarnaise sauce). Baldovino also serves pasta dishes and grilled meat until the wee hours. ⊠ *Via San Giuseppe 22/r, Santa Croce* ☎*055/241773* ⊟*MC, V.*

$$$$ ✕ Cibrèo. The food at this upscale trattoria is fantastic, from the creamy
Fodor's Choice   crostini *di fegatini* (a savory chicken-liver spread) to the melt-in-your-
★   mouth desserts. Many Florentines hail this as the city's best restaurant, and Fodor's readers tend to agree—though some take issue with the prices and complain of long waits for a table (even with a reservation). If you thought you'd never try tripe—let alone like it—this is the place to lay any doubts to rest: the *trippa in insalata* (cold tripe salad) with parsley and garlic is an epiphany. The food is traditionally Tuscan, impeccably served by a staff that's multilingual—which is a good thing, because there are no written menus. Around the corner is Cibreino, Cibrèo's budget version, with a shorter menu and a no-reservations policy. ⊠ *Via A. del Verrocchio 8/r, Santa Croce* ☎*055/2341100* ⌖*Reservations essential* ⊟*AE, DC, MC, V* ⊘ *Closed Sun. and Mon. and July 25–Sept. 5.*

¢   ✕ da Rocco. At one of Florence's biggest markets you can grab lunch to go, or you could cram yourself into one of the booths and pour from the straw-cloaked flask (wine here is *da consumo,* which means they charge you for how much you drink). Food is abundant, Tuscan, and fast; locals pack in. The menu changes daily, and the prices are great. ⊠ *In Mercato Sant'Ambrogio, Piazza Ghiberti, Santa Croce* ☎*No phone* ⌖*Reservations not accepted* ⊟*No credit cards* ⊘ *Closed Sun. No dinner.*

$$$ ✕**La Giostra.** This clubby spot, whose name means "carousel" in Ital-
★   ian, is owned and run by Prince Dimitri Kunz d'Asburgo Lorena, and
his way with mushrooms is as remarkable as his charm. The unusually
good pastas may require explanation from Soldano, one of the prince's
good-looking twin sons. In perfect English he'll describe a favorite dish,
taglierini con tartufo bianco, a decadently rich pasta with white truffles.
Leave room for dessert: this might be the only show in town with a
sublime tiramisu *and* a wonderfully gooey Sacher torte. ✉ *Borgo Pinti
12/r, Santa Croce* ☎*055/241341* ▭*AE, DC, MC, V.*

$$ ✕**La Mucca sul Tetto.** The strangely named "Cow on the Roof" has an
equally odd, but pleasing, interior: anthracite-sponged walls adorned
with Moorish-style stencil work are bounded by 15th-century vaulting. The menu, which changes every few weeks, features Tuscan seasonal classics, as well as some unusual, tasty variations. Start with their
light-as-a-feather *coccoli* (fried, coin-size discs of dough) served with
stracchino (a soft, mild cheese) and prosciutto on the side. Meat lovers
should not miss the fried lamb chops, whose batter is laden with pista-
chios. The bilingual staff is happy to guide you through the well-culled
wine list, which caters to all budgets and all tastes. ✉ *Via Ghibellina
134/r, near Santa Croce* ☎*055/2344810* ▭*AE, DC, MC, V* ⊘*Closed
Sun. No lunch.*

$$-$$$ ✕**Osteria de'Benci.** A few minutes from Santa Croce, this charming oste-
ria serves some of the most eclectic food in Florence. Try the spaghetti
degli eretici (in tomato sauce with fresh herbs). The grilled meats are justifiably famous; the *carbonata* is a succulent piece of grilled beef served
rare. When it's warm, you can dine outside with a view of the 13th-cen-
tury tower belonging to the prestigious Alberti family. Right next door
is Osteria de'Benci Caffè (¢–$), serving selections from the menu from 8
AM to midnight. ✉ *Via de'Benci 11–13/r, Santa Croce* ☎*055/2344923*
▭*AE, DC, MC, V* ⊘*Closed Sun. and 2 wks in Aug.*

$$$$ ✕**Simon Boccanegra.** Florentine food cognoscenti flock to this place
named for a condottiere (mercenary) hero in a Verdi opera. Under
high ceilings, candles on every table cast a rosy glow; the fine wine list
and superb service make a meal here a true pleasure. The chef has a deft
hand with fish dishes, as well as an inventiveness when it comes to rein-
terpreting such classics as risotto with chicken liver—he adds leek and
saffron to give it a lift. Remember to save room for dessert. A less expensive, less formal wine bar serving a basic Tuscan menu is also on the
premises. ✉ *Via Ghibellina 124/r, Santa Croce* ☎*055/2001098* ⋒*Reservations essential* ▭*AE, DC, MC, V* ⊘*Closed Sun. No lunch.*

THE OLTRARNO

$$$ ✕**Beccofino.** Forget that the noise level here often reaches the pitch of
the Tower of Babel, and ignore the generic urban decor. Come here for
the food: chef Robbie Pepin, who's worked with such heavy hitters as
Gordon Ramsey and Alain Ducasse, has breathed life into this very cool
place. His cooking, while wholly Italian, has a crisp simplicity remi-
niscent of Japanese food. He can do just about everything, but shines
with fish and shellfish. He takes the Florentine classic gnudi and tops it
with prawns, calamari, and fresh tomatoes; it creates a beautiful blend
in your mouth. The menu changes frequently, the wine list is divine,

10

and service is exceptional. ✉ *Piazza Scarlatti 1/r, Lungarno South* ☎ *055/2790076* ⚱*Reservations essential* ▤*MC, V* ⊘*No lunch.*

$ ✗**La Casalinga.** *Casalinga* means "housewife," and this place has the nostalgic charm of a 1950s kitchen with Tuscan comfort food to match. If you eat *ribollita* anywhere in Florence, eat it here—it couldn't be more authentic. Mediocre paintings clutter the semipaneled walls, tables are set close together, and the place is usually jammed. The menu is long, portions are plentiful, and service is prompt and friendly. Save room for dessert: the lemon sorbet perfectly caps off the meal. ✉ *Via Michelozzi 9/r, Santo Spirito* ☎*055/218624* ▤*AE, DC, MC, V* ⊘*Closed Sun., 1 wk at Christmas, and 3 wks in Aug.*

$ ✗**Osteria Antica Mescita San Niccolò.** It's always crowded, always good, and always cheap. The osteria is next to the church of San Niccolò, and if you sit in the lower part you'll find yourself in what was once a chapel dating from the 11th century. The subtle but dramatic background is a nice complement to the food, which is simple Tuscan at its best. The *pollo con limone* is tasty pieces of chicken in a lemon-scented broth. In winter try the *spezzatino di cinghiale con aromi* (wild boar stew with herbs). Reservations are advised. ✉*Via San Niccolò 60/r, San Niccolò* ☎*055/2342836* ▤*AE, MC, V* ⊘*Closed Sun. and Aug.*

WHERE TO STAY

No stranger to visitors, Florence is equipped with hotels for all budgets; for instance, you can find both budget and luxury hotels in the *centro storico* (historic center) and along the Arno. Florence has so many famous landmarks that it's not hard to find lodging with a panoramic vista. The equivalent of the genteel *pensioni* of yesteryear still exist, though they are now officially classified as hotels. Generally small and intimate, they often have a quaint appeal that usually doesn't preclude modern plumbing.

Florence's importance not only as a tourist city but as a convention center and the site of the Pitti fashion collections guarantees a variety of accommodations. The high demand also means that, except in winter, reservations are a must. If you find yourself in Florence with no reservations, go to **Consorzio ITA** (✉*Stazione Centrale, Santa Maria Novella* ☎*055/282893*). You must go there in person to make a booking.

THE DUOMO TO THE ARNO

$$$$ ⊞ **Hotel Helvetia and Bristol.** Painstaking care has gone into making this hotel one of the prettiest and most intimate in town. It has the extra plus of being in the center of the centro storico, making it a luxurious base from which to explore the city. From the cozy yet sophisticated lobby with its stone columns to the guest rooms decorated with prints, you might feel as if you're a guest in a sophisticated manor house. The restaurant serves sumptuous fare in a romantic setting. **Pros:** central location; superb staff. **Cons:** rooms facing the street get some noise. ✉ *Via dei Pescioni 2, Piazza della Repubblica* ☎*055/26651* ☒*055/288353* ⊕*www.hbf.royaldemeure.com* ⤷*54 rooms, 13 suites* ⚿*In-room: safe, refrigerator, VCR, Wi-Fi. In-hotel: restaurant, room service, bar, con-*

cierge, laundry service, parking (fee), some pets allowed ⊟*AE, DC, MC, V* ⏚*EP.*

$$-$$$
Fodor'sChoice
★
⛶ **In Piazza della Signoria.** Proprietors Alessandro and Sonia Pini want you to use their house—in this case, part of a 15th-century palazzo—as if it were your own. Such warm sentiments extend to the cozy feeling created in the rooms, all of which are uniquely decorated and lovingly furnished; some have sweeping damask curtains, others fanciful frescoes in the bathroom. **Pros:** marvelous staff; tasty breakfast with a view of Piazza della Signoria. **Cons:** short flight of stairs to reach elevator. ⊠ *Via dei Magazzini 2, near Piazza della Signoria* ☎*055/2399546* ⊕*www. inpiazzadellasignoria.com* ⇗*10 rooms, 3 apartments* ⌂*In-room: safe, kitchen (some), refrigerator (some), Wi-Fi. In hotel: laundry service, public Internet, parking (fee)* ⊟*AE, DC, MC, V* ⏚*BP.*

SAN LORENZO

$
★
⛶ **Residenza Johanna I.** Savvy travelers and those on a budget should look no farther, as this *residenza* is a tremendous value for quality and location. Though it's very much in the centro storico, the place is rather homey. You're given a large set of keys to let yourself into the building after 7 PM, when the staff goes home. Simple rooms have high ceilings and pale pastel floral prints. Morning tea and coffee (but no breakfast) are served in your room. **Pros:** great value. **Cons:** staff goes home at 7; no credit cards. ⊠ *Via Bonifacio Lupi 14, San Marco* ☎*055/481896* 🖷*055/482721* ⊕*www.johanna.it* ⇗*11 rooms* ⌂*In-room: no a/c, no phone, no TV. In-hotel: parking (fee)* ⊟*No credit cards* ⏚*EP.*

SANTA MARIA NOVELLA TO THE ARNO

$-$$
⛶ **Alessandra.** The location, a block from the Ponte Vecchio, and the clean, ample rooms make this a good choice. The building, known as the Palazzo Roselli del Turco, was designed in 1507 by Baccio d'Agnolo, a contemporary of Michelangelo. Though little remains of the original design save for the high wood ceilings, there's still an aura of grandeur. Friendly hosts Anna and Andrea Gennarini speak fluent English. **Pros:** several rooms have views of the Arno; the spacious suite is a bargain. **Cons:** stairs to elevator; some rooms share bath. ⊠ *Borgo Santi Apostoli 17, Santa Maria Novella* ☎*055/283438* 🖷*055/210619* ⊕*www. hotelalessandra.com* ⇗*26 rooms, 19 with bath; 1 suite; 1 apartment* ⌂*In-room: safe, refrigerator, dial-up, Wi-Fi. In-hotel: laundry service, parking (fee)* ⊟*AE, MC, V* ⊘*Closed Dec. 10–26* ⏚*BP.*

$$$
⛶ **Beacci Tornabuoni.** Florentine pensioni don't get any classier than this. It has old-fashioned style and enough modern comfort to keep you happy, and it's in a 14th-century palazzo. The sitting room has a large fireplace, the terrace has a tremendous view of some major Florentine monuments, and the wallpapered rooms are inviting. On Monday, Wednesday, and Friday nights from May through October, the dining room opens, serving Tuscan specialties. **Pros:** multilingual staff; flower-filled terrace. **Cons:** Fodor's readers advise to request rooms away from reception area, which can be noisy. ⊠ *Via Tornabuoni 3, Santa Maria Novella* ☎*055/212645* 🖷*055/283594* ⊕*www.tornabuonihotels.com* ⇗*28 rooms* ⌂*In-room: refrigerator. In- hotel: restaurant, bar, laundry*

10

service, *public Internet, parking (fee), some pets allowed* ⊟*AE, DC, MC, V* ⦿⏐*BP.*

$$$$ ⊞**JK Place.** Ori Kafri, the manager of this boutique hotel, refers to
Fodor's Choice it as a house, and indeed it is a sumptuously appointed home away
★ from home. A library serves as the reception room; buffet breakfast
is laid out on a gleaming chestnut table in an interior atrium. Soothing earth tones prevail in the rooms, some of which have chandeliers,
others canopied beds. A secluded rooftop terrace makes a perfect setting for an aperitivo, as do the ground-floor sitting rooms with large,
pillow-piled couches. The place is favored by young fashionistas, their
entourages, and other beautiful people. **Pros:** intimate feel; stellar staff.
Cons: breakfast at a shared table. ⊠*Piazza Santa Maria Novella 7*
☎*055/2645181* 🖷*055/2658387* ⊕*www.jkplace.com* ⇆*14 doubles,
6 suites* 🖧*In-room: safe, refrigerator, VCR, dial-up, Wi-Fi. In-hotel:
bar, concierge, laundry service, parking (fee), some pets allowed* ⊟*AE,
DC, MC, V* ⦿⏐*BP.*

$$ ⊞**Torre Guelfa.** If you want to get a taste of medieval Florence, try this
hotel hidden within a former 13th-century tower. The Torre Guelfa once
protected the obscenely wealthy Acciaiuoli family; now it's one of the
best small hotels in the center of Florence. Each guest room is differ-
ent, some with canopied beds, some with balconies. Those on a budget
might consider one of the six less expensive rooms on the second floor,
which are comparable to the rest of the rooms but have no TV. **Pros:**
wonderful staff; some family-friendly triple rooms. **Cons:** stairs to eleva-
tor. ⊠*Borgo Santi Apostoli 8, Santa Maria Novella* ☎*055/2396338*
🖷*055/2398577* ⊕*www.hoteltorreguelfa.com* ⇆*24 rooms, 2 suites*
🖧*In-room: safe (some), no TV (some). In-hotel: laundry service, public
Wi-Fi, parking (fee), some pets allowed* ⊟*AE, MC, V* ⦿⏐*BP.*

SANTA CROCE

¢ ⊞**Istituto Oblate dell'Assunzione.** Twelve nuns run this convent, which is
minutes from the Duomo. Rooms are spotlessly clean and simple; some
of them have views of the cupola, and others look out onto a carefully
tended garden where you are welcome to relax. Several rooms have
three and four beds, making them well suited for families. Curfew is at
11:30 PM. You can join mass every morning at 7:30. For an additional
three euros, you can get a simple continental breakfast, and the nuns
provide half or full pension for groups of 10 or more. None of the nuns
speak English, and they don't have a Web presence, so unless you speak
Italian, the best way to book is by fax. **Pros:** bargain price. **Cons:** cur-
few, no credit cards. ⊠*Borgo Pinti 15, Santa Croce* ☎*055/2480582*
🖷*055/2346291* ⇆*28 rooms, 22 with bath* 🖧*In-room: no a/c (some),
no phone, no TV. In-hotel: parking (fee)* ⊟*No credit cards* ⦿⏐*EP.*

$$$$ ⊞**Monna Lisa.** Housed in a 15th-century palazzo, with parts of the
building dating from the 13th century, this hotel retains some of its
original wood-coffered ceilings from the 1500s, as well as its original
marble staircase. Though some rooms are small, they are tasteful, and
each is done in different floral wallpaper. The public rooms retain a
19th-century aura, and the intimate bar, with its red velveteen wallpa-
per, is a good place to unwind. **Pros:** annex is wheelchair accessible.
Cons: rooms in annex are much less charming than those in palazzo.

⊠*Borgo Pinti 27, Santa Croce* ☎*055/2479751* 🖴*055/2479755* ⊕*www.monnalisa.it* ⮐*45 rooms* ♿*In-room: safe, refrigerator. In-hotel: bar, concierge, laundry service, parking (fee), some pets allowed* ▭*AE, DC, MC, V* ⦿*BP.*

$$-$$$ 🔟 **Morandi alla Crocetta.** You're made to feel like privileged friends of the family at this charming and distinguished residence near Piazza Santissima Annunziata. The former convent is close to the sights but very quiet, and it's furnished comfortably in the classic style of a gracious Florentine home. One room retains original 17th-century fresco fragments, and two others have small private terraces. The Morandi is not only an exceptional hotel but also a good value. It's very small, so book well in advance. **Pros:** interesting, offbeat location; terrific staff. **Cons:** extra charge for breakfast; two flights of stairs to reach reception and rooms. ⊠*Via Laura 50, Santissima Annunziata* ☎*055/2344747* 🖴*055/2480954* ⊕*www.hotelmorandi.it* ⮐*10 rooms* ♿*In-room: safe, refrigerator, dial-up, Wi-Fi. In-hotel: no elevator, concierge, laundry service, parking (fee), some pets allowed* ▭*AE, DC, MC, V* ⦿*EP.*

SHOPPING

Window-shopping in Florence is like visiting an enormous contemporary-art gallery. Many of today's greatest Italian artists are fashion designers, and most keep shops in Florence. Discerning shoppers may find bargains in the street markets. ■ **TIP→ Do not buy any knockoff goods from any of the hawkers plying their fake Prada (or any other high-end designer) on the streets.** It's illegal, and fines are astronomical if the police happen to catch you. (You pay the fine, not the vendor.)

Shops are generally open 9 to 1 and 3:30 to 7:30 and are closed Sunday and Monday mornings most of the year. Summer (June to September) hours are usually 9 to 1 and 4 to 8, and some shops close Saturday afternoon instead of Monday morning.

SHOPPING DISTRICTS

Florence's most fashionable shops are concentrated in the center of town. The fanciest designer shops are mainly on **Via Tornabuoni** and **Via della Vigna Nuova.** The city's largest concentrations of antiques shops are on **Borgo Ognissanti** and the Oltrarno's **Via Maggio.** The **Ponte Vecchio** houses reputable but very expensive jewelry shops, as it has since the 16th century. The area near **Santa Croce** is the heart of the leather merchants' district.

10

TUSCANY

Midway down the Italian peninsula, Tuscany (Toscana in Italian) is distinguished by rolling hills, snowcapped mountains, dramatic cypress trees, and miles of coastline on the Tyrrhenian Sea—which all adds up to gorgeous views at practically every turn. The beauty of the landscape proves a perfect foil for the region's abundance of superlative art and architecture. It also produces some of Italy's finest wines and olive oils. The combination of unforgettable art, sumptuous views, and eminently drinkable wines that pair beautifully with its simple food makes a trip to Tuscany something beyond special.

Many of Tuscany's cities and towns have retained the same fundamental character over the past 500 years. Civic rivalries that led to bloody battles centuries ago have given way to soccer rivalries. Renaissance pomp lives on in the celebration of local feast days and centuries-old traditions such as the Palio in Siena and the Giostra del Saracino (Joust of the Saracen) in Arezzo. Often, present-day Tuscans look as though they might have served as models for paintings produced hundreds of years ago. In many ways, the Renaissance still lives on in Tuscany.

PLANNING YOUR TIME

Tuscany isn't the place for a jam-packed itinerary. One of the greatest pleasures here is indulging in rustic hedonism, marked by long lunches and show-stopping sunsets. Whether by car, bike, or foot, you'll want to get out into the glorious landscape, but it's smart to keep your plans modest. Set a church or a hill town as your destination, knowing that half the pleasure is in getting there—admiring as you go the stately palaces, the tidy geometry of row upon row of grape vines, the fields vibrant with red poppies, sunflowers, and yellow broom.

You'll need to devise a Siena strategy. The place shouldn't be missed; it's compact enough that you can see the major sights on a day trip, and that's what many people do. Spend the night, and you'll get to see the town breathe a sigh and relax upon the day-trippers' departure. The flip side is, your favorite Tuscan hotel isn't likely to be in Siena.

You face similar issues with Pisa and Lucca in the northwest. Pisa's famous tower is worth seeing, but ultimately Lucca has greater charms, making it a better choice for an overnight.

GETTING HERE & AROUND

Driving is the only way (other than hiking or biking) to get to many of Tuscany's small towns and vineyards. The cities west of Florence are easily reached by the A11, which leads to Lucca and then to the sea. Florence and Siena are connected by a superstrada and also the panoramic SS222, which threads through Chianti.

The Florence–Siena Superstrada (no number) is a four-lane, divided road with exits onto smaller country roads. The Via Cassia (SR2) winds its way south from Florence to Siena, along the western edge of the Chianti region. The superstrada is more direct, but much less scenic, than the SR2, and it can have a lot of traffic, especially on Sunday evenings. The Strada Chiantigiana (SR222) cuts through the center of Chianti, to the east of the superstrada, in a curvaceous path past vineyards and countryside.

Trains on Italy's main north–south rail line stop in Florence. Another major line connects Florence with Pisa, and the coastal line between Rome and Genoa passes through Pisa as well. There's regular, nearly hourly service from Florence to Lucca, and several trips a day between Florence and Siena. Siena's train station is 2 km (1 mi) north of the centro storico, but cabs and city buses are readily available.

For other parts of Tuscany—Chianti for example—you are better off going by car. Stations, when they exist, are far from the historic centers, and service is infrequent.

VISITOR INFORMATION
The tourist information office in Greve is an excellent source for general information about the Chianti wine region and its hilltop towns. In Siena the centrally located tourist office, in Piazza del Campo, has information about Siena and its province. Both offices book hotel rooms for a nominal fee. Offices in smaller towns can also be a good place to check if you need last-minute accommodations.

Tourist bureaus in larger towns are typically open from 8:30 to 1 and 3:30 to 6 or 7; bureaus in villages are generally open from Easter until early November, but usually remain closed on Saturday afternoon and Sunday.

LUCCA

Ramparts built in the 16th and 17th centuries enclose a charming town filled with churches (99 of them), terra-cotta-roof buildings, and narrow cobblestone streets, along which local ladies maneuver bikes to do their daily shopping. Here Caesar, Pompey, and Crassus agreed to rule Rome as a triumvirate in 56 BC. Lucca was later the first Tuscan town to accept Christianity, and it still has a mind of its own: when most of Tuscany was voting communist as a matter of course, Lucca's citizens rarely followed suit. The famous composer Giacomo Puccini (1858–1924) was born here; his work forms the nucleus of the summer Opera Theater and Music Festival of Lucca. The ramparts circling the center city are the perfect place to take a stroll, ride a bicycle, kick a ball, or just stand and look down upon Lucca.

GETTING HERE
You can reach Lucca easily by train from Florence; the historic center is a short walk from the station. If you're driving, take the A11/E76.

VISITOR INFORMATION
Lucca tourism office (⊠*Piazza Santa Maria 35* ☎*0583/91991* ⊕*www. lucca.turismo.toscana.it*).

EXPLORING LUCCA
The historic center of Lucca, 51 km (31 mi) west of Florence, is walled, and motorized traffic is restricted. Walking and biking are the most efficient and most enjoyable ways to get around. You can rent bicycles, and the flat center makes biking easy. A combination ticket costing €6.50 gains you admission to both the Museo Nazionale di Villa Guinigi and the Pinacoteca Nazionale di Palazzo Mansi.

The round-arch facade of Lucca's **Duomo** is a fine example of the rigorously ordered Pisan Romanesque style, in this case happily enlivened by an extremely varied collection of small carved columns. Take a closer look at the decoration of the facade and that of the portico below; they make this one of the most entertaining church exteriors in

10

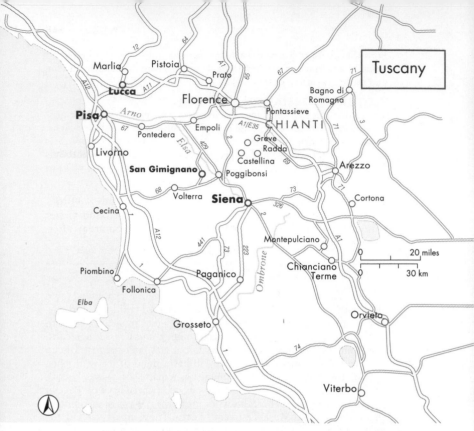

Tuscany. The Gothic interior contains a moving Byzantine crucifix—called the Volto Santo, or Holy Face—brought here, according to legend, in the eighth century (though it probably dates from between the 11th and early 13th centuries). The masterpiece of the Sienese sculptor Jacopo della Quercia (circa 1371–1438) is the marble *Tomb of Ilaria del Carretto* (1407–1408). ✉*Piazza del Duomo* ☎*0583/490530* 🖼€*2* ⊙*Duomo: weekdays 7–5:30, Sat. 9:30–6:45, Sun. 11:30–11:50 and 1–5:30. Tomb: Nov.–Mar., weekdays 9:30–4:45, Sat. 9:30–6:45, Sun. 11:30–11:50 and 1–5; Apr.–Oct., weekdays 9:30–5:45, Sat. 9–6:45, Sun. 9–10 and 1–5:45.*

Any time of day when the weather is clement, you can find the citizens of Lucca cycling, jogging, strolling, or kicking a soccer ball on the **Passeggiata delle Mura,** a green, beautiful, and very large park. It's neither inside nor outside the city but rather right on the ring of ramparts that defines Lucca. Sunlight streams through two rows of tall plane trees to dapple the *passeggiata delle mura* (walk on the walls), which is 4.2 km (2½ mi) in length. Ten bulwarks are topped with lawns, many with picnic tables, and some with play equipment for children. Be aware at all times of where the edge is—there are no railings and the drop to the ground outside the city is a precipitous 40 feet.

Torre Guinigi, the tower of the medieval Palazzo Guinigi, contains one of the city's most curious sights: a grove of ilex trees has grown at the top of the tower and their roots have pushed their way into the room below. From the top you have a magnificent view of the city and the surrounding countryside. (Only the tower is open to the public, not the palazzo.) ⊠ *Palazzo Guinigi, Via Sant'Andrea* 📞 *No phone* 🖅 *€3.50* ⊘ *Mar. and Apr., daily 9:30–6; May–Sept., daily 9–midnight; Oct.–Feb., daily 9–5.*

WHERE TO EAT & STAY

$$ ✕ **Buca di Sant'Antonio.** The staying power of Buca di Sant'Antonio—
★ it's been around since 1782—is the result of superlative Tuscan food brought to the table by waitstaff that doesn't miss a beat. The menu includes the simple-but-blissful, like *tortelli lucchesi al sugo* (meat-stuffed pasta with a tomato-and-meat sauce), and more daring dishes such as roast *capretto* (kid) with herbs. A white-wall interior hung with copper pots and brass musical instruments creates a classy but comfortable dining space. ⊠ *Via della Cervia 3* 📞 *0583/55881* 🖃 *AE, DC, MC, V* ⊘ *Closed Mon., 1 wk in Jan., and 1 wk in July. No dinner Sun.*

$ ✕ **Trattoria da Leo.** A few short turns away from the facade of San Michele, this noisy, informal, traditional trattoria delivers *cucina alla casalinga* (home cooking) in the best sense. Try the typical minestra di farro to start or just go straight to *secondi piatti* (entrées); in addition to the usual roast meats, there's excellent chicken with olives and a good cold dish of boiled meats served with a sauce of parsley and pine nuts. Save some room for a dessert, such as the rich, sweet, fig-and-walnut torte or the lemon sorbet brilliantly dotted with bits of sage, which tastes almost like mint. ⊠ *Via Tegrimi 1, at corner of Via degli Asili* 📞 *0583/492236* 🖃 *No credit cards* ⊘ *No lunch Sun. Closed Sun. Nov.–Mar.*

$$$–$$$$ 🏨 **Hotel Ilaria.** The former stables of the Villa Bottini have been transformed into a modern hotel within the historic center. A second-floor terrace, overlooking the villa, makes a comfortable place to relax, and there's a hot tub for the adventurous. Rooms are done in a warm wood veneer with blue and white fittings. The availability of free bicycles is a nice bonus in this bike-friendly city, and the sumptuous buffet breakfast could see you through dinner. Residenza dell'Alba, the hotel's annex across the street, was originally part of a 14th-century church; now it's a luxe accommodation with in-room hot tubs. **Pros:** a Fodor's reader sums it up as a "nice modern small hotel," free bicycles. **Cons:** though in city center, it's a little removed from main attractions. ⊠ *Via del Fosso 26* 📞 *0583/47615* 📠 *0583/991961* 🌐 *www.hotelilaria.com* 🛏 *36 rooms, 5 suites* 🔑 *In-room: safe, refrigerator. In-hotel: bar, bicycles, concierge, laundry service, public Internet, parking (no fee), some pets allowed (fee)* 🖃 *AE, DC, MC, V* ⏝ *BP.*

10

$ ⚏ **Piccolo Hotel Puccini.** Steps away from the busy square and church of San Michele, this little hotel is quiet and calm—and a great deal. Wallpaper, hardwood floors, and throw rugs are among the handsome decorations. Paolo, the genial manager, speaks fluent English and dispenses great touring advice. Pros: cheery, English-speaking staff. Cons: breakfast costs extra, some rooms are on the dark side. ⊠ *Via di Poggio 9* ☎*0583/55421* 📠*0583/53487* ⊕*www.hotelpuccini.com* ⟳*14 rooms* ⚲*In-room: no a/c, safe. In-hotel: bar, laundry service, some pets allowed, no-smoking rooms* ⊟*AE, MC, V* ❢❢*EP.*

PISA

When you think Pisa, you think Leaning Tower. Its position as one of Italy's most famous landmarks is a heavy reputation to bear, and it comes accompanied by abundant crowds and kitschy souvenirs. But the building *is* interesting and novel, and even if it doesn't captivate you, Pisa has other treasures that make a visit worthwhile. Taken as a whole, the Campo dei Miracoli (Field of Miracles), where the Leaning Tower, Duomo, and Baptistery are located, is among the most dramatic architectural complexes in Italy.

GETTING HERE

Pisa is an easy hour train ride from Florence. By car it's a straight shot on the Fi-Pi-Li autostrada. The Pisa–Lucca train runs frequently and takes about 30 minutes.

VISITOR INFORMATION

Pisa tourism office (⊠*Piazza Vittorio Emanuele II* ☎*050/42291*).

EXPLORING PISA

Pisa is 84 km (52 mi) west of Florence. Like many other Italian cities, the town is best seen on foot. The views along the Arno are particularly grand and shouldn't be missed—there's a sense of spaciousness here that the Arno in Florence lacks. You should weigh the different options for combination tickets to sights on the Piazza del Duomo when you begin your visit. Combination tickets are sold at the ticket office behind the Duomo opposite the Leaning Tower; one monument costs €5, two monuments €6, up to €8 for all the main sights, excluding the Leaning Tower.

The lovely Gothic **Battistero** (baptistery), which stands across from the Duomo's facade, is best known for the pulpit carved by Nicola Pisano (circa 1220–84; father of Giovanni Pisano) in 1260. Ask one of the ticket takers if he'll sing for you inside; the acoustics are remarkable. ⊠*Piazza del Duomo* ☎*050/3872210* ⊕*www.opapisa.it* ⛶*€5, discounts available if bought in combination with tickets for other monuments* ☉*Mar. 1–13, daily 9–6; Mar. 14–20, daily 9–7; Mar. 21–Sept., daily 8–8; Oct., daily 9–7; Nov.–Feb., daily 10–5.*

Pisa's **Duomo** brilliantly utilizes the horizontal marble stripe motif (borrowed from Moorish architecture) that became common to Tuscan cathedrals. It is famous for the Romanesque panels on the transept door facing the tower that depict scenes from the life of Christ. The beautifully carved 14th-century pulpit is by Giovanni Pisano (son of Nicola). ✉*Piazza del Duomo* ☎*050/3872210* ⊕*www.opapisa.it* 🎫*€2, discounts available if bought in combination with tickets for other monuments* ⊘*Mar. 1–13, daily 9–6; Mar. 14–20, daily 10–7; Mar. 21–Sept., daily 10–8; Oct., daily 10–7; Nov.–Feb., daily 10–1 and 2–5.*

Work on the **Leaning Tower** *(Torre Pendente)*, built as a campanile (bell tower) for the Duomo, started in 1173: the lopsided settling began when construction reached the third story. The tower's architects attempted to compensate through such methods as making the remaining floors slightly taller on the leaning side, but the extra weight only made the problem worse. The settling continued, and by the late 20th century it had accelerated to such a point that many feared the tower would simply topple over, despite all efforts to prop it up. The structure has since been firmly anchored to the earth. The final phase to restore the tower to its original tilt of 300 years ago was launched in early 2000 and finished two years later. The last phase removed some 100 tons of earth from beneath the foundation. Reservations, which are essential, can be made online or by calling the Museo dell'Opera del Duomo; it's also possible to arrive at the ticket office and book for the same day. Note that children under eight years of age are not allowed to climb. ✉*Piazza del Duomo* ☎*050/3872210* ⊕*www.opapisa.it* 🎫*€17* ⊘*Mar. 21–Sept., daily 8:30–8:30; Oct., daily 9–7; Nov.–Feb., daily 10–5; Mar. 1–Mar. 13, daily 9–6; Mar. 14–Mar. 20, daily 9–7.*

WHERE TO EAT & STAY

$$ ✕**Osteria dei Cavalieri.** This charming white-wall restaurant, a few steps
★ from Piazza dei Cavalieri, is reason enough to come to Pisa. They can do it all here—serve up exquisitely grilled fish dishes, please vegetarians, and prepare *tagliata* (thin slivers of rare beef) for meat lovers. Three set menus, from the sea, garden, and earth, are available, or you can order à la carte. For dinner there's an early seating (around 7:30) and a later one (around 9); opt for the later if you want time to linger over your meal. ✉*Via San Frediano 16* ☎*050/580858* ⌦*Reservations essential* ▭*AE, DC, MC, V* ⊘*Closed Sun., 2 wks in Aug., and Dec. 29–Jan. 7. No lunch Sat.*

$$ 🏨**Royal Victoria.** In a pleasant palazzo facing the Arno, a 10-minute walk from the Campo dei Miracoli, this comfortably furnished hotel has been in the Piegaja family since 1837. That continuity may help explain why such notables as Charles Dickens and Charles Lindbergh enjoyed staying here. Antiques and reproductions are in the lobby and in some rooms, whose style ranges from the 1800s, complete with frescoes, to the 1920s. Ask for a room in the charming old tower. There's also a pretty rooftop garden where you can order cocktails. **Pros:** friendly staff, free use of a Lancia that seats five—a great vehicle for tooling around Pisa. **Cons:** rooms vary significantly in size; all are a little worn. ✉*Lungarno Pacinotti 12* ☎*050/940111* 🖷*050/940180* ⊕*www.royalvictoria.it* 🛏*48 rooms, 40 with bath* ⌑*In-room: no a/c (some), dial-up. In-hotel: room service, bicycles, concierge, laundry service, parking (fee), some pets allowed* ▭*AE, DC, MC, V* ⍵*BP.*

10

CHIANTI

Chianti, directly south of Florence, is one of Italy's most famous wine-producing areas; its hill towns, olive groves, and vineyards are quintessential Tuscany. Many British and northern Europeans have relocated here, drawn by the unhurried life, balmy climate, and charming villages; there are so many Britons, in fact, that the area has been nicknamed Chiantishire. Still, it remains strongly Tuscan in character, with drop-dead views of vine-quilted hills and elegantly elongated cypress trees.

The sinuous SS222 highway, known as the Strada Chiantigiana, runs from Florence through the heart of Chianti. Its most scenic section connects Strada in Chianti, 16 km (10 mi) south of Florence, and **Greve in Chianti.** If there's an unofficial capital of Chianti, it's Greve, a friendly market town with no shortage of cafés, *enoteche* (wine bars), and craft shops lining its main square. The gently sloping, asymmetrical Piazza Matteotti is an attractive arcade whose center holds a statue of the discoverer of New York harbor, Giovanni da Verrazano (circa 1480–1527). Check out the lively market held here on Saturday morning.

South of Greve on the SR222, **Radda in Chianti** sits on a hill separating two valleys, Val di Pesa and Val d'Arbia. It's one of many tiny Chianti villages that invite you to stroll their steep streets; follow the signs pointing you toward the *camminamento,* a covered medieval passageway circling part of the city inside the walls.

★ If you only have time for one castle, visit the stunning **Castello di Brolio.** At the end of the 12th century, when Florence conquered southern Chianti, Brolio became Florence's southernmost outpost, and it was often said, "When Brolio growls, all Siena trembles." Brolio was built about AD 1000 and owned by the monks of the Badia Fiorentina; the "new" owners, the Ricasoli family, have been in possession since 1141. Bettino Ricasoli (1809–80), the so-called Iron Baron, was one of the founders of modern Italy, and is said to have invented the original formula for Chianti wine. Brolio, one of Chianti's best-known labels, is still justifiably famous. Its cellars may be toured by appointment. There's a sign at the Brolio gate that translates as RING BELL AND BE PATIENT. You pull a rope and the bell above the ramparts peals, and in a short time, the caretaker arrives to let you in. The grounds are worth visiting, even though the 19th-century manor house is not open to the public. (The current baron is very much in residence.) There are two apartments here available for rent by the week. ⊠*Località Brolio* ⊕ *2 km (1 mi) southeast of Gaiole* ☎*0577/730227* ☜*€5* ⊙*June–Sept., daily 9–noon and 2–6:30; Oct.–May, Sat.–Thurs. 9–noon and 2–6:30.*

WHERE TO EAT & STAY

$ ✕**Enoteca Fuoripiazza.** Detour off Greve's flower-strewn main square for food that relies heavily on local ingredients (especially those produced by nearby makers of cheese and salami). The lengthy wine list provides a bewildering array of choices to pair with *affettati misti* (a plate of cured meats) or one of their primi—the *pici* (a thick, short noodle) is deftly prepared here. All the dishes are made with great care. ⊠*Via I Maggio 2, Piazza Trenta* ☎*055/8546313* ⊟*AE, DC, MC, V* ⊙*Closed Mon.*

$$$$ ✕ **Osteria di Passignano.** Sophisticated country dining may not get better than at this deceptively simple restaurant next to a Vallombrosan abbey. A tiny sampling (maybe *sformatino di pecorino di fosso*, a flan made with aged pecorino) whets the appetite for what's to come. The young chefs in the kitchen can do traditional as well as whimsical Tuscan—and then divine things such as the *maccheroni del Martelli al ragù bianco di agnelli e carciofi morellini* (tubular pasta with a lamb and artichoke sauce), which really isn't Tuscan at all. The wine list is unbeatable, as is the service. ⊠ *Via Passignano 33, Località Badia a Passignano* ✛*15 km (9 mi) east of Greve in Chianti* ☎*055/8071278* ⊟*AE, DC, MC, V* ⊗*Closed Sun., Jan. 7–Feb. 1, and 15 days in Aug.*

$–$$ ✕ **Osteria Le Panzanelle.** Silvia Bonechi's experience in the kitchen—and a
★ few precious recipes handed down from her grandmother—is one of the reasons for the success of this small restaurant. The other is the front-room hospitality of Nada Michelassi. These two *panzanelle* (women from Panzano) serve a short menu of tasty and authentic dishes at what the locals refer to as *prezzi giusti* (the right prices). Both the *pappa al pomodoro* (tomato soup) and the *peposo* (peppery beef stew) are exceptional. Whether you are eating inside or under large umbrellas on the terrace near a tiny stream, the experience is always congenial. "The best food we had in Tuscany," writes one user of fodors.com. Reservations are essential in July and August. ⊠*Località Lucarelli 29* ✛*8 km (5 mi) northwest of Radda on road to Panzano,* ☎*0577/733511* ⊟*MC, V* ⊗*Closed Mon. and Jan. and Feb.*

¢ 🛏 **La Bottega di Giovannino.** The name is actually that of the wine bar run by Giovannino Bernardoni and his daughter Monica, who also rent rooms in the house next door. This is a fantastic place for the budget-conscious traveler, as rooms are immaculate. Most have a stunning view of the surrounding hills. All have their own bath, though most of them necessitate taking a short trip outside one's room. **Pros:** great location in the center of town, close to restaurants and shops, super value. **Cons:** some rooms are small, some bathrooms are down the hall, basic decor. ⊠ *Via Roma 6–8* ☎*0577/738056* ⊕*www.labottegadigiovannino.it* ⬎*10 rooms, 2 apartments* ᝍ*In-room: no a/c, no phone. In-hotel: bar, no elevator* ⊟*AE, MC, V* ⊓*EP.*

$$$–$$$$ 🛏 **Relais Fattoria Vignale.** On the outside it's a rather plain manor house
★ with an annex across the street. Inside it's a refined and comfortable country house with numerous sitting rooms that have terra-cotta floors and nice stonework. Guest rooms have exposed-brick walls and wood beams and are filled with simple wooden furnishings and handwoven rugs. The grounds, flanked by vineyards and olive trees, are equally inviting, with lawns, terraces, and a pool. The sophisticated Ristorante Vignale ($–$$$) serves excellent wines and local specialties like *cinghiale in umido con nepitella e vin cotto* (wild boar stew flavored with catmint and wine). **Pros:** intimate public spaces, excellent restaurant, helpful and friendly staff. **Cons:** north-facing rooms blocked by tall cypress trees, single rooms are small, annex across a busy road. ⊠ *Via Pianigiani 9* ☎*0577/738300 hotel, 0577/738094 restaurant, 0577/738012 enoteca* ⊕*www.vignale.it* ⬎*37 rooms, 5 suites* ᝍ*In-room: safe, refrigera-*

10

tor. In-hotel: restaurant, bar, pool, concierge, laundry service, public Internet ▭AE, DC, MC, V ⊗Closed Nov.–Mar. 15. ⟨○⟩BP.

SAN GIMIGNANO

27 km (17 mi) east of Volterra, 57 km (35 mi) southwest of Florence.

GETTING HERE

You can reach San Gimignano by car from the Florence–Siena Superstrada. Exit at Poggibonsi Nord and follow signs for San Gimignano. Although it involves changing buses in Poggibonsi, getting to San Gimignano by bus is a relatively straightforward affair. SITA operates the service between Siena or Florence and Poggibonsi, while Tra-In takes care of the Poggibonsi to San Gimignano route. You cannot reach San Gimignano by train.

VISITOR INFORMATION

San Gimignano tourism office (✉Piazza Duomo 1 ☎0577/940008 ⊕www. sangimignano.com).

EXPLORING SAN GIMIGNANO

When you're on a hilltop surrounded by soaring medieval towers silhouetted against the sky, it's difficult not to fall under the spell of San Gimignano. Its tall walls and narrow streets are typical of Tuscan hill towns, but it's the medieval "skyscrapers" that set the town apart from its neighbors. Today 14 towers remain, but at the height of the Guelph–Ghibelline conflict there was a forest of more than 70, and it was possible to cross the town by rooftop rather than by road. The towers were built partly for defensive purposes—they were a safe refuge and useful for pouring boiling oil on attacking enemies—and partly for bolstering the egos of their owners, who competed with deadly seriousness to build the highest tower in town.

Today San Gimignano isn't much more than a gentrified walled city, touristy but still very much worth exploring because, despite the profusion of cheesy souvenir shops lining the main drag, there's some serious Renaissance art to be seen here. Tour groups arrive early and clog the wine-tasting rooms—San Gimignano is famous for its light white Vernaccia—and art galleries for much of the day, but most sights stay open through late afternoon, when all the tour groups have long since departed.

WHERE TO EAT & STAY

The **Cooperativa Hotels Promotion** (✉Via di San Giovanni 125 ☎0577/ 940809 ⊕www.hotelsiena.com) provides commission-free booking for local hotels and farmhouses.

$–$$ ✗**La Mangiatoia.** Multicolored gingham tablecloths provide an interesting juxtaposition with rib-vaulted ceilings dating from the 13th century. The lighthearted touch might be explained by the influence of chef Susi Cuomo, who has been presiding over the kitchen for more than 20 years. The menu is seasonal—in autumn, don't miss her sacottino di pecorino al tartufo (little packages of pasta stuffed with pecorino and seasoned with truffles). In summer eat lighter fare on the intimate, flower-bedecked terrace in the back. ✉ *Via Mainardi 5, off Via San Matteo* ☎*0577/941528* ☐*MC, V* ⊗*Closed Tues., 3 wks in Nov., and 1 wk in Jan.*

$–$$ 🛏 **Pescille.** A rambling farmhouse has been transformed into a handsome hotel with understated contemporary furniture in the bedrooms and country-classic motifs such as farm implements hanging on the walls in the bar. From this charming spot you get a splendid view of San Gimignano's towers. **Pros:** splendid views, quiet atmosphere, 10-minute walk to town. **Cons:** furnishings a bit austere, there's an elevator for luggage but not for guests. ✉ *Strada Provinciale Castel San Gimignano, Località Pescille* ✛*4 km (2½ mi) south of San Gimignano town center* ☎*0577/940186* ⊕*www.pescille.it* 🛏*38 rooms, 12 suites* 🛠*In-room: refrigerator, Wi-Fi. In-hotel: bar, tennis court, pool, gym, no elevator, public Internet, public Wi-Fi, parking (no fee)* ☐*AE, DC, MC, V* ⊗*Closed Nov.–Mar.* 🍴*BP.*

SIENA

With its narrow streets and steep alleys, a stunning Gothic Duomo, a bounty of early Renaissance art, and the glorious Palazzo Pubblico overlooking its magnificent Campo, Siena is often described as Italy's best-preserved medieval city. Victory over Florence in 1260 at Montaperti marked the beginning of Siena's golden age. During the following decades Siena erected its greatest buildings (including the Duomo); established a model city government presided over by the Council of Nine; and became a great art, textile, and trade center. Siena succumbed to Florentine rule in the mid-16th century, when a yearlong siege virtually eliminated the native population. Ironically, it was precisely this decline that, along with the steadfast pride of the Sienese, prevented further development, to which we owe the city's marvelous medieval condition today.

GETTING HERE

From Florence, the quickest way to Siena is via the Florence–Siena Superstrada. Otherwise, take the Via Cassia (SR2), for a scenic route. Coming from Rome, leave the A1 at Valdichiana, and follow the Siena–Bettole Superstrada. SITA provides excellent bus service between Florence and Siena. Because buses are direct and speedy, they are preferable over the train, which sometimes involves a change in Empoli.

VISITOR INFORMATION

Siena tourism office (✉*Piazza del Campo 56* ☎*0577/280551* ⊕*www. comune.siena.it*).

EXPLORING SIENA

If you come by car, you're better off leaving it in one of the parking lots around the perimeter of town. Driving is difficult or impossible in most parts of the city center. Practically unchanged since medieval times, Siena is laid out in a "Y" over the slopes of several hills, dividing the city into *terzi* (thirds). Although the most interesting sites are in a fairly compact area around the Campo at the center of town in the neighborhoods of Città, Camollìa, and San Martino, be sure to leave

10

some time to wander into the narrow streets that rise and fall steeply from the main thoroughfares, giving yourself at least two days to really explore the town. At the top on the list of things to see is the Piazza del Campo, considered by many to be the finest public square in Italy. The Palazzo Pubblico sits at the lower end of the square and is well worth a visit. The Duomo is a must-see, as is the nearby Cripta.

Fodor'sChoice
★
Siena's **Duomo** is beyond question one of the finest Gothic cathedrals in Italy. The multicolored marbles and painted decoration are typical of the Italian approach to Gothic architecture—lighter and much less austere than the French. The amazingly detailed facade has few rivals in the region. It was completed in two brief phases at the end of the 13th and 14th centuries.

The Duomo's interior, with its black-and-white striping throughout and finely coffered and gilded dome, is simply striking. There are magnificent Renaissance frescoes in the **Biblioteca Piccolomini,** off the left aisle. Painted by Pinturicchio (circa 1454–1513) and completed in 1509, they depict events from the life of native son Aeneas Sylvius Piccolomini (1405–64), who became Pope Pius II in 1458. The frescoes are in excellent condition and have a freshness rarely seen in work so old. ⊠ *Piazza del Duomo, Città* ☎ *0577/283048* 🖼 *€3 Nov.–Aug.; €5 Sept. and Oct.; €10 combined ticket includes the Cripta, Battistero, and Museo dell'Opera Metropolitana* ⊙ *Mar.–Oct., Mon.–Sat. 10:30–7:30, Sun. 1:30–6:30; Nov.–Feb., Mon.–Sat. 10:30–6:30, Sun. 1:30–5:30.*

After it had lain unseen for possibly 700 years, a **Cripta** (crypt) was rediscovered under the grand *pavimento* (floor) of the Duomo during routine excavation work and was opened to the public in 2003. An unknown master executed the breathtaking frescoes here sometime between 1270–80; they retain their original colors and pack an emotional punch even with sporadic damage. ⊠ *Piazza del Duomo, Città* ☎ *0577/283048* 🖼 *€6; €10 combined ticket includes the Duomo, Battistero, and Museo dell'Opera Metropolitana* ⊙ *June–Aug., daily 9:30–8; Sept.–May, daily 9:30–7.*

The fan-shaped **Piazza del Campo,** known simply as il Campo (The Field), is one of the finest squares in Italy. Constructed toward the end of the 12th century on a market area unclaimed by any contrada, it's still the heart of town. The bricks of the Campo are patterned in nine different sections—representing each member of the medieval Government of Nine. On Palio horse race days (July 2 and August 16), the Campo and all its surrounding buildings are packed with cheering, frenzied locals and tourists craning their necks to take it all in. ⊠ *Piazza del Campo, Città*

The Gothic **Palazzo Pubblico,** the focal point of the Piazza del Campo, has served as Siena's town hall since the 1300s. It now also contains the **Museo Civico,** with walls covered in early Renaissance frescoes. The nine governors of Siena once met in the Sala della Pace, famous for Ambrogio Lorenzetti's frescoes called *Allegories of Good and Bad Government,* painted in the late 1330s to demonstrate the dangers of tyranny. The **Torre del Mangia,** the palazzo's famous bell tower, is named after one of its first bell ringers, Giovanni di Duccio (called Mangiaguadagni, or earnings eater). The climb up to the top is long and steep, but the view makes it worth every step. ⊠*Piazza del Campo 1, Città* ☎*0577/41169* ⊠*Museo €7, Torre €6, combined ticket €10* ⊙*Museo Nov.–Mar. 15, daily 10–6:30; Mar. 16–Oct., daily 10–7. Torre Nov.–Mar. 15, daily 10–4; Mar. 16–Oct., daily 10–7.*

WHERE TO EAT & STAY

$$$–$$$$ ✕**Antica Trattoria Botte ganova.** Along the road that leads to Chianti is arguably the best restaurant in Siena. Chef Michele Sorrentino's cooking is all about clean flavors, balanced combinations, and inviting presentation. Look for inspiring dishes such as spaghetti *alla chitarra in salsa di astice piccante* (with a spicy lobster sauce), or ravioli *di ricotta con ragù d'agnello* (with sheep's-milk cheese and lamb sauce). The interior, with high vaulting, is relaxed yet elegant, and the service is first-rate. ⊠*Strada per Montevarchi 29, ĵ 2 km (1 mi) northeast of Siena* ☎*0577/284230* ⚘*Reservations essential* ☰*AE, DC, MC, V* ⊙*Closed Sun.*

$–$$ ✕**Osteria del Coro.** Chef-owner Stefano Azzi promotes local produce,
★   uses age-old Sienese recipes, and backs it all up with a stellar wine list. His *pici con le briciole al modo mio* (thick spaghetti with breadcrumbs), liberally dressed with fried *cinta senese* (a bacon made from a long-snouted pig), dazzles. The place was once a pizzeria, and it retains its unadorned, unpretentious air—you certainly wouldn't come because of the decor. ⊠*Via Pantaneto 85/87, Città,* ☎*0577/222482* ☰*DC, MC, V* ⊙*Closed Mon.*

$$$ ⊞**Palazzo Ravizza.** This romantic palazzo exudes a sense of genteel shabbiness. Rooms have high ceilings, antique furnishings, and bathrooms decorated with hand-painted tiles. The location is key: from here it's just a 10-minute walk to the Duomo. Il Capriccio ($$–$$$), ably run by chef Fabio Tozzi, specializies in traditional Tuscan fare. In warm weather, enjoy your meal in the garden with a trickling fountain. "We have only positive things to say about Palazzo Ravizza . from the amazing Tuscan view, to the proximity to Il Campo this hotel was by far the best one we stayed at throughout our Italy vacation," says one traveler on Fodors.com. **Pros:** 10-minute walk to the center of town, pleasant garden with a view beyond the city walls, professional staff. **Cons:** not all rooms have views, some of the rooms are a little cramped. ⊠*Pian dei Mantellini 34, Città* ☎*0577/280462* ⊕*www.palazzoravizza.it* ↩*38 rooms, 4 suites* ⚭*In-room: safe, refrigerator, Wi-Fi (some). In-hotel: restaurant, bar, concierge, laundry service, public Internet, public Wi-Fi, parking (no fee), some pets allowed* ☰*AE, DC, MC, V* ⏐◎⏐*BP.*

10

MILAN

Milan is Italy's business hub and crucible of chic. Between the Po's rich farms and the industrious mountain valleys, it has long been the country's capital of commerce, finance, fashion, and media. Rome may be bigger and have the political power, but Milan and the affluent north are what really make the country go. It's also Italy's transport hub, with the biggest international airport, the most rail connections, and the best subway system. Leonardo da Vinci's *The Last Supper* and other great works of art are here, as well as a spectacular Gothic Duomo, the finest of its kind. Milan even reigns supreme where it really counts (in the minds of many Italians), routinely trouncing the rest of the nation with its two premier soccer teams.

PLANNING YOUR TIME

Milan's main streets radiate out from the massive Duomo, a late-Gothic cathedral that was started in 1386. Leading north is the handsome Galleria Vittorio Emanuele, an enclosed walkway that takes you to the world-famous opera house known as La Scala. Beyond are the winding streets of the elegant Brera neighborhood, once the city's bohemian quarter. Here you'll find many art galleries, as well as the academy of fine arts. Heading northeast from La Scala is Via Manzoni, which leads to the Quadrilatero della moda, or fashion district. Its streets are lined with elegant window displays from the world's most celebrated designers—the Italians taking the lead, of course.

If the part of the city to the north of the Duomo is dominated by its shops, the section to the south is famous for its works of art. The most famous is *Il Cenacolo*—known in English as *The Last Supper*. If you have time for nothing else, make sure you see this masterwork, which has now been definitively restored, after many, many years of work. Reservations will be needed to see this fresco, housed in the refectory of Santa Maria delle Grazie. Make these at least three weeks before you depart for Italy, so you can plan the rest of your time in Milan.

GETTING HERE & AROUND

Aeroporto Malpensa, 50 km (31 mi) northwest of Milan, is the major northern Italian hub for intercontinental flights and also sees substantial European and domestic traffic. Milan's central station (Stazione Centrale), 3 km (2 mi) northwest of the Duomo, is one of Italy's major passenger-train hubs, with frequent direct service

Milan's city center is compact and walkable, while the efficient Metropolitana (subway), as well as buses and trams, provides access to locations farther afield. Transit runs from 6 AM to 12:30 AM. For more information, check the Web site of **ATM (Azienda Trasporti Milanesi)** (⊕*www.atm-mi.it*), which has an English-language version, or visit the information office at the Duomo stop.

Driving the streets of Milan is difficult at best, and parking can be downright miserable, so leave the car behind. In addition, drivers entering the second ring of streets (the so-called *bastioni)* have to pay a €2 charge between 7:30 and 7:30, weekdays (⊕*www.comune.milano.it/*

ecopass). To park on the street (only in blue areas; yellow is for residents), purchase scratch-off cards from tobacconists or parking attendants who are often near busy areas.

VISITOR INFORMATION

The **tourism office** (⊠*Piazza Duomo 19/A, Piazza Duomo* ☎*02/ 74043431* ⊕*www.visitamilano.it* ⊗*Mon.–Sat. 8:45–1 and 2–6, Sun. 9–1 and 2–5*) in the Piazza del Duomo is an excellent place to begin your visit. It is now accessible by a stairway under the arches on the north side of Piazza Duomo. You can also enter from the Galleria in front of the Hyatt hotel. There are free maps on a variety of themes and a selection of brochures about smaller museums and cultural initiatives. Pick up a copy of the English-language *Hello Milano* (ask, if it is not on display). This monthly magazine includes a day-to-day schedule of events of interest to visitors and a comprehensive map.

EXPLORING MILAN

❶ **Duomo.** This intricate Gothic structure has been fascinating and exasperating visitors and conquerors alike since it was begun by Galeazzo Visconti III (1351–1402), first duke of Milan, in 1386. Consecrated in the 15th or 16th century, it was not completed until just before the coronation of Napoléon as king of Italy in 1809. Whether or not you concur with travel writer H. V. Morton's 1964 assessment that the cathedral is "one of the mightiest Gothic buildings ever created," there is no denying that for sheer size and complexity it is unrivaled. It is the second-largest church in the world—the largest being St. Peter's in Rome. The capacity is reckoned to be 40,000. Usually it is empty, a sanctuary from the frenetic pace of life outside and the perfect place for solitary contemplation. The building is adorned with 135 marble spires and 2,245 marble statues. ⊠*Piazza del Duomo* ☎*02/86463456* ⛛*Stairs to roof €3.50, elevator €5* ⊗*Mid-Feb.–mid-Nov., daily 9–5:45; mid-Nov.–mid-Feb., daily 9–4:15* Ⓜ*Duomo.* Exhibits at the **Museo del Duomo** shed light on the cathedral's history and include some of the treasures removed from the exterior for preservation purposes. ⊠*Piazza del Duomo 14* ☎*02/860358* ⛛*€6, €7 including ticket for elevator to Duomo roof* ⊗*Daily 10–1:15 and 3–6.*

❷ **Galleria Vittorio Emanuele.** This spectacular, late-19th-century glass-top, barrel-vaulted tunnel is essentially one of the planet's earliest and most select shopping malls. Like its suburban American cousins, the Galleria Vittorio Emanuele fulfills numerous social functions. This is the city's heart, midway between the Duomo and La Scala. It teems with life, inviting people-watching from the tables that spill from the bars and restaurants, where you can enjoy an overpriced coffee. Even in poor weather the great glass dome above the octagonal center is a splendid sight. And the floor mosaics are a vastly underrated source of pleasure, even if they are not to be taken too seriously. They represent Europe, Asia, Africa, and the United States; those at the entrance arch are devoted to science, industry, art, and agriculture. ⊠*Piazza del Duomo* Ⓜ*Duomo.*

10

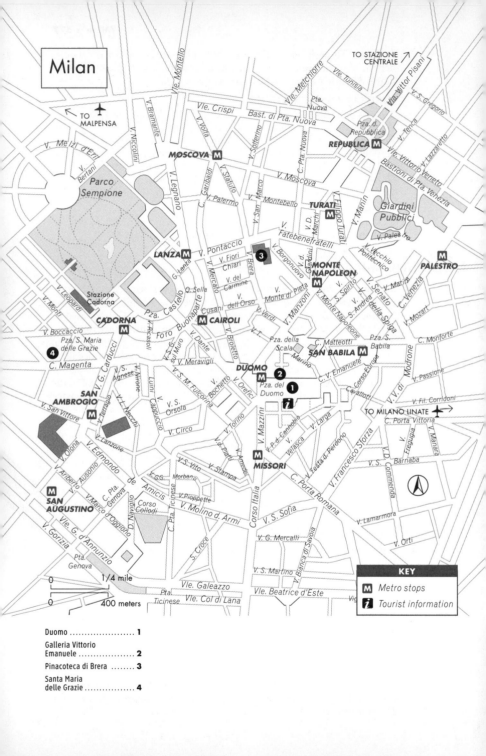

★ ❸ **Pinacoteca di Brera** *(Brera Gallery).* The collection here is star-studded even by Italian standards. The entrance hall (Room I) displays 20th-century sculpture and painting, including Carlo Carrà's (1881–1966) confident, stylish response to the schools of cubism and surrealism. The museum has nearly 40 other rooms, arranged in chronological order— pace yourself. The somber, moving *Cristo Morto (Dead Christ)* by Mantegna dominates Room VI, with its sparse palette of umber and its foreshortened perspective. Room XXIV offers two additional highlights of the gallery. Raphael's (1483–1520) *Sposalizio della Vergine,* with its mathematical composition and precise, alternating colors, portrays the betrothal of Mary and Joseph. *La Vergine con il Bambino e Santi (Madonna with Child and Saints)*, by Piero della Francesca (1420–92), is an altarpiece commissioned by Federico da Montefeltro. ⊠ *Via Brera 28* ☎*02/722631* ⊕*www.brera.beniculturali.it* ⊠*€5* ⊙*Tues.–Sun. 8:30–7:15; last admission 45 mins before closing* Ⓜ*Montenapoleone.*

❹ **Santa Maria delle Grazie.** Leonardo da Vinci's *The Last Supper,* housed in the church and former Dominican monastery of Santa Maria delle Grazie, has had an almost unbelievable history of bad luck and neglect— its near destruction in an American bombing raid in August 1943 was only the latest chapter in a series of misadventures, including, if one 19th-century source is to be believed, being whitewashed over by monks. Well-meant but disastrous attempts at restoration have done little to rectify the problem of the work's placement: it was executed on a wall unusually vulnerable to climatic dampness. Yet Leonardo chose to work slowly and patiently in oil pigments—which demand dry plaster—instead of proceeding hastily on wet plaster according to the conventional fresco technique.

Reservations are required to view the work. Viewings are in 15-minute, timed slots, and visitors must arrive 15 minutes before their assigned time if they are not to lose their slot. Reservations can be made via phone (☎*02/89421146*) or online (⊕*www.cenacolovinciano.it*); it is best to call, because more tickets are set aside for phone reservations. Call about three weeks ahead to be sure of getting the Saturday slot you want; two weeks before for a weekday slot. The telephone reservation office is open 9 AM–6 PM weekdays and 9 AM–2 PM on Saturday. Operators do speak English, though not fluently, and to reach one, you must wait for the Italian introduction to finish and then press "2." However, you can sometimes get tickets from one day to the next. Some city bus tours include a visit in their regular circuit, which may be a good option. ⊠*Piazza Santa Maria delle Grazie 2, off Corso Magenta, Sant'Ambrogio* ☎*02/89421146* ⊕*www.cenacolovinciano. org* ⊠*€6.50 plus €1.50 reservation fee* ⊙*Weekdays 9–6, Sat. 9–2* Ⓜ*Cadorna.*

10

WHERE TO EAT

$–$$ ✕**Da Abele.** If you love risotto, then make a beeline for this neighborhood trattoria. The superb risotto dishes change with the season, and there may be just two or three on the menu at any time. It is tempting to try them all. The setting is relaxed, the service informal, the prices strikingly reasonable. Outside the touristy center of town but quite convenient by subway, this trattoria is invariably packed with locals. ⊠ *Via Temperanza 5, Loreto* ☎*02/2613855* ⊟*AE, DC, MC, V* ⊘*Closed Mon., Aug., and Dec. 22–Jan. 7. No lunch* Ⓜ*Pasteur.*

$$$$ ✕**Don Carlos.** One of the few restaurants open after La Scala lets out, Don Carlos, in the Grand Hotel et de Milan, is nothing like its indecisive operatic namesake (whose betrothed was stolen by his father). Flavors are bold, their presentation precise and full of flair: broiled red mullet floats on a lacy layer of crispy leeks. Walls are blanketed with sketches of the theater, and the opera recordings are every bit as well chosen as the wine list, setting the perfect stage for discreet business negotiation or, better yet, refined romance. A gourmet menu costs €75 for six courses (two-person minimum), excluding wine. ⊠ *Grand Hotel et de Milan, Via Manzoni 29, Duomo* ☎*02/723141* ⚐*Reservations essential* ⊟*AE, DC, MC, V* ⊘*Closed Aug. No lunch* Ⓜ*Montenapoleone; Tram 1, 2.*

$$–$$$ ✕**Trattoria Montina.** Twin brothers Maurizio and Roberto Montina have
★ turned this restaurant into a local favorite. Don't be fooled by the "trattoria" name. The sage-green paneling makes it airy and cozy on a gray Milan day. Chef Roberto creates exquisite modern Italian dishes such as warmed risotto with merlot and taleggio cheese, while Maurizio chats with guests, regulars, and local families. Milan's famous cotoletta is light and tasty. Try fish or the *frittura impazzita,* a wild-and-crazy mix of delicately fried seafood. Unlike many Italian menus, there's a fine selection on the hard-to-choose dessert cart. ⊠ *Via Procaccini 54, Procaccini* ☎*02/3490498* ⊟*AE, DC, MC, V* ⊘*Closed Sun., Aug., and Dec. 25–Jan. 7. No lunch Mon.* Ⓜ*Tram 1, 19, 29, 33.*

WHERE TO STAY

$$–$$$ 🏨**Antica Locanda dei Mercanti.** On a quiet side street off Via Dante, this
★ 14-room hotel is minutes—and light-years—away from Milan's bustling downtown. Rooms are on the second and third floors (four have private terraces), but you check in at ground-floor reception and take breakfast in the dining room at No. 8. Reserve early for the terrace rooms. **Pros:** central and cozy. **Cons:** rooms are scattered around floors. ⊠ *Via San Tomaso 6, Duomo* ☎*02/8054080* 🖷*02/8054090* ⊕*www.lalocanda.it* ↩*14 rooms* ⚐*In-room: Wi-Fi. In-hotel: bar* ⊟*MC, V* ◉*EP* Ⓜ*Cordusio; Tram 1, 12, 20, 27.*

$–$$ 🏨**Hotel Casa Mia Milan.** Easy to reach from the central train station (a few blocks away) and easy on the budget, this tiny hotel, up a flight of stairs, is family-run. Rooms are simple and clean with individual (small) baths. Although not in the center of things, it is two blocks from transport center Piazza Repubblica (tram and metro lines), which also hosts the doyenne of Milan's palace hotels, the Principe di Savoia. **Pros:** clean, good value. **Cons:** neighborhood is not the nicest in Milan. ⊠ *Viale Vittorio Veneto 30, Piazza Repubblica* ☎*02/6575249* ⊕*www.casamiahotel.it* ↩*15 rooms* ⚐*In-hotel: no elevator* ⊟*MC, V* ◉*BP* Ⓜ*Republica.*

$$$$ **⊞ Principe di Savoia.** Milan's grande dame has all the trappings of an exquisite traditional hotel: lavish mirrors, drapes, and carpets, and Milan's largest guest rooms, outfitted with eclectic fin de siècle furnishings. Forty-eight Deluxe Mosaic rooms (named for the glass mosaic panels in their ample bathrooms) are even larger, and the three-bedroom Presidential Suite features its own marble pool. The Winter Garden is an elegant aperitivo spot, and the Acanto restaurant has garden seating. Lighter food is served in the Lobby Lounge. **Pros:** probably the most serious spa/health club (considered very chic by Milanese) in town. **Cons:** overblown luxury in a not-very-central or attractive neighborhood; close enough to the train station to attract pickpockets. ⊠ *Piazza della Repubblica 17, Porta Nuova* ☎ *02/62301* 📠 *02/653799* ⊕ *www. hotelprincipedisavoia.com* ⇆ *269 rooms, 132 suites* ⎈ *In-room: Wi-Fi. In-hotel: 2 restaurants, room service, bar, pool, gym, spa, laundry service* ☰ *AE, DC, MC, V* ⎰⎱*EP* Ⓜ *Repubblica.*

NIGHTLIFE & THE ARTS

Milan's hallowed **Teatro alla Scala** (⊠ *Piazza della Scala* ☎ *02/72003744* ⊕ *www.teatroallascala.org* Ⓜ *Duomo*) has undergone a complete renovation, with everything refreshed, refurbished, or replaced except the building's exterior walls. Special attention was paid to the acoustics, which have always been excellent. The season runs from December 7, the feast day of Milan patron St. Ambrose, through June. Plan well in advance, as tickets sell out quickly. For tickets, visit the **Biglietteria Centrale** (⊠ *Galleria del Sagrato, Piazza Del Duomo* ⊙ *Daily noon–6* Ⓜ *Duomo*), which is in the Duomo subway station. To pick up tickets for performances from two hours prior until 15 minutes after the start of a performance, go to the box office at the theater, which is around the corner in Via Filodrammatici 2. Although you might not get seats for the more popular operas with big stars, it is worth trying; ballets are easier. The theater is closed from the end of July through August and on national and local holidays.

SHOPPING

The heart of Milan's shopping reputation is the **Quadrilatero della moda** district north of the Duomo. Here the world's leading designers compete for shoppers' attention, showing off their ultrastylish clothes in stores that are works of high style themselves. You won't find any bargains, but regardless of whether you're making a purchase, the area is a great place for window-shopping and people-watching. But fashion is not limited to one neighborhood, and there is a huge and exciting selection of clothing that is affordable, well made, and often more interesting than what is offered by the international luxury brands with shops in the Quadrilatero.

10

VENICE

It's called La Serenissima, "the most serene," a reference to the majesty, wisdom, and monstrous power of this city that was for centuries the unrivaled mistress of trade between Europe and the Orient and the bulwark of Christendom against the tides of Turkish expansion. "Most serene" could also describe the way lovers of this miraculous city feel when they see it, imperturbably floating on its calm blue lagoon.

Built entirely on water by men who defied the sea, Venice is unlike any other town. No matter how many times you've seen it in movies or on TV, the real thing is more dreamlike than you could ever imagine. Its landmarks, the Basilica di San Marco and the Palazzo Ducale, seem hardly Italian: delightfully idiosyncratic, they are exotic mixes of Byzantine, Gothic, and Renaissance styles. Shimmering sunlight and silvery mist soften every perspective here, and you understand how the city became renowned in the Renaissance for its artists' rendering of color.

You'll see Venetians going about their daily affairs in *vaporetti* (water buses), aboard the *traghetti* (traditional gondola ferries) that carry them across the Grand Canal, in the *campi* (squares), and along the *calli* (narrow streets). They are nothing if not skilled—and remarkably tolerant—in dealing with the veritable armies of tourists from all over the world who fill the city's streets for most of the year.

PLANNING YOUR TIME

A great introduction to Venice is a ride on *vaporetto* (water bus) Line 1 from the train station all the way down the Grand Canal. If you've just arrived and have luggage in tow, you'll need to weigh the merits of taking this trip right away versus getting settled at your hotel first. (Crucial factors: your mood, the bulk of your bags, and your hotel's location.)

Seeing Piazza San Marco and the sights bordering it can fill a day, but if you're going to be around awhile, consider holding off on your visit here—the crowds can be overwhelming, especially when you're fresh off the boat. Instead, spend your first morning at Santa Maria Gloriosa dei Frari and the Scuola Grande di San Rocco, then wander through the Dorsoduro sestiere, choosing between visits to Ca' Rezzonico, the Gallerie dell'Accademia, the Peggy Guggenheim Collection, and Santa Maria della Salute—all A-list attractions. End the afternoon with a gelato-fueled stroll along the Zattere boardwalk. Then tackle San Marco on Day 2.

If you have more time, make these sights your priorities: the Rialto fish and produce markets; Ca' d'Oro and the Jewish Ghetto in Cannaregio; Santa Maria dei Miracoli and Santi Giovanni e Paolo in Castello; and, across the water from Piazza San Marco, San Giorgio Maggiore. (In Venice, there's a spectacular church for every day of the week, and then some.) A day on the outer islands of Murano, Burano, and Torcello is good for a change of pace.

GETTING HERE

Venice's **Aeroporto Marco Polo** (☎*041/2609260* ⊕*www.veniceairport.it*) is 10 km (6 mi) north of the city on the mainland. It's served by domestic and international flights, including connections from 21 European cities, plus direct flights from New York's JFK.

From Marco Polo terminal it's a €10 taxi ride or a 10-minute walk to the dock where public and private boats depart for Venice's historic center. **Alilaguna** (☎*041/2401701* ⊕*www.alilaguna.it*) has regular ferry service from predawn until nearly midnight. The charge is €12 per person, including bags, and it takes about an hour to reach the landing near Piazza San Marco, with a stop at the Lido on the way. A *motoscafo* (water taxi) carries up to four people and four bags to the city center in a sleek, modern powerboat. The base cost is €90, and the trip takes about 25 minutes. Each additional person, bag, and stop costs extra, so it's essential to agree on a fare before boarding.

Blue buses run by **ATVO** (☎*0421/383672* ⊕*www.atvo.it*) make a less scenic but quicker (20-minute) and cheaper (€3) nonstop trip from the airport to Piazzale Roma, where you can get a vaporetto to the landing nearest your hotel. Tickets are sold at the airport ticket booth (open daily 9 to 7:30), and on the bus when the booth is closed. A land taxi to Piazzale Roma costs about €40.

Venice is on the east–west A4 autostrada, which connects with Padua, Verona, Brescia, Milan, and Turin. If you bring a car to Venice, you will have to pay for a garage or parking space.

Venice has rail connections with every major city in Italy and Europe. Note that Venice's station is **Stazione Ferroviaria Santa Lucia**, not to be confused with Stazione Ferroviaria Venezia-Mestre, which is located on the mainland 12 km (7 mi) outside of town. Some continental trains stop only at the Mestre station; in such cases you can catch the next Venice-bound train. Be aware that if you change from a regional train to an Intercity or Eurostar, you'll need to upgrade with a *supplemento* (extra charge) or be liable for a hefty fine. You're also subject to a fine if before boarding you don't validate your ticket in one of the yellow machines found on or near platforms.

10

GETTING AROUND

Venice's primary means of public transportation is by vaporetto (water bus). **ACTV** (☎*041/2424* ⊕*www.hellovenezia.it*) operates vaporetti on several routes through and around the city. Beginning at 11 PM there is limited service through the night. Landing stages are clearly marked with name and line number, but check before boarding to make sure the boat is going in your direction. Line 1 is the Grand Canal local, calling at every stop and continuing via San Marco to the Lido. The trip takes about 35 minutes from Ferrovia to Vallaresso, San Marco.

A vaporetto ticket for all lines costs €6 one-way (children under four ride free). Another option is a Travel Card: €15 buys 24 hours and €30 buys 72 hours of unlimited travel. For travelers between ages 14 and 29, the 72-hour pass is €18 with the Rolling Venice card. Ask for the card

(€4) before buying your tickets. A shuttle ticket allows you to cross a canal, one stop only, for €2.

As your gondola glides away from the fondamenta, a transformation takes place. To some it feels like a Disney ride, but if you insist that your gondolier take you through the tiny side canals, you'll get an intimate glimpse of the city that can't be experienced any other way.

San Marco is loaded with gondola stations, but to get off the circuit, try the San Tomà or Santa Sofia (near Ca' d'Oro) stations. The price of a 40-minute ride is supposed to be fixed at €80 for up to six passengers, rising to €100 between 7:30 PM and 8 AM, but these are minimums and you may have difficulty finding a gondolier who will work for that unless the city is empty. Come to terms on cost and duration before you start, and make it clear that you want to see more than just the Grand Canal.

Many tourists are unaware of the two-man gondola ferries that cross the Grand Canal at numerous strategic points. At €.50, they're the cheapest and shortest gondola ride in Venice, and they can save a lot of walking. Look for TRAGHETTO signs and hand your fare to the gondolier when you board.

VISITOR INFORMATION
The multilingual staff of the **Venice tourism office** (☎*041/5298711* ⊕*www. turismovenezia.it) can help you out with directions and up-to-the-minute information about events in the city and sight closures. There are office branches at Marco Polo Airport; the train station; Procurate Nuove, near Museo Correr on Piazza San Marco; Garage Comunale, on Piazzale Roma; the Venice Pavilion, near Ghardini Reali in San Marco; and Santa Maria Elisabetta 6/a, on the Lido. The train-station branch is open daily 8–6:30; other branches generally open at 9:30.*

PIAZZA SAN MARCO

One of the world's most evocative squares, Piazza San Marco (St. Mark's Square) is the heart of Venice, a vast open space bordered by an orderly procession of arcades marching toward the fairy-tale cupolas and marble lacework of the Basilica di San Marco. Perpetually packed by day with people and fluttering pigeons, it can be magical at night, especially in winter, when mists swirl around the lampposts and the Campanile.

Piazzetta San Marco, the "little square" leading from Piazza San Marco to the waters of Bacino San Marco (St. Mark's Basin), is a *molo* (landing) that was once the grand entryway to the republic. It's distinguished by two columns towering above the waterfront. One is topped by the winged lion, a traditional emblem of St. Mark that became the symbol of Venice itself; the other supports St. Theodore, the city's first patron, along with his dragon. Between these columns the republic traditionally executed convicts.

EXPLORING PIAZZA SAN MARCO

6 **Basilica di San Marco.** An opulent synthesis of Byzantine and Romanesque styles, Venice's gem is laid out in a Greek-cross floor plan and topped with five plump domes. It didn't become the cathedral of Venice until 1807, but its role as the Chiesa Ducale (doge's private chapel) gave it immense power and wealth.

FodorsChoice
★

The basilica is famous for its 43,055 square feet of mosaics, which run from floor to ceiling thanks to an innovative roof of brick vaulting. Many of the original windows were filled in to make room for even more artwork. At midday, when the interior is fully illuminated, the mosaics truly come alive, the shimmer of their tiny gold tiles becoming nothing short of magical. The earliest mosaics are from the 11th and 12th centuries, and the last were added in the early 1700s.

Climb the steep stairway to the **Galleria** and the **Museo di San Marco** for the best overview of the basilica's interior. From here you can step outdoors for a sweeping panorama of Piazza San Marco and out over the lagoon to San Giorgio. The displays focus mainly on the types of mosaic and how they have been restored over the years. But the highlight is a close-up view of the original gilt bronze horses that were once on the outer gallery.

Be aware that guards at the basilica door turn away anyone with bare shoulders or knees; no shorts, short skirts, or tank tops are allowed. If you want a free guided tour in English during summer months (less certain in winter, as the guides are volunteers), look for groups forming on the porch inside the main door. You may also arrange tours by appointment. ⊠ *Piazza San Marco* ☎ *041/2708311 basilica, 041/2702421 for free tours Apr.–Oct. (call weekday mornings)* ⌨ *Basilica free, Tesoro €2, Santuario and Pala d'Oro €1.50, Galleria and Museo di San Marco €3* ⏰ *May–Sept., Mon.–Sat. 9:45–5:30, Sun. 2–4; Oct.–Apr., Mon.– Sat. 9:45–4:30, Sun. 2–4. Last entry ½ hr before closing* Ⓥ *Vallaresso/ San Zaccaria.*

7 **Palazzo Ducale** *(Doge's Palace).* Rising above the Piazzetta San Marco, this Gothic-Renaissance fantasia of pink-and-white marble is a majestic expression of the prosperity and power attained during Venice's most glorious period. Some architectural purists find the building top-heavy—its hulking upper floors rest upon a graceful ground-floor colonnade—but the design is what gives the palace its distinctive identity; it's hard to imagine it any other way. Always much more than a residence, the palace was Venice's White House, Senate, torture chamber, and prison rolled into one.

Though a fortress for the doge stood on this spot in the early 9th century, the building you see today was begun in the 12th century, and, like the basilica next door, was continually remodeled over the centuries. The palace's sumptuous chambers have walls and ceilings covered with works by Venice's greatest artists. The ceiling of the **Sala del Senato** (Senate Chamber), featuring *The Triumph of Venice* by Tintoretto, is magnificent, but it's dwarfed by his masterpiece *Paradise* in the **Sala del Maggiore Consiglio** (Great Council Hall). A vast work commissioned

10

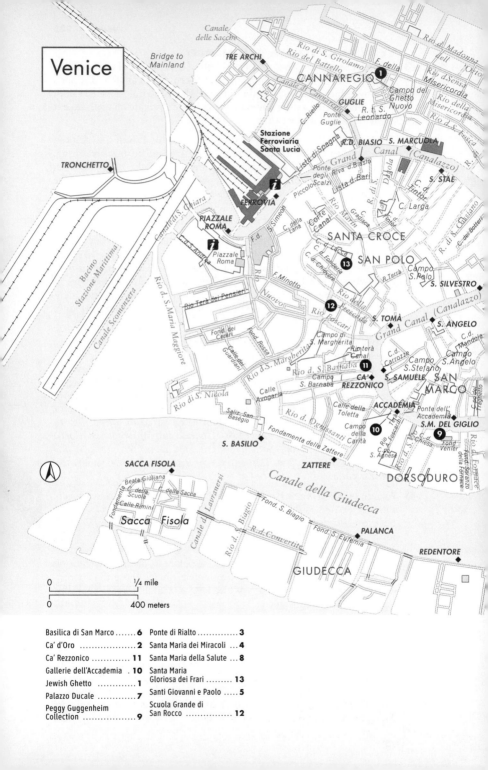

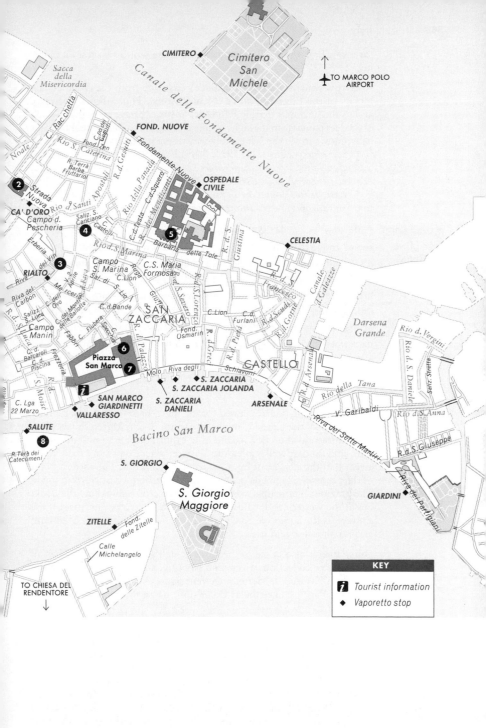

Sacca della Miséricordia

CIMITERO

Cimitero San Michele

TO MARCO POLO AIRPORT

Canale delle Fondamente Nuove

FOND. NUOVE

Noale

C. Racchetta

Fond. Zen

C.lo dei Gesuiti

R. Terrà Barba Fruttariol

Rio S. Caterina

R.d. Gesuiti

Strada Nuova

CA' D'ORO

Campo d. Pescheria

Rio d. Santi Apostoli

Saliz. S. Canciano

C.d. Testa

Rio della Panada

Fondamente Nuove

C.d. Squero

Mendicanti

OSPEDALE CIVILE

CELESTIA

Castelli

Erberia

del Vin

Rio di S. Marina

Barbaria

delle Tole

Giustina

R. d. S.

RIALTO

Riva del Carbon

Campo S. Marina

C.S. Maria Formosa

Rio d.S. Lio

Sal. di S. Lio

C. Lion

Campo S. Luca

C. dell' Ovo

Merceria

S. Aprile

R. Francesco

R. d. Scudi

Canale d. Galeazze

Darsena Grande

Rio d. Vergini

Rio di S. Daniele

Saliz. Stretta

R.d. Saliz. S. Luca

Campo Manin

C. d. Bande

C. de Mori della Ballotte

SAN ZACCARIA

S. Severo

R. d. S. Lorenzo

C. Lion

C.d. Furlani

R. d. Corte

R. dl Osmarin

CASTELLO

C.d. Piscina

C. d. Barcaroli

Frezzeria

C. Fabbri

C. Flubera

Spadaria

R. d. Palazzo

Fond. Osmarin

R.d. Greci

R. d. Pietà

R. d. Arsenale

Piazza San Marco

Molo

Riva degli

Schiavoni

Rio della Tana

V. Garibaldi

Rio di S. Anna

R.d. S. Giuseppe

SAN MARCO GIARDINETTI

S. ZACCARIA

S. ZACCARIA JOLANDA

S. ZACCARIA DANIELI

ARSENALE

Riva dei Sette Martiri

Riva dei Partigiani

C. Lga 22 Marzo

VALLARESSO

SALUTE

R.Terà dei Catecumeni

Bacino San Marco

S. GIORGIO

S. Giorgio Maggiore

GIARDINI

ZITELLE

Fond. delle Zitelle

Calle Michelangelo

TO CHIESA DEL RENDENTORE

KEY

i Tourist information

♦ Vaporetto stop

for a vast hall, this dark, dynamic piece is the world's largest oil painting (23 by 75 feet).

A narrow canal separates the palace's east side from the cramped cell blocks of the **Prigioni Nuove** (New Prisons). High above the water arches the enclosed marble **Ponte dei Sospiri** (Bridge of Sighs), which earned its name from the sighs of those being led to their fate. Look out its windows to see the last earthly view these prisoners beheld. ✉ *Piazzetta San Marco* ☎*041/2715911, 041/5209070 "Secret Itinerary" tour* 🖃*Piazza San Marco museum card €12, Musei Civici museum pass €18, "Secret Itinerary" tour €16* ⊙ *Apr.–Oct., daily 9–7; Nov.–Mar., daily 9–5. Last tickets sold 1 hr before closing. English "Secret Itinerary" tours in morning; reservations advisable* Ⓥ *Vallaresso/San Zaccaria.*

NEED A BREAK?

Caffè Florian (☎*041/5205641*), located in the Procuratie Nuove, has served coffee to the likes of Casanova, Charles Dickens, and Marcel Proust. It's Venice's oldest café, continuously in business since 1720 (though you'll find it closed Wednesday in winter). Counter seating is less expensive than taking a table, especially when there's live music. In the Procuratie Vecchie, **Caffè Quadri** (☎*041/5289299*) exudes almost as much history as Florian across the way, and is similarly pricey. It was shunned by 19th-century Venetians when the occupying Austrians made it their gathering place. In winter it closes Monday.

DORSODURO

The sestiere Dorsoduro (named for its "hard back" solid clay foundation) is across the Grand Canal to the south of San Marco. It is a place of monumental churches, meandering canals, the city's finest art museums, and a boardwalk called the Zattere, where on sunny days you'll swear half the city is out for a *passeggiata,* or stroll. The eastern point of the peninsula, Punta della Dogana, has one of the best views in town. The Stazione Marittima, where in summer cruise ships line the dock, lies at the western end. Midway between these two points, just off the Zattere, is the Squero di San Trovaso, where gondolas have been built and repaired for centuries.

Dorsoduro is also home to the Gallerie dell'Accademia, which has an unparalleled collection of Venetian painting, and Ca' Rezzonico, which houses the Museo del Settecento Veneziano. Another of its landmark sites, the Peggy Guggenheim Collection, has a fine selection of 20th-century art.

EXPLORING DOSODURO

⑪ Ca' Rezzonico. Designed by Baldassare Longhena in the 17th century, this palace was completed nearly 100 years later by Giorgio Massari and became the last home of English poet Robert Browning (1812–89). Elizabeth Taylor and Richard Burton danced in the Baroque ballroom in the 1960s. Today Ca' Rezzonico is the home of the **Museo del Settecento** (Museum of Venice in the 1700s). Its main floor is packed with period furniture and tapestries in gilded salons (note the four

Tiepolo ceiling frescoes) and successfully retains the feel of an old Venetian palazzo. Upper floors contain hundreds of paintings, most from Venetian schools of artists. There's even a restored apothecary, complete with powders and potions. ✉ *Fondamenta Rezzonico, Dorsoduro 3136* ☎*041/2410100* 🎫*€6.50, Musei Civici museum pass €18* ⊙ *Apr.–Oct., daily 10–6; Nov.–Mar., daily 10–5. Last entry 1 hr before closing* Ⓥ *Ca' Rezzonico.*

★ ⑩ **Gallerie dell'Accademia.** Napoléon founded these galleries in 1807 on the site of a religious complex he'd suppressed, and what he initiated now amounts to the world's most extraordinary collection of Venetian art. Jacopo Bellini is considered the father of the Venetian Renaissance, and in Room 2 you can compare his *Madonna and Child with Saints* with such later works as *Madonna of the Orange Tree* by Cima da Conegliano (circa 1459–1517) and *Ten Thousand Martyrs of Mt. Ararat* by Vittore Carpaccio (circa 1455–1525).

In Room 10, *Feast in the House of Levi,* commissioned as a Last Supper, got Veronese dragged before the Inquisition over its depiction of dogs, jesters, and German (therefore Protestant) soldiers. The artist saved his neck by simply changing the title, so that the painting represented a different biblical feast. Titian's *Presentation of the Virgin* (Room 24) is the collection's only work originally created for the building in which it hangs. Don't miss Rooms 20 and 21, with views of 15th- and 16th-century Venice by Carpaccio and Gentile Bellini (1429–1507), Giovanni's brother—you'll see how little the city has changed.

Booking tickets in advance isn't essential, but helps during busy seasons and costs only an additional €1. Booking is necessary to see the **Quadreria,** where additional works cover every inch of a wide hallway. A free map names art and artists, and the bookshop sells a more-informative English-language booklet. In the main galleries a €4 audio guide saves reading but adds little to each room's excellent annotation. ✉ *Campo della Carità, Dorsoduro 1050* ☎*041/5222247, 041/5200345 reservations* ⊕*www.gallerieaccademia.org* 🎫*€6.50, €11 includes Ca' d'Oro and Museo Orientale* ⊙*Tues.–Sun. 8:15–7:15, Mon. 8:15–2* Ⓥ *Accademia.*

10

NEED A BREAK? There's no sunnier spot in Venice than **Fondamenta delle Zattere,** along the southern edge of Dorsoduro. It's the city's gigantic public terrace, with bustling bars and gelato shops; come here to stroll, read in the open air, and play hooky from sightseeing. The Zattere's most decadent treat is found at **Gelateria Nico** (✉*Dorsoduro 922* ☎*041/5225293*)—order their famous *gianduiotto,* a nutty slab of chocolate ice cream floating on a cloud of whipped cream, and relax on the big, welcoming deck.

⑨ **Peggy Guggenheim Collection.** A small but choice selection of 20th-century painting and sculpture is on display at this gallery in the heiress Guggenheim's former Grand Canal home. Through wealth and social connections, Guggenheim (1898–1979) became a serious art patron, and her collection here in Palazzo Venier dei Leoni includes works by Picasso, Kandinsky, Pollock, Motherwell, and Ernst (at one time her husband).

The museum serves beverages, snacks, and light meals in its refreshingly shady, artistically sophisticated garden. On Sunday at 3 PM the museum offers a free tour and art workshop for children 12 and under. ✉ *Fondamenta Venier dei Leoni, Dorsoduro 701* ☎ *041/5209083* ⊕ *www.guggenheim-venice.it* ✆ *€10* ⓢ *Wed.–Mon. 10–6* Ⓥ *Accademia.*

8 **Santa Maria della Salute.** The view of La Salute (as this church is commonly called) from the Riva degli Schiavoni at sunset or from the Accademia bridge by moonlight is unforgettable. Baldassare Longhena was 32 years old when he won a competition to design a shrine honoring the Virgin Mary for saving Venice from a plague that killed 47,000 residents. Outside, this simple white octagon is adorned with a colossal cupola lined with snail-like buttresses and a Palladian-style facade; inside are a polychrome marble floor and six chapels. The Byzantine icon above the main altar has been venerated as the Madonna della Salute (of health) since 1670, when Francesco Morosini brought it here from Crete. For the Festa della Salute, held November 21, Venetians make a pilgrimage here and light candles in thanksgiving for another year's health. ✉ *Punta della Dogana, Dorsoduro* ☎ *041/2743928* ✆ *Church free, sacristy €1.50* ⓢ *Apr.–Sept., daily 9–noon and 3–6:30; Oct.–Mar., daily 9–noon and 3–5:30* Ⓥ *Salute.*

SAN POLO & SANTA CROCE

The two smallest of Venice's six sestieri, San Polo and Santa Croce were named after their main churches, though the Chiesa di Santa Croce was demolished in 1810. The city's most famous bridge, the Ponte di Rialto, unites sestiere San Marco (east) with San Polo (west). The Rialto Bridge takes its name from Rivoaltus, the high ground on which it was built. San Polo has two other major sites, Santa Maria Gloriosa dei Frari and the Scuola Grande di San Rocco, as well as some worthwhile but lesser-known churches.

Shops abound in the area surrounding the Rialto Bridge. On the San Marco side you'll find fashions, on the San Polo side food. Chiesa di San Giacometto, where you see the first fruit vendors as you come off the bridge on the San Polo side, was probably built in the 11th and 12th centuries, about the time the surrounding market came into being. Public announcements were traditionally read in the church's campo; its 24-hour clock, though lovely, has rarely worked.

EXPLORING SAN POLO & SANTA CROCE

3 **Ponte di Rialto** *(Rialto Bridge)*. The competition to design a stone bridge across the Grand Canal (replacing earlier wooden versions) attracted the late-16th-century's best architects, including Michelangelo, Palladio, and Sansovino, but the job went to the less famous but appropriately named Antonio da Ponte. His pragmatic design featured shop space and was high enough for galleys to pass beneath; it kept decoration and cost to a minimum at a time when the republic's coffers were low due to continual wars against the Turks and the opening of oceanic trade routes. Along the railing you'll enjoy one of the city's most famous views: the Grand Canal vibrant with boat traffic. Ⓥ *Rialto.*

⑬ **Santa Maria Gloriosa dei Frari.** This immense Gothic church of russet-
★ color brick, completed in the 1400s after more than a century of work,
is deliberately austere, befitting the Franciscan brothers' insistence on
spirituality and poverty. However, *I Frari* (as it's known locally) contains some of the most brilliant paintings in any Venetian church. Visit
the sacristy first, to see Giovanni Bellini's 1488 triptych *Madonna and
Child with Saints* in all its mellow luminosity, painted for precisely this
spot. The Corner Chapel on the other side of the chancel is graced by
Bartolomeo Vivarini's (1415–84) 1474 altarpiece *St. Mark Enthroned
and Saints John the Baptist, Jerome, Peter, and Nicholas,* of similarly
exquisite detail and color.

Titian's beautiful *Madonna di Ca' Pesaro,* in the left aisle, was modeled
after his wife, who died in childbirth. The painting took almost 10 years
to complete, and in it Titian totally disregarded the conventions of his
time by moving the Virgin out of center frame and making the saints
active participants. ✉*Campo dei Frari, San Polo* ☎*041/2728618,
041/2750462 Chorus* 🖰*€3, Chorus pass €9* ⊗*Mon.–Sat. 9–6, Sun.
1–6* Ⓥ*San Tomà.*

⑫ **Scuola Grande di San Rocco.** St. Rocco's popularity stemmed from his
miraculous recovery from the plague and his care for fellow sufferers.
Throughout the plague-filled Middle Ages, followers and donations
abounded, and this elegant example of Venetian Renaissance architecture was the result. Although it is bold and dramatic outside, its contents are even more stunning—a series of more than 60 paintings by
Tintoretto. In 1564 Tintoretto edged out competition for a commission
to decorate a ceiling by submitting not a sketch, but a finished work,
which he moreover offered free of charge. *Moses Striking Water from
the Rock, The Brazen Serpent,* and *The Fall of Manna* represent three
afflictions—thirst, disease, and hunger—that San Rocco and later his
brotherhood sought to relieve. ✉*Campo San Rocco, San Polo 3052*
☎*041/5234864* ⊕*www.scuolagrandesanrocco.it* 🖰*€7* ⊗*Apr.–Oct.,
daily 9–5:30; Nov.–Mar., daily 10–5. Last entry ½ hr before closing*
Ⓥ*San Tomà.*

10

CASTELLO & CANNAREGIO

Twice the size of tiny San Polo and Santa Croce, Castello and Cannaregio combined spread east to west from one end of Venice to the other.
From working-class shipbuilding neighborhoods to the world's first
ghetto, here you see a cross section of city life that's always existed
beyond the palace walls. There are churches that could make a Renaissance pope jealous and one of the Grand Canal's prettiest palaces, Ca'
d'Oro, as well as detour options for leaving the crowds behind.

EXPLORING CASTELLO & CANNAREGIO

❷ **Ca' d'Oro.** This exquisite Venetian Gothic palace was once literally
★ a "Golden House," when its marble traceries and ornaments were
embellished with pure gold. Created in 1434 by the enamored patrician Marino Contarini for his wife, Ca' d'Oro became a love offering
a second time when a 19th-century Russian prince gave it to Maria

Taglioni, a celebrated classical dancer who collected palaces along the Grand Canal. The last proprietor, perhaps more taken with Venice than with any of his lovers, left Ca' d'Oro to the city, after having had it carefully restored and filled with antiquities, sculptures, and paintings that today make up the **Galleria Franchetti**. Besides Andrea Mantegna's celebrated *St. Sebastian* and other first-rate Venetian works, the Galleria Franchetti contains the type of fresco that once adorned the exteriors of Venetian buildings (commissioned by those who could not afford a marble facade). One such detached fresco displayed here was made by a young Titian for the (now grayish-white) facade of the Fondaco dei Tedeschi, now the main post office. ⊠*Calle Ca' d'Oro, Cannaregio 3933* ☎*041/5222349* ⊕*www.cadoro.org* ✑*€6 includes Museo Orientale, €11 includes Gallerie dell'Accademia and Museo Orientale* ⊗*Tues.–Sun. 8:15–7, Mon. 8:15–2; last entry ½ hr before closing* Ⓥ*Ca' d'Oro.*

❶ **Jewish Ghetto.** The neighborhood that gave the world the word *ghetto* is today a quiet warren of backstreets that is still home to Jewish institutions, a kosher restaurant, a rabbinical school, and five synagogues. Though Jews may have arrived earlier, the first synagogues weren't built and a cemetery wasn't founded until the Askenazim, or Eastern European Jews, came in the late 1300s. Dwindling coffers may have prompted the republic to sell temporary visas to Jews, but over the centuries they were alternately tolerated and expelled. The Rialto commercial district, as vividly recounted in Shakespeare's *The Merchant of Venice,* depended on Jewish merchants and moneylenders for trade, and to help cover ever-increasing war expenses.

In 1516 relentless local opposition forced the Senate to confine Jews to an island in Cannaregio, named for its *geto* (foundry), which produced cannons. Although the gates were pulled down after Napoléon's 1797 arrival, the Jews realized full freedom only in the late 19th century with the founding of the Italian state.

The area has Europe's highest density of Renaissance-era synagogues, and visiting them is a unique cross-cultural experience. Though each is marked by the tastes of its individual builders, Venetian influence is evident throughout. Women's galleries resemble those of theaters from the same era, and some synagogues were decorated by artisans who were simultaneously active in local churches.

The small but well-arranged **Museo Ebraico** highlights centuries of Jewish culture with splendid silver Hanukkah lamps and Torahs, and handwritten, beautifully decorated wedding contracts in Hebrew. Tours of the ghetto in Italian and English leave hourly from the museum. ⊠*Campo del Ghetto Nuovo, Cannaregio 2902/b* ☎*041/715359* ⊕*www.museo ebraico.it* ✑*Museum €3, museum and synagogues €8.50* ⊗*June–Sept., Sun.–Fri. 10–7, last tour 5:30; Oct.–May, Sun.–Fri. 10–6, last tour 3:30* Ⓥ*San Marcuola/Guglie.*

❹ **Santa Maria dei Miracoli.** Tiny yet perfectly proportioned, this early-Renaissance gem is sheathed in marble and decorated inside with exquisite marble reliefs. Architect Pietro Lombardo (circa 1435–1515) miraculously compressed the building into its confined space, then created the illusion of greater size by varying the color of the exterior, adding extra pilasters on the building's canal side, and offsetting the arcade windows to make the arches appear deeper. The church was built in the 1480s to house *I Miracoli*, an image of the Virgin Mary that is said to perform miracles—look for it on the high altar. ⊠ *Campo Santa Maria Nova, Cannaregio* ☎ *041/2750462 Chorus* ⊠ *€3, Chorus pass €9* ⊙ *Mon.–Sat. 10–5, Sun. 1–5* Ⓥ *Rialto.*

> ### WORD OF MOUTH
>
> "The narrow *calle* of Venice could strike one as either charming or claustrophobic. At different times, we had both reactions."
>
> –Sue xx yy

★ ❺ **Santi Giovanni e Paolo.** This massive Dominican church, commonly called San Zanipolo, contains a wealth of art. The second official church of the republic after San Marco, San Zanipolo is the Venetian equivalent of London's Westminster Abbey, with a great number of important people, including 25 doges, buried here. Artistic highlights include an outstanding polyptych by Giovanni Bellini (right aisle, second altar); Alvise Vivarini's *Christ Carrying the Cross* (sacrestia); and Lorenzo Lotto's *Charity of St. Antonino* (right transept). Don't miss the Cappella del Rosario (Rosary Chapel), off the left transept, built in the 16th century to commemorate the 1571 victory of Lepanto, in western Greece, when Venice led a combined European fleet to defeat the Turkish Navy. However quick your visit, don't miss the Pietro Mocenigo tomb to the right of the main entrance, a monument built by the ubiquitous Pietro Lombardo and his sons. ⊠ *Campo dei Santi Giovanni e Paolo, Castello* ☎ *041/5235913* ⊠ *€2.50* ⊙ *Mon.–Sat. 9:30–6:30, Sun. noon–5:30* Ⓥ *Fondamente Nuove/Rialto.*

WHERE TO EAT

The catchword in Venice, at both fancy restaurants and holes-in-the-wall, is fish, often at its tastiest when it looks like nothing you've seen before. How do you learn firsthand about the catch of the day? An early-morning visit to the Rialto's *pescheria* (fish market) is more instructive than any book.

There's no getting around the fact that Venice has more than its share of overpriced, mediocre eateries that prey on tourists. Avoid places with cajoling waiters standing outside, and beware of restaurants that don't display their prices. At the other end of the spectrum, showy *menu turistico* (tourist menu) boards make offerings clear in a dozen languages, but for the same 15–20 euros you'd spend at such places you could do better at a *bacaro* (the local version of a wine bar) making a meal of *cicchetti* (savory snacks).

CANNAREGIO

$$$ ✕ **Al Fontego dei Pescaori.** Having had a stall at the Rialto fish market for over 25 years, Lolo, the proprietor, really knows fish, and diners fill two cheerful dining rooms to savor what might just be the freshest fish

10

in Venice. There are several spectacular offerings of pesce crudo (raw fish) among the antipasti. Pastas are excellent and the fish entrées are prepared simply but with a twist. Branzino (sea bass) may be topped with its own crispy skin and a frizzle of zucchini or wrapped around itself with the succulent skin becoming the stuffing. Meat dishes are available, but the wine list is built around local wines that go best with fish. ⊠*Sottoportego del Tagiapier, Cannaregio 3711* ☎*041/5200538* ⊟*MC, V* ☉*Closed Mon., 3 wks in Jan., 2 wks in Aug.* Ⓥ*Ca' d'Oro.*

$ ✕**Alla Vedova.** This warm trattoria not far from the Ca' d'Oro (it's also known as Trattoria Ca' d'Oro) was opened as a *bacaro* by the owner's great-grandparents. A Venetian terrazzo floor, old marble counter, and rustic furnishings lend a pleasant authenticity that's matched by the food and service. Cicchetti include tender *seppie roste* (grilled cuttle-fish), *polpette* (meatballs), and *baccalà mantecato* (cod creamed with milk and olive oil). The house winter pasta is the *pastisso de radicio rosso* (lasagna with sausage, radicchio, and béchamel sauce). In spring the chef switches to pastisso *de asparagi* (with asparagus). ⊠*Calle del Pistor, Cannaregio 3912* ☎*041/5285324* ⊟*No credit cards* ☉*Closed Thurs. No lunch Sun.* Ⓥ*Ca' d'Oro.*

$$ ✕**Anice Stellato.** Hidden away on one of the most romantic *fondamente* (canal-side streets) of Cannaregio, this family-run *bacaro*-trattoria is the place to stop for fairly priced, great-tasting food, though service can feel indifferent. The space has plenty of character: narrow columns rise from the colorful tile floor, dividing the room into cozy sections. Traditional Venetian fare is enriched with such offerings as *carpacci di pesce* (thin slices of raw tuna, swordfish, or salmon dressed with olive oil and fragrant herbs), tagliatelle with king prawns and zucchini flowers, and several tasty fish stews. Meat dishes are also served, including a tender beef fillet stewed in Barolo wine with potatoes. ⊠*Fondamenta de la Sensa, Cannaregio 3272* ☎*041/720744* ⊟*MC, V* ☉*Closed Mon. and Tues., 1 wk in Feb., and 3 wks in Aug.* Ⓥ*S. Alvise.*

$$–$$$ ✕**Vini da Gigio.** This family-run trattoria on the San Felice Canal is
★   deservedly popular with Venetians and visitors. Homemade pastas, such as rigatoni with duck sauce and arugula-stuffed ravioli nestled in a rich cheese sauce, are excellent. Fish is well represented on the menu, but the meat dishes steal the show: the Burano-style duck is a flavorful fricassee, the steak with red-pepper sauce and the lamb with a heavenly crusty coating are both superb, and the *fegato alla Veneziana* (Venetian style liver with onions) is among the best in Venice. Desserts are worth every luscious calorie. The wine list of over one thousand bottles is a major attraction; an oenophile will be in ecstasy here. ⊠*Fondamenta de la Chiesa, Cannaregio 3628/a* ☎*041/5285140* ⊟*DC, MC, V* ☉*Closed Mon. and Tues., 2 wks in Jan., and 3 wks in Aug.* Ⓥ*Ca' d'Oro.*

DORSODURO

¢   ✕**Cantinone Già Schiavi.** This beautiful 19th-century *bacaro* opposite the *squero* (gondola repair shop) of San Trovaso has original furnish-ings and one of the best wine selections in town—the walls are cov-ered floor to ceiling by bottles for purchase. Cicchetti here are some of the most inventive in Venice: try the crostini-style layers of bread, smoked swordfish, and slivers of raw zucchini, or pungent slices of parmeggiano, fig, and toast. They also have a creamy version of baccalà mantecato spiced with herbs. There are nearly a dozen open bottles of wine for experimenting at the bar. ⊠*Fondamenta* Maravegiei, *Dorso-duro 992* ☏*041/5230034* ⊟*No credit cards* ☾*Closed 2 wks in Aug.* Ⓥ*Zattere.*

★ $$$$ ✕**Ristorante Riviera.** Two lovely dining rooms and a canal-side terrace with an exquisite view, combined with truly inspired cuisine, make a visit to Riviera one to remember. Chef Monica Scarpa brings her creative touch to both traditional and contemporary dishes. Fish lovers will enjoy the tuna tartare, seafood risotto, or a mixed fish platter, while carnivores can dig into prosciutto with figs and pecorino cheese followed by a plate of succulent lamb chops with blueberry sauce. Host Luca excels at selecting the perfect wine for any combination of foods. Desserts include a plate of homemade cookies served with vin santo (sweet wine). A simple but appealing children's menu is offered. ⊠*Zattere, Dorsoduro 1473* ☏*041/5227621* ⌕*Reservations essential* ⊟*MC, V* ☾*Closed Mon., 4 weeks in Jan. and Feb.* Ⓥ*San Basilio.*

SAN POLO

$$$–$$$$ ✕**Al Paradiso.** In a small dining room made warm and cozy by its pleasing and unpretentious decor, proprietor Giordano makes all diners feel like honored guests. Pappardelle "al Paradiso" takes pasta with seafood sauce to new heights, while risotto with shrimp, champagne, and grapefruit puts a delectable twist on a traditional dish. The inspired and original array of entrées includes meat and fish selections such as a salmon with honey and balsamic vinegar in a stunning presentation. Desserts include a perfect panna cotta. There's an inspired wine list, but the house wines are infinitely better than those in other restaurants. ⊠*Calle dei Paradiso, San Polo 767* ☏*041/5234910* ⌕*Reservations essential* ⊟*AE, MC, V* ☾*Closed Mon. and 3 wks in Jan. and Feb.* Ⓥ*San Silvestro.*

$–$$ ✕**Antica Birreria La Corte.** Locals, students, and tourists flock here daily not only for the dazzling list of pizzas (including one topped with porcini mushrooms and wild-boar salami) but also for starters such as a salad of arugula and pecorino with a drizzle of chestnut honey. Gnocchi with white meat sauce or a rich creamy risotto can be followed with one of several excellent meat and fish entrées. Two kitchens—one for pizza and one for everything else—can result in courses arriving haphazardly. Beer's a better bet than wine here, thanks to the large selection on tap. ⊠*Campo San Polo, San Polo 2168* ☏*041/2750570* ⊟*MC, V* Ⓥ*San Silvestro/San Tomà.*

$–$$$ ✕**Bancogiro.** Come to this casual spot in the heart of the Rialto Market in a 15th-century loggia for a change from standard Venetian food. Yes, fish is on the menu, and some of the dishes are Venice classics; but highlights such as mousse *di gamberoni con salsa di avocado* (shrimp mousse with an avocado sauce) and Sicilian-style *sarde incinte* (stuffed, or "pregnant," sardines) are far from typical fare, though portions can be small. The wine list and cheese plate are both divine. There are tables upstairs in a carefully restored room with a partial view of the Grand Canal; when it's warm you can sit outdoors and get the full

10

canal view. ⊠ *Campo San Giacometto, San Polo, 122 under the porch* ☎*041/5232061* ⊟*No credit cards* ⊘*Closed Mon.* Ⓥ*Rialto.*

$-$$ ✕**Ostaria al Garanghelo.** Superior quality, competitive prices, and great ambience means this place is often packed with Venetians, especially for lunch and an after-work *ombra* (small glass of wine) and cicchetti. Chef Renato takes full advantage of the fresh ingredients from the Rialto Market, located a few steps away, bakes his own bread daily, and prefers cooking many dishes *al vapore* (steamed). The spicy *fagioli al uciletto* (literally beans, bird-style) has an unusual name and Tuscan origins; it's a perfect companion to a plate of fresh pasta. Don't confuse this centrally located restaurant with one of the same name in Via Garibaldi. ⊠*Calle dei Boteri, San Polo 1570* ☎*041/721721* ⊟*MC, V* ⊘*Closed Sun.* Ⓥ*Rialto.*

$$$$ ✕**Osteria da Fiore.** Tucked away on a little calle near Campo San Polo, **Fodor'sChoice** da Fiore is a favorite among high-end diners for its superbly prepared ★ Venetian cuisine and refined yet relaxed atmosphere. The Martin family are hands-on owners, with Mara in the kitchen and Maurizio running every aspect of the dining room. A superlative seafood lunch or dinner here might include delicate hors d'oeuvres of soft-shell crab, scallops, and tiny octopus, followed by a succulent risotto or pasta *con scampi e radicchio* (with shrimp and radicchio), and a perfectly cooked main course of *rombo* (turbot) or *tagliata di tonno* (tuna steak). The formerly all-fish menu has been expanded to include dishes such as a sublime risotto made with butternut squash and balsamic vinegar and a buffalo burger. A jacket is not required, but is highly recommended. ⊠*Calle del Scaleter, San Polo 2202* ☎*041/721308* ⚐*Reservations essential* ⊟*AE, DC, MC, V* ⊘*Closed Sun. and Mon., Aug., and Dec. 24–Jan. 15* Ⓥ*San Silvestro/San Stae.*

SANTA CROCE

$$ ✕**La Zucca.** The simple place settings, lattice-wood walls, canal window, and mélange of languages make this place feel as much like a typical vegetarian restaurant as you could expect to find in Venice. Though the menu does have superb meat dishes such as the *piccata di pollo ai caperi e limone con riso* (sliced chicken with capers and lemon served with rice), more attention is paid to dishes from the garden: try the radicchio *di Treviso con funghi e scaglie di Montasio* (with mushrooms and shavings of Montasio cheese) or the *finocchi piccanti con olive* (fennel in a spicy tomato-olive sauce). ⊠*Calle del Tintor, Santa Croce 1762* ☎*041/5241570* ⚐*Reservations essential* ⊟*AE, DC, MC, V* ⊘*Closed Sun. and 1 wk in Dec.* Ⓥ*San Stae.*

$$$ ✕**Vecio Fritolin.** At this tidy *bacaro con cucina* (with kitchen) you can have a traditional meal featuring such dishes as *bigoli in salsa* (thick spaghetti with anchovy sauce), baked fish with herbs, and ravioli with scampi and chicory. The name, which translates as "Old Fry Shop," refers to a bygone Venetian tradition of shops selling fried fish "to go,"as in London, except paired with polenta rather than chips. For €8, you can still get a paper cone of *fritto* here. ⊠*Calle della Regina, Santa Croce 2262* ☎*041/5222881* ⊟*AE, DC, MC, V* ⊘*Closed Mon.* Ⓥ*San Stae.*

WHERE TO STAY

Most of Venice's hotels are in renovated palaces, but space is at a premium—and comes for a price—and even relatively ample rooms may seem cramped by American standards. Also, not all hotels have lounge areas, and because of preservation laws, some hotels are not permitted to install elevators, so if these features are essential, ask ahead of time.

Many travelers assume that a hotel near Piazza San Marco will give them the most convenient location, but keep in mind that Venice is scaled to humans (on foot) rather than automobiles; it's difficult to find a location that's *not* convenient to most of the city. Areas away from San Marco may also offer the benefit of being less overrun by day-trippers whose primary destination is the Piazza.

It is essential to have detailed directions to your hotel when you arrive. Arm yourself with not only a detailed map and postal address (Dorsoduro 825), but the actual street name (Fondamenta San Trovaso).

Venezia Sì (☏ *39/041/5222264 from abroad, 199/173309 from Italy* ⏲ *Mon.–Sat. 9 AM–11 PM* 🌐 *www.veneziasi.it*) can help for last-minute reservations, as their Web site lists most hotels in town (with some photographs), and they offer a free reservation service over the phone. It's the public relations arm of **AVA** *(Venetian Hoteliers Association)* and has booths where you can make same-day reservations at **Piazzale Roma** (☏ *041/5231397* ⏲ *Daily 9 AM–10 PM*), **Santa Lucia train station** (☏ *041/715288 or 041/715016* ⏲ *Daily 8 AM–9 PM*), and **Marco Polo Airport** (☏ *041/5415133* ⏲ *Daily 9 AM–10 PM*).

CANNAREGIO

$$ **3749 Ponte Chiodo.** This cheery, homey bed-and-breakfast takes its name from the bridge leading to its entrance (one of the only two left in the lagoon without hand railings). Attentively appointed rooms with geranium-filled window boxes overlook either the bridge and expansive canals below or the spacious enclosed garden. It's a family-owned operation, and service is accommodating and friendly; you'll get lots of suggestions for dining and sightseeing. The private garden and patio are perfect for a relaxing breakfast or scribbling postcards or e-mails to the folks back home. Some bathrooms are smallish, but overall it's an excellent value. The location is also handy to the Ca' d'Oro vaporetto. **Pros:** highly attentive service; warm, relaxed atmosphere; canal views. **Cons:** no elevator will be a problem for some. ✉ *Calle Racchetta, Cannaregio 3749* ☏ *041/2413935* 🌐 *www.pontechiodo.it* *6 rooms* *In-room: no phone, safe, refrigerator, Wi-Fi. In-hotel: room service, bar, private kitchen for guest use, no elevator, public Internet, public Wi-Fi* *MC, V* *BP* Ⓥ *Ca' d'Oro.*

CASTELLO

$$ **Santa Maria della Pietà.** Though this *casa per ferie* (vacation house) is more spartan than sumptuous, there's more light and space here than in many of Venice's four-star hotels. The hotel, which occupies the upper floors of two historic palaces, opened 10 years ago; it has big windows, restored Venetian terrazzo floors, and a huge rooftop terrace

10

with a coffee shop, bar, and unobstructed lagoon views. On top of these advantages, it's well situated—just 100 yards from the main waterfront and about a 10-minute walk from St. Mark's—which means you'll have to book early to stay here. The shared bathrooms are plentiful, spacious, and scrupulously clean. Some rooms have been remodeled to include en-suite baths, and family rooms with up to six beds are available. **Pros:** space, light, and views at a bargain price. **Cons:** not luxurious. ⊠ *Calle della Pietà, Castello 3701* ☎ *041/2443639* ⊕ *www.pietavenezia.org/casaferie.htm* ☞ *15 rooms* ⌂ *In-room: no phone, no TV. In-hotel: bar* ⊟ *No credit cards* ⏐○⏐ *BP* Ⓥ *Arsenale/San Zaccaria.*

DORSODURO

$$ 🖾 **Casa Rezzonico.** Rooms here are the rarest site in Venice: good value. A bright canal graces the hotel entrance, and a private garden (where breakfast is served in temperate weather) makes the inner courtyard particularly inviting. Rooms vary in size but are pleasant and comfortable, and overlook either the garden or the canal. Young owners Matteo and Mattia are attentive and helpful, and the location is convenient for exploring the sights from the Rialto to the Salute, hopping the vaporetto at Ca' Rezzonico for any San Marco location. The hotel is easily reachable on foot from Piazzale Roma as well, for coming and going by car. **Pros:** a garden for relaxing, canal views at a reasonable rate, convenient to many locations, great for families. **Cons:** the six rooms fill up early, especially on weekends. ⊠ *Fondamenta Gherardini, Dorsoduro 2813* ☎ *041/2770653* ⊕ *www.casarezzonico.it* ☞ *6 rooms, from single to quad* ⌂ *In-room: safe, dial-up. In-hotel: room service, no elevator* ⊟ *AE, MC, V, cash preferred* ⏐○⏐ *BP* Ⓥ *Ca' Rezzonico.*

$$$$ 🖾 **Hotel American–Dinesen.** This quiet, family-run hotel has a yellow stucco facade typical of Venetian houses. A hall decorated with reproduction antiques and Oriental rugs leads to a breakfast room reminiscent of a theater foyer, with red velvet chairs and gilt wall lamps. Guest rooms are spacious and tastefully furnished in sage-green and delicate pink fabrics with lacquered Venetian-style furniture throughout. Some front rooms have terraces with canal views. A water taxi can deposit you directly in front of the hotel on arrival, and although the four-story building has no elevator, you'll have assistance with your luggage if needed. The exceptional service will help you feel at home at the hotel and in Venice. **Pros:** high degree of personal service; located on a quiet, exceptionally picturesque canal. **Cons:** lack of elevator will be a problem for some. ⊠ *San Vio, Dorsoduro 628* ☎ *041/5204733* ⊕ *www.hotelamerican.com* ☞ *28 rooms, 2 suites* ⌂ *In-room: safe, refrigerator, Wi-Fi. In-hotel: room service, bar, no elevator, concierge, laundry service, public Wi-Fi, some pets allowed* ⊟ *AE, MC, V* ⏐○⏐ *BP* Ⓥ *Accademia/Salute.*

★ **$$–$$$$**   🖾 **La Calcina.** In 1877, *Stones of Venice* author John Ruskin lodged at the eclectic La Calcina, which sits in an enviable position along the sunny Zattere, and has front rooms offering heady vistas across the expansive Giudecca Canal. You can sunbathe on the *altana* (wooden roof terrace) or enjoy an afternoon tea in one of the lounge's reading corners with flickering candlelight and barely perceptible classical music. A stone staircase leads to the rooms upstairs, which have parquet floors, original Art Deco furniture, and firm beds. Besides full meals at lunch and dinner, the Piscina bar and restaurant offers drinks and fresh snacks all day in the elegant dining room or on the waterside terrace. A variety of apartments are also available. One single room does not have a private bath. **Pros:** a historic and perennial favorite, rare rooftop altana, panoramic views from some rooms. **Cons:** not for travelers who want for contemporary surroundings, no elevator. ⌗*Zattere, Dorsoduro 780* ☏*041/5206466* ⊕*www.lacalcina.com* ⌀*27 rooms, 5 suites* ⌂*In-room: safe, refrigerator, dial-up, Wi-Fi. In-hotel: restaurant, room service, bar, no elevator, concierge, laundry service, public Wi-Fi* ▤*AE, DC, MC, V* ⊚*BP* ☑*Zattere.*

$$–$$$$ ⊡**Pensione Accademia Villa Maravege.** Aptly nicknamed "Villa of the **Fodor's**Choice Wonders," this patrician retreat once served as the Russian embassy and
★ was the fictional residence of Katharine Hepburn's character in the film *Summertime.* Outside, a secret garden awaits just beyond an iron gate, complete with a mini Palladian-style villa, flower beds, stone cupids, and verdant trees—all rarities in Venice. The hotel is located on a peaceful promontory where two side canals converge with the Grand Canal. The conservative rooms are outfitted with Venetian-style antiques and fine tapestry. Book well in advance. **Pros:** a historic, classic Venetian property. **Cons:** formal surroundings with lots of antiques are not well suited to families with young children. ⌗*Fondamenta Bollani, Dorsoduro 1058* ☏*041/5210188* ⊕*www.pensioneaccademia.it* ⌀*27 rooms, 2 suites* ⌂*In-room: safe, dial-up. In-hotel: bar, no elevator, concierge, laundry service* ▤*AE, DC, MC, V* ⊚*BP* ☑*Accademia.*

SAN MARCO

★ **$$$$** ⊡**Bauer Il Palazzo.** Il Palazzo, under the same management as the larger Bauer Hotel, is the ultimate word in luxury. Tufted Bevilacqua and Rubelli fabrics cover the walls, and no two rooms are decorated the same. What they have in common, however, are high ceilings, Murano glass, marble bathrooms, and damask drapes. Many have sweeping views. Breakfast is served on Venice's highest rooftop terrace, appropriately named Il Settimo Cielo (Seventh Heaven). The outdoor hot tub, also on the seventh floor, offers views of La Serenissima that will leave you breathless, and personable, professional staff will accommodate your every whim. **Pros:** Il Palazzo will pamper you while making you feel right at home. **Cons:** located in one of the busiest areas of the city. ⌗*Campo San Moisè, San Marco 1413/d* ☏*041/5207022* ⊕*www.ilpalazzovenezia.com* ⌀*44 rooms, 38 suites* ⌂*In-room: safe, refrigerator, DVD, Wi-Fi. In-hotel: restaurant, room service, bars, gym, concierge, laundry service, public Internet, public Wi-Fi, some pets allowed* ▤*AE, DC, MC, V* ⊚*EP* ☑*San Marco/Vallaresso.*

$$ ⊡**Ca' dei Dogi.** In the crush of hotels in and around Piazza San Marco, there are many undesirables, since the location alone attracts lodgers. This delightful gem, eked out of a 15th-century palace and located in a quiet courtyard secluded from the melee, is one notable exception. The thoughtful, personal touches added by owners Stefano and Susanna are evident everywhere, from the six individually decorated rooms (some with private terraces), to the carefully chosen contemporary furniture, to classic Venetian elements such as wall tapestries and mosaic tiles.

10

There's highly personal service; guests are often welcomed by one of the owners. There's a courtyard where you can enjoy breakfast or an evening interlude, and one attic apartment is available. **Pros:** terraces, with views of the Doge's Palace, are a definite plus. **Cons:** rooms are not expansive. ⊠ *Corte Santa Scolastica, Castello 4242* ☎ *041/2413751* ⊕ *www.cadeidogi.it* ⤶ *6 rooms* &*In-room: safe, dial-up. In-hotel: room service, no elevator, public Internet, public Wi-Fi, some pets allowed* ⊟*AE, DC, MC, V* ⭤*BP* ☑*San Zaccaria.*

NIGHTLIFE & THE ARTS

CARNEVALE

The first historical evidence of Carnevale (Carnival) in Venice dates from 1097, and for centuries the city marked the days preceding *quaresima* (Lent, the 40 days of abstinence leading up to Palm Sunday) with abundant feasting and wild celebrations. Carnevale was revived in the 1970s, and each year over the 10- to 12-day Carnevale period more than a half-million people attend concerts, theater and street performances, masquerade balls, historical processions, fashion shows, and contests. *A Guest in Venice* (⊕*www.aguestinvenice.com*) gives free advertising to public and private event festivities and is therefore one of the most complete Carnevale guides. For general Carnevale information, contact **Consorzio Comitato per il Carnevale di Venezia** (⊠*Santa Croce 1714* ☎*041/717065, 041/2510811 during Carnevale* ⛫*041/5200410* ⊕*www.carnevale.venezia.it*).

SHOPPING

Alluring shops abound in Venice. You'll find countless vendors of trademark Venetian wares such as glass and lace; the authenticity of some goods can be suspect. For more sophisticated tastes (and deeper pockets), there are jewelers, antiques dealers, and high-fashion boutiques on a par with those in Italy's larger cities. There are also some interesting craft and art studios, where you can find high-quality, one-of-a-kind articles, from handmade shoes to decorative lamps and mirrors.

It's always a good idea to mark on your map the location of a shop that interests you; otherwise you may not be able to find it again in the maze of tiny streets. Regular store hours are usually 9–12:30 and 3:30 or 4–7:30; some stores are closed Saturday afternoon or Monday morning. Food shops are open 8–1 and 5–7:30, and are closed Wednesday afternoon and all day Sunday. Many tourist-oriented shops are open all day, every day.

SHOPPING DISTRICTS

The **San Marco** area is full of shops and couture boutiques. **Le Mercerie,** along with the Frezzeria and Calle dei Fabbri, leading from Piazza San Marco, are some of Venice's busiest shopping streets. Other good shopping areas surround Calle del Teatro and Campi San Salvador, Manin, San Fantin, and San Bartolomeo. Less-expensive shops are between the Rialto Bridge and San Polo.

The Netherlands

The canals of Amsterdam

WORD OF MOUTH

"Amsterdam as a city was beautiful. So much to see that we are disappointed that we limited ourselves to just a couple of days. We WILL be going back and spending a longer amount of time there."

—Stacy321

WHAT'S WHERE

1 Amsterdam. Built on concentric rings of canals bordered by time-burnished, step-gabled houses, Amsterdam, the principal city of the Netherlands, is custom-made for sightseeing. You almost have to get to know the city from the water to be properly introduced, and glass-roof canal boats make that possible. Helpfully, the city is held together by the linchpins of its great public squares: the Dam, the Rembrandtplein, the Munt, and the Leidseplein.

2 The Bulb Fields. West of Amsterdam, the Bloemen Route (Flower Road) leads from Aalsmeer—one of the greatest floral villages in Europe—to the famed Keukenhof gardens and the town of Lisse. This is the Holland of tulips, hyacinths, and narcissi, aglow with the colors of Easter in spring and generally a rainbow of color year-round.

3 Haarlem. It is just a short hop from the ocean of annual color that is Holland's Bulb Route to this haven of perennial color. Haarlem's historic center is beautiful, dotted with charming *hofjes* (historic almshouse courtyards), and has a lively population—often the overspill of students who can't find lodgings in Amsterdam or Leiden. The city is also home to fine museums filled with art by masters of the Haarlem School

4 Delft. The tree-lined canals, humpbacked bridges, and step-gabled houses of Delft preserve the atmosphere of the 16th and 17th centuries better than any other city in the Netherlands. Visit here and you'll recognize it as the scene of paintings by native sons Vermeer and Pieter de Hooch.

5 The Hague. Called 's-Gravenhage or Den Haag by the Dutch (and "the Largest Village in Europe" by residents), The Hague is a royal and regal city—filled with patrician mansions and gracious parks, and home to Queen Beatrix. Its downtown is filled with fine restaurants and posh antiques shops. Although Amsterdam is the nation's constitutional capital, The Hague is the seat of the Dutch government and the International Court of Justice.

0		20 miles
0		30 km

North Sea

Overflakkee

Schouwen

Duiveland

Walcheren — Noord Beveland — Westerschelde

Vlissingen — Zuid Beveland — Westerschelde

Terneuzen

Schiermonnikoog

Ameland

Terschelling

Delfzijl

Vlieland

Leeuwarden   Groningen

Texel   Waddenzee

Den Helder   Heerenveen   Assen

IJsselmeer

Enkhuizen   Steenwijk   Emmen

Alkmaar   Hoorn   Meppel   Hoogeveen

Edam   Lelystad   *Oostelijk Flevoland*

IJmuiden   Zaandam   *Zuidelijk Flevoland*   Zwolle   Almelo

Haarlem   ⭐ AMSTERDAM   Deventer   Hengelo

3   **2**   **1**   Harderwijk   Enschede

5   Leiden   Alphen   Hilversum   Apeldoorn

⭐ DEN HAAG   Amersfoort   Doetinchem   Winterswijk
(THE HAGUE)

4   Delft   Gouda   Utrecht

Lek   Arnhem

Rotterdam   Nijmegen

borne   *Waal*

Beijerland   Dordrecht   *Rhein*

holen   's Hertogenbosch

Breda   Tilburg

Roosendaal

Eindhoven   *Maas*

Antwerpen
(Antwerp)

GERMANY

BELGIUM

Bruxelles
⭐ Brussel   Maastricht
(Brussels)

Bonn
⭐

THE NETHERLANDS (ONLY THE TWO provinces that surround Amsterdam and The Hague are technically "Holland") is every cliché you imagine and more. While the clogs may be largely confined to the souvenir shops, this really is a land of windmills, tulips, canals, and bicycles, albeit today with the modern backdrop of a fast-paced 21st-century nation. At its heart is one of Europe's most important capitals, a famously open and tolerant place where almost anything goes, and the pragmatic business-like approach of the Dutch has even turned its red-light district and coffee shops into tourist attractions and profitable industries.

The Netherlands only assumed its current form in 1830, when Belgium broke away as an independent state, but the country has existed in one form or another for around a thousand years. A proud seafaring nation that built its wealth on international trade, it has also waged a war on the sea itself that is still ongoing. With much of the land lying below sea level, it owes its continued existence to a complex series of dykes, barriers, and polders reclaimed from the waters. This fight, coupled with a population that has always been slightly too large for the available land, has turned the Dutch into perhaps the most pragmatic and practical of all Europeans, as they have learnt through the years to make the best of what they had.

While Amsterdam has all the waterways, gabled townhouses, and rusty pushbikes you could possibly shake a stick at, it is only one aspect of the Netherlands. To get the full picture you'll need to head out to the other towns, or to the countryside that is just as flat as you've been told. The country's best-known city may be the national capital, but The Hague is where you'll find both the queen and the government. Haarlem and Delft are two wonderful, dollhouse-like cities that shouldn't be missed either. And in between, the fields become a brightly colored patchwork quilt of flowers if you time your visit to coincide with the spring blooms.

WHEN TO GO

The Netherlands is at its best when the temperatures climb, and cafés and restaurants spill across sidewalks to invite leisurely alfresco meals. Unfortunately, because such weather is so transient, you may find yourself sharing your sun-dappled experience with many others. Spring is the driest time of year, and since it's also when the famous tulip fields bloom (April and May are the prime bloom-viewing months), this is the most popular time to visit Holland.

With the approach of summer, museums, galleries, and tourist sights heave with visitors. Some say that if you're making an extended tour of Europe, you should consider scheduling Holland for the beginning or end of your itinerary, saving July and August for exploring less crowded countries.

If you have to visit in high summer, be sure to take a vacation from your Amsterdam vacation with some side trips to outer towns that have

TOP REASONS TO GO

Great Art. In the country that gave the world Rembrandt, Hals, Vermeer, Van Gogh, and Mondrian, you simply cannot leave without stopping by an art gallery or two—Amsterdam's Rijksmuseum and Van Gogh Museum alone will keep you occupied all day, and the Mauritshuis in The Hague is unmissable.

Saying It with Flowers. Visit the Keukenhof, the world's largest flower gardens, and home to millions of colorful blooms during its annual spring season.

Taking to the Water. Water is crucial to Dutch society. There are 50 miles of canals in Amsterdam alone, and what better way to see them than from a boat?

Pottery in Delft. De Koninklijke Porceleyne Fles, established in 1653, is the only remaining factory producing Delft's famous blue-and-white porcelain.

Biking. Go native by renting a bike and taking to two wheels, the preferred form of transportation in this flat land. Cycling Amsterdam is a superb way to avoid tram crams and pricey taxis.

historic, quaint Dutch beauty without the crush. The main cultural calendar runs from September through June, but happily there are so many festivals and open-air events scheduled during the summer that no one really notices.

GETTING HERE & AROUND

BY AIR

Flying time to Amsterdam is 7 hours from New York, 8 hours from Chicago, 10½ hours from Los Angeles, and 9 hours from Dallas.

AIRPORTS Located 17 km (11 mi) southeast of Amsterdam, **Luchthaven Schiphol** (pronounced "Shh-kip-hole") is the main passenger airport for the Netherlands. There are several regional airports, but these largely cater to the short-haul and charter routes. With the annual number of passengers using Schiphol approaching 40 million, it is ranked among the world's top five best-connected airports. A hotel, a service to aid passengers with disabilities, parking lots, and a main office of the Netherlands tourist board can prove most useful.

Amsterdam Airport Schiphol (✉ *17 km [11 mi] southwest of Amsterdam* ☎ *0900/0141* ⊕ *www.schiphol.nl*).

GROUND TRANSPOR-TATION The Schiphol Rail Link operates between the airport and the city 24 hours a day, with service to Amsterdam Centraal Station (usually abbreviated to Amsterdam CS). From 6:30 AM to 12:30 AM, there are four trains each hour; other hours, there is one every hour. The trip takes about 15 minutes and costs €3.80. Schiphol Station is beneath Schiphol Plaza.

Connexxion Schiphol Hotel Shuttle operates a shuttle-bus service between Amsterdam Schiphol Airport and all of the city's major hotels. The trip takes about a half-hour and costs €13.50 one-way, or €22 return. Hours for this shuttle bus are 6:20 AM to 8:20 PM, every half hour.

Finally, there is a taxi stand directly in front of the arrival hall at Amsterdam Schiphol Airport. A service charge is included, but small additional tips are not unwelcome. New laws determine that taxi fares are now fixed from Schiphol to Amsterdam; depending on the neighborhood, a trip will cost around €40 or more.

Contacts **Connexxion Schiphol Hotel Shuttle** (☏ *038/339–4741* ⊕ *www. schipholhotelshuttle.nl*). **Schiphol Rail Link** (☏ *0900/9292* ⊕ *www.9292ov.nl*).

BY BUS
Several bus companies provide services across the country and within cities. The country is divided into zones, and the fare you pay depends on the number of zones you travel through. A small city is one zone (two strips), but to travel across The Hague takes you through four (five strips) zones. These zones are displayed on transport maps. Each journey you make costs one strip plus the number of zones you travel through. Buy a *strippenkaart,* available with 15 or 45 strips, from newsagents or train or bus stations in advance, as this works out far cheaper than buying tickets on board. When you get on a bus, show the driver your *strippenkaart* and say where your final destination is, or the number of zones you plan to travel through, and let him or her stamp the strips. Two or more people can travel on the same *strippenkaart.* Trams in Amsterdam have ticket control booths in the center of the tram. You may only board the tram there, unless you already have a valid stamp on your ticket, in which case you may board at the front and show your ticket to the driver. The stamp indicates the zone where the journey started, and the time, and remains valid for one hour, so you can travel within the zones you have stamped until the hour is up.

Bus Information Information on all public transportation, including schedules, fares for **trains, buses, trams, and ferries** in the Netherlands (☏ *0900/9292* ⊕ *www.9292ov.nl*).

BY CAR
A network of well-maintained highways and other roads covers the Netherlands, making car travel convenient, although traffic is exceptionally heavy around the bigger cities. There are no tolls on roads or highways.

Many of the gas stations in the Netherlands (especially those on the high-traffic motorways) are open 24 hours.

BY FERRY
International ferries link Holland with the United Kingdom. There are two daily Stena Line crossings between the **Hoek van Holland** and Harwich, on a car ferry taking approximately six hours. There is one PO North Sea overnight crossing between the Europoort in Rotterdam and Hull, which takes about 14 hours, and one DFDS Seaways overnight crossing from Newcastle to IJmuiden, in Amsterdam, taking 15 hours.

DFDS Seaways (☎ *0255/546–666* ⊕ *www.dfdsseaways.com*). **PO North Sea Ferries** (*In Holland* ☎ *020/200–8333* In the UK ☎ *08705/202–020* ⊕ *www.poferries. com*). **Stena Line** (☎ *0900/8123* ⊕ *www.stenaline.nl*).

BY TRAIN

Dutch trains are modern, and the quickest way to travel between city centers. Services are relatively frequent, with a minimum of two departures per hour for each route. Although many Dutch people complain about delays, the trains usually run roughly on time. Most staff speak English. Reserving a seat is not possible. Intercity trains can come double-decker; they only stop at major stations. *Sneltreins* (express trains) also have two decks but take in more stops, so they are a little slower. *Stoptreins* (local trains) are the slowest. Smoking is not permitted on trains, and only permitted in designated zones in stations. On the train you have the choice of first or second class. First-class travel costs 50% more, and on local trains gives you a slightly larger seat in a compartment that is less likely to be full. At peak travel times first-class train travel is worth the difference.

Train tickets for travel within the country can be purchased at the last minute. Normal tickets are either *enkele reis* (one-way) or *retour* (round-trip). Round-trip tickets cost approximately 75% of two single tickets. They are valid only on the day you buy them, unless you ask specifically for a ticket with a different date. You can get on and off at will at stops in between your destinations until midnight. You can also buy tickets at the yellow touch-screen ticket machines in every railway station. These machines accept cards with a four-digit PIN code. Fares are slightly lower than if you visit a manned ticket desk. Note that you cannot buy domestic train tickets in the Netherlands with credit cards or traveler's checks, and you can't buy tickets aboard the trains, and you risk a hefty fine if you board and travel without one.

Intercity trains link Amsterdam and Brussels in around 3 hours. Thalys high-speed trains link Brussels (in 1½ hours) and Amsterdam (4 hours) with Paris. Eurostar operates high-speed passenger trains between stations in London and Brussels (Midi) in 2½ hours.

Eurostar (☎ *0900/10–366* ⊕ *www.eurostar.com*). **NS–Nederlandse Spoorwegen/ Dutch Railways** (⊕ *www.ns.nl*). **Thalys** (☎ *0900/10–177* ⊕ *www.thalys.com*).

Train Information Holland-wide **Public Transport Information** (☎ *0900/9292 information officer*)

ABOUT THE RESTAURANTS

Most restaurants are open for lunch and dinner only. Cafés usually also have a snacks menu (*kleine kaart*), which is available all day. A set-price, three- or four- course menu for lunch is offered in many restaurants. Dinner menus are usually more elaborate and slightly more expensive. Smoking is prohibited in Dutch cafés and restaurants.

MEALS & MEAL TIMES

Traditional Dutch cuisine is very simple and filling. A typical Dutch *ontbijt* (breakfast) consists of *brood* (bread), *kaas* (cheese), *hard gekookte ei* (hard-boiled eggs), ham, yogurt, jams, and fruit.

Lunch is usually a *boterham* (sandwich) or a *broodje* (soft roll or a baguette). Salads and warm dishes are also popular. One specialty is an *uitsmijter*: two pieces of bread with three fried eggs, ham, and cheese, garnished with pickles and onions. *Pannenkoeken* (pancakes) are a favorite lunch treat topped with ham and cheese or fruit and a thick *stroop* (syrup).

A popular afternoon snack is *frites* (french fries); try them with curry ketchup and onions (*frites speciaal*), with a *kroket* (a fried, breaded meat roll) on the side. Another snack is whole *haring* (herring) served with raw onions.

Diner (dinner) usually consists of three courses: an appetizer, main course, and dessert, and many restaurants have special prix-fixe deals. Beverages are always charged separately. Dutch specialties include *erwtensoep* (a thick pea soup with sausage), *gerookte paling* (smoked eel), and *hutspot* (beef stew). Steamed North Sea mussels are popular. In general, the standard of the once dull Dutch cuisine is improving steadily. Chefs have in recent years become more adventurous and you will find many other more exciting choices (usually French-influenced) on menus than were seen a decade ago.

Holland is famous for its cheeses, including Gouda, Edam, and Limburger. Indonesian cuisine is also very popular here, and a favorite lunch or dinner is *rijsttafel*, which literally means "rice table" and refers to a prix-fixe meal that includes a feast of 10–20 small spicy dishes.

Restaurants open for lunch start at 11 AM, while restaurants opening for dinner will accept guests as early as 5 or 6 PM, closing at 11.

PAYING

Tipping 15% of the cost of a meal is not common practice in the Netherlands. Instead, round off the total to a convenient figure, to reward good service. If paying with a credit card, pay the exact amount with your card, and leave a few euros in cash on the table for the waiting staff.

WINES, BEER & SPIRITS

When you ask for a beer in Holland, you will get a small (200 milliliters) glass of draft lager with 5% alcohol, known as *pils*. A number of national breweries turn out similar fare—in Amsterdam it will usually be Heineken, but you may encounter Amstel, Oranjeboom, Grolsch, Bavaria, or another smaller outfit. The argument for serving beer in small glasses is that you can drink it before it gets warm. Many bars will serve you a pint (500 milliliters) if you ask. A number of smaller artisanal breweries attempt different beer styles with varying success— look out for the La Trappe and 't Ij names—but in general specialist brewing is left to the Belgians. You will find several Belgian standards in most Dutch cafés, including Hoegaarden "white" beer, Leffe (which comes in brown and blond versions), Kriek, a fruit-flavored beer, and Duvel, a strong blond beer.

WHAT IT COSTS IN EUROS					
	¢	$	$$	$$$	$$$$
Restaurants	under €10	€10 –€15	€15 –€22	€22 –€30	over €30

Restaurant prices are per person for a main course at dinner.

ABOUT THE HOTELS

The Netherlands has a range of options from major international hotel chains to family-run restored inns. Accommodations in Amsterdam are at a particular premium at any time of year, so book well in advance. Should you arrive without a hotel room, the tourist offices can help you find a room.

CLASSIFICATIONS

Dutch hotels are awarded stars (one to five) by the Benelux Hotel Classification System, an independent agency that inspects properties based on their facilities and services. Those with three or more stars feature en suite bathrooms where a shower is standard, whereas a tub is a four-star standard. Rooms in lodgings listed in this guide have a shower unless otherwise indicated.

RATES

Room rates for deluxe and four-star rooms are on a par with those in other European cities. Most cheaper hotels quote room rates including breakfast, while for those at the top end it usually costs extra.

Many hotels in Amsterdam appear to be permanently full, so book as far in advance as you can to be sure of getting what you want.

WHAT IT COSTS IN EUROS					
	¢	$	$$	$$$	$$$$
Hotels	under €75	€75 –€120	€120 –€165	€165 –€230	over €230

Hotel prices are for two people in a standard double room in high season, excluding tax.

PLANNING YOUR TIME

The majority of visitors will be headed for **Amsterdam**, and with good reason—it's one of Europe's most popular and laid-back capitals, and the canals, sights, and museums here will keep you occupied for several days if you want to do more than dip a toe. If you only have one or two days, you would do best to concentrate your efforts here. With a week, you can get a taste of everywhere mentioned here–all are worth spending a few nights getting to know if you can.

The Hague is not only home to the royal family and the parliament, it's also the world's legal headquarters. And the Count's Hedge, as the city's official Dutch name translates, also does some serious justice to arts and culture. The Mauritshuis is visited more than ever for its recent pop-star of a piece, Vermeer's *Girl with a Pearl Earring*, while the Gemeetemuseum holds the most Mondrians under one roof, and the Escher collection in Het Paleis Museum will literally send you bug-eyed.

Haarlem and **Delft** are both picture-book examples of how small Dutch cities should be, and with their centuries-old charm it is easy to see how Frans Hals (in Haarlem) and Johannes Vermeer (in Delft) could have found inspiration there.

Meanwhile, what could be more Dutch than tulips? So if you arrive in the right season (late March to May), be sure to trip out to see the country burst into color, and in particular make a beeline for the **Keukenhof**, the world's largest flower gardens located in Lisse, just to the south of Amsterdam.

AMSTERDAM

Amsterdam is a cornucopia of cafés, coffee shops, cozy bars, and outdoor markets. Set on 160 man-made canals (stretching 75 km [50 mi]), Amsterdam also has the largest historic inner city in Europe. The French writer J.K. Huysmans once called Amsterdam "a dream, an orgy of houses and water." It's true: when compared with other major European cities, this one is uniquely defined by its impressive gabled houses, rather than palaces, estates, and other aristocratic folderol. Most of the 7,000 registered monuments here began as residences and warehouses of humble merchants.

With a mere 730,000 friendly souls and with almost everything a scant 10-minute bike ride away, Amsterdam is actually like a village that happens to pack the cultural wallop of a megalopolis. This is an endlessly fascinating city, where it's remarkably easy to relax and enjoy yourself—just take on the characteristics of the local waterways and go with the flow.

PLANNING YOUR TIME

There is high humidity in the summer and a fair amount of rain, especially in the winter. But moisture aside, Amsterdam's weather is ultimately comfortable, and temperatures are rarely extreme. In the summer Amsterdam can be the most fascinating city in the world; a sun-bleached blend of old and new, crazy and subdued. From October to May, lines for most museums and attractions are smaller, and off-season accommodations are cheaper, but it's colder, rainier, and windier.

The electronic *I amsterdam Card* provides free and discounted admissions to many of Amsterdam's top museums, plus a free canal round-trip, free use of public transport, and a 25% discount on various attractions and restaurants; savings can amount to more than €100. A one-day pass costs €33, a two-day costs €43, and a three-day costs €53.

Anyone planning to visit a lot of museums in Amsterdam and the Netherlands should consider investing in a *Museum Jaarkaart* (Museum Year Card), or MJK. This gives you free entry to more than 440 museums throughout the country for a year, including all the top draws in Amsterdam. It is available on showing ID at VVV offices and participating museums for €35.

GETTING HERE & AROUND

Amsterdam is connected to Schiphol Airport by regular trains that run several times every hour, taking around 15 minutes.

There are no straight lines in central Amsterdam, but once understood, it's an easy city to navigate—or get lost in. Think of it as an onion whose layers come together at the stem to make a cohesive whole. With Centraal Station as the stem, the Center folds out as layers of the onion, each on a somewhat circular path under the guidance of the Canal Ring. To stay safe, always watch out for bikes and trams. Do not walk on bike paths, which are well paved and often mistaken for sidewalks. Bikers have the right-of-way, so if you hear a bell, move quickly. Trams function similarly, and will also ring their bell (a much louder one) before they move. Just look both ways, and look both ways again before crossing streets.

The best way to see Amsterdam is either by bike or on foot. The city is very small, and most places are easily accessible. Otherwise, the city's public transport system, GVB, is extremely reliable. It operates the buses, trams, and metro with service 24 hours a day. The most frequently used trams by visitors are the 1, 2, and 5, which start at Centraal Station and stop at the big central Dam Square and, along with 6, 7, and 10, also stop at Leidseplein square. The numbers 2, 3, 5, and 12 will get you from the station to Museumplein and the Museum District. The GVB also sells 24-, 48-, and 72-hour passes, and family passes. If you choose to take a taxi, make sure it is licensed and regulated by the city to avoid being scammed – licensed cabs have blue-colored license plates.

Afternoon bus tours of Amsterdam operate daily. Itineraries vary, and prices range from €18 to €47. However, it must be said that this city of narrow alleys and canals is not best appreciated from the window of a coach.

From April through October, guided 1½- to 3-hour bike trips through the central area of Amsterdam are available through Yellow Bike.

To see the city from the water, boat tours lasting one hour leave from various locations across the center at regular intervals, costing around €11.

ESSENTIALS

Boat Contacts Amsterdam Canal Cruises (✉ *Nicolaas Witsenkade, opposite the Heineken Brewery, De Pijp* ☎ *020/626–5636*). **Canal Bus** (✉ *Weteringschans 26–1, Leidseplein* ☎ *020/623–9886* ⊕ *www.canal.nl*). **Holland International** (✉ *Prins Hendrikkade, opposite Centraal Station, Centrum* ☎ *020/625–3035* ⊕ *www.hir.nl*). **Meyers Rondvaarten** (✉ *Damrak 4, Dam* ☎ *020/623–4208* ⊕ *www.meyersrond-*

vaarten.nl). **Museumboot Rederij Lovers** (⊠ *Prins Hendrikkade, opposite Centraal Station, Centrum* ☎ *020/530–1092* ⊕ *www.lovers.nl*).

Tram & Bus Contacts GVB (⊠ *Prins Hendrikkade 108–114, Centrum* ☎ *0900/9292* ⊕ *www.gvb.nl*).

Taxi Contacts Taxicentrale ☎ *020/677–7777* **Wielertaxi** "(☎ *020/672–1149*

Visitor & Tour Information VVV—Tourist Information Offices (⊕ *www. vvvamsterdam.nl* ⊠ *Spoor 2/Platform 2, Centraal Station, Centrum* ⊠ *Stationsplein 10, Centraal Station* ⊠ *Leidseplein 1, at Leidsestraat, Leidseplein* ☎ *0900/400–4040*

Bike Rentals Yellow Bike (⊠ *Nieuwezijds Kolk 29, Centrum* ☎ *020/620–6940* ⊕ *www.yellowbike.nl*).

EXPLORING AMSTERDAM

⑮ Amsterdams Historisch Museum *(Amsterdam Historical Museum)*. Any city that began in the 13th century as a sinking bog to eventually become the 17th century's most powerful trading city has a fascinating story to tell, and this museum does it superbly. It's housed in a rambling amalgamation of buildings. The centerpiece is the **Schutters Gallery.** This atrium—which used to be a narrow canal—is filled with huge, historic portraits of city militias. As portrait art in the 1600s was a symbol of wealth, power, and most importantly, bragging rights. These paintings, which are free to see, are impressive. Elsewhere, be sure to take in the grand Regents' Chamber, adorned with a magnificent 1656 ceiling painting. Also notable are the paintings of the great Golden Age, along with 17th-century city maps and dour Burgomeister, or mayoral, portraits, and a stirring photographic collage that captures the triumphs and tragedies of the modern-day metropolis. ⊠ *Kalverstraat 92 and Nieuwezijds Voorburgwal 357, Centrum* ☎ *020/523–1822* ⊕ *www. ahm.nl* ☜ *€8* ⊙ *Weekdays 10–5, weekends 11–5.*

㉑ **Anne Frankhuis** *(Anne Frank House)*. In the pages of *The Diary of Anne*
FodorsChoice *Frank* (published in 1947 as *The Annex* by her father after her death)
★ the young Anne kept her sad record of two increasingly fraught years living in hiding from the Nazis. Along with the van Daan family, the Frank family felt the noose tighten, and so decided to move into this 1635-built canal house.

Anne Frank was born in Germany in 1929; when she was four her family moved to the Netherlands to escape growing anti-Jewish sentiment. Otto Frank operated a pectin business and decided to stay in his adopted country when the war finally reached the Netherlands in 1940. In July 1942 the five adults and three children sought refuge in the attic of the annex "backhouse," or *achterhuis*, of Otto's business in the center of Amsterdam, in a hidden warren of rooms screened behind a hinged bookcase. Here, as one of many *onderduikers* ("people in hiding") throughout all of Amsterdam, Anne dreamed her dreams, wrote her diary, and pinned up movie-star pictures to her wall (still on view). The van Pelsen family, including their son, Peter (van Daan in Anne's

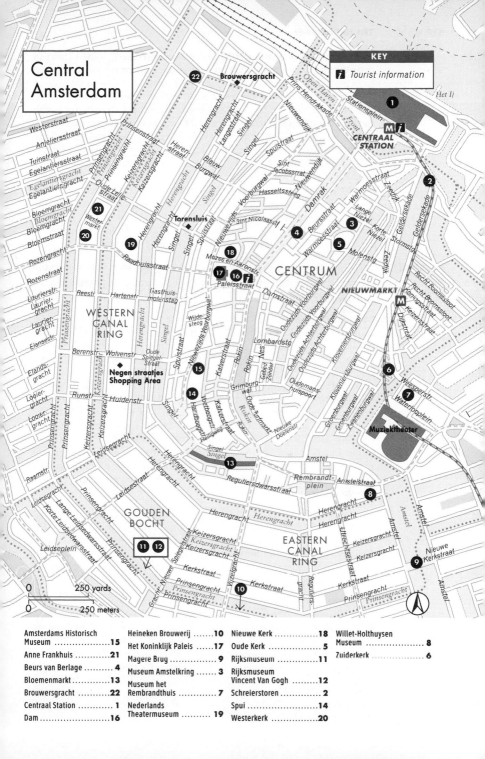

Central Amsterdam

KEY

🛈 *Tourist information*

Brouwersgracht

Het Ij

Oben Haven

Stationsplein

1

M 🛈

CENTRAAL STATION

Het Ij

Westerstraat

Anjeliersstraat

Tuinstraat

Egelantiersstraat

Egelantiersgracht

Bloemgracht

Bloemstraat

Rozengracht

Rozenstraat

Laurierstr.

Laurier-gracht

Laurier-gracht

Elansstr.

WESTERN CANAL RING

Reestr

Hartenstr

Gasthuis-molensteeg

Berenstr. Wolvenstr

Oude Spiegel-Straat

Elands-gracht

Looier-gracht

Looier-gracht

Runstr

Huidenstr

Raamstr.

GOUDEN BOCHT

Leidseplein

Prinsenstraat

Keizersgracht

Herengracht

Singel

Oude Leliestr.

Herenstraat

Blauw Burgwal

Torensluis

Singel

Nieuwezijds Voorburgwal

Mozes en Aaronstr.

Paleisstraat

Raadhuisstraat

Wijde-steeg

Lombardstg

Lombardstg

Nes

Rokin

Gebed Zonder

Grimburg-wal

Oude Turfmarkt

Nieuwe Doelenstr.

Negen straatjes Shopping Area

Voetboogstr.

Kalverstraat

Heiligeweg

Nieuwe Spiegelstraat

Singel Singel

Reguliersdwarsstraat

Herengracht

Herengracht

Kerkstraat

Prinsengracht

Kerkstraat

Prinsengracht

Prins Hendrikkade

Nieuwendijk

Nieuwendijk

Singel

Spuistraat

Singel

Damrak

Sint Jacobsstraat

Nieuwezijds Voorburgwal

Sint Nicolaasstr.

Hasselssteeg

Warmoesstraat

Beursstraat

Warmoesstraat

Molensteg

Damstraat

CENTRUM

Oudezijds Voorburgwal

Oudezijds Voorburgwal

Oudezijds Achterburgwal

Oudezijds Achterburgwal

Kloveniersburgwal

Kloveniersburgwal

Oudemans-huispoort

Groenburgwal

Groenburgwal

NIEUWMARKT

M

Warmoesstraat

Front

Zeedijk

Lange Niezel

Korte Niezel

Zeedijk

Stormst.

Recht Boomssloot

Koningsstraat

Dijkstraat

Keizersstraat

Recht Boomssloot

Weesperstr.

Waterlooplein

Muziektheater

Warmoerburgwal

Nieuwmarkt

Amstel

Reguliersdwarsstraat

Rembrandt-plein

Amstelstraat

8

Amstel

Herengracht

Herengracht

Herengracht

Herengracht

EASTERN CANAL RING

Keizersgracht

Keizersgracht

Keizersgracht

Keizersgracht

Utrechtsestraat

Amstel

Amstel

Nieuwe Kerkstraat

9

Kerkstraat

Prinsengracht

Prinsengracht

Amstel

Leidsegracht

Lange Leidsedwarsstraat

Korte Leidsedwarsstraat

Prinsengracht

Prinsengracht

Keizersgracht

Keizersgracht

Nieuwe Spiegelstraat

Kerkstraat

Vijzelgracht

Reguliers gracht

Stationsplein

Schreierstoren

2

Geldersekade

Gelderskade

22 **21** **20** **19** **18** **17** **16** **15** **14** **13** **12** **11** **10** **9** **8** **7** **6** **5** **4** **3** **2** **1**

0 250 yards

0 250 meters

journal), along with the dentist Fritz Pfeffer (Dussel) joined them in their cramped quarters. Four trusted employees provided them with food and supplies. In her diary Anne chronicles the day-to-day life in the house: her longing for a best friend, her crush on Peter, her frustration with her mother, her love for her father, and her annoyance with the petty dentist, Dussel. In August 1944 the Franks were betrayed and the Gestapo invaded their hideaway. All the members of the annex were transported to camps, where Anne, aged just 15, and her sister, Margot, died of typhoid fever in Bergen Belsen a few months before the liberation. Otto Frank was the only survivor of the annex. Miep Gies, one of the friends who helped with the hiding, found Anne's diary after the raid and kept it through the war. Now millions of children read it and its tale of humanity's struggle with fascism. ✉*Prinsengracht 267, Centrum* ☎*020/556–7105* ⊕*www.annefrank.nl* ✎*€8.50* ☉*Oct.–Mar., Sun.— Fri. 9–9, Sat. 9am–10pm; Apr.–Sept., daily 9am–10pm.*

BE AWARE

The line to get into the Anne Frank House is extremely long, especially in the summer. It moves (sort of) quickly, but it's best to arrive early and avoid the worst crowds.

❹ **Beurs van Berlage** *(Berlage's Stock Exchange).* Even though some people think the Beurs looks a bit blocky, it is revered as Amsterdam's first modern building and the country's most important piece of 20th-century architecture. Built in 1903 by H. P. Berlage, the building became a template for the style of a new century. Gone were all the ornamentations of the 19th-century "Neo" styles. The new Beurs, with its simple lines and the influence it had on the Amsterdam School architects who followed Berlage, earned him the reputation of being the "Father of Modern Dutch Architecture." Today the Beurs serves as a true Palazzo Publico, with concert halls and space for exhibitions of architecture and applied arts. Stop in at the café to admire the stunning tile tableaux over a coffee (Mon.–Sat. 10–6, Sun. 11–6). ✉*Damrak 277, Centrum* ☎*020/530–4141* ⊕*www.beursvanberlage.nl* ✎*Varies based on exhibition* ☉*Varies based on exhibition.*

⓭ **Bloemenmarkt** *(Flower Market).* This is the last of the city's floating markets. In days gone by, merchants would sail up the Amstel loaded down with blooms from the great tulip fields to delight patroons and housewives. Today the flower sellers stay put, but their wares are still offered on stalls-cum-boats. ✉*Singel (between Muntplein and Koningsplein), Centrum* ☉*Mon.–Sat. 9:30–5.*

㉒ **Brouwersgracht** *(Brewers' Canal).* One of the most photographed spots in town, this pretty, tree-lined canal at the northern border of the Jordaan district is bordered by residences and former warehouses of the brewers who traded here in the 17th century, when Amsterdam was the "warehouse of the world." Without sacrificing the ancient vibe, most of the buildings have been converted into luxury apartments. Of particular note are the houses at Nos. 188 to 194. The canal is blessed with long views down the main canals and plenty of sunlight, perfect for photoops. ✉*Centrum.*

11

❶ Centraal Station *(Central Station).* The main hub of transportation in the Netherlands, this building was designed as a major architectural statement by P. J. H. Cuypers. Although sporting many Gothic motifs (including a unique wind vane disguised as a clock in its left tower), it is now considered a landmark of Dutch Neo-Renaissance style. The building of the station required the creation of three artificial islands and the ramming of 8,600 wooden piles to support it. Completed in 1885, it represented the psychological break with the city's seafaring past, as its erection slowly blocked the view to the IJ river. ✉*Stationsplein, Centrum* ☎*0900–9292 (public transport information).*

❻ Dam *(Dam Square).* Home to the Koninklijk Paleis (Royal Palace) and the Nieuwe Kerk, this is Amsterdam's official center. The square traces its roots to the 12th century, when wanderers from central Europe came floating in their canoes down the Amstel River and decided to stop to build a dam. It became the focal point of the small settlement and the location of the local weigh house. Folks came here to trade, talk, protest, and be executed. The towering white obelisk in the center of the square was erected in 1956 as a memorial to the Dutch soldiers who died in World War II. Designed by architect J. J. P. Oud, it's the national focal point for Remembrance Day on May 4. It is also the best place in the city to meet people. Just schedule meetings next to the giant phallus. ✉*Follow Damrak south from Centraal Station. Raadhuisstraat leads from Dam to intersect main canals.*

❿ Heineken Brouwerij *(Heineken Brewery).* Founded by Gerard Heineken in 1863, the Heineken label quickly became one of the world's most famous (and popular) beers. So popular, in fact, that this factory couldn't keep up with the enormous demand—today most production rolls out of vast plants in The Hague and Den Bosch. The original brewery has now been transformed into the "Heineken Experience," an interactive center that offers tours of the more than 100-year-old facilities. (Note: this tour is open only to visitors over the age of 18.) ✉*Stadhouderskade 78, De Pijp* ☎*020/523–9222* ⊕*www.heinekenexperience.com* ▢*€15* ☉*Daily 11–7.*

❼ Het Koninklijk Paleis *(Royal Palace).* From the outside, it is somewhat hard to believe that this gray-stained building was once called the "Eighth Wonder of the World." It was built between 1648 and 1665 as the largest nonreligious building on the planet. From the inside, its magnificent interior inspires another brand of disbelief: this palace was actually built as a mere city hall. Golden Age artistic greats such as Ferdinand Bol, Govert Flinck (Rembrandt's sketches were rejected), and Jan Lievens were called in for the decorating. In the building's public entrance hall, the **Burgerzaal,** the world was placed quite literally at one's feet: two maps inlaid in the marble floor show Amsterdam as the center of the world, and as the center of the universe. The building became the Royal Palace after Napoléon's brother squatted there in 1808. Today Queen Beatrix stays here occasionally. At this writing, the palace was closed for reonvations. It is expected to reopen by the of 2009. ✉*Dam, Centrum* ☎*020/620–4060* ⊕*www.koninklijkhuis.nl*

❾ Magere Brug *(Skinny Bridge).* Of Amsterdam's 60-plus drawbridges, the Magere Brug is the most famous. It is one of Amsterdam's prettiest bridges, and offers a gorgeous view of the Amstel and surrounding area. The Magere Brug was purportedly built in 1672 by two sisters living on opposite sides of the Amstel, who wanted an efficient way of sharing that grandest of Dutch traditions: the midmorning coffee break. ✉ *Between Kerkstraat and Nieuwe Kerkstraat, Centrum.*

❸ Museum Amstelkring *(Our Lord in the Attic Museum).* With its elegant gray-and-white facade and spout gable, this appears to be just another lovely canal house, and on the lower floors it is. But tucked away in the attic is the only surviving *schuilkerk* (clandestine church) that dates from the Reformation, when open worship by Catholics was outlawed. The Oude Kerk was de-catholicized and stripped of its patron, St. Nicholas, so this little church was dedicated to him until the Sint Nicolaaskerk was built. The chapel itself is a triumph of Dutch classicist taste, with magnificent marble columns, gilded capitals, a colored-marble altar, and the *Baptism of Christ* (1716) painting by Jacob de Wit presiding over all. Sunday services and weddings are still offered here. The lower floors are also beautifully preserved and shouldn't be missed. ✉ *Oudezijds Voorburgwal 40, Centrum* ☎ *020/624–6604* ⊕ *www.museum amstelkring.nl* 🎫 *€7* ⊙ *Mon.–Sat. 10–5, Sun. 1–5.*

❼ Museum het Rembrandthuis *(Rembrandt's House).* One of Amsterdam's
★ more remarkable relics, this house was bought by Rembrandt, flush with success, for his family, and is where he lived and worked between 1639 and 1658. Rembrandt chose this house on what was once the main street of the Jewish Quarter because he thought he could then experience daily and firsthand the faces he would use in his Old Testament religious paintings. Later Rembrandt lost the house to bankruptcy when he fell from popularity after the death of Saskia, his wife.

The house interior has been restored to its original form—complete with one of Rembrandt's printing presses, his rarities collection, and fully stocked studio (which is occasionally used by guest artists). The new gallery wing, complete with shop, café, and information center, is the only place in the world where his graphic work is on permanent display. ✉ *Jodenbreestraat 4–6, Centrum* ☎ *020/520–0400* ⊕ *www. rembrandthuis.nl* 🎫 *€8* ⊙ *Daily 10–5.*

⓳ Nederlands Theatermuseum *(Netherlands Theater Museum).* Amsterdam
★ has dozens of Golden Age house museums, but few are as gilded as this one. Currently home to part of the Theater Instituut Nederland (Netherlands Theater Institute), the **Bartolotti Huis** (Nos. 170–172) is made up of two spectacular examples of Hendrick de Keyser's work. The rest of the museum takes up the equally delectable White House (No. 168), built in 1638. Its interior of marble-lined corridors, sweeping monumental staircases, densely rendered plasterwork, and ceiling paintings by Jacob de Wit, provide a lush backdrop for exhibitions about the history of theater in all its forms: circus, opera, musical, puppetry, and drama. Its stellar back garden—alone worth the price—is the perfect place to sip a coffee from the café. ✉ *Herengracht 168–170,*

Centrum ☎*020/551–3300* ⊕*www.tin.nl* ⌨*€4.50* ⊙*Mon.–Fri. 11–5, weekends 1–5.*

⑱ **Nieuwe Kerk** *(New Church).* Begun in the 14th century, the Nieuwe Kerk is a soaring Late Gothic structure whose tower was never completed because the authorities ran out of money. Don't miss the magnificently sculpted pulpit by Albert Vinckenbrinck. It took him 19 years to complete. Other features include the unmarked grave of the poet Vondel (the "Dutch Shakespeare"), and the extravagantly marked grave of naval hero Admiral Michiel de Ruyter, who daringly sailed his invading fleet up the river Medway in England in the 17th century. The Nieuwe Kerk has also been the National Church since 1815, when it began hosting the inauguration ceremony for monarchs. ⊠*Dam, Centrum* ☎*020/638–6909* ⊕*www.nieuwekerk.nl* ⌨*Admission varies according to exhibition* ⊙*During exhibitions open daily 10–5. In between exhibitions hrs vary.*

❺ **Oude Kerk** *(Old Church).* The Oude Kerk is Amsterdam's oldest church and its location never ceases to shock first-time visitors. It's smack-dab in the middle of the carnal circus of the red-light district, literally surrounded by scantily clad hookers eyeing the action in the square. It began as a wooden chapel in 1306 but was built up in to a hall church and then a cross basilica between 1366 and 1566 (and fully restored between 1955 and 1979). It was violently looted during the Reformation, and the church was stripped of its altars and images of saints— although the revolutionaries did leave the 14th-century paintings still visible on its wooden roof, as well as the Virgin Mary stained-glass windows that had been set in place in 1550. In the 17th century it was fitted with its famed Vater-Muller organ. Don't miss the inscription on the Bridal Chamber, which translates to: "Marry in Haste, Mourn in Leisure." ⊠*Oudekerksplein 23, Centrum* ☎*020/625–8284* ⊕*www. oudekerk.nl* ⌨*€5.00* ⊙*Mon.–Sat. 11–5, Sun. 1–5.*

⑪ **Rijksmuseum** *(State Museum).* The Rijksmuseum is home to Rembrandt's
Fodor'sChoice *Night Watch,* Vermeer's *The Kitchen Maid,* and world-famous master-
★ pieces by Steen, Ruisdael, Brouwers, Hals, Hobbema, Cuyp, Van der Helst, and their Golden Age ilk. Sadly, this national treasure is closed until 2010 for extensive renovations. Happily, the South (Philips) Wing is open to showcase the museum's "Best of" works. When the museum reopens, you can look forward to more than 150 rooms of paintings, sculpture, and objects with Western and Asian roots, dating from the 9th through the 19th century. The bulk of the collection is of 15th- to 17th-century paintings, mostly by Dutch masters, as well as drawings and prints from the 15th to 20th century. Designed by P.J.H. Cuypers in the late 1880s, the Rijksmuseum is a magnificent, turreted building that glitters with gold leaf and is textured with sculpture—a fitting palace for a national art collection. ⊠*Stadhouderskade 42; entrance during renovations: Jan Luijkenstraat 1, Museum District* ☎*020/674–7000* ⊕*www.rijksmuseum.nl* ⌨*€10* ⊙*Sat.–Thurs. 9–6, Fri. 9—8.30. Ticket counter closes at 5:30 PM (Fri. at 8 PM). Infocenter (The New Rijksmuseum): Tues.–Sun. 11–4. Library, Print Room, and Reading Room: Tues.–Sat. 10–5. ID required.*

⑫ **Rijksmuseum Vincent Van Gogh** *(Vincent Van Gogh Museum).* Opened
Fodor'sChoice in 1973, this remarkable, light-infused building, based on a design by
★   famed De Stijl architect Gerrit Rietveld, venerates the short, certainly
not sweet, but highly productive career of everyone's favorite tortured
19th-century artist. First things first: Vincent was a Dutch boy, so his
name is not pronounced like the "Go" in Go-Go Lounge but rather
like the "Go" uttered when one is choking on a whole raw herring.
Although some of the Van Gogh paintings scattered throughout the
world's high-art temples are of dubious provenance, this collection's
authenticity is indisputable: its roots trace directly back to brother Theo
van Gogh, Vincent's artistic and financial supporter. The 200 paintings
and 500 drawings on display here begin in 1880, when Van Gogh was
27 and end in 1890, when he took his own life. The *Potato Eaters,* the
series of *Sunflowers* and landscapes such as *Irises* and *Wheatfield with a
Reaper,* are some of Van Gogh's most famous pieces. A bonus of the Van
Gogh Museum is that it holds temporary exhibits of other important
19th-century artists and collections of art, graphic design, photography, and sculpture related to Van Gogh's development as a painter. A
modern oval extension, opened in 1999, connects the main galleries by
an underground walkway. ⊠*Paulus Potterstraat 7, Museum District*
☎*020/570–5200* ⊕*www.vangoghmuseum.nl* ⊠*€12.50* ☉*Sat.–Thurs.
10–6, Fri. 10–10.*

❷ **Schreierstoren.** This is Amsterdam's most distinctive fortress tower.
Today it's home to a café, but it began life in 1486 as the end point of
the city wall. The term *schreien* suggests the Dutch word for wailing.
As lore would have it, this "Weeping Tower" was where women came
to cry when their sailor husbands left for sea and to cry again when
they did not return. It's also famous as the point from which Henry
Hudson set sail to America. He sailed on behalf of the Dutch East India
Company to find a shorter route to the East Indies. In his failure, he
came across Canada's Hudson Bay and later New York harbor and the
Hudson River. He eventually landed on Manhattan and named it New
Amsterdam. ⊠*Prins Hendrikkade 94–95, Centrum.*

⑭ **Spui** *(Spui Square).* This beautiful and seemingly tranquil tree-lined
square hides a lively and radical recent past. Journalists and bookworms
have long favored its many cafés, and the Atheneum News Center (Nos.
14–16) and its adjoining bookstore are the city's best places to peruse
an international array of literature, magazines, and newspapers. More
cultural browsing can be enjoyed on the Spui's book market on Friday
and its art market on Sunday. ⊠*Bounded by Spuistraat and Kalverstraat, Centrum.*

▌ **NEED A
BREAK?**   Several of the bar-cafés and eateries on Spui square are good places to take
a break. The ancient **Hoppe** (⊠ *Spui 18–20, Centrum* ☎ *020/420–4420*) has
been serving drinks between woody walls and on sandy floors since 1670.

⑳ **Westerkerk** *(Western Church).* Built between 1602 and 1631 by Hendrick de Keyser, the Dutch Renaissance Westerkerk was the largest Protestant church in the world until the St. Paul's Cathedral in London was
built. Its tower is topped by a gaudy copy of the crown of the Habsburg

emperor Maximilian I (or, rather, to avoid a potential bar brawl, a later model of the crown used by Rudolph II). The tower rates as the city's highest. Its gigantic bell rings every half hour but with a different tone to mark the half before the hour—in other words, the 12 rings of 11:30 are different from the rings of 12. ⊠ *Prinsengracht 281 (corner of Westermarkt), Centrum* ☎ *020/624–7766* ⊕ *www.westerkerk.nl* ⊙ *Tower Apr.–Oct. Mon.–Sat. 11–4.30 (tours every 30 mins); interior Apr.–Sept., Mon.–Fri. 11–3; tower by appointment* ☎ *020/689–2565* 🎫 *Free; €6 tower.*

❽ **Willet-Holthuysen Museum.** Few houses are open to the public along the Herengracht, so make a beeline to this mansion to see Grachtengordel (Canal Ring) luxury at its best. In 1895 the widow Sandrina Louisa Willet-Holthuysen donated the house and contents—which included her husband's extensive art collection—to the city of Amsterdam. You can wander through this 17th-century canal house, now under the management of Amsterdam's Historisch Museum, and discover all its original 18th-century interiors, complete with that era's mod cons from ballroom to *cabinet des merveilles* (rarities cabinet). ⊠ *Herengracht 605, Centrum* ☎ *020/523–1822* ⊕ *www.willetholthuysen.nl* 🎫 *€5* ⊙ *Weekdays 10–5, weekends 11–5.*

❻ **Zuiderkerk** *(South Church).* Gorgeous enough to have inspired both Sir Christopher Wren and Monet, this famous church was built between 1603 and 1611 by Hendrick de Keyser, one of the most prolific architects of Holland's Golden Age. It was one of the earliest churches built in Amsterdam in the Renaissance style, and was the first in the city to be built for the Dutch Reformed Church. The church's hallowed floors—under which three of Rembrandt's children are buried—are now under the reign of the City Planning Office and as such are filled with detailed models of Amsterdam's ambitious future building plans. The church tower—a soaring accumulation of columns, brackets, and balustrades—is one of the most glorious exclamation points in Amsterdam. Tours of the tower take place every 30 minutes from noon when the church is open. ⊠ *Zuiderkerkhof 72, Centrum* ☎ *020/552–7987* ⊕ *www.zuiderkerk.amsterdam.nl* 🎫 *Free; €6 (tower)* ⊙ *Mon.-Fri. 9–4, Sat. 12–4.*

WHERE TO EAT

$–$$ ✕ **Amsterdam.** Getting here requires going west of the Jordaan, and beyond the Westergasfabriek cultural complex. This spot is an industrial monument—for a century, this plant pumped water from coastal dunes. Now, under a sky-high ceiling, one can dine on honestly rendered French and Dutch dishes—from steak tartare to grilled tuna—in a bustling atmosphere favored by families and larger groups. To escape the noise, seek refuge on the peaceful terrace. ⊠ *Watertorenplein 6, Jordaan* ☎ *020/682–2666* ☱ *AE, DC, MC, V.*

¢–$ ✕ **Bakkerswinkel.** This genteel yet unpretentious bakery/tearoom evokes an English country kitchen, one that lovingly prepares and serves breakfasts, high tea, hearty-breaded sandwiches, soups, and divine (almost manly) slabs of quiche. The closely clustered wooden tables don't make for much privacy, but this place is a true oasis if you want to indulge in a healthful breakfast or lunch. It opens at 8 AM daily. There's a second location, complete with garden patio, in the Museum District. ⊠ *Warmoestraat 69, Red Light District 1012 HX* ☎*020/489–8000* ▤*No credit cards* ⊘*Closed Mon. No dinner.* ⊠*Roelof Hartstraat 68, Museum District & Environs 1071 VM* ☎*020/662–3594* ▤*No credit cards* ⊘*Closed Mon. No dinner.*

$$–$$$ ✕**Blue Pepper.** One of the city's most widely acclaimed restaurants,
★   Blue Pepper features the inspired cooking of award-winning chef Sonja Pereira. If you're lucky, the ever-changing menu might include *Kambing kecap,* where panfried tender pieces of lamb are cooked with lime leaves, lemongrass, garlic, soy sauce, and chili peppers. Unlike many other Indonesian restaurants, you won't have a thousand different dishes piled on your plate here—just a few obsessively prepared ones. ⊠*Nassaukade 366, Leidseplein 1054 AB* ☎*020/489–7039* ⚑*Reservations essential* ▤*AE, DC, MC, V* ⊘*Closed Fri.—Sun. No lunch.*

$$$–$$$$ ✕**D' Vijff Vlieghen.** The "Five Flies" is a rambling dining institution that takes up five adjoining Golden Age houses. Yet the densely evocative Golden Age vibe—complete with bona fide Rembrandt etchings, wooden *jenever* (Dutch gin) barrels, crystal and armor collections, and an endless array of old-school bric-a-brac—came into being only in 1939. You'll find business folk clinching deals in private nooks here, but also busloads of tourists who have dibs on entire sections of the restaurant: book accordingly. The overpriced menu of new Dutch cuisine emphasizes local, fresh, and often organic ingredients in everything from wild boar to purely vegetarian dishes. Lack of choice is not an issue here: the menus, the wine list, and the flavored jenever are—like the decor—all of epic proportions. ⊠*Spuistraat 294–302, Centrum 1012 VX* ☎*020/530–4060 Jacket and tie* ▤*AE, DC, MC, V* ⊘*No lunch.*

$–$$ ✕**Haesje Claes.** Groaning with pewter tankards, stained glass, leaded-glass windows, rich historic paneling, Indonesian paisley *fabriks,* and betasseled Victorian lamps, this restaurant's "Old Holland" ambience and matching menu attract lots of tourists. And why change a winning formula? The Pieter de Hooch–worthy interiors eclipse the food, although the dishes include a selection of *stampotten* (mashed dishes that combine potato with a variety of vegetables and/or meats). ⊠*Spuistraat 273-275, Centrum* ☎*020/624–9998* ▤*AE, DC, MC, V.*

$–$$ ✕**Harkema.** This brasserie along the city's premier theater strip has infused a former tobacco factory with light, color, and general design savvy. The kitchen, which is open between 11 AM and 11 PM daily, pumps out reasonably priced lunches and French classics, and a wall of wine is on hand to appeal to all tastes. ⊠*Nes 67, Red Light District* ☎*020/428–2222* ▤*MC, V.*

$$–$$$ ✕**Kantjil en de Tijger.** The interior of this large and spacious Indonesian restaurant is a serene take on Jugendstil (a sort of Austrian Art Nouveau). Although you can order à la carte, the menu is based on three different *rijsttafel* (rice tables), with an abundance of meat, fish, and vegetable dishes varying in flavor from coconut-milk sweet to distressingly spicy. You can also opt to hit the counter at the adjacent Kantjil To

Go (Nieuwezijds Voorburgwal 352, open noon–9 daily) for cheap boxes of noodley goodness. ✉ *Spuistraat 291/293, Centrum* ☎ *020/620–0994* ✉ *AE, DC, MC, V* ⊘ *No lunch weekdays.*

$$ ✗ **Mamouche.** This North African teahouse takes delight in the smallest
★ details. Romantic and posh, this spot has been a hit with locals for dishes such as couscous with saffron-baked pumpkin. Chocoholics will say a heartfelt amen when rounding off their meal with the Ahram, a dark, mysterious pyramid embellished with a nut caramel sauce. ✉ *Quelijnstraat 104, The Pijp* ☎ *020/673–6361* ✉ *MC, V* ⊘ *No lunch.*

$$$$ ✗ **Supperclub.** The concept is simple but artful. Over the course of an evening, diners casually lounge on mattresses while receiving endless courses of food marked by irreverent flavor combinations. DJs, VJs, and live performances enhance the relentlessly hip vibe. Go in a large group if you can; otherwise you run the risk of being overwhelmed by one of the same. ✉ *Jonge Roelensteeg 21, Centrum 1012 PL* ☎ *020/344–6400* ⚭ *Reservations essential* ✉ *AE, DC, MC, V* ⊘ *No lunch.*

$$$$ ✗ **Vermeer.** With its milk-white walls, dramatic black-and-white pat-
Fodor'sChoice terned floors, Delft plates, fireplace hearths, and old chandeliers, this
★ stately place does conjure up the amber canvases of the great Johannes. Current chef Chris Naylor aspires to equal heights as his predecessors with such dishes as turbot with saffron gnocchi and lobster coulis. An army of waiters is on hand to ensure that the service is always impeccable. ✉ *Prins Hendrikkade 59–72, Red Light District 1012 AD* ☎ *020/556–4885* ✉ *AE, DC, MC, V* ⊘ *Closed Sun. No lunch Sat.*

$–$$ ✗ **Walem.** As if ripped from the pages of *Wallpaper* magazine, this sleekly hip and trendy all-day grand café serves elegant breakfast and brunch options—as well as plenty of both cappuccino and champagne. The dinner menu includes daily-changing specials. In the summer you can relax in the formal garden or on the canal-side terrace. Late at night, guest DJs spin hip lounge tunes for an appreciative crowd. ✉ *Keizersgracht 449, Canal Ring* ☎ *020/625–3544* ✉ *AE, DC, MC, V.*

WHERE TO STAY

$$$ 🏨 **Ambassade.** Ten 17th- and 18th-century houses have been folded into this hotel on the Herengracht near the Spui square. Two lounges—one of which functions as breakfast room—and a library are elegantly decorated with Oriental rugs, chandeliers, clocks, paintings, and antiques. The canal-side rooms are spacious, with large floor-to-ceiling windows and solid, functional furniture. The rooms at the rear are quieter but smaller and darker; attic rooms have beamed ceilings. Service is attentive and friendly. **Pros:** on a picturesque canal. **Cons:** rooms at rear can be small and dark. ✉ *Herengracht 341, 1016 AZ Western Canal Ring* ☎ *020/555–0222* ⊕ *www.ambassade-hotel.nl* ⇥ *51 rooms, 7 suites, 1 apartment* ⚭ *In-room: kitchen (some), DVD (some),VCR (some), dial-up. In-hotel: restaurant, room service, bicycles, no elevator, laundry service, public Internet, public Wi-Fi, some pets allowed, no-smoking rooms* ✉ *AE, MC, V.*

$$$$ ✗🏨 **Dylan Amsterdam.** Known for her chic London properties, Anouska
★ Hempel opened this Amsterdam outpost as the city's first "designer" hotel. It's located at (and incorporates a stone-arch entranceway from)

the site of the historic Municipal Theater, which burned down in the 17th century. Today the elegant rooms here are decorated with lacquered trunks, mahogany screens, modernist hardwood tables, and luxurious upholstery. One suite commands a view of the canal; many other rooms overlook a serene central courtyard. **Pros:** a taste of old Amsterdam, updated business facilities. **Cons:** not all rooms have water views. ⊠ *Keizersgracht 384, 1016 GB Western Canal Ring* ☎ *020/530–2010* ⊕ *www.dylanamsterdam.com* ⤴ *33 rooms, 8 suites* ⚷ *In-room: safe, refrigerator, DVD (some), Wi-Fi. In-hotel: restaurant, room service, bar, gym, spa, bicycles, concierge, laundry service, public Internet, public Wi-Fi, parking (fee), no-smoking rooms* ⊟ *AE, DC, MC, V.*

$–$$$$ ⊡ **Lloyd Hotel.** From the outside, the Art Deco–style Lloyd Hotel looks
Ⓒ slightly severe, but its appearance fits with its history. Built in 1921 as a
★ hotel for Eastern European immigrants, it then became a prison, then a detention center, before finally emerging as accommodations for artists. The vast café-cum-lobby is effortlessly stylish, with colossal white walls and plenty of natural light streaming in through windows. Its rooms are quirkily and almost all uniquely designed, with unusual furniture that has been featured in many fashion magazine spreads. Most rooms have extra-large tables, grand pianos, and kitchens. **Pros:** historic building, quirky interior, rooms priced for all budgets. **Cons:** out-of-the-way location, some of the more popular rooms are difficult to reserve. ⊠ *Oostelijke Handelskade 34, 1019 BN Eastern Docklands* ☎ *020/561–3636* ⊕ *www.lloydhotel.com* ⤴ *117 rooms, 16 with shared bath, 14 suites* ⚷ *In-room: no a/c, kitchen (some), no TV. In-hotel: restaurant, room service, bar, laundry service, concierge, public Internet, public Wi-Fi, parking (fee), no-smoking rooms* ⊟ *AE, MC, V.*

$–$$$$ ⊡ **Seven Bridges.** One of the famous canal sights in Amsterdam is the lineup of seven consecutive bridges that can be seen gracing Reguliersgracht. This atmospheric little retreat also looks over these. Occupying an 18th-century house just a few blocks from Rembrandtplein, this hotel offers uniquely stylish guest rooms, all meticulously decorated with dark woods, Oriental rugs, handcrafted and inlaid bed frames, and Art Deco tables. The proud owner scouts the antiques stores and auction houses for furnishings, and all have thorough documentation. The top-floor, beam-ceilinged rooms are the smallest and are priced accordingly; the first-floor room No. 5 is practically palatial, with its own private terrace. Reserve well in advance. **Pros:** friendly owners, wonderful view. **Cons:** no public areas, next door to a coffee shop. ⊠ *Reguliersgracht 31, 1017 LK Eastern Canal Ring & Rembrandtplein* ☎ *020/623–1329* ⊕ *www.sevenbridgeshotel.nl* ⤴ *8 rooms* ⚷ *In-room: no a/c (some), Wi-Fi. In-hotel: no elevator, public Internet, public Wi-Fi, no-smoking rooms* ⊟ *AE, MC, V* ⊙⏐CP.

$ ⊡ **Smit.** Despite its location, at the foot of the exclusive P. C. Hooftstraat and south entrance to the Rijksmuseum, this hotel is anything but pretentious. It's a lively and friendly place and a good choice for those who want to enjoy the Leidseplein nightlife. The neighboring restaurant is open for lunch and afternoon snacks but closes at 6 PM. The rooms are very plain, and the bathrooms are spacious. **Pros:** friendly staff, close to museums. **Cons:** rooms facing the tram lines are a bit noisy, rooms can be cramped. ⊠*P. C. Hooftstraat 24, 1071 BX Museum District & Environs* ☎*020/671–4785* ⊕*www.hotelsmit.com* ⌁*51 rooms* ☖*In-room: no a/c, safe, Wi-Fi. In-hotel: restaurant, laundry service, public Internet, public Wi-Fi, no-smoking rooms* ⊟*AE, MC, V* ⦿*CP.*

$$$$ ✕⊡ **Sofitel The Grand Amsterdam.** For captivating elegance, nothing tops the facade of the Grand, with its neoclassical courtyard, white sash windows, carved marble pediments, and roof abristle with chimneys and gilded weather vanes. If it seems lifted from a Rembrandt painting, that's because this hotel's celebrated city-center site has a long and varied history: it was built in the 14th century as a convent, then went on to house the offices of the Amsterdam Admiralty. After being rezoned by Napoléon, it became Amsterdam's city hall from 1808 to 1988, and then finally reopened in 1992 as one of the city's most deluxe hotels, where guests like Mick Jagger and President Jacques Chirac of France have made their home-away-from-home. The guest rooms here feature traditional-luxe furniture, fine fabrics, and quiet hues, plus every manner of business mod con. **Pros:** beautiful courtyard, a good chance of spotting a celebrity. **Cons:** run-down neighborhood, noisy location. ⊠*Oudezijds Voorburgwal 197, 1012 EX Centrum* ☎*020/555–3111* ⊕*www.thegrand.nl* ⌁*178 rooms and suites* ☖*In-room: safe, kitchen (some), refrigerator (some), DVD (some), VCR (some), Wi-Fi. In-hotel: restaurant, room service, bar, pool, gym, spa, bicycles, laundry service, concierge, public Internet, public Wi-Fi, parking (fee), no-smoking rooms* ⊟*AE, DC, MC, V.*

¢ ⊡ **Stayokay Amsterdam-Vondelpark.** Word of mouth has made this hostel so popular that more than 75,000 backpackers stay here every year. Hidden on a small side path within the Vondelpark, the location is almost like being in a secret forest, despite being only minutes away from the hustle and bustle of the city. Put your bike in the hostel's covered shed, breakfast on the terrace, ogle the parrots in the trees, then do a few rounds of the park (a great place to connect with new people). Accommodations range from rooms that sleep two to dormitories for 20, and sheets are included in the price. In the spacious lounge, you can use the Internet, watch TV, play pool, or get acquainted with backpackers from around the world. Some rooms are available for those with disabilities. This is probably the cleanest hostel anywhere—your mother would definitely approve. **Pros:** quiet location in the Vondelpark, clean rooms. **Cons:** no particular Dutch flavor, harried staff. ⊠*Zandpad 5, 1054 GA Museum District & Environs* ☎*020/589–8996* ⊕*www.stayokay.com* ⌁*100 rooms, 536 beds* ☖*In-room: no a/c, no phone, no TV. In-hotel: restaurant, bar, bicycles, no elevator, laundry facilities, public Internet, no-smoking rooms* ⊟*AE, MC, V* ⦿*CP.*

$–$$ ⊡ **Washington.** Just a stone's throw from the Museumplein, this hotel
★ often attracts international musicians in town to perform at the nearby Concertgebouw—except perhaps those who play the cello (the steep staircase is hard to navigate with bulky baggage). Owner Johan Boelhouwer is helpful and will lend from his collection of guidebooks. The breakfast room and lounge are filled with antiques and marvelous brass chandeliers, and the hotel is meticulously polished and sparkling clean. The rooms are simply and charmingly decorated in white and

pastel shades. Large windows let in a flood of light. There are also four comfortable and cozy apartments with their own kitchens; some also have living rooms, bathtubs, and pianos. **Pros:** laid-back atmosphere, friendly staff. **Cons:** no elevator. ✉ *Frans van Mierisstraat 10, 1071 RS Museum District* ☎ *020/679–7453* ⊕ *www.hotelwashington.nl* ↪ *22 rooms, 4 with shared bath, 1 suite, 4 apartments* ♿ *In-room: no a/c, safe, Wi-Fi. In-hotel: no elevator* ⊟ *AE, V* ⧖|*CP.*

NIGHTLIFE

Amsterdam's nightlife can have you careening between smoky coffee shops, chic wine bars, mellow jazz joints, laid-back lounges, and clubs either intimate or raucous. The bona fide local flavor can perhaps best be tasted in one of the city's ubiquitous brown café-bars—called "brown" because of their woody walls and nicotine-stained ceilings.

't Smalle. Set with Golden Age chandeliers, leaded-glass windows, and the patina of centuries, this charmer is one of Amsterdam's most glorious spots. The after-work crowd always jams the waterside terrace here, though you do just as well to opt for the historic interior. ✉ *Egelantiersgracht 12, Jordaan* ☎ *020/623–9617.*

Wynand Fockink. This is Amsterdam's most famous—and miraculously least hyped—*proeflokaal* (tasting room). Opened in 1679, this dim-lit, blithely cramped little bar has a menu of over 60 Dutch spirits. ✉ *Pijlsteeg 31, The Old City Center (Het Centrum)* ☎ *020/639–2695* ⊕ *www.wynand-fockink.nl* ⊙ *Daily 3* PM*–9* PM.

De Rokerij. For over a decade, this coffee shop has managed to maintain a magical-grotto feel that, ironically enough, requires no extra indulgences to induce a state of giddy transcendence. Dim lights, Indian-inspired murals, and low-to-the-ground seating keep the ambience chill regardless of how busy the Leidseplein headquarters can get. ✉ *Lange Leidsedwarsstraat 41, Leidseplein* ☎ *020/622–9442* ⊕ *www.rokerij.net.*

SHOPPING

Just down the road from Centrale Station is **Nieuwendijk.** Besides the national chains, this street has a busy pedestrian mall catering to bargain hunters and a younger crowd. To the south of the Dam is **Kalverstraat** (one of the only areas open on Sundays), where you'll find the international chains and favorite Dutch franchises. **Leidsestraat** offers a scaled-down version of Kalverstraat. Just east is the **Spiegelkwartier,** one of Europe's most fabled agglomerations of antiques shops.

Alternatively, go where the locals go. Explore the unique clothing and jewelry boutiques, crafts ateliers, and funky consignment stores dotted along the **Nine Streets,** which radiate from behind the Royal Palace to the periphery of the **Jordaan.** Take time to browse this neighborhood's art galleries, jewelry shops, and purchasable homages to interior design. **P. C. Hooftstraat** is the Madison Avenue of Amsterdam: all the main fashion houses are here, from Armani to Vuitton. Most shops close at 6, but remain open until 9 on Thursdays (*koopavonden*).

THE BULB FIELDS OF SOUTH HOLLAND

In the spring (late March until mid-May) the bulb fields of South Holland are transformed into a vivid series of Mondrian paintings through the colors of millions of tulips and other flowers. The bulb fields extend from just north of Leiden to the southern limits of Haarlem, with the greatest concentration beginning at the village of Sassenheim and ending between Hillegom and Bennebroek. Floral HQ is the town of Lisse and the fields and glasshouses of the Keukenhof Gardens. It is an unmissable and unforgettable sight. Timing can be volatile, but there's a general progression from crocus in the middle of March, daffodils and narcissi from the end of March to the middle of April, early tulips and hyacinths from the second week of April to the end of the month, and late tulips immediately afterward. An early or late spring can move these approximate dates forward or backward by as much as two weeks.

The **Bollenstreek Route** *(Bulb District Route)*, more popularly known as the Bloemen Route (Flower Route), is a series of roads that meander through the bulb-growing region. It was originally designed by Dutch motoring organization ANWB, which began life as a a cycling association. Look out for the small blue-and-white signs marked Bollenstreek. Driving from Amsterdam, take the A4 towards Leiden then the N207 signposted Lisse. By train, head for Haarlem and take bus 50 or bus 51, which allows you to embark and disembark along the route. Tour companies and the local VVVs (Tourist Information Offices) also organize walking and bicycle tours that usually include a visit to Keukenhof.

The heart of tulip country, the town of Lisse is home to the famous 17-acre **Keukenhof** park and greenhouse complex. Founded in 1950 by Tom van Waveren and other leading bulb growers, the Keukenhof is one of the largest open-air flower exhibitions in the world, and draws steady crowds between the end of March and the end of May. As many as 7 million tulip bulbs bloom here every spring, either in hothouses (where they may reach a height of nearly 3 feet) or in flower beds along the sides of a charming lake. In the last weeks of April you can catch tulips, daffodils, hyacinths, and narcissi all flowering simultaneously. In addition there are 50,000 square feet of more exotic blooms under glass.

This is the Netherlands' most popular springtime attraction, which is easy to reach from all points of the country. Traveling independently rather than in an organized group should present no problem: just follow the crowds. By car from Amsterdam take the A4 in the direction of Schiphol and Den Hague then take exit 4. Continue on the N207 to Lisse and follow the signs for the Keukenhof. Parking costs €6. You can buy a ticket in advance from the Web site ⊕*www.keukenhof.nl*. You can also take the train to Leiden Centraal and then bus 54 (aka "Keukenhof Express"). For bus departure times, call ☎0900/9292. There are also bus connections from Haarlem (bus 50 or bus 51) and Lisse (bus 57). ✉*N207, Lisse* ☎*0252/465-555* ⊕*www.keukenhof.nl* 💶*€13.50* ☉*Late Mar.–May, daily 8–7:30.*

HAARLEM

Walking past the charming *hofjes* (historic almshouse courtyards), and between the red brick gabled facades lining Haarlem's historic streets, it is easy to feel transported back to the Netherlands' Golden Age, especially around the central market square where the hulking form of Sint Bavo's church dominates the city skyline and evokes a bygone age. The intrusive motorized transport apart, much of Frans Hals' hometown appears unchanged for centuries. Yet despite its many picturesque monuments and rich supply of fascinating museums, Haarlem isn't a city rooted in the past. It is home to a lively population of students who bring with them a youthful vibrancy, especially at night. With its close proximity to the dunes, Haarlem also attracts hordes of beach-goers every summer. The result is an intoxicating mix of old and new that makes the town well worth checking out.

PLANNING YOUR TIME

Haarlem is at its best in late spring or early autumn. High summer means too many visitors, and touring in winter often puts you at the mercy of the weather (bring your umbrella year-round). For flora lovers, mid- to late April is ideal for a trip around Haarlem, as the fields are bright with spring bulbs. Many restaurants are closed Sunday (also Monday); museums tend to close Monday. The city is compact, and you can easily cover the main sights in one day.

GETTING HERE & AROUND

Haarlem is 20 km (12 mi) west of Amsterdam and 41 km (26 mi) north of The Hague. Getting to Haarlem by rail is a simple matter. Around six trains make the 15 minute trip from Amsterdam's Centraal Station every hour during the day. Driving will take around 20–25 minutes— you'll need to head west out of Amsterdam on the N200/A200. If you have the energy, you can bike.

Haarlem is compact city and easy to cover on foot. From the main railway station it is about five minutes' walk south to the Grote Markt. The Frans Hals Museum is another five minutes beyond that.

ESSENTIALS

Bike Hire Contacts Fietsverhuur Haarlem Station *(023/531–7066)*.

Taxi Contacts Taxicentrale Haarlem (☎ *023/540–0600)*.

Train Contacts Intercity Information (☎ *0900/9292)*.

Visitor Information VVV Haarlem (✉ *Stationsplein 1, 2011 LR* ☎ *0900/616–1600)*.

EXPLORING HAARLEM

② **De Hallen** *(The Halls).* A branch of the Frans Hals Museum, De Hallen has an extensive collection, with the works of Dutch impressionists and expressionists, including sculpture, textiles, and ceramics, as well as paintings and graphics. The complex consists of two buildings— the Vleeshal and the Verweyhal House. The **Vleeshal** (Meat Market) building is one of the most interesting cultural legacies of the Dutch Renaissance, with a fine sweep of stepped gables that seems to pierce the scudding clouds. It was built in 1602–03 by Lieven de Key, Haarlem's

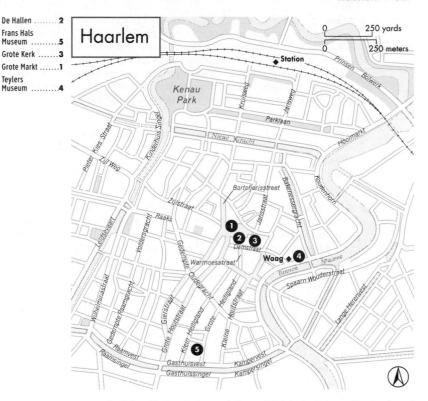

master builder. Today it is used for exhibitions—generally works of modern and contemporary art, usually by local artists. Note the early landscape work by Piet Mondrian, *Farms in Duivendrecht,* so different from his later De Stijl shapes.

The **Verweyhal Gallery of Modern Art** was built in 1879 as a gentlemen's club, originally named *Trou moet Blijcken* (Loyalty Must Be Proven). The building now bears the name of native Haarlem artist Kees Verwey, who died in 1995. It is used as an exhibition space for selections from the Frans Hals Museum's enormous collection of modern and contemporary art. ⊠ *Grote Markt 16* ☎ *023/511–5775* ⊕ *www. dehallen.com* ⊠ *€5* ⊙ *Tues.–Sat. 11–5, Sun. noon–5.*

⑤ Frans Hals Museum. This not-to-be-missed museum holds a collection of amazingly virile and lively group portraits by the Golden Age painter, depicting the merrymaking civic guards and congregating regents for which he became world famous. The building itself is one of the town's smarter hofjes: an entire block of almshouses grouped around an attractive courtyard. They form a sequence of galleries for paintings, period furniture, antique silver, and ceramics. But the focal point is the collection of 17th-century paintings that includes the works of Frans Hals and other masters of the Haarlem School.

Many of the works on display represent Hals at his jovial best—for instance, the *Banquet of the Officers of the Civic Guard of St. Adrian* (1624–27) or the *Banquet of the Officers of the St. George Militia* (1616), where the artist cunningly allows for the niceties of rank (captains are more prominent than sergeants, and so on down the line) as well as emotional interaction: he was also the first painter to have people gaze and laugh at each other in these grand portraits.

As respite from nearly 250 canvases, step into the museum's courtyard—lovely, and planted with formal-garden baby hedges. In one room, with curtains drawn for extra protection, is **Sara Rothè's Dolls' House**; nearby is an exquisitely crafted miniature version of a merchant's canal house. ⊠ *Groot Heiligland 62* ☎ *023/511–5775* ⊕ *www. franshalsmuseum.com* ☜ *€7.50* ☉ *Tues.–Sat. 11–5, Sun. noon–5.*

③ **Grote Kerk** *(Great Church).* Late Gothic Sint Bavo's, more commonly called the Great Church, dominates the main market square. It was built in the 14th century, but severe fire damage in 1370 led to a further 150 years of rebuilding and expansion. This is the burial place of Frans Hals—a lamp marks his tombstone behind the brass choir screen. Laurens Coster is buried here too. It is rumored that he was the first European to use movable type in 1423 (sorry, Gutenberg), which he discovered while carving letters for his children; he was inspired when one of the bark letters fell into the sand and made an imprint. The church is the home of the Müller organ, on which both Handel and Mozart played. Installed in 1738, and for centuries considered the finest in the world, it has been meticulously restored. Between May and October organists perform free concerts every Tuesday at 8:15 PM, and occasionally on Thursday at 3 PM. ⊠ *Grote Markt* ☎ *023/533–2040* ☜ *€2* ☉ *Mon.–Sat. 10–4.*

① **Grote Markt.** Around this great market square the whole of Dutch architecture can be traced in a chain of majestic buildings ranging from the 14th to the 19th century (with a smile and a little bravado, you can enter most of them for a quick look), but it is the imposing mass of Sint Bavo's church that catches the eye and towers over everything.

④ ★ **Teylers Museum.** Just north of the **Waag** (Weigh House)—built entirely of stone in 1598 and now a café—Teylers is the best sort of small museum: it is based on the eclectic whims of an eccentric private collector, in this case the 18th-century merchant Pieter Teyler van der Hulst. Founded in 1784, it's the country's oldest museum and has a mixture of exhibits—fossils and minerals sit alongside antique scientific instruments, such as a battery of 25 Leiden jars, dating from 1789 and used to store an electric charge. Its major artistic attraction is the legendary collection of drawings and prints by Old Masters, such as Michelangelo, Rembrandt, and Raphael. ⊠ *Spaarne 16* ☎ *023/516–0960* ⊕ *www.teylersmuseum. nl* ☜ *€7* ☉ *Tues.–Sat. 10–5, Sun. noon–5.*

WHERE TO STAY & EAT

$-$$ ✕ **De Lachende Javaan.** Stepping into "The Laughing Javanese" off an old Haarlem street that hasn't changed in centuries, you are hit with a flash of color and pungent smells. You can sit upstairs at one of the window tables and look out over the sober gabled houses while eating *kambing saté* (skewers of lamb in soy sauce) and *kipkarbonaade met sambal djeroek* (grilled chicken with a fiery Indonesian sauce), but the menu options are enormous, so you can mix and match, choosing a meal of 12 small dishes if you want. ⊠ *Frankestraat 27* ☎ *023/532–8792* ⊟ *AE, DC, MC, V* ⊘ *Closed Mon. No lunch.*

¢-$$ ✕ **Jacobus Pieck.** One of Haarlem's best *eetlokaals* (dining spots), this attracts locals with its long bar, cozy tables, and lovely sun trap of a garden. The menu offers standards but with a twist: try the Popeye Blues Salad—a wild spinach, blue cheese, and bacon number, with creamy mustard dressing for a lighter option—or, for dinner, lamb with ratatouille and rosemary jus. This restaurant-café is very popular, so get here early or book ahead to snag a table. ⊠ *Warmoestraat 18* ☎ *023/532–6144* ⊟ *No credit cards* ⊘ *Closed Sun. No dinner Mon.*

¢-$$ ✕ **XO.** A very funky restaurant-bar, XO has chunky silver graphics,
★ purple-and-gray walls, and oversize but softly lighted lamps. Throw in some fun touches—"king" chairs, complete with claw feet and red cushions; nifty recesses at the bar for extra intimacy; big stone candlesticks—and you've got an alluring setting for lunch and evening edibles. The dinner menu changes regularly but always contains mouthwatering and exquisitely presented dishes, such as cod filet baked in a sun-dried tomato-and-truffle crust, with black pasta, spinach, and a white-wine cream sauce. For a lunchtime snack try the imaginative bread rolls. ⊠ *Grote Markt 8* ☎ *023/551–1350* ⊟ *AE, MC, V.*

¢-$ ▦ **Carillon.** This is an old-fashioned hotel with a friendly staff, set in the shadow of Sint Bavo's across the Grote Markt. Small rooms are spartan but fresh and comfortable, with impeccable bathrooms that include showers but not tubs. The central location and reasonable rates make it a top spot to accommodate a day of exploring and then a night out. The café-bar has a nice terrace on the square. **Pros:** great central location; friendly. **Cons:** some rooms quite small; can be noisy on weekend evenings; no elevator. ⊠ *Grote Markt 27 2011 RC* ☎ *023/531–0591* ▦ *023/890–1285* ⊕ *www.hotelcarillon.com* ⇆ *21 rooms, 15 with bath* ♨ *In-room: no a/c Wi-Fi. In-hotel: restaurant, bar, no elevator* ⊟ *AE, DC, MC, V* ⬩❙CP.

$$-$$$ ▦ **Golden Tulip Lion d'Or.** This modern hotel is in a pretty 18th-century building just 50 yards from the railway station and within walking distance of major downtown sights. Rooms are spacious, with good lighting and upscale chain-hotel-style furnishings. The bathrooms all have tubs as well as showers. Downstairs are meeting rooms, and a reasonably priced restaurant and bar. A jogging path runs behind the hotel. **Pros:** good for transport connections; spacious rooms. **Cons:** a little away from the sights. ⊠ *Kruisweg 34–36 2011 LC* ☎ *023/532–1750* ▦ *023/532–9543* ⊕ *www.goldentulip.com* ⇆ *32 rooms, 2 suites* ♨ *In-room: dial-up. In-hotel: restaurant, bar, parking (fee), some pets allowed* ⊟ *AE, DC, MC, V* ⬩❙BP.

11

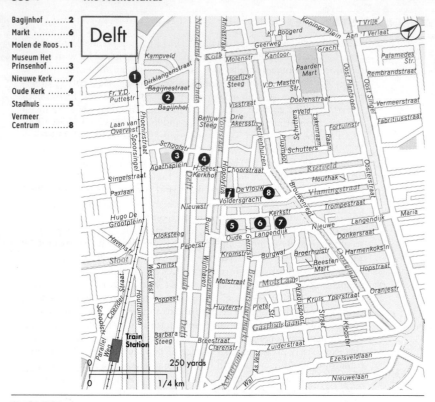

DELFT

For many travelers, few spots in Holland are as intimate and attractive as this town. With time-burnished canals and cobblestone streets, Delft possesses a peaceful calm that recalls the quieter pace of the 17th-century Golden Age, back when Johannes Vermeer was counted among its citizens. Imagine a tiny Amsterdam, with smaller canals and narrower bridges, and you have the essence of Old Delft. But even though the city has one foot rooted in the past, another is planted firmly in the present: Delft teems with hip cafés, and being a college town, revelers pile in and out of bars almost every day of the week.

PLANNING YOUR TIME

Delft is lovely at any time of year, but high summer means hordes of visitors; spring and fall can be more pleasant. Most museums tend to close Monday. The city is compact, and you can easily visit the sights on a day trip from Amsterdam. However, staying overnight to experience Delft after the trippers have left can be a real joy.

GETTING HERE & AROUND

Delft is 14 km (9 mi) southeast of The Hague, 71 km (44 mi) southwest of Amsterdam.

11

Direct trains leave Amsterdam Central Station for Delft every half-hour throughout the day; the journey time is a little under one hour. If driving, take the A10 then the A4 south from Amsterdam. The drive will take between 45 minutes and an hour.

Compact and easy to traverse despite its web of canals, Delft is best explored on foot, although water taxis are available in summer. Everything you might want to see is in the old center. If arriving by train, look for the computer information terminals outside by the bus station, which will print out a map with directions to any sight you request.

ESSENTIALS

Bike Hire Contacts **Fietsverhuur Delft Station** (☎ *015/214–3033*).

Boat Contacts **Rondvaart Delft** (✉ *Koornmarkt 113* ☎ *015/212–6385* ⊕ *www. rondvaartdelft.nl*).

Train Contacts **Intercity Information** (☎ *0900/9292*).

Visitor Information **Toeristen Informatie Punt Delft (Delft Tourist Information Point)** (✉ *Hippolytusbuurt 4, 2611 HN* ☎ *0900/515–1555*).

EXPLORING DELFT

❷ **Bagijnhof.** On the Oude Delft, just north of the Lambert van Meerten Museum, is a weather-beaten 13th-century Gothic gate, with ancient-looking stone relief, that leads through to a small courtyard. The city sided with the (Protestant) Dutch rebels during the Eighty Years' War, and when the (Catholic) Spanish were driven out in 1572, the city reverted to Protestantism, leaving many Catholic communities in dire straits. One group of women was permitted to stay and practice their religion, but according to a new law, their place of worship had to be very modest: a drab exterior in the Bagijnhof hides their sumptuously Baroque church.

❻ **Markt.** Delft's main square is bracketed by two town landmarks, the Stadhuis (Town Hall) and the Nieuwe Kerk. Here, too, are cafés, restaurants, and souvenir shops (most selling imitation Delftware) and, on Thursday, a busy general market. Markt 52 is the site of Johannes Vermeer's house, where the 17th-century painter spent much of his youth. Not far away is a statue of Grotius, or Hugo de Groot, born in Delft in 1583 and one of Holland's most famous humanists and lawyers.

❶ **Molen de Roos** *(Rose Windmill).* Just to the west of Oude Delft is Phoenixstraat, where you'll find this former flour mill that originally stood on the town ramparts. The hexagonal base dates back to 1728. The platform encircling the mill about halfway up was restored in 1990. The mill sails get going every Saturday, when you can climb up the vertiginous stairs to get a view from the platform as the sails swoosh by. ✉ *Phoenixstraat 112* ☎ *015/212–1589* ⊕ *www.molenderoos.nl* 🎫 *Free* ☉ *Sat.–Sun. 10–4, but only when a blue flag is flying from the sails.*

❸ ★ **Museum Het Prinsenhof.** A former dignitary-hosting convent of St. Agatha, the Prinsenhof Museum is celebrated as the residence of Prince William the Silent, beloved as *Vader des Vaderlands* (Father of the Nation) for his role in the Spanish Revolt and a hero whose tragic end here gave

CLOSE UP

Buying Delftware

It's corny, even sometimes a little tacky (miniature clogs, anyone?), but no visit to Delft would be complete without stopping at a Delft porcelain factory, to see plates and tulip vases being painted by hand and perhaps picking up a souvenir or two. **De Porceleyne Fles** (✉ *Royal Delftware Factory, Rotterdamseweg 196* ☎ *015/251–2030*) is the original and most famous home to the popular blue-and-white pottery. Regular demonstrations of molding and painting pottery are given by the artisans.

Another favorite place for picking up Delftware is at the factories of **De Delftse Pauw** (✉ *Delftweg 133* ☎ *015/212–4920*), which, although not as famous as De Porceleyne Fles, produce work of equally high quality. **Atelier de Candelaer** (✉ *Kerkstraat 14* ☎ *015/213–1848*) is a smaller pottery, and its city-center location makes it a convenient stop-off for comparisons of Delftware with other pottery.

this structure the sobriquet "cradle of Dutch liberty." The complex of buildings was taken over by the government of the new Dutch Republic in 1572 and given to William of Orange for his use as a residence. On July 10, 1584, Bathasar Gerard, a Catholic fanatic, gained admittance to the mansion and shot the prince on the staircase hall, since known as Moordhal (Murder Hall). The fatal bullet holes—the *teykenen der koogelen*—are still visible in the stairwell. Today, the imposing structure is a museum, with a 15th-century chapel, a quaint courtyard, and a number of elegantly furnished 17th-century rooms. ✉ *Sint Agathaplein 1* ☎ *015/260–2358* ⊕ *www.gemeentemusea-delft.nl* 🎫 *combined ticket to Het Prinsenhof, Nusantara, and Lambert van Meerten museums €6* ☉ *Tues.–Sat. 10–5, Sun. 1–5.*

❼ **Nieuwe Kerk** *(New Church.)* Presiding over the Markt, this Late Gothic edifice was built between 1483 and 1510. It represents more than a century's worth of Dutch craftsmanship—it's as though its founders knew it would one day be the last resting place of the man who built the nation, William the Silent, and his descendants of the House of Orange. In 1872 the noted architect P. J. H. Cuypers raised the tower to its current height. The ornate black-marble and alabaster tomb of William of Orange was designed by Hendrick de Keyser and his son. The small dog you see at the prince's feet is rumored to have starved to death after refusing to eat following his owner's death. In summer it is possible to climb the 380-odd steps of the church tower for an unparalleled view that stretches as far as Scheveningen to the north and Rotterdam to the south. ✉ *Markt 2* ☎ *015/212–3025* 🎫 *Combined ticket for Oude Kerk and Nieuwe Kerk €3.20, tower €2.70* ☉ *Apr.–Oct., Mon.–Sat. 9–6; Nov.–Mar., Mon.–Fri. 11–4, Sat. 11–5.*

❹ **Oude Kerk** *(Old Church).* At the very heart of historic Delft, the Gothic Oude Kerk, with its tower 6 feet off-kilter, is the last resting place of Vermeer. The tower seems to lean in all directions at once, but then, this is the oldest church in Delft, having been founded in 1200. Building went on until the 15th century, which accounts for the combination of architectural styles, and much of its austere interior dates from the latter part of the work. The tower, dating to 1350, started leaning in the Middle Ages. It holds the largest carillon bell in the Netherlands, weighing nearly 20,000 pounds. ⊠*Heilige Geestkerkhof* ☎*015/212–3015* ✉*Combined ticket to Oude Kerk and Nieuwe Kerk €3.20* ⊗*Apr.– Oct., Mon.–Sat. 9–6; Nov.–Mar., Mon.–Fri. 11–4, Sat. 10–5.*

❺ Stadhuis *(Town Hall).* At the west end of the Markt, only the solid 13th-century tower remains from the original medieval town hall building. The gray-stone edifice that looms over has picturesque red shutters and lavish detailing. It was designed in 1618 by Hendrick de Keyser, one of the most prolific architects of the Golden Age. Inside are a grand staircase and the Council Chamber with a famous old map of Delft. You can view the Town Hall interior only by making arrangements through the Delft tourist office. ⊠*Markt 87* ⊗*By appointment only.*

❽ Vermeer Centrum. Opened in 2007, and housed in the former St. Lucas Guild, where Delft's favorite son was dean for many years, the Vermeer Center takes visitors on a multimedia journey through the life and work of Johannes Vermeer. Touch screens, projections, and other interactive features are interspersed with giant reproductions of the master's work, weaving a tale of 17th-century Delft and drawing you into the mind of the painter. The centerpiece is a huge model of the city as it would have looked in Vermeer's day. ⊠*Voldersgracht 21* ☎*015/213–8588* ⊕*www.vermeerdelft.nl* ✉*€6* ⊗ *daily 10–5.*

WHERE TO STAY & EAT

¢–$$ ✕**Café Vlaanderen.** Board games keep you entertained on a rainy day inside the extensive café, but sunny skies will make you head for the tables set under leafy lime trees out front on the Beestenmarkt. Out back is an equally shady garden. The deluxe fish wrap makes a delicious light lunch. ⊠*Beestenmarkt 16* ☎*015/213–3311* ▤*MC, V.*

¢–$ ✕**De Wijnhaven.** This Delft staple has loyal regulars, drawn by the many terrace tables on a small square overlooking a narrow canal, and a mean Indonesian satay. There's a smart restaurant on the first floor, but the bar and mezzanine have plenty to offer, with lunch snacks, a reasonable menu for dinner with the latest tracks on the speakers, and great fries and salads. ⊠*Wijnhaven 22* ☎*015/214–1460* ▤*MC, V.*

$$$ ✕**L'Orage.** In cool shades of blue, with pristine white linen, Restaurant ★ L'Orage has a sublime aura; as soon as you walk through the door, you anticipate the sensational dining options on offer. It is owned and run by Denmark-born Jannie Munk—Delft's very own prizewinning lady chef. Her architect-husband, Pim Hienkans, was the mastermind behind the look of the place, which is accented by a huge, hinged glass roof to create an indoors-outdoors feeling. Munk creates delicious fish dishes, many based on recipes from her native country. ⊠*Oude Delft 111b* ☎*015/212–3629* ✍*Reservations essential* ▤*AE, DC, MC, V* ⊗*Closed Mon. No lunch.*

$-$$ ✕**Stadscafé de Waag.** The ancient brick-and-stone walls of this cavern-ous former weigh house are adorned with hulking 17th-century balance scales. Tables on the mezzanine in the rear overlook the Wijnhaven canal, while those on the terrace in front nestle under the magnificent, looming, town clock tower. All the while, tastefully unobtrusive music creates a cool vibe for a mixed clientele. Happily, dishes such as Flemish asparagus with ham and egg, or *parelhoen* (guinea fowl) in a rich dark broth, are equal to the fabulous setting. ⊠*Markt 11* ☎*015/213–0393* ▤*AE, MC, V.*

$-$$$ ⊡**Bridges House.** The history of this hotel goes back to Jan Steen—one of the great painters of The Hague School—who lived and painted here. His contemporaries didn't recognize his talent, so he opened an inn and operated a brewery to supplement his income. The current owner has re-created a patrician's house in a tasteful refurbishment. Antiques grace each spacious room, all adorned with extra-long beds with bespoke Pullman mattresses. The bathrooms are fitted with enormous shower-heads for a wake-up blast, and all have tubs. The breakfast room over-looks the canal. For longer stays, consider one of the apartments. **Pros:** historic building; good location. **Cons:** no elevator. ⊠*Oude Delft 74 2611 CD* ☎*015/212–4036* ▤*015/213–3600* ⊕*www.bridges-house. com* ⇆*10 rooms, 2 studio apartments* ⌂*In-room: no a/c, dial-up. In-hotel: no elevator* ▤*MC, V* ¡◎¡*BP.*

$$ ⊡**Johannes Vermeer.** It's surprising that no one else thought of it before, ★ but this is the first Delft hotel to pay homage to the town's most famous local son. The buildings of this former cigar factory were completely modernized and turned into a sumptuous hotel in 2000. You'll be spoiled for choice of Old Master views: rooms at the front overlook a canal, while rooms at the back have a sweeping city view that takes in three churches. In tasteful greens and yellows, the decor is unobtru-sive, and the staff are pleasantly friendly. The garden behind the hotel is a mellow place to have a drink. **Pros:** historic building; good loca-tion. **Cons:** no elevator. ⊠*Molslaan 18–22 2611 RM* ☎*015/212–6466* ▤*015/213–4835* ⊕*www.hotelvermeer.nl* ⇆*24 rooms, 1 suite* ⌂*In-room: Wi-Fi. In-hotel: no elevator* ▤*AE, DC, MC, V* ¡◎¡*BP.*

$-$$ ⊡**Leeuwenbrug.** Facing one of Delft's quieter waterways, this traditional and well-maintained hotel has an Old Dutch–style canal-side lounge, an ideal spot to sip a drink and rest up aching feet after a hard day's touring and shopping. Most rooms are large, airy, and tastefully contemporary in decor; those in the annex are particularly appealing. Rooms at the front have canal views. The staff are very friendly and helpful, and often go out of their way to make guests feel welcome. **Pros:** historic building; friendly staff. **Cons:** some rooms quite small. ⊠*Koornmarkt 16 2611 EE* ☎*015/214–7741* ▤*015/215–9759* ⊕*www.leeuwenbrug. nl* ⇆*36 rooms* ⌂*In-room: no a/c, dial-up. In-hotel: bar* ▤*AE, MC, V* ¡◎¡*BP.*

THE HAGUE

In certain ways The Hague is Amsterdam's prissy maiden aunt—it's Holland's seat of government, and also home to the Dutch royal family and the International Court of Justice. Yet it is also a lively metropolis that is both elegant and quirky. Explore the 25-plus public parks and the narrow winding streets where contemporary architecture sits comfortably beside grand 17th-century mansions. Relax at sidewalk cafés and watch as they fill with civil servants spilling from the offices around the 13th-century Ridderzaal. Or visit the galleries and museums to find masterpieces by Johannes Vermeer, or the dazzling optical conundrums of Dutch graphic artist M. C. Escher.

The Hague's official name is 's-Gravenhage (literally "the Count's Hedge"), harking back to the 13th century when the Count of Holland's hunting lodge was based in a village called Die Haghe. But to the Dutch the city is known simply as Den Haag, and that's the name you'll hear used on the street.

PLANNING YOUR TIME

Done at a pace that will allow you to soak up The Hague's historical atmosphere, a minimal tour around the city center should take about three or four hours. If you stop to visit the main sights, it will be a very full day.

For a city that sees so much political and diplomatic action, The Hague can seem surprisingly quiet, and a pleasure to those who want to escape the crowds. Bear in mind that most museums and galleries close at 5 PM, and many sites are also closed Monday.

GETTING HERE & AROUND

To reach The Hague directly from Amsterdam by car, take E19 via Amsterdam Schiphol Airport. Once you're approaching the city, follow the signs for the central parking route. This is an extremely helpful ring road that covers the many inexpensive parking lots within the city center.

There are two railway stations in The Hague: one is in the central business district, the Station Hollands Spoor (⊠ *Stationsweg*). The other station, Centraal Station (⊠ *Koningin Julianaplein*), is in the residential area. Trains from Amsterdam run directly to both, but the Centraal stop is an end stop. Many other Intercity (express) trains stop only at Hollands Spoor, and require a transfer to reach Centraal.

The Hague is a flat, compact city, and most of the sights in the town center are within a 15-minute walk from either of the city's train stations. Tram lines 3 and 17 cover many of the sights in town, and Tram No. 10 will get you to the outlying Statenkwartier museums. Tram No. 9 goes to Madurodam. For information on specific lines, ask at the HTM offices in The Hague's stations, or at offices listed below. For information on public transport (trains, buses, trams, and ferries), call the national information line.

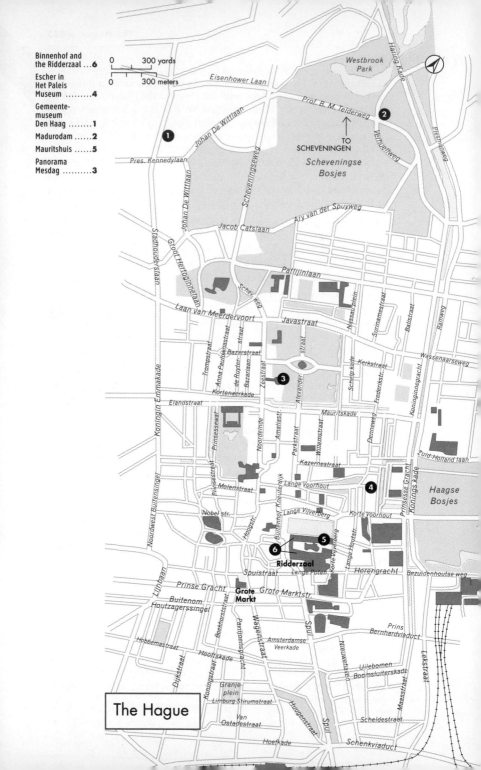

0   300 yards

0   300 meters

Westbrook
Park

Haring Kade

Eisenhower Laan

Prof. B. M. Telderweg

Verhulftweg

Plesmanweg

1

2

TO
SCHEVENINGEN

Scheveningse
Bosjes

Johan De Wittlaan

Scheveningseweg

Pres. Kennedylaan

Johan De Wittlaan

Ary van der Spuyweg

Jacob Catslaan

Stadhouderslaan

Groot Hertoginnelaan

Schev. weg

Pattijnlaan

Nassau-plein

Surinamestraat

Balistraat

Ramweg

Laan van Meerdervoort

Javastraat

straat

Wassenaarseweg

Koningin Emmakade

Trompstraat

Anna Paulownastraat

de Ruyter straat

Bazarstraat

Bazarlaan

Zeestraat

straat

Alexander-

Kerkstraat

Frederikstr.

Schelp kade

Koninginnegracht

3

Kortenaerkade

Elandstraat

Mauritskade

Dennenweg

Prinsessew

eg

Noordeinde

Amaliastr.

Parkstraat

Willemstraat

Zuid-Holland laan

Nederlei

Prinsestraat

Molenstraat

Kazernestraat

Lange Voorhout

4

Prinsesse Gracht

Konings Kade

Haagse
Bosjes

Noordwest Buitensingel

Nobel str.

Hoogstr.

Buitenhof

Lange Vijverberg

Korte Voorhout

Korte Vijverberg

Lange Houtstr.

6

5

Ridderzaal

Herengracht

Bezuidenhoutse weg

Lijnbaan

Spuistraat

Lange Poten

Korte Poten

Spui

Prinse Gracht

**Grote
Markt**

Grote Marktstr.

Prins
Bernhardviaduct

Buitenom

Boekhorststraat

Pavilijoensgracht

Wagenstraat

Amsterdamse
Veerkade

Nieuwehaven

Uilebomen

Houtzagerssingel

Hobbemastraat

Hooftskade

Koningstraat

Dijkstraat

Granje-
plein

Limburg Stirumstraat

Van
Ostadestraat

Hoefkade

Boomsluiterskade

Maasstraat

Scheldestraat

Lekstraat

Huijgenstraat

Spui

Schenkviaduct

The Hague

ESSENTIALS

Bus & Tram Contacts **HTM** (☎ *070/374–9000*). **Public Transportation Information** (☎ *0900/9292* ⊕ *www.9292ov.nl*).

Train Contact **Intercity Express Trains** (☎ *0900/9292*).

Visitor Information **VVV City Mondial** (⊠ *Wagenstraat 193* ⊙ *Tues.–Sat. 10–5* ☎ *070/402–3336*).

EXPLORING THE HAGUE

❻ Binnenhof and the Ridderzaal *(Inner Court and the Knights' Hall)*. The governmental heart of the Netherlands, the Binnenhof (or Inner Court) complex is in the very center of town yet tranquilly set apart from it, thanks to the charming Hofvijver (court lake). The setting creates a poetic contrast to the endlessly dull debates that go on within its walls—the basis of everyday Dutch politics.

For many centuries the Binnenhof was the court for the Counts of Holland; it is now a complex of buildings from several eras. As you enter, the twin-turreted former castle of the Earls of Holland dominates the scene. It was originally built by Count Floris V and became a meeting hall for the Knights of the Order of the Golden Fleece (one of the most regal societies of the Middle Ages). The interior of the Great Hall simply drips with history: there are vast wooden beams, flags of the Dutch provinces, and a massive rose window bearing coats of arms. It is still called Knights' Hall, and you can almost feel the feasts and revelries that took place there.

The Binnenhof also incorporates the halls used by the First and Second Chambers of Parliament (equivalent to the U.S. Senate and House of Representatives). You can wander freely around the open outer courtyard, but entrance to the Knights' Hall and other rooms is by guided tour only. The vaulted reception area is below the Knights' Hall. ⊠ *Binnenhof 8a* ☎ *070/364–6144* 🎟 *€8* ⊙ *Mon.–Sat. 10–4 (some areas may be closed when government meetings are taking place)*.

❹ Escher in Het Paleis Museum *(Escher Museum)*. First known as the Lange
☺ Voorhout Palace, this lovely building was originally the residence of Caroline of Nassau, daughter of Prince Willem IV—in 1765 Mozart performed for her here. In 2001 the palace was transformed into a museum devoted to Dutch graphic artist M. C. Escher (1892–1972), whose prints and engravings of unforgettable images—roofs becoming floors, water flowing upward, fish transforming into birds—became world famous in the 1960s and '70s. Replete with ever-repeating Baroque pillars, Palladian portals, and parallel horizons, Maurits Cornelis Escher's visual trickery presages the "virtual reality" worlds of today. Fittingly, the museum now features an Escher Experience, where you don a helmet and take a 360-degree digital trip through his unique world. Don't forget to look up as you walk around—the latest addition to the museum is a series of custom-designed chandeliers by Dutch sculptor Hans van Bentem that are inspired by Escher's work. These delightfully playful creations include umbrellas, sea horses, birds, and even a giant skull and

crossbones. A family ticket for €20 makes this an even more attractive museum for kids. ⊠*Lange Voorhout 74* ☎*070/427–7730* ⊕*www. escherinhetpaleis.nl* ▣*€7.50* ⊙*Tues.–Sun. 11–5.*

❶ Gemeentemuseum Den Haag *(Hague Municipal Museum).* Designed by
★ H.P. Berlage in 1935, this is considered one of the finest examples of 20th-century museum architecture. Although its collection ranges from A to Z—Golden Age silver, Greek and Chinese pottery, historic musical instruments, and paintings by Claude Monet and Vincent van Gogh—it is best known for the world's largest collection of works by Piet Mondrian (1872–1944), the greatest artist of the Dutch De Stijl movement. The crowning masterpiece, and widely considered one of the landmarks of modern art, is Mondrian's *Victory Boogie Woogie*—an iconic work, begun in 1942 but left unfinished at the artist's death. ⊠*Stadhouderslaan 41* ☎*070/338–1111* ⊕*www.gemeentemuseum.nl* ▣*€9* ⊙*Tues.–Sun. 11–5.*

❷ Madurodam. Statistically, the Dutch are the tallest people in Europe, and
🄲 never must they be more aware of their size than when they visit this miniature version of their own land. Set in a sprawling "village" with pathways, tram tracks, and a railway station, every important building of the Netherlands is reproduced here, on a scale of 1:25. Many aspects of Dutch life ancient and modern are also on view: windmills turn; the famous cheese-weighing ritual is carried out in Alkmaar; a harbor fire is extinguished; the awe-inspiring Delta Works storm surge barrier holds the ocean at bay; and planes land at Schiphol Airport. The world's longest miniature railway is here, too. The sunset hour is a fairy-tale experience as some 50,000 lights are turned on in the little houses. Madurodam is in the woods that separate The Hague from the port of Scheveningen to the north. To get there take Tram No. 9 from either railway station in the city center. ⊠*George Maduroplein 1* ☎*070/416–2400* ⊕*www.madurodam.nl* ▣*€13.75* ⊙*Sept.–mid-Mar., daily 9–6; mid-Mar.–June, daily 9–8; July and Aug., daily 9* AM*–11* PM.

❺ Mauritshuis. One of Europe's greatest museums, it's an incomparable
Fodor's Choice feast of art in only a dozen rooms and includes 14 Rembrandts, 10 Jan
★ Steens, and 3 Vermeers. The latter's remarkable *View of Delft* takes pride of place; its rediscovery in the late 19th century assured the artist's eternal fame. In the same room is Vermeer's (1632–75) most haunting work, *Girl with a Pearl Earring,* which inspired Tracy Chevalier's 1999 best-selling novel as well as the 2003 filmed version.

As an added treat, the building itself is worthy of a 17th-century master's brush: a cream-color mansion tucked into a corner behind the Parliament complex and overlooking the Hofvijver. It was built around 1640 for one Johan Maurits, Count of Nassau-Siegen and governor-general of Dutch Brazil. The pair behind its creation, Jacob van Campen and Pieter Post, were the two most important Dutch architects of their era. ⊠*Korte Vijverberg 8* ☎*070/302–3456* ⊕*www.mauritshuis.nl* ▣*€9.50* ⊙*Mon.–Sat. 10–5, Sun. 11–5; Sept.—Mar. Tues.–Sat. 10–5, Sun. 11–5.*

❸ Panorama Mesdag. The *Panorama Mesdag*, painted in 1880 by the renowned marine artist Hendrik Willem Mesdag and a team including his wife, Sientje Mesdag-van Houtenback, is one of the largest and finest surviving examples of its genre. The cinematic vision is a sweeping view of the sea, the dunes, and the picturesque fishing village of Scheveningen. To enhance the effect of the painting, you are first led through a narrow, dark passage, then up a spiral staircase, and out onto a "sand dune" viewing platform. So lifelike is the 45-foot-high panorama with a 400-foot circumference that it's hard to resist the temptation to step across the guardrail onto the dune and stride down to the water's edge. ⊠ *Zeestraat 65* ☎ *070/364–4544* ⊕ *www.panorama-mesdag.nl* 🎫 *€6* 🕐 *Mon.–Sat. 10–5, Sun. noon–5.*

WHERE TO EAT

$-$$ ✕ **Dudok Brasserie.** These days, Dudok is *the* in place in The Hague.
★ It's ideal for people-of-every-stripe-watching, from politicians debating over a beer, to the fashionistas toying with their salads, to pensioners tucking into an afternoon tea of cream cakes and salmon sandwiches. The vast granite-and-metal interior looks like a cross between a 1930s railway station and an ultracontemporary factory, and besides the countless small tables and roomy bar area, there's a communal central table and a packed magazine rack to keep solo diners busy. The menu combines international dishes—carpaccio of beef, steaks, and grilled chicken—with traditional Dutch fare such as mustard soup and sausage with cabbage. ⊠ *Hofweg 1a* ☎ *070/890–0100* ⊕ *www.dudok.nl* 🖃 *AE, DC, MC, V.*

$$-$$$ ✕ **Garoeda.** Named after a golden eagle in Indonesian mythology, a symbol of happiness and friendship, Garoeda is something of an institution among Hagenaars, many of whom consider it the best Indonesian spot in town. Established in 1949 and spread over five floors, the restaurant is decorated with Eastern art, and filled with wicker chairs and lush plants to give it a unique "colonial" atmosphere. Waiters are dressed in traditional costume and are more than happy to advise patrons new to the Indonesian dining experience. In addition to a choice of no less than seven different *rijsttafels* (an exotic smorgasbord of Indonesian dishes), there is also an extensive à la carte menu. ⊠ *Kneuterdijk 18a* ☎ *070/346–5319* ⊕ *www.garoeda.com* 🖃 *AE, DC, MC, V.*

$$-$$$$ ✕ **It Rains Fishes.** Crown Prince Willem Alexander has been known to
★ pop in here, so you know it must be good. A gleaming eggshell, ivory, and mirrored jewel box, It Rains Fishes is run by a team of five international chefs, whose predominantly aquatic specialties combine Thai, Malaysian, Indonesian, and French flavors. Its name, taken from a Thai folktale of fishes jumping from the river after a heavy rainfall, finds a few echoes in the restaurant's decor, with the occasional painted fish leaping around on the ceiling and walls. Specialties include sea bass with lemon and tarragon oil and king crab in the shell with Malay black pepper sauce. Outdoor dining is available in good weather. ⊠ *Noordeinde 123* ☎ *070/365–2598* ⊕ *www.itrainsfishes.nl* 🖃 *AE, DC, MC, V* 🕐 *No lunch Sat. and Sun.*

$–$$$ ✗ **Le Haricot Vert.** In a 17th-century building that once housed the staff of the nearby Noordeinde palace, Le Haricot Vert is a popular haunt for locals who come to enjoy good food in an intimate, candlelit atmosphere. Every possible wall surface is hung with china, sections of stained glass, pictures, and mirrors, and the overall effect is one of beguiling, romantic clutter. Dishes such as grilled sardines with ratatouille, and lamb fillet served with rosemary and sweet peppers, combine Dutch classics with French flair. ✉ *Molenstraat 9a–11* ☎ *070/365–2278* ☐ *AE, MC, V* ☉ *No lunch Mon.–Wed.*

WHERE TO STAY

$$$$ **Le Méridien Hotel Des Indes.** Des Indes has a graciousness that makes it one of the world's premier hotels. The interior is a harmonious blend of Belle Époque elements: marble fluted columns, brocaded walls, a good deal of gilding. Luxurious and ample bedrooms have all the best facilities—there are even Jacuzzis in some. The former inner courtyard is now a towering domed lounge leading to the superb formal dining room—all crystal and linen—called Le Restaurant. **Pros:** historic building; central location. **Cons:** such luxury doesn't come cheap. ✉ *Lange Voorhout 54–56 2514 EG* ☎ *070/361–2345* 🖷 *070/361–2350* ⊕ *www.hoteldesindes.nl* ⇱ *79 rooms, 13 suites* ⏦ *In-room: refrigerator, Wi-Fi. In-hotel: public Wi-Fi, restaurant, pool, gym, parking (fee), no-smoking rooms* ☐ *AE, DC, MC, V.*

$$–$$$$ 🖪 **Parkhotel Den Haag.** Situated in lovely Molenstraat, a boutique- and
★   café-busy street with a bohemian feel, the Parkhotel has been sheltering visitors since 1912. The building still exults in plenty of Art Nouveau detailing; architecture buffs won't want to miss its fabulous five-story brick-and-stone stairway. Today friendly staff plus light, airy rooms complete with all the modern conveniences add to its charms. **Pros:** historic building; friendly; good location. **Cons:** limited parking (reserve in advance). ✉ *Molenstraat 53 2513 BJ* ☎ *070/362–4371* 🖷 *070/361–4525* ⊕ *www.parkhoteldenhaag.nl* ⇱ *120 rooms* ⏦ *In-room: no a/c, Wi-Fi. In-hotel: restaurant, bar, parking (fee)* ☐ *AE, DC, MC, V* ⏍*BP.*

$ 🖪 **Petit.** This quiet, family-style hotel, operated by a young couple and fronted by a pretty garden, is on a residential boulevard between the Peace Palace and The Hague Municipal Museum. Occupying two large houses that date from 1895, Petit is tastefully furnished in warm shades of red and gold, with the occasional period stained-glass accent. The wood-paneled bar-lounge is a nice place to relax. **Pros:** friendly; good value; central location. **Cons:** some rooms quite small. ✉ *Groothertoginnelaan 42 2517 EH* ☎ *070/346–5500* 🖷 *070/346–3257* ⊕ *www.hotelpetit.nl* ⇱ *20 rooms* ⏦ *In-room: no a/c, refrigerator, Wi-Fi. In-hotel: bar, parking (fee)* ☐ *AE, DC, MC, V* ⏍*BP.*

Portugal

Wine harvest festival, Portugal

WORD OF MOUTH

"Friends who had been to Portugal many times convinced us to go to Porto as we had not planned to include the city. We loved it and are so glad we visited. The setting is pretty and the city has a real [un-touristy] feel to it. Again, like in all of Portugal, the local people were very helpful and friendly."

—HappyTrvlr

WHAT'S WHERE

1 Lisbon. Portugal's capital, founded more than three millennia ago, is an engaging mixture of modernity and mellow age. It moved into the international limelight by hosting Expo '98, the last great World Exposition of the 20th century, and then the final of soccer's 2004 European championship. A regeneration program has improved the city center, its transportation, and public buildings. The former Expo site—reclaimed shore to the northeast now renamed Parque das Nações (Park of the Nations)—hosts riverside restaurants, shows, a cable-car ride, and the stupendous Oceanarium.

2 Sintra. Along the coastal region west of Lisbon, Sintra is undoubtedly the biggest draw. Described by Lord Byron as "a glorious Eden," this hilly former royal retreat is studded with magnificent palaces, gardens, and luxury *quintas* (manor houses), and is a UNESCO World Heritage Site. The Atlantic coast to its west is often windswept, which means that, while it may not be so conducive to sunbathing, it is excellent for wind- and kite-surfing and sailboarding, as well as stunning coastal drives.

3 Porto. Portugal's northern region is a dramatic patchwork of soaring mountains, rolling hills, and dense forests, centered on Porto. The city is a captivating mix of the medieval and modern, combining a slick commercial hub with the charmingly dilapidated riverfront district—another well-deserved World Heritage Site. Across the water, Vila Nova de Gaia is the headquarters of the thriving Port wine trade.

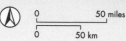

0		50 miles
0	50 km	

ATLANTIC OCEAN

← TO THE AZORES

↙ TO MADEIRA ISLAND

PORTUGAL'S LANDSCAPE UNFOLDS IN ASTONISHING variety from a mountainous, green interior to a sweeping coastline. Celtic, Roman, and Islamic influences are evident in the land, its people, and their tongue. The long Atlantic coastline means that most of Portugal's tumultuous history has centered on the sea. From the charting of the Azores archipelago in 1427 to their arrival in Japan in 1540, Portuguese explorers unlocked sea routes to southern Africa, India, eastern Asia, and the Americas. The great era of exploration, known as the *Descobrimentos,* reached its height during the 15th century under the influence of Prince Henry the Navigator. But the next several centuries saw dynastic instability, extravagant spending by monarchs, natural disasters, and foreign invasion. Order came in the 20th century in the form of a right-wing dictatorship that lasted more than 40 years, until a near-bloodless coup established democracy in 1974.

Today Portugal is politically stable, its people enjoying the prosperity brought by inegration into the European Union (EU). The highway system, in particular, has been overhauled with the help of EU money.

WHEN TO GO

If you're planning to visit in summer, particularly July and August, you *must* reserve a hotel room in advance. The best time to experience Lisbon and the south is spring or early fall: the crowds are much thinner than in summer, and even if you want to spend time on a beach, it could be warm enough for a brisk swim in April and October. As for Porto and the north, it's best to visit in summer, when the region is comfortably warm, but be prepared for drizzling rain at any time. Coastal temperatures are a few degrees cooler than in the south, but still mild in comparison to the rest of Europe.

Most festivals in Portugal are held in summer. The season starts in June, with the Festa de Santo António (Saint Anthony's Day), celebrated above all in Lisbon. Porto's big day is that of São João, its patron, on June 24. São Pedro de Sintra is a good place to mark the Festa de São Pedro (St. Peter's Day) on June 29.

GETTING HERE & AROUND

BY AIR
The flying time to Lisbon is 6½ hours from New York, 9 hours from Chicago, and 15 hours from Los Angeles. The flight from London to Lisbon is about 2½ hours. Continental Airlines has one daily nonstop flight from Newark to Lisbon's Aeroporto Internacional de Lisboa (LIS) (☎21/841–3500),as does TAP Air Portugal (☎800/221–7370 *in U.S.* ⊕*www.tap.pt*), but with connections to Porto's Aeroporto Francisco Sá Carneiro (OPO) (☎22/943–2400). It may be cheaper flying to London and picking up a budget airline or charter flight. Domestic flights are expensive. From Lisbon, TAP serves Porto and Faro.

TOP REASONS TO GO

World Treasures. Located a stone's throw from each other, Lisbon's Mosteiro dos Jerónimos and Torre de Belém, both UNESCO World Heritage sites, are monuments reflecting Portugal's proud seafaring past.

City Sophistication. Lisbon's Museu Colecção Berardo and Porto's Casa da Musica are just two of the ultra-modern institutions that make both cities major cultural centers.

Victorian Style. Explore Lisbon on ancient street trams that wind around narrow cobbled streets where washing hangs from the windows of pastel-colored houses and sardines sizzle on barbecue grills.

Trams of a similar vintage ply routes in both Sintra and Porto, too.

Old-Fashioned Hospitality. Even in a modern city such as Lisbon, or the bustling northern business capital of Porto, shopkeepers and café owners tend to move at a slower pace than their counterparts elsewhere in Europe. But even when there's a language barrier, old-fashioned courteousness also tends to prevail.

Buzzing Nightlife. Lisbon and Porto have earned reputations in recent years as great places to hit the town, with bars and dance clubs often located in stunning riverside settings such as adapted former warehouses.

12

BY BUS

Within Portugal, *expressos* are the best cheap long-distance option—they're comfortable, direct buses, some with video and food service. Operators include Rede Expressos (⊕*www.rede-expressos.pt*); Rodonorte (⊕*www.rodonorte.pt*), in the north; and Eva Transportes (⊕*www.eva-bus.com*), in the south. Book ahead. Tourism offices can help with schedules, and most travel agents sell tickets.

BY CAR

Your home-country license is valid in Portugal. Roads are mostly good, but drivers alarmingly cavalier. Wear a seatbelt, and note that one glass of wine can put you over the limit. Four-lane *autoestradas* (labeled "A" plus a number) save a lot of time—except late on Sunday when weekenders flock home—but have hefty tolls (Almot €20 between Lisbon and Porto). Lanes marked "Via Verde" are for those with a special payment device.

At intersections, traffic from the right has the right of way; at traffic circles you must yield to vehicles already in the circle. Speed limits are 120 kph (74 mph) on autoestradas, 90 kph (56 mph) on other highways, and 50 kph (30 mph) in urban areas.

Theft is common with rental cars. Contact the agency and police if yours is stolen. Never leave luggage or anything else of value visible in an unattended vehicle.

BY TRAIN

CP-Caminhos de Ferro Portugueses (☎*808/208–208, 21/318–5990* ⊕*www.cp.pt*), the national railway, has fast Alfa and Alfa Pendular trains—the latter with air-conditioning, food service, and electrical sockets—linking Porto, Lisbon, and Faro. Slower InterCidade trains serve other cities; regional lines, and *suburbanos* in Greater Lisbon (serving Sintra) and Porto, stop more frequently. All are no-smoking.

A nightly train departs from Madrid Chamartín at 10:45 PM and arrives at Lisbon Santa Apolónia (via Gare do Oriente) at 8:15 the following morning; in the other direction, it departs at 10 PM, and arrives at 8:25 AM. Berths must be reserved. There's also a daily service to and from Paris, switching trains at the French border.

A one-way ticket is an *ida*, a return *ida e volta*. First class costs 40% more than second. Advance booking is recommended for long distances. Traveler's checks are not always accepted, but major credit cards are. Eurail passes are valid, and CP's own *bilhetes turísticos* (tourist tickets) offer unlimited travel on 7, 14, or 21 consecutive days. You must book seats. CP's information lines are of help only if you speak Portuguese; the Web site is more useful.

ABOUT THE RESTAURANTS

The best dining in Portugal often is in moderately priced spots, including *churrasqueiras*, serving charcoal-grilled meats and fish. *Marisqueiras* serving fresh fish and shellfish are pricier.

Restaurant menus invariably include a *prato do dia* (dish of the day). An *ementa turística* (tourist menu) can be 80% of the cost of three courses ordered separately, but limits choice. Main dishes are large, and at lunchtime you can request a *meia dose* (half portion). Upmarket restaurants and those in tourist areas will have menus in English.

MEALS & MEAL TIMES
Breakfast (*pequeno almoço*) is often just a pastry washed down with coffee, either a dark *bica* or a milky *meia de leite*. Lunch (*almoço*) is served between noon and 2:30, dinner from 7 to 10. Unless otherwise noted, restaurants listed are open daily for both.

SPECIALTIES
Thanks to the sea's proximity, *caldeirada* (seafood stew) and *sardinhas grelhadas* (grilled sardines) are usually good choices. Tasty fresh fish includes *salmão grelhado* (grilled salmon), *dourada* (sea bream) and *peixe espada* (scabbard fish). *Bacalhau* (salt cod) served in a reputed 365 different ways, may come *à brás* (with eggs, onions and potatoes), *com natas* (finely flaked, with cream), and *assado com batatas à murro* (baked with small potatoes, garlic and olive oil). *Açorda com gambas* is a bread stew with prawns, garlic and cilantro.

Porco à alentejana mixes marinated pork and clams. You can go whole hog with *leitão da bairrada* (roast suckling pig) or *plumas do porco preto,* from black pigs fed on acorns. Sautéed or grilled *bife à portuguesa* (steak) comes in a port-wine sauce. Steak usually comes rare—*mal passado*; *to avoid this,* say *"bem passado."*

Cafés serve *tosta mista* (toasted cheese and ham sandwich) and usually also *bifana* (braised pork sandwich) or *prego* (steak sandwich).

Desserts include *baba de camelo* (literally "camel's spit," condensed milk and egg), *molotov* (baked egg whites with caramel), *maçã assada* (baked apple), *arroz doce* (rice pudding), *mousse de chocolate*, and fruit.

WINES, BEER & SPIRITS

Red wine accompanies most meals, with the *vinho da casa* (house wine) invariably drinkable. Periquita from the Setúbal region is a bargain. Bairrada, Dão, and sparkling *vinhos verdes* (green wines, so named for their youth) are popular. Portuguese beers such as Super Bock and Sagres are on tap and bottled. They have a good, clean flavor. Local brandies (Macieira, Constantino) are cheap. You must be over 16 to buy alcohol.

12

WHAT IT COSTS IN EUROS					
	¢	$	$$	$$$	$$$$
RESTAURANT	under €9	€9–€15	€15–€20	€20–€25	over €25

Restaurant prices are per person for a main course at dinner.

ABOUT THE HOTELS

Though international chains are present in Portugal, *residenciais* and *pensões* (simple accommodations that only serve breakfast) in former private homes are usually comfortable and affordable. *Pousadas* (inns), many housed in renovated castles or convents, are more atmospheric.

HOTELS

Hotels are graded with one to five stars or with a category rating, based on the amenities offered; a faded establishment with cable television might be rated higher than a new one without. Most rooms have private bathrooms. You generally have a choice of twin beds or a double (never king-size). High season means the summer months, Easter week, and during local festivals. In the off-season (generally November through March), rates may tumble by 20%.

COUNTRY HOUSES

Throughout the country, *solares* (manors) and *casas de campo* (country houses) have been remodeled to receive guests in a venture called Turismo de Habitação or Turismo Rural. Breakfast is included.

Contact Central Nacional de Turismo no Espaço Rural (⊕ *www.center.pt*). **TURIHAB** (⊕ *www.turihab.pt*).

POUSADAS

There are 45 of these four- or five-star hotels in historic buildings, tastefully furnished with regional crafts and antiques. Their restaurants serve local specialties. Some have only a handful of rooms, so reserve well in advance.

Information Pousadas de Portugal (☎ *21/844-2000* ⊕ *www.pousadas.pt*).

WHAT IT COSTS IN EUROS				
¢	$	$$	$$$	$$$$
HOTELS	under €60	€60–€100	€100–€175	€175–€275	over €275

Hotel prices are for two people in a standard double room, including tax and service.

PLANNING YOUR TIME

Portugal is one of Europe's smaller countries—you could drive from one end to the other in seven hours. However, it's also one of one of Europe's more diverse, and to appreciate land and people you will need to take things slowly.

The main population centers cluster along the coast, above all Lisbon and Porto. Though Porto was never the national capital, it has sought to rival Lisbon for centuries. The centralizing tendencies of the modern era have sapped the northern city's influence, but it remains a vibrant cultural center.

Each city has a different feel. If you can, you should overnight in both (they're only some 3 hours apart by car or train). But if you're in Portugal for less than a week, it may be best to focus on one and, if you have time, explore the surrounding region from there.

The culture of Lisbon is firmly rooted in the south. Moorish traces remain in the layout of the older quarters, in lifestyle, and even food (northerners profess to be disgusted by the snails served in Lisbon snack bars). It was from this city that the first ships set out to ply the sea routes to India and the East Indies, and to Brazil. Many—though by no means all—came back, bringing spices, gold, and other plunder, including slaves. These riches funded the building of many monuments, while the culture absorbed myriad influences. Despite its grand sights, Lisbon is also a fine city for aimless wandering, so allow for a day or two of exploring its nooks and corners.

Near Lisbon, Sintra is the only must-see. Indeed, many visitors find it so delightful—and restful—that they make it their regional base. Romantics swoon over its castles and palaces, gardeners love the mixture of indigenous and exotic flowers and other plants to be found in its gardens, and walkers make the most of marked trails of varying difficulty in the surrounding hills.

A worthwhile stop on the rail line or highway from Lisbon is Queluz, with its Baroque palace set in charming formal gardens. Beyond Sintra are aristocratic follies and pretty villages, spectacular beaches, and a looming cape that is Europe's westernmost point.

Porto, the beating heart of the industrial north, also thrived on international trade, though booming mainly thanks to exports to northern Europe, particularly Britain. The port wine industry based here—and whose cellars you can visit—still accounts for a large slice of Portugal's exports. Porto's setting, on the steep banks of the River Douro, is if anything even more stunning than Lisbon's, and there are sights enough to fill three or four days.

As in Lisbon, there are beaches to hand north and south of the city; from Porto you can also take scenic boat or rail trips up the Douro.

12

LISBON

Lisbon bears the mark of an incredible heritage with laid-back pride. Spread over seven hills north of the Rio Tejo (Tagus River) estuary, the city also presents a variety of faces to those who negotiate its switch-back streets. In the oldest *bairros* (neighborhoods), stepped alleys are lined with pastel-color houses decked with laundry; here and there *miradouros* (vantage points) afford spectacular views. *Eléctricos* (trams) clank through the streets, and blue-and-white *azulejos* (and glazed ceramic tiles) adorn churches and fountains.

Of course, parts of Lisbon lack charm. Even some downtown areas have lost their classic Portuguese appearance as the city has become more cosmopolitan: shiny office blocks have replaced some 19th- and 20th-century Art Nouveau buildings. And centenarian trams share the streets with "fast trams" and smoke-belching automobiles.

Some modernization has improved matters, though. In preparing to host the 1998 World Exposition, Lisbon spruced up public buildings, overhauled its subway system, and completed an impressive second bridge across the river. Today the Expo site is an expansive riverfront development known as Parque das Nações, and the city is a popular port of call for cruises, whose passengers disembark onto a revitalized waterfront.

PLANNING YOUR TIME

It's best not to visit at the height of summer, when the city is hot and steamy and lodgings are expensive and crowded. Winters are generally mild and usually accompanied by bright blue skies, and there are plenty of bargains to be had at hotels. For optimum Lisbon weather, visit on either side of summer, in May or late September through October. The city's major festivals are in June; the so-called *santos populares* (popular saints) see days of riotous celebration dedicated to saints Anthony, John, and Peter.

You'll want to give yourself a day at least exploring the *bairro* of Alfama, climbing up to the Castelo de São Jorge (Saint's George's castle) for an overview of the city; another in the monumental downtown area, the Baixa, and in the neighboring fancy shopping district of Chiado, and perhaps also in the funkier shops of the Bairro Alto. Another again could be spent in historic Belém, with its many museums and monuments. Note that many are closed Monday, and that churches often close for a couple of hours at lunchtime.

There are other attractions dotted around the modern city, and families will appreciate the child-friendly attractions of the Parque das Nações, the former Expo site. All in all, there's enough to do and see to fill a week—though if you're staying that long you should think about visiting Sintra or other sights in the hinterland.

GETTING HERE & AROUND
BY AIR
Lisbon's small, modern airport, sometimes known as Aeroporto de Portela, is just 7 km (4½ mi) north of the center, and getting downtown is simple and inexpensive. A special service, Aerobus 91, departs every 20 minutes between 7:45 AM and 8:15 PM. Tickets from the driver cost €4. It stops near major downtown hotels, at Praça Marquês de Pombal, Avenida da Liberdade, Rossio, Praça do Comércio, and Cais do Sodré train station. Cheaper (€1.40) city buses 44 and 45 bound for Cais do Sodré via Rossio depart every 15 to 30 minutes between 5 AM and 1:40 AM from the main road in front of the terminal. For a taxi, you'll pay €15 to €20 to get downtown, plus a €1.80 surcharge per item of luggage in the trunk.

BY BUS
Lisbon's main bus terminal is the Gare do Oriente, adjacent to Parque das Nações, also served by rail and metro. Most international and domestic express buses operate from the Sete Rios terminal, beside the metro and suburban train stations of the same name.

BY CAR
Heading in or out by car, there's rapid access to and from points south and east via the Ponte 25 de Abril bridge across the Rio Tejo (Tagus River), although in rush hour the 17-km-long (11-mi-long) Ponte Vasco da Gama is a better option. To and from Porto, the A1 is the fastest route.

The capital's drivers are notorious and parking is difficult, so your rental car is best left in a lot while in town.

BY FERRY
Ferries across the Rio Tejo are run by Transtejo, from terminals at Belém, Cais do Sodre, and Terreiro do Paço. They offer unique views of Lisbon, and their top decks are a nice way to catch the sun. The 85-cent passenger ticket for the prettiest trip, on the car ferry between Belém and Cacilhas, contrasts favorably with the €20 price of the Transtejo cruises that depart daily at 3 from Terreiro do Paço between April and October.

BY PUBLIC TRANSPORT
The best way to see central Lisbon is on foot; most points of interest are within the well-defined older quarters. The city's cobblestone sidewalks make walking tiring, even with comfortable shoes, so at some point you'll want to use the public-transportation system, if only to experience the old trams and *elevadores*: funicular railways and elevators linking high and low parts of the city. Like the buses, they are operated by the public transportation company, Carris.

For all these forms of transport, paying as you board means paying twice as much (€1.40 a ride), in cash, as when you use a 7 Colinas card. This nontransferable debit card, also usable on the metro and ferries, can be purchased at ticket offices and at Carris kiosks, such as in Praça de Figueira, and at the foot of the Elevador de Santa Justa.

Lisbon's modern metro system (station entrances are marked with a red "M") is cheap and speedy, though it misses out many sights and gets crowded during rush hour and for big soccer matches. You can purchase single tickets or cards for multiple journeys.

The Lisboa Card, a special pass that allows free travel on all public transportation and entry into 27 museums, monuments, and galleries, is valid for 24 hours (€15), 48 hours (€26), or 72 hours (€32). It's sold all over the city.

BY TRAIN

International and long-distance trains arrive at Santa Apolónia station, to the east of Lisbon's center, after passing through Gare do Oriente, where fast trains from the Algarve also stop. Services to Sintra use Rossio station, a neo-Manueline building just off Rossio square itself. Trains along the Estoril coast terminate at the waterfront Cais do Sodré station.

TOURS

Carris operates two tourist trams, tickets for each of which are €17: one rattles through the Old Town, the other takes you out to Belém. It also runs two different hop-on, hop-off routes in open-top buses, starting at Praça de Comércio, and costing €14. One circles downtown and stops at the Belém Tower and the Jerónimos Monastery, the other heads east to the Military Museum, Ceramic Tile Museum, and Parque das Nações. Gray Line offers coach tours covering Lisbon and the surrounding area.

ESSENTIALS

Bus & Tram Contact **Carris** (☎ *21/361–3054* ⊕ *www.carris.pt*).

Ferry Contact **Transtejo** (☎ *808/203050* ⊕ *www.transetjo.pt*).

Metro Contact **Metropolitano de Lisboa** (☎ *21/361–3054* ⊕ *www.metrolisboa. pt*).

Visitor & Tour Information **Gray Line** (☎ *21/319–1090* ⊕ *www.grayline.com*). **ITP (National Tourism Office)** (✉ *Palácio Foz, Praça dos Restauradores, Baixa* ☎ *21/346–3314, 21/845–0660 airport branch*). **Lisbon Welcome Center** (✉ *Praça do Comércio, Baixa* ☎ *21/031–2810*).

THE ALFAMA

The Alfama's timeless alleys and squares have a notoriously confusing layout, but the Alfama is relatively compact, and you'll keep circling back to the same buildings and streets. In the Moorish period this area thrived, and in the 15th century—as evidenced by the ancient synagogue on Beco das Barrelas—it was an important Jewish quarter.

The Alfama's streets and alleys are very steep, and its levels are connected by flights of stone steps, which means it's easier to tour the area from the top down (give yourself two hours, or three if you plan to visit the Museu-Escola de Artes Decorativas). Take a taxi up to the castle or approach it by Tram 28 from Rua Conceição in the Baixa or Bus 37 from Praça da Figueira. The large terrace next to the church of Santa Luzia, just below the castle, gives a fine overview of the Alfama and the river.

EXPLORING THE ALFAMA

❹ Castelo de São Jorge. Although St. George's Castle was constructed by Fodor'sChoice the Moors, the site had previously been fortified by Romans and Visig- ★ oths. At the main entrance is a statue of Dom Afonso Henriques, whose forces in 1147 besieged the castle and drove the Moors from Lisbon. The ramparts offer panoramic views of the city's layout as far as the towering Ponte 25 de Abril suspension bridge; be careful of the uneven footing. Remnants of a palace that was a residence of the kings of Portugal until the 16th century house a cozy, stately restaurant, and a multimedia exhibit on the city's history that brings to life the drama of such episodes as the Great Earthquake of 1755. From the Câmara Escura in the Torre de São Lourenço, in the castle's keep, you can spy on visitors going about their business below. The outer walls encompass a small neighbourhood, Castelo, the medieval church of Santa Cruz, restaurants, and souvenir shops. ⊠*Entrances at Largo do Chão da Feira, Alfama* ☎*21/880–620* ⊠*Castle €5* ☉*Mar.–Oct., daily 9–9; Nov.–Feb., daily 9–6.*

❺ Sé. Lisbon's austere Romanesque cathedral, Sé (which stands for *Sedes Episcopalis),* was founded in 1150 to commemorate the defeat of the Moors three years earlier; to rub salt in the wound, the conquerors built the sanctuary on the spot where Moorish Lisbon's main mosque once stood. Note the fine rose window, and be sure to visit the 13th-century cloister and the treasure-filled sacristy, which, among other things, contains the relics of the martyr St. Vincent. According to legend, the relics were carried from the Algarve to Lisbon in a ship piloted by ravens. ⊠*Largo da Sé, Alfama* ☎*21/886–6752* ⊠*Cathedral free, cloister and sacristy €2.50* ☉*Cathedral daily 10–7, cloister and sacristy daily 10–1 and 2–6.*

THE BAIXA

The earthquake of 1755, the massive tidal wave, and subsequent fires killed thousands of people and reduced 18th-century Lisbon to rubble. But within a decade frantic rebuilding under the direction of the king's minister, the Marquês de Pombal, had given the Baixa, or downtown, a neoclassical look. Today full of shops, restaurants, and other commercial enterprises, it stretches from the riverfront Praça do Comércio to the square known as the Rossio. Pombal intended the various streets to house workshops for certain trades and crafts, something that's still reflected in street names such as Rua dos Sapateiros (Cobblers' Street) and Rua da Prata (Silversmiths' Street). Near the neoclassical arch at the bottom of Rua Augusta you'll find street vendors selling jewelry. Northeast of Rossio, the Rua das Portas de Santo Antão has seafood

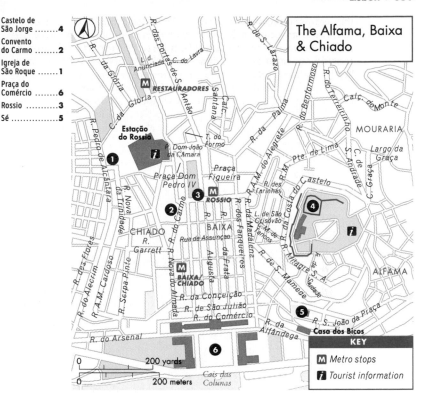

The Alfama, Baixa & Chiado

KEY

Ⓜ *Metro stops*

ℹ️ *Tourist information*

restaurants and two surviving *ginginha* bars—cubbyholes where local characters throw down shots of cherry brandy.

EXPLORING THE BAIXA

6 Praça do Comércio. Known also as the Terreiro do Paço, after the royal palace (the Paço) that once stood here, the Praça do Comércio is lined with 18th-century buildings. Down by the river, steps—once used by occupants of the royal barges that docked here—lead up from the water. On the north side, the Arco Triunfal (Triumphal Arch) was the last structure to be completed, in 1873. The equestrian statue in the center is of Dom José I, king at the time of the earthquake and subsequent rebuilding. In 1908, amid unrest that led to the declaration of a republic, King Carlos and his eldest son, Luís Filipe, were assassinated as they rode through the square in a carriage. On Sunday morning a market of old coins and banknotes takes place in the arcades. On the northwest corner the smart **Lisbon Welcome Center** (☎21/031–2700) has an information desk, craft shops, café, and deli. It's open daily from 9 to 8. The building also houses the **Sala Ogival,** a showroom for wine producers' association Vini Portugal, where you can taste Portuguese wines for free. ☎21/342–0690 ☼ *Tues.–Sat. 10 AM–8 PM.*

3 Rossio. Lisbon's main square since the Middle Ages is popularly known as the Rossio, although its official name is Praça Dom Pedro IV (whom the central statue commemorates). Although rather overwhelmed by traffic, it is a grand space, with ornate French fountains. Public *autos-da-fé* of heretics were once carried out here; the site of the Palace of the Inquisition, which oversaw these, is now occupied by the 19th-century Teatro Nacional (National Theater). On nearby Largo de São Domingos, where thousands were burned, is a memorial to Jewish victims of the Inquisition. You'll probably do what the locals do when they come here, though: pick up a newspaper and sit at one of the cafés that line the square, or perhaps have a shoe shiner give your boots a polish—just agree on a price first.

CHIADO & BAIRRO ALTO

West of the Baixa is the fashionable shopping district of Chiado. A decade after the calamitous 1988 fire destroyed much of the area, an ambitious rebuilding program restored some fin de siècle facades. And a chic retail complex on the site of the old Armazéns do Chiado—once Lisbon's largest department store—has given the district a modern focus. Along Rua Garrett and Rua do Carmo are fine shoe stores, glittering jewelry shops, hip boutiques, and a host of cafés, the most famous being **Café A Brasileira** (⊠ *Rua Garrett 120, Chiado* ☎ *21/346–9541*), which has a life-size statue of the modernist poet Fernando Pessoa seated at an outside table.

Uphill, the Bairro Alto dates back to the 17th century, but most of its buildings are from the 18th and 19th: an appealing mixture of old grocery stores, art galleries, and town houses with wrought-iron balconies. In the daytime, children scuffle amid drying laundry, and old men clog the doorways of bars; at night the area's restaurants, discos, and fado clubs come to life. The neighborhood has always been seen as rather rough-and-ready, and there are alleys where it would be unwise to venture after dark, but on the whole it's safe to walk around this remarkably compact but fascinating area.

EXPLORING CHIADO & BAIRRO ALTO

❷ **Convento do Carmo.** The Carmelite Convent—once Lisbon's largest—was all but ruined by the 1755 earthquake. Its sacristy houses the **Museu Arqueológico do Carmo** (Archaeological Museum), a small collection of ceramic tiles, medieval tombs, ancient coins, and other city finds. The lovely square outside is a great place to dawdle over a coffee. ⊠ *Largo do Carmo, Chiado* ☎ *21/347–8629* ☞ *€2.50* ⊙ *Apr.–Sept., Mon.–Sat. 10–6; Oct.–Mar., Mon.–Sat. 10–5.*

❶ **Igreja de São Roque.** Filippo Terzi, the architect who designed São Vicente on the outskirts of the Alfama, also designed this Renaissance church, at the Jesuits' behest. It was completed in 1574. Several side chapels contain statuary and art dating from the early 17th century. The last one on the left is the extraordinary 18th-century Capela de São João Baptista (Chapel of St. John the Baptist): built in Rome, decorated with mosaics that resemble oil paintings, the chapel was taken apart, shipped to Lisbon, and reassembled here in 1747. Adjoining the church, the **Museu de Arte Sacra** (Museum of Sacred Art) displays an engaging collection of rich clerical vestments and liturgical objects. ⊠*Largo Trindade Coelho, Bairro Alto* ☎*21/323–5381* ⊜*Church free; museum €1.50 Tues.– Sat., free Sun.* ⊙*Church weekdays 8:30–5, weekends 9:30–5; museum Tues.–Sun. 10–5* Ⓜ*Baixa-Chiado.*

12

THE MODERN CITY

The 10 parallel rows of trees along the Avenida da Liberdade, which was laid out in 1879, make Lisbon's downtown axis a pleasant place to linger, despite the traffic. Beyond it is the city's central park, Parque Eduardo VII, and then modern Lisbon, stretching into residential suburbs with the occasional attraction. It could take three hours to do justice to the Gulbenkian alone—especially if you have lunch there; add another for walking; and perhaps a fifth for shopping and a coffee.

EXPLORING THE MODERN CITY

Fodor'sChoice **Museu Calouste Gulbenkian.** On its own lush grounds, the museum of the
★ celebrated Calouste Gulbenkian Foundation, a cultural trust, houses treasures collected by Armenian oil magnate Calouste Gulbenkian (1869–1955) and donated to Portugal in return for tax concessions. The collection is split in two: one part is devoted to Egyptian, Greek, Roman, Islamic, and Asian art and the other to European acquisitions. Both holdings are relatively small, but the quality of the pieces is magnificent, and you should aim to spend at least two hours here. English-language notes are available throughout.

In the gardens outside, sculptures are found in every recess. Follow signs to the Centro de Arte Moderna, which has one of the finest collections of Portuguese modern art. If it's all too much to take in at one time, break up your visit with a stop in the main museum's basement café-restaurant. There's also a large shop that sells posters and postcards. ⊠*Av. de Berna 45, São Sebastião* ☎*21/782–3000* ⊕*www.museu.gulbenkian.pt* ⊠*€3, combined ticket with Modern Art Center €5; free Sun.* ⊙*Tues.–Sun. 10–5:45* Ⓜ*São Sebastião or Praça de Espanha.*

Ⓒ **Oceanário de Lisboa.** Europe's largest indoor aquarium wows children and adults alike with a vast salt-water tank featuring an array of fish, including several types of shark. Along the way you pass through habitats representing the North Atlantic, Pacific, and Indian oceans, where puffins and penguins dive into the water, sea otters roll and play, and tropical birds flit past you. You then descend to the bottom of the tank to watch rays float past gracefully and schools of silvery fish darting this way and that. To avoid the crowds, come during the week or early in the day. ⊠*Esplanada D. Carlos I (Doca dos Olivais), Parque das Nações* ☎*21/891–7002 or 21/891–7006* ⊕*www.oceanario.pt* ⊠*€11* ⊙*Apr.–Oct., daily 10–7; Nov.–Mar., daily 10–7.*

BELÉM

Some of Lisbon's grandest monuments and museums are in the district of Belém (Portuguese for Bethlehem), at the city's western edge. It was from here that explorers set out during the period of the discoveries. The wealth brought back helped pay for many neighborhood structures, some of which are fine examples of the uniquely Portuguese late-Gothic architecture known as Manueline. Several buses come here from Lisbon's center, but the 30-minute ride on Tram 15 from the Baixa district's Praça do Comércio is scenic and passes other attractions in the Santos and Alcântara districts along the way. Note that most sights are closed Monday, while Sunday sees free or reduced admission to many.

EXPLORING BELÉM

2 Mosteiro dos Jerónimos. Conceived
Fodor's Choice and commissioned by Dom Man-
★ uel I, who petitioned the Holy See for permission to build it in 1496, Belém's famous Jerónimos Monastery was financed largely by treasures brought back from Africa, Asia, and South America. Construction began in 1502 under the supervision of Diogo de Boitaca.

> **BULLFIGHTS**
>
> **Praça de Touros de Campo Pequeno.** Nothing grabs your attention quite so suddenly as the city's circular, redbrick, Moorish-style bullring, built in 1892. The recently renovated ring holds about 9,000 people who crowd in to watch Portuguese-style bullfights (in which the bull is never killed in the ring), held every Thursday at 10 PM from Easter through September. It's also used as a venue for concerts and other events. *Av. da República* ☎ *21/793-2093* ⊕ *www. campopequeno.com* Ⓜ *Campo Pequeno.*

This UNESCO World Heritage Site is a supreme example of the Manueline style of building (named after King Dom Manuel I), which represented a marked departure from the prevailing Gothic. Much of it is characterized by elaborate sculptural details, often with a maritime motif. João de Castilho was responsible for the southern portal, which forms the main entrance to the church: the figure on the central pillar is Henry the Navigator. Inside, the spacious interior contrasts with the riot of decoration on the six nave columns and complex latticework ceiling. This is the resting place of both explorer Vasco de Gama and national poet Luís de Camões. Don't miss the Gothic- and Renaissance-style double cloister, also designed to stunning effect by Castilho. The Hieronymite community lived in the monastery for more than 400 years until the dissolution of religious orders in 1833. ⊠ *Praça do Império, Belém* ☎ *21/362–0034* ⊕ *www.mosteirojeronimos.pt* 🏛 *Cloister €6, €10 combination ticket includes Torre de Belém and Palacio de Ajuda; free Sun.* ☉ *May–Sept., Tues.–Sun. 10–6; Oct.–Apr., Tues.–Sun. 10–5.*

▌ NEED A BREAK? For a real taste of Lisbon, stop at the **Antiga Confeitaria de Belém** (⊠ *Rua de Belém 84–92, Belém* ☎ *21/363-7423* ⊕ *www.pasteisdebelem.pt*), a bakery shop–café that serves delicious, warm custard pastries sprinkled with cinnamon and powdered sugar. Such *pastéis de nata* are sold throughout Lisbon, but those made here, since 1837, are reputed to be the best.

4 Museu de Arte Antiga. On the route from the center of Lisbon to Belém
★ is the Ancient Art Museum, the only institution in the city to approach

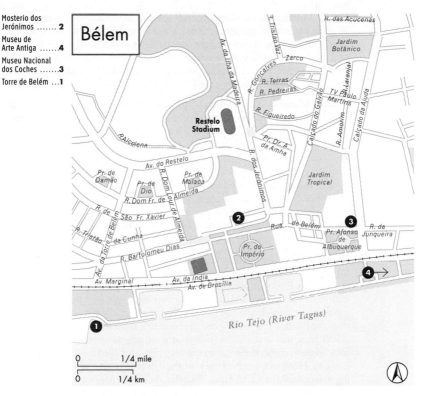

the status of the Gulbenkian. Housed in a 17th-century palace once owned by the Counts of Alvor and vastly enlarged in 1940 when it took over the Convent of St. Albert, the museum has a beautifully displayed collection of Portuguese art—mainly from the 15th through 19th century

The religious works of the Flemish-influenced Portuguese school stand out, especially Nuno Gonçalves' masterpiece, the *St. Vincent Panels.* Painted between 1467 and 1470, the altarpiece has six panels believed to show the patron saint of Lisbon receiving the homage of king, court, and citizens (although there are other theories). Sixty figures have been identified, including Henry the Navigator; the archbishop of Lisbon; and sundry dukes, fishermen, knights, and religious figures. In the top left corner of the two central panels is a figure purported to be Gonçalves himself.

The museum also boasts early Flemish works that influenced the Portuguese, and other European artists are well represented, such as Hieronymous Bosch, Hans Holbein, Brueghel the Younger, and Diego Velázquez. There are also extensive collections of French silver, Portuguese furniture and tapestries, Asian ceramics, and items fashioned from Goan ivory.

Tram 15 from Praça do Comércio drops you at the foot of a steep flight of steps below the museum. Otherwise, Buses 27 and 49 from Praça Marquês de Pombal run straight to Rua das Janelas Verdes, via Rossio; coming from Belém, you can pick them up across from the Jerónimos monastery. ⊠ *Rua das Janelas Verdes, Lapa* ☎ *21/391–2800* ⊕ *www.mnarteantiga-ipmuseus.pt* ⌧ *€3* ⊘ *Tues. 2–6, Wed.–Sun. 10–1, 2–6.*

❸ **Museu Nacional dos Coches.** In a former royal riding school, the National Coach Museum has dazzling collection of gloriously painted and gilded Baroque horse-drawn carraiges. The oldest on display was made for Philip II of Spain in the late 1500s; the most stunning are three conveyances created in Rome for King John V in 1716. The museum is right next door to the official residence of the President of the Republic, whose Museu da Presidência tells the story of the presidency, profiles the office holders, and displays gifts they have received on state visits. ⊠ *Praça Afonso de Albuquerque, Belém* ☎ *21/361–0850* ⊕ *www.museudoscoches-ipmuseus.pt* ⌧ *€4, free Sun. until 2* ⊘ *Tues.–Sun. 10–6.*

❶ **Torre de Belém.** The openwork balconies and domed turrets of the fanciful Belém Tower make it perhaps the country's purest Manueline structure. It was built between 1514 and 1520 on what was an island in the middle of the Rio Tejo, to defend the port entrance, and dedicated to St. Vincent, the patron saint of Lisbon. Today the chalk-white tower stands near the north bank—evidence of the river's changing course. Cross the wood gangway and walk inside, not so much to see the plain interior but rather to climb the steps to the very top for a bird's-eye view of river and city. However, the best view of the tower is from the nearby Padrão dos Descobrimentos. ⊠ *Av. de Brasília, Belém* ☎ *21/362–0034* ⊕ *www.mosteirojeronimos.pt/index_torre.html* ⌧ *€4* ⊘ *Oct.–Apr., Tues.–Sun. 10–5; May–Sept., Tues.–Sun. 10–6.30.*

WHERE TO EAT

ALFAMA

$$$$ ✕ **Bica do Sapato.** A favorite among in-the-know locals, this riverfront restaurant is known for its stylish interior design and furnishings: Knoll, Eero Saarien, and Mies van der Rohe all feature. Choose between a café serving light meals, a restaurant offering tasty (and expensive) nouvelle cuisine, and an upstairs sushi bar. ⊠ *Av. Infante D. Henrique, Armazém B, Cais da Pedra, Alfama* ☎ *21/881–0320* ⊕ *www.bicadosapato.com* ▭ *AE, DC, MC, V* ⊘ *Closed Sun. No lunch Mon.*

$$$–$$$$ ✕ **Casa do Leão.** Located within the castle, this restaurant affords diners an incredible view of Lisbon from its terrace. The dining room, with its vaulted ceiling, has an open fireplace for the winter months. You could start with grilled sardines with sea salt on corn bread, then move on to pork with clams and shrimp. Note: to eat here during the day you must pay to enter the castle. With a reservation you get a discount. ⊠ *Entrance to castle at Largo do Chão da Feira, Alfama* ☎ *21/888–0154* ▭ *AE, DC, MC, V.*

$$$$ ✕ **Santo António de Alfama.** Up some steps from the Travessa Terreiro do Trigo, you'll find this restaurant hung with black-and-white photos of famous artists, including a signed one of pop singer Nelly Furtado. The mushrooms stuffed with Gorgonzola and *joaquinzinhos fritos* (whitebait fried in batter) are tasty starters. Steak, fish, or duck accompanied by steamed vegetables are the most popular main dishes. ✉*Beco de São Miguel 7, Alfama* ☎*21/888–1328* ⊟*AE, DC, MC, V* ⊘*Closed Tues.*

12

AVENIDA DA LIBERDADE

$$$$ ✕ **Luca.** Noted for its excellent service and delicious food, this restaurant a couple of blocks off Avenida de Liberdade is very much in fashion, so reserve a table or arrive early to avoid the rush. Consider pasta with chunks of seafood or leg of lamb braised in its own juice, accompanied with a bottle of red wine. ✉*Rua Santa Marta, 35, Liberdade* ☎*21/315-0212* ⊕*www.luca.pt* ⊟*AE, DC, MC, V* ⊘*Closed Sun. No lunch Sat.*

$$ ✕ **Os Tibetanos.** Delicious dishes such as *bife de seitan com cogumelos* (wheat gluten with mushrooms), *tofu gratinado com queijo de cabra* (bean curd au gratin with goat cheese), and *tarte de papaia e requeijão* (papaya cheesecake) mean that even carnivores are among those who wait in line for a table in the dining room or pleasant garden here. The restaurant is part of a Buddhist center where you can purchase incense made by Nepalese monks, homeopathic medicine, and other natural products. ✉*Rua do Salitre 117, Liberdade* ☎*21/314-2038* ⊕*www. tibetanos.com* ⊟*No credit cards* ⊘*Closed weekends.*

BAIRRO ALTO

$$ ✕ **Cantinho da Paz.** This place is on an alley off the Tram 28 route from Chiado to Estrela, but take a taxi if you're worried about getting lost. It's a joyful mom-and-pop establishment that specializes in the cuisine of Goa; the shrimp curry is particularly rich and flavorful. The English-speaking owner will guide you through the menu. ✉*Rua da Paz 4, off Rua dos Poiais de São Bento, Bairro Alto* ☎*21/396-9698* ⊕*www. restaurantecantinhodapaz.com* ⚑*Reservations essential* ⊟*MC, V* ⊘*Closed Sun.*

$$ ✕ **Casa Faz Frio.** This convivial adega—complete with wood beams, stone floors, paneled booths, and bunches of garlic suspended from the ceiling—is of a type that's fast disappearing. The list of Portuguese dishes on the prix-fixe menu changes daily, although you'll usually find steak, pork, and quail. ✉*Rua de Dom Pedro V 96–98, Bairro Alto* ☎*21/346-1860* ⊟*No credit cards.*

$$–$$$ ✕ **Cervejaria Trindade.** The colourful wall tiles and vaulted ceiling of this ★ former monastery hint at its long history, and it's popular with both locals and tourists alike. A homey bar at the entrance will quench your thirst as you wait. You might start with *ameijoas Trindade* (clams in a garlic butter and coriander sauce) before moving on to *bife vazia Trindade* (steak in a thick onion gravy) or *bacalhau a brás* (flaked cod with potato and onion). It all tastes great with the house wine. ✉*Rua Nova da Trindade 20, Bairro Alto* ☎*21/342-3506* ⊕*www.cervejaria trindade.pt* ⊟*AE, DC, MC, V.*

$$$$ ✗**Olivier.** Named after its owner, a famous chef like his father, this restaurant has successfully won the hearts of Lisbon's gourmets. You go through a big white door into the cozy, sophisticated black-and-red interior. As a starter, try crab guacamole served on corn bread, tomato and feta cheese on the spit, foie gras with onion and port wine, or mushrooms with pesto and cheese; main dishes include braised veal shanks, and sea scallops in a white butter sauce. ⊠*Rua do Teixeira 35, Bairro Alto* ☎*21/342–1024* ⊕*www.restaurante-olivier.com* ▤*AE, DC, MC, V* ◎*Closed Sun.*

$$$–$$$$ ✗**Tavares Rico.** Established as a café in 1784, the city's oldest restau-
   ★ rant pleases its customers with a handsome Edwardian dining room, outstanding service, French-inspired fare, and an excellent wine list. The sole cooked in champagne sauce is a classic, and there are game birds available in season, served roasted in a rich wine sauce. Portugal is represented with bacalhau or *sopa alentejana* (a concoction of garlic, bread, and egg). ⊠*Rua Misericórdia 35–37, Bairro Alto* ☎*21/342–1112* ⊕*www.tavaresrico.pt* ⌖*Reservations essential* ▤*AE, DC, MC, V* ◎*Closed Sun. and Mon. No lunch Sat.*

$–$$ ✗**Vá e Volte.** In a few tile-lined dining rooms, staff keep the meals coming with speed and good humor. Fried or grilled fish or meat dishes are served with enough salad, potatoes, and vegetables to keep the wolf from the door. The *arroz doce* (rice pudding) is homemade. Even if you choose a fine regional wine, the price won't break the bank. ⊠*Rua Diário de Notícias 100, Bairro Alto* ☎*21/342–7888* ⊕*www.restaurante vaevolte.com* ▤*AE, MC, V* ◎*Closed Mon.*

BAIXA-CHIADO

$$$–$$$$ ✗**Tagide.** In a fine old house that looks out over the Baixa and the Rio Tejo (reserve a table by the window), you can have one of Lisbon's great food experiences. The dining room lined with 17th-century tiles is a lovely backdrop for sampling regional Portuguese fare. Try the famous *presunto* (smoked ham) from Chaves, stuffed squid from the Algarve, or the classic *porco à alentejana* (Alentejo-style pork with clams). ⊠*Largo Academia das Belas Artes 18–20, Chiado* ☎*21/340–4010* ⊕*www. restaurantetagide.com* ⌖*Reservations essential* ▤*AE, DC, MC, V* ◎*Closed Sun. and Mon.*

$$$–$$$$ ✗**Terreiro do Paço.** On the site of the old Royal Palace, this restaurant
   ★ has a discreet entrance leading to a subtly lit vaulted space. The lower level, which includes tables on the esplanade in the summer, has a contemporary design. The upper level is more traditional, with earthy tones reflecting the colours of the restored stone and brick ceiling. Under the direction of chef Vitor Sobral, the kitchen creates incredibly creative starters like oysters with purée of baked eggplant and such main dishes as caramelized duck breast in a ginger cream sauce. The set tasting menus offer a wonderful combination of textures and flavors. ⊠*Praça do Comércio, Baixa* ☎*21/031–2850* ⊕*www.terreiropaco.com* ▤ *AE, MC, V* ◎*No lunch weekends.*

WHERE TO STAY

ALFAMA

$$ **Albergaria Senhora do Monte.** If you want expansive views of the castle and river, book a room on one of the upper floors of this hotel. If it's summer, ask for a balcony. The top-floor dining room has huge windows, making breakfast a real pleasure, and a terrace where guests gather for drinks at sunset. Though the hotel is on Lisbon's highest hill, Tram 28 runs nearby. **Pros:** pretty views, helpful staff, off the beaten track. **Cons:** on a steep hill, rooms on top floor can get noisy. ⊠ *Calçada do Monte 39, Alfama* ☎ *21/886–6002* ⊕ *www.maisturismo. pt/sramonte* ⬐ *24 rooms, 4 suites* ⧉ *In-hotel: room service, bar, laundry service, Internet terminal, Wi-Fi* ⊟ *AE, DC, MC, V* ⦿|*CP.*

$$ **Olissipo Castelo.** Just below the castle, this small, elegant hotel pampers guests with luxurious linens, thick carpeting, elegantly furnishings, and marble bathrooms. Rooms on the second and third floors have lovely terraces where you can breakfast or sip an afternoon drink. Those on the fourth floor have full-length windows so you can take in the views of the city. **Pros:** great views, quiet area, away from the most touristy areas. **Cons:** on a steep hill, sometimes a wait for breakfast seating. ⊠ *Rua Costa do Castelo 112–126, Alfama* ☎ *21/882–0190* ⊕ *www.olissippohotels.com* ⬐ *22 rooms, 2 suites* ⧉ *In-room: safe, Internet. In-hotel: room service, bar, laundry service, parking (paid), Wi-Fi* ⊟ *AE, DC, MC, V* ⦿|*BP.*

$$$$ **Solar do Castelo.** What's better than staying in an 18th-century mansion? How about if that mansion is within the walls of a castle, with Roman ruins below? In this, one of the city's most unusual lodgings, numerous original architectural features have been lovingly restored, including elegant masonry and tile work. Featuring classical furnishings and subtle color schemes, the standard rooms in the original building offer nice views of the Rio Tejo; rooms in the newer wing incorporate parts of the castle wall. A sun-drenched courtyard acts as a breakfast area and is home to a family of peacocks. There's no restaurant, but there are plenty of them a short walk away. **Pros:** lovely architecture, charm to spare, quiet location. **Cons:** up a steep cobbled road, some rooms only have showers. ⊠ *Rua das Cozinhas 2, Alfama* ☎ *21/880–6050* ⊕ *www.heritage.pt* ⬐ *14 rooms* ⧉ *In-room: safe, DVD, Wi-Fi. In-hotel: room service, bar, laundry, Internet terminal, Wi-Fi* ⊟ *AE, DC, MC, V* ⦿|*BP.*

$$$ **Solar dos Mouros.** This melon-colored town house has a great location near the Castelo de São Jorge. The decor, in a contemporary style with bright colors and minimalist furnishings, is a pleasant contrast to the traditional facade. For the best views, request a room on the upper floors overlooking the Rio Tejo: those with castle views are slightly cheaper. The attic room is up a flight of stairs and has low ceilings, but has a private terrace with great views across the city. **Pros:** close to the castle, lovely views, funky decor. **Cons:** up a steep hills, stairs to climb. ⊠ *Rua do Milagre de Santo Antonio 6, Alfama* ☎ *21/885–4940* ⊕ *www.solardosmouros.com* ⬐ *11 rooms, 1 suite* ⧉ *In-room: safe, Wi-Fi. In-hotel: room service, bar, laundry service, Wi-Fi* ⊟ *AE, DC, MC, V* ⦿|*EP.*

AVENIDA DA LIBERDADE

$$$ 🏨 **Britânia.** Hidden away just behind Avenida da Liberdade, this Art
★ Deco masterpiece has been lovingly restored to its original splendor,
including original artwork in the marbled lobby and wood-paneled
bar that was discovered during renovation. The spacious guest rooms
feature high ceilings, marble bathrooms, and 1940s-style furniture. The
staff treat returning guests like members of the family. **Pros:** period
charm, outgoing staff. **Cons:** decor not to everyone's taste, a bit old-
fashioned. ⊠*Rua Rodrigues Sampaio 17, Liberdade* 🕾*21/315–5016*
⊕*www.heritage.pt* ➳*32 rooms, 1 suite* ⌂*In-room: safe, DVD, Wi-Fi.
In-hotel: room service, bar, laundry service, Internet terminal, Wi-Fi*
☰*AE, DC, MC, V* ⎜⎡⎜*BP* Ⓜ*Avenida.*

$$$–$$$$ 🏨 **Tivoli Lisboa.** There's enough marble in the public areas to make you
fear for the future supply of the stone, but grandness gives way to com-
fort in the pleasant guest rooms. In warmer months the outdoor pool
and garden offer respite from the bustling city; the top-floor Terraço
grill (where you may take breakfast) presents wonderful views of the
castle. **Pros:** close to public transportation, walking distance to many
restaurants, rooftop restaurant with great views. **Cons:** more expensive
than surrounding hotels, some small rooms. ⊠*Av. da Liberdade 185,
Liberdade* 🕾*21/319–8900* ⊕*www.tivolihotels.com* ➳*308 rooms, 15
suites* ⌂*In-room: safe, Internet. In-hotel: 2 restaurants, room service,
bars, tennis courts, pool, gym, laundry service, Internet terminal, Wi-Fi,
parking (paid)* ☰*AE, DC, MC, V* ⎜⎡⎜*BP* Ⓜ*Avenida.*

BAIRRO ALTO

$$$$ 🏨 **Bairro Alto Hotel.** Lisbon's first contemporary boutique hotel, with
sleek contemporary design, "the BA" is in the heart of the city. In the
guest rooms the color scheme and atmosphere reflects the traditional
Lisbon streets outside. The best are on the upper floors facing Praça
Luis de Camões; don't worry about street noise, as double-glazed win-
dows keep things quiet. In the popular Flores restaurant, the menu fuses
traditional and modern flavors. The rooftop terrace bar, which over-
looks the Rio Tejo and Ponte 25 de Abril, is a photographer's dream.
Pros: cutting-edge design, central location, attentive staff. **Cons:** some
small rooms, few amenities for business travelers. ⊠*Praça Luís de
Camões 2, Bairro Alto* 🕾*21/340–8288* ⊕*www.bairroaltohotel.com*
➳*51 rooms, 4 suites* ⌂*In-room: safe, DVD, Wi-Fi. In-hotel: restau-
rant, room service, bar, gym, spa, laundry service* ☰*AE, DC, MC, V*
⎜⎡⎜*BP* Ⓜ*Baixa Chiado.*

¢ 🏨 **Camões.** Typical of the guesthouses in Bairro Alto, the Camões has
simple rooms spread out over a couple of floors of an apartment build-
ing. Don't expect luxury; just clean, bright rooms with beds that don't
sag. Rooms facing the street have little balconies—which can make
for noisy nights. There's a small breakfast room (although breakfast is
only served in high season), or step out for coffee and pastries. **Pros:**
rock-bottom prices, near nightlife. **Cons:** can be noisy on weekends,
small bathrooms. ⊠*Travessa do Poço da Cidade 38, Bairro Alto*
🕾*21/346–7510* ➳*19 rooms, 7 with bath* ☰*No credit cards* ⎜⎡⎜*CP*
Ⓜ*Baixa-Chiado.*

$ ⌘ **Londres.** This modest bed-and-breakfast is a surprisingly agreeable choice in the "you-get-what-you-pay-for" category. Expect a modest but indisputably clean room with dated furniture and decor—singles, doubles, or triples—with or without bath. Rooms are on the third floor and above: the higher you go, the better the view from your large window or balcony. **Pros:** budget rates, not far from the sites. **Cons:** can be noisy at night, basic rooms. ✉*Rua Dom Pedro V 53, Bairro Alto* ☎*21/346–2203* ⊕*www.pensaolondres.com.pt* ⇄*40 rooms, 13 with bath* ♿*In-room: no a/c* ▤*DC, MC, V* ⦿*CP* Ⓜ*Avenida.*

12

BAIXA-CHIADA

$$ ⌘ **Lisboa Regency Chiado.** Attention, shoppers: the Lisboa Regency sits high atop of the Armazens do Chiado shopping mall. But that's hardly its only attribute. Because of their lofty position, rooms look out over the city's terra-cotta rooftops to the castle. For even better views, request a room with a private terrace. Breakfast is served in a public lounge bathed in the glow of the morning sun. **Pros:** ideal location, informal feel, nice views. **Cons:** not many amenities, some noise from mall. ✉*Rua Nova de Almada 114, Chiado* ☎*21/325–6100 or 21/325–6200* ⊕*www.lisboaregencychiado.com* ⇄*38 rooms, 2 suites* ♿*In-room: safe, Wi-Fi. In-hotel: room service, bar, laundry service, Wi-Fi, parking (paid)* ▤*AE, DC, MC, V* ⦿*BP* Ⓜ*Baixa-Chiado.*

¢ ⌘ **Lisbon Lounge Hostel.** A "designer hostel" might sound like a con-
Fodor's Choice tradiction in terms, but that's just what you get at this lodging run by
★ four young artists. With polished wood floors, original architectural details, and funky eclectic furniture, this place looks like a boutique hotel. You have a choice of dorm rooms with shared bathrooms and two-person twin rooms (all to yourself). The hostel attracts backpackers, but also older travelers and families, and is a great place to meet people. **Pros:** cheapest rates in town, central location, energetic staff. **Cons:** no air-conditioning, can be very noisy. ✉*Rua Sao Nicolau 41, Baixa* ☎*21/346–2061* ⊕*www.lisbonloungehostel.com* ⇄*9 rooms* ♿*In-room: no a/c (some), no phone, safe, no TV, Wi-Fi. In-hotel: laundry service, Internet terminal, Wi-Fi* ▤*AE, DC, MC, V* ⦿*BP* Ⓜ*Baixa Chiado.*

LAPA

$$$$ ⌘ **Lapa Palace.** Combining the elegance of a 19th-century manor house
★ with the modern amenities of a luxury resort, Lapa Palace satisfies a wide range of travelers. The spectacular gardens are dotted with lakes and waterfalls and have an expansive swimming pool, children's plunge pool, and sundeck. The spa has a heated indoor pool, fully equipped gym, steam baths, and massage rooms. The rooms have sun-soaked balconies and views of the garden below: the higher you are, the better the view. The renowned Cipriani restaurant offers Italian and Portuguese dishes such as lobster ravioli, seafood risotto, and roasted suckling pig. The comfortable bar is a great place for drinks and conversation. **Pros:** exclusive feel, delicious food, lovely gardens. **Cons:** away from tourist sites, need a taxi to get around. ✉*Rua Pau de Bandeira 4, Lapa* ☎*21/394–9494* ⊕*www.lapapalace.com* ⇄*109 rooms and suites* ♿*In-room: safe, DVD, Internet. In-hotel: restaurant, room service, bar,*

2 pools, gym, spa, laundry service, Internet terminal, Wi-Fi, parking (free) ☰AE, DC, MC, V ⏐◯⏐BP.

NIGHTLIFE

Lisbon has a thriving nightlife scene, and there are listings of concerts, plays, and films in the monthly *Agenda Cultural* and the quarterly *Unforgettable Lisboa* booklets, both available from the tourist office.

Lisbon bars don't get going until after midnight, and clubs even later. On weekends, mobs stand shoulder to shoulder in the streets. For a less boisterous night out, visit an *adega típica* (traditional tavern) that has fado shows, or a venue that hosts live music.

BARS

The Bairro Alto, long the center of Lisbon's nightlife, is the best place for barhopping. Most bars here are fairly small, and stay open until 2 AM or so. Larger designer bars can be found along Avenida 24 de Julho and in the Santos neighborhood, where—because this isn't a residential area—they may stay open until 5 or 6 AM. Farther along the riverbank, under the bridge in Alcântara, the Doca do Santo Amaro has terrace-bars and restaurants converted from old warehouses. For an intriguing evening, take a walk to the **Pavilhão Chinês** (⊠ *Rua Dom Pedro V 89, Bairro Alto* ☎21/342-4729).It's filled to the brim with fascinating junk collected over the years, from old toys to statues.

CAFÉ-BARS & PASTELARIAS

Lisbon's older cafés have rich interiors of burnished wood, mirrors, and tiles. Many have outdoor seating, so you can sip your coffee and watch the city pass by, in many cases until late. Those specializing in sticky Portuguese pastries are known *pastelarias*.

DANCE CLUBS

Most clubs are in Alcântara and along the Avenida 24 de Julho. Some charge a cover of €10–€15 (more on weekends), including one drink; if you come early you may get in free. Clubs are open from about 10 or 11 PM until 4 or 5 AM; a few stay open until 8 AM. **Lux** (⊠ *Av. Infante D. Henrique near Sta. Apolónia, Alfama* ☎21/882–0890 ⊕*www.luxfragil. com*) is undoubtedly the most stylish club in Lisbon, with two dance floors favored by big-name DJs.

FADO CLUBS

Fado is a haunting music that emerged in Lisbon from hotly disputed roots: African, Brazilian, and Moorish are among the contenders. Today most *casas de fado* (fado houses) are in the Bairro Alto or Alfama. Traditional Portuguese food is served in the fado clubs, though it's rarely anything special, and the singing starts at 10 or 11 and may continue until 3 AM.

SHOPPING

Family-owned stores remain common in Lisbon, especially in Baixa, Chiado, and Bairro Alto, and salespeople are courteous almost everywhere. Apart from designer fashions and high-end antiques, prices are moderate. Most shops are open weekdays 9–1 and 3–7 and Saturday 9–1; malls and supermarkets are often open until 10 and on Sunday. Credit cards—Visa in particular—are widely accepted.

One of the main shopping attractions is the **Feira da Ladra** (✉ *Campo de Santa Clara, Graça*), a flea market held on Tuesday morning and all day Saturday. It's fun, but watch your wallet.

12

SINTRA

It was the Moors who first built a castle northwest of the capital at Sintra as a defense against Christian forces, which, under Dom Afonso Henriques, moved steadily southward after the victory at Ourique in 1139. The castle fell to the Christians in 1147, a few days after Lisbon. Sintra's lush hills and valleys later became the summer residence of Portuguese kings and aristocrats, its late medieval palace the greatest expression of royal wealth and power of the time. In the 18th and 19th centuries English travelers, poets, and writers—including an enthusiastic Lord Byron—were drawn by the area's beauty. The poet Robert Southey described Sintra as "the most blessed spot on the whole inhabitable globe." Its historic importance in the Romantic movement in 1995 brought it UNESCO recognition as a World Heritage Site.

Sintra's main attractions are within walking distance or accessible by bus or horse-drawn carriages. There are several marked walks in the surrounding countryside (ideal for escaping the summer crowds), which is crisscrossed by minor roads and marked by old monastic buildings, estates, gardens, and market villages. But it is most easily covered by car, particularly if you want to range as far north as Mafra, with its giant palace-convent. You could also take a guided tour (arranged through the tourist office) or see sights by taxi.

To the west, the Atlantic makes itself felt in windswept beaches and capes, including Cabo da Roca—the westernmost point in Europe, topped by a lighthouse. In the other direction, the town of Queluz, halfway betweeen Lisbon and Sintra, is dominated by its magnificent Baroque palace, in gardens dotted with statuary.

GETTING HERE

Sintra is 30 km (18 mi) northwest of Lisbon. Trains from Lisbon's Rossio station, between Praça dos Restauradores and Rossio square, run every 15 minutes to Queluz (a 20-minute trip to Queluz-Belas station, then turn left outside and follow the signs for the 1-km (½-mi) walk to the palace) and on to Sintra (40 minutes total). The service operates 6 AM–2:40 AM, and one-way tickets cost €1.20 to Queluz-Belas, €1.70 to Sintra. Rail operator offers information on (☎ *808/208–208* ⊕ *www.cp.pt*).

Buses are a good way to explore the Sintra area, including Cabo da Roca. Tickets are cheap (less than €3.50 for most journeys), more so if bought in advance. Regional operator Scotturb (⊠*Av. Miguel Bombarda 59* ☎*21/923–0381*).has one-day passes and also a combined pass that includes train travel to and from Lisbon. From outside Sintra train station there are half-hourly departures in summer to the resorts of Praia das Maçãs (also reached by antique tram) and Azenhas do Mar (30 minutes) in the west, and north to Mafra (one hour). There's also regular year-round service to Cascais and Estoril (one hour).

By car, Queluz is 20 minutes from Lisbon, signposted off route N249/IC19, making this a good half-day option, or a fine stop on the way to or from Sintra (40 minutes from Lisbon).

In Sintra itself, for those who don't want climb the steep hills, you can take Scotturb's bus 434 (ticket €3.50), which you can hop on and off so long as you don't backtrack. It stops at the two national palaces and the Moorish castle.

Sintratur offers old-fashioned **horse-and-carriage rides** (⊠*Rua João de Deus 82* ☎*21/924–1238* ⊕*www.sintratur.com*) in and around the town. A short tour costs €30 for up to four people; longer trips run between €60 and €100 and go as far afield as Pena Palace and Monserrate.

VISITOR INFORMATION
The local tourist office, the Turismo ⊠*Praça da República 23* ☎*21/923–6932* ⊠*Free* ☉*Tues.–Fri. 9–noon and 2–6, weekends 2:30–7.* ⊠*Sintra train station* ☎*21/924–1623*),has full information on opening hours and prices, on walking trails in the countryside, and on tour companies. The Turismo also houses an art gallery, the **Galeria do Museu Municipal,** specializing in works associated with Sintra.

EXPLORING SINTRA

FodorsChoice
★
The conical twin white chimneys of the **Palácio Nacional de Sintra** *(Sintra Palace)* are the town's most recognizable landmarks. There has probably been a palace here since Moorish times, although the current structure, also known as the Paço Real, dates from the late 14th century. It is the only surviving royal palace in Portugal from the Middle Ages, and displays a fetching combination of Moorish, Gothic, and Manueline architectural styles. Bilingual descriptions in each room let you enjoy them at your own pace. The chapel has Mozarabic (Moorish-influenced) azulejos from the 15th and 16th centuries. The ceiling of the Sala das Armas is painted with the coats of arms of 72 noble families, and the grand Sala dos Cisnes has a remarkable ceiling of painted swans. The Sala das Pegas (magpies) figures in a well-known tale about Dom João I (1385–1433) and his dalliance with a lady-in-waiting. The king had the room painted with as many magpies as there were chattering court ladies, thus satirizing the gossips as loose-tongued birds. ⊠*Largo Rainha D. Amélia* ☎*21/910–6840* ⊠*€4, free Sun. 10–2* ☉*Thurs.–Tues. 10–5:30 (last admission 5).*

The Disney-like **Palácio Nacional da Pena** is a glorious conglomeration of turrets and domes awash in pastels. In 1503 the Monastery of Nossa Senhora da Pena was constructed here, but fell into ruins after religious orders were expelled from Portugal in 1832. Seven years later the ruins were purchased by Maria II's consort, Ferdinand of Saxe-Coburg. Inspired by the Bavarian castles of his homeland, Ferdinand commissioned a German architect, Baron Eschwege, to build the castle of his fantasies, in styles that range from Arabian to Victorian. Work was finished in 1885 when he was Fernando II. The surrounding park is filled with trees and flowers from every corner of the Portuguese empire. Portugal's last monarchs lived in the Pena Palace, the last of whom—Queen Amália—went into exile in England after the Republic was proclaimed on October 5, 1910. Inside is a rich, sometimes vulgar, and often bizarre collection of Victorian and Edwardian furniture, ornaments, and paintings. Placards explain each room.

A mini-train takes you from the park gate up to the palace. A path beyond an enormous statue (thought to be Baron Eschwege, cast as a medieval knight) on a nearby crag leads to the **Cruz Alta,** a 16th-century stone cross 1,782 feet above sea level, with stupendous views. ⊠*Estrada da Pena* ☎*21/910–5340, advance booking 21/923–7300* ⊕*www.parquesdesintra.pt* ☏*Park €6 mid-Sept.–Mar., €8 Apr.–mid-Sept.; combined ticket for park and palace €8 mid-Sep.-Mar., €11 Apr-mid-Sep. Mini-train €1.50* ⊗*Mid-Sept.–Mar., daily 10–6 (last admission 5); Apr.–mid-Sept., daily 9:45–7 (last admission 6:15).*

The battlemented ruins of the 9th-century **Castelo dos Mouros** or Moorish Castle still give a fine impression of the fortress that finally fell to Christian forces led by Dom Afonso Henriques in 1147. It's visible from various points in Sintra itself, but for a closer look follow the steps that lead up to the ruins from the back of the town center (40 minutes going up, 25 minutes coming down), or catch the Scotturb's 434 bus or rent a horse-drawn carriage in town. Panoramic views from the serrated walls explain why the Moors chose the site. ⊠*Estrada da Pena* ☎*21/923–7300* ⊕*www.parquedesintra.pt* ☏*€5, guided tours €10* ⊗*Apr.–mid-Sept., daily 9:30–8; mid-Sep.–Mar., daily 10–6. Last admission 1 hr before closing.*

<table>
<tr><td>

▌**NEED A
BREAK?**

</td><td>

Sintra is known for its *queijadas* **(cottage-cheese cakes), and one baker with two outlets on the same street is their most renowned purveyor. Periquita dois (** ⊠ *Rua das Padarias 18* ☎ *21/923–1595* ⊗ *Closed Tues.***) , the larger of the two, has fine views from its terrace.**

</td></tr>
</table>

℧ The former fire-station headquarters has been transformed into the **Museu do Brinquedo** *(Toy Museum).* Based on the collection of João Arbués Moreira, who began hoarding his toys when he was 14, the museum occupies more than four floors and contains thousands of toy planes, trains, and automobiles; dolls' furniture; rare lead soldiers; and puppets. There's a playroom for kids with Legos—and computers—and a café. ⊠*Rua Visconde de Monserrate* ☎*21/924–2171* ⊕*www.museu-do-brinquedo. pt* ☏*€4* ⊗*Tues.–Sun. 10–6. Last admission 5:30.*

Among Sintra's many privately owned mansions is the intriguing **Quinta da Regaleira**, a five-minute walk along the main road past the tourist office. Laid out in the early 20th century for a Brazilian mining magnate with a vivid imagination and a keen interest in freemasonry and the Knights Templars (who made their 11th-century headquarters on this very site), the estate includes gardens where almost everything—statues, water features, grottoes, lookout towers—is linked to freemasonry or the Knights Templars. Spookiest of all is the 100-foot-deep Poço do Iniciático (Initiation Well)—an inverted underground "tower". The house has an uninspired exhibit on freemasonry, a café, and a restaurant. ⊠ *Rua Barbosa do Bocage 5* ☎*21/910–6650* ⊕*www.regaleira.pt* 💰*€6, guided tours (call ahead for tours in English) €10* ⊙ *Apr–Sept., 10–8 (last admission 7); Nov.–Dec., 10–5.30 (last admission 5); Oct., Feb and Mar., 10–6.30 (last admission 6).* regaleira@mail.telepac.pt

In a former palace, the **Sintra Museu de Arte Moderna–Colecção Berardo** *is one of several institutions (the main one in the Lisbon suburb of Belém) showcasing the eclectic taste* of Madeiran-born magnate Joe Berardo. The modern art collection, parts of which are often on show here, includes works by Andy Warhol, Pablo Picasso, Roy Lichtenstein, and Francis Bacon. ⊠*Av. Heliodoro Salgado* ☎*21/924–8170* ⊕*www. berardocollection.com* 💰*€3, free Sun. to 2.* ⊙*Tues.–Sun. 10–6.*

OUTSIDE SINTRA

MONSERRATE
4 km (2½ mi) west of Sintra.

The **estate** here was laid out by Scottish gardeners in the mid-19th century at the behest of a wealthy Englishman, Sir Francis Cook. The centerpiece is the Moorish-style, three-domed **Palácio de Monserrate**. The original palace was built by the Portuguese viceroy of India, and was later home to Gothic novelist William Beckford. A regular ticket allows you to visit the park and part of the palace (there are also combination tickets with the Pena Palace, Castelo dos Mouros and Convento dos Capuchos), but full guided tours are at 10 AM and 3 PM; book several days in advance. The gardens, with their streams, waterfalls, and Etruscan tombs, are famed for their array of tree and plant species, though labels are lacking. ⊠*Estrada da Monserrate* ☎*21/923–7300* ⊕*www. parquesdesintra.pt* 💰*€5, guided tours of palace and garden (reserve in advance) €10* ⊙*April.–mid-Sept., daily 10–1 and 2–7; mid-Sep.–Mar., daily 10.30–1 and 2–5. Last admission 30 mins before closing.*

CONVENTO DOS CAPUCHOS
13 km (8 mi) southwest of Sintra.

★ From 1560 until 1834, when it was abandoned, seven monks—never any more, never any less—inhabited the bare, cork-lined cells in this remote, extraordinarily austere convent, and prayed in the tiny chapel hewn out of the rock. Impure thoughts meant a spell in the Penitents' Cell, an excruciatingly small space. Guides for the 45-minute tour bring the history of the place to life with zest and humor. ⊠*Convento dos*

Capuchos ☎*21/923-7300* ⊕*www.parquesdesintra.pt* 🎫*€5, guided tour €10* ⊙*Apr.–mid-Sept, daily 9.30–8; mid-Sep.–Mar., daily 10–6. Last admission 1 hr before closing.*

SÃO PEDRO DE SINTRA
2 km (1 mi) southeast of Sintra.

This little hillside village is most famous for its fair, the Feira de São Pedro, which dates from the time of the Christian Reconquest. It's held every second and fourth Sunday of the month in the vast Praça Dom Fernando II (also called the Largo da Feira), but it's worth stopping by on other days to see the village church in its enclosed little square, or for a lunch far from the tourist crowds.

The gardens of the **Parque Liberdade** (⊙*June–Sept., daily 9–8; Oct.–May, daily 9–6*), off the road between Sintra train station and the National Palace, are a short cut to São Pedro, but you can also catch a local bus from outside Sintra station.

CABO DA ROCA
15 km (9 mi) west of Sintra, 20 km (12 mi) northwest of Cascais.

★ The windswept Cabo da Roca and its lighthouse, set in a protected natural park a 40 minute bus ride from Sintra, mark continental Europe's westernmost point, topped by a cross bearing an inscription by Portuguese national poet Luís de Camões. Even if you don't buy a certificate at the gift shop to verify your visit, the memory of this desolate granite cape will linger.

| OFF THE BEATEN PATH

The Atlantic Coast. North of Cabo da Roca, the natural parkland extends through the villages of Praia Grande, Praia das Maçãs, and Azenhas do Mar. The first two have good beaches, and all have seafood restaurants. A fun way to reach Praia das Maçãs is on the Eléctrico de Sintra, a hundred-year-old tram that departs roughly hourly from 9:30 to 5:25, Friday through Sunday, from a stop behind the Museu de Arte Moderna, plying a scenic route via Colares. The fare is €1 one-way. ☎*21/923-8789 for Eléctrico de Sintra information.*

QUELUZ
15 km (9 mi) east of Sintra, 15 km (9 mi) northwest of Lisbon.

Fodor'sChoice
★ The **Palácio Nacional de Queluz** *(Queluz National Palace)* was inspired, in part, by the palace at Versailles. The salmon-pink rococo edifice was ordered as a royal summer residence by Dom Pedro III in 1747. Architect Mateus Vicente de Oliveira took five years to make the place habitable; Frenchman Jean-Baptiste Robillon spent 40 more executing a detailed Baroque plan that also comprised imported trees and statues, and azulejo-lined canals and fountains. You can tour the apartments and elegant staterooms, including the frescoed Music Salon, the Hall of Ambassadors, and the mirrored Throne Room with its crystal chandeliers and gilt trim. Some are now used for concerts and state visits, while the old kitchens have been converted into an ordinary café and a fancy restaurant with an imposing open fireplace and a vast oak table. ⊠*IC19* ☎*21/434-3860* 🎫*€5, free Sun. to 2.* ⊙*Wed.–Mon. 9–5 (last admission 4:30).*

WHERE TO EAT

$–$$$ ✕**Curral dos Caprinos.** On the site of a former sheep corral, this rustic restaurant has clay pots, smoked hams, onions and dried corn cobs hanging from its ceiling, while the walls are lined in cork. The most spectacular meat dish is the *cabrito à moda de Oleiros*, a whole lamb roasted over laurel branches. Order in advance. ⊠ *Rua 28 de Setembro 13, Cabriz* ☎ *21/923–3113* ⊟ *AE, DC, MC, V.*

$$–$$$$ ✕**Tacho Real.** Locals climb a steep hill to this restaurant for traditional dishes cooked with panache, such as bacalhau *à brás* (with eggs, onions, and sliced potato), steaks, and game in season. On warm days the small terrace is delightful. ⊠ *Rua do Ferraria 4* ☎ *21/923–5277* ⊟ *AE, DC, MC, V* ☉ *Closed Wed.*

WHERE TO STAY

$–$$ 🏨 **Casa Miradouro.** The owners of this candy-stripe 1890s house at the
★ edge of Sintra have a keen eye for style and comfort. Rooms have grand views, wrought-iron bedsteads, and polished tile floors. The downstairs breakfast room opens onto a terrace. **Pros:** all rooms have views, in-room double glazing and heating an unusual a winter bonus in this category, special week and five-night deals in winter. **Cons:** requires very early booking, no phone or TV in rooms. ⊠ *Rua Sotto Mayor 55* ☎ *21/923–5900* ⊕ *www.casa-miradouro.com* 📞 *6 rooms* 🛏 *In-room: no a/c, no phone, no TV, Wi-Fi (free). In-hotel: bar.* ⊟ *DC, MC, V* ⦿*BP* ☉ *Closed mid-Jan.–Feb.*

$$$ ✕🏨 **Lawrence's Hotel.** When this 18th-century inn, the oldest on the
Fodor's Choice peninsula, reopened in 1999, the U.S. secretary of state and the Neth-
★ erlands' Queen Beatrix were among the first guests. The intimate rooms—with wood and terra-cotta predominating—are bathed in light from French windows, and deluxe touches abound. Staff can arrange anything from jeep tours to babysitting. In the Old World restaurant ($$$–$$$$; reservations recommended) specialties are served on Portugal's Vista Alegre porcelain. **Pros:** rich in historical associations, cozy refuge from at times chilly local climate, charming rear terrace. **Cons:** no pool, gym or garden, some rooms little bigger than their bathrooms. ⊠ *Rua Consiglieri Pedroso 38-40* ☎ *21/910–5500* ⊕ *www.lawrences hotel.com* 📞 *11 rooms, 5 suites* 🛏 *In-room: safe, DVD (some), Internet (free), Wi-Fi (free). In-hotel: restaurant, bar, laundry service, Wi-Fi (free).* ⊟ *AE, DC, MC, V* ⦿*BP.*

PORTO

Portugal's second-largest city, with a population of roughly 250,000, considers itself the north's capital and, more contentiously, the country's economic center. Locals support this claim by quoting a typically down-to-earth maxim: "Coimbra sings, Braga prays, Lisbon shows off, and Porto works." There's poverty here, of course, primarily down by the river in the ragged older areas, parts of which are positively medieval.

But in the shopping centers, the stately old stock exchange building, and the port-wine trade, Porto oozes confidence.

This emphasis on worth rather than beauty has created a solid rather than graceful city. Largely unaffected by the great earthquake of 1755, while Porto has some fine Baroque architecture, its public buildings are generally sober. But its location on a steep hillside above the Rio Douro affords exhilarating perspectives.

12

The river has influenced the city's development since pre-Roman times, when the town of Cale on the left bank prospered sufficiently to support a trading port, called Portus, on the site of today's city. The 1703 Methuen agreement with England, giving commercial preference to Portuguese wines in detriment to French ones, provided the Douro Valley vineyards with a new market and Porto with a further boost. It was here that Douro wine was first mixed with brandy to preserve it during the journey, and to improve its taste over time. The port wine trade is still big business, based across the river in Vila Nova de Gaia; downtown, the two banks are linked by the impressive two-tier Ponte Dom Luís I (King Luís I Bridge), which was completed in 1886.

Porto is also a cultural hub, thanks to the Serralves Contemporary Art Museum and numerous commercial galleries, many clustered along Rua Miguel Bombarda, and now to the stunning Casa da Musica, or House of Music, designed by Dutch architect Rem Koolhaas and opened in 2005. The restaurants and nightclubs along the riverfront are almost all designed by young Portuguese architects, and Foz do Douro, where the river flows into the Atlantic, is a fashion and design hot spot.

PLANNING YOUR TIME
You'll need a couple of days to experience Porto and its wine lodges, and the nearby coastal resorts. Make sure you visit the port-wine lodges, and leave yourself an afternoon or evening free to relax at a riverside bar or restaurant. Art lovers may end up spending hours at the Serralves National Contemporary Art Museum, whose extensive gardens will also charm visitors. And to really appreciate the new Casa da Música, you should take in a concert.

Several more days here would permit a trip out to one of the region's beautiful beaches; up the lovely Douro Valley—rail or boat are options, or rental car, if you want to visit a *quinta* (wine estate); or an excursion to the history-rich towns of Braga, Guimarães, or Amarante.

GETTING HERE & AROUND
BY AIR
Porto's Aeroporto Francisco Sá Carneiro, 13 km (8 mi) north of the city, is the gateway to northern Portugal. There's direct service from many European cities, though not from the United States, and TAP Portugal runs regular flights from Lisbon. The airport is now served by the expanding metro system (a 30 minute trip downtown). Taxis are also available outside the terminal; the metered fare into town should run €18 to €20, including €1.50 for baggage. Outside the city limits, tariffs are based on kilometers traveled: €1.08 per kilometer until 10 PM and 20% more at night and on weekends.

BY CAR

Porto is 3½ hours north of Lisbon by highway (via the A1 toll highway) or by express train, so even a short trip to Portugal can include a night or two here. From Porto it's another 2 hours up the coast to the Spanish border, or 3 to 4 hours east through the less visited Trás-os-Montes region to the border there. The densely populated north itself is well served with roads.

Downtown streets are congested or out of bounds, and local drivers manic, so leave your car at your hotel. You can walk around most of the center (though be prepared for steep hills), reaching outlying attractions by bus, taxi or metro.

BY BUS

Rede Expressos operates frequent bus service to and from Lisbon, while Rodonorte serves the northern region. The best source of information is the local tourist office.

BY PUBLIC TRANSPORT

Porto has a good network of buses and trams, run by Sociedade dos Transportes Colectivos do Porto (STCP). The tourist office can provides a bus map. The Metro do Porto—actually a light rail service—has five lines that converge at the Trindade stop. The English-language *Transport Guide* from the tourist office has full information; they'll also sell you a Porto Card, which is valid for public transportation and entrance to 21 city sights, and discounts for others, during 24 hours (€7.50), 48 hours (€11.50), or 72 hours (€15.50).

BY TRAIN

Long-distance trains arrive at Porto Campanhã station, east of the center. From here you can take a five-minute connection to the central São Bento station. From Spain, the Vigo–Porto train crosses at Tuy/Valença do Minho and then heads south towards Porto, usually stopping at both Campanhã and São Bento. From Porto some of the most scenic lines in the country stretch out into the river valleys and mountain ranges to the northeast. Even if you rent a car, try to take a day trip on one. For reservations and schedules, visit São Bento station or the tourist office.

ESSENTIALS

Air Contact Aeroporto F. Sá Carneiro (☎ 22/943–2400 ⊕ www.ana-aeroportos. pt).

Bus & Tram Contacts Rede Expressos (✉ Rua Alexandre Herculano 370, Porto ☎ 969/502050 ⊕ www.rede-expressos.pt). **Rodonorte** (✉ Rua Ateneu Comercial 19, Porto ☎ 22/200–5637). **STCP** (✉ Av. Fernão de Magalhães 1862, Porto ☎ 22/507–1000 or 808/200166 ⊕ www.stcp.pt).

Visitor Information Centro de Informação Turística do Porto (✉ Praça Dom João I 43 ☎ 22/205–7514 ⊕ www.portoturismo.pt). **Posto de Turismo Municipal** (✉ Rua Clube dos Fenianos 25 ☎ 22/339–3470 ✉ Rua do Infante Dom Henrique 63 ☎ 22/200–9770 ⊕ cm-porto.pt).

EXPLORING PORTO

8 Cais da Ribeira *(Ribeira Pier)*. A string of fish restaurants and *tascas* (taverns) are built into the street-level arcade of timeworn buildings along this pier. In the Praça da Ribeira, people sit and chat around an odd, modern, cube-like sculpture; farther on, steps lead to a walkway above the river that's backed by tall houses. The pier also provides the easiest access to the lower level of the middle bridge across the Douro. Boats docked at Cais da Ribeira offer various cruises around the bridges and up the river to Peso da Régua and Pinhão.

6 Estação de São Bento. This train station was built in the early 20th century (King D. Carlos I laid the first brick himself in 1900) and inaugurated in 1915. It sits precisely where the Convent of S. Bento de Avé-Maria was located, and therefore inherited the convent's name—Saint Bento. The atrium is covered with 20,000 azulejos painted by Jorge Colaço (1916) depicting scenes of Portugal's history as well as ethnographic images. It is one of the most magnificent artistic undertakings of the early 20th century. The building was designed by architect Marques da Silva. ⊠*Praça Almeida Garret* ☎*22/205–1714* ☎*808/208208 national call center* ⊕*www.cp.pt.*

4 Igreja da Misericórdia *(Mercy Church)*. Today's building represents a compromise between the church first built during the late 16th century and its reconstruction between 1749 and 1755 by painter and architect Nicolau Nasoni. At the church museum next door you can see *Fons Vitae* (Fountain of Life), a vibrant, anonymous, Renaissance painting depicting the founder of the church, Dom Manuel I, his queen, and their eight children kneeling before a crucified Christ. ⊠*Rua das Flores 5* ☎*22/207–4710* ⊕*www.scmp.pt* ⊠*Church free, museum €1.50* ⊙*Church Tues.–Fri. 8–12:30 and 2–5:30, museum weekdays 9:30–12:30 and 2–5:30.*

2 Igreja de São Francisco *(Church of St. Francis)*. During the last days of Porto's siege by the absolutist army (the *miguelistas*) in July 1842, there was gunfire by the nearby São Francisco Convent. These shootings caused a fire that destroyed most parts of the convent, sparing only this church. The church is an undistinguished, late-14th-century Gothic building on the outside, but inside is an astounding interior: gilded carving—added in the mid-18th century—runs up the pillars, over the altar, and across the ceiling. An adjacent museum (Museu de Arte Sacra) houses furnishings from the Franciscan convent. A guided tour (call the day before) includes a visit to the church, museum, and catacombs. ⊠*Rua do Infante Dom Henrique 93* ☎*22/206–2100* ⊠*€3* ⊙*Nov.– Mar., daily 9–5:30; Apr.–Oct., daily 9–7; May–Sept., daily 9–8.*

★ Museu de Arte Contemporânea. Designed by Siza Vieira, a winner of the Pritzker Architecture Prize, the Contemporary Art Museum is part of the Serralves Foundation and is surrounded by lovely gardens. It has changing international exhibitions, as well as displaying the work of Portuguese painters, sculptors, and designers. Check with the tourist office for the latest information. You can take either a taxi or Bus 78 from Praça da Liberdade; it's about 30 minutes from downtown. ⊠*Rua D. João*

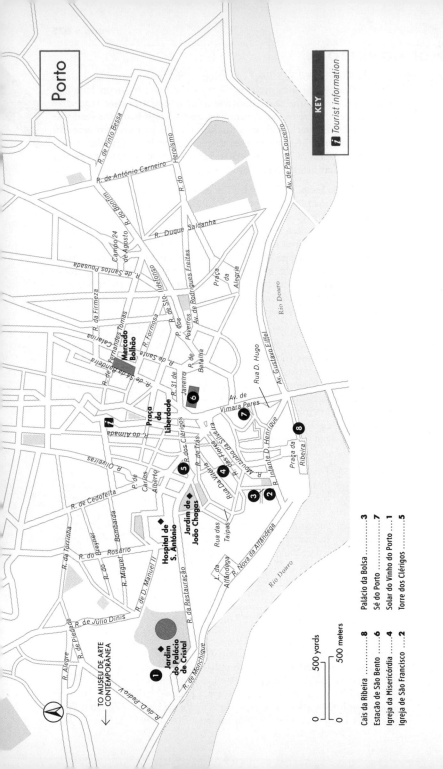

Porto

de Castro 210 ☎*22/615–6500 or 808/200543* ⊕*www.serralves.pt* 🏛*Museum and garden €5, garden €2.50* 🕐*Tues., Wed., and Fri.–Sun. 10–7, Thurs. 10–10.*

❸ **Palácio da Bolsa.** Porto's 19th-century, neoclassical stock exchange takes
Fodor's Choice up much of the site of the former Franciscan convent at the Igreja de
★ São Francisco. Guided tours are the only way to see the interior of this
masterpiece of 19th-century Portuguese architecture. The Arab-style
ballroom, in particular, is one of the most admired chambers and was
designed by civil engineer Gustavo Adolfo Gonçalves e Sousa. ✉*Rua
Ferreira Borges* ☎*22/339–9013* ⊕*www.palaciodabolsa.pt* 🏛*Tours €5*
🕐*Apr.–Oct., daily 9–6:30; Nov.–Mar., daily 9–12:30 and 2–5:30.*

❼ **Sé do Porto** *(Cathedral).* Originally constructed in the 12th century by
the parents of Afonso Henriques (Portugal's first king), Porto's granite
cathedral has been rebuilt twice: first in the late 13th century and again
in the 18th century, when the architect of the Torre dos Clérigos, Nicolau Nasoni, was among those commissioned to work on its expansion.
Despite the renovations, it remains a fortress-like structure—an uncom-
promising testament to medieval wealth and power. Notice a low relief
on the northern tower, depicting a 14th-century vessel and symbolizing
the city's nautical vocation. Size is the only exceptional thing about the
interior; when you enter the two-story, 14th-century cloisters, however,
the building comes to life. Decorated with gleaming azulejos, a staircase
added by Nasoni leads to the second level and into a richly furnished
chapter house, from which there are fine views through narrow windows. Nasoni also designed the Paço dos Arcebispos (Archbishops'
Palace) behind the cathedral. It has been converted to offices, so you can
only admire its 197-foot-long facade. ✉*Terreiro da Sé* ☎*22/205–9028*
🏛*Cathedral free; cloisters €3* 🕐*Mon.–Sat. 8:45–12:30 and 2:30–7,
Sun. 8:30–12:30 and 2:30–7.*

❶ **Solar do Vinho do Porto** *(Port Wine Institute).* Located in a 19th-century
country house called the Quinta da Macieirinha, the institute offers
relaxed tastings of Porto's famous wine in much the same fashion as
its counterpart in Lisbon, but it has a much friendlier reputation—and
the wine has only had to travel across the river before being served.
Tasting prices start at less than €1 per glass. The Quinta da Macieirinha
is home to the **Museu Romântico da Quinta da Macieirinha** (Romantic Museum), with displays of period furniture. ✉*Quinta da Macier-
inha, Rua de Entre Quintas 220* ☎*22/609–4749 Port Wine Institute,
22/605–7033 museum, 22/606–6207 for guided tours* ⊕*www.ivp.pt*
🏛*Port Wine Institute free. Museum €1* 🕐*Port Wine Institute Mon.–
Sat. 2–11 and Sun. 4–11; museum Tues.–Sun. 10–12:30 and 2–5:30.*

❺ **Torre dos Clérigos.** Designed by Italian architect Nicolau Nasoni and
🌀 begun in 1754, the tower of the church Igreja dos Clérigos reaches an
impressive height of 249 feet. There are 225 steep stone steps to the
belfry, and the considerable effort required to climb them is rewarded
by stunning views of the Old Town, the river, and beyond to the mouth
of the Douro. The church itself, also built by Nasoni, predates the tower
and is an elaborate example of Italianate Baroque architecture. ✉*Rua*

CLOSE UP

Port Wine

Many of the more than 16 companies with caves in Vila Nova de Gaia are still foreign owned. They include such well-known names as Sandeman, Osborne, Cockburn, Kopke, Ferreira, Calém, Taylor's, Barros, Ramos-Pinto, Real Companhia Velha, Fonseca, Rozès, Burmester, Offley, Noval, and Graham's. All are signposted and within a few minutes' walk of the bridge and each other; their names are also displayed in huge white letters across their roofs. Each company offers free guided tours of its facility, which always end with a tasting of one or two wines and an opportunity to buy bottles from the company store. Children are usually welcome and are often fascinated by the huge warehouses and all sorts of interesting machinery. The major lodges are open weekdays 9–12:30 and 2–7, Saturday 9–12:30, from June through September; the rest of the year, tours end at 5 and are conducted only on weekdays. Tours begin regularly, usually when enough visitors are assembled. The tourist office at Vila Nova de Gaia offers a small map of the main lodges and can advise you on hours of the smaller operations.

S. Filipe Nery ☎*22/200–1729* *Tower €1.50* ⏲*Tower Sept.–May, daily 10–1 and 2–5; June and July, daily 9:30–1 and 2:30–7; Aug., daily 10–7. Church 8:45–12:30 and 3:30–7.*

WHERE TO EAT

$$$–$$$$ ✕ **Bull and Bear.** Chef-owner Miguel Castro Silva gives his northern Portugal dishes touches of French, Italian, and even Japanese flavors at this sleek dining room in the Porto stock-exchange building. The results are such unusual and successful combinations as *ameijoas com feijão manteiga* (clams with butter beans) and *linguado com molho de amêndoa* (sole with almond sauce). ✉*Av. da Boavista 3431* ☎*22/610–7669* *AE, DC, MC, V* ⏲*Closed Sun. No lunch Sat.*

$$ ★ ✕ **Chez Lapin.** At this Cais da Ribeira restaurant overlooking the river, the service may be slow and the folksy decor may be overdone, but the food is excellent. Grab a table on the attractive outdoor terrace and order generous portions of such uncommon Porto dishes as *bacalhau e polvo assado no forno* (salt cod baked and with octopus) and *caldeirada de peixe* (fish stew). The restaurant also offers river excursions on its five traditional boats docked at the quay. ✉*Rua Canastreiros 40–42* ☎*22/200–6418* *Reservations essential* *AE, DC, MC, V.*

$–$$$ ✕ **Cufra.** Named after the biggest oasis in the Sahara Desert, this longtime favorite is one of the best places in Porto to try the famous *francesinha* (rye bread, ham, sirloin steak, sausage, and Dutch cheese, all seasoned with a special sauce). The seafood specialties are a good value. The more informal dining room has benches and tables, and the other area has individual tables, wood paneling, and a few atmospheric paintings. ✉*Av. da Boavista 2504* ☎*22/617–2715* *AE, DC, MC, V* ⏲*Closed Mon. No lunch.*

$$$ ✗ **Dom Tonho.** Seafood is the specialty of this riverfront restaurant, which
★ occupies a beautiful and historic building that dates back to the 16th
century. Try one of the codfish dishes, the *robalo ao sal* (rock bass
baked in salt), *arroz de tamboril malandro com camarão* (monkfish,
shrimp, and coriander rice stew), or *pescada da Póvoa grelhada* (grilled
whiting from Póvoa). ✉ *Cais da Ribeira 13–15* ☎ *22/200–4307* ▤ *AE,
DC, MC, V.*

$$ ✗ **Foz Velha.** Nestled in the heart of the old Foz neighborhood, this lovely
restaurant provides one of the best fine-dining experiences in town. Chef
Marco Gomes is a whiz with meat and seafood, and also has a way
with vegetarian dishes. The contemporary Portuguese menu offers six-
courses and nine-course options, as well as à la carte. ✉ *Esplanada do
Castelo 141* ☎ *22/615-4178* ▤ *No credit cards* ⊘ *Closed Sun.*

$$$–$$$$ ✗ **O Escondidinho.** In business since 1934, this beloved restaurant opened
during the first great Portuguese Colonial Exhibition that took place in
the Palácio de Cristal. Its long history is evident in the entrance, where
hand-painted tiles from the 17th century announce a country-house decor.
The menu has French-influenced dishes as well as very creative Douro
dishes. Steak is prepared no less than six ways (try the smoky version
with truffles), and the sole is always deliciously fresh. The specialty is sea-
food, namely codfish, whiting, and lobster au gratin. The *pudim flan* (egg
custard) is outstanding. ✉ *Rua dos Passos Manuel 144* ☎ *22/200–1079*
⚖ *Reservations essential* ▤ *DC, MC, V* ⊘ *Closed Sun.*

$$–$$$ ✗ **Sessenta Setenta.** Hidden in the ruins of the Monchique Monastery
and at the bottom of a winding street, this restaurant is a bit hard
to find. The meals make it worth the effort, however. Chef Francisco
Meireles's large menu features Mediterranean and contemporary Por-
tuguese cuisine, and offers about a dozen desserts. ✉ *Rua de Sobre-o-
Douro, 1A* ☎ *22/340-6093* ▤ *No credit cards* ⊘ *Closed Sun.*

$$ ✗ **Shis.** On Ourigo beach out at Foz, Shis lures in diners with its waterfront views. Chef Antonio Silva Vieira creates a variety of interna-
tional dishes from sushi to Italian favorites, as well as old Portuguese
classics including cod roasted with bread and olives. ✉ *Esplanada do
Castelo* ☎ *22/618-9593* ▤ *www.shisrestaurante.com* ▤ *No credit
cards* ⊘ *Closed Sun.*

$$$–$$$$ ✗ **Tripeiro.** This spacious restaurant is just the place to try the ubiqui-
tous *tripas á moda do Porto* (Porto-style tripe) or the famous *cozido
à portuguesa* (boiled meat with vegetables), which are nearly always
on the menu in one form or another. In case you don't appreciate the
city's favorite food, the menu has several meat and fish specialties,
too. Along with the typically Portuguese food come typically Portu-
guese details: wooden ceiling beams, whitewashed walls, and potted
plants add plenty of charm. There's an adjacent bar where you can eat
cheaper. ✉ *Rua de Passos Manuel 195* ☎ *22/200–5886* ▤ *AE, DC,
MC, V* ⊘ *Closed Sun.*

WHERE TO STAY

$$ ⬚ **Grande Hotel do Porto.** If you enjoy shopping, you can't do better than the stately Grande Hotel do Porto, as it sits on the city's best shopping street. The hotel has just the right mix of old-fashioned charm and new-fangled amenities. Public areas are full of turn-of-the-last-century details; streamlined guest rooms are small but loaded with modern amenities. **Pros:** good location, efficient staff, near public transportation. **Cons:** rooms are small and dark. ⊠*Rua de Santa Catarina 197* ☎*22/207–6690* ⊕*www.grandehotelporto.com* ☏*100 rooms* ⒮*In-room: safe, refrigerator, Wi-Fi. In-hotel: restaurant, room service, bar, laundry service, parking (paid), no-smoking rooms* ☰*AE, DC, MC, V* �*BP.*

$$$ ⬚ **Hotel Infante de Sagres.** Intricately carved wood details, rare area rugs
Fodor'sChoice and tapestries, stained-glass windows, and 18th- and 19th-century
★ antiques fill the public areas. In guest rooms, shades of beige, cream, and white complement dark-wood furnishings and lend a contemporary character; bathrooms are marble from floor to ceiling and have sophisticated lighting. The Boca do Lomo restaurant serves updated versions of classic dishes and emphasizes local ingredients. **Pros:** beautiful views, central location, nice spa. **Cons:** no pool, few in-room amenities. ⊠*Praça D. Filipa de Lencastre 62* ☎*22/339–8500* ⊕*www.hotelinfante sagres.pt* ☏*73 rooms* ⒮*In-room: refrigerator. In-hotel: restaurant, room service, bar, parking (paid)* ☰*AE, DC, MC, V* ◉*BP.*

$$$ ⬚ **Hotel Mercure Porto Central.** Next door to the Sao João Theatre, the Mercure has a great location only a block or two from Avenida dos Aliados. Rooms are elegantly appointed in lovely shades of cocoa and cinnamon. You can get sweeping views over the city from a wide terrace at the top of the building. **Pros:** central location, cozy rooms. **Cons:** reception seems understaffed, small parking lot. ⊠*Praça da Batalha 116* ☎*22/204–3300* ⊕*www.mercure.com* ☏*149 rooms* ⒮*In-room: safe, refrigerator, Wi-Fi. In-hotel: restaurant, bar, laundry service, parking (paid)* ☰*AE, DC, MC, V* ◉*BP.*

$$ ⬚ **Pestana Porto.** Right in Porto's historic heart, the Pestana Porto is
★ in a restored old building abutted by a medieval wall. Rooms have city or water views; all are contemporary, cozy, and almost cluttered with vibrant fabrics, plush carpets, throw pillows, and upholstered chairs. Ask for a room with a balcony. **Pros:** historic building, plenty of charm. **Cons:** not a good choice for families, bus stop is up a steep hill. ⊠*Praça da Ribeira 1* ☎*22/340–2300* ⊕*www.pestana.com* ☏*48 rooms* ⒮*In-room: safe, refrigerator, Wi-Fi. In-hotel: restaurant, room service, bar, laundry service, parking (paid), no-smoking rooms* ☰*AE, DC, MC, V* ◉*BP.*

$ ⬚ **Residencial Pão de Açúcar.** Just off Avenida dos Aliados, this Art Nouveau pensão offers a lot of amenities for relatively modest rates. You can choose from among dark and simple rooms, suites, or a top-floor room opening onto a terrace. The owner also operates a car-rental agency. **Pros:** affordable rates, good location. **Cons:** furnishings are worn, downstairs rooms can be noisy. ⊠*Rua do Almada 262* ☎*22/200–2425* ⊕*www.residencialpaodeacucar.com* ☏*51 rooms* ⒮*In-room: Wi-Fi. In-hotel: room service, bar, laundry service* ☰*AE, MC, V* ◉*CP.*

Scandinavia

The sauna, a Scancinavian staple

WORD OF MOUTH

"3 days is enough to do Oslo. I would leave 5 days for Stockholm—
more if you want a couple of day trips. Frankly I think Copenhagen
is much more charming and has more to see/do than Oslo and I
would give it at least 4 days, more if you do day trips to the local
castles."

—nytraveler

WHAT'S WHERE

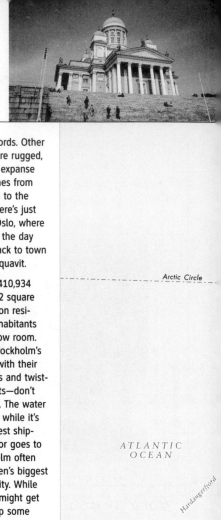

1 Denmark. The Kingdom of Denmark dapples the Baltic Sea in an archipelago of some 450 islands and the arc of one peninsula. Coziness is a Danish trait, and you'll find lots of it in Copenhagen's canals, cafés, and narrow streets. But don't let the low-slung skyline fool you: downtown Copenhagen is a sophisticated cultural hub. Beyond this hub, Denmark is divided into three regions: the two major islands of Zealand and Funen and the peninsula of Jutland. To the east, Zealand is Denmark's largest and most populated island, with Copenhagen as its focal point. Denmark's second-largest island, Funen, is a pastoral, undulating land of farms and beach villages, with Odense as its one major town. To the west, the vast Jutland connects Denmark to the continent.

2 Norway. Roughly 400,000 square km (155,000 square mi), long and narrow Norway is about 30% clear lakes, lush forests, and rugged mountains. Oslo, the capital and eastern Norway's hub, has a population of about a half million and is a friendly, manageable city. Some areas of the country might trump this region in majestic scenery: mountainous western Norway, where you'll find Bergen, is home to some of the country's longest, deepest fjords. Other areas might be more rugged, like the rocky, thin expanse of land that stretches from bustling Trondheim to the North Cape. But there's just something about Oslo, where you can hike away the day and still make it back to town for a nightcap of aquavit.

3 Sweden. With 410,934 square km (158,662 square mi) for only 9 million residents, Sweden's inhabitants have plenty of elbow room. Even capital city Stockholm's 14 small islands—with their bustling boulevards and twisting medieval streets—don't seem too crowded. The water is a different story: while it's not Sweden's biggest shipping city (that honor goes to Göteborg), Stockholm often feels like it's Sweden's biggest pleasure-boating city. While in Stockholm, you might get a chance to pick up some crystal glassware from the Småland province to the south, or taste something from Skåne province, defined by its farmland, castles, golden beaches, and unique dialect. Finally, if you're eager to chat with locals but not sure what to talk about, you might start with Dalarna, the central region of Sweden and the focal point of most of the country's myth, symbolism, and tradition.

Arctic Circle

ATLANTIC
OCEAN

Hardangerfjord

North
Sea

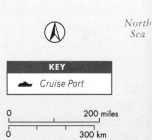

KEY
🚢 Cruise Port

```
0                    200 miles
├────────┬───────────┤
0                    300 km
```

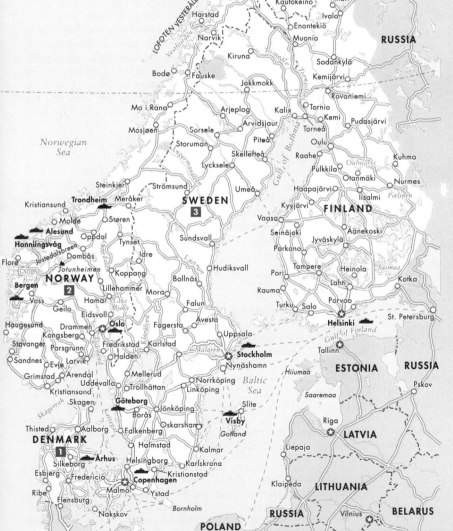

TO SVALBARD

Barents
Sea

Hammerfest

Alta
Karasjok
Kautokeino
Ufsjoki
Inari

Tromsø
Harstad
Narvik

Ivalo
Enontekiö
Muonio

RUSSIA

LOFOTEN VESTERÅLEN
Vestfjorden
Kiruna

Sodankylä

Bodø
Fauske
Jokkmokk
Kemijärvi

Rovaniemi

Norwegian
Sea

Mo i Rana
Arjeplog
Mosjøen
Sorsele
Storuman
Kalix
Tornio
Kemi
Torneå
Pudasjärvi

Arvidsjaur
Piteå
Oulu
Raahe

Skellefteå
Lycksele
Pulkkila

Kuhmo

Oulujärvi
Otanmäki
Nurmes

Steinkjer
Strömsund
Umeå
Haapajärvi
Iisalmi
Pielinen

Kristiansund
Trondheim
Meråker
SWEDEN
3
Kyyjärvi
FINLAND

Molde
Støren
Vaasa

Alesund
Opdal
Tynset
Seinäjoki
Äänekoski

Honningsvåg
Jostedalsbreen
Dombås
Idre
Parkano
Jyväskylä

Florø
Totunheimen
Koppang
Sundsvall
Pori
Tampere
Heinola
Saimaa

Bergen
2
Lillehammer
Mora
Bollnäs
Hudiksvall
Lahti
Kotka

Voss
Hamar
Lake
Mjøsa
Kauma
Turku
Salo
Porvoo

Geilo
Eidsvoll
Falun

Hougesund
Drammen
Oslo
Fagersta
Avesta
Helsinki
St. Petersburg

Kongsberg
Karlstad
Uppsala
Gulf of Finland

Stavanger
Porsgrunn
Fredrikstad
Tallinn

Sandnes
Evje
Larvik
Halden
Stockholm
ESTONIA
RUSSIA

Grimstad
Arendal
Mellerud
Nynäshamn
Hiiumaa
Pskov

Uddevalla
Trollhättan
Norrköping
Baltic
Saaremaa

Kristiansand
Göteborg
Linköping
Sea
Slite

Skagen
Jönköping
Visby
Riga
LATVIA

Thisted
Borås
Oskarshamn
Gotland
Liepaja

Aalborg
Falkenberg

DENMARK
1
Halmstad
Kalmar

Silkeborg
Århus
Helsingborg
Karlskrona
Klaipeda
LITHUANIA

Esbjerg
Fredericia
Kristianstad

Ribe
Copenhagen
Malmö
Ystad

Flensburg
Vilnius
BELARUS

Nakskov
Bornholm
RUSSIA

POLAND

THE ISLANDS OF STOCKHOLM, MIRRORED in the water; the ships and Little Mermaid of Copenhagen; Oslo and its majestic fjord: the capitals of Scandinavia are unthinkable without the water that surrounds and sustains them. What is true of the capitals is true of the countries. Denmark consists of one peninsula and more than 400 islands, only half of them inhabited. An island summer in the archipelago is part of every Stockholmer's childhood memory. The mail packets of Norway's Hurtigruten sail north from Bergen along the fjord-indented coast and turn around at Kirkenes on the Russian border, 2,000 km (1,242 mi) later.

Water has never separated the Scandinavian nations. It was their mastery of shipbuilding that enabled the Vikings to rule the waves 1,000 years ago. Viking explorations and conquests ranged from North America to the Black Sea and from Greenland to Majorca. They developed the angular Runic alphabet, ideal for carving in stone. In Sweden alone, more than 2,000 runic stones still stand, in memory of Vikings who fell in faraway battles. You might think that with so much in common the Scandinavians would keep peace among themselves. But by the 11th century the passion that had inflamed the Vikings was spent and the region became factioned and fractured, along one line or another, until the first half of the 20th century.

You're still likely to see differences reflected along the national boundary lines of today's Scandinavia, but these days they're much more peaceable. Notably, while Denmark and Sweden have chosen to join the EU, Norway is still a non-member. And some might argue that similarities outnumber the differences: all three excel where design is concerned, and each nation's capital city, while maintaining its own flavor, has found a way to successfully marry the financial successes of the last decade and a half with a state of mind that remains purely Scandinavian.

COPENHAGEN

The Kingdom of Denmark is the geographical link between Scandinavia and Europe. Half-timber villages and tidy farms rub shoulders with towns and a few cities, where pedestrians set the pace, not traffic. In the capital, Copenhagen—København in Danish—mothers safely park baby carriages outside bakeries while outdoor cafés fill with cappuccino-sippers, and lanky Danes pedal to work in lanes thick with bicycle traffic. The town was a fishing colony until 1157, when Valdemar the Great gave it to Bishop Absalon, who built a castle on the site of what is now the parliament, Christiansborg. It grew as a center on the Baltic trade route and became known as *købmændenes havn* (merchants' harbor) and eventually København.

In the 15th century it became the royal residence and the capital of Norway and Sweden. From 1596 to 1648 Christian IV, a Renaissance king obsessed with fine architecture, began a building boom that crowned the city with towers and castles, many of which still stand. They're almost all that remain of the city's 800-year history; much of Copenhagen was

TOP REASONS TO GO

Tickle your Taste Buds (Sweden): Industry investment, the finest raw ingredients, and a thirst for the exotic have seen new Swedish cuisine become competitive with the absolute best of Europe's kitchens.

Get Outside (Sweden): The right to roam freely is part of the Swedish constitution, and a couple of days right in Stockholm's archipelago is hard to beat.

Delve into Danish Design (Denmark): Denmark's capital is *the* place to experience one of the nation's top exports—in museums like the Dansk Design Center and in shops like Bang & Olufsen, Royal Copenhagen, and Georg Jensen.

Tivoli Gardens (Denmark): It's filled with amuseuments, restaurants, and people-watching ops. Visit twice: once by day and once by night.

Explore the Fjord (Norway): The Norwegian fjords are known for their beauty, and should top your agenda. One of the most accessible is the Oslofjord, which runs south from Oslo to the sea and is abuzz with locals and visitors all summer long.

Ski from the City (Norway): Whether you're after miles upon miles of well-lit cross-country skiing trails or just some time on a ski simulator at Holmenkollen, Oslo's the place to base yourself.

13

destroyed by two major fires in the 18th century and by British bombing during the Napoleonic Wars.

Today's Copenhagen has no glittering skylines and little of the high-stress bustle of most capitals. The morning air in the pedestrian streets of the city's core is redolent of baked bread and soap-scrubbed storefronts. If there's such a thing as a cozy city, this is it.

PLANNING YOUR TIME

With just one day in Copenhagen, start at Kongens Nytorv and Nyhavn and walk along the pedestrian street of Strøget in the direction of Rådhus Pladsen. You can see Christiansborg and/or Rosenborg Slot along the way. If you're not up for a walk, one of the guided canal tours will give you a good sense of the city. In summer or around Christmas time, round off your day with a relaxed stroll and nightcap in Tivoli.

With additional days, plan to spend time inside one or more of the following: Nationalmuseet, Dansk Design Center, Statens Museum for Kunst, and Kastellet. You could also head over to Christianshavn, for its café-lined canals and for Christiania, with its hippie culture.

GETTING HERE & AROUND
BY AIR

Kastrup International Airport (CPH), 10 km (6 mi) from the center of Copenhagen, is Denmark's air hub. SAS, the main carrier, flies here from several North American cities. The 20-minute taxi ride from the airport to downtown costs DKr 190–DKr 250. A sleek subterranean train zips you from the airport the city's main train station in about 14 minutes. Buy a ticket (DKr 28.50) upstairs in the airport train station at Terminal 3.

BY PUBLIC TRANSPORT

Copenhagen's Hovedbanegården (Central Station) is the hub of the DSB rail network and is connected to most major cities in Europe. Intercity trains run regularly (usually every hour) from 6 AM to midnight for principal towns in Funen and Jutland.

Most trains and buses operate from 5 AM (Sunday 6 AM) to midnight. Night buses run every half-hour from 1 AM to 4:30 AM from the main bus station at Rådhus Pladsen to most areas. Trains and buses operate on the same ticket system and divide Copenhagen and surrounding areas into three zones.

MONEY & EXCHANGE

The monetary unit in Denmark is the krone (DKr), divided into 100 øre. Even though Denmark hasn't adopted the euro, the Danish krone is firmly bound to it at about DKr 7.5 to 1€, with only minimal fluctuations. At this writing, the krone stood at 5.40 to the U.S. dollar and 7.45 to the euro. ATMs are located around most towns and cities. Look for the red signs for KONTANTEN/ DANKORT AUTOMAT. Many, but not all, machines are open 24 hours.

Unlimited travel within two zones (inner city area) for one hour costs DKr 20 for an adult. A discount *klippe kort* (clip card), good for 10 rides, costs DKr 125 for two zones. The card must be stamped in the automatic ticket machines on buses or at stations. (If you don't stamp your clip card, you can be fined up to DKr 600.) Cards can be stamped multiple times for multiple passengers and/or longer rides.

The harbor buses are small ferries that travel along the canal, with stops along the way. The boats are a great way to sightsee and get around the city. They run from 7 AM to 11 PM (10 AM to 11 PM on weekends). Standard bus fares and tickets apply.

The Metro system runs from 5 AM to midnight, and all night on weekends. There are currently two Metro lines in operation. The major Metro hubs in central Copenhagen are Noøreport Station and Kongens Nytorv. Stations are marked with a dark-red Metro logo.

BY TAXI

The computer-metered Mercedes and Volvo cabs aren't cheap. The base charge is DKr 24–40, plus DKr 11.50–15.80 per kilometer, depending on the hour. A cab is available when it displays the sign FRI (free); you can hail cabs, pick them up at stands, or call for one (more expensive). The latter option is your best bet outside the city center.

ESSENTIALS

Air Contact **SAS Scandinavian Airlines** (⊕ *www.flysas.com*).

Emergency Services **Police, fire, and ambulance** (☎ *112*).

Taxi Contacts **Amager Øbro Taxi** (☎ *32/51-51-51*). **Koøbenhavns Taxa** (☎ *35/35-35-35*).

Visitor Information **Danmarks Turistråd** (*Danish Tourist Board* ☎ *32/88-99-00, 212/885-9700 in New York* ⊕ *www.visitdenmark.com*). **Scandinavian Tourist Board** (⊕ *www.goscandinavia.com*). **Wonderful Copenhagen** (✉ *Vesterbrog. 4C, Vesterbro* ☎ *70/22-24-42* ⊕ *www.visitcopenhagen.com*).

EXPLORING COPENHAGEN

Be it sea or canal, water surrounds Copenhagen. A network of bridges and drawbridges connects the two main islands—Zealand and Amager—on which Copenhagen is built. The seafaring atmosphere is indelible, especially around the districts of Nyhavn and Christianshavn.

Copenhagen is small, with most sights within 2½ square km (1 square mi) at its center. Sightseeing, especially downtown, is best done on foot. Or follow the example of the Danes and rent a bike.

13

CENTRUM

Centrum (central Copenhagen, aka downtown and city center) is packed with shops, restaurants, and businesses, as well as the crowning architectural achievements of Christian IV. Its boundaries roughly match the fortified borders under his reign (1588–1648), when the city was surrounded by fortified walls and moats.

Centrum is cut by the city's pedestrian spine, called Strøget (pronounced *Stroy*-et), Europe's longest pedestrian shopping street (about 2 km/1 mi). It's actually a series of five streets: Frederiksberggade, Nygade, Vimmelskaftet, Amagertorv, and Østergade. By mid-morning, particularly on Saturday, it's congested with people, baby strollers, and motionless-until-paid mimes. To the north of Strøget, you will find smaller, more peaceful shopping streets.

6 ★ Christiansborg Slot, Surrounded by canals on three sides, the massive granite Christiansborg Castle is where the queen officially receives guests. From 1441 until the fire of 1795, it was used as the royal residence. Even though the first two castles on the site were burned, Christiansborg remains an impressive neo-Baroque and neoclassical compound. Free tours of the **Folketinget** (*Parliament House* ☎*33/37–55–00* ⊕*www.folketinget.dk*) are given weekdays from July until mid-September. English-language tours begin at 2. Additional tours are offered on Sunday. At the **Kongelige Repræsantationlokaler** (*Royal Reception Chambers* ☎*33/92–64–92*), you're asked to don slippers to protect the floors. Admission is DKr 65; entry is via guided tour only. Tours are given daily May through September. English-language tours are at 11, 1, and 3. From October through April, there are tours every day at 3 PM except Monday. The **Højesteret** (*Supreme Court* ⊠*Prins Jørgens Gård, Copenhagen K, Centrum*) was built on the site of the city's first fortress. The guards at the entrance are knowledgeable and friendly; ask them about the court's complicated opening hours. While the castle was being rebuilt around 1900, the national museum excavated the **ruins of Bishop Absalon's castle** (☎*33/92–64–92*) beneath it. The resulting dark, subterranean maze contains fascinating models and architectural relics. The ruins are open daily 10–4, and admission is DKr 40. ⊠*Slotsholmen (area around Christiansborg; bordered by Boørsgade, Vindebrogade, and Frederiksholms Kanal), Centrum.*

3 Dansk Design Center (*Danish Design Center*). This sleek, glass-panel structure looms in sharp contrast to the Old World ambience of Tivoli just across the street. More a design showroom than a museum, the

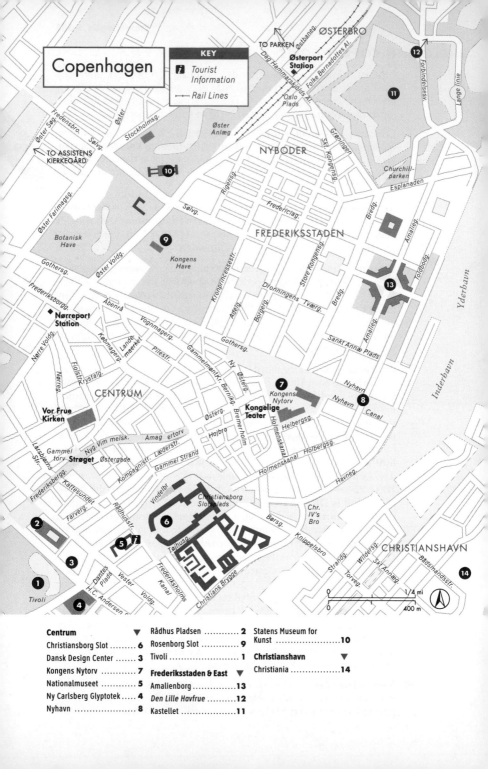

center's highlights are the innovative temporary exhibits (some great, others less so) on the main floor. One-third of these showcase Danish design; the rest focus on international design. The semipermanent collection on the ground floor (renewed every other year) often includes samples from the greats, including chairs by Arne Jacobsen, several artichoke PH lamps (designed by Poul Henningsen), and Bang & Olufsen radios and stereos. Wall labels are in English. The center's shop carries a wide range of Danish design items and selected pieces from the temporary exhibits. You can enjoy light organic meals in the café. ⊠ *H. C. Andersens Blvd. 27, Centrum* ☎ *33/69–33–69* ⊕ *www.ddc.dk* ⊠ *DKr 50* ☽ *Mon.–Fri. 10–5; Wed. 10–9; weekends 11–4.*

❼ Kongens Nytorv. An equestrian statue of Christian V dominates King's New Square. Crafted in 1688 by the French sculptor Lamoureux, the king is conspicuously depicted as a Roman emperor. Every year at the end of June graduating high-school students arrive in truckloads and dance beneath the furrowed brow of the sober statue.

Charlottenborg (⊠ *Nyhavn 2, Centrum* ☎ *33/13–40–22* ⊕ *www.kunsthal charlottenborg.dk*), a Dutch Baroque–style castle on the square, was built by Frederik III's half-brother in 1670. Since 1754 the garden-flanked property has housed the faculty and students of the Danish Academy of Fine Art. A section of the building is devoted to exhibitions of contemporary art and is open to the public Tuesday through Sunday noon to 5. Admission is DKr 60.

❺ Nationalmuseet *(National Museum).* An 18th-century royal residence, with massive overhead windows has contained—since the 1930s—what is regarded as one of the best national museums in Europe. Extensive permanent exhibits chronicle Danish cultural history from prehistoric to modern times. The museum has one of the largest collections of Stone Age tools in the world, as well as Egyptian, Greek, and Roman antiquities. The exhibit on Danish prehistory features a great section on Viking times. The children's museum, with replicas of period clothing and a scalable copy of a real Viking ship, makes history fun for the under-12 set. Displays have English labels, and the do-it-yourself walking tour "History of Denmark in 60 Minutes" offers a good introduction to Denmark; the guide is free at the information desk. ⊠ *Ny Vesterg. 10, Centrum* ☎ *33/13–44–11* ⊕ *www.natmus.dk* ⊠ *Free* ☽ *Tues.–Sun. 10–5.*

❹ Ny Carlsberg Glyptotek. Among Copenhagen's most important museums—thanks to its exquisite antiquities and a world-class collection of impressionist masterpieces—the neoclassical New Carlsberg Museum was donated in 1888 by Carl Jacobsen, son of the founder of the Carlsberg Brewery. Surrounding its lush indoor garden, a series of rooms house works by Pissarro, Degas, Monet, Sisley, Rodin, and Gauguin. The museum is also renowned for its extensive assemblage of Egyptian and Greek pieces, not to mention Europe's finest collection of Roman portraits and the best collection of Etruscan art outside Italy. A modern wing, designed by the acclaimed Danish architect Henning Larsen, provides a luminous entry to the French painting section. From June to September guided English-language tours start at 2. The café overlooking

FodorśChoice
★

13

the winter garden is well known among Copenhageners for its Sunday brunch. ✉ *Dantes Pl. 7, Centrum* ☎ *33/41–81–41* ⊕ *www.glyptoteket. dk* ⊠ *DKr 50; free Sun.* ☉ *Tues.–Sun. 10–4.*

❽ Nyhavn *(New Harbor).* This harbor-front neighborhood was built 300 years ago to attract traffic and commerce to the city center. Until 1970 the area was a favorite haunt of sailors. Though restaurants, boutiques, and antiques stores now outnumber tattoo parlors, many old buildings have been well preserved and retain the harbor's authentic 18th-century maritime character; you can even see a fleet of old-time sailing ships from the quay. Hans Christian Andersen lived at various times in the Nyhavn houses at numbers 18, 20, and 67.

❷ Rådhus Pladsen. City Hall Square is dominated by the 1905 mock-Renaissance Rådhus (City Hall). Architect Martin Nyrop's creation was popular from the start, perhaps because he envisioned that it should give "gaiety to everyday life and spontaneous pleasure to all . . ." A statue of Copenhagen's 12th-century founder, Bishop Absalon, sits atop the main entrance.

Besides being an important ceremonial meeting place for Danish VIPs, the intricately decorated Rådhus contains the first world clock. The multidial, superaccurate astronomical timepiece has a 570,000-year calendar and took inventor Jens Olsen 27 years to complete before it was put into action in 1955.

Topped by two Vikings blowing an ancient trumpet called a *lur,* the Lurblæserne (Lur Blower Column) displays a good deal of artistic license—the lur dates from the Bronze Age, 1500 BC, whereas the Vikings lived a mere 1,000 years ago. City tours often start at this landmark, which was erected in 1914. Look up to see one of the city's most charming bronze sculptures, created by the Danish artist E. Utzon Frank in 1936. Across H. C. Andersens Boulevard, atop a corner office building, are an old neon thermometer and a gilded barometer. On sunny days there's a golden sculpture of a girl on a bicycle; come rain, a girl with an umbrella appears. ✉ *Between H. C. Andersens Blvd., Vester Voldgade, and Bag Rådhuset Centrum* ☎ *33/66–25–82* ⊠ *Free; guided tours DKr 20–DKr 30* ☉ *Mon.–Sat. 10–4; English-language tours weekdays at 3, Sat. at 10.*

❾ Rosenborg Slot. The Dutch Renaissance Rosenborg Castle contains
★ ballrooms, halls, and reception chambers, but for all of its grandeur there's an intimacy that makes you think the king might return any minute. Thousands of objects are displayed, including beer glasses, gilded clocks, golden swords, family portraits, a pearl-studded saddle, and gem-encrusted tables; an adjacent treasury contains the crown jewels. The castle's setting is equally welcoming: it's in the middle of the Kongens Have (King's Garden), amid lawns, park benches, and shady walking paths.

King Christian IV built Rosenborg Castle as a summer residence but loved it so much that he ended up living and dying here. In 1849, when the absolute monarchy was abolished, all the royal castles became state property, except for Rosenborg, which is still passed down from monarch to monarch. Once a year, during the fall holiday, the castle stays open until midnight, and visitors are invited to explore its darkened interior with bicycle lights. Textual information is also in English. ⊠ *Øster Voldg. 4A, Centrum* ☏ *33/15–32–86* ⌨ *DKr 70* ⊙ *Castle: May.–Oct., daily 10–4; Nov.–Dec., Tues.–Sun. 11–2. Treasury: Tues.– Sun., 11–4.*

① **Tivoli.** Copenhagen's best-known attraction, conveniently next to its
Ⓒ main train station, attracts an astounding 4 million people from mid-
Fodor's Choice April to mid-September. Tivoli is more sophisticated than a mere amuse-
★ ment park: among its attractions are a pantomime theater, an open-air stage, 38 restaurants (some of them very elegant), and frequent concerts, which cover the spectrum from classical to rock to jazz. Fantastic flower exhibits color the lush gardens and float on the swan-filled ponds.

The park was established in the 1840s, when Danish architect George Carstensen persuaded a worried King Christian VIII to let him build an amusement park on the edge of the city's fortifications, rationalizing that "when people amuse themselves, they forget politics." The Tivoli Guard, a youth version of the Queen's Royal Guard, performs every day. Try to see Tivoli at least once by night, when 100,000 colored lanterns illuminate the Chinese pagoda and the main fountain. Some evenings there are also fireworks displays. Call to check the season's opening and closing dates as well as family discounts. Tivoli is also open select hours around Halloween and from late November until late December. ⊠ *Vesterbrog. 3, Centrum (on border of Vesterbro district)* ☏ *33/15–10–01* ⊕ *www.tivoli.dk* ⌨ *Grounds DKr 85, unlimited ride pass DKr 200* ⊙ *Mid-Apr.–mid-Sept., Sun.–Wed. 11–11, Fri. 11* AM–*12:30* AM, *Sat. 11* AM–*midnight.*

FREDERIKSSTADEN & EAST

Northeast of Kongens Nytorv is the posh thoroughfare of Bredgade, which intersects Frederiksstaden, a royal quarter commissioned by Frederik V in the mid-1700s. It's home to the castle of Amalienborg. Time your visit with the noon changing of the guard. The old sailors' neighborhood of Nyboder is west of the fortification of Kastallet.

⑬ **Amalienborg.** The four identical rococo buildings occupying this square have housed royals since 1784. It's still the queen's winter residence. The Christian VIII palace across from the royal's wing houses the Amalienborg Museum, which displays the second part of the Royal Collection (the first is at Rosenborg Slot) and chronicles royal lifestyles between 1863 and 1947. Here you can view the study of King Christian IX (1818–1906) and the drawing room of his wife, Queen Louise. Rooms are packed with royal heirlooms and treasures.

In the square's center is a magnificent equestrian statue of King Frederik V by the French sculptor Jacques François Joseph Saly. It reputedly cost as much as all the buildings combined. Every day at noon, the Royal Guard and band march from Rosenborg Slot through the city for the changing of the guard. At noon on Queen Margrethe's birthday, April 16, crowds of Danes gather to cheer their monarch, who stands and

13

waves from her balcony. On Amalienborg's harbor side is the garden of Amaliehaven, at the foot of which the queen's ship often docks. Since the royal family leaves Amalienborg during the summer months, guided tours of Christian VII's Palace are available July–September. English tours depart at 1 and 2:30 pm, DKr 75. ⊠ *Christian VIII's Palace–Amalienborg Pl., Frederiksstaden* ☎ *33/12–21–86* ☒ *Museum: DKr 55* ☉ *Museum: Tues.–Sun. 10–4.*

⑫ Den Lille Havfrue *(The Little Mermaid).* On the Langelinie promenade, this somewhat overhyped 1913 statue commemorates Hans Christian Andersen's lovelorn creation. Donated to the city by Carl Jacobsen, the son of the founder of Carlsberg Breweries, the innocent waif has also been the subject of some cruel practical jokes, including decapitation and the loss of an arm, but she's currently in one piece. Especially on a sunny Sunday, the Langelinie promenade is thronged with Danes and visitors making their pilgrimage to the statue. On this occasion, you may want to read the original Hans Christian Andersen tale; it's a heart-wrenching story that's a far cry from the Disney animated movie. Although the statue itself is modest, the views of the surrounding harbor are not. ⊠ *Langelinie promenade, Østerbro.*

⑪ Kastellet. At the end of Amaliegade, the beautiful Churchill Park surrounds the spired Anglican (or Episcopal) church St. Alban's. From here, walk north on the main path to reach the fortification of Kastellet. The peaceful walking paths, grazing sheep, and greenery welcome joggers and lovebirds to this still-operative military structure. Built in the aftermath of the Swedish siege of the city on February 10, 1659, the double moats were among the improvements made to the city's defense. The Citadel served as the city's main fortress into the 18th century; in a grim reversal during World War II, the Germans used it as headquarters during their occupation. ⊠ *Kastellet 68, Østerbro* ☒ *Free* ☉ *Daily 6 AM–10 PM.*

⑩ Statens Museum for Kunst. Old Master paintings—including works by Rubens, Rembrandt, Titian, El Greco, and Fragonard—as well as a comprehensive array of antique and 20th-century Danish art make up the National Art Gallery collection. Also notable is the modern art, which includes pieces by a very small but select group of artists, including Henri Matisse, Edvard Munch, Henri Laurens, Emil Nolde, and Georges Braque. The space also contains a children's museum, which puts on shows for different age groups at kids' eye level. Wall texts are in English. The bookstore and café are also worth a visit. ⊠ *Sølvg. 48–50, Østerbro* ☎ *33/74–84–94* ⊕ *www.smk.dk* ☒ *Free for permanent collection, DKr 80 for special exhibitions* ☉ *Tues. and Thurs.–Sun. 10–5, Wed. 10–8.*

CHRISTIANSHAVN

Across the capital's main harbor, Inderhavn, is Christianshavn. In the early 1600s this area was mostly a series of shallows between land, which were eventually dammed. Today Christianshavn's colorful boats, cobbled avenues, antique street lamps, shops, and cafés make it one of the toniest parts of town. It's ramparts are edged with green areas and walking paths, making it the perfect neighborhood for an afternoon or evening amble.To get here, walk from the Christiansborg area in Centrum across the Knippelsbro Bridge.

⑭ Christiania. If you're nostalgic for 1960s counterculture, head to this anarchists' commune. You can walk here from Christianshavn: take Torvegade and make a left on Prinsessegade, which takes you to the main gate. You can also take Bus 2A from Rådhuspladsen, Tivoli, Christiansborg, and Christianshavn Station. Founded in 1971, when students occupied army barracks, it's now a peaceful community of nonconformists who run a number of businesses, including a bike shop, a rockmusic club, and good organic eateries. Wall cartoons preach drugs and peace, but the inhabitants are less fond of cameras—picture-taking is forbidden. A group of residents recount their experiences as well as the history of Christiania on daily English-language tours conducted from June 26 through August 31. Tours depart at 3 from the main gate and are 1- to 1½-hours long. They cost DKr 30 per person and are a great way to discover the nooks and crannies of this quirky community. ⊠ *Prinsesseg. and Bådsmansstr., Christianshavn* 🕾 *32/57–60–05 guided tours* ⊕ *www.christiania.org.*

WHERE TO EAT

Copenhagen has experienced a gastronomical revolution over the past decade. A rising interest in new Nordic cooking emphasizes using locally sourced raw materials and high-quality seasonal ingredients. Wild game, cured or smoked fish and meats, Limfjord oysters, Læsø langoustine, eel, and plaice are a few examples.

There's also been a revival of authentic Danish fare. Most such meals begin with *sild*, pickled herring of various flavors, served on *rugbrød,* a very dark and dense rye-based bread. This bread is also the basis for *smørrebrød*—open-face sandwiches piled high with various meats, vegetables, and condiments. For dinner, try *flæskesteg,* pork roast with a crispy rind, which is commonly served with *rødkål,* stewed red cabbage, and potatoes.

There are plenty of bistros serving moderately priced meals, and for inexpensive savory noshes in stylish surroundings, consider lingering in a café. Many restaurants offer fixed-priced meals with wine-pairing menus, and most restaurants require reservations. Many restaurants tack a surcharge of between 3.75% and 5.75% onto the bill for the use of foreign credit cards.

WHAT IT COSTS IN DANISH KRONER					
	¢	$	$$	$$$	$$$$
Restaurants	under 100	100–200	200–300	300–400	over 400

Restaurant prices are based on the median main course price at dinner.

CENTRUM

$–$$ ✕**Custom House.** British entrepreneur Terrance Conran expanded his empire with the renovation of the Art Deco harborfront customs office. The complex now houses three restaurants and a trendy lounge-bar frequented by expats. The Italian restaurant, **Bacino,** offers simple dishes: think fresh pastas and risottos. Try the braised veal cheeks in Barolo with truffles or the *panna cotta* (caramel custard) with cherries and blood oranges. There's a five-course tasting menu, a theater menu, and an à la carte menu. **Ebisu,** the Japanese restaurant, is modeled after an Izakayan-type establishment where you're encouraged to share dishes. An open kitchen offers a glance into the preparation of such dishes as miso-marinated sea bass as well as tempura, sushi, and sashimi. You can choose from either an à la carte or one of several set menus. **Custom House Bar & Grill** is a European brasserie with a Scandinavian bent that's particularly good for lunch (try an open-face sandwich) or a late-night nosh, as the kitchen is open until midnight every day. ✉*Havnegade 44, Centrum* 🕿*33/31–01–30* ⊕*www.customhouse.dk* ⚑*Reservations essential* ▤*AE, DC, MC, V* ⊗*Bacino and Ebisu closed Sun.*

$ ✕**Ida Davidsen.** This five-generations-old, world-renowned lunch spot is
★ synonymous with smørrebrød. The often-packed dining area is dimly lighted, with worn wooden tables and news clippings of famous visitors on the walls. Creative sandwiches include the H. C. Andersen, with liver pâté, bacon, and tomatoes. The terrific duck is smoked by Ida's husband, Adam, and served alongside a horseradish-spiked cabbage salad. ✉*Store Kongensg. 70, Centrum* 🕿*33/91–36–55* ⊕*www.idadavidsen. dk* ⚑*Reservations essential* ▤*AE, DC, MC, V* ⊗*No dinner. Closed weekends and July.*

$$$$ ✕**Kong Hans Kælder.** Five centuries ago this was a Nordic vineyard. Now it's one of Scandinavia's finest restaurants. Chef Thomas Rode Andersen's French-Danish–inspired dishes employ the freshest local ingredients and are served in a medieval subterranean space with white-washed walls and vaulted ceilings. Try the foie gras with raspberry-vinegar sauce or the Belgian oysters from Marenne and Baerii caviar served with horseradish and rye croutons. ✉*Vingårdstr. 6, Centrum* 🕿*33/11–68–68* ⊕*www.konghans.dk* ▤*AE, D, MC, V* ⊗*No lunch. Closed Sun.*

$ ✕**Peder Oxe.** On a 17th-century square, this lively, countrified bistro has rustic tables and 15th-century Portuguese tiles. All entrées—among them grilled steaks, fish, and the best burgers in town—come with salad from the excellent self-service bar. Tables are set with simple white linens, heavy cutlery, and opened bottles of hearty French wine. A clever call-light for the waitress is above each table. In spring, when the high northern sun is shining but the warmth still hasn't kicked in, you won't do badly sitting outside in the Gråbrødretorv (Gray Friars' Square) sipping drinks wrapped in one of the blankets left out on the wicker chairs. ✉*Gråbrødretorv 11, Centrum* 🕿*33/11–00–77* ⊕*www. pederoxe.dk* ▤*DC, MC, V.*

$$$$ ✕**Restaurant Herman.** Thomas Herman is one of Denmark's most talented young chefs and the former head chef at the praised restaurant
Fodor'sChoice
★ Kong Hans Kælder. Herman's philosophy is that taste is attached to

memories and emotions. At his restaurant in the Nimb hotel, he set out to honor the old Danish kitchen, and his meticulously crafted modern remakes of classic country-style dishes delight all the senses. The menu changes seasonally, but you might find smoked duck served with brined walnuts, marjoram, red cabbage, and morel mayonnaise. Four-, five-, and six-course tasting menus are available at dinner with matching wines; lunch sees two- and three-course menus starting at DKr 395. ⊠*Nimb Hotel, Tivoli Gardens, Bernstorffsgade 5, Centrum* ☎*88/70–00–00* ⊕*www.nimb.dk* ⚖*Reservations essential* ▤*AE, DC, MC, V* ✆*No lunch Sat. Closed Sun.*

13

$$ ✕The Royal Café. Tucked between the Royal Copenhagen and Georg Jensen shops, this eatery is part Danish design museum, part shop, and part café. High ceilings, Holmegaard glass chandeliers, and a whimsical mural evoke *Alice's Adventures in Wonderland*. Created in collaboration with design legends like Fritz Hansen, Arne Jacobsen, Royal Copenhagen, and Bang & Olufsen, the café is truly a showcase for what is quintessentially Danish. It's perhaps most known for it's modern twist on traditional smørrebrød called "smushi." The staff delicately assembles these artful, sushi-ish–size, open-face sandwiches, and a pastry and cake bar tempts sweet tooths. ⊠*Amagertorv 6, Centrum* ☎*38/14–95–27* ⊕*www.theroyalcafe.dk* ⚖*Reservations not accepted* ▤*AE, DC, MC, V* ✆*No dinner Sun.*

FREDERIKSSTADEN

$ ✕BioM. The country's only government-certified organic restaurant takes cooking and operating ecologically seriously. Everything here is organic, from the food, wine, and spirits to the paper on which the menu is printed to the earth-tone paint on the walls. It's in a quiet residential area, just beside the old sailors' neighborhood of Nyboder, and it has a street-corner terrace. The French-inspired kitchen prepares seasonal hearty dishes made with local and fair-trade ingredients. Try the weekend brunch, or come for lunch, when the menu has the most choices for under 100 DKr. ⊠*Fredericiagade 78, Frederiksstaden* ☎*33/32–24–66* ⊕*www.biom.dk* ⚖*Reservations essential* ▤*AE, MC, V* ✆*No dinner Sun. Closed Mon.*

$$$$ **✕Geranium.** Located in the beautiful Kongens Have, "the King's Garden," is this modern northern European kitchen. You can dine in the simple white interior, with its rustic detailing and abundant windows, or on a sculpture-laden terrace with its open fire. Award-winning chefs Rasmus Kofoed and Søren Ledet put a modern touch on classic Scandinavian cooking by using advanced techniques including intriguing molecular configurations. They source products from biodynamic farmers (that is, those who follow a system of organic and holistic cultivation) to create vegetable-centric masterpieces. A seven-course menu features venison covered with a thin layer of smoked lard and served with beet root, mushrooms, and forest herbs. For dessert, there's elderberry jelly. An organic vegetarian menu and individual courses are also on offer. All are served with matching wines or juices. ⊠*Kronprinsessegade 13, Frederiksstaden* ☎*33/11–13–04* ⊕*www.restaurantgeranium. com* ⚖*Reservations essential* ▤*AE, DC, MC, V* ✆*No lunch Sat. Closed Sun.–Mon.*

Fodor's Choice
★

$ ✕**Madklubben.** The city's best-value kitchen offers meals of between one and four courses for as little as DKr 100. It's known for its satisfying traditional Danish dishes with a twist: *brændende kælighed* (literally, "burning love," but actually glazed pork cheeks, pickled pearl onions, and chives in a foamy potato puree) or *smilende økoæg* ("smiling organic egg;" cured ham from Skågen, peanut mayo, and watercress). Be aware of added charges and a timed seating schedule. Service can be slow due to crowds. A sister restaurant, Den Anden, meaning "The Second," serves traditional French cuisine in a historic building dating from 1750. It's where H. C. Andersen once dined. ⊠*Store Kongensgade 66, Frederiksstaden* ☎*33/32–32–34* ⚐*Reservations essential* ▤*MC, V* ⊙*No lunch. Closed Sun.*

CHRISTIANHAVN

¢   ✕**Lagkagehuset.** Most everyone is familiar with Danish pastries, but did you know that they have their origin in Vienna, and the Danes call them *weinerbrød* meaning Vienna bread? This bakery is considered one of the city's best. Besides the scrumptious varieties of weinerbrød, fresh baked breads, and cakes, there are also delicious sandwiches, tea, and coffee available. This branch is on the picturesque Christianhavns' canal, but there's also a location in the Wonderful Copenhagen tourist office in Centrum. ⊠*Torvegade 45, Christianshavn* ☎*32/57–36–07.*

WHERE TO STAY

Copenhagen has a variety of hotel options, but rates are consistently high side and rooms are small. The city has increased its capacity with new design hotels, a luxury all-suite hotel in Tivoli Gardens, and a youth hostel in the city center. Many existing properties have undergone renovation that allows for eco-friendly, sustainable business practices. Note that in Copenhagen, as in the rest of Denmark, most rooms only have showers (while some have showers and tubs); state your preference when booking.

WHAT IT COSTS IN DANISH KRONER				
	¢	$	$$	$$$	$$$$
Hotels	under 1,000	1,000–1,500	1,500–2,000	2,000–2,500	over 2,500

Hotel prices are for two people in a standard double room in high season.

CENTRUM

¢   ▦**Danhostel Copenhagen Downtown.** This modern member of a hostel chain has a variety of room configurations, including double rooms. Its location next to Strøget and City Hall means that you can be close to sights, restaurants, and bars even if you're on a tight budget. The hostel also hosts events and exhibitions, making it something of a cultural hub. The street-side café serves breakfast, lunch, and dinner and offers free fruit during the day. **Pros:** central location, inexpensive breakfast. **Cons:** small rooms, quiet time required 11 PM–4 AM, potential for lots of street noise. ⊠*Vandkunsten 5, Centrum* ☎*70/23–21–10* ⊕*www.danhostel.*

dk ⮐*280 rooms* ⟐*In-hotel: restaurant, bicycles, no-smoking rooms* ▭*AE, DC, MC, V* ⦿*EP.*

$$$ –$$$$ ⊡ **First Hotel Skt. Petri.** For the better part of a century, a beloved budget department store nicknamed Dalle Valle occupied this site. It has been supplanted by this luxury hotel that's a hit with interior designers, fashionistas, and celebrities. It has everything you'd expect from a member of the Design Hotels, a collection of properties committed to design and cultural authenticity: a talking elevator telling you how fabulous the place is, contemporary Danish furnishings throughout, front desk staffers who could be models. Guest rooms, designed by Per Arnoldi, have a functional, modern aesthetic that's softened by bright, cheery colors. Many units have a terrace or balcony. The breakfast buffet and weekend brunch are among the city's best. **Pros:** great design everywhere; beautiful terrace; sleek cocktail bar. **Cons:** on the pretentious side; small rooms; street noise. ✉*Krystalg. 22, Centrum,* ☎*33/45–91–00* ⊕*www. hotelsktpetri.com* ⮐*241 rooms, 27 suites* ⟐*In-room: safe, Internet. In-hotel: 2 restaurants, room service, bar, gym, laundry service, parking (paid), no-smoking rooms* ▭*AE, DC, MC, V* ⦿*EP.*

$$$$ ⊡ **Hotel D'Angleterre.** The famed 250-year-old hotel welcomes royalty,
Fodor's Choice   politicians, and rock stars—from Margaret Thatcher to Madonna. An
★   imposing New Georgian facade leads into an English-style sitting room. Standard guest rooms are individually decorated, many in pastels with overstuffed chairs and a mix of modern and antique furniture. The spit-and-polish staff accommodates every wish. The elegant Restaurant D'Angleterre serves excellent French cuisine. In winter the square in front of the hotel is converted into a skating rink. **Pros:** superb location; rich in history; full-service spa; large fitness center; decent-quality restaurant. **Cons:** expensive; formal and straightlaced; some rooms could use a face-lift. ✉*Kongens Nytorv 34, Centrum* ☎*33/12–00–95* ⊕*www. dangleterre.com* ⮐*104 rooms, 19 suites* ⟐*In-room: safe, Internet. In-hotel: restaurant, room service, bar, pool, gym, spa, bicycles, laundry service, Internet terminal* ▭*AE, DC, MC, V* ⦿*EP.*

$$$$ ⊡ **Hotel Nimb.** It's the first hotel in Tivoli Gardens and the most exclusive one in the city, with prices to match. Each of the 13 country-style, individually appointed suites has a view over the gardens; fine art, antiques, and textiles; and such amenities as Egyptian cotton towels and robes, a working fireplace, four-poster beds, and Bang & Olufsen electronics. **Pros:** very comfortable; superb location; great views. **Cons:** awkward spaces throughout due to building limitations; only a few guest rooms. ✉*Bernstorffsgade 5, Centrum* ☎*88/70–00–00* ⊕*www.nimb.dk* ⮐*13 suites* ⟐*In-room: Wi-Fi, DVD (some), In-hotel: restaurant, bar, Wi-Fi, no-smoking rooms* ▭*AE, DC, MC, V* ⦿*EP.*

$$ –$$$ ⊡ **Hotel Twentyseven.** This stylish Scandinavian lifestyle hotel is on a relatively quiet street, yet right across from the Rådhus Pladsen and a block from Strøget. Swedish interior designers shopped at Fritz Hansen to outfit this hotel with things like Series 7 bar stools, Arne Jacobsen Egg and Swan chairs, and Poul Henningsen PH-lamps. Vending machines offer everything from snacks to liquor to sex toys. Rooms have black, gray, and brown fabrics; wooden floors; plump bedding; slate bathrooms; and the occassional piece of red-lacquer furniture. The three on-site

drinking establishments include The Wine Room, with 40 varieties by the glass; the Honey Ryder Cocktail Lounge, with a *Saturday Night Fever*–theme bathroom; and The Absolut Icebar. An organic breakfast and a light dinner buffet are included in the price. **Pros:** superb location; modern look and feel; meals included in rates. **Cons:** clock tower across the way rings on the hour 8 AM–midnight; not ideal for small children. ⊠ *Løngangstræde 27, Centrum* ☎ *70/27–56–27* ⊕ *www.hotel27.dk* ⇱ *200 rooms* ⚴ *In-room: safe, Wi-Fi. In-hotel: restaurant, Wi-Fi, no-smoking rooms* ⊟ *AE, DC, MC, V* ¶⊙¶ *MAP.*

FREDERIKSSTADEN

$$
★
Copenhagen Admiral Hotel. A five-minute stroll from Nyhavn, overlooking old Copenhagen and Amalienborg Palace, the massive Admiral was once a grain warehouse (circa 1787). Today it's one of the least expensive top hotels, cutting frills and prices but retaining charm. Thick stone walls are broken by rows of windows; guest rooms mix maritime accents with modern furnishings and prints. Each room has a sitting area with leather sofas surrounded by 200-year-old exposed beams. Rooms on the first through fourth floors also have French balconies. The SALT bar and restaurant lends Nordic touches to modern French brasserie food. A beautiful harborfront café offers great views. **Pros:** renovated rooms; great restaurant; quiet waterfront location. **Cons:** short walk to main attractions and other conveniences. ⊠ *Toldbodg. 24–28, Frederiksstaden* ☎ *33/74–14–14* ⊕ *www.admiralhotel. dk* ⇱ *314 rooms, 52 suites* ⚴ *In room: Internet. In-hotel: restaurant, room service, bar, bicycles, laundry service, parking (paid), some pets allowed, no-smoking rooms* ⊟ *AE, DC, MC, V* ¶⊙¶ *EP.*

$$–$$$
Front. Huge purple flower pots stand at the entrance to this funky harborside boutique property. Inside, a chalkboard on the wall welcomes you into the lounge with hot pink Danish-design chairs, tall black candle holders, and floral-pattern sofas. There's also an on-site American-style diner that serves milk shakes, burgers, and fries. Simple, modern guest rooms—many with harbor views—have bold-colored walls, black wooden accents, coordinating bedspreads, and pebble-stone bathroom floors. Free mineral water, soda, and beer from the minibar are a nice touch. The hotel is a showcase for Danish-design, with pieces from Normann Copenhagen, Ikea, and Gub, to name a few; some of the items are for sale in the on-site shop. **Pros:** great views; good-size rooms; laid-back. **Cons:** street noise during rush hour. ⊠ *Sankt Annæ Plads 21, Frederiksstaden* ☎ *33/13–34–00* ⊕ *www. front.dk* ⇱ *131 rooms* ⚴ *In-room: Internet. In-hotel: restaurant, gym, laundry service, Internet terminal, parking (paid), some pets allowed* ⊟ *AE, D, MC, V* ¶⊙¶ *EP.*

NIGHTLIFE

Nightspots are concentrated on and around Strøget. Restaurants, cafés, bars, and clubs stay open after midnight, a few until 5 AM. Check out *Copenhagen This Week* (⊕ *www.ctw.dk*) and the English newspaper *The Copenhagen Post* (⊕ *www.cphpost.dk*) for listings.

BARS & LOUNGES

Absolut Icebar Copenhagen (⊠ *Løngangstræde 27, Centrum,* ☎ *70/27–56–27* ⊕ *www.hotel27.dk/icebar*) is literally one of the coolest bars in Copenhagen. Part of the trendy Hotel Twentyseven (which also houses the Honey Ryder lounge serving "molecular" cocktails), it's basically a –31°C (–23°F) ice box (don't worry, a coat is provided during your 40-minute visit), where you drink vodka concoctions in glasses made of ice. **Hviids Vinstue** (⊠ *Kongens Nytorv 19, Centrum* ☎ *33/15–10–64* ⊕ *www.hviidsvinstue.dk*) dates from the 1720s and attracts all kinds, young and old, singles and couples, for a glass of wine or cognac. **Y's Café and Cocktailbar** (⊠ *Nørre Voldgade 102, Centrum* ☎ *33/14–20–44*) is a low-key cocktail bar with a 110 drinks on its menu, each one concocted by award-winning mixologist and owner Yvonne Kubach.

CASINO

The **Casino Copenhagen** (⊠ *Amager Blvd. 70, Amager* ☎ *33/96–59–65* ⊕ *www.casinocopenhagen.dk*), at the SAS Scandinavia Hotel, has American roulette, blackjack, poker, and slot machines. You must be 18 years old to enter, and there's a strictly enforced dress code—jackets are required and no athletic clothing is allowed. Outerwear must be left at the coat check, for a fee. Dealers and croupiers aren't shy about reminding winners that a tip of a certain percentage is customary. The casino is open daily 2 PM to 4 AM, and admission is DKr 90.

DANCE & ROCK CLUBS

Most discos open at 11 PM, charging covers of about DKr 75 and selling drinks at steep prices. **K3** (⊠ *Knabrostræde 3, Centrum* ☎ *33/11–37–84*) is a four-room club with two separate dance floors in the formerly gay Pan Club. Now a mixed crowd—men and women, straight and gay (though all over age of 24)—enjoys electronica, DJs, and disco from the '70s, '80s, and '90s.

Lades Kælder (⊠ *Kattesundet 6, Centrum* ☎ *33/14–00–67* ⊕ *www.lades.dk*), a local hangout just off Strøget, hosts good old-fashioned rock-and-roll bands. It's one of the few places with live music every night.

SHOPPING

A showcase for world-famous Danish design and craftsmanship, Copenhagen seems to have been set up with shoppers in mind. In fact, the city's name means the "merchant's harbor." The best buys are crystal, porcelain, and silver. Throughout summer and into autumn, there are six major markets every weekend, many of which sell antiques and secondhand porcelain, silver, and glassware. Bargaining is expected. Check with the tourist office or the magazine *Copenhagen This Week* (⊕ *www.ctw.dk*) for street markets.

The **Information Center for Danish Crafts and Design** (⊠ *Amagertorv 1, Centrum* ☎ *33/12–61–62* ⊕ *www.danishcrafts.dk*) provides helpful information on galleries, shops, and workshops specializing in Danish crafts and design—from jewelry to ceramics to furniture.

SPECIALTY STORES

AUDIO
EQUIPMENT

For high-tech design and acoustics, **Bang & Olufsen** (⊠ *Kongens Nytorv 26, Centrum* ☎*33/11–14–15* ⊕*www.bang-olufsen.dk*) is so renowned that its products are in the permanent design collection of New York's Museum of Modern Art. (Check prices at home first to make sure you are getting a deal.)

GLASSWARE
& PORCELAIN

Bodum Hus (⊠ *Østerg. 10, on Strøget, Centrum* ☎*33/36–40–80* ⊕*www. bodum.com*) shows off a wide variety of reasonably priced Danish-designed, functional—and especially kitchen-oriented—accoutrements. The French-press is a must for true coffee lovers.

The flagship store for **Royal Copenhagen** (⊠ *Amagertorv 6, Centrum* ☎*33/13–71–81* ⊕*www.royalcopenhagen.dk*) beautifully displays its famous porcelain ware and settings fit for a king. The shop also has a museum on the second floor where you can see the painters in action. The **Royal Copenhagen Factory Outlet** (⊠ *Søndre Fasanvej 9, Frederiksberg* ☎*38/34–10–04* ⊕*www.royalcopenhagen.com*) has a good deal of stock, often at reduced prices, and is open on weekdays from 10 to 5 and Saturday 10 to 2. You can also buy Holmegaard Glass at the Royal Copenhagen store in Centrum and at this factory outlet.

SILVER

Georg Jensen (⊠ *Amagertorv 4, Centrum* ☎*33/11–40–80* ⊕*www.georg jensen.com*) is one of the most recognized names in international silver, and his elegant, austere shop is aglitter with sterling. Jensen has its own museum next door.

STOCKHOLM

Sweden requires the visitor to travel far, in both distance and attitude. Approximately the size of California, Sweden reaches as far north as the arctic fringes of Europe, where glacier-topped mountains and thousands of acres of forests are broken only by wild rivers, pristine lakes, and desolate moorland. In the more populous south, roads meander through miles of softly undulating countryside, skirting lakes and passing small villages with sharp-pointed church spires.

Stockholm itself is a city in the flush of its second youth. In the last 15 years Sweden's capital has emerged from its cold, Nordic shadow to take the stage as a truly international city. What started with entry into the European Union in 1995 gained pace with the extraordinary IT boom of the late 1990s, strengthened with the Skype-led IT second wave of 2003, and solidified with the hedge-fund invasion of the mid-noughties is still happening today as Stockholm gains even more global confidence. And despite more recent economic turmoil, Stockholm's one million or so inhabitants have, almost as one, realized that their city is one to rival Paris, London, New York, or any other great metropolis.

Stockholm also has plenty of history. Positioned where the waters of Lake Mälaren rush into the Baltic, it's been an important Baltic trading site and a wealthy international city for centuries. Built on 14 small islands joined by bridges crossing open bays and narrow channels, Stockholm boasts the story of its history in its glorious medieval old town, grand palaces, ancient churches, sturdy edifices, public parks, and 19th-century museums—its history is soaked into the very fabric of its airy boulevards, built as a public display of trading glory.

PLANNING YOUR TIME

You can manage to see a satisfying amount of Stockholm in a day, though it would be tough to get too much of this place. Start near Stadhuset (City Hall) for a morning trip up to the top of its 348-foot tower. Make your way to Kulturehuset for some art, then relax before heading to Gamla Stan and the Kungliga Slottet. To save on dinner, try picnicking in the beautiful Kungsträdgården, just across Strömsbron.

CURRENCY & EXCHANGE

The unit of currency is the krona (plural kronor), which is divided into 100 öre and is written as SKr or SEK. At press time some exchange rates for the krona were SKr 6.5 to the U.S. dollar, SKr 6.09 to the Canadian dollar, SKr 11.78 to the British pound sterling, and SKr 9.4 to the euro. ATMs are located throughout Stockholm; Many, but not all, machines are open 24 hours.

If you can linger here for a few days, take a day trip into the archipelago. Whether it be a landlubber's stroll along the docks at Strandvägen, venturing onto a commuter ferry for a bit of island hopping, or sea kayaking as far as your arms will let you, get thee to the water.

GETTING HERE & AROUND
BY AIR

Stockholm's Arlanda International Airport, 42 km (26 mi) from the city center, is Sweden's air hub. The main regional carrier SAS flies from several North American cities. *Flygbussarna* (airport buses) leave every 10–15 minutes from 6:30 AM to 11 PM and terminate at Klarabergsviadukten, next to the central railway station.

If you take a taxi, be sure to ask about a *fast pris* (fixed price) between Arlanda and the city. It should be between SKr 490 and SKr 510, depending on the final destination. Watch out for unregistered cabs, which charge high rates and won't provide the same service.

Alternatively, the yellow-nosed Arlanda Express train takes 20 minutes and leaves every 15 minutes (and every 10 minutes during peak hours). Single tickets cost SKr 220.

BY PUBLIC TRANSPORT

The subway system, known as T-banen (Tunnelbanan, with stations marked by a blue-on-white T), is the easiest and fastest way to get around. Servicing more than 100 stations and covering more than 96 km (60 mi) of track, trains run frequently between 5 AM and 3 AM. In 2000 the subway system was bought from SL by Connex, the same company that runs the subways in Paris and London. Tickets for Stockholm subways and buses are interchangeable. Maps and timetables for all city transportation networks are available from the SL information desks at Sergels Torg, the central station, Slussen, and online.

Both long-distance and commuter trains arrive at the central station in Stockholm on Vasagatan. All the major bus services, including Flygbussarna, Swebus Express, Svenska Buss, and Interbus, arrive at Cityterminalen (City Terminal), next to the central railway station. Stockholm has an excellent bus system operated by SL (Stockholm Local Traffic). Tickets work interchangeably on buses and subways in the city. Latenight buses connect certain stations when trains stop running.

Waxholmsbolaget (Waxholm Ferries) offers the Båtluffarkortet (Inter Skerries Card), a discount pass for its extensive commuter network of archipelago boats; the price is SKr 380 for five days of unlimited travel. The Strömma Kanalbolaget operates a fleet of archipelago boats that provide excellent sightseeing tours and excursions.

BY TAXI

If you call a cab, ask the dispatcher to quote you a *fast pris* (fixed price), which is usually lower than the metered fare. A trip of 10 km (6 mi) should cost about SKr 110 between 6 AM and 7 PM, SKr 115 at night, and SKr 123 on weekends.

ESSENTIALS

Airport Contacts SAS Scandinavian Airlines (⊕ *www.flysas.com*).

Emergency Services Police, Fire & Ambulance (☎ *112*).

Taxi Contacts Taxi 020 (☎ *020/202020*). **Taxi Kurir** (☎ *08/300000*). **Taxi Stockholm** (☎ *08/150000*).

Visitor Information Stockholm Information Service (*Sweden House* ⊠ *Hamng. 27, Box 7542, Stockholm* ☎ *08/50828508*). **Swedish Travel and Tourism Council** (⊠ *Box 3030, Kungsg. 36, Stockholm* ☎ *08/7891000* 🖷 *08/7891038* ⊕ *www. visit-sweden.com*).

EXPLORING STOCKHOLM

For the inhabitants there's a tribal status to each of the city's islands. But for the visitor, Stockholm's archipelago location primarily helps to dissect the city, both in terms of history and in terms of Stockholm's different characteristics, conveniently packaging the capital into easily handled, ultimately digestible, areas.

The central island of Gamla Stan wows visitors with its medieval beauty, winding, narrow lanes and small café-lined squares. To the south, Södermalm challenges with contemporary boutiques, hip hangouts, and left-of-center sensibilities. North of Gamla Stan is Norrmalm, the financial and business heart of the city. Travel west and you'll find Kungsholmen, site of the Stadshuset. Turn east from Norrmalm and Östermalm awaits, an old residential neighborhood with the most money, the most glamor, and the most expensive street on the Swedish Monopoly board. Finally, between Östermalm and Södermalm lies the island of Djurgården, once a royal game preserve, now the site of lovely parks and museums.

MODERN STOCKHOLM

The area bounded by Stadshuset, Hötorget, Stureplan, and the Kungliga Dramatiska Teatern (nicknamed Dramaten) is essentially Stockholm's downtown. Shopping, nightlife, business, traffic, dining—all are at their most intense in this part of town. Much of this area was razed to the ground in the 1960s as part of a social experiment to move people to the new suburbs. What came in its place, a series of modernist buildings, concrete public spaces, and pedestrianized walkways, garners support and derision in equal measure.

13

② **Hallwylska Museet** *(Hallwyl Museum).* This private late-19th-century palace, one of the first in Stockholm to have electricity and a telephone installed, has imposing wood-panel rooms and a collection of furniture, paintings, and musical instruments that can be best described as eclectic. The palace is decked out in a bewildering mélange of styles assembled by the apparently spendaholic Countess von Hallwyl, who left it to the state on her death. ⊠ *Hamng. 4, Norrmalm* ☎ *08/4023099* ⊕ *hwy. lsh.se* ✉ *SKr 70* ☉ *Guided tours only. Tours in English July and Aug., Tues.–Sun. at 1; Sept.–June, Sun. at 1.*

① **Kulturhuset** *(Culture House).* Since it opened in 1974, architect Peter
⊙ Celsing's cultural center, a glass-and-stone monolith on the south side of Sergels Torg, has become a symbol of modernism in Sweden. Stockholmers are divided on the aesthetics of this building—most either love it or hate it. Here there are exhibitions for children and adults, a library, a theater, a youth center, an exhibition center, and a restaurant. Head to Café Panorama, on the top floor, to savor traditional Swedish cuisine and a great view of Sergels Torg down below. ⊠ *Sergels Torg 3, City* ☎ *08/50831508* ⊕ *www.kulturhuset.stockholm.se.*

Kungsträdgården. Once the Royal kitchen garden, this is now Stockholm's smallest but most central park. It is often used to host festivals and events, but is best seen in its everyday guise: as a pleasant sanctuary from the pulse of downtown. Diseasesd trees removed in 2004 have been replaced by neat little glass-cube cafés selling light lunches, coffee, and snacks. ⊠ *Between Hamng. and the Operan.*

GAMLA STAN & SKEPPSHOLMEN

Gamla Stan (Old Town) sits between two of Stockholm's main islands, and is the site of the medieval city. Just east of Gamla Stan is the island of Skeppsholmen, whose twisting cobbled streets are lined with superbly preserved old buildings. As the site of the original Stockholm, history, culture, and a dash of Old Europe come thick and fast here. Understandably, Gamla Stan is also a magnet for tourists. Consequently there are plenty of substandard shops and restaurants ready to take your money for shoddy goods and bad food. Because of this, locals often make a big show of dismissing the area, but don't believe them. Secretly they love Gamla Stan and Skeppsholmen. And who wouldn't? Its divine alleys and bars, gorgeous architecture, shops, and restaurants are irresistable.

⑤ **Kungliga Slottet** *(Royal Palace).* Designed by Nicodemus Tessin, the
Fodor'sChoice Royal Palace was completed in 1760 and replaced the previous pal-
★ ace that had burned here in 1697. The four facades of the palace each

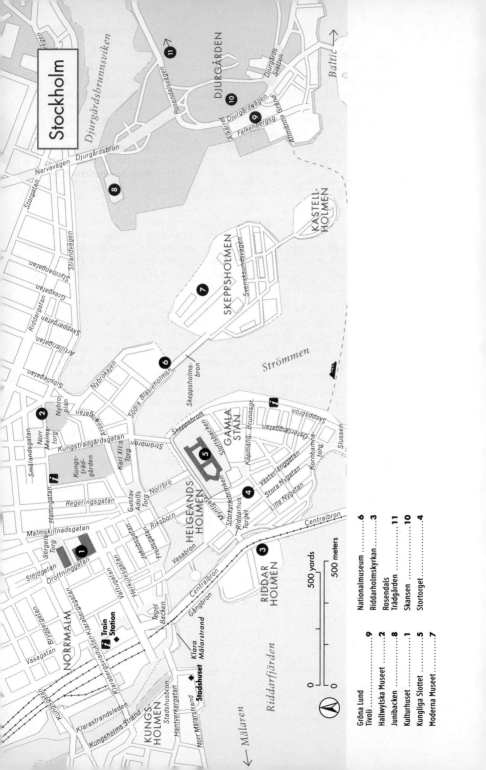

Stockholm

500 yards
500 meters

have a distinct style: the west is the king's, the east the queen's, the south belongs to the nation, and the north represents royalty in general. Watch the changing of the guard in the curved terrace entrance, and view the palace's fine furnishings and Gobelin tapestries on a tour of the **Representationsvän** (State Apartments). To survey the crown jewels, which are no longer used in this self-consciously egalitarian country, head to the **Skattkammaren** (Treasury). The **Livrustkammaren** (Royal Armory) has an outstanding collection of weaponry, coaches, and royal regalia. Entrances to the Treasury and Armory are on the Slottsbacken side of the palace. ⊠ *Gamla Stan* ☎ *08/4026130* ⊕ *www.royalcourt.se* ⊠ *State Apartments SKr 90, Treasury SKr 90, Royal Armory SKr 90, combined ticket for all areas SKr 130* ☉ *State Apartments and Treasury May–Aug., daily 10–4; Sept.–Apr., Tues.–Sun. noon–3. Armory May–Aug., daily 11–4; Sept.–Apr., Tues.–Sun. 11–4.*

❼ **Moderna Museet** (*Museum of Modern Art*) The museum's excellent collection includes works by Picasso, Kandinsky, Dalí, Brancusi, and other international artists. You can also view examples of significant Swedish painters and sculptors and an extensive section on photography. The building itself is striking. Designed by the well-regarded Spanish architect Rafael Moneo, it has seemingly endless hallways of blond wood and walls of glass. ⊠ *Skeppsholmen, City* ☎ *08/51955200* ⊕ *www.modernamuseet.se* ⊠ *SKr 80* ☉ *Tues. 10–8, Wed.–Sun. 10–6.*

❻ **Nationalmuseum.** The museum's collection of paintings and sculptures
★ is made up of about 12,500 works, so allow at least a few hours if you want to see the highlights. The emphasis is on Swedish and Nordic art, but other areas are well represented. Look especially for some fine works by Rembrandt. The print and drawing department is also impressive, with a nearly complete collection of Edouard Manet prints. ⊠ *Södra Blasieholmshamnen, City* ☎ *08/51954300* ⊕ *www.nationalmuseum.se* ⊠ *SKr 100* ☉ *Jan.–Aug., Tues. 11–8, Wed.–Sun. 11–5; Sept.–Dec., Tues. and Thurs. 11–8, Wed., Fri., and weekends 11–5.*

❸ **Riddarholmskyrkan** (*Riddarholm Church*). Dating from 1270, the Grey Friars monastery is the second-oldest structure in Stockholm, and has been the burial place for Swedish kings for more than 400 years. The redbrick structure, distinguished by its delicate iron-fretwork spire, is rarely used for services: it's more like a museum now. The most famous figures interred within are King Gustavus Adolphus, hero of the Thirty Years' War, and the warrior King Karl XII, renowned for his daring invasion of Russia, who died in Norway in 1718. The most recent of the 17 Swedish kings to be put to rest here was Gustav V, in 1950. The different rulers' sarcophagi, usually embellished with their monograms, are visible in the small chapels dedicated to the various dynasties. ⊠ *Riddarholmen* ☎ *08/4026130* ⊕ *www.royalcourt.se* ⊠ *SKr 30* ☉ *Jun–Aug., daily 10–5; May and Sept., daily 10–4.*

❹ **Stortorget** (*Great Square*). Here in 1520 the Danish king Christian II ordered a massacre of Swedish noblemen. The slaughter paved the way for a national revolt against foreign rule and the founding of Sweden as a sovereign state under King Gustav Vasa, who ruled from 1523 to 1560. One legend holds that if it rains heavily enough on the anniversary of the massacre, the old stones still run red. ⊠*Near Kungliga Slottet, Gamla Stan.*

DJURGÅRDEN & SKANSEN

Throughout history, Djurgården has been Stockholm's pleasure island. There was time when only the king could enjoy this enormous green space. Today everyone comes here to breathe fresh air, visit the many museums, stroll through the forests and glades, get their pulses racing at the Gröna Lund amusement park, or just relax by the water. You can approach Djurgården from the water aboard the small ferries that leave from Slussen at the southern end of Gamla Stan. In summer, ferries also leave from Nybrokajen, or New Bridge Quay, in front of the Kungliga Dramatiska Teatern.

9 **Gröna Lund Tivoli.** Smaller than Copenhagen's Tivoli or Göteborg's Liseberg, this amusement park has managed to retain much of its historical charm, while making room for some modern, hair-raising rides among the pleasure gardens, amusement arcades, and restaurants. If you're feeling especially daring, try the Power Tower. At 350 feet, it's Europe's tallest free-fall amusement-park ride and one of the best ways to see Stockholm, albeit for about three seconds before you plummet. There isn't an adult who grew up in Stockholm who can't remember the annual excitement of Gröna Lund's April opening. Go and you will see why. ⊠*Allmänna Gränd 9, Djurgården* ☎*08/58750100* ⊕*www. tivoli.se* ⊠*SKr 70, not including tickets or passes for rides* ☉*Late Apr.–mid-Sept., daily. Hrs vary but are generally noon–11* PM. *Call ahead for specific information.*

8 **Junibacken.** In this storybook house you travel in small carriages through the world of children's book writer Astrid Lindgren, creator of the irrepressible character Pippi Longstocking, among others. Lindgren's tales come alive as various scenes are revealed. Parents can enjoy a welcome moment of rest after the mini-train ride as the children lose themselves in the near-life-size model of Pippi Longstocking's house. It's perfect for children ages five and up. ⊠*Galärvarsv., Djurgården* ☎*08/58723000* ⊕*www.junibacken.se* ⊠*SKr 110* ☉*Jan.–May and Sept.–Dec., Tues. to Sun. 10–5; June and Aug. daily 10–5; July daily 9–6.*

11 **Rosendals Trädgården** *(Rosendal's Garden).* This gorgeous slice of greenery is a perfect place to spend a few hours on a late-summer afternoon. When the weather's nice, people flock to the garden café, which is in one of the greenhouses, to enjoy tasty pastries and salads made from the locally grown vegetables. Pick your own flowers from the vast flower beds (paying by weight), stroll through the creative garden displays, or take away produce from the farm shop. ⊠*Rosendalsterrassen 12, Djurgården* ☎*08/54581270* ⊕*www.rosendalstradgard.se* ⊠*Free* ☉*May–Sept., weekdays 11–5, weekends 11–6; Oct.–Apr. call ahead for specific information.*

Fodor's Choice ★

10 **Skansen.** The world's first open-air museum, Skansen was founded in 1891 by philologist and ethnographer Artur Hazelius, who is buried here. He preserved examples of traditional Swedish architecture brought from all parts of the country, including farmhouses, windmills, barns, a working glassblower's hut, and churches. Not only is Skansen a delightful trip out of time in the center of a modern city, but it also provides insight into the life and culture of Sweden's various regions. In addition, the park has a zoo, carnival area, aquarium, theater, and cafés. ⊠ *Djurgårdsslätten 4951, Djurgården* ☎ *08/4428000* ⊕ *www. skansen.se* ✉ *Park and zoo: Sept.–Apr. SKr 65; May–Aug. SKr 100. Aquarium SKr 75* ⊙ *Nov.–Feb., daily 10–3; Mar.–Apr. and Oct., daily 10–4; May and Sept., daily 10–8; June–Aug., daily 10–10.*

13

WHERE TO EAT

What was once a dour landscape of overpriced, uninspiring eateries is now a creative hotbed of culinary achievement to rival any major European capital. Industry investment in training, receptivity to international influence, and a flair for creativity all mean that Stockholm's best chefs have stayed way ahead of the game. Increasingly, this achievement is rubbing off on their mid-price colleagues and in terms of culinary experience per krona, mid-range restaurants reperesent the best value for money in town. Two recent trends have seen many of the city's better restaurants pick up on this and offer more set-priced tasting menus and increasing numbers of wines by the glass—making even the most expensive restaurants relatively affordable. In terms of food, *New Swedish* remains the buzzword, with chefs looking no further than their backyards for fine, seasonal, traditional ingredients, served with a modern twist. Of course, there are also many less expensive restaurants with traditional Swedish cooking. Among Swedish dishes, the best bets are wild game and fish, particularly salmon, and the smorgasbord buffet, which usually offers a good variety at an inexpensive price. Reservations are often necessary.

WHAT IT COSTS IN SWEDISH KRONER					
	¢	$	$$	$$$	$$$$
Restaurants	under SKr 100	SKr 100–SKr 150	SKr 150–SKr 250	SKr 250–SKr 420	over SKr 420

Restaurant prices are for a main course at dinner.

DOWNTOWN STOCKHOLM & BEYOND

¢ ✕ **Birkastans Restaurang & Pizzeria.** Sweden has made the pizza its own, with a shabby, but usually good take-away pizza place on every street corner. This, though, is the best in town. It's diminutive size is inversely proportional to the owner's ambitions for offering choice, and there are more than 80 different pizza combinations on the menu. You may have to wait a while for a table, but it's worth it. ⊠ *Vikingag. 16, Vasastan* ☎ *08/321790* ⚇ *Reservations not accepted* ⊟ *MC, V.*

$$ ✕ **Cassi.** It doesn't get any better than this for authentic French-inspired cuisine. Think grilled cuts of meat with the finest french fries in town. It's counter service here, so queue up, order, and watch while the chef cooks your dinner. Don't expect any frills; save for a few French film posters and shots of Paris, the interior design of this place isn't the

hippest. But that's not why you come: that would be the food. Dinner service ends at eight, so this is not the best choice for night owls, but Cassi is busiest and best at lunchtime anyway, when the daily set lunch can reduce the price dramatically. And those guys in the corner—with the cool suits, carafe of wine, and copies of *Le Figaro*—they probably come from the French Embassy right next door. Now that's a good sign. ✉ *Naravägen 30* ☎ *08/6617461* ⌕ *Reservations not accepted* ▤ *AE, MC, V* ⊘ *Closed Sat.*

$$$ ✕ **Fredsgatan 12.** Without a doubt, this is one of the most creative res-
★ taurants in town. The showpieces are the two seven-course tasting menus: Tradition and Innovative, where dishes such as duck parfait with cherry and pistachio (tradition) and chicken popcorn with truffle and curry (innovative) delight, confuse, and surprise in equal measure. The elegant, neutral-toned dining room oozes class and style; the refreshingly friendly, impressively knowledgable staff add a pleasant down-to-earth touch to the sky-high prices. This is haute cuisine at its very best. ✉ *Fredsg. 12, City* ☎ *08/248052* ⌕ *Reservations essential* ▤ *AE, DC, MC, V* ⊘ *Closed Sun. No lunch Sat.*

$ ✕ **Systrarna Lundberg.** A perfectly relaxed, down-to-earth, and friendly neighborhood restaurant. You are just as welcome here for a coffee as you are for one of their globally inspired main courses. Try the Japanese-style beef with jasmine rice, lamb with feta cheese, or the delicious Thai green curry. ✉ *Rörstrandsg. 12* ☎ *08/305747* ⌕ *No reservations* ▤ *AE, DC, MC, V* ⊘ *No lunch.*

GAMLA STAN, SKEPPSHOLMEN & SÖDERMALM

$ ✕ **Hermans.** Hermans is a haven for vegetarians out to get the most bang for their kronor. The glassed-in back deck and open garden both provide breathtaking vistas across the water of Stockholm harbor, Gamla Stan, and the island of Djurgården. The food is always served buffet style, and includes various vegetable and pasta salads, warm casseroles, and such entrées as Indonesian stew with peanut sauce and vegetarian lasagna. The fruit pies, chocolate cakes, and cookies are delicious. ✉ *Fjällg. 23A, Södermalm* ☎ *08/6439480* ▤ *MC, V.*

$$$ ✕ **Mathias Dahlgren.** It seemed like all of Stockholm was holding its
Fodor's Choice breath for Mattias Dahlgren to open his new eponymous restaurant at
★ the end of 2007 (his first since he shuttered the legendary Bon Lloc). When the doors finally opened, a collective sigh of relief was audible: success! From the elegant modern dining room to the food—simple, artistically rendered local food which Dahlgren's dubs "natural cuisine"—this place doesn't disappoint. For his trouble he picked up a Michelin star in his first six months. Don't miss this place. ✉ *Grand Hotel, S Blasieholmshamen* ☎ *08/6793584* ⌕ *Reservations essential* ▤ *AE, DC, MC, V* ⊘ *Lunch served Mon.–Fri. in the bar. No lunch weekends. Closed Sun.*

$$ ✕ **Pelikan.** Beer, beer, and more beer is the order of the day at Pelikan, a traditional working-class drinking hall, a relic of the days when Södermalm was the dwelling place of the city's blue-collar brigade. Today's more bohemian residents find it just as enticing, with the unvarnished wood-paneled walls, faded murals, and glass globe lights fulfilling all their down-at-the-heel pretensions. The food here is some of the best traditional Swedish fare in the city. The herring, meatballs, and salted bacon with onion sauce are not to be missed. ✉*Blekingeg. 40, Södermalm* ☎*08/55609090* ♨*Reservations not accepted* ▤*MC, V* ⊘*No lunch Sun.–Thurs.*

WHERE TO STAY

Although Stockholm has a reputation for prohibitively expensive hotels, great deals can be found in summer. More than 50 hotels offer the "Stockholm Package," which includes accommodations for one night, breakfast, and the Stockholmskortet, or Stockholm Card, which entitles the cardholder to free admission to museums and travel on public transport. Details are available from travel agents, tourist bureaus, and the **Stockholm Information Service** (✉*Box 7542, 103 93 Stockholm* ☎*08/50828500* 🖷*08/508289510*). Also try **Hotellcentralen** (✉*Centralstation, Stockholm* ☎*08/7892425* 🖷*08/7918666*); the service is free if you go in person, but a fee applies if you call.

All rooms in the hotels reviewed below are equipped with shower or bath unless otherwise noted. Unless otherwise stated, hotels do not have air-conditioning. Some hotels close during the winter holidays; call ahead if you expect to travel during that time.

WHAT IT COSTS IN SWEDISH KRONER					
	¢	$	$$	$$$	$$$$
Hotels	under SKr 1,000	SKr 1,000–SKr 1,500	SKr 1,500–SKr 2,300	SKr 2,300–SKr 2,900	over SKr 2,900

Hotel prices are for two people in a standard double room in high season.

DOWNTOWN STOCKHOLM

$$$$ 🖳**Berns Hotel.** This ultramodern hotel was a hot spot when it opened its doors in the late 19th century, and it retains that status today. Rooms here have hardwood floors, white walls, feather-stuffed white quilts and fabrics in cobalt-blue, chocolate-brown, moss-green, and stone—a lesson in comfortable modernism. All feature a rotating wooden tower containing TV, CD player, and minibar. The restaurant/bar is a joint venture with restaurant entrepreneur and designer Terence Conran. Hotel rates include the use of a nearby fitness center with a pool. **Pros:** stylish rooms; fantastic restaurant; great bath products. **Cons:** some rooms are a little small; the bar gets rowdy on weekend nights. ✉*Näckströmsg. 8, City* ☎*08/56632000* 🖷*08/56632201* ⊕*www.berns.se* ☎*65 rooms, 3 suites* ♨*In-room: refrigerator, Internet. In-hotel: restaurant, room service, bar, Wi-Fi, no-smoking rooms* ▤*AE, DC, MC, V* ⊙I*BP.*

$$ 🖳**Hotel Gustav Wasa.** The Gustav Wasa is in a 19th-century residential building and has fairly large, bright rooms with herringbone hardwood floors, original trim and details along the ceilings, and a funky blend of antiques and furniture that's more modern. Some rooms have wonderful original tiled fireplaces. Ask for a room with a window out to the street in order to get a direct view of the grand Gustav Wasa Church and the Odenplan. The other available view, of the inner courtyard, is much less exciting. The downtown location and lower prices make this an excellent place for budget travelers who prefer a friendly hotel. **Pros:** good location; very friendly staff; rooms are of ample size. **Cons:** basic facilities; small bathrooms. ✉ *Västmannag. 61, Vasastan* ☎*08/54544805* 🖷*08/307372* ⊕*www.gustavvasahotel.se* ⟲*41 rooms* ▤*AE, DC, MC, V* ⦿*BP.*

$$$ 🖥 **Hotel Stureplan.** Following the demise of the Lydmar Hotel, the undis-
Fodor's Choice   puted best boutique to have ever graced Stockholm's sidewalks, the city's
★   hotel watchers were left wondering if they would ever recover. Then along came Hotel Stureplan. Housed in a beautiful 18th century mansion, Stureplan has pitched itself just right: it's the perfect mix between modern design, comfortable living, and functional hotel. Rooms come in small, medium, large, or extra large and are further categorized as classic (Gustavian furniture, stucco features, balconies, fireplaces) and loft (modern, minimal and light-filled). Whichever you choose, Stureplan has perfected the elusive art of making guests feel truly at home. **Pros:** to-die-for design; great service; perfect location. **Cons:** no restaurant; small rooms are very small. ✉*Birger Jarlsg. 24* ☎*08/4406600* 🖷*08/4406611* ⊕*www.hotelstureplan.se* ⟲*102 rooms* ⅙*In-room: safe, refrigerator, Internet. In-hotel: room service, bar, laundry service, Internet terminal, no-smoking rooms* ▤*AE, DC, MC, V* ⦿*BP.*

GAMLA STAN & SKEPPSHOLMEN

$$$$ 🖥 **Grand Hotel.** At first glance the Grand seems like any other world-
★   class international hotel, and in many ways it is. Its location is one of the best in the city, on the quayside just across the water from the Royal Palace. The large rooms are sumptuous and decadent, with robes so fluffy, beds so soft, and antiques so lovely you may never want to leave. But the Grand offers something else: a touch of the uniquely Scandinavian. You can feel it in the relaxed atmosphere that pervades the hotel, you can smell it in the fresh, salt-tinged air that wafts through the open windows, and you can see it in the purity of the light that penetrates all corners of the hotel. If there is a more exquisite hotel anywhere in town, it is yet to be found. **Pros:** unadulterated luxury; world-class service; great bar. **Cons:** some rooms are small; faded in parts. ✉*Södra Blasieholmshamnen 8, Box 16424, City* ☎*08/6793500* 🖷*08/6118686* ⊕*www.grandhotel.se* ⟲*386 rooms, 21 suites* ⅙*In-room: safe, refrigerator, Wi-Fi. In-hotel: 2 restaurants, room service, bar, gym, spa, laundry service, Wi-Fi, no-smoking rooms* ▤*AE, DC, MC, V* ⦿*BP.*

$$ 🖥 **Rica Hotel Gamla Stan.** The feel of historical Stockholm living is rarely more prevalent than in this quiet hotel tucked away on a narrow street in one of the Gamla Stan's 17th-century houses. All rooms are decorated in the Gustavian style, with hardwood floors, Oriental rugs, and antique furniture. A short walk from the Gamla Stan metro stop, it's a perfect home base for later exploring. **Pros:** personal service; most rooms are comfortable. **Cons:** some rooms are small; basic facilities. ✉*Lilla Nyg. 25, Gamla Stan* ☎*08/7237250* 🖷*08/7237259* ⊕*www.rica.se* ⟲*51 rooms* ⅙*In-room: refrigerator, Internet. In-hotel: no-smoking rooms.* ▤*AE, DC, MC, V* ⦿*BP.*

NIGHTLIFE

Birger Jarlsgatan, Stureplan, and the city end of Kungsträdgården are more upscale and trendy, and thus more expensive. To the south, in Södermalm, things are a bit wilder. Anywhere, a safe bet is wearing black, Stockholm's hue of choice. Things wind down around 3 AM. The tourist guide *What's On* (⊕*www.stockholmtown.com*) lists the month's events in both English and Swedish. The Thursday editions of the daily newspapers *Dagens Nyheter* (⊕*www.dn.se*) and *Svenska Dagbladet* (⊕*www.svd.se*) carry listings.

BARS & NIGHTCLUBS

★ **Berns Salonger** (✉*Berns Hotel, Berzelii Park, City* ☎*08/56632000*) has three bars—one in 19th-century style and two modern rooms—plus a huge veranda that's spectacular in summer. Don't let the name of **Hotellet** (✉*Linneg. 18, Östermalm* ☎*08/4428900*) fool you. Although originally designed as a hotel, it is now a very chic bar that has managed to retain that open lobby feel for its hot crowd.

Sumptuous **Le Rouge** (✉*Brunnsgränd 2, Gamla Stan* ☎*08/50524430*) has one of the most interesting cocktail menus in town. **Mosebacke Etablissement** (✉*Mosebacke Torg 3, Södermalm* ☎*08/6419020*) is a combined indoor theater, comedy club, and outdoor café with a spectacular view of the city. The crowd here leans toward over-30 hipsters. A trendy youngish crowd props up the long bar at **WC** (✉*Skåneg. 51, Södermalm* ☎*08/7022963*), with ladies' drink specials on Sunday.

DANCE CLUBS

Café Opera (✉*Operahuset, City* ☎*08/6765807*), at the waterfront end of Kungsträdgården, is a popular meeting place for young and old alike. It has the longest bar in town, fantastic 19th-century ceilings and details, plus dining and roulette, and major dancing after midnight. The kitchen offers a night menu until 2:30 AM. **Debaser** (✉*Karl Johans torg 1, Södermalm* ☎*08/4629860*) is the perfect place for those who like their dancing a bit wilder. The epicenter of Stockholm's rock music scene, this is where denim-clad legions come to shake their stuff. Down on Stureplan is **Sturecompagniet** (✉*Stureg. 4, Östermalm* ☎*08/6117800*), a galleried, multi-floor club where the crowd is young, the dance music is loud, and the lines are long.

BOATING

From May to September sailboats large and small and gorgeous restored wooden boats cruise from island to island. Both types of boats are available for rental. Walk along the water on Strandvägen, where many large power yachts and sailboats (available for charter) are docked. Sea kayaking has also become increasingly popular and is a delightful way to explore the islands.

Contact **Svenska Seglarförbundet** (*Swedish Sailing Association* ✉*Af Pontins väg 6, Djurgården* ☎*08/4590990* ⊕*www.ssf.se*) for information on sailing. **Svenska Kanotförbundet** (*Swedish Canoeing Association* ✉*Rosvalla, Nyköping* ☎*0155/209080* ⊕*www.kanot.com*) has information on canoeing and kayaking. At the end of Strandvägen, before the bridge to Djurgården, is **Tvillingarnas Båtuthyrning** (⊠ *Strand-vägskajen 27, City* ☎ *08/58815580*), which has large and small motor-boats and small sailboats.

SHOPPING

For souvenirs and crafts, peruse the boutiques and galleries in Väster-långgatan, the main street of Gamla Stan. For jewelry, crafts, and fine art, hit the shops that line the raised sidewalk at the start of Hornsga-tan on Södermalm. Drottninggatan, Birger Jarlsgatan, Biblioteksgatan, Götgatan, and Hamngatan also offer some great shopping.

MARKETS

For a good indoor market hit **Hötorgshallen** (⊠ *Hötorget, City*), directly under Filmstaden. The market is filled with butcher shops, coffee and tea shops, and fresh-fish markets. It's also open daily and closes at 6 PM. **Street** (⊠ *Hornstulls Strand 1, Södermalm*) is a waterside street market with stalls selling fashionable clothing, design, books, and other artsy and creative wares. If you're interested in high-quality Swedish food, try the classic European indoor market **Östermalms Saluhall** (⊠ *Öster-malmstorg, Östermalm*), where you can buy superb fish, game, bread, vegetables, and other foodstuffs—or just have a glass of wine at one of the bars and watch the world go by.

SPECIALTY STORES

GLASS Kosta Boda and Orrefors produce the most popular and well-regarded lines of glassware. The **Crystal Art Center** (⊠ *Tegelbacken 4, City* ☎ *08/217169*), near the central station, has a great selection of smaller glass items. **Duka** (⊠ *Sveav. 24–26, City* ☎ *08/104530*) specializes in crystal and porcelain at reasonable prices. **NK** carries a wide representa-tive line of Swedish glasswork in its Swedish Shop, downstairs.

INTERIOR DESIGN Sweden is recognized globally for its unique design sense and has con-tributed significantly to what is commonly referred to as Scandinavian design. All of this makes Stockholm one of the best cities in the world for shopping for furniture and home and office accessories.

You can't do better than **Modernity** (⊠ *Sibylleg. 6, Östermalm* ☎ *08/208025*). This is *the* place for ultimate 20th-century Scandinavian design, with names like Arne Jacobsen, Alvar Aalto, and Poul Hen-ningsen represented in full force.

WOMEN'S CLOTHING Swedish designer **Anna Holtblad** (⊠ *Grev Tureg. 13, Östermalm* ☎ *08/54502220*) sells her elegant designs at her own boutique. She spe-cializes in knitted clothes. **Filippa K** (⊠ *Grev Tureg. 18, Östermalm* ☎ *08/54588888*) has quickly become one of Sweden's hottest designers. Her stores are filled with young women grabbing the latest fashions.

Hennes & Mauritz (*H&M* ⊠ *Hamng. 22, City* ⊠ *Drottningg. 53 and 56, City* ⊠ *Sergelg. 1 and 22, City* ⊠ *Sergels torg 12, City* ☎ *08/7965500*) is one of the few Swedish-owned clothing stores to have achieved interna-tional success. Here you can find updated designs at rock-bottom prices.

OSLO

One of the world's most beautiful countries, Norway has long been a popular cruising destination, famed for its stunning fjords. Formed during the last ice age's meltdown when the inland valleys carved by huge glaciers filled with seawater, fjords are undoubtedly Norway's top attractions—they shape the country's unique landscape and never fail to take your breath away.

Oslo itself, Norway's capital, is in the east, only a few hours from the Swedish border. What sets Oslo apart from other European cities is not so much its cultural traditions or its internationally renowned museums as its simply stunning natural beauty. How many world capitals have subway service to the forest, or lakes and hiking trails within city limits? But Norwegians will be quick to remind you that Oslo is a cosmopolitan metropolis with prosperous businesses and a thriving nightlife.

Once overlooked by travelers to Scandinavia, Oslo is now a major tourist destination and the gateway to what many believe is Scandinavia's most scenic country. That's just one more change for this town of 500,000—a place that has become good at survival and rebirth throughout its nearly 1,000-year history. In 1348 a plague wiped out half the city's population. In 1624 a fire burned almost the whole of Oslo to the ground. It was redesigned and renamed Christiania by Denmark's royal builder, King Christian IV. After that it slowly gained prominence as the largest and most economically significant city in Norway.

During the mid-19th century, Norway and Sweden were ruled as one kingdom, under Karl Johan. It was then that the grand main street that's his namesake was built, and Karl Johans Gate has been at the center of city life ever since. In 1905 the country separated from Sweden, and in 1925 an act of Parliament finally changed the city's name back to Oslo. Today Oslo is Norway's political, economic, industrial, and cultural capital.

PLANNING YOUR TIME

The Norwegian capital is home to just over 500,000 inhabitants, but it boasts great museums, top restaurants, and a stunning new Opera House. Check out the Royal Palace, at the end of Karl Johans Gate (Oslo's main thoroughfare) before ambling down to Aker Brygge, the trendy area by the harbor. Then visit Vigeland's statue park or the Holmenkollen ski jump, before ending your day in one of Grünerløkka's many buzzing restaurants.

GETTING HERE & AROUND

BY AIR

Oslo Airport in Gardermoen, 45 km (28 mi) north of the city, is a 50-minute car or taxi ride (around NKr 700 a trip) from Oslo's city center. From Oslo S Station, it's a 19-minute ride by Flytoget (express train, NKr 170 one-way, or NKr 160 if booked online), with trains scheduled every 10 minutes (from 5:36 AM to 12:56 AM every day).

Flybussen buses, operated by SAS, depart from Oslo Bussterminalen Galleriet daily every 20 minutes and reach Oslo Airport approximately

40 minutes later (NKr 140 one-way, NKr 240 round-trip).

BY BUS & TRAIN

The main bus station, Oslo Bussterminalen, is across from the Oslo S Station. You can buy local bus tickets at the terminal or on the bus. Tickets for long-distance routes on Nor-Way Bussekspress can be purchased here or at travel agencies.

Norway's state railway, NSB (Norges Statsbaner), has two train stations downtown—Oslo Sentralstasjon (Oslo S) and a station at Nationaltheatret. Long-distance trains arrive at and leave from Oslo S Station. Suburban commuter trains use one or the other station.

> ### CURRENCY & EXCHANGE
>
> The Norwegian *krone* (plural: *kroner*) translates as "crown," written officially as NOK. Price tags are seldom marked this way, but instead read "Kr" followed by the amount, such as Kr 10. (In this book, the Norwegian krone is abbreviated NKr.) One krone is divided into 100 øre. At this writing, the rate of exchange was NKr 5.82 to the U.S. dollar and NKr 8.33 to the euro. ATMs are found throughout the city, and many are open 24 hours.

BY PUBLIC TRANSIT

Within Oslo subways and most buses and tramways (*trikk*) start running at 5:30 AM, with the last run after midnight. On weekends there's night service on certain routes. Trips on all public transportation within Oslo cost NKr 34 (NKr 24 if purchased from the machine before boarding), with a one-hour free transfer; tickets that cross municipal boundaries have different rates. It often pays to buy a pass or multiple-travel card, which includes transfers. A day card *(dagskort)* costs NKr 60 and a seven-day pass costs NKr 200. Tickets can be used on subway, bus, or tramway. Trafikanten provides transit information.

The NKr 160 *flexikort*—available at Narvesen newsstands, 7-Eleven stores, tourist offices, T-bane stations, and on some routes—is valid for eight trips by subway, bus, or tramway. The Oslo Pass (from NKr 220 for one day, NKr 320 for two days and NKr 410 for three days) offers unlimited travel on all public transport in greater Oslo, free admission to several sights, discounts at specified restaurants, and other perks. Buy the cards at tourist offices and hotels.

BY TAXI

Taxis are radio dispatched from a central office, and it can take up to 30 minutes to get one during peak hours. There are also taxi stands all over town, usually near Narvesen newsstands and kiosks. It's not unheard-of to wait for more than an hour at a taxi stand in the wee hours of the morning. Never take pirate taxis; all registered taxis should have their roof lights on when they're available. Rates start at around NKr 40 for hailed or rank cabs and NKr 60 for ordered taxis, depending on the time of day and the company.

ESSENTIALS

Air Contacts **SAS Scandinavian Airlines** (⊕ *www.flysas.com*).

Emergency Services **Police, fire, and ambulance** (☎ *112*).

Taxi Contacts Oslo Taxi (☎ *02323*). Taxi 2 (☎ *800–TAXI2*).

Visitor Information Visit Norway (⊕ *www.visitnorway.com*).

EXPLORING OSLO

Karl Johans Gate, starting at Oslo Sentralstasjon (Oslo Central Station, also called Oslo S Station and simply *Jernbanetorget,* or "railway station" in Norwegian) and ending at the Royal Palace, forms the backbone of downtown Oslo. Many major museums and historic buildings lie between the parallel streets of Grensen and Rådhusgata. West of downtown are Frogner and Majorstuen, residential areas with fine restaurants, shopping, cafés, galleries, and the Vigeland sculpture park. Southwest is the Bygdøy Peninsula, with a castle and five interesting museums that honor aspects of Norway's taste for exploration.

Northwest of town is Holmenkollen, with its stunning bird's-eye view of the city and the surrounding fjords, a world-famous ski jump and museum, and three historic restaurants. On the more multicultural east side, where a diverse immigrant population lives alongside native Norwegians, are the Munch Museum and the Botanisk Hage og Museum (Botanical Gardens and Museum). The trendy neighborhood of Grünerløkka, with lots of cafés and shops, is northeast of the center.

DOWNTOWN: THE ROYAL PALACE TO CITY HALL

Although the city region is huge (454 square km [175 square mi]), downtown Oslo is compact, with shops, museums, historic buildings, restaurants, and clubs concentrated in a small, walkable center that's brightly illuminated at night.

➐ Det Kongelige Slottet *(The Royal Palace).* Located at one end of Karl Johans Gate, this vanilla-and-cream-color neoclassical palace was completed in 1848. Although generally closed to the public, the palace is open for guided tours (in English) in summer Monday to Thursday and Saturday at 12:00, 2 and 2:20 PM, and Friday and Sunday at 2, 2:30, and 4 PM. The rest of the time, you can simply admire it from the outside. An equestrian statue of Karl Johan, King of Sweden and Norway from 1818 to 1844, stands in the square in front of the palace. ✉*Drammensvn. 1, Sentrum* ☎*22–04–89–25* ⊕*www.kongehuset.no* 🎫*Tour NKr 95* ⊘*Mid-June–mid-Aug. (guided tours only).*

➎ Ibsenmuseet. Famed Norwegian dramatist Henrik Ibsen, known for *A Doll's House, Ghosts,* and *Peer Gynt,* among other classic plays, spent his final years here, in the apartment on the second floor, until his death in 1906. Take a guided tour by well-versed and entertaining Ibsen scholars. Afterward, visit the museum's exhibition of Ibsen's drawings and paintings and first magazine writings. ✉*Henrik Ibsens gate 26, Sentrum* ☎*22–12–35–50* ⊕*www.norskfolkemuseum.no/ibsenmuseet* 🎫*NKr 85* ⊘*Tues.–Sun., guided tours at 11, noon, 1, 2 and 3; June–Aug., additional guided tours at 4 and 5.*

➑ Nasjonalgalleriet *(National Gallery.)* The gallery, part of the National ★ Museum of Art, Architecture and Design, houses Norway's largest

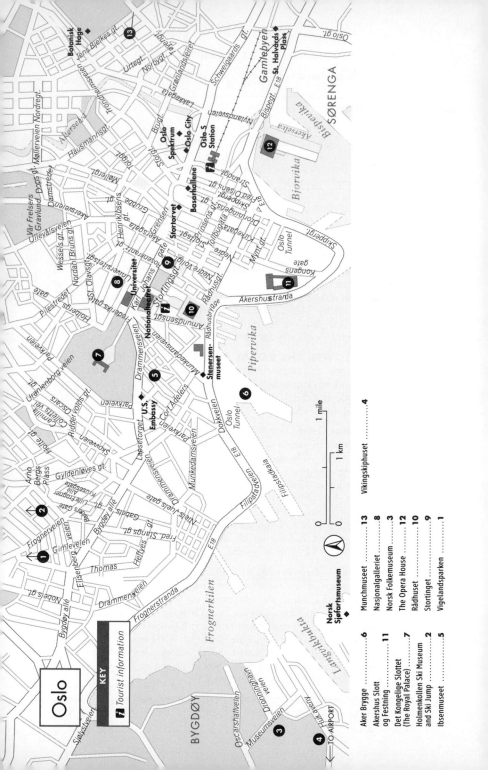

collection of art created before 1945. The deep-red Edvard Munch room holds such major paintings as *The Dance of Life,* one of two existing oil versions of *The Scream,* and several self-portraits. Classic landscapes by Hans Gude and Adolph Tidemand—including *Bridal Voyage on the Hardangerfjord*—share space in galleries with other works by major Norwegian artists. The museum also has works by Monet, Renoir, Van Gogh, and Gauguin. ⊠ *Universitetsgt. 13, Sentrum* ☎ *21–98–20–00* ⊕ *www.nasjonalmuseet.no* ⊠ *Free* ⊙ *Tues., Wed., and Fri. 10–6; Thurs. 10–7; weekends 11–5.*

13

⑩ **Rådhuset** *(City Hall).* This redbrick building is best known today for the awarding of the Nobel peace prize, which takes place here every December. In 1915 the mayor of Oslo made plans for a new City Hall, and ordered the clearing of slums that stood on the site. The building was finally completed in 1950. Inside, many museum-quality master-pieces are on the walls. After viewing the frescoes in the Main Hall, walk upstairs to the Banquet Hall to see the royal portraits. In the East Gallery, Per Krogh's mosaic of a pastoral scene covers all four walls, making you feel like you're part of the painting. On festive occasions the Central Hall is illuminated from outside by 60 large spotlights that simulate daylight. ⊠ *Rådhuspl., Sentrum* ☎ *23–46–16–00* ⊕ *www. radhusets-forvaltningstjeneste.oslo.kommune.no* ⊠ *NKr 40* ⊙ *May–Aug., daily 9–6; Sept.–Apr., daily 9–4.*

FodorśChoice
★

⑨ **Stortinget** *(Norwegian Parliament).* Informative guided tours of this clas-sic 1866 building are conducted daily in summer, and on Saturday the rest of the year. In front of the Parliament building the park benches of Eidsvolls plass are a popular meeting and gathering place. ⊠ *Karl Johans gate 22, Sentrum* ☎ *23–31–31–80* ⊕ *www.stortinget.no* ⊠ *Free* ⊙ *Guided tours in English and Norwegian July–mid-Aug., weekdays at 10, 11:30, and 1; mid-Aug.–June, Sat. at 10, 11:30, and 1.*

KVADRATUREN, AKERSHUS CASTLE & AKER BRYGGE
The Kvadraturen is the oldest part of Oslo still standing. Aker Brygge, on the other side of Pipervika, is one of the trendiest areas in Oslo, with several shopping centers and dozens of bars and restaurants lining the waterfront. On a sunny summer day you can sit and relax at one of the many terraces, or hop on a boat for a trip on the Oslo Fjord. The new Opera House, a bit farther to the east in Bjørvika, opened in April 2008. Designed by renowned Norwegian architect firm Snøhetta, the white-marble and glass building has been an instant hit with the public, and quickly established itself as Oslo's new must-see landmark.

⑥ **Aker Brygge.** This area was the site of a disused shipbuilding yard until redevelopment saw the addition of residential town houses and a com-mercial sector. Postmodern steel and glass buildings dominate the sky-line now. The area has more than 40 restaurants and 60 shops, including upmarket fashion boutiques, as well as pubs, cinemas, theaters, and an indoor shopping mall. There is outdoor dining capacity of 2,500 as well as an open boulevard for strolling. Service facilities include banks, drug-stores, and a parking lot for 1,600. ⊠ *Aker Brygge* ☎ *22–83–26–80*

⊕*www.akerbrygge.no* ✉*Free* ⊙*Shopping hrs weekdays 10–8, Sat. 10–6.*

⓫ **Akershus Slott og Festning** *(Akershus Castle and Fortress).* Dating to 1299, this stone medieval castle and royal residence was developed into a fortress armed with cannons by 1592. After that time, it withstood a number of sieges and then fell into decay. It was finally restored in 1899. Summer tours take you through its magnificent halls, the castle church, the royal mausoleum, reception rooms, and banqueting halls. ✉*Akershus Slott, Festningspl., Sentrum* ☎*23–09–35–53* ⊕*www. nasjonalefestningsverk.no/akershus* ✉*Grounds and concerts free, castle NKr 65* ⊙*Grounds: daily 6 AM–9 PM. Castle: May–end Aug., Mon.–Sat. 10–6, Sun. 12:30–4; mid-Sept.–Apr., Thurs. tours at 1. Guided tours: May–mid-Sept., daily at 11, 1, and 3; mid-Sept.–Apr., Thurs. at 1.*

⓭ **Munchmuseet** *(Munch Museum).* Edvard Munch, Norway's most famous artist, bequeathed his enormous collection of works (about 1,100 paintings, 3,000 drawings, and 18,000 graphic works) to the city when he died in 1944. The museum (east of the city center in Tøyen, an area in which Edvard Munch spent many of his years in Oslo) is a monument to his artistic genius, housing the largest collection of his works and changing exhibitions. ✉*Tøyengt. 53, Tøyen* ☎*23–49–35–00* ⊕*www. munch.museum.no* ✉*NKr 75* ⊙*June–Aug., daily 10–6; Sept.–May, Tues.–Fri. 10–6, weekends 11–5.*

⓬ **The Opera House.** Oslo's brand-new opera house opened with great fan-
★ fare on April 12, 2008, in the presence of the Norwegian King and a host of celebrities. The white marble and glass building, designed by renowned Norwegian architect firm Snøhetta, is a stunning addition to the Oslo waterfront, and the pride of Norwegians. It doesn't just look good; accoustics inside the dark-oak auditorium are excellent too. The program includes ballet, orchestra concerts, rock, and opera. ✉*Kirsten Flagstads pl. 1* ☎*21–42–21–00 or 815–444–88* ⊕*www.operaen.no* ✉*Free* ⊙*Guided tours available every day.*

FROGNER, MAJORSTUEN & HOLMENKOLLEN

Frogner and Majorstuen combine classic Scandinavian elegance with contemporary European chic. Hip boutiques and galleries coexist with embassies and ambassadors' residences on the streets near and around Bygdøy Allé. Holmenkollen, the hill past Frogner Park, has the famous ski jump and miles of ski trails.

❷ **Holmenkollen Ski Museum and Ski Jump.** A distinctive part of the city's skyline, Oslo's ski jump holds a special place in the hearts of Norwegians. Originally built in 1892, it has been rebuilt 18 times since, the last time for the World Championships in 1982, and is still a popular site for international competitions. It attracts a million visitors, both skiers and non, every year. The ski museum and jump tower are currently closed because the hill is being rebuilt for the Nordic World Ski Championships 2011, and Holmenkollen will reopen in January 2010. In the meantime, you can stop at the nearby **visitor center** (✉*Kollenstua* ☎*22–92–32–00*) in Kollenstua, where you'll be able to learn more about the history of Holmenkollen, watch archive movies taken during earlier competitions, and see models of the hill over the years, as well as the impressive model of the new Holmenkollen Ski Jump currently under construction. ✉*Kongevn. 5, Holmenkollen* ☎*22–92–32–00* ⊕*www.skiforeningen.no* ✉*NKr Free* ☉*Oct.–Apr., Mon.–Fri. 10–3, Sat.–Sun. 10–4; May–Sept., daily 10–4.*

1 Vigelandsparken *(Vigeland's Park).* Also known as Frogner Park, Vigelandsparken has 212 bronze, granite, and wrought-iron sculptures by Gustav Vigeland (1869–1943). Most of the stunning park sculptures are placed on a nearly 1-km-long (½ mi-long) axis and depict the stages of life: birth to death, one generation to the next. There is also a museum on-site for those wishing to delve deeper into the artist's work. ✉*Kirkevn., Frogner* ☎*23–49–37–00* ⊕*www.vigeland.museum. no* ✉*Free; NKr 50 for the museum* ☉*Daily.*

13

BYGDØY

Several of Oslo's best-known historic sights are concentrated on the Bygdøy Peninsula (west of the city center), as are several beaches, jogging paths, and the royal family's summer residence. The most pleasant way to get to Bygdøy—available from May to September—is to catch Ferry 91 from the rear of the Rådhuset on Pier 3. Times vary, so check with Trafikanten (☎177) for schedules. Year-round, Bus 30 will take you there from Stortingsgata at Nationaltheatret.

3 Norsk Folkemuseum *(Norwegian Folk Museum).* One of the largest openair museums in Europe, this is a perfect way to see Norway in a day. From the stoic stave church to farmers' houses made of sod, the old buildings here span Norway's regions and history as far back as the 14th century. Indoors, there's a fascinating display of folk costumes. The displays of richly embroidered, colorful *bunader* (national costumes) from every region includes one set at a Telemark country wedding. The museum also has stunning dragon-style wood carvings from 1550 and some beautiful *rosemaling,* or decorative painted floral patterns. If you're visiting in summer, inquire about Norwegian Evening, a summer program of folk dancing, guided tours, and food tastings. On Sundays in December, the museum holds Oslo's largest Christmas market. ✉*Museumsvn. 10, Bygdøy* ☎*22–12–37–00* ⊕*www.norsk folke.museum.no* ✉*NKr 95* ☉*Mid-Sept.–mid-May, weekdays 11–3, weekends 11–4; mid-May–mid-Sept., daily 10–6.*

4 Vikingskiphuset *(Viking Ship Museum).* The Viking legacy in all its glory lives on at this classic Oslo museum. Chances are you'll come away fascinated by the three blackened wooden Viking ships *Gokstad, Oseberg,* and *Tune,* which date to AD 800. Discovered in Viking tombs around the Oslo fjords between 1860 and 1904, the boats are the best-preserved Viking ships ever found and have been exhibited since the museum's 1957 opening. Avoid summertime crowds by visiting at lunchtime. ✉*Huk Aveny 35, Bygdøy* ☎*22–13–52–80* ⊕*www.ukm. uio.no/vikingskipshuset* ✉*NKr 50* ☉*May–Sept., daily 9–6; Oct.–Apr., daily 10–4.*

WHERE TO EAT

Many Oslo chefs have developed menus based on classic Norwegian recipes but with exciting variations, like Asian or Mediterranean cooking styles and ingredients. You may read about "New Scandinavian" cuisine on some menus. It combines seafood and game from Scandinavia with spices and sauces from any other country.

Spend at least one sunny summer afternoon harborside at Aker Brygge eating in one of the many seafood restaurants and watching the world go by. Or buy steamed shrimp off the nearby docked fishing boats and plan a picnic in the Oslo fjords or Vigeland or another of the city's parks. Note that some restaurants close for a week around Easter, in July, and during the Christmas holiday season. Some restaurants are also closed on Sundays.

WHAT IT COSTS IN NORWEGIAN KRONER					
	¢	$	$$	$$$	$$$$
Restaurants	under 130	130—200	200–270	270–350	over 350

Restaurant prices are based on the median main course price at dinner, excluding tip.

DOWNTOWN: ROYAL PALACE TO THE PARLIAMENT

$$$$ ✕ **Baltazar Ristorante & Enoteca.** Celebrating its 10th anniversary in 2008, this gem of a restaurant, tucked away in the arcades behind the cathedral, is well worth seeking out. There is a gourmet venue upstairs, serving top modern Italian food, and a more informal enoteca downstairs (with more informal prices; think $ to $$), offering simpler, more traditional dishes. In summer, tables spill out on the big outside terrace and you can enjoy your meal alfresco. Whichever floor you decide to visit, the antipasti are always superb, and so is the home-made pasta; veal with tuna sauce and Parmesan is a delicious starter. The stunning wine list features some 450 Italian wines, with all regions well represented, and a choice of vintages for several labels. Our favorite Italian in Oslo. ✉Dronningensgt. 27, Domkirkeparken ☎23–35–70–60 ⊕www.baltazar.no ⊟AE, DC, MC, V ⊘Closed Sun., July, and for Easter and Christmas.

$ ✕ **Dinner.** The simple name belies the fact that this is one of the best places in Oslo for Chinese food, particularly spicy Szechuan and Cantonese dishes, and seafood in general. Peking duck is a specialty here, or, for a lighter meal, try the delectable dim sum basket. ✉Stortingsgt. 22, Sentrum ☎23–10–04–66 ⊕www.dinner.no ⊟AE, DC, MC, V ⊘No lunch Sun.

¢ ✕ **Vegan.** This innovative buffet-style vegetarian restaurant was established in 1938, and is one of Europe's oldest. Its success has been such that it recently had to move to bigger premises, and it now accommodates 100 customers. Vegan is a godsend for vegetarians in a town with meat- and fish-centric menus. A wide variety of meals are on offer here, including vegetarian pasta dishes, pizza, curries, salads, soups and quiches. ✉Akersgt. 74, Sentrum ☎91–18–88–32 ⊕www.vegano.no ⊟AE, DC, MC, V ⊘Closed Sat.

KVADRATUREN & AKER BRYGGE

$$ ✕**Det Gamle Rådhus.** Housed in Oslo's first town hall, in a building dating back to 1641, this is the city's oldest restaurant. Its reputation is based mostly on traditional fish and game dishes such as the moose entrecote or the Røros reindeer. An absolute must, if you're lucky enough to be visiting at the right time, is the house specialty, the pre-Christmas lutefisk platter. The backyard has a charming outdoor area for dining in summer. ✉*Nedre Slottsgt. 1, Sentrum* ☎*22–42–01–07* ⊕*www.gamle raadhus.no* ⊟*AE, DC, MC, V* ⊘*Closed Sun.*

> ## GRÜNERLØKKA
>
> Once a simple working-class neighborhood north of the center, Grünerløkka has undergone a revival since the '90s and now hosts a number of trendy bars, cafés, eateries, eclectic galleries, and gift stores. Popular with young people, the area is now known as Oslo's little Greenwich Village. Take a shopping tour here during the day or come for dinner and a drink at night; the two main drags are Markveien & Thorvald Meyers Gate.

13

$$–$$$ ✕**Solsiden.** With its high ceiling and huge windows, this restaurant,
★ housed in a former warehouse right by the harbor, is the perfect place for dinner on a sunny summer evening. Heed the locals and splash out on a *plateau de fruits de mer* (the house specialty) or opt for the well-priced menu of the day. Dishes like turbot with mustard purée and lobster sauce, or halibut with mushroom risotto and blue mussel sauce, come highly recommended. The desserts, from passionfruit Pavlova to strawberry clafoutis, don't disappoint either. There is also a good wine list with decent by-the-glass options. The restaurant attracts the odd celebrity—the Rolling Stones and Bruce Springsteen all ate here recently. Fifteen years since opening it still draws sizeable crowds, so book ahead. ✉*Søndre Akershus Kai 34* ☎*22–33–36–30* ⊕*www.solsiden.no* ⊟*AE, DC, MC, V* ⊘*Open in summer only, from mid-May to end of Aug., dinner only.*

TØYEN & GRØNLAND

¢ ✕**Asylet.** This popular pub right by Grønland Torg serves homemade
☉ traditional Norwegian food in an atmospheric setting. The building, which dates from the 1730s, was once an orphanage. The big lunch menu features a good selection of smørbrød, and Christmas specialties are served in December. There is a fireplace inside, and a beer garden in which to enjoy the sun in summer. ✉*Grønland 28* ☎*22–17–09–39* ⊕*www.asylet.no* ⊟*AE, DC, MC, V.*

GRÜNERLØKKA

$$ ✕**Markveien Mat og Vinhus.** This restaurant in the heart of the Grünerløkka district serves fresh French-inspired cuisine. It's a relaxed, artsy place with a bohemian clientele. Paintings cover the yellow walls, and the tables are laid with white linen. Veal and baked halibut are both house specialties, but it's the stunning wine list that draws the crowds—it was recently singled out by Wine Spectator magazine as among the best in Oslo. ✉*Tor-*

vbakkgt. 12, entrance on Markvn. 57, Grünerløkka ☎22–37–22–97 ⊕*www.markveien.no* ⊟*AE, DC, MC, V* ⊗*Closed Sun.*

FROGNER & MAJORSTUEN

$$$$ ✕**Bagatelle.** Chef and owner Eyvind Hellstrøm has established an inter-
Fodor'sChoice   national reputation for his modern Norwegian cuisine and superb ser-
★   vice. Bagatelle attracts the who's who of Oslo society, and is widely
recognized as the city's best restaurant. Artworks by contemporary
artists accent the understated, elegant dining room. Three-, five-, and
seven-course menus change daily. The lobster is always a standout.
⊠*Bygdøy Allé 3, Frogner* ☎22–12–14–40 ⊕*www.bagatelle.no* ⊟*AE,
DC, MC, V* ⊗*Closed Sun. Mid-July–mid-Aug. No lunch.*

$$ ✕**Hos Thea.** An intimate yet lively dining experience awaits in this
white-and-blue restaurant that recently celebrated 20 years in busi-
ness. From the open kitchen, owner Sergio Barcilon and the other chefs
often serve the French and Spanish food themselves. The small menu
lists four or five choices for each course, but every dish is superbly
prepared. Noise levels can be high late at night, as can smoke levels
on the terrace. ⊠*Gabelsgt. 11, entrance on Drammensvn., Skillebekk*
☎22–44–68–74 ⊕*www.hosthea.no* ⊗*Reservations essential* ⊟*AE,
DC, MC, V* ⊗*No lunch.*

HOLMENKOLLEN

$$$–$$$$ ✕**De Fem Stuer.** Near the famous Holmenkollen ski jump, in the historic
★   Holmenkollen Park Hotel Rica, this restaurant serves first-rate food in
a grand setting, with stunning views over Oslo. Chef Are Nortvedt's
modern Norwegian dishes blend classic ingredients with more exotic
ones; just try not to be intrigued by the pigeon with Japanese noodles
or the pan-fried Arctic char with pickled shiitake mushrooms and caviar
sauce. For something a bit more traditional, opt for the four-course
menu called A Taste of Norway—you'll get exactly that. ⊠*Holmen-
kollen Park Hotel Rica, Kongevn. 26, Holmenkollen* ☎22–92–27–34
Jacket and tie ⊟*AE, DC, MC, V.*

WHERE TO STAY

Most lodgings are central, just a short walk from Karl Johans Gate.
Many are between the Royal Palace and Oslo S Station, with the newer
ones closer to the station. For a quiet stay, choose a hotel in either
Frogner or Majorstuen, elegant residential neighborhoods behind the
Royal Palace and within walking distance of downtown. Television and
phones can be expected in most Oslo hotel rooms, and Internet con-
nection is found in all but budget hotels. Most hotels in Oslo include
either a full or continental breakfast in their rates.

WHAT IT COSTS IN NORWEGIAN KRONER				
¢	$	$$	$$$	$$$$
HOTELs	under 900	900–1,300	1,300–1,700	1,700–2,100	over 2,100

Hotel prices are for two people in a standard double room in high season.

DOWNTOWN: ROYAL PALACE TO THE PARLIAMENT

¢ ⊡ **Cochs Pensjonat.** A stone's throw from the Royal Palace, this no-frills guesthouse has reasonably priced, comfortable, but rather spartan rooms. Most of the 88 rooms have private bathrooms, but check when you make your reservation; some also have kitchenettes. **Pros:** central location; good value for money. **Cons:** basic facilities; value rooms are tiny; no on-site restaurant. ⊠*Parkvn. 25, Majorstuen* ☎*23–33–24–00* ⊕*www.cochspensjonat.no* ⋑*88 rooms* ☖*In-room: no phone, no TV (some)* ▤*MC, V* ⦿*EP.*

$$$–$$$$ ⊡ **Hotel Continental.** With its elegant early-20th-century facade, the
Fodor'sChoice Continental is an Oslo landmark that continues to attract with stylish
★ rooms, gracious service, and two wonderful restaurants—Theatercafeen, an Oslo landmark, and since 2006, Annen Etage, another great choice for dinner. Opposite Nationaltheatret and close to many cafés, clubs, and movie theaters, the hotel is ideal for leisure as well as business travelers. Dagligstuen (The Sitting Room) has original Munch lithographs on the walls, and is a popular meeting place for drinks and quiet conversation. **Pros:** exemplary service; beautiful, well appointed rooms; brand-new gym. **Cons:** steep prices; corridors are a bit dated (though they're due to begin refurbishment by press time). ⊠*Stortingsgt. 24–26, Sentrum* ☎*22–82–40–00* ⊕*www.hotel-continental.no* ⋑*155 rooms, 23 suites* ☖*In-room: Internet. In-hotel: 2 restaurants, bars, gym* ▤*AE, DC, MC, V* ⦿*EP.*

$ ⊡ **Thon Hotel Cecil.** A short walk from Parliament, this modern hotel is a relatively inexpensive option in the center of town. Although the rooms are basic, they are perfectly suited to the active, on-the-go traveler. The second floor opens onto a plant-filled atrium, the hotel's "activity center." In the morning it's a breakfast room, but in the afternoon it becomes a lounge, serving coffee, juice, and fresh fruit. **Pros:** friendly staff; good value for money; the heated shower floors are a nice touch. **Cons:** Internet connection is not included in the rate; facilities are limited. ⊠*Stortingsgt. 8, Sentrum* ☎*23–31–48–00* ⊕*www.thonhotels.no/cecil* ⋑*111 rooms, 2 suites* ☖*In-room: Internet. In-hotel: bar* ▤*AE, DC, MC, V* ⦿*BP.*

KVADRATUREN AND OSLO S STATION

$$–$$$ ⊡ **Clarion Royal Christiania Hotel.** What was once bare-bones hous-
★ ing for 1952 Olympians is now a luxury, 100% no-smoking hotel. Although the original plain exterior remains, the interior is more modern, designed using feng shui principles. Rooms have white walls and mahogany furniture. **Pros:** welcoming lobby; organic breakfast; on-site parking. **Cons:** the size can seem daunting to some; the location—right by a busy intersection—is convenient but not particularly charming. ⊠*Biskop Gunnerus gt. 3* ☎*23–10–80–00* ⊕*www.royalchristiania.no* ⋑*412 rooms, 91 suites* ☖*In-hotel: restaurant, bar, pool, gym, spa* ▤*AE, DC, MC, V* ⦿*BP.*

$$$–$$$$ ⊡ **Radisson SAS Plaza Hotel.** Standing out from other buildings on the city's skyline, northern Europe's largest hotel is the jewel of the Radisson SAS chain. The understated, elegant rooms have gilded fixtures and marble, and many have spectacular views. Since it's next to Oslo S Station, buses and other local transit are convenient. **Pros:** great top-

13

floor bar; fit-for-a-king breakfast buffet; luxuriously grand bathtubs **Cons:** crowds outside the Oslo Spektrum, right opposite the hotel, a nuisance when there is a concert on; elevators seem to have a mind of their own when it comes to heading up or down; the huge reception area looks more like a station concourse than a hotel lobby. ⊠ *Sonja Henies pl. 3* ☎ *22–05–80–00* ⊕ *www.radissonsas.com* ⇥ *673 rooms, 20 suites* ⚐ *In-room: Internet. In-hotel: 2 restaurants, bars, pool, gym* ⊟ *AE, DC, MC, V* ⊙| *BP.*

NIGHTLIFE

Into the early hours, people are usually out on Karl Johans Gate. Aker Brygge, the wharf area, has many bars and some nightclubs, attracting mostly tourists, couples on first dates, and other people willing to spend extra for the waterfront location. Grünerløkka and Grønland have even more bars, pubs, and cafés catering to a younger crowd. A more mature upmarket crowd ventures out to the less busy west side of Oslo, to Frogner and Bygdøy.

Drinking out is very expensive, starting at around NKr 70 for a beer or a mixed drink. Some bars in town remain quiet until 11 PM or midnight when the first groups of *forschpiel* partiers arrive. For nightlife listings, pick up a copy of the free monthly paper *Natt og Dag* or Friday's edition of *Avis 1.*

BARS & LOUNGES

With its 1970s theme, **Café Con Bar** (⊠ *Brugt. 11, Grønland* ☎ *22–05–02–00* ⊕ *www.cafeconbar.no*) is one of Oslo's trendy crowd-pleasers. The kitchen closes at 10 and guest DJs spin on weekends. For cheap beer and an informal crowd, visit the popular student hangout **Stargate Pub** (⊠ *Grønlandsleiret 33, Grønland* ☎ *22–04–13–77*) at Brugata, just alongside the bridge. The **Bibliotekbaren og Vinterhaven** at the Hotel Bristol (⊠ *Kristian IVs gt. 7, Sentrum* ☎ *22–82–60–00*) is a stylish hanghout with old-fashioned leather armchairs, huge marble columns, and live piano music.

Serious beer drinkers may find **Oslo Mikrobryggeriet** (⊠ *Bogstadvn. 6, Majorstuen* ☎ *22–56–97–76* ⊕ *www.omb.no*) worth a stop. Eight different beers are brewed on the premises, including the increasingly popular Oslo Pils. The **Underwater Bar** (⊠ *Dalsbergstien 4, St. Hanshaugen* ☎ *22–46–05–26* ⊕ *www.underwater.no*) is a pub with an undersea theme, complete with fish tanks and scuba gear, and live opera on Tuesday and Thursday at 9 PM.

CAFÉS

As a mark of Oslo's growing cosmopolitanism, the city now has a continental café culture, with bohemian coffeehouses and chic cafés. Grünerløkka especially has lots of cafés to suit every taste; they're great for people-watching and whiling away summer afternoons.

Following in the tradition of the grand continental cafés, the **Theatercafe** in the Continental Hotel (⊠ *Stortingsgt. 24–26, Sentrum* ☎ *22–82–40–50* ⊕ *www.theatercafeen.no*) is an Oslo institution. **Kaffebrenneriet**

(⊠*Storgt. 2, Sentrum* ☎*22–42–01–31* ⊕*www.kaffebrenneriet.no*) is Oslo's answer to Starbucks, with good coffee and shops throughout town. The **Tea Lounge** (⊠*Thorvald Meyers gt. 33B, Grünerløkka* ☎*22–37–07–07* ⊕*www.tealounge.no*) is stylish and serves alcoholic and nonalcoholic tea drinks. Bohemian **Fru Hagen** (⊠*Thorvald Meyers gt. 40, Grünerløkka* ☎*45–49–19–04* ⊕*www.fruhagen.no*) has classical-looking chandeliers and elegant velvet sofas.In the west of the city, **Clodion Art Café** (⊠*Bygdøy Allé 63, Frogner* ☎*22–44–97–26* ⊕*www.clodion.no*) with its children's play area, is popular with families.

13

DANCE CLUBS

Most dance clubs open late, so the beat doesn't really start until midnight. Many establishments have a minimum age for entry, which can be as high as 25. There's also usually a cover of around NKr 50–NKr 100.

Oslo's beautiful people congregate at **Cosmo** (⊠*Ruseløkkvn. 14, Sentrum* ☎*40–00–33–97*), Norway's biggest club, bar, and lounge, spread over three floors. Another one of Oslo's best clubs is **Sikamikanico** (⊠*Mollergata 2, Sentrum* ☎*22—41—44–09* ⊕*www.sikamikanico.no*), with DJs playing anything from hip-hop to progressive house and jazz. Expect big crowds and a big party atmosphere.Serious clubbers should try **Skansen** (⊠*Rådhusgt. 25, Sentrum* ☎*22–42–28–88*) for house and techno music.

SHOPPING

Oslo is the best place in the country for buying anything Norwegian. Popular souvenirs include knitwear, wood and ceramic trolls, cheese slicers, boxes with rosemaling, gold and silver jewelry, items made from pewter, smoked salmon, caviar, *akvavit* (a white spirit), chocolate, and goat cheese. Established Norwegian brands include Porsgrund porcelain, Hadeland and Magnor glass, David Andersen jewelry, and Husfliden handicrafts. You may also want to look for popular, classical, or folk music CDs; English translations of Norwegian books; or clothing by a Norwegian designer.

Prices in Norway, as in all of Scandinavia, are generally much higher than in other European countries. Prices of handmade articles, such as knitwear, are controlled, making comparison shopping useless. Otherwise, shops have both sales and specials—look for the words *salg* and *tilbud*.

SHOPPING NEIGHBORHOODS

Basarhallene, the arcade behind the cathedral, is worth a browse for glass and crystal and handicrafts made in Norway. Walk 15 minutes west of the city center and you can wander up the tree-lined Bygdøy Allé and browse the fashionable **Frogner** and **Bygdøy** areas, which are brimming with modern and antique furniture stores, interior design shops, food shops, art galleries, haute couture, and Oslo's beautiful people. The streets downtown around **Karl Johans Gate** draw many of Oslo's shoppers. The concentration of department stores is especially high in this part of town. **Majorstuen** starts at the T-bane station with the same name and proceeds down Bogstadveien to the Royal Palace. Every Saturday a flea market is open at **Vestkanttorget,** at Amaldus Nilsens plass near Frognerparken. **Grünerløkka,** a 15-minute walk north of the center, is blooming with trendy new and bohemian fashion boutiques, and many quirky little shops.

KNITWEAR Norway is famous for its colorful hand-knit wool sweaters, and even mass-produced (machine-knit) models are of top quality. Prices are regulated, and they are always lower than buying a Norwegian sweater abroad. **Maurtua Husflid** (⊠ *Akershusstranda, Sentrum* ☎ *22–41–31–64* ⊕ *www.maurtua.no*), on the waterfront beneath Akershus Castle, has a large selection of sweaters and blanket coats.

Spain

Parque del Buen Retiro, Madrid

WORD OF MOUTH

"Just returned [from a] two-week trip to Spain. . . . My wish list of things to visit was, I thought, extremely modest, but we ended up hitting just a few major sights and opting for more time to sit at cafés, stroll, and relax. In more than a dozen trips to Europe, this might be the most reluctant I've ever been to leave somewhere or for a trip to be finished. Spain absolutely surpassed all of the high expectations . . . the scenery, the food, the people, the architecture . . . all of it was truly spectacular."

—Chicago Heather

WHAT'S WHERE

1 Madrid. Its boundless energy makes sights and sounds larger than life. The Prado, Reina Sofia, and Thyssen-Bornemisza museums pack thousands of Spanish and European masterworks into half a mile of art heaven, while the cafes and wine bars of Plaza Mayor and Cava Baja are always buzzing. Sunday's crowded flea market in El Rastro is thick with overpriced oddities. Toledo, an hour from Madrid by bus, is a city of dreamy spires and rambling, narrow streets perched on the banks of the Río Tajo.

2 Barcelona. Its Rambla is a mass of strollers, artists, street entertainers, vendors, and vamps, all preparing you for the city's startling architectural landmarks. Antoni Gaudí's sinuous Casa Milà and unique Sagrada Familia church are masterpieces of the Moderniste movement.

3 Bilbao. Greener, cloudier and stubbornly independent in spirit, the Basque region is a country within a country, proud of its own language, one of Europe's oldest. Its capital, Bilbao, overlooking the Bay of Biscay, is a hotbed of architectural endeavour, exciting urban regeneration projects, and culinary excellence.

4 Andalusia. Eight provinces, five of which are coastal (Huelva, Cádiz, Málaga, Granada, and Almería) and three that are landlocked (Seville, Córdoba, and Jaén) compose this southern autonomous community known for its Moorish influences. Highlights are the romantic Alhambra and seductive Seville.

FRANCE

Bay of Biscay

Gijón
Oviedo
Ribadesella Santander
San Sebastián
Roncesvalles
ANDORRA
Figueres

PICOS DE EUROPA
León
Bilbao **3**
Vitoria
Logroño
Pamplona
Jaca
PYRENEES
Huesca
Manresa
Vic
COSTA BRAVA

Benavente
Palencia
Burgos
Soria
Tudela
Zaragoza
Lleida
Montserrat
Barcelona **2**

Valladolid
Zamora
Tordesillas
Duero
SIERRA DE GUADARRAMA
Calatayud
Daroca
Alcañiz
Tarragona
COSTA DORADA

Salamanca
Adanero
Segovia
Medinaceli
Caminreal
Tortosa

Ávila
Guadalajara
Monreal del Campo
Vinaròs
La Jana

SIERRA DE GREDOS
MADRID **1**
Teruel
Vinaròs
TO MINORCA →

Tajo
Toledo
Cuenca
Castellón de la Plana
COSTA DEL AZAHAR
Balearic Sea
Palma

Talavera de la Reina
Aranjuez
Tarancón
Sagunto
Majorca

Trujillo Guadalupe
Alcázar de San Juan
Requena
Valencia
Ibiza
BALEARIC ISLANDS

Tajo
Guadiana
Abenójar
Valdepeñas
Albacete
Eivissa

Almadén
Alcaraz
Hellín
COSTA BLANCA
Formentera

SIERRA MORENA
Ubeda
Alicante
Minorca
Ciutadella
Mahón

Córdoba
Linares
Bailén Baeza
Jaén
Cazorla
Orihuela
Elche
Murcia
Manga del Mar Menor

Guadalquivir
Écija
Baena
Granada **4**
SIERRA NEVADA
Cartagena
Mediterranean Sea

Antequera
Loja
Nerja
Almería
COSTA DE ALMERIA

Ronda
Málaga
Motril
COSTA DEL SOL
ALGERIA

Marbella
Algeciras
Gibraltar

MOROCCO

0   100 miles
0   150 km

THE WORD *SPAIN* CONJURES IMAGES of flamenco dancers, bullfighters, and white hillside villages. Beyond these traditional associations you'll find that Spain is really several countries within a country, with cutting-edge art museums, green highland valleys, soaring cathedrals, medieval towns, designer cuisine, raucous nightlife, and an immense treasury of paintings and sculptures.

At the center of it all, sprawling over the parched plains of Castille, is one of Europe's liveliest capitals, Madrid. Beyond its designer boutiques and chic restaurants, you'll discover the noisy cafés and rustic taverns of a typical Castilian town. Food lovers will appreciate the fact that delicious seafood is packed into lorries and imported daily from the coast. Arts lovers will swoon over the world-famous Prado, Reina Sofía, and Thyssen-Bornemisza museums, all collected on one half-mile stretch of leafy promenade. Madrid inherited its capital status from Toledo, a short side trip away, in whose labyrinthine *casco antiguo* (Old Town) Jews, Moors, and Christians lived and worked together to inspire Europe's intellectual and cultural renaissance. A virtual open-air museum, Toledo is often referred to as Spain's spiritual capital.

Nowhere are tradition and history more beautifully preserved than in Andalusia, where rolling hills dotted with whitewashed villages and olive trees seem to encapsulate the romance of Spain. Jutting out into the Atlantic, Cadiz, with its gold-domed cathedral and ramshackle streets, is almost African in appearance, while Cordoba, center of Western art and culture between the 8th and 11th centuries, is dominated by the ochre-red archways of its mosque-cum-cathedral, scene of an epic clash of Baroque and Moorish styles. Granada is synonymous with the opulent, frescoed rooms, and the spectacular snow-capped backdrop of its Alhambra Palace. Seville is known for flamenco, for beautiful women in ruffled polka-dot dresses at its April Fair, and the solemn procession of penitents during Semana Santa (Holy Week). Go to Andalusia's famous tiled bars and you can expect generous mounds of fried fish and shellfish—called *frituras*—olives, and serrano ham, all washed down with the sherries of Jerez.

Catalonia, with a population of 6 million Catalan speakers, is Spain's richest and most industrial region. Its capital, Barcelona, rivals Madrid for power, and edges it in culture and style. Its tree-lined streets, Art Nouveau architecture, and renovated waterfront still gleam from a facelift received for the 1992 Olympic Games, an event that not only focused the world's attention on this Mediterranean port but also provided the city with new museums, sports facilities, and restaurants. Barcelona's museums, including the recently revamped Picasso Museum and innovative science extravaganza, CosmoCaixa, receive around 14 million visitors a year. The spirit of Moderniste architect Antoni Gaudí lives on in the surreal spires of his work-in-progress cathedral, La Sagrada Familia, and in the Catalan passion for radical, playful design, illustrated in the MACBA modern art center.

Industrious, artistic Bilbao, famous for its cuisine and fierce sense of local identity, is now beginning to emerge from the shadows of Barcelona and

Madrid. Here you'll find one of the world's most talked-about buildings, Frank Gehry's Guggenheim, as well as mouthwatering culinary concoctions—Bilbao's pintxo chefs are taking the world by storm with their innovative cooking.

Since joining the European Union (EU) in 1986, Spain has come up to speed technologically with rest of Western Europe. The most obvious improvement for travellers are the nationwide network of superhighways and the high-speed AVE trains linking Madrid with Barcelona and Còrdoba and Seville. Spain's progress, happily, has not nudged aside cherished old traditions: Shops still shut at around 2 PM for a siesta and three-hour lunches are commonplace. Young adults often still live with their parents until marriage. Bullfights continue despite protests from animal-rights activists. And flamenco is being fused successfully with everything from rock music to rap.

14

Most exciting for any visitor is the national insistence on enjoying life. Whether it be strolling in the park with the family on a Sunday afternoon, lingering over a weekday lunch, or socializing with friends until dawn, living life to its fullest is what Spain does best.

GETTING HERE AND AROUND

BY AIR
Most flights into Spain go to Madrid or Barcelona, though certain destinations in Andalusia are popular with carriers travelling from England and other European countries. Flying time from New York to Madrid is about 7 hours; from London, it's just over two hours. Regular nonstop flights serve Spain from major cities in the eastern United States; flying from other North American cities usually involves a stop. There are a few solid package flight options for travel to and within Spain. If you buy a round-trip transatlantic ticket on Iberia, you might want to purchase an Iberiabono air pass, which provides access to economy-class travel across Spain. The pass must be purchased before arrival in Spain and all flights must be booked in advance.

Contacts Air Europa (☎ *888/238–7672 or 902/401501* ⊕ *www.air-europa.com*). **FlightPass** (☎ *888/321–4737 EuropebyAir* ⊕ *www.europebyair.com*). **Iberia** (☎ *800/ 772–4642* ⊕ *www.iberia.com*).

BY BOAT
Regular car ferries connect the United Kingdom with northern Spain. Brittany Ferries sails from Plymouth to Santander, P&O European ferries from Portsmouth to Bilbao. You can catch a ferry or catamaran from Morocco into southern Spain, or on a cruise Barcelona is Spain's main port-of-call, but other ports-of-call include Málaga, Cádiz, Gibraltar, Valencia, A Coruña, and stops on the Balearic Islands.

U.K. to Spain Brittany Ferries (☎ *0870/907–6103 in U.K., 94/236–0611 in Spain* ⊕ *www.brittany-ferries.com*). **Direct Ferries (booking site)** (⊕ *www.directferries. co.uk*). **P&O European Ferries** (☎ *0871/664–5645 in U.K., 902/020461 in Spain* ⊕ *www.poferries.com*).

TOP REASONS TO GO

La Alhambra. Nothing can prepare you for the Moorish grandeur of Andalusia's greatest monument. The ornamental palace is set around sumptuous courtyards and gardens with bubbling fountains, magnificent statues, and fragrant flower beds.

Toledo. Castile's crowning glory, Toledo is often cited as Spain's spiritual capital. This open-air city is an architectural tapestry of medieval buildings, churches, mosques, and synagogues threaded by narrow cobbled streets and squares.

La Sagrada Familia, Barcelona. *The* symbol of Barcelona, Gaudí's extraordinary unfinished cathedral should be included on everyone's must-see list. The pointed spires, with organic shapes that resemble a honeycombed stalagmite, give the whole city a fairytale quality.

Guggenheim, Bilbao. All swooping curves and rippling forms, the innovative museum—one of architect Frank Gehry's most breathtaking projects—was built on the site of the city's former shipyards, its inspiration the shape of a ship's hull.

Museo del Prado, Madrid. Set in a magnificent neoclassical building on one of the capital's most elegant boulevards, the Prado is Spain's answer to the Louvre and a regal home to Spanish masterpieces.

Festa de Sant Jordi, Barcelona. Valentine's Day with a Catalan twist. Celebrating St. George, the patron saint of Barcelona, who saved a princess from a dragon, local tradition dictates that men buy their true love a rose and, since the festival shares a date with International Book Day, women reciprocate by buying their beau a book.

Drink like a Madrileño. In the capital an aperitif is a crucial part of daily life. In fact, there are more bars per square mile than in any other capital in Europe, so finding a venue poses no great challenge.

Feria de Abril, Seville. Seville's April Fair features sultry, foot-stomping señoritas wearing traditional, brilliantly colored dresses. From 1 to 5 every afternoon, Sevillan society parades around in carriages drawn by glossy high-stepping horses.

In Spain Balearia (☎ 902/160180 ⊕ www.balearia.com). **FRS** (☎ 956/681830 ⊕ www.frs.es). **Trasmediterránea** (☎ 902/454645 ⊕ www.trasmediterranea.com). **Grimaldi** (☎ 902/531333 ⊕ www.grimaldi-ferries.com).

BY BUS

The bus is usually much faster than the train, and bus fares tend to be lower. Service is extensive, though less frequent on weekends. Various bus companies service the country, but Spain's major national bus line is Alsa-Enatcar (tel:902/422242)

In Spain Alsa-Enatcar (⊠ Estación Sur de Autobuses, Calle Méndez Álvaro, Madrid ☎ 902/422242 ⊕ www.enatcar.com). **Eurolines Spain** (☎ 902/405040 ⊕ www.eurolines.es). **Movelia (booking site)** (☎ 902/335533 ⊕ www.movelia.es).

Bus Tours Marsans (⊠ Gran Vía 59, Madrid ☎ 902/306090). **Pullmantur** (⊠ Pl. de Oriente 8, Madrid ☎ 91/541–1805 ⊕ www.pullmantur-spain.com).

BY TRAIN

RENFE trains are economical if they're short routes with convenient schedules (such as the commuter trains around Madrid and Barcelona); or take the AVE, Spain's high-speed train, which is wonderfully fast—it can go from Madrid to Seville in under three hours. Tip-Rail passes like the Eurailpass must be purchased before you leave for Europe.

Contacts RENFE (☎ *902/157507* ⊕ *www.renfe.es*).

BY CAR

Large chain car-rental companies all have branches in Spain, though the online outfit Pepe Car may have better deals. Its modus operandi is the earlier you book, the less you pay. In Spain most vehicles have a manual transmission. Children under 10 may not ride in the front seat and seat belts are mandatory for all passengers. Follow speed limits. Rental cars are frequently targeted by police monitoring speeding vehicles.

14

National Car Rental/Atesa (☎ *800/227–7368, 902/100101 in Spain* ⊕ *www.nationalcar.com*). **Pepe Car** (☎ *807/414243 in Spain* ⊕ *www.pepecar.com*)

ABOUT THE RESTAURANTS

MEALS & MEALTIMES

Most restaurants in Spain do not serve breakfast (*desayuno*); for coffee and carbs, head to a bar or *cafetería*. Outside major hotels, which serve morning buffets, breakfast in Spain is usually limited to coffee and toast or a roll. Lunch (*comida* or *almuerzo*) traditionally consists of an appetizer, a main course, and dessert, followed by coffee and perhaps a liqueur. Between lunch and dinner the best way to snack is to sample some *tapas* (appetizers) at a bar; normally you can choose from quite a variety. Dinner (*cena*) is somewhat lighter, with perhaps only one course. In addition to an à la carte menu, most restaurants offer a daily fixed-price menu (*menú del día*) consisting of a starter, main plate, drink (wine, beer, water, soda, etc), and usually either coffee or dessert at a very attractive price (usually between €6 and €12). If your waiter does not suggest the menú del día when you're seated, ask for it—"*Hay menú del día, por favor?*" Restaurants in many of the larger tourist areas will have the menú del día posted outside. The menú del día is traditionally offered only at lunch, but increasingly it's also offered at dinner in popular tourist destinations.

Mealtimes in Spain are later than elsewhere in Europe, and later still in Madrid and the southern region of Andalusia. Lunch starts around 2 or 2:30 (closer to 3 in Madrid), and dinner after 9 (later in Madrid). Weekend eating times, especially dinner, can begin upward of about an hour later. In areas with heavy tourist traffic, some restaurants open a bit earlier.

PAYING

Credit cards are widely accepted in Spanish restaurants, but some smaller establishments do not take them. If you pay by credit card and you want to leave a small tip above and beyond the service charge, leave it in cash.

RESERVATIONS & DRESS

Regardless of where you are, it's a good idea to make a reservation. For popular restaurants, book as far ahead as you can (often 30 days), and reconfirm as soon as you arrive. We mention dress only when men are required to wear a jacket or a jacket and tie.

WINES, BEER & SPIRITS

Apart from its famous wines, Spain produces many brands of lager, the most popular of which are San Miguel, Moritz, Cruzcampo, Aguila, Voll Damm, Mahou, and Estrella. Jerez de la Frontera is Europe's largest producer of brandy, and is a major source of sherry. Catalonia produces most of the world's *cava* (sparkling wine). Spanish law prohibits the sale of alcohol to people under 18.

WHAT IT COSTS IN EUROS				
¢	$	$$	$$$	$$$$
Restaurants in Madrid & Barcelona	Under €8	€8–€12	€13–€18	€19–€25	over €25
Restaurants elsewhere	Under €6	€6–€10	€11–€15	€16–€20	over €20

Prices are per person for a main course at dinner.

ABOUT THE HOTELS

For a slice of Spanish culture, check out the paradores; to indulge your pastoral fantasies, a *casa rural* (country house), Spain's version of a bed-and-breakfast. On the other end of the spectrum are luxurious high-rise hotels along the coastline, and chain hotels in the major cities.

In big cities or popular tourist areas it's best to book in advance. In smaller towns and rural areas you can usually find something on the spot, except when local fiestas are on—for those dates you may have to book months in advance.

WHAT IT COSTS IN EUROS				
¢	$	$$	$$$	$$$$
Hotels in Madrid & Barcelona	Under €50	€50–€80	€81–€150	€151–€225	over €225
Hotels elsewhere	Under €40	€40–€60	€61–€100	€101–€180	over €180

Prices are for two people in a standard double room in high season, including taxes and service. Assume that hotels operate on the European Plan (EP, with no meals provided) unless we note that they use the Breakfast Plan (BP).

PLANNING YOUR TIME

Spain is anchored by two great cities, Madrid and Barcelona. If you have time you should visit both, but if you're in Spain for a week or less, you're better off choosing one and planning excursions to the surrounding region. Madrid will give you world-class art and much more of a sense of a workaday Spanish city. From here you can also make a short side trip to Spain's capital of old, Toledo, where two thousand years of architectural styles clash, from the Roman to the Visigothic to the Baroque and beyond. Cosmopolitan Barcelona has Gaudí, Catalan cuisine, and its special Mediterranean atmosphere. This city is in itself worth longer than just a several-day sojourn, and has the Pyrenees at hand for side trips. The northern city of Bilbao, across the Pyrenees, is a must for foodies and culture vultures, thanks to its pintxo bars and cutting-edge architecture.

14

If you're interested in the Moorish influence on Spain or seduced by the rhythm of flamenco, make time for a trip south to Andalusia. The area is large, however, and if you don't have more than a week, it will be hard to visit all of its principal attractions, but absolutely essential are stops in the old Moorish strongholds of Granada, Seville, and Cordoba, all easily accessible to each other by car, bus, or rail.

An ideal way to organize a trip around Spain if arriving by air in Madrid would be to start in Madrid before moving south to discover Andalusia and then heading north-east to Barcelona and Bilbao, before returning to Madrid. If arriving by car or train from France, begin with Bilbao, before heading to Barcelona and then doing Madrid and the South.

MADRID

Sitting on a plateau 2,165 feet above sea level and bordered to the north by a mountain range, swashbuckling Madrid celebrates itself and life in general around the clock. A vibrant crossroads, Madrid—the Spanish capital since 1561—has an infectious appetite for art, music, and epicurean pleasure, and it's turned into a cosmopolitan, modern urban center while fiercely preserving its traditions. The rapid political and economic development of Spain following the arrival of democracy in 1977, the integration of the country in the European Union a decade later, and the social upheaval brought in by the many immigrants settling here after the new millennium have put Madrid back on the world stage with an energy redolent of its 17th-century golden age, when painters and playwrights swarmed to the flame of Spain's brilliant royal court.

PLANNING YOUR TIME

Madrid's most valuable art treasures are all on display within a few blocks of Paseo del Prado. This area is home to the Prado, with its astounding selection of masterworks from Velázquez, Goya, El Greco, and others; the Centro de Arte Reina Sofía, with an excellent collection of contemporary art; and the Thyssen Museum, with a singular collection that stretches from the Renaissance to the 21st century. Each can take a number of hours to explore, so it's best to alternate museum visits

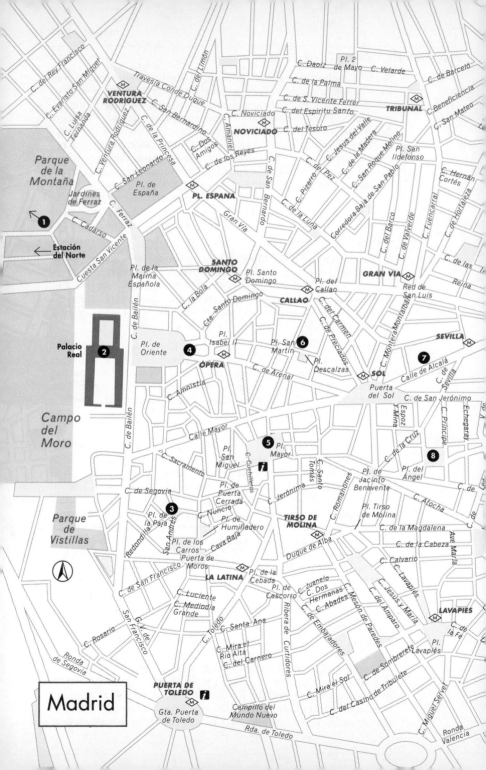

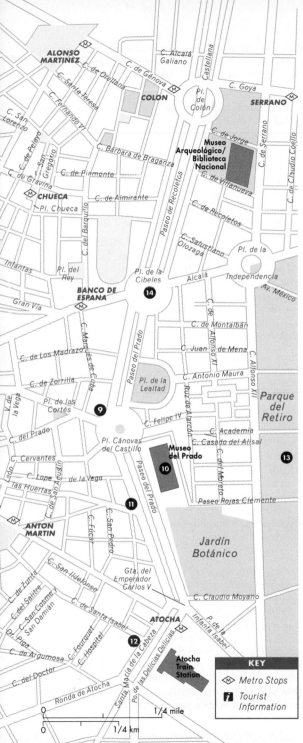

CaixaForum **11**

Centro de Arte Reina Sofía **12**

Convento de las Descalzas Reales **6**

Ermita de San Antonio de la Florida
(Goya's tomb) **1**

Museo del Prado **10**

Museo Thyssen-Bornemisza **9**

Palacio Real **2**

Parque del Buen Retiro **13**

Plaza de la Cibeles **14**

Plaza de la Paja **3**

Plaza Mayor **5**

Plaza Santa Ana **8**

Real Academia de Bellas Artes
de San Fernando **7**

Teatro Real **4**

with less overwhelming attractions. If you're running short on time and want to pack everything in, replenish your energy at any of the tapas bars or restaurants in the Barrio de las Letras (behind the Paseo del Prado, across from the Prado Museum).

Any visit to Madrid should include a walk in the old area between Puerta del Sol and the Royal Palace.

GETTING HERE & AROUND
BY AIR
Madrid is served by Madrid Barajas Airport (12 km [7 mi] east of the city), which, with a capacity of up to 70 million passengers a year, is Europe's fourth-largest airport. It has four terminals and a bus service, *lanzadera,* that connects all of them, departing every three minutes. It goes from Terminal 1 to Terminal 4 in 10 minutes.

The fastest way to get to all four terminals is the subway line number 8 (*Línea 8*). Terminal 2 (T-2) and the more remote Terminal 4 (T-4) each have a subway stop, and from Terminal 2 you can walk or take the bus to the other two terminals. The metro runs every few minutes between Nuevos Ministerios (where you can check your luggage) and Barajas Airport; it costs €1 plus a €1 airport supplement that you can pay at any subway stop or once you get on or leave from either of the two airport subway stops. The journey takes 20–30 minutes.

For a mere €1 there's also a convenient bus to Avenida de América, where you can catch the subway or a taxi to your hotel. From Avenida de América you can also take Bus 204, which takes you straight to T-4, or Bus 200, which takes you to the other three terminals. Buses leave every 15 minutes between 5:20 AM and 11:30 PM (slightly less often very early or late in the day).

In bad traffic, the 20-minute taxi ride to Madrid can take the better part of an hour, but it makes sense if you have a lot of luggage. Taxis normally wait outside the airport terminal near the clearly marked bus stop; expect to pay up to €25, more in heavy traffic (and more from Terminal 4, which is farther out), including a surcharge that goes up each year. Make sure the driver is on the meter—off-the-meter "deals" will surely cost you more. Some hotels offer shuttle service in vans; check with yours when you reserve.

BY BUS
Madrid has no central bus station; buses are generally less popular than trains (though they sometimes can be faster). Most of southern and eastern Spain (including Toledo) is served by the Estación del Sur. Auto Res also operates buses from there to other destinations such as Cuenca, Extremadura, Salamanca, and Valencia. From the Estación de Avenida de América, two companies, Continental Auto and Alsa (which also has buses departing from the south station), serve mostly the north and the east, respectively. Alsa, for instance, runs two buses to Barcelona daily from Estación del Sur, and almost 20 from Avenida de América. There are also several smaller stations in Madrid, so inquire at travel agencies for the one serving your destination.

Estación de Avenida de América and Estación del Sur have subway stops (Avenida de América and Méndez Álvaro) that leave you right at the station. If you intend to go to Segovia, take the subway to the Príncipe Pío stop, get the Paseo de la Florida exit, and walk on the left-hand side of the street until you get to La Sepulvedana bus station. La Sepulvedana bus company serves Segovia, Ávila, and La Granja. Herranz goes to El Escorial (it leaves from the Intercambiador de Moncloa; that is, the Moncloa bus station) and from there to the Valle de los Caídos. La Veloz has service to Chinchón, and Aisa goes to Aranjuez and from there to Chinchón.

Red city buses run from about 6 AM to 11:30 PM and cost €1 per ride. After midnight, buses called *búhos* ("night owls") run out to the suburbs from Plaza de Cibeles for the same price. Signs at every stop list all other stops by street name, but they're hard to comprehend if you don't know the city well. Pick up a free route map from the transportation authority's (EMT) kiosks on the Plaza de Cibeles or the Puerta del Sol, where you can also buy a 10-ride ticket called a Metrobus (€6.15)—it's also valid for the subway.

14

Bus Stations Estación del Avenida de América (✉ *Av. de América, 9, Salamanca* ☎ *No phone* Ⓜ *Avenida de América*). **Estación del Sur** (✉ *Méndez Álvaro s/n, Atocha* ☎ *91/468-4200* ⊕ *www.estaciondeautobuses.com* Ⓜ *Méndez Álvaro*). **Intercambiador de Moncloa** (✉ *Princesa 89, Moncloa* ☎ *No phone* Ⓜ *Moncloa*).

BY CAR

Felipe II made Madrid the capital of Spain because it was at the very center of his peninsular domains, and to this day many of the nation's highways radiate from Madrid like the spokes of a wheel. Originating at Kilometer 0—marked by a brass plaque on the sidewalk of the Puerta del Sol—these highways include the A6 (Segovia, Salamanca, Galicia); A1 (Burgos and the Basque Country); the A2 (Guadalajara, Barcelona, France); the A3 (Cuenca, Valencia, the Mediterranean coast); the A4 (Aranjuez, La Mancha, Granada, Seville); the A42 (Toledo); and the A5 (Talavera de la Reina, Portugal). The city is surrounded by the M30 (the inner ring road), and the M40 and M50 (the outer ring roads), from which most of these highways are easily picked up. To fight the heavy traffic leaving and getting into Madrid, the government set up an infrastructure plan that includes radial toll highways (marked R1, R2, R3, R4, and R5) that bypass the major highways by 50 to 60 km (31 to 37 mi), as well as the A41, a new toll highway connecting Madrid and Toledo. These options are worth considering, especially if you're driving on a summer weekend or a holiday.

That said, driving in Madrid is best avoided. Parking is nightmarish, traffic is heavy almost all the time, and the city's daredevil drivers can be frightening. August is an exception; the streets are then largely emptied by the mass exodus of madrileños on vacation.

BY FOOT, METRO & TAXI

Once in Madrid you'll find that all the historic neighborhoods are in close proximity and can best be enjoyed when explored on foot. However, the metro, which runs frequently (open 6 AM–1:30 AM), is a fast and—at

€1 no matter how far you travel—cheap alternative. Taxis are another good deal, and are easily hailed on the street—except when it rains or on weekend nights, when they're exceedingly hard to come by.

BY TRAIN

Madrid has three main train stations: Chamartín, Atocha, and Norte, the last primarily for commuter trains. Remember to confirm which station you need when arranging a trip. Generally speaking, Chamartín, near the northern tip of Paseo de la Castellana, serves destinations north and west, including San Sebastián, Burgos, León, Oviedo, La Coruña, and Salamanca, as well as France and Portugal and the night train to Barcelona. Atocha, at the southern end of Paseo del Prado, serves towns near Madrid, including El Escorial, Segovia, and Toledo, and southern and eastern cities such as Seville, Málaga, Córdoba, Valencia, and Castellón, and the daily trains to Barcelona. Atocha also sends AVE (high-speed) trains to Córdoba, Seville, Zaragosa, Toledo, Segovia, Huesca, Lleida, Málaga, and Barcelona. For some destinations, however, you can depart from either Atocha or Chamartín (this is the case for Toledo, Segovia, El Escorial, and Alcalá de Henares).

Train Information **Estación de Atocha** (⊠ *Glorieta del Emperador Carlos V, Atocha* ☎ *91/528–4630* Ⓜ *Atocha*). **Estación Chamartín** (⊠ *Agustín de Foxá s/n, Chamartín* ☎ *91/315–9976* Ⓜ *Chamartín*). **Estación de Príncipe Pío (Norte)** (⊠ *Paseo de la Florida s/n, Moncloa* ☎ *902/240202 RENFE* Ⓜ *Príncipe Pío*). **RENFE** (☎ *902/240202* ⊕ *www.renfe.es*).

EXPLORING MADRID

The real Madrid is not to be found along major arteries like the Gran Vía and the Paseo de la Castellana. To find the quiet, intimate streets and squares that give the city its true character, duck into the warren of villagelike byways in the downtown area that extends 2 km (1 mi) from the Royal Palace to the Parque del Buen Retiro and from Plaza de Lavapiés to the Glorieta de Bilbao. Broad *avenidas,* twisting medieval alleys, grand museums, stately gardens, and tiny, tile taverns are all jumbled together, creating an urban texture so rich that walking is really the only way to soak it in.

⓫ **CaixaForum** An early 20th-century power station turned into an arts complex by Swiss architects Jacques Herzog and Pierre de Meuron—who also transformed a factory into London's Tate Modern—is the fourth vortex in what was formerly Madrid's triangle of great art institutions—the Prado, the Reina Sofía, and the Thyssen-Bornemisza museums. ⊠ *Paseo del Prado 36, Cortes* ☎ *91/330–7300* ⊕ *obrasocial. lacaixa.es/centros/caixaforummadrid_es.html* ⊠ *Free* ☉ *Daily 10–8*

⓬ **Centro de Arte Reina Sofía** *(Queen Sofía Art Center).* Madrid's museum of modern art is in a converted hospital, the classical granite austerity of which is somewhat relieved (or ruined, depending on your point of view) by the playful pair of glass elevator shafts on its facade. The museum's showpiece is Picasso's *Guernica,* in the center hall on the second floor. The huge black-and-white canvas depicts the horror of the

Nazi Condor Legion's bombing of the ancient Basque town of Gernika in 1937, during the Spanish civil war. The room in front of *Guernica* has surrealist works, with six canvases by Miró. Room 10 belongs to Salvador Dalí, hung in three *ámbitos* (areas). ⊠*Santa Isabel 52, Atocha* ☎*91/467–5062* ⊕*museoreinasofia.mcu. es* 🖭*€6, free Sat. after 2:30 and all day Sun.* ☉*Mon. and Wed.–Sat. 10–9, Sun. 10–2:30.*

❻ Convento de las Descalzas Reales *(Convent of the Royal Discalced, or Barefoot, Nuns)*. This 16th-century building was restricted for 200 years to women of royal blood. Its plain, brick-and-stone facade hides paintings by Zurbarán, Titian, and Brueghel the Elder—all part of the dowry the novices had to provide when they joined the monastery—as well as a hall of sumptuous tapestries crafted from drawings by Peter Paul Rubens. ⊠*Plaza de las Descalzas Reales 3, Palacio* ☎*91/454–8800* 🖭*€5, €6 combined ticket with Convento de la Encarnación* ☉*Tues.–Thurs. and Sat. 10:30–12:45 and 4–5:30, Fri. 10:30–12:30, Sun. 11–1:30.*

❶ Ermita de San Antonio de la Florida (Goya's tomb). Built from 1792 to 1798 by the Italian architect Francisco Fontana, this neoclassical church was financed by King Carlos IV, who also commissioned Goya to paint the vaults and the main dome: he took 120 days to complete his assignment, painting alone, with only the help of a little boy who would stir the pigments for him. ⊠*Glorieta de San Antonio de la Florida 5, Príncipe Pío* ☎*91/542–0722* 🖭*Free* ☉*Tues.–Fri. 9:30–8, Sun. 10–2.*

❿ Museo del Prado *(Prado Museum)*. When the Prado was commissioned FodorśChoice by King-Mayor Carlos III, in 1785, it was meant to be a natural-science ★ museum. The king wanted the museum, the adjoining botanical gardens, and the elegant Paseo del Prado to serve as a center of scientific enlightenment. By the time the building was completed in 1819, its purpose had changed to exhibiting the art gathered by Spanish royalty since the time of Ferdinand and Isabella. The museum was completed in 2007, after five years of work. It features a massive new wing together with a new building around the remains of the Cloister of the San Jerónimo el Real, designed by Rafael Moneo, that has resurrected long-hidden works by Zurbarán and Pereda and more than doubled the number of paintings on display from the permanent collection.

The Prado's jewels are its works by the nation's three great masters: Francisco Goya, Diego Velázquez, and El Greco. The museum also holds masterpieces by Flemish, Dutch, German, French, and Italian artists, collected when their lands were part of the Spanish Empire. The museum benefited greatly from the anticlerical laws of 1836, which forced monasteries, convents, and churches to forfeit many of their artworks for public display.

Enter the Prado via the Goya entrance, with steps opposite the Ritz hotel, or by the less-crowded Murillo door opposite the Jardín Botánico. The layout varies (grab a floor plan), but the first halls on the left, coming from the Goya entrance (7A to 11 on the second floor, or *planta primera*), are usually devoted to **17th-century Flemish painters,** including

Peter Paul Rubens (1577–1640), Jacob Jordaens (1593–1678), and Antony van Dyck (1599–1641).

Room 12 introduces you to the meticulous brushwork of **Velázquez** (1599–1660) in his numerous portraits of kings and queens. Look for the magnificent *Las Hilanderas (The Spinners)*, evidence of the artist's talent for painting light. The Prado's most famous canvas, Velázquez's *Las Meninas (The Maids of Honor)*, combines a self-portrait of the artist at work with a mirror reflection of the king and queen in a revolutionary interplay of space and perspectives. Picasso was obsessed with this work and painted several copies of it in his own abstract style, now on display in the Picasso Museum in Barcelona.

The south ends of the second and top floors (*planta primera* and *planta segunda*) are reserved for **Goya** (1746–1828), whose works span a staggering range of tone, from bucolic to horrific. Among his early masterpieces are portraits of the family of King Carlos IV, for whom he was court painter—one glance at their unflattering and imbecilic expressions, especially in the painting *The Family of Carlos IV,* reveals the loathing Goya developed for these self-indulgent, reactionary rulers. His famous side-by-side canvases, *The Clothed Maja* and *The Nude Maja,* may represent the young duchess of Alba, whom Goya adored and frequently painted. No one knows whether she ever returned his affection. The adjacent rooms house a series of idyllic scenes of Spaniards at play, painted as designs for tapestries.

Goya's paintings took on political purpose starting in 1808, when the population of Madrid rose up against occupying French troops. *The 2nd of May* portrays the insurrection at the Puerta del Sol, and its even more terrifying companion piece, *The 3rd of May,* depicts the nighttime executions of patriots who had rebelled the day before. The garish light effects in this work typify the romantic style, which favors drama over detail, and make it one of the most powerful indictments of violence ever committed to canvas.

Goya's "black paintings" are dark, disturbing works, completed late in his life, that reflect his inner turmoil after losing his hearing and his deep embitterment over the bloody War of Independence. These are copies of the monstrous hallucinatory paintings Goya made with marvelously free brushstrokes on the walls of his house by southern Madrid's Manzanares River, popularly known as *La Quinta del Sordo* (the deaf one's villa). Having grown gravely ill in his old age, Goya was deaf, lonely, bitter, and despairing; his terrifying *Saturn Devouring One of His Sons* (which Goya displayed in his dining room!) communicates the ravages of age and time.

Near the Goya entrance, the Prado's ground floor (*planta baja*) is filled with 15th- and 16th-century Flemish paintings, including the bizarre proto-surrealist masterpiece *Garden of Earthly Delights* by Hieronymus Bosch (circa 1450–1516). Next come Rooms 60A, 61A, and 62A, filled with the passionately spiritual works of **El Greco** (Doménikos Theotokópoulos, 1541–1614), the Greek-born artist who lived and worked in Toledo. El Greco is known for his mystical, elongated forms and faces—a style that was shocking to a public accustomed to strictly representational images. Two of his greatest paintings, *The Resurrection* and *The Adoration of the Shepherds*, are on view here. Before you leave, stop in the 14th- to 16th-century Italian rooms to see Titian's *Portrait of Emperor Charles V* and Raphael's exquisite *Portrait of a Cardinal.* ⊠*Paseo del Prado s/n, Cortes* ☎*91/330–2800* ⊕*www.TK.org* ✉ *€6, free Mon.-Sat., 6pm-8pm, Sun. 5am-8pm* ☉*Tues.–Sat., 9am-8pm, Sun, 9am-7pm. Closed Monday.*

❾ Museo Thyssen-Bornemisza. The newest—it first opened in 1992; the second part of the collection, that of Baron Thyssen's wife, which is of a lesser quality, was added in 2004—of Madrid's three major art centers, the Thyssen occupies spacious galleries washed in salmon pink and filled with natural light in the late-18th-century Villahermosa Palace, finished in 1771. This ambitious collection of almost 1,000 paintings traces the history of Western art with examples from every important movement, from the 13th-century Italian Gothic through 20th-century American pop art.

Fodor's Choice ★

⊠*Paseo del Prado 8, Cortes* ☎*91/369–0151* ⊕*www.museothyssen. org* ✉*Permanent collection €6, temporary exhibition €5, combined €9* ☉*Tues.–Sun. 10–7.*

❷ Palacio Real. The Royal Palace was commissioned in the early 18th century by the first of Spain's Bourbon rulers, Felipe V, on the same strategic site where Madrid's first Alcázar (Moorish fortress) was built in the 9th century. Outside, you can see the classical French architecture on the graceful **Patio de Armas:** King Felipe was obviously inspired by his childhood days at Versailles with his grandfather Louis XIV. ⊠*Calle Bailén s/n, Palacio* ☎*91/454–8800* ✉*€8, guided tour €9; Royal Armory only €3.40* ☉*Apr.–Sept., Mon.–Sat. 9–6, Sun. 9–3; Oct.–Mar., Mon.–Sat. 9–5, Sun. 9–2.*

Fodor's Choice ★

⓭ Parque del Buen Retiro *(The Retreat).* Once the private playground of royalty, Madrid's crowning park is a vast expanse of green encompassing formal gardens, fountains, lakes, exhibition halls, children's play areas, outdoor cafés, and a **Puppet Theater.** The park is especially lively on weekends, when it fills with street musicians, jugglers, clowns, gypsy fortune-tellers, and sidewalk painters along with hundreds of Spanish families out for a walk. ⊠*Puerta de Alcalá, Retiro* ✉*Free.*

⓮ Plaza de la Cibeles. A tree-lined walkway runs down the center of Paseo del Prado to the grand Plaza de la Cibeles, where the famous Fuente de la Cibeles (Fountain of Cybele) depicts the nature goddess driving a chariot drawn by lions. Even more than the officially designated bear and arbutus tree of Madrid's coat of arms, this monument, beautifully lighted at night, has come to symbolize Madrid—so much so that during the civil war patriotic madrileños risked life and limb to sandbag it as Nationalist aircraft bombed the city. ⊠*Plaza de la Cibeles, Cortes.*

❸ Plaza de la Paja. At the top of the hill, on Costanilla San Andrés, the Plaza de la Paja was the most important square in medieval Madrid. The plaza's jewel is the **Capilla del Obispo** (Bishop's Chapel), built between

1520 and 1530; this was where peasants deposited their tithes, called *diezmas*—literally, one-tenth of their crop. The stacks of wheat on the chapel's ceramic tiles refer to this tradition. Architecturally, the chapel marks a transition from the blockish Gothic period, which gave the structure its basic shape, to the Renaissance, the source of the decorations. ⊠*Plaza de la Paja, La Latina.*

❺ Plaza Mayor. Austere, grand, and often surprisingly quiet compared with the rest of Madrid, this 360-foot-by-300-foot public square—finished in 1620 under Felipe III, whose equestrian statue stands in the center—is one of the largest in Europe. ⊠*Plaza Mayor, Sol.*

❽ Plaza Santa Ana. This plaza was the heart of the theater district in the 17th century—the golden age of Spanish literature—and is now the center of Madrid's thumping nightlife. ⊠*Plaza de Santa Ana s/n, Barrio de las Letras.*

❼ Real Academia de Bellas Artes de San Fernando *(St. Ferdinand Royal Academy of Fine Arts).* Designed by Churriguera in the waning Baroque years of the early 18th century, this museum showcases 500 years of Spanish painting, from Ribera and Murillo to Sorolla and Zuloaga. The tapestries along the stairways are stunning. ⊠*Alcalá 13, Sol* ☎*91/524–0864* ⌨*€3, free Wed.* ☉*Tues.–Fri. 9–7, Sat.–Mon. 9–2:30; free guided tour Wed. 5–7.*

❹ Teatro Real *(Royal Theater).* Built in 1850, this neoclassical theater was long a cultural center for madrileño society. A major restoration project has left it filled with golden balconies, plush seats, and state-of-the-art stage equipment for operas and ballets. ⊠*Plaza de Isabel II, Palacio* ☎*91/516–0660* ⊕*www.teatro-real.com.*

WHERE TO EAT

$$$ ✕**Casa Botín.** The *Guinness Book of Records* calls this the world's oldest
SPANISH restaurant (1725), and Hemingway called it the best. The latter claim may be a bit over the top, but the restaurant *is* excellent and extremely charming (and so successful that the owners opened a "branch" in Miami, Florida). There are four floors of tile and wood-beam dining rooms, and, if you're seated upstairs, you'll pass ovens dating back centuries. Musical groups called *tunas* (mostly made up of students dressed in old costumes) often drop in. Specialties are *cochinillo* (roast pig) and *cordero* (roast lamb). It's rumored that Goya washed dishes here before he made it as a painter. ⊠*Cuchilleros 17, off Plaza Mayor, La Latina* ☎*91/366–4217* ▤*AE, DC, MC, V.*

$$ ✕**Casa Ciriaco.** One of Madrid's most traditional restaurants—host to
SPANISH a long list of Spain's illustrious, from royalty to philosophers, painters, and bullfighters—simple home cooking in an unpretentious environment is the attraction here. You can get a flask of Valdepeñas or a split of a Rioja reserve to accompany the *perdiz con judiones* (partridge with broad beans). The *pepitoria de gallina* (hen in an almond sauce) is another favorite. ⊠*C. Mayor 84, La Latina* ☎*91/559–5066* ▤*DC, MC, V* ☉*Closed Wed. and Aug.*

$$ ✕**Casa Lastra.** Established in 1926, this Asturian tavern is popular with
SPANISH Lavapiés locals. The rustic, half-tile walls are strung with relics from
the Asturian countryside, including wooden clogs, cow bells, sausages,
and garlic. Specialties include *fabada* (Asturian white beans stewed with
sausage), *fabes con almejas* (white beans with clams), and *queso de
cabrales,* aromatic cheese made in the Picos de Europa. Great hunks of
crisp bread and hard Asturian cider complement a hearty meal; desserts
include tangy baked apples. There's an inexpensive fixed-price lunch
menu on weekdays. ✉*Olivar 3, Lavapiés* ☎*91/369–0837* ▭*MC, V*
⊙*Closed Wed. and July. No dinner Sun.*

$$$ ✕**Casa Paco.** This Castilian tavern wouldn't have looked out of place
★ two or three centuries ago and today you can still squeeze past the old,
STEAK zinc-top bar, crowded with madrileños downing shots of Valdepeñas
red wine, and into the tile dining rooms. Feast on thick slabs of red
meat, sizzling on plates so hot the meat continues to cook at your table.
The Spanish consider overcooking a sin, so expect looks of dismay if
you ask for your meat well done (*bien hecho*). You order by weight,
so remember that a *medio kilo* is more than a pound. To start, try the
pisto manchego (La Mancha version of ratatouille) or the Castilian *sopa
de ajo* (garlic soup). ✉*Puerta Cerrada 11, La Latina* ☎*91/366–3166*
⚑*Reservations essential* ▭*DC, MC, V* ⊙*Closed Sun. and Aug.*

$$$ ✕**Citra.** Young cooking wizard Elías Murciano understands that today's
MEDITERRANEAN youngsters can be tomorrow's customers. That's why his sober yet ele-
gant restaurant is separated into two well-defined areas. The bar and the
tables next to the entrance allow casual dining: customers are offered a
selection of sophisticated tapas (smaller portions of the regular courses),
and a five-tapas sampler for €25. The upper floor is where the dar-
ing but balanced creations of this young Venezuelan chef, trained in
top-notch Spanish and French restaurants, achieve their greatest splen-
dor: highlights include red snapper with a light cauliflower purée and
mushroom risotto, superb venison steak, and scallops over caramelized
mushroom. For dessert, don't miss the chocolate soufflé. ✉*C. Castelló,
18, Salamanca* ☎*91/575–2866* ⚑*Reservations essential* ▭*AE, MC,
V* ⊙*Closed Sun.*

$$ ✕**El Cenador del Prado.** The name means "The Prado Dining Room,"
MEDITERRANEAN and the space includes a boldly painted dining room as well as a plant-
filled conservatory, also for dining. There is a separate Baroque salon,
too: a sitting area, mainly occupied by large groups. The innovative
menu has French and Asian touches, as well as exotic Spanish dishes.
The house specialty is *patatas a la importancia* (sliced potatoes fried in
a sauce of garlic, parsley, and clams); other options include black rice
with baby squid and prawns, and sirloin on a pear pastry puff. For dessert, try the *bartolillos* (custard-filled pastries). ✉*C. del Prado 4, Retiro*
☎*91/429–1561* ▭ *DC, V* ⊙*Closed 1 wk in Aug. No dinner Sun.*

$$$$ ✕**Gastro.** At the end of 2007 celebrity chef Sergi Arola—Ferran Adrià's
★ most popular disciple—left La Broche, the restaurant where he vaulted
ECLECTIC to the top of Madrid dining, to go solo. The result is a smaller, less
minimalist though equally modern bistro space crafted to enhance the
dining experience, just thirty customers at a time. At the height of
his career and surrounded by an impeccable team—which now also

Continued on page 748

MINIATURE FOOD, MAXIMUM FLAVOR
TAPAS

An Introduction to

Virtually every day, coworkers head to a tapas bar after work for a *caña* (a 4–6 oz beer) that's almost always paired with a tapa or two. On weeknights, families crowd around tables with drinks and tapas, filling up on several *raciones* or small *cazuelas*. In the evenings, couples out on the town do "tapas crawls," the Spanish version of a pub crawl where *croquetas*

Defining tapas as merely a snack is, for a Spaniard, like defining air as an occasional breathable treat. If that sounds a little dramatic, consider how this bite-sized food influences daily life across all regions and classes throughout Spain.

THE HISTORY OF SHRINKING PORTIONS

The origin of tapas is the stuff of heated tapas bar debates. Various reports cloud the history of when and how it started. Some credit Alfonso X's diet for his delicate stomach. However, the most commonly accepted explanation is that a flat object (be it a slice of bread or a flat card with some nuts or sunflower seeds) was used to cover the rim of wine glasses and keep dive-bombing fruit flies out. (To cover something up is "tapar" in Spanish.)

balance out rich wine. And sometimes the spread for a *pica-pica* (a nibbling marathon) with *tortilla de patata, aceitunas, chorizo,* and *jamon* will cause Spaniards to replace their lunch or dinner outright with tapas. These tiny dishes are such a way of life that a verb had to be created for them: *tapear* (to eat tapas) or *"ir a tapeo"* (to go eat tapas). The staff of life in Spain isn't bread. It's finger food.

TAPAS ACROSS SPAIN

MADRID

It is often difficult to qualify what is authentically from Madrid and what has been gastronomically cribbed from other regions thanks to Madrid's melting-pot status for people and customs all over Spain. While *croquetas, tortilla de patata,* and even *paella* can be served as tapas, *patatas bravas* and *calamares* can be found in almost any restaurant in Madrid. The popular *patatas* are a very simple mixture of fried or roasted potatoes with a "Brava" sauce. The sauce is slightly spicy, which is surprising given a country-wide aversion for dishes with the slightest kick. The *calamares*, fried in olive oil, can be served alone or with alioli sauce, mayonnaise, or—and you're reading correctly—in a sandwich. A slice of lemon usually accompanies your serving.

Tortilla de patata

Calamares

ANDALUSIA

Known for the warmth of its climate and its people, Andalusian bars tend to be very generous with their tapas—maybe in spite of the fact that they aren't exactly celebrated for their culinary inventiveness. But tapas here are traditional and among the best. Many times ordering a drink will bring you a sandwich large enough to make a meal, or a bowl of gazpacho that you could swim in. Seafood is also extremely popular in Andalusia, and you will find tapas ranging from sizzling prawns to small anchovies soaked in vinegar or olive oil.

Pescado frito (fried fish) and *albondigas* (meatballs) are two common tapas in the region, and it's worth grazing multiple bars to try the different preparations. The fish usually includes squid, anchovies, and other tiny fish, deep fried and served as is. Since the bones are very small, they are not removed and considered fine for digestion. If this idea bothers you, sip some more wine. The saffron-almond sauce (*salsa de almendras y azafrán*) that accompanies the meatballs might very well make your eyes roll to the back of your head. And since saffron is not as expensive in Spain as it is in the United States, the meatballs are liberally drenched in it.

Fried anchovy fish

Not incidentally, Spain's biggest export, olives, grows in Andalusia, so you can expect many varieties among the tapas served with your drinks.

Albondigas

BASQUE COUNTRY

More than any other community in Spain, the Basque Country is known for its culinary originality. The tapas, like the region itself, tend to be more expensive and inventive. And since the Basques insist on doing things their way, they call their unbelievable bites *pintxos* (or *pinchos* in Spanish) rather than tapas. *Gildas*, probably the most ordered *pintxo* in the Basque Country, is a simple toothpick skewer composed of a special green pepper, (called *Guindilla Vasca*), an anchovy, and a pitted olive. All the ingredients must be of the highest quality, especially the anchovy, which should be marinated in the best olive oil and not be too salty. Pimientos *Rellenos de Bacalao* (roasted red peppers with cod) is also popular, given the Basque Country's adjacency to the ocean. The festive color of the red peppers and the savoriness of the fish make it a bite-sized Basque delicacy.

Red and green peppers *pintxos*

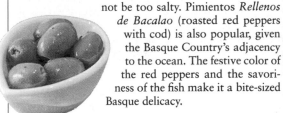

A spread of tapas selections

GET YOUR TAPAS ON

Madrid

El Bocaíto. Here you'll find the best *pescaito frito* (deep-fried whitebait) and a huge assortment of *tostas* (toast points with different toppings). ⊠ *Libertad 6, Chueca.* ☎ *91/532–1219.*

Estay. You'll find delicious *tortilla Espanola con atun y lechuga* (Spanish omelet with tuna and lettuce) and excellent *rabas* (fried calamari). ⊠ *Hermosilla 46, Salamanca* ☎ *91/578–0470.*

Andalusia

El Churrasco. With a name like this, you would expect the meats to be delicious, and they are. But don't miss the *berenjenas crujientes con salmorejo* (crispy fried eggplant slices with thick gazpacho). ⊠ *Romero 16, Judería, Córdoba* ☎ *95/729–0819.*

El Rinconcillo. It's great for the view of the Iglesia de Santa Catalina and a *caldereta de venado* (venison stew). ⊠ *C. Gerona 40, Barrio de la Macarena, Seville* ☎ *95/422–3183.*

The Basque Country

Aloña Berri Bar. The repeat winner of tapas championships, its *contraste de pato* (duck à l'orange) and *bastela de pichón* (pigeon pie) makes foodies swoon. ⊠ *C. Bermingham 24, Gros, San Sebastián* ☎ *94/329–0818.*

Bernardo Etxea. Straight up, freshly prepared classics like fried peppers, octopus, and pimientos with anchovies are served here. ⊠ *C. Puerto 7, Parte Vieja* ☎ *94/342–2055.*

Bite-sized food and drink

A wine pairing

includes a talented and talkative bartender in the lounge—Arola offers only three sampler menus (a short one, a long one, and one entirely made up of cheeses) and more than 600 different wines mostly from small producers, all available by the glass. ⊠ *Zurbano 31, Chamberí* ☎*91/310–2169* ⚑*Reservations essential* ⊟*AE, DC, MC, V.*

$$$$
Fodor's Choice
★
ECLECTIC
✕ **La Terraza—Casino de Madrid.** This rooftop terrace just off Puerta del Sol is in one of Madrid's oldest, most exclusive clubs (the *casino* is a club for gentlemen, not gamblers; the club is for members only, but the restaurant is open to everybody). The food is inspired and overseen by Ferran Adrià, who runs his own famous restaurant, El Bullí, near Roses in Catalonia, and Francisco Roncero's creations closely follow Adrià's trademarks: try any of the light and tasty mousses, foams, and liquid jellies, or indulge in the unique tapas—experiments of flavor, texture, and temperature. There's also a sampler menu. ⊠*Alcalá 15, Sol* ☎*91/521–8700* ⚑*Reservations essential* ⊟*AE, DC, MC, V* ⊘*Closed Sun. and Aug. No lunch Sat.*

$–$$
MEDITERRANEAN
✕ **Nina.** One of the first restaurants to bring sophistication and refinement to a neighborhood best known for its wild and unrestricted spirit, Nina has an airy loftlike interior with high ceilings, exposed brick-and-alabaster walls, and dark hardwood floors. Waiters dressed in black serve the creative Mediterranean cuisine with an Eastern touch to a mostly young, hip crowd. Highlights include goat cheese *milhojas* (pastry puffs), glazed codfish with honey sauce, and venison and mango in a mushroom sauce. There is a good weekday fixed-price lunch menu, and brunch is served on weekends. ⊠*Manuela Malasaña 10, Malasaña* ☎*91/591–0046* ⊟*AE, DC, MC, V.*

$$$–$$$$
SPANISH
✕**Pedro Larumbe.** This restaurant is literally the pinnacle of the ABC shopping center between Paseo de la Castellana and Calle Serrano. Dining quarters include a summer roof terrace (it turns into a lively bar after dinner) and an Andalusian patio. For over a decade chef-owner Pedro Larumbe has built a reputation for market food that respectfully breaks away from tradition, and his menu features such contemporary dishes as veal meatballs with truffle and king prawns, or roasted sea bass with bacon and tomato. The dessert buffet is an art exhibit, and a good wine list complements the fare. ⊠*Paseo de la Castellana 34, at Calle Serrano 61, Salamanca* ☎*91/575–1112* ⊟*AE, DC, MC, V* ⊘*Closed Sun., Holy Week, and 2 wks in Aug. No dinner Mon.*

$$$$
Fodor's Choice
★
SPANISH
✕ **Zalacaín.** This restaurant introduced nouvelle Basque cuisine to Spain in the 1970s and has since become a Madrid classic. It's particularly known for using the best and freshest seasonal products available, as well as for having the best service in town. From the variety of fungi and game meat to hard-to-find seafood, the food here tends to be unusual—you won't find many of these sorts of ingredients, or dishes, elsewhere. The restaurant has a deep-apricot color scheme that is made more dramatic by dark wood and gleaming silver. You'll feel like you're in an exclusive villa. ⊠*Alvarez de Baena 4, Salamanca* ☎*91/561–4840* ⚑*Reservations essential. Jacket and tie* ⊟*AE, DC, V* ⊘*Closed Sun., Aug., and Holy Week. No lunch Sat.*

WHERE TO STAY

CHAMBERÍ, RETIRO & SALAMANCA

$$$$

Fodor'sChoice

★

AC Palacio del Retiro. An early-20th-century restored palatial building owned by a noble family with extravagant habits (the elevator carried the horses up and down from the exercise ring on the roof), this spectacular hotel closely follows the path of the first AC Santo Mauro with its tasteful, modern decor in a historic building. Palacio preserves even more of its grandiose past: baseboards and fountains covered with ceramics from Talavera, original Parisian stained-glass windows, marble floors and columns, and original moldings. All rooms have superb views of the nearby Retiro Park. Pros: spacious, stylish rooms; within walking distance of the Prado; bathrooms stocked with all sorts of complimentary products. Cons: pricey, lower rooms facing the park can get noisy. ⊠*Alfonso XII 14, Retiro,* ☎*91/523–7460* ⊕*www. ac-hotels.com* ☞*51 rooms* &*In-room: safe, Wi-Fi. In-hotel: restaurant, bar, gym, spa, public Wi-Fi, parking (fee)* ⊟*AE, DC, MC, V.*

$$$$

Puerta de América. Inspired by Paul Eluard's *La Liberté* (whose verses are written across the facade), the owners of this hotel granted an unlimited budget to 19 of the world's top architects and designers. The result: 12 hotels in one, with floors by Zaha Hadid, Norman Foster, Jean Nouvel, David Chipperfield, and more. There's also a reputed restaurant and two bars (one on the rooftop), which are all just as impressive in design. The only snag: you'll need a taxi or the subway to get to the city center. Pros: an architect's dreamland, top-notch restaurant and bars. Cons: less than convenient location. ⊠*Avenida de América 41, Prosperidad* ☎*91/744–5400* ⊕*www.hotelpuertamerica.com* ☞*294 rooms, 21 junior suites, 12 suites* &*In-room: safe, Wi-Fi. In-hotel: 2 restaurants, bars, pool, gym, public Wi-Fi, parking (fee)* ⊟*AE, DC, MC, V.*

BARRIO DE LAS LETRAS & SANTA ANA

$$$$

Hotel Vincci Centrum. The combination of orange, steel, and dark tones is repeated throughout this small boutique hotel, providing a bold welcome to guests arriving at the counter. Shades of orange are present in the paintings, the iron columns enclosed in acrylic, the curtains, the lamps, and the sleek, velvety couches and armchairs in the two adjacent small and dimly lighted common areas, as well as in the coffee shop. Pros: comfortable and quiet, good location. Cons: a bit dark, rather pricey. ⊠*Cedaceros, 4, Centro* ☎*91/360–4720* ⊕*www.vinccihoteles. com* ☞*85 rooms, 2 junior suites* &*In-room: safe, dial-up, Wi-Fi. In-hotel: restaurant* ⊟*AE, DC, MC, V.*

$$

Inglés. Virginia Woolf was among the first luminaries to discover this hotel in the middle of the old city's bar-and-restaurant district. Since then, the Inglés has attracted more than its share of less celebrated artists and writers. Half of the rooms were tiled and painted in 2005, and new bathrooms were installed, but the decor still resembles the ornate and outdated lobby. If your room faces Calle Echegaray, you can get an unusual aerial view of the medieval quarter, which is all red tiles and ramshackle gables. Pros: huge rooms by local standards, centrally located. Cons: outdated decor, noisy street. ⊠*Echegaray 8, Santa*

14

Ana ☎91/429–6551 ☞58 *rooms* ⚷*In-room: no a/c (some). In-hotel: restaurant, bar, gym, parking (fee)* ☐*AE, DC, MC, V.*

$ 🏨 **Mora.** This cheery hotel with a sparkling, faux-marble lobby and bright, carpeted hallways is within meters of the CaixaForum and across from the Botanical Garden. Guest rooms are modestly decorated (those on the third and fourth floors are newer) but are large and comfortable; those facing the street have great views of the gardens and the Prado, and double-pane windows keep them fairly quiet. For breakfast and lunch, the café is excellent, affordable, and popular with locals. **Pros:** close to all major museums. **Cons:** busy and touristy street, uninspiring decor. ⊠*Paseo del Prado 32, Centro* ☎91/420–1569 ⊕*www.hotel mora.com* ☞62 *rooms* ⚷*In-hotel: restaurant* ☐*AE, DC, MC, V.*

$$$$ 🏨 **Westin Palace.** Built in 1912, Madrid's most famous grand hotel is a Belle Époque creation of Alfonso XIII, and has hosted the likes of Salvador Dalí, Marlon Brando, Rita Hayworth, and Madonna. Guest rooms are high-tech and generally impeccable; banquet halls and lobbies have been beautified, and the facade has been restored. The Art Nouveau stained-glass dome over the lounge remains exquisitely original, and guest-room windows are double-glazed against street noise. Suites are no less luxurious than the opulent public spaces, with Bang & Olufsen CD players, spacious bathrooms, and hot tubs. The hotel also houses the popular Asia Gallery restaurant. **Pros:** grand hotel with tons of history, weekend brunch with opera performances. **Cons:** fourth floor has not been renovated yet, standard rooms face a back street. ⊠*Plaza de las Cortés 7, Retiro* ☎91/360–8000 ⊕*www.palacemadrid.com* ☞465 *rooms, 45 suites* ⚷*In-room: dial-up, Wi-Fi. In-hotel: 2 restaurants, bar, gym, public Wi-Fi, parking (fee)* ☐*AE, DC, MC, V.*

SOL & THE ROYAL PALACE

$$$ 🏨 **Hotel Intur Palacio San Martín.** In an unbeatable location across from
Fodor'sChoice   one of Madrid's most celebrated monuments (the Convent of Des-
★   calzas), this hotel, once the old U.S. embassy and later a luxurious residential building crowded with noblemen, still exudes a kind of glory. The entrance leads to a glass-dome atrium that serves as a tranquil sitting area. There's an antique elevator, and many of the ceilings are carved and ornate. Rooms are spacious and carpeted; request one facing the big plaza. **Pros:** charming location, spacious rooms. **Cons:** no restaurant. ⊠*Plaza de San Martín 5, Palacio* ☎91/701–5000 ⊕*www. intur.com* ☞93 *rooms, 8 suites* ⚷*In-room: safe, Wi-Fi. In-hotel: gym, public Wi-Fi, parking (fee)* ☐*AE, DC, MC, V.*

$$ 🏨 **Liabeny.** Although unassuming in style and a bit outdated, this 1960s hotel near a plaza (and several department stores) between Gran Vía and Puerta del Sol has large, comfortable rooms with floral fabrics and big windows. Interior and top-floor rooms are the quietest. **Pros:** centrally located, near Princesa's shopping area. **Cons:** small rooms and bathrooms, crowded and noisy neighborhood. ⊠*Salud 3, Sol* ☎91/531–9000 ⊕*www.liabeny.es* ☞220 *rooms* ⚷*In-room: dial-up, Wi-Fi. In-hotel: restaurant, bar, gym, public Wi-Fi, parking (fee)* ☐*AE, DC, MC, V.*

$$$ 🏨 **Tryp Ambassador.** On an old street between Gran Vía and the Royal Palace, the Ambassador occupies the renovated 19th-century palace of

the Dukes of Granada. The facade (restored in 2007), a magnificent front door, and a graceful three-story staircase recall the building's aristocratic past. The rest has been transformed into elegant, somewhat soulless lodgings favored by executives. Large guest rooms have sitting areas, wooden floors, and mahogany furnishings. The greenhouse restaurant, filled with plants and songbirds, is especially pleasant on cold days. **Pros:** grand building, central location, the better rooms have big balconies with good views. **Cons:** some rooms need to be revamped. ⊠*Cuesta Santo Domingo 5 and 7, Palacio* ☎*91/541–6700* ⊕*www.solmelia.com* ⇨*183 rooms, 25 suites* ⚲*In-room: Wi-Fi. In-hotel: restaurant, bar, airport shuttle, public Wi-Fi, parking (fee)* ⊟*AE, DC, MC, V.*

NIGHTLIFE & THE ARTS

14

THE ARTS

As Madrid's reputation as a vibrant, contemporary arts center has grown, artists and performers have been arriving in droves. Consult the weekly *Guía del Ocio* (published Friday) or the daily listings and Friday supplements in any of the leading newspapers—*El País, El Mundo,* or *ABC,* all of which are fairly easy to understand even if you don't read much Spanish.

DANCE & MUSIC PERFORMANCES

The modern **Auditorio Nacional de Música** (⊠*Príncipe de Vergara 146, Salamanca* ☎*91/337–0100* ⊕*www.auditorionacional.mcu.es*) is Madrid's main concert hall, with spaces for both symphonic and chamber music. The resplendent **Teatro Real** (⊠*Plaza de Isabel II, Ópera* ☎*91/516–0660* ⊕*www.teatro-real.com*) is the site of opera and dance performances.

The **Matadero Madrid** (⊠*Paseo de la Chopera 14, Legazpi* ☎*91/517–7309*) is the city's newest and the biggest arts center. It sits in the city's old slaughterhouse—a massive early-20th-century *neomudejar* compound of 13 buildings. It has a theater, multiple exhibition spaces, workshops, and a lively bar. It's so large that it won't be completely finished until 2011, but some of the exhibition spaces and the theater are now open.

FILM

Of Madrid's 60 movie theaters, only 12 show foreign films, generally in English, with original soundtracks and Spanish subtitles. These are listed in newspapers and in the *Guía de Ocio* under "v. o."—*versión original,* that is, undubbed. Your best bet for catching a new release is the **Ideal Yelmo Cineplex** (⊠*Doctor Cortezo 6, Centro* ☎*902/220922*). The excellent, classic v. o. films at the **Filmoteca Cine Doré** (⊠*Santa Isabel 3, Lavapiés* ☎*91/369–1125*) change daily. There are also good theaters (Alphaville, Renoir Plaza de España, and Princesa) around the Plaza de España.

FLAMENCO

Although the best place in Spain to find flamenco is Andalusia, there are a few possibilities in Madrid. Note that *tablaos* (flamenco venues) charge around €25–€35 for the show only (with a complimentary drink included), so save money by dining elsewhere.

Café de Chinitas. It's expensive, but the flamenco is the best in Madrid. Reserve in advance; shows often sell out. The restaurant opens around 8:30 PM and performances begin at 10:15 PM Monday through Saturday. ⊠ *Torrija 7, Ópera* ☎ *91/559–5135.*

Casa Patas. Along with tapas, this well-known space offers good, relatively authentic (according to the performers) flamenco. Prices are more reasonable than elsewhere. Shows are at 10:30 PM Monday through Thursday, and at 9 PM and midnight on Friday and Saturday. ⊠ *Canizares 10, Lavapiés* ☎ *91/369–0496.*

Las Carboneras. A prime flamenco showcase, this venue rivals Casa Patas as the best option in terms of quality and price. Performing here are young and less commercial artists as well as more established stars on tour. Nightly shows are staged at 9 and 10:30 Monday through Thursday and at 8:30 and 11 Friday and Saturday. ⊠ *Plaza del Conde de Miranda 1, Centro* ☎ *91/542–8677.*

NIGHTLIFE

Nightlife—or *la marcha*—reaches legendary heights in Madrid. It's been said that madrileños rarely sleep, largely because they spend so much time in bars—not drunk, but socializing in the easy, sophisticated way that's unique to this city. This is true of old as well as young, and it's not uncommon for children to play on the sidewalks past midnight while multigenerational families and friends convene over coffee or cocktails at an outdoor café.

BARS & NIGHTCLUBS

Bar Cock. Resembling a room at some very exclusive club, it caters to an older, more classic crowd. ⊠ *C. Reina 16, Chueca* ☎ *91/532–2826.*

Café Belén. The handful of tables here are rarely empty on weekends, thanks to the candlelight and cozy atmosphere—it attracts a young, mixed, postdinner crowd. ⊠ *C. Belen 5, Chueca* ☎ *91/308–2747.*

Café Central. Madrid's best-known jazz venue is chic, and the musicians are often internationally known. Performances are usually from 10 PM to midnight. ⊠ *Plaza de Ángel 10, Santa Ana* ☎ *91/369–4143.*

Del Diego. Arguably Madrid's trendiest cocktail bar, this place is frequented by a variety of crowds from movie directors to moviegoers. ⊠ *Calle de la Reina 12, Centro* ☎ *91/523–3106* ☉ *Closed Sun.*

Museo Chicote. Recently refurbished and regaining popularity, this landmark cocktail bar–lounge is said to have been one of Hemingway's haunts. ⊠ *Gran Vía 12, Centro* ☎ *91/532–6737* ☉ *Closed Sun.*

Reina Bruja. Magical and chameleonlike, thanks to a sleek design that makes good use of LED lighting and the seemingly undulating shapes of the columns and walls, this is the place to go if you want to a latenight drink—it opens at 11 and closes at 5:30 AM—without the thunder of a full–blown disco. ⊠ *Jacometrezo 6, Palacio* ☎ *91/445–6886* ☉ *Closed Sun.–Wed.*

DISCOS

Madrid's oldest disco, and one of the hippest clubs for all-night dancing to an international music mix, is **El Sol** (⊠ *C. Jardines 3, Centro*

☎91/532–6490), open until 5:30 AM. There's live music starting at around midnight, Thursday through Saturday. **Pachá** (✉*Barceló 11, Centro* ☎*91/447–0128* ☾*Closed Mon.–Wed.*) is always energetic. Salsa has become a fixture in Madrid; check out the most spectacular moves at **Azúcar** (✉*Paseo Reina Cristina 7, Atocha* ☎*91/501–6107*). **Clamores** (✉*Albuquerque 14, Chamberí* ☎*91/445–7938* ☾*Closes at 11 PM Sun.*) usually plays live music until 2:30 AM. **Golden Boite** (✉*Duque de Sesto 54, Retiro* ☎*91/573–8775*) is always hot from midnight on. For funky rhythms, try **Stella** (✉*C. Arlabán 7, Centro* ☎*91/531–6378* ☾*Closed Sun.–Wed.*). On Thursday it's called Mondo (electronic and house music); on Friday and Saturday it's the Room—a more mainstream scene. Show up late. An indie and hip crowd flocks to **Elástico** (✉*C. Montera 25 [entrance on Plaza del Carmen], Sol* ☎*91/531–6378*), the Saturday night pop session at Wind club. It has two different spaces and a new DJ every week.

14

SHOPPING

Spain has become one of the world's centers for design of every kind. You'll have no trouble finding traditional crafts, such as ceramics, guitars, and leather goods, albeit not at countryside prices—at this point, the city is more like Rodeo Drive than the bargain bin. Known for contemporary furniture and decorative items as well as chic clothing, shoes, and jewelry, Spain's capital has become stiff competition for Barcelona. Keep in mind that many shops, especially those that are small and family run, close during lunch hours, on Sunday, and on Saturday afternoon. Shops generally accept most major credit cards.

DEPARTMENT STORES

El Corte Inglés. Spain's largest department store carries the best selection of everything, from auto parts to groceries, electronics, lingerie, and designer fashions. ✉*Preciados 1, 2, and 3, Sol* ☎*91/379–8000, 901/122122 general information, 902/400222 ticket sales* ⊕*www.elcorteingles.es* ✉*Callao 2, Centro* ☎*91/379–8000* ✉*Calle Goya 76 and 85, Salamanca* ☎*91/432–9300* ✉*Princesa 41, 47, and 56, Centro* ☎*91/454–6000* ✉*Calle Serrano 47 and 52, Salamanca* ☎*91/432–5490* ✉*Raimundo Fernández Villaverde 79, Chamartín* ☎*91/418–8800.*

FASHION

Mango. The Turkish brothers Isaac and Nahman Andic opened their first store in Barcelona in 1984. Two decades later Mango has stores all over the world, and the brand rivals Zara as Spain's healthiest fashion venture. Mango's target customer is the young, modern, and urban woman. In comparison with Zara, Mango has fewer formal options. ✉*Fuencarral 70, Malasña* ☎*91/523–0412* ⊕*www.mango.com* ✉*Fuencarral 140, Bilbao* ☎*91/445–7811* ✉*Calle Goya 83, Salamanca* ☎*91/435–3958* ✉*Hermosilla 22, Salamanca* ☎*91/576–8303.*

Zara. For those with young, functional, and designy tastes but slim wallets (picture hip clothes that won't last you more than one or two seasons), Zara—whose minimalist window displays are hard to miss—carries the latest looks for men, women, and children. Zara is self-made entrepreneur Amancio Ortega's textile empire flagship, which you will find all over the city. Zara's clothes are considerably cheaper in Spain than in the United States or the UK. There are also two outlet stores in Madrid—in the Gran Vía store and in Calle Carretas; both are called Lefties. If you choose to try your luck at the outlets, keep in mind that Monday and Thursday are when new deliveries arrive—and therefore the days when you have the best chance of finding good stuff. ⊠ *Centro Comercial ABC, Calle Serrano 61, Salamanca* ☎*91/575–6334* ⊠ *Gran Vía 34, Centro* ☎*91/521–1283* ⊠ *Velázquez 49, Salamanca* ☎*91/575–1476* ⊠ *Carretas 6, Sol* ☎*91/522–6945* ⊠ *Princesa 63, Centro* ☎*91/543–2415* ⊠ *Conde de Peñalver 4, Salamanca* ☎*91/435–4135.*

FLEA MARKET

On Sunday morning Calle de Ribera de Curtidores is closed to traffic and jammed with outdoor booths selling everything under the sun—the weekly transformation into the **El Rastro** flea market, Madrid's most popular outdoor market.

SPECIALTY STORES
BOUTIQUES & FASHION

SALAMANCA **Adolfo Domínguez** (⊠ *Calle Serrano 18 and 96, Salamanca* ☎*91/576–7053*) is a Galician designer with simple, sober, and elegant lines for both men and women. Of his eight other locations in the city, the one at Calle Fuencarral 5, a block away from Gran Vía, is geared toward a younger crowd, with more affordable and colorful clothes. Also popular is the Madrileño designer **Pedro del Hierro** (⊠ *Calle Serrano 24 and 63, Salamanca* ☎*91/575–6906*), who has built himself a good reputation for his sophisticated but uncomplicated clothes for both sexes.

Sybilla (⊠ *Jorge Juan 12, at end of one of two cul-de-sacs, Salamanca* ☎*91/578–1322*) is the studio of Spain's best-known female designer. Her fluid dresses and hand-knit sweaters have made her a favorite with Danish former supermodel and now editor and designer Helena Christensen. Next to Sybilla is **Jocomomola** (⊠ *Jorge Juan 12, Salamanca* ☎*91/575–0005*), Sybilla's younger and more affordable second brand. Here you'll find plenty of informal and provocative colorful pieces as well as some accessories.

CHUECA & Brothers Custodio and David Dalmau are the creative force behind the
MALASAÑA success of **Custo** (⊠ *Mayor 37, Sol* ☎*91/578–1322* ⊠ *Fuencarral 29, Chueca* ☎*91/360–4636*), whose eye-catching T-shirts can be found in the closets of such stars as Madonna and Julia Roberts.

Chueca's trademark are its multi-brand boutiques and small multi-brand fashion shops, often managed by eccentric and outspoken characters. A good example of this is **H.A.N.D** (⊠ *Hortaleza 26, Chueca* ☎*91/521–5152*), a cozy, tasteful store owned by two Frenchmen: Stephan and Thierry. They specialize in feminine, colorful, and young French prêt-à-porter designers (Stella Forest, La Petite, Tara Jarmon).

CERAMICS
Antigua Casa Talavera (✉ *Isabel la Católica 2, Centro* ☎ *91/547–3417*) is the best of Madrid's many ceramics shops. Despite the name, the finest wares sold here are from Manises, near Valencia, but the blue-and-yellow Talavera ceramics are also excellent.

LEATHER GOODS
The owners of **Boxcalf** (✉ *Jorge Juan 34, Salamanca* ☎ *91/531–5343*), on the corner of one of Calle Jorge Juan's alleys, sell exclusive suede, nappa, and leather coats for women, as well as accessories, made in Majorca. On a street full of bargain shoe stores, or *muestrarios*, **Caligae** (✉ *Augusto Figueroa 18, 20, and 31, Chueca* ☎ *91/531–5343*) is probably the best of the bunch.

14

TOLEDO

Long the spiritual capital of Spain, Toledo perches atop a rocky mount with steep ocher hills rising on either side, bound on three sides by the Río Tajo (Tagus River). When the Romans came in 192 BC they fortified the highest point of the rock, where you now see the Alcázar. This stronghold was later remodeled by the Visigoths. In the 8th century, the Moors arrived.

Today the Moorish legacy is evident in Toledo's strong crafts tradition, the mazelike arrangement of the streets, and the predominance of brick rather than stone.

Alfonso VI, aided by El Cid ("Lord Conqueror"), captured the city in 1085 and styled himself emperor of Toledo. Under the Christians, the town's strong intellectual life was maintained, and Toledo became famous for its school of translators, who spread to the West knowledge of Arab medicine, law, culture, and philosophy. Today Toledo is conservative, prosperous, and expensive.

EXPLORING TOLEDO

5 **Alcázar.** Closed for renovations until late 2008 or early 2009, the Alcázar ("fortress" in Arabic) was originally a Moorish citadel that stood here from the 10th century to the Reconquest. A tour around the exterior reveals the south facade, the building's most severe—the work of Juan de Herrera, of El Escorial fame. The east facade incorporates a large section of battlements. The finest facade is the northern, one of many Toledan works by Alonso de Covarrubias, who did more than any other architect to introduce the Renaissance style here. The Alcázar's architectural highlight is Covarrubias's Italianate courtyard, which, like most other parts of the building, was largely rebuilt after the civil war, when the Alcázar was besieged by the Republicans. ✉ *Calle Cuesta Carlos V 2* ☎ *925/221673* 🎟️ *€5* 🕐 *Tues.–Sun. 9:30–2:30.*

10 **Casa de El Greco** (*El Greco's House*). This house is on the property that belonged to Peter the Cruel's treasurer, Samuel Levi. El Greco once lived in a house owned by Levi, but it's pure conjecture that the artist

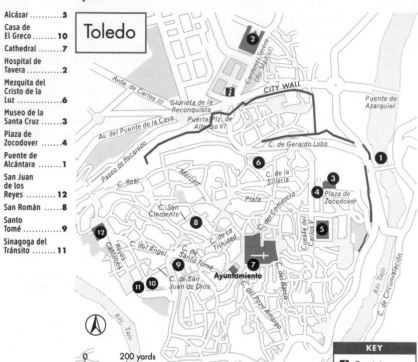

Toledo

KEY

i Tourist
Information

0   200 yards
0   200 meters

lived here. The interior, decorated in the late 19th century to resemble a "typical" house of El Greco's time, is a fake, albeit a pleasant one. The museum next door has a few of El Greco's paintings, including a panorama of Toledo with the Hospital of Tavera in the foreground. ⊠ *Calle Samuel Levi s/n* ☎ *925/224046* ✑ *€2.50, free Sat. afternoon and Sun. morning* ☉ *Tues.–Sat. 10–2 and 4–9, Sun. 10–2.*

❼ **Cathedral.** Jorge Manuel Theotokópoulos was responsible for the cathedral's Mozarabic chapel, the elongated dome of which crowns the right-hand side of the west facade. The rest of this facade is mainly early 15th century and has a depiction of Mary presenting her robe to Toledo's patron saint, the Visigothic Ildefonsus. Enter the cathedral from the 14th-century cloisters to the left of the west facade. The primarily 13th-century architecture was inspired by Chartres and other Gothic cathedrals in France, but the squat proportions give it a Spanish feel, as do the wealth and weight of the furnishings and the location of the elaborate choir in the center of the nave. Immediately to your right as you enter the building is a beautifully carved plateresque doorway by Covarrubias, marking the entrance to the Treasury. The latter houses a small Crucifixion by the Italian painter Cimabue and an extraordinarily intricate late-15th-century monstrance by Juan del Arfe, a silversmith of German descent; the ceiling is an excellent example of Mudejar (11th- to 16th-century Moorish-influenced) workmanship.

In the middle of the ambulatory is an example of baroque illusionism by Narciso Tomé known as the *Transparente*, a blend of painting, stucco, and sculpture. Finally, off the northern end of the ambulatory, you'll come to the sacristy and several El Grecos, including one version of *El Espolio* (Christ Being Stripped of His Raiment). This painting is considered to be the first recorded instance of the painter in Spain. ⊠*Cardenal Cisneros, 1* ☎*925/222241* ⊆*€7* ☉*Mon.–Sat. 10–6:30, Sun. 2–6:30.*

2 Hospital de Tavera. You can find this hospital, Covarrubias's last work, outside the walls beyond Toledo's main northern gate, Covarrubias's imposing Puerta de Bisagra. Unlike the former Hospital of Santa Cruz, this complex is unfinished and slightly dilapidated, but it is nonetheless full of character and has the evocatively ramshackle **Museo de Duque de Lema** in its southern wing. The most important work in the museum's miscellaneous collection is a painting by the 17th-century artist José Ribera. The hospital's monumental chapel holds El Greco's *Baptism of Christ* and the exquisitely carved marble tomb of Cardinal Tavera, the last work of Alonso de Berruguete. ⊠*Calle Cardenal Tavera 2* ☎*925/220451* ⊆*€4* ☉*Daily 10–1:30 and 3:30–5:30.*

6 Mezquita del Cristo de la Luz *(Mosque of Christ of the Light).* A gardener will show you around this mosque-chapel, in a park above the ramparts; if he's not around, ask at the house opposite. Originally a tiny Visigothic church, the chapel was transformed into a mosque during the Moorish occupation; the Islamic arches and vaulting survived, making this the most important relic of Moorish Toledo. ⊠*Calle Cuesta de los Carmelitas Descalzas 10* ☎*925/254191* ⊆*€2.30* ☉*Oct. 1–Mar. 1, daily 10–5:45; Mar. 2–Sept. 30, daily 10–7.*

3 Museo de la Santa Cruz. This museum is in a beautiful Renaissance hospital with a stunning classical-plateresque facade; unlike Toledo's other sights, it's open all day without a break. The light and elegant interior has changed little since the 16th century, the main difference being that works of art have replaced the hospital beds; among the displays is El Greco's *Assumption* of 1613, the artist's last known work. A small **Museo de Arqueología** (Museum of Archaeology) is in and around the hospital's delightful cloister. ⊠*Calle de Miguel de Cervantes 3* ☎*925/221036* ⊆*Free* ☉*Mon.–Sat. 10–6, Sun. 10–2.*

4 Plaza de Zocodover. Toledo's main square was built in the early 17th century as part of an unsuccessful attempt to impose a rigid geometry on the chaotic Moorish ground plan. This teeny plaza is also home to the largest and oldest marzipan store in town, Santo Tomé—and Toledo's only McDonald's. You can catch inner-city buses here and the tourist office is just around the corner. Nearby, you can find **Calle del Comercio,** the town's narrow and lively pedestrian thoroughfare, lined with bars and shops and shaded in summer by awnings.

14

① **Puente de Alcántara.** Roman in origin, this is the town's oldest bridge. Next to it is a heavily restored castle built after the Christian capture of 1085 and, above this, a vast and depressingly severe military academy, a typical example of fascist architecture under Franco.

⑫ **San Juan de los Reyes.** This convent church in western Toledo was erected by Ferdinand and Isabella to commemorate their victory at the Battle of Toro in 1476 and was intended to be their burial place. The building is largely the work of architect Juan Guas, who considered it his masterpiece and asked to be buried here himself. In true plateresque fashion, the white interior is covered with inscriptions and heraldic motifs. ⊠ *Calle de Reyes Católicos 17* ☎ *925/223802* ⊠ *€2.30* ⊙ *Oct. 1–Mar. 1, daily 10–5:45; Mar. 2–Sept. 30, daily 10–7.*

⑧ **San Román.** A virtually unspoiled part of Toledo hides this early-13th-century Mudejar church with extensive remains of frescoes inside. It has been deconsecrated and is now the **Museo de los Concilios y de la Cultura Visigótica,** and has statuary, manuscript illustrations, and jewelry. ⊠ *Calle de San Román s/n* ☎ *925/227872* ⊠ *Free* ⊙ *Tues.–Sat. 10–2 and 4–6:30, Sun. 10–2.*

⑨ **Santo Tomé.** Topped with a Mudejar tower, this chapel was specially built to house El Greco's most famous painting, *The Burial of Count Orgaz,* and remains devoted to that purpose. The painting portrays the benefactor of the church being buried with the posthumous assistance of St. Augustine and St. Stephen, who have miraculously appeared at the funeral to thank him for all the money he gave to religious institutions named after them. ⊠ *Pl. del Conde 4* ☎ *925/256098* ⊕ *www.santotome.org* ⊠ *€2.30* ⊙ *Mar.–mid-Oct., daily 10–6:45; mid-Oct.–Feb., daily 10–5:45.*

⑪ **Sinagoga del Tránsito.** Financed by Samuel Levi, this 14th-century rectangular synagogue is plain on the outside, but the inside walls are covered with intricate Mudejar decoration, as well as Hebraic inscriptions glorifying God, Peter the Cruel, and Levi himself. It's said that Levi imported cedars from Lebanon for the building's construction, à la Solomon when he built the First Temple in Jerusalem. Adjoining the main hall is the **Museo Sefardí,** a small museum of Jewish culture in Spain. ⊠ *Samuel Levi s/n* ☎ *925/223665* ⊠ *€2.40, free Sat. afternoon and Sun.* ⊙ *Mar.–Nov., Tues.–Sat. 10–9, Sun. 10–2; Dec.–Feb., Tues.–Sat. 10–2 and 4–9, Sun. 10–2.*

WHERE TO EAT

$$$–$$$$ ✗ **Asador Adolfo.** Steps from the cathedral but discreetly hidden away, this restaurant has an intimate interior with a coffered ceiling painted in the 14th century. Game, fresh produce, and traditional Toledan recipes are prepared in innovative ways. The *tempura de flor de calabacín* (fried zucchini blossoms in saffron sauce) makes for a tasty starter; King Juan Carlos I has declared Adolfo's partridge stew the best in Spain. Finish with a Toledan specialty, *delicias de mazapán* (marzipan delights). ⊠ *Calle de La Granada 6, corner of Calle Hombre de Palo*

☎*925/227321* ⚐*Reservations essential* ▭*AE, DC, MC, V* ✆*Closed Mon. No dinner Sun.*

$$$-$$$$ ✕ **Casón de los López de Toledo.** A vaulted foyer leads to a patio with marble statues, twittering caged birds, a fountain, and abstract religious paintings; in the dining room, carved wood abounds. The menu might include garlic-ravioli soup, braised rabbit with sesame sauce and mashed potatoes, or cod with manchego cheese, onions, and olive oil. Try the almond *mazapán* (marzipan) cake topped with cream cheese. Make reservations. ⊠*Calle Sillería 3* ☎*902/198344* ▭*AE, DC, MC, V* ✆*No dinner Sun.*

$-$$ ✕ **Enebro Tapas Bar.** The motto here is, "Don't drink if you're not going to eat." Every drink ordered comes with an ample serving of *patatas bravas* (roast potatoes) and some combination of pizza, olives, and *croquetas* (croquettes). An enormous terrace offers gas lamps and umbrellas to provide heat in the winter and shade in the summer. It's popular with locals, but more of a place to take a break than have a full meal. ⊠*Pl. Santiago de los Caballeros 1* ☎*No phone* ▭*No credit cards.*

$-$$$ ✕ **Restaurante Maravilla.** Partridge, quail, and seafood stand out at this homey, modestly priced spot, though the roast leg of lamb is hard to resist. ⊠*Pl. Barrio Rey 7* ☎*925/228582* ▭*AE, DC, MC, V.*

WHERE TO STAY

$$-$$$ 🏨 **Hostal del Cardenal.** Built in the 18th century (restored in 1972) as a
★ summer palace for Cardinal Lorenzana, this quiet and beautiful hotel is fully stocked with antique furniture. Some rooms overlook the hotel's enchanting wooded garden, which lies at the foot of the town's walls. The restaurant, popular with tourists, has a long-standing reputation; the dishes are mainly local, and in season you can find delicious asparagus and strawberries from Aranjuez. ■TIP→ If you have a car, reserve a parking spot when you book your room, or you may not be guaranteed a spot. Pros: lovely courtyard, convenient parking. Cons: restaurant often full and somewhat pricey. ⊠*Paseo de Recaredo 24* ☎*925/224900* ⊕*www.hostaldelcardenal.com* ⤆*27 rooms* ⚅*In-hotel: restaurant, no elevator, laundry service, public Wi-Fi (some), parking (no fee), some pets allowed* ▭*AE, DC, MC, V.*

$$-$$$ 🏨 **Hotel Pintor El Greco Sercotel.** Next door to the painter's house, this friendly hotel occupies what was once a 17th-century bakery. The modern interior is warm and clean, with tawny colors and antique touches, such as exposed-brick vaulting. The elevator goes to the second floor only. Pros: parking garage adjacent. Cons: street noise in most rooms. ⊠*Alamillos del Tránsito 13* ☎*925/285191* ⊕*www.hotel-pintorelgreco. com* ⤆*33 rooms* ⚅*In-hotel: laundry service, public Wi-Fi, parking (fee)* ▭*AE, DC, MC, V.*

$$$ ✕🏨 **Parador de Toledo.** This modern building on Toledo's outskirts has an unbeatable panorama of the town. The architecture and furnishings nod to traditional style, emphasizing brick and wood. The restaurant ($$$-$$$$) is stately and traditional, with top-quality regional wines and products. Pros: breathtaking views, newly renovated. Cons: austere setting can be dark. ⊠*Calle Cerro del Emperador s/n,* ☎*925/221850*

14

⊕*www.parador.es* ✑ *80 rooms* &*In-hotel: no elevator until renovation completed* ☰*AE, DC, MC, V.*

SHOPPING

The Moors established silver work, damascening (metalwork inlaid with gold or silver), pottery, embroidery, and marzipan traditions here, and next to San Juan de los Reyes a turn-of-the-20th-century art school keeps these crafts alive. For inexpensive pottery, stop at the large emporia on the outskirts of town, on the main road to Madrid. Most of the region's pottery is made in Talavera la Reina, 76 km (47 mi) west of Toledo. At **Museo Ruiz de Luna** (⊠*Pl. de San Augustín* ☎*925/800149* ☜*Museum €0.60, weekends free* ☉*Tues.–Sat. 10–2 and 4–6:30, Sun. 10–2*), watch artisans throw local clay, and trace the development of Talavera's world-famous ceramics—chronicled through 1,500 tiles, bowls, vases, and plates dating back to the 15th century.

BILBAO

397 km (247 mi) north of Madrid, 610 km (380 mi) northwest of Barcelona.

Time in Bilbao (Bilbo, in Euskera) may soon need to be identified as BG or AG (Before Guggenheim, After Guggenheim). Never has a single monument of art and architecture so radically changed a city—or, for that matter, a nation, and in this case two: Spain and Euskadi. Frank Gehry's stunning museum, Norman Foster's sleek subway system, the glass Santiago Calatrava footbridge, and the leafy park and commercial complex in Abandoibarra have all helped foment a cultural revolution in the commercial capital of the Basque Country. Greater Bilbao encompasses almost 1 million inhabitants, nearly half the total population of the Basque Country.

Bilbao's new attractions get more press, but the city's old treasures still quietly line the banks of the rust-color Nervión River. The Casco Viejo (Old Quarter)—also known as Siete Calles (Seven Streets)—is a charming jumble of shops, bars, and restaurants on the river's Right Bank, near the Puente del Arenal bridge. Throughout the old quarter are ancient mansions emblazoned with family coats of arms, noble wooden doors, and fine ironwork balconies. Bilbao's cultural institutions include, along with the Guggenheim, a major museum of fine arts (the Museo de Bellas Artes) and an opera society (ABAO: Asociacion Bilbaina de Amigos de la Opera) with 7,000 members from all over Spain and parts of southern France. In addition, epicureans have long ranked Bilbao's culinary offerings among the best in Spain.

EXPLORING BILBAO

❺ Near the Ayuntamiento Bridge is the riverside **ayuntamiento** *(city hall)*, built in 1892. Ⓜ*Casco Viejo.*

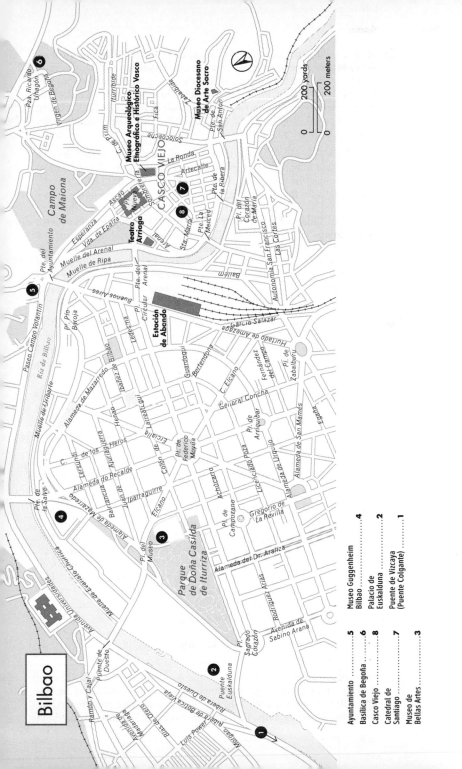

Bilbao

Museo Guggenheim Bilbao **5**
Palacio de Euskalduna **2**
Puente de Vizcaya (Puente Colgante) **1**

Ayuntamiento **5**
Basílica de Begoña **6**
Casco Viejo **8**
Catedral de Santiago **7**
Museo de Bellas Artes **3**

6 Stop at Calle Esperanza 6 and take the elevator to Bilbao's iconic **Basílica de Begoña** overlooking the city. The church's three-nave Gothic hulk was begun in 1511 on a spot where the Virgin Mary had supposedly appeared long before. Partly destroyed in the First Carlist War of 1835, the facade, tower, and sacristy were rebuilt in the early 20th century. ⊠*C. Virgen de Begoña 38* ☎*94/412–7091* ⊕*www.basilicadebegona. com* Ⓜ*Casco Viejo.*

8 The **Casco Viejo** *(Old Quarter)* is folded into an elbow of the Nervión River behind Bilbao's grand, elaborately restored theater. While exploring, don't miss the colossal food market **El Mercado de la Ribera** at the edge of the river, the Renaissance town house **Palacio Yohn** at the corner of Sant Maria and Perro, and the library and cultural center **Biblioteca Municipal Bidebarrieta** at Calle Bidebarrieta 4. Inaugurated in 1890, **Teatro Arriaga** was a symbol of Bilbao's industrial might and cultural vibrancy by the time it burned nearly to the ground in 1914. Styled after the Paris Opéra, the theater defies easy classification: although its symmetry suggests neoclassicism, its ornamentation defines the Belle Époque style. Walk around to see the stained-glass windows in the back. ⊠*Plaza Arriaga 1* ☎*94/479–2036* Ⓜ*Casco Viejo.*

7 **Catedral de Santiago** *(St. James's Cathedral).* Bilbao's earliest church, this was a pilgrimage stop on the coastal route to Santiago de Compostela. Work on the structure began in 1379, but fire destroyed most of it in 1571; it has a notable outdoor arcade. ⊠*Plaza de Santiago* Ⓜ*Casco Viejo.*

3 Don't let the Guggenheim eclipse the **Museo de Bellas Artes** *(Museum of*
Fodor'sChoice *Fine Arts).* Depending on your tastes, you may find the art here more
★ satisfying. The museum's fine collection of Flemish, French, Italian, and Spanish paintings includes works by El Greco, Goya, Velázquez, Zurbarán, Ribera, and Gauguin. ⊠*Plaza del Museo 2* ☎*94/439–6060* ⊕*www.museobilbao.com* ⊠€*5.50, free Wed., combined ticket with Guggenheim (valid 1 yr)* €*12.50 plus* €*2 additional on admittance to 2nd museum* ⊙*Tues.–Sat. 10–1:30 and 4–7:30, Sun. 10–2* Ⓜ*Moyúa.*

4 Covered with a dazzling 30,000 sheets of titanium, the **Museo Guggen-**
Fodor'sChoice **heim Bilbao** opened in October 1997 and became Bilbao's main attrac-
★ tion overnight. The shimmering effect of this finned and fluted titanium whale next to the rusty waters of the Nervión is difficult to over-describe, especially for anyone familiar with the smoldering industrial heap that occupied this space not so long ago. An enormous atrium, more than 150 feet high, is connected to the 19 galleries by a system of suspended metal walkways and glass elevators. ⊠ *Avenida Abandoibarra 2* ☎*94/435–9080* ⊕*www.guggenheim-bilbao.es* ⊠€*12.50; combined ticket with Museo de Bellas Artes (valid 1 yr)* €*14.50 plus* €*2 additional on admittance to 2nd museum* ⊙*July and Aug., daily 10–8; Sept.–June, Tues.–Sun. 10–8* Ⓜ*Moyúa.*

2 **Palacio de Euskalduna.** In homage to the Astilleros Euskalduna (Basque Country shipbuilders) who operated shipyards here beside the Euskalduna Bridge into the mid-'80s, this music venue and convention hall resembles a rusting ship. Designed by Federico Soriano, Euskalduna opened in 1999 and is Bilbao's main opera venue and home of the Bilbao Symphony Orchestra. ⊠ *Abandoibarra 4, El Ensanche* ☎ *94/403–5000* ⊕ *www.euskalduna.net* 📧 *Tour €3* ⊙ *Office weekdays 9–2 and 4–7; box office Mon.–Sat. noon–2 and 5–8:30, Sun. noon–2; guided tours Sat. at noon or by fax appointment* Ⓜ *San Mamés.*

❶ Dubbed Bilbao's Eiffel Tower (albeit a horizontal version) the **Puente de Vizcaya** is commonly called the Puente Colgante (Hanging Bridge). Spanning the Nervión, this transporter hung from cables unites two distinct worlds: exclusive, quiet Las Arenas and Portugalete, a much older, working-class town that spawned Dolores Ibarruri, the famous Republican orator of the Spanish civil war, known as La Pasionaria for her ardor. ☎ *94/480–1012* ⊕ *www.puente-colgante.org* 📧 *€0.30 to cross on foot, €1.10 by car; €4 for visit to observation deck* Ⓜ *Areeta.*

14

WHERE TO EAT

$$$–$$$$ ✕ **Aizian.** Euskera for "in the wind," the Sheraton Bilbao restaurant—under the direction of chef José Miguel Olazabalaga—has in record time become one of the city's most respected dining establishments. Typically Bilbaino culinary classicism doesn't keep Mr. Olazabalaga from creating surprising reductions and contemporary interpretations of traditional dishes such as *la marmita de chipirón,* a stew of sautéed cuttlefish with a topping of whipped potatoes covering the sauce of squid ink. ⊠ *C. Lehendakari Leizaola 29, El Ensanche* ☎ *94/428–0035* ☰ *AE, DC, MC, V* ⊙ *Closed Sun. and Aug. 1–15* Ⓜ *San Mamés.*

$$$–$$$$ ✕ **El Perro Chico.** Named for the toll once charged here for crossing
★ the footbridge below Bilbao's Mercado de la Ribera (a *perro chico* was the colloquial name for an ancient coin), this restaurant became a Frank Gehry favorite during his time in Bilbao supervising the construction of the Guggenheim. Try the *pato a la naranja* (duck à l'orange) or the *bacalao con berenjena* (salt cod with eggplant). ⊠ *Aretxaga 2* ☎ *94/415–0519* ☰ *AE, DC, MC, V* ⊙ *Closed Sun. No lunch Mon.* Ⓜ *Casco Viejo.*

$$$–$$$$ ✕ **Guggenheim Bilbao.** The museum's restaurant-in-residence has a lot to live up to, but easily succeeds. Famous for his eponymous restaurant outside San Sebastián, Martín Berasategui (or his staff) will install you at a table overlooking the Nervión and the green heights of Artxanda, then feed you such exciting creations as *pichón de Bresse* (wild pigeon) and *ensalada de bogavante* (lobster salad). ⊠ *Av. Abandoibarra 2* ☎ *94/423–9333* ⚑ *Reservations essential* ☰ *AE, DC, MC, V* ⊙ *Closed Mon. and Jan. 1–19. No dinner Sun. or Tues.* Ⓜ *Moyúa.*

$–$$ ✕ **Kiskia.** A modern version of the traditional cider house, this rambling
Fodor's Choice tavern near the San Mamés soccer stadium serves the classical *sidrería*
★ menu of chorizo sausage cooked in cider, codfish omelet, *txuleta de buey* (beef chops), Idiazabal cheese with quince jelly and nuts, and as much cider as you can drink, all for €28. Actors, sculptors, writers, soccer stars, and Bilbao's (and Spain's) who's who frequent this boisterous marvel. ⊠ *Pérez Galdós 51, San Mamés* ☎ *94/442–0032* ☰ *AE, DC, MC, V* ⊙ *No dinner Sun.–Tues.* Ⓜ *San Mamés.*

WHERE TO STAY

$$$-$$$$ ⌂ **Lopez de Haro.** Because it's just five minutes from the Guggenheim, this top hotel has become quite a scene. The converted 19th-century building has an English feel and all the comforts your heart desires. Club Náutico, a handy place for dinner on one of Bilbao's many rainy evenings, serves modern and classical Basque dishes, ranging from a simple *besugo* (sea bream) or one of the city's famous *bacalao* (codfish) preparations to sleek, contemporary interpretations of traditional favorites. **Pros:** quintessential Bilbao style and comfort, small enough to be clubby. **Cons:** a little too quiet, not a young vibe. ⌂ *Obispo Orueta 2* ☎ *94/423–5500* ⊕ *www.hotellopezdeharo.com* ✐ *49 rooms, 4 suites* ♿ *In-room: Wi-Fi. In-hotel: restaurant, bar, parking (fee)* ▤ *AE, DC, MC, V* Ⓜ *Moyúa.*

$$$-$$$$ ⌂ **Carlton.** Luminaries who have trod the halls of this grande dame include Orson Welles, Ava Gardner, Ernest Hemingway, Lauren Bacall, and most of Spain's great bullfighters. During the civil war it was the seat of the Republican Basque government; later it housed a number of Nationalist generals. It remains high-ceilinged and elegant, with creaky wooden floorboards and floor-to-ceiling windows swathed in heavy drapes. **Pros:** historic location, famous ghosts, a sense of history. **Cons:** surrounded by noisy streets, antique infrastructure and equipment. ⌂ *Pl. Federico Moyúa 2, El Ensanche* ☎ *94/416–2200* ⊕ *www.aranzazu-hoteles.com* ✐ *137 rooms, 7 suites* ♿ *In-room: Wi-Fi. In-hotel: restaurant, bar, parking (fee)* ▤ *AE, DC, MC, V* Ⓜ *Moyúa.*

$$$-$$$$ ⌂ **Gran Hotel Domine Bilbao.** Half modern design festival, half hotel, this member of the Silken chain, directly across the street from the Guggenheim, showcases the conceptual wit of Javier Mariscal, creator of Barcelona's 1992 Olympic mascot Cobi, and the structural know-how of Bilbao architect Iñaki Aurreroextea. With adjustable window-panes reflecting Gehry's titanium leviathan and every lamp and piece of furniture reflecting Mariscal's playful whimsy, this is the brightest star in Bilbao's design constellation. Comprehensively equipped and comfortable, it's the next best thing to moving into the Guggenheim. **Pros:** exciting design and decor, highly professional service. **Cons:** slightly self-conscious runway vibe, noisy streets require closed windows. ⌂ *Alameda de Mazarredo 61, El Ensanche* ☎ *94/425–3300* ⊕ *www.granhoteldominebilbao.com* ✐ *139 rooms, 6 suites* ♿ *In-room: Wi-Fi. In-hotel: restaurant, bar, parking (fee)* ▤ *AE, DC, MC, V* Ⓜ *Moyúa.*

$$$ ⌂ **Miró Hotel.** Across from the Guggenheim and a block from Bilbao's
Fodor'sChoice   Museo de Bellas Artes, this boutique hotel, designed by Barcelona fash-
★   ion and interior designer Antonio Miró, is exciting, comfortable, and daringly innovative. Rooms are quiet, spacious, and contemporary, with lots of high-tech design touches. Public rooms are simple and unpretentious; the hip downstairs bar is punctuated with canary-yellow walls. Expect excellent service throughout your stay, and, if you opt for it, a lavish breakfast with fresh-squeezed orange juice, bacon, eggs, and more— enough to keep you going until dinner. There's a CD and DVD library, in addition to plenty of books. **Pros:** all the Guggenheim eyeful you could ever ask for, sexy clientele and staff. **Cons:** over-designed, certain practicalities such as bedside tables and closet space seem to have been

overlooked. ✉ *Alameda de Mazarredo 77, El Ensanche* ☎ *94/661–1880*
⊕ *www.mirohotelbilbao.com* ⟿ *45 rooms, 5 suites* ☾ *In-room: Wi-Fi.
In-hotel: restaurant, room service, bar, gym, spa, laundry service, airport
shuttle, parking (fee)* ☰ *AE, DC, MC, V* Ⓜ *Moyúa.*

BARCELONA

Capital of Catalonia, 2,000-year-old Barcelona commanded a vast
Mediterranean empire when Madrid was still a dusty Moorish outpost on the Spanish steppe. One of Europe's most visually stunning
cities, Barcelona balances the medieval intimacy of its Gothic Quarter
with the grace and distinction of the wide boulevards in the Moderniste
Eixample—just as the Mediterranean Gothic elegance of the church of
Santa Maria del Mar provides a perfect counterpoint to Gaudí's riotous Sagrada Família. Mies van der Rohe's pavilion seems even more
minimalist after a look at the Art Nouveau Palau de la Música Catalana, while such exciting contemporary creations as Bofill's neoclassical
Parthenon-under-glass Teatre Nacional de Catalunya, Frank Gehry's
waterfront goldfish, Norman Foster's Torre de Collscrola, and Jean
Nouvel's Torre Agbar all add spice to Barcelona's visual soup. Meanwhile, Barcelona's fashion industry is pulling even with those of Paris
and Milan, and FC (Futbol Club) is Barcelona's perennial contender for
European championships and the world's most glamorous soccer club.

14

PLANNING YOUR TIME

The Rambla is the focal point of most trips to Barcelona, from Plaça
Catalunya, and moving toward the Port, and don't miss the Boqueria
market with all its colors and aromas of Mediterranean life. Other
must-sees include the Liceu opera house, Plaça Reial, and Gaudí's masterworks, the Palau Güell and the Sagrada Família church.

The Gothic Quarter is a warren of Roman and medieval alleys. Once
the Roman forum, Plaça Sant Jaume opens up between the municipal
and Catalonian government palaces. Across Via Laietana, the Ribera-
Born neighborhood is centered on the exquisite Mediterranean Gothic
Santa Maria del Mar basilica, a step away from the Picasso Museum. A
15-minute walk east from Santa Maria del Mar is Barceloneta, the traditional fisherman's quarter, with a dozen good seafood restaurants.

El Raval, home of the medieval hospital, one of the city's finest Gothic
spaces, is a good morning's hike. Gràcia, and Sarrià are each interesting
half-day explorations, while Montjuïc has the Museu Nacional d'Art de
Catalunya, the Miró Fundació, and the Mies van der Rohe Pavilion.

WHEN TO GO

Summer can be uncomfortably hot in Barcelona, and many of the finest restaurants and musical venues are closed. On the other hand, El
Grec, the summer music festival, is a delight, and the August Gràcia
Festa Major is a major block party, while the whole city becomes an
extension of the Barceloneta beach, which is not without its attractions.
October through June is the time to come to observe Barcelona's daily
hum, with mid-November–early April pleasantly cool and the rest of
the time ideally warm. Late September's Festa de la Mercé is a fiesta

not to miss; winter's Carnaval and *calçot* (long-stemmed onions) season are spectacular and delicious, and April and May are best of all: the Sant Jordi lovers' day on April 23 and the Sant Ponç celebration of natural produce on May 11 are among the most magical moments of the year.

GETTING HERE & AROUND

Barcelona's El Prat de Llobregat Airport, 7 km (4½ mi) south of the city, receives international flights from all over the world. Low-cost flights such as Ryanair land in Girona, an hour north of Barcelona. Getting to the city from the airport is easiest by taxi (€20–€28), but the bus to Plaça Catalunya (€4.95) leaves from directly in front of each terminal and is about as fast as a taxi—and a fraction of the cost. From Plaça Catalunya a taxi to your hotel (€5–€10) can be easily flagged down.

Long-distance trains arrive and depart from Estació de Sants. En route to or from Sants, some trains stop at another station on Passeig de Gràcia at Carrer Aragó; this can be a good way to avoid the long lines that form at Sants during holidays, though even better is dealing directly with www.renfe.es. For schedules and fares, call RENFE at ☎ 902/240202.

For trips outside of town, car-rental agencies in Barcelona are at the airport and at Sants train station. Within the city, a car is more liability than an asset; you're better off with taxis, your feet, the metro, or the bus.

For getting around in Barcelona, the Targeta-10 (€7.20), valid for metro or bus, is an essential resource. The FCG (Ferrocarril de la Generalitat) train from Plaça Catalunya through the center of town to Sarrià and outlying cities is a commuter train that gets you to within walking distance of nearly everything in Barcelona. Transfers to the regular city metro are free. A major taxi stand is at the head of the Rambla on Plaça Catalunya, though lines often form there. A better choice is the one at Plaça Sant Jaume, at the center of the Gothic Quarter. City buses run daily from 5:30 AM to 11:30 PM. The fare is €1.35. Route maps are displayed at bus stops.

Daily bus service connects the major cities to Madrid, Zaragoza, and Barcelona (and with a layover or transfer to Spain's other destinations). From Madrid, call the bus company Continental Auto for details, or go to the station at Calle Alenza 20. Even better, reserve online at ⊕*www. alsa.es*. Bus service between cities and smaller towns is comprehensive, but few have central bus stations; most have numerous bus lines leaving from various points in town.

ESSENTIALS

Air Contacts Aeroport del Prat (☎ *902/404704*).

Bus Schedules Schedules are available at bus and metro stations or at ⊕ *www. bcn.es/guia/welcomea.htm.*

Subway Contact Transports Metropolitans de Barcelona (TMB) (☎ *93/298–7000* ⊕ *www.tmb.net*).

Taxi Contact **City Taxis** (☎*93/387–1000, 93/490–2222, or 93/357–7755 24 hours a day*).

City Tourist Offices Institut de Cultura (✉*La Rambla 99, Rambla* ☎*93/316–1000*). **Institut de Cultura Centro de Arte Santa Mónica** (✉*La Rambla 7, Rambla* ☎*93/316–2811*). **Palau de Congressos** (✉*Av. María Cristina s/n, Eixample* ☎*902/233200*). **Turisme de Barcelona** (✉*Pl. de Catalunya 17 bis, Eixample* ☎*807/117222* ⊕*www.barcelonaturisme.com* ✉*Pl. Sant Jaume 1, Barri Gòtic* ☎*906/301282*).

Regional Tourist Offices El Prat Airport (☎*93/478–4704*). **Palau Robert** (✉*Passeig de Gràcia 107, at Diagonal, Eixample* ☎*93/238–4000*).

EXPLORING BARCELONA

Barcelona has long had a frenetically active cultural life. It was the home of architect Antoni Gaudí, whose buildings are the most startling statements of Modernisme. Other leading Moderniste architects of the city include Lluís Domènech i Montaner and Josep Puig i Cadafalch, and the painters Joan Miró, Salvador Dalí, and Antoni Tàpies are also strongly identified with Catalonia. Pablo Picasso spent his formative years in Barcelona, and one of the city's treasures is a museum devoted to his works. Barcelona's opera house, the Liceu, is the finest in Spain, and the city claims such native Catalan musicians as cellist Pablo (Pau, in Catalan) Casals, opera singers Montserrat Caballé and José (Josep) Carreras, and early-music viola da gamba master Jordi Savall.

THE RAMBLA

Barcelona's best-known promenade is a constant and colorful flood of humanity that flows past flower stalls, bird vendors, mimes, musicians, newspaper kiosks, and outdoor cafés; traffic plays second fiddle to the endless *paseo* (stroll) of locals and travelers alike. Federico García Lorca called this street the only one in the world that he wished would never end. The whole avenue is referred to as Las Ramblas (Les Rambles, in Catalan) or La Rambla, but each section has its own name: Rambla Santa Monica is at the southeastern, or port, end; Rambla de les Flors in the middle; and Rambla dels Estudis is at the top, near Plaça de Catalunya.

㉔ **Antic Hospital de la Santa Creu.** The 15th-century medieval hospital, now
★ housing the Biblioteca de Catalunya (the "Library of Catalunya") cultural institutions, and the Escola Massana art school, is one of the four finest Gothic spaces in Barcelona (along with Drassanes, Santa Maria del Mar, and La Llotja). ✉*Carrer del Carme 45, or Carrer Hospital 56, Raval* Ⓜ*Catalunya, Liceu.*

㉓ **Gran Teatre del Liceu.** Along with Milan's La Scala, Barcelona's opera house has long been considered one of the most beautiful in Europe. First built in 1848, it was burned down in 1861, bombed in 1893, and once again gutted by a blaze of mysterious origins in early 1994. ✉*La Rambla 51–59, Rambla* ☎*93/485–9900* ⊕*www.liceubarcelona.com* 🎫*Guided tours €8.50, 20-min self-guided express tour €4* ☉*Tours daily at 10 AM in Spanish and English, self-guided express tours daily at*

14

KEY

- •••• *Funicular*
- Ⓜ *Metro Stations*
- ⊢—⊢ *Railway Lines*
- •••• *Telefèric*
- 🛈 *Tourist Information*
- ↗ *Tram stops*

11:30, noon, 12:30, and 1. The backstage tour at 9:30 AM *(€10) must be arranged by reservation (☎ 93/485–9900 or visites@liceubarcelona. com).* Ⓜ*Liceu.*

㉕ **Museu d'Art Contemporani de Barcelona** *(Barcelona Museum of Contemporary Art, MACBA).* Designed in 1992 by American architect Richard Meier, this gleaming explosion of glass and planes of white contains 20th-century masters including Calder, Rauschenberg, Oteiza, Chillida, and Tàpies. ✉*Pl. dels Àngels 1, Raval* ☎93/412–0810 ⊕*www.macba. es* 🖃*€7.50, Wed. €3.50* ☉*Mon. and Wed.–Fri. 11–7:30, Sat. 10–8, Sun. 10–3; free guided tours daily at 6, Sun. at noon* Ⓜ*Catalunya.*

❺ **Museu Marítim.** The superb Maritime Museum is in the 13th-century **Drassanes Reials** (Royal Shipyards), to the right at the foot of the Rambla. This vast medieval space, one of Barcelona's finest Gothic structures, seems more like a cathedral than a boatyard, and is filled with ships, including a life-size reconstructed galley, figureheads, and early navigational charts. ✉ *Av. de les Drassanes s/n, Rambla* ☎93/342–9920 ⊕*www.museumaritimbarcelona.org* 🖃*€6.50; free 1st Sat. of month after 3* ☉*Daily 10–7* Ⓜ*Drassanes.*

㉒ **Palau Güell.** Antoni Gaudí built this mansion during the years 1886–89 for his patron, textile baron Count Eusebi de Güell, and soon found himself in the international limelight. The dark facade is a dramatic foil for the treasure house inside, where spear-shape Art Nouveau columns frame the windows and prop up a series of intricately coffered wood ceilings. ✉*Carrer Nou de la Rambla 3–5, Rambla* ☎93/317–3974 ⊕*www.palauguell.cat* ☉*Tues.–Sat. 10–2:30.* Ⓜ*Drassanes, Liceu.*

㉖ **Plaça de Catalunya.** Barcelona's main transport hub, the Plaça de Catalunya, is the frontier between the old city and the post-1860 Eixample. Café Zurich, at the head of the Rambla and the mouth of the metro, is a classic rendezvous point.

❻ **Port.** Beyond the Monument a Colom—behind the Duana, or former customs building (now site of the Barcelona Port Authority)—is the **Rambla de Mar,** a boardwalk with a drawbridge. The Rambla de Mar extends out to the **Moll d'Espanya,** with its Maremagnum shopping center, IMAX theater, and aquarium.

CIUTAT VELLA: EL BARRI GÒTIC & RIBERA-BORN

⑰ **Catedral de la Seu.** On Saturday afternoons, Sunday mornings, and occasional evenings, Barcelona folk gather in the Plaça de la Seu to dance the *sardana,* a somewhat demure circular dance and a great symbol of Catalan identity. The Gothic cathedral was built between 1298 and 1450, with the spire and neo-Gothic facade added in 1892. Architects of Catalan Gothic churches strove to make the high altar visible to the entire congregation, hence the unusually wide central nave and slender side columns. ✉*Pl. de la Seu, Barri Gòtic* ☎93/342–8260 ⊕*www. catedralbcn.org* 🖃*1–5* PM *Special Visit: €5.50; the rest of the time free* ☉*Daily 7:45* AM*–7:45* PM Ⓜ*Catalunya, Liceu, Jaume I.*

⑫ **El Born.** Once the site of medieval jousts, the Passeig del Born is at the end of Carrer Montcada behind the church of Santa Maria del Mar.

The numbered cannonballs under the benches are in memory of the 1714 siege of Barcelona that concluded the 14-year War of the Spanish Succession. ⊠ *Born-Ribera* ☎ *93/315–1111 Museu de Història de la Ciutat* Ⓜ *Jaume I.*

⑲ **Museu d'Història de la Ciutat** *(City History Museum)*. This fascinating museum traces the evolution of Barcelona from its first Iberian settlement to its alleged founding by the Carthaginian Hamilcar Barca in about 230 BC, to Roman and Visigothic times and beyond. ⊠ *Plaça del Rei s/n, Barri Gòtic* ☎ *93/256–2100* ⊕ *www.museuhistoria.bcn. cat* ⊞ *€5.50 (includes admission to Monestir de Pedralbes, Centre d'Interpretació del Park Güell, Centre d'Interpretació del Call, Centre d'Interpretació Històrica, Refugi 307, and Museu-Casa Verdaguer)* ⊙ *Oct.–May, Tues.–Sat. 10–2 and 4–7; June–Sept., Tues.–Sat. 10–7; Sun. 10–3* Ⓜ *Catalunya, Liceu, Jaume I.*

⑬ **Museu Picasso.** Picasso spent key formative years (1895–1904) in Barcelona, when he was a young Bohemian, and never forgot these good times. (His *Demoiselles d'Avignon* was, in fact, inspired by the eponymous Barcelona street known for its brothels, not by the French city.) A collection of his work can be found in Carrer Montcada, known for Barcelona's most elegant medieval and Renaissance palaces, five of which are occupied by the Picasso Museum. ⊠ *Carrer Montcada 15–23, Born-Ribera* ☎ *93/319–6310* ⊕ *www.museupicasso.bcn.cat* ⊞ *€9.50; free 1st Sun. of month* ⊙ *Tues.–Sun. 10–8.* Ⓜ *Catalunya, Liceu, Jaume I.*

Fodor'sChoice ★

⑯ **Palau de la Música Catalana.** A riot of color and form, Barcelona's Music Palace is the flagship of the city's Moderniste architecture. Designed by Lluís Domènech i Montaner in 1908, it was originally conceived by the Orfeó Català musical society as a vindication of the importance of music at a popular level—as opposed to the Liceu opera house's identification with the Catalan (often Castilian-speaking monarchist) aristocracy. *Ticket office* ⊠ *Carrer Sant Francesc de Paula 2, just off Via Laietana, around corner from hall, Sant Pere* ☎ *902/442882* ⊕ *www. palaumusica.org* ⊞ *Tour €10* ⊙ *Sept.–June, tours daily 10–3:30, July and Aug., tours daily 10–7* Ⓜ *Catalunya.*

Fodor'sChoice ★

⑱ **Plaça del Rei.** As chronicled in legend, song, and painting, this austere medieval square has long been believed to be the scene of Columbus's triumphal return from his first voyage to the New World, with Ferdinand and Isabella receiving "the discoverer" on the stairs. (It turns out that the king and queen were actually at a summer palace outside of town.) The **Palau Reial Major** was the Catholic Monarchs' official residence in Barcelona. Ⓜ *Catalunya, Liceu, Jaume I.*

㉑ **Plaça Reial.** Pungent and seedy around the edges but elegant and neoclassical in design, this symmetrical mid-19th-century arcaded square is bordered by ocher facades with balconies overlooking the **Fountain of the Three Graces** and lampposts designed by Gaudí. Ⓜ *Catalunya, Liceu.*

⑳ **Plaça Sant Jaume.** Two thousand years ago, this formal square was the center of the Roman forum, which seems fitting for the modern-day site of both Catalonia's and Barcelona's government seats. The 15th-century *ajuntament* (City Hall) contains impressive black-and-burnished-gold murals (1928) by Josep Maria Sert and the historic Saló de Cent, where the Council of One Hundred, Europe's earliest proto-democratic body founded in 1372, governed until Felipe V abolished Catalonia's autonomous institutions in 1715. The **Palau de la Generalitat,** seat of

the Catalan government, is a majestic 15th-century palace—through the front windows you can see the gilded ceiling of the Saló de Sant Jordi (Hall of St. George), named for Catalonia's dragon-slaying patron saint. ⊠*Pl. Sant Jaume 1, Barri Gòtic* ☎*93/402–7000* ⊕*www.bcn.es* ⊙*Sun. 10–1* Ⓜ*Catalunya, Liceu, Jaume I.*

⓫ **Santa Maria del Mar.** The most breathtakingly symmetrical and grace-
★ ful of all Barcelona's churches is on the Carrer Montcada end of Passeig del Born. It's an early Gothic basilica with Romanesque echoes and overtones; simple and spacious, this pure, classical space enclosed by soaring columns is something of an oddity in ornate and complex Moderniste Barcelona. Santa Maria del Mar (Saint Mary of the Sea) was built from 1329 to 1383, an extraordinarily prompt construction time in that era, in fulfillment of a vow made a century earlier by Jaume I to build a church to watch over all Catalan seafarers. ⊠ *Pl. de Santa Maria, Born-Ribera* ☎*93/310–2390* ⊙*Daily 9–1:30 and 4:30–8* Ⓜ*Catalunya, Jaume I.*

BARCELONETA, LA CIUTADELLA & PORT OLIMPIC

⓯ **Arc del Triomf.** This imposing, exposed-redbrick arch on Passeig de Sant Joan was built by Josep Vilaseca as the grand entrance for the Universal Exposition of 1888. Similar in size and sense to the triumphal arches of ancient Rome, this one refers to Jaume I El Conqueridor's 1229 conquest of the Moors in Mallorca—the bats, on either side of the arch, are always part of Jaume I's coat of arms.

❼ **Barceloneta.** Once Barcelona's pungent fishing port, Barceloneta retains much of its salty maritime flavor. It's an exciting and colorful place to walk through, with narrow streets with lines of laundry snapping in the breeze. Barceloneta's surprisingly clean and sandy **beach,** though over-crowded in midsummer, offers swimming, surfing, and a lively social scene from late May through September.

⓮ **Castell dels Tres Dragons** (*Castle of the Three Dragons*). Built by Domènech i Montaner as a restaurant for the Universal Exposition of 1888, this arresting structure was named in honor of a popular mid-19th-century comedy by the father of the Catalan theater, Serafí Pitarra. ⊠*Passeig Picasso 5, La Ciutadella* ☎*93/319–6912* ⊕*www.bcn.es/medciencies* ⊡*€4.50* ⊙*Tues., Wed., Fri.–Sun. 10–2:30, Thurs. 10–6:30* Ⓜ*Arc de Triomf.*

❿ Parc de la Ciutadella *(Citadel Park).*
Ꮯ Once a fortress designed to consolidate Madrid's military occupation of Barcelona, the Ciutadella is now the city's main downtown park. ✉ *Bounded by Passeig Picasso, Passeig Pujades, Carrer de Wellington, and Born-Ribera* Ⓜ *Barceloneta.*

❾ Port Olímpic. Choked with yachts, restaurants, and tapas bars of all kinds, the Olympic Port is 2 km (1 mi) up the beach, marked by the mammoth Frank Gehry goldfish sculpture in front of Barcelona's first real skyscraper, the Hotel Arts. ✉ *Carrer de la Marina/Passeig Marítim, Born-Ribera* Ⓜ *Ciutadella, Vila Olimpica.*

❽ Port Vell *(Old Port).* Barcelona's
Ꮯ marina stretches the length of Passeig de Joan de Borbó, and encompasses the large pedestrian wharves (molls). Just beyond the Lichtenstein sculpture *Barcelona Head*, the modern Port Vell complex stretches up the grassy hill to the wood-panel *Ictineo II* reproduction of the submarine created by Narcis Monturiol (1819–85). ✉ *Passeig d'Ítaca s/n, Barceloneta Port Vell* Ⓜ *Barceloneta.*

> **CATALAN FOR BEGINNERS**
>
> Catalan is derived from Latin and Provençal French, whereas Spanish is heavy on Arabic vocabulary and phonetics. For language exchange *(intercambios),* check the bulletin board at the central university Philosophy and Letters Faculty on Gran Via or any English bookstore for free half-hour exchanges of English for Catalan (or Spanish), a great way to get free private lessons and meet locals. Who knows? With the right chemistry, intercambios can lead to cross-cultural friendships and even romance. Who said the language of love is French?

14

THE EIXAMPLE

㉘ Casa Milà. Gaudí's Casa Milà, usually referred to as **La Pedrera** (The
★ Stone Quarry), has a curving stone facade that bobs around the corner of the block. When the building was unveiled, in 1905, residents weren't enthusiastic about the cavelike balconies. Don't miss Gaudí's rooftop chimney park, especially in late afternoon, when the sunlight slants over the city into the Mediterranean. ✉ *Carrer Provença 261–265, Eixample* ☎ *902/400973* ☞ *€8.50* ☉ *Daily 9–6:30; guided tours weekdays at 6* PM, *weekends at 11* AM. *Espai Gaudí roof terrace open for drinks evenings June–Sept.* Ⓜ *Diagonal, Provença.*

㉚ Hospital de Sant Pau. Certainly one of the most beautiful hospital complexes in the world, a 10-minute walk down Avinguda Gaudí from the Sagrada Família, the Hospital de Sant Pau is notable for its Mudejar motifs and sylvan plantings. Begun in 1900, this monumental production won Lluís Domènech i Montaner his third Barcelona "Best Building" award, in 1912. ✉ *Carrer Sant Antoni Maria Claret 167, Eixample* ☎ *93/291–9000* ⊕ *www.santpau.es* ☞ *Free; tour €5* ☉ *Daily 9–8; tours weekends 10–2, weekdays by advance arrangement* Ⓜ *Hospital de Sant Pau.*

㉗ Manzana de la Discòrdia. A pun on the Spanish word *manzana,* meaning
★ both city block and apple, the reference is to the classical myth of the Apple of Discord, in which Eris, goddess of strife, drops a golden apple

with the inscription "to the fairest." Hera, Athena, and Aphrodite all claim the apple; Paris is chosen to settle the dispute and awards the apple to Aphrodite, who promises him Helen, the most beautiful of women, triggering the Trojan War. On this city block you can find the architectural counterpoint, where the three main Moderniste architects go hand to hand, drawing steady crowds of architecture buffs. **Casa Lleó Morera** (No. 35) was extensively rebuilt (1902–06) by Palau de la Música Catalana architect Domènech i Montaner and is a treasure chest of Modernisme.

The pseudo-Flemish **Casa Amatller** (No. 41) was built by Josep Puig i Cadafalch in 1900 when the architect was 33 years old. At No. 43, the colorful and bizarre **Casa Batlló**—Gaudí at his most spectacular—with its mottled facade resembling anything from an abstract pointillist painting to rainbow sprinkles on an ice-cream cone, is usually easily identifiable by the crowd of tourists snapping photographs on the sidewalk. ⊠ *Passeig de Gràcia 43, between Carrer Consell de Cent and Carrer Aragó, Eixample* ☎ *93/216–0306* ⊕ *www.casabatllo.es* ⊠ *€17* ☉ *Daily 9–8* Ⓜ *Passeig de Gràcia.*

㉙ **Temple Expiatori de la Sagrada Família.** Looming over Barcelona like a
Fodor'sChoice   magical mid-city massif of needles and peaks left by eons of wind ero-
★   sion and fungal exuberance, Barcelona's most unforgettable landmark, Antoni Gaudí's Sagrada Família, was conceived as nothing short of a Bible in stone. This landmark is one of the most important architectural creations of the 19th to 21st centuries, though it's still under construction. ⊠ *Mallorca 401, Eixample* ☎ *93/207–3031* ⊕ *www. sagradafamilia.org* ⊠ *€9, bell tower elevator €2.* ☉ *Oct.–Mar., daily 9–6; Apr.–Sept., daily 9–8* Ⓜ *Sagrada Família.*

UPPER BARCELONA

㉛ **Park Güell.** Güell Park is one of Gaudí's, and Barcelona's, most pleas-
Fodor'sChoice   ant and visually stimulating places to spend a few hours; it's light and
★   playful, alternately shady, green, floral, and sunny. Named for and commissioned by Gaudí's main patron, Count Eusebio Güell, the park was intended as a hillside garden suburb on the English model. Barcelona's bourgeoisie seemed happier living closer to "town," however, so only two of the houses were ever built and the Güell family eventually turned the land over to the city as a public park. ⊠ *Carrer d'Olot s/n; take Metro to Lesseps; then walk 10 min uphill or catch Bus 24 to park entrance, Gràcia* ☉ *Oct.–Mar., daily 10–6; Apr.–June, daily 10–7; July–Sept., daily 10–9* Ⓜ *Lesseps.*

㉜ **Tibidabo.** On clear days the views from this hill are legendary, particularly from the 850-foot communications tower, Torre de Collserola. Created by Norman Foster, the Collserola Tower was erected for the 1992 Olympics amid controversy over defacement of the traditional mountain skyline. ⊠ *Plaça del Doctor Andreu s/n Take Tibidabo train (U-7) from Pl. de Catalunya or buses 24 and 22 to Pl. Kennedy. At Av. Tibidabo, catch Tramvía Blau (Blue Trolley), which connects with funicular to summit. Take the funicular up to Tibidabo; from Pl. Tibidabo there is free transport to the tower.* ☎ *93/406–9354* ⊕ *www.*

torredecollserola.com ⌨€6 ⊘ *Wed.–Fri. 11–2:30 and 3:30–6, week-ends 11–6* Ⓜ*Tibidabo.*

MONTJUÏC

❹ **Castell de Montjuïc.** Built in 1640 by rebels against Felipe IV, the star-shape pentagon has been stormed several times, most famously in 1705 by Lord Peterborough for Archduke Carlos of Austria. ⊠*Ctra. de Montjuïc 66, Montjuïc* ☎93/329–8613 ⌨€4.50 ⊘*Tues.–Sun. 9:30–8.*

❷ **Estadi Olímpic.** The Olympic Stadium was originally built for the International Exposition of 1929, with the idea that Barcelona would then be the site of the 1936 Olympics (ultimately staged in Hitler's Berlin). After failing twice, Barcelona celebrated the attainment of its long-cherished goal by renovating the semi-derelict stadium in time for 1992, providing seating for 70,000. ⊠*Passeig Olímpic 17–19, Montjuïc* ☎93/426–0660 ⊕*www.fundaciobarcelonaolimpica.es* ⌨*Gallery €4.50* ⊘*Tues.–Sat. 10–2 and 4–7.*

❸ **Fundació Miró.** The Miró Foundation was a gift from the artist Joan Miró
★ to his native city and is one of Barcelona's most exciting showcases of contemporary art. The airy, white building was designed by Josep Lluís Sert and opened in 1975; an extension was added by Sert's pupil Jaume Freixa in 1988. ⊠*Av. Miramar 71, Montjuïc* ☎93/443–9470 ⊕*www.bcn.fjmiro.es* ⌨€8.50 ⊘*Tues., Wed., Fri., and Sat. 10–7, Thurs. 10–9:30, Sun. 10–2:30.*

❶ **Museu Nacional d'Art de Catalunya** *(MNAC, Catalonian National Museum of*
Fodor's Choice *Art).* Housed in the imposingly domed, towered, frescoed, and columned
★ **Palau Nacional,** built in 1929 as the centerpiece of the World's Fair, this superb museum was renovated in 1995 by Gae Aulenti, architect of the Musée d'Orsay in Paris. ⊠*Mirador del Palau 6, Montjuïc* ☎93/622–0375 ⊕*www.mnac.es* ⌨€10 ⊘*Tues.–Sat. 10–7, Sun. 10–2:30.*

WHERE TO EAT

CIUTAT VELLA (OLD CITY)

$–$$ ✕**Agut.** This is no-frills classical Catalan fare at a fantastic value. Agut
CATALAN was founded in 1924, and its popularity has never waned, despite the enormous changes in Barcelona's dining scene. Wood paneling and oil paintings provide the background for the mostly Catalan crowd in this homey restaurant in the lower reaches of the Gothic Quarter. In season (September through May), try the *pato silvestre agridulce* (sweet-and-sour wild duck). ⊠*Gignàs 16, Barri Gòtic* ☎93/315–1709 ▤*AE, MC, V* ⊘*Closed Mon. and July. No dinner Sun.* Ⓜ*Jaume I.*

$$$$ ✕**Ca l'Isidre.** Gourmets, gourmands, cognoscenti, and epicureans of
Fodor's Choice all stripes recognize Ca l'Isidre as the finest restaurant in Barcelona.
★ Just off Avinguda del Paral.lel in the darkest Raval, this is a favorite
MEDITERRANEAN with Barcelona's art crowd. Paintings and engravings by Miró, Dalí, Joan Pere Viladecans, and other stars line the walls. The traditional yet contemporary Catalan cooking draws on fresh produce from the Boqueria and has a slight French accent. The homemade foie gras is

superb. ⊠*Carrer de les Flors 12, Raval* ☎93/441–1139 ♨*Reservations essential* ☰*AE, MC, V* ⊘*Closed Sun., Easter wk, and mid-July–mid-Aug.* Ⓜ*Paral.lel.*

$$$$ ✗**Comerç 24.** Artist, aesthete, and chef Carles Abellan playfully reinter-
LA NUEVA prets traditional Catalan favorites at this sleek, designer dining spot.
COCINA Try the deconstructed *tortilla de patatas* (potato omelet), or the *huevo kinder* (an egg with surprises inside, based on a popular children's toy). For dessert, prepare for a postmodern version of the traditional after-school snack of chocolate, olive oil, salt, and bread. ⊠*Carrer Comerç 24, Born-Ribera* ☎93/319–2102 ♨*Reservations essential* ☰*AE, DC, MC, V* ⊘*Closed Sun.* Ⓜ*Jaume I.*

$$–$$$ ✗**Cometacinc.** This stylish spot in the Barri Gòtic, an increasingly chic
CATALAN neighborhood, is a fine example of Barcelona's taste and technology with new-over-old architecture and interior design. The floor-to-ceiling wooden shutters are a visual feast, but the carefully prepared interpre-tations of old standards, such as the *carpaccio de toro de lidia* (carpac-cio of fighting bull) with basil sauce and pine nuts, are also brilliant. ⊠*Carrer Cometa 5, Barri Gòtic* ☎93/310–1558 ☰*AE, DC, MC, V* ⊘*Closed Tues.* Ⓜ*Jaume I.*

BARCELONETA & THE PORT OLÍMPIC

Barceloneta and the Port Olímpic (Olympic Port) have little in common beyond their seaside location: the former is a traditional fishermen's quar-ter, the latter is a crazed disco strip with thousand-seat restaurants.

$$$–$$$$ ✗**Can Majó.** One of Barcelona's premier seafood restaurants, Can
SEAFOOD Majó combines fine cooking and a cosmopolitan vibe. House special-ties include *caldero de bogavante* (a cross between paella and lobster bouillabaisse) and *suquet* (fish stewed in its own juices), but what-ever you choose will be excellent. ⊠*Almirall Aixada 23, Barceloneta* ☎93/221–5455 ☰*AE, DC, MC, V* ⊘*Closed Mon. No dinner Sun.* Ⓜ*Barceloneta.*

$–$$ ✗**Can Manel la Puda.** The first choice for a non-wallet-knocking paella in
SEAFOOD the sun, year-round, Can Manel is near the end of the main road out to the Barceloneta beach. *Arròs a banda* (rice with peeled shellfish), paella marinera (seafood and rice), or *fideuá* (with noodles instead of rice) are all delicious. ⊠*Passeig Joan de Borbó 60, Barceloneta* ☎93/221–5013 ☰*AE, DC, MC, V* ⊘*Closed Mon.* Ⓜ*Barceloneta.*

EIXAMPLE

$$$–$$$$ ✗**Alkimia.** Chef Jordi Vilà makes news with his inventive creations and
★ tasting menus at €40 and €54 that pass for a bargain in top Barcelona
LA NUEVA culinary culture. It's usually packed, but the alcoves are intimate. Vilà's
COCINA deconstructed *pa amb tomaquet* (in classical usage, toasted bread with olive oil and squeezed tomato) in a shot glass gives a witty culinary wink before things get serious with raw tuna strips, baby squid, or turbot. ⊠*Indústria 79, Eixample* ☎93/207–6115 ☰*AE, DC, MC, V* ⊘*Closed Sat. lunch, Sun., Easter wk, and Aug. 1–21* Ⓜ*Sagrada Família.*

$$$–$$$$ ✗**Casa Calvet.** This Art Nouveau space in Antoni Gaudí's 1898–1900
MEDITERRANEAN Casa Calvet, just a block from the Hotel Palace, is an opportunity to break bread in one of the great Moderniste's creations. The dining room is a graceful and spectacular display featuring signature Gaudí-esque

ornamentation from looping parabolic door handles to polychrome stained glass, and wood carved in floral and organic motifs. The menu is Mediterranean, with an emphasis on light, contemporary fare. ⊠ *Casp 48, Eixample* ☎ *93/412–4012* ⊟ *AE, DC, MC, V* ⊘ *Closed Sun. and last 2 wks of Aug.* Ⓜ *Urquinaona.*

$$$$
FodorsChoice
★
MEDITERRANEAN

✗ **Drolma.** Chef Fermin Puig's blend of tradition, innovation, and inspiration produces classical Mediterranean excellence based on peerless products and painstakingly perfect execution. Named (in Sanskrit) for Buddha's female side, this intimate refuge has been a success since the doors first opened. Fermin's foie gras *a la ceniza con ceps* (cooked over wood coals with wild mushrooms) is a typical example of a childhood favorite reinvented in the big city. ⊠ *Majestic Hotel, Passeig de Gràcia 70, Eixample* ☎ *93/496–7710* ⚠ *Reservations essential* ⊟ *AE, DC, MC, V* ⊘ *Closed Sun. and Aug.* Ⓜ *Provença, Passeig de Gràcia.*

14

GRÁCIA

$$$$
SPANISH

✗ **Botafumeiro.** Fleets of waiters in white outfits flash by at the speed of light in Barcelona's best Galician restaurant, which specializes in seafood medleys from shellfish to finfish to cuttlefish to caviar. An assortment of *media ración* (half-ration) selections is available at the bar, where *pulpo a feira* (squid on potato) and *jamón bellota de Guijuelo* (acorn-fed ham) make peerless late-night fare. People-watching is tops here, and the waiters are better than stand-up comics. ⊠ *Carrer Gran de Gràcia 81, Gràcia* ☎ *93/218–4230* ⊟ *AE, DC, MC, V* Ⓜ *Gràcia.*

SARRIA-PEDRALBES & SANT GERVASI

$$$$
LA NUEVA
COCINA

✗ **El Racó d'en Freixa.** Chef Ramón Freixa's original riffs on traditional recipes, all using the best ingredients, have established his work as *cuina d'autor* (designer cuisine). A typical specialty is *peus de porc en escabetx de guatlle* (pig's trotters with quail in a garlic-and-parsley gratin). Four textures (raw, freeze-fried, stewed, transparent) of tomato with Palamós jumbo shrimp is another original creation. The minimalist, clean-lined design of the dining room perfectly matches the aesthetic of Freixa's cuisine. ⊠ *Sant Elíes 22, Sant Gervasi* ☎ *93/209–7559* ⊟ *AE, DC, MC, V* ⊘ *Closed Mon., Easter wk, and Aug. No dinner Sun.* Ⓜ *Sant Gervasi.*

$$$–$$$$
★
MEDITERRANEAN

✗ **Tram-Tram.** Isidre Soler and his wife Reyes have put together one of Barcelona's finest culinary offerings at what was once the end of the old tram line above the village of Sarrià. Try the *menú de degustaciòn* and you might score marinated tuna salad, cod medallions, and venison filets mignon. Perfect portions and a streamlined reinterpretation of space within this traditional Sarrià house—especially in or near the garden out back—make this a memorable dining experience. ⊠ *Major de Sarrià 121, Sarrià* ☎ *93/204–8518* ⊟ *AE, DC, MC, V* ⊘ *Closed Sun. and late Dec.–early Jan. No lunch Sat.* Ⓜ *Reina Elisenda.*

WHERE TO STAY

CIUTAT VELLA (OLD CITY)

$–$$

🛏 **Hotel Market.** A wallet-friendly boutique hotel and yet another Barcelona design triumph, the Hotel Market is named for the Mercat de Sant Antoni, the first city market built outside the medieval walls after they were torn down in 1860. On a small alleyway one block from the market and within walking distance of all of the Raval and Gothic Quarter attractions, this ultramodern, high-tech, minimalist lodging is one of Barcelona's best bargains. The hotel restaurant offers superlative fare and excellent value, too. **Pros:** well equipped, designed and positioned for a low-cost Barcelona visit, young and friendly staff. **Cons:** rooms are a bit cramped, the area comes alive at dawn on weekends when the Mercat de Sant Antoni market is setting up. ⊠ *Carrer Comte Borrell 68 (entrance on Passage Sant Antoni Abat 10), Raval* ☎ *93/325–1205* ⊕ *www.markethotel.com.es* ⤳ *37 rooms* ⚿ *In-room: refrigerator, Wi-Fi. In-hotel: restaurant, bar, public Internet.* ⊟ *AE, DC, MC, V* Ⓜ *Sant Antoni*

BARCELONETA & THE PORT OLÍMPIC

$$$$ 🏨 **Hotel Arts.** This luxurious Ritz-Carlton monolith overlooks Barcelona from the Olympic Port, providing unique views of the Mediterranean, the city, and the mountains behind. The hotel's main drawback is that it's somewhat in a world of its own, a short taxi ride from the center of the city. That said, its world is an exciting one. True to its name, fine art—from Chillida drawings to Susana Solano sculptures—hangs everywhere. There are three restaurants; Sergi Arola's eponymous dining spot is a chic, postmodern culinary playground. **Pros:** excellent views over Barcelona, fine restaurants and general comfort and technology. **Cons:** a 20-minute hike from Barri de la Ribera, a colony of (mostly American) tourists, not very Spanish (it could be anywhere). ⊠ *Calle de la Marina 19, Port Olímpic* ☎ *93/221–1000* ⊕ *www.harts.es* ⤳ *397 rooms, 59 suites, 27 apartments* ⚿ *In-room: refrigerator, Wi-Fi. In-hotel: 3 restaurants, room service, bar, pool, beachfront, parking (fee)* ⊟ *AE, DC, MC, V* Ⓜ *Ciutadella–Vila Olímpica.*

EIXAMPLE

$$$$ 🏨 **Claris.** Widely considered one of Barcelona's best hotels, this mid-
★ town refuge is a fascinating mélange of design and tradition. The rooms come in 60 modern layouts, some with restored 18th-century English furniture, some with contemporary furnishings from Barcelona's endless legion of playful lamp and chair designers. The restaurant, East 47, is stellar. **Pros:** elegant service and furnishings, central location for shopping and Moderniste architecture. **Cons:** street side can be noisy, Internet sometimes unavailable in rooms. ⊠ *Carrer Pau Claris 150, Eixample* ☎ *93/487–6262* ⊕ *www.derbyhotels.es* ⤳ *80 rooms, 40 suites* ⚿ *In room: refrigerator, Wi-Fi. In-hotel: 2 restaurants, bar, pool, gym, laundry service, parking (fee)* ⊟ *AE, DC, MC, V* Ⓜ *Passeig de Gràcia.*

$$$–$$$$ 🏨 **Condes de Barcelona.** Reserve well in advance—this is one of Barcelo-
★ na's most popular hotels. The pentagonal lobby has a marble floor and the original columns and courtyard from the 1891 building, while the newest rooms have hot tubs and terraces overlooking interior gardens. An affiliated fitness club nearby has golf, squash, and swimming. The hotel's two restaurants, Lasarte and the less formal, bistrolike Loidi, serve excellent Basque-influenced cuisine. **Pros:** elegant Moderniste building with chic contemporary furnishings, prime spot in the middle

of the Eixample. **Cons:** too large to have much of a personal touch, the staff sometimes seem overextended. ✉*Passeig de Gràcia 75, Eixample* ☎*93/445–0000* ⊕*www.condesdebarcelona.com* ⤴*181 rooms, 2 suites* ☐*In room: safe, refrigerator, Wi-Fi. In-hotel: restaurant, bar, pools, gym, parking (fee)* ☐*AE, DC, MC, V* Ⓜ*Passeig de Gràcia.*

$$–$$$ 📷**Gran Via.** A Moderniste enclave with an original chapel, a hall-of-mirrors breakfast room, and a sweeping staircase, this slightly down-at-the-heel 19th-century town house has an antique charm that compensates for absent technology and extra comforts. Guest rooms have plain alcoved walls, bottle-green carpets, and Regency-style furniture; those overlooking Gran Via itself have better views but are noisy. **Pros:** a chance to sleep inside Moderniste architecture. **Cons:** somewhat antiquated, service a little tourist-weary. ✉*Gran Via 642, Eixample* ☎*93/318–1900* ⊕*www.nnhotels.com* ⤴*53 rooms* ☐*In-room: refrigerator, Wi-Fi. In-hotel: public Internet, parking (fee)* ☐*AE, DC, MC, V* Ⓜ*Passeig de Gràcia.*

$$$–$$$$
Fodor'sChoice
★
📷**Hotel Granados 83.** Built with an exposed-brick, steel, and glass factory aesthetic, with Buddhist and Hindu art supplying a sense of peace and tranquillity, this relative newcomer to the city hotel panorama has established itself as one of Barcelona's best design hotels. A few steps below the Diagonal and well situated for exploring the Eixample and the rest of the city, the hotel, named for Barcelona's famous composer and pianist Enric Granados (1867–1916), is an interesting compendium of materials and taste. The first-rate Mediterranean on-site dining options and the rooftop pool and solarium are the icing on the cake. **Pros:** quiet semi-pedestrian street, elegant building with chic design, polished service. **Cons:** room prices vary wildly according to availability and season. ✉*Carrer Enric Granados 83, Eixample* ☎*93/492–9670* ⊕*www.derbyhotels.es* ⤴*70 rooms, 7 suites* ☐ *In-room: safe, refrigerator, Wi-Fi. In-hotel: restaurant, bar, pools, spa, gym, parking (fee)* ☐*AE, DC, MC, V* Ⓜ *Provenca*

$$$$
★
📷**Hotel Palace.** Founded in 1919 by Caesar Ritz, this grande dame of Barcelona hotels has been restored to the splendor of its earlier years. The imperial lobby is at once rambling and elegant; guest rooms contain Regency furniture, and some have Roman baths and mosaics. The restaurant, Caelis, serves superb French and Catalan cuisine. **Pros:** equidistant from Gothic Quarter and central Eixample, elegant and polished service, consummate Old World luxury in rooms. **Cons:** a little stuffy, excessively expensive. ✉*Gran Via de les Corts Catalanes 668, Eixample* ☎*93/510–1130* ⊕*www.hotelpalacebarcelona.com* ⤴*122 rooms* ☐*In room: refrigerator, Wi-Fi. In-hotel: restaurant, bar, gym* ☐*AE, DC, MC, V* Ⓜ*Passeig de Gràcia.*

$$$$
Fodor'sChoice
★
📷 **Majestic.** On Barcelona's most stylish boulevard is this near-perfect place to stay. The building is part Eixample town house and part modern extension; pastels and Mediterranean hues warm each room, and the furnishings are all state-of-the-art contemporary. The superb restaurant ($$$$), Fermin Puig's internationally acclaimed Drolma, is a destination in itself. **Pros:** perfectly situated in the center of the Eixample, good balance between technology and charm, one of Barcelona's best restaurants. **Cons:** faces one of the city's widest, brightest,

noisiest, most commercial thoroughfares. ⊠*Passeig de Gràcia 68, Eixample* ☎*93/488–1717* ⊕*www.hotelmajestic.es* ↩*273 rooms, 30 suites* ♿*In-room: Wi-Fi. In-hotel: 2 restaurants, bar, pool, gym, parking (fee)* ⊟*AE, DC, MC, V* Ⓜ*Passeig de Gràcia.*

TIBIDABO

$$$$ 🖾 **Gran Hotel la Florida.** This gem of a hotel has unparalleled views over Barcelona, water sculptures everywhere but in your bed, a superb restaurant (L'Orangerie), and designer suites that are difficult to leave. Twenty minutes (and euros) from the port, this design hotel first opened in 1925 has roared back to the forefront of Barcelona's most stylish lodgings. **Pros:** panoramic views, artistic design and horizon pool, friendly and attentive service. **Cons:** a half-hour taxi ride from the center of town. ⊠*Ctra. Vallvidrera al Tibidabo 83–93, Tibidabo* ☎*93/259–3000* ⊕*www.hotellaflorida.com* ↩*74 rooms, 22 suites* ♿*In-room: safe, refrigerator, Wi-Fi. In-hotel: restaurant, bar, pool, gym, spa, parking (fee)* ⊟*AE, DC, MC, V* Ⓜ*Tibidabo.*

NIGHTLIFE & THE ARTS

Barcelona's art and nightlife scenes start early and never quite stop. To find out what's on, look in newspapers or the weekly *Guía Del Ocio,* which has a section in English, and is available at newsstands all over town.

THE ARTS

FESTIVALS AND CLASSICAL MUSIC

Barcelona's most famous concert hall is the Moderniste **Palau de la Música Catalana** (⊠*Sant Francesc de Paula 2, Sant Pere* ☎*93/295–7200*), with performances September–June. Tickets range from €6–€100 and are best purchased well in advance, though a last-minute *palco sin vistas* (box seat with no sight of the stage) is a good way to get into the building for a concert. The contemporary **Auditori de Barcelona** (⊠*Carrer Lepant 150, near Plaça de les Glòries, Eixample* ☎*93/247–9300*) has classical music, with occasional jazz and pop thrown in. Barcelona's **Gran Teatre del Liceu** (⊠*La Rambla 51–59 [box office: La Rambla de Capuchinos 63], Rambla* ☎*93/485–9900 box office*) stages operas and recitals.

DANCE

L'Espai de Dansa i Música de la Generalitat de Catalunya (⊠*Travessera de Gràcia 63, Eixample* ☎*93/414–3133*)—generally listed as L'Espai, or "The Space"—is the prime venue for ballet and modern dance, as well as some musical offerings. **El Mercat de les Flors** (⊠*Carrer Lleida 59, Eixample* ☎*93/426–1875*), near Plaça de Espanya, is a traditional venue for modern dance and theater.

FILM

Though many foreign films are dubbed, Barcelona has a full complement of original-language cinema; look for listings marked "v.o." (*versión original*). **Verdi** (⊠*Carrer Verdi 32, Gràcia*) screens current releases with original-version soundtracks in a fun neighborhood for pre- and post-movie eating and drinking. The **Icaria Yelmo** (⊠*Salvador Espriu*

61, Port Olímpic) complex in the Olympic Port has the city's largest selection of English-language films.

THEATER

Barcelona is known for avant-garde theater and troupes that specialize in mime, large-scale performance art, and special effects (La Fura dels Baus, Els Joglars, Els Comediants). Most plays are performed in Catalan, though some are in Spanish. **Teatre Lliure** has English subtitles on Wednesday, to make theater accessible for visitors, and other theaters are beginning to follow this lead. Call ahead for details. Several theaters along Avinguda Parallel specialize in musicals. The **Teatre Nacional de Catalunya** (⊠ *Pl. de les Arts 1* ☏ *93/306–5700*) covers everything from Shakespeare to ballet to avant-garde theater. The **Teatre Poliorama** (⊠ *La Rambla Estudios 115, Rambla* ☏ *93/317–7599*) is below Plaça de Catalunya. The **Teatre Romea** (⊠ *Carrer Hospital 51, Raval* ☏ *93/301–5504*) is behind the Boqueria. The **Teatre Tívoli** (⊠ *Carrer Casp 8, Eixample* ☏ *93/412–2063*), above Plaça de Catalunya, has theater and dance performances. Gràcia's **Teatre Lliure** (⊠ *Carrer Montseny 47, Gràcia* ☏ *93/218–9251*) stages theater, dance, and musical events. The **Mercat de les Flors** (⊠ *Lleida 59, Montjuïc* ☏ *93/426–1875*), near Plaça d' Espanya, is the city's most traditional dance and theater venue.

NIGHTLIFE
CABARET

Bcn Seven Dreams (⊠ *Plaza Mayor 9, Poble Espanyol, Avda. Marquès de Comillas s/n, Montjuïc* ☏ *93/325–4604*), in Montjuïc's Poble Espanyol, is Barcelona's last true cabaret show, featuring a chorus line, song and dance, and light erotic innuendo.

JAZZ, BLUES, & LIVE MUSIC VENUES

The Palau de la Música Catalana holds an **international jazz festival** in November. The Gothic Quarter's **Harlem Jazz Club** (⊠ *Carrer Comtessa Sobradiel 8, Barri Gòtic* ☏ *93/310–0755*) is small but atmospheric, with good jazz and country bands. **Jamboree-Jazz & Dance-Club** (⊠ *Pl. Reial 17, Rambla* ☏ *93/301–7564*) is a center for jazz, rock, and flamenco. **Luz de Gas** (⊠ *Carrer Muntaner 246, Eixample* ☏ *93/209–7711*) hosts every genre from Irish fusion to Cuban sounds.

LATE NIGHT BARS

Almirall. This Moderniste bar in the Raval is quiet, dimly lit, and dominated by the Art Nouveau mirror and frame behind the marble bar. It's an evocative spot, romantic and mischievous. ⊠ *Carrer Joaquín Costa 33, Raval* ☏ *93/302–4126* Ⓜ *Catalunya, Liceu, Sant Antoni.*

El Copetín. Right on Barcelona's best-known cocktail avenue, this bar has good drinks and Irish coffee. Dimly lit, it has a romantic South Seas motif. ⊠ *Passeig del Born 19, La Ribera* ☏ *93/319–4496* Ⓜ *Jaume I.*

El Bitxo. An original wine list and ever-changing choices of interesting cava selections accompany creative tapas and small dishes from *foie* (duck or goose liver) to Ibérico (native Iberian pigs fattened on acorns) hams and cheeses, all in a rustic wooden setting 50 yards from the Palau de la Música. ⊠ *Verdaguer i Callis 9, Sant Pere* ☏ *93/268–1708.*

El Xampanyet. Hanging *botas* (wineskins) mark this lively saloon, just down Carrer Montcada from the Picasso Museum. Caveat: The sparkling wine served here is not cava but a sweet brew of indeterminate origin. Stick with beer or one of their excellent wines. ✉ *Carrer Montcada 22, La Ribera* ☎ *93/319–7003* ⊙ *Closed Mon.*

L'Ovella Negra (✉ *Carrer Sitjàs 5, Raval* ☎ *93/317–1087*) is the top student tavern. **Glaciar** (✉ *Pl. Reial 13, Rambla* ☎ *93/302–1163*) is *the* spot for young out-of-towners. Downtown, deep in the Barrio Chino, try the **London Bar** (✉ *Carrer Nou de la Rambla 34, Raval* ☎ *93/302–3102*), an Art Nouveau circus haunt with a trapeze suspended above the bar. **Bar Muy Buenas** (✉ *Carrer del Carme 63, Raval* ☎ *93/442–5053*) is an Art Nouveau gem.

NIGHTCLUBS & DISCOS

Still popular, though not to the heights it once was, is the prisonesque nightclub **Otto Zutz** (✉ *Carrer Lincoln 15, Eixample* ☎ *93/238–0722*), off Via Augusta. The nearly classic **Up and Down** (✉ *Carrer Numancia 179, Eixample* ☎ *93/280–2922*), pronounced "Pen-*dow*," is a good choice for elegant carousers. A line forms at **Bikini** (✉ *Carrer Deu i Mata 105, at Entença, Eixample* ☎ *93/322–0005*) on festive Saturday nights. **Danzatoria** (✉ *Av. Tibidabo 61, Tibidabo* ☎ *93/211–6261*), a fusion of Salsitas and Partycular (two former clubs), is a "multispace" with five venues (disco, hall, dance, chill-out, garden) and fills with models and hopeful guys. **Sala Razzmatazz** (✉ *Carrer Almogavers 122, Poble Nou* ☎ *93/320–8200*) offers Friday and Saturday disco madness until dawn. Weeknight concerts have international stars like Ani DiFranco and Enya. The beachfront **CDLC** (✉ *Passeig Maritim 32, Port Olímpic* ☎ *93/224–0470*) has compartmentalized *sofa-camas* (sofa beds of a sort) for prime canoodling. **DosTrece** (✉ *Carrer del Carme 40, Raval* ☎ *93/443–0341*) packs in young internationals for dancing and carousing. **Shôko** (✉ *CPasseig Marítim 36, Port Olímpic* ☎ *93/225–9200*) is an excellent Asian-fusion restaurant until midnight, when it morphs into the beachfront's wildest dance and lounge club.

For big-band tango in an old-fashioned *sala de baile* (dance hall), head to **La Paloma** (✉ *Carrer Tigre 27, Raval* ☎ *93/301–6897*), with kitschy 1950s furnishings.

SHOPPING

Barcelona's prime shopping districts are the Passeig de Gràcia, Rambla de Catalunya, Plaça de Catalunya, Porta de l'Àngel, and Avinguda Diagonal up to Carrer Ganduxer.

For high fashion, browse along **Passeig de Gràcia** and the **Diagonal** between Plaça Joan Carles I and Plaça Francesc Macià. There are two-dozen antiques shops in the Gothic Quarter, another 70 shops off Passeig de Gràcia on Bulevard dels Antiquaris, and still more in Gràcia and Sarrià. For old-fashioned Spanish shops, prowl the Gothic Quarter, especially **Carrer Ferran**. The area surrounding **Plaça del Pi**, from the Boqueria to Carrer Portaferrissa and Carrer de la Canuda, is thick with boutiques, jewelry, and design shops. The **Barri de la Ribera,** around Santa Maria del Mar, especially El Born area, has a cluster of design, fashion, and food shops.

SPECIALTY STORES
ANTIQUES
The headquarter of antiques shopping is the Gothic Quarter, where **Carrer de la Palla** and **Carrer Banys Nous** are lined with shops full of prints, maps, books, paintings, and furniture. An antiques market is held in front of the Catedral de la Seau every Thursday from 10 to 8.

CLOTHING BOUTIQUES & JEWELRY
El Bulevard Rosa (⊠*Passeig de Gràcia 53–55, Eixample*) is a collection of boutiques with the latest outfits.

14

Adolfo Domínguez (⊠*Passeig de Gràcia 35, Av. Diagonal 570, Eixample*) is one of Spain's leading designers. The two locations of Toni Miró's **Groc** (⊠*C. Muntaner 382, Eixample* ⊠*La Rambla de Catalunya 100, Eixample*) have the latest looks for men, women, and children. **David Valls** (⊠*C. Valencia 235, Eixample*) represents new, young Barcelona fashion design. **May Day** (⊠*C. Portaferrissa 16, Barri Gòtic*) carries cutting-edge clothing, footwear, and accessories. **Joaquim Berao** (⊠*C. Rosselló 277, Eixample*) is a top jewelry designer.

DEPARTMENT STORES
Spain's ubiquitous **El Corte Inglés** (⊠Plaça de Catalunya 14, *Eixample* ⊠*Porta de l'Angel 19-21, Barri Gòtic* ⊠*Avinguda Francesc Macià 58, Sant Gervasi* ⊠*Avinguda Diagonal 617, Les Corts*) has four locations in Barcelona. On Plaça de Catalunya you can also find the international book and music store **FNAC** and the furniture and household design goods store **Habitat,** also on Carrer Tuset at the Diagonal.

FOOD & FLEA MARKETS
The **Boqueria** (⊠*La Rambla 91, Rambla*) is Barcelona's most colorful food market and the oldest of its kind in Europe. Open Monday to Saturday 8 to 8, it's most active before 3 PM. Barcelona's largest flea market, **Els Encants** (⊠ *Dos de Maig, on Plaça de les Glòries, Eixample* Ⓜ*Glòries*) is held Monday, Wednesday, Friday, and Saturday, from 8 to 7. The **Mercat Gòtic** (⊠ *Pl. de la Seu, Barri Gòtic*) fills the area in front of the Catedral de la Seu on Thursday. The **Mercat de Sant Antoni** (⊠ *Ronda Sant Antoni, Eixample*) is an old-fashioned food, clothing, and used-book (many in English) market that's best on Sunday.

GIFTS & MISCELLANY
La Manual Alpargartera (⊠*Carrer d'Avinyó 7, Barri Gòtic*), off Carrer Ferran, specializes in handmade rope-sole sandals and espadrilles. **Solé** (⊠*C. Ample 7, Barri Gòtic*) makes shoes by hand and sells others from all over the world. **La Lionesa** (⊠*C. Ample 21, Barri Gòtic*) is an old-time grocery store. Barcelona's best music store is **Discos Castelló** (⊠*Carrer Tallers 3, Raval*). For textiles, try **Teranyina** (⊠*C. Notariat 10, Raval*). **Baclava** (⊠*C. Notariat 10, Raval*) shares an address with Teranyina and sells artisanal textile products. **Les Muses del Palau** (⊠*Sant Pere Més Alt 1, Sant Pere*), next to the Palau de la Música Catalana,

shows and sells Palau de la Música-themed gifts from neckties to pencils, posters, models, jigsaw puzzles, and teacups.

ANDALUSIA

Andalusia—for 781 years (711–1492) a Moorish empire and named for Al-Andalus (Arabic for "Land of the West")—is where the authentic history and character of the Iberian Peninsula and Spanish culture are most palpably, visibly, audibly, and aromatically apparent.

Though church- and Franco regime–influenced historians endeavor to sell a sanitized, Christians-versus-infidels portrayal of Spanish history, what most distinctively imprinted and defined Spanish culture—and most singularly marked the art, architecture, language, thought, and even the cooking and dining customs of most of the Iberian Peninsula— was the almost eight-century reign of the Arabic-speaking peoples who have become known collectively as the Moors.

All the romantic images of Andalusia, and Spain in general, spring vividly to life in Seville. Spain's fourth-largest city is a cliché of matadors, flamenco, tapas bars, gypsies, geraniums, and strolling guitarists. So tantalizing is this city that many travelers spend their entire Andalusian time here. It's a good start, for an exploration of Andalusia must begin with the cities of Seville, Córdoba, and Granada as the fundamental triangle of interest and identity. The smaller cities of Cádiz—the Western world's oldest metropolis, founded by Phoenicians more than 3,000 years ago—and Jerez, with its sherry cellars and purebred horses, have much to recommend themselves as well.

PLANNING YOUR TIME

A week in Andalusia should include visits to Córdoba, Seville, and Granada to see, respectively, the Mezquita, the Cathedral and its Giralda, and the Alhambra. Two days in each city nearly fills the week, though the extra day would be best spent in Seville, by far Andalusia's most vibrant concentration of art, architecture, culture, and excitement.

A week or more in Seville alone would be well spent, especially during the *Semana Santa* celebration when the city, though crowded, becomes a giant street party. With more time on your hands, Cádiz and Jerez de la Frontera form a three- or four-day jaunt through flamenco, sherry, Andalusian equestrian culture, and tapas emporiums.

GETTING HERE AND AROUND

Seville is easily reached by air, although from the U.S. you need to connect in Madrid or London. Domestically, airlines such as Air Europa, Spanair, and Vueling connect Madrid, Barcelona, Valencia, and other major Spanish cities with Seville, Granada, Málaga, and Gibraltar, while Iberia flies from Jerez de la Frontera to Almería, Madrid, Barcelona, Bilbao, Valencia, Ibiza, and Zaragoza.

From Madrid, the best approach to Andalusia is via the high-speed railroad connection, the AVE. In under three hours, the spectacular ride winds from Madrid's Atocha Station through the olive groves and rolling fields of the Castilian countryside to Córdoba and on to Seville. Another option, especially if you plan to go outside Seville, Granada, and Córdoba, is to travel by car. The main road south from Madrid is the A4/E5.

Once in the region, buses are the best way (other than driving) to get around Andalusia. Buses serve most small towns and villages and are faster and more frequent than trains. From Granada, Alsina Gräells serves Alcalá la Real, Almería, Almuñecar, Cazorla, Córdoba, Guadix, Jaén, Lanjarón, Motril, Órgiva, Salobreña, Seville, and Úbeda.

Autocares Bonal operates buses between Granada and the Sierra Nevada. Granada's bus station is on the highway to Jaén. Buses serve Córdoba as well, but the routes are covered by myriad companies. For schedules and details, go to Córdoba's bus station (next to the train station) and inquire with the appropriate company. Alsina Gräells connects Córdoba with Granada, Seville, Cádiz, Badajoz, and Málaga. Alsa long-distance buses connect Seville with Madrid; and with Córdoba, Granada, and Málaga in Andalusia.

14

ESSENTIALS

Airports Aeropuerto de Granada (Aeropuerto Federico García Lorca) (☎ *958/245200*). **Aeropuerto de Sevilla** (Aeropuerto San Pablo) (☎ *95/444–9000*).

Airport Tranfers J. González (☎ *958/490164*).

Bus Stations Cádiz–Estación de Autobuses Comes (✉ *Pl. de la Hispanidad 1* ☎ *956/342174*). **Córdoba** (✉ *Glorieta de las Tres Culturas, Córdoba* ☎ *957/404040*). **Granada** (✉ *Ctra. Jaén, Granada* ☎ *958/185480*). **Jerez de la Frontera** (✉ *Calle de la Cartuja* ☎ *956/345207*). **Seville–Estación del Prado de San Sebastián** (✉ *Prado de San Sebastián s/n* ☎ *95/441–7111*). **Seville–Estación Plaza de Armas** (✉ *Calle Cristo de la Expiración* ☎ *95/490–7737*).

Taxi Companies Asociació de RadioTaxi (✉ *Granada* ☎ *958/132323*). **Radio Taxi** (✉ *Córdoba* ☎ *957/764444*). **Radio Teléfono Giralda** (✉ *Seville* ☎ *95/467–5555*). **Tele Radio Taxi** (✉ *Granada* ☎ *958/280654*). **Tele Taxi** (✉ *Jerez de la Frontera* ☎ *956/344860*). **Tele Taxi** (✉ *Huelva* ☎ *959/250022*). **Unitaxi** (✉ *Cádiz* ☎ *956/212121*).

Train Stations Cádiz (✉ *Pl. de Sevilla s/n* ☎ *956/251010*). **Córdoba** (✉ *Glorieta de las Tres Culturas s/n* ☎ *957/403480*). **Granada** (✉ *Av. de los Andaluces s/n* ☎ *958/271272*). **Jerez de la Frontera** (✉ *Pl. de la Estación s/n, off Calle Diego Fernández Herrera* ☎ *956/342319*). **Seville–Estación Santa Justa** (✉ *Av. Kansas City* ☎ *95/454–0202*).

Tourist Offices Cádiz (✉ *Pl. San Juan de Dios 11* ☎ *956/241001* ⊕ *www.cadiz turismo.com*). **Córdoba** (✉ *Pl. Juda Levi, Judería* ☎ *957/200522* 🖷 *957/200277*). **Granada** (✉ *Pl. Mariana Pineda 10, Centro* ☎ *958/247128*). **Jerez de la Frontera** (✉ *Calle Larga 39* ☎ *956/350129* ⊕ *www.turismojerez.com*). **Seville** (✉ *Av. de la Constitucíon 21, Arenal* ☎ *95/422–1404* ⊕ *www.sevilla.org* ✉ *Costurero de la Reina, Paseo de las Delicias 9, Arenal* ☎ *95/423–4465*).

SEVILLE

550 km (340 mi) southwest of Madrid.

Seville's whitewashed houses bright with bougainvillea, its ocher-colored palaces, and its Baroque facades have long enchanted both sevillanos and travelers. Lord Byron's well-known line, "Seville is a pleasant city famous for oranges and women," may be true, but is far too tame. Yes, the orange trees are pretty enough, but the fruit is too bitter to eat except as Scottish-made marmalade. As for the women, stroll down the swankier pedestrian shopping streets and you can't fail to notice just how good-looking *everyone* is. Aside from being blessed with even features and flashing dark eyes, sevillanos exude a cool sophistication of style about them that seems more Catalan than Andalusian.

EXPLORING SEVILLE

❼ Alcázar. The Plaza Triunfo forms the entrance to the Mudejar palace
★ built by Pedro I (1350–69) on the site of Seville's former Moorish *alcázar* (fortress). Don't mistake the Alcázar for a genuine Moorish palace, like Granada's Alhambra—it may look like one, and it was indeed designed and built by Moorish workers brought in from Granada, but it was commissioned and paid for by a Christian king more than 100 years after the reconquest of Seville. In its construction, Pedro the Cruel incorporated stones and capitals he pillaged from Valencia, from Córdoba's Medina Azahara, and from Seville itself. The palace serves as the official Seville residence of the king and queen.

You enter the Alcázar through the Puerta del León (Lion's Gate) and the high, fortified walls. You'll first find yourself in a garden courtyard, the **Patio del León** (Courtyard of the Lion). Off to the left are the oldest parts of the building, the 14th-century **Sala de Justicia** (Hall of Justice) and, next to it, the intimate **Patio del Yeso** (Courtyard of Plaster), the only part of the original 12th-century Almohad Alcázar. Cross the **Patio de la Montería** (Courtyard of the Hunt) to Pedro's Mudejar palace, arranged around the beautiful **Patio de las Doncellas** (Court of the Damsels), resplendent with delicately carved stucco.Opening off this patio, the **Salón de Embajadores** (Hall of the Ambassadors), with its cedar cupola of green, red, and gold, is the most sumptuous hall in the palace. It was here that Carlos V married Isabel of Portugal in 1526.

In the **gardens,** inhale jasmine and myrtle, wander among terraces and baths, and peer into the well-stocked goldfish pond. From the gardens, a passageway leads to the **Patio de las Banderas** (Court of the Flags), which has a classic view of the Giralda.

Tours depart in the morning only, every half hour in summer and every hour in winter. ⊠ *Pl. del Triunfo, Santa Cruz* ☎ *95/450–2323* ⊕ *www. patronato-alcazarsevilla.es* 🎫 *€8* ⊘ *Tues.–Sat. 9:30–7, Sun. 9:30–5.*

❶ Cathedral. The cathedral can be described only in superlatives: it's the
★ largest and highest cathedral in Spain, the largest Gothic building in the world, and the world's third-largest church, after St. Peter's in Rome and St. Paul's in London. After Ferdinand III captured Seville from the Moors in 1248, the great mosque begun by Yusuf II in 1171 was

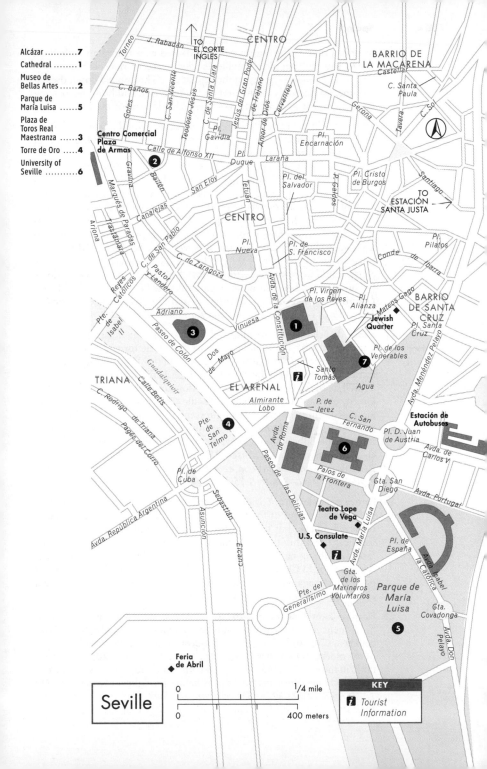

CENTRO

J. Rabadán

TO
EL CORTE
INGLES

BARRIO DE
LA MACARENA

Castellar

C. Santa
Paula

C. Sol

Torneo

C. Baños

Gotes

C. de San Vicente

Teodosio Jesús

Jesús del Gran Poder

C. de Santa Clara

C. de Trajano

Amor de Dios

Cervantes

Gerona

Tavera

Pl.
Gavidia

Calle de Alfonso XII

Centro Comercial
Plaza
de Armas

2

Pl.
Duque

Laraña

Pl.
Encarnación

Pl. Cristo
de Burgos

Santiago

Grauina

Bailén

San Eloy

Tetuán

P. Gallos

Marqués de Paradas

Trastámara

Ariona

Canalejas

C. de San Pablo

C. de Zaragoza

Pl.
Nueva

Pl. del
Salvador

CENTRO

Pl. de
S. Francisco

TO
ESTACIÓN
SANTA JUSTA

Pl.
Pilatos

Conde de Ibarra

Reyes Católicos

Pastor
y Landero

Pte.
de
Isabel
II

Adriano

Paseo de Colón

3

Vinuesa

Pl. Virgen
de los Reyes

Pl.
Alianza

Mateos Gago

BARRIO
DE SANTA
CRUZ

TRIANA

C. Rodrigo de Triana

Calle Betis

Guadalquivir

Dos de Mayo

1

Jewish
Quarter

Pl. Santa
Cruz

Pl. de los
Venerables

7

Santo
Tomás

ℹ

EL ARENAL

Agua

Pagés del Corro

Pte.
de
San
Telmo

4

Almirante
Lobo

P. de
Jerez

C. San
Fernando

Estación de
Autobuses

Avda. Menéndez Pelayo

Pl. de
Cuba

Avda. de Roma

6

Pl. D. Juan
de Austria

Avda. de
Carlos V

Paseo de las Delicias

Palos de
la Frontera

Avda. República Argentina

Sebastián

Asunción

Elcano

Teatro Lope
de Vega

U.S. Consulate

ℹ

Gta. San
Diego

Avda. Portugal

Gta.
de los
Marineros
Voluntarios

Avda. María Luisa

Pl. de
España

Avda. Isabel la Católica

Pte. del
Generalísimo

Parque de
María
Luisa

5

Gta.
Covadonga

Avda. Don Pelayo

Feria
de Abril

◆

Seville

0   1/4 mile

0   400 meters

KEY

ℹ *Tourist
Information*

reconsecrated to the Virgin Mary and used as a Christian cathedral. But in 1401 the people of Seville decided to erect a new cathedral, one that would equal the glory of their great city. They pulled down the old mosque, leaving only its minaret and outer court, and built the existing building in just over a century—a remarkable feat for the time.

Once the minaret of Seville's great mosque, the **Giralda,** from which the faithful were summoned to prayer, was built between 1184 and 1196, just 50 years before the reconquest of Seville. The Christians could not bring themselves to destroy this tower when they tore down the mosque, so they incorporated it into their new cathedral. In 1565–68 they added a lantern and belfry to the old minaret and installed 24 bells, one for each of Seville's 24 parishes and the 24 Christian knights who fought with Ferdinand III in the reconquest. Inside, instead of steps, 35 sloping ramps—wide enough for two horsemen to pass abreast—climb to a viewing platform 230 feet up. It is said that Ferdinand III rode his horse to the top to admire the city he had conquered. If you follow his route, you'll be rewarded with a view of tile roofs and the Guadalquivir shimmering beneath palm-lined banks. ⊠*Pl. Virgen de los Reyes, Centro* ☎*95/421–4971* ⊠*Cathedral and Giralda €7.50* ☼*Cathedral Mon.–Sat. 11–5, Sun. 2:30–6, and for mass (8:30, 9, 10, noon, 5).*

❷ **Museo de Bellas Artes** (Museum of Fine Arts). This museum is second
Fodor's Choice only to Madrid's Prado in Spanish art. It's in the former convent of La
★ Merced Calzada, most of which dates from the 17th century. The collection includes works by Murillo and the 17th-century Seville school, as well as by Zurbarán, Velázquez, Alonso Cano, Valdés Leal, and El Greco; outstanding examples of Seville Gothic art; and Baroque religious sculptures in wood (a quintessentially Andalusian art form). In the rooms dedicated to Sevillian art of the 19th and 20th centuries, look for Gonzalo Bilbao's *Las Cigarreras,* a group portrait of Seville's famous cigar makers. ⊠*Pl. del Museo 9, El Arenal/Porvenir* ☎*95/478–6482* ⊕*www.museosdeandalucia.es* ⊠*€2, free for EU citizens* ☼*Tues. 2:30–8:15, Wed.–Sat. 9–8:15, Sun. 9–2:15.*

❺ **Parque de María Luisa.** Formerly the garden of the Palacio de San Telmo, the park is a blend of formal design and wild vegetation. In the burst of development that gripped Seville in the 1920s, it was redesigned for the 1929 Exhibition, and the impressive villas you see now are the fair's remaining pavilions, many of them consulates or schools. Note the **statue of El Cid** by Rodrigo Díaz de Vivar (1043–99), who fought both for and against the Muslim rulers during the Reconquest. ⊠*Main entrance: Glorieta San Diego, El Arenal.*

❸ **Plaza de Toros Real Maestranza** (Royal Maestranza Bullring). Sevillanos have spent many a thrilling Sunday afternoon in this bullring, built between 1760 and 1763. Painted a deep ocher, the stadium is the one of the oldest and loveliest *plazas de toros* in Spain. The 20-minute tour takes in the empty arena, a museum with elaborate costumes and prints, and the chapel where matadors pray before the fight. ⊠*Paseo de Colón 12, El Arenal* ☎*95/422–4577* ⊠*Plaza and bullfighting museum €5 with English-speaking guide* ☼*Daily 9:30–7 (bullfighting days 9:30–3).*

4 **Torre de Oro** (Tower of Gold). A 12-sided tower on the banks of the Guadalquivir built by the Moors in 1220 to complete the city's ramparts, it served to close off the harbor when a chain was stretched across the river from its base to another tower on the opposite bank. In 1248, Admiral Ramón de Bonifaz broke through this barrier, and Ferdinand III captured Seville. The tower houses a small naval museum. ⊠*Paseo Alcalde Marqués de Contadero s/n, El Arenal* ☎*95/422–2419* ⊡*€1* ⊙*Tues.–Fri. 10–2, Sat.–Sun. 11–2.*

6 **University of Seville.** At the far end of the Jardines de Murillo, opposite Calle San Fernando, stands what used to be the **Real Fábrica de Tabacos** (Royal Tobacco Factory). Built in the mid-1700s, the factory employed some 3,000 *cigarreras* (female cigar makers) less than a century later, including Bizet's opera heroine *Carmen*, who reputedly rolled her cigars on her thighs. ⊠*C. San Fernando s/n, Parque Maria Luisa* ☎*95/455–1000* ⊡*Free* ⊙*Weekdays 9–8:30.*

14

WHERE TO EAT

$$$–$$$$
★ ✕**Abades Triana.** With panoramic views across the Guadalquivir River to the Torre de Oro and the Maestranza bullring, Willy Moya's new place offers the best of both worlds: a large space for brasserie fare and a smaller gastronomical enclave for more sophisticated dining. Chef Moya trained in Paris and blends local Andalusian and cosmopolitan cuisine in creations such as the *salmorejo encapotado* (thick, garlic-laden gazpacho topped with diced egg and ham), or the *besugo con gambitas* (sea bream with shrimp). Desserts include a Moorish-derived riff on French toast, with slivered almonds and cinnamon ice cream. ⊠*C. Betis 69, Triana* ☎*95/428–6459* ⊟*AE, DC, MC, V* ⊙*Closed Sun. No dinner Mon.*

$$$$
★ ✕**Egaña-Oriza.** Owner José Mari Egaña is Basque, but he is considered one of the fathers of modern Andalusian cooking. The restaurant, on the edge of the Murillo Gardens opposite the university, has spare contemporary decor with high ceilings and wall-to-wall windows. The menu might include *lomos de lubina con salsa de erizos de mar* (sea bass with sea urchin sauce) or *solomillo con foie natural y salsa de ciruelas* (fillet steak with foie gras and plum sauce). On the downside, the service can be slow. You can always drop into the adjoining Bar España for tapas such as stuffed mussels with béchamel sauce. ⊠*San Fernando 41, Santa Cruz Jardines de Murillo* ☎*95/422–7211* ⊟*AE, DC, MC, V* ⊙*Closed Sun. and Aug. No lunch Sat.*

$–$$$
✕**El Corral del Agua.** Abutting the outer walls of the Alcázar on a narrow pedestrian street in the Santa Cruz neighborhood is a restored 18th-century palace, with a patio filled with geraniums and a central fountain. Andalusian specialties, such as *cola de toro al estilo de Sevilla* (Seville-style bull's tail), are prepared with contemporary flair. ⊠*Callejón del Agua 6, Santa Cruz* ☎*95/422–4841* ⊟*AE, DC, MC, V* ⊙*Closed Sun. and Jan. and Feb.*

$$–$$$$
Fodor's Choice
★ ✕**Enrique Becerra.** Excellent tapas and a lively bar await at this restaurant run by the fifth generation of a family of celebrated restaurateurs (Enrique's brother Jesus owns Becerrita). The menu focuses on traditional, home-cooked Andalusian dishes, such as *pez espada al*

amontillado (swordfish cooked in dark sherry) and *cordero a la miel con espinacas* (honey-glazed lamb stuffed with spinach and pine nuts). Don't miss the cumin seed–laced *espinacas con garbanzos* (spinach with chickpeas). ⊠*Calle Gamazo 2, El Arenal* ☎*95/421–3049* ▭*AE, DC, MC, V* ☺*Closed Sun. and last 2 wks of July.*

$$$–$$$$ ✕**La Albahaca.** Overlooking one of Seville's prettiest small plazas in
★   the Barrio de Santa Cruz, this wonderful old manor house was built by the celebrated architect Juan Talavera for his own family; inside, four dining rooms are decorated with tiles, oil paintings, and plants. There's a Basque twist to many dishes—consider the *lubina al horno con berenjenas y yogur al cardamomo* (baked sea bass with eggplant in a yogurt-and-cardamom sauce) or *foie de oca salteado* (lightly sautéed goose liver) followed by the delicious fig mousse. There's an excellent €27 daily menu. ⊠*Pl. Santa Cruz 12, Santa Cruz* ☎*95/422–0714* ⌖*Reservations essential* ▭*AE, DC, MC, V* ☺*Closed Sun.*

$–$$ ✕**Mesón Don Raimundo.** Tucked into an alleyway off Calle Argote de Molina near the cathedral, this former 17th-century convent with its eclectic decor of religious artifacts tends to attract the tour buses. Still, it's worth the trip for its generous portions of traditional fare, including Mozarab-style wild duck (braised in sherry) and solomillo *a la castel-lana* (Castilian-style steak). Start with the crisp *tortillitas de camarones* (batter-fried shrimp pancakes) or stuffed peppers. ⊠*Argote de Molina 26, Santa Cruz* ☎*95/422–3355* ▭*AE, DC, MC, V.*

$$$ ✕**San Marco.** In a 17th-century palace in the shopping district, this Italian restaurant has original frescoes, a gracious patio, and a menu that combines Italian, French, and Andalusian cuisine. Pasta dishes, such as ravioli stuffed with shrimp and pesto sauce, are notable. The restaurant has four satellites, but this one, the original, is the most charming. ⊠*Calle Cuna 6, Centro* ☎*95/421–2440* ⌖*Reservations essential* ▭*AE, DC, MC, V.*

WHERE TO STAY

$$$$ ▦**Alfonso XIII.** Inaugurated by King Alfonso XIII in 1929, this grand
Fodor's Choice   hotel is a splendid, historical Mudejar-style palace, built around a central
★   patio and surrounded by ornate brick arches. Public rooms have marble floors, wood-panel ceilings, heavy Moorish lamps, stained glass, and ceramic tiles in typical Seville colors. There are Spanish and Japanese restaurants, and an elegant bar. **Pros:** both stately and hip, impeccable service. **Cons:** a tourist colony, colossally expensive. ⊠*San Fernando 2, El Arenal,* ☎*95/491–7000* ⊕*www.westin.com/hotelalfonso* ⌁*127 rooms, 19 suites* ⌂*In-room: Wi-Fi. In-hotel: 2 restaurants, bar, pool, parking (fee)* ▭*AE, DC, MC, V.*

$$$$ ▦ **Casa Imperial.** Adjoining the Casa de Pilatos, and once connected to it via underground tunnel, this 16th-century palace is the former residence of the Marquis of Tarifa. Public areas surround four plant-filled patios. The 24 suites are approached by a stairway adorned with trompe-l'oeil tiles. Each suite is different—one has a private courtyard with a trick-ling fountain—but all have kitchenettes. There's a roof terrace with gorgeous views. **Pros:** elegant and historic, quirky and exciting. **Cons:** rooms on patios are noisy, bathrooms small. ⊠*Calle Imperial 29, Santa Cruz/Santa Catalina* ☎*95/450–0300* ⊕*www.casaimperial.com* ⌁*24*

suites ₰ *In-room: kitchen, Wi-Fi. In-hotel: restaurant, bar, parking (no fee)* ⊟*AE, DC, MC, V* ⏀|*BP.*

$$$–$$$$ ⬚ **Doña María.** In a 14th-century former mansion, one of Seville's most charmingly old-fashioned hotels is near the cathedral. Some rooms have been refurbished in minimalist chic, but most are more ornate and furnished with antiques. Bathrooms are spacious. There's also a rooftop pool with a view of the Giralda. **Pros:** traditional old Seville hotel, elegant service, perfect location. **Cons:** hard to find, old-fashioned decor, erratic air-conditioning. ⊠*Calle Don Remondo 19, Santa Cruz* ☎*95/422–4990* ⊕*www.hdmaria.com* ⬚*64 rooms* ₰*In-room: Wi-Fi. In-hotel: pool* ⊟*AE, DC, MC, V.*

$$$$ **El Bulli Hotel Hacienda Benazuza.** This luxury hotel is in a rambling 10th-
★ century country palace near Sanlúcar la Mayor, 15 km (9 mi) outside Seville. Surrounded by olive and orange trees and in a courtyard with towering palms, the building incorporates an 18th-century church. The interior has clay-tile floors and ocher walls. The acclaimed restaurant, La Alquería, serves Spanish and international dishes, creative variations on the recipes of superstar Catalan chef (and hotel owner) Ferrán Adrià. **Pros:** nonpareil beauty and taste, polished service. **Cons:** too far from Seville, budget unfriendly. ⊠*C. Virgen de las Nieves, Sanlúcar la Mayor,* ☎*95/570–3344* ⊕*www.elbullihotel.com* ⬚*26 rooms, 18 suites* ₰*In-room: Wi-Fi. In-hotel: 2 restaurants, tennis court, pool, public Internet, parking (no fee), some pets allowed* ⊟*AE, DC, MC, V* ⊘*Closed Jan.*

$$$ ⬚ **Hostería del Laurel.** A small tree-lined square in the heart of the Barrio de Santa Cruz makes an unbeatable setting for this hotel. It's known for its bodega, which is mentioned in Zorilla's popular 19th-century play *Don Juan Tenorio,* and for the adjoining restaurant, which specializes in traditional local cuisine, such as *pollo a la Sevillana* (chicken in a rich gravy) and *espinacas* (spinach) and squid in garlic. The rooms are a relatively recent addition, and are spotlessly clean and simply furnished. **Pros:** exciting location in the thick of the Jewish Quarter, pretty square and rooms, reasonably priced. **Cons:** rooms small, street side rooms noisy, some interior rooms airless. ⊠*Pl. de los Venerables 5, Santa Cruz* ☎*95/422–0295* ⊕*www.hosteriadellaurel.com* ⬚*21 rooms* ₰*In-hotel: restaurant, bar, public Internet* ⊟*MC, V* ⏀|*BP.*

$$$ ⬚ **Las Casas de la Judería.** This labyrinthine hotel occupies three of the barrio's old palaces, each arranged around inner courtyards. The spacious guest rooms are painted in subdued pastel colors and decorated with prints of Seville. The hotel is tucked into a passageway off the Plaza Santa María. **Pros:** lovely ancient Barrio de Santa Cruz houses, at the end of a quiet alley, charming rooms. **Cons:** slightly dark and damp, some rooms get almost no natural light. ⊠*Callejón de Dos Hermanas 7, Santa Cruz* ☎*95/441–5150* ⊕*www.casasypalacios.com* ⬚*103 rooms, 3 suites* ₰*In-room: Wi-Fi. In-hotel: restaurant, bar, parking (fee)* ⊟*AE, DC, MC, V.*

$$ ⬚ **Simón.** In a rambling turn-of-the-19th-century town house, this hotel is a good choice for inexpensive, comfortable accommodations near the cathedral. The spacious, fern-filled, azulejo-tile patio makes a fine initial impression; the marble stairway and high-ceiling and pillared dining

14

room are cool, stately spaces. The rooms are less grand, but the mansion's style permeates the house. **Pros:** ideal location, breezy Andalusian decor. **Cons:** rooms plain, service pleasant but lackadaisical. ⊠ *Calle García de Vinuesa 19, El Arenal* ☎ *95/422–6660* ⊕ *www.hotelsimonsevilla.com* ⤢ *29 rooms* ♢ *In room: Wi-Fi. In-hotel: restaurant, some pets allowed* ☰ *AE, DC, MC, V.*

$$$ ✕⛶ **Taberna del Alabardero.** Near the Plaza Nueva, this highly regarded mansion-hotel and restaurant is a superb mid-Seville retreat in a traditional setting. A courtyard and bar precede the dining area, which is decorated in Sevillian tiles. Modern dishes include *bacalao a la parrilla triija de hongos sobre pil-pil y aceite de jamón* (grilled cod with mushrooms in a spicy chili-and-ham sauce). **Pros:** gorgeous house, rooms aesthetically perfect, intimate and romantic. **Cons:** air-conditioning not up to battling the summer heat, rooms pretty but quirky. ⊠ *Calle Zaragoza 20, El Arenal* ☎ *95/456–0637* ⊕ *www.tabernadelalabardero.com* ⤢ *7 rooms* ♢ *In-hotel: bar, public Wi-Fi, public Internet, parking (fee)* ☰ *AE, DC, MC, V* ☽ *Closed Aug.*

NIGHTLIFE & THE ARTS
NIGHTLIFE

FLAMENCO CLUBS Seville has a handful of commercial *tablaos* (flamenco clubs), patronized more by tourists than locals. Spontaneous flamenco is often found for free in *peñas flamencas* (flamenco clubs) and flamenco bars in Triana.

Casa Anselma is a semi-secret (unmarked) bar on the corner of Antillano Campos where Anselma and her friends sing and dance for the pure joy and catharsis that are at the heart of flamenco. ⊠ *Calle Pagés del Corro 49, Triana* ☎ *No phone* ✉ *Free* ☽ *Shows nightly after 11.*

★ **Casa de la Memoria de Al-Andaluz,** housed in an 18th-century palace, has a nightly show plus classes for the intrepid. ⊠ *Calle Ximenez de Enciso 28, Santa Cruz* ☎ *95/456–0670* ✉ *€12* ☽ *Shows nightly at 9.*

El Tamboril is a late-night bar in the heart of the Barrio de Santa Cruz noted for its great glass case in which the Virgin of Rocío sits in splendor. At 11 each night, locals pack in to sing the *Salve Rociera,* an emotive prayer to her. Afterward everything from flamenco to salsa continues until the early hours. ⊠ *Pl. Santa Cruz, Santa Cruz* ✉ *Free.*

La Carbonería—when it gets packed, which is most Thursdays, the flamenco is spontaneous. ⊠ *C. Levíes 18, Santa Cruz* ☎ *95/421–4460.*

THE ARTS

☾ Long prominent in the opera world, Seville is proud of its opera house, the **Teatro de la Maestranza** (⊠ *Paseo de Colón 22, Arenal* ☎ *95/422–3344* ⊕ *www.teatromaestranza.com*). Classical music and ballet are performed at the **Teatro Lope de Vega** (⊠ *Av. María Luisa s/n, Parque de María Luisa* ☎ *95/459–0853*). The modern **Teatro Central** (⊠ *José de Gálvez s/n, Isla de la Cartuja* ☎ *95/503–7200* ⊕ *www.teatrocentral.com*) stages theater, dance, and classical and contemporary music.

BULLFIGHTING Bullfighting season is Easter through Columbus Day; most *corridas* (bullfights) are held on Sunday. The highlight is the April Fair, with Spain's leading toreros; other key dates are Corpus Christi (date varies; about seven weeks after Easter), Assumption (August 15), and the last weekend in September. Bullfights take place at the **Maestranza Bullring** (✉*Paseo de Colón 12, Arenal* ☎*95/422–4577*). Bullfighting tickets are expensive; buy them in advance from the official *despacho de entradas* (*ticket office* ✉*Calle Adriano 37, Arenal* ☎*95/450–1382*), alongside the bullring. Other despachos sell tickets on Calle Sierpes, but these are unofficial and charge a 20% commission.

JEREZ DE LA FRONTERA

★ *97 km (60 mi) south of Seville.*

Jerez, world headquarters for sherry, is surrounded by vineyards of chalky soil, whose Palomino grapes have funded a host of churches and noble mansions. Names such as González Byass, Domecq, Harvey, and Sandeman are inextricably linked with Jerez. The word "sherry," first used in Great Britain in 1608, is an English corruption of the town's old Moorish name, Xeres. Both sherry and horses are the domain of Jerez's Anglo-Spanish aristocracy, whose Catholic ancestors came here from England centuries ago.

14

EXPLORING JEREZ DE LA FRONTERA

The 12th-century **Alcázar** was once the residence of the caliph of Seville. Its small, octagonal **mosque** and **baths** were built for the Moorish governor's private use. The baths have three sections: the *sala fria* (cold room), the larger *sala templada* (warm room), and the *sala caliente* (hot room), for steam baths. In the midst of it all is the 17th-century **Palacio de Villavicencio**, built on the site of the original Moorish palace. A camera obscura, a lens-and-mirrors device that projects the outdoors onto a large indoor screen, offers a 360-degree view of Jerez. ✉*Alameda Vieja* ☎*956/350129* 💶*€3, €5.40 including camera obscura* ☉*Mid-Sept.–Apr., daily 10–6; May–mid-Sept., daily 10–8.*

Across from the Alcázar and around the corner from the González Byass winery, the **cathedral** (✉*Pl. de la Encarnación* ☉ *Weekdays 11–1 11–1 and 6–8, Sat. 11–2 and 6–8, Sun. 11–2*) has an octagonal cupola and a separate bell tower, as well as Zurbarán's canvas *La Virgen Niña* (the Virgin as a young girl).

Diving into the maze of streets that form the scruffy San Mateo neighborhood east of the town center, you come to the **Museo Arqueológico**, one of Andalusia's best archaeological museums. The collection is strongest on the pre-Roman period. The star item, found near Jerez, is a Greek helmet dating from the 7th century BC. ✉*Pl. del Mercado s/n* ☎*956/341350* 💶*€3.50* ☉*Sept.–mid-June, Tues.–Fri. 10–2 and 4–7, weekends 10–2:30; mid-June–Aug., Tues.–Sun. 10–2:30.*

☾ The **Real Escuela Andaluza del Arte Ecuestre** *(Royal Andalusian School of* **Fodor'sChoice** *Equestrian Art)* operates on the grounds of the Recreo de las Cadenas, ★ a 19th-century palace. This prestigious school was masterminded by Alvaro Domecq in the 1970s. Every Thursday (and at various other times throughout the year) the Cartujana horses—a cross between the native Andalusian workhorse and the Arabian—and skilled riders in 18th-century riding costume demonstrate intricate dressage techniques and jumping in the spectacular show "Cómo Bailan los Caballos Anda-luces" (roughly, "The Dancing Horses of Andalusia"). Reservations are essential. ✉ *Av. Duque de Abrantes s/n* ☎*956/319635* ⊕*www. realescuela.org* ✏*€18–€25, €10 for rehearsals* ☉*Shows Mar.–Dec. 14, Tues. and Thurs. at noon (also Fri. at noon in Aug.); Dec. 15–Feb., Thurs. at noon. Check locally for additional late-April Feria de Caballo exhibitions, museum visits, and the rehearsal schedule.*

WHERE TO STAY & EAT

$$ ✕**La Mesa Redonda.** Owner José Antonio Valdespino spent years
★ researching the classic recipes once served in aristocratic Jerez homes, and now his son, José, presents them in this small, friendly restau-rant off Avenida Alcalde Alvaro Domecq, around the corner from the Hotel Avenida Jerez. Don't be put off by the bland exterior—within, the eight tables are surrounded by watercolors and shelves lined with cookbooks; the round table at the end of the room gave the restaurant its name. Ask the chef's mother, Margarita—who has an encyclopedic knowledge of Spanish wines—what to order. ✉*Calle Manuel de la Quintana 3* ☎*956/340069* ▭*AE, DC, MC, V* ☉*Closed Sun. and mid-July–mid-Aug.*

$$$ ▦**Hotel Sherry Park.** Set back from the road in an unusually large, tree-
★ filled garden, this modern hotel is designed around several patios filled with exotic foliage. The sunny hallways are hung with contemporary paintings. Rooms are bright and airy and decorated in sunny peach and blue; most have balconies overlooking the garden and pool. There are good deals out of season, as well as special weekend packages. **Pros:** midtown convenience, polished service, next to the equestrian school. **Cons:** busy highway nearby, modern and antiseptic architecture. ✉*Av. Alvaro Domecq 11* ☎*956/317614* ⊕*www.hipotels.com* ↩*174 rooms* ☖ *In-room: Wi-Fi. In-hotel: restaurant, bar, pools, gym* ▭*AE, DC, MC, V* ⊖*BP.*

CÁDIZ

★ *32 km (20 mi) southwest of Jerez, 149 km (93 mi) southwest of Seville.*

Surrounded by the Atlantic Ocean on three sides, Cádiz was founded as Gadir by Phoenician traders in 1100 BC and claims to be the old-est continuously inhabited city in the Western world. Hannibal lived in Cádiz for a time, Julius Caesar first held public office here, and Columbus set out from here on his second voyage, after which the city became the home base of the Spanish fleet. In the 18th century, when the Guadalquivir silted up, Cádiz monopolized New World trade and became the wealthiest port in Western Europe. Most of its buildings—including the cathedral, built in part with gold and silver from the New World—date from this period.

EXPLORING CÁDIZ

On the east side of the Plaza de Mina, a large, leafy square, is the **Museo de Cádiz** (Provincial Museum). Notable pieces include works by Murillo and Alonso Cano as well as the *Four Evangelists* and set of saints by Zurbarán, which have much in common with his masterpieces at Guadalupe, in Extremadura. The archaeological section contains Phoenician sarcophagi from the time of this ancient city's birth. ✉ *Pl. de Mina* ☎ *956/212281* 🎫 *€2, free for EU citizens* ⊘ *Tues. 2:30–8, Wed.–Sat. 9–8, Sun. 9–2.*

Backtrack along Calle Sacramento toward the city center to **Torre Tavira**. At 150 feet, the Torre Tavira, attached to an 18th-century palace that's now a conservatory of music, is the highest point in the old city. More than a hundred such watchtowers were used by Cádiz ship owners to spot their arriving fleets. A camera obscura gives a good overview of the city and its monuments; the last show is a half hour before closing time. ✉ *Calle Marqués del Real Tesoro 10* ☎ *956/212910* 🎫 *€5* ⊘ *Mid-June–mid-Sept., daily 10–8; mid-Sept.–mid-June, daily 10–6.*

Cádiz's gold-domed baroque **cathedral** was begun in 1722, when the city was at the height of its power. The Cádiz-born composer Manuel de Falla, who died in 1946 at the age of 70, is buried in the **crypt**. The cathedral **museum**, on Calle Acero, displays gold, silver, and jewels from the New World, as well as Enrique de Arfe's processional cross, which is carried in the annual Corpus Christi parades. ✉ *Pl. Catedral* ☎ *956/259812* 🎫 *€5* ⊘ *Mass Sun. at noon; museum Tues.–Fri. 10–2 and 4:30–7:30, Sat. 10–1.*

WHERE TO STAY & EAT

$$–$$$$ ✕ **El Faro.** This famous fishing-quarter restaurant is deservedly known
Fodor's Choice   as the best in the province. Outside, it's one of many low-rise, white
★   houses with bright-blue flowerpots; inside it's warm and inviting, with half-tile walls, glass lanterns, oil paintings, and photos of old Cádiz. Fish dominates the menu, but alternatives include *cebón al queso de cabrales* (venison in blue-cheese sauce). If you don't want to go for the full splurge, there's an excellent tapas bar as well. ✉ *Calle San Felix 15* ☎ *956/211068* ▭ *AE, DC, MC, V.*

$$$ 🏨 **Parador de Cádiz.** Cádiz's modern Parador Atlántico has a privileged position on the headland overlooking the bay and is the only hotel in its class in the old part of Cádiz. The spacious indoor public rooms have gleaming marble floors, and tables and chairs surround a fountain on the small patio. The cheerful, bright-green bar, decorated with ceramic tiles and bullfighting posters, is a popular meeting place for Cádiz society. Most rooms have small balconies facing the sea. **Pros:** panoramic and central location, bright and cheerful. **Cons:** large, characterless modern building. ✉ *Av. Duque de Nájera 9* ☎ *956/226905* ⊕ *www.parador.es* 🛏 *143 rooms, 6 suites* ♿ *In-room: dial-up, Wi-Fi. In-hotel: restaurant, bar, pool, gym, parking (no fee), some pets allowed* ▭ *AE, DC, MC, V* ⊙ *BP.*

14

CÓRDOBA

166 km (103 mi) northwest of Granada, 407 km (250 mi) southwest of Madrid, 239 km (143 mi) northeast of Cádiz, 143 km (86 mi) northeast of Seville.

Strategically located on the north bank of the Guadalquivir River, Córdoba was the Roman and Moorish capital of Spain, and its old quarter, clustered around its famous mosque (Mezquita), remains one of the country's grandest and yet most intimate examples of its Moorish heritage.

The city's artistic and historical treasures begin with the *mezquita-catedral* (mosque-cathedral), as it is ever-more-frequently called, and continue through the winding, whitewashed streets of the Judería (the medieval Jewish quarter); the jasmine-, geranium-, and orange blossom–filled patios; the Renaissance palaces; and the two-dozen churches, convents, and hermitages built by Moorish artisans directly over former mosques.

EXPLORING CÓRDOBA

Alcázar de los Reyes Cristianos *(Fortress of the Christian Monarchs)*. Built by Alfonso XI in 1328, the Alcázar is a Mudejar-style palace with splendid gardens. (The original Moorish Alcázar stood beside the Mezquita, on the site of the present Bishop's Palace.) This is where, in the 15th century, the Catholic Monarchs held court and launched their conquest of Granada. The most important sights here are the Hall of the Mosaics and a Roman stone sacrophagus from the 2nd or 3rd century. ⊠ *Pl. Campo Santo de los Mártires, Judería* ☎ *957/420151* 🖼 *€5, free Fri.* ☉ *May–Sept., Tues.–Sat. 10–2 and 6–8, Sun. 9:30–3; Oct.–Apr., Tues.–Sat. 10–2 and 4:30–6:30, Sun. 9:30–2:30.*

Calleja de las Flores. You'd be hard pressed to find prettier patios than those along this tiny street, a few yards off the northeastern corner of the Mezquita. Patios, many with ceramics, foliage, and iron grilles, are key to Córdoba's architecture, at least in the old quarter, where life is lived behind sturdy white walls—a legacy of the Moors, who honored both the sanctity of the home and the need to shut out the fierce summer sun.

Iglesia de San Miguel. Complete with Romanesque doors built around Mudejar horseshoe arches, the San Miguel Church, the square and café terraces around it, and its excellent tavern, Taberna San Miguel-Casa El Pisto, form one of the city's finest combinations of art, history, and gastronomy. ⊠ *Pl. San Miguel, Centro.*

Fodor'sChoice ★ **Mezquita** *(Mosque)*. Built between the 8th and 10th centuries, Córdoba's mosque is one of the earliest and most transportingly beautiful examples of Spanish Muslim architecture. As you enter through the **Puerta de las Palmas** (Door of the Palms), some 850 columns rise before you in a forest of jasper, marble, granite, and onyx. The pillars are topped by ornate capitals taken from the Visigothic church that was razed to make way for the mosque. Crowning these, red-and-white-stripe arches curve away into the dimness. The ceiling is carved of delicately tinted cedar.

The Mezquita has served as a cathedral since 1236, but its origins as a mosque are clear.

Al Hakam II (961–76) built the beautiful **Mihrab** (prayer niche), the Mezquita's greatest jewel. Make your way over to the **Qiblah**, the south-facing wall in which this sacred prayer niche was hollowed out. (Muslim law decrees that a Mihrab face east, toward Mecca, and that worshippers do likewise when they pray. Because of an error in calculation, the Mihrab here faces more south than east.

After the Reconquest, the Christians left the Mezquita largely undisturbed, dedicating it to the Virgin Mary and using it as a place of Christian worship. In the 13th century Christians had the **Capilla de Villaviciosa** built by Moorish craftsmen, its Mudejar architecture blending with the lines of the mosque. Not so the heavy, incongruous baroque structure of the **cathedral,** sanctioned in the very heart of the mosque by Charles V in the 1520s. To the emperor's credit, he was supposedly horrified when he came to inspect the new construction, exclaiming to the architects, "To build something ordinary, you have destroyed something that was unique in the world".

★ **Museo Regina.** You can watch craftsmen at work here creating the delicate silver filigree pieces for which Córdoba is famous. Construction unearthed the Roman and Moorish archaeological remains that are on display on the ground floor. ⊠*Pl. Luís Venegas 1, Centro* ☎*957/496889* ⊕*www.museoregina.com* ⊠*€3.50* ☉*June–mid-Sept., daily 9–2 and 5:30–9; mid-Sept.–May, daily 10–3 and 5–8.*

Museo Taurino (Museum of Bullfighting). Two adjoining mansions on the Plaza Maimónides (or Plaza de las Bulas) house this museum. It's worth a visit, as much for the chance to see a restored mansion as for the posters, Art Nouveau paintings, bull's heads, suits of lights (bullfighter outfits), and memorabilia of famous Córdoban bullfighters, including the most famous of all, Manolete. To the surprise of the nation, Manolete, who was considered immortal, was killed by a bull in the ring at Linares in 1947. ⊠*Pl. Maimónides, Judería* ☎*957/201056* ⊠*€3.50, free Fri.* ☉*Tues.–Sat. 10–2 and 6–8 (4:30–6:30 Oct.–May), Sun. 9:30–3.*

Synagogue. The only Jewish temple in Andalusia to survive the expulsion and inquisition of the Jews in 1492, Córdoba's synagogue is also one of only three ancient synagogues left in all of Spain (the other two are in Toledo). Though it no longer functions as a place of worship, it's a treasured symbol for Spain's modern Jewish communities. The outside is plain, but the inside, measuring 23 feet by 21 feet, contains some exquisite Mudejar stucco tracery. ⊠*C. Judíos, Judería* ☎*957/202928* ⊠*€1, free for EU citizens* ☉*Tues.–Sat. 9:30–2 and 3:30–5:30, Sun. 9:30–1:30.*

Zoco. Zoco is the Spanish word for the Arab souk, the onetime function of this courtyard near the synagogue. It now is the site of a daily crafts market, where you can see artisans at work and evening flamenco in summer. ⊠*Calle Judíos 5, Judería* ☎*957/204033* ⊠*Free.*

14

WHERE TO EAT

$$$–$$$$ ✗**Bodegas Campos.** A block east of the Plaza del Potro, this restaurant in a traditional old wine cellar is the epitome of all that is great about Andalusian cuisine and service. The dining rooms are in barrel-heavy and leafy courtyards. Regional dishes include *ensalada de bacalao y naranja* (salad of salt cod and orange with olive oil) and *solomillo con salsa de setas* (sirloin with a wild mushroom sauce). The *menu degustacíon* (taster's menu) is a good value at €35. ⊠ *Calle Los Lineros 32, San Pedro* ☎957/497643 ☐*AE, MC, V* ⊘*No dinner Sun.*

$$$–$$$$ ✗**El Caballo Rojo.** This is one of the most famous traditional restaurants
Fodor's Choice   in Andalusia, frequented by royalty and society folk. The interior resem-
★   bles a cool, leafy Andalusian patio, and the dining room is furnished with stained glass, dark wood, and gleaming marble. The menu mixes traditional specialties, such as *rabo de toro* (oxtail stew) and *salmorejo* (a thick version of gazpacho), with dishes inspired by Córdoba's Moorish and Jewish heritage, such as *alboronia* (a cold salad of stewed vegetables flavored with honey, saffron, and anise), *cordero a la miel* (lamb roasted with honey), and *rape mozárabe* (grilled monkfish with Moorish spices). ⊠ *Calle Cardenal Herrero 28, Judería* ☎957/475375 ⊕*www.elcaballorojo.com* ☐*AE, DC, MC, V.*

$$$–$$$$ ✗**El Churrasco.** The name suggests grilled meat, but this restaurant in the heart of the Judería serves much more than that. Try tapas such as the *berenjenas crujientes con salmorejo* (crispy fried eggplant slices with thick gazpacho) in the colorful bar. The grilled fish is also supremely fresh, *and* the steak is the best in town. On the inner patio, there's alfresco dining when it's warm outside (covered in winter). ⊠ *Calle Romero 16, Judería* ☎957/290819 ⊕*www.elchurrasco.com* ☐*AE, DC, MC, V* ⊘*Closed Aug.*

$$–$$$ ✗**Taberna San Miguel-Casa El Pisto.** This central Córdoba hot spot behind
★   Plaza de las Tendillas is always booming with happy diners, most of them Córdobans, enjoying a wide range of typical pinchos and raciones accompanied by chilled glasses of Moriles, the excellent local sherrylike wine. The heavy wooden bar is as good a spot as any, but the tables in the back rooms crackle with conviviality. ⊠ *Pl. de San Miguel 1, Centro* ☎957/470166 ☐*AE, DC, MC, V* ⊘*Closed Sun.*

WHERE TO STAY

$$$–$$$$ 🖫**Amistad Córdoba.** Two 18th-century mansions that look out on the
★   Plaza de Maimónides in the heart of the Judería are now a stylish hotel. (You can also enter through the old Moorish walls on Calle Cairuán.) There's a cobblestone Mudejar courtyard, carved-wood ceilings, and a plush lounge area; the newer wing across the street is done in blues and grays and Norwegian wood. Guest rooms are large and comfortable. **Pros:** perfect design and comfort, pleasant and efficient service. **Cons:** parking near the hotel difficult. ⊠ *Pl. de Maimónides 3, Judería* ☎957/420335 ⊕*www.nh-hoteles.com* ☞*84 rooms* �*In-room: Wi-Fi. In-hotel: restaurant, room service, bar, laundry service, parking (fee)* ☐*AE, DC, MC, V.*

$$$ 🖫**Casa de los Azulejos.** Although renovated in 1934, this 17th-century house still has its underground rooms with vaulted ceilings. Decorated with colorful tiles, it mixes Andalusian and Latin American influences.

All rooms, painted in warm, pastel colors and filled with antique furnishings, open onto the central patio. There's an Andalusian–Latin American restaurant and a Mexican cantina on the premises. Pros: interesting and unusual environment, friendly staff and clientele. Cons: hyper-busy decor, limited privacy. ✉ *Calle Fernando Colón 5, Centro* ☎ *957/470000* ⊕ *www.casadelosazulejos.com* ⤴ *7 rooms, 1 suite* ☃ *In-room: Wi-Fi. In-hotel: 2 restaurants, no elevator, public Internet* ▤ *MC, V.*

$$$ ⊡ **Conquistador.** Ceramic tiles and inlaid marquetry adorn the bar and public rooms at this contemporary, Andalusian Moorish–style hotel next to the Mezquita. The reception area overlooks a colonnaded patio, fountain, and small enclosed garden. Rooms are comfortable and classically Andalusian; those at the front have small balconies overlooking the mosque, which is floodlighted at night. Pros: views into Mezquita, central location. Cons: bells, busy street at the door. ✉ *Magistral González Francés 17, Judería* ☎ *957/481102 or 957/481411* ⊕ *www.hotelconquistador cordoba.com* ⤴ *99 rooms, 3 suites* ☃ *In-room: Wi-Fi. In-hotel: room service, bar, laundry service, parking (fee)* ▤ *AE, DC, MC, V.*

$–$$ ⊡ **Hotel Maestre.** Rooms here overlook a gracious inner courtyard framed by arches. The Castilian-style furniture, gleaming marble, and high-quality oil paintings add elegance to excellent value. The hotel is around the corner from the Plaza del Potro. The management also runs an even cheaper lodging, the Hostal Maestre, and two types of apartments down the street; the best apartments are large and clean and offer one of the best deals in town. Pros: location, value. Cons: beds flimsy and lumpy, plumbing functional but ancient. ✉ *Calle Romero Barros 4–6, San Pedro* ☎ *957/472410* ⊕ *www.hotelmaestre.com* ⤴ *26 rooms* ☃ *In-hotel: parking (fee)* ▤ *AE, MC, V.*

$$$ ⊡ **La Hospedería de El Churrasco.** As should be expected from a place associated with the nearby restaurant of the same name, this small hotel is one of the town's most beautiful and tasteful places to stay. Each room is individually furnished with fine antiques, but also comes with such modern facilities as plasma TVs. The terrace-solarium has fine views of the Mezquita. Pros: excellent combination of traditional design and contemporary comfort, intimate and personal service. Cons: lengthy baggage haul from car, tumultuous street on weekends. ✉ *Calle Romero 38, Judería* ☎ *957/294808* ⊕ *www.elchurrasco.com* ⤴ *9 rooms* ☃ *In-room: Wi-Fi. In-hotel: parking (fee)* ▤ *AE, DC, MC, V* ⦿ *BP.*

$$$$ ⊡ **Palacio del Bailío.** A beautiful 17th-century mansion built over the
Fodor's Choice ruins of a Roman house in the heart of the historic center jumped to
★ the top of the city's lodging options as soon as it opened. The company in charge specializes in tastefully renovating impressive and historic buildings to the highest of expected modern standards, and this is another exemplary example of its work. Archaeological remains mixed with contempory features, such as clever lighting and a relaxing spa, complete the contemporary-antiquity mélange. Pros: dazzling lines and decor, impeccable comforts. Cons: not easy to reach by car. ✉ *Calle Ramírez de las Casas Deza 10–12, Plaza de La Corredera* ☎ *957/498993* ⊕ *www.hospes.es* ⤴ *53 rooms* ☃ *In-room: Ethernet, Wi-Fi. In-hotel: restaurant, bar, pools, spa, bicycles, laundry facilities, public Internet* ▤ *MC, V.*

14

$$$ **Parador de Córdoba.** A peaceful garden surrounds this modern parador on the slopes of the Sierra de Córdoba, 5 km (3 mi) north of town. Rooms are sunny, with wood or wicker furnishings, and the pricier ones have balconies overlooking the garden or facing Córdoba. **Pros:** wonderful views from south-facing rooms, sleek decor. **Cons:** characterless modern building, far from city's main sights. ✉*Av. de la Arruzafa, El Brillante* ☎*957/275900* 🌐*www.parador.es* *89 rooms, 5 suites* *In-room: dial-up, Wi-Fi. In-hotel: restaurant, room service, tennis court, pool, parking (no fee)* 💳*AE, DC, MC, V.*

NIGHTLIFE & THE ARTS

FLAMENCO Córdoba's most popular flamenco club, the year-round **Tablao Cardenal** (✉*Calle Torrijos 10, Judería* ☎*957/483320* 🌐*www.tablaocardenal.com*) is worth the trip just to see the courtyard of the 16th-century building, which was Córdoba's first hospital. Admission is €20.

THE ARTS

During the **Patio Festival,** held the second and third weeks of May, the city fills with flamenco dancers and singers. The **Festival de Córdoba-Guitarra** attracts Spanish and international guitarists for more than two weeks of great music in July. Orchestras perform in the Alcázar's garden on Sunday throughout the summer. The **Feria de Mayo** (the last week of May) draws popular musical performers to the city. See concerts, ballets, and plays year-round in the **Gran Teatro** (✉*Av. Gran Capitán 3, Centro* ☎*957/480644* 🌐*www.teatrocordoba.com*).

GRANADA

430 km (265 mi) south of Madrid, 261 km (162 mi) east of Seville, and 160 km (100 mi) southeast of Córdoba.

The Alhambra and the tomb of the Catholic Monarchs are the pride of Granada. The city rises majestically from a plain onto three hills, dwarfed—on a clear day—by the Sierra Nevada. Atop one of these hills perches the reddish-gold Alhambra palace. The stunning view from the palace promontory takes in the sprawling medieval Moorish quarter, the caves of the Sacromonte, and, in the distance, the fertile *vega* (plain), rich in orchards, tobacco fields, and poplar groves.

Granada was the Moors' last stronghold; the city fell to Catholic monarchs in January 1492.

SACROMONTE

The third of Granada's three hills, the **Sacromonte** rises behind the Albayzín. The hill is covered with prickly pear cacti and riddled with caverns. These caves may have sheltered early Christians; 15th-century treasure hunters found bones inside and assumed they belonged to San Cecilio, the city's patron saint. Thus the hill was sanctified—*sacro monte* (holy mountain)—and an abbey built on its summit, the **Abadía de Sacromonte** (✉*C. del Sacromonte, Sacromonte* ☎*958/221445* *€3* *Tues.–Sat. 11–1 and 4–6, Sun. 4–6; guided tours every ½ hr*). The Sacromonte has long been notorious as a domain of Granada's gypsies and a thus den of thieves and scam artists, but its reputation is largely undeserved. The quarter is more like a quiet Andalusian *pueblo* (village). Many of the quarter's colorful *cuevas* (caves) have been restored as middle-class homes, and some of the old spirit lives on in a handful of *zambras*—flamenco performances in caves garishly decorated with brass plates and cooking utensils.

ALBAYZÍN

Fodor's Choice
★

Covering a hill of its own, across the Darro ravine from the Alhambra, this ancient Moorish neighborhood is a mix of dilapidated white houses and immaculate *carmenes* (private villas in gardens enclosed by high walls). It was founded in 1228 by Moors who fled Baeza after Saint King Ferdinand III captured the city. Full of cobblestone alleyways and secret corners, the Albayzín guards its old Moorish roots jealously, though its 30 mosques were converted to Baroque churches long ago. A stretch of the Moors' original city wall runs beside the Cuesta de la Alhacaba. If you're walking—the best way to explore—you can enter the Albayzín from either the Cuesta de Elvira or the Plaza Nueva. One of the highest points in the quarter, the plaza in front of the church of San Nicolás—called the **Mirador de San Nicolás**—has one of the finest views in all of Granada: on the hill opposite, the turrets and towers of the Alhambra form a dramatic silhouette against the snowy peaks of the Sierra Nevada.

El Bañuelo *(Little Bath House).* These 11th-century Arab steam baths might now be a little dark and dank, but try to imagine them filled, some 900 years ago, with Moorish beauties. Back then, the dull brick walls were backed by bright ceramic tiles, tapestries, and rugs. Light comes in through star-shape vents in the ceiling, à la the bathhouse in the Alhambra. ⊠ *Carrera del Darro 31, Albayzín* 🕾 *958/027800* 🖼️ *Free* ☉ *Tues.–Sat. 10–2.*

CENTRO

Capilla Real *(Royal Chapel).* This ornate Gothic masterpiece is the burial shrine of Ferdinand and Isabella, placed here since 1521. The sacristy holds Ferdinand's sword, Isabella's crown and scepter, and a fine collection of Flemish paintings once owned by Isabella. ⊠ *Calle Oficios, Centro* 🕾 *958/229239* ⊕ *www.capillarealgranada.com* 🖼️ *€3* ☉ *Apr.–Oct., Mon.–Sat. 10:30–1 and 4–7, Sun. 11–1 and 4–7; Nov.–Mar., Mon.–Sat. 10:30–1 and 3:30–5:30, Sun. 11–1 and 3:30–6:30.*

Cathedral. Granada's cathedral was commissioned in 1521 by Charles V, who considered the Royal Chapel "too small for so much glory" and wanted to house his illustrious late grandparents someplace more worthy. Charles undoubtedly had great designs, as the cathedral was created by some of the finest architects of its time: Enrique Egas, Diego de Siloé, Alonso Cano, and sculptor Juan de Mena. Alas, his ambitions came to little, for the cathedral is a grand and gloomy monument, not completed until 1714, and never used as the crypt for his grandparents (or parents). ⊠ *Gran Vía s/n, Centro* 🕾 *958/222959* 🖼️ *€3.50* ☉ *Apr.–Oct., Mon.–Sat. 10:30–1:30 and 4–8, Sun. 4–8; Nov.–Mar., Mon.–Sat. 10:45–1:30 and 4–7, Sun. 4–7.*

Corral del Carbón *(Coal House).* This building was used to store coal in the 19th century, but its history goes further back. Dating from the 14th century, it was used by Moorish merchants as a lodging house, and then later by Christians as a theater. It's one of the oldest Moorish buildings in the city, and is the only Arab structure of its kind in Spain. ⊠*Pl. Mariana Pineda s/n, Centro* ☎*958/221118* ⊡*Free* ☉ *Weekdays 10–1:30 and 5–8, weekends 10:30–2.*

OUTSKIRTS OF TOWN

Casa-Museo Federico García Lorca. Granada's most famous native son, the poet Federico García Lorca, gets his due here, in the middle of a park devoted to him on the southern fringe of the city. Lorca's onetime summer home, **La Huerta de San Vicente,** is now a museum—run by his niece Laura García Lorca—with such artifacts as his beloved piano and changing exhibits on specific aspects of his life. ⊠*Parque García Lorca, Virgen Blanca s/n, Arabial* ☎*958/258466* ⊕*www.huertadesanvicente. com* ⊠*€3, free Wed.* ☉*July and Aug., Tues.–Sun. 10–3; Apr., May, June, and Sept., Tues.–Sun. 10–1 and 5–8; Oct.–Mar. Tues.–Sun. 10–1 and 4–7. Guided tours every 45 min until 30 min before closing.*

Monasterio de La Cartuja. This Carthusian monastery in northern Granada (2 km [1 mi]) from the center and reached by the number 8 bus) was begun in 1506 and moved to its present site in 1516, though construction continued for the next 300 years. The exterior is sober and monolithic, but inside are twisted, multicolor marble columns; a profusion of gold, silver, tortoiseshell, and ivory; intricate stucco; and the extravagant sacristy—it's easy to see why Cartuja has been called the Christian answer to the Alhambra. Among the wonders of the Cartuja are the trompe-l'oeil spikes, shadows and all, in the Sanchez Cotan cross over the Last Supper painting at the west end of the refectory. If you're lucky you may see small birds attempting to land on these faux perches. ⊠*C. de Alfacar, Cartuja* ☎*958/161932* ⊠*€4* ☉*Apr.–Oct., Mon.–Sat. 10–1 and 4–8, Sun. 10–noon and 4–8; Nov.–Mar., daily 10–1 and 3:30–6.*

WHERE TO EAT

$$–$$$$ ✕**Carmen Verde Luna.** This intriguingly named restaurant, Carmen (Arabic for "summer cottage") Green Moon, a reference to Federico García Lorca's famous poem "Romance Somnámbulo" (Sleepwalking Ballad), has a terrace with views across to the Alhambra and Sierra Nevada. Regional dishes might include toasted and stuffed eggplants with pâté, stuffed sea bass and vegetables, and hake with prawns. ⊠*Calle Nuevo de San Nicolás 16, Albayzín* ☎*958/291794* ⊟*MC, V.*

$$–$$$$ ✕**Mirador de Morayma.** Buried in the Albayzín, this place is hard to find and might appear to be closed (ring the doorbell). Once inside, you'll have unbeatable views across the gorge to the Alhambra, particularly from the wisteria-laden outdoor terrace. The adequate menu has some surprises, such as smoked *esturión* (sturgeon) from Riofrío, served cold with cured ham and a vegetable dip, and the *ensalada de remojón granadino,* a salad of cod, orange, and olives. ⊠*Calle Pianista García Carrillo 2, Albayzín* ☎*958/228290* ⊟*AE, MC, V* ☉*No dinner Sun.*

$$$-$$$$ ✕ **Ruta del Veleta.** It's worth the short drive 5 km (3 mi) out of town to
★   this Spanish restaurant, which serves some of the best food in Granada.
House specialties include *carnes a la brasa* (succulent grilled meats)
and fish dishes cooked in rock salt, as well as seasonal dishes such as
solomillo de jabalí con frutos de otoño y salsa de vinagre (wild boar
fillet with autumn fruits in a vinegar-and-honey sauce). Dessert might
be *morito de chocolate templado con helado de gachas* (warm choco-
late sponge cake with ice cream). ✉ *Ctra. de la Sierra 136, on road to
Sierra Nevada, Cenes de la Vega* ☎*958/486134* ▤*AE, DC, MC, V*
🌙*No dinner Sun.*

$$-$$$$ ✕ **Sevilla.** Open since 1930, this colorful, central two-story restaurant
has fed the likes of composer Manuel de Falla and poet Federico García
Lorca. There are four dining rooms and an outdoor terrace overlooking
the Royal Chapel and Cathedral, as well as a small but superb tapas
bar. The dinner menu includes Granada favorites such as *sopa sevillana*
(soup with fish and shellfish) and *tortilla al Sacromonte* (with bull's
brains and testicles), along with more elaborate dishes. ✉ *Calle Oficios
12, Centro* ☎*958/221223* ▤*AE, DC, MC, V* 🌙*No dinner Sun.*

WHERE TO STAY

$$$$ 🏨 **Alhambra Palace.** Built by a local duke in 1910, this neo-Moorish
Fodor'sChoice   hotel is on leafy grounds at the back of the Alhambra hill. The interior
★   is very Arabian Nights, with orange-and-brown overtones, multicolor
tiles, and Moorish arches and pillars. Even the bar is decorated as a
mosque. Rooms overlooking the city have majestic views, as does the
terrace, a perfect place to watch the sun set. **Pros:** bird's-eye views, location near but not in the Alhambra. **Cons:** steep climb up from Granada, certain rooms somewhat threadbare. ✉ *Plaza Arquitecto García
de Paredes 1, Alhambra* ☎*958/221468* ⊕*www.h-alhambrapalace.es*
⮑*113 rooms, 13 suites* ᐃ*In-room: Wi-Fi. In-hotel: restaurant, bars,
parking (no fee)* ▤*AE, DC, MC, V.*

$$$-$$$$ 🏨 **Casa Morisca.** The architect-owner of this 15th-century building
transformed it into a hotel and received the 2001 National Restoration
Award for the project. The brick building has many original architec-
tural elements, three floors, and a central courtyard with a small pond
and well. The rooms aren't large, but they get a heady Moorish feel
through wonderful antiques and views of the Alhambra and Albayzín.
Even if you don't stay in it, ask for a look at the bridal suite, with its
intricately carved and painted wooden ceiling. **Pros:** handy to Albayzín,
easy free parking in front of the hotel. **Cons:** breakfast expensive and
mediocre, interior rooms are stuffy and airless. ✉*Cuesta de la Victo-
ria 9, Albayzín* ☎*958/221100* ⊕*www.hotelcasamorisca.com* ⮑*12
rooms, 2 suites* ᐃ*In-room: Wi-Fi.* ▤*AE, DC, MC, V.*

$$-$$$ 🏨 **Palacio de Santa Inés.** It's not often you stay in a 16th-century palace,
and this one in has a stunning location in the heart of the Albayzín.
Rooms on the two upper floors are centered on a courtyard with frescoes
painted by a disciple of Raphael. Each room is magnificently decorated
with antiques and modern art; some have balconies with Alhambra
views. **Pros:** perfect location for exploring the Albayzín, gorgeous decor.
Cons: can't get there by car as it's in a pedestrianized zone, service slow
and sloppy. ✉*Cuesta de Santa Inés 9, Albayzín* ☎*958/222362* ⊕*www.*

14

palaciosantaines.com 🛏*15 rooms, 20 suites* ᏟᏥ*In-room: Wi-Fi. In-hotel: restaurant, parking (fee)* 🚭*AE, DC, MC, V.*

$$$$ 🏨**Parador de Granada.** This is Spain's most expensive and popular para-
★ dor, and it's right in the Alhambra precinct. The building, a former Franciscan monastery built in the 15th century by the Catholic Monarchs
after they captured Granada, is soul-stirringly gorgeous. If possible, go
for a room in the old section where there are beautiful antiques, woven
curtains, and bedspreads. Rooms in the newer wing are also charming
but simple. **Pros:** location, decor, garden restaurant. **Cons:** no views
of Granada or the Albayzín, removed from city life. ✉*Calle Real de
la Alhambra s/n, Alhambra* ☎*958/221440* ⊕*www.parador.es* 🛏*34
rooms, 2 suites* ᏟᏥ*In-room: dial-up. In-hotel: restaurant, bar, parking
(no fee)* 🚭*AE, DC, MC, V.*

$$$ 🏨**Reina Cristina.** In the former family residence of the poet Luis Rosa-
les, where poet Federico García Lorca was arrested after taking refuge
when the Spanish civil war broke out, the Reina Cristina is near Plaza
de la Trinidad. Plants trail from the windowsills of the reception area
and from a patio with a small marble fountain. A marble stairway leads
to the simply but cheerfully furnished guest rooms. The restaurant,
El Rincón de Lorca, is excellent. **Pros:** like staying in a private home,
quiet street, fine cuisine. **Cons:** not easy to drive to because of one-way
streets, air-conditioning unreliable, some rooms have no views at all.
✉*Calle Tablas 4, Centro* ☎*958/253211* ⊕*www.hotelreinacristina.
com* 🛏*43 rooms* ᏟᏥ*In-room: Wi-Fi. In-hotel: restaurant, bar, parking
(fee)* 🚭*AE, DC, MC, V* 🍴❙*BP.*

Switzerland

A Swiss Alpine chateau

WORD OF MOUTH

"I spent 3 nights in Switzerland last summer as part of my honeymoon and only got a small sampling. I'd love to have a whole week there; it was an amazing country."

—jenblase

WHAT'S
WHERE

1 Zurich. This rich banking center and bastion of Swiss-Germanism has actually become cool and found its voice with a vibrant restaurant, art and design scene that offers lively counterpoints to its fascinating history. Straddling the Limmat River, Zurich's center is made up primarily of medieval churches, guildhalls, and town houses.

2 Berner Oberland. Valleys, lakes and peaks—including the Jungfraujoch, an almost alien landscape slathered in whipped-cream snow all year round, and at 11,400 feet the most accessible high-altitude peak in Europe. This is among the most popular destinations in Switzerland, and with good reason.

3 Geneva. Gleaming with cosmopolitan wealth, home to international organizations like the UN, Geneva's cathedral, International Museum of the Reformation, and monuments bear witness to the city's former incarnation as the Protestant Rome. Its manageable size is a blessing for visitors—any point in the city is accessible on foot from almost anywhere else.

4 Lucerne. A mere 9 square miles in size, it's many of Switzerland's cities in a nutshell: a well-preserved medieval old town, a lakeshore promenade with breathtaking Alpine views, great shops, restaurants and museums. It also boasts a world-class concert hall.

5 Central Switzerland. This is where it all started, on a meadow overlooking the Lake of Lucerne where in 1291 rebels swore an oath and sowed the seeds of the Swiss Confederation. And it's smack dab in the heart of William Tell country. It's the most visited region in the country.

6 Zermatt. A fairy-tale version of the typical Alpine village, with carriage rides, chalet restaurants and hotels, shops galore. The Matterhorn, Switzerland's trademark Alp and the world's most recognizable peak, hovers over the pedestrian-only resort.

FRANCE

JURA MOUNTAINS

La Chaux-de-Fonds

Neuchâtel

Lac de Neuchâtel

Yverdon

Payerne

Lausanne

Gruyères

Nyon

Vevey

Lac Léman

Montreux

3 Geneva

Martigny

| 0 | | 40 miles |
| 0 | | 60 km |

THE PARADOX OF SWITZERLAND PITCHES rustic homeyness against high-tech urban efficiency. While digital screens tick off beef futures in Zurich, the crude harmony of cowbells echoes in the velvet mountain pastures of the Berner Oberland. While fur-clad socialites raise jeweled fingers to bid at auctions in Geneva, the women of Appenzell, in Central Switzerland, stand beside the men on the Landsgemeindeplatz and raise their hands to vote—a right not won until 1991.

Switzerland is a haven of private banking, serious shopping, major music festivals, fabulous art collections, palace hotels, state-of-the-art spas, some of the finest gastronomy in the world—from the hautest French and even molecular cuisine to traditional foods like fondue and *Rösti*—and a burgeoning contemporary scene of filmmakers, architects, artists, and designers making international names for themselves.

The country's Roman ruins, decorated medieval facades in towns and cities, castles, churches, and ornately carved wooden chalets point to its rich history, as do folk traditions like "banishing winter," where bell ringing, whip cracking, fire, and fearsome costumes are meant to frighten off the old spirits and usher in the spring

This home of William Tell, heartland of the Reformation, birthplace of the Red Cross, and one of the world's oldest democracies also boasts extraordinary scenery – lakes and valleys, craggy peaks.

WHEN TO GO

Ski season starts before Christmas, with the peak season being over the Christmas and New Year holidays, carrying through to about the end of March.

Otherwise, any time of year is good to travel in Switzerland. You may wish to check ahead if you're planning to visit cities, because a big event—like the annual car show in March in Geneva—can mean hotels are full for miles around and even if you find space it'll be for top-most dollar.

Spring and fall weather can be rainy but is usually mild.

Summers tend to last into October and bring out a "Riviera" feel in many Swiss cities, giving them a laid-back, sometimes almost Mediterranean ambience, with people sunbathing along lake and river shores, and filling sidewalk cafés.

City winters are relatively mild with little snow (although watch out for occasional glacial winds, like the *Bise*) but the higher you go into the mountains the colder it gets, particularly at night. It can be chilly at night up there in the summer, too.

GETTING HERE & AROUND

BY AIR
The major gateways are the Unique Zurich Airport (ZRH) and Geneva's Cointrin Airport (GVA), 10 km (8 mi) and 5 km (3 mi) outside the

TOP REASONS TO GO

Scenery. Whether you're on the water, in the air, lowlands or mountains, the scenery is breathtaking—and from cities, the sight of silent snowy peaks rising up over urban buildings offers a poignant contrast to cosmopolitan concerns.

Food and Wine. Some of the highest concentrations of Michelin-starred restaurants anywhere are here, but if gastronomic French is not your thing, then discover Swiss cuisine, which, like the country's excellent wines, is characterized by strong regional differences.

Museums. There are world-class collections of art in Switzerland. For Impressionists and classical moderns like Picasso, Chagall, Miró: in Zurich alone, there's the art museum and the Bührle Collection, with the Hahnloser and Reinhart collections in nearby Winterthur.

Great Outdoors. Winter and mountain sports aside, this is a country where detailed maps are available for walkers, hikers, cyclists, and even those touring on horseback. There's

rafting on the rivers, sailing on the lakes, and paragliding and hang gliding for some of the most stupendous takes ever on all that glorious scenery.

Shopping. Swiss contemporary design (sometimes using the Swiss flag as an iconic feature) just keeps getting better and better. Whether its lifestyle accessories, clothes or watches from Swatch to Patek Philippe (Geneva is the luxury watch capital of the world), the shopping's great—if not necessarily cheap.

Diversity. Finding such distinct regions with their own languages and traditions in such a compact country exercises a fascination of its own—multiplied by the startling contrasts between urban sophistication and the time-warp, rural simplicity of mountain folk.

Festivals and Folk Traditions. World-class music festivals are huge drawing cards—as are increasingly folk traditions that take place largely in Central Switzerland.

respective cities. You can connect to the cities (and the rest of the country) via train from the airport, or have a rental car waiting for you.

BY CAR

If you want to explore more remote areas of the country, driving is certainly the best option. Road maps are available at gas stations, but a rule of thumb if you're looking for the fastest way to get from place to place is follow the *autoroute* signs.

There are no tolls, however to use semi-expressways and expressways, you must display a sticker, or *vignette,* on the windshield. You can buy one at the border or in gas stations for 40 SF. Cars rented within Switzerland already have these stickers.

Have some 10 SF and 20 SF notes available, as many gas stations (especially in the mountains) have vending-machine pumps that operate even when they're closed. Simply slide in a bill and fill your tank. Many of these machines also accept major credit cards with precoded PIN numbers. You can request a receipt (*Quittung* in German, *quittance* in French) from the machine.

BY BUS

Switzerland's famous yellow post-buses (called *Postautos* or *cars postaux*), with their stentorian tritone horns, link main cities with villages off the beaten track and even crawl over the highest mountain passes.

Both postbuses and city buses follow posted schedules to the minute: you can set your watch by them. You can pick up a free schedule for a particular route in most post-buses; full schedules are included in train schedule books.

> **MONEY & EXCHANGE**
>
> The unit of currency in Switzerland is the Swiss franc (SF), available in notes of 10, 20, 50, 100, 200, and 1,000. Francs are divided into centimes (in Suisse Romande) or Rappen (in German Switzerland). There are coins for 5, 10, 20, and 50 centimes or Rappen. Larger coins are the 1-, 2-, and 5-franc pieces. At this writing, the exchange rate stood at 1.16 SF to the U.S. dollar and 1,15 SF to the euro.

Postbuses cater to hikers: walking itineraries are available at some post-bus stops.

Be sure to ask whether reservations are required, as is the case for some Alpine pass routes.

BY TRAIN

Trains described as Inter-City or Express are the fastest, stopping only in principal towns. Regional trains stop at all the small stations along the way. There are numerous train passes available. The Swiss Pass is the best value, offering unlimited travel on Swiss Federal Railways, post-buses, lake steamers, and the local bus and tram services of 38 cities.

ABOUT THE RESTAURANTS

While the standard Swiss breakfast consists of coffee, bread, jam, and sometimes Birchermüesli (oat flakes mixed with berries, nuts and yoghurt), many hotel restaurants offer a larger spread, which can include eggs, toast, cheese, cold cuts and sausage, potatoes, and pancakes or waffles.

Popular specialties for lunch and dinner include cheese fondue and raclette (melted cheese served with potatoes in their skins, and pickles); order a plate of air-dried beef from Graubünden or Valais to enjoy beforehand. You can get fondue in most parts of the country, but it is not customary for Swiss to eat it during the warmer months. However—especially for tourists—some restaurants serve it anyway.

The French-speaking cantons pride themselves on *filets de perche* (fried perch fillets), served with various sauces, or just lemon, and French fries.

German-speaking Switzerland made its mark in culinary history with the ubiquitous Rösti, a grated potato pancake. If served on its own as a main dish, it is often spruced up with herbs, bacon, or cheese. Just plain, it is served with nearly any meat but tastes particularly good with *Leberli* (sautéed calf's liver) or *Geschnezeltes*, a Zurich specialty of veal strips in cream sauce.

Risotto, gnocchi, polenta, and pasta dishes that reflect both Italian and Swiss-Italian cooking are available in eateries all over the nation, as are some of the better known Graubünden specialties like air-dried beef (*Bündnerfleisch* or *viande des Grisons*) and walnut tart.

MEALS AND MEAL TIMES

Restaurants serve lunch between noon and 2, and dinner usually from 7 to 10, but in some places (especially the farther out in the countryside you are) service may stop earlier than that.

RESERVATIONS AND DRESS

It's a good idea to reserve a table, but essentially (do it several months ahead) for a famed restaurant—even if said restaurant is in a hotel that you are a guest at.

Casual smart will be fine for almost any restaurant, even the gastronomic venues.

MONEY-SAVING TIPS

Müesli is available in most supermarkets (such as Migros and Coop) and can make a hearty lunch, especially when eaten with plain or fruit yogurt instead of milk and fresh fruit.

Lunch is also a good opportunity to sample the fare at some of the more expensive venues, as almost all restaurants offer a fixed-price lunch special that includes soup or salad and a main course at way less than dinner prices.

Food halls like Globus delicatessan in Zurich, or Manor Food or the Halle de Rive in Geneva, can be great places to wander through buying small quantities of cheese, sausage, breads, and baked goods that make it possible to sample a lot of prime Swiss specialties for very little money.

WHAT IT COSTS IN SWISS FRANCS				
¢	$	$$	$$$	$$$$
Restaurants under 15 SF	15 SF–25 SF	25 SF–45 SF	45 SF–65 SF	over 65 SF

Restaurant prices are per person for a main course at dinner.

ABOUT THE HOTELS

When selecting a place to stay, an important resource can be the Swiss Hotel Association (SHA), a rigorous and demanding organization that maintains a specific rating system for lodging standards. Four out of five Swiss hotels belong to this group and take their stars seriously.

In contrast to more casual European countries, stars in Switzerland have precise meaning: a five-star hotel is required to have a specific staff–guest ratio, a daily change of bed linens, and extended hours for room service. In contrast, a two-star hotel must have telephones in the rooms, soap in the bathrooms, and fabric tablecloths in the restaurant.

But the SHA standards cannot control the quality of the decor and the grace of service. Thus you may find a five-star hotel that meets the technical requirements but has shabby appointments, leaky plumbing, or a rude concierge, or a good, family-run two-star pension that makes you feel like royalty.

INNS

Travelers on a budget can find help from the *Check-in E & G Hotels* guide, available through Switzerland Tourism. It lists comfortable little hotels that offer simple two-star standards in usually very atmospheric inns.

Other organizations can help you find unusual properties: the Relais & Châteaux group seeks out manor houses, historic buildings, and generally atmospheric luxury, with most of its properties falling into the $$$ or $$$$ range. A similar group, Romantik Hotels and Restaurants, combines architectural interest, historic atmosphere, and fine regional food. Relais du Silence hotels are usually isolated in a peaceful, natural setting, with first-class comforts.

BED & BREAKFASTS

You can get information about B&Bs from the user-friendly site of Bed & Breakfast Switzerland, www.bnb.ch. You can make reservations online through the site.

FARM STAYS

An unusual option for families seeking the local experience: stay on a farm with a Swiss family, complete with children, animals, and the option to work in the fields. You should be reasonably fluent in French or German, depending on the region of your stay. More information is available through Switzerland Tourism.

WHAT IT COSTS IN SWISS FRANCS				
¢	$	$$	$$$	$$$$
Hotels	under 100 SF	100 SF–200 SF	100 SF–200 SF	300 SF–450 SF	over 450 SF

Hotel prices are for two people in a standard double room in high season, including tax and service.

PLANNING YOUR TIME

Since Switzerland's two major airports are located in Zurich and Geneva, it makes sense to arrive at one and depart from the other.

In French-speaking Geneva, try to stay at one of the palace hotels along the lake or river, and make a point of exploring the Old Town with its cathedral and International Museum of the Reformation—and check out the shopping district at the bottom of the hill. Visiting the Red Cross Museum in the International Quarter, right across the street from the UN, is also worth it.

Take the train or a rental car to Zermatt; this takes you through lake and wine country in the canton of Vaud, with scenery getting positively breathtaking in the Lavaux area after Lausanne. As you move into the Rhône Valley in the canton of Valais, look out for steep vineyards—steep as in: require a helicopter to harvest the grapes—with dry stone walls and a special irrigation system called *bisses*. Pedestrian-only Zermatt combines both a high-altitude mountain experience and a pretty, jet-setty scene.

If mountains have a "home," it is truly Switzerland—a summit of summits. In the Berner Oberland, you have the Lauterbrunnen Valley, which looks more like a painting than real life, with the jaw-dropping vista threaded by 72 waterfalls that plummet from sky-high cliffs.

15

Moving on to Lucerne and Central Switzerland: this is gentler country, with the lake and rolling hills surrounded by Alps. A must here is a steamer cruise to explore the William Tell legend, but also just how the Swiss Confederation began way back in 1291. Check the concert schedules—world-class symphony orchestras and soloists perform here.

In Zurich: explore the Old Town, its hip shops and galleries, the Fraumünster church with stained-glass windows by Marc Chagall, and stroll down Bahnhofstrasse—Zurich's equivalent to 5th Avenue. Stop in for coffee and pastry at Sprüngli, on Paradeplatz where the big banks are located. Art lovers will want to check out not only the Kunstmuseum but the Bührle Collection, and may even want to take a day trip to Winterthur to see the world famous Reinhart and Hahnloser collections.

ZURICH

Zurich, located by the Limmat River at the point where it emerges from the Zürichsee (Lake of Zurich), is a beautiful city with vistas of snowy mountains in the distance and a charming *Altstadt* (Old Town). The Romans came here in the 1st century BC, but were expelled in the 5th century by the Germanic Alemanni, ancestors of present-day Zurichers. Zurich was renowned as a center of commerce from the 12th century. The Reformation defined its soul: from his pulpit in the Grossmünster, Ulrich Zwingli ingrained in Zurichers a devotion to thrift and industriousness. Today the Zurich stock exchange is the fourth-largest in the world, and the city's extraordinary museums and galleries and luxurious shops along Bahnhofstrasse, Zurich's 5th Avenue, attest to its position as Switzerland's money and cultural—if not political—capital. The latest addition to the city's profile is Zurich West, where former factories now house restaurants, bars, art galleries, and dance clubs.

PLANNING YOUR TIME

The Limmat River neatly bisects Zurich, crisscrossed by lovely, low bridges. On the left bank are the grander, more genteel part of the Old Town; the main train station; and Bahnhofplatz, an urban crossroads off which the world-famous luxury shopping street, Bahnhofstrasse, feeds. The right bank constitutes the livelier old section, divided into the Oberdorf (Upper Village) and the Niederdorf (Lower Village). Scattered throughout the town are 13 medieval guildhalls, or *Zunfthäuser,* which once formed the backbone of Zurich's commercial society.

Just walk around the city, on both sides of the river: it's the best way to take it all in—see most of the listed sites even if only from the outside, and the shops. Museum buffs may want to think not only in terms of the Kunstmuseum and the Bührle Collection, but of a day-trip to Winterthur to see the Reinhart and Hahnloser collections.

GETTING HERE & AROUND

Zurich Airport is Switzerland's most important airport and the 10th-busiest in the world. Some 60 airlines, including American, United, and, of course, Swiss Air Lines, known as Swiss, serve this airport, located 11 km (7 mi) north of the city.

Zurich ZVV, the tram service in Zurich, runs from 5:30 AM to midnight, every 6 minutes at peak hours, every 12 minutes at other times.

Switzerland's highway system also networks through Zurich: If you're traveling by car, it's best to leave it parked, since those streets that aren't pedestrian zones are liable to be one-way—you'll get fewer headaches on foot, and the city's public transit system (ZVV, 0840/988988, www.zvv.ch) is excellent.

For train travel, the Swiss Federal Railways (SBB, 0900/300300, www.sbb.ch) manages everything—check them out when planning your trip. Trains arrive hourly from Geneva (80 SF one-way) and Lucerne (23 SF one-way).

ESSENTIALS

Tourist information (⊠ *Hauptbahnhof, Kreis 1 CH-8023* ☎ *044/2154000*)

EXPLORING ZURICH

❶ **Fraumünster** *(Church of Our Lady).* Of the church spires that are Zurich's signature, the Fraumünster's is the most delicate. It was added to the Gothic structure in 1732; the remains of Louis the German's original 9th-century abbey are below. Its Romanesque choir is a perfect spot for meditation beneath the ocher, sapphire, and ruby glow of the 1970 stained-glass windows by the Russian-born Marc Chagall, who loved Zurich. Augusto Giacometti, the Graubünden sculptor Alberto Giacometti's cousin, executed the fine painted window, made in 1930, in the north transept. ⊠ *Stadthausquai, Kreis 1* ⊙ *Daily 10–4.*

❷ **Zunfthaus zur Meisen.** Set on the bank of the Limmat across the river from the towering Fraumünster is Zurich's most beautiful guildhall, comprising a magnificent suite of reception salons, several of which

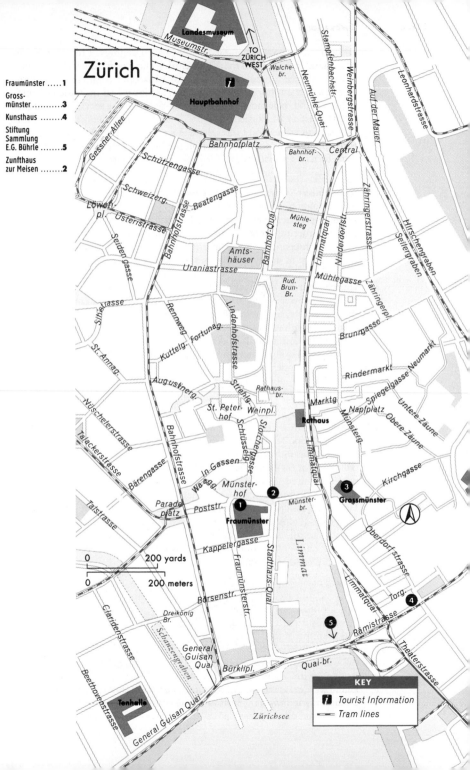

Zürich

Landesmuseum

Museumstr.

TO
ZÜRICH
WEST

Walche-
br.

Stampfenbachstr.

Weinbergstrasse

Leonhardstrasse

Neumühle-Quai

Auf der Mauer

Hauptbahnhof

Bahnhofplatz

Bahnhof-
br.

Central

Zähringerstrasse

Hirschengraben

Seilergraben

Gessner-Allee

Schützengasse

Schweizerg.

Beatengasse

Bahnhofstrasse

Löwen-
pl.

Usteristrasse

Seidengasse

Uraniastrasse

Amts-
häuser

Bahnhof-Quai

Mühle-
steg

Niederdorfstr.

Limmatquai

Mühlegasse

Zähringerpl.

Rud.
Brun-
Br.

Brunngasse

Sihlstrasse

St. Annag.

Rennweg

Kuttelg.-fortunag.

Augustnerg.

Lindenhofstrasse

Strehlg.

Rathaus-
br.

St. Peter-
hof

Weinpl.

Schlüsselg.

Storchengasse

Marktg.

Rathaus

Rindermarkt

Spiegelgasse

Neumarkt

Untere Zäune

Obere Zäune

Napfplatz

Münsterg.

Nüschelerstrasse

Talackerstrasse

Bärengasse

Bahnhofstrasse

Wa ag

In Gassen

Münster-
hof

2

3

Grossmünster

Kirchgasse

Parade
platz

Poststr.

1

Fraumünster

Münster-
br.

Limmatquai

Oberdorfstrasse

Talstrasse

Kappelergasse

Fraumünsterstr.

Stadthaus-Quai

Limmat

Limmatquai

Torg.

4

0   200 yards

0   200 meters

Börsenstr.

Claridenstrasse

Dreikönig
Br.

Schanzengraben

General
Guisan
Quai

Bürklipl.

5

Quai-br.

Rämistrasse

Theaterstrasse

Beethovenstrasse

Tonhalle

General Guisan Quai

Zürichsee

are topped by extravagant Baroque stucco ceilings. Erected for the city's wine merchants in the 18th century, the Zunfthaus today is a fitting showplace for the Swiss National Museum's ceramics collection. The Kilchberg-Schooren porcelain works flourished in Zurich during 1763–90 and their masterwork—a 300-piece dining service created for the Monastery of Einsiedeln in 1775—takes center stage, along with exquisite figurines and table decor. Also on view are Nyon porcelains, Swiss pottery, and faience. Enter on the Fraumünster side. ⊠ *Münsterhof 20, Kreis 1* ☎ *044/2212807* ⊕ *www.musee-suisse.com/e/index2. html* 🎫 *3 SF* ☉ *Tues.–Sun. 10:30–5.*

❸ Grossmünster *(Great Church).* This impressive cathedral is affectionately known to English speakers as the "Gross Monster." Executed on the plump twin towers (circa 1781) are classical caricatures of Gothic forms bordering on the comical. The core of the structure was built in the 12th century on the site of a Carolingian church dedicated to the memory of martyrs Felix and Regula, who allegedly carried their severed heads to the spot. Charlemagne is said to have founded the church after his horse stumbled over their burial site. On the side of the south tower an enormous stone Charlemagne sits enthroned; the original statue, carved in the late 15th century, is protected in the crypt. In keeping with what the 16th-century reformer Zwingli preached from the Grossmünster's pulpit, the interior is spare, even forbidding, with all luxurious ornamentation long since stripped away. The only artistic touches are modern: stained-glass windows by Augusto Giacometti, and ornate bronze doors in the north and south portals, dating from the late 1940s. ⊠ *Zwinglipl., Kreis 1* ☎ *044/2525949* ☉ *Daily 9–6; tower weekdays 9:15–5; cloister weekdays 9–6.*

❹ Kunsthaus *(Museum of Art).* With a varied and high-quality permanent collection of paintings—medieval, Dutch and Italian Baroque, and Impressionist—the Kunsthaus is possibly Zurich's best art museum. The collection of Swiss art includes some fascinating works; others might be an acquired taste. Besides works by Ferdinand Hodler, with their mix of realism and stylization, there's a superb room full of Johann Heinrich Füssli paintings, which hover between the darkly ethereal and the grotesque. And then there's Picasso, Klee, Degas, Matisse, Kandinsky, Chagall, and Munch, all satisfyingly represented. ⊠ *Heimpl. 1, Kreis 1* ☎ *044/2538484* ⊕ *www.kunsthaus.ch* 🎫 *Varies with exhibition* ☉ *Wed.–Fri. 10–8, Sat., Sun.,Tues 10—6.*

❺ Stiftung Sammlung E. G. Bührle. A stunning array of Cézannes, Manets, ★ Monets, and Degases makes this eye-knocking collection one of the best art museums in Europe. Unfortunately, visits are now by appointment only after a spectacular robbery in February 2008. Amazingly, it was all put together in the space of a single decade. During the 1950s, Zurich industrialist E.G. Bührle purchased the finest offerings from the world's most prestigious art dealers, winding up with a collection studded with legendary Impressionist and Postimpressionist works, including Cézanne's *Self Portrait with Palette,* Renoir's *Little Irene,* and Degas's *Little Dancer.* The core of the collection remains French 19th-century, and all the great names are here, from Courbet and Manet to

Picasso, with forays into the Nabi, Fauve, and Cubist schools. Housed in an 1886 villa, there is little period splendor on view but nothing could outshine these masterpieces. Take Tram 11 from Bellevue, then Bus 77 from Hegibachplatz to the Altenhofstrasse stop. ⊠ *Zollikerstr. 172, Kreis 8* ☎ *044/4220086* ⊕ *www.buehrle.ch* ⬚*25 SF.*

WHERE TO EAT

$$ ✕ **Bierhalle Kropf.** Under the mounted boar's head and restored century-old murals depicting gallivanting cherubs, businesspeople, workers, and shoppers share crowded tables to feast on generous hot dishes and a great selection of sausages. The *Leberknödli* (liver dumplings) are tasty, the potato croquettes are filled with farmer's cheese and garnished with a generous fresh salad, and the *Apfelküchli* (fried apple slices) are tender and sweet. The bustle and clatter provide a lively, sociable experience, and you'll more than likely get to know your neighbor. ⊠ *In Gassen 16, Kreis 1* ☎ *044/2211805* ▤ *AE, DC, MC, V* ☉ *Closed Sun.*

$$$$ ✕ **Haus zum Rüden.** The most culinarily ambitious of Zurich's many Zunfthaus (historic guildhall) dining places, this fine restaurant is also the ★ most architecturally spectacular, combining a wooden barrel-vaulted ceiling and 30-foot beams. Slick modern improvements—including a glassed-in elevator—manage to blend intelligently with the ancient decor and Old World chandeliers. Innovative entrées might include clear beef soup with vegetable strips and black Perigord truffles, or duck breast in honey ginger sauce. The river views are especially impressive at night; ask for a window table. ⊠ *Limmatquai 42, Kreis 1* ☎ *044/2619566* ▤ *AE, DC, MC, V.*

$$ ✕ **Kronenhalle.** From Stravinsky, Brecht, and Joyce to Nureyev, Deneuve, **Fodor's**Choice and Saint-Laurent, this beloved landmark has always drawn a stellar ★ crowd. Every panel of gleaming wood wainscoting frames works by Picasso, Braque, Miró, Chagall, or Matisse, collected by patroness-hostess Hulda Zumsteg, who owned the restaurant from 1921 until her death in 1985. The tradition is carried on by the family trust, and robust cooking is still served in hefty portions: fish in sage butter, veal steak in morel sauce, duck *à l'orange* with red cabbage and Spätzli. There's no shame in ordering the sausage and Rösti just to take in the animated and genial scene. ⊠ *Rämistr. 4, Kreis 1* ☎ *044/2516669* ⊕ *www.kronenhalle.com* ⚑ *Reservations essential* ▤ *AE, DC, MC, V.*

$$$$ ✕ **Petermann's Kunststuben.** Set in an 1879 house with rooms replete with aubergine-hued walls, gigantic bouquets, Venetian glass lanterns, and modern paintings ("Kunststuben" means art studio), Petermann's is 9 km (5 mi) south of Zurich in Küsnacht, a village near Rapperswil. Though it's south of the city center, this formal restaurant is more than worth the time and effort to get here. Chef Horst Petermann never rests on his laurels: the ever-changing international French menu may include garlic lamb with jellied vegetables, with presentation so fantastic it looks more like art than food. On the small side, the restaurant nearly doubles in summer thanks to the flower-fragrant outdoor terrace. ⊠ *Seestr. 160, Küsnacht, CH-8700* ☎ *044/9100715* ⊕ *www.kunststuben.com* ⚑ *Reservations essential* ▤ *AE, DC, MC, V* ☉ *Closed Sun. and Mon., 2 wks in Feb., and 3 wks in late summer.*

15

WHERE TO STAY

$$$$ ⚏ **Baur au Lac.** Austria's Empress Elisabeth paved the way (spending an entire summer here with a retinue of 60 people). The Russian Tsarina and German Emperor Wilhelm II followed; Richard Wagner arrived and premiered the first act of his *Die Walküre* here, accompanied on the piano by his father-in-law, Franz Liszt. Kings and queens, empresses and dukes took turns visiting (and let's not forget Arthur Rubinstein, Marc Chagall, Henry Moore, and Placido Domingo), making this hotel a truly upper-crust establishment ever since it opened its doors in 1844. Today there is nary an empress in sight. This is still one highbrow patrician—it even goes so far as to turn its broad back to the commercial center; its front rooms overlook the lake, the canal, and the manicured lawns of its own private park. Le Hall, the vast lobby, has a Jugendstil flavor and is just the place to apertif the late afternoon away. Upstairs, the signature classic room decor gleams with rich fabrics and Empire mirrors. In summer, meals (including breakfast) are served in the glassed-in pavilion along the canal; in winter, in the glowing Restaurant Français. **Pros:** Old World style plus ultramodern comforts such as triple-glazed windows and CD players. **Cons:** service can get a little sniffy. ⊠ *Talstr. 1, Kreis 1 CH-8022* ☎*044/2205020* ☏*044/2205044* ⊕*www.bauraulac.ch* ⊲*84 rooms, 42 suites* ♿*In-room: refrigerators, safe, dial-up. In-hotel: 2 restaurants, bar, gym, Wi-Fi.* ⊟*AE, DC, MC, V.*

$$–$$$ ⚏ **Haus zum Kindli.** This charming little bijou hotel is as artfully styled as a magazine ad, with subtle grays and beiges underscoring the inviting white bed linens, and original bath fixtures refurbished to match modern needs. The result is welcoming, intimate, and less contrived than many hotels' cookie-cutter decors. An added attraction is "revitalized" water throughout the hotel—a process said to provide healthier water than the stuff fresh out of the tap. **Pros:** pretend you live in the middle of the Old Town, just steps away from where the town was founded; run home to the bathroom while you're shopping—it's that close! **Cons:** no parking; a little dark during winter. ⊠*Pfalzg. 1, Kreis 1 CH-8001* ☎*043/8887676* ☏*043/8887677* ⊕*www.kindli.ch* ⊲*16 rooms* ♿*In-room: refrigerators, no a/c. In-hotel: restaurant, Wi-Fi, no elevator.* ⊟*AE, DC, MC, V* ⏍*BP.*

¢–$ ⚏ **Kafischnaps.** Away from the throb of downtown but still only a 15-minute walk back, this is the best deal in town for those on a budget. Each room has its own color scheme, taken from a local schnapps. Beds are very comfy, with down quilts and soft pillows. The smoky café downstairs doubles as the reception area and breakfast room. Reservations can only be made online. **Pros:** beautifully designed rooms; very hip café; great value. **Cons:** far from the madding crowd; check-in can be annoying if the café is busy. ⊠*Kornhausstr. 57, Kreis 6 CH-8037* ☎*043/5388116* ⊕*www.kafischnaps.ch* ⊲*5 rooms* ♿*In-room: no a/c, no phone, no TV (some), Wi-Fi.* ⊟*AE, DC, MC, V* ⏍*BP.*

$$–$$$ ⚏ **Seehof.** Offering the best of both worlds, this lodging is in a quiet neighborhood, yet conveniently close to the opera, movie theaters, and the lake. It's a favorite of hip business executives and travelers looking for seclusion. The interior's leitmotif is modern, minimal; the bright rooms' parquet floors and white walls and furnishings give them a fresh, crisp look. The bar downstairs has a good selection of wines; in summer a garden terrace adds to the charm. **Pros:** small but very nice bathrooms; a good in-house sushi restaurant. **Cons:** on a narrow and charmless side street. ✉ *Seehofstr. 11, Kreis 1 CH-8008* ☎ *044/2545757* 🖷 *044/2545758* ⊕ *www.hotelseehof.ch* ⚲ *19 rooms* ⚲ *In-room: refrigerator, no a/c, safe. In-hotel: bar, Wi-Fi.* ⊟ *AE, DC, MC, V* ⎪⎪*BP.*

$$$$
Fodor'sChoice
★

🏨 **Widder.** Zurich's most captivating hotel was created when 10 adjacent medieval houses were gutted and combined—now steel fuses with ancient stone and timeworn wood. Behind every door is a fascinating mix of old and new; a guest room could mix old restored 17th-century frescoes and stone floors with a leather bedspread and halogen bell jars. Set in the heart of Zurich's historic quarter, many of the houses look out into a communal courtyard, while others flaunt views of the Rennweg or the Augustinerkirche. Four suites have private roof terraces. **Pros:** the spectacular Room 210; the more modern Room 509. **Cons:** there is no con, this place is perfect. ✉ *Rennweg 7, Kreis 1 CH-8001* ☎ *044/2242526* 🖷 *044/2242424* ⊕ *www.widderhotel.ch* ⚲ *42 rooms, 7 suites* ⚲ *In-room: refrigerator, safe, dial-up, Wi-Fi. In-hotel: 2 restaurants, bar.* ⊟ *AE, DC, MC, V.*

15

NIGHTLIFE & THE ARTS

NIGHTLIFE

Of all the Swiss cities, Zurich has the liveliest nightlife. The Niederdorf is Zurich's well-known nightlife district, but the locales are a shade hipper in Zurich West. In winter things wind down between midnight and 2 AM, but come summer most places stay open until 4 AM.

BARS

DOWNTOWN **Barfüsser** (✉ *Spitalg. 14, Kreis 1* ☎ *044/2514064*), established in 1956, claims to be one of the oldest gay bars in Europe. It has comfortable lounge chairs and space to mix and mingle. There's also excellent sushi. **Barrique** (✉ *Marktg. 17, Kreis 1* ☎ *044/2525941*) is a vinotheque featuring a world-renowned wine list. **Café Central Bar** (✉ *Central 1, Kreis 1* ☎ *044/2515555*), in the Hotel Central, is a popular neo–Art Deco café by day and a piano bar by night. **Cranberry** (✉ *Metzgerg. 3, Kreis 1* ☎ *044/2612772*) stocks broad selections of rum and port; it also has an upstairs cigar room. The narrow bar at the **Kronenhalle** (✉ *Rämistr. 4, Kreis 1* ☎ *044/2511597*) draws mobs of well-heeled locals and internationals for its prize-winning cocktails. At **Purpur** (✉ *Seefeldstr. 9, Kreis 2* ☎ *044/4192066*), a Moroccan-style lounge, you can take your drinks lying down on a heap of throw pillows while DJs mix ambient sound.

THE ARTS

Despite its small population, Zurich is a big city when it comes to the arts; it supports a top-rank orchestra, an opera company, and a theater. Check *Zürich News,* published weekly in English and German, or "Züri-tipp," a German-language supplement to the Friday edition of the daily newspaper *Tages Anzeiger.*

SHOPPING

Many of Zurich's designer boutiques lie hidden along the narrow streets between Bahnhofstrasse and the Limmat River. Quirky bookstores and antiques shops lurk in the sloping cobblestone alleyways leading off Niedorfstrasse and Oberdorfstrasse. The fabled Bahnhofstrasse is dominated by large department stores and extravagantly priced jewelry shops.

GENEVA

Today the world's largest center for multicultural diplomacy, and a hotbed of luxury shopping, Geneva was a postcard-perfect city known for enlightened tolerance long before Henry Dunant founded the International Red Cross here (1864), the League of Nations moved in (1919), the World Health Organization (WHO) set up shop after World War II, or the World Wide Web was invented here at CERN, the European Center for Nuclear Research. Once a place of refuge for the religious reformers Jean Calvin and John Knox, it has sheltered many others, and today a whopping 40% of the city's 187,000 inhabitants are not Swiss. Four hundred years ago it was wave after wave of Protestant refugees—and Geneva flourished, under the iron yoke of its 16th century reformer, as a multilingual stronghold of Protestant reform.

PLANNING YOUR TIME

The République et Canton de Genève (Republic and Canton of Geneva) commands sweeping views of the French Alps and the French Jura from its fortuitous position at the southwestern tip of Lac Léman (Lake Geneva). The water flows straight through the city center and into the River Rhône en route to Lyon and the Mediterranean, leaving museums, shops, restaurants, and parks to jostle for space on its history-laden south shore, known as Rive Gauche (Left Bank). Busy shopping streets underline the hilltop Vieille Ville (Old Town). The *quartier international* (International Area), the Gare Cornavin (main train station), and sumptuous waterfront hotels dominate the north shore, or Rive Droite (Right Bank). Try to divide whatever time you have in the city equally between an extended stroll along the waterfront and a thorough exploration of the Vieille Ville.

GETTING HERE & AROUND

British Airways, easyJet, and Swiss fly direct between London and Geneva; Swiss and Continental operate direct service from New York. Swiss also schedules frequent connections to its hub in Zurich. Cointrin International Airport, Switzerland's second-largest, lies 5 km (3 mi) northwest of downtown Geneva.

Express trains from most Swiss cities arrive at and depart from the Right Bank Gare Cornavin every hour. Zurich is roughly three hours away.

The Compagnie Générale de Navigation operates steamship connections between Geneva and Nyon, Lausanne, Vevey, Montreux, and assorted smaller lake towns in Switzerland, as well as some in France.

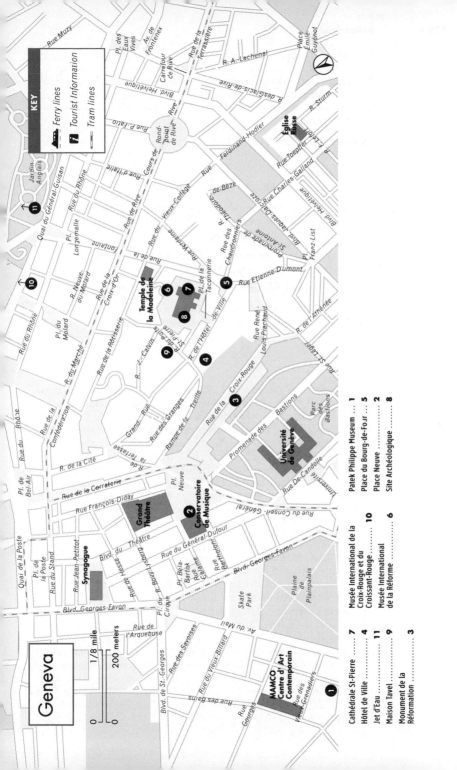

Geneva

KEY

⛴ Ferry lines

i Tourist Information

══ Tram lines

Cathédrale St-Pierre **7**

Hôtel de Ville **4**

Jet d'Eau **11**

Maison Tavel **9**

Monument de la
Réformation **3**

Musée International de la
Croix-Rouge et du
Croissant-Rouge **10**

Musée International
de la Réforme **6**

Patek Philippe Museum ... **1**

Place du Bourg-de-Four ... **5**

Place Neuve **2**

Site Archéologique **8**

0 ── 1/8 mile

0 ── 200 meters

The Swiss A1 expressway, along the north shore, connects Geneva to the rest of Switzerland by way of Lausanne. Traffic along the quays clogs easily, and parking in town is both restricted and expensive; look for electric signs on major incoming roads that note the whereabouts of (immaculate) municipal parking garages and their current number of empty spaces.

Local buses and trams operate every few minutes on all city routes from 5 AM to midnight.

ESSENTIALS

Air Contacts Cointrin (☎022/7177111 ⊕ www.gva.ch).

Boat & Ferry Contacts Compagnie Générale de Navigation (*CGN* ☎0848/811848 ⊕ www.cgn.ch). **Mouettes Genevoises** (⊠4 quai du Mont-Blanc, Les Pâquis ☎ 022/7322944 ⊕ www.mouettesgenevoises.ch).

Bus & Tram Contacts Transports Publics Genevois (*TPG;* ☎0900/022021 ⊕ www.tpg.ch and www.unireso.com).

Train Contacts Gare Cornavin (⊠7 pl. Cornavin ☎0900/300300 ⊕ www.cff.ch).

Visitor Information Genève Tourisme (⊠18 rue du Mont-Blanc, Les Pâquis, Case Postale 1602, CH-1211Genève 1 ☎022/9097070 ☎022/9097075 ⊕ www. geneve-tourisme.ch)

EXPLORING GENEVA

❼ **Cathédrale St-Pierre** *(St. Peter's Cathedral).* A stylistic hybrid scarred by centuries of religious upheaval and political turmoil, this imposing cathedral somehow survived the ages with its dignity intact. The massive neoclassical facade was an 18th-century addition meant to shore up 12th-century Romanesque-Gothic walls; stained-glass windows, the Duke of Rohan's tomb, a few choir stalls, and the 15th-century **Chapel of the Maccabees** hint at lavish alternatives to Calvin's plain chair. Fifteenth-century bells and bird's-eye city views reward those who climb the **north tower.** ⊠ Cour St-Pierre, Vieille Ville ☎022/3117575 ⊕ www.saintpierre-geneve.ch ☜North tower 4 SF ◷ June–Sept., Mon.–Sat. 9:30–6:30, Sun. noon–6:30; Oct.–May, Mon.–Sat. 10–5:30, Sun. noon–5:30.

❹ **Hôtel de Ville** *(City Hall).* Sixteen countries signed the first Geneva Convention in the ground-floor **Alabama Hall** on August 22, 1864, making it the birthplace of the International Red Cross, and the League of Nations convened its first assembly here, on November 15, 1920. The canton's executive and legislative bodies meet here; until 1958 city functionaries lived here. But the history of this elegant vaulted compound begins in 1455, when the city built a large fortified tower, the **Tour Baudet,** to house the State Council Chamber. Its circular ramp, an architectural anomaly added during the Reformation, was used by at least one lawmaker to reach the second-floor meeting place without dismounting his horse. ⊠2 rue de l'Hôtel-de-Ville, Vieille Ville ☎022/3272118 ⊕ www.geneve.ch ☜Free ◷ Daily; information booth weekdays 9–noon, 2–5.

⓫ **Jet d'Eau** *(Water Jet)*. The direct descendant of a late-19th-century
☾ hydroelectric safety valve, Europe's tallest fountain shoots 132 gallons
of water 390 feet into the air every second at 120 mph (wind conditions
permitting). The water is aerated on the way up by a special nozzle,
making it white. ⊠*Off quai Gustave-Ador, Eaux-Vives.*

❾ **Maison Tavel** *(Tavel House)*. Vaulted cellars and ground-floor kitchens
display medieval graffiti, local coins, 15th-century tiles, and a guil-
lotine in Geneva's oldest house, now a museum focused on life in the
city from 1334 to the 1800's. Seventeenth-century ironwork, doors,
and other fragments of long-demolished houses fill the first floor; a
bourgeois home complete with 18th-century wallpaper is re-created
on the second. The enormous Magnin Model (which depicts Geneva
as it looked before its elaborate defense walls came down in 1850), is
housed in the attic; temporary exhibits rotate through the basement.
⊠*6 rue du Puits-St-Pierre, Vieille Ville* ☎*022/4183700* ⊕*mah.ville-ge.
ch* ⊒*Free* ⊗*Tues.–Sun. 10–5.*

❸ **Monument de la Réformation** *(Wall of the Reformers)*. Conceived on a
★ grand scale and erected between 1909 and 1917, this solemn 325- by
30-foot swath of granite pays homage to the 16th-century religious
movement spearheaded by Guillaume Farel, Jean Calvin, Théodore de
Bèze, and John Knox. Smaller statues of major Protestant figures, bas-
reliefs, and inscriptions connected with the Reformation flank the lifelike
giants as they hover over Bern, Geneva, and Edinburgh's coats of arms;
Oliver Cromwell is surrounded by Pilgrims praying on the deck of the
Mayflower and the 1689 presentation of the Bill of Rights to King William and Queen Mary by the English Houses of Parliament. The Reformation's—and Geneva's—motto, *Post Tenebras Lux* (After Darkness,
Light), spreads over the whole. ⊠*Parc des Bastions, Centre Ville.*

❿ **Musée International de la Croix-Rouge et du Croissant-Rouge** *(International
★ Red Cross and Red Crescent Museum)*. Powerful mute statues speak
to the need for human kindness in the face of disaster, and balanced
but often grim exhibits trace the history of the struggle to provide it in
this carefully nonjudgmental museum buried in the hillside beneath the
world headquarters of the International Committee of the Red Cross.
Audiovisuals show the postbattle horrors at Solferino that moved Henry
Dunant to form the Red Cross; endless aisles of file boxes hold 7 million records of World War I prisoners. Good deeds are dramatized,
from the proverbial Samaritan's to Clara Barton's. There's a replica of
a 6½-foot by 6½-foot concrete cell in which Red Cross workers discovered 17 political prisoners; the **Mur du Temps** (Wall of Time), a simple
timeline punctuated by armed conflicts and natural disasters in which
more than 10,000 people died, puts the overall story into sobering perspective. Good news, in the form of disaster-relief kits and snapshots
used to reunite Rwandan families after the 1994 genocide, is also on
display, however; signage and audio guides are in English. ⊠*17 av. de
la Paix, International Area* ☎*022/7489525* ⊕*www.micr.org* ⊒*10 SF*
⊗*Wed.–Mon. 10–5.*

15

⑥ Musée International de la Réforme *(International Museum of the Reforma-*
★ *tion)*. Engaging audiovisuals, period artifacts, and carefully preserved
documents explain the logic behind the Protestant Reformation, explore
its impact as a religious, cultural, and philosophical phenomenon, and
trace its roots from the early 16th century through today in this sophisticated, modern, and remarkably friendly museum. The sparkling 18th-
century premises, on the site where Geneva voted to adopt the Reform,
connect by underground passage to the *site archéologique*; all signage
and audioguide material is in English. ✉ *4 rue du Cloître, Vieille Ville*
☎ *022/3102431* ⊕ *www.musee-reforme.ch* 💶 *10 SF, 16 SF with cathedral towers and site archéologique* ⊗ *Tues.–Sun. 10–5.*

❶ Patek Philippe Museum. Geneva's renown as a center for watchmaking
Fodor's Choice and enameling, sustained since the 16th century, finds full justification
★ in this breathtaking private collection of delicate gold watch cases, complicated watch innards, lifelike portrait miniatures, and softly lighted
enameled fans, pens, pocket knives, snuffboxes, telescopes, and vanity
pistols that shoot singing birds. Most of the objects displayed in this
former watchmaking workshop are hundreds of years old; many were
created in Geneva by Patek Philippe, one of the city's most venerable
watchmaking companies. Meticulously restored workbenches, audiovisual displays, classical music, and a horological library complete the
picture; the 2½-hour guided tour (in English at 2:30 on Saturday) puts
it all in context. All signage is in English. ✉ *7 rue des Vieux-Grenadiers,
Plainpalais* ☎ *022/8070910* ⊕ *www.patekmuseum.com* 💶 *10 SF (tour
15 SF)* ⊗ *Tues.–Fri. 2–6, Sat. 10–6.*

❺ Place du Bourg-de-Four. Ancient roads met in this layered Vieille Ville
square before heading south to Annecy and Lyon, east to Italy and the
Chablais, north to the Rues-Basses, and west through the center of town
to the bridge. Once a Roman cattle market, later flooded with refugees,
it's still the quintessential Genevois crossroads where shoppers, lawyers, workers, and students all meet for drinks around an 18th-century
fountain. ✉ *Intersection of Rue de la Fontaine, Rue Verdaine, Rue des
Chaudronniers, Rue Etienne-Dumont, Rue Saint-Léger, and Rue de
l'Hôtel-de-Ville, Vieille Ville.*

❷ Place Neuve. Aristocratic town houses now overlook Geneva's opera
house, the Musée Rath, the Conservatoire de Musique, and the gilded
wrought-iron entrance to the Parc des Bastions, but until 1850 this
wide-open space was the city's heavily fortified main southern gate. The
equestrian statue at the center of the square honors Guillaume-Henri
Dufour, the first general of Switzerland's federal army and the first person to map the country. The large bust of Henry Dunant, founder of the
International Red Cross, marks the spot where public executions once
took place. ✉ *Intersection of Blvd. du Théâtre, Rue de la Corraterie,
Rue de la Croix-Rouge, and Rue Bartholoni, Centre Ville.*

❽ Site Archéologique. Archaeologists found multiple layers of history under-
⊙ neath the Cathédrale St-Pierre when its foundations began to falter in
1976. Excavations have so far yielded remnants of two 4th-century Christian sanctuaries, mosaic floors from the late Roman Empire, three early

churches, and an 11th-century crypt. The first Romanesque cathedral on the site was built in 1000; today audio guides in English and careful lighting help navigate the (reinforced) underground maze that remains. ⊠6 *cour St-Pierre, Vieille Ville* ☎*022/3117574* ⊕*www.site-archeologique. ch* 🖃*8 SF* ◷*Tues.–Sun. 10–5.*

WHERE TO EAT

$–$$ ✗**Café Léo.** Trendy locals descend for lunch, then linger over coffee at this atmospherically tiny, sunny corner bistro whose highlights include avocado and Roquefort salad, homemade ravioli, veal *piccata* with mustard sauce, and a noteworthy *tarte au citron* (lemon tart). Before and after lunch you can join the oldtimers inside drinking small cups of strong coffee and perusing local newspapers mounted onto anti-theft wooden sticks, or sit outside in season watching the streams of people walking by—Rive is one of Geneva's Left Bank hubs. ⊠*9 cours de Rive, Centre VilleCH-1204* ☎*022/3115307* ⊕*www.cafeleo.com* 🖃*MC, V* ◷*Closed Sun. No dinner Sat.*

$$$$ ✗**Domaine de Châteauvieux.** Philippe Chevrier's expansive kitchen, out in

Fodor'sChoice the heart of Geneva's wine country, draws inspiration and the culinary

★ equivalent of spun gold from local and regional foods (many of which are sold on-site in a little *épicerie*). The restaurant is the focal point of a 16th century *domaine,* or château complex, that was once attacked by the Genevois; these days they come in peace to find antique wine-presses, kitchen gardens, weathered stone, ancient beams, a leafy summer terrace with sweeping hilltop views, and a gastronomic experience that can stretch to seven courses and cost 300 SF per person. Exquisite seasonal dishes rarely repeat from year to year but reliably transform asparagus in spring, game come October, and truffles in winter; the Menu Surprise, at 270 SF, is an invitation to sit back, relax, and let the kitchen sing. The cellar houses top Swiss and French wines and there's a humidor off the bar; take a boat up the Rhône to Peney or drive 20 minutes—about 16 km (10 mi)—from Geneva. Café de Peney down the hill also belongs to Chevrier; it is much less pricey and it's open 7/7. ⊠*16 chemin de Châteauvieux, Peney-Dessus, CH-1242Satigny* ☎*022/7531511* ⊕*www.chateauvieux.ch* ᐊ*Reservations essential* 🖃*AE, DC, MC, V* ◷*Closed Sun. and Mon.*

$$$–$$$$ ✗**Il Lago.** Risotto with lobster and basil, risotto with calamari and champagne, and tortelli with cheese, lemon, and mint are some of the northern Italian creations Carrara native and unabashed lover of pasta Marco Garfagnini has road-tested on diners then added to his menu. Set in the Four Seasons des Bergues hotel, the green and blue-tinted dining room, split in half by gilt French doors, is decorated with brocades, chandeliers, and sweeping hand-painted scenery—if seared scallops with wild mushrooms in a shellfish reduction or braised veal cheek with semolina gnocchi and asparagus were served at Versailles, this is what it might be like. In season, there's a gorgeous sidewalk terrace complete with olive trees and aromatic herbs. ⊠*Four Seasons des Bergues, 33 quai des Bergues, Centre VilleCH-1201* ☎*022/9087110* ⊕*www.fourseasons. com/geneva* 🖃*AE, DC, MC, V* ᐊ*Reservations essential.*

15

$$–$$$ ✕ **La Favola.** Lace curtains, embroidered tablecloths, antique silver, collections of tea pots and Murano glass, a sponge-painted ceiling, and a vertiginous spiral staircase strike a delicate balance between rustic and fussy in this wood-paneled dollhouse located on the same street where Jean Calvin, the Protestant reformer, used to live. The food echoes the decor: part country-simple, part city-chic. Homemade pastas come drizzled with herbs, the carpaccio is paper-thin, the tiramisu divine; seasonal risottos, creamy polenta, and regional wines reflect the Ticinese chef's roots in Ascona, near Locarno. ✉ *15 rue Jean-Calvin, Vieille Ville* *CH-1204* ☎ *022/3117437* ⊕ *www.lafavola.com* ☐ *No credit cards* ⌫ *Reservations essential* ⊘ *Closed weekends June–Aug., Sat. lunch and Sun. Sept.–May.*

$$$–$$$$ ✕ **Le Chat Botté.** The dining room of the Beau-Rivage's elegant hotel restaurant has just a hint of the library about it—book cases, framed prints, reading lamps—and is generally used only when the weather's cold. Between May and September, service is moved to the flower-filled terrace upstairs with its majestic harbor views. The menu also evolves with the seasons: chef Dominique Gauthier tweaks the details of his line-up every few months, and highlights range from classics like the fillets of Austrian venison with quince and cinnamon compote or the roast Scottish woodcock served up with sweet chestnuts and ceps from the Voirons to the nouvelle—one winner are the scampi roasted in Kadaïf, citrus vinaigrette, and basil chiffonade. That noted, French classics like foie gras, salt- and freshwater fish, roasted rack of lamb, and lobster put in regular appearances. Vegetarians will always find something here; the wine cellar, Geneva's largest, has 40,000 hand-picked bottles. ✉ *Beau-Rivage Hotel, 13 quai du Mont-Blanc, Les Pâquis* *CH-1201* ☎ *022/7166920* ⊕ *www.beau-rivage.ch* ⌫ *Reservations essential* ☐ *AE, DC, MC, V.*

$$ ✕ **Le Relais de l'Entrecôte.** It is rare to find a line of people waiting for a
Fodor's Choice table anywhere in Geneva, so the fact that it's commonplace outside
★ this bustling wood-paneled Parisian import means the tender strips of grilled steak drenched in herb-based *sauce maison* (house sauce) are a true cut above. A crisp green salad sprinkled with walnuts, robust house wine, and thin, golden fries complete the only option on the menu; but don't worry, there's a second portion on the way, and desserts—like the flower bouquets adorning the restaurant—remain fabulous. ✉ *49 rue du Rhône, Centre Ville* *CH-1204* ☎ *022/3106004* ⊕ *www.relaisentrecote.fr* ⌫ *Reservations not accepted* ☐ *MC, V* ⊘ *Closed July.*

$–$$ ✕ **Les Armures.** A robust Swiss menu has made this Vieille Ville institution a magnet for local street sweepers, foreign heads of state, and everyone in between. Before tucking into a fondue or raclette (melted cheese served with small potatoes in their skins, pickled pearl onions, and cornichons), order a plate of air-dried meat cut paper thin—a specialty of the canton of Grisons—for starters. Other specialties include *Schübling* (sausage), and veal strips in cream sauce: both come with sinfully delicious *Rösti,* a buttery cake of grated potatoes. The kitchen serves until 11:30 PM (11 on Sunday) and in season you can sit outdoors and soak up the Old Town's historic vibe. ✉ *1 rue du Puits-St-Pierre,*

Vieille VilleCH-1204 🕾*022/3103442* ⊕*www.hotel-les-armures.ch* ⊟*AE, DC, MC, V.*

¢–$ ✕**Taverne de la Madeleine.** The sunny, elevated stone terrace looks across at the 15th-century Temple de la Madeleine, homemade fruit tarts sell for 3:50 SF per slice between 3 and 6 PM, and the lunch-only kitchen in this big, plain, friendly canteen serves wholesome *plats du jour*—reasonably priced lunch specials served by most Geneva restaurants on weekdays— but must-trys include the *filets de perches* (a dish that is ubiquitous in the French-speaking part of Switzerland), chocolate mousse, or lemon pie. The city's temperance league owns and operates the Taverne, so it serves no wine or beer. ✉*20 rue Toutes-Âmes, Vieille VilleCH-1204* 🕾*022/3106070* ⊟*AE, DC, MC, V* ⊙*Closed Sun. No dinner.*

WHERE TO STAY

$$$$ 📺**Beau-Rivage.** While luxuriously contemporary where it counts, and with that all-important crisp feel, guest rooms of this gracious, history-rich landmark hotel are awash in swathes of tasseled drape and Louis Something furniture; standard rooms may be less *époque* but still bask in the vibe, and all rooms (and public spaces) feed off from a grand five-story atrium. Sotheby's Geneva offices are here; there's an elegant bar and world-class Thai restaurant, along with Le Chat Botté, the French restaurant that moves to an upstairs terrace in summer. Savoring a meal on its awning-shielded balcony with cascades of flowers in planters—not to mention lake, mountain, and Jet d'Eau views to die for—continues to be a Best of Geneva experience. **Pros:** family-owned; not to worry that there's no spa on-site—if you feel the need for extra pampering, they have a deal with the Spatio day spa. **Cons:** the plants and the incongruously dated "modern" furniture surrounding the burbling lobby fountain could use a little feng shui. ✉*13 quai du Mont-Blanc, Les Pâquis, CH-1201* 🕾*022/7166666* 🖶*022/7166060* ⊕*www. beau-rivage.ch* ⇄*82 rooms, 11 suites* ⅏*In-room: safe, refrigerator, free Wi-Fi. In-hotel: 2 restaurants, room service, bar, gym, laundry service, pay Internet terminal, free Wi-Fi, parking (pay), no-smoking rooms.* ⊟*AE, DC, MC, V.*

$ 📺**Bel'Espérance.** Rooftop views of Lake Geneva, bright yellow-and-blue rooms, tile baths, impeccable upkeep, and a graceful Louis-Philippe-style salon and breakfast room put this Salvation Army-run former *foyer pour dames* (ladies' boarding house) on a par with much pricier hotels. Large doubles connect to form "suites" for parents and children, the communal kitchen has a fridge with lockers, the whole hotel is off-limits to smokers, and Place du Bourg-de-Four is right up the hill. **Pros:** sitting on the roof terrace, soaking up spectacular views; the clean, airy vibe. **Cons:** street entrance could use a spiff-up; neither access nor pay-parking favor those arriving by car. ✉*1 rue de la Vallée, Vieille VilleCH-1204* 🕾*022/8183737* 🖶*022/8183773* ⊕*www.hotel-bel-esperance.ch* ⇄*37 rooms, 3 studios* ⅏*In-room: no a/c, kitchen (studios only), free Wi-Fi. In-hotel: safe at reception desk, laundry facilities, free Internet terminal and Wi-Fi, all rooms are no-smoking.* ⊟*AE, DC, MC, V* ⏝*BP.*

15

$ ▣ **De Genève.** A small hotel, this spot has its own brand of charm and exceptionally caring staffers. Rustic stone, carved wood, and a thoroughly cozy chalet-style lobby give way to cheery rooms full of eclectic modern and antique furnishings, original art, and delicate stenciling in this family-run establishment housed in a block-long Belle Époque building. Corner doubles with bay windows and parquet floors face the 15th-century Temple de Saint-Gervais, double-glazing ensures silence, and breakfast comes with a backdrop of plane trees. Pros: very personal, original decor; they take pride in good service. Cons: chalet lobby-cum-breakfast area can get very crowded; need for pay parking makes it less of an option for drivers. ⊠*1 pl. Isaac-Mercier, St-Gervais CH-1201* ☎*022/7323264* 📠*022/7328264* ⊕*www.hotel-de-geneve. ch* ➾*39 rooms* ⅏*In-room: no a/c, pay Wi-Fi. In-hotel: bar, laundry facilities, laundry service, pay Internet terminal and Wi-Fi, no-smoking rooms.* ☰*AE, DC, MC, V* ⎮◎⎮*BP.*

$$$–$$$$ ▣ **EastWest.** Take a small hotel and convert it into a town-house-y bijou with a world traveler feel. Add a signature restaurant and "tapas" bar driven by globe-trotting three-star Michelin chefs (the Pourcel brothers), and you have something unique—a Geneva first. The contemporary taste, and mix of art and design objects in guest and public rooms alike, is exquisite here; so is the food at Sens, the restaurant part of which overlooks a lovely small court where bamboo riffles in the breeze against a water wall. The "tapas" bar has nothing to do with hearty Spanish nibbles but rather with rarefied gourmet delights that take their references from all over. Pros: aesthetics, sophistication, luxurious sensuality. Cons: space (closets et al.) can be a little tight; this place is definitely not for the "I know what I like" meat-and-potatoes type. ⊠*6 rue des Pâquis, Les Pâquis CH-1201* ☎*022/7081717* 📠*022/7081718* ⊕*www.eastwesthotel.ch* ➾*37 rooms, 4 suites.* ⅏*In-room: safe, refrigerator, free Wi-Fi. In-hotel: restaurant, room service, bar, gym, free Internet terminal and Wi-Fi, laundry service, parking (pay), no-smoking rooms* ☰*AE, DC, MC, V.*

$$$$ ▣ **Four Seasons des Bergues.** Unpretentious service gives the first Four Seasons in Switzerland and the oldest (1834), least self-conscious, of Geneva's grand hotels an inner glow. Louis-Philippe opulence, ornamental stucco, and Portuguese marble mesh seamlessly with perfect maintenance and modern comforts like flat-screen TVs that turn toward you, luxuriously thick mattresses, in-room spa treatments, and breakfast menus that stretch from Asia to the Alps. Guest rooms booked for children have pint-sized bathrobes and slippers, milk and cookies, and a smorgasbord of toys. Not to mention that the views—Jet d'Eau, Old Town—from this swooningly impressive, yet so personal, hotel are superb. Or that the restaurant, Il Lago, features northern Italian cuisine that many say is the best in Geneva. Pros: What can you say about perfection? Cons: even the issue of "no spa" is temporary, as a full Four Seasons spa with large pool is scheduled for 2010. ⊠*33 quai des Bergues, Centre Ville CH-1201* ☎*022/9087000* 📠*022/9087400* ⊕*www.fourseasons. com/Geneva* ➾*68 rooms, 35 suites* ⅏*In-room: safe, refrigerator, pay Wi-Fi. In-hotel: restaurant, room service, bar, gym, laundry service, pay Wi-Fi, parking (pay), no-smoking rooms.* ☰*AE, DC, MC, V.*

Fodor's Choice
★

LUCERNE

With the mist rising off the waves and the mountains looming above the clouds, it's easy to understand how Wagner could have composed his *Siegfried Idyll* here. It was on Lake Lucerne, after all, that Wilhelm Tell—the beloved, if legendary, Swiss national hero—supposedly leaped from the tyrant Gessler's boat to freedom. And it was in a meadow on the western shore of Lake Lucerne that the world's oldest still-extant democracy was born. Every August 1, the Swiss national holiday, citizens gather in the meadow in remembrance, and the sky glows with the light of hundreds of mountaintop bonfires.

Wilhelm Tell played an important role in that early rebellion, and here, around the villages of Altdorf, Bürglen, and the stunningly picturesque lakeside Tell Chapel, thousands come to honor the memory of the rebellious archer.

Yet for all its potential for drama, central Switzerland and the area surrounding Lake Lucerne are tame enough turf: neat little towns, accessible mountains, smooth roads, resorts virtually glamour-free—and modest, graceful Lucerne astride the River Reuss much as it has been since the Middle Ages.

15

PLANNING YOUR TIME

Lucerne is a convenient home base for excursions all over central Switzerland. The countryside here is tame, and the vast Vierwaldstättersee offers a prime opportunity for the lake steamer cruise. Where the River Reuss flows out of Lake Lucerne, the Old Town straddles the narrow waters. There are a couple of discount passes available for museums and sites in the city to take advantage of.

GETTING HERE & AROUND

The nearest airport to Lucerne is Unique Zürich Airport, which is approximately 54 km (33 mi) to the northeast.

Lucerne's centrally located main station brings hourly trains in from Zurich (23 SF one way). Geneva trains arrive through Bern or Olten (72 SF one way). Directly outside the station's entrance is the quay where lake boats that form part of the public transit system can take you to a variety of towns along the Vierwaldstättersee.

It's easy to reach Lucerne from Zurich by road, approaching from national expressway A3 south, connecting to A4 via the secondary E41 in the direction of Zug, and continuing on A4, which turns into the A14, to the city. Parking is limited, and the Old Town is pedestrian only; it is best to park your car and walk. All destinations in this region mentioned here are small, reachable by train or boat, and can easily be traveled on foot once you get there.

It would be a shame to see this historic region only from the shore; some of its most impressive landscapes are framed along the waterfront, as seen from the decks of one of the cruise ships that ply the lake. Rides on these are included in a Swiss Pass or a Swiss Boat Pass. Individual tickets can be purchased at Lucerne's departure docks; the fee is based on the length of your ride.

ESSENTIALS

Boat & Ferry Contacts **Schiffahrtsgesellschaft des Vierwaldstättersees** (✉ *Quay in front of train station* ☎ *041/3676767* ⊕ *www.lakeluzern.ch*).

Train Contacts (✉ *Bahnhof (Train Station): Zentralstr. 5, CH-6002* ☎ *041/2271717* ⊕ *www.luzern.com*).

VISITOR INFORMATION

The principal tourist bureau for the whole of central Switzerland, including the lake region, is Zentralschweiz Tourismus (Central Switzerland Tourism; www.lakeluzern.ch). There are also local tourist offices and in many of the region's towns, often near the train station.

EXPLORING LUCERNE

❸ **Altes Rathaus** *(Old Town Hall).* In 1606 the Lucerne town council held its first meeting in this late-Renaissance-style building, built between 1602 and 1606. It still meets here today. ✉ *Rathausquai, facing the north end of Rathaus-Steg.*

❶ **Historisches Museum** *(Historical Museum).* Housed in the late-Gothic armory dating from 1567, this stylish institution exhibits numerous city icons, including the original Gothic fountain that stood in the Weinmarkt. Reconstructed rooms depict rural and urban life. ✉ *Pfisterg. 24* ☎ *041/2285424* ⊕ *www.hmluzern.ch* ☒ *10 SF* ⊗ *Tues.–Sun. and holidays 10–5.*

❹ **Jesuitenkirche** *(Jesuit Church).* Constructed in 1666–77, this Baroque
★ church with a symmetrical entrance is flanked by two onion-dome towers, added in 1893. Inside, its vast interior, restored to its original splendor, is a dramatic explosion of gilt, marble, and epic frescoes. Nearby is the Renaissance **Regierungsgebäude** (Government Building), seat of the cantonal government. ✉ *Bahnhofstr., just west of Rathaus-Steg* ☎ *041/2100756* ⊕ *www.jesuitenkirche-luzern.ch* ⊗ *Daily 6 AM–6:30 PM.*

❻ **Kapellbrücke** *(Chapel Bridge).* The oldest wooden bridge in Europe
Fodor'sChoice snakes diagonally across the Reuss. When it was constructed in the early
★ 14th century, the bridge served as a rampart in case of attacks from the lake. Its shingle roof and grand stone water tower are to Lucerne what the Matterhorn is to Zermatt, but considerably more vulnerable, as a 1993 fire proved. Almost 80% of this fragile monument was destroyed, including many of the 17th-century paintings inside. However, a walk through this dark, creaky landmark will take you past polychrome copies of 110 gable panels, painted by Heinrich Wägmann in the 17th century and depicting Lucerne and Swiss history, stories of St. Leodegar and St. Mauritius, Lucerne's patron saints, and coats of arms of local patrician families. ✉ *Between Seebrücke and Rathaus-Steg, connecting Rathausquai and Bahnhofstr..*

❼ **Kultur- und Kongresszentrum** *(Culture and Convention Center).* Architect
★ Jean Nouvel's stunning glass-and-steel building manages to both stand

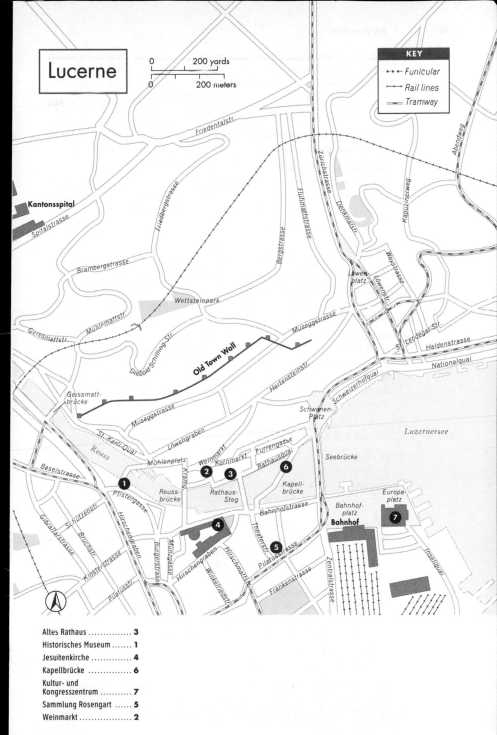

Lucerne

0	200 yards
0	200 meters

KEY

←•→ Funicular

←—→ Rail lines

⋯⋯ Tramway

out from and fuse with its ancient milieu. The lakeside center's roof is an oversized, cantilevered, flat plane; shallow water channels thread inside, and immense glass plates mirror the surrounding views. The main draw is the concert hall, which opened in 1998. Although the lobbies are rich in blue, red, and stained wood, the hall itself is refreshingly pale, with acoustics so perfect you can hear the proverbial pin drop. Among the annual music events is the renowned International Music Festival. A museum focuses on rotating exhibits of new international artists. ⊠ *Europapl. 1* ☎ *041/2267070* ⊕ *www.kkl-luzern.ch.*

⑤ **Sammlung Rosengart** *(Rosengart Collection).* A father-and-daughter team amassed this amazing group of works by major late-19th- and 20th-century artists. Now housed in a former bank building, the collection, opened to the public in 2002, reveals their intensely personal approach; the Rosengarts acquired according to their own tastes instead of investment potential. Here you can see Miro's *Dancer,* Léger's *Contraste de formes,* and works by Cézanne, Monet, Matisse, Klee, and Chagall. There's an especially rich selection of Picassos; the artist painted the daughter, Angela Rosengart, five times. ⊠ *Pilatusstr. 10* ☎ *041/2201660* ⊕ *www.rosengart.ch* 🎟 *18 SF* ☉ *Apr.–Oct., daily 10–6; Nov.–Mar., daily 11–5.*

② **Weinmarkt** *(Wine Market).* What is now the loveliest of Lucerne's several fountain squares drew visitors from all across Europe in the 15th to 17th centuries with its passion plays. Its Gothic central fountain depicts St. Mauritius (patron saint of warriors), and its surrounding buildings are flamboyantly frescoed in 16th-century style. ⊠ *Square just west of Kornmarkt, north of Metzgerainli.*

ON & AROUND LAKE LUCERNE

WEGGIS

Boats come from Lucerne every 1 to 1 ½ hours during daylight hours. Weggis is a summer resort town known for its mild, almost subtropical climate The famed **Mt. Rigi** (1,798 meters [5,900 feet]) is just a cable-car ride away: follow signs for the Rigibahn, a station high above the resort (a 15-minute walk). From here you can ride a large cable car to **Rigi-Kaltbad,** a small resort on a spectacular plateau; walk across to the electric rack-and-pinion railway station and ride the steep tracks of the Vitznau–Rigi line to the summit of the mountain. Take an elevator to the **Rigi-Kulm** hotel to enjoy the views indoors or walk to the crest (45 minutes) to see as far as the Black Forest in one direction and Mt. Säntis in the other. Or consider climbing to the top, staying in the hotel, and getting up early to see the sun rise over the Alps—a view that astounded both Victor Hugo and Mark Twain.

RÜTLI MEADOW

The lake steamers from Lucerne make frequent stops here.

About 10 minutes beyond the **Schillerstein,** a spectacular natural rock obelisk extending nearly 85 feet up out of the lake, the steamer pulls up at the quaint, 19th-century landing dock for perhaps the most historically significant site in central Switzerland: the Rütli Meadow, where the confederates of Schwyz, Unterwalden, and Uri are said to have met in 1307 to renew the 1291 Oath of Eternal Alliance.

Head up the hillside for a five-minute walk to emerge on a grassy plateau where you'll find a rock and flagpole to honor the sacred spot. Afterwards, head back down, watch the video presentation, and stop in the time-burnished, 19th-century chalet snack shop, with its lovely stained-glass salons and picturesque wood verandas.

THE TELLSKAPELLE

This magnificently picturesque lakeside chapel at the foot of the Axen mountain is a shrine to Wilhelm Tell. The adjacent **Tellsplatte**, was the rocky ledge onto which Tell, the rebellious archer, leaped to escape from Gessler's boat, pushing the boat back into the stormy waves as he jumped. Originally built in 1500, the chapel contains frescoes of the Tell legend. This is but one of the many scenic highlights that line the lake shore, some of which are incorporated into "The Swiss Way" (Der Weg der Schweiz; www.weg-der-schweiz.ch/), an historic foot trail, which covers 35 km (21½ mi) of lakefront lore offering spectacular vistas and lakeside perches.

15

ALTDORF

Schiller's play *Wilhelm Tell* sums up the tale for the Swiss, who perform his play religiously in venues all over the country—including the town of Altdorf, just up the road from the Rütli Meadow. Leave the steamer at Flüelen, the farthest point of the boat ride around the lake, and connect by postbus to Altdorf, the capital of the canton Uri and, by popular if not scholarly consensus, the setting for Tell's famous apple-shooting scene.

There's an often-reproduced **Tell monument** in the village center, showing a proud father with crossbow on one shoulder, the other hand grasping his son's hand.

BÜRGLEN

Tell was supposedly from the tiny, turreted town of Bürglen, just up the road from Altdorf. The **Tell-Museum** devoted to him displays documents and art related to the legend. ⊠*Postpl.* ☎*041/8704155* ⊕*www.tellmuseum.ch* ⊠*5 SF* ⊙*Jul.–Aug., daily 10–5 and Sept.–Oct., daily 10–11:30, 1:30–5; otherwise by appointment only.*

WHERE TO EAT

$$ ✕**Galliker.** Step past the ancient facade and into a room roaring with local action. Brisk waitresses serve up the dishes *Mutti* (Mom) used to make: fresh *Kutteln* (tripe) in rich white-wine sauce with cumin seeds; real *Kalbskopf* (chopped fresh veal head) served with heaps of green onions and warm vinaigrette; and authentic Luzerner Kügelipaschtetli. Occasional experiments in a modern mode—such as steak with wasabi sauce—prove that Peter Galliker's kitchen is no museum. Desserts may include raspberries with peppermint ice cream. ⊠*Schützenstr. 1*

☎041/2401002 ▤AE, DC, MC, V ⊘*Closed Sun., Mon., and mid-July–mid-Aug.*

$$$ ✕**Old Swiss House.** This popular establishment has been feeding travelers since 1931. Originally built as a farmhouse in 1858, it pleases crowds with its beautifully contrived collection of 17th-century antiques, leaded glass, and an Old World style now pleasantly burnished by more than 77 years of service. The standing menu includes specialties from around the country: cubed fillet of beef in a green pepper mustard sauce with fresh buttered noodles, lake fish with spinach and lemon ricotta ravioli, and chocolate mousse. In warm weather, enjoy your meal in the outdoor seating area, which spills out into the pedestrian zone. ⊠*Löwenpl. 4* ☎*041/4106171* ▤*AE, DC, MC, V* ⊘*Closed Mon. and Feb.*

$$ ✕**Pfistern.** One of the architectural focal points of the Old Town waterfront, this floridly decorated guildhall—the guild's origins can be traced back to 1341—provides an authentic medieval setting in which to sample reasonably priced local fare. Lake fish with steamed new potatoes or *pastetli* (meat pies with puff pastry) are worthy local options. Inside, it's woody and publike, if slightly down-at-the-heels, but in summer the small first-floor balcony and the airy cobblestone riverside arcade provide some of the best seats in town. ⊠*Kornmarkt 4* ☎*041/4103650* ▤*AE, DC, MC, V.*

$$ ✕**Rebstock/Hofstube.** Formerly a 16th-century tavern, this spot is now a meeting place for Lucerne's art and media set. The lively brasserie hums with locals lunching by the bar, and the more formal old-style restaurant glows with wood and brass under a low-beamed parquetry ceiling. Fresh market ingredients are combined for modern, international fare, including chicken simmered in white wine, rabbit stewed with rosemary, and classic garlic snails, as well as East Asian and vegetarian specialties. There is ample outside seating when it's warm, including a small garden. ⊠*St. Leodegarpl. 3* ☎*041/4103581* ▤*AE, MC, V.*

WHERE TO STAY

$$$–$$$$ ▦**Des Balances.** Built in the 19th century on the site of two ancient guildhalls, this waterfront property is full of style. State-of-the-art tile baths, up-to-date pastel furnishings, and one of the best sites in the heart of the Old Town make this the slickest in its price class. Rotes Gatter ($$–$$$$), the hotel's chic restaurant, has a combination as desirable as it is rare: a soigné interior, shimmering river views, and a sophisticated menu. The restaurant has a more casual, less expensive bistro area as well. **Pros:** all rooms have great views; the river terrace is exceptional. **Cons:** top-floor rooms tend to be rudimentary. ⊠*Weinmarkt CH-6000* ☎*041/4182828* ▤*041/4182838* ⊕*www.balances.ch* ⇗*50 rooms, 7 suites* ⌂*In-room: no a/c, safe, refrigerator. In-hotel: restaurant, Wi-Fi.* ▤*AE, DC, MC, V* ⎮⊙⎮*BP.*

$$$$ ▦**Palace Hotel.** This waterfront hotel drinks in the broadest possible lake views. Built in 1906, it has been brilliantly refurbished so that its classical look has a touch of postmodernism. Rooms are large enough for a game of badminton, and picture windows afford sweeping views of Mt. Pilatus. The hotel's elegance also seeps into its restaurant, Jasper ($$–$$$$). The contemporary cuisine—think veal with

celery mousse and truffle sauce—is faultlessly prepared and formally presented. The bar has a clubby look—leather chairs, brass fixtures, and a long oak bar. **Pros:** lakefront setting, right off the promenade; grand interiors. **Cons:** backs onto a main thoroughfare. ⊠*Haldenstr. 10 CH-6002* ☎*041/4161616* 📠*041/4161000* ⊕*www.palace-luzern.com* 🛏*178 rooms, 45 suites* ᕱ*In-room: no a/c, safe, refrigerator, dial-up. In-hotel: 2 restaurants, bar, gym, laundry service, public Wi-Fi, parking (fee).* ⊟*AE, DC, MC, V.*

$-$$ 🏨**Schlüssel.** This crisp, no-nonsense lodging on the Franziskanerplatz attracts young bargain hunters. It's a pleasant combination of tidy modern touches (quarry tile, white paint) and antiquity: you can admire the fine old beams in the lobby or in the low, cross-vaulted "crypt"-esque restaurant. Locals come here for Swiss specialties like cheese fondue or *Fleischvögel*—pounded beef steaks wrapped around stuffing in a sausage shape. Two of the rooms overlooking the square's Franciscan church have small balconies. **Pros:** staff makes that extra effort. **Cons:** be prepared for insistent morning church bells. ⊠*Franziskanerpl. 12 CH-6003* ☎*041/2101061* 📠*041/2101021* ⊕*www.luzern-schluessel. ch* 🛏*10 rooms* ᕱ*In-room: no a/c. In-hotel: restaurant, public Wi-Fi.* ⊟*MC, V.*

$$$-$$$$ 🏨**Wilden Mann.** The city's best-known hotel creates a gracious and
★ authentic experience of old Lucerne, with stone, beams, brass, and burnished wood everywhere. Even the street is atmospheric—across the way is a 16th-century pharmacy. The hotel's reputation extends to its restaurants: the Burgerstube is cozy with its dark beams and family crests, whereas vaulting and candlelight make the Liedertafel more formal. Both menus strike a fine balance between local cooking and French cuisine, with main dishes such as pike-perch with chanterelle mushroom ravioli and desserts like port-wine cherries. **Pros:** friendly service; medieval architecture straight out of Middle Earth. **Cons:** some ceilings are a bit low. ⊠*Bahnhofstr. 30 CH-6003* ☎*041/2101666* 📠*041/2101629* ⊕*www.wilden-mann.ch* 🛏*42 rooms, 8 suites* ᕱ*In-room: no a/c, refrigerator. In-hotel: 2 restaurants, public Wi-Fi.* ⊟*AE, DC, MC, V* ⧓*BP.*

ZERMATT & THE MATTERHORN

Zermatt lies in a hollow of meadows and trees ringed by mountains—among them the broad **Monte Rosa** and its tallest peak, the **Dufourspitze** (at 15,200 feet, the highest point in Switzerland)—plus 36 others that tower above 13,000 feet—of which visitors hear relatively little, so all-consuming is the cult of the Matterhorn. Despite its fame—which stems from that mythic mountain and from its excellent ski facilities—Zermatt is a resort with its feet on the ground. It protects its regional quirks along with its wildlife and its tumbledown mazots, which crowd between glass-and-concrete chalets like old tenements between skyscrapers. Streets twist past weathered-wood walls, flower boxes, and haphazard stone roofs until they break into open country that slopes, inevitably, uphill. Despite the crowds, you're never far from the wild roar of the silty river and the peace of a mountain path.

15

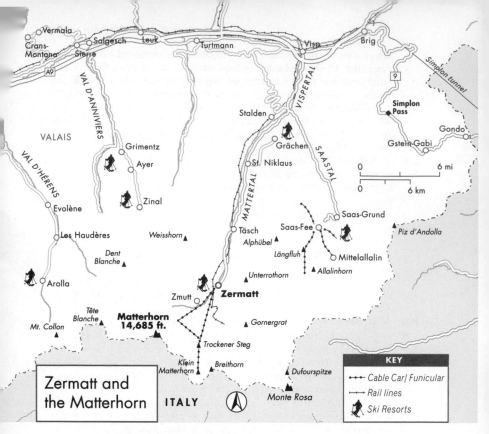

Zermatt and
the Matterhorn

ITALY

KEY

•••••• *Cable Car/ Funicular*

——— *Rail lines*

🎿 *Ski Resorts*

PLANNING YOUR TIME

Skiing or hiking will presumably be the Number One Priorities, around which to fit good food, perhaps some spa time, shopping, and nightlife—all of which Zermatt offers in abundance.

GETTING HERE & AROUND

The airports of Zurich and Geneva are roughly equidistant from the nearby town of Brig, which is well connected by train, but by approaching from Geneva you can avoid crossing mountain passes.

Zermatt, the world's most famous car-free Alpine village, requires that residents and guests leave their vehicles in the village of Täsch. Shuttle service (12 min., 16 SF round-trip) is provided by train via a state-of-the-art station with adjacent decks of covered parking. Access to the commuter trains that run every 20 minutes is eased with ramps and luggage carts that roll onto the passenger cars.

There are straightforward rail connections to the region by way of Geneva/Lausanne to the west and Brig/Brigue to the east. The two are connected by one clean rail sweep that runs the length of the valley. In winter a special extension of the high-speed train from France, TGV Neige, terminates in Brig. (Information is available through the SBB.)

Zermatt electric taxis shuttles and horse-drawn carriages operated by hotels are the only means of transportation, but the village is relatively small and easily covered on foot. A sophisticated network including cable cars, lifts, and railways carries you above the village center into the wilderness for hiking and skiing.

ESSENTIALS

Tourist Information ⊠ *CH-3920* 🕾 *027/9668100* ⊕ *www.zermatt.ch).*

EXPLORING ZERMATT

Fodor'sChoice
★
Hordes of package-tour sightseers push shoulder to shoulder to get yet another shot of the **Matterhorn** (14,685 feet). Called one of the wonders of the Western world, the mountain deserves the title, though it has become an almost self-parodying icon, like the Eiffel Tower or the Empire State Building. Its peculiar snaggletooth form, free from competition from other peaks on all sides, rears up over the village, larger than life and genuinely awe-inspiring. As you leave the train station and weave through pedestrian crowds, aggressive electric taxi carts, and aromatic horse-drawn carriages along the main street, Bahnhofstrasse, you're assaulted on all sides by Matterhorn images—on postcards, sweatshirts, calendars, beer steins, and candy wrappers—though not by the original, which is obscured by resort buildings (except from the windows of pricier hotel rooms). But break past the shops and hotels onto the main road into the hills, and you'll reach a slightly elevated spot where you'll probably stop dead in your tracks. There it is at last, its twist of snowy rock blinding in the sun, weathered mazots scattered romantically at its base. Surely more pictures are taken from this spot than from anywhere else in Switzerland. It was Edward Whymper's spectacular—and catastrophic—conquest of the Matterhorn, on July 14, 1865, that made Zermatt a household word. Whymper and six others got to the top, but then tragedy struck. On the descent, a safety rope snapped and pulled the party to their death. One of the bodies was never recovered, but the others lie in little cemeteries behind the park near the village church.[esc]

It's quite simple to gain the broader perspective of high altitudes without risking life or limb. A train trip on the **Gornergrat–Monte Rose Bahn** functions as an excursion as well as ski transport. Part of its rail system was completed in 1898, and it's the highest open-air rail system in Europe (the tracks to the Jungfraujoch, though higher, bore through the face of the Eiger). It connects out of the main Zermatt train station and heads sharply left, at a right angle to the track that brings you into town. Its stop at the **Riffelberg,** at 8,469 feet, offers wide-open views of the Matterhorn. Farther on, from **Rotenboden,** at 9,246 feet, a short downhill walk leads to the **Riffelsee,** which obligingly provides photographers with a postcard-perfect reflection of the famous peak. At the end of the 9-km (5½-mi) line, the train stops at the summit station of **Gornergrat** (10,266 feet), and passengers pour onto the observation terraces to take in the majestic views of the Matterhorn, Monte Rosa, Gorner Glacier, and an expanse of scores of peaks and 24 other glaciers. Make sure

15

to bring warm clothes, sunglasses, and sturdy shoes, especially if you plan to ski or hike down. ⊠*Zermatt station* ☎*027/9214711* 🖼*76 SF round-trip, 38 SF one-way* ⊙*Departures daily every 24 min, 7–7.*

SKIING

Zermatt's skiable terrain lives up to its reputation: the 63 lift installations, 73 lifts, and mountain railways are capable of moving well above 50,000 skiers per hour to reach its approximately 313 km (194 mi) of marked pistes—if you count those of Cervinia in Italy. Among the lifts are the cable car that carries skiers up to an elevation of 12,746 feet on the Matterhorn Glacier Paradise (previously known as Klein Matterhorn), the small Gornergratbahn that creeps up to the Gornergrat, and a subway through an underground tunnel that gives more pleasure to ecologists than it does to sun-loving skiers.

The skiable territory on this royal plateau was once separated into three separate sectors, but the installation of a gondola to Riffelberg has linked the three together. The first sector is **Sunegga-Blauherd-Rothorn,** which culminates at an elevation of 10,170 feet. **Gornergrat-Stockhorn** (11,155 feet) is the second. The third is the region dominated by the **Matterhorn Glacier Paradise (MGP),** which goes to Italy. The best way to prioritize your ski day is still to concentrate on one or two areas, especially during high season. Thanks to snowmaking machines and the eternal snows of the Klein Matterhorn Glacier, Zermatt is said to guarantee skiers 7,216 feet of vertical drop no matter what the snowfall—an impressive claim. Gravity Park, a snowboarding center on Theodul glacier below the MGP, has pipes, kickers, and rails to thrill. A one-day lift ticket costs 71 SF; a six-day pass costs 350 SF; if you want to ski to Italy it costs 80 SF and 394 SF. Ask for the hands-free "Smart Card" or "Swatch Access Key" with computer chip gate activation and billing. A **ski and snowboard school** (⊠*Skischulbüro, Bahnhofstr.* ☎*027/9662466)* operates seven ski schools from mid-December until April and in July and August.

WHERE TO EAT

$$ ✗**Elsie's Bar.** This tiny log cabin of a ski haunt, directly across from the Zermatt church, draws an international crowd as soon as it opens it doors at 4 o'clock. They come to select from an extensive list of aged scotches and mixed cocktails. Light meals include cheese dishes, oysters, escargots, and would you believe spaghetti with caviar and crème fraîche? ⊠*Kirchepl. 16* ☎*027/9672431* 🖃*AE, DC, MC, V* ⊙*Closed May and mid-Oct to Dec.*

$$ ✗**Findlerhof.** This mountain restaurant is ideal for long lunches between sessions on the slopes or for a panoramic break on an all-day hike. It's perched in tiny Findeln, between the Sunnegga and Blauherd ski areas; the Matterhorn views are astonishing. The food is decidedly fresh and creative. Franz and Heidi Schwery tend their own Alpine garden to provide lettuce for their salads and berries for vinaigrettes and hot desserts. The fluffy *Matterkuchen,* a bacon and leek quiche, will fortify you for the 30- to 40-minute walk down to the village.

✉ *Findeln CH-3920* ☎*027/9672588* ▭*MC, V* ☉*Closed May–mid-June and mid-Oct.–Nov.*

$$ ✗**Grill-Room Stockhorn.** The moment you step across the threshold into this low-slung, two-story restaurant decked with mountaineering memorabilia, tantalizing aromas of cheese melting should sharpen your appetite. Downstairs, you can watch your meat roasting on the open grill while enjoying the chalet-style decor. Upstairs, a mélange of Mediterranean tiles and traditional Valaisan exposed dark-wood beams creates a romantic atmosphere. This is a great place for regional dishes and meat specialties like juicy Chateaubriand grilled to perfection dripping with a creamy Béarnaise sauce, served by lively staff. ✉*Hotel Stockhorn, Riedstr. 22* ☎*027/9671747* ▭*AE, MC, V* ☉*Closed mid-May–mid-June and Oct.*

$$ ✗**Whymperstube.** At this little restaurant in the Hotel Monte Rosa, plates of melted raclette and bubbling pots of fondue are delivered to tightly packed tables by an agile waitstaff. Be sure to try the unusual variations on cheese dishes like the fresh mushroom or pear-laced fondue. The restaurant is named for Edward Whymper, the first man to reach the Matterhorn summit—imagine the climbers' stories that must have echoed within these walls. In the winter season, the place stays open until 1 AM. ✉*Bahnhofstr. 80* ☎*027/9672296* ⚲*Reservations essential* ▭*AE, DC, MC, V.*

15

WHERE TO STAY

$$$$ ✗**Mont Cervin Hotel Palace.** Part of the Seiler dynasty, this Leading Hotels
Fodor's Choice of the World property is luxurious, genteel, and one of Zermatt's grandes
★ dames. The main lounge has a soaring three-story sash-window view of the town and Matterhorn that is to die for. Guest rooms are decorated with tasteful stripes and plaids in primary colors, while suites have luxe rustic touches and fabrics; most rooms have Matterhorn views. The Residence, across the street, offers spacious apartments. The main restaurant ($$$) has a light, modern ambience with dishes to match, including sea bass with white tomato mousse on lemon risotto. There's also a more casual dining option in-hotel ($–$$), and others at the hotel's sister properties. The hotel will reserve covered parking and transportation from Täsch. **Pros:** station pick-up in a red antique horse-drawn carriage; wellness and spa facilities that are tops. **Cons:** big-city luxury removes you somewhat from the village atmosphere. ✉*Bahnhofstr. 31 CH-3920* ☎*027/9668888* ⊕*www.seilerhotels.ch* ⇨*87 rooms, 31 suites, 15 apartments* ⚐*In-room: safe, refrigerator, Wi-Fi. In-hotel: 2 restaurants, bar, pool, gym, spa.* ▭*AE, DC, MC, V* ☉*Closed May–mid-June, Oct. and mid-Nov.* ⦿|*MAP.*

$$$$ ⛰**Riffelalp Resort 2222m.** Accessed by a little mountainside railway and enjoying a stunning location—with the Matterhorn posing directly in front of your balcony—this hotel is a winner in many respects. Set at 7,288 feet amid fields and Alpine forests, this mountaintop option offers both direct views of the Matterhorn—especially breathtaking in the orange glow of early morning—and enchantingly stylish decor. Guest rooms are storybook in ambience, with Heidi-esque woodwork, couture fabrics, sumptuous sofas, Jacuzzi tubs, and Bose sound systems.

Dining ranges from pizza to plush: the Alexandre restaurant has elegant wood paneling, the Walliser Keller is a cut-stone tavern, while the Al Bosco sun terrace is just the place to enjoy a "Matterhorn pizza." Bliss out with chilling footbaths and organic saunas in the spa center, which is crowned by an indoor pool that is a whirlpool extravaganza and an outdoor pool that is no less than Europe's highest—wow. Even transit is made memorable, as you can ride a private restored tram to and from the train station. **Pros:** far from the village hubbub; no better skiing location in Zermatt. **Cons:** no train service from the village after 11; remote location means dining is limited to the hotel's three options. ⊠ *CH-3920* ☎ *027/9660555* ⊕ *www.seilerhotels.ch* ⏎ *65 rooms, 5 suites, 2 apartments* ☐ *In-room: safe, refrigerator, Wi-Fi. In-hotel: 3 restaurants, bar, 2 pools.* ☐ *AE, DC, MC, V* ⊗ *Closed mid-Apr.–late-June and mid-Oct.–mid-Dec.* ⏐◎⏐ *MAP.*

$–$$ ⊡ **Romantica.** Among the scores of anonymously modern hotels along the Zermatt plain, this modest structure offers an exceptional location directly above the town center, a block up a narrow, mazot-lined lane. Its tidy, bright gardens, game trophies, and granite stove give it personality. You can also stay in one of the two Walliserstadel, charming, 200-year-old huts in the garden. Keep in mind that this is a *garni* hotel (no restaurant), so only breakfast is served. **Pros:** quiet, yet only a stone's throw from the trendiest nightlife; big balconies and windows. **Cons:** overly kitschy murals in lobby; most double beds are two twins side by side—leaving lovebirds divided ⊠ *Churm 21 CH-3920* ☎ *027/9662650* ⊕ *www.reconline.ch/romantica* ⏎ *13 rooms, 1 apartment, 2 cabins* ☐ *In-hotel: bar.* ☐ *AE, DC, MC, V* ⏐◎⏐ *CP.*

$–$$ ⊡ **Touring.** Reassuringly traditional architecture, sunny guest rooms full of pine, and an elevated position apart from town with excellent Matterhorn views make this an appealing, informal alternative to the chic downtown scene. Hearty daily menus are served to pension guests in the cozy dining room (the same menu is available in the Stübli). **Pros:** excellent rapport quality/price; delicious, comprehensive breakfast buffet includes local specialties. **Cons:** lacking modern amenities—no elevator, no Wi-Fi. ⊠ *Riedstr. 45 CH-3920* ☎ *027/9671177* ⊕ *www.touring. buz.ch* ⏎ *20 rooms* ☐ *In-hotel: restaurant, bar, public Internet, no elevator.* ☐ *MC, V* ⏐◎⏐ *CP.*

BERNER OBERLAND: THE JUNGFRAU REGION

There are times when the reality of Switzerland puts postcard idealization to shame, and those times happen most often in the Berner Oberland, with its awesome mountain panoramas, massive glaciers, crystalline lakes, gorges and waterfalls, chic ski resorts, dense pine forests, and charming gingerbread chalets.

The region's main resort city, Interlaken, lies in green lowlands between the gleaming twin pools of the Brienzersee and the Thunersee. Behind them to the south loom craggy, forested foothills, and behind those foothills stand some of Europe's noblest peaks, most notably the snowy crowns of the Eiger (13,022 feet), the Mönch (13,445 feet), and the fiercely beautiful Jungfrau (13,638 feet). The area offers an efficient

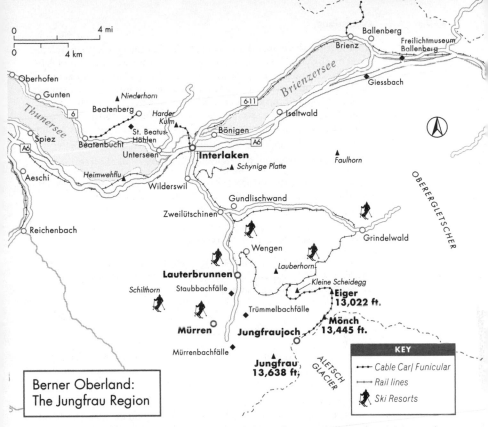

Berner Oberland:
The Jungfrau Region

KEY

- ●—● Cable Car/ Funicular
- ●—● Rail lines
- 🎿 Ski Resorts

network of boats, trains, and funiculars, a variety of activities and attractions, and a wide range of accommodations.

PLANNING YOUR TIME
The central, urban-Victorian resort of Interlaken makes a good base for excursions for visitors who want to experience the entire Jungfrau region, which includes the craggy, bluff-lined Lauterbrunnen Valley and the opposing resorts that perch high above it: car-free Mürren and Wengen.

GETTING HERE & AROUND
Belp Airport in Bern brings you within an hour via train of Interlaken, the hub of the Berner Oberland. The Unique Zürich Airport is 2½ hours away. Geneva's Cointrin is less than three hours away.

From Zurich, a direct line leads through Bern to Interlaken and takes about 3 hours, departing hourly; a more scenic trip over the Golden Pass route via Lucerne takes about two hours. Trains run hourly from Geneva (a 2 ½-hour ride).

The Berner Oberland is riddled with railways, funiculars, cogwheel trains, and cable lifts designed with the sole purpose of getting you closer to its spectacular views. A Swiss Pass lets you travel free on federal trains and lake steamers.

From Zurich, the planned autoroute link with Lucerne is incomplete; travel by Highway E41 south, then pick up the autoroutes A4 and A14 in the direction of Lucerne. South of Lucerne, pick up the A4 again in the direction of Interlaken. From Geneva, the autoroute leads through Lausanne and Fribourg to Bern, where you catch A6 south, toward Thun. A long, winding, scenic alternative: continue on the autoroute from Lausanne to Montreux, then to Aigle; then, head northeast up the mountain on A11 from Aigle through Château-d'Oex to Gstaad.

Remember that Wengen, Mürren, and Gstaad are all car-free.

Postbuses (called postautos or postcars) travel into much of the area not served by trains, including most smaller mountain towns.

ESSENTIALS

Bus & Train Contacts Swiss Rail (☎ *0900/300300* ⊕ *www.sbb.ch*) is the leading company, and even offers private motor-coach tours to many points of interest.

Visitor Information Berner Oberland Tourismus (✉ *Jungfraustr. 38, CH-3800 Interlaken* ☎ *033/8283737* 🖷 *033/8283734* ⊕ *www.berneroberland.ch*). **Interlaken Tourist Office** (✉ *Höheweg 37, CH-3800* ☎ *033/8265300* 🖷 *033/8265375* ⊕ *www. interlaken.ch*).

INTERLAKEN

As a gateway to the entire Berner Oberland, this bustling Victorian resort town is the obvious home base for travelers planning to visit both the region's two lakes and the mountains towering behind them.

WHERE TO STAY & EAT

$$-$$$ ✗**Im Gade.** This welcoming hybrid of carved-wood coziness and sleek formality fills up with appreciative locals who recognize fresh, fine cooking and alert service. Details count here: even that dab of smoky sauerkraut in your crisp mixed salad is made on the premises. Choose seasonal specialties such as salmon with lime mousse and ratatouille, pork fillet with truffles. A new owner has taken over, but has succeeded in maintaining the high standards, especially with the fishy favorites. ✉ *Hotel du Nord, Höheweg 70CH-3800* ☎ *033/8275050* ▭ *AE, DC, MC, V* ⊗ *Closed mid-Nov.–mid-Dec.*

$$-$$$ ✗**Schuh.** With a luxurious shady terrace spilling into the Höhematte in summer and mellow piano sounds enhancing the old-fashioned elegance inside, this sweet shop and café-restaurant serves everything from tea to rich, hot Swiss meals. No matter that recipes are used that date all the way back to 1818—most of the ingredients and dishes are freshly made in-house on a daily basis. Leave room for the chocolate specialties and pastries, like the glossy strawberry tarts, which you'll also find in the adjoining shop. ✉ *Höheweg 56* ☎ *033/8229441* ▭ *AE, DC, MC, V.*

$ 🏠**Alphorn.** Comfortably old-fashioned, this lovely family-run Victorian bed-and-breakfast sits on a quiet side street between Interlaken West and the Heimwehfluh. Some rooms have tapestry wallpaper, waxed parquet floors, and original plaster moldings; florals and other patterns abound. Service is warm and welcoming. The bar/breakfast room is bright and light with an alphorn adorning the wall. Do not expect high class, but do expect affordability and savor the age-old Swiss guarantee of clean comfort. **Pros:** free Internet in lobby; peaceful location; ideal for budget seekers. **Cons:** some rooms are tiny; the single beds pushed together to make a double with two separate covers can surprise those not used to this Swiss tradition. ✉*Rothornstrasse 29a CH-3800* ☎*033/8223051* 📠*033/8233069* 🌐*www.hotel-alphorn.ch* *10 rooms* *In-room: no a/c, safe. In-hotel: bar, public Internet (free), Wi-Fi (free), parking (free), some pets allowed, no-smoking rooms* *AE, MC, V* *BP.*

$$–$$$ **Hotel Interlaken.** When they say this is the oldest hotel in town, they don't fool around: it's been hosting overnight guests since 1323—first as a hospital, then as a cloister, and by the early 15th century as a tavern-hotel. Felix Mendelssohn and Lord Byron may have once slept here but today the comfortable guest rooms are quite up-to-date, with sleek furnishings and pastel accents. A multicultural air is added by the elaborate Japanese garden and the Italian, Swiss, and excellent Cantonese menus on offer. It's a short walk to the Interlaken East train station, making excursions a snap. **Pros:** location in historic part of Interlaken and close to train station; friendly helpful service. **Cons:** no air-conditioning; no leisure/wellness facilities. ✉*Höheweg 74 CH-3800* ☎*033/8266868* 📠*033/8266869* 🌐*www.interlakenhotel.ch* *60 rooms* *In-room: no a/c, safe, refrigerator, Wi-Fi (fee). In-hotel: restaurant, room service on request, bar, laundry service, public Internet (fee), Wi-Fi (fee), free parking, some pets allowed, no-smoking rooms.* *AE, DC, MC, V* *BP.*

$$$$ Fodor's Choice ★ **Victoria-Jungfrau Grand Hotel & Spa.** Grand says it all. Mark Twain may have slept in this 1865 landmark, but its restoration has taken it firmly into the 21st century, with glitzy postmodern touches such as the burled-wood entryway. The vast Belle Époque atrium lobby spirals off into innumerable bars, tea salons, and the concierge desks, where the front-desk staff may seem frenzied by the awesome demands of 400 occupied beds. There are plenty of facilities, including indoor master golf, and a knockout spa. Guest rooms are gorgeous, from fresh gingham fabrics and waxed wood floors to marble columns. Nearly all take in the obligatory view over the central Interlaken meadow and on to the Cinerama-wide range of Alps, with the snowy peak of the Jungfrau crowning the far distance. Don't forget to check out the Brasserie, a mammoth, leaded-glass-and-carved-wood Victorian concoction almost as delicious as its meals. **Pros:** location with view across to Jungfrau and two lakes; wonderful spa. **Cons:** this is such a gargantuan place that you can feel like a mouse among many; some say it is overpriced. ✉*Höheweg 41* ☎*033/8282828* 📠*033/8282880* 🌐*www.victoria-jungfrau.ch* *212 rooms, 95 suites* *In-room: no a/c (some), safe, refrigerator, Wi-Fi (fee). In-hotel: 3 restaurants, room service, bars, 2 tennis courts, pool, gym, spa, bicycles, children's programs (4-10 yrs), laundry service, public Internet (fee), Wi-Fi (fee), parking (free), some pets allowed (fee), no-smoking rooms.* *AE, DC, MC, V* *BP, MAP.*

THE ARTS

THEATER Fodor's Choice ★ For a real introduction to the local experience, don't miss the **Tellfreilichtspiele,** an outdoor pageant presented in Interlaken every summer by a cast of Swiss amateurs. Wrapped in a rented blanket—which you'll need, since evenings can be chilly, even from June to September—and seated in a 2,200-seat sheltered amphitheater that opens onto illuminated woods and a permanent "medieval" village set, you'll see 250 players in splendid costumes acting out the epic tale of Swiss hero Wilhelm Tell. The text is Schiller's famous play, performed in German with the guttural singsong of a Schwyzerdütsch accent—but don't worry; with galloping horses, flower-decked cows, bonfires, parades, and, of course, the famous apple-shooting climax, the operatic story tells itself. Tickets range from 26 SF to 48 SF and are available through the **Tellbüro** (⊠*Bahnhofstr. 5A* ☎*033/8223722* ⊕*www.tellspiele.ch*). Travel agents and hotel concierges can also secure tickets. (⊠*Höheweg 37, CH-3800* ☎*033/8265300* 🖷*033/8265375* ⊕*www.interlaken.ch*).

LAUTERBRUNNEN

The Lauterbrunnen Valley is often ranked as one of the five most beautiful places in Switzerland. What really sets this mountainous masterpiece apart are the more than 70 waterfalls (Lauterbrunnen means "only springs") that line the length of the 2-mi-long valley. The relentlessly picturesque panorama opens up as you get off the train. This tidy town of weathered chalets also serves as a starting point for the region's two most famous excursions: to the Schilthorn and to the Jungfraujoch. Super-efficient parking and a rail terminal allow long- and short-term parking for visitors heading for Wengen, Mürren, and the Jungfraujoch. Consider choosing this valley as a home base for day trips by train, funicular, or cable, thereby saving considerably on hotel rates. But don't ignore its own wealth of hiking options through some of the most awe-inspiring scenery in Europe.

Magnificent waterfalls adorn the length of the Lauterbrunnen Valley, the most famous being the 984-foot **Staubbachfälle** *(Staubbach Falls)* , which are illuminated at night and visible from town. These falls draw you like a magnet through the village of Lauterbrunnen itself, past a bevy of roadside cafés and the town center (marked by a church and a small Museum of the Lauterbrunnen Valley) and they are found just opposite a centuries-old, flower-bedecked graveyard. At the other side of the valley is the Mürrenbachfälle, which at 250 meters (820 feet) are among the tallest in Europe (the tourist office has a brochure outlining a hike to the top 10 waterfalls). Five minutes by car and forty minutes by foot beyond the Staubbachfälle are the spectacular **Trümmelbachfälle** (Trümmelbach Falls), a series of 10 glacier waterfalls hidden deep inside rock walls at the base of the Jungfrau, which you can access by a tunnel lift. Approach the departure point via a pretty, creek-side walkway and brace yourself for some steep stair climbing. Be sure to bring along a light jacket—the spray can be more than refreshing in the cool Alpine air. ⊠*Follow signs from town* ☎*033/8553232* ⊕*www. truemmelbach.ch* 🎫*11 SF* ☉*Apr.–early Nov., daily 9–5; July and Aug., daily 8:30–6.*

MÜRREN

Birthplace of downhill and slalom skiing (in the 1920s), Mürren offers extraordinarily peaceful mountain nights and an unrivaled panorama of the Jungfrau, Mönch, and Eiger, all set so close you feel you can almost reach out and touch them. Skiers may want to settle here for daredevil year-round skiing at the top (the annual Inferno Race in January is the longest downhill in the world); hikers can combine bluff-top trails with staggering views. Mürren is usually accessed from the center of Lauterbrunnen village by an aerial cable car and Bergbahn cogwheel rail (round-trip 25 SF) from Grütschalp; alternatively, take the bus to Stechelberg—located at the far end of the valley—where two even more dizzying cable cars (round-trip 21 SF) have you reaching for the sky in no time. Upon arrival, Mürren splays out along a long mountain ridge road lined with hotels, restaurants, shops, a few historic châlets, and a large **Sportzentrum** sports center. The village is not overly picturesque, but having your *Kaffee und Kuchen* on a nearly levitating restaurant terrace will give you that top-of-the-world feeling.

15

Visitor Information **Wengen-Mürren-Lauterbrunnen** (⊠ *CH-3822, Lauter-brunnen* ☎ *033/8568568* ⊕ *www.wengen-muerren.ch*).

Mürren boasts some of the longest downhill runs because it is at the foot of the **Schilthorn** (9,742 feet) mountain, famed for its role in the James Bond thriller *On Her Majesty's Secret Service*. The peak of this icy Goliath is accessed by a four-stage cable-lift ride past bare-rock cliffs and stunning slopes. At each level you step off the cable car, walk across the station, and wait briefly for the next cable car. At the top is the much-photographed revolving restaurant, **Piz Gloria**, where you can see clips of the film thriller in the Touristorama—if you can tear yourself away from the restaurant panorama, which slowly rolls past your window (sit here for 50 minutes and you'll go full circle). The cable-car station is in the town of Stechelberg, near the spectacular Mürrenbachfälle (Mürrenbach Falls). ⊠ *Stechelberg* ☎ *033/8260007* ⊕ *www.schilthorn.ch* ☜ *Round-trip cable car Stechelberg–Schilthorn 96 SF; 72 SF 7:25–8:55 or after 3:25 in May and mid-Oct.–mid-Nov.* ☉ *Departures daily yr-round, twice hourly 6:25 AM–4:25 PM; last departure from the top 6:03 PM in summer, 5:03 PM in winter.*

A more affordable way to Mürren is the **aerial cable car** built in 2006, whose station sits across the street from Lauterbrunnen's train station. You then connect to the cogwheel rail from Grütschalp, which runs along the cliff and affords some magnificent views. The whole trip takes about 30 minutes and drops you at the Mürren rail station, at the opposite end of town from the cable-car stop. There are departures every 15 to 20 minutes. As you ascend, point your binoculars at the gleaming dome on the Jungfraujoch across the valley: you can almost hear the winds howling off the Aletsch Glacier. ⊠ *Lauterbrunnen* ☎ *0900/300300* ⊕ *www.sbb.ch* ☜ *25 SF.*

SKIING

Mürren provides access to the **Schilthorn,** where you'll find a 15-km (9-mi) run that drops all the way through Mürren to Lauterbrunnen. At 5,413 feet, the resort has one funicular railway, two cable cars, seven lifts, and 65 km (40 mi) of downhill runs. A one-day pass covering the Schilthorn region costs 56 SF; a seven-day pass costs 265 SF.

For lessons, contact Mürren's **Swiss Ski & Snowboard School** (☎*033/ 8551247*) at Chalet Finel, directly behind the Hotel Jungfrau.

WHERE TO STAY & EAT

$ ⊡ **Alpenruh.** Clad in time-burnished pine, fitted out with cute gables and some great gingerbread wood trim, the Alpenruh is as picturesque a hotel as you can get in Mürren. Its perch is spectacular, nearly cantilevered over the vast valley and with reach-out-and-touch vistas of the great Jungfrau and Eiger. No place in Mürren has such a fetching and gorgeous dining terrace. Because the prices here are on the gentle side, the guest rooms verge on plain. The owners also run the Mürren cable car up to the Schilthorn, and you can trade in the hotel's buffet for breakfast atop the revolving Piz Gloria. During key weeks, room rates are upped to include board. **Pros:** picturesque house with jaw-dropping views straight out of a postcard; simple, tasteful interiors at low prices. **Cons:** nearby cable-car girders may mar the view from some rooms; only three bathrooms have bathtubs—if you like a long hot soak après-ski be sure to book one of them. ⊠*CH-3825 Mürren* ☎*033/8568800* 🖶*033/8568888* ⊕*www.alpenruh-muerren.ch* ⇗*26 rooms* ⌂*In-room: no a/c, safe, refrigerator. In-hotel: 2 restaurants, bar, spa, laundry service, public Internet, some pets allowed (fee), no-smoking rooms.* ⊟*DC, MC, V* ⓧ*BP & MAP.*

$$$–$$$$ ⊡ **Hotel Eiger.** Set on a hilly flank with a front-row perch directly across
Fodor's Choice   from the Eiger, Mönch, and Jungfrau, this is the most stylish hotel in
★   Mürren. With one five-story wing dating back to the 1920s and an even larger, snazzier wing from the early 1990s, most rooms flaunt balconies with "peak" views. In addition, the hotel has room to spare for a spa replete with an indoor pool with staggering views of the ermine-mantled mountains. Inside, all is *Gemütlichkeit*-elegant: the adorable bar has a big fireplace hood, while regular guest rooms come with elegant pine wainscotting and suites can go all out with exposed timber beams and gorgeous fabrics. If you want to enjoy the high life—in more ways than one—head here. **Pros:** fantastic views; plush and cosy environment; adjacent to the Bergbahn clifftop station. **Cons:** the windows do not open for safety reasons, so claustrophobics beware; the location is all about peace and tranquillity; if you are looking for cosmopolitan lifestyle, this hotel is not for you. ⊠*CH-3825 Mürren* ☎*033/8565454* 🖶*033/8565456* ⊕*www.hoteleiger.com* ⇗*49 rooms* ⌂*In-room: no a/c, safe, refrigerator (some), Wi-Fi (fee). In-hotel: 2 restaurants, room service, bar, pool, spa, laundry service, public Internet (free), Wi-Fi (fee), some pets allowed (fee), no-smoking rooms* ⊟*AE, D, MC, V* ⓧ*BP & MAP.*

JUNGFRAUJOCH

The granddaddy of all high-altitude excursions, the famous journey to the Jungfraujoch, site of the highest railroad station in Europe, is one of the most popular rides in Switzerland. From the station at Lauterbrunnen you take the green cogwheel Wengernalp Railway nearly straight up the wooded mountainside, and watch as the valley and the village shrink below. From the hilltop resort of **Wengen** the train climbs up steep grassy slopes past the timberline to **Kleine Scheidegg**, a tiny, isolated resort settlement surrounded by vertiginous scenery. Here you change to the **Jungfraubahn**, another train, which tunnels straight into the rock of the Eiger, stopping briefly for views out enormous picture windows blasted through its stony face.

The **Jungfraujoch terminus** stands at an elevation of 11,400 feet; you may feel a bit light-headed from the altitude. Follow signs to the Top of Europe restaurant, a gleaming white glass-and-steel pavilion. The expanse of rock and ice you see from here is simply blinding.

If you're not sated with the staggering views from the Jungfraujoch terminus, you can reach yet another height by riding a high-tech 90-second elevator up 364 feet to the **Sphinx Terrace**: to the south crawls the vast Aletsch Glacier, to the northeast stand the Mönch and the Eiger, and to the southwest—almost close enough to touch—towers the tip of the Jungfrau herself. Note: even in low season you may have to wait in line for the elevator.

More than views are offered to the hordes that mount the Jungfraujoch daily. From June to the middle of September you can sign up for a beginner's ski lesson or a dogsled ride, or tour the chill blue depths of the **Ice Palace**, a novelty reminiscent of a wax museum, full of incongruous and slightly soggy ice sculptures. Admission to the attraction is included in the price of the excursion.

15

INDEX

Photo Credits: Chapter 1: Experience Italy: 7, *Stefano Brozzi/age fotostock.* 8, *Richard Cummins/viestiphoto.com.* 9, *(left) Kurt De Bruyn/Shutterstock.* 9, *(right) E.A. Janes/age fotostock.* 10, *SGM/age fotostock.* 11, *(left) Martin Siepmann/age fotostock.* 11 *(right), Switzerland Tourism.* 12, *Walter Bibikow/age fotostock.* 13 *(left), JLImages/Alamy.* 13 *(right), Nils-Johan Norenlind/age fotostock.* 18 *(left), Corbis.* 18 *(top center), Rostislaw/Shutterstock.* 18 *(top right), Foucras G./age fotostock.* 18 *(bottom right), Corbis RF.* 19 *(left) Marc C. Johnson/Shutterstock.* 19 *(top center), Bruno Morandi/age fotostock.* 19 *(top right), Atlantide S.N.C./age fotostock.* 19 *(bottom right), Yuri Yavnik/Shutterstock.* 20 *(left), Wikipedia. org.* 20 *(top center), Bruno Morandi/age fotostock.* 20 *(top right), Eduardo Ripoll/age fotostock.* 20 *(bottom right), German National Tourist Board.* 21 *(left) Adriaan Thomas Snaaijer/Shutterstock.* 21 *(top center), travelstock44/Alamy.* 21 *(top right), Wikipedia.org.* 21 *(bottom right), Wikipedia.org.* 22 *(left), Jan Kranendonk/Shutterstock.* 22 *(top center), Julius Honnor.* 22 *(top right), Bryce Newell/Shutterstock.* 22 *(bottom right), Philip Lange/Shutterstock.* 23 *(left), Marlene Challis/Shutterstock.* 23 *(left), Jan Kranendonk/Shutterstock.* 23 *(bottom), Photodisc.* 24 *(left), Regien Paassen/Shutterstock.* 24 *(top center), Gary718/Shutterstock.* 24 *(top right), David Hughes/Shutterstock.* 24 *(bottom right), Cork Kerry Tourism.* 25 *(left), Edward L. Ewert/age fotostock.* 25 *(top center), Senorcampesino/Shutterstock.* 25 *(top right), Anyka/Shutterstock.* 25 *(right bottom), Lazar Mihai-Bogdan/Shutterstock.* 26, *WoodyStock/ Alamy.* 27 *(left), Cro Magnon/Alamy.* 27 *(right), Martin Siepmann/age fotostock.* Chapter 2: Austria: 29, *Sylvain Grandadam/age fotostock.* 30, *Pigneter/Austria Tourism.* 31 *(left), Paul M. R. Maeyae/age fotostock.* 31 *(right), Sylvain Grandadam/age fotostock.* Chapter 3: Belgium: 63, *Belgian Tourist Office NYC/USA, www.visitbelgium.com.* 64, *Jan Kranendonk/Shutterstock.* 65 *(left), Belgian Tourist Office NYC/USA, www.visitbelgium.com.* 65 *(right), Peter Adams/age fotostock.* Chapter 4: Czech Republic: 103, *Hemis /Alamy.* 104, *Doug Scott/age fotostock.* 105 *(left), Miroslav Kro/age fotostock.* 105 *(right), Jon Arnold/age fotostock.* Chapter 5: France: 141, *Doug Scott/age fotostock.* 142, *Robert Fried/Alamy.* 143 *(left), Chuck Pefle/Alamy.* 143 *(right), Kader Meguedad/Alamy.* 156, *Directphoto.org/Alamy.* 157 *(top left), The Print Collector/Alamy.* 157 *(top right), Scott S. Warren/Aurora Photos.* 157 *(center), www. tour-eiffel.fr.* 157 *(bottom right), Gabrielle Chan/Shutterstock.* 157 *(bottom left), Directphoto.org/Alamy.* Chapter 6: Germany: 233 and 234, *Martin Siepmann/age fotostock.* 235 *(left), Picture Finders/age fotostock.* 235 *(right), Corbis.* Chapter 7: Great Britain: 313, *Doug Scott/age fotostock.* 314, *Peter Phipp/ age fotostock.* 315 *(left), E.A. Janes/age fotostock.* 315 *(right), Bill Terry/Viesti.* 333 *(left), F. Monheim/R. von G't/Bildarchiv Monheim/age fotostock.* 333 *(top right), Dean and Chapter of Westminster, London.* 333 *(center right), Mark Thomas/Alamy..* 333 *(bottom right) and 335, Dean and Chapter of Westminster.* 337, *British Tourist Authority.* Chapter 8: Greece: 399, *Maro Kouri/IML Image Group/Aurora Photos.* 400, *Danita Delimont/Alamy.* 401 *(left), Roberto Meazza/IML Image Group/Aurora Photos.* 401 *(right), Deco Images/Alamy.* 414, *SIME s.a.s/eStock Photo.* 416, *Vidler/age fotostock.* 417 *(top), Kord.com/age fotostock.* 420, *Juha-Pekka Kervinen/Shutterstock.* Chapter 9: Ireland: 455, *Richard Cummins/viestiphoto.com.* 456, *Ken Welsh/age fotostock.* 457 *(left), Joe Viesti/viestiphoto.com.* 457 *(right), Kevin O'Hara/ age fotostock.* 481 *(top center), Richard Cummins/viestiphoto.com.* 481 *(bottom left), Alvaro Leiva/age fotostock.* 481 *(bottom right), Richard Cummins/viestiphoto.com.* 482 and 483, *Joe Viesti/viestiphoto. com.* 484 *(top left), Chloe Johnson/Alamy.* 484 *(top right), ImageState/Alamy.* 484 *(center left), Murphy Brewery.* 484 *(bottom left), Beamish & Crawford.* 485 *(top and bottom), David Sanger Photography/ Alamy.* Chapter 10: Italy: 505, *Javier Larrea/age fotostock.* 506, *Alan Copson/Agency Jon Arnold Images/ age fotostock.* 507 *(left), Atlantide S.N.C./age fotostock.* 507 *(right), Bruno Morandi/age fotostock.* 549 *(left), Classic Vision/age fotostock.* 459 *(center), SuperStock/age fotostock.* 459 *(right), Classic Vision/ age fotostock.* 550 *(left), Chie Ushio.* 550 *(right), Planet Art.* 551 *(top left), Classic Vision/age fotostock.* 551 *(center left), SuperStock/age fotostock.* 551 *(bottom left), Photodisc.* 551 *(bottom right), Corbis.* 552 *(left) Fototeca ENIT.* 552 *(center), SuperStock/age fotostock.* 552 *(right), Bruno Morandi/age fotostock.* 553 *(left and center), SuperStock/age fotostock.* 553 *(right), PTE/age fotostock.* 554 *(all), Planet Art.* Chapter 11: The Netherlands: 601, *Javier Larrea/age fotostock.* 602, *Atlantide S.N.C. /age fotostock.* 603 *(left), Killroy Productions/Shutterstock.* 603 *(right), April Gertler.* Chapter 12: Portugal: 641, *Joe Viesti/ viestiphoto.com.* 642, *José Manuel-ITP.* 643 *(left), Regiao de Turismo do Algarve/ICP.* 643 *(right), Cro Magnon/Alamy.* Chapter 13: Scandinavia: 679, *D. Guilloux/viestiphoto.com.* 680, *Photodisc.* 681 *(left), José Fuste Raga/age fotostock.* 681 *(right), Sylvain Grandadam/age fotostock.* Chapter 14: Spain: 725, *David Noton/age fotostock.* 726, *Corbis.* 727 *(left), J.D. Dallet/age fotostock.* 727 *(right), Juan Manuel Silva/age fotostock.* 744-45 *(top), Alan Copson City Pictures/Alamy.* 744 *(bottom), Jon Arnold Images/ Alamy.* 746 *(top), Tim Hill /Alamy.* 746 *(top center), Mediacolor's/Alamy.* 746 *(bottom center), Ramon Grosso Dolarea/Shutterstock.* 746 *(bottom), Peter Cassidy/age fotostock.* 747 *(top), Mark Baynes/Alamy.* 747 *(top center), Alex Segre/Alamy.* 747 *(left center), Kathleen Melis/Shutterstock.* 747 *(bottom center), Peter Cassidy/age fotostock.* 747 *(bottom), Frank Heuer/Laif/Aurora Photos.* Chapter 15: Switzerland: 805, *BL Images Ltd/Alamy.* 806, *Basel Tourismus.* 807 *(left), Bern Tourismus.* 807 *(right), Grindelwald Tourismus.*

NOTES

NOTES

ABOUT OUR WRITERS

Fodor's aims to give you the best local insights by using writers who live in the destinations they cover. *Essential Europe* is the work of the following Europe-based team:

Austria: Daniela Lettner, Diane Naar-Elphee, Giambattista Pace, Horst E. Reischenböck.

Belgium: Tim Skelton (lead contributor), Nicola Smith

The Czech Republic: Mark Baker, Alexander Basek, Mindy Kay Bricker, Evan Rail.

France: Sarah Fraser (lead contributor), Jennifer Ditsler-Ladonne, Linda Hervieux, Rosa Jackson, Lisa Pasold, Nicole Pritchard, Heather Stimmler-Hall, Simon Hewit.

Germany: Ted Shoemaker (lead contributor), Uli Ehrhardt, Lee A. Evans, Jürgen Scheunemann.

Great Britain: Robert Andrews (lead contributor); Christi Daugherty, Jack Jewers, James Knight, Shona Main, Katrina Manson, Michelle Rosenberg, Alex Wijeratna.

Greece: Adrian Vrettos (lead contributor), Jeffrey Carson, Angelike Contis, Natasha Giannousi, Joanna Kakissis.

Ireland: Alannah Hopkin, Anto Howard.

Italy: Peter Blackman, Shannon Essa, Ruth Edenbaum, Erica Firpo, Dana Klitzberg, Jen Laskey, Nan McElroy, Patricia Rucidlo, Pamela Santini, Megan K. Williams.

The Netherlands: Tim Skelton (lead contributor), Nicole Chabot, Madelon Evers, Ann Maher, Shain Shapiro.

Portugal: Alison Roberts (lead contributor), Matthew Wilkinson, Sarah Wyatt.

Scandinavia: Rob Hincks, Sarah Lookofsy, Laura Stadler-Jensen, Marie Peyre.

Spain: Paul Cannon, Ignacio Gómez, George Semler.

Switzerland: Gail Mangold (lead contributor), Katrin Gygax, Suzanne Hégelé, Alexis Munier.